AA

TRAVELLERS' GUIDE TO EUROPE

Editor: Barbara Littlewood
Designer: Elizabeth Baldin

Gazetteer: compiled by the Publications Research Unit of the Automobile Association
Maps: prepared by the Cartographic Services Unit of the Automobile Association
Cover picture: Venice, gondolas (International Photobank)

Head of Advertisement Sales: Christopher Heard Tel 0256 20123 (ext 2020)

Advertisement Production: Karen Weeks Tel 0256 20123 (ext 3525)

Filmsetting by Vantage Photosetting Co. Ltd., Eastleigh and London
Printed and bound in Great Britain by William Collins, Glasgow

ISBN 0 86145 251 8

Published by the Automobile Association, Basingstoke, Hampshire RG21 2EA

Contents

There's a certain freedom you get when you leave the country by car.

Basically you're free to motor along wherever you fancy.

But if you're smart, your plans will take you towards a hotel you already know and feel comfortable with.

For us, that means Crest.

The reception you get is in plain English. Literally. Whether you are in Belgium, Holland, Germany or Italy.

The Crest staff are every bit as friendly as the ones we've encountered here.

"It's enough to drive you out of the country."

You even find the same tea, coffee and biscuits in your room.

And being AA members, we get what's already a really good deal for even less.

Not just at a few Crest Hotels. But at all the 36 throughout Europe.

Crest Hotels
International

Nobody works harder to make your stay better.

ABC of European motoring regulations and general information

The ABC provides a wide background of motoring regulations and general information and is designed to be read in conjunction with the relevant country section(s).

Motoring laws in Europe are just as wide and complicated as those in the UK but they should cause little difficulty to the average British motorist. He should however, take more care and extend greater courtesy than he would normally do at home, and bear in mind the essentials of good motoring – avoiding any behaviour likely to obstruct traffic, to endanger persons or cause damage to property. It is also important to remember that when travelling in a country the tourist is subject to the laws of that country.

Road signs are mainly international and should be familiar to the British motorist, but in every country there are a few exceptions. One should particularly watch for signs indicating crossings and speed limits. Probably the most unusual aspect of motoring abroad to the British motorist is the universal and firm rule giving priority to traffic coming from the right and unless this rule is varied by signs, it must be strictly observed.

As well as a current passport, a tourist temporarily importing a motor vehicle should always carry a valid national driving licence, even when an International Driving Permit is held, the registration document of the car and evidence of insurance. The proper international distinguishing sign should be affixed to the rear of the vehicle. The appropriate papers must be carried at all times and secured against loss. The practice of spot checks on foreign cars is widespread and to avoid inconvenience or an *on-the-spot* fine, ensure that your papers are in order and that the international distinguishing sign is of the approved standard design.

Make sure that you have clear all-round vision. See that your seat belts are securely mounted and not damaged, and remember that in most European countries their use is compulsory.

If you are carrying skis, remember that their tips should point to the rear. You must be sure that your vehicle complies with the regulations concerning dimensions for all the countries you intend to pass through (see *ABC* and *Country sections*). This is particularly necessary if you are towing a trailer of any sort. If you are planning to tow a caravan, you will find advice and information in the AA guide *Camping and Caravanning in Europe*.

We know as well as anyone how expensive mechanical repairs and replacement parts can be abroad. While not all breakdowns are avoidable, a vast number of those we deal with occur because the vehicle has not been prepared properly before the start of the journey. A holiday abroad involves many miles of hard driving over roads completely new to you, perhaps without the facilities you have come to take for granted in this country. Therefore you should give serious thought to the business of *preparing your vehicle for a holiday abroad*.

We recommend that your car undergoes a major service by a franchised dealer shortly before your holiday or tour abroad. In addition, it is advisable to carry out your own general check for any audible or visible defects.

It is not practicable to provide a complete list of points to look for but the ABC contains information under the following headings:

Automatic gearboxes
Automatic transmission fluid
Brakes
Cold weather touring
Direction indicators
Electrical

Engine and mechanical
Lights
Spares
Tyres
Warm climate touring

which, if used in conjunction with the manufacturer's handbook, should ensure that no obvious faults are missed.

If AA members would like a thorough check of their car made by one of the AA's experienced engineers, any AA Centre can arrange this at a few days' notice. Our engineer will then submit a written report complete with a list of repairs required. There is a fee for this service. For more information please ask for our leaflet Tech 8.

AA Agents including Port Agents (See also *Country sections*)

The Association does not maintain any offices outside Britain but is represented by allied motoring clubs throughout Europe. Additionally it has appointed port agents at the more popular *Belgian, French* and *Spanish* ports whose particular function is to assist and advise motorists embarking and disembarking. European motoring clubs allied to the AA will extend a courtesy service to AA members but this will be commensurate with their facilities.

Accidents (See also *Country sections*)

The country sections give individual country regulations and information on summoning the emergency services. The international regulations are similar to those in the UK; the following recommendations are usually advisable.

If you are involved in an accident you *must* stop. A warning triangle should be placed on the road at a suitable distance to warn following traffic of the obstruction. The use of hazard warning lights in no way affects the regulations governing the use of warning triangles. Medical assistance should be obtained for persons injured in the accident. If the accident necessitates calling the police, leave the vehicle in the posi-

tion in which it came to rest; should it seriously obstruct other traffic, mark the position of the vehicle on the road and get the details confirmed by independent witnesses before moving it.

The accident must be reported to the police; if it is required by law; if the accident has caused death or bodily injury; or if the unoccupied vehicle or property has been damaged and there is no one present to represent the interests of the party suffering damage. Notify your insurance company by letter, if possible, within 24 hours of the accident; see the conditions of your policy. If a third party is injured, the insurance company or bureau, whose address is given on the back of your Green Card or frontier insurance certificate, should be notified; the company or bureau will, if necessary, pay compensation to the injured party.

Make sure that all the essential particulars are noted, especially details concerning third parties, and co-operate with police or other officials taking on-the-spot notes by supplying your name, address or other personal details as required. It is also a good idea to take photographs of the scene, endeavouring to get good shots of other vehicles involved, their registration plates and any background which might help later enquiries. This record may be useful when completing the

insurance company's accident form.

If you are not involved in the accident but feel your assistance as a witness or in any other useful capacity would be helpful, then stop and park your car carefully, well away from the scene. If all the help necessary is at the scene, then do not stop out of curiosity and do not park your car at the site.

Automatic gearboxes
When towing a caravan the fluid in the automatic gearbox becomes hotter and thinner so there is more slip and more heat generated in the gearbox. Many manufacturers recommend the fitting of a gearbox oil cooler. Check with the manufacturer what is suitable for your car.

Automatic transmission fluid
Automatic transmission fluid is not always readily available especially in some of the more remote areas of Western Europe and tourists are advised to carry an emergency supply with them.

BBC World Service
If you wish to receive English language broadcasts whilst travelling abroad, BBC World Service transmissions can be heard in many European countries. A full programme including current affairs, sport and music is available, with

world news at approximately every hour. Most car radios operate on medium and long waves and BBC World Service programmes may normally be obtained in north-western Europe by tuning to the following frequencies between the times mentioned.

KHz	Metres	Summer broadcasting times – GMT
1296	231	03.00–03.30, 06.00–06.30, 16.00–18.00, 22.00–23.15.
648	463	04.45–05.30, 05.45–10.30, 11.00–16.45, 20.00–03.30.
200	1500	02.00–04.30.

For more comprehensive information on BBC World Service transmissions throughout Europe write to BBC World Information Centre and Shop, Bush House, Strand, LONDON WC2B 2PH.

Boats

Tourists taking any type of boat by car to France, or the German Federal Republic (West Germany), Greece, Italy, the Netherlands, Spain or Yugoslavia are strongly advised to obtain a Helmsman's Certificate of Competence, also boat registration documentation from the Royal Yachting Association, Victoria Way, Woking, Surrey, GU21 1EQ tel (048 62)5022. Applications should be made well in advance. See also *Carnet de Passages* under *Customs regulations*, page 11, *Identification Plate*, page 16, and *Insurance*, page 16.

Brakes

Car brakes must always be in peak condition. Check especially the level in the brake fluid reservoir and the thickness of the brake lining/pad material. The brake fluid should be completely changed in accordance with the manufacturer's instructions, or at intervals of not more than 18 months or 18,000 miles.

However it is advisable to change the brake fluid, regardless of the foregoing, before departing on a Continental holiday, particularly if the journey includes travelling through a hilly or mountainous area.

Breakdown (See also *Country sections*)

If your car breaks down, endeavour to move it to the side of the road or to a position where it will obstruct the traffic flow as little as possible. Place a warning triangle at the appropriate distance on the road behind the obstruction. Bear in mind road conditions and if near or on a bend the triangle should be placed where it is clearly visible to following traffic. If the car is fitted with hazard warning lights these may be switched on but they will only warn on the straight and will have no effect at bends or rises in the road. If the fault is electrical, the lights may not operate and it is for these reasons that they cannot take the place of a triangle. Having taken these first precautions, seek assistance if you cannot deal with the fault yourself.

Motorists are advised to purchase AA 5-Star Service which provides a wide range of services, insurance and credit

vouchers which offer security and peace of mind when travelling in Europe. Cover may be purchased by all motorists. However, a small additional premium must be paid by non-members. Details and brochures may be obtained from travel agents and AA Centres, or by telephoning 021-550 7648.

Note Members who have not purchased AA 5-Star Service prior to departure and who subsequently require assistance may request spare parts or vehicle recovery, but in this case the AA will require a deposit to cover estimated costs and a service fee prior to providing the service. All expenses must be reimbursed to the AA in addition to the service fee.

British Consulates

Consulates overseas will help or advise British travellers only if they are in serious trouble or distress. They will not advance money or finance a traveller for any reason, nor will they do the work of travel agents, information bureaux, banks or police. The loss of valuables, including passports, is a police matter and should be reported to them, not a consulate. In most countries there is usually more than one British Consulate and degrees of status vary. In the *Country sections* the address of the most important is given, together with the towns in which others are located.

Camping and caravanning

Information is given separately in the AA guide *Camping and Caravanning in Europe*, a copy of which may be purchased from most AA Centres.

Take the fresh approach to Europe

Don't wait until you reach the Continent to start your holiday, start it at Dover. With over 100 sailings a day in Summer, we make the "going" as good as the getting there.

You can choose from 4 different operators, Sealink, P & O Ferries, Townsend Thoresen and Hoverspeed. There is also the Sealink Jetfoil service to Ostend for foot passengers. No other port gives you so many ways to leave, or places to go.

You can drive off at Boulogne, Calais, Dunkirk, Ostend or Zeebrugge, and come back the same way, all year round. Slip out from Dover and make the crossing part of the holiday, remember — even *without* a prior booking during the *peak* Summer periods, you'll find yourself on a ferry within an hour or so.

go through Dover -it's plain sailing all the way

The Travellers Guide to Dover provides a wealth of information to help you make the most of your journey through Dover. Information and sailing schedules on Prestel 344119.

Please send me a free copy of the Travellers Guide to Dover.

Name _____ TGE

Address _____

_____ Postcode

Dover Harbour Board, Harbour House, Dover, Kent CT17 9BU.
Telephone: 0304 206560. Telex: 965619.

Caravan and luggage trailers

Carry a list of contents, as this may be required at a frontier. A towed vehicle should be readily identifiable by a plate in an accessible position showing the name of the maker of the vehicle and his production or serial number. If the vehicle does not have an identification plate see page 16. See also Principal mountain passes page 40.

Claims against Third Parties

The law and levels of damages in foreign countries are generally different to our own. It is important to remember this when considering making a claim against another motorist arising out of an accident abroad. Certain types of claims invariably present difficulties, the most common probably being that relating to the recovery of car-hiring charges. Rarely are they recoverable in full and in some countries they may be drastically reduced or not recoverable at all. General damages for pain and suffering are not recoverable in certain countries but even in those countries where they are recoverable the levels are, in most cases, lower than our own.

The negotiation of claims against foreign insurers is extremely protracted and translation of all documents slows down the process. A delay of three months between sending a letter and receiving a reply is not uncommon!

If you have taken out the AA's 5-Star Service cover this includes a discretionary service in respect of matters arising abroad requiring legal assistance including the pursuit of uninsured loss claims against third parties arising out of a road accident. In this event, members should seek guidance and/or assistance from the AA.

Cold weather touring

If you are planning a winter tour, make sure that you fit a high-temperature (winter) thermostat and make sure that the strength of your anti-freeze mixture is correct for the low temperatures likely to be encountered.

If you are likely to be passing through snow-bound regions, it is important to remember that for many resorts and passes the authorities insist on wheel chains, spiked or studded tyres, or snow tyres. In some countries, however, spiked or studded tyres are banned.

In fair weather, wheel chains, spiked or studded tyres, or snow tyres are only necessary on the higher passes, but in severe weather you will probably need them (as a rough guide) at altitudes exceeding 2,000ft.

If you think you will need wheel chains, it is better to take them with you from home. They may be hired from the AA and further details are available from your nearest AA Centre.

Information on hiring wheel chains (where such a service exists) in the countries where they are most needed is given in the country sections.

Wheel chains and spiked or studded tyres can damage the road surface if it is free of snow or ice; there are definite periods when these may be used and in certain countries the use of spiked or studded tyres is illegal. If wheel chains, spiked or studded tyres, or snow tyres are compulsory, this is usually signposted.

Wheel chains fit over the tyres to enable the wheels to grip on snow or icy surfaces. They are sometimes called snow chains or anti-skid chains. Full-length chains which fit right round the tyre are the most satisfactory, but they must be fitted correctly. Check that the chains do not foul your vehicle bodywork; if your vehicle has front-wheel-drive, then put the steering on full lock while checking. If your vehicle has radial tyres it is essential that you contact the manufacturers of your vehicle and tyres for their recommendations in order to avoid damage to your tyres. Chains should only be used when compulsory or necessary as prolonged use on hard surfaces will damage the tyres. See also Country sections for Andorra, Austria, France, Italy and Switzerland.

Spiked or studded tyres are sometimes called snow tyres. They are tyres with rugged treads on to which spikes or studs have been fitted. For the best grip they should be fitted to all wheels. The correct type of spiked or studded winter tyres will generally be more effective than chains. See also Country sections.

Note The above comments do not apply where severe winter conditions prevail. It is doubtful whether the cost of preparing a car, normally used in the UK, would be justified for a short period. However, the AA's Technical Services Department will be pleased to advise on specific enquiries.

Compulsory equipment

All countries have differing regulations as to how vehicles circulating on their roads should be equipped but generally domestic laws are not enforced on visiting foreig-

ners. However, where a country considers aspects of safety or other factors are involved, they will impose some regulations on visitors and these will be mentioned in the country sections.

Crash or safety helmets

All countries in this guide (except Belgium and Italy where they are strongly recommended) require visiting motorcyclists and their passengers to wear crash or safety helmets.

Credit cards

Credit cards may be used abroad but their use is subject to the 'conditions of use' set out by the issuing company who, on request, will provide full information. Establishments display the symbols of cards they accept, but it is not possible to produce any detailed lists. See also *Country sections* under *Petrol* for information as to whether credit cards may be used to purchase fuel.

Currency and banking hours

(See also *Country sections*)

There is no limit to the amount of sterling notes you may take abroad. However, it is best to carry only enough currency for immediate expenses.

As many countries have regulations controlling the import and export of currency, you are advised to consult your bank for full information before making final arrangements.

Customs regulations for European countries (other than the United Kingdom)

Bona fide visitors to the countries listed in this guide may assume as a general rule that they may *temporarily import*

personal articles duty free, providing the following conditions are met:

   a that the articles are for personal use and are not to be sold or otherwise disposed of;

   b that they may be considered as being in use and in keeping with the personal status of the importer;

   c that they are taken out when the importer leaves the country;

   d that the importer stays less than 6 in any 12 months, for *EEC member states.*

All dutiable articles must be declared when you enter a country, otherwise you will be liable to penalties. Should you be taking a large number of personal effects with you, it would be a wise measure to prepare in advance an inventory to present to the Customs authorities on entry. Customs officers may withhold concessions at any time and ask the traveller to deposit enough money to cover possible duty, especially on portable items of apparent high value such as television sets, or radios, cassette recorders, pocket calculators, and musical instruments, etc, all of which must be declared. Any deposit paid (for which a receipt must be obtained) is likely to be high; it is recoverable (but only at the entry point at which it was paid) on leaving the country and exporting the item. Alternatively the Customs may enter the item in the traveller's passport and in these circumstances it is important to remember to get the entry cancelled when the item is exported. Duty and tax free allowances may not apply (except for EEC countries) if the traveller

enters the country more than once a month, or if he is under 17 years of age (an alternative age may apply in some countries).

A *temporarily imported motor vehicle, caravan, boat* or any other type of *trailer* is subject to strict control on entering a country, attracting Customs duty and a variety of taxes; much depends upon the circumstances and the period of the import and also upon the status of the importer. A person entering a country in which he has no residence, with a private vehicle for holiday or recreational purposes, and intending to export the vehicle within a short period, enjoys special privileges and the normal formalities are reduced to an absolute minimum in the interests of tourism. However, a *Customs Carnet de Passages en Douane* is required to import temporarily certain vehicles, boats and outboard engines into some countries (see *Country sections* for *Belgium, France* and *Luxembourg*). The *Carnet*, for which a charge is made, is a valuable document issued by the AA to its members or as part of the AA 5-Star Service – further information may be obtained from most AA Centres. If you are issued with a *Carnet* you must ensure that it is returned to the AA correctly discharged in order to avoid inconvenience and expense, possibly including payment of customs charges, at a later date. A temporarily imported vehicle, etc, should not:

   a be left in the country after the importer has left;

   b be put at the disposal of a resident of the country;

c be retained in the country longer than the permitted period;

d be lent, sold, hired, given away, exchanged or otherwise disposed of.

A person entering a country with a motor vehicle for a period of generally more than three months or to take up residence, employment, any commercial activity or with the intention of disposing of the vehicle should seek advice concerning his position well in advance of his departure. Most AA Centres will be pleased to help.

you bought in the UK, it is a good idea to carry the retailer's receipts with you if they are available. In the absence of such receipts you may be asked to make a written declaration of where the goods were obtained.

The exportation of certain goods *from the United Kingdom* is prohibited or restricted. These include: controlled drugs; most animals, birds and some plants; firearms and ammunition; strategic and technological equipment (including computers); photographic material over 60 years

ces (see below) which you have obtained outside the United Kingdom or on the journey and everything previously obtained free of duty or tax in the United Kingdom. You may not mix allowances between duty-free and non-duty-free sources within each heading eg Tobacco, Alcohol etc. Currently as a concession only, travellers may use their entitlement of alcoholic drinks not over 22% vol to import table wine in addition to the set table wine allowance. You must also declare any prohibited or restricted goods and goods for commercial purposes. Don't be tempted to hide anything or to mislead the Customs. The penalties are severe and in addition articles which are not properly declared may be forfeited. If articles are hidden in a vehicle, that too becomes liable to forfeiture. The Customs officer is legally entitled to examine your luggage. Please co-operate with him if he asks to examine it. You are responsible for opening, unpacking and repacking your luggage.

The importation of certain goods into the United Kingdom is prohibited or restricted. These include controlled drugs such as opium, morphine, heroin, cocaine, cannabis, amphetamines and LSD (lysergide); counterfeit currency; firearms (including gas pistols and similar weapons), ammunition, explosives (including fireworks) and flick knives; horror comics, indecent or obscene books, magazines, films, video tapes and other articles; most animals* and all birds, whether alive or dead (eg stuffed); certain articles derived from endangered species including furskins, ivory, reptile

From non-EEC country or goods bought in duty-free shop	Duty and tax free allowances	From ECC country and goods not bought in duty-free shop
	Tobacco	
200	Cigarettes	300
	or	
100	Cigarillos	150
	or	
50	Cigars (large)	75
	or	
250g	Tobacco	400g
	Alcohol	
1 litre	Over 22% vol	1.5 litres
	or	
2 litres	Under 22% vol	3 litres
	and	
2 litres	Still table wine	4 litres
	Perfume	
50g		75g
	Toilet water	
250ml		375ml
	Other goods	
£28		£163

Customs regulations for the United Kingdom

If, when leaving Britain, you export any items of new appearance, as for example watches, items of jewellery, cameras etc, particularly of foreign manufacture, which

old; and antiques and collectors' items more than 50 years old.

When you *enter the United Kingdom* you will pass through Customs. You must declare everything in excess of the duty and tax free allowan-

*Note: cats, dogs and other mammals must not be landed unless a British import licence (rabies) has previously been issued.

leather and goods made from them; meat and poultry and most of their products (whether or not cooked), including ham, bacon, sausage, pâté, eggs and milk; plants, parts thereof and plant produce, including trees and shrubs, potatoes and certain other vegetables, fruit, bulbs and seeds; wood with bark attached; radio transmitters (*eg* citizens' band radios, walkie-talkies etc) not approved for use in the United Kingdom.

Customs Notice No. 1 is available to all travellers at the point of entry or on the boat and contains useful information of which returning tourists should be aware. Motorists should obtain a copy of Customs Notice No. 15 on the ferry or ship, and display the appropriate red or green sticker that can be found in the notice, on arrival. Advance copies of Customs Notices 1 and 15 can be obtained from HM Customs and Excise, Dorset House, Stamford Street, London SE1 9PS.

Dimensions and weight restrictions

For an ordinary private car a height of 4 metres and a width limit of 2.5 metres is generally imposed. However, see *Country sections* for full details. Apart from a laden weight limit imposed on commercial vehicles, every vehicle, private or commercial, has an individual weight limit and as this affects private cars see *Overloading* page 19. See also *Major road tunnels* page 38, as some dimensions are restricted by the shape of tunnels. If you have any doubts consult the AA.

Direction indicators

All direction indicators should

be working at between 60 and 120 flashes per minute. Most standard car-flasher units will be overloaded by the extra lamps of a caravan or trailer and a special heavy duty unit or a relay device should be fitted.

Drinking and driving

There is only one safe rule – if you drink, don't drive. The laws are strict and penalties severe.

Driving licence and International Driving Permit

You should carry your national driving licence with you when motoring abroad. If an International Driving Permit is necessary (see *IDP requirements* below) it is recommended that you still carry your national driving licence. In most of the countries covered by this guide a visitor can drive a temporarily imported car without formality for up to three months with a valid licence (not provisional) issued in the United Kingdom or Republic of Ireland, subject to the minimum age requirements of the country concerned (see *Country sections*). If you wish to drive a hired or borrowed car in the country you are visiting, make local enquiries. The minimum age limit at which visitors may ride motorcycles varies according to the cylinder capacity of the machine. Therefore, persons under 21 intending to travel by motorcycle are recommended to make the appropriate enquiries either through the AA or relevant national tourist office.

If your licence is due to expire before your anticipated return, it should be renewed in good time prior to your departure. The Driver and Vehicle

Licensing Centre will accept an application two months before the expiry of your old licence (in Northern Ireland and the Republic of Ireland licensing authorities will accept an application one month before the expiry of your old licence).

An International Driving Permit (IDP) is an internationally recognised document which enables the holder to drive for a limited period in countries where their national licences are not recognised (see Austrian, Greek and Spanish *Country sections* under *Driving licence*). The permit, for which a charge is made, is issued by the AA to an applicant who holds a valid British driving licence and who is over 18 years old. It has a validity of 12 months, cannot be renewed, and application forms are available from any AA Travel Agency or AA Centre. The permit cannot be issued to the holder of a foreign licence who must apply to the appropriate authority in the country where the driving licence was issued. *Note* Residents of the Republic of Ireland, Channel Islands and the Isle of Man should apply to their local AA Centre.

Electrical information

General The public electricity supply in Europe is predominantly AC (alternating current) of 220 volts (50 cycles) but can be as low as 110 volts. In some isolated areas low voltage DC (direct current) is provided. European circular two-pin plugs and screw-type bulbs are usually the rule. Useful electrical adaptors (not voltage transformers) which can be used in Continental shaver points and light bulb sockets

are available in the United Kingdom, usually from the larger electrical appliance retailers.

Vehicle Check that all the connections are sound and that the wiring is in good condition. Should any problem arise with the charging system, it is essential to obtain the services of a qualified auto-electrician.

Emergency messages to tourists

In cases of emergency the AA will assist in the passing on of messages to tourists in Austria, Belgium, Denmark, France, Germany, Greece, Italy, Netherlands, Norway, Portugal, Spain, Sweden, Switzerland and Yugoslavia.

The AA can also arrange for messages to be published in overseas editions of the *Daily Mail* and in an extreme emergency (death or serious illness concerning next-of-kin) can arrange to have personal messages broadcast on overseas radio networks. Anyone wishing to use this service should contact their nearest AA Centre.

Before you leave home make sure your relatives understand the procedure to follow should an emergency occur.

If you have reason to expect a message from home, information about which frequencies you should tune in to and at what time such messages are normally broadcast are given in the *Country sections*. If you require further information contact the tourist office or motoring club of the country you are staying in.

No guarantee can be given, either by the AA or by the *Daily Mail*, to trace the person con-

cerned, and no responsibility can be accepted for the authenticity of messages.

Engine and mechanical

Consult your vehicle handbook for servicing intervals. Unless the engine oil has been changed recently, drain and refill with fresh oil and fit a new filter. Deal with any significant leaks by tightening up loose nuts and bolts and renewing faulty joints and seals. Brands and grades of *engine oil* familiar to the British motorist are usually available in Western Europe but may be difficult to find in remote country areas. When available they will be much more expensive than in the UK and generally packed in 2-litre cans ($3\frac{1}{2}$ pints). A motorist can usually assess the normal consumption of his car and is strongly advised to carry with him what oil he may require for his trip. If you suspect that there is anything wrong with the engine, however insignificant it may seem, it should be dealt with straight away. Even if everything seems in order, don't neglect such commonsense precautions as checking valve clearances, sparking plugs, and contact breaker points, and make sure that the distributor cap is sound. The fan belt should be checked for fraying and slackness. If any of the items mentioned previously are showing signs of wear you should replace them.

Any obvious mechanical defects should be attended to at once. Look particularly for play in steering connections and wheel bearings and, where applicable, ensure that they are adequately greased. A car that has covered a high mileage will have absorbed a certain amount of dirt into the fuel system and as break-

downs are often caused by dirt, it is essential that all filters (petrol and air) should be cleaned or renewed.

Owners should think twice about towing a caravan with a car that has already given appreciable service. Hard driving on motorways and in mountainous country puts an extra strain on ageing parts and items such as a burnt-out clutch can be very expensive.

The cooling system should be checked for leaks and the correct proportion of anti-freeze and any perished hoses or suspect parts replaced.

Eurocheques

The Eurocheque scheme is a flexible money-transfer system operated by a network of European banks. If you wish to cash your personal cheques abroad at banks, hotels or shops displaying the blue and red Eurocheque 'EC' symbol you must obtain a separate Eurocheque encashment card from your bankers. Additionally, if your bankers are part of the uniform Eurocheque scheme you will also be able to obtain a multi-currency chequebook enabling you to write cheques in the currency of the country you are visiting. Ask your bank for further information.

Ferry crossings

From Britain the shortest sea crossing from a southern port would be the obvious but it might not always be the best choice, bearing in mind how it places you on landing for main roads to your destination. Your starting point is important because if you have a long journey to a southern port then a service from an eastern port might be more

14

Sealink.
More services.
With more service.

You may already know about Sealink's services

We offer you more than any other ferry company. More sailings, day and night… to more places in France, Belgium, Holland, Ireland, the Channel Islands, the Isle of Man and the Isle of Wight. From more places in England, Scotland and Wales.

But do you know about Sealink's service?

A fleet that includes some of the newest and best equipped ships on the Channel, the Irish Sea and the North Sea.

Higher, and still rising standards of cuisine, comfort, entertainment, politeness, friendliness and care.

Comfort that approaches luxury on longer routes. Video lounges.

Cinemas. Children's play-care centres. Discos. Stylish restaurants serving excellent food and wines. Smart cafeterias for swifter eating. Good bars. Well stocked duty free shops. Comfortable cabins.

Service that extends from quay to quay and can, if you wish, go on to provide a choice of high quality, good value weekend, mid-week and longer holidays when you arrive.

Please send me a copy of   Car Ferry Guide '85 ☐   Motoring Holidays '85 ☐

Name_____

Address_____

County_____Post Code_____

Post to: Sealink UK Limited, Hudson's Place, PO Box 29, London SW1V 1JX, or call into your travel agent.   TGE

☲ SEALINK
Determined to give you a better service

convenient. Perhaps the Motorail service to the south might save time and possibly an overnight stop? In some circumstances the south-western ports may offer a convenient service and before making bookings it may be worth seeking advice so that the journey can be as economic and as comfortable as possible. The AA provides a full information and booking service on all sea, motorail and hovercraft services and instant confirmation is available on many by ringing one of the numbers listed below (Monday to Friday, 09.00–17.00). Ask also if you want information and booking on Continental car-sleeper and ferry services.

The South-East
01-891 4791
The West & Wales
Bristol (0272) 24417
The Midlands
021-550 7648
The North 061-486 0777
Scotland 041-812 2888
Northern Ireland
Belfast (0232) 228924
Republic of Ireland
Dublin (0001) 777004

Fire extinguisher

It is a wise precaution (compulsory in Greece) to equip your vehicle with a fire extinguisher when motoring abroad. An AA Fire Extinguisher may be purchased from your nearest AA Centre.

First aid kit

It is a wise precaution (compulsory in Austria, Greece and Yugoslavia) to equip your vehicle with a first-aid kit when motoring abroad. An AA First-Aid Kit may be purchased from your nearest AA Centre.

Holiday traffic

For information relating to holiday traffic see *Road conditions*, page 23, and the Austrian, French, German, Spanish and Swiss *Country sections* under the *Roads and holiday traffic* heading.

Identification plate

If a boat, caravan or trailer is taken abroad it must have a unique chassis number for identification purposes. If your boat, caravan or trailer does not have a number an *identification plate* may be purchased from the AA.

Insurance including caravan insurance

Motor insurance is compulsory by law in all the countries covered in this Guide and you are strongly advised to ensure that you are adequately covered for all countries in which you will travel. Temporary policies may be obtained at all frontiers except the Greek, but this is a most expensive way of effecting cover. It is best to seek the advice of your insurer regarding the extent of cover and full terms of your existing policy. Some insurers may not be willing to offer cover in the countries that you intend to visit and it may be necessary to seek a new, special policy for the trip from another insurer. Should you have any difficulty, AA Insurance Services will be pleased to help you. *Note* Extra insurance is recommended when visiting Spain (See *Bail Bond* page 317). Third-party insurance is compulsory for certain boats with engines in Italian waters (See also *Boats* page 8) and is recommended elsewhere for all boats used abroad. It is compulsory for

trailers temporarily imported into Austria (See page 60).

An international motor-insurance certificate or Green Card is recognised in most countries as evidence that you are covered to the minimum extent demanded by law. Compulsory in Greece*, Portugal, Spain and Yugoslavia, *the AA strongly recommends its use elsewhere*. It will be issued by your own insurer upon payment of the additional premium for extension of your UK policy cover to apply in those countries you intend visiting. It will name all the countries for which it is valid. The document will not be accepted until you have signed it. Green Cards are internationally recognised by police and other authorities and may save a great deal of inconvenience in the event of an accident. If you are towing a caravan or trailer it will need separate insurance, and to be mentioned on your Green Card. Remember, the cover on a caravan or on a trailer associated with a Green Card is normally limited to third-party risks, so a separate policy (see *AA Leisureplan*, below) is advisable to cover accidental damage, fire or theft.

In accordance with a Common Market Directive, the production and inspection of Green Cards at the frontiers of Common Market countries is no longer a legal requirement and the principle has been accepted by other European countries who are not members of the EEC. However, the fact that Green Cards will not be inspected does not remove the necessity of having insurance cover as required by law in the countries concerned.

16

Motorists can obtain expert advice through AA Insurance Services for all types of insurance. Several special schemes have been arranged with leading insurers to enable motorists to obtain wide insurance cover at economic premiums. One of these schemes, *AA Leisureplan*, includes damage cover for caravans, their contents, including personal effects and, while detached from the towing vehicle, protection against your legal liability to other persons arising out of the use of the caravan. Cover is extended to most European countries for up to 6 weeks without extra charge. *AA Leisureplan* also provides cover for camping equipment. Full details of *AA Leisureplan* may be obtained from any AA Centre or direct from AA Insurance Services Ltd, PO Box 2AA, Newcastle upon Tyne NE99 2AA.

Finally, make sure you are covered against damage in transit (eg on ferry or motorail). Most comprehensive motor insurance policies provide adequate cover, but check with your insurer to be certain.

*Although Greece is now a member of the EEC a Green Card is, for the time being, still a compulsory requirement for entry and travel in Greece.

International distinguishing sign

An international distinguishing sign of the approved pattern, oval with black letters on a white background, and size (GB at least 6.9in by 4.5in), must be displayed on a vertical surface at the rear of your vehicle (and caravan or trailer if you are towing one). On the Continent checks are made to ensure that a vehicle's nationality plate is in order. In Italy, Luxembourg, Netherlands, Norway, Portugal, Spain and Switzerland (See also *Country sections*) fines are imposed for failing to display a nationality plate, or for not displaying the correct nationality plate.

Level crossings

Practically all level crossings are indicated by international signs. Most guarded ones are of the lifting barrier type, sometimes with bells or flashing lights to give warning of an approaching train.

Lights (See also *Country sections*)

For driving abroad, headlights should be adjusted so that they do not dip to the left. This can be achieved by the use of beam deflectors which may be purchased from your nearest AA Centre. However, don't forget to remove the deflectors as soon as you return to the UK.

Dipped headlights should be used in conditions of fog, snowfall, heavy rain, and when passing through a tunnel, irrespective of its length and lighting. In some countries police will wait at the end of a tunnel to check this requirement. Headlight flashing is used only as a warning of approach or a passing signal at night. In other circumstances it is accepted as a sign of irritation and should be used with caution lest it is misunderstood.

It is a wise precaution (compulsory in France, Spain and Yugoslavia) to equip your vehicle with a set of replacement bulbs when motoring abroad. An AA Emergency Auto Bulb Kit suitable for most makes of car can be purchased from your nearest AA Centre.

Note Remember to have the lights set to compensate for the load being carried.

Liquefied Petroleum Gas/ LPG

The availability of this gas in Europe makes a carefully planned tour, with a converted vehicle, limited but feasible. The gas is retailed by several companies in Europe who will supply information as to where their product may be purchased. A motorist regularly purchasing the fuel in UK could possibly obtain lists of European addresses from his retailer.

Hours of opening of filling stations vary from country to country but generally they operate during normal business hours, except for holidays and saints'-days. At weekends LPG users are well advised to fill up on Saturdays and not rely on Sunday opening. It is recommended that a reducer nipple be carried as a precautionary measure. This accessory can normally be obtained from the importer/manufacturer of the LPG unit at minimal cost.

LPG is available in all the countries covered by this guide except Portugal and Spain. When booking a ferry crossing it is advisable to point out to the booking agent/ferry company that the vehicle runs on a dual fuel system.

Medical treatment

Travellers who are in the habit of taking certain medicines should make sure that they have a sufficient supply to last for their trip since they may be

very difficult to get abroad.

Those who suffer from certain diseases (diabetes or coronary artery diseases, for example) should get a letter from their doctor giving treatment details. Some Continental doctors will understand a letter written in English, but it is better to have it translated into the language of the country that it is intended to visit. The AA cannot make such a translation.

Travellers, who for legitimate health reasons carry drugs or appliances (eg hypodermic syringe etc) may have difficulty with Customs or other authorities. Others may have a diet problem which would be understood in hotels but for a language problem. The letter which such persons carry should therefore supply treatment details, a statement for Customs, and diet requirements.

The National Health Service is available in the United Kingdom only and medical expenses incurred overseas cannot generally be reimbursed by the United Kingdom Government. There are reciprocal health agreements with most of the countries covered by this guide, but you should not rely exclusively on these arrangements as the cover provided under the respective national schemes is not always comprehensive. The full costs of medical care must be paid in Andorra, Liechtenstein, Monaco, San Marino, Spain and Switzerland. Therefore, as facilities and financial cover can differ considerably between the various countries, you are strongly advised to take out comprehensive and adequate insurance cover before leaving the UK, such as that offered by Personal Security under the AA 5-Star Service.

Urgently needed medical treatment can be obtained by most visitors, free of charge or at reduced cost, from the health care schemes of those countries with whom the UK has health care arrangements. Details are in leaflet SA30 which is available from local social security offices of the Department of Health and Social Security or from its Leaflets Unit at PO Box 21, Stanmore, Middlesex HA7 1AY. In some of these countries a visitor can obtain urgently needed treatment by showing his UK passport but in some an NHS medical card must be produced and in most European Community countries a certificate of entitlement (E111) is necessary. A form to obtain this certificate is included in the DHSS leaflet. Applicants should allow at least one month for the form to be processed, although in an emergency the E111 can be obtained over the counter of the local DHSS office (residents of the Republic of Ireland should apply to their Regional Health Board for the E111). The DHSS will also supply on request a leaflet SA35 Notice to Travellers – Health Protection which gives advice on health precautions and guidance about international vaccination requirements. This may be obtained by writing to the DHSS at the address given below or telephoning ext 6711.

Further information about health care arrangements overseas is obtainable from the Department of Health and Social Security, Alexander Fleming House, Elephant and Castle, London SE1 6BY, tel 01-407 5522 ext 6641 (non-EEC countries), ext 6737 (EEC countries).

Minibus

If you plan to tour in EEC countries with a minibus equipped to carry 10 or more persons (including the driver) you should contact the local Traffic Area Office of the Department of Transport, or, if in Northern Ireland, The Department of the Environment for Northern Ireland, Vehicle Inspection and Driving Tests Headquarters, Balmoral Road, Belfast 12. In the Republic of Ireland information regarding EEC regulations may be obtained from Government Publications, Sales Office, Molesworth Street, Dublin 2 and details about the tachographs from the Department of Labour, Mespil Road, Dublin 4. Note When contacting any of the above authorities, do so well in advance of your departure.

Motoring Clubs in Europe

The Alliance Internationale de Tourisme (AIT) is the largest confederation of touring associations in the world and it is through this body that the AA is able to offer its members the widest possible touring information service. Its membership consists not of individuals, but of associations or groups of associations having an interest in touring. The Alliance was formed in 1919 – the AA was a founder member and is represented on its Administrative Council and Management Committee. The General Secretariat of the AIT is in Geneva.

Tourists visiting a country where there is an AIT club may avail themselves of its touring advisory services upon furnishing proof of membership of

their home AIT club. AA members making overseas trips should, whenever possible, seek the advice of the AA before setting out and should only approach the overseas AIT clubs when necessary.

Motorways (See also *Country sections*)

Most of the countries in this guide have motorways, varying from a few short stretches to a comprehensive system. Tolls are payable on many of them. Motorway leaflets (containing information on tolls etc) for France, Italy, Portugal and Spain are available to AA members. See also *Tolls* page 24.

Orange badge scheme for disabled drivers

Some European countries, operating national schemes of parking concessions for the disabled, have reciprocal arrangements whereby disabled visitors can enjoy the concessions of the host country by displaying the badge of their own scheme. Information, where available, is given in the appropriate *Country section*. However, it should be noted that in some countries responsibility for introducing the concessions rests with individual local authorities and in some cases they may not be generally available. Under these circumstances badge holders should enquire locally, as they should whenever they are in any doubt as to their entitlement. As in the UK the arrangements apply only to badge holders themselves and the concessions are not for the benefit of able-bodied friends or relatives. A non-entitled person who seeks to take advantage of the concessions in Europe by wrongfully dis-

playing an orange badge will be liable to whatever penalties apply for unlawful parking in the country in question.

Overloading

This can create safety risks, and in most countries committing such an offence can involve *on-the-spot* fines (see *Police fines* page 21). It would also be a great inconvenience if your car was stopped because of overloading – you would not be allowed to proceed until the load had been reduced. The maximum loaded weight, and its distribution between front and rear axles is decided by the vehicle manufacturer and if your owner's handbook does not give these facts you should seek the advice of the manufacturer direct. There is a public weighbridge in all districts and when the car is fully loaded (not forgetting the passengers, of course) use this to check that the vehicle is within the limits. When loading a vehicle, care should be taken that no lights, reflectors or number plates are masked and that the driver's view is in no way impaired. All luggage loaded on a roof-rack must be tightly secured and should not upset the stability of the vehicle. Any projections beyond the front, rear, or sides of a vehicle that might not be noticed by other drivers must be clearly marked.

Overtaking

When overtaking on roads with two lanes or more in each direction, always signal your intention in good time, and after the manoeuvre, signal and return to the inside lane. Do *not* remain in any other lane. Failure to comply with this regulation, particularly in France, will incur an *on-the-*

spot fine (see *Police fines* page 21).

Always overtake on the left and use your horn as a warning to the driver of the vehicle being overtaken (except in areas where the use of the horn is prohibited). Do not overtake whilst being overtaken or when a vehicle behind is preparing to overtake. Do not overtake at level crossings, at intersections, the crest of a hill or at pedestrian crossings. When being overtaken keep well to the right and reduce speed if necessary – never increase speed. See also *Luxembourg* page 271, *Portugal* page 307 and *Spain* page 321.

Parking (See also *Country sections*)

Parking is a problem everywhere in Europe and the police are extremely strict with offenders. Heavy fines are inflicted as well as the towing away of unaccompanied offending cars. This can cause inconvenience and heavy charges are imposed for the recovery of impounded vehicles. You should acquaint yourself with local parking regulations and endeavour to understand all relative signs. As a rule always park on the right-hand side of the road or at an authorised place. As far as possible park off the main carriageway but not on cycle tracks or tram tracks.

Passengers (See also *Country sections*)

It is an offence in all countries to carry more passengers in a car than the vehicle is constructed to seat, but some have regulations as to how the passengers shall be seated. Where such regulations are

applied to visiting foreigners it will be mentioned in the *Country Sections*.

For passenger-carrying vehicles constructed and equipped to carry more than 10 passengers including the driver there are special regulations. See *Minibus* page 18.

Passports

Each person must hold, or be named on, an up-to-date passport valid for all the countries through which it is intended to travel. Passports should be carried at all times and, as an extra precaution, a separate note kept of the number, date and place of issue. There are various types of British passports including the standard or regular passport and the limited British Visitor's Passport.

Standard UK passports are issued to United Kingdom Nationals, ie, British citizens, British Dependent Territories citizens, British Overseas citizens, British subjects, and British Protected Persons. Normally issued for a period of 10 years, a standard UK passport is valid for travel to all countries in the world. A family passport may cover husband, wife and children under 16, but only the first person named on the passport may use it to travel alone. Children under 16 may be issued with a separate passport valid for 5 years and renewable for a further 5 years on application. Full information and application forms in respect of the standard UK passport may be obtained from a main Post Office or from one of the Passport Offices in Belfast, Douglas (Isle of Man), Glasgow, Liverpool, London, Newport (Gwent), Peterborough, St Helier (Jersey) and St Peter

Port (Guernsey). Application for a standard passport should be made to the Passport Office appropriate for the area concerned, allowing at least four weeks for passport formalities to be completed, and should be accompanied by the requisite documents and fees.

British Visitor's Passports are issued to UK Nationals over the age of 8, resident in the UK, Isle of Man or Channel Islands. Valid for one year only and acceptable for travel in Western Europe and West Berlin but not for Yugoslavia, they cannot be used for a business trip or overland travel through the German Democratic Republic to West Berlin. A British Visitor's Passport issued to cover husband, wife and children under 16 may only be used by the first person named on the passport to travel alone. Children under 8 cannot have their own Visitor's Passport. Full information and application forms may be obtained from main Post Offices in Great Britain (England, Scotland and Wales) or Passport Offices in the Channel Islands, Isle of Man and Northern Ireland. However, Visitor's Passports or application forms for Visitor's Passports are NOT obtainable from Passport Offices in Great Britain. All applications for a Visitor's Passport must be submitted in person to a main Post Office or Passport Office as appropriate. Provided the documents are in order and the fee is paid the passport is issued immediately.

Irish citizens resident in the Dublin Metropolitan area or in Northern Ireland should apply to the Passport Office, Dublin; if resident elsewhere in the

Irish Republic they should apply through the nearest Garda station. Irish citizens resident in Britain should apply to the Irish Embassy in London.

Petrol (See also *Country sections*)

In Western Europe, and indeed throughout the world, grades of petrol compare favourably with those in the UK. Internationally-known brands are usually available on main tourist and international routes, but in remote districts familiar brands may not be readily available. The minimum amount of petrol which may be purchased is usually five litres (just over one gallon). It is advisable to keep the petrol tank topped up, particularly in remote areas or if wishing to make an early start when garages may be closed, but when doing this use a lockable filler cap as a security measure. Some garages may close between 12.00 and 15.00hrs for lunch. Generally petrol is readily available and in most of the countries featured in this guide you will find that petrol stations on motorways provide a 24hr service.

The international method of denoting the grade of petrol is by an octane number. In Britain this rating is related to a star method, 2-Star–90 octane; 3-Star–94 octane and 4-Star–97 octane.

In Britain the motorist uses a fuel recommended by the vehicle manufacturer and this is expressed by an octane number. Overseas he should use a grade in the recommended range. If a car requires a fuel in the high octane range (100 or higher) and he is visiting a country where he sus-

pects that this may not be available then it is possible that engine adjustments may have to be made for a satisfactory performance on a lower grade. If such adjustments are contemplated then the advice of the vehicle manufacturer or his agent must be sought. If a lower grade petrol than that recommended by the manufacturer is used then the speed of the car must be restricted and engine loads reduced.

Petrol prices at filling stations on motorways will be higher than elsewhere whilst at self-service pumps it will be slightly cheaper. Although petrol prices are not quoted, the current position can be checked with the AA. At the time of going to press petrol price concessions in the form of petrol coupons are available for Italy (see page 242) and compulsory for Yugoslavia (see page 392) – check with the AA to ascertain the latest position.

The petrol contained in a vehicle tank may be imported duty-free. In some countries an additional quantity may be imported duty-free in cans whilst others impose duty or forbid the carrying of petrol in cans in a vehicle, see *Country sections* for further information. If you intend carrying a reserve supply of petrol in a can remember that on sea and air ferries and European car-sleeper trains operators insist that spare cans must be empty.

Note A roof-rack laden with luggage increases petrol consumption, which should be taken into consideration when calculating the mileage per gallon.

Photography

Photography in European countries is generally allowed without restriction, with the exception of photographs taken within the vicinity of military or government establishments.

Signs are usually prominent where the use of cameras is prohibited. These are obvious – mostly a picture of a camera crossed by a diagonal line.

Police fines

Some countries impose *on-the-spot* fines for minor traffic offences which vary in amount according to the offence committed and the country concerned. Other countries *eg* France, impose an immediate deposit and subsequently levy a fine which may be greater or lesser than this sum, but which usually matches it. Fines are either paid in cash to the police or at a local post office against a *ticket* issued by the police. They must usually be paid in the currency of the country concerned, and can vary in amount from £3–£690 (approximate amounts). The reason for the fines is to penalise and at the same time keep minor motoring offences out of the courts. Disputing the fine usually leads to a court appearance and delays and additional expense.

If the fine is not paid then legal proceedings will usually follow. Some countries immobilise vehicles until a fine is paid and may sell it to pay the penalty imposed.

Once paid, a fine cannot be recovered, but a receipt should always be obtained as proof of payment. Should AA members require assistance in any motoring matter involving local police they should apply to the legal department of the

relevant national motoring organisation.

Pollution

Tourists should be aware that pollution of the sea water at European coastal resorts, particularly on the shores of the Mediterranean, represents a severe health hazard. Not many popular resorts wish to admit to this, but many now realise the dangers and erect signs, albeit small ones, forbidding bathing. These signs would read as follows:

	French
No bathing	*Défense de se baigner*
Bathing prohibited	*Il est défendu de se baigner*

	Italian
No bathing	*Vietato bagnàrsi*
Bathing prohibited	*È vietato bagnàrsi*

	Spanish
No bathing	*Prohibido bañarse*
Bathing prohibited	*Se prohíbe bañarse*

Postcheques (See also *Country sections*)

National Girobank current account holders who have a cheque guarantee card can use the National Girobank Postcheque service when travelling in all of the countries covered by this guide. The service enables account holders to cash Postcheques, up to the local currency equivalent of about £50, at most post offices. Further information may be obtained from International Division, National Girobank, Bridle Road, BOOTLE, Merseyside G1R 0AA.

Poste restante

If you are uncertain of having a precise address, you can be contacted through the local *poste restante*. Before leaving

the United Kingdom, notify your friends of your approximate whereabouts abroad at given times. If you expect mail, call with your passport at the main post office of the town where you are staying. To ensure that the arrival of correspondence will coincide with your stay, your correspondent should check with the Post Office before posting, as delivery times differ throughout Europe, and appropriate allowance must be made. It is most important that the recipient's name be written in full: *eg* Mr Lazarus Perkins, Poste Restante, Turnhout, Belgium. Do not use Esq.

Italy Correspondence can be addressed c/o post office by adding *Fermo in Posta* to the name of the locality. It will be handed over at the local central post office upon identification of the addressee by passport.

Spain Letters should be addressed as follows: name of addressee, *Liste de Correos*, name of town or village, name of province in brackets, if town or village, name of province in brackets, if necessary. Letters can be collected from the main post office in the town concerned upon identification of the addressee by passport.

For all other countries letters should be addressed as in the example.

Priority including Roundabouts (See also *Country sections*)

The general rule is to give way to traffic entering a junction from the right, but this is sometimes varied at roundabouts (see below). This is one aspect of European driving which may cause the British driver the most confusion because his whole training

and experience makes it unnatural. Road signs indicate priority or loss of priority and tourists are well advised to make sure that they understand such signs.

Great care should be taken at intersections and tourists should never rely on receiving the right of way, particularly in small towns and villages where local traffic, often slow-moving, such as farm tractors, etc, will assume right of way regardless of oncoming traffic. Always give way to public services and military vehicles. Blind or disabled people, funerals and marching columns must always be allowed right of way. Vehicles such as buses and coaches carrying large numbers of passengers will expect and should be allowed priority.

Generally priority at roundabouts is given to vehicles entering the roundabout unless signposted to the contrary (See *France* page 00). This is a complete reversal of the United Kingdom rule and particular care should be exercised when manoeuvring while circulating in an anticlockwise direction on a roundabout. It is advisable to keep to the outside lane on a roundabout, if possible, to make your exit easier.

Public holidays

Public holidays, on which banks, offices and shops are closed, vary from country to country, but generally fall into two categories; those which are fixed on the calendar by some national festival or religious date and those which are movable. The latter, usually religious, are based on a movable Easter Sunday, and the actual dates are given in the respective *Country sec-*

tions. For information about annual holidays and festivals contact the appropriate Tourist Office, see *Country section* for address.

Radio telephones/Citizens' band radios and transmitters in tourist cars abroad

Many countries exercise controls on the temporary importation and subsequent use of radio transmitters and radio telephones. Therefore if your vehicle contains such equipment, whether fitted or portable, you should approach the AA for guidance.

Rear view mirror

If your vehicle is not equipped with a rear view mirror on the left external side it is recommended that you fit one before travelling abroad. However, if it is your intention to visit Italy see page 242.

Registration document

You must carry the vehicle registration document with you. If the vehicle is not registered in your name, you should have a letter from the owner (for Yugoslavia this must be countersigned by a motoring organisation; for Portugal a special certificate is required, available *free* from the AA) authorising you to use it.

If you are using a UK registered hired or leased vehicle for touring overseas the registration document will not be available and a Hire Car Registration Certificate (VE103), which may be purchased from the AA, should be used in its place.

If for any reason your registration document has to be sent to the licensing authorities you should bear in mind that,

as processing can take some time, the document may not be available in time for your departure. Under these circumstances a certificate of registration (V379) will normally be issued and can be obtained free of charge from your nearest Local Vehicle Licensing Office to cover the vehicle for international circulation purposes.

Religious services

Refer to your religious organisations in the British Isles. A directory of British Protestant churches in Europe, North Africa and the Middle East entitled *English Speaking Churches*, can be purchased from Intercon (Intercontinental Church Society), 175 Tower Bridge Road, London SE1 2AQ *tel* 01-407 4588. See also the Belgian, French, Dutch, Spanish and Swiss *Country sections* for details of English-speaking church services in those countries.

Report forms

We would appreciate your comments on accommodation, garages and roads to help us to prepare future publications. Please list your comments on the report forms provided at the back of the guide. The accommodation report form is for your comments on hotels and motels which you have visited, whether they are listed in the guide or not.

Similarly, the garage report form can be used for your reports on garages which you have visited. The road report form can be used for particularly bad stretches and road works.

Road conditions

Main roads are usually in good condition but often not finished to our standards. The camber is often steeper than that usually found in the United Kingdom and edges may be badly corrugated and surfaces allowed to wear beyond the customary limits before being repaired. In France such stretches are sometimes signposted *Chaussée déformée*. However, there are extensive motorway systems in France, Germany and Italy, and many miles of such roads in other countries. When roads under repair are closed, you must follow diversion signs – often inadequate – such as *déviation* (French) and *Umleitung* (German). To avoid damage to windscreens or paintwork, drive slowly over loose grit and take care when overtaking.

The months of July and August are the peak of the touring season particularly in Austria, Belgium, France and Germany when the school holidays start, and during this period motorways and main roads are heavily congested. Throughout the summer there is a general exodus from the cities, particularly at weekends when tourists should be prepared for congested roads and consequent hold-ups. See also *Roads* and *Motorways* in *Country sections*.

Road Signs

Most road signs through Europe are internationally agreed and the majority would be familiar to the British motorist. Watch also for road markings – do not cross a solid white or yellow line marked on the road centre. In *Belgium* there are two official languages and signs will be in Flemish or French, see *Roads*,

page 83 for further information. In the Basque and Catalonian areas of *Spain* local and national place-names appear on signposts, see *Road signs* (page 322) for further information. For *Germany, Greece, Netherlands* and *Yugoslavia* see also *Country sections*.

Rule of the road

In all European countries, drive on the right and overtake on the left.

Seat belts

All countries in this guide (except *Italy* where they are strongly *recommended*) require visitors to wear seat belts. If your car is fitted with belts, then in the interest of safety, wear them, otherwise you may run the risk of a police fine.

Signals

Signals of a driver's intentions must be given clearly, within a reasonable distance, and in good time. In built-up areas, the general rule is not to use horns unless safety demands it; in many large towns and resorts, as well as in areas indicated by the international sign, the use of the horn is totally prohibited.

Spares

The problem of what spares to carry is a difficult one; it depends on the vehicle and how long you are likely to be away. However, you should consider hiring an AA Spares Kit for your car; full information about this service is available from any AA Centre. AA Emergency Windscreens are also available for hire. In addition to the items contained in the

spares kit, the following would also prove useful:

A pair of windscreen wiper blades;
a torch;
a length of electrical cable;
a fire extinguisher;
an inner tube of the correct type;
a tow rope;
a roll of insulating or adhesive tape

Remember that when ordering spare parts for dispatch abroad you just be able to identify them as clearly as possible and by the manufacturer's part numbers if known. When ordering spares, always quote the engine and chassis numbers of your car. See also *Lights*, page 17.

Speed limits (See also *Country sections*)

It is important to observe speed limits at all times. Offenders may be fined and driving licences confiscated on the spot, thus causing great inconvenience and possible expense. The limits may be varied by road signs and where such signs are displayed the lower limit should be accepted. At certain times limits may also be temporarily varied and information should be available at the frontier. It can be an offence to travel at so slow a speed as to obstruct traffic flow without good reason.

Tolls

Tolls are charged on most motorways in France, Italy, Portugal, Spain and on sections in Austria, Greece and Yugoslavia. Over long distances the toll charges can be quite considerable. It is advisable to weight the cost against time and convenience

(eg overnight stops), particularly as some of the all-purpose roads are often fast. Always have some currency of the country in which you are travelling ready to pay the tolls, as travellers' cheques etc, are not acceptable at toll booths. *Note* All toll charges quoted in this publication should be used as a guide only as they are subject to change.

Tourist information offices
(See also *Country sections*)

National tourist offices are especially equipped to deal with enquiries relating to their countries. They are particularly useful for information on current events, tourist attractions, car hire, equipment hire and information on specific activities such as skin-diving, gliding, horse-riding etc.

The offices in London are most helpful but the local offices overseas merit a visit because they have information not available elsewhere and tourists are advised to visit the office when they arrive at their destination. Hotels etc, will be able to supply the address.

Traffic lights

In principal cities and towns traffic lights operate in a way similar to those in the United Kingdom, although they are sometimes suspended overhead. The density of the light may be so poor that lights could be missed. There is usually only one set on the right-hand side of the road some distance before the road junction, and if you stop too close to the corner the lights will not be visible. Watch out for 'filter' lights which will enable you to turn right at a junction against the main

lights. If you wish to go straight ahead do not enter a lane leading to 'filter' lights otherwise you may obstruct traffic wishing to turn right. See also the *Country sections* for *Austria, Belgium, France, Germany* and *Spain*.

Trams

Trams take priority over other vehicles. Always give way to passengers boarding and alighting. Never position a vehicle so that it impedes the free passage of a tram. Trams must be overtaken on the right except in one-way streets. See also *Country sections* for *Norway* and *Sweden*.

Travellers cheques

We recommend that you carry travellers cheques, offering a high degree of security. Barclay's Visa Travellers Cheques can be used as cash or exchanged for currency in just about any country in the world. In the event of loss a reverse-charge telephone call will put you in touch with Visa's worldwide instant refund service. Call in to any AA Travel Agency for these Barclay's Visa Travellers Cheques. With cash payment, these can be purchased on demand

Tyres

Inspect your tyres carefully; if you think they are likely to be more than three-quarters worn before you get back, it is better to replace them before you start out. Expert advice should be sought if you notice uneven wear, scuffed treads or damaged walls, on whether the tyres are suitable for further use. In some European countries, drivers can be fined if tyres are badly worn. The regulations in the UK governing tyres call for a minimum

FERRY DIRECT.

FERRY STYLISH

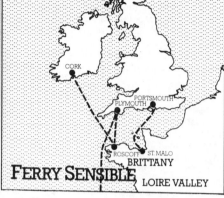

CORK

PORTSMOUTH
PLYMOUTH

ROSCOFF   ST MALO
BRITTANY

FERRY SENSIBLE
LOIRE VALLEY

Our spacious modern, fully-stabilized ships;
the relaxing way to Brittany,
Spain and Portugal.

Only Brittany Ferries sail <u>direct</u> to.Brittany,
landing you often hundreds of miles
nearer your destination.

FERRY BEAUTIFUL

DORDOGNE

AQUITAINE

SANTANDER

PORTUGAL

SPAIN

FERRY COST-SAVING

We bring all the holiday areas of The West
of France within easy reach. And we've an
unbeatable range of value-for-money Inclusive
Car Holidays and Short Breaks to France,
Spain and Portugal.

From Brittany itself, to The Loire Valley,
The Dordogne, Aquitaine and beyond.
Or direct to Spain in just 24 hours,
saving the costly 1,000 mile drive
through France.

Brittany Ferries
The Holiday Ferry

Millbay Docks, Plymouth PL1 3EW. Telephone: (0752) 21321.
The Brittany Centre, Wharf Road, Portsmouth PO2 8RU. Telephone: (0705) 827701.
Tourist House, 42 Grand Parade, Cork. Telephone: (021) 507666.

tread depth of 1mm over 75% of the width of the tyre all around the circumference, with the original tread pattern clearly visible on the remainder. European regulations are tougher, a minimum tread depth of 1mm or 1.6mm over the whole width of the tyre around the circumference.

When checking tyre pressures, remember that if the car is heavily loaded the recommended pressures may have to be raised; this may also be required for high-speed driving. Check the recommendations in your handbook but remember pressures can only be checked accurately when the tyres are cold and don't forget the spare tyre.

Using the telephone abroad

(See also *Country sections*)

It is no more difficult to use the telephone abroad than it is at home, it only appears to be so because of unfamiliarity with the language and equipment. In most Continental countries the ringing tone consists of a single tone of about $1-1\frac{1}{2}$ seconds repeated at intervals of between 3 and 10 seconds (depending upon the country). The engaged tone is similar to UK or faster. The information in the *Country sections* will be helpful with elementary principles when making calls from public callboxes, but try to get assistance in case you encounter language difficulties.

International Direct Dial (IDD) calls can be made from many public callboxes abroad thus avoiding the addition of surcharges imposed by most hotels. Types of callboxes from which IDD calls can be made are identified in the *Country sections*. You will need to dial the international code, international country code (for the UK it is 44), the STD code (omitting the initial '0'), followed by the number. For example to call the AA Basingstoke (STD 0256) 20123 from Italy, dial 00 44 256 20123. Use higher-denomination coins for IDD calls to ensure reasonably lengthy periods of conversation before coin-expiry warning. The equivalent of £1 should allow a reasonable period of uninterrupted conversation.

Valuables

Tourists should pay particular attention to the security of their money and items of value while touring. Whenever possible, any excess cash and travellers cheques should be left with the hotel management **against a receipt**. In some areas, children and youths cause a diversion to attract tourists' attention while pickpockets operate in organised gangs. Unusual incidents, which are more likely to occur in crowded markets or shopping centres, should be avoided.

It cannot be stressed too strongly that all valuables should be removed from a parked car even if it is parked in a supervised car park or lock-up garage.

Visas

A visa is not normally required by United Kingdom and Republic of Ireland passport holders, when visiting Western European countries for periods of three months or less. However if you hold a passport of any other nationality, a UK passport not issued in this country, or are in any doubt at all about your position, check with the embassies or consulates of the countries you intend to visit.

Visitors' registration

All visitors to a country must register with local police which is a formality usually satisfied by the completion of a card or certificate when booking into an hotel, camp site or place offering accommodation. If staying with friends or relations then it is usually the responsibility of the host to seek advice from the police within 24 hours of the arrival of his guests.

For short holiday visits the formalities are very simple but most countries place a time limit on the period that tourists may stay, after which a firmer type of registration is imposed.

Therefore, if you intend staying in any one country for longer than three months, you should make the appropriate enquiries before departure from the UK.

Warm-climate touring

In hot weather and at high altitudes, excessive heat in the engine compartment can cause carburation problems. It is advisable, if you are towing a caravan, to consult the manufacturers about the limitations of the cooling system, and the operating temperature of the gearbox fluid if automatic transmission is fitted. See also *Automatic gearboxes* page 7.

Warning triangles/Hazard warning lights (See also *Country sections*)

Warning triangles are not required for two-wheeled vehicles. The triangle should be placed on the road behind a stopped vehicle to warn traffic approaching from the rear of an obstruction ahead. Warning triangles should be used when a vehicle has stopped

for any reason – not only breakdowns. The triangle should be placed in such a position as to be clearly visible up to 100m (109yds) by day and by night, about 2ft from the edge of the road but not in such a position as to present a danger to on-coming traffic. It should be set about 30m (33yds) behind the obstruction but this distance should be increased up to 100m (109yds) on motorways. An AA Warning Triangle, which complies with the latest international and European standards, can be hired from the AA or bought in AA Travel Agencies, AA Centres or by mail order.

Although four flashing indicators are allowed in the countries covered by this guide, they in no way affect the regulations governing the use of warning triangles. Generally hazard warning lights should not be used in place of a triangle although they may complement it in use, but see *France* page 105 and *Switzerland* page 363.

Weather information including Winter conditions

Members of the public may telephone or call at one of the Meteorological Office Weather Centres listed below for information about local, national and continental weather forecasts. The centres **do not** provide information about road conditions:

Cardiff
Southgate House, Wood Street, tel (0222) 397020

Glasgow
118 Waterloo Street, tel 041-248 3451
London
284–286 High Holborn, tel 01-836 4311
Manchester
56 Royal Exchange, tel 061-832 6701
Newcastle upon Tyne
7th Floor, Newgate House, Newgate Street, tel (0632) 326453
Nottingham
Main Road, Watnall, tel (0602) 384092
Southampton
160 High Street, Below Bar, tel (0703) 28844

If you require forecasted weather information as a guide when planning your holidays, you should contact the national tourist offices of the countries concerned (see *Country sections*). When you are abroad, you should contact the nearest office of the appropriate national motoring club. It is advisable to check on conditions ahead as you go along and hotels and garages are often helpful in this respect.

Winter conditions Motoring in Europe during the winter months is restricted because of the vast mountain ranges – the Alps sweeping in an arc from the French Riviera, through Switzerland, Northern Italy and Austria to the borders of Yugoslavia, the Pyrenees which divide France and Spain – as well as extensive areas of Spain, France and Germany which are at an altitude of well over 1,000ft. However matters have been eased with improved com-

munications and modern snow clearing apparatus.

Reports on the accessibility of mountain passes in Austria, France, Italy and Switzerland are received by the AA from the European Road Information Centre in Geneva. Additionally during the winter months and also under certain weather conditions, the AA Port Agents in Belgium and France collect information regarding the state of approach roads to the continental Channel ports. To obtain information ring the AA Overseas Routes Unit at Basingstoke during office hours, tel (0256) 20123, or the AA London Operations Centre (24-hr service), tel 01-954 7373 or enquire at the AA Port Service Centre before embarking.

Details of road and rail tunnels which can be used to pass under the mountains are given on pages 38–40 and the periods when the most important mountain passes are usually closed are given on pages 41–49. If you want a conventional seaside holiday between October and March, you will probably ·have to travel at least as far south as Lisbon, Valencia, or Naples to be reasonably certain of fine weather. See also *Country sections* for *Austria, Belgium, France, Germany, Italy, Norway, Spain, Sweden* and *Switzerland*. Further information on this subject is given in the leaflet entitled *Motoring in Winter and Continental Weather* which is available from the AA.

When you've seen something to write home abou
have to do is pick up a pay-phone and dial. It does

British
TELECOM
International

Route planning

The AA European Route Planning Service consists of a series of route planning maps, route books and town plans for which a charge is made. The Country Map, Town Plan and Route Book series are complementary to each other (see map below) and can be supplied as a complete pack or separately. They may be obtained by **completing the application form on pages 31-32** and sending it, with the appropriate remittance, to the address given.

A Throughroute Maps: (scale approximately 33 miles to 1 inch)
A series of six maps each based on a different main European cross-Channel port. These maps are not ordinary road maps but are specially designed to give guidance on straightforward journeys by indicating the easiest and quickest AA-recommended route plus the mileage from each port to a large number of nations in Western Europe.

B European Tour Planning Map: (scale approximately 33 miles to 1 inch)
Suitable for general planning purposes, this map covers Western Europe excluding Scandinavia. It shows motorways, main roads, distances and road numbers and includes an index of placenames.

C Country Maps: (scale approximately 16 miles to 1 inch unless otherwise stated)
A series of motorists' maps covering France (No 1), Spain and Portugal (No 2), Benelux and Germany (No 3), Switzerland, Austria and Italy (No 4), South East Europe (scale 20 miles to 1 inch) covering Yugoslavia, Greece, Hungary, Romania and Bulgaria (No 5) and Scandinavia (No 6) covering Denmark, Finland, Norway and Sweden (scale approximately 24 miles to 1 inch). They show classification of roads, road numbers, distance in kilometres, mountain pass information, toll roads, bridges and tunnels, ferries, airports, scenic roads etc.

Remember, if you want a marked map, our experts will indicate a route for you on either B or C.

D Town plans
Six books of town plans are availa-

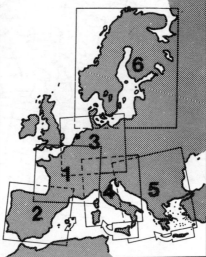

ble, drawn by the AA to help you get into, out of, or around the larger towns in Europe with the minimum fuss and bother. So often the problem-related areas of your journey centre on the towns and cities across your route. It is here that you can find those places of interest that makes your journey an experience. It is here that your accommodation needs to be found. Even if you simply wish to avoid the congested centre the clear easy-to-read two colour AA Plans of the larger towns and cities in Europe are invaluable. They make finding your way so easy. One-way systems, public buildings, places of interest, information offices, and those vital throughroutes you need are all shown clearly. Save time, petrol and money.

Paris—the AA map of Paris is now produced in full colour for increased clarity. The ring road signs of the central plan benefit particularly from the introduction of colour and simlify the task of driving around Paris.

E Route Books
These remarkable fact-filled books of routes can make so much difference to your holiday abroad and make your journey more interesting. Each book features several hundred full itineraries for all main routes and a large proportion of other routes. Each itinerary usually starts and ends at a town prominently situated at the junction of several roads and provides details of towns, villages, landmarks, and other road junctions on route, and the road numbers and mileages between. The descriptive heading of each itinerary describes the topography of the road and the scenery passed through. It mentions hills particularly those with gradients of more than 10%. Comparative notes help you to choose between the alternative routes that are frequently given. Finally the Gazetteer describes hundreds of places of special interest along the route.

Application for route planning service

The publications available are described on the previous page. A suggested route can be marked on the Country maps, European Tour Planning maps or on the key map to the route books. For this service, please complete section **(F)** overleaf. Please state also if your vehicle is other than a private car. When you have completed the application form please send with your remittance, which should be by crossed cheque or postal order payable to *The Automobile Association*, to: **The Automobile Association, Fanum House, Basingstoke, Hants RG21 2EA** at least **21 days** before your departure date.

Please complete in BLOCK CAPITALS
Mr/Mrs/Miss Initials: Surname:
Address to which publications should be sent:

County/Postcode:

Date of application:	Telephone numbers: Home: Business:
Membership number: (If you are not a Member of the AA a fee of £2.00 is payable)	Continental port of landing:

A) European Throughroute Maps – each map extends as far north as Copenhagen, eastwards as far as Berlin, Prague, Budapest, Bucharest, Athens and Istanbul and southwards as far as Gibraltar and Sicily. Specially suitable for journeys using direct routes from the ports listed, using motorways where applicable.

Routes from other ports can be marked on the Country or European Tour planning maps. Please complete Section **(F)** overleaf.

Please tick box(es) of map(s) required	Sale price	Total price
		£ p
☐ **Boulogne**		
☐ **Calais/Dunkerque**		
☐ **Cherbourg**	80p	
☐ **Dieppe**	each	
☐ **Le Havre**		
☐ **Ostende/Zeebrugge**		
B) European Tour Planning Map – covers same areas as the Throughroute maps described above. ☐	80p each	

continued overleaf

31

	Please tick box(es) required	Sale price	Total price
C) Country Route Planning Maps			£ p
Map 1 France			
Map 2 Spain & Portugal			
Map 3 Belgium, Netherlands, Luxembourg & Germany		80p each	
Map 4 Switzerland, Austria & Italy			
Map 5 S E Europe			
Map 6 Scandinavia			
D) Town Plans **Paris**		40p each	
Book 1 France			
Book 2 Spain & Portugal			
Book 3 Belgium, Netherlands, Luxembourg & Germany		80p each	
Book 4 Switzerland, Austria & Italy			
Book 5 S E Europe			
Book 6 Scandinavia			
E) Route Books			
Book 1 France			
Book 2 Spain & Portugal			
Book 3 Belgium, Netherlands, Luxembourg & Germany		£1.60p each	
Book 4 Switzerland, Austria & Italy			
Book 5 S E Europe			
Book 6 Scandinavia			
Total			:
Add for postage & packing			: 50
Non-members requiring route service please add £2.00 service fee			:
Total remittance enclosed			:

F) If you require us to suggest a route and indicate it on the map(s), please list the placenames (in BLOCK CAPITALS) in the order in which they will be visited. If you require route information for countries other than those listed above, please give details here.

Date of departure	Please tick (✔) this box if a caravan is being towed	VAT Reg. No. 198 962 9 79
	☐ TGE	For office use only: A/C No. 7710/768/40

FEAST ACROSS THE CHANNEL. FAST TO THE SUN.

Cross the Channel with the Sally Line from Ramsgate and you can really make a meal of it.

Even though it's usually the cheapest way to cross the Channel to France at peak time, the Sally Line doesn't lower its standards to keep fares down.

Take your seat in our luxurious restaurant and you'll see exactly what we mean. Because on the Sally ferry you don't have to splash out to enjoy our delicious smorgasbord buffet.

In plain English that's a vast selection of hot and cold meats, fish, cheese and desserts.

Help yourself to as much as you can carry, as many times as you like, for a very reasonable price. And half price for children.

If you've time after your meal, a stroll round our enormous duty-free supermarket will help your digestion, with prices which are very easy to swallow.

Then before you can say 'smorgasbord' you'll be docking in Dunkirk. Which is closer to the continental motorway network than any other Channel port.

So after loosening your belt in the restaurant, fasten your safety belt for the quickest, easiest drive to the sun.

Pick up a Sally brochure from your Travel Agent, or phone 01-858 1127 or Thanet (0843) 595522.

SALLY LINE LIMITED, 54 HARBOUR PARADE, RAMSGATE, KENT CT11 8LN.

Customs offices

Many Customs offices at the main frontier crossings are open 24 hours daily to deal with touring documents.

Major offices with restricted opening times are listed below. During these hours the Customs handle normal tourist entry into their country. However, persons with dutiable items to declare or other business to transact should cross the frontier during normal business hours only. For additional information see also **Customs regulations for European countries** page 11.

The table can be read in either direction eg for France–Belgium read from left to right, for Belgium–France read from right to left.

Nearest town	Road No.	Frontier post	Opening times		Frontier post	Road No.	Nearest town
France					**Belgium**		
Dunkirk	D916A	Oost-Cappel	06.00-22.00		Kapelhoek (Stavele)	N9	**Ypres (Ieper)**
Lille	D941	Baisieux	08.00-12.00 14.00-18.00 Mon-Fri	08.20-21.00	Hertain	N8	**Tournai**
Valenciennes	D169	Maulde	06.00-22.00		Bléharies	N71	**Tournai**
Maubeuge	D936	Cousoire	09.00-21.00		Leugnies	N36	**Beaumont**
Avesnes	D962	Hestrud	07.00-22.00	07.00-22.00 Mon-Fri 08.00-21.00 Sat-Sun	Grandrieu	N21	**Beaumont**
Givet	D949	Givet	08.00-21.00		Petit Doische	N46	**Philippeville**
Givet	D949	Givet	08.00-21.00		Dion	N46	**Beauraing**
France					**Germany**		
Metz	D954	Villing	06.00-22.00 (1 Oct-31 Mar)	00.00-24.00	Ittersdorf Villinger Strasse	269	**Saarlouis**
France					**Spain**		
Bayonne	D20	Ainhoa	1May-30Sep 1Oct-30Apr	07.00-24.00 07.00-22.00	Dancharinea	N121	**Pamplona**
St-Jean-Pied-de-Port	D933	Arnéguy	as above		Valcarios	C135	**Pamplona**
Oloron-Ste-Marie	N134	Urdos		16-Jun-30Sep Always 1Oct-15Jun 08.00-21.00	Canfranc	N330	**Jaca**
Pau	D934	Eaux-Chaudes	1Jun-31Oct 1Nov-31May	07.00-24.00 08.00-21.00	Sallent-de Gállego	C136	**Huesca**
Bagnères de Luchon	D618	Bagnères de Luchon	08.00-22.00		Bosost-El Portillón	C141	**Viella**
Montréjeau	N125	Fos	As above	1May-30Sep Always 31Oct-30Apr 08.00-24.00	Lés	N230	**Viella**
Amélie-les Bains	D115	Prats-de-Mollo	1Jun-30Sep Always 1Oct-31May 08.00-16.30		Camprodón	C151	**Ripoll**
Belgium					**Netherlands**		
Maldegem	N310	Strooibrug	07.00-21.00	1Apr-30Sep 07.00-24.00 1Oct-31Mar 07.00-21.00	Eede	Unclass	**Breskens**

Nearest town	Road No.	Frontier post	Opening times		Frontier post	Road No.	Nearest town
Gent	N56	Watervliet	07.00-19.00	as above	Veldzicht	Unclass	Breskens
Turnhout	N20	Weelde	06.00-24.00	07.00-24.00	Baarle-	Unclass	Breda
			Mon-Fri		Nassau		
			07.00-17.00				
			Sat				
			09.00-17.00				
			Sun				

Netherlands / Germany

Nearest town	Road No.	Frontier post	Opening times	Frontier post	Road No.	Nearest town
Emmen	Unclass	Coevorden	06.00-24.00	Eschebrügge	403	Nordhorn
Zutphen	Unclass	's-Heeren-berg	06.00-22.00 (08.00-22.00 Sundays)	Heerenber-gerbrücke	220	Emmerich
Venlo	Unclass	Herungerweg	06.00-22.00	Niderdorf	60	Moere

Italy / Switzerland

Nearest town	Road No.	Frontier post	Opening times		Frontier post	Road No.	Nearest town
Domodóssola	SS337	Ponte Ribellasca	05.00-24.00		Cámedo	69	Locarno
Luino	SS394	Zenna	06.00-24.00 Mon-Fri 06.00-13.00 Sat-Sun	05.00-24.00 Mon-Fri 06.00-24.00 Sat-Sun	Dirinella	Unclass	Locarno
Luino	Unclass	Formasette	06.00-23.00	1May-30Sept 06.00-01.00 1Oct-30Apr 06.00-23.00	Fornasette	Unclass	Lugano
Chiavenna	SS36	Montespluga	08.00-20.00	1Jun-30Jun 06.00-22.00 1Jul-30Sept 05.00-24.00 1Oct-Autumn 06.00-22.00	Splügen Pass	64	Thusis
Tirano	SS38A	Piattamala	8Jan-22Dec 05.00-00.30 23Dec-7Jan 05.00-22.00		Campo-cologno	29 via Bernina Pass	Pontresina
Bórmio	SS38	Giogo di Santa Maria (Stelvio)	05.00-24.00	1June-30June 06.00-20.00 1Jul-30Sept 06.00-22.00 1Oct-Autumn 06.00-20.00 (closed during winter)	Umbrail Pass	66	Santa Maria
Giorenza	SS41	Tubre	08.00-20.00	1May-31Oct 04.00-24.00 Mon-Fri 00.00-24.00 Sat-Sun 1Nov-30Apr 05.00-24.00	Müstair	28	Santa Maria

Switzerland / Austria

Nearest town	Road No.	Frontier post	Opening times	Frontier post	Road No.	Nearest town
Zernez	27	Martina	05.00-24.00	Nauders (Zollhaus)	185	Nauders

Italy / Austria

Nearest town	Road No.	Frontier post	Opening times	Frontier post	Road No.	Nearest town
Merano	SS44b	Passo del Rombo	07.00-20.00 (when pass is open)	Timmelsjoch	186	Sölden

Portugal / Spain

Nearest town	Road No.	Frontier post	Opening times	Frontier post	Road No.	Nearest town
Porto	N13	Valença do Minho	00.00-24.00	1Apr-31Oct 07.00-01.00 1Nov-31Mar 08.00-24.00	Tuy	N550	Vigo

Nearest town	Road No.	Frontier post	Opening times		Frontier post	Road No.	Nearest town
Villa Real	N103-5	Vila Verde da Raia	4Jan-11Apr 26Apr-30Jun 1Oct-17Dec 07.00-24.00 Otherwise 24hr	May-Oct 07.00-24.00 Nov-Apr 08.00-21.00	Feces de Abajo	C532	**Orense**
Bragança	N218-1	Quintanilha	1Mar-31Oct 07.00-24.00 1Nov-28Feb 07.00-21.00	Apr-Oct 07.00-24.00 Nov-Mar 08.00-21.00	San Martin del Pedroso/ Alcañices	N122	**Zamora**
Guarda	N16	Vilar Formoso	00.00-24.00	Apr-Oct 07.00-01.00 Nov-Mar 08.00-24.00	Fuentes de Oñoro	N620	**Salamanca**
Castelo Branco	N355	Segura	1Mar-31Oct 07.00-24.00 1Nov-28Feb 07.00-24.00	1May-1Oct 07.00-24.00 2Oct-30Apr 09.00-21.00	Piedras Albas	C523	**Cáceres**
Portalegre	N246-1	Galegos Marvão	1Mar-31Oct 07.00-24.00 1Nov-28Feb 07.00-21.00	1Apr-31Oct 07.00-24.00 1Nov-31Mar 08.00-21.00	Valencia de Alcàntara	N251	**Cáceres**
Elvas	N4	Caia	00.00-24.00	Apr-Oct 07.00-01.00 Nov-Mar 08.00-24.00	Caya	NV	**Mérida**
Mouráo	N256	São Leonardo	1Mar-31Oct 07.00-24.00 1Nov-28Feb 07.00-24.00	1Apr-31Oct 07.00-24.00 1Nov-31Mar 08.30-21.00	Villanueva del Fresno	C436	**Zafra**
Beja	N260	Vila Verde de Ficalho	1Mar-31Oct 07.00-24.00 1Nov-28Feb 07.00-24.00	1Apr-30Sep 07.00-24.00 1Oct-31Mar 08.00-21.00	Rosal de la Frontera	N433	**Seville**
Faro	N125	Vila Real de Santo António	1May-31Oct 08.00-23.00 1Nov-30Apr 08.00-20.00	1May-31Oct 08.00-24.00 1Nov-30Apr 09.00-21.00	Ayamonte	N431	**Huelva**

Denmark

Åbenrå	Unclass	Padborg	06.00-24.00	

Germany

Harrislee	Unclass	**Flensburg**	

Sweden*

Hällavadsholm	165	Vassbotten	09.00-16.00 Mon-Fri 09.00-13.00 Sat
Torsby	Unclass	Vittjärn	07.00-21.00 Mon-Fri 09.00-16.00 Sat
Sälen	Unclass	Grundforsen	07.00-21.00
Idre	295	Flötningen	08.00-18.00 Mon-Sat
Östersund	32	Ådalsvollen	09.00-16.00
Gäddede	342	Gäddede	07.00-21.00
Tärnaby	E79	Strimasund	07.00-21.00
Arjeplog	375	Merknes	08.00-21.00 Mon-Fri 08.00-15.00 Sat

Norway*

Vassbotten	22	**Halden**
Vittjärn	204	**Kongsvinger**
Støa	25	**Elverum**
Flötningen	218	**Drevsjo**
Ådalsvollen	72	**Levanger**
Gäddede	74	**Grong**
Umbukta	E79	**Mo-I-Rana**
Junkerdal	77	**Storjord**

*Note All Customs offices on the Swedish/Norwegian frontier may be passed at any time of the day, regardless of whether they are open or not, on condition that the visitor has no goods to declare.

Journey times

As there are several aspects of a journey to consider it will be difficult accurately to estimate how long a journey will take. Customs clearance, traffic and weather conditions, the time of day, the negotiating of mountain passes and other factors will affect calculations. However, an approximate travelling time can be arrived at by considering the kilometre distance as minutes: ie 60 Km (37½ miles) takes about 60 minutes. Thus to travel 300 Km will take about 300 minutes or 5 hours. Allowance will, of course, have to be made in the light of your experience when travelling along motorways (where an average speed of 55 mph is possible) and secondary roads.

The table below is a guide to journey times at average speeds expressed in kilometres.

Distance in kilometres	Average speed in mph									
	30		40		50		60		70	
	hrs	mins	hrs	mins	hrs	mins	hrs	mins	hrs	mins
20		25		19		15		13		11
30		37		28		22		19		16
40		50		37		30		25		21
50	1	2		47		37		31		27
60	1	15		56		45		38		32
70	1	25	1	5		52		43		36
80	1	39	1	15	1	0		50		42
90	1	52	1	24	1	7		56		48
100	2	4	1	33	1	15	1	2		53
150	3	6	2	20	1	52	1	33	1	20
200	4	8	3	6	2	30	2	4	1	46
250	5	10	3	53	3	7	2	35	2	13
300	6	12	4	40	3	44	3	6	2	40
350	7	14	5	27	4	21	3	37	3	7
400	8	16	6	12	5	0	4	8	3	32
450	9	18	6	59	5	37	4	39	3	59
500	10	20	7	46	6	14	5	10	4	26

Major road tunnels

See *Lights* page 17. There are also minimum and maximum speed limits in operation in the tunnels. All charges listed below should be used as a guide only

Pyrénées France–Spain
The trans-Pyrenean tunnel is 3km (2 miles) long, and runs nearly 6,000ft above sea level between Aragnouet and Bielsa. The tunnel is usually closed from October to Easter.

Fréjus France–Italy
This tunnel (opened July 1980) is over 4,000ft above sea level; it runs between Modane and Bardonecchia. The tunnel is 12.8km (8 miles) long, 4.5m (14ft 9in) high, and the two-lane carriageway is 9m (29ft 6in) wide. Toll charges as Mont Blanc Tunnel (see below).

Mont Blanc Chamonix (France)–Courmayeur (Italy)
The tunnel is over 4,000ft above sea level. It is 11.6km (7 miles) long. Customs and passport control are at the Italian end. The permitted maximum dimensions of vehicles are: height 4.15m (13ft 7in); length 18m (59ft); width 2.5m (8ft 2in). Total weight 35 metric tons (34 tons 9cwt); axle weight 13 metric tons (12tons 16cwt). The minimum speed is 50kph (31mph) and the maximum 80kph (49mph). Do not stop or overtake. There are breakdown bays with telephones. From November to March wheel chains may occasionally be required on the approaches to the tunnel.

Charges (in *French francs*)
The tolls are calculated on the wheelbase.

cars	wheelbase up to 2.30m (7ft 6½in)	50
	wheelbase from 2.30m to 2.63m (7ft 6½in to 8ft 7½in)	80
	wheelbase from 2.64m to 3.30m (8ft 7½in to 10ft 10in) and cars with caravans	105
	wheelbase over 3.30m (10ft 10in)	270
vehicles	with three axles	400
	with four, or more axles	535

Grand St Bernard Switzerland–Italy
The tunnel is over 6,000ft above sea level; although there are covered approaches, wheel chains may be needed to reach it in winter. The Customs, passport control, and toll offices are at the entrance. The tunnel is 5.9km (3½ miles) long. The permitted maximum dimensions of vehicles are: height 4m (13ft 1in), width 2.5m (8ft 2½in). The minimum speed is 40kph (24mph) and the maximum 80kph (49mph). Do not stop or overtake. There are breakdown bays with telephones on either side.

Charges (in *Swiss francs*)
The toll charges are calculated according to the wheelbase.

motorcycles		5
cars	wheelbase up to 2.08m (6ft 10in)	15
	wheelbase from 2.08m to 3.20m (6ft 10in to 10ft 6in)	22.50
	wheelbase over 3.20m	
	(10ft 6in)	34
	with caravan	34
minibuses		34
coaches		62–103

St Gotthard Switzerland
The world's longest road tunnel opened in September 1980. The tunnel is about 3,800ft above sea level; it runs under the St Gotthard Pass from Goschenen, on the northern side of the Alps, to Airolo in the Ticino. The tunnel is 16.3km (10 miles) long, 4.5m (14ft 9in) high, and the two-lane carriageway is 7.5m (25ft) wide. Forming part of the Swiss national motorway network, the tunnel is toll-free.

From December to February wheel chains may occasionally be required on the approaches to the tunnel, but they are NOT allowed to be used in the tunnel. (Lay-bys are available for the removal and refitting of wheel chains).

San Bernardino Switzerland
This tunnel is over 5,000ft above sea level. It is 6.6km (4 miles) long, 4.8m (15ft 9in) high, and the carriageway is 7m (23ft) wide. Do not stop or overtake in the tunnel. Keep 100m (110yd) between vehicles. There are breakdown bays with telephones. No tolls. From November to March wheel chains may occasionally be required on the approaches to the tunnel.

Arlberg Austria
This tunnel is 14km (8¾ miles) long and runs at about 4,000ft above sea level, to the south of and parallel to the Arlberg Pass.

Charges
The toll charges for cars (with or without caravans) are 140 *Austrian Schillings* each way.

Bosruck Austria
This tunnel (opened October 1983) is 2,434ft above sea level. It is 5.5km (3½ miles) long and runs between Spital am Pyhrn and Selzthal, to the east of the Pyhrn Pass. With the Gleinalm Tunnel (see below) it forms an important part of the A9 Pyhrn Autobahn between Linz and Graz, now being built in stages.

Charges
The toll charges for cars (with or without caravans) are 60 *Austrian schillings* for a single journey.

Falbertauern Austria
This tunnel is over 5,000ft above sea level; it runs between Mittersill and Matrei, to the west of and parallel to the Grossglockner Pass. The tunnel is 5.2km (3¼ miles) long, 4.5m (14ft 9in) high, and the two-lane carriageway is 7m (23ft) wide. From November to April wheel chains may be

needed on the approach to the tunnel

Charges (in *Austrian schillings*)

		Single
cars	summer rate	180
	winter rate	100
caravans		free
motorcycles		180

Gleinalm Austria
This tunnel is 2,680ft above sea level, it is 8.3km (5 miles) long and runs between St Michael and Friesach, near Graz. The tunnel forms part of the A9 Pyhrn Autobahn which will, in due course, run from Linz via Graz to Yugoslavia.

Charges
The toll charges for cars (with or without caravan) are 120 *Austrian schillings* for a single journey.

Katschberg Austria
This tunnel is 3,642ft above sea level, and forms an impor-

tant part of the Tauern Autobahn (toll) between Salzburg and Carinthia. The tunnel is 5.4km (3½ miles) long, 4.5m (14ft 9in) high, and the two-lane carriageway is 7.5m (25ft) wide.

Charges
The toll charges for cars (with or without caravan) are 90 *Austrian schillings* for a single journey.

Radstädter Tauern Austria
This tunnel is 4,396ft above sea level. It is 6.4km (4 miles) long, and runs to the east of and parallel to the Tauern railway tunnel. With the Katschberg Tunnel (see above) it forms an important part of the Tauern Autobahn between Salzburg and Carinthia.

Charges
The toll charges for cars (with or without caravan) are 90 *Austrian schillings* for a single journey.

Major rail tunnels

Switzerland and Switzerland–Italy

Vehicles are conveyed throughout the year through the **Simplon** Tunnel (Brig-Iselle) and the **Lötschberg** Tunnel (Kandersteg-Goppenstein). It is also possible to travel all the way from Kandersteg to Iselle by rail via both the Lötschberg and Simplon Tunnels. Services are frequent and no advance booking is necessary and although the actual transit time is 15/20 minutes, some time may be taken by the loading and unloading formalities.

The operating company issues a full timetable and tariff list which is available from the AA, the Swiss National Tourist Office or at most Swiss frontier crossings.

Albula Tunnel Switzerland
Thusis(2,372ft)**Tiefencastel** (2,821ft) – **Samedan** (5,650ft)
The railway tunnel is 5.9km (3½ miles) long. Motor vehicles can be conveyed through the

tunnel, but you are recommended to give notice. Thusis *tel* (081) 811113, Tiefencastel (081) 711112, Samedan (082) 65404.

Services
9 trains daily going south; 6

trains daily going north.

Charges
These are given in *Swiss francs* and are likely to increase.
cars – 82 (up to eight passengers, including driver)
car and caravan – 155

Furka Tunnel Switzerland
Oberwald (4,482ft) – **Realp** (5,046ft).
The railway tunnel is 15.3km (9¼ miles) long. Journey duration 20 minutes.

Services
Hourly from 07.00–20.00hrs.

Charges
Cars including passengers 33 *Swiss francs.*

Oberalp Railway

Switzerland

Andermatt (4,737ft) – **Sedrun** (4,728ft).
Journey duration 50 minutes.

Services

Three trains daily.

Charges

Cars including driver 60 *Swiss francs*. Additional passengers 8 *Swiss francs*.

Tauern Tunnel Austria
Böckstein (3,711ft) (near Badgastein) – **Mallnitz** 8.5km (5½miles) long.

Maximum dimensions for caravans and trailers are height 8ft 10½in, width 8ft 2½in.

Booking

Advance booking is unecessary (except for request trains), but motorists must report at least 30 minutes before the train is due to start. The driver must drive his vehicle on and off the wagon.

Services

In summer, trains run approximately every half-hour in both directions, 07.40–23.00hrs; and every hour during the night providing there is sufficient traffic; additional trains are run during the day when necessary. In winter, there is a service approximately every hour 04.45–22.05hrs.
Duration 10 minutes.

Charges

These are given in *Austrian schillings* and are for a single journey.
cars (including passengers) 160
motorcycles (with or without sidecar) 50
caravans free

Karawanken Tunnel
Yugoslavia
Rosenbach – Jesenice
This tunnel is 8.5km (5½ miles) long. Since the opening of the Loibl Tunnel, see page 45, assuring an all-year-round link between Klagenfurt and Ljubljana, the use of the Karawanken Tunnel by motorists is not an economic proposition.

Principal mountain passes

It is best not to attempt to cross mountain passes at night, and daily schedules should make allowance for the comparatively slow speeds inevitable in mountainous areas.

Gravel surfaces (such as grit and stone chips) vary considerably; they are dusty when dry, slippery when wet. Where known to exist, this type of surface has been noted. Road repairs can be carried out only during the summer, and may interrupt traffic. Precipitous sides are rarely, if ever, totally unguarded; on the older roads stone pillars are placed at close intervals. Gradient figures take the mean on hairpin bends, and may be steeper on the insides of the curves, particularly on the older roads.

Before attempting late evening or early morning journeys across frontier passes, check the times of opening of the Customs offices. A number of

offices close at night, eg the Timmelsjoch border crossing is closed between 20.00 and 07.00hrs.

Always engage a low gear before either ascending or descending steep gradients, keep well to the right side of the road and avoid cutting corners. Avoid excessive use of brakes. If the engine overheats, pull off the road, making sure you do not cause an obstruction, leave the engine idling, and put the heater controls, including the fan, into the maximum heat position. Under no circumstances remove the radiator cap until the engine has cooled down. Do not fill the coolant system of a hot engine with cold water.

Always engage a lower gear before taking a hairpin bend, give priority to vehicles ascending and remember that as your altitude increases so your engine power decreases. Priority must always be given

to postal coaches travelling in either direction. Their route is usually signposted.

Caravans

Passes *suitable for caravans* are indicated in the table (pages 41–49). Those shown to be *negotiable by caravans* are best used by experienced drivers driving cars with ample power. The remainder are probably best avoided. A correct power-to-load ratio is always essential.

Conditions in winter

Winter conditions are given in italics in the last column. *UO* means usually open although a severe fall of snow may temporarily obstruct the road for 24–48 hours, and wheel chains are often necessary; *OC* means occasionally closed between the dates stated and *UC* usually closed between the dates stated. Dates for opening and closing the passes are approximate only. Warning notices are usually posted at the foot of a

pass if it is closed, or if chains or snow tyres should or must be used.

Wheel chains may be needed early and late in the season, and between short spells (a few hours) of obstruction. At these times conditions are usually more difficult for caravans.

In fair weather, wheel chains or snow tyres are only necessary on the higher passes, but in severe weather you will probably need them (as a rough guide) at altitudes exceeding 2,000ft.

Conversion table gradients

All steep hill signs show the grade in percentage terms. The following conversion table may be used as a guide:

30%	1	in	3
25%	1	in	4
20%	1	in	5
16%	1	in	6
14%	1	in	7
12%	1	in	8
11%	1	in	9
10%	1	in	10

Pass and height	From To	Distances from summit and max gradient		Min width of road	Conditions (See page 40 for key to abbreviations)
*Albula 7,595ft Switzerland	Tiefencastel (2,821ft) La Punt (5,546ft)	31km 9km	1 in 10 1 in 10	12ft	UC Nov–early June. An inferior alternative to the Julier; tar and gravel; fine scenery. Alternative rail tunnel.
Allos 7,382ft France	Barcelonnette (3,740ft) Colmars (4,085ft)	20km 24km	1 in 10 1 in 12	13ft	UC early Nov–early June. Very winding, narrow, mostly unguarded but not difficult otherwise; passing bays on southern slope, poor surface (maximum width vehicles 5ft 11in).
Aprica 3,875ft Italy	Tresenda (1,220ft) Edolo (2,264ft)	14km 15km	1 in 11 1 in 16	13ft	UO. Fine scenery; good surface, well graded; suitable for caravans.
Aravis 4,915ft France	La Clusaz (3,412ft) Flumet (3,008ft)	8km 12km	1 in 11 1 in 11	13ft	OC Dec–Mar. Outstanding scenery, and a fairly easy road.
Arlberg 5,912ft Austria	Bludenz (1,905ft) Landeck (2677ft)	33km 35km	1 in 8 1 in 7½	20ft	OC Dec–Apr. Modern road; short steep stretch from west easing towards the summit; heavy traffic; parallel toll road tunnel available. Suitable for caravans, using tunnel. Pass road closed to vehicles towing trailers.
Aubisque 5,610ft France	Eaux Bonnes (2,461ft) Argelès-Gazost (1,519ft)	11km 32km	1 in 10 1 in 10	11ft	UC mid Oct–June. A very winding road; continuous but easy ascent; the descent incorporates the Col de Soulor (4,757ft); 8km of very narrow, rough, unguarded road, with a steep drop.
Ballon d'Alsace 3,865ft France	Giromagny (1,830ft) St-Maurice-sur-Moselle (1,800ft)	17km 9km	1 in 9 1 in 9	13ft	OC Dec–Mar. A fairly straightforward ascent and descent, but numerous bends; negotiable by caravans.
Bayard 4,094ft France	Chauffayer (2,988ft) Gap (2,382ft)	18km 8km	1 in 12 1 in 7	20ft	UO. Part of the Route Napoléon. Fairly easy, steepest on the southern side; negotiable by caravans from north to south.
*Bernina 7,644ft Switzerland	Pontresina (5,915ft) Poschiavo (3,317ft)	15.5km 17km	1 in 10 1 in 8	16ft	OC Dec–Mar during the day, but closed at night. A good road on both sides; negotiable by caravans.

*Permitted maximum width of vehicles 7ft 6in

Pass and height	From To	Distances from summit and max gradient		Min width of road	Conditions (See page 40 for key to abbreviations)
Bonaigua 6,797ft Spain	Viella (3,150ft) Esterri d'Aneu (3,140ft)	23km 21km	1 in 12 1 in 12	14ft	*UC Nov–Apr.* A sinuous and narrow road with many hairpin bends and some precipitous drops; the alternative route to Lleida (Lérida) through the Viella tunnel is open in winter.
Bracco 2,018ft Italy	Riva Trigoso (141ft) Borghetto di Vara (318ft)	15km 18km	1 in 7 1 in 7	16ft	*UO.* A two-lane road with continuous bends; passing usually difficult; *negotiable by caravans;* alternative toll motorway available.
Brenner 4,508ft Austria–Italy	Innsbruck (1,885ft) Vipiteno (3,115ft)	39km 14.5km	1 in 12 1 in 7	20ft	*UO.* Parallel toll motorway open; heavy traffic may delay at Customs; *suitable for caravans;* Resia Pass and Felbertauern Tunnel possible alternatives.
†Brünig 3,304ft Switzerland	Brienzwiler Station (1,886ft) Giswil (1,601ft)	6km 13km	1 in 12 1 in 12	20ft	*UO.* An easy but winding road; heavy traffic at weekends; *suitable for caravans.*
Bussang 2,365ft France	Thann (1,115ft) St-Maurice-sur-Moselle (1,800ft)	22km 8km	1 in 10 1 in 14	13ft	*UO.* A very easy road over the Vosges; beautiful scenery; *suitable for caravans.*
Cabre 3,871ft France	Luc-en-Diois (1,870ft) Aspres-sur-Buëch (2,497ft)	22km 17km	1 in 11 1 in 14	18ft	*UO.* An easy pleasant road; *suitable for caravans.*
Campolongo 6,152ft Italy	Corvara in Badia (5,145ft) Arabba (5,253ft)	6km 4km	1 in 8 1 in 8	16ft	*OC. Dec–Mar.* A winding but easy ascent; long level stretch on summit followed by easy descent; good surface; *suitable for caravans.*
Cayolle 7,631ft France	Barcelonnette (3,740ft) Guillaumes (2,687ft)	32km 33km	1 ln 10 1 in 10	13ft	*UC early Nov–early June.* Narrow and winding road with hairpin bends; poor surface and broken edges; steep drops. Long stretches of single-track road with passing places.
Costalunga (Karer) 5,751ft Italy	Cardano (925ft) Pozza (4,232ft)	23km 10km	1 in 8 1 in 7	16ft	*OC Dec–Apr.* A good, well-engineered road but mostly winding; *caravans prohibited.*
Croix 5,833ft Switzerland	Villars-sur-Ollon (4,111ft) Les Diablerets (3,789ft)	8km 9km	1 in 7½ 1 in 11	11ft	*UC Nov–May.* A narrow and winding route but extremely picturesque.
Croix-Haute 3,858ft France	Monestier-de Clermont (2,776ft) Aspres-sur-Buëch (2,497ft)	36km 28km	1 in 14 1 in 14	18ft	*UO.* Well-engineered; several hairpin bends on the north side; *suitable for caravans.*
Envalira 7,897ft Andorra	Pas de la Casa (6,851ft) Andorra (3,375ft)	5km 29km	1 in 10 1 in 8	20ft	*OC Nov–Apr.* A good road with wide bends on ascent and descent; fine views; *negotiable by caravans* (max height vehicles 11ft 6in on northern approach near L'Hospitalet).

*Permitted maximum width of vehicles 7ft 6in
†Permitted maximum width of vehicles 8ft 2½in

Pass and height	From To	Distances from summit and max gradient		Min width of road	Conditions (See page 40 for key to abbreviations)
Falzarego 6,945ft Italy	Cortina d'Ampezzo (3,958ft) Andraz (4,622ft)	17km 9km	1 in 12 1 in 12	16ft	OC Dec–May. Well-engineered bitumen surface; many hairpin bends on both sides; negotiable by caravans.
Faucille 4,341ft France	Gex (1,985ft) Morez (2,247ft)	11km 28km	1 in 10 1 in 12	16ft	UO. Fairly wide, winding road across the Jura mountains; negotiable by caravans but it is probably better to follow La Cure–St-Cerque–Nyon.
Fern 3,967ft Austria	Nassereith (2,742ft) Lermoos (3,244ft)	9km 10km	1 in 10 1 in 10	20ft	UO. An easy pass but slippery when wet; suitable for caravans.
Flexen 5,853ft Austria	Lech (4,747ft) Rauzalpe (near Arlberg Pass) (5,341ft)	6.5km 2km	1 in 10 1 in 10	18ft	UO. The magnificent 'Flexenstrasse', a well-engineered mountain road with tunnels and galleries. The road from Lech to Warth, north of the pass, is usually closed between November and April due to danger of avalanches.
*Flüela 7,818ft Switzerland	Davos-Dorf (5,174ft) Susch (4,659ft)	13km 13km	1 in 10 1 in 8	16ft	OC Nov–May Easy ascent from Davos; some acute hairpin bends on the eastern side; bitumen surface; negotiable by caravans.
†Forclaz 5,010ft Switzerland France	Martigny (1,562ft) Argentière (4,111ft)	13km 19km	1 in 12 1 in 12	16ft	UO Forclaz; Montets OC Dec–early Apr. A good road over the pass and to the frontier; in France narrow and rough over Col des Montets (4,793ft); negotiable by caravans.
Foscagno 7,516ft Italy	Bormio (4,019ft) Livigno (5,958ft)	24km 14km	1 in 8 1 in 8	11ft	OC Nov–Apr. Narrow and winding through lonely mountains, generally poor surface. Long winding ascent with many blind bends; not always well guarded. The descent includes winding rise and fall over the Passo d'Eira (7,218ft).
Fugazze 3,802ft Italy	Rovereto (660ft) Valli del Pasubio (1,148ft)	27km 12km	1 in 8 1 in 8	10ft	UO. Bitumen surface; several hairpin bends, narrow on northern side
*Furka 7,976ft Switzerland	Gletsch (5,777ft) Realp (5,046ft)	10km 13km	1 in 10 1 in 10	13ft	UC Oct–Jun. A well-graded modern road, but with narrow sections and several sharp hairpin bends on both ascent and descent. Fine views of the Rhône Glacier. Alternative rail tunnel.
Galibier 8,678ft France	Lautaret Pass (6,752ft) St-Michel-de-Maurienne (2,336ft)	7km 34km	1 in 14 1 in 8	10ft	UC Oct–Jun. Mainly wide, well-surfaced but unguarded. Ten hairpin bends on descent then 5km narrow and rough. Rise over the Col du Télégraphe (5,249ft), then eleven more hairpin bends. (Tunnel under the Galibier summit is closed).
Gardena (Grödner-Joch) 6,959ft Italy	Val Gardena (6,109ft) Corvara in Badia (5,145ft)	6km 10km	1 in 8 1 in 8	16ft	UC Jan–Jun. A well-engineered road, very winding on descent.
Gavia 8,599ft Italy	Bormio (4,019ft) Ponte di Legno (4,140ft)	25km 16km	1 in 5½ 1 in 5½	10ft	UC Oct–Jul. Steep and narrow but with frequent passing bays; many hairpin bends and a gravel surface; not for the faint-hearted; extra care necessary.

*Permitted maximum width of vehicles 7ft 6in
†Permitted maximum width of vehicles 8ft 2½in

Pass and height	From To	Distances from summit and max gradient		Min width of road	Conditions (See page 40 for key to abbreviations)
Gerlos 5,341ft Austria	Zell am Ziller (1,886ft) Wald (2,890ft)	29km 15km	1 in 12 1 in 11	14ft	UO. Hairpin ascent out of Zell to modern toll road; the old, steep narrow, and winding route with passing bays and 1-in-7 gradient is not recommended, but is negotiable with care.
†**Grand St Bernard** 8,114ft Switzerland Italy	Martigny (1,562ft) Aosta (1,913ft)	44km 33km	1 in 9 1 in 9	13ft	UC late Oct–Jun. Modern road to entrance of road tunnel (usually open; see page 38) then bitumen surface over summit to frontier; also good in Italy; suitable for caravans, using tunnel. Pass road closed to vehicles towing trailers.
*****Grimsel** 7,100ft Switzerland	Innertkirchen (2,067ft) Gletsch (5,777ft)	25km 6km	1 in 10 1 in 10	16ft	UC mid Oct–late Jun. A fairly easy, modern road, but heavy traffic at weekends. A long ascent, finally hairpin bends; then a terraced descent with six hairpins into the Rhône valley.
Grossglockner 8,212ft Austria	Bruck an der Glocknerstrasse (2,480ft) Heiligenblut (4,268ft)	33km 15km	1 in 8 1 in 8	16ft	UC late Oct–early May. Numerous well-engineered hairpin bends; moderate but very long ascents; toll road; very fine scenery; heavy tourist traffic; negotiable preferably from south to north, by caravans.
Hochtannberg 5,510ft Austria	Schröcken (4,163ft) Warth (near Lech) (4,921ft)	5.5km 4.5km	1 in 7 1 in 11	13ft	OC Jan–Mar. A reconstructed modern road.
Ibañeta (Roncesvalles) 3,468ft France–Spain	St-Jean-Pied-de-Port (584ft) Pamplona (1,380ft)	26km 52km	1 in 10 1 in 10	13ft	UO. A slow and winding, scenic route; negotiable by caravans.
Iseran 9,088ft France	Bourg-St-Maurice (2,756ft) Lanslebourg (4,587ft)	49km 33km	1 in 12 1 in 9	13ft	UC mid Oct–late Jun. The second highest pass in the Alps. Well graded with reasonable bends, average surface; several unlit tunnels on northern approach.
Izoard 7,743ft France	Guillestre (3,248ft) Briançon (4,396ft)	32km 20km	1 in 8 1 in 10	16ft	UC late Oct–mid Jun. A fairly easy but winding road with many hairpin bends. Several unlit tunnels near Guillestre.
*****Jaun** 4,948ft Switzerland	Broc (2,378ft) Reidenbach (2,769ft)	25km 8km	1 in 10 1 in 10	13ft	UO. A modernised but generally narrow road; some poor sections on ascent, and several hairpin bends on descent; negotiable by caravans.
†**Julier** 7,493ft Switzerland	Tiefencastel (2,821ft) Silvaplana (5,958ft)	36km 7km	1 in 10 1 in 7½	13ft	UO. Well-engineered road approached from Chur by Lenzerheide Pass (5,098ft); suitable for caravans.
Katschberg 5,384ft Austria	Spittal (1,018ft) St Michael (3,504ft)	35km 6km	1 in 5½ 1 in 6	20ft	UO. Steep though not particularly difficult; parallel toll motorway, including tunnel available; negotiable by light caravans, using tunnel.
*****Klausen** 6,391ft Switzerland	Altdorf (1,512ft) Linthal (2,126ft)	25km 23km	1 in 11 1 in 11	16ft	UC late Oct–early Jun. Easy in spite of a number of sharp bends; no through route for caravans as they are prohibited on part of road in Canton of Glarus.

*Permitted maximum width of vehicles 7ft 6in
†Permitted maximum width of vehicles 8ft 2½in

44

Pass and height	From To	Distances from summit and max gradient		Min width of road	Conditions (See page 40 for key to abbreviations)
Larche (dalla Maddalena) 6,542ft France–Italy	Condamine (4,291ft) Vinadio (2,986ft)	19km 32km	1 in 12 1 in 12	10ft	OC Nov–Mar. An easy, well-graded road; narrow and rough on ascent, wider with better surface on descent; suitable for caravans.
Lautaret 6,752ft France	Le Bourg-d'Oisans (2,359ft) Briançon (4,396ft)	38km 28km	1 in 8 1 in 10	14ft	OC Dec–Mar. Modern, evenly graded, but winding, and unguarded in places; very fine scenery; suitable for caravans.
Loibl (Ljubelj) 3,500ft Austria– Yugoslavia	Unterloibl (1,699ft) Kranj (1,263ft)	10km 29km	1 in 5½ 1 in 8	20ft	UO. Steep rise and fall over Little Loibl Pass to tunnel (1.6km long) under summit; from south to north just negotiable by experienced drivers with light caravans. The old road over the summit is closed to through traffic.
*Lukmanier (Lucomagno) 6,286ft Switzerland	Olivone (2,945ft) Disentis (3,772ft)	18km 22km	1 in 11 1 in 11	16ft	UC early Nov–late May. Rebuilt, modern road; suitable for caravans.
†Maloja 5,955ft Switzerland	Silvaplana (5,958ft) Chiavenna (1,083ft)	11km 32km	level 1 in 11	13ft	UO. Escarpment facing south; fairly easy but many hairpin bends on descent; negotiable by caravans, possibly difficult on ascent.
Mauria 4,258ft Italy	Lozzo Cadore (2,470ft) Ampezzo (1,837ft)	14km 31km	1 in 14 1 in 14	16ft	UO. A well-designed road with easy, winding ascent and descent; suitable for caravans.
Mendola 4,475ft Italy	Appiano (1,365ft) Sarnonico (3,208ft)	15km 8km	1 in 8 1 in 10	16ft	UO. A fairly straightforward, but winding road; well guarded; suitable for caravans.
Mont Cenis 6,834ft France–Italy	Lanslebourg (4,587ft) Susa (1,624ft)	11km 28km	1 in 10 1 in 8	16ft	UC Nov–May. Approach by industrial valley. An easy broad highway but with poor surface in places; suitable for caravans. Alternative Fréjus road tunnel available (see page 38).
Monte Croce di Comélico (Kreuzberg) 5,368ft Italy	San Candido (3,847ft) Santo Stefano di Cadore (2,978ft)	15km 22km	1 in 12 1 in 12	16ft	UO. A winding road with moderate gradients; beautiful scenery; suitable for caravans.
Montgenèvre 6,100ft France–Italy	Briançon (4,396ft) Cesana Torinese (4,429ft)	12km 8km	1 in 14 1 in 11	16ft	UO. An easy, modern road; suitable for caravans.
Monte Giovo (Jaufen) 6,870ft Italy	Merano (1,063ft) Vipiteno (3,115ft)	41km 19km	1 in 8 1 in 11	13ft	UC Nov–May. Many well-engineered hairpin bends; caravans prohibited.
Montets (see Forclaz)					
Morgins 4,491ft France– Switzerland	Abondance (3,051ft) Monthey (1,391ft)	14km 15km	1 in 11 1 in 7	13ft	UO. A lesser used route through pleasant, forested countryside crossing the French/Swiss border.

*Permitted maximum width of vehicles 7ft 6in
†Permitted maximum width of vehicles 8ft 2½in

Pass and height	From To	Distances from summit and max gradient		Min width of road	Conditions (See page 40 for key to abbreviations)
*Mosses 4,740ft Switzerland	Aigle (1,378ft) Château-d'Oex (3,153ft)	18km 15km	1 in 12 1 in 12	13ft	UO. A modern road; suitable for caravans
Nassfeld (Pramollo) 5,020ft Austria–Italy	Tröpolach (1,972ft) Pontebba (1,841ft)	10km 12km	1 in 5 1 in 10	13ft	OC late Nov–Feb. The Austrian section is mostly narrow and winding, with tight, blind bends; the winding descent in Italy has been improved.
Nufenen (Novena) 8,130ft Switzerland	Ulrichen (4,416ft) Airolo (3,747ft)	13km 24km	1 in 10 1 in 10	13ft	UC mid Oct–mid Jun. The approach roads are narrow, with tight bends, but the road over the pass is good; negotiable by light caravans (limit 1.5 tons).
*Oberalp 6,706ft Switzerland	Andermatt (4,737ft) Disentis (3,772ft)	10km 22km	1 in 10 1 in 10	16ft	UC early Nov–late May. A much improved and widened road with a modern surface; many hairpin bends but long level stretch on summit; negotiable by caravans. Alternative rail tunnel.
*Ofen (Fuorn) 7,051ft Switzerland	Zernez (4,836ft) Santa Maria im Münstertal (4,547ft)	22km 14km	1 in 10 1 in 8	12ft	UO. Good, fairly easy road through the Swiss National Park; suitable for caravans.
Petit St Bernard 7,178ft France–Italy	Bourg-St-Maurice (2,756ft) Pré St-Didier (3,335ft)	31km 23km	1 in 20 1 in 12	16ft	UC mid Oct–Jun. Outstanding scenery; a fairly easy approach but poor surface and unguarded broken edges near the summit; good on the descent in Italy; negotiable by light caravans.
Peyresourde 5,128ft France	Arreau (2,310ft) Luchon (2,067ft)	18km 14km	1 in 10 1 in 10	13ft	UO. Somewhat narrow with several hairpin bends, though not difficult.
*Pillon 5,072ft Switzerland	Le Sépey (3,212ft) Gsteig (2,911ft)	14km 7km	1 in 11 1 in 11	13ft	OC Jan–Feb. A comparatively easy modern road; suitable for caravans.
Plöcken (Mont Croce Carnico) 4,468ft Austria–Italy	Kötschach (2,316ft) Paluzza (1,968ft)	14km 16km	1 in 7 1 in 14	16ft	OC Nov–May. A modern road with long reconstructed sections; heavy traffic at summer weekends; delay likely at the frontier; negotiable by caravans.
Pordoi 7,346ft Italy	Arabba (5,253ft) Canazei (4,806ft)	9km 12km	1 in 10 1 in 10	16ft	OC Dec–Apr. An excellent modern road with numerous hairpin bends; negotiable by caravans.
Port 4,098ft France	Tarascon (1,555ft) Massat (2,133ft)	18km 13km	1 in 10 1 in 10	14ft	OC Nov–Mar. A fairly easy road but narrow on some bends; negotiable by caravans.
Portet-d'Aspet 3,507ft France	Audresseiri (1,625ft) Fronsac (1,548ft)	18km 29km	1 in 7 1 in 7	11ft	UO. Approach from the west by the easy Col des Ares (2,611ft) and Col de Buret (1,975ft); well-engineered road, but calls for particular care on hairpin bends; rather narrow.

*Permitted maximum width of vehicles 7ft 6in

Pass and height	From To	Distances from summit and max gradient		Min width of road	Conditions (See page 40 for key to abbreviations)
Pötschen 3,221ft Austria	Bad Ischl (1,535ft) Bad Aussee (2,133ft)	17km 8km	1 in 11 1 in 11	23ft	UO. A modern road; *suitable for caravans.*
Pourtalet 5,879ft France– Spain	Eaux-Chaudes (2,152ft) Biescas (2,821ft)	23km 34km	1 in 10 1 in 10	11ft	UC late Oct–early Jun. A fairly easy, unguarded road, but narrow in places; poor but *being rebuilt on Spanish side.*
Puymorens 6,283ft France	Ax-les-Thermes (2,362ft) Bourg-Madame (3,707ft)	28km 27km	1 in 10 1 in 10	18ft	OC Nov–Apr. A generally easy modern tarmac road, but narrow, winding, and with a poor surface in places; not suitable for night driving; *suitable for caravans* (max height vehicles 11ft 6in). Alternative rail service available between Ax-les-Thermes and Latour-de-Carol.
Quillane 5,623ft France	Quillan (955ft) Mont-Louis (5,135ft)	63km 5km	1 in 12 1 in 12	16ft	OC Nov–Mar. An easy, straightforward ascent and descent; *suitable for caravans.*
Radstädter-Tauern 5,702ft Austria	Radstadt (2,808ft) St Michael (3,504ft)	21km 26km	1 in 6 1 in 7	16ft	OC Jan–Mar. Northern ascent steep but not difficult otherwise; parallel toll motorway including tunnel available; *negotiable by light caravans, using tunnel.*
Résia (Reschen) 4,934ft Italy–Austria	Spondigna (2,903ft) Pfunds-Stuben (3,182ft)	30km 20km	1 in 10 1 in 10	20ft	UO. A good straightforward alternative to the Brenner Pass; *suitable for caravans.*
Restefond (La Bonette) 9,193ft France	Jausiers (near Barcelonnette) (3,986ft) St-Etienne-de-Tinée (3,766ft)	23km 27km	1 in 9 1 in 9	10ft	UC Oct–Jun. The highest pass in the Alps, completed in 1962. Narrow, rough, unguarded ascent with many blind bends, and nine hairpins. Descent easier; winding with twelve hairpin bends.
Rolle 6,463ft Italy	Predazzo (3,337ft) Mezzano (2,126ft)	21km 25km	1 in 11 1 in 14	16ft	OC Dec–Mar. Very beautiful scenery; bitumen surface; a well-engineered road; *negotiable by caravans.*
Rombo (see Timmelsjoch)					
Route des Crêtes 4,210ft France	St-Dié (1,125ft) Cernay (902ft)	— —	1 in 8 1 in 8	13ft	UC Nov–Apr. A renowned scenic route crossing seven ridges, with the highest point at Hôtel du Grand Ballon.
†St Gotthard (San Gottardo) 6,916ft Switzerland	Göschenen (3,629ft) Airolo (3,747ft)	19km 15km	1 in 10 1 in 10	20ft	UC mid Oct–early Jun. Modern, fairly easy two or three lane road. Heavy traffic; *negotiable by caravans* (max height vehicles 11ft 9in). Alternative road tunnel available (see page 38).
***San Bernardino** 6,778ft Switzerland	Mesocco (2,549ft) Hinterrhein (5,328ft)	22km 8km	1 in`10 1 in 10	13ft	UC Oct–mid Jun. Easy, modern roads on northern and southern approaches to tunnel (see page 38); narrow and winding over summit; via tunnel *suitable for caravans.*
Schlucht 3,737ft France	Gérardmer (2,182ft) Munster (1,250ft)	15km 17km	1 in 14 1 in 14	16ft	UO. An extremely picturesque route crossing the Vosges mountains, with easy, wide bends on the descent; *suitable for caravans.*

*Permitted maximum width of vehicles 7ft 6in
†Permitted maximum width of vehicles 8ft 2½in

Pass and height	From To	Distances from summit and max gradient	Min width of road	Conditions (See page 40 for key to abbreviations)
Seeberg (Jezersko) 3,990ft Austria– Yugoslavia	Eisenkappel (1,821ft) Kranj (1,263ft)	14km 1 in 8 33km 1 in 10	16ft	*UO.* An alternative to the steeper Loibl and Wurzen passes; moderate climb with winding, hairpin ascent and descent.
Sella 7,349ft Italy	Plan (5,269ft) Canazei (4,806ft)	9km 1 in 9 13km 1 in 9	16ft	*UC. Jan–early Jun.* A finely engineered, winding road; exceptional views of the Dolomites.
Semmering 3,232ft Austria	Mürzzuschlag im Mürztal (2,205ft) Gloggnitz (1,427ft)	13km 1 in 16 16km 1 in 16	20ft	*UO.* A fine, well-engineered highway; *suitable for caravans.*
Sestriere 6,660ft Italy	Cesana Torinese (4,429ft) Pinerolo (1,234ft)	12km 1 in 10 55km 1 in 10	16ft	*UO.* Mostly bitumen surface; *negotiable by caravans.*
Silvretta (Bielerhöhe) 6,666ft Austria	Partenen (3,451ft) Galtür (5,195ft)	15km 1 in 9 10km 1 in 9	16ft	*UC late Oct–early Jun.* For the most part reconstructed; thirty-two easy hairpin bends on western ascent; eastern side more straightforward. Toll road; *caravans prohibited.*
†Simplon 6,578ft Switzerland– Italy	Brig (2,231ft) Domodóssola (919ft)	22km 1 in 9 41km 1 in 11	23ft	*OC Nov–Apr.* An easy reconstructed modern road, but 13 miles long, continuous ascent to summit; *suitable for caravans.* Alternative rail tunnel.
Somport 5,354ft France– Spain	Bedous (1,365ft) Jaca (2,687ft)	31km 1 in 10 30km 1 in 10	12ft	*UO.* A favoured, old established route; generally easy, but in parts narrow and unguarded; fairly good-surfaced road; *suitable for caravans.*
***Splügen** 6,932ft Switzerland– Italy	Splügen (4,780ft) Chiavenna (1,083ft)	9km 1 in 9 30km 1 in 7½	10ft	*UC Oct–May.* Mostly narrow and winding, with many hairpin bends, and not well guarded; care also required at many tunnels and galleries (max height vehicles 9ft 2in).
††Stelvio 9,045ft Italy	Bormio (4,019ft) Spondigna (2,903ft)	22km 1 in 8 28km 1 in 8	13ft	*UC Oct–Jun.* The third highest pass in the Alps; the number of acute hairpin bends, all well-engineered, is exceptional – from forty to fifty on either side; the surface is good, the traffic heavy. Hairpin bends are too acute for long vehicles.
†Susten 7,297ft Switzerland	Innertkirchen (2,067ft) Wassen (3,005ft)	28km 1 in 11 19km 1 in 11	20ft	*UC Nov–Jun.* A very scenic route and a good example of mountain road engineering; easy gradients and turns; heavy traffic at weekends; *negotiable by caravans.*
Tenda (Tende) 4,334ft Italy–France	Borgo S Dalmazzo (2,103ft) La Giandola (1,010ft)	24km 1 in 11 29km 1 in 11	18ft	*UO.* Well guarded, modern road with several hairpin bends; road tunnel at summit; *suitable for caravans; but prohibited during the winter.*

*Permitted maximum width of vehicles 7ft 6in
†Permitted maximum width of vehicles 8ft 2½in
††Maximum length of vehicles 30ft

Pass and height	From To	Distances from summit and max gradient		Min width of road	Conditions (See page 40 for key to abbreviations)
Thurn 4,180ft Austria	Kitzbühel (2,500ft) Mittersill (2,588ft)	19km 11km	1 in 12 1 in 16	16ft	UO. A good road with narrow stretches; northern approach rebuilt; suitable for caravans.
Timmelsjoch (Rombo) 8,232ft Austria–Italy	Obergurgl (6,322ft) Moso (3,304ft)	14km 23km	1 in 7 1 in 8	12ft	UC mid Oct–late Jun. Roadworks on Italian side still in progress. The pass is open to private cars (without trailers) only as some tunnels on the Italian side are too narrow for larger vehicles; toll road.
Tonale 6,181ft Italy	Edolo (2,264ft) Dimaro (2,513ft)	30km 27km	1 in 14 1 in 8	16ft	UO. A relatively easy road; suitable for caravans.
Toses (Tosas) 5,905ft Spain	Puigcerdá (3,708ft) Ribes de Freser (3,018ft)	25km 25km	1 in 10 1 in 10	16ft	UO. Now a fairly straightforward, but continuously winding two-lane road with many sharp bends; some unguarded edges; negotiable by caravans.
Tourmalet 6,936ft France	Luz (2,333ft) Ste-Marie-de-Campan (2,811ft)	19km 17km	1 in 8 1 in 8	14ft	UC Oct–mid Jun. The highest of the French Pyrénées routes; the approaches are good though winding and exacting over summit; sufficiently guarded.
Tre Croci 5,935ft Italy	Cortina d'Ampezzo (3,983ft) Pelos (2,427ft)	7km 48km	1 in 9 1 in 9	16ft	OC Dec–Mar. An easy pass; very fine scenery; suitable for caravans.
Turracher Höhe 5,784ft Austria	Predlitz (3,024ft) Ebene-Reichenau (3,563ft)	20km 8km	1 in 5½ 1 in 4½	13ft	UO. Formerly one of the steepest mountain roads in Austria; now much improved; steep, fairly straightforward ascent, followed by a very steep descent; good surface and mainly two lane width; fine scenery.
*Umbrail 8,205ft Switzerland–Italy	Santa Maria im Müstertal (4,547ft) Bormio (4,019ft)	13km 19km	1 in 11 1 in 11	14ft	UC early Nov–early Jun. Highest of the Swiss passes; narrow; mostly gravel surfaced with thirty-four hairpin bends but not too difficult.
Vars 6,919ft France	St-Paul-sur-Ubaye (4,823ft) Guillestre (3,248ft)	8km 20km	1 in 10 1 in 10	16ft	OC Dec–Mar. Easy winding ascent with seven hairpin bends; gradual winding descent with another seven hairpin bends; good surface, negotiable by caravans..
Wurzen (Koren) 3,520ft Austria–Yugoslavia	Riegersdorf (1,775ft) Kranjska Gora (2,657ft)	7km 6km	1 in 5½ 1 in 5½	13ft	UO. A steep two-lane road which otherwise is not particularly difficult; caravans prohibited.
Zirler Berg 3,310ft Austria	Seefeld (3,870ft) Zirl (2,041ft)	7km 5km	1 in 7 1 in 6½	20ft	UO. An escarpment facing south, part of the route from Garmisch to Innsbruck; a good modern road but heavy tourist traffic and a long steep descent, with one hairpin bend, into the Inn Valley. Steepest from the hairpin bend down to Zirl.

*Permitted maximum width of vehicles 7ft 6in

About the Gazetteer

Accommodation

AA signs
The AA issues signs on request to hotels listed in this Guide. You are advised, however, not to rely solely on the sign, but to check that the establishment still appears in this edition.

Charges
The gazetteer normally quotes terms minimum and maximum for one and two persons with Continental breakfast price added to the room tariff to give inclusive terms for bed and breakfast with and without private facilities.

DPn indicates *demi-pension* (half-board) terms only available which means that in addition to the charge for rooms, guests are expected to pay for one main meal whether it is taken or not.

Pn indicates *full pension* (full board) terms only available. Both these terms are shown minimum and maximum with and without private facilities for one and two persons.

Hotels are not required by law to exchange travellers cheques for guests, and many small hotels are unable to do so. You must expect to pay a higher rate of commission for this service at a hotel than you would at a bank.

All prices quoted in this guide refer to 1984 and are shown purely as a guide to the relative cost of the hotels listed.

Classification
Although the system of classification in Europe is similar to the AA system in this country, the variations in the traditions and customs of hotelkeeping abroad often make identical grading difficult.

Hotels and motels are classified by stars. The definitions are intended to indicate the type of hotel rather than the degree of merit. Meals, service, and hours of service should be in keeping with the classification, and all establishments with restaurants must serve meals to non-residents and are expected to give good value for money.

★ Hotels simply furnished but clean and well kept; all bedrooms with hot and cold running water; adequate bath and lavatory facilities.

★★ Hotels offering a higher standard of accommodation; adequate bath and lavatory facilities on all main floors and some private bathrooms and/or showers.

★★★ Well-appointed hotels; with a large number of bedrooms with private bathrooms/showers.

★★★★ Exceptionally well-appointed hotels offering a very high standard of comfort and service with the majority of bedrooms providing private bathrooms/showers.

★★★★★ Luxury hotels offering the highest international standards.

Complaints
You are advised to bring any criticism to the notice of the hotel management immediately. This will enable the matter to be dealt with promptly to the advantage of all concerned. If a personal approach fails, members should inform the AA. You are asked to state whether or not your name may be disclosed in any enquiries we may make.

Gazetteer entry and example
The gazetteer entry is compiled from information supplied by the proprietor. *The establishments shown in italics indicate that particulars have not been confirmed by management.*

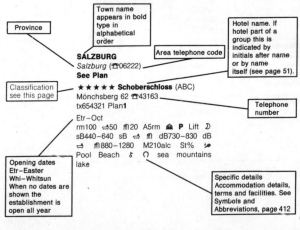

Province

Town name appears in bold type in alphabetical order

Area telephone code

Hotel name. If hotel part of a group this is indicated by initials after name or by name itself (see page 51).

SÁLZBURG
Salzburg (☎06222)
See Plan

Classification see this page

★★★★★ **Schoberschloss** (ABC)
Mönchsberg 62 ☎43163
tx654321 Plan1

Telephone number

Etr–Oct
rm100 ⇌50 ⋔20 A5rm ☎ **P** Lift ♪
sB440–640 sB ⇌ ⋔ dB730–830 dB
⇌ ⋔880–1280 M210alc St% ✍
Pool Beach ⅃ Ω sea mountains
lake

Opening dates
Etr–Easter
Whi–Whitsun
When no dates are shown the establishment is open all year

Specific details
Accommodation details, terms and facilities. See Symbols and Abbreviations, page 412

50

Hotel Groups

Most of the hotel groups shown below have agreements with AA Travel. If you want to reserve accommodation and make payment in advance, any AA Travel Agency will be happy to undertake these arrangements. A full list of AA Travel Agencies is shown on page 26 of the current AA Members' Handbook. If you would prefer to make your reservations by telephone a special unit is operated at the AA Travel Agency in Brighton, and payment by Access or Visa credit cards is accepted. Please telephone (0273) 24934 Mon–Fri 09.00–17.00hrs and Sat 09.00–12.30hrs.

Key to abbreviations and company reservation telephone numbers:

Company	tel
Alba (AL)	01-221 2626
Ambassador (Amb)	01-940 9766
Astir	01-636 0818
Best Western (BW)	01-940 9766
Campanile	0953-883713
Climat de France	01-630 9161
Comfort Hotels (Comfort)	01-221 2626
Crest* (Crest)	01-236 3242
Scandic	01-903 6422

Company	tel
ETAP/PLM/Euromotels (ETAP)	01-367 5175
Eurotel	01-221 2626
Forum	01-491 7181
France Accueil (FAH)	0273-731908
Frantel	01-568 9144
Gast im Schloss (GS)	01-370 2702
Golden Tulip (GT)	01-568 0071
Hilton International	01-631 1767
Holiday Inns	01-722 7755
IBIS	01-724 1000
Inter	01-370 2702
Inter Continental (Intercont)	01-491 7181
Inter DK	01-940 9766
Inter Scan (Inter S)	01-940 9766
Italian Grand Hotels (CIGA)	01-930 4147
Katag (KA)	01-221 2626
L'Horset	01-951 3990
MAP Hotels (MAP)	01-940 9766
Melia	01-636 5242
Mercure	01-724 1000
Minotels (MIN)	0273-731908
Mövenpick	01-940 9766
Novotels International	01-724 1000
Romantik (Rom)	01-373 0681
Sheraton	01-636 6411
Sofitel	01-724 1000
Steigenberger (SRS)	01-486 5754
Trusthouse Forte	01-567 3444

*Crest Hotels offer AA members the opportunity to book a double room at the normal single rate (for double occupancy). For details of terms and conditions please see the special leaflet obtainable from Crest Hotels or the AA.

Hotels and motels

The lists of hotels and motels for each country have been compiled from information given by members, by the motoring organisations and tourist offices of the countries concerned, and from many other sources.

Motels, motor hotels and some purpose-built hotels are indicated by white stars (eg ☆☆). These establishments conform to the major requirements of their star classification but their facilities are designed to cater particularly for overnight stays. In some cases porterage and room service may be rather restricted for the classification, but this is offset by studio-type bedrooms, a higher proportion of private bathrooms to bedrooms, extended meal hours, and more parking space. A list of motels, published by the European Motel Federation, is obtainable by AA members from Hotel and Information Services, AA, Basingstoke, Hants RG21 2EA.

Your comments concerning the whole range of hotel information – whether included in this Guide or not, and whether in praise or in criticism – will always be most welcome; a special form will be found at the back of this book, and all information will be treated in the strictest confidence.

Location maps

The location maps are at the beginning of each country section except those for Luxembourg, Portugal and Sweden where they are incorporated in the Belgian, Spanish and Norwegian maps respectively. These maps are intended to assist the reader who wishes to stay in a certain area by showing only those towns for which there is an entry in the gazetteer. Thus someone wishing to stay in the Innsbruck area will be able to select suitable towns by looking at the map. All location maps in this book use the

following symbols to indicate adjoining countries:
It must be emphasised that these maps are not intended to be used to find your way around the country and we recommend readers to buy the AA Big Road Atlas of Europe, available at £4.95, or the individual maps offered under the AA European Route Planning Service (see page 30).

grettably, many hotels will not accept bookings for one or two nights only. Sometimes a deposit is required which can be arranged through your bank. Many hotels do not hold reservations after 19.00hrs, and you should advise hotels if you anticipate a late arrival or if you are unable to take up your booking for any reason. Unwanted rooms can then often be relet and you will be

found on page 51 together with the telephone numbers for reservations. Most of the hotel groups listed have agreements with AA Travel and reservations may also be made at any AA Travel Agency.

The AA regrets that it cannot make reservations on your behalf at other hotels, except in conjunction with a holiday scheme, details of which are available from any AA Travel Agency.

When writing direct to hotels abroad, it is advisable to enclose an international reply coupon; these are available from any post office.

When reservations are made on the spot, it is the custom to inspect the rooms offered and to ask for the price before accepting them. No embarrassment is caused by this practice, and British visitors are urged to adopt it also, as it will be in their own interests.

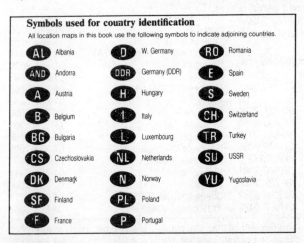

Symbols used for country identification

All location maps in this book use the following symbols to indicate adjoining countries.

AL Albania	**D** W. Germany	**RO** Romania
AND Andorra	**DDR** Germany (DDR)	**E** Spain
A Austria	**H** Hungary	**S** Sweden
B Belgium	**1** Italy	**CH** Switzerland
BG Bulgaria	**L** Luxembourg	**TR** Turkey
CS Czechoslovakia	**NL** Netherlands	**SU** USSR
DK Denmark	**N** Norway	**YU** Yugoslavia
SF Finland	**PL** Poland	
F France	**P** Portugal	

Reservations

The practice is the same on the Continent as it is in this country; rooms are booked subject to their still being available when confirmation is received. It is therefore most important that confirmation should be sent to the hotel as soon as possible after the rooms have been offered. Re-

saved the expense of paying for them, as a confirmed booking represents a legal contract.

Hotel telephone numbers are given in the gazetteer. In some entries the name of the group operating the hotel is indicated and a key to the abbreviations used may be

Double rooms may not be reduced in price when let to one person; however, a double room is generally cheaper than two rooms. Accommodation in an annexe may be of a different standard from rooms in the main hotel building; it is advisable to check the exact nature of the accommodation at the time of reservation.

Specimen letters for booking hotels

Please use **block letters** and enclose an **International Reply Coupon**, obtainable from the post office. Be sure to include your own name and address, clearly written.

English

Dear Sir
Please send me by return your terms with tax and service included, and confirm availability of accommodation with: Full Board/Half Board/Bed and Breakfast*
I would arrive on ....
and leave on ....
I would need .... rooms with single bed with/without* bath/shower*
.... rooms with double bed with/without* bath/shower*
.... rooms with twin beds with/without* bath/shower*
.... cots in parents' room
We are .... Adults
Our party also includes .... Children; ....
boys aged .... years and .... girls aged
.... years.
I look forward to receiving your reply and thank you in advance.
*delete where inapplicable.

French

Monsieur
Pourriez vous m'indiquer par retour si vous pouvez réserver et à quel tarif, taxe et service compris, pour un séjour en: Pension/Demi-pension/Chambre et petit déjeuner*
J'arriverais le ....
et je repartirais le ....
Il me faudrait .... Chambres à un lit d'une personne avec/sans*
.... bain/douche*
.... Chambres à grand lit avec/sans* bain/douche*
.... Chambres à deux lits avec/sans* bain/douche*
.... Lits d'enfants dans la chambre des parents.
Nous sommes .... Adultes
Accompagnés de .... Enfants; ....
Garçons de .... ans et ....Filles de ....
ans
J'attends vos renseignements et vous remercie par avance.
*delete where inapplicable.

German

Sehr geehrte Damen und Herren
Bitte senden Sie mir umgehend Angaben Ihrer Preise, einschl. Steuer-und Bedienungskosten, und bestätigen, ob Sie Zimmer frei haben, für eine Unterbringung mit: Vollpension/Halb-pension/Zimmer mit Frühstück*
Ankunftsdatum ....
Abfahrtsdatum ....
Ich möchte .... Einzelzimmer mit/ohne* Bad/Dusche*
.... Zimmer mit Doppelbett mit/ohne* Bad/Dusche*
.... Zimmer mit zwei Betten mit/ohne* Bad/Dusche*
.... Kinderbettchen im Elternzimmer
Wir sind .... Erwachsene
und zusätzlich .... Kinder .... Jungen
.... Jahre und .... Mädched .... Jahre.
Ich sehe Ihrer Antwort gern entgegen und danke Ihnen im voraus für Ihre Bemühungen.
*delete where inapplicable.

Italian

Egregio Direttore
Potrebbe indicarmi a ritorno di posta le condizioni d'alloggio con tasse e servizio inclusi, e se é posssibile riservare con:
Pensione completa/mezza pensione/camera e colazione*
Data d'arrivo ....
dat di partenza ....
Vorrei riservare .... camere con letto singolo e con/senza* bagno doccia*
.... camere con letto matrimoniale e con/senza * bagno/doccia*
.... camere a due letti e con/senza* bagno/doccia*
.... lettino neela camera dei genitori
Siamo .... adulti
Accompagnati da .... bambini di
.... anni e .... bambine di .... anni.
Resto in attesa di una sua cortese risposta e la ringrazio.
*delete where inapplicable.

Spanish

Muy Señor mio
Sirvase comunicarme a vuelta de correo sus condiciones de alojamiénto con impuestos y servicio incluidos, y si puedo reservar con:
Pensión completa/media pensión/habitación y desayuno*

Fecha de ilegada ....
fecha de salida ....
Necesitaría .... habitaciones de
una sola cama con/sin* bano/ducha*
.... habitaciones con
cama de matrimonio con/sin* baño/
ducha*
.... habitaciones de dos
camas con/sin* baño/ducha*
.... camita en la
habitación de los padres
Somos .... adultos
Acompañados por .... niños de ....
años y .... niñas de .... años.
Quedo a là espera de sus noticias y le doy las
gracias.
*delete where inapplicable.

Town plans

Listed below are major towns and cities for which there are town plans, followed by page numbers. A list of hotels showing the plan number can be found adjacent to the relevant plan. In addition, the appropriate plan number will appear following the telophone number in the hotel entry. These numbers correspond to the number on the plan thereby giving the location of the hotel.

Villas and chalets

An AA Travel Agency can give you details of many Villas and Chalet arrangements.

Garages

(See also *France* page 112 and *Spain* page 320)

The garages listed in the gazetteer for each country are those which are most likely to be of help to members on tour, because of their situation and the services they have stated they can provide. Although the AA cannot accept responsibility for difficulties over repairs to members' cars, any unsatisfactory cases will be noted for amendment in future editions of the guide.

It cannot be emphasised too strongly that disputes with garages on the Continent must be settled on the spot. It has been the AA's experience that subsequent negotiations can seldom be brough to a satisfactory conclusion.

In selecting garages, preference has been given to those which provide a breakdown service (see opposite) and those accepting AIT Credit Vouchers. The number of garages holding each agency reflects, as far as possible, the relative popularity of the various makes of cars. Although firms normally specialise in the makes for which they are accredited agents, they do not necessarily hold stocks of spare parts. Certain garages will repair only the make of car for which they are officially agents as indicated in the text.

A complete list of service agencies for your own make of car is generally available through your own dealer. It has been found on occasions that some garages in Europe make extremely high charges for repairing tourists' cars; always ask for an estimate before authorising a repair.

Breakdown service

The breakdown service of garages listed in the gazetteer is not free and any assistance obtained must be paid for. The AA's free breakdown service for members operates in the United Kingdom and Republic of Ireland only. Therefore

motorists travelling in Europe are advised to purchase AA 5-Star Service, see *Breakdown* page 8 for further information.

Hours of opening

In most European countries business hours are 08.00–18.00hrs; these times may be altered on Sundays and public holidays, when repairs, breakdown service, and petrol are often unobtainable.

In many countries, especially France, it may be difficult to get a car repaired during August because many garages close down for annual holidays.

Service Agencies

The service agencies held by garages are indicated by the following abbreviations:

AM	Aston Martin
AR	Alfa Romeo
Aud	Audi
†Bed	See Vau
BL	Austin, MG, Morris, Vanden Plas, Wolseley
BMW	BMW
Chy	Commer, Hillman, Humber, Singer, Sunbeam
Cit	Citroën
Dat	Datsun, Nissan
DJ	Daimler and Jaguar
Fia	Fiat
Frd	Ford
Hon	Honda
Lnc	Lancia
Lot	Lotus
Maz	Mazda
MB	Mercedes-Benz
MG	MG

Opl	Opel
Peu	Peugeot
Por	Porsche
Ren	Renault
RR	Rolls-Royce, Bentley
RT	Rover/Triumph
Sab	Saab
Sim	Simca
Sko	Skoda
Tal	Talbot – See Chy
Toy	Toyota
† Vau	Vauxhall/Bedford
VW	Volkswagen
‡ Vlo	Volvo, Daf

†Where no Vau or Bed dealer is available owners could approach the nearest Opl agency listed.

‡All Daf dealers are now incorporated into the Volvo network.

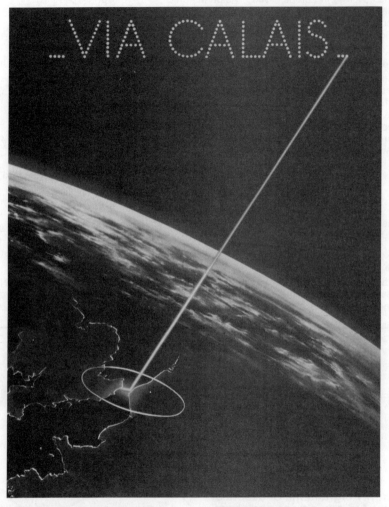

CALAIS—So close you could touch it. Once the only landfall for Britons bound for the continent and far and away the best route today.

Modern jumbo car ferries plus giant hovercraft provide a choice of over 100 crossings daily during the summer and never less than 50 off peak.

Take the shortest crossing between Dover and Calais. From 75 minutes by car ferry and from 30 minutes by hovercraft.

VIA

By far the <u>fastest</u> and the <u>best</u> way to go and come back

AUSTRIA

Austria is a land of chalet villages and beautiful cities bordered by six countries: Czechoslovakia, German Federal Republic, Hungary, Italy, Switzerland and Yugoslavia. The scenery is predominantly Alpine, an enchanting mix of mountains, lakes and pine forests. The splendour of the mountains is seen in the imposing Dachstein region of Upper Austria and the massive Tyrolean peaks. The lakes of Burgenland and Salzkammergut, the River Danube, the forest and woods of Styria and the world-famous city of Wien are outstanding features of the landscape. The other large cities are Salzburg and Innsbruck.

Most of the country enjoys a moderate climate during the summer, although eastern areas are sometimes very hot. The heaviest rainfall occurs in midsummer. The cold winters and the beautiful mountains attract large numbers of visitors for winter sports. The language of Austria is German.

Kitzsteinhorn and Zell am See

Area 32,389 sq miles
Population 7,520,000
Local time GMT + 1
(Summer GMT + 2)

National flag Horizontal tricolour, red, white and red

How to get there

The usual approach from Calais, Oostende and Zeebrugge is via Belgium to Aachen to join the German *Autobahn* network, then onwards via Köln (Cologne) to Frankfurt. Here the routes branch southwards via Karlsruhe and Stuttgart for Innsbruck and the Tirol or eastwards via Nürnberg and München (Munich) to Salzburg for central Austria. The distance to Salzburg is about 700 miles and usually requires two night stops. Wien (Vienna) the capital is a further 200 miles east. Travelling via the Netherlands is a straightforward run joining the German *Autobahn* system near Arnhem. Alternatively, Austria can be reached via northern France to Strasbourg and Stuttgart or via Basel and northern Switzerland. This is also the route if travelling from Dieppe, Le Havre and Cherbourg. Car sleeper services operate during the summer from Brussels and 's-Hertogenbosch to Salzburg and Villach.

Motoring regulations and general information

This information should be read in conjunction with the general content of the European ABC (pages 6–27). **Note** As certain regulations and requirements are common to many countries they are covered by one entry in the ABC and the following headings represent some of the subjects dealt with in this way:
AA Agents
Crash or safety helmets
Customs regulations for European countries
Drinking and driving
Fire extinguisher
International distinguishing sign
Medical treatment
Overtaking
Police fines
Radio telephones/Radio transmitters
Road signs
Rear view mirror
Seat belts
Tyres
Visitors' registration

Accidents

Fire ☎ 122 **police** ☎ 133 **ambulance** ☎ 144.
A driver who is involved in an accident must stop and exchange particulars with the other party. If personal injury is sustained it is obligatory that you obtain medical assistance for the injured persons and immediately report the incident to the police. All persons who arrive at the scene of an accident are obliged to render assistance unless it is obvious that everything necessary has already been done. See also *Accidents* page 7.

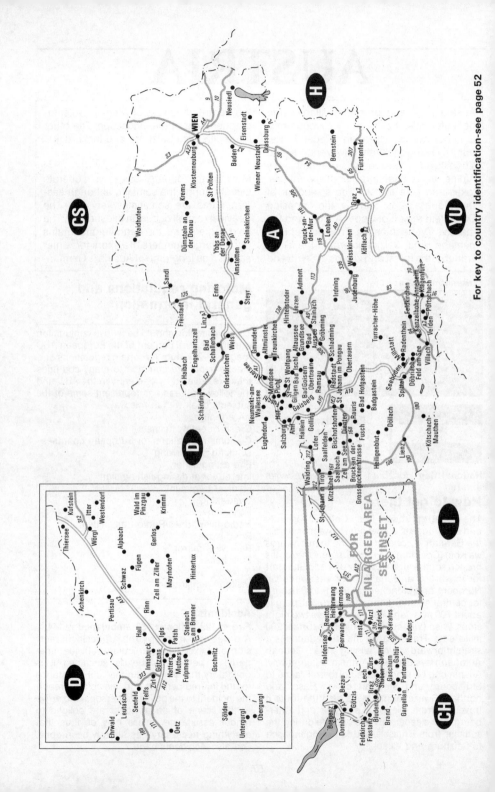

For key to country identification-see page 52

Salzburg: the castle

Accommodation
The official guide giving details of hotel classifications is available from the Tourist Office in London. Additional information on accommodation at small inns, in private homes and at farmhouses may be obtained from local and regional tourist information offices. Hotels are officially classified from A1 (luxury) to D (simple hotels). Room, pension, service and heating charges are exhibited in bedrooms.

Boats
(See also page 8)
Motorboats are not allowed on most of Austria's lakes. It is advisable to check with the Tourist Office before taking boats to Austria.

Breakdown
If your car breaks down, try to move it to the side of the road so that it obstructs the traffic flow as little as possible. The Austrian motoring club Österreichischer Automobil-, Motorrad-und Touring club (ÖAMTC) maintains a roadside assistance service (Pannenhilfe) and a towing service (Abschleppdienst). A patrol service (Strassenwacht) operates around Wien and on the south and west motorways when the volume of traffic demands it. See also *Breakdown* page 8, *Motorways* page 60 and *Warning triangles* page 62.

British Consulates
(See also page 8)
1030 Wien Reisnerstrasse 40 ☎(0222)756117/8.
There are also consulates in Graz, Innsbruck and Salzburg.

Currency and banking hours
(See also page 11)
The unit of currency is the Austrian schilling, divided into 100 groschen. There is no restriction on the amount of foreign or Austrian money that a *bona fide* tourist may import into the country. However, a maximum of 15,000 Austrian *Sch* may be exported and there is no restriction of foreign currency.

Banks are open Monday, Tuesday, Wednesday and Friday 08.00–12.30hrs, 13.30–15.00hrs; Thursday 08.00–12.30hrs, 13.30–17.30hrs. The bank counter at the ÖAMTC head office is open during office hours; exchange offices at some main railway stations are open on Saturdays, Sundays and public holidays.

Dimensions and weight restrictions
Vehicles must not exceed– height: 4 metres; width: 2.5 metres; length: vehicle/trailer combination 12 metres, articulated vehicles 18 metres; weight: trailers without brakes may weigh up to 750kg and may have a total weight up to 50% of the towing vehicle.

Driving licence
A valid British licence is acceptable in Austria and although language difficulties may give rise to misunderstanding in a few isolated cases, it is legally valid. The minimum age at which a visitor may drive a temporarily imported car or motorcycle (exceeding 50cc) is 18 years. The Austrian motoring club (ÖAMTC) will supply a free translation of your licence into German, but this is only available from their head office in Vienna and therefore will only be of use if touring in eastern Austria. However, an International Driving Permit is required by the holder of a licence issued in the Republic of Ireland. See under *Driving Licence and International Driving Permit* page 13 for further information.

Emergency messages to tourists
(See also page 14)
Emergency messages to tourists are broadcast daily by Austrian Radio in the *Autofahrer unterwegs* programme. These messages are transmitted in German on short wave Monday–Saturday between 11.30–12.45hrs and on Sunday and public holidays between 12.03–13.00hrs.

First-aid kit
(See also page 16)
In Austria all motorists are required to carry a first-aid kit by law and visitors are expected to comply. This item will not be checked at the frontier and foreigners will not be penalised if

59

they are not carrying one. However, at the scene of an accident any motorist can be stopped and his first-aid kit demanded; if this is not forthcoming the police may take action.

Hitch-hiking
In Austria, hitch-hiking is generally prohibited on motorways and highways. In Upper Austria, Styria and Vorarlberg hitch-hiking is prohibited for persons under the age of 16.

Insurance
(See also page 16)
All temporarily imported trailers must be covered by a separate policy, not the policy covering the towing vehicle.

Lights
(See also page 17)
Although it is prohibited to drive with undipped headlights in built-up areas, motorists may give warning of approach by flashing their lights. It is prohibited to drive on illuminated urban motorways with sidelights only. In poor visibility motorists may use fog lamps in conjunction with both sidelights and dipped headlights. Parking lights are not required if the vehicle can be seen from 50 metres (55yds). Lights on lampposts which are ringed with red do not stay on all night and parking lights will be required. It is compulsory for *motorcyclists* to use dipped headlights during the day.

Motoring club
(See also page 18)

 The **Österreichischer Automobil-, Motorrad-und Touring Club** (ÖAMTC) which has its headquarters at 1/3 Schubertring, 1010 Wien 1 ☎(0222)72990 has offices at the major frontier crossings and is represented in most towns either direct or through provincial motoring clubs. The offices are usually open between 08.30 and 18.00hrs weekdays, 09.00 to 12.00hrs on Saturdays and are closed on Sundays and public holidays.

Motorways
About 700 miles of motorway (Autobahn) are open and more stretches are under construction. A network of 1167 miles is planned. Only three motorways carry a toll; the Brenner Autobahn, the Tauern Autobahn and the Pyhrn Autobahn (Gleinalm and Bosruck Tunnels). The toll for the Brenner Autobahn is *Sch* 120 and return toll tickets *Sch* 200.

There are *emergency telephone posts* sited at 2km (1¼m) intervals. Small triangles on the guardrails or limitation posts point towards the nearest emergency telephone. To use the telephone lift the speaking flap and you will be automatically connected to the motorway control. The location of the post is printed inside the speaking flap; read this into the telephone, standing from 6 to 8in away from the microphone. If you ask for help and then find you do not need it, you must tell the motorway control. On the Brenner motorway emergency callposts of a different type have been installed. They are coloured red and orange and are furnished with a speaking tube and four levers bearing the symbols for police, Red Cross, repair service and telephone connection. By pressing the appropriate lever, a motorist will be connected with the required emergency service. When one of the first three levers is used, sufficient indication of what type of help is needed is conveyed to the headquarters in Innsbruck; when the telephone connection lever is used a motorist can talk direct to headquarters which will send help if required.

At the top of each telephone post there is an orange/yellow light which flashes if there is danger on that stretch of the motorway.

Orange badge scheme for disabled drivers
(See also page 19)
In Austria badge holders are allowed to park without any time limit in areas where restricted or prohibited standing and parking signs appear (red ring and bars with blue background). In some areas the local authority provides special parking places for disabled people's vehicles near hospitals and public service facilities.

Parking
(See also page 19)
Before you leave your vehicle make sure it does not contravene parking regulations.

Parking is forbidden on a main road or one carrying fast-moving traffic. In addition, parking is prohibited wherever there is a sign reading *Beschränkung für Halten oder Parken* (restriction for stopping or parking).

There is a total ban on stopping on roads which have priority (as a rule Federal roads), fog or any other impediment to visibility.

Cars must be parked facing in the direction of traffic flow.

In *Blue zones* or restricted parking areas there are no signs other than those on entering the zone, so tourists unfamiliar with the area should be alert to the fact they will have no reminders.

In Wien, parking on roads with tram lines is prohibited at all times from 15 December to 31 March. There is no parking in the centre of the city as it is a pedestrian zone.

In some towns short-term parking is allowed in areas known as *blue zones*. Here parking is free but a parking disc must be used. In Wien a charge is made for parking and tickets are available from Viennese traffic authorities, some banks, tobacco shops and the ÖAMTC. These tickets allow parking for periods of $\frac{1}{2}$, 1 or $1\frac{1}{2}$ hours.

In Wien parked vehicles which obstruct traffic will be towed away and their drivers made to pay costs arising.

Spending the night in a vehicle or trailer on the roadside is prohibited.

Passengers

(See also page 19)
Children under 12 are not permitted to travel in a vehicle as front-seat passengers unless they are using special seats or safety belts suitable for children.

Petrol

(See also page 20)
Credit cards Petrol stations generally accept recognised credit cards.
Duty-free petrol In addition to the petrol in the vehicle tank, up to 10 litres in a can may be imported free of customs duty and tax.
Octane rating Normal benzin (89) and Super benzin (96).

Postal information

Mail Postcards *Sch* 4; letters up to 20gm *Sch* 6.
Post offices There are 2,300 post offices in Austria. Opening hours in major towns are from 08.00-17.00hrs Monday to Friday and 08.00-10.00hrs Saturday. Elsewhere they are open 08.00-12.00hrs and 14.00-16.00hrs Monday to Friday.

Postcheques

(See also page 21)
Postcheques may be cashed at all post offices for any amount up to *Sch* 1,500 per cheque. Counter positions are identified by the words *Auszahlungen* or *Scheck und Auszahlungverkehr*. See above for post office opening hours.

Priority

See also *Priority including Roundabouts* p22)
Vehicles which continue straight ahead or make a right-hand turn at a crossroads or intersection have priority over oncoming vehicles turning left, provided that there are no signs to the contrary; in this case, even trams cede priority.

If you wish to turn across the flow of traffic at a junction controlled by a policeman, pass in front of him unless otherwise directed.

Public holidays

Official public holidays in Austria for 1985 are given below. See also *Public holidays* page 22.

January 1 (New Year's Day)
January 6†(Epiphany)
April 8 (Easter Monday)
May 1 (Labour Day)
May 16 (Ascension Day)
May 27 (Whit Monday)
June 6 (Corpus Christi)
August 15 (Assumption)
October 26* (National Day)
November 1 (All Saints' Day)
December 8†(Immaculate Conception)
December 25 (Christmas Day)
December 26 (St Stephen's Day)

* Saturday † Sunday

Roads including holiday traffic

(See also *Road conditions* page 23)
The motorist crossing into Austria from any frontier enters a network of well-engineered roads.

The main traffic artery runs from Bregenz in the west to Wien (Vienna) in the east, via the Arlberg Tunnel (Toll: see page 38), Innsbruck, Salzburg and Linz. Most of the major Alpine roads are excellent, and a comprehensive tour can be made through the Tirol, Salzkammergut and Carinthia without difficulty. Service stations are fairly frequent, even on mountain roads.

In July and August, several roads across the frontier become congested. The main points are on the Lindau – Bregenz road; at the Brenner Pass (possible alternative - the Resia Pass); at Kufstein; on the München (Munich) – Salzburg *Autobahn* and on the Villach – Tarvisio road. For details of mountain passes, see page 40.

Shopping hours

Shops are generally open from 08.00-18.00hrs with a 2-4hr break around midday. They close at 12.00hrs on Saturdays.

Some shops operate a tax-free service whereby, on leaving the country, visitors are reimbursed for VAT paid. A special form (U34) must be obtained, completed and stamped, from the shop and presented to the Austrian

Customs when crossing the border. Look for shops displaying the blue 'Tax-free Shopping' sign, or go to the local tourist information or ÖAMTC office for address lists.

Speed limits
(See also page 25)
The beginning of a built-up area is indicated by the placename sign and the end by a sign bearing the inscription *Ortsende von* (end of area) followed by the name of the place. In these areas the maximum speed for all vehicles (except mopeds) is 50kph (31mph); mopeds 40kph (24mph). Outside built-up areas, private cars are subject to a speed limit of 100kph (62mph) which is increased to 130kph (80mph) on motorways unless lower speed limits are indicated. Private vehicles towing trailers with a total weight of less than 750kg* (1,650lb) are restricted to 100 kph (62mph) on all roads, including motorways, outside built-up areas. If the trailer is over 750kg* then the limit is 100kph on motorways and 80kph (49mph) on main roads outside built-up areas. At certain periods during the summer, lower speed restrictions are imposed.

*If the weight of the trailer exceeds that of the towing vehicle or if the total weight of the two vehicles exceeds 3,500kg the limit outside built-up areas is 60kph (37mph) and 70kph (43mph) on motorways. **Note** When the total weight of the two vehicles exceeds 3,500kg it is not permissable to tow with a motorcar driving licence.

Spiked, studded or snow tyres
(See also page 10)
Spiked tyres may be used between 1 November and 30 April, although local regulations may extend this period. They may only be used on vehicles with a maximum total authorised weight not exceeding 3,500kg. Spiked tyres must be fitted on all wheels or on two wheels if the drive wheels are fitted with snow chains. However, speed must be restricted to 80kph (49mph) outside built-up areas and 100kph (62mph) on motorways.

Tourist information offices
(See also page 25)
The Austrian National Tourist organisation maintains an information office in London at 30 St George Street, W1R 9FA ☎01-629 0461 and will be pleased to assist you with any information regarding tourism. In most towns in Austria there will be found a local or regional tourist office which will supply detailed local information.

Traffic lights
(See also page 25)
A flashing green light indicates that the green phase is about to end.

Using the telephone
(See also page 26)
Insert coin **after** lifting receiver (instructions in English in many callboxes). Use *Sch* 1 coins for local calls and *Sch* 10 or 20 coins for national and international calls.
International callbox identification Boxes with three/four coin slots.
Telephone rates A telephone call to the UK costs *Sch* 14 for 1 minute.
What to dial for the Irish Republic 00 353.
What to dial for the UK 00 44.

Warning triangle
The use of a warning triangle is compulsory for all vehicles except two-wheelers. The triangle must be placed on the road 50 metres (55yds) behind the vehicle or obstacle and must be clearly visible from 200 metres (219yds). See also *Warning triangles/Hazard warning lights* page 26.

Wheel chains
(See also page 10)
If you plan to motor in areas of high altitude during winter you may find wheel chains are compulsory in certain local conditions. It is probably better to consider hiring (see page 10) or purchasing these at home prior to departure; they can be ordered from multiple car accessory retailers but allow 6-8 weeks for delivery. This will have the advantage of ensuring a proper fit and their availability when you want them. Further, they may be useful at home in certain winter conditions. Alternatively they may be hired from the ÖAMTC for a maximum period of 60 days but a deposit will have to be paid. They are delivered in a packed condition and if they are returned unused then the deposit is returned, less a percentage reduction, according to the length of hire.

The conditions of hire are fully described in a leaflet issued by the ÖAMTC from any of their offices.

Winter conditions
(See also page 27)
Entry from southern Germany The main approaches to Innsbruck and to Salzburg and Wien (Vienna) are not affected.

Entry from Switzerland The approach to Vorarlberg and Tirol is available at all times through the Arlberg Tunnel (toll).

From Austria into Italy The Resia and Brenner Passes are usually open throughout the year, but snow chains may be necessary in severe weather. The Plöcken Pass is occasionally closed in winter. Roads entering Italy at Dobbiaco and Tarvisio are usually clear, providing an unobstructed throughroute from Wien (Vienna) to Venice.

From Austria into Yugoslavia It is best to travel via Tarvisio (Italy) and Jesenice, via Lavamünd and Dravograd, or via Graz and Maribor. Entry via the Wurzen and Seeberg Passes and the Loibl Pass road tunnel is possible but not advised.

Within Austria in the provinces of Upper Austria, Lower Austria and Burgenland motoring is unaffected by winter conditions; elsewhere, because of the altitude, it is restricted.

When the Grossglockner Pass is closed, Ost Tirol and Carinthia can be reached by either the Felbertauern road tunnel, the Tauern Autobahn or the Tauern railway tunnel between Böckstein (near Badgastein) and Mallnitz (see page 39).

Winter-sports resorts The main approach roads are swept and are closed only in the most severe weather. Zürs and Lech can be reached via the Arlberg Pass only.

Prices are in Austrian Schillings
Abbreviations
pl   platz
str   strasse

ACHENKIRCH AM ACHENSEE
Tirol(☎05246)

★**Sporthotel Imhof** ☎6309

15 Dec–20 Oct
rm30 ⇔10 ⋒20 🏛 P Lift sB ⇔
⋒310–370 dB480–600 mountains lake

ADMONT
Steiermark (☎03613)
★ ★**Post** ☎2416

rm35 ⇔4 ⋒11 🏛 P sB150–170 sB
⇔ ⋒250–270 dB300–340 dB ⇔
⋒440–400 M90–120 mountains

AIGEN See **SALZBURG**

ALPBACH
Tirol (☎05336)

★ ★ ★**Böglerhof** Dorfpl ☎5227
tx051160

15 Dec–Mar & 20 May–15 Dec
⇔48 🏛 P Lift sB ⇔510–930 dB
⇔980–1720 ⚓ Pool mountains

★ ★**Alpbacher-Hof** ☎5237
Jan–Mar & May–Aug
rm33 ⇔30 ⋒3 🏛 P Lift sB ⇔
⋒410–480 dB ⇔ ⋒720–1050
M150–200 Pool mountains

ALTAUSSEE
Steiermark (☎06152)

★ ★ ★**Tyrol** ☎71636
15 Apr–15 Oct
⇔22 🏛 P Lift 𝄞 sB ⇔350–460
dB ⇔700–920 M190 mountains lake

★ ★**Hubertushof** Puchen 86 ☎71280
Jun–Oct
rm8 ⇔5 ⋒3 A1rm P sB ⇔ ⋒ 410
dB ⇔ ⋒ 720–760 mountains lake

★ ★**Kitzer** Hauptstr 21 ☎71227
rm21 ⇔4 ⋒5 🏛 P 𝄞 sB180–200
sB ⇔ ⋒220–250 dB360–400
dB ⇔ ⋒ 400–500 mountains lake

⊗**E Plasonig** Puch 269 ☎7327 Maz

ALTMÜNSTER
Oberösterreich (☎07612)

★ ★**Reiberstorfer** Ebenzweier 27 ☎8338
rm37 ⇔19 ⋒18 🏛 P Lift
sB ⇔ ⋒290–380 dB ⇔ ⋒480–660
M80–120 mountains lake

AMSTETTEN
Niederösterreich (☎07472)

★ ★ ★**Hoffman** Bahnhofstr 2 ☎2516
tx19212

rm60 ⇔19 ⋒20 🏛 P Lift 𝄞
sB210–230 sB ⇔ ⋒240–290
dB400–440 dB ⇔ ⋒480–700 M90–130

⊗**OK Laumer** Linzer Str 112 ☎2525 Peu

ANIF
Salzburg (☎06246)

★ ★**Schlosswirt** (ROM) ☎2175
rm36 ⇔23 ⋒3 A17m 🏛 P
sB ⇔ ⋒590 dB ⇔ ⋒860–960
mountains

ARZL IM PITZTAL
Tirol (☎05412)

★ ★**Post** ☎3111 tx58240
10 May–10 Oct
rm70 ⇔35 ⋒10 A32rm 🏛
sB ⇔ ⋒252–287 dB ⇔ ⋒434–600
Lift Pool mountains lake

ATTERSEE
Oberösterreich (☎07666)

★ ★**Oberndorfer** ☎364 tx026597
Mar–Oct
rm22 ⇔6 ⋒16 🏛 P sB ⇔ ⋒400
dB ⇔ ⋒620–1160 M100–200
mountains lake

AUSSEE (BAD)
Steiermark (☎06152)

★ ★**Eurotel Erzherzog Johann**
Kurhausplatz 62 ☎2507 tx3817527
⇔63 P Lift sB ⇔460–580
dB ⇔760–920 Pool

★ ★**Kristina** Altausseerstr 54 ☎2017
rm12 ⇔7 ⋒5 P mountains

★ ★**Stadt Wien** ☎2068
rm20 ⋒4 P mountains

H Adlmannseder Grundlseerstr 236
☎2106 MB

Bad Each name preceded by 'Bad' is listed under the name that follows it.

BADEN BEI WIEN
Niederösterreich (☎02252)

★ ★ ★**Herzoghof** (BW) Theresiengasse 5
☎48395 tx014480
86rm ⇔82 ⋒4 P Lift 𝄞
sB ⇔475–830 dB ⇔880–1150 Mfr145

★ ★ ★**Krainerhütte** Helenental ☎4511
tx14303
rm68 ⇔55 ⋒13 🏛 P Lift 𝄞 ↝
sB ⇔ ⋒565–785 dB ⇔ ⋒940–1220
Pool

★ ★ ★**Schloss Wiekersdorf**
Schlossgasse 9–11 ☎48301 tx014420
⇔76 A26rm P Lift 𝄞 sB ⇔410–680
dB ⇔640–1090 M alc ↝ Pool

M Bierbaum Vöslauerstr 73 ☎3252 Vlo

BADGASTEIN
Salzburg (☎06434)

★ ★ ★**Elisabethpark** ☎25510
tx67518
Dec–Mar & May–Sep
⇔135 🏛 P Lift sB ⇔ ⋒825–925
dB1550–1750 Pool

★ ★**Eurotel** ☎25260 tx67556
⇔146 P Lift sB ⇔620–900 dB
⇔960–1440 Pool mountains

★ ★**Parkhotel Bellevue** ☎2571
tx67524
4 Dec–20 Oct
rm123 ⇔105 A44rm P Lift 𝄞
sB550–600 sB ⇔ ⋒600–700
dB1100–1200 dB ⇔ ⋒1300–1400 Pool
mountains

★ ★**Savoy** ☎2588 tx67668
Dec–mid Oct
rm59 ⇔31 ⋒14 🏛 P Lift 𝄞
Pn500–710 Pool mountains

★ ★**Bristol** ☎2219
Dec–15 Apr & 20 June–Sep
rm23 ⇔12 ⋒25 A25rm 🏛 P →

63

sB ⇌ 🏠260–280 dB ⇌ 🏠460–500
mountains

★★Grüner Baum (ROM) ☎25160
tx67516

May–17 Oct & 20 Dec–Mar
rm80 ⇌50 🏠27 🏛 P Pn500–920
Pool mountains

★★Kurhotel Eden ☎2076

rm37 ⇌11 P Lift Pn310–430
mountains

BERNSTEIN
Burgenland (☎03354)

★★★Burg Bernstein

Etr–Sep
rm10 ⇌9 🏠1 🏛 P sB ⇌ 🏠465
dB ⇌ 🏠930 M150 Pool mountains

BERWANG
Tirol (☎05674)

★★★Singer Haus Am Sonnenhang
☎8181 tx05544

25 May–25 Sep & 10 Dec–20 Apr
rm53 ⇌40 🏠3 🏛 P Lift sB290–510
sB ⇌ 🏠390–630 dB540–960
dB ⇌ 🏠700–1260 mountains

BEZAU
Vorarlberg (☎05514)

★★Post Hauptstr ☎2207

20 Dec–Oct
rm42 ⇌26 🏠16 P Lift
sB ⇌ 🏠480–550 dB ⇌ 🏠960–1070
M120–170 Pool mountains

BISCHOFSHOFEN
Salzburg (☎06462)

★Tirolerwirt Gasteinerstr 3 ☎2776
rm10 A2m 🏛 P

BLUDENZ
Vorarlberg (☎05552)

★★Schlosshotel ☎3016 tx52175
rm36 ⇌15 🏠18 A3m 🏛 P sB
⇌ 🏠360–500 dB ⇌ 🏠520–720
mountains

F Koch Wichner-Str 11 ☎2032 Fia

BRAND
Vorarlberg (☎05559)

★★★Scesaplana ☎221 tx52193
⇌ 🏠42 P Lift sB ⇌ 🏠540
dB ⇌ 🏠1000 Pool mountains

★★Hämmerle ☎213
Dec–Mar & May–Sep
rm36 ⇌13 🏠19 P Lift DPn300–500
M100–200 mountains

★Zimba ☎219
Jun–Sep
rm21 ⇌12 🏠4 🏛 P Pn310–400
mountains

BRAZ
Vorarlberg (☎05552)

★Landhaus Walch ☎8102
Dec–Sep
rm10 ⇌1 🏠9 🏛 P sB ⇌ 🏠315–342
dB ⇌ 🏠344–369 M75–110 mountains

Austria

BREGENZ
Vorarlberg (☎05574)

★★Weisses Kreuz (BW) Römerstr 5
☎22488 tx057741
rm44 ⇌27 🏠17 🏛 P Lift D
sB ⇌ 🏠380–550 dB ⇌ 🏠660–890
M120–130 mountains

🅖G Böhler Weiherstr 13 ☎22208 MB

**BRUCK AN DER GROSS-
GLOCKNERSTRASSE**
Salzburg (☎06545)

★★Lukashansi ☎458
rm81 ⇌66 🏛 P Lift mountains

★Höllern ☎240
⇌45 🏛 P Lift sB ⇌250–300
dB ⇌400–500 Pool mountains

BRUCK AN DER MUR
Steiermark (☎03862)

★★Bauer 'Zum Schwarzen Adler'
Mittergasse 23 ☎51331
rm60 ⇌33 🏠19 🏛 P sB160–185
sB ⇌ 🏠265–340 dB270–360
dB ⇌ 🏠446–530

★★Bayer ☎51218
rm33 ⇌12 🏠4 P sB230–270
sB ⇌ 🏠310–450 dB380–420
db ⇌ 🏠520–660 mountains

🅡R Reichl Grazer Str 17 ☎51633 Frd

DIENTEN AM HOCHKÖNIG
Salzburg (☎06416)

★Pesentheiner ☎207
Jun–Sep & 18 Dec–20 Apr
rm25 ⇌1 🏠17 P Pool

DÖBRIACH
Kärnten (☎04246)

🅕F Burgstaller Hauptstr 49 ☎7736 Frd

DÖLLACH
Kärnten (☎04825)

★★Schlosswirt ☎211 tx048180
Closed 3wks fr mid Apr & 1 wk Oct
rm24 ⇌17 🏠7 P sB ⇌ 🏠515
dB ⇌ 🏠930 Pool mountains

DORNBIRN
Voralberg (☎05572)

★★★Park Goethestr 6 ☎62691
tx059109
rm35 ⇌17 🏠14 P Lift D sB250–280
sB ⇌ 🏠430–480 dB450
dB ⇌ 🏠680–780

★★Hirschen Marktpl 12 ☎66363
rm38 ⇌4 🏠18 A15rm D
sB ⇌ 🏠270–290 dB ⇌ 🏠980–1000
mountains

L Winder Hartlerstr 27 ☎62094 Fia

DRASSBURG
Burgenland (☎02686)

★★★Schloss ☎2220
15 Mar–Dec
⇌34 🏛 P Lift D sB ⇌655
dB ⇌1130 M alc Pool 🅞

DÜRNSTEIN AN DER DONAU
Niederösterreich (☎02711)

★★★Schloss Dürnstein ☎212
tx071147
20 Mar–20 Nov
rm37 ⇌33 🏠4 P Lift D sB ⇌
🏠680–780 dB ⇌ 🏠840–1600 Pool

★★Richard Löwenherz ☎222
tx071199
Mar–Nov
rm46 ⇌36 🏠10 P D
sB ⇌ 🏠470–790 dB ⇌ 🏠780–1100
Pool

EHRWALD
Tirol (☎05673)

★★Halalli ☎2101
Dec–Oct
rm15 ⇌4 🏠10 🏛 P
sB ⇌ 🏠260–295 dB ⇌ 🏠500–590
mountains

★★Schönruh ☎2322
15 Dec–Mar & May–Sep
rm45 ⇌35 🏠2 🏛 P Lift sB300–350
sB ⇌ 🏠360–410 dB 540–640
dB ⇌ 🏠660–740 mountains

★★Sonnenspitze Kirchpl 14 ☎2208
Dec 18–Mar & May–10 Oct
rm32 ⇌3 🏠20 🏛 P Pn420–630
mountains

★★Spielmann Wettersteinstr 24 ☎2225
15 Dec–15 Oct
rm30 ⇌24 🏠4 🏛 P sB300–350
sB ⇌350–400 dB500–600
dB ⇌600–760 M100–180 Pool 🅞
mountains

EISENSTADT
Burgenland (☎02682)

★Elsenstadt Sylvester 5 (n.rest) ☎3350
15 May–15 Nov
rm14 ⇌2 🏠3 🏛 P

ENGELHARTSZELL
Oberösterreich (☎07717)

★★Ronthalerhof Nibelungenstr ☎7717
⇌21 🏛 P sB ⇌ 🏠295–345
dB ⇌ 🏠465–540

ENNS
Oberösterreich (☎07223)

★★Lauriacum (BW) Wiener Str 5–7
☎2315
⇌ 🏠30 🏛 P Lift sB ⇌ 🏠420–450
dB ⇌ 🏠650–700 M80

EUGENDORF
Salzburg (☎06212)

☆☆Wallersee ☎8282
🏠12 🏛 P sB 🏠280–380
dB 🏠460–540 mountains

M Neuhofer Eugenbach 29 ☎8242 Frd

FELD AM SEE
Kärnten (☎04246)

★★**Lindenhof** ☎2274
rm26 🛁5 🚿21 sB🛁🚿260–350 dB🛁🚿480–660 🐕 mountains lake

FELDKIRCH
Vorarlberg (☎05522)

★★★**Central-Löwen** Neustadt 17 ☎22070 tx52311
rm59 🛁27 🚿12 **P** Lift ☽ sB🛁🚿330–380 dB🛁🚿600–700 mountains

★★★**III Park** ☎24600 tx2119
🛁92 **P** Lift ☽ sB🛁670 dB🛁1860 M130 Pool mountains

★★**Alpenrose** Rosengasse 6 ☎22175
rm16 🛁8 🚿7 **P** ☽ sBfr220 sB🛁🚿300–350 dB450–460 dB🛁🚿500–540

P Fehr Bundesstre 1 ☎23373 Frd

FELDKIRCHEN
Kärnten (☎04276)

★★**Dauke** ☎2413
rm24 🛁12 🚿12 **P** ☽ sB🛁🚿250 dB🛁🚿480 mountains

FRASTANZ
Vorarlberg (☎05522)

★★**Stern** ☎51517
rm54 🛁6 🚿42 🏠 sB275 sB🛁🚿290–385 dB420 dB🛁🚿480–640 mountains

FRIESTADT
Oberösterreich (☎07942)

★**Goldener Hirsch** Böhmerg 8 ☎2258
rm23 🛁10 🚿8 **P** sBfr230 sB🛁🚿fr300 dBfr420 dB🛁🚿fr560 M80–100

FÜGEN
Tirol (☎05288)

★**Post** ☎3212
15 Dec–15 Oct
rm60 🛁54 🚿6 **P** Lift sB🛁🚿370–440 dB🛁🚿680–780 Pool mountains

FULPMES
Tirol (☎05225)

★★**Alphof** Herrengasse ☎3163
🛁🚿25 **P** sB🛁🚿290–350 dB🛁🚿1080–1320 M70–150 🐕 mountains

FÜRNITZ See **VILLACH**

FÜRSTENFELD
Steiermark (☎03382)

★★**Hitzl** ☎2144
rm35 🛁30 **P** sB200 sB🛁260 dB376 dB🛁480

M Koller Fehringer Str 13 ☎2527 Frd

Marth Ledergasse 27 ☎3293 Cit

FUSCH
Salzburg (☎06546)

★★**Post Hofer** ☎226
20 Dec–15 Oct
rm47 🛁15 🚿32 🏠 **P**

Austria

sB🛁🚿190–210 dB🛁🚿320–400 M60–100 🐕 mountains

★**Lampenhäusl** ☎302
Dec–Oct
rm38 🛁1 🚿20 A18rm 🏠 **P** sB175 sB🛁🚿200 dB300 dB🛁🚿350 mountains

FUSCHL AM SEE
Salzburg (☎06226)

★★★**Parkhotel Waldhof** ☎264 tx632795
Mar 20–Oct
🛁🚿65 **P** Lift sB🛁🚿320–390 dB🛁🚿620–1060 Pool mountains lake

★★**Seehotel Schlick** ☎237 tx632795
rm42 🛁8 🚿24 🏠 **P** sB250–300 sB🛁🚿280–360 dB900–1000 dB🛁🚿1020–1320 M95–140 Pool Beach mountains lake

GAISBERG
Salzburg (☎06222)
See Salzburg Plan

★★★**Zistelaim** ☎20104 Plan **12**
15 Jul–15 Sep & 15 Dec–7 Jan
rm24 🛁3 🚿12 🏠 **P** ☽ Pool mountains

GALTÜR
Tirol (☎05443)

★★**Berghaus Franz Lorenz** ☎206
Dec–Apr & 15Jun–Sep
rm22 🛁15 🚿7 🏠 **P** Lift mountains

★★**Fluchthorn** ☎202
15 Dec–Apr & Jun–Sep
rm50 🛁23 🚿27 🏠 **P** Lift ☽ sB🛁🚿330–550 dB🛁🚿560–940 mountains

GARGELLEN
Vorarlberg (☎05557)

★★**Alpenrose** ☎6314
Dec–Apr & Jun–15 Oct
rm19 🛁8 🚿11 🏠 **P** **Pn**560–730 mountains

GASCHURN
Vorarlberg (☎05558)

★★★**Sporthotel Epple** ☎251 tx52389
Dec–Apr
rm70 🛁41 🚿29 🏠 **P** Lift ☽ 🐕 Pool mountains

GERLOS
Tirol (☎05284)

★★**Kroller & Aimhof** ☎5202
Dec–Oct
rm80 🛁50 **P** Lift sB180–220 sB🛁300–350 dB320–380 dB🛁560–720 🐕 Pool mountains lake

★**Jägerhof** ☎5203
rm35 🛁4 🚿21 A14rm **P** ☽ mountains

GMUNDEN
Oberösterreich (☎07612)

★★★**Parkhotel am See** Schiffslände 17 ☎4230
26 May–Sep
rm50 🛁19 🚿18 🏠 **P** Lift sB300–410 sB🛁🚿420–490 dB500–720 dB🛁🚿740–880 M110–130 alc mountains lake

J Beham Georgstr 5 ☎3838 Ren

GOISERN (BAD)
Oberösterreich (☎06135)

★★**Agathawirt** ☎8342 tx68186
rm43 🛁20 🏠 **P** sB245–280 sB🛁330–410 dB330–400 dB🛁500–660 M80–120 Pool mountains

GOLLING
Salzburg (☎06244)

★**Goldener Stern** ☎2200
🛁22 🏠 **P** sB🛁205–225 dB🛁🚿370–460 mountains

GÖTZENS
Tirol (☎05227)

★***Haus Elisabeth*** ☎8209
rm30 🛁9 🚿2 🏠 **P** mountains

GÖTZIS
Vorarlberg (☎05523)

M Mayer Im Buch 27 ☎2539 Opl

GRAZ
Steiermark (☎0316)

★★★**Daniel** (BW) Europapl 1 ☎911080 tx31182
rm100 🛁51 🚿43 🏠 **P** Lift ☽ sB🛁🚿585–730 dB🛁🚿880–990 M150

★★★**Park** Leonhardstr 8 ☎33511 tx031498
🛁65 **P** Lift ☽ sB🛁600–670 dB🛁840–950 M alc

★★★***Steirerhof*** Jackominipl 12 ☎76356 tx031282
rm98 🛁57 🚿41 Lift ☽

★★★**Weitzer Goldener Ochs** Griesgasse 15 ☎913801 tx31284
rm174 🛁73 🚿54 🏠 **P** Lift ☽ sB350–435 sB🛁🚿690–875 dB650–750 dB🛁🚿960–1400

★★★**Wiesler** Grieskai 4 ☎913241 tx031130
rm90 🛁65 **P** Lift ☽ sB330–410 sB🛁🚿550–810 dB640–710 dB🛁🚿830–1250

★★**Mariahilf** Mariahilfer Str 9 ☎913163 tx031087
rm44 🛁15 🚿16 🏠 **P** Lift ☽ sB270–300 sB🛁🚿440–600 dB480–550 dB🛁🚿700–800 M120

W Denzel Wetzelsdorferstr 35 ☎53580 BMW Vlo

J Jacomini Kärntnerstr 115 ☎(93)22474 BL Hon

&H Krajacic Idlhofgasse 17
☎(93)912823 BL

&Dr K Repitsch Harnsdorfer Gasse 44
☎42111 Maz

&Sails & Braunstein (Autozentrale)
Wiener Str 35 ☎9880 Opl

GRIESKIRCHEN
Oberösterreich(☎07248)

At **NEUMARKT IM HAUSRUCKKELS**
(5.5km NW)

&H Edtstadler Marktplatz 22
☎(07733) 127 BMW Vlo

GRÖBMING
Steiermark(☎03685)

&A Franz Nr Bundesstr 324 ☎2359 Fia
MB

GRUNDLSEE
Steiermark(☎06152)

★**Backenstein** ☎8545
rm28 ⇨15 🛏13 **P** mountains lake

GSCHNITZ
Tirol(☎05276)

★★**Gschnitzer Hof** ☎213
18 Dec–20 Apr
rm30 ⇨10 🛏10 **P** sB270 sB ⇨ 🛏310
dB480 dB ⇨ 🛏660 M100–120 Pool
mountains

HAIBACH
Oberösterreich(☎07713)

★★**Donauhotel Faberhof** ☎8144
Mar–Oct
rm20 ⇨7 🛏13 🛏 **P** ☽
sB ⇨195–315 dB ⇨395–495

HALDENSEE
Tirol(☎05675)

★**Rot–Fluh** ☎6465 tx05546
15 Dec–Oct
rm85 ⇨70 🛏10 🛏 **P** Lift ☽ ⤳
Pool mountains lake

HALL IN TIROL
Tirol(☎05223)

★★**Maria Theresia** Reimmichlstr 25
☎6313
rm15 **P** Lift

★**Tyrol** ☎6621 tx54223
rm36 ⇨13 🛏23 🛏 **P** Lift
sB ⇨ 🛏350–370 dB ⇨ 🛏600–640
M80 Pool mountains

HALLEIN
Salzburg(☎06245)

★**Stern** (n.rest) ☎2610
May–Sep
rm35 ⇨2 🛏3 🛏 **P**

HEILIGENBLUT
Kärnten(☎04824)

★★★**Glocknerhof** ☎2244 tx048154
20 May–10 Oct & 20 Dec–20 Apr
rm73 ⇨32 🛏20 A10rm 🛏 **P** Lift
sB ⇨ 🛏630–680 dB ⇨ 🛏1110–1360
Pool mountains

Austria

★★★**Post** ☎2245
Jan–Oct
rm50 ⇨28 🛏22 🛏 **P** Lift ☽
sB ⇨ 🛏335–375 dB ⇨ 🛏610–690
M90–140 Pool mountains

★★**Rupertihaus** ☎2247
May–26 Oct
rm30 ⇨12 🛏16 **P** Pool mountains

HEITERWANG
Tirol(☎05674)

★**Fischer-Am-See** ☎5116
Dec, Feb & Mar & May–Oct
⇨11 🛏 **P** M alc mountains

HINTERSTODER
Oberösterreich(☎07564)

★★★**Berghotel** ☎5421 tx023379
15 Dec–Apr
🛏26 **P** Lift sB ⇨ 🛏490–600
dB ⇨ 🛏680–900 ⤳ Pool mountains

★**Dietigut** ☎5248
rm29 ⇨12 🛏9 A4rm 🛏 **P**
Pn410–500 ⤳ Pool mountains

HINTERTUX
Tirol(☎05287)

★★**Berghof** ☎304
Closed Jun
rm28 ⇨20 A5rm 🛏 **P** mountains

HOF BEI SALZBURG
Salzburg(☎06229)

★★★**Schloss Fusch** (BW) ☎253
tx0633454
Apr–Oct
rm57 ⇨47 🛏10 A40rm 🛏 **P** ☽
sB ⇨ 🛏1000–1100 dB ⇨ 🛏1800–3700
⤳ Pool 🐟 mountains lake

HOFGASTEIN (BAD)
Salzburg(☎06432)

★★★**Grand Park** Kurgarten Str 26
☎350 tx67756
rm92 ⇨79 🛏8 🛏 **P** Lift ☽ Pool
mountains

★★**Österreichischer Hof** Kurgartenstr 9
☎2160
7 May–10 Oct & 20 Dec–26 Mar
rm58 ⇨25 🛏33 🛏 **P** Lift
sB ⇨ 🛏415–560 dB ⇨ 🛏710–1000
M90–105 Pool mountains

&P Schober Anger 104 ☎532 Fia

IGLS
Tirol(☎05222)

★★★**Aegidihof** Bilgeristr 1 ☎77108
tx054123
Dec–Oct
rm28 ⇨26 🛏 **P** Lift ☽ sB270–280
sB ⇨335–520 dB460–680
dB ⇨590–960 mountains

★★★**Alpenhof** Iglerstr 47 ☎77491
tx054119

---

15 May–Sept & 15 Dec–March
rm38 ⇨35 🛏 **P** Lift ☽ sB350–400
sB ⇨ 🛏410–510 dB620–720
dB ⇨ 🛏760–950 M100–110 mountains

★★★**Park** ☎77305 tx053576
Closed Nov
rm60 ⇨55 🛏 **P** Lift ☽ ⤳ Pool
mountains

★★★**Sport** ☎77241 tx053314
18 Dec–Sep
⇨ 🛏100 🛏 **P** Lift ☽
sB ⇨ 🛏650–1100 dB ⇨ 🛏1200–2000
⤳ Pool mountains

★★**Batzenhäusl** ☎77104 tx053495
Dec–Oct
rm28 ⇨22 🛏4 🛏 **P** Lift sB450
sB ⇨ 🛏510–640 dB760
dB ⇨ 🛏860–1080 M100–150
mountains

★★**Waldhotel** ☎77272
Dec–Oct
rm19 ⇨10 🛏9 **P** Lift
sB ⇨ 🛏540–600 dB ⇨ 🛏920–1080
Pool mountains

★**Bon-Alpina** Hilberstr 8 ☎77219
15 Dec–Oct
rm52 ⇨5 A6rm mountains

★**Gothensitz** (n.rest) ☎77211
rm15 ⇨3 🛏6 🛏 **P** sB170–250
sB ⇨ 🛏255–295 dB340–440
dB ⇨ 🛏460–540 mountains

★**Romedihof** ☎77141
Dec–Sep
rm22 ⇨16 🛏6 **P** mountains

IMST
Tirol(☎05412)

★★**Post** (ROM) Postpl 3 ☎2554
15 Dec–20 Oct
rm40 ⇨25 🛏 **P** Lift ☽ sB260–330
sB ⇨310–360 dB470–570
dB ⇨620–700 M120–200 Pool
mountains

INNSBRUCK
Tirol(☎05222)

See Plan page 67
The area around the Herzog–Friedrich Str
is a pedestrian precinct.and only open to
vehicular traffic at certain times of the day.

☆☆☆**Holiday Inn** Salurnerstr 15
☎36501 tx053484 Plan **1**
⇨ 🛏194 🛏 **P** Lift ☽
sB ⇨ 🛏950–1450 dB ⇨ 🛏1600–2400
M110–180 Pool mountains

★★**Europa Tyrol** (SRS) Südtirolerpl 2
☎35571 tx53424 Plan **2**
⇨166 A35rm 🛏 **P** Lift ☽
sB ⇨975–1435 dB ⇨1320–2420 M fr
165 mountains

★★★**Goldener Adler**
Herzog–Friedrich Str 6 ☎26334
tx053415 Plan **4**
rm37 ⇨15 🛏22 **P** Lift ☽
sB ⇨ 🛏500–700 dB ⇨ 🛏800–1000
mountains

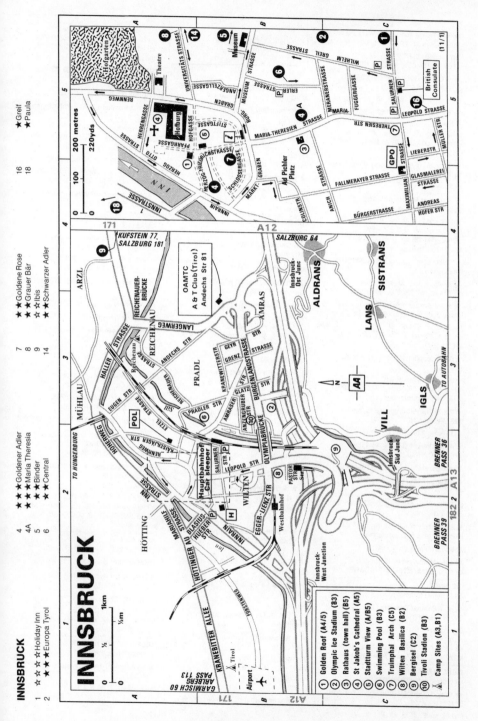

INNSBRUCK

1	☆ ☆ ☆ Holiday Inn
2	★ ★ ★ Europa Tyrol
4	★ ★ ★ Goldener Adler
4A	★ ★ ★ Maria Theresia
5	★ ★ Central
6	★ ★ Binder
7	★ ★ Goldene Rose
8	★ ★ Grauer Bär
9	☆ ★ Ibis
14	★ ★ Schwarzer Adler
16	★ Greif
18	★ Paula

1 Golden Roof (A4/5)
2 Olympic Ice Stadium (B3)
3 Rathaus (town hall) (B5)
4 St Jakob's Cathedral (A5)
5 Stadtturm View (A/B5)
6 Swimming Pool (B3)
7 Truimphal Arch (C5)
8 Wilten Basilica (B2)
9 Bergisel (C2)
10 Camp Sites (A3,B1)

OAMTC
A & T Club (Tirol)
Andechs Str 81

British Consulate

★ ★ ★**Maria Theresia** (BW) Maria
Theresienstr 31 ☎35615 tx53300 Plan **4A**
rm77 ⇌50 ▥17 **P** Lift ♪
sB ⇌ ▥580–890 dB ⇌ ▥920–1400

★ ★**Binder** Dr. Glatzstr 20 ☎42236
tx054404 Plan **5**
rm36 ⇌4 ▥12 🏠 **P** ♪ mountains

★ ★**Central** Erlerstr 11 ☎24866 tx53824
Plan**6**
rm94 ⇌23 ▥25 A23rm **P** Lift ♪
sB ⇌ ▥700–900 dB ⇌ ▥900–1280
Pool

★ ★**Goldene Rose** Herzog–Friedrichstr
39 ☎22041 Plan **7**
rm27 ⇌7 **P** Lift ♪

★ ★**Grauer Bär** Universitätstr 5–7
☎34531 tx53387 Plan **8**
rm160 ⇌67 ▥40 🏠 **P** Lift ♪
sB490–550 sB ⇌ ▥590–680
dB780–840 dB ⇌ ▥980–1100
M120–130 mountains

☆ ☆**Ibis** Schützenstrasse 43 ☎65544
tx4433 Plan **9**
▥96 🏠 **P** Lift ♪ sB ▥590
dB ▥1580 M100–200 mountains

★ ★**Schwarzer Adler** (ROM)
Kaiserjägerstr 2 ☎27109 Plan **14**
rm20 ⇌16 ▥4 **P** ♪
oB ⇌ ▥500–600 dB ⇌ ▥800--1000
M130–150 mountains

★**Greif** Leopoldstr 3 ☎27401 tx053111
Plan **16**
rm66 ⇌19 ▥47 **P** Lift
sB ⇌ ▥420–680 dB ⇌ ▥720–1100
M130 St% mountains

★**Paula** Weiherburggasse 15 (n.rest)
☎37795 Plan **18**
rm13 ⇌1 ▥4 **P** mountains

🖐**Auto-Linser KG** Haller Str 116a
☎62421 Opl Vau

🖐**W Denzel** Gumppstr 82 ☎45441 Vlo

🖐**F Niederkofler** Grassmayrstr 23
☎25759 Dat Sko

🖐**G Plörer** Griesauweg 33 ☎95/45451
BWM Vlo

M Steger Haymongasse 9A ☎27377
Electrical repairs (Lucas agent)

At **VÖLS** (5km W on No 1A)
🖐**Auto-Meisinger** (M Meisinger)
Innsbruckstr 57 ☎(95)34516 DJ RR

IRDNING
Steiermark (☎03682)

★ ★ ★**Schloss Pichlarn** Gatschen 28
☎2841 tx38190
Closed Nov–16 Dec
rm76 ⇌72 ▥4 🏠 **P** Lift ♪
sB ⇌ ▥770–1270 dB ⇌ ▥720–2420
M220–350 ⊌ Pool ∩ mountains

ISCHL (BAD)
Oberösterreich (☎06132)

★ ★ ★ ★**Kurhotel** (BW) Voglhuberstr 10
☎4271 tx68127
rm115 ⇌82 ▥33 🏠 **P** Lift ♪

Austria

---

sB ⇌ ▥630–680 dB ⇌ ▥1160–1260
M145–165 Pool mountains

★ ★**Freischütz** Rottenbach 96 ☎3354
Apr–Oct
rm25 ⇌8 🏠 **P** sB160–200 sB ⇌300
dB330–480 dB ⇌500–600 mountains

ITTER
Tirol (☎05332)

★ ★**Tirolerhof** ☎2690
Jun–Sep & Dec–Mar
rm63 ⇌40 ▥23 A12rm **P** Lift
mountains

JUDENBURG
Steiermark (☎03572)

🖐**W Denzel AG** Wiesenweg 4 ☎2477
BMW Vlo

JUDENSTEIN See **RINN**

KANZELHOHE–ANNENHEIM
Kärnten (☎04248)

★ ★ ★**Sonnenhotel** ☎2713
Jun–Sep & Dec–Apr
rm34 ⇌34 **P** Lift M100–150
Pn530–710 ⊌ Pool mountains lake

KITZBÜHEL
Tirol(☎05356)

★ ★ ★ ★**Hirzingerhof** Schwarzser Str 8
☎3211 tx05117124
Dec–Mar
rm26 ⇌24 ▥2 🏠 **P** Lift ♪
sB ⇌600–800 dB ⇌500–700
mountains

★ ★ ★**Tennerhof** (ROM)
Griesenauweg ☎3181 tx5118426
Jun–Sep & 17 Dec–April
rm50 ⇌47 A6rm **P** ♪ sB ⇌580–750
dB ⇌1020–1300 Pool mountains

★ ★ ★**Goldener Greif** ☎4311
tx(51)17118
Seasonal
rm56 ⇌54 ▥2 **P** Lift ♪ mountains

★ ★ ★**Schloss Lebenberg** Lebenbergstr
17 ☎4301 tx5118414
Feb–15 Oct
⇌96 🏠 **P** Lift ♪ sB ⇌705–2240
dB ⇌1150–2440 Pool mountains

★ ★**Erika** J–Pirchistr 21 ☎4885
tx051264
Dec–Oct
⇌36 🏠 **P** Lift DPn430–530 Pool
mountains

★ ★**Klausner** Bahnhofstr ☎2136
tx05118418
Dec–Apr & Jun–Sep
rm47 ⇌25 ▥19 🏠 **P** Lift ♪
sB ⇌440–500 dB ⇌ ▥800–920
mountains

★ ★**Schweizerhof** Hahnenkampstr 4
☎2735 tx51370

---

12 May–7 Oct & 8 Dec–10 Apr
rm38 ⇌18 ▥15 🏠 **P** sB300–350
sB ⇌ ▥350–450 dB ⇌ ▥700–900
mountains

🖐**Herz KG** J–Pirchler Str 30 ☎4638 Frd

KLAGENFURT
Kärnten (☎04222)

★ ★ ★**Sandwirt** (BW) Pernhartgasse 9
☎56209 tx422329
rm55 ⇌28 ▥12 🏠 **P** Lift ♪
sB320–380 sB ⇌ ▥600–650 dB600
dB ⇌ ▥900–1080 Mfr170

★ ★**Dermuth** Kohlderferstr 52 ☎21247
rm46 ⇌42 ▥4 🏠 **P** sB ⇌ ▥490–530
dB ⇌ ▥820–840 Pool mountains

★ ★**Kurhotel Carinthia** 8 Maistr 41
(n.rest) ☎511645 tx422399
⇌24 **P** Lift ♪ sB ⇌400–600
dB ⇌1100–1700

★ ★**Moser Verdino** Domgasse 2
☎57878 tx422110
rm271 ⇌271 ▥6 🏠 **P** Lift ♪
sB ⇌ ▥540–800 dB ⇌ ▥720–1100

🖐**W Denzel** Morogasse 39 ☎(94)84756
BMW

🖐**W Denzel** St–Veiterstr 209 ☎43220 Vlo

K Kroplunig Reinholdweg 7 ☎22796 Toy

Porsche–Inter Auto Villacher Str 213
☎21521 Por

🖐**J Sintachnig** Südbahngürtel 8
☎32144 Frd

K Umschaden Völkermarkterstr 233
☎33455 Cit

🖐**A Wiesner** Rosentalerstr 205
☎(94)22206 BL MG RT

🖐**R Wurm KG** St–Veiter Ring 27 ☎80991
Ren

KLOSTERNEUBURG
Niederöstereich (☎02243)

★ ★ ★**Martinschloss** Martinstr 34–36
☎7426 tx1174257
Apr–Oct
rm31 ⇌22 ▥2 A5rm **P** ♪
sB550–1350 sB ⇌ ▥950–1350 dB2000
dB ⇌ ▥2200–3300 M alc Pool
mountains

KÖFLACH
Steiermark (☎03144)

P Kainbacher Grazerstr 12 ☎491 Fia

KÖTSCHACH–MAUTHEN
Kärnten (☎04715)

★ ★**Post** ☎221
Apr–15 Oct & 15 Dec–Feb
rm30 ⇌8 ▥17 🏠 **P** sB ⇌ ▥280
dB ⇌ ▥240 mountains

KREMS AN DER DONAU
Niederösterreich (☎02732)

★ ★**Park** E–Hofbauerstr 19 ☎3266
tx071130
rm72 ⇌48 ▥24 **P** Lift ♪
sB ⇌ ▥400–450 dB ⇌ ▥630–700

68

★★**Weisse Rose** Obere Landstr 19 (n.rest) ☎3457
Apr–Oct
rm25 ⇔9 🍴3 P
&⊙**Auer** Wiener Str 82 ☎3501 Opl
&⊙**H Starkl** Wienerstr 48 ☎3030 Peu Ren

KRIMML
Salzburg (☎06564)
★★**Klockerhaus** ☎208
Closed Nov
rm40 ⇔4 🍴24 P sB255 sB ⇔ 🍴295
dB290–350 dB ⇔ 🍴420—430
mountains

KUFSTEIN
Tirol (☎05372)
&⊙**Krimbacher** K–Kraft Str 13 ☎2236 Frd
&⊙**A Reibmayr** Fischergriesgries 16 ☎2141 Opl
F–Unterberger Endach 32 ☎3652 Vlo

LANDECK
Tirol (☎05442)
★★**Post** Maiserstr 19 ☎2383
⇔75 P Lift ☽ sB ⇔430–450
dB ⇔720–750 mountains
At **ZAMS** (2km NE)
Auto–Plaselier Buntweg 8 ☎2304 Frd

LECH AM ARLBERG
Vorarlberg (☎05583)
★★★**Post** ☎22060 tx5239118
25 Jun–Sep & Dec–20 Apr
rm40 ⇔32 🍴8 A6rm 🛁 P Lift
sB ⇔ 🍴590–1500 dB ⇔ 🍴900–2400
M150–420 Pool mountains

★★★**Tannbergerhof** ☎2202 tx5239117
Jun–Sep & Dec–Apr
rm30 ⇔25 🍴5 🛁 P(summer only)
Lift ☽ (winter only) sB ⇔ 🍴445–480
dB ⇔ 🍴790–860 mountains

★★**Arlberg** ☎2134 tx05239122
rm43 ⇔32 🍴9 P Lift
sB ⇔ 🍴520–650 dB ⇔ 🍴940–1180
🏊 Pool mountains

★★**Schneider** ☎3500 tx5239115
Nov–Apr
rm64 ⇔61 P Lift ☽ 🏊 Pool
mountains

LEOBEN
Steiermark (☎03842)
★★**Baumann** F–Josef Str 10 ☎42565 tx33402
May–Oct
rm44 ⇔15 🍴16 P Lift ☽ sB190–280
sB ⇔ 🍴365–385 dB305–405
dB ⇔ 🍴460–770 Mfr60 mountains

J Puntinger Kerpelystr 14 ☎2206 Fia

LEONDING See **LINZ AN DER DONAU**

LERMOOS
Tirol (☎05673)
★★★**Drei Mohren** Haupstr 25 ☎2362 tx05558

Austria

17 Dec–Mar & May–Oct
rm50 ⇔39 🍴5 🛁 P Lift Pn340–620
mountains
★★**Post** ☎2281
15 May–15 Oct
rm60 ⇔45 🛁 P sB220–250
sB ⇔ 300–380 dB400–460
dB ⇔ 560–660 Pool mountains
★**Loisach** Unterdorf 6 ☎2394
10 May–14 Oct
rm47 ⇔25 🍴21 A22rm 🛁 P Lift
sB ⇔ 🍴350–395 dB ⇔ 🍴620–650
mountains

LEUTASCH WEIDACH
Tirol (☎05214)
★**Waldheim** ☎6288
rm12 ⇔6 P mountains

LIENZ
Tirol (☎04852)
★★★**Traube** (ROM) Haupt Pl 14 ☎2551 tx46618
15 Dec–15 Oct
rm57 ⇔49 🍴8 🛁 P Lift ☽
sB ⇔ 🍴540 dB ⇔ 🍴1100 Pool
mountains
★★**Glocknerhof** Schillerster 4 ☎2167
20 Dec–15 Oct
rm16 ⇔6 🍴10 P sB ⇔ 🍴250–270
dB ⇔ 🍴404–484 Pool mountains
★★**Post** Südtirolerpl 7 ☎2505
rm26 ⇔2 🍴19 P ☽ sB ⇔ 🍴360
dB ⇔ 🍴620 mountains
★★**Sonne** (BW) Südtirolerpl ☎3311 tx4666
Dec–Oct
rm57 ⇔42 🍴9 🛁 P Lift ☽
sB400–440 sB ⇔ 🍴450–490
dB680–760 dB ⇔ 🍴780–800
mountains
H Pfeifhofer Pustertalerstr 12 ☎2727 Vlo
&⊙**E Plössnig** Beim Neuen Sportstadion ☎3110 Ren
&⊙**W Rogen** Kärntner Str 36 ☎2335 Opl
&⊙**G Troger** Dr–K–Renner Str 12 ☎3411 Frd

LIEZEN
Steiermark (☎03612)
★★**Karow** Bahnhofstr 4 ☎2381
rm33 ⇔8 🍴1 🛁 P sB190–220
sB ⇔ 🍴270–300 dB360–400
dB ⇔ 🍴480–520 mountains
&⊙**A Böhm** Ausserstr 29 ☎2330 Ren
&⊙**T Manner** Salzburger Str 30 ☎2313 Maz MG

LINZ AN DER DONAU
Oberösterreich (☎0732)

★★★★**Schillerpark** (AL) Rainerstr 2-4 ☎554050 tx022107
⇔ 🍴111 🛁 Lift ☽
★★★**Tourotel** Untere Donaulände 9 ☎275075 tx021962
⇔176 🛁 P Lift ☽ sB ⇔790–870
dB ⇔990–1050 Pool river
★★**Ebelsbergerhof** Wiener Str 485 ☎42125 tx022415
rm40 ⇔36 🍴4 🛁 P Lift ☽
sB ⇔ 🍴650 dB ⇔ 🍴800 Pool
★★**Waldegg** (AL) Wankmüllerhofstr 39 ☎42361 tx021795
rm105 ⇔56 🍴46 🛁 P Lift ☽
sB ⇔ 🍴670 dB ⇔ 🍴840 M130–150
☆☆☆**Novotel** Wankmüllerhofstr 37 ☎47281 tx22618
⇔115 P Lift ☽ sB ⇔775 dB ⇔950
🏊 Pool
★★**Woifinger** ☎73291
rm22 ⇔9 🛁 P Lift ☽ sB265–290
sB ⇔340–360 dB470–490
dB ⇔570–580
W Danzel Humboldstr 49 ☎54411 Vlo
&⊙**H Günther KG** Hamerlingstr 13-15 ☎(0732)55025 Chy Opl
Pichler KG Wienerstr 430 ☎(0732)46216 Cit
At **LEONDING** (5km SW)
&⊙**Schoeller Auto–Vertrieb** Kremstaler Bundesstr ☎55586 Ren

LOFER
Salzburg (☎06588)
★★**Bräu** Haupstr ☎2070 tx66535
⇔27 P Lift sB ⇔550–600
dB ⇔900–1000 mountains
★★**Post** Hauptpl ☎3030 tx66535
20 Dec–Oct
rm31 ⇔12 🍴9 P sB265–375
sB ⇔ 🍴365–475 dB390–610
dB ⇔ 🍴590–810 mountains
★★**St–Hubertus** ☎266
15 May–20 Oct
rm17 ⇔11 🍴6 🛁 P
sB ⇔ 🍴270–310 dB ⇔ 🍴460–580
mountains
★**Lintner** ☎240
Dec–Oct
rm25 ⇔6 🍴6 🛁 P sB160–190
sB 🍴240–270 dB320–380
dB 🍴480–540 mountains

MAYRHOFEN
Tirol (☎05285)
★★★**Krammerwirt** ☎2615 tx53841
15 Dec–5 Nov
rm70 ⇔42 🍴20 P Lift
sB ⇔ 🍴456–706 dB ⇔ 🍴356–606

MILLSTATT
Kärnten (☎04766)
★★**Forelle** ☎2050
Apr–Oct
rm55 ⇔30 🍴12 🛁 P Lift ☽ →

sB330-370 sB ⇄ 🛏570-650
dB660-740 dB ⇄ 🛏1000-1680 🍴
Pool mountains lake

MONDSEE
Oberösterreich(☎06232)

☆ ☆ ☆ **Euromotel Mondsee** (ETAP)
Innerschwandt 150 ☎2876 tx633357
⇄46 **P** Lift) mountains lake

☆ ☆ ☆ **Mondsee** ☎2154
⇄ 🛏22 A11rm ⚐ **P** sB ⇄ 🛏445-490·
dB ⇄ 🛏770-860

★**Leitnerbräu** Marktpl 9 ☎2219
rm19 ⇄1 🛏5 A10rm **P** sB196 dB392
dB ⇄ 🛏455-472 M70-140

&♡W **Berger** Poststr 2-4 ☎2303 Opl

W **Widlroither** Südtiroler Str 4 ☎2612 BL
Toy

MUTTERS
Tirol(☎05222)

★ ★**Mutterhof** ☎27491

20 Dec-Mar & May-20 Oct
rm21 ⇄14 🛏13 ⚐ **P** sBfr400
sB ⇄ 🛏fr420 dBfr720 dB ⇄ 🛏fr780
M95-105 Pool mountains

NATTERS
Tirol(☎05222)

★**Eichhof** ☎266555

Apr-Oct
rm40 **P** mountains

★**Steffl** ☎29402

15 Jun-15 Sep
🛏12 ⚐ **P** mountains

NAUDERS
Tirol(☎05473)

★ ★**Tirolerhof** ☎255 tx58172

18 Dec-23 Apr & 19 May-Sep
rm70 ⇄41 🛏19 ⚐ **P** Lift)
sB ⇄ 🛏540-760 dB ⇄ 🛏470-690
Pool mountains

★**Post** ☎202

7 Jun-Sep
rm37 ⇄4 🛏16 A32rm ⚐ **P**
sB230-265 sB ⇄ 🛏275-345
dB420-490 dB ⇄ 🛏510-650 M90-120
mountains

★**Verzasca** (n.rest) ☎237

15 Dec-25 Apr & Jun-Sep
rm18 ⇄1 🛏9 ⚐ **P** mountains

NEUMARKT AM WALLERSEE
Salzburg(☎06216)

★**Lauterbacher** ☎456

rm10 ⇄5 🛏4 ⚐ **P** dB ⇄ 🛏320-360
mountains lake

&♡**Poller** Hauptstr 12 ☎207 Fia

NEUMARKT IM HAUSRUCKKELS See
GRIESKIRCHEN

NEUSIEDL AM SEE
Burgenland(☎02167)

★ ★ ★**Wende** (BW) Seestr 40-42 ☎8111
tx18182
rm106 ⇄18 🛏88 ⚐ **P** Lift)

Austria

---

sB ⇄ 🛏410-460 dB ⇄ 🛏700-800
M95 🍴 Pool

OBERGURGL
Tirol(☎05256)

★ ★ ★**Edelweiss & Gurgl** ☎233

rm96 ⇄55 🛏21 ⚐ **P** Lift Pool
mountains

OBERTAUERN
Salzburg(☎06466)

★ ★ ★**Pohl** ☎209

Jul-Sep & Nov-Apr
rm17 ⇄5 🛏12 **P** sB ⇄ 🛏285-405
dB 🛏490-690 mountains

OBERTRAUN
Oberösterreich(☎06135)

★ ★**Berghotel Krippenstein** ☎7129
tx068143

22 Dec-15 Oct
rm40 🛏11 ⚐ **P** Lift mountains

OETZ
Tirol(☎05252)

★ ★**Alpenhotel Oetz** Bielefeldstr 4
☎6232

May-Sep & 18 Dec-23 Apr
rm45 ⇄28 🛏17 **P** Lift
sB ⇄ 🛏310-350 dB ⇄ 🛏560-640
M90 mountains

★ ★**Drei Mohren** Haupstr ☎6301
rm30 ⇄14 🛏13 ⚐ **P** Lift 🍴
mountains

PARTENEN
Vorarlberg(☎05558)

★ ★ ★**Bielerhohe** ☎246

12 May-6 Oct
rm50 ⇄19 🛏12 ⚐ **P** Lift sB260
sB ⇄ 🛏270-290 dB440-480
dB ⇄ 🛏500-540 Pool mountains lake

PATSCH
Tirol(☎05222)

★ ★**Grünwalderhof** ☎77304

15 May-Sep & 18 Dec-15 Mar
rm30 ⇄19 🛏3 ⚐ **P** sB250-350
sB ⇄ 🛏320-400 dB400-620
dB ⇄ 🛏560-800 M100-150 🍴 Pool
mountains

PERTISAU AM ACHENSEE
Tirol(☎05243)

★ ★**Pfandler** ☎5223

15 Dec-15 Oct
rm53 ⇄40 🛏14 **P** Lift mountains lake

PICHL-AUHOF AM MONDSEE
Oberösterreich(☎06224)

★ ★**Seehof am Mondsee** ☎(06232)2550

15 May-20 Sep
⇄22 **P** mountains lake

PÖRTSCHACH AM WÖRTHERSEE
Kärnten(☎04272)

★ ★ ★ ★**Park** Elisabethstr 22 ☎2621
tx422344

May-15 Oct
rm182 ⇄172 🛏10 ⚐ **P** Lift)
DPn610-890 M185 🍴 Pool mountains
lake

★ ★ ★**Schloss Leonstein** ☎2816
tx422019

May-Sep
rm37 ⇄30 🛏2 ⚐ **P**) sB350-380
sB ⇄ 🛏700-730 dB700-760
dB ⇄ 🛏1360-1400 Pool

★ ★ ★**Sonnengrund** Annastr 9 ☎2343

20 Apr-10 Oct
rm47 ⇄22 🛏21 ⚐ **P** Lift)
sB520-580 sB ⇄ 🛏680-720
dB ⇄ 🛏1160-1300 Pool mountains
lake

★ ★**Schloss Seefels** Töschling 1
☎2377 tx0422153

15 Apr-15 Oct
rm80 ⇄70 🛏10 ⚐ **P**)
sB ⇄ 🛏670-1350 dB ⇄ 🛏1340-2500
M200-350 🍴 Pool 🛇 ∩
lake mountains

★ ★**Werzer Astoria** Werzer Promenade
8 ☎2231 tx422940

May-Oct
rm126 ⇄99 🛏10 ⚐ **P** Lift)
sB430-720 sB ⇄ 🛏740-800
dB1100-1380 dB ⇄ 🛏1360-1660

RADENTHEIN
Kärnten(☎04246)

★ ★**Metzgerwirt** ☎2052

rm18 🛏15 ⚐ **P** Pn550-572 mountains

&♡W **Flath** Millstätter Str ☎2171 Opl

&♡G **Tusch** Schattseite 101 ☎2214 Hen

RADSTADT
Salzburg(☎06465)

&♡W **Pfleger KG** Salzburger Str 228
☎312 Frd

RAMSAU AM DACHSTEIN
Steiermark(☎03687)

K **Knaus** Am Dachstein 149 ☎2941 BMW
Vlo

RAURIS
Salzburg(☎06544)

★ ★**Rauriserhof** ☎213

rm94 ⇄23 🛏33 Lift sB ⇄ 🛏455
dB ⇄ 🛏830 Pool

REUTTE
Tirol(☎05672)

★ ★**Tirolerhof** Bahnhofstr 16 ☎2557

rm37 ⇄3 🛏12 ⚐ **P** Lift mountains

&♡**Auto-Schiaffer** Allgäuer Str 68 ☎2622
Cit Toy

&♡J **Breschjak** Innsbruckerstr 27 ☎2627
BMW

&♡K **Hiebl** Lindenstr 3 ☎2385 MB

RINN
Tirol(☎05223)

At **JUDENSTEIN** (1km N)

70

★★Judenstein ☎8168
rm32 ⇌15 ▥5 ⩲ P Lift sB250-260
sB ⇌ ▥350-360 dB420-440
dB ⇌ ▥620-640 Pool

SAALBACH
Salzburg(☎06541)

★★★Kendler ☎225
Dec-Mar & May-Sep
⇌52 ⩲ P Lift ☽ DPn340-520
mountains

★★Berger's Sporthotel ☎577 tx66504
May-Sep & Dec-Apr
rm55 ⇌40 ▥15 ⩲ P Lift ☽
DPn350-820 M80-120 Pool mountains

★★Saalbacherhof ☎7111 tx66502
Dec-10 Oct
rm100 ⇌75 ▥25 ⩲ P Lift ☽
sB ⇌ ▥470-520 dB ⇌ ▥810-1380
⅍ Pool mountains

SAALFELDEN
Salzburg(☎06582)

★★Dick Bahnhofstr 106 ☎2215
rm30 ⇌14 ▥8 ⩲ P sB220-270
sB ⇌ ▥270-340 dB440-440
dB ⇌ ▥500-580 M110-140 Pool ∩
mountains

★★Schoerhof ☎2210
rm34 ⇌6 ▥29 A5rm ⩲ P
sB ⇌ ▥195-230 dB ⇌ ▥370-420
Pool

⅍Rieger KG Bundesstr 64 ☎2031 Frd
MB

ST ANTON AM ARLBERG
Tirol(☎05446)

★★★Mooserkreuz ☎2730
May-Oct
rm42 ⇌27 ▥15 ⩲ P Lift ☽
sB ⇌ ▥350-450 dB ⇌ ▥540-820
M100-150 Pool mountains

★★★Post & Alte Post ☎2213
Dec-Oct
rm56 ⇌40 ▥16 P Lift ☽ mountains

★★Arlberg Haupstr ☎2210
Jun-15 Sep
rm60 ⇌45 ⩲ Lift Pn630-890 ⅍

★★Montjola ☎2302
5 Dec-15 Apr
rm20 ⇌10 ▥2 A9rm P sB250
sB ⇌ ▥320 dB440 dB ⇌ ▥640
mountains

★★Rendlhof (n.rest) ☎2951
Jun-Sep & Nov-Apr
rm20 ⇌4 ▥16 ⩲ P mountains

★Bergheim (n.rest) ☎2255
Dec-Apr
rm30 ⇌14 ▥11 ⩲ P sB240-310
sB ⇌ ▥340-620 dB400-560
dB ⇌ ▥640-840 mountains

M Hauser Nr 361 ☎2708 Cit

ST GILGEN AM WOLFGANGSEE
Salzburg(☎06227)

Austria

★★★Parkhotel Billroth ☎217
15 May-15 Sep
rm39 ⇌24 ▥15 sB365-490
sB ⇌ ▥537-595 dB868-980
dB ⇌ ▥1098-1190 mountains lake

★★Alpenland am See (n.rest) ☎330
Jun-Sep
rm16 ⇌2 ▥14 ⩲ P
sB ⇌ ▥140-180 dB ⇌ ▥260-440
mountains lake

★★Hollweger Mondseer Bundesstr 2
☎226
15 Dec-Oct
rm30 ⇌20 ▥17 A8rm ⩲ P sB340
sB ⇌ ▥405-440 dB500-600
dB ⇌ ▥670-850 mountains lake

★★Post ☎239 tx632607
15 Dec-Nov
rm48 ⇌19 ▥2 A14rm ⩲ P
sB190-230 dB ⇌ ▥370 dB380-460
dB ⇌ ▥700-760 Pool mountains lake

★★Radetzky Streicherpl 1 ☎232
Apr-Oct
rm25 ⇌4 ▥10 P sB260-270
dB480-500 dB ⇌ ▥620-650
mountains lake

★Mozartblick (n.rest) ☎403
rm40 ⇌4 ▥20 A12rm ⩲ sB120-135
⅋B ⇌ ▥135-155 dB240-280
dB ⇌ ▥260-310 mountains lake

ST JOHANN IM PONGAU
Salzburg(☎06412)

★Prem ☎207
rm54 ⇌15 ▥15 ⩲ P
sB ⇌ ▥280-340 dB ⇌ ▥490-620 ⅍
mountains

ST JOHANN IN TIROL
Tirol(☎05352)

★★Kaiserhof ☎25770
May-Sep
rm36 ⇌25 ⩲ P Lift mountains

⅍E Foidl Pass Thurn Str 11 ☎20912 Dat

ST PÖLTEN
Niederösterreich(☎02742)

Auto-Dinstl Stifterstr 1 ☎2644 Cit

⅍W Denzel AG Linzerstr 52a ☎63281
BMW Vlo

⅍F Lutzenberger (Jnr) Kremser Landstr
8-10 ☎2475 Sab Toy

F Lutzenberger (Snr) Linzerstr 33 ☎2024
Dat Sko

ST WOLFGANG AM WOLFGANGSEE
Oberösterreich(☎06138)

★★★Weisses Rossl (ROM) ☎2306
tx68148
Nov-18 Dec
rm67 ⇌49 ▥15 P Lift ☽ sB390-490
sB ⇌ ▥590-640 dB880

---

dB ⇌ ▥880-1180 M110-160 ⅍ Pool
mountains lake

★★Appesbach ☎2209
15 Apr-15 Oct
rm21 ⇌15 ▥10 A7rm P ⅍
mountains lake

★★Post & Schloss Elbenstein ☎2346
Etr-Oct
rm170 ⇌111 ▥8 P Lift sB285 dB520
dB ⇌ ▥600 Pool mountains lake

SALZBURG
Salzburg(☎0662)
See Plan page 72

See also **GAISBERG**

★★★★SchlossMönchstein(BW) am
Mönchsberg 26 ☎41363 tx632080 Plan 1
rm17 ⇌15 ▥2 ⩲ P Lift ☽
sB ⇌1300-1500 dB ⇌2000-3300 ⅍

★★★Europa (AL) Rainerstr 31
☎73293 tx06-33424 Plan 3
rm104 ⇌65 ▥39 P Lift ☽
sB ⇌ ▥870 dB ⇌ ▥1400

★★★Österreichischer Hof (SRS)
Schwarzstr 5-7 ☎72541 tx633590 Plan 5
⇌120 ⩲ P Lift ☽ sB ⇌855-1045
dB ⇌1640-1860 M230-280

★★★Winkler F-Josefstr 7-9
☎73513 tx633961 Plan 6
⇌103 P Lift ☽ sB ⇌685-810
dB ⇌1160-1360 M140-150

★★Auersperg Auerspergstr 61
☎71721 tx633817 Plan 6A
rm61 ⇌20 ▥41 ⩲ P Lift ☽
sB ⇌ ▥365-690 dB ⇌ ▥1380-2180
M100-250 mountains

★★★Gablerbräu Linzergasse 9
☎73441 tx631067 Plan 7
rm60 ⇌26 ▥14 P Lift ☽ sB390
sB ⇌ ▥550 dB740 dB ⇌ ▥960

★★★Kasererhof (BW) Alpenstr 6
☎21265 tx633477 Plan 8
rm48 ⇌40 ▥8 P Lift ☽
sB ⇌ ▥780-1130 dB ⇌ ▥1355-2155
M alc mountains

★★★Schlosshotel St-Rupert
Morzgerstr 31 ☎43231 Plan 10
Apr-Oct
rm30 ⇌22 ▥1 ⩲ P mountains

★★Carlton M-Sittikusstr 3 ☎74343
Plan 13
8 Jan-20 Dec
rm50 ⇌10 ▥10 ⩲ P ☽ sB320
sB ⇌ ▥370 dB560 dB ⇌ ▥640-770

★★Eden Gaisbergstr 38 ☎20118
Plan 14
⇌12 ▥10 A3rm ⩲

★★Gastein Ignaz Rieder Kai 5 (n.rest)
☎22565 Plan 15
⇌12 ⩲ ☽ sB ⇌1000-1100
dB ⇌2800-3000 mountains

★★Markus Sittikus M-Sittikusstr 20
(n.rest) ☎71121 Plan 17
rm40 ⇌11 ▥21 P Lift ☽ sB295-370 →

SALZBURG

1	★★★★★Schloss Mönchstein
3	★★★★Europa
5	★★★★Österreichischer Hof
6	★★★★Winkler
6A	★★★Auersperg
7	★★★Gablerbräu
7A	★★★Doktorwirt(At Aigen)
8	★★★Kasererhof
10	★★★Schlosshotel St–Rupert
12	★★★Zistelalm
	(Listed under Gaisberg)
13	★★Carlton
14	★★Eden
15	★★Gastein
17	★★Markus Sittikus
19	★★Pitter
20	★★Schwarzes Rössl
21	★★Stein
22	★★Traube
22A	★★Weisse Taube
24	★Elefant

sB ⇄ 🛏 410–540 dB490–640
dB ⇄ 🛏 690–890

★★**Pitter** Rainerstr 6-8 ☎78571
tx633532 Plan **19**
rm220 ⇄180 🛏40 **P** Lift ♪
sB ⇄ 🛏 470–700 dB ⇄ 🛏 800–1300
M155–165 mountains

★★**Schwarzes Rössl** Priesterhausgasse
6 ☎74426 Plan **20**
Jul–Sep
rm51 ⇄4 **P** ♪ sB280 sB ⇄345
dB440 dB ⇄570 M115–230

★★**Stein** Staatsbrücke ☎74348 Plan **21**
22 Dec–Oct
rm80 ⇄41 Lift ♪

★★**Traube** Linzergasse 4 (n.rest)
☎74062 Plan **22**
Jul–Sep
rm40 ⇄20 **P** Lift ♪ sB300 sB ⇄400
dB500 dB ⇄700

★★**Weisse Taube** Kalgasse 9 (n.rest)
☎42404 tx633065 Plan **22A**
rm32 ⇄16 🛏9 **P** Lift sB350–400
sB ⇄ 🛏 500–620 dB550–650
dB ⇄ 🛏 850–1100

★**Elefant** S–Haffnergasse 4 ☎43397
tx632725 Plan **24**
rm36 ⇄15 🛏21 **P** Lift ♪
sB ⇄ 🛏 350–380 dB ⇄ 🛏 550–950

Auto–Grasser Sterneckstr 28-30
☎73679 BL Maz

🕉**Automobilvertriebges** (G Pappas)
Siebenstädterstr 46 ☎31531 MB

🕉**W Denzel** Innsbrucker Bundesstr 79
☎44184 BMW Vlo

🕉**Intermotor** Imbergstr 23 ☎75302 Dat
Sab Sko

🕉**ÖAF–Gräf & Stift AG** Plainstr 41
☎77202 Lada

ÖFAG Innsbrucker Bundesstr 128
☎44501 Opl Vau

🕉**Porsche–Inter Auto** Alpenstr 175
☎20911 Por

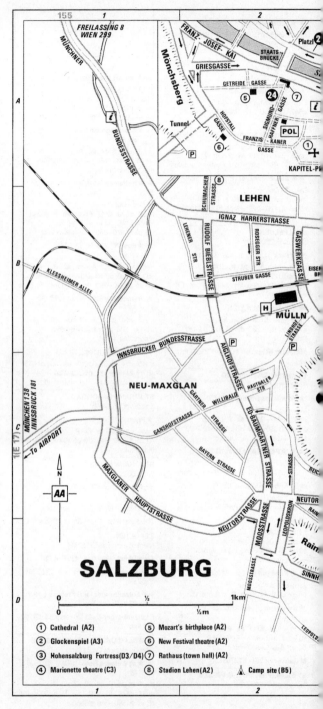

① Cathedral (A2)
② Glockenspiel (A3)
③ Hohensalzburg Fortress(D3/D4)
④ Marionette theatre (C3)
⑤ Mozart's birthplace (A2)
⑥ New Festival theatre (A2)
⑦ Rathaus (town hall) (A2)
⑧ Stadion Lehen (A2)
⛺ Camp site (B5)

SALZBURG

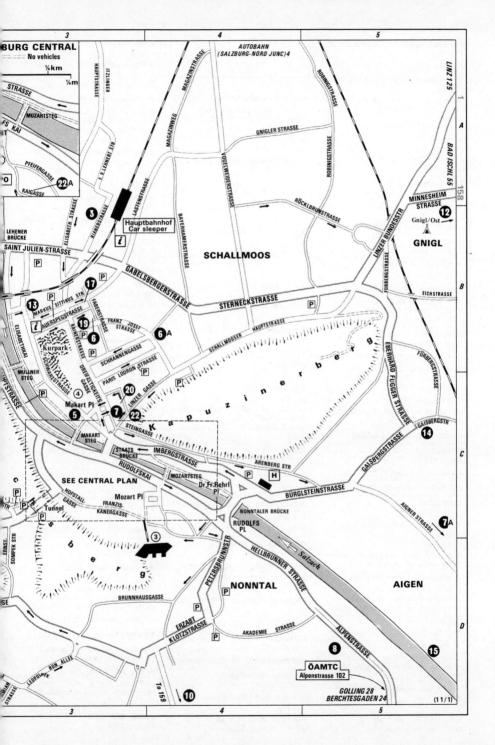

&⅁E Scheidinger Schallmoser Haupstr 24 ☎71176 Frd

At **AIGEN** (3km SE)

★ ★ ★*Doktorwirt* Glaserstr 9 ☎22973 Plan **7A**

rm49 ⇆29 ⋔4 A10rm 🚗 **P**

SANDL
Oberösterreich(☎07944)

★ ★**Braun** ☎250

Closed Apr & Nov
rm18 ⇆2 ⋔16 **P** sB ⇆ ⋔215
dB ⇆ ⋔430

SCHALLERBACH (BAD)
Oberösterreich(☎07249)

★ ★**Grünes Türl** ☎8163

rm23 ⇆9 ⋔14 🚗 **P**
sB ⇆ ⋔249–260 dB ⇆ ⋔254–520

SCHÄRDING
Oberösterreich(☎07712)

★ ★*Forstinger* ☎2302

⇆23 **P** Pool

★ ★**Schärdinger Hof** ☎2651 tx027459

rm32 ⇆3 ⋔18 🚗 **P** sB200–310
sB ⇆ ⋔200–310 dB380–540
dB ⇆ ⋔440–540

SCHLADMING
Steiermark(☎03687)

★ ★ ★**Alte Post** ☎22571 tx038/282

rm34 ⇆10 ⋔24 **P** Lift
sB ⇆ ⋔475–575 dB ⇆ ⋔1410–1810
M100–110 mountains

★ ★**Grogger** ☎22105

rm30 ⇆14 ⋔12 **P** Lift sB ⇆ ⋔300
dB ⇆ ⋔460–520

SCHUTTDORF See **ZELL AM SEE**

SCHWAZ
Tirol(☎05242)

H Arnold Münchnerstr 30 ☎2567 Dat

SCHWECHAT See **WIEN (VIENNA)**

SEEBODEN
Kärnten (☎04762)

★ ★ ★**Royal Hotel Seehof** ☎81714 tx48122

Apr–2 Oct
rm85 ⇆70 ⋔15 A35rm 🚗 **P** Lift ⅃
Pn750–980 Pool mountains lake

★ ★**Seehotel Steiner** ☎81713

May–10 Oct
rm50 ⇆5 ⋔40 A5rm 🚗 **P** ⅅ
DPn416–531 ⅃ Pool mountains lake

SEEFELD
Tirol(☎05212)

★ ★ ★**Astoria** ☎2272 tx5-385523

17 Dec–Mar & Jun–Sep
rm49 ⇆46 ⋔3 Lift ⅅ Pn680–920
mountains

★ ★ ★**Gartenhotel Tümmlerhof** ☎2571

Dec–Oct
rm66 ⇆65 ⋔1 🚗 **P** Lift ⅅ
Pn760–990 Pool mountains

Austria

★ ★ ★**Klosterbräu** ☎2621 tx5385517

15 Dec–20 Mar & 20 May–20 Sep
rm105 ⇆88 ⋔17 A10rm 🚗 **P** Lift ⅅ
sB580–1330 sB ⇆ ⋔770–1650
dB1020–2260 dB ⇆ ⋔1220–2660 ⅃
Pool mountains

★ ★**Dreitorspitze** Speckbacherstr 182 ☎2951 tx385525

15 Dec–Mar & 25 May–5 Oct
rm55 ⇆43 ⋔9 🚗 **P** Lift sB480–790
sB ⇆ ⋔620–1020 dB800–1540
dB ⇆ ⋔940–1940 M130–220 Pool
mountains

★ ★ ★**Philipp** Münchnerstr 68 ☎2301

May–Sep
⇆ ⋔60 🚗 **P** Lift ⅅ
sB ⇆ ⋔400–500 dB ⇆ ⋔600–800
mountains

★ ★**Kurhotel** ☎2671 tx053453

Dec–1 Oct
rm50 ⇆35 🚗 **P** Lift Pn440–700 Pool
mountains

★ ★*Regina* Claudiastr 171 ☎2270

17 Dec–Apr & 15 Jun–20 Sep
rm29 ⇆5 ⋔2 🚗 **P** mountains

SERFAUS
Tirol (☎05476)

★**Furgler** ☎6201

Dec–Oct
rm42 ⇆36 ⋔6 🚗 **P** Lift sB445–795
sB485–795 dB530–770
dB ⇆ ⋔550–920 M75–240 Pool
mountains

SÖLDEN
Tirol (☎05254)

★ ★ ★**Central** ☎2260 tx053353

Jul–Apr
⇆70 **P** Lift ⅅ sB ⇆ ⋔550–700
dB ⇆900–1240 ⅃ Pool mountains

★ ★ ★**Sonne** ☎2203

rm128 ⇆12 ⋔42 🚗 **P** DPn400–600 ⅃

SPITTAL AN DER DRAU
Kärnten (☎04762)

★ ★**Salzburg** Tirolerstr 12 ☎3165

rm55 ⇆16 ⋔11 A26rm 🚗 **P** ⅅ
mountains

&⅁N Nowak Villacherstr 72 ☎3447 BMW Vlo

&⅁W Riebler Koschatstr 13 ☎2561 Frd

STAINACH
Steiermark (☎03684)

&⅁W Denzel AG Nr 246 ☎2304 BMW Vlo

STEINACH AM BRENNER
Tirol(☎05272)

★ ★**Post** ☎6239 tx53245

Nov–Sep
rm34 ⇆10 ⋔19 A4rm 🚗 **P** ⅅ
sB254–274 sB ⇆ ⋔294–314

dB438–498 dB ⇆ ⋔548–588 M85–200
mountains

★ ★**Steinacherhof** ☎6241 tx54440

Dec–Oct
⇆60 🚗 **P** Lift ⅃ Pool mountains

★ ★**Weisses Rossl** ☎6206

20 Dec–25 Mar & 7 May–10 Oct
rm44 ⇆29 ⋔15 A27rm 🚗 **P** Lift
sB ⇆ ⋔330–350 dB ⇆ ⋔600–640
Pool mountains

★ ★**Wilder Mann** ☎6210

15 Dec–Oct
rm54 ⇆41 ⋔13 A8rm 🚗 **P** Lift Pool
mountains

STEINAKIRCHEN AM FORST
Niederösterreich (☎07488)

★ ★ ★**Schloss Ernegg** ☎214 tx019289

May–Oct
rm22 ⇆16 ⋔2 **P** sB320–420
sB ⇆ ⋔450–550 dB500–700
dB ⇆ ⋔640–960 ♣ ∩ mountains
river

STEYR
Oberösterreich (☎07252)

★ ★ ★*Mader* Stadtpl 36 ☎23358
tx28302

rm41 ⇆10 ⋔26 🚗 **P** Lift

★ ★**Minichmayr** Haratzmüllerstr 1
☎23410 tx028134

rm51 ⇆18 ⋔24 🚗 **P** Lift ⅅ sB183
sB ⇆ ⋔370–423 dB306
dB ⇆ ⋔416–596

J-Raiser Pachergasse 8 ☎23256 Frd

STUBEN
Voralberg (☎05582)

★ ★**Post** ☎761

15 Dec–Apr & Jun–15 Sep
rm55 ⇆20 ⋔14 A23rm **P**
DPn320–640 mountains

TELFS
Tirol (☎05262)

★**Hohe Munde** Untermarkstr 17 ☎2408
rm23 ⇆10 ⋔10 🚗 sB205
sB ⇆ ⋔295 dB350 dB ⇆ ⋔470 Pool

&⅁H Härting Bundesstr 1 ☎2854 MB

THIERSEE
Tirol (☎05376)

★ ★**Haus Charlotte** ☎5500

15 Dec–15 Oct
rm36 ⇆12 ⋔16 🚗 **P** Lift sB272–332
sB ⇆ ⋔367–430 sB444–564
dB ⇆ ⋔624–774 Pool mountains lake

&⅁S Mairhofer Nr 111 ☎4155 Ren

THUMERSBACH See **ZELL AM SEE**

TRAUNKIRCHEN AM TRAUNSEE
Oberösterreich (☎07617)

★ ★**Post** ☎307 tx24555

rm60 ⇆30 ⋔30 **P** Lift
sB ⇆ ⋔270–300 dB ⇆ ⋔500–580
mountains lake

TURRACHER-HÖHE
Kärnten (☎04275)

★ ★ ★ **Hochschober** ☎8213 tx42152
12 Apr – 6 Oct
rm72 ⇄35 ▥23 ▥ **P** sB370
sB ⇄ ▥490 dB750 – 790 dB ⇄ ▥1000
✒ Pool

UNTERGURGL
Tirol (☎05256)

★ ★ **Alpenglühn** (n.rest) ☎301
Nov – Apr & 15 Jun – Sep
rm12 ⇄5 ▥7 **P** mountains

VELDEN AM WÖRTHERSEE
Kärnten (☎04274)

★ ★ ★ **Schloss Velden** am Corso 24
☎2655 tx4294515
May – Sep
rm160 ⇄140 ▥ Lift ♪ sB490 – 560
sB ⇄ ▥610 – 730 dB940 – 1080
dB ⇄ ▥1160 – 1320

★ ★ ★ **Seehotel Europa** (BW) Wrannpark
1 ☎2770 tx422608
May – Oct
rm82 ⇄50 ▥32 A15rm ▥ **P** Lift ♪
Pn650 – 750 mountains lake

★ ★ ★ **Seehotel Veldnerhof-Mösslacher**
am Corso 17 ☎2018
rm107 ⇄47 ▥34 **P** Lift ♪
sB330 – 470 sB ⇄ ▥410 – 620
dB660 – 940 dB ⇄ ▥760 – 1000
M105 – 125 ✒ lake

★ ★ **Alte Post-Wrann** Europapl 4
☎2141 tx4294522
May – Oct
rm40 ⇄7 ▥17 ▥ **P** ✒ Pool

★ ★ **Seehotel Hubertushof** ☎2676
Etr – 15 Oct
rm50 ⇄22 ▥25 **P** sB490
sB ⇄ ▥560 – 660 dB420 dB ⇄
▥1120 – 1320 Pool mountains lake

▥**O Matachnig** am Corso 18 ☎2067 Ren

VIENNA See **WIEN**

VILLACH
Kärnten (☎04242)

★ ★ ★ **City** Bahnhof pl 3 ☎27897
tx045602
rm61 ⇄33 ▥28 **P** Lift ♪
sB ⇄ ▥400 – 560 dB ⇄ ▥570 – 840
M100 mountains

★ ★ ★ **Parkhotel** Moritzschstr 2 ☎23300
tx045582
⇄165 ▥ **P** Lift ♪ sB ⇄320 – 560
dB ⇄550 – 1020 M110 – 165 mountains

★ ★ **Mosser** Bahnhofstr 9 ☎24115
rm30 ⇄3 ▥27 **P** ♪ sB ⇄ ▥445
dB ⇄ ▥790

★ ★ **Post** (ROM) Hauptpl 26 ☎26101
tx45723
rm77 ⇄50 ▥27 **P** Lift ♪
sB ⇄ ▥350 – 510 dB ⇄ ▥550 – 820
mountains

▥**Brüder Brodnik** Klagenfurterstr 37
☎24388 Sko

S Papp KG Steinwenderstr 15 ☎24826
Frd

Austria

R Prohinig St-Georgen 117 ☎28186 BL

At **FÜRNITZ** (7km S on 85)

▥**W Denzel** Kärntenerstr 50a
☎(04257)271 Vlo

At **WARMBAD** (5km S)

★ ★ ★ **Josefinenhof** ☎25531 tx045563
rm61 ⇄42 ▥8 **P** Lift ♪ sB475 – 570
sB ⇄ ▥520 – 840 dB780 – 880
dB ⇄ ▥1060 – 1540 ✒ Pool mountains

VÖLS See **INNSBRUCK**

VÖSENDORF See **WIEN (VIENNA)**

WAIDHOFEN-AN-DER-THAYA
Niederösterreich (☎02842)

F Streicher Heldenreichsteinerstr 25
☎2352 Ren

WAIDRING
Tirol (☎05353)

★ ★ **Tiroler Adler** ☎5311
Closed Nov
rm33 ⇄33 ▥6 ▥ **P** Lift mountains

WALD IN PINZGAU
Salzburg (☎06565)

★ ★ **Jagschloss Graf Recke** ☎417
tx66659
19 May – Sep
rm33 ⇄19 ▥3 ▥ **P** sB385 – 415
sB ⇄ ▥495 – 515 dB670 – 770
dB ⇄ ▥930 – 950 M120 – 140 Pool
mountains

WARMBAD See **VILLACH**

WEISSKIRCHEN IN STEIERMARK
Steiermark (☎03577)

▥**Kocher** Bahnhofstr 21 ☎2567 Vau

WELS
Oberösterreich (☎07242)

E Fribl Eferdingerstr 69 ☎4432 BL

WESTENDORF
Tirol (☎05334)

★ **Jakobwirt** ☎6245
mid Dec – Mar & May – Sep
⇄50 **P** Lift sB ⇄360 – 390
dB ⇄620 – 680 mountains

WIEN (VIENNA) (☎0222)
See Plan page 76

Bezirk I

★ ★ ★ ★ ★ **Ambassador** Neuer Markt 5
☎527511 tx111906 Plan 1
rm107 ⇄103 ▥2 **P** Lift ♪
sB ⇄870 – 1090 dB ⇄1500 – 1850

★ ★ ★ ★ ★ **Bristol** (SRS) Kärntner Ring 1
☎529552 tx112474 Plan 2
⇄130 **P** Lift ♪ sB ⇄1200 – 1900
dB ⇄1900 – 2600

★ ★ ★ ★ ★ **Imperial** Kärtner Ring 16
☎651765 tx112630 Plan 3

rm150 ⇄140 ▥10 **P** Lift ♪ sB ⇄
▥1200 – 1900 dB ⇄ ▥1900 – 2800

★ ★ ★ ★ ★ **Sacher** Philharmonikerstr 4
☎525575 tx012520 Plan 5
rm 119 ⇄113 ▥3 **P** Lift ♪ sB500
sB ⇄ ▥800 – 1400 dB ⇄ ▥1700 – 2800

★ ★ ★ **Europa** (AL) Neuer Markt 3
☎521594 tx112292 Plan 6
⇄102 **P** Lift ♪ sB ⇄980 – 1020
dB ⇄1260 – 1590 M240

★ ★ ★ **Parkring** (BW)9 Parkring 12
☎526524 tx113420 Plan 7
⇄64 ▥ **P** Lift ♪ sB ⇄890 – 980
dB ⇄1190 – 1380

★ ★ ★ **Royal** Singerstr 3 ☎524631
tx112870 Plan 9
⇄66 Lift ♪ sB ⇄ ▥730 – 970
dB ⇄ ▥830 – 1300 Mfr110

★ ★ ★ **Stephansplatz** Stephanspl 9
☎635605 tx114334 Plan 9A
rm66 ⇄48 ▥14 Lift ♪ sB460
sB ⇄ ▥760 – 940 dB ⇄ ▥1140 – 1380

★ ★ **Amadeus** Wildpretmarkt 5
☎638738 Plan 10A
8 Jan – 23 Dec
rm30 ⇄22 ▥8 Lift ♪
sB ⇄ ▥1340 – 1760 dB ⇄ ▥1314

★ ★ **Astoria** (AL) Kärnterstr ☎526585
tx112856 Plan 11
rm108 ⇄103 **P** Lift ▥ sB500
sB ⇄ ▥980 – 1050 dB900
dB ⇄ ▥1360 – 1700

★ ★ **Kärntnerhof** Grashofgasse 4
(n.rest) ☎521923 tx112535 Plan 16
rm45 ⇄22 ▥12 **P** Lift ♪
sB ⇄ ▥450 – 620 dB ⇄ ▥650 – 960

★ ★ **Römischer Kaiser** (BW) Anngasse
16 (n.rest) ☎527751 tx113696 Plan 19
rm27 ⇄25 ▥12 **P** Lift ♪
sB ⇄ ▥850 – 950 dB ⇄ ▥1200 – 1550

★ ★ **Wandl** Peterspl 9 (n.rest)
☎636317 Plan 22
rm136 ⇄51 ▥70 **P** Lift ♪ sB320
sB ⇄ ▥450 – 560 dB550
dB ⇄ ▥760 – 880

★ ★ **Austria** Wolfengasse 3 (n.rest)
☎526724 tx112848 Plan 24
rm51 ⇄28 ▥12 **P** Lift ♪ sB410 – 500
sB ⇄ ▥620 – 770 dB610 – 710
dB ⇄ ▥930 – 1150

★ ★ **Graben** Dorotheegasse 3
☎521531 tx114700 Plan 25
rm46 ⇄40 ▥6 Lift ♪ sB ⇄
▥550 – 850 dB ⇄ ▥760 – 1080 Mfr110

F Augustin Laxenburgerstr 96A ☎641638
RR

Bezirk II

H Rischer Breitenfurterstr 89 ☎92852148
M/c BMW

Bezirk III

★ ★ ★ ★ ★ **Hilton International** am
Stadtpark ☎752652 tx136799 Plan 2A
⇄620 ▥ **P** Lift ♪ sB ⇄1190 – 1780
dB ⇄1600 – 2400

WIEN (VIENNA)

1	★★★★★Ambassador Bezirk	I
2	★★★★★Bristol	I
2A	★★★★★Hilton International	III
3	★★★★★Imperial	I
4	★★★★★Inter-Continental	III
5	★★★★★Sacher	I
6	★★★★Europa	I
7	★★★★Parkring	I
8	★★★★Prinz Eugen	IV
9	★★★★Royal	I
9A	★★★★Stephansplatz	I
10	★★★Alba	V
10A	★★★Amadeus	I
11	★★★Astoria	I
12	★★★Bellevue	IX
13	★★★Erzherzog Rainer	IV
13A	★★★ETAP Vienna	III
14	★★★Kahlenberg	XIX
15	★★★Kaiserhof	IV
16	★★★Kärntnerhof	I
17	★★★Palais Schwarzenberg	III
18	★★★Parkhotel Schönbrunn	XIII
18A	★★★Regina	IX
19	★★★Römischer Kaiser	I
21	★★★Tyrol	VI
22	★★★Wandl	I
23	★★★Weisser Hahn	VIII
24	★★Austria	I
25	★★Graben	I
26	★★Madeleine	XVII
28	★★Stieglbräu	XV

★★★★★Inter-Continental
Johannesgasse 28 ☎7505 tx131235
Plan 4

⇥498 🏛 P Lift ♪ sB 1450–1900
dB ⇥1840–2440 ⅃⅄

★★★ETAP Vienna am Heumarkt Ecke
Lisztstr ☎752535 tx11822 Plan 13A

⇥212 🏛 P Lift sB ⇥675–850
dB ⇥950–1180 Malc

★★★Palais Schwarzenberg
Schwarzenbergpl 9 ☎784515 tx136124
Plan 17

⇥42 🏛 P Lift ♪ sB ⇥1350–1680
dB ⇥1850–3450

⅃⅄F Ecki Untere Viadukstr 3 ☎738105
Ren

Bezirk IV

★★★★Prinz Eugen (ETAP) Wiedner
Gürtel 14 ☎651741 tx132483 Plan 8
rm106 ⇥65 🛏41 P Lift ♪
sB ⇥ 🛏891–975 dB ⇥ 🛏1470–1600
M180

★★★Erzherzog Rainer (BW) Wiedner
Hauptstr 27–29 ☎6546460 tx132329
Plan 13
rm84 ⇥70 🛏14 🏛 P Lift ♪
sB ⇥ 🛏765–965 dB ⇥ 🛏1310–1470

★★★Kaiserhof(BW)Frankenberggasse
10 ☎651701 tx136872 Plan 15
rm74 ⇥28 🛏46 Lift sB ⇥ 🛏680–750
dB ⇥ 🛏1040–1140

E Köstler Cumberlandstr 29 ☎92824388
BMW

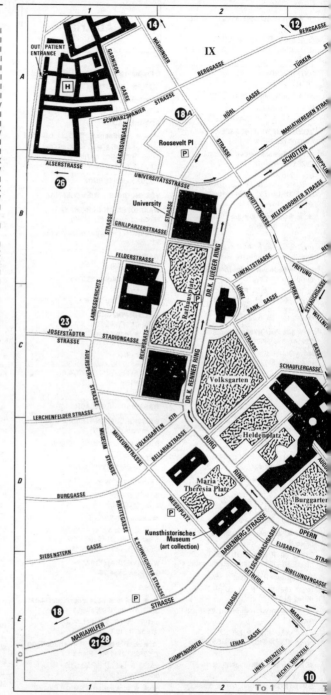

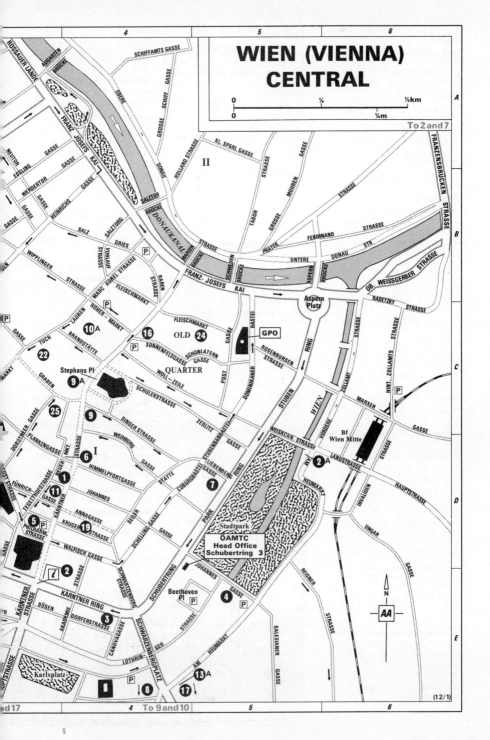

Austria

Bezirk V

★ ★ ★**Alba** Margarethenstr 53
☎575585 tx113264 Plan **10**
rm46 ⇌43 🛏3 🏛 **P** Lift ◐
sB ⇌ 🛏785−910 dB ⇌ 🛏1010−1290

Bezirk VI

★ ★ ★**Tyrol** Mariahilferstr 15 ☎575416
tx11185 Plan **21**
rm36 ⇌18 🛏18 **P** Lift ◐
sB ⇌ 🛏600−750 dB ⇌ 🛏840−1080

♨W **Denzel AG** Gumpendorferstr 19
☎92571571 BMW Vlo

♨G **Wittek** Liniengasse 28−30 ☎564283
Frd

Bezirk VIII

★ ★ ★**Weisser Hahn** Josefstädter Str 22
(n.rest) ☎423648 tx115533 Plan **23**
rm66 ⇌25 🛏29 Lift ◐ sB430−480
sB ⇌ 🛏550−735 dB ⇌ 🛏1000−1260

Bezirk IX

★ ★ ★**Bellevue** Althanstr 5 ☎345631
tx11906 Plan **12**
rm160 ⇌150 🛏10 🏛 **P** Lift ◐
sB ⇌ 🛏560−850 dB ⇌ 🛏800−1200
M140−160

★ ★ ★**Regina** Rooseveltpl 15 ☎427681
tx114700 Plan **18A**
rm128 ⇌90 🛏31 Lift ◐ sB360−460
sB ⇌ 🛏530−850 dB ⇌ 🛏670−1500
Mfr110

K Richter OHG Lazarettgasse 6
☎426521 Frd

Bezirk X

♨**Ing Felber** Jagdgasse 6 ☎641674 Opl
Vau

♨**J Manhardt** Himbergerstr 32 ☎685310
Frd

♨**F M Tarbuk** Davidgasse 90 ☎641631
Dat Sab Sko

Bezirk XIII

★ ★ ★**Parkhotel Schönbrunn** (SRS)
Hietzinger Hauptstr 10−14
☎822676 tx132513 Plan **18**
rm490 ⇌364 🛏81 A52rm **P** Lift ◐
sB ⇌ 🛏785−1125 dB ⇌ 🛏1520−1990
Pool

Bezirk XIV

☆ ☆ ☆**Novotel Wien West**
Autobahnstation Auhof ☎972542
tx135585 Not on plan
⇌116 **P** Lift ◐ sB ⇌780 dB ⇌1000
Pool

Bezirk XV

★ ★**Stieglbräu** Mariahilferstr 156 (n.rest)
☎833621 tx133636 Plan **28**
rm54 ⇌36 🛏5 Lift ◐ sB385
sB ⇌ 🛏600−650 dB660−680
dB ⇌ 🛏950−1050

♨W **Denzel** Tautenhayngasse 22
☎920306 Vlo

Bezirk XVII

★ ★**Madeleine** Geblergasse 21 (n.rest)
☎434741 tx115121 Plan **26**
rm80 ⇌60 🛏13 🏛 **P** Lift ◐
sB ⇌ 🛏650−900 dB ⇌ 🛏950−1150
lake

Bezirk XIX

★ ★ ★**Kahlenberg** Kahlenberg
☎321251 tx74970 Plan **14**
rm32 ⇌13 🛏15 **P** Lift

Bezirk XXII

I Bader KG Langobardenstr 145
☎221365 Frd

At **SCHWECHAT** (Airport) (10kmSE)

☆ ☆ ☆**Novotel** ☎776666 tx111566 Not
on plan
⇌ 🛏127 **P** Lift ◐ sB ⇌ 🛏780
dB ⇌ 🛏1000 Pool

At **VÖSENDORF** (10kmS)

☆ ☆ ☆**Novotel Wien Süd** ☎676506
tx134793 Not on plan
⇌102 **P** Lift ◐ sB ⇌780 dB ⇌1000
Pool

WIENER NEUSTADT
Niederösterreich (☎02622)

♨W **Denzel AG** Neunkirchnerstr 129
☎3766 Vlo

WÖRGL
Tirol (☎05332)

☆ ☆ ☆**Angath** (AL) ☎4375 tx51135
⇌45 **P** Lift ◐ mountains

★ ★**Central** Bahnhofstr 27 ☎2459
rm55 ⇌9 🛏19 A7rm **P** Lift sB180 sB
⇌ 🛏210 dB300 dB ⇌ 🛏330 M80
Pool mountains

YBBS AN DER DONAU
Niederösterreich (☎07412)

★ ★**Royal Weisses Rössel** ☎2292

Belvedere Palace, Vienna

May−Oct
rm32 ⇌4 🛏14 **P** Lift sB180
sB ⇌ 🛏250−290 dB300
dB ⇌ 🛏350−420

★**Steiner** Burgpl 2 ☎2629
rm20 ⇌11 🛏11 A40rm 🏛 **P** sB160
sB ⇌ 🛏200 dB300 dB ⇌ 🛏800

ZAMS See **LANDECK**

ZELL AM SEE
Salzburg (☎06542)

★ ★**Berner** N-Gassner-Promenade 1
☎2557
Closed Nov
rm28 ⇌26 🛏2 **P** Lift
sB ⇌ 🛏360−440 dB ⇌ 🛏640−800
lake mountains

♨G **Altendorfer OHG** Brücker Bundesstr
108 ☎3283 Opl

♨F **Gottwald** Flugplatzstr 3 ☎2490 Ren

At **SCHÜTTDORF** (2km S)

H Kirchner Bundesstr 441 ☎3826 Frd

At **THUMERSBACH** (2km E)

★ ★**Bellevue** ☎3104
May−Oct
rm51 ⇌11 🛏7 A18rm **P**
sB ⇌ 🛏160−240 dB ⇌ 🛏390−550

ZELL AM ZILLER
Tirol (☎05282)

★ ★ ★**Tirolerhof** ☎2227
22 Dec−9 Oct
🛏40 **P** Lift sB 🛏270−290
dB 🛏500−540 mountains

ZIRL
Tirol (☎05238)

★ ★**Goldener Löwe** (BW) Hauptpl
☎2330 tx053350
15 Feb−Dec
rm19 ⇌12 🏛 **P** sB260−290
sB ⇌430−510 dB465−505
dB ⇌705−940 M120−250 mountains

ZÜRS AM ARLBERG
Vorarlberg (☎05583)

★ ★ ★**Zürserhof** ☎513 tx5239114
24 Nov−15 Apr
⇌120 🏛 **P** Lift ◐

78

BELGIUM

Belgium is a varied, charming country where the rivers and gorges of the Ardennes contrast sharply with the rolling plains which make up the rest of the countryside. It is small and densely populated, bordered by France, German Federal Republic, Luxembourg and the Netherlands. Despite the fact that it is heavily industrialised, it possesses some beautiful scenery, notably the great forest of the Ardennes. The resorts in the Oostende area offer a selection of wide, safe, sandy beaches and cover about forty miles of coastline. The climate is temperate and similar to that of Britain, with the variation between summer and winter lessened by the effects of the Gulf Stream. French is spoken in the south, Flemish in the north and a German dialect in the eastern part of the province of Liège.

Area *11,775 sq miles*
Population *9,800,000*
Local time *GMT + 1*
(Summer GMT + 2)

National flag *Vertical tricolour of black, yellow and red*

How to get there

Many cross-Channel ferries operate direct from Dover and Folkestone to Oostende or from Dover, Felixstowe and Hull to Zeebrugge. Alternatively, it is possible to use the shorter Channel crossings from Dover or Folkestone to France and drive along the coastal road to Belgium. Fast hovercraft services operate from Dover to Calais and Boulogne.

Ypres: les Halles

Motoring regulations and general information

This information should be read in conjunction with the general content of the European ABC (pages 6–27). **Note** As certain regulations and requirements are common to many countries they are covered by one entry in the ABC and the following headings represent some of the subjects dealt with in this way:
Crash or safety helmets
Drinking and driving
Fire extinguisher
First-aid kit
Insurance
International distinguishing sign
Medical treatment
Overtaking
Police fines
Radio telephones/Radio transmitters
Rear view mirror
Road signs
Seat belts
Tyres
Visitors' registration

AA Port agent
(See also *AA Agents* page 7)
8400 Oostende G E Huyghe & Son, Zuidstraat 10 ☎(059)702855.

Accidents
Fire and **ambulance** ☎900 **police** ☎901 but in Bruxelles, Brugge, Gent, Mechelen, Charleroi and Antwerpen ☎906. The police must be called if an unoccupied stationary vehicle is damaged or if injuries are caused to persons; in the latter case the car must not be moved, see recommendations under *Accidents* page 7.

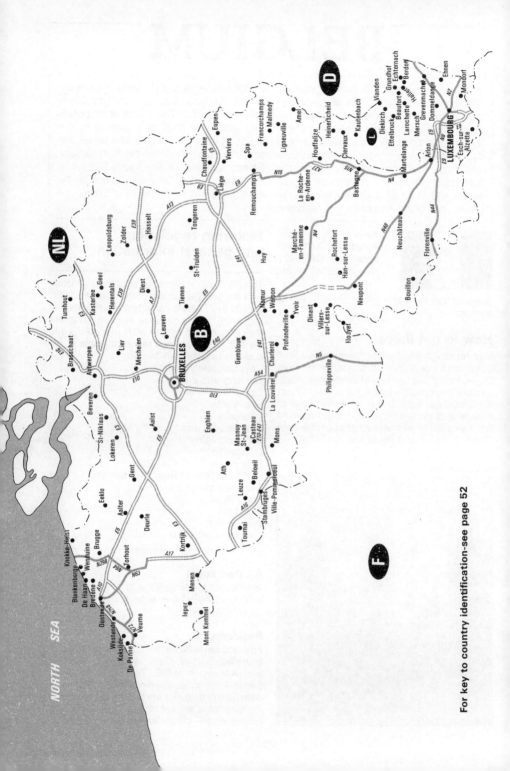

NORTH SEA

NL

B

D

L

LUXEMBOURG

F

For key to country identification—see page 52

Accommodation

The official hotel guide classifies hotels 1–5 according to their degree of comfort. Standards for amenities and comfort are laid down by law for establishments designated as *Hotel*, *Pension*, *Hostellerie*, *Auberge*, *Gasthof* and *Motel*. Such hotels exhibit the distinctive sign issued by the Belgian National Tourist Office.

Room prices are exhibited in hotel reception areas and full details of all charges including service and taxes are shown in each room. They are subject to approval by the Ministry of Economic Affairs.

There is a reservation service operated by Belgium Tourist Reservations (BTR), BP41 Bruxelles 23, 1000 Bruxelles ☎(02)2305029 or telex 65888 who provide a free hotel booking service throughout the country. Once in Belgium tourist offices in major towns can also arrange hotel bookings for visitors; the service is free but a deposit is payable in advance which will be deducted from the final bill.

Boats

When temporarily importing boats into Belgium documentation, in addition to the *Customs regulations* referred to below, may be required if your route takes you through France. See *Boats* page 8 for further information.

Breakdown

The Belgian motoring club, Touring Club Royal de Belgique (TCB), maintains an efficient breakdown service known as Touring Secours/Touring Wegenhulp. The Touring Secours/Touring Wegenhulp operates a 24 hour breakdown service throughout the year.

The Flemish Automobile Club (VAB-VTB operates only in the Flemish area) and the Royal Automobile Club of Belgium (RACB) each have patrol cars displaying the signs 'Wacht op de Weg'or 'RACB'. However, neither is associated with the AA and motorists will have to pay for all services. See also *Breakdown* page 8 and *Warning triangles* page 84.

British Consulates

(See also page 8)
1040 Bruxelles Britannia House, 28 rue Joseph II, ☎(02)2179000. There are also Consulates in Antwerpen, Gent and Liège.

Currency and banking hours

(See also page 11)
The unit of currency is the Belgian franc, divided into 100 centimes. There is no restriction on the amount of currency which may be taken into or out of Belgium, whether in the form of travellers' cheques or Belgian and foreign banknotes.

Banks are generally open from 09.00–15.30hrs from Monday to Friday and closed all day Saturday. Many also close for lunch. Outside banking hours currency can be exchanged in Bruxelles at the Gare du Nord and the Gare du Midi, open 07.00–22.00hrs daily and at Zaventem Airport open 07.30–22.00hrs daily.

Customs regulations

A *Customs Carnet de Passages en Douane* is required for all pleasure craft temporarily imported by road, except craft without motors not exceeding 18ft (5.5 metres) in length, and for trailers not accompanied by the towing vehicle. See also *Customs regulations for European countries* page 11 for further information.

Dimensions and weight restrictions

Vehicles must not exceed-height: 4 metres; width: 2.5 metres; length: vehicle/caravan combination 18 metres. Trailers without brakes may have a total weight of up to 50% of the towing vehicle with a maximum of 750kg.

Driving licence

(See also page 13)
A valid British driving licence is acceptable in Belgium. The minimum age at which a visitor may drive a temporarily imported car or motorcycle is 18 years.

Emergency messages to tourists

(See also page 14)
Emergency messages to tourists are broadcast daily on Belgian Radio in French and Dutch.

Radio Television Belge transmitting on 483 metres medium wave broadcasts these messages in French before the news at 14.00hrs and after the news at 19.00hrs Monday to Friday and after the news at 14.00 and 19.00hrs on Saturday and Sunday.

Belgische Radio en Televisie (BRT1) transmitting on 323.6 metres medium wave broadcasts the messages daily in Dutch after the news at 07.00, 08.00, 12.00, 17.00, 19.00 and 22.00hrs.

Radio Television Belge (RTBF) transmitting on 16 and 49 metres short wave broadcasts the messages daily in French at 12.45hrs.

Belgische Radio en Televisie (BRT) transmitting on 25.65 metres medium wave and 49.91 metres short wave broadcasts the messages in Dutch after the news at 10.00hrs.

Lights
(See also page 17)

Between dusk and dawn and in all cases where visibility is restricted to 200m, dipped or full headlights must be used. However, headlights must be dipped: where street lighting is continuous permitting clear vision for 100m; at the approach of oncoming traffic (including vehicles on rails); when following another vehicle at a distance of less than 50 metres and, where the road is adjacent to water, at the approach of oncoming craft if the pilot is likely to be dazzled. It is compulsory for *motorcyclists* to use dipped headlights during the day.

Vehicles parked on the public highway must use position lights (parking lights) both day and night if vehicles are not visible from 100 metres.

In built-up areas the position lights may be replaced by a single parking light displayed on the side nearest to the centre of the road providing the vehicle is not more than 6 metres long and 2 metres wide, has no trailer attached to it and its maximum carrying capacity is not more than eight persons excluding the driver.

Motoring Club
(See also page 18)

The **Touring Club Royal de Belgique** (TCB) has its head office at 44 rue de la Loi, 1040 Bruxelles ☎(02)2332211 and branch offices in most towns.

The Bruxelles head office is open weekly 09.00–18.00hrs; Saturday 09.00–12.00hrs. Regional offices are open weekdays 09.00–12.30hrs (Monday from 09.30hrs) and 14.00–18.00hrs; Saturday 09.00–12.00hrs. All offices are closed on Saturday afternoons and Sundays.

Motorways
There is a comprehensive system of toll free motorways linking major towns and adjoining countries.

Orange badge scheme for disabled drivers
(See also page 19)

In Belgium special parking places are reserved for disabled drivers and are indicated by parking sign (white letter on blue panel) with the international disabled symbol added. Badge holders may also park without time limit by road signs and in *blue zones* where parking time is otherwise restricted. In addition many local authorities do not require badge holders to pay at parking meters. However, badge holders are not allowed to park in places where parking is otherwise prohibited.

Parking
(See also page 19)

Regulations differentiate between *waiting* (long enough to load or unload goods or for passengers to get in or out) and *parking*. Vehicles must be left on the right-hand side of the road, except in one-way streets when they can be left on either side. Where possible the vehicle must be left on the level shoulder inside built-up areas and on the shoulder, level or otherwise, outside these areas. If the shoulder is used by pedestrians, then at least 1 metre must be left for them on the side farthest away from the traffic. Parking restrictions are similar to those in the UK. Before leaving your vehicle make sure it does not restrict the movement of other road users and do not park on major roads outside built-up areas; on a carriageway marked in traffic lanes or where broken yellow lines are painted; opposite another stationary vehicle if this would hamper the crossing of **two** other vehicles and on the central reservation of dual carriageways.

Bruxelles: Royal Palace

In many towns and cities there are short-term parking areas known as *blue zones* where parking discs must be displayed. Outside these areas a parking disc must be used where the parking sign has an additional panel showing a parking disc. In some areas parking meters may also be found, in which case the parking disc is not valid in the meter bay.

Where these are used the instructions for use will be on the meter.

Passengers
(See also page 19)
Children under 12 are not permitted to travel in a vehicle as front seat passengers when rear seating is available.

Petrol
(See also page 20)
Credit cards Some petrol stations will accept Diners Club International and Visa.
Duty free petrol In addition to the petrol in the vehicle tank up to 10 litres in a can may be imported free of customs duty and tax.
Octane rating Normal (92–94) and Super (98–100).

Postal information
Mail Postcards BFr10.00, letters up to 20g BFr14.00
Post Offices There are 1,800 post offices in Belgium. The opening hours of larger offices are from 09.00–17.00hrs Monday to Friday. The smaller offices open from 09.00–12.30hrs and 14.00–16.00hrs Monday to Friday.

Postcheques
(See also page 21)
Postcheques may be cashed for any amount up to a maximum of BFr4,000 per cheque, but only at main post offices. Counter positions are identified by the words *Chèques Postaux* or *Postchecks*. See above for post office opening hours.

Priority
(See also *Priority including Roundabouts* page 22)
In built-up areas, a driver must give way to bus drivers who have used their direction indicators to show they intend driving away from a bus stop. Trams have priority from both right and left.

Public holidays
Official public holidays in Belgium for 1985 are given below. See also *Public holidays* page 22
January 1 (New Year's Day)
April 5 (Good Friday)
April 8 (Easter Monday)
May 1 (Labour Day)
May 16 (Ascension Day)
May 27 (Whit Monday)
July 21† (National Day)
August 15 (Assumption Day)
November 1 (All Saints' Day)
November 11 (Armistice Day)
December 25 (Christmas Day)
† Sunday

Religious services
(See also page 23)
The Intercontinental Church Society welcomes visitors from any denomination to English language services in the following centres: *8000 Brugge* The Revd Merry Hart, Niklaas Desparstraat 6 ☎(050)341194
1050 Bruxelles The Ven John Lewis, 38 Avenue Guillaume Gilbert ☎(02)5117183

Roads
(See also *Road conditions* page 23)
A good road system is available. However, one international route that has given more cause for complaints than any other is, without doubt, that from Calais (France) to Köln (Cologne) (Germany). The problem is aggravated by the fact that there are two official languages in Belgium: in the Flemish part of Belgium all signs are in Flemish only, while in the French half of the country the signs are all in French. Bruxelles (Brussels) seems to be the only neutral ground where the signs show the two alternative spellings of place names (Antwerpen-Anvers; Gent-Gand; Liège-Luik; Lille-Rijsel; Mons-Bergen; Namur-Namen; Oostende-Ostende; Paris-Parijs; Tournai-Doornik).

Shopping hours
All shops are usually open 09.00–18.00, 19.00 or 20.00hrs from Monday to Saturday, however, *food shops* may close 1hr later.

Speed limits
(See also page 25)
The following limits apply even if they are not indicated unless there are signs to the contrary. A placename denotes the start of a built-up area:

Car/caravan/trailer
Built-up area 60kph (37mph)
Other roads 90kph (56mph)
Motorways & 4 lane roads 120kph (74mph)

Minimum on motorways on straight level stretches is 70kph (43mph). Vehicles being towed after an accident or breakdown are limited to 25kph (15mph) on all roads and, if on a motorway, must leave at the first exit.

Spiked, studded or snow tyres
(See also page 10)
Spiked tyres are permitted between 1 November and 31 March on vehicles under 3.5tonnes. They must be fitted to all four wheels and also to a trailer over 500kg. Speed should not exceed 90kph (56mph) on motorways and other roads having four or more lanes and 60kph (37mph) on all other public roads.

Tourist information offices

(See also page 25)
The Belgian National Tourist Office is at 38 Dover St, London W1X 3RB. Their telephone number is 01-499 5379 and they will be pleased to supply information on all aspects of tourism. In Belgium the National Tourist organisation is supplemented by the Provincial Tourist Federation, whilst in most towns there are local tourist offices. These organisations will help tourists with information and accommodation.

Traffic lights

(See also page 25)
The three-colour traffic light system operates in Belgium. However, the lights may be replaced by arrows of the individual colours and these have the same meaning as the lights, but only in the direction in which the arrow points.

Using the telephone

(See also page 26)
Insert coin **after** lifting receiver, dialling tone same as UK. When making calls to subscribers within Belgium precede number with relevant area code. (shown in parentheses against town entry in gazetteer) Use BFr5 coins for local calls and BFr5, 10 or 20 coins for national and international calls.

International callbox identification Boxes identified with European flags.
Telephone rates A telephone call to the UK costs BFr25 for each minute with a minimum of BFr75.
What to dial for the Irish Republic 00 *353.
What to dial for the UK 00 *44.
*Wait for second dialling tone

Warning triangle

The use of a warning triangle is compulsory for all vehicles except two-wheelers. The triangle must be placed 30 metres (33yds) behind the vehicle on ordinary roads and 100 metres (109yds) on motorways to warn following traffic of any obstruction; it must be visible at a distance of 50 metres (55yds). See also *Warning triangles/Hazard warning lights* page 26.

Winter conditions

(See also page 27)
From 1 November to 31 March, motorists may telephone (02)2305775 (French), 2308333 (Dutch) at any time of the day or night for a pre-recorded general report on road conditions. They might obtain information concerning the specific section of road in Belgium or a main route abroad by telephoning (02)2332211 between 07.00 and 21.00hrs.

Prices are in Belgian Francs

St% Service and tax charge
Supplementary local taxes are payable in addition to the charges shown. These vary from town to town.

Abbreviations:
av	avenue	r	rue
bd	boulevard	rte	route
esp	espalanade	str	straat
pl	place, plein		

Belgium is divided into the Flemish region in the north and the French-speaking Walloon region in the south. Some of the town names in the gazetteer show both languages, and that shown first is the one used locally. Brussels (Bruxelles/Brussel) is officially bi-lingual.

AALST (ALOST)
Oost-Vlaanderen (☎053)

★**Borse van Amsterdam** Grote Markt 26 ☎211581
Closed 2–14 Jul
rm6 ⇄1 sB500 sB⇄580 dB1000 dB⇄1150

AALTER
Oost-Vlaanderen (☎091)

★★**Memling** Markt 11 (n.rest) ☎741013
rm9 ⇄3 ⋔6 sB ⇄ ⋔850–950 dB⇄ ⋔1300–1500

AARLEN See **ARLON**

ALBERT PLAGE See **KNOKKE-HEIST**

AMEL (AMBLEVE)
Liège (☎080)

★**Oos Heem** Deidenberg 124 ☎349692
rm19 ⋔2 **P** sB890 sB ⋔955 db1400 dB ⋔1540 Pool

ANTWERPEN (ANVERS)
Antwerpen (☎03)

☆ ☆ ☆**Crest (See page 51)** G-Lagrellelaan 10 ☎2372900 tx33843
⇄245 **P** Lift ♪ sB ⇄2650 dB ⇄3200

☆ ☆ ☆**Eurotel Antwerpen** (GT)
Copernicuslaan 2 ☎2316780 tx33965
rm350 ⇄350 ⋔128 ⓜ **P** Lift
sB ⇄ ⋔2390–3140 dB⇄ ⋔3480–3980 ⅏ Pool

☆ ☆ ☆**Novotel Antwerpen Nord**
Luithagen-Haven 6 ☎5420320 tx32488
⇄119 **P** Lift sB⇄1750 dB⇄2300 ⅏ Pool

★ ★ ★**Plaza** Charlottalei 43 (n.rest) ☎2395970 tx31531
rm79 ⇄75 ⋔4 ⓜ Lift
sB ⇄ ⋔2135–3200 dB ⇄ ⋔3125–4905

★ ★ ★**Waldorf** (GT) Belgielei 36 ☎2309950 tx32948
⇄74 ⓜ **P** Lift sB ⇄1500 dB ⇄2200

🅢**Antwerp Car Service** Ijzerlaan 52 ☎2329830 Peu Tal

🅢**J Lins** Tunnelpl 3–7 ☎2339928 **P** BL Dat Vau

🅢**Vleminckveld** Vleminckveld 42 ☎2319088 Fia

At **BERCHEM** (1 km S)

🅢**Singel Motors** Uitbreidingstr 94–6 ☎2309999 Vlo

At **BORGERHOUT**

☆ ☆ ☆**Holiday Inn** Lippenslaan 66 ☎2359191 tx34479
⇄ ⋔179 **P** Lift ♪ sB ⇄ ⋔2400 dB ⇄ ⋔3050 Pool

ARLON (AARLEN)
Luxembourg (☎063)

★ ★**Nord** r des Faubourgs ☎220283
rm24 ⇄7 ⋔3 **P** sB655 sB ⇄ ⋔855 dB860 dB ⇄ ⋔1260

🅢**Beau Site** av de Longwy 163–167 ☎220389 Frd

ATH
Hainaut (☎068)

🅢**Center** Chaussée de Bruxelles 45 ☎224283 **P** BL

BALMORAL See **SPA**

BASTOGNE
Luxembourg (☎062)

84

★★Lebrun (DPn) r de Marché 8
☎211193

Feb–Dec
rm26 ⇔15 ᵐ6 ᵐ sB615 sB ⇔ ᵐ765
dB985 dB ⇔ ᵐ1200–1615

Luxembourg (DPn) pl MacAuliffe 25
☎211226

rm9

⑩F Luc-Nadin r des Scieries 16
☎211806 BL

BELOEIL
Hainaut (☎069)

★★Couronne r Durieu 8 ☎679567
rm7 ⇔4 P

BERCHEM See **ANTWERPEN (ANVERS)**

BERGEN See **MONS**

BEVEREN-WAAS
Oost-Vlaanderen (☎03)

☆☆☆Beveren Gentseweg 280
☎7758623
rm29 ⇔7 ᵐ22 P sB ⇔ ᵐ900–1050
dB ⇔ ᵐ1000–1300 Pool

BLANKENBERGE
West-Vlaanderen (☎050)

★★★Ideal Zeedijk 244 ☎411691

Apr–20 Sep
⇔50 ᵐ Lift sB ⇔1140 dB ⇔2025
Pool

★★Marie-José av Maria-José 2
☎411639
rm53 ⇔12 ᵐ17 Lift sB600–700
sB ⇔ ᵐ700–900 dB1200 dB ⇔ ᵐ1400

★★Pacific J-de-Troozlaan 48 ☎411542

Closed 16–31 Oct
rm24 ᵐ12 Lift sB950–1050
sBᵐ1160–1260 dB1300–1500
dB ᵐ1720–1920

★★Petit Rouge Zeedijk Bakkerstr 1
☎411032

Apr–15 Sep & 5 Oct–15 Nov
rm60 ⇔20 ᵐ10 P Lift sB805–925
sB ⇔ ᵐ1100–1250 dB1500–1800
dB ⇔ ᵐ2100–2400

BOUILLON
Luxembourg (☎061)

★★Panorama r av Dessus de la Ville
☎466138

21 Mar–15 Nov
rm49 ⇔11 ᵐ14 ᵐ P Lift sB650
sB ⇔ ᵐ850 dB1050 dB ⇔ ᵐ1350

★Semois r du Collège 46 ☎466027
rm45 ⇔14 ᵐ22 ᵐ Lift sB425–545
sB ⇔ ᵐ725–850 dB770–875
dB ⇔ ᵐ1035–1350

BOUVIGNES See **DINANT**

BRASSCHAAT-POLYGOON
Antwerpen (☎031)

Belgium

☆☆Dennenhof Bredabaan 940
☎6630509
ᵐ20 P sB ᵐ850 dB ᵐ1000 Pool

BREDENE
West-Vlaanderen (☎059)

★Zomerlust P-Benoitlaan 26 ☎320340
rm20 dB774–877

BRUGGE (BRUGES)
West-Vlaanderen (☎050)

☆☆☆☆Holiday Inn Boeveeriestr 2
☎335341 tx81369
⇔ ᵐ128 ᵐ Lift sB ⇔ ᵐ2800
dB ⇔ ᵐ3500 Pool

☆☆☆Novotel Chartreuseweg 20
☎312851 tx81507
⇔ ᵐ101 P Lift sB ⇔ ᵐ1900
dB ⇔ ᵐ2300–2375

★★★Park t'Zand Vrydagmarkt 5
(n.rest) ☎333364 tx81686
⇔61 Lift sB ⇔2100 dB ⇔2500–2800

★★Duc de Bourgogne Huidenvetterspl
12 ☎332038

Closed Jan & Jul
⇔9 sB ⇔1800 dB ⇔2300–3600

★★Europ Augustynerei (n.rest)
☎337956

3 Mar–18 Nov
rm28 ⇔6 ᵐ19 ᵐ Lift sB ⇔ ᵐ1690
dB ⇔ ᵐ2380

★★Jacobs Baliestr 1 (n.rest) ☎339831

Feb–Dec & New Year
rm28 ⇔12 ᵐ9 Lift

★★Sablon Noordzandstr 21 ☎333902
rm46 ⇔19 ᵐ6 Lift

★Févéry Collaert Mansionstr 3 (n.rest)
☎331269
ᵐ10 Lift dB ᵐ1230–1350

★Lybeer Korte Vuldersstr 31 (n.rest)
☎334355

Mar–Oct
rm24 sB580 dB990

⑩Canada St-Pieterskaai 15 ☎317370
Frd

BRUXELLES-BRUSSEL
Brabant (☎02)
See Plan page 86

★★★★★Brussels Sheraton pl Rogier
3 ☎2193400 tx26887 Plan **1**
⇔474 P ⅅ sB ⇔3050–5000
dB ⇔3500–5000 Pool

★★★★★Hilton International 38 bd de
Waterloo ☎5138877 tx22744 Plan **2**
⇔369 P Lift ⅅ sB ⇔3120–4720
dB ⇔4165–5890

★★★★Amigo r de l'Amigo 1–3
☎5115910 tx21618 Plan**3**
rm183 ⇔173 ᵐ10 ᵐ Lift

---

sB ⇔ ᵐ3000–3900 dB ⇔ ᵐ3500–4350
M600

★★★★Astoria (ETAP) r Royale 103
☎2176290 tx25040 Plan **4**
⇔125 Lift sB ⇔2750 dB ⇔3555

★★★Brussels Europa (Forum) r de la
Loi 107 ☎2301333 tx25121 Plan **5**
⇔245 P Lift ⅅ sB ⇔3275 dB ⇔4450

★★★Mayfair Crest (See page 51) av
Louise 381–383 ☎6499800 tx24821
Plan **7**
⇔99 ᵐ Lift sB ⇔3385 dB ⇔4255

★★★Palace pl C-Rogier 22
☎2176200 tx65604 Plan **8**
⇔ ᵐ352 Lift sB ⇔ ᵐ2350
dB ⇔ ᵐ2800

★★★Royal Windsor (SRS)
Duquesnoystr 5–7 ☎5114215 tx62905
Plan **9**
⇔ ᵐ275 ᵐ Lift sB ⇔ ᵐ4900
dB ⇔ ᵐ5900

★★Arenberg r d'Assaut 15 (n.rest)
☎5110770 tx25660 Plan **11**
rm158 ⇔123 ᵐ35 ᵐ Lift
sB ⇔ ᵐ1250 dB ⇔ ᵐ1700

★★Bedford (MAP) r du Midi 135
☎5127840 tx24059 Plan **12**
⇔250 ᵐ Lift sB ⇔2475–2650
dB ⇔3090–3310

★★Delta chaussée de Charleroi
☎5390160 tx63225 Plan **13**
⇔ ᵐ253 ᵐ Lift sB ⇔ ᵐ2150
dB ⇔ ᵐ2650

★★Jolly Atlanta bd A-Max 7 (n.rest)
☎2170120 tx21475 Plan **14**
⇔240 ᵐ Lift sB ⇔3000–3500
dB ⇔4090–4400

★★Président Nord (MAP) bd A-Max
107 (n.rest) ☎2190060 tx61417 Plan **16**
rm63 ⇔49 ᵐ14 Lift
sB ⇔ ᵐ2120–2330 dB ⇔ ᵐ2240–2540

★★Ramada Charleroisesteenweg 38
☎5393000 tx25539 Plan **17**
⇔ ᵐ201 ᵐ Lift sB ⇔ ᵐ3515–3715
dB ⇔ ᵐ4380–4590

☆☆Arcade pl Ste-Catherine ☎5137620
tx22476 Plan **18**
⇔234

★★Noga r de Béguinage (n.rest)
☎2186763 Plan **19**
rm19 ⇔10 ᵐ7 Lift

★★Queen Anne bd E-Jacqmain 110
(n.rest) ☎2171600 Plan **20**
rm59 ⇔54 Lift sB ⇔ ᵐ1145–1260
dB ⇔1525–1650

★★Scheers (Inter) bd A-Max 132
☎2177760 tx21675 Plan **21**
rm62 ⇔46 ᵐ16 Lift
sB ⇔ ᵐ2186–2408 dB ⇔ ᵐ2416–2638

★★Van Belle Chaussée de Mong 39
☎5213516 tx63840 Not on plan
rm146 ⇔71 ᵐ65 ᵐ Lift sB825 →

sB ⇄ 🛏1330 dB1140
dB ⇄ 🛏1510–2000

★**Albergo** av de la Toison d'Or 58
☎5382960 Plan **22**

rm58 ⇄55 🛏3 🚾 **P** Lift

★**Concorde-Louise** r de la Concorde 59
(n.rest) ☎5128610 Plan **23**

rm20 ⇄12 🛏8 🚾 Lift sB⇄ 🛏1030
dB ⇄ 🛏1345

★**Pacific** r A-Dansaert 57 ☎5118459
Plan **24**

rm15 🚾 **P** Lift sB435 dB670
dB ⇄ 🛏920

🚗**Anio Motors** Chaussée de Waterloo
567 ☎3451950 M/c Frd

🚗**Demaeyer Motors** r de Hennin 18–22
☎6492020 BL

🚗**Group Motors** av Gl-Médecin Derache
120–122 ☎6470780 Opl Vau

🚗**Leon** r de Koninck 81–83 ☎4253827
P All makes

🚗**Moranville** r de Moranville 66
☎4254099 **P** AR

BRUXELLES-BRUSSEL AIRPORT
At **DIEGEM** (8km NE)

☆ ☆ ☆**Holiday Inn** Holidaystr 7
☎7205865 tx24285 Plan **6**

⇄ 🛏300 **P** Lift ☽
sB ⇄ 🛏1835–3680 dB⇄ 🛏2900–4725
Pool

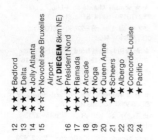

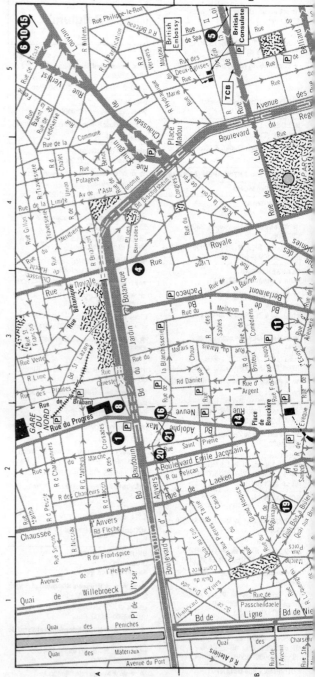

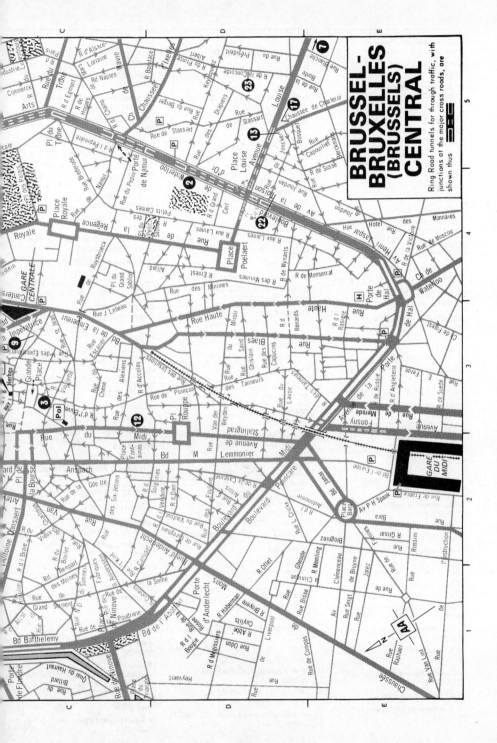

BRUSSEL-
BRUXELLES
(BRUSSELS)
CENTRAL

Ring Road tunnels for through traffic, with
junctions at the major cross roads, are
shown thus

☆ ☆ ☆ ★**Sofitel** Bessenveldstr 15
☎7206050 tx26595 Plan **10**
⇌125 🚗 sB⇌fr2850 dB⇌fr3100
Pool

☆ ☆ ☆**Novotel Brussels Airport**
Olmenstr ☎7205830 tx26751 Plan **15**
⇌ 🛏158 **P** Lift sB⇌ 🛏2450
dB⇌ 🛏2580 Pool

CASTEAU
Hainaut (☎065)

☆ ☆ ☆**Crest (See page 51)** Chaussée de
Bruxelles 38 ☎728741 tx57164
rm71 ⇌35 🛏36 **P** ⅅ sB⇌ 🛏1775
dB⇌ 🛏2590

CHARLEROI
Hainaut (☎071)

⅏**Leteren Charleroi** r Montignies 145
☎3222232 **P** Aud VW

CHAUDFONTAINE
Liège (☎041)

★ ★**Palace** esp 2 ☎650070
rm32 ⇌27 **P** Lift sB925 sB⇌ 🛏1290
dB1565 dB⇌ 🛏1565

COQ (LE) See HAAN (DE)

COURTRAI See KORTRIJK

COXYDE-SUR-MER See KOKSIJDE

DEURLE
Oost-Vlaanderen (☎091)

★ ★**Auberge de Pêcheur** Pontstr 42
☎824444
⇌11 **P** sB⇌950–1500 dB⇌950–1500

DIEGEM See BRUXELLES-BRUSSEL AIRPORT

DIEST
Brabant (☎013)

★ ★**Modern** Leuvensesteenweg 93
☎331066
Closed Jul
rm13 ⇌5 🛏8 **P** sB⇌ 🛏685
dB⇌ 🛏970–1290

⅏**Meelbergs NV** Leuvensesteenweg 108
☎333386 **P** Frd

DINANT
Namur (☎082)

★ ★**Couronne** r A-Sax 1 ☎222441
rm24 ⇌6 🛏4 **P** Lift sB600–650
sB⇌ 🛏900 dB1050 dB⇌ 🛏1500

★**Belle Vue** r de Philippeville 1–3
☎222924
rm7 ⇌5 **P** sB750–850 sB⇌800–900
dB950–1000 dB⇌1000–1200

★**Gare (DPn)** r de la Station 39–41
☎222056
rm25 ⇌7 🚗 **P** Lift sB600 dB1000
dB⇌1400

⅏**Dinant Motors** rte de Bouvignes 53
☎223026 **P** Opl

At **BOUVIGNES** (2km NW)

★ ★**Auberge de Bouvignes** r Fetis 112
☎611600

Belgium

rm6 ⇌3 🚗 **P** sB890 sB⇌980
dB1040 dB⇌1260

DOORNIK See TOURNAI

EEKLO
Oost-Vlaanderen (☎091)

★**Rembrandt** Koningin Astridpl 2
☎772570
rm8 🛏2 sB560 dB🛏775

⅏**B de Baets** Markt 85 ☎771285 **P**
Aud VW

ENGHIEN
Hainaut (☎02)

⅏**Chapelle** r d'Hoves 132 ☎3951509 Cit

EUPEN
Liège (☎087)

★ ★**Bosten** Verviersestr 2 ☎552209
rm14 ⇌6 🚗 **P** sB540 sB⇌755
dB1060 dB⇌1180

FLORENVILLE
Luxembourg (☎061)

★ ★**France** r Généraux Cuvelier 26
☎311032
16 Feb–Dec
rm38 ⇌8 🚗 **P** Lift sB725 sB⇌850
dB1000–1100 dB⇌1250

⅏**Mauxhin & Fils** r de la Station 326
☎311055 **P** Cit

FRANCORCHAMPS
Liège (☎087)

★ ★ ★**Roannay (DPn** at wknds) rte de
Spa 155 ☎275311 tx49031
Closed 15 Nov–15 Dec
rm21 ⇌10 🛏5 🚗 **P** sB940
sB⇌ 🛏1470–1645 dB1250
dB⇌ 🛏2140–2635

FURNES See VEURNE

GEEL
Antwerpen (☎014)

⅏**Dierckx** Pas 170 ☎588020 **P** BMW

GEMBLOUX
Namur (☎081)

Croisée (A Dennis) Chaussée de Namur
18 ☎611626 **P** Frd

GENT (GAND)
Oost-Vlaanderen (☎091)

☆ ☆ ☆**Holiday Inn**
Ottergernsesteenweg 600 ☎225885
tx11756
⇌120 **P** Lift sB⇌2295 dB⇌3365 🏊
Pool

★ ★ ★**Europa** Gordunakaai 59
☎226071 tx11547
⇌37 🚗 **P** Lift sB⇌1300
dB⇌1650–2150

★ ★**St-Jorishof** Botermarkt 1 ☎242424
tx12738

9 Jan–23 Dec
rm66 ⇌45 🛏2 🚗 **P** Lift sB1240
sB⇌ 🛏1450 dB1500 dB⇌ 🛏3000

⅏**Center & Docks Motors** Doornzelestr
21 ☎234567

⅏**Leyland Vernaeve** Doornzelestr 31
☎230384 BL

⅏**A Vandersmissen** Flevestr 26
☎236723 Frd

HAAN (DE) (LE COQ)
West-Vlaanderen (☎059)

★ ★ ★**Dunes** Leopoldpl 5 (n.rest)
☎233146
15 Mar–Sep
rm27 ⇌23 🛏4 **P** Lift
sB⇌ 🛏1000–1200 dB⇌ 🛏1250–1900

★ ★**Auberge des Rois** Zeedijk 1
☎233018
rm28 ⇌15 🛏9 **P** Lift dB1760–1860
dB⇌ 🛏1860–2160 sea

★ ★**Bellevue** Koningspl 5 ☎233439
Etr–15 Oct
rm51 ⇌15 🛏15 **P** Lift sB650–825
dB1100–1200 dB⇌ 🛏1400–1500

HAN-SUR-LESSE
Namur (☎084)

★ ★**Voyageurs (DPn)** rte de Rochefort 1
☎377237 tx42079
rm42 ⇌11 🛏12 **P** Lift sB550–600
sB⇌ 🛏700–750 dB950–1150
dB⇌ 🛏1250

HASSELT
Limburg (☎011)

★**Century** Leopoldpl 1 ☎2247499
rm10 sB500–600 dB1000–1200

⅏**Hoffer** Demerstr 66 ☎224911 Ren

HERENTALS
Antwerpen (☎014)

⅏**Tuerlinx** St-Janstr 116 ☎272372 Opl
Vau

HERSTAL See LIÈGE (LUIK)

HOEI See HUY

HOUFFALIZE
Luxembourg (☎062)

★**Clé des Champs** rte de Libramont
☎288044
Apr–5 Nov
rm9 🛏4 🚗 **P** sB650 sB🛏750 dB950
dB 🛏1150

⅏**Lambin** rte de Liège 10 ☎288035 **P**
RL

HOUYET
Namur (☎082)

★**Marquisette** rte de Dinant (4km NE)
☎666429
Closed 20 Jun–10 Jul
rm10 ⇌2 🛏8 🚗 **P** sB⇌ 🛏550–650
dB⇌ 🛏650–1000

HUY (HOEI)
Liège (☎085)

★ ★**Fort** Chaussée Napoléon 5–6
☎212403

rm22 ⇌12 sB505 sB ⇌720–915
dB695–780 dB ⇌1080–1430

IEPER (YPRES)
West-Vlaanderen (☎057)

★**St Nicolas** G-de Stuerstr 6 ☎200622
Closed 18 Jul–8 Aug
rm8 ⇌4 sB ⇌850 dB ⇌1200

JAMBES See **NAMUR**

KASTERLEE
Antwerpen (☎014)

★★**Dennen** Lichtaarsebaan 73
☎556107
Closed 1–14 Jan
rm12 ⇌9 **P** sB660 sB ⇌835 dB935
dB ⇌1085

KNOKKE-HEIST
West-Vlaanderen (☎051)

At **ALBERT PLAGE**

★★★**Lido** Zwalluwenlaan 18 ☎601925
Jun–Sep
rm40 ⇌34 🏶6 🍴 **P** Lift
sB ⇌ 🏶1300 dB ⇌ 🏶3260

At **KNOKKE**

★★**Cecil** Elizabethlaan 20 ☎601033
15 Apr–Sep & 22 Dec–4 Jan
rm12 ⇌3 🏶9

At **ZOUTE (LE)**

★★★**Majestic** Zeedijk 697 ☎611144
Mar–24 Sep & 23 Dec–2 Jan
rm61 ⇌48 🏶4 🍴 Lift sB1000–1025
sB ⇌ 🏶1050–1075 dB1900–1950
dB ⇌ 🏶2000–2500

KOKSIJDE (COXYDE-SUR-MER)
West-Vlaanderen (☎058)

★★**Royal Plage** Zeedijk 65 ☎511300
Apr–Sep
rm30 ⇌7 Lift sB650–1100
dB900–1250 dB ⇌1300–1600

KORTRIJK (COURTRAI)
West-Vlaanderen (☎056)

★★**Damier** Grote Markt 41 ☎221547
rm43 ⇌20 Lift sB490–580
sB ⇌900–1050 dB830–900
dB ⇌1170–1250

LA Each name preceded by 'La' is listed
under the name that follows it.

LAC-DE-WARFAZ See **SPA**

LE Each name preceded by 'Le' is listed
under the name that follows it.

LEOPOLDSBURG
Limburg (☎011)

🏠**W Heesen Heeren** Diestersteenweg
144 ☎341295 **P** Dat

LEUVEN (LOUVAIN)
Brabant (☎016)

At **WINKSELE** (3km NW)

🏠**Hergon** Brusselsesteenweg 57
☎223506 Frd

Belgium

LEUZE
Hainaut (☎069)

★**Couronne** pl de la Gare 18 ☎662166
Closed Aug
rm10

LIÈGE (LUIK)
Liège (☎041)

☆ ☆ ☆ ☆**Holiday Inn** esp de l'Europe 2
(n.rest) ☎426020 tx41156
⇌224 🍴 **P** Lift sB ⇌2350–2530
dB3080–3325 Pool

☆ ☆ ☆ ☆**Ramada** bd de la Sauvenière
100 ☎224910 tx4896
⇌105 🍴 Lift sB ⇌2500 dB ⇌3180

★★**Cygne d'Argent** r Beekman 49
☎237001
rm27 ⇌6 🏶19 sB1065
sB ⇌ 🏶1185–1465 dB1380
dB ⇌ 🏶1565–1765

🏠**Brondeel** quai de coronmeuse 28
☎271820 Chy Sab

🏠**S A Sodia** r L-Boumal 24 ☎526862 BL

At **HERSTAL** (8km NE on E5)

★★★**Post House** (THF) r Hurbise (SE5 at
exit 34 Hermée-Hauts-Sarts) ☎646400
tx41103
⇌ 🏶100 **P** Lift sB ⇌ 🏶2235
dB ⇌ 🏶2980 Pool

LIER
Antwerpen (☎031)

🏠**G Guwry** F-Van Cauwenbergstr 19–21
☎800962 Frd

LIGNEUVILLE
Liège (☎080)

★★**Moulin** r de Centre 91 ☎570081
Closed 10 Nov–20 Dec
rm19 ⇌7 🍴 **P**

LOKEREN
Oost-Vlaanderen (☎091)

★★**Park** Antwerpsesteenweg 1
☎482046
18 Jan–14 Jul & 31 Jul–8 Jan
rm9 ⇌4 🏶5 🍴 **P** sB ⇌ 🏶975–1750
dB ⇌ 🏶1250–2150

🏠**Slau** Weverslaan 14 ☎481400 BWM

LOUVAIN See **LEUVAN**

LOUVIÈRE (LA)
Hainaut (☎064)

J Dupire et fils r L-Dupuis 10 ☎224031
P BL

LUIK See **LIÈGE**

MALINES See **MECHELEN**

MALMÉDY
Liège (☎080)

At **XHOFFRAIX** (5km N on N28)

★★**Trôs Marets (DPn)** rte de Mont 1
☎337917
Closed 16 Nov–21 Dec
rm11 ⇌9 🏶2 **P** sB ⇌ 🏶2000–3250
dB ⇌ 🏶2250–3800 Pool

MARCHE-EN-FAMENNE
Luxembourg (☎084)

★★**Cloche** r de Luxembourg 2 ☎311579
⇌6 **P** sB ⇌1166 dB ⇌1325

🏠**Leunen** rte de Bastogne 51A
☎311582 **P** Fia Lnc

MARTELANGE
Luxembourg (☎063)

★**Maison Rouge** rte d'Arlon 5 ☎64006
Closed Oct
rm12 🍴 **P**

MASNUY-ST-JEAN
Hainaut (☎065)

★★★**Amigo** Chaussée Brunehault 4
☎728721 tx57313
rm56 ⇌48 🏶8 **P** Lift
sB ⇌ 🏶1300–1700 dB ⇌ 🏶2100–3200
Pool

MECHELEN (MALINES)
Antwerpen (☎015)

★**Claes** O.L-Vroowstr 51 (n.rest)
☎412866
rm15 🏶9 sB630 sB 🏶800 dB1100
dB 🏶1200

🏠**Festraets** M-Sabbestr 123 ☎202752
Fia Lnc Vau

🏠**Mato** Liersesteenweg 26 ☎208015 **P**
Peu

MENEN (MENIN)
West-Vlaanderen (☎056)

🏠**Imecar** Kortrijk Str 269 ☎513535 Ren

MONS (BERGEN)
Hainaut (☎065)

🏠**Automons** (G Vienne) r du Chemin de
Fer 163 ☎311126 Fia

🏠**A Wattier** r du Grand Jour 3 ☎335173
Frd

MONTKEMMEL
West-Vlaanderen (☎057)

★★★**Mont Kemmel** Berg 4 ☎444145
1 Mar–15 Jan
rm16 ⇌15 🏶1 🍴 **P** Sea

NAMUR (NAMEN)
Namur (☎081)

🏠**Carco** chaussée de Louvain 320
☎212711 **P** BL

At **JAMBES**

🏠**SA Jambes** pl-Charlotte 18 ☎301451
Frd

NEUFCHÂTEAU
Luxembourg (☎061)

🏠**Michaux** av de la Gare 43 ☎277444
Frd

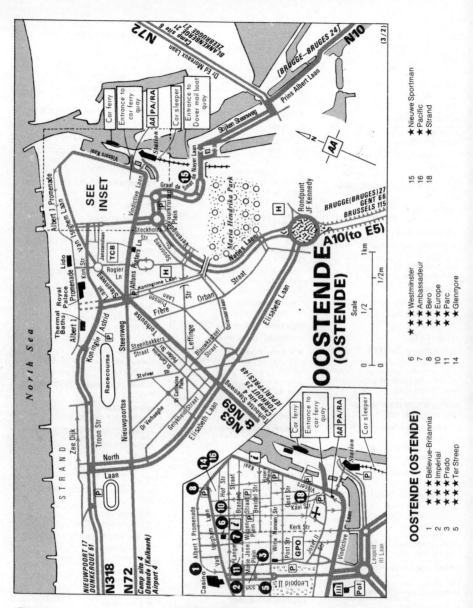

OOSTENDE (OSTENDE)

★ Nieuwe Sportman 15
★ Pacific 16
★ Strand 18

6 ★★★ Westminster
7 ★★★ Ambassadeur
8 ★★ Bero
10 ★★ Europe
11 ★★ Parc
14 ★ Glennore

OOSTENDE (OSTENDE)

1 ★★★ Bellevue-Britannia
2 ★★★ Imperial
3 ★★★ Prado
5 ★★★ Ter Streep

NEUPONT
Luxembourg (☎084)

★**Ry des Glands** rte de Libin 93
☎388133
Mar–Jan
rm12 **P DPn**900–1000

NIVELLES (NIJVEL)
Brabant (☎067)

🏍**Auto Parc** Chaussée de Namur 52
☎228050 Ren

OOSTENDE (OSTENDE)
West-Vlaanderen (☎059)

See Plan

★★★**Bellevue-Britannia** Prom Albert T
55–56 (n.rest) ☎706373 Plan **1**
16 Dec–14 Nov
rm58 ⇆🛏49 **P** Lift sB825
sB ⇆🛏1025–1160 dB1250
dB ⇆🛏1650–1920

★★**Imperial** van Iseghemiaan 74–76
☎705481 tx81167 Plan **2**

---

rm61 ⇆51 🛏7 🛗 Lift
sB ⇆🛏980–1100 dB1500
dB ⇆🛏1700–2080

★★★**Prado** Leopold II Laan 22 (n.rest)
☎705306 tx82237 Plan **3**
rm31 ⇆🛏27 🛗 Lift dB1000–1100
dB ⇆🛏1600–1800

★★★**Ter Streep** Leopold II Laan 14
(n.rest) ☎700912 tx82261 Plan **5**
⇆35 Lift sB ⇆1000–1700
dB ⇆1400–2290

★ ★ ★**Westminster** van Iseghemlaan 22
☎702411 Plan **6**

rm60 ⇌18 ▥42 **P** Lift sB ⇌ ▥1000
dB ⇌ ▥1600

★ ★**Ambassadeur** Wapenpl 8A
☎700941 Plan **7**

rm23 ⇌18 ▥5 ▥ Lift sB ⇌ ▥1500
dB ⇌ ▥1800

★ ★**Bero** Hofstr 1A ☎702335 tx82163
Plan **8**

⇌60 ▥ Lift sB ⇌1000 dB ⇌1350

★ ★**Europe** Kapucijnenstr 52 (n.rest)
☎701012 tx81659 Plan **10**

Mar–Oct
rm65 ⇌15 ▥38 ▥ **P** Lift sB750–800
sB ⇌ ▥1100–1250 dB1350–1500
dB ⇌ ▥1500–1750

★ ★**Parc** Marie Josépl 3 (n.rest)
☎706580 Plan **11**

rm53 ⇌7 ▥5 ▥ Lift

★**Glenmore** Hofstr 25 ☎702022 Plan **14**

20 Apr–1 May & 25 May–20 Sep
rm50 ⇌21 ▥8 Lift sB625
sB ⇌ ▥775–875 dB1050–1250
dB ⇌ ▥1350–1550 sea

★**Nieuwe Sportman** de Smet de
Naeyerlaan 9 ☎702384 Plan **15**

rm10 sB400 dB800

★**Pacific** Hofstr 11 ☎701507 Plan **16**

Apr–15 Oct
rm51 ▥35 ▥ Lift sB ▥900 dB ▥1300

★**Strand** Visserskaai 1 ☎703383
tx81357 Plan **18**

Feb–Nov
rm21 ⇌18 ▥2 Lift sB ⇌ ▥1500
dB ⇌ ▥1900

♫**Casino Kursaal** Torhoutsesteenweg
684 ☎703240 Peu Tal

♫**Delta** Steenweg op Torhout 529
☎801503 Frd

♫**Royal-Auto** Koninginnelaan 52
☎707635 Chy Fia

♫**St-Christophe** Warschaustr 29
☎701759 Fia

♫**F Stoops** chaussée de
Torthoutsteenweg 54 ☎702472 AR Toy

PANNE (DE) (LA PANNE)
West-Vlaanderen (☎508)

★ ★**Regina Maris** Bortierlaan 11
☎411222

Closed 6 Jan–4 Feb
rm72 ⇌22 ▥30 Lift sB750–800
sB ⇌ ▥800–850 dB1200–1300
dB ⇌ ▥1300–1400 Pool

☆ ☆**Strand** Nieuwpoortlaan 153
☎411196

Apr–Sep
rm51 ⇌2 ▥41 ▥ **P** sB800–1020
dB1265–1575 dB ⇌ ▥1365–1675 sea

PHILIPPEVILLE
Namur (☎071)

★**Croisée** r de France 45 ☎666231

rm12 ⇌5 ▥ **P** dB820 dB ⇌930–1030

Belgium

PROFONDEVILLE
Namur (☎081)

★**Auberge d'Alsace** av Gl-Garcia 42
☎412228

Closed 17 Aug–6 Sep
⇌6 **P**

REMOUCHAMPS
Liège (☎041)

★ ★**Royal Étrangers (DPn)** r de la Reffe
26 ☎724006

rm10 ⇌5 ▥ **P**

ROCHE-EN-ARDENNE (LA)
Luxembourg (☎084)

★ ★ ★**Air Pur (DPn)** rte d'Houffalize 11,
Villez ☎411223

Apr–15 Nov & 15–31 Dec
rm11 ⇌10 ▥ **P** dB ⇌3500–3780

★ ★ ★**Ardennes (DPn)** r de Beausaint 2
☎411112

15 Mar–20 Nov & 20 Dec–2 Jan
⇌12 ▥ **P**

★ ★**Belle Vue** av de la Gare 10 ☎411187

rm18 ⇌5 ▥1 **P** sB900 dB1165
dB⇌ ▥1350

ROCHEFORT
Namur (☎084)

★**Central** pl Albert 1er 30 (n.rest)
☎211044

Closed Oct
rm7 ⇌2 **P**

★**Fayette** r Jaquet 87 ☎211024

Closed 16 Sep–5 Oct
rm21 ⇌5 ▥7 **P**

SINT NIKLAAS (ST-NICOLAS)
Oost-Vlaanderen (☎03)

★ ★**Serwir** Koningen Astridlaan 49
☎765311 tx32422

Closed 8–22 Jul
rm28 ⇌19 ▥9 **P** Lift
sB ⇌ ▥1250–1600 dB ⇌ ▥2000

★**Central** Dalstr 28 ☎7763830 Frd

♫**Sint-Christoffel** Wegvoeringstr 88
☎7761338 BL

SINT TRUIDEN (ST-TROND)
Limburg (☎011)

♫**Cella** Naamestweg 239 ☎677951 M/c
BL Vlo

♫**Milou Palms** Tiensesteenweg 109
☎683941 **P** Ren

SPA
Liège (☎087)

★ ★**Grand Cerf** r de la Sauvenière 111
☎772565

16 Jan–14 Dec
⇌7 **P**

At **BALMORAL** (3km N)

★ ★ ★**Dorint Ardennes** rte de Balmoral
33 ☎772581 tx49209

⇌96 **P** Lift ☽ sB ⇌1450–1750
dB ⇌2300–2700 ♨ Pool ♂

At **LAC-DE-WARFAZ** (2.5km NE)

★ ★**Lac (DPn)** av A-Hesse 45 ☎771074

rm12 ⇌4 ▥1 ▥ **P** DPn780–980

At **TIÈGE-LEZ-SPA** (5km NE)

★ ★ ★**Charmille** r de Tiège 44 ☎474313

Apr–15 Nov
rm35 ⇌22 ▥3 ▥ **P** Lift sB823
sB ⇌ ▥914 dB1096 dB ⇌ ▥1210

STAMBRUGES-GRANDGLISE
Hainaut (☎069)

★ ★**Vert Gazon** rte de Mons 1 ☎575984

15 Jan–15 Jun & Jul–Dec
rm6 ⇌5 ▥1 ▥ **P** sB ⇌ ▥950–1190
dB ⇌ ▥1190–1490

THOUROUT See **TORHOUT**

TIÈGE-LEZ-SPA See **SPA**

TIENEN (TIRLEMONT)
Brabant (☎016)

♫**Dalaisse** Leuvensestr 115–117
☎811077 **P** Toy

TONGEREN
Limburg (☎012)

★**Lido** Grote Markt 19 ☎231948

rm9 ⇌4 ▥1 sB450–550 sB ⇌ ▥700
dB700–850

TORHOUT (THROUROUT)
West-Vlaanderen (☎050)

♫**Deketelaere** Vredelaan 69 ☎212623
Hon Vau

At **WYNENDAELE** (3km)

★ ★**t'Gravenhof** Oostendestr 343
☎212314

rm8 ⇌2 ▥2 **P**

TOURNAI (DOORNIK)
Hainaut (☎069)

♫**American** av Van Cutsem 23 ☎221921
Frd

TURNHOUT
Antwerpen (☎014)

♫**Perfect** Nieuwekaal 9–11 ☎413588
Ren

VERVIERS
Liège (☎087)

★ ★ ★**Amigo** r Herla 1 ☎221121
tx49128

rm51 ⇌43 ▥8 **P** Lift
sB ⇌ ▥1130–1700 dB ⇌ ▥2100–3200
Pool

★ ★**Grand** r du Palais 145 ☎223177

rm35 ⇌11 ▥2 Lift

♫**Colard** r de Limbourg 26 ☎332859 **P**
Dat

At **WEGNEZ** (4km SW)

♫**Stevens** Vovegnez 69 ☎460317 **P**
Ren

VEURNE (FURNES)
West-Vlaanderen (☎058)

§⊘R Popeller Pannestr 116 ☎311869 M/c
P Fia

§⊘R Sierens D-de-Haenelaan 2
☎311205 Aud VW

VILLE-POMMEROEUL
Hainaut (☎065)

★★Relais rte de Mons 10 ☎620561

Closed 24 Aug–14 Sep
⊷6 🏠 P sB⊷905–995
dB⊷1030–1120

VILLERS-SUR-LESSE
Namur (☎084)

★Beau Séjour r du Village 15 ☎377115

Mar–15 Jan
rm22 ⊷9 🛏8 🏠 P
sB⊷ 🛏935–1175 dB⊷ 🛏1150–1390
Pool

WEGNEZ See **VERVIERS**

WENDUINE
West-Vlaanderen (☎050)

Belgium

★★Mouettes Zeedijk 7 ☎411514

15 Apr–Sep
rm30 ⊷8 🛏16 Lift sB750–900
sB⊷ 🛏1400–1700 dB800–1000
dB⊷ 🛏1000–2000 sea

WEPION
Namur (☎081)

☆☆☆☆Sofitel Chaussée de Dinant
1149 ☎460811 tx59031
⊷118 🏠 Lift sB⊷2295 dB⊷2840
Pool

★Frisia Chaussée de Dinant 311 (n.rest)
☎411106
rm10 ⊷2 🛏5 P sB700 sB⊷ 🛏800
dB800 dB⊷ 🛏1050 sea

WESTENDE
West-Vlaanderen (☎059)

★★Rotonda Zeedijk 300 ☎300495
Mar–Dec
rm18 ⊷10 🏠 P

WINKSELE See **LEUVEN (LOUVAIN)**

WYNEDAELE See **TORHOUT (THOUROUT)**

XHOFFRAIX See **MALMÉDY**

YPRES See **IEPER**

YVOIR
Namur (☎082)

★★Vachter Chaussée de Namur 140
☎611314

Closed 16 Jan–Feb
rm10 ⊷9 🏠 P

ZOLDER
Limburg (☎011)

★Pits Omloop Terlaemen ☎580318
⊷12 P sB⊷1050 dB⊷1585 Pool

ZOUTE (LE) See **KNOKKE HEIST**

The Meuse, Lustin

Flea Market, Brussels

DENMARK

Denmark is the smallest of the Scandinavian countries consisting of the peninsula of Jutland and over 500 islands of various sizes, some inhabited and linked to the mainland by ferry or bridge. It is a constitutional monarchy, whose capital is Copenhagen. The countryside is low-lying, its fertile lands broken up by beech woods, small lakes and numerous fjords.

It has a very efficient agricultural industry, as well as fishing and the export of specialised industrial manufactures.

The climate is mild and equable similar to that of southern Scotland, although a little more extreme. Danish is the national language, but English is widely spoken as a second language. German and French will often be understood, but less frequently spoken, particularly in country areas.

Area *16,631 sq miles*
Population *5,119,155*
Local time *GMT + 1*
(Summer GMT + 2)

National flag *White upright cross on a red field*

Canals at Christianshavn

How to get there

The two main ways of reaching Denmark are either by using the direct ferry services from Newcastle or Harwich to Esbjerg in western Jutland or by using one of the short Channel crossings to France or Belguim and driving through the Netherlands and northern Germany to Denmark. The distance from the Channel ports to København (Copenhagen) is roughly 660 miles and the journey would require one or two night stops.

Another possibility is to use the ferry operating between Harwich and Hamburg and drive the short distance to southern Denmark.

Inter-island travel is made easy by either bridge links or frequent vehicle ferries.

Motoring regulations and general information

This information should be read in conjunction with the general content of the European ABC (pages 6–27). **Note** As certain regulations and requirements are common to many countries they are covered by one entry in the ABC and the following headings represent some of the subjects dealt with in this way:
AA Agents
Crash or safety helmets
Customs regulations for European countries
Drinking and driving
Fire extinguisher
First-aid kit
Insurance
International distinguishing sign
Medical treatment
Overtaking
Passengers
Police fines
Radio telephones/Radio transmitters
Rear view mirror
Road signs
Seat belts
Traffic lights
Tyres
Visitors' registration

Accidents

Fire, police, ambulance ☎000. If you are involved in a collision or other traffic accident you must stop and exchange particulars with any other person concerned. If personal injury is sustained, it is obligatory to obtain medical assistance for the injured persons. The incident should then be reported to the police. See also *Accidents* page 7.

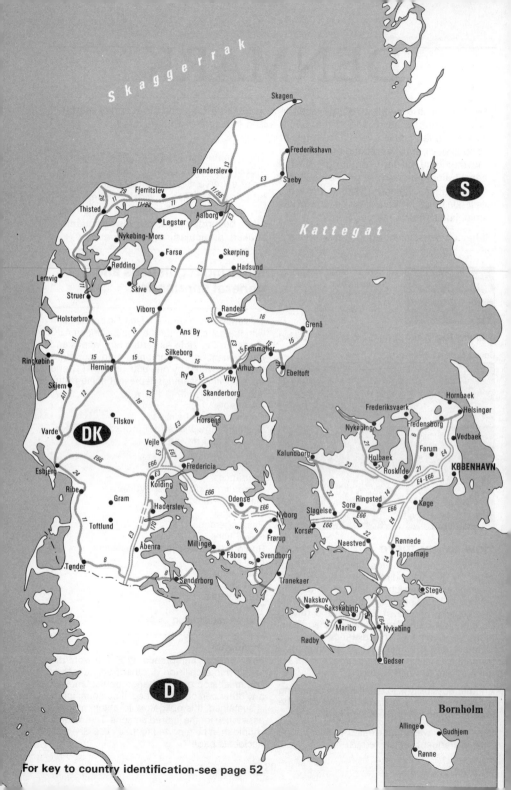

Accommodation

A list of hotels, pensions, inns and motels is available from the Tourist Office in London with full details of charges, but there is no official classification. Prices generally include VAT (22%) and service (15%).

Visitors arriving in København without accommodation are advised to make personal application to the Accommodation Service, Kiosk P, Central Railway Station, where assistance will be given in finding accommodation in an hotel or, failing that, a private home.

Provincial tourist associations will also provide information on accommodation in their area and will effect reservations in response to written applications. Accommodation is also available at farmhouses and the renting of summer cottages can be arranged through tourist associations on written application.

Hotel cheques are generally available in Denmark from Tourist Offices (see page 97) and FDM Travel Agencies and, if purchased by AA members from the FDM (see page 96) a discount of 5% is given on production of a valid membership card. The cheques cover accommodation for one person, breakfast, service and taxes and charges are as follows:
Budgetcheck *Dkr* 120 (without private facilities)
Kro (Inn) check *Dkr* 170
Dancheck *Dkr* 210

Breakdown

If your car breaks down, try to move it to the verge of the road so that it obstructs the traffic flow as little as possible. The Danish Motoring Club, FDM, is unable to provide roadside assistance. In the event of a breakdown assistance may be obtained from one of the following organisations who operate a 24hr service, Road Watch (*Vejvagt*), FALCK and the Danish Automobile Assistance (*Dansk Autohjaelp* or *DAH*). Any service received must be paid for. See also *Breakdown* page 8 and *Warning triangles* page 97.

British Consulates

(See also page 8)
DK-2100 København 36-40 Kastelsvej ☎(01)264600. There are also Consulates in Åbenrå, Ålborg, Århus, Esbjerg, Fredericia and Odense.

Currency and banking hours

(See also page 11)
The unit of currency is the krone, divided into 100 øre. There is no limit to the amount of foreign or Danish currency which may be imported. Visitors may export any amount of foreign currency provided the amounts have been declared to the Customs on entry. If the amount exceeds *DKr*50,000 the traveller must be able to prove that it was brought into the country or acquired by exchange of foreign currency in Denmark.

In København banking hours are 09.30-16.00hrs Monday, Tuesday, Wednesday and Friday and Thursday 09.30-18.00hrs. At the Central Railway Station and the Air Terminal banks are open until 22.00hrs. Outside København banking hours are generally 09.30-12.00hrs and 14.00-16.00hrs.

All banks are closed on Saturday, except Exchange offices on the Danish/German border which close between 13.00 and 15.00hrs. These offices may also open on Sundays during the summer.

Dimensions and weight restrictions

Vehicles must not exceed — height: 4 metres; width: 2.5 metres; length: vehicle/trailer combination 18 metres; weight: trailers without brakes may have a total weight of up to 50% of the weight of the towing vehicle; trailers with brakes may have a total weight up to 90% of the towing vehicle's weight.

Driving licence

(See also page 13)
A valid British driving licence is acceptable in Denmark. The minimum age at which a visitor may drive a temporarily imported car or motorcycle is 17 years.

Old street in København

Emergency messages to tourists
(See also page 14)
Emergency messages to tourists are broadcast daily on *Radio Denmark* in English. The messages are transmitted on 1224 metres long wave after the news at 08.15hrs.

Lights
(See also page 17)
Headlights should be dipped early when meeting another vehicle as the lighting of Danish-registered vehicles is of lower density than that of UK-registered vehicles. Driving with only one headlight or spotlight is not allowed. Fog lamps may be used in pairs in conjunction with sidelights (but not headlights). It is compulsory for *motorcyclists* to use dipped headlights during the day.

Motoring club
(See also page 18)

 The **Forenede Danske Motor-ejere** (FDM) has its headquarters at Blegdamsvej 124, 2100 København Ø ☎(01)382112 and branch offices are maintained in major towns throughout the country. The offices are usually open between 09.00 and 17.00hrs from Monday to Friday. During the summer the headquarters and many branch offices are open on Saturday to personal callers between 09.00-12.00hrs.

Motorways
Approximately 350 miles of toll-free motorways (motorvej) are at present open and more stretches of the planned 560 mile network are under construction. Nearly all motorways are part of the European international network *ie* E3, E4 and E66.

Orange badge scheme for disabled drivers
(See also page 19)
Concessions are extended to badge holders who are allowed to park for up to 1 hour where a shorter time limit applies to other motorists. Unlimited parking is permitted where a time limit of 1 hour or longer would otherwise apply,

Parking
(See also page 19)
Regulations are similar to those in the UK but it is advisable to use public car parks. In central København, kerbside parking is restricted to one hour; three hours where there are parking meters. Vehicles illegally parked will be removed by the police at the owner's expense and a fine will be imposed. Parking discs which are obtained from the police, FDM offices or service stations are obligatory. These discs are set at the time of parking and show when the parking time expires according to the time limit allowed in the district. Failure to observe zonal regulations could result in a fine or the vehicle being towed away.

Parking lights must be used in badly lit areas and when visibility is poor.

Petrol
(See also page 20)
Credit cards Diners Club International accepted at Gulf petrol stations
Duty-free petrol In addition to the petrol in the vehicle tank up to 10 litres in a can may be imported free of customs duty and tax.
Octane rating Normal Benzin (92) and Super Benzin (96-98)

Postal information
Mail Postcards *Dkr*2.70, letters up to 20gm *Dkr*2.70.

Post offices There are 300 post offices in Denmark. Opening hours are from 09.00-17.00hrs Monday to Friday and 09.00-12.00hrs Saturday. In København the Head Post Office is open from 09.00-19.00hrs and the Central Station post office from 08.00-23.00hrs.

Postcheques
(See also page 21)
Postcheques may be cashed for any amount up to a maximum of *DKr*700 per cheque, but only at post offices in major towns. Counter positions are identified by the word *Udbetaling*. See above for post office opening hours.

Priority
(See also *Priority including Roundabouts* page 22)
A line of white triangles painted across the road indicates that you must **stop** and give way to traffic on the road you are entering.

Public holidays
Official public holidays in Denmark for 1985 are given below. See also *Public holidays* page 22.
January 1 (New Year's Day)
April 4 (Maundy Thursday)
April 5 (Good Friday)
April 8 (Easter Monday)
May 3 (Store Bededag or Great Prayer Day)
May 16 (Ascension Day)
May 27 (Whit Monday)
June 5 (Constitution Day)*
December 24 (Christmas Eve)

December 25 (Christmas Day)
December 26 (Boxing Day)
December 31 (New Year's Eve)*
* Officially a public holiday from noon

Roads
(See also *Road conditions* page 23)
The roads in Denmark are generally of a very high standard and well signposted. They are classified into three categories, showing E-roads (green and white signs with prefix 'E'), primary roads (one or two digit black numbers on yellow boards) and secondary roads (three digit black numbers on white boards).

Shopping hours
Shops are usually open between 09.00hrs and 17.30hrs (19.00 or 20.00hrs on Friday). Most shops are closed on Saturday afternoons.

Speed limits
(See also page 25)
Unless indicated by signs the following limits apply:

	Built-up area (indicated by the placename)
Car	60 kph (37 mph)
Car/caravan/trailer	60 kph (37 mph)
	Other roads
Car	80 kph (49 mph)
Car/caravan/trailer	70 kph (43 mph)
	Motorways
Car	100 kph (62 mph)
Car/caravan/trailer	70 kph (43 mph)

Even minor infringement of these limits can result in a heavy fine.

Spiked, studded or snow tyres
(See also page 10)
Spiked and studded tyres may be used between 1 October and 30 April. When spiked tyres are used no special speed limits apply but the spiked tyres must be fitted to all wheels. Generally, motoring in Denmark is rarely restricted by bad weather.

Tourist information offices
(See also page 25)
The Danish Tourist Board has offices in all the main towns. They also have an office in London: The Danish Tourist Board, Sceptre House, 169/173 Regent Street (entrance New Burlington Street), London W1R 8PY ☎01-734 2637/8.

Using the telephone
(See also page 26)
Insert coin **after** lifting receiver, dialling tone continuous tone. When making calls to subscribers within Denmark precede number with relevant area code (shown in parentheses against town entry in gazetteer). Use *DKr*1 coin or two 25øre coins for local calls and *DKr*1 or 5 coins for national and international calls. Coins inserted in a callbox are not returned even if the number is engaged, but repeat attempts may be made until the time runs out.
International callbox identification All callboxes.
Telephone rates A telephone call to the UK costs *DKr*3.60 for each minute.
What to dial for the Irish Republic 009 353.
What to dial for the UK 009 44.

Warning triangle
The use of a warning triangle is compulsory for all vehicles except two-wheelers. The triangle must be placed at least 50 metres (55yds) behind the vehicle on ordinary roads and 100 metres (109yds) on motorways to warn following traffic of any obstruction. See also *Warning triangles/Hazard warning lights* page 26.

Prices are in Danish Kroner
The Danish alphabet differs from the English one in that the last letters after **Z** are **AE, Ø, Å**; this must be borne in mind when using Danish reference books.

Abbreviations:
bd   boulevard
pl   plads

AALBORG
Jylland(☎08)

★ ★ ★ ★**Hvide Hus** Vesterbro 2
☎138400 tx69690
⇌202 **P** Lift ⅅ sB ⇌445–490
dB ⇌600–690 Pool

★ ★ ★**Limfjordshotellet** Ved Stranden 14–16 (n.rest) ☎164333
⇌85 🏛 **P** Lift ⅅ sB ⇌330–350
dB ⇌500

☆ ☆ ☆**Phønix** Vesterbro 77 ☎120011
tx69782
⇌150 🏛 **P** Lift ⅅ sB ⇌420
dB ⇌540

☆ ☆ ☆**Scheelsminde** (Inter DK)
Scheelsmindevej 35 ☎183233 tx27459
⇌54 🏛 **P** ⅅ sB290 dB440

★ ★**Central** Vesterbro 38 ☎126933
rm70 ⇌12 🍴9 **P** Lift ⅅ sB190–225
sB ⇌ 🍴285 dB375 dB ⇌ 🍴430–460

🗱*Autocentralen* Ny Kaervej 47
☎128777 VW

🗱*Vilh Nellemann* Jyllandsgade 28
☎126377 **P** BL DJ MG RT

ÅBENRA
Jylland(☎04)

★ ★ ★**Hvide Hus** Flensborgvej 50
☎624700
⇌69 🏛 **P** ⅅ sB ⇌330 dB ⇌475 sea

🗱*E Grodt* Vestermarksvej 7-9 ☎622028
Chy Peu Sim

🗱*IM Jensen* Flensborgvej 2 ☎621355
Cit Vau

ᔆ0Skifter Andersen Bil Langrode, Vestvejen ☎621333 Vlo

At **KLIPLEV**

★ ★ ★**Søgårdhus** ☎687780
rm40 ᔕ8 🏨15 🍴

ALBERTSLUND See **KØBENHAVN (COPENHAGEN)**

ALLINGE
Bornholm(☎03)

★**Højers** Østergade 32 ☎980003
rm38

ANS BY
Jylland (☎06)

At **KONGENSBRO** (5km SE)

★ ★**Kongensbro Kro** Gl–Kongevej 70
☎870177
rm17 ᔕ10 🍴 P sB145–170
sB ᔕ215–250 dB270–300 dB ᔕ330–380

ÅRHUS
Jylland(☎06)

★ ★ ★**Atlantic** Europapl ☎131111
tx64301
ᔕ102 🍴 P Lift 𝄞 sB ᔕ450
dB ᔕ600 M150 sea

★ ★ ★**Marselis** Strandvejen 25
☎144411 tx68751
ᔕ72 P Lift 𝄞 sB ᔕ450 dB ᔕ600
Beach sea

★ ★ ★**Ritz** Banegaardsplads 12
☎134444
rm62 ᔕ22 🏨40 🍴 P Lift 𝄞
sB ᔕ 🏨300–325 dB ᔕ 🏨425–450

★ ★**Ansgar** Banegårdspl 14 ☎124122
rm184 ᔕ114 🍴 P Lift 𝄞 sB140–185
sB ᔕ215–240 dB270–280 dB ᔕ315–360

★ ★**Royal** Store Torv 4 ☎120011
rm206 ᔕ110 🍴 P Lift sB150
sB ᔕ210 dB250 dB ᔕ330

ᔆ0**Århus Motor Co** Skolebakken 2
☎133833 Frd

ᔆ0**Skandinavisk Motor Co** G–Clausensvej 5 ☎147500 Por VW

At **HØJBJERG** (3km SE)

★ ★ ★**Scanticon** Skaade Maesgardvej Bakker ☎273233 tx68715
ᔕ110 P 𝄞 sB ᔕ385 dB ᔕ465 Pool sea

BLOMMENSLYST See **ODENSE**

BORNHOLM (ISLE OF) See **ALLINGE, GUDHJEM, RØNNE**

BRØNDERSLEV
Jylland (☎08)

ᔆ0**J Andersen** Østergade ☎820588 M/c Opl Vau

COPENHAGEN See **KØBENHAVN**

EBELTOFT
Jylland(☎06)

★ ★ ★**Ebeltoft Strand** Nordre Strandvej 3 ☎343300 tx60872

Denmark

ᔕ68 P 𝄞 sB ᔕ330 dB ᔕ475 Beach
𝄞 sea

★ ★ ★**Hvide Hus** Strandgaardshøj
☎341466 tx60872
ᔕ63 P Lift 𝄞 sB ᔕ330 dB ᔕ475
Pool 𝄞 sea

★ ★**Vigen** Adelgade 5 ☎341433
rm30 ᔕ8 🏨1 sB155 sB ᔕ 🏨180
dB250 dB ᔕ 🏨280

ELSINORE See **HELSINGØR**

ESBJERG
Jylland(☎05)

★ ★ ★**Britannia** Torvet ☎130111
rm48 ᔕ48 A40rm P Lift 𝄞 sB ᔕ320
dB ᔕ410–550

★ ★**Bangs** Torvet 21 (n.rest) ☎126933
rm40 ᔕ20 🏨5 P Lift 𝄞 sB210
sB ᔕ 🏨240 dB270 dB ᔕ 🏨350

★ ★**Missionshotellet Ansgar**
Skolegaade 36 ☎128244
rm69 ᔕ46 🍴 Lift P 𝄞 sB160
sB ᔕ200–240 dB ᔕ 🏨280–360

★ ★**Palads** Skolegade 14 ☎123000
rm48 🏨27 P Lift 𝄞 sB145 sB 🏨185
dB270 dB 🏨340

ᔆ0**A/S Ejvin Hansen** Hovedvej 12
☎127400 Ren Vlo

ᔆ0**K S Kristensen** Hovedvej 1 ☎142111
Frd

Langtidsparkering Englandskajen
☎123240 P

FÅBORG
Fyn(☎09)

ᔆ0**T Oddershede** Assensvej 2-4
☎611501 Frd

FARSØ
Jylland(☎08)

ᔆ0**M Nielsen** Norregade 18-20 ☎631600
M/c Opl Vau

FARUM
Sjaelland(☎07)

ᔆ0**H Wiingård** Rugmarken 13 ☎952210 P
Fia

FEMMØLLER
Jylland(☎06)

★ ★**Molskroen** Femmøller Strand
☎362200
rm26 ᔕ13 🏨13 P 𝄞 sea

★ ★**Vaegtergarden** ☎362211
rm26 ᔕ13 P

FILSKOV
Jylland(☎05)

★**Filskov Kro** ☎348111
Closed 24–25 Dec & New Year
rm45 ᔕ42 A3rm P Pool

FJERRITSLEV
Jylland(☎08)

ᔆ0**Auto–Centralen** (C Ronnow Nielsen)
Sondergrade 15 ☎211666 Opl

FREDENSBORG
Sjælland (☎02)

★ ★ ★**Store Kro** Slotsgade 6
☎280047
rm65 ᔕ49 🏨11 A16rm P Lift 𝄞
sB ᔕ370 dB ᔕ560 M99–150

FREDERICIA
Jylland(☎05)

★ ★ ★**Landsoldaten** Norgesgade 1
☎921555
2 Jan–23 Dec
rm62 ᔕ 🏨40 P Lift 𝄞 sB170–205
sB ᔕ245–265 dB275–295 dB ᔕ355–380
M60

★ ★ ★**Postgaarden** Oldenborggade 4
☎921855
rm66 ᔕ40 P 𝄞 sB130–170
sB ᔕ190–250 dB230 dB ᔕ270–335
M50

★ ★**Ny Missionshotel Postgaarden**
Oldenborggade 4 ☎921855
rm44 ᔕ14 🏨1 P Lift

ᔆ0**Autohuset** Vejlevej 38 ☎923402 Opl
Vau

ᔆ0**Fredericia Automobilhandel** Vejlvej 30
☎920211 Frd

FREDERIKSHAVN
Jylland(☎08)

★ ★ ★**Jutlandia** Havnepladsen 1
☎424200 tx67142
Closed Xmas
ᔕ102 🍴 P Lift 𝄞 sB ᔕ290–395
dB ᔕ485–605

★ ★**Hoffmans** Danmarksgade 62
☎422168
rm72 ᔕ37 🍴 P Lift 𝄞

ᔆ0**Bangsbostrand Motor Co** Soebyvej
3–7 ☎423300 P Frd Opl VW

ᔆ0**A Precht-Jensen** Hjørringvej 12–14
☎423366 Ren Sab

ᔆ0**B Sørensen** Grønlandsvej 10
☎422877 P BL

FREDERIKSVAERK
Sjaelland(☎02)

ᔆ0**Toft & Larsen** Vinderød Skov 9
☎121488 VW

ᔆ0**Thorkild Sørensen** Hillerødvej 103,
Kregme ☎121800 BL

FRØRUP
Fyn(☎09)

☆ ☆**Øksendrup Kro** Svendborg Landevej
30, Øksendrup ☎371057
🏨15 P sB 🏨165–205 dB 🏨255–350
M45–75

GAMMEL SKAGEN See **SKAGEN**

GEDSER
Falster(☎03)

★**Gedser** Langgade 59 ☎879302
rm16 ⇄6 sB165 dB250 dB ⇄280

GENTOFTE See **KØBENHAVN (COPENHAGEN)**

GLOSTRUP See **KØBENHAVN (COPENHAGEN)**

GRAM
Jylland(☎04)

☆☆**Gamle Kro** Slotsvej 47 ☎821620
rm18 ▥12 **P** sB80–130 sB ▥150
dB150–280 dB ▥245–345

GRENÅ
Jylland(☎06)

★★★**Nord** (Inter DK) Kystvej 25
☎322500 tx63480
⇄100 **P** Lift ☽ sB ⇄340 dB ⇄480
Pool

GUDHJEM
Bornholm(☎03)

★**Jantzens** Broddegade 33 ☎985017
Mar–Oct
rm15 ▥10 **P** sea

HADERSLEV
Jylland(☎04)

★★★**Norden** Storegade 55 ☎524030
rm43 ⇄34 **P** sB158 sB ⇄190–235
dB296 dB ⇄351–406

☆☆**Haderslev** Damparken ☎526010
⇄30 A3rm Lift sB175 sB ⇄220 dB275
dB ⇄375

ಿ**E Grodt** Sønderbro 10 ☎521750 M/c
Cit

HADSUND
Jylland(☎08)

★**Øster Hurup** Kystvegen 57, Øster
Hurup ☎588014
rm13 🏛 **P** sB80 dB160

ಿ**Autogarden** Østergade 14 ☎571677
M/c **P** Opl Vau

HELSINGØR (ELSINORE)
Sjælland(☎02)

★★★**Marienlyst** (SRS) Nordre
Strandvej 2 ☎211801 tx41116
⇄215 **P** Lift ☽ sB ⇄460 dB ⇄740
Pool sea

★**Meulenborg** Bogebakken 5 (n.rest)
☎215220
May–Sep
rm30 ⇄4 🏛 **P** ☽ Pool

★**Missions** (Temperance) Bramsstraede
5 ☎210591
rm46 ⇄14 ▥14 **P** Lift ☽ sB120–150
sB ⇄240 dB260 dB ⇄360

ಿ**Aurogården** Marienlyst alle 1
☎210123 **P** Frd MB Opl

HERNING
Jylland(☎07)

★★★**Eyde** (Inter DK) Torvet 1
☎221800 tx62195
rm64 ⇄52 ▥2 Lift sB100–210

Denmark

sB ⇄ ▥275–325 dB260
dB ⇄ ▥395–440

HIMMELEV See **ROSKILDE**

HØJBJERG See **ÅRHUS**

HOLBAEK
Sjælland(☎03)

★★**Strandparken** Kalundborvej 58
☎430616
⇄31 **P** ☽ sB ⇄270 dB ⇄380–410
Beach sea

Auto Centralen Østre Havnevej 12
☎434300 BL Sab

ಿ**Holbaek Autolager** Smedelundsgade
21 ☎433500 Frd

ಿ**'Trekanten'** (F O Frederiksen) Taastrup
Møllevej 6 ☎431313 Cit Ren Vau

HOLSTEBRO
Jylland (☎07)

★★★**Bel Air** ☎426666
⇄57 **P** Lift ☽ sB ⇄260 dB ⇄410

★★**Schaumburg** Norregade 26
☎423111
Closed 24–31 Dec
rm35 ⇄20 **P** ☽ sB185 sB ⇄245
dB290 dB ⇄390

ಿ**Biler** Lundholmvej 1 ☎423411 BL Toy

HORNBAEK
Sjælland (☎02)

★★★**Trouville** Kystvej 20 ☎202200
tx41241
⇄50 **P** Lift ☽ sB ⇄395 dB ⇄576
Pool Beach Sea

HORNDRUP See **SKANDERBORG**

HORSENS
Jylland (☎05)

★★★**Bygholm Park** Schuttesvej 6
☎622333
rm70 ⇄50 🏛 **P** ☽ sB180
sB ⇄230–245 dB295–315
dB ⇄375–395

★★**Missionshotellet** Gl- Jernbanegade
6 ☎621800
rm50 🏛 **P**

ಿ**Bilforum** Silkeborgvej 2 ☎626000 Opl
Vau

HVIDOVRE See **KØBENHAVN (COPENHAGEN)**

KALUNDBORG
Sjælland (☎03)

ಿ**Autohallen** Slagelsevej 242 ☎510982
BL

KASTRUP See **KØBENHAVN (COPENHAGEN)**

KLIPLEV See **ÅBRENÅ**

KØBENHAVN (COPENHAGEN)
(☎01)
See Plan page 100

★★★★**Angleterre** (Intercont)
Kongens Nytorv 34 ☎120095 tx15877
Plan 1
⇄144 **P** Lift ☽ sB ⇄930 dB ⇄1515

★★★★**SAS Royal** (SRS)
Hammerichsgade 1 ☎141412 tx27155
Plan 2
⇄300 🏛 **P** Lift ☽ sB ⇄580–840
dB ⇄950–1070

★★★★**Sheraton** Vester Søgade 6
☎143535 tx27450 Plan 2A
⇄474 **P** Lift ☽ sB ⇄690–870
dB ⇄935–985

★★★**Codan** St Annae Pl ☎133400
tx15815 Plan 3
⇄134 **P** Lift ☽ sB ⇄500 dB ⇄600

★★★**Imperial** (THF) Vester
Farimagsgade 9 ☎128000 tx15556
Plan 6
⇄176 🏛 Lift sB ⇄515 dB ⇄650–770

★★★**Mercur** Vester Farimagsgade
17 ☎125711 tx19767 Plan 6A
⇄108 **P** Lift ☽ sB ⇄510
dB ⇄685–790 Mfr130 ✆

★★★**Palace** (Comfort) Raadhuspl57
☎144050 tx19693 Plan 7
⇄170 Lift ☽ sB ⇄510 dB ⇄690 M149

★★★**Richmond** Vester Farimagsgade
33 ☎123366 tx19767 Plan9
rm133 ⇄56 ▥77 **P** Lift ☽
sB ⇄ ▥510 dB ⇄ ▥685–790 Mfr130

★★**Alexandra** H-C-Andersens bd 8
(n.rest) ☎142200 Plan 10
⇄65 A1rm 🏛 Lift sB ⇄365–525
dB ⇄520–715

★★**Astoria** Banegaardspladsen 4
☎141419 tx16319 Plan 11
rm91 ⇄83 **P** Lift ☽ sB ⇄375–460
dB ⇄525–750

★★**Comfort** Løngangstraede 27
☎126570 tx16488 Plan 13
rm200 ⇄40 ▥160 **P** Lift ☽
sB ⇄ ▥310 dB ⇄ ▥490 M115

★★**Grand** Vesterbrogade 9
☎313600 tx15343 Plan 15
rm108 ⇄86 ▥10 Lift ☽
sB ⇄ ▥350–450 dB ⇄ ▥520–680

★★**71 Nyhavn** Nyhavn 71 ☎118585
tx27558 Plan 16
rm81 ⇄13 ▥68 **P** Lift ☽
sB ⇄ ▥518–608 dB ⇄ ▥648–758

★★**SAS Globetrotter** 171 Engvej
☎551433 tx31222 Plan 17
⇄156 **P** Lift ☽ sB ⇄460 dB ⇄600 M
alc

★★**Tre Falke** (Inter DK) Falconer Alle
9 ☎198001 tx15550 Plan 19
⇄162 🏛 Lift sB ⇄575 dB ⇄700

★★Missionhotellet Hebron
Helgolandsgade 4 (n.rest) ☎316906
tx27416 Plan **20**

rm130 ⇌64 Lift ♪ sB155–255
sB ⇌260–335 dB265–350
dB ⇌420–500

★★Viking Bregade 65 ☎124550
tx19590 Plan **21**

rm91 ⋔18 **P** Lift ♪ sB225–275
sB ⋔275–325 dB375 dB ⋔500

★Vestersøhus Vestersøgade 58 (n.rest)
☎113870 Plan **22**

rm53 ⇌20 ⋔7 ⌂ Lift ♪ sB280
sB ⇌ ⋔450 dB450 dB ⇌ ⋔550

å⅋N Baunsoe Middelfartgade 15
☎297711 Chy Peu

å⅋BMW City Lautrupsgade 2–4
☎209560 M/c BWM

å⅋H Lystrup Herlev Hovedgade 147
☎949200 Dat Vau

å⅋V Nelleman Vodroffsvej 55–57
☎353333 BL

å⅋B P Parkeringshuset Nyropsgade 6
☎126765 **P** Toy

At **ALBERTSLUND** (15km W on N1)

☆ Wittrup Rosklidevej 251 ☎(02)649551
Plan **23**

Closed Xmas
rm56 ⇌48 **P** ♪ sB170 sB ⇌210
dB ⇌275

At **GENTOFTE** (5km N)

KØBENHAVN
(COPENHAGEN)

1	★★★ Angleterre
2	★★★ SAS Roya
2A	★★ Sheraton
3	★★★ Codan
4	★★★ Dan (At Kastrup/ Airport 9 km SE)
6	★★★ Imperial
6A	★★★ Mercur
7	★★★ Palace
9	★★★ Richmond
10	★★★ Alexandra
11	★★ Astoria
12	★★ Bel Air (At Kastrup/Airport 9 km SE)
13	★★★ Comfort
14	★★★ Gentofte (At Gentofte 5 km N)
15	★★★ Grand
16	★★★ 71 Nyhavn
17	★★★ SAS Globetrotter
18	☆ ☆ Scandic (At Hvidovre)
19	★★★ Tre Falke
20	★★ Missionshotellet Hebron
21	★★ Viking
22	★ Vestersøhus
23	☆ Wittrup (At Albertslund 15 km W on N1)

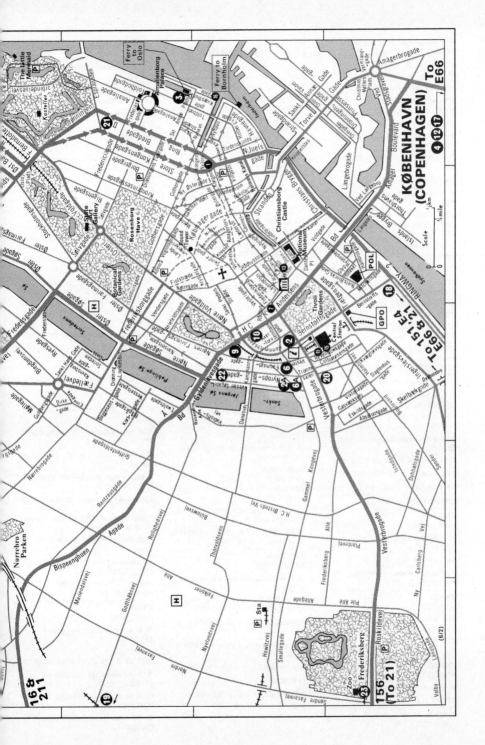

KØBENHAVN (COPENHAGEN)

★ ★ ★Gentofte Gentoftegade 29
☎680911 tx15812 Plan 14

⇦70 P Lift ☽ sB ⇔335 – 385
dB ⇔445 – 535

At GLOSTRUP (11km W on N1)

♨Monk's Automobiler Vibeholmsvej
26 – 28 ☎(02)459000 Toy

At HVIDOVRE (6km SW)

☆ ☆ ☆Scandic Kettevej 4 ☎498222
tx15517 Plan 18

🏨150 P Lift ☽ sB 🏨370 dB 🏨480
Pool

At KASTRUP/Airport (9km SE)

★ ★ ★ ★Dan Kastruplundgade 15
☎511400 tx31111 Plan 4

rm271 ⇔200 🏨71 P Lift ☽
sB ⇔ 🏨390 – 490 dB ⇔ 🏨580 – 720
M100 Beach Sea

★ ★ ★Bel Air Løjtegårdsvej 99 ☎513033
tx31240 Plan 12

⇔215 P ☽ sB ⇔390 dB ⇔490 Pool

KØGE
Sjælland (☎03)

★ ★ ★Hvide Hus Strandvejen 111
☎653690 tx43501

⇦118 A12rm 🛁 P ☽ sB ⇔330
dB ⇔425 – 475 sea

♨G Due Tangmosevej 105 ☎653400
Maz Opl

KOLDING
Jylland (☎05)

★ ★ ★Saxildhus Banegaardspl
☎521200 tx51446

rm88 ⇦78 P Lift ☽ sB180
sB ⇔200 – 350 dB270 dB ⇔330 – 400

☆ ☆ ☆Tre Roser Dyrehavegårdsvej
☎532122

🏨83 P ☽ sB 🏨265 dB 🏨385 Pool

A E Jensen Monten 1 ☎520944 Cit

♨H G Nielsen Vejlevej 108 ☎522555 Frd

KONGENSBRO See ANS BY

KORSØR
Sjælland (☎03)

☆ ☆Halskov Tårnborgvej 180, Halskov
☎571616

rm22 ⇦12 P ☽

♨Bilhuset T Nielsen Tårnborgvej 170
☎572900 BL Sko Vlo

LEMVIG
Jylland (☎07)

★ ★ ★Niørre Vinkel Søgårdevejen 6,
Vinkelhage ☎822211

⇦26 P Lift ☽ sB ⇔220 dB ⇔350
lake

LØGSTØR
Jylland (☎08)

★ ★Nord Havnevej 38 ☎671711

rm25 ⇦2 🏨1 🛁 sea

MARIBO
Lolland (☎03)

Denmark

★ ★ ★Hvide Hus Vestergade 27
☎881011 tx40880

⇦69 A6rm P Lift ☽ sB ⇔330
dB ⇔450 – 475 Pool lake

MILLINGE
Fyn (☎09)

★ ★Falsled Kro Assensvej 513, Falsled
☎681111

Mar – Dec
rm11 ⇦11 P sB ⇔ 🏨340 dB ⇔ 🏨700
M alc

NÆSTVED
Sjælland (☎03)

★ ★ ★Mogenstrup Kro Praestø
Landevej, Mogenstrup ☎761130 tx27459

rm53 ⇦30 A9rm P ☽ sB ⇔295
dB ⇔395 – 460 Pool

★ ★ ★Vinhuset St-Peders Kirkepl 4
☎720807

rm42 ⇦30 🛁 P ☽ sB180 sB⇔225
dB310 dB⇔395

NAKSKOV
Lolland (☎03)

★ ★Harmonien Nybrogade 2 ☎922100

rm39 ⇦28 🏨5 sB175 sB ⇔ 🏨210
dB290 dB ⇔ 🏨330

★ ★Skovrider Gaarden Svingelen
☎920355

⇦10 P sB ⇔250 dB ⇔380 M alc

NYBORG
Fyn (☎09)

★ ★ ★Hesselet Christianslundsvej
119 ☎313029

4 Jan – 22 Dec
⇦46 🛁 P ☽ sB ⇔400
dB ⇔583 – 700 M alc ☙ Pool Beach
δ sea lake

★ ★Nyborg Strand (Inter DK) Osterovej 2
☎313131 tx50371

rm260 ⇦160 🛁 P Lift ☽ sB125 – 175
sB ⇔310 dB250 dB ⇔400 – 475 sea

NYKØBING
Falster (☎03)

★ ★ ★Baltic Jernbanegade 45 (n.rest)
☎853066

rm70 ⇦27 🏨5 🛁 P Lift ☽ sB190
sB ⇦ 🏨220 dB315 dB ⇔ 🏨370

♨Auto Co Frisegade 31 ☎853155 Aud
VW

♨Breitenstein Randersvej 4 ☎852266
BL Sab

♨A Hansen Randersvej 8 ☎850600 Frd

At SUNDBY (2km N)

☆Liselund Lundevej 22 ☎851566

⇦25 P sB ⇔210 dB ⇔300

NYKØBING-MORS
Jylland (☎07)

♨H D Pedersen Limfjordvej 44 ☎723044
Ren Vlo

NYKØBING-SJÆLLAND
Sælland (☎03)

♨P Tamstort Kirkestraede 5 ☎411400
Frd

ODENSE
Fyn (☎09)

★ ★ ★Grand Jernbanegade 18
☎117747 tx59972

rm150 ⇦112 🛁 P Lift ☽
sB ⇔315 – 355 dB ⇔500 M50 – 400

★ ★ ★H C Andersen C-Bergsgade 7
☎147800 tx59694

🏨148 P Lift ☽

★ ★Ny Missions Østre Stationsvej 24
☎117745

rm81 ⇦21 P Lift ☽ sB160 – 190
sB ⇔210 – 250 dB280 – 310
dB ⇔330 – 350

☆ ☆Odense (Inter DK) Hunderupgade 2
☎114213 tx27459

⇦ 🏨46 P Lift ☽ sB ⇔ 🏨275 – 295
dB ⇔ 🏨375 – 400 M65 – 110

★ ★Windsor Vindegade 45 ☎120652
tx59662

⇦ 🛁 P Lift ☽ sB ⇔225 – 450
dB ⇔425 – 600

☆Ansgarhus Kirkegårds allé 17 – 19
☎128800

Closed Oct
rm17 ⇦4 🛁 sB125 sB ⇦150 dB200
dB ⇔250

♨Bilhuset R Carlsen Svendborgvej 247
☎131113 Opl Peu

♨V Hansen Odensevej 121 ☎117255
Ren Vlo

♨EM Jensen Odensevej 101 ☎115810
BL RT Sab Sko

♨Odense Dalumvej 67 ☎140400 BMW
Hon

♨Skandinavisk Motor Co Middelfartvej
50 ☎118500 Aud VW

At BLOMMENSLYST (10km W on A1
[E66])

☆ ☆Brasilia (Inter DK)) Middelfartvej
420 ☎967012 tx27459

⇦52 P ☽ sB ⇔ 🏨285 – 385
dB ⇔ 🏨390 – 490

RANDERS
Jylland(☎06)

★ ★ ★Randers Torvegade 11
☎423422

3 Jan – 23 Dec
⇦83 🛁 P Lift ☽ sB ⇔300 dB⇔450

★ ★Kogens Ege Hadsundvej 2
☎430300 tx65130

⇦88 🛁 P Lift ☽ sB ⇔295 dB ⇔460
M118 sea

★ ★Westend Vestergade 53 (n.rest)
☎425388

102

rm22 ⇋4 **P** 𝄞

⬧J Madson Århusvej 108 ☏427800 Opl Vau

⬧R Nellemann Strømmen 27, Grenåvej ☏423233 Frd

RIBE
Jylland(☏05)

★ ★ ★**Dagmar** (Inter DK) Torvet 1 ☏420033
rm42 ⇋20 sB160–220 sB ⇋300 dB290–390 dB ⇋475

⬧Auto Forum Industrivej 36 ☏422811 **P** Opl Vau

⬧Fredegods Autogård Bohrsvej 1 ☏421611 BL

⬧V Veirup Industrivej 1 ☏420600 **P** Aud VW

RINGKØBING
Jylland(☏07)

★ ★ ★**Fjordgaarden** (Inter DK) Vesterkaer 28 ☏321400
rm60 ⇋47 **P** 𝄞 sB ⇋245–300 dB ⇋350–425

⬧N Hansens Motorcompagni Enghavevej 11 ☏321133 Frd

RINGSTED
Sjælland (☏03)

⬧H Larsen Nørregade 90–92 ☏612518 Frd

RØDBY
Lolland(☏03)

★ ★ ★**Danhotel** Havnegade 2 ☏905366 tx40890
⇋39 **P** Lift 𝄞 sB ⇋270–320 dB ⇋375–450 sea

RØDDING
Jylland(☏04)

⬧P Henriksen Gramvej ☏841022 Opl Vau

RØNNE
Isle of Bornholm(☏03)

⬧F Jorgensen Ringvejen ☏950250 Opl Vau

⬧G Larsen Åkirkebyvej 51 ☏950804 **P** Frd

RØNNEDE
Sjælland (☏03)

☆**Axelved** Ronnedevej 1, Axelved ☏711401
rm8 sB110 dB180

ROSKILDE
Sjælland (☏02)

★ ★**Prindsen** Algade 13 ☏358010
rm41 ⇋37 **P** 𝄞 sB210 sB ⇋240 dB320 dB ⇋380

At **HIMMELEV** (3km N on N6)

☆ ☆ **B P Motel** Hovedvej A1 ☏354385 tx43145
rm42 ⇋16 A13rm **P** sB155 sB ⇋220 dB200 dB ⇋330

Denmark

RY
Jylland(☏06)

★ ★**Ry** Kyhnsvej 2 ☏891911
rm60 ⇋ 🖩55 A30rm **P** sB ⇋ 🖩158–208 dB ⇋ 🖩282–382

SAEBY
Jylland(☏08)

⬧O Christensen Ålborgvej 32–34 ☏462255 **P** Chy Peu

SAKSKØBING
Lolland(☏03)

⬧M Skotte Sakskøbing Nykøbingvej 8 ☏894285 Opl Vau

SILKEBORG
Jylland(☏06)

★ ★ ★**Dania** Torvet 5 ☏820111 tx63269
rm48 ⇋35 **P** 𝄞 sB160–180 sB ⇋245–285 dB280–310 dB ⇋370–410 lake

★ ★ ★**Impala** (Inter DK) Vester Ringvej ☏820300
rm41 ⇋36 **P** 𝄞 sB ⇋370 dB ⇋535 Pool lake

SKAGEN
Jylland(☏08)

★ ★ ★**Skagen** Gammel Landevej ☏442233
⇋ 🖩47 **P** sB ⇋ 🖩280–320 dB ⇋ 🖩450–675 Pool

⬧G A Hylander Øresundsvej 8 ☏445200 Fia

At **GAMMEL SKAGEN** (2km W)

★**Ruth's** H–Ruthsvej 1 ☏441124
Jun–Aug
rm110 A20rm 🖩 sB210 dB420 sea

SKANDERBORG
Jylland(☏06)

★ ★ ★**Skanderborghus** Dyre Haven ☏520955
rm50 ⇋28 🖩14 **P** Lift 𝄞 sB160 sB ⇋ 🖩215–270 dB260 dB ⇋ 🖩335–355

★**Slotskroen** Adelgade 23 ☏520012
rm16 ⇋8 🖩 **P** sB100 sB ⇋140 dB200 dB ⇋280

⬧Skanderborg Motor Nørregade 1 ☏520566 BL

At **HORNDRUP** (10km S)

☆ ☆ **Oasen** ☏579228
⇋12 🖩 dB ⇋130 lake

SKIVE
Jylland(☏07)

★ ★**Gl Skivehus** (Inter DK) Sdr 1, Østertorv ☏521144 tx66755
rm66 ⇋46 A6rm 🖩 **P** Lift 𝄞 sB170 sB ⇋200–260 dB240 dB ⇋400

★ ★**Hilltop** Sondre-Boulevard ☏523711
⇋71 A15rm **P** 𝄞 sB ⇋270 dB ⇋410

⬧J Fogh Sdr Boulevard 9 ☏522100 **P** Frd

SKJERN
Jylland(☏07)

⬧Skjern Motor Co Bredgade 3 ☏371300 Frd

⬧A B Sørensen Nygade 54 ☏350950 M/c **P** Fia Lnc Sab

SKØRPING
Jylland(☏08)

★ ★ ★**Rold Stor-Kro** (Inter DK) Storegade 27 ☏375100 tx16600
rm53 ⇋42 🖩 **P** 𝄞 sB125 sB ⇋295 dB250 dB ⇋420–460

SLAGELSE
Sjælland (☏03)

⬧G Kjeruiff Sverigesvej 12 ☏520815 **P** Opl

SØNDERBORG
Jylland(☏04)

★ ★**City** Kongevej 64 ☏421626 tx16600
rm13 ⇋11 **P** 𝄞 sB170–180 sB ⇋220–250 dB ⇋350

⬧Automobiler APS (B Kock) Alsgade 33 ☏427878 Opl Vau

⬧Nybol Autovaerksted Amtsvejen 9 ☏467943 **P** Ren

Skifter Anderson Bil A/s Ellegårdsvej 5 ☏425155 Ren Vlo

SORØ
Jylland(☏03)

★ ★**Kong Frederik d, VII** Storgade 10, Torvet ☏630063
rm10 ⇋5 🖩 sB120 sB ⇋ 🖩150 dB230 dB ⇋ 🖩260

★ ★**Postgården** Storgade 27 ☏632222
8 Jan–22 Dec
rm26 ⇋9 **P** sB150 sB ⇋200 dB280 dB ⇋340
J Frandsen Holbaekvej 1–3 ☏630100 Frd

STEGE
Møn(☏03)

⬧H P Hansen Kostervej 19 ☏815024 Cit Vau

STRUER
Jylland(☏07)

★ ★**Grand** Østergade 24 ☏850400
rm39 ⇋14 **P** sB160 sB ⇋195 dB260 dB ⇋330

⬧W Laursen Bredgade ☏851500 **P** BL DJ MG RT

SUNDBY See **NYKØBING**

SVENDBORG
Fyn(☏09)

★ ★ ★**Svendborg** (Inter DK) Voldgade 10 ☏211700 tx58149
⇋60 **P** Lift 𝄞 sB ⇋280 dB ⇋420

&OBilhuset Grønnemosevej 6 ☎221111 P
BL Fia RT Sab

&OC Bukkehave Lerchesvej 11 ☎211313
M/c P All makes

&ON Kjær Bilcentret Odensvej 94
☎212323 P Frd

&OS Nauerby Odensevej 42 ☎213811
Ren Vlo

TAPPERNØJE
Sjælland (☎03)

&OTappernøje Autoservice Hovedvejen
67 ☎765099 BL

THISTED
Jylland(☎07)

★ ★ ★Ålborg Storegade 29 ☎923566
rm32 ⇄17 🏛 P ♪ sB150 sB ⇄190
dB260 dB ⇄310 sea

&OA P Anderson Rosenkrantzgade 1
☎921600 P Opl Vau

TOFTLUND
Jylland(☎04)

&OP Henriksen Østergade 23 ☎831122
Opl Vau

TØNDER
Jylland(☎04)

★ ★ ★Tønderhus Jomflustien 1
☎722222
rm32 ⇄15 🏛

★ ★Hostrups Søndergade 30 ☎722129
3 Jan–22 Dec
rm27 ⇄13 🛏13 A6rm 🏛 P
sB120–140 dB210–250 dB ⇄ 🛏250–300

&OM Wollesen Sønderport ☎721179 P
Dat Sko

Denmark

TRANEKAER
(*Island of Langeland*)(☎09)

★Gjaestgivergaarden Slotsgade 74
☎591204
Closed Feb
rm16 ⇄12 P sB145 sB ⇄217 dB324
dB ⇄362

VARDE
Jylland(☎05)

★ ★ ★Varde Torvet 3 ☎220500
rm50 ⇄35 🛏30

&OVarde Motor Compagni V Landevej 78
☎220499 P Frd

VEDBÆK
Sjælland (☎02)

★ ★ ★Marina Vedbaek Strandvej 391
☎891711 tx37217
rm106 ⇄97 🛏9 🏛 P Lift ♪
sB ⇄ 🛏400 dB ⇄ 🛏535 ⤢ Beach
sea

VEJLE
Jylland(☎05)

★ ★ ★ ★Australia Daemningen 6
☎824311 tx61104
2 Jan–23 Dec
⇄108 🏛 P Lift ♪ sB ⇄248–415
dB ⇄375–530

★ ★ ★ ★Munkebjerg Munkebjergvej 125
☎827500 tx61103
2 Jan–23 Dec
⇄124 P Lift ♪ sB ⇄340
dB ⇄465–550 M85–150 ⤢ Pool sea

★ ★ ★Grand Oria Lehmannsgade 1
☎829400
rm63 ⇄33 P Lift ♪ sB155 sB ⇄185
dB290 dB ⇄340

★ ★Missionshotellet 'Caleb'
Daemningen 52 (n.rest) ☎823211
Closed Jan
rm40 ⇄16 🛏3 A5rm P Lift ♪ sB165
sB ⇄ 🛏200–230 dB300
dB ⇄ 🛏380–430

&OBøje & Brechner Boulevarden
☎826000 Frd

&OM Kjae Boulevarden 54 ☎828255
Lada Opl Vau

&ONeergaard Vestre Engvej 7 ☎823366
M/c BMW Hon

&OVejle Motor Co Boulevarden 13
☎822110 BL Sko

VIBORG
Jylland(☎06)

☆ ☆ ☆Søndersø Randersvej 2 (n.rest)
☎610222

⇄53 P ♪ sB ⇄225 dB ⇄325

★ ★Missionshottellet St–Matthiasgade
5 ☎623700
rm45 ⇄5 🛏30 A15rm 🏛 P Lift ♪
sB180–210 sB ⇄ 🛏230–270 dB270–300
dB ⇄ 🛏340–400

&OCitröen Viborg Randersvej 51–53
☎626000 Cit

&OF Jørgensen Skivevej ☎623511 Frd

&OP Wraa Falkevej 23 ☎624600 Aud VW

VIBY
Jylland(☎06)

★ ★ ★Mercur Viby Torv ☎141411
tx68746
⇄110 🏛 P Lift ♪

Fåborg, on the island of Funen

Møn's Cliffs, south of Sealand

FRANCE
AND MONACO

France, rich in history and natural beauty, is bordered by six countries, Belgium, German Federal Republic, Italy, Luxembourg, Spain and Switzerland. The country offers a great variety of scenery from the mountain ranges of the Alps and the Pyrénées to the attractive river valleys of the Loire, Rhône and Dordogne. With some 1,800 miles of coastline which includes the golden sands of the Côte d'Azur, there is countryside appealing to everyone's taste. The climate of France is temperate but varies considerably. The Mediterranean coast enjoys a sub-tropical climate with hot summers, whilst along the coast of Brittany the climate is very similar to that of Devon and Cornwall. The language is, of course, French and this is spoken throughout the country, although there are many local dialects and variations.

Area *213,000 sq miles*
Population *53,400,000*
Local time *GMT + 1*
(Summer GMT + 2)

National flag *Vertical tricolour of blue, white and red*

A leaflet entitled *Motoring in Corsica* is available to AA members.

How to get there

Motorists can cross the Channel by ship or hovercraft services. Short sea crossings operate from Dover and Folkestone to Boulogne and Calais ($1\frac{1}{4}-1\frac{3}{4}$hrs). Longer Channel crossings operate from Dover and Ramsgate to Dunkerque ($2\frac{1}{2}$hrs). Newhaven to Dieppe (4hrs), Portsmouth to Le Havre ($5\frac{1}{2}$hrs) or Cherbourg ($4-6\frac{1}{2}$hrs) or St-Malo ($9-9\frac{1}{2}$hrs), Southampton to Le Havre ($6\frac{1}{2}-8\frac{1}{2}$hrs) Plymouth to Roscoff ($6-6\frac{1}{2}$hrs) and Weymouth to Cherbourg (4hrs). Fast hovercraft services operate between Dover and Boulogne or Calais (30–35 mins).

Château de Villandry

Motoring regulations and general information

This information should be read in conjunction with the general content of the European ABC (pages 6–27). **Note** As certain regulations and requirements are common to many countries they are covered by one entry in the ABC and the following headings represent some of the subjects dealt with in this way:
Crash or safety helmets
Drinking and driving
Fire extinguisher
First-aid kit
Insurance
International distinguishing sign
Medical treatment
Overtaking
Police fines
Radio telephones/Radio transmitters
Rear view mirror
Road signs
Seat belts
Tyres
Visitors' registration

AA Port agents
(See also *AA Agents* page 7)
62201 Boulogne-sur-Mer G A Gregson & Sons, The Automobile Association, Tour Damremont (18 eme), Boulevard Chanzy BP No. 21 ☎(21)302222.
62100 Calais G A Gregson & Sons, The Automobile Association, Terminal Est ☎(21)964720

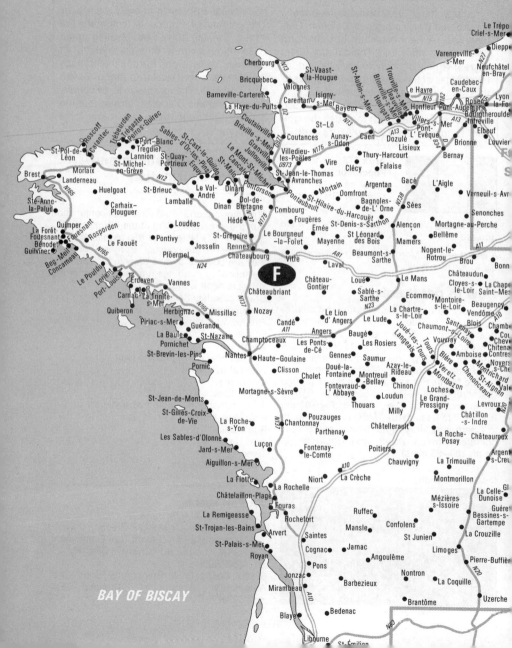

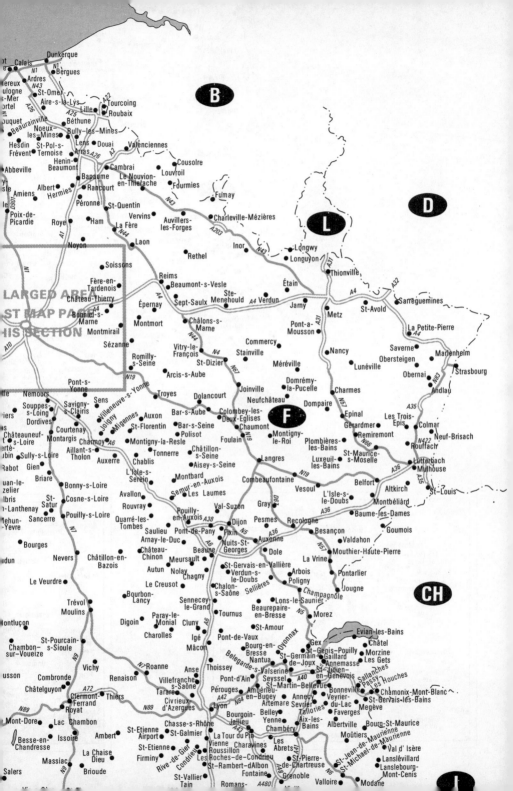

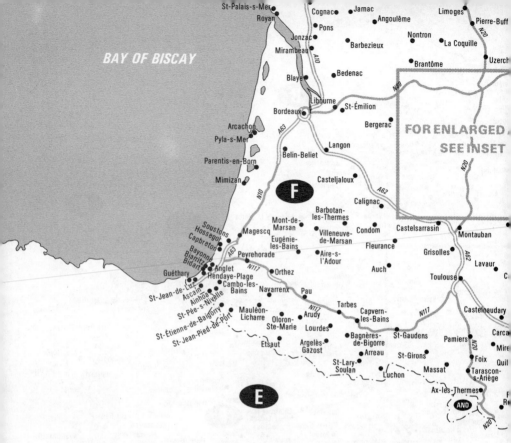
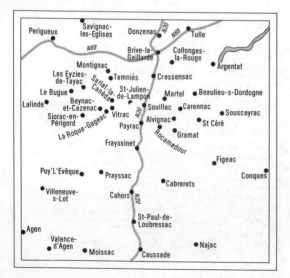

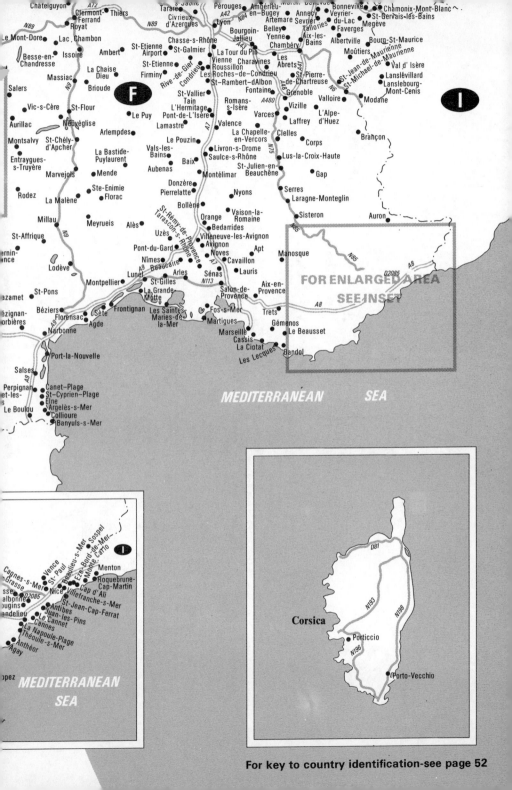

For key to country identification-see page 52

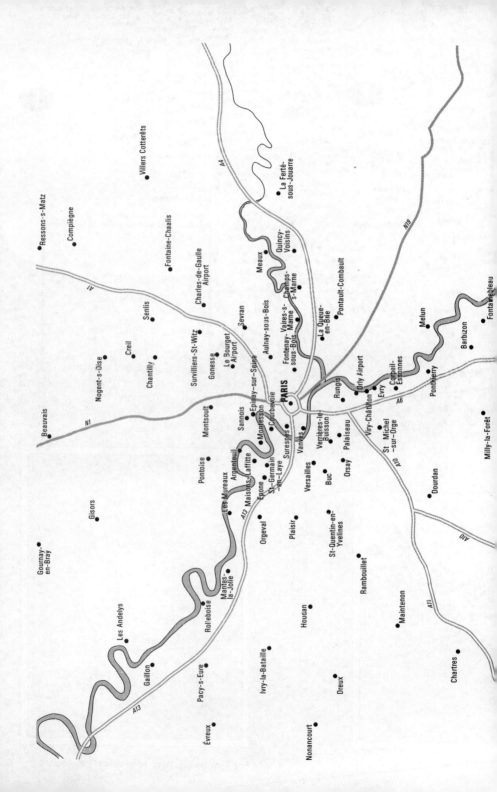

50100 Cherbourg Agence Maritime Tellier, Gare Maritime ☎(33)204338; Port office (when ferries operating), car ferry terminal ☎(33)204274.
76200 Dieppe G A Gregson & Sons, The Automobile Association, Car Ferry Terminal, Esplanade ☎(35)841941.
76600 Le Havre G A Gregson & Sons, The Automobile Association, 47 Boulevard John Kennedy ☎(35)420566.

Accidents

Fire☎18 **police** and **ambulance**☎17. Contact the police (*brigade de gendarmerie*) particularly in cases of injury. Emergency telephone boxes are stationed every 20 km on some roadways and are connected direct to the local police station. In the larger towns emergency help can be obtained from the *police secours* (emergency assistance department).

Motorists involved in a traffic accident must complete a *constat à l'amiable* before the vehicle is moved. If the vehicle has been seriously damaged an expert's examination is advised prior to the return to the UK. The *constat à l'amiable* was introduced by the French insurance companies and represents the 'European Accident Statement Form'. It must be signed by the other party, but if a dispute arises and one of the parties involved should refuse to complete the *constat à l'amiable* then the other party should immediately obtain a written report from a bailiff (*huissier*), which is known as a *constat d'huissier*. A bailiff can usually be found in any large town and charges a fee of Fr400 for preparing the report. Normally the police are only called out to accidents where persons are injured, a driver is under the influence of alcohol or the accident impedes traffic flow. When attending an accident the police prepare a report known as a *procès verbal.*

After an accident the French authorities, at their discretion, may request a surety payment to cover the court costs or fines. See also *Accidents* page 7.

Accommodation

There is a large selection of hotels of all categories. The French Ministry of Tourism classifies hotels in five categories: one-star to *de luxe*. Local tourist information offices (see page 115) can provide details of hotels and restaurants in the area.

Rates for rooms are usually officially controlled and must be displayed in each room but this does not apply to the cost of meals. Many hotels offer half-board terms only, as indicated in the gazetteer (**DPn**).

Accueil de France Tourist offices showing this sign will make hotel bookings **only for personal callers** and only for up to a week ahead. Bookings are made in the same town or at one of some 35 major towns and cities, including Calais, Le Havre and Rouen (open to 18.30hrs weekdays, sometimes later in season). The head office in Paris is the Office de Tourisme, 127 avenue des Champs-Elysées, Paris 6, open every day from 09.00–20.00hrs, Sundays and Bank Holidays from 09.00–18.00hrs.

Gites de France. This is furnished accommodation in rural France, often at farms, for those who prefer to cater for themselves. There are some 23,000 Gites in 4,000 villages, created with the financial support of the French Government and governed by a charter laid down by the Fédération National de Gites de France. For information on membership write to Gites de France, 178 Piccadilly, London W1V 0PQ enclosing details of preferred regions and choice of dates.

Logis de France These are privately owned, mostly family run hotels equivalent to the one-star or two-star categories. They are generally located off the beaten track and offer a high standard for their type and good value for money. There are nearly 4,000 Logis, some of which are listed in the gazetteer, and they are marked by the symbol **L**. A copy of the Logis Hotel Guide may be obtained from the French Government Tourist Office, 178 Piccadilly, London W1V 0AL (against payment of 50p in stamps to cover postage and packing).

Relais Routiers These are restaurants situated on main roads offering simple accommodation and providing a good meal at a reasonable price. The *Relais Routiers Guide* issued each year can be purchased through bookshops.

Boats

A Helmsman's Certificate of Competence is recommended for France. See page 8 for further information about this and boat documentation.

Breakdown

If your car breaks down, try to move it to the verge of the road so that it obstructs the traffic flow as little as possible. Place a warning triangle to the rear of the vehicle to warn following traffic.

You are advised to seek local assistance as, at the time of going to press, there is no nationwide road assistance service in France. See also *Breakdown* page 8 and *Warning triangle/ Hazard warning lights* page 116.

British Consulates
(See also page 8)

75008 Paris 109 rue du Faubourg St-Honoré
☎(1)2669142. There are also consulates in
Bordeaux, Boulogne-sur-Mer, Calais, Cherbourg, Dunkerque, Le Havre, Lille, Lyons, Mar-
seilles, Nantes, Nicé, Perpignan, St. Malo-Din-
ard and Toulouse.

Currency and banking hours
(See also page 11)

The unit of currency is the French franc, which
is divided into 100 centimes. There is no restriction on the amount of foreign currency which
may be taken into France. Travellers are,
however, restricted to taking Fr5,000 with them
when leaving the country, unless, of course,
they imported more currency on entry and
completed the appropriate form at the time.

In most large towns banks are open from
Monday to Friday 09.00–noon and 14.00–
16.30hrs; they close on Saturday, Sunday and
some on Monday. Banks close at midday on the
day prior to a national holiday and all day on
Monday if the holiday falls on a Tuesday.

The *Crédit Lyonnais* has offices at the Invalides
air terminal in Paris for cashing travellers'
cheques and the *Société Générale* has two
offices at Orly airport whilst at the Charles de
Gaulle airport exchange facilities are available.

Customs regulations

A *Customs Carnet de Passages en Douane* is
required for temporarily imported outboard
engines, exceeding 92cc (5cv as applied to
marine engines), imported without the boats
with which they are to be used, and for cycles
with auxiliary motors up to 50cc which are new
or show no signs of use. See also *Customs
regulations for European countries* page 11 for
further information.

Dimensions and weight restrictions

Private cars and trailers are restricted to the
following dimensions – height: no restrictions
but 4 metres is the recommended maximum;
width: 2.50 metres; length: Vehicle/trailer combinations 18 metres.

Vehicle/trailer combinations of more than
3,500 kg in weight or 7 metres (22 ft 9 in) in
length must travel at least 50 metres behind a
similar combination. They must also keep to the
two right-hand lanes on roads with three or
more lanes in each direction.

Driving licence

A valid British driving licence is acceptable in
France. The minimum age at which a visitor

may drive a temporarily imported car or motorcycle (exceeding 80cc) is 18 years. See also
page 13 and *Speed limits* page 115.

Emergency messages to tourists
(See also page 14)

Emergency messages to tourists are broadcast
daily on *Radio France*. These messages are
transmitted in French on 1829 metres long
wave and precede the news at 08.00, 12.00 and
20.00hrs.

Garages
(See also page 54)

All prices must be displayed on the premises so
that they are clearly visible and legible. When
you have had a repair carried out you should
receive an invoice stating the labour charge, *ie*
the hourly rate (displayed) multiplied by the
time spent or the time shown on the time
schedule for each operation and not just a
lump sum. The price of supplies and spares
should be shown separately. Parts which have
been replaced must be returned to you unless it
is a routine replacement or the repair is carried
out free during the guarantee period.

The River Rhône

Lights
(See also page 17)

It is obligatory to use headlights as driving on
sidelights only is not permitted. In fog, mist or
poor visibility during the day either two fog
lamps or two dipped headlights must be switched on in addition to two sidelights. It is also
compulsory for *motorcyclists* riding machines
exceeding 125cc to use dipped headlights
during the day. Failure to comply with these
regulations will lead to an *on the spot* fine (see
Police fines page 21).

It is compulsory for visiting motorists to equip their vehicle with a set of replacement bulbs. Visiting motorists are also advised to comply with the French law which requires all vehicles to be equipped with headlights which emit a yellow beam. Amber lens converters may be used or, alternatively, the outer surface of the headlamp glass can be coated with yellow plastic paint which is removable with a solvent.

Motoring club

(See also page 18) The AA is affiliated to the **Association Française des Automobilistes** (AFA) whose office is at 9 rue Anatole-de-la-Forge, F-75017 Paris ☎(1)2278200.

Motorways

There are about 3,862 miles of motorway (Autoroute) open, and more are under construction or in preparation. To join a motorway follow signs with the international motorway symbol, or signs with the words 'par Autoroute' added. Signs with the added words 'Péage' or 'par péage' lead to toll roads. With the exception of a few sections into or around large cities, all motorways (autoroutes) have a toll charged according to the distance travelled; eg for a journey from Calais to Nice and return the toll charges amount to Fr554 for a car, or for a car towing a caravan the toll is Fr841.

On the majority of the toll motorways a travel ticket is issued on entry and the toll is paid on leaving the motorway. The travel ticket gives all relevant information about the toll charges including the toll category of your vehicle. At the exit point the ticket is handed in and the amount due shows up on an illuminated sign at the toll booth. On some motorways the toll collection is automatic; have the correct amount ready to throw into the collecting basket. If change is required use the marked separate lane.

For assistance on a motorway, use one of the *telephone boxes* sited at 2.4km (1½ mile) intervals; they are connected to police stations.

A leaflet entitled *Motorways in France* is available to AA members.

Orange badge scheme for disabled drivers

(See also page 19)
There is no formal system of concessions in operation and responsibility for parking in built-up areas rests with the local authorities. Any parking places reserved for the disabled are indicated by the international symbol.

However, the police are instructed to show consideration where parking by the disabled is concerned. In some towns and cities including Paris, badge holders may be allowed to park at meter bays and pay only the initial charge.

Parking

(See also page 19)
Regulations are similar to those in the UK. As a general rule all prohibitions are indicated by road signs or by yellow markings on the kerb. It is prohibited to leave a vehicle parked in the same place for more than 24 consecutive hours in Paris and surrounding departments.

On some roads in built-up areas, parking is allowed from the 1st to the 15th day of each month on the side of the road where the numbers of the buildings are odd and from the 16th to the last day of the month on the side with even numbers. This is called alternate unilateral parking.

There are short-term parking areas known as *blue zones* in most principal towns; in these areas discs must be used (placed against the windscreen) every day, except Sundays and public holidays, between 09.00 and 12.30hrs and 14.30 and 19.00hrs. They permit parking for up to one hour. Discs are sold at police stations, but at tourist offices and some clubs and commercial firms they are available free of charge. There are *grey zones* where parking meters are in use; in these zones a fee must be paid between 09.00 and 19.00hrs. Motorists using a ticket issued by an automatic machine must display the ticket behind the windscreen or nearside front window of their car.

In *Paris* cars towing caravans are prohibited from the *blue zone* between 14.00 and 20.30hrs. Cars towing trailers with an overall surface of 10 square metres or more may neither circulate nor park in the central *green zone* between 14.00–20.30hrs, except on Sundays and public holidays. Vehicle combinations with an overall surface exceeding 16 square metres may neither circulate nor park in the *green zone* between 08.00–20.30hrs. Those wishing to cross Paris during these hours with vehicle/trailer combinations can use the boulevard Périphérique, although the route is heavily congested, except during public holiday periods. In some parts of the *green zone* parking is completely forbidden. It is prohibited to park caravans, even for a limited period, not only in the *green zone* but in almost all areas of Paris.

Vehicles which are parked contrary to regulations are liable to be removed by the police at

the owner's risk and the driver will be liable for any costs incurred including a heavy fine.

Passengers
(See also page 19)
Children under 10 are not permitted to travel in a vehicle as front seat passengers.

Petrol
(See also page 20)
Credit cards The most widely accepted credit cards at petrol stations in France are Eurocard/ Mastercard and Visa which can be used for purchases of petrol at many main garages.
Duty-free petrol The petrol in the vehicle tank may be imported free of customs duty and tax.
Octane rating Essence Normale (90) and Essence Super (98).

Postal information
Mail Postcards *Fr*1.70; letters up to 20gm *Fr*2.40.

Post offices There are 17,500 post offices in France. They are open from 08.00–12.00hrs and 14.00–18.00hrs Monday to Friday and 08.00–12.00hrs Saturday. In Paris the office at 52 rue du Louvre is open 24 hours a day.

Postcheques
(See also page 21)
Postcheques may be cashed at all post offices for any amount up to a maximum of *Fr*600 per cheque. Counter positions are identified by the words *Paiement des mandats, Mandats à encaisser* or *Retraits à vue*. See this page for post office opening hours.

Priority including Roundabouts
(See also page 22)
In built-up areas drivers must slow down and be prepared to stop at all road junctions. If there are no priority signs give way to traffic from the right, but you have priority on roads bearing the sign *Passage Protégé*. On steep gradients, vehicles travelling downhill must give way to vehicles travelling uphill. Give way to street-cleaning vehicles.

Motorists should be extra careful when negotiating roundabouts as new priorities have been introduced. At unsigned roundabouts traffic entering has priority; at signed roundabouts bearing the words *Vous n'avez pas la priorité* or *Cédez le passage*, traffic on the roundabout has priority.

Public holidays
Official public holidays in France for 1985 are given below. See also *Public holidays* page 22.
January 1 (New Year's Day)
April 7 (Easter Sunday)
April 8 (Easter Monday)
May 1 (Labour Day)
May 8 (VE Day)
May 16 (Ascension Day)
May 26 (Whit Sunday)
May 27 (Whit Monday)
July 14† (National Holiday)
August 15 (Assumption)
November 1 (All Saints' Day)
November 11 (Armistice Day)
December 25 (Christmas Day)
†Sunday

Religious services
(See also page 23)
The Intercontinental Church Society welcomes visitors from any denomination to English language services in the following centres:
06400 Cannes The Revd Ian Watts, Chaplain's Apartment, 'Residence Kent', rue General Ferrie *tel*945461
60500 Chantilly The Revd Anthony Creery-Hill, 5 Residence Sylvie *tel*582012
59140 Dunkerque The Revd David Dicker, 130 rue de l'Ecole Matemelle *tel*650420
78600 Maisons-Laffitte The Revd Russel Avery, 15 Avenue Carnot (Paris area) *tel*623497
75008 Paris The Revd Peter Sertin, 5 rue d'Aguesseau *tel*427008
64000 Pau The Revd Kenneth Forrester, Apartment 11, 43 rue Montpensier *tel*625645
69110 Sainte Foy-Les-Lyon The Revd Brian Bradley, Le Coteau, 38 Chemin de Taffignon (serving Lyon and Grenoble) *tel*596706
31500 Toulouse The Revd Arthur Harvey, 5 Impasse Joseph Anglade *tel*543005
78140 Velizy-Villacoublay The Revd Jonathan Wilmot, 126 rue Lavoisier (Nr Versailles) *tel*461386

Roads including holiday traffic
(See also *Road conditions* page 23)
France has a very comprehensive network of roads, the surfaces of which are normally good; exceptions are usually signposted *Chaussée déformée*. The camber is often severe and the edges rough.

During July and August and especially at weekends traffic on main roads is likely to be very heavy. Special signs are erected to indicate alternative routes with the least traffic congestion. Wherever they appear it is usually advantageous to follow them although you cannot be absolutely sure of gaining time. The alternative routes are quiet but they are not as wide as the main roads. They are **not** suitable for caravans.

A free road map showing the marked alternative routes, plus information centres and

petrol stations open for 24hrs, is available from service stations displaying the *Bison Futé* poster (a Red Indian chief in full war bonnet). These maps are also available from *Syndicats d'Initiative* and Information offices.

Road number changes Following the 1974–78 decentralisation, when many secondary National highways were transferred to the Departments ('N' – to 'D' roads; when N315 became D915, and N16 became D916 etc), further modifications to the road system are taking place. These latest changes involve about 4,000–5,000km on N-roads throughout France, and some irregularities may occur during the changeover period when the same road may have signs showing two different numbers.

Traffic lanes (Paris) There are special lanes for buses and taxis only in some streets; they are marked by a continuous yellow line painted one vehicle width from the kerb. Usually, buses and taxis in the special lane travel in the opposite direction to other traffic.

Shopping hours

Department stores are usually open from Monday to Saturday, 10.00–13.00hrs and 15.00–19.00hrs although *food shops* open at 08.30hrs and may also open on Sunday mornings.

Speed limits

(See also page 25)
The beginning of a built-up area is indicated by a sign bearing the placename in blue letters on a light background; the end by the placename sign with a thin red line diagonally across it. Unless otherwise signposted speed limits are;

Built-up areas 60 kph (37 mph)
Outside built-up areas on normal roads 90 kph (56 mph)
On dual carriageways separated by a central reservation and toll-free motorways 110 kph (68 mph)
On toll motorways 130 kph (80 mph)
In wet weather speed limits outside built-up areas are reduced to 80 kph (49 mph), 100 kph (62 mph) and 110 kph (68 mph) on toll motorways.

These limits also apply to private cars towing a trailer or caravan if the latter's weight exceeds the towing vehicle's weight by less than 30%. If the trailer exceeds the towing vehicle's weight by more than 30% the vehicle must not be driven at more than 45 kph (28 mph) and must display a plate at the rear bearing the figure 45. They must not be driven in the fast lane of a 3-

lane motorway. (See also Parking *Green Zone* page 113).

Both French residents and visitors to France, who have held a driving licence for less than one year, must not exceed 90 kph (56 mph) or any lower signposted limit when driving in France.

Spiked, studded or snow tyres

(See also page 10)
Spiked or studded tyres may be used from 15 November to 15 March provided that a speed of 90 kph (56 mph) is not exceeded. A speed limitation disc bearing the figure 90 must be displayed at the rear of the vehicle.

Tourist information offices

(See also page 25)
The French Government Tourist Office maintains a full information service in London at 178 Piccadilly, London W1V 0AL (Mon–Fri) and will be pleased to answer any enquiries on touring in France. The telephone number is 01-491 7622 for urgent enquiries and 01-449 6911 for the 24hr recorded information service.

Once in France you should contact the local tourist office, *Syndicat d'Initiative* which will be found in all larger towns and resorts. They are pleased to give advice on local events, amenities and excursions and can also answer specific local queries such as bus timetables and local religious services (all denominations) not available in the UK.

A further source of information within the country, is the *Accueil de France* (welcome office) who will also book hotel reservations within their area for the same night, or up to seven days in advance for personal callers only. There are not so many of these offices and mainly they are located at important stations and airports.

The hours of operating vary considerably depending upon the district and the time of year. Generally the offices are open between 09.00–12.00hrs and 14.00–18.00hrs from Monday to Saturday but in popular resort areas *Syndicats d'Initiative* are sometimes open later and on Sunday mornings.

Traffic lights

(See also page 25)
The three-colour system, as in the United Kingdom, is in operation, with the addition of miniatures set at eye-level and with the posts placed in irregular positions, sometimes overhead and possibly without a set on the opposite side of the junction. It must be stressed that the

lights themselves are extremely dim, and easily missed.

A flashing amber light is a warning that the intersection or junction is particularly dangerous. A flashing red light indicates no entry, or may be used to mark obstacles.

Using the telephone
(See also page 26)
Insert coin **after** lifting receiver, dialling tone is a continuous tone. Generally to make a local call use Fr1 coin or jeton (special telephone coin) bought from the point where the call is made, but 2 × 50 centimes are required in some callboxes. For toll or trunk calls you will need to go to a post office. Highest value coin accepted is Fr5.

When making a telephone call within France you must first dial 16 to obtain the dialling tone, then the area code (shown in parentheses against town entry in gazetteer) followed by the number. However, if you wish to make a local call to a town within the same department (ie Boulogne-sur-Mer and Calais are both in the Pas de Calais) omit 16 and the area code.

International callbox identification Metallic grey.
Telephone rates The charge for a call to the UK is Fr0.5 for 11 seconds with a surcharge if the call is made from an hotel. Calls are usually cheaper after 20.00hrs.
What to dial for the Irish Republic 19 *353.
What to dial for the UK 19 *44.
*Wait for second dialling tone

Warning triangle/Hazard warning lights
The use of a warning triangle or hazard warning lights is compulsory for all vehicles except two-wheelers. As hazard warning lights may be damaged or inoperative it is recommended that a warning triangle be carried. The triangle must be placed on the road 30 metres (33yds) behind the vehicle and clearly visible from 100 metres (109yds). For vehicles over 3,500kg warning must be given by at least a warning triangle. See also *Warning triangles/Hazard warning lights* page 26.

Wheel chains
(See also page 10)
These can be purchased from vehicle accessory shops in large towns. Wheel chains can be hired from some garages; however, they have only small supplies.

Winter conditions
Although there are five mountain regions – the Vosges, Jura, Central Plateau, Alps and Pyrénées – motoring in winter is not severely restricted. The main channels for south-bound traffic wanting to avoid the Alps and Central Plateau are the A7 and N7 route along the Rhône Valley, the N20 from Limoges to Toulouse, and the highways farther west. Roads into Belgium, Luxembourg and Germany are generally not affected by road closures in winter.

All-the-year-round approaches to Strasbourg and Basle avoiding the Vosges and Jura are the Paris–Strasbourg Motorway A4, and the Paris–Beaune–Belfort motorway A6–A36 respectively. The approach to Switzerland via Pontarlier is very seldom obstructed, and during very severe weather is a better route to Geneva than over the Faucille Pass; alternatively the road via Bourg to Geneva is always open. Italy can be entered via the Mont Blanc road tunnel, the Fréjus road tunnel, or along the French Riviera via Menton. The main routes to Spain via Biarritz and Perpignan avoid the Pyrénées.

Whenever possible roads are swept and kept clear. However, during periods of thaw some barred roads may be used by certain classes of traffic at the driver's risk; passenger vehicles without trailers being used privately may proceed provided they do not exceed 80 kph (49 mph).

Monaco

National flag
Red over white in two strips of equal breadth.

The Principality of Monaco has a population of 24,000 and an area of 8 sq miles. The official Monaco Information Centre in the UK is at 34 Sackville Street, London W1X 1DB ☎01-437 3660. Although a sovereign state, it is very much under the influence of France and its laws are similar to those of the major country. Monaco is one large city/state but Monaco Town and Monte Carlo are the two towns of the State.

Motoring regulations are the same as in France but it should be stated that whilst caravans are permitted to pass through the Principality they are not allowed to stop or park.

Prices are in French Francs (F Frs)
For additional information on French hotels, see page 111.
The department name follows the town name.
For information on making internal local telephone calls see page 116.

Abbreviations;
av   avenue
bd   boulevard
cpt   Capitaine
Cdt   Commandant
espl   esplanade
fbg   faubourg
Gl   Général
Ml   Marshal, Maréchal
Mon   Monseigneur
pl   place
Prés   Président
Prof   Professeur
prom   promenade
r   rue
rte   route
sq   square

ABBEVILLE
Somme(☎22)

★**Conde (DPn)** 14 pl de la Libération ☎240633
Closed Aug
rm8 sB63 dB90

★**Jean Bart** 5–7 r Ste-Catherine ☎242171
rm16 ⋔5 **P** sB60–112 dB90–120 dB ⋔110–150

&D**SADRA** (M Thomas) 53 av R-Schumann ☎243481 Closed Sat Aud VW

ABRETS (LES)
Isère(☎76)

★**Belle Etoile** ⌶ 4 r V-Hugo ☎320497
rm15 ⇆3 ⋔1 🏠 **P** dB90–176
dB ⇆ ⋔138–176 M50–95 mountains

★**Hostellerie Abrésienne** 75 rte de Grenoble (N75) ☎320428
rm22 ⇆1 ⋔4 🏠 **P** sB63–68
sB ⇆ ⋔83–90 dB81–85
dB ⇆ ⋔111–136 M40–90 mountains

&D**Gadou** (N6) ☎320155 Closed Sun Ren

AGAY
Var(☎94)

&D**Agay** av du Gratadis ☎440616 M/c Ren

At **DRAMONT (LE)** (2km SW)

★ ★ ★**Sol et Mar (DPn)** ☎952560
Apr–15 Oct
⇆47 **P** Lift ♪ sB ⇆255–330
dB ⇆255–330 Pool Beach sea

AGDE
Hérault(☎67)

★ ★**Tamarissière** (Inter) quai Théophile Cornu ☎942087
15 Mar–15 Dec
rm32 ⇆28 ⋔4

&D**Four** 12 av Gl-de-Gaulle ☎941141 & 941783 Closed Sat & Sun Aud VW

France

&D**Gare** (A Gilbert) 1 av V-Hugo ☎943368 Closed Sun Opl Peu

&D**Midi** 46 r de République ☎941354 Closed Sun All makes

At **CAP D'AGDE** (7km SE)

★ ★ ★**Matago** r Trésor Royal ☎260005 tx480979
⇆67 **P** Lift ♪ sB ⇆236–277
dB ⇆277–347 Pool sea

★ ★ ★**Delfis** llot St-Martin (n.rest) ☎944847
Apr–Oct
⇆144 **P** sea

★ ★ ★**Sablotel** Plage du Môle ☎260004 tx480980
Apr–Oct
⇆131 **P** Lift sB ⇆213–268
dB ⇆271–358 Mfr75 Pool sea

AGEN
Lot-et-Garonne(☎53)

☆ ☆**Ibis** llot 5, bd Carnot ☎473123 tx541331
⇆39 **P** sB ⇆176 dB ⇆206

★ ★**Périgord (DPn)** 42 pl XIV Juillet ☎661001
rm23 ⇆20 **P** Lift sB82–126
sB ⇆82–126 dB ⇆89–155

★ ★**Résidence Jacobins** ⌶ 1 pl Jacobins ☎470331 tx560800
rm17 ⇆15 ⋔2 **P** dB ⇆ ⋔124–300

F Tastets 182 bd de la Liberté ☎471063 Closed Sat & Sun pm BL

AIGLE (L')
Orne(☎33)

★ ★ ★**Dauphin** (MAP) pl de la Halle ☎244312 tx170979
rm24 ⇆ ⋔18 🏠 **P** ♪ sB220–245
sB220–258 dB270–301
dB ⇆ ⋔270–448

AIGUEBELLE
Var(☎94)

★ ★ ★**Roches Fleuries (DPn)** (4km on N599 to Le Lavandu) ☎710507
20 May–20 Sep
rm48 ⇆42 ⋔6 🏠 **P** ♪ Pool Beach sea

★ ★**Plage** ☎058074
25 May–24 Sep
rm52 ⇆8 ⋔40 A29rm sea

AIGUILLON-SUR-MER
Vendée(☎51)

★ ★**Port** ⌶ **(DPn** summer only) 2 r Belle Vue ☎564008
Apr–Sep
rm33 ⇆12 ⋔11 **P** dB ⇆ ⋔95–190
M45–100 🍴 Pool

AILLANT-SUR-THOLON
Yonne(☎86)

&D**St-Antoine** 10 Grande r, St-Antoine ☎634681 M/c Closed Sun Fia

AINHOA
Pyrénées-Atlantiques(☎59)

★ ★ ★**Argi-Eder** (MAP) rte de la Chapelle ☎299104 tx570067
Apr–15 Nov
rm36 ⇆34 ⋔2 A4rm **P** 🍴 Pool mountains

AIRE-SUR-L'ADOUR
Landes(☎58)

&D**Saema** rte de Bordeaux ☎766001 Closed Sat pm, Sun & Mon am Ren

&D**Tolerie** (A-Dalla Barba) 65 av de Bordeaux ☎76621 M/c Cit MB Opl

AIRE-SUR-LA-LYS
Pas-de-Calais(☎21)

★**Europ** 14 Grand Pl (n.rest) ☎390432
rm16 ⋔9 🏠 **P** sB60 dB73 dB ⋔86

&D**H Delgery** 5 pl J-d'Aire ☎390298 Closed Sat pm Ren

AISEY-SUR-SEINE
Côte-d'Or(☎80)

★**Roy** ⌶ ☎932163
rm10 ⇆2 ⋔5 **P** dB90–120
dB ⇆ ⋔106–146

AIX-EN-PROVENCE
Bouches-du-Rhône(☎42)

★ ★ ★ ★**PLM le Pigonnet** 5 av Pigonnet (off rd N8 towards Marseille) ☎590290 tx410629
rm49 ⇆38 ⋔11 🏠 **P** Lift ♪
sB ⇆ ⋔300–375 dB ⇆ ⋔410–510
M115 Pool

★ ★ ★**Manoir** ⌶ r d'Entrecasteaux 8 (n.rest) ☎262720
15 Feb–Dec
rm43 ⇆21 ⋔22 **P** Lift ♪

☆ ☆ ☆**Novotel Beaumanoir** Résidence Beaumanoir (A8) ☎274750 tx400244
⇆102 **P** Lift sB ⇆240–265
dB ⇆299–319 Pool

☆ ☆ ☆**Novotel Sud** Périphérique Sud, Arc de Meyran ☎279049 tx420517
⇆80 **P** Lift sB ⇆246–261
dB ⇆304–320 Pool

★ ★ ★**Paul Cézanne** 40 av V-Hugo (n.rest) ☎263473
rm44 ⇆29 ⋔13 🏠 **P** Lift ♪ sB343
sB423 dB376 dB ⇆ ⋔656

☆ ☆**Campanile** ZAC du Jas de Bouffan ☎594073 tx420588
⇆50 **P** dB ⇆206–222 M55–80

☆ ☆**Ibis** Chemin des infirmeries ☎279820 tx420519
⇆83 **P** sB ⇆203 dB ⇆241 M alc

★ ★**Renaissance** 4 bd de la République (n.rest) ☎260422
rm35 ⇆15 sB81–157 sB ⇆157
dB83–159 dB ⇆159

★★Résidence Rotunde 15 av des Belges (n.rest) ☎262988

rm45 ⇌15 ⋔30 🛆 **P** Lift

🅟J **Mavel** R N Luynes ☎240580 Closed Sun & Jul BL Lada

🅟**Michelon** r des Milles ☎277598 Closed Sat & Sun Cit

🅟**Monjo** Montée d'Avignon ☎234908 Closed Sat & Sun Maz

At **EGUILLES** (11km NW)

★★Belvedere quartier des Landons ☎925292

rm70 ⇌29 ⋔9 A32rm **P** sB ⇌ ⋔180–237 dB ⇌ ⋔200–295 Pool

At **MILLES (LES)** (5km S off D9)

☆ ☆**Climat de France** r Ampère, ZI ☎203077 tx612241

⇌38 **P** dB ⇌216–220

AIX-LES-BAINS
Savoie(☎79)

★★★Iles Britanniques pl de l'Etablissement Thermal ☎610377 May–Sep

rm90 ⇌46 ⋔19 A10rm 🛆 **P** Lift 𝄞 **DPn**190–330 mountains lake

★★★International Rivollier 18 av C-de-Gaulle ☎352100 tx320410

rm61 ⇌37 ⋔17 🛆 Lift 𝄞 **DPn**190–330 mountains

★★★Manoir 233 r Georges Ier ☎614400 tx980793 Feb–24 Dec

rm72 ⇌30 ⋔30 🛆 **P** Lift sB ⇌ ⋔140–220 dB ⇌ ⋔160–290

☆ ☆**Campanile** av du Golf ☎613066 tx610016

⇌43 **P** dB ⇌207 M55–80

★★Cecil 20 av Victoria (n.rest) ☎350412

rm18 ⇌11 Lift dB100–190 dB ⇌100–190 mountains

★★Parc 28 r de Chambéry ☎612911 24 Apr–25 Oct

rm42 ⇌13 A8rm 🛆 Lift 𝄞

★★Pavillion Rivollier pl Gare ☎351904 May–Oct

rm40 ⇌22 ⋔15 Lift 𝄞 **DPn**160–270 mountains

ALBERT
Somme(☎22)

★Basilique 🅛 **(DPn)** 3–5 r Gambetta ☎750471

rm10 ⇌6 sB53–95 sB ⇌95–104 dB80–116 dB ⇌107–116 M39–100 & alc

★Paix 43 r V-Hugo ☎750164

rm15 ⇌2 ⋔2 🛆

ALBERTVILLE
Savoie(☎79)

★★Costaroche 1 chemin P-du-Roy ☎320202

⇌20 **P** sB ⇌134–169 dB ⇌177–190 M65–115 mountains

France

★★Million 8 pl de la Liberté ☎322515

Closed 25 Apr–15 May, 29 Sep–10 Oct, rest. closed Sun pm & Mon

rm29 ⇌26 ⋔1 🛆 **P** Lift sB145–230 sB ⇌ ⋔210–230 dB ⇌ ⋔260–290

ALBI
Tarn(☎63)

★★★Chiffre 50 r Séré de Rivières ☎540460 tx51794

rm39 ⇌16 ⋔20 🛆 **P** Lift 𝄞 sB120–150 sB ⇌ ⋔170–270 dB ⇌ ⋔230–340 M60–160 & alc

★★★Grand St-Antoine (MAP) 17 r St-Antoine ☎540404 tx520850

rm56 ⇌39 ⋔17 🛆 **P** Lift 𝄞 sB ⇌ ⋔248–348 dB ⇌ ⋔306–476 M80–200

★★Orléans (FAH) pl Stalingrad ☎541656 tx521605 15 Jun–20 Dec

rm64 ⇌21 ⋔43 Lift 𝄞

★Vieil Alby 🅛 25 r Toulouse-Lautrec ☎541469

rm9 ⇌5 **P** dB88–150 dB ⋔101–150

🅟**Albi Auto** 22 av A-Thomas ☎607903 Closed Aug, Sat & Sun Frd

At **FONVIALANE** (3km N on N606)

★★★Réserve (DPn) rte de Cordes ☎607979 tx520850 Apr–Oct

rm20 ⇌17 ⋔3 **P** 𝄞 sB ⇌ ⋔285–415 dB ⇌ ⋔400–570 M80–200 🏊 Pool

ALENÇON
Orne(☎33)

See also **ST-LÉONARD-DES-BOIS**

★★★Grand Cerf 21 r St-Blaise ☎260051 tx170296 15 Jan–15 Dec

rm33 ⇌15 ⋔10 Lift sB ⇌ ⋔200 dB95–200 dB ⇌ ⋔95–200

☆ ☆**Campanile** rte de Paris ☎295385 tx610016

⇌35 **P** dB ⇌197 M55–80

★★France 3 r St-Blaise (n.rest) ☎262636

rm31 ⇌9 ⋔5 **P** 𝄞 sB52–105 sB ⇌ ⋔102–120 dB89–130 dB ⇌ ⋔129–154

★★Gare 🅛 50 av Wilson ☎290393 5 Jan–20 Dec

rm22 ⇌6 ⋔10 🛆 **P** sB94–114 sB ⇌ ⋔146–180 dB208 dB ⇌ ⋔178–220

★Industrie 🅛 20–22 pl du Gl-de-Gaulle ☎290651

rm12 ⇌1 ⋔4 **P** sB70–95 sB ⇌ ⋔95 dB105–140 sB ⇌ ⋔130–150

★Paris 26 r D-Papin (opposite station) (n.rest) ☎290164

Closed 8–28 Aug

rm16 ⋔6 🛆 **P** sB84–100 sB ⋔104–115 dB93–140 dB ⋔128–180

ALÈS
Gard(☎66)

☆ ☆ ☆**Mercure** 18 r E-Quinet ☎522707 tx480830

⇌75 **P** Lift sB ⇌203–218 dB ⇌265–280

🅟**Auto Service** (J Maniez) 914 rte d'Uzès ☎302569 M/c Closed Sat & Sun BL Hon Lada

ALPE-D'HUEZ(L')
Isère(☎76)

★★★Chamois d'Or (DPn) r de Fontbelle ☎803132 Xmas–Etr

rm40 ⇌23 ⋔12 **P** Lift sB162–182 sB ⇌ ⋔182–202 dB244–264 dB ⇌ ⋔284–320 mountains

★★★Ours Blanc (MAP) av des Jeux ☎803111 tx320807 20 Dec–15 Apr

⇌37 🛆 **P** M140 **DPn**385–450 mountains

ALTKIRCH
Haut-Rhin(☎89)

★Sundgovienne 🅛 (3.5km W on N19) rte de Belfort ☎409718 Feb–24 Dec

rm31 ⇌19 ⋔4 🛆 **P** Lift mountains

★Terrasse 🅛 44–46 r du 3e-Zouave ☎409802

rm20 ⇌10 ⋔5 🛆 **P**

At **WALHEIM** (3.5km NE off D432)

🅟**Schmitt** ☎409162 M/c All makes

ALVIGNAC
Lot(☎65)

★★★Palladium (DPn) av de Padirac ☎336023 May–Sep

rm27 ⇌21 ⋔6 **P** 𝄞

AMBÉRIEU-EN-BUGEY
Ain(☎74)

★★Savoie (Inter) (2km N on D36) ☎380690 Feb–23 Dec

⇌45 **P** Lift sB ⇌180 dB ⇌200

AMBERT
Puy-de-Dôme(☎73)

★★Livradois (DPn) 1 pl du Livradois ☎821001

rm14 ⇌3 ⋔3 🛆 **P** mountains

★Gare 17 av de la Gare ☎820022 Nov–Oct

rm21 ⇌4 ⋔2 **P** mountains

AMBOISE
Indre-et-Loire(☎47)

☆ ☆ ☆**Novotel** 17 r des Sabionnières ☎574207 tx 751203

⇌82 **P** Lift sB ⇌227–251 dB ⇌307–318

★★**Château de Pray** (2km NE on N751) ☎572367
10 Feb–Dec
rm16 ⇌14 🚗 P

★★**Lion d'Or** 🅛 (DPn) 17 quai C-Guinot ☎570023
15 Mar–2 Nov
rm23 ⇌13 🛏3 🚗 sB96–106
sB ⇌ 🛏164 dB159 dB ⇌ 🛏190

★**Brèche** (DPn) 26 r J-Ferry ☎570079
rm15 ⇌4 🛏2 🚗 P sB64–120
sB ⇌ 🛏140 dB123–145 dB ⇌ 🛏173

★**France et Cheval Blanc** (DPn) 6–7 quai C-de-Gaulle ☎570244
Mar–mid Nov
rm26 ⇌8 🛏12 🚗 P sB68–100
sB ⇌ 🛏97–112 dB80–150
dB ⇌ 🛏109–174

★**Parc** 🅛 8 r L-de-Vinci ☎570693
Mar–Oct
rm17 ⇌13 🛏4 P

AMIENS
Somme(☎22)

★★★**Grand Hotel de l'Universe** 2 r Noyon (n.rest) ☎915251 tx150409
rm41 ⇌25 🛏16 Lift 🄓 sB125–227
sB ⇌ 🛏188–227 dB ⇌ 🛏210–250

★★**Carlton-Belfort** 42 r de Noyon ☎922644 tx140754
rm40 ⇌32 🛏8 P Lift 🄓
sB ⇌ 🛏205–260 dB ⇌ 🛏295–350

★★**Gritti** 8 pl A-Fiquet ☎913632 tx14075
rm23 ⇌3 🛏16 🚗 P

☆ **Ibis** 'Le Centrum', r MI-de-Lattre-de-Tassigny ☎925733 tx140765
⇌94 P Lift sB ⇌180 dB ⇌ 🛏217

★★**Nord-Sud** 11 r Gresset ☎915903
rm26 ⇌20 sB99–180 sB ⇌135–180
dB124–180 dB ⇌150–200

★★**Paix** 8 r de la République (n.rest) ☎913921
20 Jan–15 Dec
rm26 ⇌11 🛏11

★**Normandie** 1 bis r Lamartine (n.rest) ☎917499
rm26 ⇌9 🛏5 🚗 P

🐶**Auto-Picardie** 1 bis chemin des Vignes ☎460417 Fia Lnc

At **BOVES** (7km SE of D934)

☆☆**Novotel Amiens Est** (CD 934) ☎462222 tx140731
⇌92 P sB ⇌226–276 dB ⇌302–347 Pool

AMMERSCHWIHR See COLMAR

ANDELYS (LES)
Eure (☎32)

★**Chaine d'Or**🅛(DPn) 27 r Grande, pl St-Sauveur ☎540031
Closed Jan
rm11 ⇌6 🛏2 A1rm P dB 166–200
dB ⇌ 🛏176–240 M58–90

France

★**Normandie** 1 r Grande ☎541052
Jan–Nov
rm11 ⇌2 🛏1 P sB71 sB ⇌ 🛏110
dB94–120 dB ⇌ 🛏151

ANDLAU
Bas-Rhin (☎88)

★★**Kastelberg** 🅛 r du GI-Koenig ☎089783
rm28 ⇌24 🛏6 A11rm P
dB ⇌ 🛏155–210 Malc mountains

ANDRÉZIEUX-BOUTHÉON See ST-ETIENNE AIRPORT

ANGERS
Maine-et-Loire (☎41)

★★★**Anjou** (MAP) 1 bd MI-Foch ☎882482 tx720521
⇌51 🚗 P Lift 🄓 sB ⇌235–255 dB ⇌250–290

☆☆☆**Mercure** bd Carnot ☎(40)603481 tx722139
⇌86 🚗 P Lift sB ⇌322–372 dB ⇌374–424

★★**Boule d'Or** 27 bd Carnot ☎437656 tx720930
rm28 ⇌10 🛏13 (A5rm) 🚗 P
sB ⇌ 🛏88–115 dB80–140
dB ⇌ 🛏125–151

☆☆**Climat de France** r du Château-d'Orgemont ☎(6)4460123 tx692844
⇌42 dB ⇌218–233

★★**Croix de Guerre** 23 r Château Gontier ☎886659 tx720930
rm28 ⇌8 🛏6 🚗 P 🚗 sB85–165
dB102–153 dB ⇌ 🛏165

★★**France** (FAH) 8 pl de la Gare ☎884942 tx720895
rm64 ⇌17 🛏29 Lift dB137–200
dB ⇌ 🛏159–259

★★**Progrès** (Inter) 26 r D-Papin (n.rest) ☎881014 tx720982
⇌41 Lift 🄓

★**Univers** 2 r de la Gare (n.rest) ☎884358 tx720930
rm45 ⇌10 🛏21 Lift 🄓 sB78–150
dB95–155 dB ⇌ 🛏116–181

🐶**Clogenson** 30 r Coste et Bellonte ☎668266 All makes

ANGLET
Pyrénées-Atlantiques (☎59)

★★★**Chibera & Golf** (Inter) 104 bd Plage ☎638830 tx550637
rm80 ⇌75 🛏5 P Lift 🄓
sB ⇌ 🛏205–308 dB ⇌ 🛏250–424 sea lake

★★**Biarritz Golf** 20 av Guynemer à la Chambre d'Amour ☎038302
Apr–Sep
rm25 ⇌7 🛏4 P

★**Fauvettes** (DPn in summer) 69 r Moulin Barbot à la Chambre d'Amour (rest for guests only) ☎037558
Apr–Sep
rm11 🛏3 🚗 sea

Auto-Durruty des Pontots ☎630968 Closed Sat & Sun Frd

🐶**J-Iribarren** quartier Sutar, av de Cambo ☎254840 Cit

ANGOULÊME
Charente (☎45)

★★★**Grand France** (Inter) 1 pl des Halles ☎954795 tx791020
rm60 ⇌34 🛏13 🚗 P Lift 🄓
sB107–180 sB ⇌ 🛏177–220
dB164–240 dB ⇌ 🛏239–290

★★**Epi d'Or** (Inter) 66 bd R-Chabasse (n.rest) ☎956764
rm32 ⇌ 🛏 P Lift

★**Flore** 414 rte de Bordeaux ☎928055
rm54 ⇌2 🛏11 A17rm 🚗 P

🐶**Boutin** 74 r de Paris ☎950493 All makes

At **CHAMPNIERS** (7km NE)

☆☆☆**Novotel Angoulême Nord** (N10) ☎885322 tx790153
⇌100 P Lift sB ⇌253–291 dB ⇌291–303 Pool

☆☆**PM16** 🅛 rte de Poitiers ☎680322 tx790345
rm41 ⇌30 🛏11 P 🄓
sB ⇌ 🛏152–164 dB ⇌ 🛏194–205

ANNECY
Haute-Savoie (☎50)
See also: **TALLOIRES; VEYRIER-DU-LAC**

☆☆☆**Mercure Annecy Sud** Le Champ Fleuri (N201) Seynod ☎510347 tx385303
⇌69 P sB ⇌219–258 dB ⇌273–303 Malc Pool mountains

★★★**Splendid** 4 quai E-Chappuis (n.rest) ☎452000 tx385233
rm50 ⇌35 🛏15 Lift sB ⇌ 🛏120–190
dB ⇌ 🛏190–220

☆☆**Campanile** Impasse des Crêts ☎677666
⇌42 P dB ⇌218–222 M55–80 mountains lake

★★**Faisan Doré** 🅛 84 av d'Albigny ☎230246
rm41 ⇌16 🛏16 🚗 Lift
sB ⇌ 🛏140–180 dB ⇌ 🛏160–270 mountains

☆☆**Ibis** quartier de la Manufacture, r de la Gare ☎454321 tx385585
⇌83 P Lift sB ⇌178 dB ⇌231 St%

🐶**Parmelan** av du Petit Port, Annecy-le-Vieux ☎231285 Closed Sta & Sun Opl Vau

ANNEMASSE
Haute-Savoie (☎50)
See also **GAILLARD**

★★**National** 10 pl J-Deffault ☎920644 →

rm45 ⇆27 🛏15 🍴 **P** Lift sB126−146
sB ⇆ 🛏157−167 dB ⇆ 🛏172−182
mountains

★ ★**Parc** (MAP) 19 r de Genève (n.rest)
☎384460

rm30 ⇆6 🛏24 🍴 Lift ♪
sB ⇆ 🛏218 dB ⇆ 🛏236 mountains

🐾**Mont-Blanc** chemin de la Chamarette
☎381575 All makes

ANSE
Rhône (☎74)

🐾**Aux Pierres Dorées** 29 av de la Gare
☎670335 Closed Aug 1−10 & Sun Opl

🐾**Centre** (M Authier) 18 r des
Marronniers ☎670196 Closed Sat pm &
Sun Cit

🐾**M Salel** 59 r Nationale ☎670368
Closed Sep 1−10 All makes

ANTHÉOR
Var (☎94)

★ ★**Réserve d'Anthéor (DPn)** (N98)
☎448005

Feb−Oct
rm13 ⇆5 🛏8 **P** sB145−180
dB ⇆ 🛏195−210 Beach sea

ANTIBES
Alpes-Maritimes (☎93)

★ ★ ★**Tananarive** rte de Nice (N7)
(n.rest) ☎333000 tx470851
rm50 ⇆28 🛏22 🍴 **P** Lift
sB ⇆ 🛏184−332 dB ⇆ 🛏231−340 🏊
Pool sea mountains

★ ★**First** 21 av des Chênes ☎618737
tx470673

rm16 ⇆9 🛏3 **P** 🍴 ♪
sB ⇆ 🛏220−320 dB ⇆ 🛏320−600 sea

☆ ☆**Mercator** chemin des Groules,
quartier de la Brague (4km N via N7)
(n.rest) ☎335075

15 Dec−15 Nov
⇆18 A4rm 🛏239−262

🐾**Dugommier** 16 bd Dugommier
☎745999 Closed Sat pm & Sun Opl

🐾**Molineri** chemin de St-Maymes
☎616203 Closed Sat pm & Sun All makes

At **CAP D'ANTIBES**

★ ★**Gardiole** chemin de la Garoupe
☎613503 tx470915

Feb−Nov
rm20 ⇆6 🛏14 sB ⇆ 🛏130−150
dB ⇆ 🛏220−280 mountains

★ ★**Résidence du Cap (DPn)** 161 bd J-
F-Kennedy ☎610944 tx470892

Apr−Oct
rm44 ⇆40 A4rm **P** Lift ♪ 🏊 Pool

★ ★**Beau Site** 141 bd Kennedy (n.rest)
☎615343

rm26 ⇆8 🛏18 A6rm **P** sea mountains

APPOIGNY See **AUXERRE**

APT
Vaucluse (☎90)

★ ★**Ventoux**🅻🄴 67 a V-Hugo ☎740758

France

Mar−15 Dec
rm13 ⇆2 🛏11 Lift sB ⇆ 🛏117−166
dB ⇆ 🛏102−166

ARBOIS
Jura (☎84)

★ ★**Messageries**🅻🄴 2 r Courcelles
(n.rest) ☎661545

Mar−Nov
rm25 ⇆10 🍴 sB57−144
sB ⇆ 🛏142−150 dB ⇆ 🛏159−188
mountains

★**Paris**🅻🄴 (FAH) (DPn) 9 r de l'Hôtel-de-
Ville ☎660567

15 Mar−15 Nov
rm18 ⇆12 🛏6 A6rm 🍴 **P**
dB ⇆ 🛏200−280

ARCACHON
Gironde (☎56)
See also **PYLA-SUR-MER**

★ ★ ★**Arc** 89 bed Plage (n.rest)
☎830685

⇆30 **P** Lift ♪ Pool sea

★ ★ ★**Tamarins** 253 bd Côte d'Argent
☎225096

20 Dec−10 Nov
rm36 ⇆4 🛏25 A8rm Lift

ARCIS-SUR-AUBE
Aube (☎25)

🐾**S Allais** r de Troyes ☎378482 Closed
Aug, Sat pm & Sun Cit

🐾**Leroy** 17 rte de Chalons ☎378452
Closed Aug 5−25 & Sun Tal

ARDRES
Pas-de-Calais (☎21)

★ ★ ★**Grand Clément** pl du Gl-Leclerc
☎354066 tx130866

15 Feb−15 Jan
rm18 ⇆12 🛏4 🍴 **P** sB75−180
sB ⇆ 🛏135−205 dB115−180
dB ⇆ 🛏155−225

★ ★**Relais**🅻🄴 (DPn) bd C-Senlecq
☎354200 tx130886

Closed Jan
rm11 ⇆3 🛏7 A1rm **P**
dB ⇆ 🛏151−211

★**Chaumière** 67 av de Rouville (n.rest)
☎354124

rm12 ⇆5 🛏6 **P** sB104−182
sB ⇆ 🛏182 dB123−201 dB ⇆ 🛏203

ARGELÈS-GAZOST
Hautes-Pyrénées (☎62)

★**Bernède**🅻🄴 (FAH) 51 r Ml-Foch
☎970664 tx531040

rm35 ⇆ 🛏6 A5rm

★**Mon Cottage (DPn)** 3 r Yser ☎970792

15 Apr−15 Oct
rm20 ⇆19 A6rm **P** Lift mountains

ARGELÈS-SUR-MER
Pyrénées-Orientales (☎68)

★ ★ ★**Plage des Pins** allée des Pins, à la
Plage ☎810905

Jun−Sep
⇆49 🍴 **P** Lift ♪ sB ⇆ 🛏245−287
dB ⇆ 🛏245−287 sea

★**Grand Commerce (DPn)** 14 rte de
Collioure (N22) ☎810033

Closed Jan
rm89 ⇆16 🛏27 A23rm **P** Lift Pool

🐾**Relais de la Grône** 114 rte Nationale
☎811317 Closed Sat pm & Sun winter Peu

ARGENTAN
Orne (☎33)

★ ★ ★**Renaissance**🅻🄴 (DPn) av de la 2E
D-B ☎671611

rm15 ⇆3 🛏9 Lift sB84−195
sB ⇆ 🛏110−195 dB ⇆ 🛏168−210

ARGENTAT
Corrèze (☎55)

★ ★**Gilbert**🅻🄴 av J-Vachal ☎280162

Feb−Dec
rm30 ⇆10 🛏4 🍴 **P** Lift ♪ dB180
dB ⇆ 🛏80−200 mountains

🐾**Manaux** 1 rte de Tulle ☎280332
Closed Sun Peu

ARGENTEUIL
Val-d'Oise (☎3)

☆ ☆**Fimotel** 148 rte de Pontoise (N 192)
☎4105200 tx215269

⇆40 Lift sB ⇆ 🛏194 dB ⇆223

ARGENTON-SUR-CREUSE
Indre (☎54)

★ ★**Manoir de Boisvilliers** 11 r Moulin de
Bord (n.rest) ☎241388

rm15 ⇆5 🛏5 **P**

★**France**🅻🄴 (DPn) 8 r J-J-Rousseau
☎240331

rm26 ⇆3 🛏10 A10rm 🍴 **P**
dB70−136 dB ⇆ 🛏101−148

🐾**Chavegrand** rte de Limoges ☎240432
Peu

ARLEMPDES
Haute-Loire (☎71)

★ ★**Manoir**🅻🄴 (DPn) ☎571714

rm16 🛏11 mountains

ARLES
Bouches-du-Rhône (☎90)

★ ★ ★**Jules César** bd des Lices
☎934320 tx400239

21 Dec−1 Nov
rm60 ⇆30 🛏30 🍴 **P** ♪
sB ⇆ 🛏250−450 dB ⇆ 🛏400−600
St15%

☆ ☆ ☆**Cantarelles** (Inter) Ville Vieille
☎964410 tx401582

Dec−Oct
rm35 ⇆34 🛏1 **P** Pool

★ ★ ★**Forum** 10 pl Forum (n.rest)
☎934895

15 Feb–15 Nov
rm45 ⇌35 🍴3 **P** Lift 🌙 Pool

★ ★ ★**Primotel** av de la 1ᵉʳ Division
Français Libre (opposite Palais du
Congrès) ☎939880 tx401001
25 Mar–Oct
⇌107 **P** Lift 🌙 sB ⇌250–300
dB ⇌300–350 🏊 Pool

★ ★ ★**Sélect** 35 bd G-Clemenceau
☎960831
rm24 ⇌21 🍴3 🚗 Lift

★ ★**Arlatan** 26 r Sauvage (n.rest)
☎935666 tx440096
rm46 ⇌30 🍴12 🚗 🌙

★ ★**Cloître** 18 r du Cloître (n.rest)
☎962950
15 Mar–15 Nov
rm33 ⇌30 🍴3 A10rm
sB ⇌ 🍴120–175 dB ⇌ 🍴150–185

☆ ★**Ibis** quartier de Fourchon ☎931674
tx440201
⇌64 **P** sB ⇌ 186–207 dB ⇌235–256
M61 & alc Pool

★ ★**Mireille** (Inter) 2 pl St-Pierre
☎937074 tx44038
Feb–Dec
rm39 ⇌ 🍴3 A4rm **P** 🌙
sB ⇌ 🍴99–261 dB ⇌ 🍴99–261 Pool

☆ ☆**Montmajour et Le Rodin** (FAH) 84 rte
de Tarascon ☎939833 tx420776
⇌20 **P** Lift dB ⇌ 🍴159–259 🏊 Pool

&🄳**Sovra** 69 rte de Crau ☎961075
Closed Sat pm & Sun AR Fia Hon Lada MB
Por Toy

ARMBOUTS CAPPEL See **DUNKERQUE**

ARNAGE See **MANS (LE)**

ARNAY-LE-DUC
Côte-d'Or (☎80)

★**Terminus** 🔠 r Arquebuse ☎900033
Closed Wed & 7 Jan–5 Feb
rm12 🍴5 **P** sB55–85 sB 🍴60–95
dB55–95 dB 🍴60–95

&🄳**Binet** (N6) ☎901007 Cit

ARRAS
Pas-de-Calais (☎21)

★ ★ ★**Univers** 3 pl Croix Rouge
☎213401
rm36 ⇌19 🍴10 A1rm 🚗 **P** 🌙
sB ⇌ 🍴115–220 dB130–140
db ⇌ 🍴220–250

★ ★**Astoria** 12 pl MI-Foch ☎210814
tx160768
24 Dec–10 Jan
rm31 ⇌8

★ ★**Commerce** 24 r Gambetta (n.rest)
☎211007
rm40 ⇌13 🍴4 🚗 **P** Lift 🌙 sB84
sB ⇌ 🍴 174 dB84

★ ★**Moderne** (Inter) 1 bd Faidherbe
(n.rest) ☎233957
Closed Xmas
rm43 ⇌40 Lift sB ⇌152–180
dB ⇌187–215

France

★**Chánzy** 🔠 8 r Chánzy ☎210202
rm23 ⇌9 🍴4 🚗 **P** Lift sB85–95
sB ⇌ 🍴135–150 dB120–150
dB ⇌ 🍴190–230

&🄳**Artois Poids Lourds** rte Nationale Ste-
Catherine (N113) ☎236822 Closed Sat &
Sun All makes

&🄳**Cyr Leroy** 75 r de Cambrai ☎732626
Closed Sun Tal

&🄳**Llevinoise Auto** 16 av P-Michonneau
☎554242 Closed Sat & Sun Frd

&🄳**Michonneau** 6 av P-Michonneau
☎553751 Closed Aug 11–25, Sat & Sun
Fia

ARREAU
Hautes-Pyrénées (☎62)

At **CADÉAC** (2km S)

★ ★**Val d'Aure** rte de St-Lary ☎986063
19 Jun–Sep
rm23 ⇌15 🍴8 **P** sB ⇌ 🍴166–200
dB ⇌ 🍴166–200 🏊 mountains

ARTEMARE
Ain (☎79)

★**Valromey** (Inter) ☎873010
rm25 ⇌13 🍴6 A16rm 🚗 **P**
mountains

ARTIGUES See **BORDEAUX**

ARUDY
Pyrénées-Atlantiques (☎59)

&🄳**M-Versavaud** rte de Pau ☎056070
Closed Sun Tal

ARVERT
Charente-Maritime (☎46)

★ ★**Villa Fantaisie** 🔠 (DPn) ☎364009
Closed Jan–Feb
rm23 ⇌7 🍴11 🚗 **P** sB130
sB ⇌ 🍴200 dB ⇌ 🍴150–250

ASCAIN
Pyrénées-Atlantiques (☎59)

★ ★**Rhune** pl d'Ascain ☎540004
Feb–15 Nov
rm42 ⇌31 🍴8 A15rm **P** Pool
mountains

ASSEVILLIERS See **PÉRONNE**

ATHIS-MONS See **PARIS AIRPORTS**
under **ORLY AIRPORT**

AUBENAS
Ardèche (☎75)

&🄳**Gounon** 22 St-Didier ☎350821 Closed
25 Aug–15 Sep, Sat pm & Sun Fia

AUBUSSON
Creuse (☎55)

★ ★**France** 🔠 (FAH) (DPn) 6 r de Portes-
Politiques ☎661022
rm25 ⇌10 🍴10 🚗 dB137–177
dB ⇌159–259

★**Lion d'Or** pl d'Espagne ☎661388
rm15 ⇌3 🍴3 **P** mountains
At **FOURNEAUX** (11km NW of D942)

★ ★**Tullerie** ☎662492
May–Sep
⇌24 **P** Pool

AUCH
Gers (☎62)

★ ★ ★**France** (MAP) pl de la Libération
☎050044 tx520474
rm30 ⇌20 🍴10 🚗 Lift 🌙
sB ⇌ 🍴216–346 dB ⇌ 🍴304–647
M130–330

★ ★**Poste** 5 r-C-Desmoulins ☎050236
tx531918
rm28 ⇌10 🍴13 🚗 sB ⇌ 🍴107–167
dB ⇌ 🍴134–224

AULNAT AÉROPORT See **CLERMONT
FERRAND**

AULNAY-SOUS-BOIS
Seine (☎1)

☆ ☆ ☆**Novotel Paris Aulnay-sous-Bois**
(N370) ☎8662297 tx230121
⇌ 🍴138 **P** Lift sB ⇌ 🍴257–287
dB ⇌ 🍴289–319 M alc Pool

AUMALE
Seine-Maritime (☎35)

★**Dauphin** (DPn) r St-Lazare ☎934192
m11 ⇌2 🍴4 🚗 **P**

&🄳**Fertun** 3 av Foch ☎934121 Closed
Sun Peu

AUNAY-SUR-ODON
Calvados (☎31)

★**St-Michel** 🔠 (DPn) 6 & 8 r Caen
☎776316
rm7 **P** sB72 dB84

AURILLAC
Cantal (☎71)

★ ★**Grand Bordeaux** 🔠 (MAP) 2 av de la
République (n. rest) ☎480184 tx990316
15 Jan–15 Dec
rm37 ⇌27 🚗 lift

AURON
Aples-Maritimes (☎93)

★ ★ ★**Pilon** ☎230015 tx470300
15 Dec–20 Apr & Jul–Aug
rm30 ⇌21 🍴9 **P** Lift
sB ⇌ 205–255 dB ⇌ 🍴275–380
Pool mountains

AUTUN
Saône-et-Loire (☎85)

★ ★**Tête Noir** 🔠 1–3 de l'Arquebuse
☎522539
rm20 ⇌3 🍴10 🚗 **P** DPn104–270

AUVILLERS-LES-FORGES
Ardennes (☎24)

★ ★**Lenoir** 🔠 ☎543011
Mar–Dec
rm21 ⇌12 🍴6 **P** Lift

France

AUXERRE
Yonne (☎86)

★ ★ ★ **Clairions** ℍ av Worms ☎468564 tx800039
⇱44 **P** Lift sB ⇱165–205 dB ⇱190–230

★ ★ ★ **Maxime** 2 quai de la Marine ☎521419
rm25 ⇱23 🛏2 ♨ **P** Lift 🌙
sB ⇱ 🛏175–230 dB⇱ 🛏185–270

★ ★ **Cygne** 14 r du 24 Août (n.rest) ☎522651
rm24 ⇱10 🛏14 ♨ **P** dB ⇱ 🛏137–220

★ ★ **Fontaine** 12 pl C-Lepère (n.rest) ☎524080
rm23 ⇱21 🛏2 ♨ Lift
sB ⇱ 🛏65–180 dB⇱ 🛏100–230

★ ★ **Normandie** 41 bd Vauban (n.rest) ☎525780
rm48 ⇱16 🛏22 ♨ **P** 🌙 sB100
sB⇱ 🛏140 dB107 dB⇱ 🛏150

★ ★ **Seignelay** 2 r Pont ☎520348
10 Feb–10 Jan
rm24 ⇱4 🛏8 ♨ sB76 dB ⇱ 🛏190

🚗**Carette** 34–36 av C-de-Gaulle ☎523715 Closed Sat pm & Sun Dat Vlo

🚗**Casimir** rte de Chablis ☎469876 Closed Sun & Mon am All makes

🚗**Grand Garage Gambetta** 8 av Gambetta ☎469718 Frd

🚗**B Jeannin** 40 av C-de-Gaulle ☎523383 Closed Sat pm Aud VW

🚗**Route de Lyon** 15 av MI-Juin ☎469805 Closed Sun Peu

🚗**Sodiva** 2 av J-Mermoz ☎527545 Closed Sat pm & Sun Ren

At **APPOIGNY** (9.5km NW via N6)

☆ ☆ ☆ **Mercure** C D 319 Lieu-dit-Le Chaumois ☎532500 tx800095
⇱ 🛏82 sB ⇱ 🛏210–242 dB ⇱ 🛏265–297 M alc Pool

AUXON
Aube (☎25)

🚗**Domagala** Le Péage (N7) ☎457012 M/c Closed Sun Peu

AUXONNE
Côte-d'Or (☎80)

★ **Corbeau** ℍ (**DPn**) 1 r de Berbis ☎381188
⇱10 **P** dB ⇱113–160

At **VILLERS-LES-POTS** (5km NW)

★ ★ **Auberge de Cheval Rouge** ℍ ☎373411
rm10 ⇱6 🛏4 **P** dB ⇱ 🛏90–122

AVALLON
Yonne (☎86)

★ ★ ★ **Poste** 13 pl Vauban ☎340612
Jan–Nov
⇱24 ♨ **P** 🌙 sB250–320 sB⇱ 🛏400 dB ⇱ 🛏750 St15%

★ ★ ★ **Moulin des Ruats** (**DPn**) (4.5km W via D957 & D427) Vallée du Cousin ☎340714
Mar–Oct
rm21 ⇱14 🛏1 **P** dB210 dB ⇱ 🛏230

★ ★ **Relais Fleuri** ℍ (5km E on N6) ☎340285 tx800084
⇱49 **P** sB ⇱170–200 dB ⇱180–220

🚗**Avallon-Autos** 15 r Carnot ☎340647 Closed Sun & Mon Frd

🚗**Gallmard** 2 rte de Paris ☎341303 Closed Xmas and New Year Toy

🚗**Gueneau** 30 r de Paris ☎341927 Closed Sun Ren

AVIGNON
Vaucluse (☎90)
See also **VILLENEUVE-LES-AVIGNON**

☆ ☆ ☆ **Mercure Avignon-Sud** rte Marseille-La Barbière ☎889110 tx431994
⇱ 🛏105 **P** Lift sB ⇱ 🛏226–257 dB ⇱ 🛏298–328 Pool

☆ ☆ ☆ **Novotel Avignon Sud** rte de Marseille (N7) ☎876236 tx432878
⇱79 **P** sB ⇱244–274 dB ⇱287–317 M alc Pool

★ ★ **Angleterre** ℍ 29 bd de Raspail (n.rest) ☎863431 tx431532
15 Jan–15 Dec
rm37 ⇱19 🛏15 **P** Lift ♨ sB93 sB ⇱ 🛏198 dB ⇱ 🛏152–198

★ ★ **Midi** (Inter) 53 r de la République (n.rest) ☎821556 tx431074
20 Jan–10 Dec
rm54 ⇱24 🛏40 Lift sB88 sB ⇱210 dB⇱222–260

★ **Jaquemart** 3 r F-David (n.rest) ☎863471
rm20 ⇱2 🛏6

🚗**C Delage** 14 bd de la Liberté ☎851320 Closed Sat pm & Sun Vlo

🚗**EGSA** Centre des affaires Cap Sud – rte de Marseille ☎876322 Closed Sat pm & Sun Aud VW

🚗**Parking** 77 av de Marseille ☎885594 Closed Sat pm & Sun BMW

🚗**Scandolera** 1 bis rte de Morieres (N7) ☎821676 Closed Sat pm & Sun Frd

At **AVIGNON NORD AUTOROUTE JUNCTION** (A7) (8km F by D942)

☆ ☆ ☆ **Sofitel** ☎311643 tx432869
⇱100 ♨ Lift sB ⇱223–403 dB ⇱441–521 ✍ Pool

At **MONTFAVET** (5.5km E)

☆ ☆ **Climat de France de l'Amandler** allée des Fenaisons ☎881300 tx692844
⇱30 **P** dB ⇱218

☆ ☆ **Climat de France de la Cristole** ZA du Clos de la Cristole ☎881500 tx612241

⇱38 **P** dB ⇱206–226 M54–70

☆ ☆ **Ibis** rte de Marseille (RN7), Zone de la Cristole ☎871100 tx432811
⇱65 **P** sB ⇱180–193 dB ⇱221–234 M55–63

Daures Shell Service Station, Cantarel (N7) ☎880295 Closed 1–15 Sep & Sun Ren

AVRANCHES
Manche (☎33)

★ ★ **Croix d'Or** (**DPn**) 83 r de la Constitution ☎580488
rm34 ⇱17 🛏8 A4rm ♨ **P** sB68–180 dB ⇱ 🛏70–250

★ ★ **St-Michel** (**DPn**) 5 pl GI-Patton ☎580191
1 Jan–Nov
rm24 ⇱10 🛏6 ♨ **P** dB ⇱ 79–166

🚗**Total Station Loisirs** (R Plaine) 182 av de la Liberté ☎581475 All makes

AX-LES-THERMES
Ariège (☎61)

★ ★ ★ **Royal Thermal** (MAP) espl de Couloubret ☎642251 tx530955
rm68 🛏54 Lift sB218–298 dB ⇱268–420 mountains

★ ★ **Moderne** ℍ (**DPn**) 20 av du Dr-Gomma ☎642024
4 Feb–Nov
rm44 ⇱5 🛏5 A22rm ♨ l ift mountains

★ ★ **Roy René** ℍ (**DPn**) 11 av du Dr-Gomma ☎642228 tx530955
Jan–25 Oct
rm30 ⇱6 🛏20 ♨ **P** Lift dB98–155 mountains

★ **Lauzerale** prom du Couloubert ☎642070 tx530806
May–Oct
rm30 ⇱5 🛏5 A6rm sB70 sB ⇱ 🛏143 dB80 dB ⇱ 🛏102–143 mountains

AZAY-LE-RIDEAU
Indre-et-Loire (☎47)

★ ★ **Grand Monarque** ℍ ☎433008
rm30 ⇱10 🛏6 ♨ **P** dB240 dB ⇱ 🛏240 M80–115

BAGNÈRES-DE-BIGORRE
Hautes-Pyrénées (☎62)

★ ★ **Résidence** Parc Thermal de Salut ☎950397
Apr–15 Oct
rm41 ⇱16 🛏25 A10rm sB160–180 sB ⇱ 🛏160–180 dB170–190 db ⇱ 🛏170–190 Pool mountains

★ ★ **Vignaux** ℍ 16 r de la République ☎950341
rm16 ⇱2 dB60–120 dB ⇱60–120

BAGNEAUX See **SAUMUR**

BAGNOLES-DE-L'ORNE
Orne (☎33)

★ ★ ★ **Lutetia-Reine Astrid** bd P-Chalvet, pl du GI-de-Gaulle ☎379477

Apr–Oct
rm30 ⇆19 **P** sB129 dB ⇆168–232

★★**Bois Joli** av P-du Rosier ☎379277
Mid Apr–Sep
rm20 ⇆13 ▥2 sB ⇆137–230
dB ⇆ ▥137–286

★★**Ermitage** 24 bd P-Chalvet (n.rest)
☎379622
Apr–Sep
rm39⇆11 ▥9 ▥ **P** dB143

BAGNOLS-EN-FORÊT
Var (☎94)

★★**Auberge Bagnolaise** ᴸᴱ rte Fayence
☎406024
Mar–Sep
⇆8 **P** mountains

BAGNOLET See **PARIS**

BAIX
Ardèche (☎75)

★★★**Cardinale** quai du Rhône
☎858040
15 Feb–2 Jan
⇆17 A10rm **P** Pool mountains

BANDOL
Var (☎94)

★★★**PLM Ile Rousse** (**DPn** Jul & Aug)
bd L-Lumière 294686 tx400372
⇆55 ▥ Lift sB ⇆285–750
dB ⇆360–880 M140–150 Pool Beach
sea

★★**Bale** 62 r Marçon (n.rest) ☎294082
⇆14 **P** 𝄞 sB ⇆198 dB306 sea

★★**Golf** Plage de Renécros (n.rest)
☎294583
Etr–mid Oct
rm24 ⇆9 ▥13 **P** Beach sea

★★**Provençal** r des Écoles ☎295211
tx400308
Feb–Oct
rm22 ⇆16 ▥6 sB ⇆ ▥140
dB ⇆ ▥200

★★**Réserve** (**DPn**) rte de Sanary
☎294271
15 Jan–Nov
rm16 ⇆12 ▥1 **P** sB126–211
sB ⇆ ▥211 dB ⇆ ▥246 sea

BANYULS-SUR-MER
Pyrénées-Orientales (☎68)

★★★**Catalan** (**DPn** Jul & Aug)
☎880280 tx500557
Apr–Oct
rm36 ⇆34 ▥2 **P** Lift
sB ⇆ ▥250–440 dB ⇆ ▥320–330 🏊
Pool sea mountains

BAPAUME
Pas-de-Calais (☎21)

★**Paix** 11 av A-Guidet ☎071103
Jan–15 Jul & Aug–20 Dec
rm15 ⇆9 **P** sB75 sB ⇆135–150
dB ⇆135–150

🅓**Greselle** 38 r de Péronne ☎071413
Closed Sat & Sun Peu

France

🅓**Piscine** av A-Guidet ☎071304 Closed
Sat pm & Sun Cit

Sellier 22 fbg d'Arras ☎071279 Tal

BARBEN (LA) See **SALON-DE-PROVENCE**

BARBEREY See **TROYES AIRPORT**

BARBEZIEUX
Charente (☎45)

★★**Boule d'Or** ᴸᴱ (**DPn**) 11 bd
Gambetta ☎782272
rm28 ⇆12 ▥22 ▥ **P** sB95
sB ⇆ ▥146 dB ⇆ ▥195

🅓**Cholet** av Vergne ☎781166 M/c
Closed Sun Peu

🅓**Gaboriaud** 13 bd Gambetta ☎781213
Closed Sun & Mon am VW

At **BOIS VERT** (11km S on N10)

★★★**Venta** ☎784095
rm23 ⇆7 ▥16 **P** 🏊 Pool

BARBIZON
Seine-et-Marne (☎6)

★★★★**Bas-Breau** (**DPn**) Grand Rue
☎0664005 tx690953
20 Feb–2 Jan
⇆19 ▥ **P** 𝄞 dB ⇆950–1500 St15%
🏊

★★★**Charmettes** (**DPn**) Grand Rue
☎0664021
rm41 ⇆34 ▥8 A5rm **P** sB90–210
sB ⇆ ▥96–174 dB ⇆ ▥96–310 St15%

BARBOTAN-LES-THERMES
Gers (☎62)

★★**Château-de-Bégue** (2km SW on
N656) ☎695008 tx531918
May–Oct
rm33 ⇆12 ▥5 ▥ **P** Pool

BARENTIN See **ROUEN**

BARNEVILLE-CARTERET
Manche (☎33)

At **BARNEVILLE PLAGE**

★★**Isles** ᴸᴱ bd Maritime ☎549076
15 Jan–15 Nov
rm36 ⇆12 ▥12 **P** dB120–230
dB ⇆ ▥230 sea

At **CARTERET**

★★**Angleterre** ᴸᴱ (**DPn**) 4 r de Paris
☎548604
Apr–Oct
rm43 ⇆23 **P** dB ⇆94–188 sea

★★**Marine** ᴸᴱ 2 r de Paris ☎548331
10 Feb–10 Nov
rm31 ⇆12 ▥12 **P** sB87–127
sB ⇆ ▥127 dB ⇆ ▥222–234 sea

★★**Plage et du Cap** ᴸᴱ (**DPn**) Le Cap
☎548696

Mar–Oct
rm15 ▥11 **P** sea

BAR-SUR-AUBE
Aube (☎25)

★**Commerce** 38 r Nationale ☎270876
Closed Jan
rm16 ⇆9 ▥4 ▥ **P** sB ⇆ ▥95–240
dB ⇆ ▥95–240

BAR-SUR-SEINE
Aube (☎25)

★★**Barséquanais** 7 av Gl-Leclerc
☎388275
24 Jan–24 Dec
rm24 ⇆3 ▥11 A14rm **P** sB72
sB ⇆ ▥98 dB85 dB ⇆ ▥160

BASTIDE-PUYLAURENT (LA)
Lozère (☎66)

★★**Pinas** ☎460007
▥25 sB ▥87–98 dB ▥109–121

BAUGÉ
Maine-et-Loire (☎41)

★**Boule d'Or** ᴸᴱ (**DPn**) 4 r du Cygne
☎898212
Closed Jan
rm14 ⇆2 ▥5 **P** sB90–175
sB ⇆ ▥105 dB140 dB ⇆ ▥190
M50–140

BAULE (LA)
Loire-Atlantique (☎40)

★★★**Majestic** espl F-André (n.rest)
☎602486
Apr–Sep
⇆67 **P** Lift 𝄞 sea

★★**Bellevue Plage** (**DPn**) 27 bd Océan
☎602855
⇆34 **P** Lift 𝄞 dB ⇆260–350 sea

★★**Concorde** 1 av de la Concorde
(n.rest) ☎602309
1 Apr–15 Oct
rm42 ⇆22 ▥20 ▥ **P** Lift
sB ⇆ ▥167–285 dB ⇆ ▥194–285 sea

★★**Palmerale** ᴸᴱ 7 allée Cormorans
☎602441
Apr–Sep
rm23 ⇆17 ▥6 dB ⇆ ▥214–249
M77–87

★★**Riviera** 16 av des Lilas ☎602897
15 May–Sep
rm20 ⇆6 ▥10 **P** dB ⇆ ▥97–195

★★**Welcome** 7 av des Impairs (n.rest)
☎603025
May–Sep
rm18 ⇆7 ▥11 sB ⇆ ▥150–178
dB ⇆ ▥180–201

🅓**Sté-Atlantic** 33 av G-Clemenceau
☎602375 Closed Sep 26–Oct 20, Sat pm
& Sun AR BL MB

BAUME-LES-DAMES
Doubes (☎81)

🅓**Duffing** av du Gl-Leclerc ☎840995
Frd

At **HYÈVRE PAROISSE** (7km E)

★★**Ziss** (N83) ☎840788
⇌21 🛏 **P** Lift mountains

BAVANS See **MONTBÉLIARD**

BAYEUX
Calvados (☎31)

★★★**Lion d'Or** 🅻 71 r St-Jean
☎920690
20 Jan – 16 Dec
rm30 ⇌13 🛁13 🛏 **P** 🌙
dB ⇌ 🍴150–240

☆☆**Pacary** 117 r St-Patrice ☎921611
tx170176
⇌65 **P** Lift 🌙 sB ⇌180–192
dB ⇌225–237 Pool

BAYONNE
Pyrénées-Atlantiques (☎59)

★★★**Agora** av J-Rostand ☎633090
tx550621
rm110 ⇌74 🍴36 **P** Lift
sB ⇌ 🍴166–213 dB* ⇌ 🍴185–258

★★**Capagorry** (MAP) 14r Thiers (n.rest)
☎254822 tx540376
rm48 ⇌25 🍴20 Lift sB200–220
sB ⇌ 🍴250–270 dB ⇌ 🍴250–270

★**Basses-Pyrénées** 12 r Tour de Sault
☎590029 tx541535
rm58 ⇌11 🍴15 A10rm 🛏 Lift
mountains

🏍**Marmande** rte de Pau ☎550561
Closed Sat & Sun BL

🏍**Sajons** 36 allée Marines ☎254579 All
makes

BEAUCAIRE
Gard (☎66)

★★★**Vignes Blanches** (Inter) rte de
Nîmes ☎591312 tx480690
Apr – 15 Oct
rm58 ⇌39 🍴19 **P** Lift
dB ⇌ 🍴199–243

★★**Robinson** 🅻 r de Pont du Gard
☎592132
rm30 ⇌16 🍴9 **P** 🏊 Pool

BEAUGENCY
Loiret (☎38)

★★**Ecu de Bretagne** 🅻 pl du Martroi
☎446760
Mar – 25 Jan
rm26 ⇌11 🛁8 A11rm 🛏 **P**
sB73–160 sB ⇌ 🍴119–180
dB ⇌ 🍴131–185

BEAULIEU-SUR-DORDOGNE
Corrèze (☎55)

★★**Central** (DPn) 910134
15 Mar – 15 Nov
rm32 ⇌10 🍴7 **P** sB62–74
sB ⇌ 🍴122–134 dB94–178
dB ⇌ 🍴144–180

★★**Chasseing Farges** 🅻 pl du Champ
de Mars ☎911104
1 Mar – 1 Nov
rm 20 ⇌2 🍴7 dB55–110
dB ⇌ 🍴84–110

· **France**

BEAULIEU-SUR-MER
Alpes-Maritimes (☎93)

★★★★★**Réserve de Beaulieu** (DPn
May – Sep) 5 bd Gl-Leclerc ☎010001
tx470301
10 Jan – Nov
⇌50 🛏 **P** Lift 🌙 sB ⇌394–944
dB ⇌588–1288 M alc St15% Pool sea

★★★**Métropole** bd Gl-Leclerc
☎010008 tx470304
20 Dec – 20 Oct
⇌50 **P** Lift 🌙 M290 **DPn**875–1155
Pool Beach sea

★★★**Victoria** (Pn) 47 bd Marinoni
☎010220 tx470303
20 Dec – Sep
rm80 ⇌49 🍴20 Lift 🌙 dB136
dB ⇌ 🍴195 sea mountains

BEAUMONT-SUR-SARTHE
Sarthe (☎43)

★**Barque** 1 pl de la Libération ☎970016
15 Jan – 15 Dec
rm25 ⇌6 🍴10 **P**

★**Chemin de Fer** 🅻 La Gare (1.5km E on
D26) ☎970005
Closed 2 wks Feb & 2 wks Oct
rm16 ⇌2 🍴4 🛏

🏍**Thureau** rte Nationale 138 ☎970033
Closed last 3 weeks Aug, Sat pm and Sun
Tal

BEAUMONT-SUR-VESLE
Marne (☎26)

★**Maison du Champagne** 🅻 (DPn)
☎616245 tx51400
rm10 ⇌6 🛁4 🛏 **P** sB ⇌ 🍴47–85
dB131

BEAUNE
Côte-d'Or (☎80)

★★★**Cep** 27 r Maufoux ☎223548
tx350690
Apr – Nov
rm21 ⇌17 🍴3 🛏 **P** 🌙

☆☆**PLM** (A6) ☎214612 tx350627
⇌150 **P** sB ⇌230 dB ⇌260 M85

★★★**Poste** 3 bd Clemenceau ☎220811
6 Apr – 19 Nov
rm25 ⇌20 🍴3 🛏 **P** Lift 🌙
mountains

★★**Bourgogne** 🅻 av C-de-Gaulle
☎222200 tx350666
24 Mar – 20 Nov
⇌120 **P** Lift sB ⇌190 dB ⇌212 Pool

★★**Central** 🅻 (DPn) 2 r V-Millot
☎247724
Mar – Nov
rm22 ⇌11 🍴6 dB120–260
dB ⇌ 🍴135–260

☆☆**Climat de France** 🅻 ZA de la
Chartreuse ☎227410 tx612241
⇌38 **P** dB ⇌206–227 M54–70

☆☆**Samotel** rte de Pommard (N74)
☎223555 tx350596
⇌66 **P** Pool mountains

🏍**Bolatre** 40 fbg Bretonnière ☎222803
Closed Sat & Sun Fia

🏍**M Marinho** rte de Seurre ☎224500
Closed Sat & Sun Ren

🏍**M Monnot** 146 rte de Dijon ☎221102
Closed Aug 8–18, Sat pm & Sun Frd

At **BROUZE-LES-BEAUNE** (6.5km NW on
D970)

🏍**Niquet Frères** ☎224059 Closed Sat
pm and Sun Tal

At **LADOIX-SERRIGNY** (5km NE)

★★**Paulands** ☎264105
rm21 ⇌20 🍴1 🛏 **P** mountains

At **LEVERNOIS** (5km SE)

☆☆**Campanile** rte de Verdun ☎226550
tx610016
⇌42 **P** dB ⇌216–222 M56–75

BEAURAINVILLE
Pas-de-Calais (☎21)

★**Val de Canche** 🅻 (DPn) ☎903222
rm10 ⇌1 🍴3 🛏 **P** dB112–192
dB ⇌ 🍴132–192

BEAUREPAIRE
Isère (☎74)

★★**Fiard** 25 r de la République
☎846202
Closed Jan
rm21 ⇌7 🍴9 sB108–180 sB ⇌ 🍴180
dB146–200 dB ⇌ 🍴196–220

BEAUSSET (LE)
Var (☎94)

★★**Auberge de la Gruppi** 🅻 46 rte
Nationale 8 ☎987018
Closed Oct
rm12 ⇌4 🍴3 **P** sB125
sB ⇌ 🍴147–175 dB144
dB ⇌ 🍴194–234 M62

BEAUVAIS
Oise (☎4)

☆☆☆**Mercure** ZAC St Lazare, av
Montaigne ☎4020336 tx150210
⇌60 **P** sB ⇌234–269 dB ⇌268–298

★**Commerce** 🅻 11 & 13 r Chambiges
☎4481784
14 Jan – 2 Dec
rm13 🍴6 🛏 **P**

★**Palais** 9 r St-Nicholas (n.rest)
☎4451258
rm14 ⇌3 🍴11 **P**

🏍**Beauvais** (M Letresse) 5 r du Pont
Laverdure ☎4450413 All makes

🏍**Boullanger** 124 r de Clemont
☎4480522 All makes

BEAUVALLON
Var (☎94)
See also **STE-MAXIME**

★**Marie Louise (DPn)** Guerrevieille (1km NE) ☎960605
🏨14 A5rm **P** sea

BEDARRIDES
Vaucluse (☎90)

☆ ☆**Motel 7** (N7) ☎392534
rm20 ⇌7 🏨6 A5rm **P** Pool mountains

BEDENAC
Charente-Maritime (☎46)

⬧🔾**Pacha** rte Nationale 10, le Jarculet ☎044548 Closed Sun pm Frd

BEG-MEIL
Finistère (☎98)

★ ★**Bretagne** ☎949804
Apr–Sep
rm48 ⇌6 🏨19 A19rm **P**
dB ⇌ 🏨66–182

★ ★**Thalamot** 🄻 **(DPn** in season) Le Chemin Creux Fouesnant ☎949738
21 Apr–10 Oct
rm35 ⇌1 🏨13 sea

BELFORT
Territoire-de-Belfort (☎84)

★ ★ ★**Grand Lion** (ETAP) r G-Clemenceau ☎211700 tx360914
rm82 ⇌44 🏨38 **P** Lift
sB ⇌ 🏨191–245 dB ⇌ 🏨213–277
M alc

⬧🔾M Dartier 86 fbg de Montbéliard ☎281970 Closed Sun All makes

⬧🔾J Wittlinger 10–15 r de Turenne ☎216399 Closed Aug 1–22, Sat & Sun Frd

At **BESSONCOURT** (7km NE)

☆ ☆**Campanile** Exchangeur Belfort Nord ☎221256 tx610016
⇌46 **P** dB ⇌ 206–209 M55–80

At **DANJOUTIN** (3km S)

☆ ☆ ☆**Mercure** r de Dr-Jacquot ☎215501 tx360801
⇌80 **P** Lift 🌙 sB ⇌249–259
dB ⇌288–300 Pool mountains

⬧🔾L Maldiney 25 r du Gl-de-Gaulle ☎282415 All makes

BELIN-BELIET
Gironde (☎56)

★**Alienor d'Aquitaine** 🄻 ☎880123
rm12 ⇌3 🏨9 🍴 **P** dB ⇌ 🏨120–160

BELLEGARDE-SUR-VALSERINE
Ain (☎50)

☆ ☆**Campanile** av de Lattre de Tassigny ☎481410 tx610016
⇌42 **P** dB ⇌194–197 M55–80

BELLÊME
Orne (☎33)

★**Relais St-Louis** 1 bd Bansart-des-Bois ☎731221

France

Mar–Dec
rm9 ⇌4 🏨3 🍴 **P** dB78–122
dB ⇌ 🏨112–134

BELLEY
Ain (☎79)

★ ★**Pernollet** 9 pl de la Victoire ☎810618
15 Dec–15 Nov
rm20 ⇌19 🍴 mountains

BÉNODET
Finistère (☎98)

★ ★ ★**Gwell-Kaer (DPn)** av de la Plage ☎910438
rm24 ⇌14 🏨10 🍴 Lift sea

★ ★**Ancre de Marine** 🄻 6 av l'Odet ☎570529
Mar–Oct
rm25 ⇌11 🏨3 dB119–220
dB ⇌ 🏨169–220 sea

BERCK-PLAGE
Pas-de-Calais (☎21)

★ ★**Comme Chez Sol** 44–48 pl de l'Entonnoir ☎090465
20 Jan–20 Dec
rm19 ⇌10 🏨6 sea

BERGERAC
Dordogne (☎53)

★ ★**Bordeaux** 🄻 (Inter) 38 pl Gambetta ☎571283 tx570418
10 Jan–10 Dec
rm42 ⇌15 🏨25 🍴 **P** Lift 🌙
sB ⇌140–160 dB155–165
dB ⇌ 🏨165–180

BERGUES
Nord (☎28)
See also **DUNKERQUE**

☆ ☆**Motel 25** (2km S at interchange Autoroute Lille-Dunkerque) ☎687900
⇌ 🏨40 **P** sB ⇌ 🏨160–170
dB ⇌ 🏨190–200

★**Tonnelier** 4 r de Mont de Piété ☎687005
rm12 ⇌1 🏨1 🍴 **P** sB70–115
sB ⇌ 🏨135 dB94–144 dB ⇌ 🏨164

BERNAY
Eure (☎32)

★ ★**Angleterre et Cheval Blanc**🄻 **(DPn)** 10 r Gl-de-Gaulle ☎431259
rm23 ⇌1 🏨2 🍴 **P** sB88–120
sB ⇌ 🏨115–150 dB120–150
dB ⇌ 🏨126–160

BESANÇON
Doubs (☎81)

★ ★ ★**Frantel** av E-Droz ☎801444
tx360268
rm96 ⇌67 🏨29 **P** Lift dB ⇌ 🏨382

☆ ☆ ☆**Novotel** 22 bis r de Trey (n.rest) ☎501466 tx360009

⇌107 **P** Lift sB ⇌ 252–272
dB ⇌303–323

☆ ☆**Ibis** 4 av Carnot ☎803311 tx361276
⇌66 **P** Lift sB ⇌193 dB ⇌229

★**Family** 13 r du Gl-Lecourbe (n.rest) ☎813392
rm23 ⇌12 **P** sB50–125 sB ⇌100–125
dB65–165 dB ⇌100–165

★**Gambetta** 13 r Gambetta ☎820233
rm26 ⇌12 🏨7 🌙 sB95 sB ⇌ 🏨160
dB123–178 dB ⇌ 🏨180

⬧🔾**Auto Dépannage** 9 r A-Fanart ☎501332 Closed Sat pm & Sun Cit

Auto Secours 119 r de Vesoul ☎504210
All makes

⬧🔾G Bever 4 r Pergaud ☎812801
Closed Sun Aud BMW Opl VW

⬧🔾J Petetin 7 r Demangel ☎501202
Closed Sat pm & Sun Opl Vau

At **CHÂTEAU-FARINE** (6km SW)

☆ ☆ ☆**Mercure** 159 r de Dôle ☎520400
tx360167
⇌59 **P** Lift sB ⇌281 dB ⇌278 M alc
Pool

At **ÉCOLE VALENTIN** (4.5km NW)

☆ ☆**Campanile** ZAC de Valentin ☎535222
⇌43 **P** dB ⇌206–209 M55–80

BESSE-EN-CHANDESSE
Puy-de-Dôme (☎73)

★ ★**Beffroy (DPn)** ☎795008
May–Sep
rm17 ⇌9 🏨3 🍴 sB60 sB ⇌ 🏨66
dB160 dB ⇌ 🏨177 mountains

BESSINES-SUR-GARTEMPE
Haute-Vienne (☎55)

☆ ☆ ☆**Toit de Chaume** (5km S on Limoges rd) ☎760102 tx580915
⇌20 Pool

★ ★**Vallée (DPn)** (N20) ☎760166
Closed Feb
rm20 ⇌8 🍴 **P** sB63–115 sB ⇌123
dB73–115 dB ⇌194–130

BESSONCOURT See **BELFORT**

BÉTHUNE
Pas-de-Calais (☎21)

★ ★**Vieux Beffroi** 48 Grand Pl ☎251500
rm65 ⇌21 🏨33 A29rm **P** Lift
sB78–106 sB ⇌ 🏨109–120 dB102–142
dB ⇌ 🏨145–155 St15%

★ ★**Bernard et Gare** 🄻 3 pl de la Gare ☎572002
rm34 ⇌10 🏨11 **P** 🌙

⬧🔾Auto-Béthunoise 225 bd Thiers ☎572430 Closed Sun All makes

At **BEUVRY** (4km SE)

★ ★**France II** r du Gl-Leclerc ☎573434
tx110691
⇌54 🍴 **P** Lift 🌙 sB ⇌220–240
dB ⇌240–260

125

BEYNAC-ET-CAZENAC
Dordogne (☎53)

★★**Bonnet** **L̃** **(DPn)** ☎295001

15 Apr–15 Oct
rm22 ⇆18 ⋔2 🖤 **P** sB85–185
sB ⇆ ⋔120–185 dB ⇆ ⋔120–185

BÉZIERS
Hérault (☎67)

★★★**Imperator** (Inter) 28 allées P-Riquet
(n.rest) 490225 tx490608

rm45 ⇆22 ⋔23 🖤 Lift ☾
dB ⇆ ⋔173–235

☆☆**Ibis** (5km S–exit Bèziers Est from A9)
☎625514 tx480938

⇆50 **P** Lift sB ⇆185 dB ⇆238

🕭**Grand Garage Foch** 117 av Ml-Foch
☎312742 Closed Sat & Sun BL

🕭**Grand Garage Rech** rte de Bessan
☎622269 Closed Sat & Sun Tal

🕭**St-Säens Auto's** 12 av St-Säens
☎763568 Closed Sat pm & Sun Aud VW

🕭**Socra** (P-Chanut) 6 r Amiral Courbet
☎765754 Closed Sat pm & Sun Maz Vlo

BIARD See POITIERS

BIARRITZ
Pyrénées-Atlantiques (☎59)

★★★★★**Palais** 1 av de l'Impératrice
☎240940 tx570000

May–Oct
⇆140 **P** Lift ☾ sB ⇆562–792
dB ⇆894–1254 M alc Pool sea

★★★**Eurotel** 19 av Perspective
☎243233 tx570014

rm60 ⇆48 ⋔12 🖤 **P** Lift ☾
sB ⇆ ⋔270–315 dB ⇆ ⋔145–580 sea

★★★**Miramar** av de l'Impératrice
☎248520 tx540831

Closed Jan
⇆126 Lift ☾ Pool sea

★★★**Regina & Golf** 52 av de
l'Impératrice (n.rest) ☎240960 tx541330

⇆50 **P** Lift ☾ sB ⇆260–300
dB⇆290–330 sea

★★★**Windsor** **(DPn** in summer) Grande
Plage ☎240852

15 Mar–10 Nov
rm37 ⇆27 ⋔10 **P** Lift ☾
sB ⇆ ⋔140–230 dB ⇆ ⋔200–330 sea

★★**Beau-Lieu** **(DPn** in summer) 3 espl du
Port-Vieux ☎242359

Mar–Dec
rm28 ⇆16 ⋔3 dB200–230
dB ⇆ ⋔200–230 sea

★**Palacito** 1 r Gambetta (n.rest)
☎240489

rm26 ⇆12 ⋔16 **P**

🕭**Biarritz Assistance Auto** 109 av de la
Marne ☎24708 Closed Sat & Sun All
makes

🕭**Paris Biarritz Auto** 48 av du Ml-Foch
☎230583 Closed Sat & Sun Aud Por VW

BIDART
Pyrénées-Atlantiques (☎59)

France

★★★**Bidartea** (MAP) rte d'Espagne
(N10) ☎549468 tx540140

Mar–Oct
rm36 ⇆32 ⋔4 **P** Lift
dB ⇆ ⋔246–326 Pool

BLAGNAC See TOULOUSE AIRPORT

BLANGY-SUR-BRESLE
Seine-Maritime (☎35)

★**Poste** 44 Grande Rue ☎935020

25 Jan–20 Dec
rm 14 🖤 **P**

★**Ville** **(DPn)** 2 r Notre Dame ☎935157

Closed Aug
rm9 ⇆1 ⋔1 A3rm

🕭**St-Denis** 61 r St-Denis ☎935042 Ren

BLAYE
Gironde (☎56)

★★**Citadelle** pl d'Armes ☎421710
tx540127

⇆ ⋔21 **P** ☾ Pool

BLÉRE
Indre-et-Loire (☎47)

★**Cher** **(DPn)** 9 r Pont ☎579515

19 Dec–15 Nov
rm19 ⇆1 ⋔18 A8rm dB ⇆ ⋔95–131

BLÉRIOT-PLAGE
Pas-de-Calais (☎21)

★**Dunes** **(DPn)** (N48) ☎345430
tx160081

Jan–15 Feb & Mar–Sep
rm12 **P**

BLOIS
Loir-et-Cher (☎54)

☆☆**Campanile** 15 r de la Vallée Maillard
☎744466

⇆42 **P** dB ⇆206–209 M55–80

☆☆**Ibis** r de la Vallée Maillard ☎746060

⇆40 sB ⇆173 dB ⇆212

★**Bellay** **L̃** 12 r Minimes (n.rest)
☎782362 tx750135

rm14 ⇆6 ⋔6 A2rm dB114–180
dB ⇆ ⋔144–180

★**Gerbe d'Or** 1 r Bourg-Neuf ☎742645

rm25 ⇆4 ⋔10 A10rm **P**

★**St-Jacques** **L̃** pl Gare ☎780415

rm28 ⇆6 sB96–134 sB ⇆ 136–139
dB122 dB ⇆ ⋔162–108

★**Viennois** **L̃** **(DPn)** 5 quai A-Coutant
☎741280

15 Jan–15 Dec
rm26 ⇆8 ⋔2 A15rm dB49–120
dB ⇆ ⋔85–135 lake

🕭**M Gueniot** 74 Levée des Tuileries
☎789463 All makes

Peigné 20 av Maunoury ☎740634
Closed Sat pm, Sun & Mon am Frd

At CHAUSSÉE ST-VICTOR (LA) (4km N)

☆☆☆**Novotel Blois l'Hermitage** 20 r des
Pontières ☎783357 tx75232

⇆116 **P** Lift sB ⇆259–269
dB ⇆305–315 Pool

At VINEUIL (4km SE)

☆☆**Cilmat de France** 48 r des Quatre-
Vents ☎467022 tx692844

⇆38 **P** dB ⇆206–221 M54–70

BLONVILLE-SUR-MERE
Calvados (☎31)

★**Mer** **L̃** 93 av de la République (n.rest)
☎879323

Apr–Sep
rm20 ⇆13 **P** sB75–85 dB ⇆176 sea

BOLLENBERG See ROUFFACH

BOLLÈNE
Vaucluse (☎90)

☆☆**Campanile** av T-Aubanel ☎300042
tx610016

⇆30 **P** dB ⇆206–209 M55–80

🕭**Carrosserie des Grès** les Grès du
Fourmillier ☎301704 All makes

🕭**R David** 1 r du Souvenir ☎301223
Closed Sun VW

🕭**Portes de Provence** ☎301046 Peu

BONDY See PARIS

BONNEIL-SUR-MARNE
Val-de-Marne (☎1)

☆☆**Campanile** ZA des Petits Carreaux, 1
av des Bleuets ☎3777029 tx211251

⇆50 **P** dB ⇆218–222

BONNEVAL
Eure-et-Loire (☎37)

★★**Bois Guibert** **(DPn** in season) (N10)
☎472233

rm14 ⇆6 ⋔ 🖤 **P** sB ⇆ ⋔100–198
dB ⇆100–198

BONNEVILLE
Haute-Savoie (☎50)

At CONTAMINE-SUR-ARVE (8km NW)

★**Tourne-Bride** ☎036218

rm8 🖤 M42–98 **DPn** fr 90 mountains

BONNY-SUR-LOIRE
Loiret (☎38)

☆☆**Fimotel-Val de Loire** (N7) ☎316462

rm46 ⇆36 ⋔10 **P** sB ⇆ ⋔178–203
dB ⇆ ⋔206–236 M42-70

🕭**Parot** 139 Grande Rue ☎316332
Closed Sun Ren

BORDEAUX
Gironde (☎56)

★★★**Aquitania Sofitel** Parc des
Expositions ☎508380 tx570557

⇆210 **P** Lift ☾ dB ⇆370–460
dB ⇆455–555 Pool lake

★★★**Frantel** 5 r R-Lateulade
☎909237 tx540565

⇆196 **P** Lift sB ⇆453 dB ⇆541

☆ ☆ ☆**Mercure Bordeaux le Lac** quartier du Lac ☎509030 tx540077

⇌108 **P** Lift sB ⇌264–316 dB ⇌300–352 lake

★ ★ **Normandie** 7 cours 30 Juillet (n.rest) ☎521680 tx570481

rm100 ⇌50 ⋒50 Lift ♪ sB ⇌ ⋒155–220 dB ⇌ ⋒200–260

☆ ☆ ☆**Novotel Bordeaux-le-Lac** quartier du Lac ☎509970 tx570274

⇌173 **P** Lift sB ⇌263–280 dB ⇌294–312 Pool

☆ ☆ ☆**Sofitel** Centre Hôtelier ☎509014 tx540097

⇌100 ⚒ **P** Lift ✒ Pool

☆ ☆**Arcade** 60 r E-le-Roy ☎909240 tx550952

⋒140 Lift sB ⋒155 dB ⋒165

★ ★**Bayonne** 15 cours de l'Intendance (n.rest) ☎480088

rm37 ⇌11 ⋒15 Lift

☆ ☆**Campanile** quartier du Lac ☎395454 tx560425

⇌50 **P** dB ⇌206–209 M55–80

☆ ☆**Ibis** quartier du Lac ☎509650 tx550346

⇌119 **P** Lift sB ⇌163 dB ⇌206

★ ★**Sèze** 23 allées Tourny (n.rest) ☎526554

rm25 ⇌12 ⋒9 Lift sB120–225 sB ⇌ ⋒180–225 dB120–245 dB ⇌ ⋒180–245

★**Etche-Ona** (Inter) 11 r Mautrec (n.rest) ☎443649

rm35 ⇌16 ⋒11 Lift sB90 sB ⇌ ⋒162–198 dB ⇌ ⋒162–198

P Mercier 162–166 r de la Benauge ☎862133 Closed Sat pm BL DJ RR

At **ARTIGUES** (7km NE)

☆ ☆**Campanile** av de la Prairie ☎327332

⇌50 **P** dB ⇌206–209 M55–80

At **BRUGES** (5km NW)

⮞**A Pigeon** 469 rte due Médoc ☎288428 Closed Sat pm & Sun Opl

At **CESTAS** (15km SW)

☆ ☆**Campanile** Aire de Service de Bordeaux Cestas, A63 ☎218068

⇌36 **P** dB ⇌206–209 M55–80

At **LORMONT** (5km NE)

☆ ☆**Climat de France** Carrefour des 4 Pavillions, N10 ☎329610 tx612241

⇌38 **P** dB ⇌197 M54–71

At **MÉRIGNAC** (5km W on D106)

☆ ☆ ☆**Novotel Bordeaux Aéroport** av du Prés-Kennedy ☎341025 tx540320

⇌100 sB ⇌267–297 dB ⇌303–323 Pool

☆ ☆**Ibis Bordeaux Aéroport** av du Prés-Kennedy ☎341019 tx541430

⇌64 **P** Lift sB ⇌191 dB ⇌221

France

BORMES-LES-MIMOSAS
Var(☎94)

★ ★**Safari** rte Stade ☎710983

Apr–15 Oct
rm33 ⇌31 ✒ Pool sea

★**Belle Vue** Ⅼ **(DPn)** pl Gambetta ☎711515

Feb–Oct
rm15 ⇌1 ⋒13 dB111–130 dB ⇌ ⋒136 sea

⮞**Pin** (B Pichou) ☎711177 Closed Nov 1–20, Sat pm & Sun All makes

BOSSONS (LES) See **CHAMONIX-MONT-BLANC**

BOULOGNE-BILLANCOURT See **PARIS**

BOULOGNE-SUR-MER
Pas-de-Calais(☎21)
See Plan page 128

AA Agent: see page 105

See also **PORTEL (LE)**

★ ★**Alexandra** 93 r Thiers (n.rest) ☎305222 Plan **1**

25 Jan–Dec
rm20 ⇌8 ⋒6

★ ★**Faidherbe** 12 r Faidherbe (n.rest) ☎316093 Plan **2**

rm35 ⇌25 ⋒5 **P** Lift ♪ sB120 sB200 dB240 dB ⇌ ⋒400 sea

☆ ☆**Ibis** quartier L-Danremont, bd Diderot ☎301240 tx160485 Plan **3**

⇌79 **P** Lift sB ⇌174 dB ⇌215

★**Lorraine** 7 pl de Lorraine (n.rest) ☎313478 Plan **4**

rm21 ⇌5 ⋒9 sB70–150 sB ⇌ ⋒140–150 dB100–150 dB ⇌ ⋒140–150

★ ★**Métropole** 51 r Thiers (n.rest) ☎315430 Plan **6**

5 Jan–16 Dec
rm27 ⇌9 ⋒13 Lift

★**Hamiot** 1 r Faidherbe ☎314420 Plan **7**

rm24 Lift

★**Londres** 22 pl de France (n.rest) ☎313563 Plan **8**

rm20 ⇌4 ⋒12 Lift sB83 sB ⇌ ⋒110 dB83 dB ⇌ ⋒110

⮞**Gare** (M Porquet) bd Diderot ☎911088 Closed Sat pm & Sun Chy Sim

⮞**Paris** 33 av Kennedy ☎920522 Closed Sat & Sun Frd

⮞**St-Christophe** 128 bd de la Liane, ZI ☎920911 Closed Sun AR Opl Vau

At **ST-LÉONARD** (4km S off N1)

⮞**Citroën** bd de la Liane, ZI ☎922111 Closed Sat & Sun Cit

⮞**J Venière** 122 bd de la Liane, ZI ☎319740 M/c Closed Sat pm & Sun Peu

BOULOU (LE)
Pyrénées-Orientales(☎68)

⮞**M Borg** 1 r E-Zola ☎833057 All makes

⮞**Perrin** 5 av J-Moulin ☎831321 Ren

BOURBON-LANCY
Seine-et-Loire(☎85)

★ ★**Raymond** Ⅼ 8 r d'Autun ☎891739

rm20 ⇌7 ⋒5 ⚒ **P** sB75–130 sB ⇌ ⋒130 dB100–160 dB ⇌ ⋒160

BOURDEILLES See **BRANTÔME**

BOURG See **LANGRES**

BOURG-EN-BRESSE
Ain(☎74)

★ ★ ★**Logis de Brou** 132 bd Brou (n.rest) ☎221155

rm30 ⇌18 ⋒12 ⚒ **P** Lift ♪ sB ⇌ ⋒100–200 dB ⇌ ⋒150–240

★ ★**Chantecler** 10 rte St-Etienne du Bois ☎224488 tx380468

⇌28 **P** sB ⇌158 dB ⇌184

☆ ☆**Ibis** ZAC de la Croix Blanche, bd Ch-de-Gaulle ☎225266 tx9900471

⇌42 **P** sB ⇌168 dB ⇌216

BOURGES
Cher(☎48)

★ ★ ★**Angleterre** 1 pl des Quatre Piliers ☎246851

rm31 ⇌27 ⚒ **P** Lift ♪ sB120 sB ⇌250–270 dB140 dB ⇌290 M80 alc

★ ★**D'Artagnan** 19 pl Séraucourt ☎246751

rm71 ⇌61 ⋒10 ⚒ **P** Lift

★ ★**Christina** 5 r Halle (n.rest) ☎705650

rm76 ⇌41 ⋒30 ⚒ **P** Lift ♪

★ ★**Poste** 22 r Moyenne (n.rest) ☎700806

rm34 ⇌4 ⋒9 A6rm ⚒ **P** Lift

★ ★**St-Jean** 23 av M-Dormoy (n.rest) ☎241348

Closed Feb
rm24 ⇌2 ⋒16 ⚒ **P** Lift sB73–134 sB ⇌ ⋒83–134 dB82–175 dB ⇌ ⋒102–175

⮞**Guerenne** rte de la Chapelle St Ursin, ZI ☎505343 Ren

BOURGET AIRPORT (LE) See **PARIS AIRPORTS**

BOURG-LÈS-VALENCE See **VALENCE**

BOURGNEUF-LA-FORÊT (LE)
Mayenne(☎43)

★**Vieille Auberge** pl de l'Église ☎015112

2 Jan–18 Sep & 30 Sep–30 Dec
rm8 ⋒2 ⚒ **P** sB83 sB ⋒93–98 dB fr 88 dB ⇌ ⋒121–126 M38–100

BOURGOIN-JALLIEU
Isère (☎74)

☆ ☆**Campanile** Zac de St-Hubert l'Isle d'Abeau Est ☎935063 tx610016 →

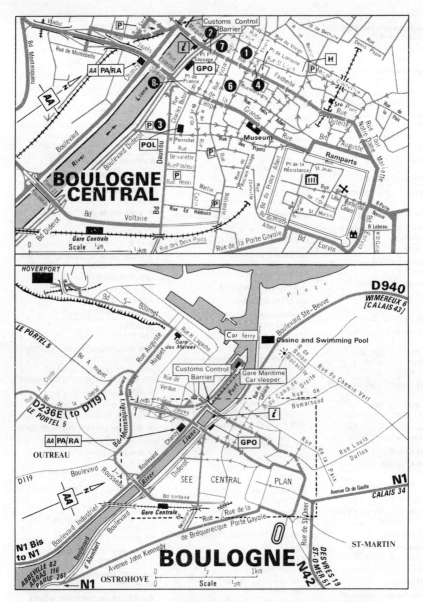

⌐50 **P** dB ⌐206–209 M55–80

☆ ☆**Climat de France** 15 r E-Branly, ZAC de la Maladière ☎(6)4460123 tx692844

⌐42

🏂**J Derud** 216 av Liberation ☎930676 Closed Aug 1–21, Sat pm & Sun Cit

BOURG-ST-MAURICE
Savoie(☎79)

★ ★**Petit St-Bernard (DPn)** 2 av Stade
☎070432

Seasonal
rm30 ⌐14 🏠3 A3rm 🏛 **P** sB90–150
sB ⌐ 🏠125–150 dB90–165
dB ⌐ 🏠150–180 mountains

BOURGTHEROULDE-INFREVILLE
Eure(☎35)

★**Corne d'Abondance** Ⅼⅎ pl de la Mairie
☎876008

BOULOGNE

1	★ ★ Alexandra
2	★ ★ Faidherbe
3	☆ ☆ Ibis
4	★ ★ Lorraine
6	★ ★ Métropole
7	★ Hamiot
8	★ Londres

rm9 ⇌1 🛁 P sB80–150 sB ⇌160
dB160–200

♨J Noyelle rte d'Elbeuf ☎776009
Closed Aug, Sat pm & Sun Ren

BOUZE-LES-BEAUNE See **BEAUNE**

BOVES See **AMIENS**

BRANTÔME
Dordogne(☎53)

★★★**Chabrol** 59 r Gambetta ☎057015
rm21 ⇌10 🍴11 sB ⇌ 🍴160
dB ⇌ 🍴200

At **BOURDEILLES** (10km SW)

★★★**Griffons (DPn)** ☎057561
Apr–Sep
⇌10 Lift 🏊 Pool ☊

BREST
Finistère(☎98)

☆☆★**Novotel de Brest** ZAC de
Kergaradec, rte du Gouesnou ☎023283
tx940470
⇌85 P sB ⇌276–292 dB ⇌332–348
Pool

★★★**Sofitel Océania** 82 r de Siam
☎806666 tx940951
⇌82 Lift sB ⇌297–367 dB ⇌342–425

Auto-Depan-Service 5 r M-Dufosset
☎020669 All makes

Sébastopol Autos 56 r Sébastopol & 231 r
J-Jaurès ☎441979 Closed Sat & Sun BL

At **PLOUGASTEL-DAOULAS** (9.5km SE)

☆☆**Ibis Brest** rte de Quimper, quartier de
Ty-Menez ☎405028 tx940731
⇌46 P Lift sB ⇌169 dB ⇌208

BRÉVILLE-SUR-MER
Manche(☎33)

★★**Mougine des Moulins à Vent** Les
Moulins à Vent (D971) (n.rest) ☎502241
⇌ 🍴7 P sB ⇌ 🍴175–214
dB ⇌ 🍴175–214 sea

BRIANÇON
Hautes-Alpes(☎92)

★★**Cristol** 🛗 **(DPn)** 6 rte d'Italie
☎202011
25 Dec–25 Oct
⇌16 P dB ⇌180–210 mountains

♨R Rignon 3 rte d'Italie ☎211073
Closed Sep 8–21, Sat pm & Sun BMW Fia

At **STE-CATHÉRINE**

★★★**Mont Brison** 1 av Gl-de-Gaulle
(n.rest) ☎211455
20 Dec–Oct
rm45 ⇌25 🍴12 P Lift sB90
sB ⇌ 🍴170 dB ⇌ 🍴90–180

★★★**Vauban (DPn)** 13 av Gl-de-Gaulle
☎211211
17 Dec–11 Nov
rm44 ⇌23 🍴14 🛁 P Lift sB130
sB ⇌ 🍴200 dB130 dB ⇌ 🍴250
mountains

BRIARE
Loiret(☎38)

France

★**Cerf** 22 bd Buyser ☎370080
15 Jan–15 Dec
rm20 ⇌4 🍴4 A8rm 🛁 P

♨SARL Relais Briarois Autos 17 av de
Lattre de Tassigny ☎370161 Closed Sat
pm & alternate Sun Tal

BRICQUEBEC
Manche(☎33)

★**Vieux Château** 🛗 **(DPn)** 4 cour du
Château ☎522449
15 Feb–Dec
rm22 ⇌13 🍴2 🛁 P dB90–200
dB ⇌ 🍴90–212

BRIDORÉ See **LOCHES**

BRIGNOLES
Var(☎94)

♨A Mangini ☎690575 M/c All makes

♨Marcel rte de Nice ☎694208 M/c
Closed Sun Aud VW

BRIONNE
Eure(☎32)

★**Logis de Brionne** 🛗 **(DPn)** 1 pl St-
Denis ☎448173
rm16 ⇌3 🍴5 🛁 P sB60–80
sB ⇌ 🍴103–116 dB82–114
dB ⇌ 🍴126–153

★**Vieux Donjon (DPn)** 19 r de la Soie
☎448062
Dec–Oct
rm9 ⇌1 🍴1 🛁 P sB70 sB ⇌ 🍴100
dB70–100 dB ⇌ 🍴100

BRIOUDE
Haute-Loire(☎71)

★★**Brivas** 🛗 (Inter) rte Puy ☎501049
rm30 ⇌8 🍴22 P dB ⇌ 🍴133–195

★★**Moderne** 🛗 (FAH) 12 av V-Hugo
☎500730
rm17 ⇌7 🍴10 🛁

BRIVE-LA-GAILLARD
Corrèze(☎55)

★★**Crémaillère** 🛗 53 av de Paris
☎743247
⇌12

★★**Truffe Noir** 22 bd A-France
☎743532
rm35 ⇌31 🍴4 P Lift 🌙

★**Montauban** 🛗 **(DPn** in season) 6 av E-
Herriot ☎240038
rm21 ⇌2 🍴12 🛁

♨G Cremoux 20 av du Ml-Bugeaud
☎236922 Closed Sat pm & Sun BL

♨Socoda av du Prés Kennedy ☎740731
Closed Sat & Sun Aud VW

♨M Taurisson 21–23 av de Toulouse
☎742542 Closed Sun BMW

At **VARETZ** (14km NW)

★★★**Château de Castel Novel** 🛗
☎850001 tx590065
8 May–20 Oct
⇌28 P Lift 🌙 sB ⇌325–380
dB ⇌380–575 🏊 Pool

BRON See **LYON**

BROU
Eure-et-Loir(☎37)

★**Plat d'Etain** 🛗 pl de Halles ☎470398
15 Jan–15 Dec
rm18 ⇌5 🍴2 A7rm 🛁 sB70 dB103
dB ⇌ 🍴137

BRUGES See **BORDEAUX**

BUC
Yvelines(☎3)

☆☆**Climat de France** r L-Pasteur
☎9564811 tx612241
⇌38 P dB ⇌206–227 M54–70

BUGUE (LE)
Dordogne(☎53)

★★★**Royal Vezère** (MAP) pl H-de-Ville
☎062001 tx540710
17 Apr–12 Oct
rm55 ⇌41 🍴12 🛁 Lift 🌙
sB280–295 sB ⇌ 🍴280–295 dB314–326
dB ⇌ 🍴314–326 Pool

BULLY-LES-MINES
Pas-de-Calais(☎21)

★**Moderne** 144 r de la Gare ☎291422
rm37 ⇌4 🍴10 🛁 P sB85–105
sB ⇌120 dB ⇌150

♨Derache 59 r R-Salengro ☎291799
Closed Sat pm & Sun Ren

CABRERETS
Lot(☎65)

★**Grottes** 🛗 **(DPn)** ☎312702
Apr–8 Oct
rm17 ⇌3 🍴5 A5rm P Pool

CADÉAC See **ARREAU**

CAEN
Calvados(☎31)

★★★★**Relais des Gourmets** 15 r
Geôle ☎860601 tx170353
rm26 ⇌16 🍴10 Lift 🌙
dB ⇌ 🍴178–264

★★★**Malherbe** pl Ml-Foch ☎844006
tx170555
rm45 ⇌33 🍴5 P Lift 🌙 sB86-228
sB ⇌ 🍴228–256 dB ⇌ 🍴228–332

★★**Moderne** (MAP) 116 bd Gl-Leclerc
☎860423 tx171106
rm57 ⇌15 🍴39 🛁 Lift 🌙
sB ⇌ 🍴241–275 dB ⇌ 🍴258–286

☆☆**Novotel** av de la Côte de Nacre
☎930588 tx170563
⇌126 P Lift sB ⇌259–274
dB ⇌295–310 M alc Pool

★**Bristol** 31 r du XI Novembre (n.rest)
☎845976 tx170353
rm25 ⇌4 🍴16 P Lift sB83–185
sB ⇌ 🍴116–185 dB100–185
dB ⇌ 🍴131–185

★★**Château** 5 av du 6-Juin (n.rest)
☎861537
rm21 ⇄5 ▥10 **P** Lift sB80–100
sB ⇄ ▥188 dB80–100 dB ⇄ ▥.188

★★**Métropole** (Inter) 16 pl de la Gare
(n.rest) ☎822676 tx170165
rm71 ⇄ ▥54 **P** Lift dB ⇄ ▥80–180

★**Bernières** 50 r Bernières (n.rest)
☎860126
5 Jan–22 Dec
rm16 ⇄1 ▥7 sB70 sB ⇄ ▥133 dB70
dB ⇄ ▥133

★**St-Jean** 20 r des Martyrs ☎862335
rm15 ⇄6 **P**

&⊃**Auto Secours** 7 bis r Marchaud
☎824555 All makes

At **HÉROUVILLE-ST-CLAIR**

☆☆**Campanile** Parc Tertaire, bd du Bois
☎952924 tx170618
⇄43 **P** dB ⇄206–209 M55–80

☆☆**Ibis Caen** 4 quartier Savary
☎935446 tx170755
⇄89 **P** Lift sB ⇄174 dB ⇄215

CAGNES-SUR-MER
Alpes-Maritimes (☎93)

★★★**Cagnard** r Pontis Long ☎207322
rm19 ⇄18 ▥1 A9rm **P** Lift
sB ⇄ ▥230–300 dB ⇄ 260–650 sea
mountains

★★★**Tierce** bd de la Plage/bd Kennedy
☎200209
Dec–24 Oct
⇄ ▥23 ⦿ **P** Lift ☽
sB ⇄ ▥190–260 dB ⇄ ▥280 sea
mountains

At **CROS-DE-CAGNES** (2km SE)

☆☆**Horizon** 111 bd de la Plage (n.rest)
☎310995 tx460938
Jan–Nov
rm44 ⇄21 ▥18 **P** sB168 sB ⇄ ▥279
dB205 dB ⇄ ▥357 sea mountains

&⊃**Grand Garage Modern** 90 av de Nice
☎310081 Closed Sun All makes

At **VILLENEUVE-LOUBET PLAGE**

☆☆**Méditerranée** (N98) (n.rest)
☎200007
Xmas–Oct
⇄16 **P** dB ⇄125–174

CAHORS
Lot (☎65)

★★★**Wilson** 72 r Prés-Wilson (n.rest)
☎354180 tx801059
⇄36 **P** Lift sB ⇄260 dB ⇄340

★★**France** Ⅼ (Inter) 252 av-J-Jaurès
(n.rest) ☎351676 tx520394
rm79 ⇄46 ▥33 ⦿ **P** Lift
sB ⇄ ▥150–195 dB ⇄ ▥250

★**Terminus** Ⅼ 5 av C-de-Freycinet
(n.rest) ☎352450
rm31 ⇄7 ▥24 ⦿ **P** Lift ☽
dB ⇄ ▥220 mountains

France

&⊃**Grandes Garages** rte de Toulouse
☎356725 Closed Sat & Sun Sim Tal

&⊃**Lacassagne** av A-de-Monsie
☎354510 Closed 19 Aug–9 Sep & Sun
All makes

&⊃**E Marcou** Rivière de Regourd
☎351880 Closed Sat & Sun BL Vlo

Recuper-Autos rte de Villefranche
☎351516 Closed Mon BL Dat Maz Toy

At **LAROQUE-DES-ARCS** (5km N)

★**Beau Rivage** ☎353058
Mar–Dec
▥14 **P**

CAISSARGUES BOUILLARGUES See
NÎMES

CALAIS
Pas-de-Calais (☎21)
See Plan page 132
AA agent; see page 105

★★★**Meurice** 5 r E-Roche (n.rest)
☎345703 Plan **1**
rm40 ⇄30 ▥10 ⦿ **P** Lift ☽
dB ⇄ ▥155–195

★★**Bellevue** 25 pl d'Armes (n.rest)
☎345375 Plan **2**
rm42 ⇄10 ▥14 ⦿ Lift sB64–146
sB ⇄104–147 dB91–179 dB ⇄132–182

★★**Capitainerie** quai du Danube
☎961010 Plan **2A**
▥48 **P** sB ▥140–160 dB ▥174–194
M42–72

★★**George V** 36 r Royale (n.rest)
☎344029 tx130764 Plan **3**
15 Mar–Nov
rm46 ⇄8 ▥6 sB75 dB174
dB ⇄ ▥215

☆☆**Ibis** r Greuze, ZUP de Beau-Marais
☎966969 tx135004 Plan **4**
⇄52 **P** sB ⇄179 dB ⇄222

★★**Pacific** 40 r de Duc de Guise
☎345024 Plan **5**
Mar–Dec
rm24 ⇄2 ▥19 A4rm ⦿

★**Beffrol** 10 r A-Gerschel (n.rest)
☎344751 Plan **7**
rm20 ⇄4 ▥7 sB78 dB101
dB ⇄ ▥148

★**Richelieu** 17 r Richelieu (n.rest)
☎346160 Plan **8**
rm18 ⇄2 ▥8 ⦿ **P** sB93–126
sB ⇄ ▥140–170 dB 126–142
dB ⇄ ▥165–220

★**Sole Meunière** 53 r de la Mer (n.rest)
☎(20)343608 Plan **9**
rm15 ⇄7 ▥8 **P** sB ⇄ ▥166–203
dB ⇄ ▥198–251 sea

&⊃**Calaisienne d'Autos** 361 av de St-
Exupéry ☎967242 Peu

CALIGNAC
Lot-et-Garonne (☎58)

★**Palmiers** ☎971102
rm24 ⇄7 ▥17 **P** sB ⇄ ▥118–153
dB ⇄ ▥139–177 Pool lake

CAMBO-LES-BAINS
Pyrénées-Atlantiques (☎59)

★**Bellevue** r des Terrasses ☎297322
rm28 ⇄14 ▥4 A3rm **P** sB67–127
sB ⇄ ▥88–127 dB87–163
dB ⇄ ▥163 mountains

CAMBRAI
Nord (☎27)

★★★**Beatus** 38 rte de Paris (n.rest)
☎814570 tx820211
rm26 ⇄24 ▥2 ⦿ **P** ☽
sB ⇄ ▥180–220 dB ⇄ ▥206–236

★★★**Château de la Motte Fenelon** sq
du Château ☎836138 tx120285
rm33 ⇄27 **P** Lift sB90–155 sB ⇄210
dB ⇄210 Pool

☆☆**Ibis** rte de Bapaume, Fontaine Notre
Dame ☎835454
⇄27 **P** sB ⇄181 dB ⇄221

★★**Mounton Blanc** 33 r Alsace-Lorraine
☎813016 tx133365
rm38 ⇄16 ▥11 ⦿ **P** Lift sBfr121
sB ⇄ ▥156–246 dBfr152
dB ⇄ ▥172–262

★★**Poste** 58–60 av de la Victoire (n.rest)
☎813469
rm33 ⇄10 ▥20 ⦿ Lift sB110
sB ⇄ ▥184 dB110 dB ⇄ ▥196

★**France** 37 r Lille (n.rest) ☎813880
Closed Aug
rm24 ⇄2 ▥5

&⊃**Bachelet** 8 av A-ler ☎812634 Closed
Sun Peu

&⊃**P Decamps** Fontaine-Notre Dame
(N30) ☎815583 All makes

CAMP ST-LAURENT See **TOULON**

CANCALE
Ille-et-Vilaine (☎99)

★★**Continental** Ⅼ **(DPn)** quai au
Thomas ☎896016
Apr–15 Nov
rm21 ⇄10 ▥6 sB88–288 dB106–306
dB ⇄106–306 sea

CANDÉ
Maine-et-Loire (☎41)

★**Tonnelles** Ⅼ 6 pl des Halles ☎927112
rm10 ⇄2

CANET-PLAGE
Pyrénées-Orientales (☎68)

★★★**Sables** (Inter) r Vallée du Rhône
(n.rest) ☎802363 tx500997
rm41 ⇄26 ▥15 A17rm **P** Lift ☽ Pool

★★**Mar-I-Cel** pl Centrale ☎803216
tx500997
Apr–Sep
rm60 ⇄57 ▥3 **P** Lift sea mountains

CANNES
Alpes-Maritimes (☎93)

★ ★ ★ ★ ★**Carlton** (Intercont) 58 bd
Croisette ☎689168 tx470720
⇔337 🏩 P Lift ♪ sB ⇔655–1160
dB ⇔885–1370 M200 St% Beach sea

★ ★ ★ ★ ★**Majestic** (SRS) 163 bd
Croisette ☎689100 tx470787
rm300 ⇔294 🍴16 🏩 P Lift ♪
sB ⇔466–1305 dB ⇔569–1483 M alc
Pool ♂ sea

★ ★ ★ ★ ★**Martinez-Concorde** 73 bd
Croisette ☎689191 tx470708
Jan–Nov
⇔400 Lift ♪ sB ⇔425–1325
dB ⇔530–1570 Beach sea

★ ★ ★ ★**Grand** 45 bd Croisette
☎381545 tx470727
⇔76 P Lift ♪ sB ⇔410–800
dB ⇔500–910 Beach sea

★ ★ ★ ★**Sofitel Méditerranée** 1 bd J-
Hibert ☎992275 tx470728
Closed Jan
⇔150 🏩 Lift sB ⇔355–485
dB ⇔480–645 Pool sea

★ ★ ★**Embassy** 6 r de Bone ☎387902
tx470081
⇔60 🏩 P Lift sB ⇔230–370
dB ⇔260–410 Beach

★ ★ ★**Frantel Beach** 13 r du Canada
☎382232 tx470034
⇔95 P Lift sB ⇔328–498
dB ⇔353–551 Pool

★ ★ ★**Savoy** 5 r F-Einsey ☎381774
20 Dec–Oct
rm55 ⇔48 Lift ♪ sB ⇔ 🍴280–380
dB ⇔ 🍴362–462

☆ ☆**Campanile** Aérodrome de Cannes-
Mandelieu ☎486941 tx470886
⇔49 P dB ⇔218–222 M55–80

★ ★**France** 85 r d'Antibes (n.rest)
☎392334 tx470673
⇔34 P Lift sB ⇔135–240
dB ⇔150–260

★ ★**Roches Fleuries** 92 r G-Clemenceau
(n.rest) ☎392878
27 Dec–12 Nov
rm24 ⇔8 🍴7 🏩 P Lift sB76–150
dB150–185 dB ⇔ 🍴162–199 sea
mountains

🏵**Carlton et du Canada** r F-Einsey
☎380451 Closed Nov–Dec 15 & Sun All
makes

Carnot Autos 48 bd Carnot ☎682025 Cit

Europa Bretelle Autoroute au Cannet
☎451700 AR

CANNET (LE)
Alpes-Maritimes (☎93)

☆ ☆**Ibis** 87 bd Carnot ☎457976
tx470095
⇔40 P sB ⇔198 dB ⇔260

🏵**Europe** Bretelle Autoroute ☎468646
Closed Sat & Sun Hon RR

France

CAPBRETON
Landes (☎58)

★ ★**Océan** ᴸ av de la Plage ☎721022
Mar–Oct
rm43 ⇔29 🍴8 A20rm P Lift
dB96–180 dB ⇔ 🍴180 sea

CAP D'AGDE See **AGDE**

CAP D'AIL
Alpes-Maritimes (☎93)

★ ★**Cigogne** ᴸ(DPn) r de la Gare
☎782960
Mar–Oct
⇔15 dB ⇔290 sea

★**Miramar** 126 av du 3 Septembre
☎780660
15 Jan–15 Nov
rm27 🍴20 P dB125–170
dB 🍴190–195 sea

CAP D'ANTIBES See **ANTIBES**

CAP FERRAT See **ST-JEAN-CAP-FERRAT**

CAP-MARTIN See **ROQUEBRUNE-CAP-MARTIN**

CAPVERN-LES-BAINS
Hautes-Pyrénées (☎62)

★ ★ ★**Laca** rte de Mauvezin ☎995206
May–15 Oct
rm60 ⇔33 🍴27 P Lift Pool
mountains

CARANTEC
Finistère (☎98)

★**Falaise** Plage du Kelenn ☎670053
Apr–17 Sep
rm26 ⇔13 P sB71–80 sB ⇔86
dB110–137 dB ⇔122 sea

CARCASSONNE
Aude (☎68)

★ ★ ★ ★**Domaine d'Auriac** (DPn) (4km
SE via D104, D42, D342) rte St-Hilaire
☎257222 tx500385
Closed Jan & Sun–Mon pm
⇔23 P Lift ♪ sB ⇔fr250
dB ⇔395 ⚓ Pool mountains

★ ★ ★**Cité** pl St-Nazaire ☎250334
Apr–Oct
rm54 ⇔50 🍴4 🏩 P Lift ♪
mountains

★ ★ ★**Donjon** ᴸ (MAP) 2 r Comte Roger
(n.rest) ☎710880 tx505012
Closed Jan
rm36 ⇔23 🍴13 🏩 P Lift ♪
sB ⇔ 🍴160–240 dB ⇔ 🍴210–260

★ ★ ★**Terminus** (Inter) 2 av Ml-Joffre
(n.rest) ☎252500 tx500198
Closed Nov
rm110 ⇔80 🍴25 🏩 P Lift 🏩
sB ⇔ 🍴78–126 dB ⇔ 🍴104–282

★ ★**Aragon** 15 Montée Cormbéléran
(n.rest) ☎471631
⇔19 P sB ⇔195 dB ⇔180–212

☆ ☆**Croque Sel** rte Narbonne (N113)
☎251415
Closed Feb
⇔11 P

☆ ☆**Ibis** rte de Berriac ☎479835
tx500376
⇔40 P sB170 dB ⇔212

★ ★**Logis de Trencavel** ᴸ (DPn in
season) 286 av du Gl-Leclerc ☎710953
10 Feb–10 Jan
rm12 ⇔3 🍴6 🏩 P ♪ sB100–190
sB ⇔ 🍴190 dB100–225
dB ⇔ 🍴190–225 mountains

★ ★**Montségur** 27 allée d'Iéna (n.rest)
☎253141
Closed 3 wks Xmas
rm21 ⇔6 🍴15 P Lift ♪
sB ⇔ 🍴120–225 dB ⇔ 🍴253

🏵**Laporta** 47 av H-Gout ☎251150
Closed Sat pm & Sun BL

CARENNAC
Lot (☎65)

★**Fenelon** ᴸ (DPN) ☎384716
6 Mar–Jan
rm23 ⇔6 🍴6 P

CARENTAN
Manche (☎33)

★**Auberge Normande** ᴸ (DPn) bd
Verdun ☎420299
Closed 11–24 Oct
rm8 ⇔1 🍴2 P

🏵**J Santini** 7 bd de Verdun ☎420266
Closed Sat Fia Frd

CARHAIX-PLOUGUER
Finistère (☎98)

★ ★**Gradlon** (Inter) 12 bd de la
République ☎931522 tx940933
⇔43 P Lift

CARNAC
Morbihan (☎97)

★ ★**Armoric** 53 av de la Poste ☎521347
20 May–15 Sep
rm27 ⇔5 🍴13 A2rm P ⚓

At CARNAC-PLAGE

★ ★ ★**Novotel Tal-Ar-Mor** av de
l'Atlantique ☎521666 tx950324
3 Jan–18 Nov
⇔106 P Lift sB ⇔298–313
dB ⇔244–259 Pool

★ ★ ★**Celtique** 17 av Kermario
☎521149
Jun–Oct
rm35 ⇔6 🍴17 P

★**Genêts (Pn)** 45 av Kermario ☎521101
Jun–Sep
rm35 ⇔18 🍴6 A4rm P sB95
sB ⇔ 🍴178 dB105–130
dB ⇔ 🍴130–245

CALAIS

CARQUEFOU See **NANTES**

CARQUEIRANNE
Var (☎94)

★★**Plein Sud** av du Gl-de-Gaulle/rte des Salettes (n.rest) ☎585286
15 Dec – 1 Nov
rm17 ⇌6 ▥11 **P** dB ⇌ ▥194

CARTERET See **BARNEVILLE-CARTERET**

CASSIS
Bouches-du-Rhône (☎42)

★★★**Plage (DPn)** pl Bestouan
☎010570
Mar – Oct
rm29 ⇌19 ▥10 Lift ♪
sB ⇌ ▥110 – 237 dB ⇌ ▥169 – 304 sea

CASTELJALOUX
Lot-et-Garonne (☎53)

★**Grand Cadets de Gascogne**🄻 pl Gambetta ☎930059
15 Feb – 15 Oct Closed Mon
rm15 ⇌7 A1rm 🏛 **P** Lift

CASTELLANE
Alpes-de-Hautes-Provence (☎92)

★**Ma Petit Auberge** pl M-Sauvaire
☎836206
Mar – Nov
rm18 ⇌4 ▥11 mountains

CASTELNAUDARY
Aude (☎68)

★★**Palmes** (MAP) 10 r Ml-Foch
☎230310 tx500372
rm20 ⇌10 ▥5 **P** Lift ..

★**Fourcade** 14 r des Carmes ☎230208
rm14 ⇌14 ▥5 sB50 – 150
sB ⇌ ▥150 dB ⇌ ▥90 – 190

CASTELSARRASIN
Tarn-et-Garonne (☎68)

★**Modern** 54 r de l'Egalité (n.rest)
☎323010
rm12 ▥3 🏛 **P** sB41 – 5/ dB41 – 57
dB ▥57

CASTRES
Tarn (☎63)

★★**Grand** (Inter) 11 r de la Libération
☎590030
15 Jan – 15 Dec
rm40 ⇌24 ▥12 🏛 Lift ♪
sB 100 – 170 sB ⇌ ▥145 – 175
dB119 – 199 dB ⇌ ▥204

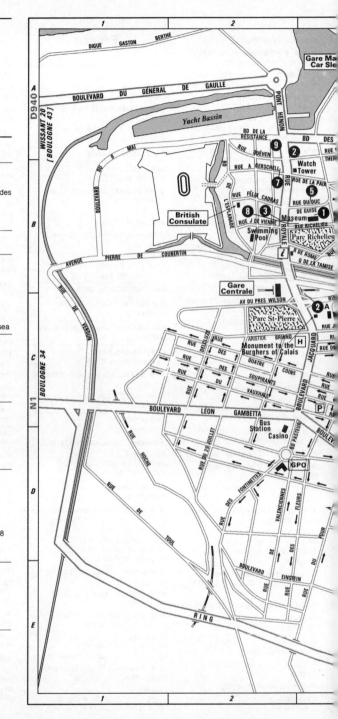

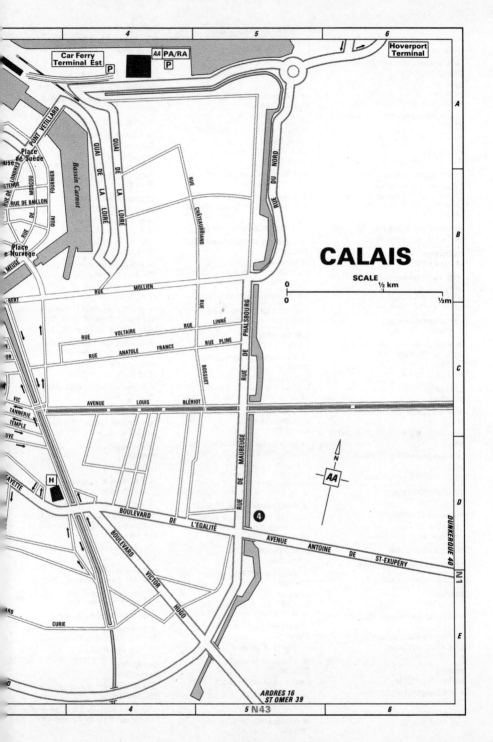

CALAIS

SCALE

½ km

½m

Car Ferry Terminal Est

AA PA/RA

Hoverport Terminal

Place de Suède

Bassin Carnot

PORT VÉTILLARD

RUE DE LONDRES

STENVE

RUE DE MOSCOU

QUAI FOURNIER

RUE DE BAILLON

QUAI DE MEUSE

RUE DE

Place de Norvège

QUAI DE LA LOIRE

RUE DE LA LOIRE

RUE CHÂTEAUBRIAND

RUE DU NORD

RUE MOLLIEN

BERT

RUE

RUE VOLTAIRE

RUE LINNÉ

RUE ANATOLE FRANCE

RUE PLINE

BOSSUET

RUE DE PHALSBOURG

AVENUE LOUIS BLÉRIOT

VIC

TANNERIE

TEMPLE

UVE

RUE DE MAUBEUGE

H

AYETTE

BOULEVARD DE L'EGALITÉ

4

N

AA

BOULEVARD VICTOR HUGO

AVENUE ANTOINE DE ST-EXUPÉRY

DUNKERQUE 40

N1

CURIE

ARD

ARDRES 16
ST OMER 39

N43

CAUDEBEC-EN-CAUX
Seine-Maritime (☎35)

★★★**Marine** 18 quai Guilbaud
☎962011 tx770404

8 Feb–3 Jan
rm34 ⇌15 ▥14 **P** Lift sB115
sB ⇌ ▥235 dB115 dB ⇌ ▥235

★★**Normandie** **L⁺** (DPn) quai Guilbaud
☎962511

rm11 ⇌3 ▥3 **P**

CAUSSADE
Tarn-et-Garonne (☎63)

★★**Dupont** 12 r Recollets ☎930502

Closed Nov & 1st week May
rm31 ⇌8 ▥15 A8rm 🅿 **P** sB76–119
sB ⇌ ▥108–119 dB89–131
dB ⇌ ▥121–131

★★**Larroque** av de la Gare ☎931014

rm25 ⇌17 ▥5 🅿 **P** Pool

CAVAILLON
Vaucluse (☎90)

★★★**Christel** Boscodomini ☎710779
tx431547

⇌109 **P** Lift sB ⇌200–270
dB ⇌220–270 Pool

CAVALAIRE-SUR-MER
Var (☎94)

★★**Bonne Auberge** 400 av des Alliés, rte
Nationale ☎640296

May–Oct
rm31 ⇌3 ▥21 **P**

CAVALIÈRE
Var (☎94)

★★★**Surplage (DPn)** ☎058419
15 May–Sep
rm63 ⇌60 ▥3 **P** Lift ☽ Pool Beach
sea

★★**Cap Nègre (DPn)** ☎058046
Etr–Sep
rm32 ⇌29 ▥3 **P** Lift sea

CELLE-DUNOISE (LA)
Creuse (☎55)

★**Pascaud** **L⁺** ☎891016

Closed Oct
rm10 ▥4 🅿 **P**

CERGY See **PONTOISE**

CESSON-SÉVIGNÉ See **RENNES**

CESTAS See **BORDEAUX**

CHABLIS
Yonne (☎86)

★**Étoile (DPn)** 4 r Moulins ☎421050

Feb–19 Dec
rm15 ⇌3 ▥6 🅿 sB72–87
sB ⇌ ▥120 dB100–140
dB ⇌ ▥134–164

CHAGNY
Saône-et-Loire (☎85)

★★**Lameloise** 36 pl d'Armes
☎870885

Closed 18–26 Jul & 5 Dec–3 Jan
rm25 ⇌17 ▥8 🅿

France

★★**Capucines** **L⁺** (DPn) 30 rte de
Châlon ☎870817

rm18 ⇌8 ▥4 A4rm **P**

★**Paris** 6 r de Beaune ☎870838

10 Feb–10 Dec
rm12 ⇌1 ▥ **P** dB65–85
dB ⇌ ▥65–85

▥**G Guyot** les Creusottes
(N6) ☎872228 Ren

▥**Thevenaut** pl du Creux des
Nazoires ☎871787 Closed Sat & Sun
All makes

At **CHASSEY-LE-CAMP** (6km W)

★★**Auberge du Camp Romain** **L⁺**
☎870991

15 Feb–5 Jan
rm25 ⇌18 ▥6 🅿 **P** sB ⇌ ▥128–220
dB ⇌ ▥102–220 mountains

CHAIGNES See **PACY-SUR-EURE**

**CHAINTRÉ-LA-CHAPELLE-DE-
GUINCHAY** See **MÂCON**

CHAISE DIEU (LA)
Haute-Loire (☎71)

★★**Tremblant** **L⁺** (DPn) (D906)
☎000185

15 Mar–Nov
rm28 ⇌8 ▥9 🅿 **P** sB85–95
sB ⇌165–185 dB100–170 dB ⇌180–200
mountains

CHALLES-LES-EAUX
Savoie (☎79)

★★★**Château de Challes** 247 r de
Château ☎852145

15 May–25 Sep
rm75 ⇌35 ▥6 A55rm 🅿 **P** ☽
sB80–180 sB ⇌ ▥180 dB120–200
dB ⇌ ▥210–240 🏊 Pool mountains

★★**Château de Trivier** ☎850727

rm30 ⇌8 ▥14 A14rm **P** sB68–265
sB ⇌ ▥189–265 dB88–265
dB ⇌ ▥216–265 mountains

CHÂLONS-SUR-MARNE
Marne (☎26)

★★**Angleterre (DPn)** 19 pl Mgr-Tissier
☎682151

15 Mar–15 Feb
rm18 ⇌9 ▥5 **P** ☽ sB117–218
sB ⇌ ▥159–218 dB ⇌ ▥159–229

★★**Bristol** // av P-Sémard (n.rest)
☎682463

rm24 ⇌11 ▥13 🅿 **P**

☆**Ibis** rte de Sedan, Complexe Agricole
☎651665

⇌40 **P** sB ⇌180 dB ⇌223

★★**Mont des Logès** La Veuve ☎673343

rm19 ⇌1 ▥18 **P**

★★**Pasteur** 46 r Pasteur (n.rest)
☎681000

rm28 ⇌11 ▥13 **P** sB59–140
sB ⇌ ▥83–140 dB ⇌ ▥100–145

▥**Raige** 17 r C-Jacquiert
☎681431 Closed Sun

At **COURTISOLS** (10.5km NE off N3)

▥**Montel** 63 rte Nationale ☎696004 M/c
Ren

At **ÉPINE (L')** (8.5km E on N3)

★★**Armes de Champagne** (N3)
☎681043

15 Feb–10 Jan
rm37 ⇌9 ▥16 A12rm 🅿 **P** ☽
sB120–241 sB ⇌ ▥241 dB139–255
dB ⇌ ▥255

CHALON-SUR-SAÔNE
Saône-et-Loire (☎85)

☆☆☆**Mercure** Centre Commercial de la
Thalie, av de l'Europe ☎465189 tx800132
⇌85 **P** Lift sB ⇌228–248
dB ⇌285–306 Pool

★★★**Royal** (MAP) 8 r du Port Villiers
☎481586 tx801510

rm50 ⇌35 ▥15 Lift ☽ sB ⇌ ▥250
dB ⇌ ▥310–350

★★★**St-Georges et Terminus** (Inter) 32
av J-Jaurès ☎482705 tx800330

rm48 ⇌14 ▥34 🅿 **P** Lift ☽

★★★**St-Régis** (MAP) 22 bd de la
République ☎480728 tx801624

rm40 ⇌20 ▥15 🅿 **P** Lift ☽
sB ⇌ ▥170 dB ⇌ ▥315

☆☆**Ibis** Carrefour des Moirots (n.rest)
☎466462 tx800132

⇌41 **P** sB ⇌173 dB ⇌227

★★**Rotonde** (n.rest) ☎483593

rm32 ▥10 🅿 **P**

★★**St-Jean** 24 quai Gambetta (n.rest)
☎484565

rm25 ⇌18

★★**St-Rémy** **L⁺** pl Pont Paron, St-Rémy
(n.rest) ☎483804 tx800175

rm40 ⇌16 ▥22 **P**

▥**Bourgogne Véhicules Industriels** (N6
Lux-Chalon Sud) ☎488857 Closed
Sun MB

▥**Duval** 10 rte de Lyon ☎487663 Closed
Sun Fia

Moderne r des P-d'Orient
☎465212 Closed Sat & Sun Cit

▥**Soreva** 4 av J-F.Kennedy
☎464945 Closed Sun Frd

At **CHAMPFORGEUIL** (4km NW)

☆☆**Climat de France** ZAC des Blettrys
☎(6)4460123 tx692844

⇌42 dB ⇌211–266

CHAMBÉRY
Savoie (☎79)

★★★★**Grand** 6 pl de la Gare
☎695454 tx320910

rm55 ⇌40 ▥15 🅿 Lift ☽ sB ⇌ ▥
216–366 dB ⇌ ▥272–492 M90–190

★ ★ ★**France** 22 fbg Reclus (n.rest)
☎335118 tx320410

rm48 ⮂42 ▥6 🏧 🌙
sB ⮂ ▥160–200 dB ⮂ ▥215–400
mountains

☆ ☆ ☆**Novotel** Le Cheminet ☎692127
tx320446

⮂103 **P** Lift sB ⮂251–267
dB ⮂283–299 **M** alc Pool mountains

★ ★ ★**Touring** 12 r Sommeiller (n.rest)
☎623726

rm43 ⮂12 ▥18 🏧 Lift 🌙 sB90–165
sB ⮂ ▥140–165 dB105–207
dB ⮂ ▥155–207

⮂**Gare** 29 av de la Baisse ☎623637
M/c Closed Sat & Sun Fia

At **CHAMNORD**

☆ ☆**Ibis Chambéry** av E-Ducretet
☎692836 tx320457

⮂89 **P** Lift sB ⮂165 dB ⮂220

CHAMBON (LAC)
Puy-de-Dôme(☎73)

★ ★**Bellevue** 🅻 **(DPn)** ☎886106

Apr–Sep
rm25 ⮂11 ▥11 A8rm Lift
dB ⮂ ▥133–243 mountains lake

★ ★**Grillon** 🅻 **(DPn)** ☎886066

Apr–Sep
rm20 ⮂5 ▥4 **P** dB60–140
dB ⮂ ▥60–140 lake mountains

CHAMBON-SUR-VOUEIZE
Creuse(☎55)

★ ★**Etonneries** 🅻 **(DPn)** 41 av G-
Clemenceau ☎821466

rm10 ⮂2 ▥4 **P** sBfr60 dB130–214
dB ⮂ ▥130–214 mountains

CHAMBORD
Loir-et-Cher(☎54)

★ ★**St-Michel** 🅻 **(DPn)** Face au
Château ☎203131

rm38 ⮂27 ▥3 🏧 **P** dB90–250
dB ⮂ ▥140–260 ⮰

CHAMBOURCY See **ST-GERMAIN-EN-
LAYE**

CHAMBRAY-LES-TOURS See **TOURS**

CHAMNORD See **CHAMBÉRY**

CHAMONIX-MONT-BLANC
Haute-Savoie(☎50)

★ ★ ★ ★**Croix Blanche** 7 r Vallot
☎530011 tx385614

Closed Jan
rm36 ⮂26 ▥10 **P** Lift
sB ⮂ ▥130–170 dB ⮂ ▥180–240
mountains

★ ★ ★**Mont Blanc (DPn)** pl d'Église
☎530564 tx385614

15 Dec–Oct
⮂51 🏧 **P** Lift 🌙 sB ⮂190–240
dB ⮂280–350 M110 ⮰ Pool
mountains

★ ★ ★**Richemond** 228 r Dr-Paccard
☎530885 tx385417

France

17 Dec–16 Apr & 16 Jun–16 Sep
rm54 ⮂36 **P** Lift 🌙 sB100 sB ⮂190
dB165 dB ⮂275 M65 mountains

★ ★ ★**Sapinière-Montana** (**DPn** in
season) 102 r Mummery ☎530763
tx385022

Dec–Sep
rm34 ⮂29 ▥1 A6rm 🏧 Lift 🌙
dB ⮂220–340 mountains

At **BOSSONS (LES)** (3.5km S)

★ ★**Aiguille du Midi** 🅻 **(DPn)** ☎530065

Xmas, Feb, Etr & May–Sep
rm50 ⮂35 ▥4 A15rm **P** Lift sB120
sB ⮂ ▥160 dB156 dB ⮂ ▥216 ⮰
Pool mountains

CHAMPAGNOLE
Jura(☎84)

★ ★ ★**Ripotot** 54 r Ml-Foch ☎521545

Apr–15 Oct
rm60 ⮂35 🏧 **P** Lift sB93–145
sB ⮂163–168 dB126–170 dB ⮂196–226
⮰

CHAMPFORGEUIL See **CHALON-
SUR-SAÔNE**

CHAMPILLON See **ÉPERNAY**

CHAMPNIERS See **ANGOULÊME**

CHAMPS-SUR-MARNE
Seine-et-Marne(☎6)

At **ÉMERAINVILLE**

☆ ☆**Climat de France** Le Pavé Neuf
(CD51) ☎0063834 tx612241

⮂38 **P** dB ⮂209–236 M54–74

CHAMPTOCEAUX
Marne-et-Loire(☎40)

★ ★**Côte** 🅻 **(DPn)** 2 r du Dr-Giffard
☎835039 tx711592

rm28 ⮂12 ▥7 🏧 **P** dB73–154
dB ⮂ ▥154

CHANAS See **ROUSSILLON**

CHANTILLY
Oise(☎4)

☆ ☆**Campanile** rte de Creil (N16)
☎4573924 tx610016

⮂50 **P** dB ⮂206–209 M55–80

★**Petit Vatel** ☎4570166

Closed 2 wks Xmas
rm13 ▥3

SADELL (M Livache) 33 av due Ml-Joffre
☎4570509

Closed Sat pm & Sun Opl

At **LAMORLAYE** (5km S)

★ ★**Hostellerie du Lys** 7th Avenue
☎4212619 tx150298

rm35 ⮂25 ▥10 **P** dB ⮂ ▥270

CHANTONNAY
Vendée(☎51)

★ ★**Moulin Neuf** 🅻 ☎943027

rm49 ⮂23 ▥23 A19rm **P**
sB ⮂ ▥128–148 dB ⮂ ▥268–368
M40–150 ⮰ ♂ lake

★**Mouton** 🅻 **(DPn)** 31 r Nationale
☎943022

Closed 2 Oct–9 Nov & Mon in Aug
rm12 ⮂2 ▥3 🏧 **P** sB82–135
sB ⮂ ▥122–150 dB94–165
dB ⮂ ▥134–200 St%

CHAPELLE-EN-VERCORS (LA)
Drôme(☎75)

★**Bellier** ☎482003

10 Jun–25 Sep
rm12 ⮂8 ▥1 A2rm **P** sB45
sB ⮂ ▥65 dB ⮂ ▥100–230 mountains

CHAPELLE-SAINT-MESMIN (LA)
Loiret(☎38)

☆ ☆**Fimotel** 7 r d'Aquitaine ☎437144

⮂42 **P** Lift sB ⮂193 dB ⮂221 M49–75

CHARAVINES
Isère(☎76)

★ ★**Hostellerie Lac Bleu** 🅻 **(DPn)**
(1.5km N on D50) ☎066048

Mar–Oct
rm15 ⮂2 ▥8 **P** sB96 sB ⮂ ▥141
dB137–180 dB ⮂ ▥157–212 Beach
mountains lake

CHARBONNIÈRES-LES-BAINS See **LYON**

CHARLES DE GAULLE AIRPORT See
PARIS AIRPORTS

CHARLEVILLE-MÉZIÈRES
Ardennes(☎24)

At **VILLERS-SEMEUSE** (5km E)

☆ ☆ ☆**Mercure** r L-Michel ☎570529
tx840076

⮂67 **P** sB ⮂234–269 dB ⮂268–298 M
alc Pool

CHARMES
Vosges(☎29)

★**Central** 🅻 **(DPn)** 4 r des Capucins
☎380240

Closed Oct
rm11 ⮂2 ▥7 🏧 **P** sB80–170
sB ⮂ ▥90–170 dB ⮂ ▥190–170

CHARMOY
Yonne(☎86)

★**Relais de Charmoy (DPn)** 2 rte de
Paris ☎732319

rm9 ⮂2 ▥3 **P**

CHAROLLES
Saône-et-Loire(☎85)

★**Moderne** 🅻 10 av de la Gare
☎240702

Feb–24 Dec
rm18 ⮂14 ▥3 A7rm 🏧. **P** dB85–250
dB ⮂ ▥85–250 Pool mountains

CHARTRES
Eure-et-Loir(☎37)

★ ★ ★**Grand Monarque** (MAP) 22 pl des
Epars ☎210072 tx760777 →

135

Closed Feb
rm42 ⊷34 ▥4 ▦ P ☾ sB210–265
sB ⇌ ▥290 dB255–325 dB ⇌ ▥357

☆ ☆ ☆Novotel av M-Proust, le Madeleire
☎348030 tx781298
⊷78 P Lift sB ⊷255–273
dB ⊷295–313 Pool

★ ★Capitainerie 5 av M-Proust
☎359111
▥48 P ☾ sB ▥126–146
dB ▥157–177 M42–72

★ ★Poste 3 r du Gl-König ☎210427
rm60 ⊷38 ▥13 ▦ P Lift ☾
sB90–123 sB ⇌ ▥138–174 dB108–180
dB ⇌ ▥211–222

★Ouest 3 pl Sémard (n.rest) ☎214327
rm26 ▥18 sB70–125 sB ▥125 dB130
dB ▥150

⅃OGARD 28 55 r des V-Capucins
☎219439 All makes

At LUCÉ (3km SW on N23)
⅃OChartres Auto Sport rte d'Illiers
☎352479 Closed Mon BL

CHARTRE-SUR-LE-LOIR (LA)
Sarthe(☎43)
★ ★France ᴸᴱ (DPn) 20 pl de la
République ☎444016
15 Dec–15 Nov
rm32 ⊷11 ▥16 A14rm ▦ P dB100
dB ⊷100–150

CHASSENEUIL-DU-POITOU See
POITIERS

CHASSE-SUR-RHÔNE
Isère(☎7)
☆ ☆ ☆Mercure Lyon Sud CD4-Les
Roues ☎8731394 tx300625
⊷115 P Lift sB ⊷219–229
dB ⊷265–282

CHASSEY-LE-CAMP See CHAGNY

CHÂTEAU-ARNOUX
Alpes-de-Hautes-Provence(☎92)
★ ★ ★Bonne Étape (DPn) (N85)
☎640009 tx430605
15 Feb–3 Jan
⊷18 ▦ P dB ⊷282–492 Pool
mountains lake

CHÂTEAUBOURG
Ille-et-Vilaine(☎99)
★ ★ ★Ar Milin (FAH) ☎003091
tx740083
15 Jan–15 Dec
rm33 ⊷23 ▥10 A20rm P Lift
sB ⇌ ▥223–243 dB ⇌ ▥200–286
M110 ⅃

CHÂTEAUBRIANT
Loire-Atlantique(☎40)
★ ★ ★Hostellerie de la Ferrière (FAH)
rte de Nantes ☎280028
rm25 ⊷24 A14rm P dB165 dB ⊷235
★Armor 19 pl Motte (n.rest) ☎811119
rm20 ⊷6 ▥7 P Lift sB53 sB ⇌ ▥65
dB89 dB ⇌ ▥113

France

CHÂTEAU-CHINON
Nièvre(☎86)
★ ★Vieux Morvan ᴸᴱ (DPn) pl Ancienne
Mairie ☎850501
10 Jan–15 Nov
rm23 ▥11 mountains

CHÂTEAU D'OLONNE See SABLES
D'OLONNE (LES)

CHÂTEAUDUN
Eure-et-Loir(☎37)
★ ★Armorial 59 r Gambetta ☎451957
rm15 ⊷4 ▥5 ▦ sB65–75
sB ⇌ ▥110–145 dB ⇌ ▥105–145

★ ★Beauce 50 r de Jallans (n.rest)
☎451475
rm24 ⊷16 ▦ P dB75 dB ⊷170

★Rose ᴸᴱ (DPn) 12 r L-Licors ☎452183
rm8 ⊷7 ▦ dB77–105 dB ⊷118

★Trois Pastoureaux 31 r A-Gillet
☎450162
15 Feb–15 Jan
rm10 ⊷1 ▥1 ▦ P sB77–111
sB ⇌ ▥91–11 dB154–222
dB ⇌ ▥182–222 M45–92

CHÂTEAU-FARINE See BESANÇON

CHÂTEAU-GONTIER
Mayenne(☎43)
★ ★Mirwault (DPn) ☎071317
rm10 ▥4 P sB91–111 dB ▥152

CHÂTEAUNEAUF (Côte-d'Or) See
POUILLY-EN-AUXOIS

CHÂTEAUNEUF-DE-GRASSE
Alpes-Maritimes(☎93)
☆ ☆Campanile Le Pré du Lac ☎425555
⊷42 P sB ⊷162 mountains

CHÂTEAUNEUF-SUR-LOIRE
Loiret (☎38)
★Nouvel du Loiretᴸᴱ (DPn) 4 pl A-Briand
☎584228
20Jan–20 Dec
rm20 ⊷4 ▥7 ▦ P

CHÂTEAUROUX
Indre (☎54)
★ ★ ★France 16 r V-Hugo ☎270080
tx751676
rm43 ⊷20 ▥20 P Lift ☾
★Central 19 av de la Gare (n.rest)
☎220100
Closed Xmas
rm11 ▥3 sB65–72 sB ▥75–82
dB69–77 dB ▥89–97
⅃OAubert & Chatein 24 r des Fontaines
☎3242672 Closed Sun Ren

CHÂTEAU-THIERRY
Aisne (☎23)

★ ★Ile de France (Inter) (3km N on N37)
☎691012 tx150666
rm56 ⊷31 ▥16 P Lift sB86
sB ⇌ ▥180 dB138–200
dB ⇌ ▥214–252 St15%

☆Girafe pl A-Briand (n.rest) ☎830206
rm30 ⊷3 ▥9 ▦ P sB72–114
sB ⇌ ▥112–114 db104–158
dB ⇌ ▥124–158

⅃OSA Aisne Auto 8 av de Montmirail
☎832380 Closed Sat pm & Sun Cit

⅃OVerdel 18 av d'Essonnes ☎832025
Closed Sat pm, Sun & Mon am Peu

At NOGENTEL (3.5km S on D15)
⅃OTourisport Carrefour Luxembourg
☎811128 Closed Sat pm & Mon am BL

CHÂTEL
Haute-Savoie (☎50)
★ ★Stella (DPn) ☎732325 tx385856
15 Dec–2 May & Jun–Sep
rm35 ⊷25 ▥10 ▦ P

CHÂTELAILLON-PLAGE
Charente-Maritime (☎46)
★ ★Grand 13 av Gl-Leclerc ☎562097
May–15 Oct
rm27 ⊷14 ▥8 P

★ ★Hostellerie Select 1 r G-Musset
☎562431
rm21 ⊷16 ▥2 P

★Majesticᴸᴱ pl de St-Marsault ☎562053
10 Jan–20 Dec
rm30 ⊷10 ▥17 ▦ sB90–125
sB ⇌ ▥145 dB105–180 dB ⇌ ▥180
M65–90

CHÂTELGUYON
Puy-de-Dôme (☎73)
★ ★ ★International r A-Punnet
☎860672
5 May–Sep
rm68 ⊷45 ▥11 lift ☾

★ ★ ★Splendid (MAP) 5–7 r
d'Angleterre ☎860480 tx990585
25 Apr–20 Oct
rm94 ⊷72 ▥12 P Lift ☾ sB236–282
sB ⇌ ▥236–282 dB386–430
dB ⇌ ▥386–473 ⅃ Pool mountains

CHÂTELLERAULT
Vienne (☎49)
★ ★ ★Moderne (MAP) (DPn) 74 bd
Blossac ☎213011 tx791801
rm39 ⊷9 ▥29 ▦ P Lift ☾
sB145–375 sB ⇌ ▥205–375 dB410–750
dB ⊷410–750 M50–150

★ ★Croissant 19 av J-F-Kennedy
☎210177
2 Jan–15 Dec
rm20 ⊷9 ▥2 P

☆ ☆Ibis av Camille Plage, quartier de la
Forêt ☎217577 tx791488
⊷72 P Lift sB ⊷173 dB ⊷214

★ ★Univers 4 av G-Clemenceau
☎212353 tx791344

15 Jan–20 Dec
rm30 ⇌6 ⋔18 🏛 Lift sB70–95
sB ⇌ ⋔135–170 dB115 dB ⇌ ⋔190

🍴Rousseau 91 av L-Ripault ☎210613
Closed Aug 15–Sep 9, 1 wk Feb & Sat pm
Pau

CHÂTILLON-EN-BAZOIS
Nièvre (☎86)

★Poste 🆑 (DPn) Grande Rue ☎841468
25 Jan–20 Dec
rm11 ⋔3 🏛 P dB84–112
dB ⋔135–139

CHÂTILLON-SUR-INDRE
Indre (☎54)

★Auberge de la Tour 🆑 (DPn) ☎387217
rm11 ⇌1 ⋔2 🏛 P sB89–94
sB ⇌ ⋔106–139 dB103–115
dB ⇌ ⋔120–188

CHÂTILLON-SUR-SEINE
Côte-d'Or (☎80)

★ ★Côte d'Or (DPn) r C-Ronot ☎911329
15 Jan–15 Dec
rm11 ⇌7 ⋔2 🏛 P sB146–266
sB ⇌ ⋔176–276 dB172–280
dB ⇌ ⋔202–337

★ ★Sylvia 9 av de la Gare (n.rest)
☎910244
rm21 ⇌7 ⋔7 A8rm 🏛 P sB70–157
sB ⇌ ⋔108–157 dB123–157
dB ⇌ ⋔152–175

★Jura 19 r Dr-Robert (n.rest) ☎912696
Closed Jan
rm10 ⇌1 ⋔3 P sB70–100 dB90–120
dB ⇌ ⋔90–150

🍴Berthier rte de Troyes ☎910560
Closed Sat pm & Sun Peu

CHATTANCOURT See VERDUN

CHAUMONT
Haute-Marne (☎25)

★ ★ ★Terminus Reine (MAP) pl de la
Gare ☎0366666 tx840920
rm70 ⇌40 ⋔20 🏛 P Lift 🌙
sB180–220 sB ⇌ ⋔180–300
dB270–320 dB ⇌ ⋔270–320

☆ ☆Étoile d'Or rte de Langres ☎030223
rm16 ⇌3 ⋔7 A4rm 🏛 P sB95
sB ⇌ ⋔135 dB ⇌ ⋔140–170
M50–100 & alc

★ ★Grand Val (Inter) (DPn in season) rte
de Langres (N19) ☎039035
rm64 ⇌6 ⋔26 🏛 P Lift

★France 25 r Toupot de Beveaux
☎030111
rm40 ⇌20 A5rm 🏛 P

🍴François rte de Langres ☎030888 M/c
Closed Sat pm & Sun Chy RT

CHAUMONT-SUR-LOIRE
Loir-et-Cher (☎54)

★ ★ ★Château 🆑 (DPn) ☎469804
15 Mar–15 Nov
⇌20 🏛 P dB ⇌205 Pool

CHAUSSÉE-ST-VICTOR See BLOIS

France

CHAUVIGNY
Vienne (☎49)

★Lion d'Or 🆑 8 r Marché ☎463028
rm27 ⇌16 ⋔5 A16m P
sB ⇌ ⋔95–190 dB ⇌ ⋔142–190
dB ⇌ ⋔80–150 M50–100 & alc

CHAVAGNÉ See CRÈCHE (LA)

CHÊNEHUTTE-LES-TUFFEAUX See SAUMUR

CHENONCEAUX
Indre-et-Loire (☎47)

★ ★Bon Laboureur et Château (DPn)
(N75) ☎299002
Apr–early Nov
rm26 ⇌17 ⋔3 🏛 P

★Roy 9 r Dr-Brenneau ☎299017
Feb–Nov
rm36 ⇌12 ⋔6 A6rm P sB63–70
dB82–111 dB ⇌ ⋔152–164

CHERBOURG
Manche (☎33)
See Plan page 138
AA agent; see page 105

☆ ☆ ☆Mercure Gare Maritime
☎440111 tx170613 Plan 1
rm79 ⇌52 ⋔27 🏛 P Lift
sB ⇌ ⋔266–385 dB ⇌ ⋔318–437 sea

★ ★Beauséjour 26 r Grande Vallée
(n.rest) ☎531030 Plan 1A
rm27 ⇌18 🏛 sB59–170 sB ⇌170
dB82–170 dB ⇌169–225

★ ★France 41 r MI-Foch ☎531024
tx170164 Plan 2
8 Jan–20 Dec
rm50 ⇌5 ⋔25 Lift dB89 dB ⇌ ⋔180

★ ★Louvre 28 r de la Paix (n.rest)
☎530228 Plan 3
rm42 ⇌9 ⋔20 🏛 Lift sB183–210
dB ⇌ ⋔83–210

★Rennaissance 4 r de l'Église (n.rest)
☎432390 Plan 4
rm12 ⋔10 P dB103–188
dB ⋔123–188 sea

★Torgistorps 14 pl de la République
(n.rest) ☎433232 Plan 5
rm14 ⇌8 ⋔4 sea

🍴Rond Point 6 av A-Briand ☎536924
Closed Sat pm & Sun BL

At GLACERIE (LA) (6km SE via N13)

☆ ☆Campanile r Montmartre
☎(1)7571111 Plan 2A
⇌43 dB ⇌218–222

CHILLY-MAZARIN See PARIS

CHINON
Indre-et-Loire (☎47)

★Boule d'Or 🆑 66 quai J-d'Arc ☎930313

Feb–Nov
rm19 ⇌2 ⋔7 Mfr55 DPnfr160

★Gargantua (DPn) 73 r Voltaire
☎930471
15 Mar–15 Nov
rm13 ⇌6 ⋔3 A3rm 🏛 P dB120–190
dB ⇌ ⋔180–234 St15%

At MARCAY (7km S on D116)

★ ★ ★Château de Marcay ☎930347
tx751475
Mar–Jan
rm26 ⇌16 ⋔10 11rm P Lift 🌙
sB ⇌ ⋔300–700 dB ⇌ ⋔336–800 🏊
Pool

CHITENAY
Loir-et-Cher (☎54)

★Clé des Champs 🆑 (DPn) rte de
Fougères ☎442203
Feb–Dec
rm10 ⇌1 ⋔2 P sB72–120 dB94–120
dB ⇌ ⋔120 M95–125

CHOLET
Maine-et-Loire (☎41)

★ ★ ★Fimotel (previously Chotel) av
Sables d'Olonne (2km S) ☎624545
⇌42 🏛 P Lift 🌙 sB ⇌179–199
dB ⇌227 M50–80

☆ ☆Campanile Parc de Carteron, sq de
la Nouvelle France ☎(1)7571111
⇌42 P dB ⇌218–222

CHONAS-L'AMBALLAN See VIENNE

CIBOURNE See ST-JEAN-DE-LUZ

CIOTAT (LA)
Bouches-du-Rhône (☎42)

★ ★ ★Rose Thé 4 bd Beau Rivage
(n.rest) ☎830923
Apr–20 Oct
rm21 ⇌6 ⋔8 🏛 P 🌙 sB95–105
sB ⇌ ⋔175–205 dB105–115
dB ⇌ ⋔175–220 sea

★ ★Rotonde 44 bd de la République
(n.rest) ☎086750
rm28 ⇌3 ⋔24 P Lift 🌙 dB120
dB ⇌ ⋔140

Coussy quartier St-Estève ☎831809

CIVRIEUX-D'AZERGUES
Rhône (☎7)

★ ★Roserale 🆑 ☎8430178
rm12 ⇌6 ⋔3 🏛 sB81–162
sB ⇌ ⋔107–162 dB93–174
dB ⇌ ⋔119–174

CLAIX See GRENOBLE

CLÉCY
Calvados (☎31)

★ ★Site Normand 🆑 (DPn) ☎697105
16 Mar–15 Nov
rm14 ⇌5 P dB100–178 dB ⇌139–184
mountains

CLELLES
Isère (☎76)

★ ★Ferrat (DPn) ☎344270 →

137

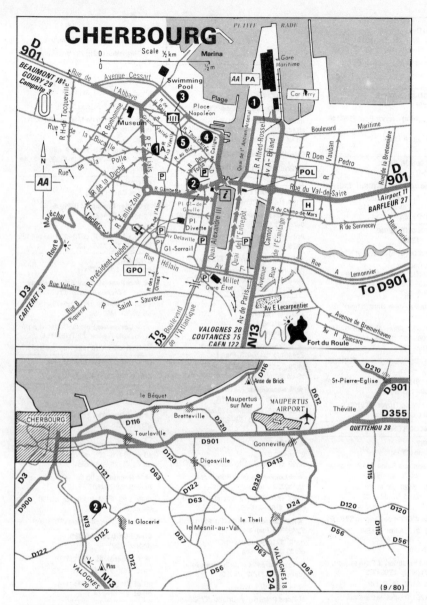

CHERBOURG

1	☆☆☆Mercure
1A	★★Beauséjour
2	★★France
2A	☆☆Campanile
	(At La Glacerie)
3	★★Louvre
4	★Renaissance
5	★Torgistorps

Mar–Nov
rm16 ⇌5 ▥2 🏠 **P** sB94 dB150–200
dB ⇌ ▥158–200 mountains

☆Trieves (N75) ☎344035 Ren

CLÉON See ELBEUF

CLERMONT-FERRAND
Puy-de-Dôme (☎73)

★★★★**Frantel** 82 bd Gergovia
☎930575 tx392658
⇌124 🏠 **P** Lift sB ⇌326 dB ⇌392

★★★**Colbert** (MAP) 19 r Colbert (n.rest)
☎932566 tx990125
rm65 ⇌17 ▥36 **P** Lift ♪ sB250
sB ⇌ ▥250 dB320 dB ⇌ ▥320
mountains

★★★**Gallieni** 51 r Bonnabaud
☎935969 tx392779
rm80 ⇌50 ▥30 **P** Lift mountains

★★★**PLM Arverne** 16 pl Delille
☎919206 tx392741

rm57 ⇆47 🍴10 🛗 P Lift
sB ⇆ 🍴245–288 dB ⇆ 🍴356 M100
mountains

☆ ☆**Campanile** r C-Guichard
☎(77)918891 tx394166
⇆43 P dB ⇆206–209

★★**Minimes** (Inter) 10 r des Minimes
(n.rest) ☎933149
rm28 ⇆13 🌙 sB ⇆ 🍴82–124
dB ⇆ 🍴82–147 mountains

★**Foch** 22 r Ml-Foch (n.rest) ☎934840
rm19 ⇆5 🍴7 sB64 ⇆ 🍴79
dB86–90 dB ⇆ 🍴96

★**Ravel** (FAH) 8 r de Maringues (n.rest)
☎915133 tx392853
rm20 ⇆3 🍴8 dB118 dB ⇆ 🍴148

🅿**Auvergne Auto** 4 r B-Palissy, Zi du
Brézet ☎917656 Closed Sat & Sun. Opl
Vau

At **AULNAT AÉROPORT** (5km E)
☆ ☆**Climat de France** ☎4460123
tx692844
⇆42 dB ⇆206–221

CLISSON
Loire-Atlantique (☎40)

★**Auberge de la Cascade** Gervaux
☎780241
rm10 ⇆4 lake

CLOYES-SUR-LE-LOIR
Eure-et-Loir (☎37)

★★**St-Jacques** (FAH) 35 r Nationale
☎984008
1 Feb–15 Nov
rm20 ⇆10 🍴8 P dB137–177
dB ⇆ 🍴167–259 M80–165

★**St-Georges** 13 r du Temple
☎985436
rm11 ⇆1 🍴6 P dB65–125
dB ⇆ 🍴65–125

CLUNY
Saône-et-Loire (☎85)

★★**Bourgogne** pl de l'Abbaye ☎590058
Mar–Nov (Closed Wed, Thu pm)
rm18 ⇆10 🍴4 🛗 P sB120–220
sB ⇆ 🍴250 dB120–220
dB ⇆ 🍴195–260

★★**Moderne** (DPn) Pont de l'Étang
☎590565
Apr–Nov
rm16 ⇆7 🍴2 🛗 P sB85–180
sB ⇆ 🍴200 dB85–180 dB ⇆ 🍴200

★**Abbaye** (DPn) av de la Gare
☎591114
5 Feb–1 Dec
rm18 ⇆5 🍴4 🛗 P 🌙 sB68–160
sB ⇆ 🍴111–160 dB96–160
dB ⇆ 🍴124–160 mountains

COGNAC
Charente (☎45)

★★**Auberge** 13 r Plumejeau ☎320870
rm26 ⇆8 🍴13

France

★★**Moderne** 24 r E-Mousnier, pl de la
S-Préfecture ☎821953
Feb–12 Dec
⇆26 P Lift

At **ST-LAURENT-DE-COGNAC** (6km W)
★★**Logis de Beaulieu** (DPn) (N141)
☎823050 tx791020
Jan–15 Dec
rm21 ⇆15 🍴2 🛗 P 🌙 dB90–350
dB ⇆ 🍴350

COGOLIN
Var (☎94)

🅿**Finet** quartier Font-Mourier ☎560412
Closed Dec & Sun Frd

COL DE CUREBOURSE See **VIC-SUR-CÈRE**

COLLIOURE
Pyrénées-Orientales (☎68)

★★**Madeloc** (Inter) r R-Rolland (n.rest)
☎820756
May–15 Oct
rm21 ⇆9 🍴12 P mountains

COLLONGES-LA-ROUGE
Corrèze (☎55)

★**Relais St-Jacques de Compostelle**
☎254102
rm12 ⇆5 🍴2 PsB65 dB75–90
dB ⇆ 🍴130–160

COLMAR
Haut-Rhin (☎89)

★★★**Champs de Mars** (ETAP) 2 av de la
Marne (n.rest) ☎41545 tx880928
⇆75 🛗 P Lift sB ⇆210 dB ⇆245

☆ ☆ ☆**Novotel** 49 rte de Strasbourg
☎414914 tx880915
⇆66 P sB ⇆247–262 dB ⇆298–308
pool

★★★**Terminus Bristol** (MAP) 7 pl de la
Gare ☎235959 tx880248
rm85 ⇆45 🍴20 P Lift 🌙 sB230
sB ⇆ 🍴250 dB351 dB ⇆ 🍴400

☆ ☆**Campanile** r des Frères Lumière, ZI
Nord ☎241818 tx880911
⇆42 P dB ⇆206–209 M55–80

★★**Turenne** 10 rte Bâle (n.rest)
☎411226
rm72 ⇆30 🍴40 🛗 P Lift 🌙

At **AMMERSCHWIHR** (7km NW)
★★**Arbre Vert** r des Cigognes
☎471223
Apr–Feb
rm3 ⇆10 M55–190 DPn130–170

At **KAYSERSBERG** (1km NW)
★★**Remparts** r de la Flieh (n.rest)
☎471212

⇆29 A6rm 🛗 P sB ⇆140–160
dB ⇆209–244

COLOMBEY-LES-DEUX-ÉGLISES
Haute-Marne (☎25)

★★★**Dhuits** (MAP) N19 ☎015010
tx840920
⇆30 🛗 P sB ⇆180 dB ⇆250 St15%

COLOMBIER See **FRÉJUS**

COMBEAUFONTAINE
Haute-Saône (☎84)

★**Balcon** rte de Paris ☎786234
rm26 ⇆11 🍴6 🛗 P
sB ⇆ 🍴115–155 dB ⇆ 🍴140–200

COMBOURG
Ille-et-Vilaine (☎99)

★**Château et Voyageurs** (FAH) (DPn)
1 pl Châteaubriand ☎730038 tx740802
rm33 ⇆18 🍴9 A9rm P
dB137–272 dB ⇆ 🍴159–288 lake

COMBRONDE
Puy-de-Dôme (☎73)

★**Family** ☎971001
15 Nov–15 Oct
rm18 🍴4 P

COMMERCY
Meuse (☎29)

★★**Stanislas** 13 r R-Grosdidier
☎911236
⇆32 A5rm Lift sB 🍴129 dB ⇆137–153

COMPIÈGNE
Oise (☎4)

☆ ☆**Campanile** av de Huy ☎4204235
tx610016
⇆43 P dB ⇆218–222 M55–80

★★**Harlay** 3 r Harlay (n.rest) ☎4230150
rm20 ⇆16 🍴4 P Lift sB ⇆ 🍴160
dB ⇆ 🍴210–230

☆ ☆**Ibis** 18 r E-Branly, quartier de
l'Université ☎4231627 tx145991
⇆40 P sB ⇆181–194 dB ⇆222–235
M70

Sova Autos 23 r du Bataillon de France
☎4403307 Closed Sat pm & Sun BL Toy
Vlo

Thiry Centre C-de-Venette ☎4400992
Closed Sat pm & Sun Aud VW

At **MARGNY** (2km W on D935)
🅿**Sari Depan'Nord** 2 r d'a-Lorraine
☎4402442 All makes

CONCARNEAU
Finistère (☎98)

★★**Grand** 1 av P-Guéguen (n.rest)
☎970028
Etr–Oct
rm33 ⇆9 🍴12 🌙 dB ⇆ 🍴220 sea

★**Sables Blancs** Plage des Sables
☎970139
Mar–Nov
rm48 ⇆8 🍴35 sB ⇆ 🍴155–240
dB ⇆ 🍴170-240 sea

France

CONDOM
Gers (☎62)

⏰C **Durrieu** 20 bd St-Jacques ☎280053
Closed Sat pm, Sun & Mon am Tal

CONDRIEU
Rhône (☎72)

★ ★ ★**Beau Rivage (DPn)** quai St-
Abdon ☎595224

15 Feb–1 Jan
rm24 ⇌20 ⬛4 A16rm ⬛ **P**
sB ⇌ ⬛270 dB ⇌ ⬛300–330

CONFOLENS
Charente (☎45)

★**Auberge Belle Étoile** ⚹ **(DPn)** 151 bis
rte Angoulême ☎840235
Closed 1–25 Oct, 1 week Feb & Thu
Oct–Jun
rm14 ⇌5 ⬛1 ⬛ **P** dB85–148
dB ⇌ ⬛148

CONQUES
Aveyron (☎65)

★**Ste-Foy** ☎698403
Apr–15 Sep
rm20 ⇌12 ⬛8 ⬛ **P**
sB ⇌ ⬛100–180 dB ⇌ ⬛140–280

CONTAMINE-SUR-ARVE See
BONNEVILLE

CONTRES
Loir-et-Cher (☎54)

★ ★**France** ⚹ 33 r P-H-Mauger
☎795014

8 Mar–Jan
rm44 ⇌19 ⬛6 A7rm **P**
sB ⇌ ⬛130–188 dB90–188
dB ⇌ ⬛155–192 ⚑

COQUILLE (LA)
Dordogne (☎53)

★**Voyageurs** ⚹ **(DPn)** r de la République
(N21) ☎528013
Apr–Oct
rm10 ⇌7 ⬛ **P** dB125–155
dB ⇌140–170

CORBEIL-ESSONNES
Essonne (☎6)
See also **ÉVRY**

⏰**Diffusion-Auto-Européenne** 27 bd de
Fontainebleau ☎0891414 Closed Sat
pm & Sun Aud VW

⏰**Grand Garage Feray** 46 av du Mai
1945 ☎0889200 Closed Sat pm & Sun
Ren

⏰**St-Jean** 17 bd de Fontainebleau
☎0881617 Closed Sat pm & Sun AD Frd

At **PLESSIS-CHENET (LE)** (4km S)

☆ ☆**Climat de France** 2 r Panhard
☎4938536 tx692844
⇌50 **P** dB⇌206–221

CORDES
Tarn (☎63)

★ ★ ★**Grand-Écuyer** r Voltaire ☎560103
2 Apr–15 Oct
⇌16 sB ⇌200–300 dB ⇌250–400

CORPS
Isère (☎76)

★ ★**Poste** ⚹ pl de la Mairie ☎300003
rm15 ⇌6 ⬛4 A6rm ⬛ **P** sB75–130
sB ⇌ ⬛120–150 dB100–150
dB ⇌ ⬛125–200 mountains

⏰R **Rivière SARL** pl Napoléon
☎300113 M/c Peu Ren

CORSE (CORSICA)
(☎95)
PORTICCIO *Corse du Sud*

★ ★ ★ ★**Sofitel Porticcio (DPn)** Pointe de
Porticcio ☎250034 tx460708
⇌100 ⬛ Lift 𝄞 sB ⇌490–990
dB ⇌360–750 ⚑ Pool Beach sea

PORTO-VECCHIO *Corse du Sud*

★ ★ ★**Ziglione (DPn)** (5km E on N198)
☎700983
15 May–15 Sep
⇌32 **P** 𝄞 Beach sea

COSNE-SUR-LOIRE
Nièvre (☎86)

★ ★**Grand Cerf (DPn)** 43 r St-Jaques
☎280446
10 Jan–10 Dec
rm21 ⇌5 ⬛8 ⬛

★**Vieux Relais** ⚹ **(DPn)** 11 r St-Agnan
☎282021
Feb–24 Dec
rm 11 ⇌4 ⬛6 ⬛ dB82–190
dB ⇌ ⬛102–190

COURBEVOIE
Hauts-de-Seine (☎1)

★ ★ ★**Paris Penta** 18 r Baudin
☎7885051 tx610470
⇌494 **P** Lift 𝄞 sB ⇌422 dB ⇌452

COUR-CHEVERNY
Loir-et-Cher (☎54)

★ ★**St-Hubert** ⚹ **(DPn)** ☎799660
rm20 ⇌14 ⬛6 **P** dB ⇌ ⬛100–177
M70–140

★ ★**Trois Marchands** ⚹ (FAH) **(DPn)** 3 pl
Église ☎799644
rm44 ⇌15 ⬛8 ⬛ **P** 𝄞

COURTABOEUF See **ORSAY**

COURTENAY
Loiret (☎38)

⏰**ACA** (M L Redon) rte de Sens
☎944371 Closed Mon Peu

⏰**Chenardière** rte de Sens ☎944194
Tal Sim

⏰**P Vinot** Esso Station, rte de Sens
☎973003 Closed Sun Fia Lnc

COURTISOLS See **CHÂLONS-SUR-
MARNE**

COUSOLRE
Nord (☎20)

★ ★**Viennois** (N49) ☎632173
rm10 ⇌5 ⬛5 ⬛ **P**

COUTAINVILLE
Manche (☎33)

★**Hardy** ⚹ **(DPn)** pl 28 Juillet ☎470411
5 Feb–5 Jan
rm13 ⇌12 ⬛1 sB ⇌ ⬛135–156
dB ⇌ ⬛170

COUTANCES
Manche (☎33)

★**Moderne** 25 bd Alsace-Lorraine
(n.rest) ☎451377
rm17 ⇌1 ⬛ **P** dB90–100 dB ⇌153

CRÈCHE (LA)
Deux-Sèvres (☎49)

☆ ☆**Campanile** rte de Paris ☎255622
tx610016
⇌33 **P**
At **CHAVAGNÉ** (4km SW)

☆ ☆ ☆**Rocs** ☎255038 tx790632
⇌51 **P** 𝄞 dB ⇌270 ⚑ Pool

CRÈCHES-SUR-SAÔNE See **MÂCON**

CREIL
Oise (☎4)

⏰**Central** (M Elbaz) 90 r J-Jaurès
☎4554197 Closed Sat & Sun BL

CRESSENSAC
Lot (☎65)

★**Chez Gilles** ⚹ (N20) ☎377006
rm25 ⇌7 ⬛6 ⬛ dB110–190
dB ⇌ ⬛145–225

CRÉTEIL See **PARIS**

CREUSOT (LE)
Saône-et-Loire (☎85)
At **MONTCHANIN** (8km E off D28)

☆ ☆ ☆**Novotel** r du Pont J-Rose
☎557211 tx800588
⇌87 **P** Lift sB ⇌265 dB ⇌321 M alc
Pool

CRIEL-SUR-MER
Seine-Maritime (☎35)

★ ★**Hostellerie de la Vielle Ferme (DPn)**
23 r de la Mer ☎867218
Closed 6 Jan–4 Feb
rm36 ⇌30 **P** sB165 sB ⇌183
dB ⇌201–266

CROIX-VALMER
Var (☎94)

★ ★ ★**Mer** (2.5km SE on N559) ☎796061
Apr–Sep
rm31 ⇌14 ⬛13 **P** Pool Beach
mountains

CROS-DE-CAGNES See **CAGNES-SUR-
MER**

CROUZILLE (LA)
Haute-Vienne (☎55)
At **NANTIAT**

☆☆**Relais St-Europe** ☎399121
⇌19 sB ⇌180 dB ⇌200 mountains

CUVILLY See **RESSONS-SUR-MATZ**

DAMMARIE-LES-LYS See **MELUN**

DANJOUTIN See **BELFORT**

DARDILY See **LYON**

DEAUVILLE
Calvados (☎31)

★★★★★**Normandy** r J-Mermoz
☎880921 tx170617
⇌306 Lift ☽ sB ⇌460-850
dB ⇌500-900 M165 sea

★★★★★**Royal** ☎881641 tx170549
Etr-mid Oct
rm309 ⇌240 ▥53 P Lift ☽
sB ⇌ ▥330-980 dB ⇌ ▥430-980
Mfr165 St15% ⊷ Pool Beach ♂ sea

★★★**PLM Port Deauville** bd Cornuché
(n.rest) ☎886262 tx170364
⇌70 ▥ P Lift ☽ sB ⇌176-291
dB ⇌256-369 sea

At **TOUQUES** (2.5km S)

☆☆**Amirauté** (N834) ☎889062
tx171665
⇌120 P Lift ☽ ⊷ Pool

DIEPPE
Seine-Maritime (☎35)

See Plan page 142
|AA| agent; see page 105

★★★★**Présidence** 1 bd de Verdun
☎843131 tx180865 Plan1
rm89 ⇌76 ▥4 A9rm ▥ P Lift
sB171-250 sB ⇌ ▥246-310
dB212-290 dB ⇌ ▥292-350 M alc sea

★★★**Aguado** 30 bd de Verdun (n.rest)
☎842700 Plan 2
rm55 ⇌33 ▥22 Lift ☽
sB ⇌ ▥178-230 dB ⇌ ▥254-296 sea

☆★**Ibis Dieppe** le Val Druel ☎826530
tx180067 Not on plan
⇌43 P sB ⇌167 dB ⇌203

★★**Select** 1 r Toustain, pl de la Barre
(n.rest) ☎841466 Plan 4
rm25 ⇌23 A3rm P Lift

★★**Windsor** ☍(DPn) 18 bd de Verdun
☎841523 Plan 6
rm47 ⇌41 P Lift ☽ sB102-162
sB ⇌ ▥192-207 dB149-190 dB ⇌
▥209-224 sea

DIGNE
Alpes-de-Haute-Provence (☎92)

★★★**Ermitage Napoléon** bd Gambetta
☎310109 tx401768
Closed Feb-21 Mar & Nov-20 Dec
rm59 ⇌36 ▥23 P Lift mountains

★★**Algion** ☍ 1 r de Provence
☎310270 tx430605
Feb-Nov
rm33 ▥12 A9rm P sB83-90
sB ⇌ ▥120-127 dB116-157
dB ⇌ ▥178-185 mountains

France

★★**Mistre** 65 bd Gassendi ☎310016
5 Jan-1 Dec
rm18 ⇌9 ▥9 ▥ P sea mountains

⅋⅁P **Thumin** pl du Gl-de-Gaulle
☎310423 Closed Sun Opl

DIGOIN
Saône-et-Loire (☎85)

★**Gare** 79 av Gl-de-Gaulle ☎530304
Feb-Dec
rm13 ⇌8 ▥5 P sB ⇌ ▥130-180
dB ⇌ ▥160-220

★**Terminus** ☍ 76 av de Gl-de-Gaulle
☎531726
Closed 14 Jan-15 Feb
rm17 ⇌5 ▥3 ▥ P sB78
sB ⇌ ▥97-105 dB90-118
dB ⇌ ▥109-123

DIJON
Côte-d'Or (☎80)

★★★**Chapeau Rouge** (MAP) 5 r
Michelet ☎302810 tx350535
4 Jan-20 Dec
rm33 ⇌28 ▥5 ▥ Lift ☽
sB ⇌ ▥300-330 dB ⇌ ▥520

★★★**Frantel** 22 bd de la Marne
☎723113 tx350293
▥124 Lift sB▥297 dB ▥389

★★★**Ibis Central** 3 pl Grangier
☎304400 tx350606
⇌90 P Lift sB ⇌177-197
dB ⇌214-234

★★**Hostellerie du Sauvage** 64 r Monge
☎413121
rm23 ⇌3 ▥6 ▥ P sB70 sB ⇌ ▥140
dB ⇌ ▥185

★★**Jura** (Inter) 14 av Ml-Foch (n.rest)
☎416112 tx350485
rm65 ⇌31 ▥33 A10rm ▥ P Lift ☽
sB134 sB ⇌ ▥209-224 dB153
dB ⇌ ▥243-278

★**Nord** 2 r Liberté ☎305858 tx350912
15 Jan-23 Dec
rm26 ⇌10 ▥6 Lift sB77-196
sB ⇌ ▥196 dB128-160
dB ⇌ ▥187-222

⅋⅁**Depan-Auto** 22 r de l'Égalité ☎415727
All makes

⅋⅁J **Faisca** 5 bis av Garibaldi ☎734690
Closed Aug 15-30 & Sun Opl

⅋⅁**Lignier** 3 r des G-Champs ☎663905
All makes

At **HAUTEVILLE-LÈS-DIJON** (7km NE on
D107)

★**Musarde** ☍ ☎562282
rm11 ⇌5 ▥3 P

At **PERRIGNY-LÈS-DIJON** (9km S on N74)

☆☆☆**Novotel Dijon Sud** rte de Beaune
(N74) ☎521422 tx350728

⇌124 P sB ⇌245-267 dB ⇌293-318
M alc Pool

☆☆**Ibis** rte de Lyon-Beaune ☎528645
tx351510

⇌48 P sB⇌175 dB ⇌212 M alc

At **QUÉTIGNY** (5km E via CD107b)

☆☆**Climat de France** 14 av de
Bourgogne ☎460446 tx692844

⇌42 P dB ⇌206-222 M48-70

At **ST-APOLLINAIRE** (3km E)

☆☆**Campanile** rte de Gray ☎724538
tx610016

⇌50 P dB ⇌206-209 M55-80

At **SENNECEY-LÈS-DIJON** (3km SW)

★★★★**Flambée** (MAP) rte de Genève
☎473535 tx350273
rm23 ⇌21 ▥2 P Lift
sB ⇌ ▥247-287 dB ⇌ ▥304-364
M55-150

DINAN
Côtes-du-Nord (☎96)

★★**Avaugour** ☍ 1 pl du Champs Clos
☎390749
rm27 ⇌25 ▥2 Lift

DINARD
Ille-et-Vilaine (☎99)

★★★**Grand** (DPn) 46 av George-V
☎461028 tx740522
Apr-Oct
rm100 ⇌50 ▥50 P Lift ☽
sB ⇌ ▥310-560 dB ⇌ ▥330-580 sea

★★**Bains** 38 av George-V ☎461371
tx740802
15 Mar-15 Oct
rm40 ⇌12 ▥13 P Lift sB80-110
dB120-170 dB ⇌ ▥200-230 sea

★★**Dunes** ☍ 5 r G-Clemenceau
☎461272
Mar-Sep
rm32 ⇌14 ▥3

★★**Emeraude Plage** 1 bd Albert ler
☎461579 tx740802
rm50 ⇌29 ▥3 A5rm ▥ P ☽

★★**Printania** (DPn) 5 av George-V
☎461307
Mid Apr-Sep
rm77 ⇌45 ▥45 sB80-250
sB ⇌80-250 dB140-250 dB ⇌250 sea

⅋⅁**Parc** 10 r Y-Verney ☎461338 Closed
1-15, Sat pm & Sun BL

DOLANCOURT
Aube (☎25)

★★**Moulin du Landion** ☍ (DPn)
☎261217
⇌16 P

DOL-DE-BRETAGNE
Ille-et-Vilaine(☎99)

★★**Bresche Arthur** ☍ bd Deminiac
☎480144 tx730808
rm24 ⇌5 ▥17 ▥ P sB110-180
sB ⇌ ▥180 dB130-170 dB ⇌ ▥190

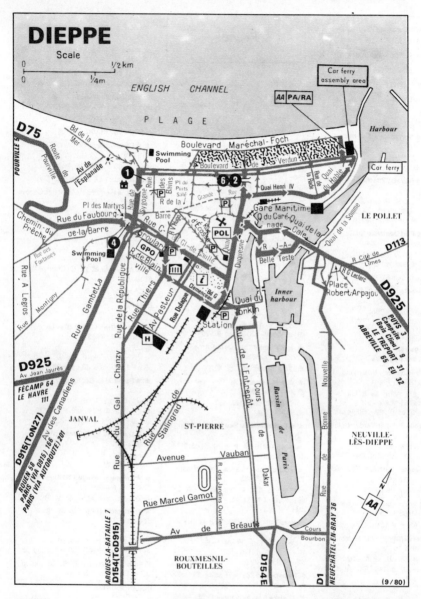

DIEPPE

Scale

ENGLISH CHANNEL

PLAGE

Car ferry assembly area

AA PA/RA

Harbour

D75

Bd de la Mer

Route de Pourville

Av de l'Esplanade

Swimming Pool

Boulevard Maréchal-Foch

Boulevard de Verdun

Rue de la Hâble

Quai du Hâble

Car ferry

❶

❻❷

Rue des Bains

Pl du Puits Salé

R de la

Quai Henri IV

Quai de la Somme

LE POLLET

Pl des Martyrs

Rue du Faubourg

de-la-Barre

Chemin du Prêche

Rue de Sygogne

Grande Rue

Barre

Rue C.

R Hugo

Rue d'Écosse

Gare Maritime

Q du Café

Quai de la nage.

Quai de la Somme

D113

Rue des Fontaines

Swimming Pool

❹

GPO

R de Blainville

Rue Thiers

Av Pasteur

Rue Dufaure

Rue G Clemenceau

Cl-de-l'aulle

POL

Bd G

ℹ

R J-A-Belle Teste

R G Leclerc

R Cité de Limes

Place Robert-Arpajou

D925

D925

Av Jean Jaurès

FÉCAMP 64

LE HAVRE 111

D915(ToN27)

ROUEN 58 (VIA D915)

PARIS (VIA D915) 165

PARIS (VIA AUTOROUTE) 201

Av des Canadiens

JANVAL

Rue A. Legros

Rue Montigny

Rue Gambetta

Rue de la République

Rue du Gal - Chanzy

Quai du Tonkin

Quai de l'Entrepôt

Station

H

Rue Stalingrad

ST-PIERRE

Avenue Vauban

Rue Dakar

R des Jardins Ouvriers

Inner harbour

Bassin de Paris

Cours de Bonne

Rue Nouvelle

NEUVILLE-LÈS-DIEPPE

AA

N

Rue Marcel Gamot

Av de Bréauté

Cours Bourbon

ARQUES-LA-BATAILLE 7

D154(ToD915)

ROUXMESNIL-BOUTEILLES

D154E

D1

NEUFCHÂTEL-EN-BRAY 36

PUYS 3

Camping

(Bois Cheu) 9 31

LE TRÉPORT

ABBEVILLE 65

EU 32

(9/80)

DIEPPE

1	★★★★Présidence
2	★★★Aguado
4	★★Select
6	★★Windsor

★★Bretagne LE 17 pl Châteaubriand
☎480203
rm30 ⇄3 ▥8 🏠 P sB55–89
dB ⇄ ▥107–113

DOLE
Jura(☎84)

★★★Chandioux (MAP) (DPn) pl Grévy
☎790066 tx360498
rm33 ⇄29 ▥4 🏠 P 𝄇 sB149–304
sB ⇄ ▥259–304 dB248–398
dB ⇄ ▥288–398 M78–250

🌢G Cuynet 8 r Sombardier
☎722334 Closed Aug 8–15, Sep &
Sun Aud VW

DOMFRONT
Orne(☎33)

★★Poste LE (DPn) 15 r Ml-Foch
☎385100

Closed 6 Jan–26 Feb
rm29 ⇄8 ▥6 🏠 P sB69–95
dB96–155 dB ⇄ ▥127–230

★**France** 🅻 r Mont-St-Michel ☎385144
9 Dec–2 Nov
rm22 ⇄2 🛏5 P dB93–130
dB ⇄ 🛏183

DOMPAIRE
Vosges(☎29)
★★**Commerce** 🅻 pl Ml-Leclerc
☎365028 tx960573
rm11 ⇄4 🛏7 sB ⇄ 🛏130 dB124–132
dB ⇄ 🛏164

DOMRÉMY-LA-PUCELLE
Vosges(☎29)
★**Basilique** (DPn) le Bois Chenu (1.5km S by D53) ☎940781 tx88300
Closed Jan
rm28 ⇄7 🛁 P sB65–100 sB ⇄65–100
dB80–120 dB ⇄80–120
★*Pucelle* (DPn) ☎940460
15 Feb–Dec
rm19 🛏6 A7rm 🛁

DONZENAC
Corrèze(☎55)
🅂**A Chamournie** av de Paris ☎857237 Closed Sat pm & Sun Cit Tal
At **ST-PARDOUX L'ORTIGLER** (9km N off N20)
🅂**M Dely** (N20) ☎857341 Closed Oct, Sun pm & Mon Peu

DONZÈRE
Drôme(☎75)
Porte Provence quartier Greo (N7) ☎986052 Closed Sat & Sun All makes
🅂**Renault** 55 B-Bourgade ☎986109 Closed Sun pm Ren
🅂**Sud** (N7) ☎986074 All makes
🅂**R Thomas** 36 B-Bourgade ☎986160 Peu

DORDIVES
Loiret(☎38)
★**César** 🅻 8 r de la République (n.rest) ☎927320 tx780523
rm20 ⇄2 🛏6 🛁 P 🌙 sB64
sB ⇄ 🛏154 dB108–160 dB ⇄ 🛏188 M40–90

DOUAI
Nord(☎27)
★**Grand Cerf** 46 r St-Jacques ☎887960
rm38 ⇄21 🛏5 P sB96–107
sB ⇄ 🛏140–187 dB112
dB ⇄ 🛏155–198

DOUÉ-LA-FONTAINE
Maine-et-Loire(☎41)
★**Dagobert** (DPn) 14 pl Champ-de-Foire ☎591444
Closed Nov
rm20 ⇄3 🛏5 P dB60–147
dB ⇄ 🛏60–147 M38–110

DOURDAN
Essonne(☎1)
★★★**Blanche de Castille** pl des Halles ☎4596892 tx690902

France

Closed 13–20 Aug
⇄40 P Lift sB ⇄220 dB ⇄260

DOUSSARD See FAVERGES

DOZULÉ
Calvados(☎31)
🅂**R Marci** fbg du Pont Mousse ☎792041 Closed Sep, Sat pm & Sun Peu
🅂**St-Christophe** 102 Grande Rue ☎792036 Closed 1–15 Sep & Sun Ren

DRAGUIGNAN
Var(☎94)
★★**Col de l'Ange** (Inter) rte de Lorgues ☎682301 tx970423
⇄ 🛏30 P sB ⇄ 🛏200–250
dB ⇄ 🛏280–350 Pool mountains
🅂**Sodra** ZI rte de Lorgues ☎688244 Closed Sat & Sun Aud VW

DRAMONT (LE) See AGAY

DREUX
Eure-et-Loire(☎37)
Ouest 51 av des Fenots ☎461145 Closed Aug BL
At **MONTREUIL** (8km NE)
★★**Auberge Gué des Grues** ☎435025
rm ⇄3 🛏2 P Lift sB ⇄ 🛏60–150
dB ⇄ 🛏75–150

DUNKERQUE (DUNKIRK)
Nord(☎28)
★★★**Europ** (MAP) 13 r de Leughenaer ☎662907 tx120084
rm130 ⇄110 🛏20 🛁 Lift sB ⇄
🛏198–218 dB ⇄ 🛏278 M80–100
★★**Frantel** r J-Jaurès (n.rest) ☎659722 tx110587
⇄126 Lift sB ⇄298 dB ⇄348
★★**Borel** (Inter) 6 r l'Hermitte (n.rest) ☎665180 tx820050
⇄40 P Lift 🌙 sB ⇄201 dB ⇄246 sea
🅂**Patfoort** 9 r du Leughenaer ☎665112 Closed Sat & Sun Fia
At **ARMBOUTS CAPPEL** (6km S)
☆☆☆**Novotel** Voie Express-Bordure du Lac ☎659733 tx820916
rm64 ⇄52 P 🛏12 P sB ⇄ 🛏247–262
dB ⇄ 🛏298–323 Pool

ÉCOLE VALENTIN See BESANÇON

ÉCOMMOY
Sarthe(☎43)
★**Commerce** 🅻 (DPn) 19 pl République ☎271034
rm13 🛏6 🛁 P sB74–80 sB ⇄ 🛏105–111
dB98–132 dB 🛏140–152

ECULLY See LYON

EGUILLES See AIX-EN-PROVENCE

ELBEUF
Seine-Maritime(☎35)
At **CLÉON** (5km N over river)
☆☆**Campanile** r de l'Église ☎813800 tx610016
⇄42 P
At **LONDE (LA)** (5km NW on unclass rd off D913)
🅂**Maison Brulée** ☎923055 M/c Closed 2 wks Jun & 2nd Tue per month Fia

ELNE
Pyrénées-Orientales(☎68)
🅂**R Jammet** 9 bd Voltaire ☎220858 Closed Sat pm & Sun Peu
🅂**Mary** 10 av de Perpignan ☎220101 Closed Sep 8–29, Sat & Sun Cit

ÉMERAINVILLE See CHAMPS-SUR-MARNE

ENGLOS See LILLE

ENTRAYGUES-SUR-TRUYÈRE
Aveyron(☎65)
★**Truyère** 🅻 (DPn) ☎445110 tx530366
15 Mar–Sep
rm26 ⇄24 🛏2 🛁 P Lift
sB ⇄ 🛏105–178 dB ⇄ 🛏145–235
M57–130 mountains

ÉPERNAY
Marne(☎26)
★★★**Berceaux** 13 r Berceaux ☎552884
⇄25 Lift sB194 sB ⇄194–224
dB ⇄220–268
★★**Pomme d'Or** 12 r E-Mercier (n.rest) ☎531144 tx841150
rm26 ⇄22 P Lift sB ⇄ 🛏84–120
dB ⇄ 🛏120–150
★**Europe** 18 r Porte-Lucas ☎518028
rm26 ⇄1 🛏14 🛁 P
At **CHAMPILLON** (6km N on 51)
★★★**Royal Champagne** Bellevue ☎511151 tx830906
rm16 ⇄14 🛏2 P 🌙 sB ⇄ 🛏260–500
dB ⇄ 🛏285–500
At **VINAY** (6km S on N51)
★★*Briqueterie* rte de Sézanne ☎541122
rm42 ⇄40 🛏2 P 🌙

EPINAL
Vosges(☎29)
★★**Résidence** 39 av des Templiers (n.rest) ☎824564
Closed Xmas & New Year
rm18 ⇄10 🛏8 P sB ⇄ 🛏105–165
dB ⇄ 🛏140–175
★★**Vosges et Terminus** 16 pl de la Gare (n.rest) ☎823578
rm48 ⇄6 🛏12 P sB51 dB76–106
dB ⇄ 🛏125
★*Azur* 54 quai des Bons Enfants (n.rest) ☎822915
rm21 ⇄2 🛏5

France

EPINAY-SUR-SEINE
Seine-et-Denis(☎1)

☆ ☆**Ibis** av du 18 Juin 1940 ☎8298341
tx614354
⇄64 **P** Lift sB ⇄238 dB ⇄276 M alc

EPONE
Yvelines(☎3)

☆ ☆**Routel** (D113) ☎0956870 tx801059
⇄49 **P** sB ⇄178–198 dB ⇄221–241 ✍

ÉPINE (L') See **CHÂLONS-SUR-MARNE**

ERDEVEN
Morbihan(☎97)

★ ★**Relais du Sous Bois** (FAH) rte de
Pont Lorois ☎553431 tx950581
Apr–15 Oct
rm22 ⇄2 ⋔20 **P DPn**175

ERNÉE
Mayenne(☎43)

★ ★ ★**Relais de Poste** 🄻 1 pl de l'Eglise
☎052033
⇄35 ⇱ **P** Lift sB ⇄175 dB ⇄220

ERQUY
Côtes-du-Nord(☎96)

★**Beauregard** 🄻 bd de la Mer ☎723003
rm17 A8rm **P** sea

⮑**P Thomas** 11 de la Corniche
☎323037 Ren

ÉTAIN
Meuse(☎29)

⮑**Beauguitte** 87 r-Poincaré
☎781290 Ren

⮑**Boulard** 6 av du Gl-de-Gaulle
☎871004 M/c Closed Sun Cit

⮑**R Thevenin** av du Gl-de-Gaulle
☎871214 Peu

ETSAUT
Pyrénées-Atlantiques(☎59)

★**Pyrénées (DPn)** ☎348862
Closed Nov
rm22 ⇄6 ⋔7 A6rm ⇱ **P** sB79
sB ⇄ ⋔116 dB80 dB ⇄ ⋔125
mountains

EUGÉNIE-LES-BAINS
Landes(☎58)

☆ ☆**Climat de France** 4 chemin
Communal ☎581414 tx692844
⇄36 dB ⇄fr208–306

EVIAN-LES-BAINS
Haute-Savoie(☎50)

★ ★ ★ ★ ★**Royal** ☎751400 tx385759
15 Feb–15 Nov
⇄200 ⇱ **P** Lift ☾ sB ⇄330–1,140
dB ⇄480–1,380 Mfr190 ✍ Pool ♨
mountains lake

★ ★ ★**Bellevue** 6 r B-Moutardier
☎750113
20 May–20 Sep
rm50 ⇄34 ⋔15 **P** Lift
sB ⇄ ⋔200–250 dB ⇄ ⋔280–350
M110–125 lake

★ ★**Mateirons** (Inter) ☎750416

15 Mar–15 Oct
rm22 ⇄18 **P** sB80–90 sB ⇄100–120
dB ⇄150–170 mountains lake

At **MAXILLY-PETITE-RIVE** (2km E on N5)

★ ★ ★**Lumina** ☎752867
⇄60 **P** Lift ☾ Pool mountains lake

ÉVREUX
Eure(☎32)

★ ★**France** 🄻 29 r St-Thomas ☎390925
rm16 ⇄11 ⋔1 ⇱ **P** dB81–254
dB ⇄ ⋔95–290

★**Grenoble** 17 r St-Pierre (n.rest)
☎330731
rm19 ⇄6 ⋔2 ⇱ **P**

☆ ☆**Ibis** av W-Churchill ☎381636
⇄42 **P** sB ⇄183 dB ⇄226

★ ★**Normandy** 37 r R-Féray ☎331440
rm26 ⇄8 ⋔12 ⇱ **P**

★ ★**Orme** 🄻 13 r Lombards (n.rest)
☎393412
rm27 ⇄9 ⋔9 ⇱ sB86–105
sB ⇄ ⋔121–195 dB102–175
dB ⇄ ⋔137–215

⮑**Lemoine** 1 r de Cocheral
ZI ☎394073 Closed Sat BL

ÉVRY
Essonne(☎6)

See also **CORBEIL-ESSONNES**

☆ ☆ ☆**Novotel Paris Evry** (A6)
☎0778270 tx600685
⇄180 **P** Lift ☾ sB ⇄256–288
dB ⇄299–330 Pool lake

★ ★**Arcade** cours B-Pascal, Butte
Creuse ☎0782990 tx691249
⋔100 Lift sB ⋔173 dB ⋔173 M15

EYZIES-DE-TAYAC (LES)
Dordogne(☎53)

★ ★ ★**Cro-Magnon** (MAP) ☎069706
24 Apr–10 Oct
rm27 ⇄24 ⋔3 A12rm **P DPn**550–785

★ ★**Centenaire** 🄻 ☎069718
Apr–Nov
⇄31 A11rm ⇱ **P** ☾

★ ★**Centre** 🄻 **(DPn)** les Sireuils
☎069713
Jan–15 Nov
⇄18 sB ⇄115 dB ⇄145–175 M63–165

★ ★**Glycines (DPn)** ☎069707
Etr–15 Oct
rm26 ⇄23 ⋔3 ⇱ **P** sB ⇄ ⋔110–216
dB ⇄ ⋔138–230

★**France – Auberge de Musée** 🄻 **(DPn**
in summer) ☎069723
Apr–3 Nov
rm16 ⇄4 ⋔5 **P** sB81 dB ⇄ ⋔160
M59–174 mountains

⮑**J C Dupuy** pl de la Porte
☎069732 Ren

ÉZE-BORD-DE-MER
Alpes-Maritimes(☎93)

★ ★ ★ ★**Cap Estel** ☎015044 tx470305
Feb–Oct
⇄43 **P** Lift ☾ **DPn**1,060–2000 (incl.2
persons) Pool Beach sea

★ ★**Bananerale** (n.rest) ☎015139
tx470305
10 Jun–Sep
rm32 ⇄21 **P**

★ ★**Cap Roux** Basse Corniche (n.rest)
☎015123
15 Mar–Sep
rm30 ⇄16 ⋔14 **P** Lift
sB ⇄ ⋔80–168 dB ⇄ ⋔126–210 sea
mountains

FALAISE
Calvados(☎31)

★ ★**Normandie** 4 r Al-Courbet ☎901826
rm30 ⇄6 ⋔9 ⇱ dB89–130
dB ⇄ ⋔134

★ ★**Poste** 🄻 38 r G-Clemenceau
☎901314
rm19 ⇄2 ⋔4 ⇱ **P** sB65
sB ⇄ ⋔105–115 dB77–110
dB ⇄ ⋔109–119

FAOUËT (LE)
Morbihan(☎97)

★**Croix d'Or (DPn)** 9 pl Bellanger
☎230733
rm16 ⇄2 ⋔2 ⇱ **P**

FARLÈDE (LA) See **TOULON**

FAVERGES
Haute-Savoie(☎50)

★**Parc** rte d'Albertville ☎445025
rm12 ⇄5 ⋔4 **P** sB ⇄ ⋔70–130
dB ⇄ ⋔75–180 mountains

At **DOUSSARD** (7km NW)

★ ★**Marceau** Marceau Dessus (2km W)
☎443011
Feb–2 Nov
rm20 ⇄14 ⋔1 A3rm ⇱ **P** dB140
dB ⇄ ⋔250–400 ✍ mountains lake

FAYENCE
Var(☎94)

⮑**Difant Georges** quartier Pré-Gaudin
☎760740 All makes

⮑**St-Eloy** (H Wolf) quartier de la
Gare ☎760072 M/c Fia MB Por

At **TOURRETTES** (1km W)

★**Grillon** (N562) ☎760296
⇄25 **P** dB ⇄170 Pool

FÈRE (LA)
Aisne(☎23)

★**Tourelles** 51 r de la République
☎563166
rm17 ⇄2 ⋔5 sB63 dB89
dB ⇄ ⋔115–130

144

FÈRE-EN-TARDENOIS
Aisne(☎23)

★ ★ ★ **Château (DPn)** ☎822113
tx145526

Mar–Dec
⇆20 **P** dB ⇆450–660 ✍

FERNEY VOLTAIRE See **GENEVA AIRPORT** Switzerland

FERTÉ-ST-AUBIN (LA)
Loiret(☎38)

★ ★ **Perron** (FAH) **(DPn)** 9 r du Gl-Leclerc
☎765336

4 Feb–20 Jan
rm30 ⇆5 ⋔8 **P** dB137–177
dB ⇆ ⋔159–259

FERTÉ-SOUS-JOUARRE (LA)
Seine-et-Marne (☎71)

⭑Condé 48 r de Condé ☎0220810
Closed Sep Frd

⭑Parc 10 av de Montmirail ☎0220136
Closed Aug, Sat pm, Sun am Cit

FIGEAC
Lot (☎65)

★ ★ **Carmes** ᴸᴱ (FAH) 18 pl XII Mai
☎342078 tx520794

8 Jan–15 Dec
rm34 ⇆26 ⋔8

FIRMINY
Loire (☎77)

★ ★ **Firm** 37 r J-Jaurès ☎560899
rm20 ⇆6 ⋔14 **P** ☽
sB ⇆ ⋔113–138 dB ⇆ ⋔138–166

★ ★ **Table du Pavillon** (FAH) 4 av de la Gare ☎569111
rm22 ⇆14 ⋔8 🏛 **P** Lift sB ⇆ ⋔160
dB ⇆ ⋔200

FIXIN
Côte-d'Or (☎80)

★ ★ **Chez Jeanette** ᴸᴱ **(DPn)** ☎524549
rm11 ⋔9 **P** sB70 sB ⋔89–92
dB90–120 dB ⋔118–139

FLEURAC See **JARNAC**

FLEURANCE
Gers (☎62)

★ ★ **Fleurance** rte d'Agen ☎061485
rm25 ⇆15 ⋔6 **P** sB103–180
sB ⇆ ⋔160–180 dB125–220
dB ⇆ ⋔185–220

FLORAC
Lozère (☎66)

★ **Gorges du Tarn** 48 r du Pecher (n.rest)
☎450063

May–Sep
rm31 ⇆13 ⋔4 A12rm **P**
mountains

★ **Parc** 47 av J-Monestier ☎450305
15 Mar–1 Dec
rm58 ⇆20 ⋔22 A26rm **P** mountains

FLORENSAC
Hérault (☎67)

France

★ ★ **Leonce** ᴸᴱ 2 pl de la République
☎770305

7 Oct–28 Jan & 18 Feb–12 Sep
rm18 ⇆6 ⋔6 **P** Lift dB80–150
dB ⇆ ⋔150

FLOTTE (LA) See **RÉ (ILE DE)**

FOIX
Ariège (☎61)

★ ★ ★ **Barbacane** 1 av de Lérida (n.rest)
☎655044

Apr–Oct
rm22 ⇆19 🏛 sB95–105 dB165–190
dB ⇆ ⋔180–215 mountains

★ ★ ★ **Tourisme** 2 cours I-Cros
☎655121 tx530955
⇆29 sB ⇆110–120 dB ⇆160–186
mountains

FONTAINE
Isère (☎76)

⭑MA Mignot 2 r Baptiste Harcet, ZI de l'Argentière ☎266946 All makes

FONTAINEBLEAU
Seine-et-Marne (☎6)

★ ★ ★ **Aigle Noir** (MAP) 27 pl N-Bonaparte ☎4223265 tx600080
rm30 ⇆28 ⋔2 🏛 Lift ☽
sB ⇆ ⋔390–595 dB ⇆ ⋔495–715

★ ★ **Ile de France** ᴸᴱ 128 r de France
☎4222117 tx692131
rm25 ⇆16 ⋔9 **P** sB ⇆ ⋔95–180
dB110–120

★ ★ **Londres (DPn)** 1 pl du Gl-de-Gaulle
☎4222021

Mar–Jan
rm22 ⇆3 ⋔4 🏛 **P** ☽ sB130–234
dB130–234

★ ★ **Toulouse** 183 r Grande (n.rest)
☎4222273

Closed 16–30 Jan & 15–30 Nov
rm18 ⇆4 ⋔11 🏛 sB74–145
sB ⇆ ⋔114–145 dB100–183
dB ⇆ ⋔138–183

★ **Forêt** 79 av Prés Roosevelt (n.rest)
☎4223926
rm30 ⇆6 ⋔11 A7rm 🏛 **P** Pool

★ **Neuville (DPn)** 196 r Grande ☎4222339
Closed Feb
rm16 ⇆4 ⋔6 A4rm 🏛 **P**

⭑Ile de France Autos 86 r de France
☎4223159 Closed Sat pm & Sun AR Lada

At **URY** (6km SW on N51)

☆ ☆ ☆ **Novotel** ☎4224825 tx600153
⇆127 **P** sB ⇆283 dB ⇆302 ✍ Pool

FONTAINE-CHAALIS
Oise (☎4)

★ **Auberge de Fontaine** Grande Rue
☎4542022

Mar–15 Jan
rm7 ⇆4 ⋔3

FONTENAY-AUX-ROSES See **PARIS**

FONTENAY-LE-COMTE
Vendée (☎51)

★ ★ **Rabelais** ᴸᴱ (Inter) rte Parthenay
☎698620 tx710703
rm35 ⇆20 ⋔15 **P**

FONTENAY-SOUS-BOIS
Val-de-Marne (☎1)

☆ ☆ **Climat de France** r Rabelais
☎8762198 tx692844
⇆42 **P** dB ⇆223–243 M48–74

FONTEVRAUD-L'ABBAYE
Maine-et-Loire (☎41)

★ ★ **Croix Blanche** ᴸᴱ 7 pl Plantagenets
☎517111
rm19 ⇆3 ⋔12 **P**

FONT-ROMEU
Pyrénées-Orientales (☎68)

★ ★ ★ **Bellevue** av du Dr-Capelle
☎300016
Rest closed 15 Sep–15 Dec
rm65 ⇆30 **P** sB ⇆195 dB90–195
dB ⇆195 mountains

★ ★ **Carlit** ☎300745 tx500802
20 May–Sep & 15 Dec–Apr
rm81 ⇆59 ⋔18 A23rm Lift
dB180–250 dB ⇆ ⋔180–250
mountains

★ ★ **Pyréenées** pl des Pyrénées
☎300149
20 Dec–4 Nov
rm37 ⇆17 ⋔20 Lift mountains

FONVIALANE See **ALBI**

FOÊT-FOUESNANT (LA)
Finistère (☎98)

★ ★ **Baie** ᴸᴱ ☎569735
Apr–Sep
rm22 ⇆12 **P** dB95 dB ⇆130–165 sea

★ ★ **Esperance** ᴸᴱ ☎569658
Apr–14 Oct
rm33 ⇆10 ⋔8 A19rm **P** sea

★ **Beauséjour** 47 r de la Baie ☎569718
Apr–Sep
rm30 ⇆12 **P** dB101–112 dB ⋔119–124

FOS-SUR-MER
Bouches-du-Rhône (☎42)

★ ★ ★ ★ **Frantel Camargue** La Bastidonne, rte d'Istres ☎050057
tx4108121
⇆146 **P** sB ⇆304 dB ⇆367 Pool

FOUESNANT
Finistère (☎98)

★ ★ **Pointe du Mousterlin (DPn)** Pointe de Mousterlin ☎560412
30 May–20 Sep
rm48 ⇆29 ⋔6 🏛 **P** dB104–222
dB ⇆125–237 sea

★ **Armorique** ᴸᴱ **(DPn)** ☎560019 →

Apr–Sep
rm25 ⇌8 ▥8 A12rm **P**

🏧⊅J **L Bourhis** rte de Quimper ☎560265
Closed Sep 15–30 Ren

FOUGÈRES
Ille-et-Vilaine (☎99)

★ ★**Voyageurs** 10 pl Gambetta (n.rest)
☎990820

9 Jan–22 Dec
rm37 ⇌12 ▥24 A10rm ⌂ **P** Lift ☽

★**Moderne** ⌷(**DPn**) 15 r Tribunal
☎990024
rm26 ⇌5 ▥14 ⌂ **P** dB75–85
dB ⇌ ▥130

FOULAIN
Haute-Marne (☎25)

★**Chalet (DPn)** (NI9) ☎311111

15 Dec–15 Nov
rm12 ⇌5 **P**

FOURAS
Charente-Maritime (☎46)

★ ★**Grand Hotel des Bains** 15 r Gl-
Bruncher ☎840344

30 May–24 Sep
rm36 ⇌3 ▥32 ⌂ dB95–132
dB ⇌ ▥146–160

FOURMETOT See **PONT-AUDEMER**

FOURMIES
Nord (☎27)

☆ ☆**Ibis** Etangs des Moines (n.rest)
☎602154

⇌31 **P** sB ⇌166 dB ⇌205

FOURNEAUX (Creuse) See **AUBUSSON**

FOURNEAUX (Savois) See **MODANE**

FRAYSSINNET
Lot (☎65)

★**Bonne Auberge** ⌷(**DPn**) ☎310002

Feb–Nov
▥10 A2rm ⌂ sB ▥91 dB ▥138–180

☆**Escale** ☎310001

15 Apr–Nov
▥18 ⌂ mountains

🏧⊅**Societé Drianne Campana** (N20)
☎310017

At PONT-DE-RHODES
(1km N on N20)

★**Relais** ☎310016
Etr–Oct
rm29 ⇌19 ▥4 ⌂ **P** Dpn130
Pool

FRÉJUS
Var (☎94)

☆ ☆ ☆**St-Aygulf** 214 rte Nationale 98
☎810123

⇌383 Lift sB ⇌200–240 dB ⇌400–480
M65 sea mountains

🏧⊅**Auge Christian** 280 av de Verdun
☎510299 Closed Oct 1–5, Sat pm & Sun
BL

Daniel Depannages 25 r d'Aubenas
☎510356

France

🏧⊅**Grand Garage de Fréjus Plage** 137 bd
de la Libération ☎512319 Closed Sat pm
& Sun Tal

🏧⊅**Satac** (N7) ☎514061 Ren

At COLOMBIER (3km W)

★ ★ ★**Residences du Colombier** (MAP)
rte de Bagnols ☎514592 tx470328

Apr–10 Oct
rm60 ⇌40 ▥20 dB ⇌ ▥400–530 🏊
Pool

FRÉVENT
Pas-de-Calais (☎21)

★**Amiens** ⌷7 r Doullens ☎042543
rm10 ⇌1 ▥3 ⌂

FRIGNICOURT See **VITRY-LE-FRANÇOIS**

FRONTIGNAN
Hérault (☎67)

★ ★**Balajan** (Inter) (4km NE on N112)
☎481399

Mar–Jan
rm21 ⇌11 ▥4 ⌂ **P** mountains

🏧⊅**Peugeot Frontignan** rte de Montpellier
☎481368 Closed Sat & Sun Peu

FUMAY
Ardennes (☎24)

★ ★**Roches** 82 av J-Jaurès ☎411012
Closed Feb
rm30 ⇌8 ▥8 ⌂ **P** sB90 sB ⇌ ▥145
dB105 dB ⇌ ▥160 mountains

GACÉ
Orne (☎33)

★ ★ ★**Champs** ⌷(**DPn**) rte d'Alençon-
Rouen ☎355145
15 Jan–15 Feb
rm14 ⇌6 ▥2 **P** sB88–158
sB ⇌ ▥118–158 dB116–200
dB ⇌ ▥136–236 Pool

★**Étoile d'Or** 60 Grande Rue ☎355003
15 Mar–10 Feb
rm12 ⌂ **P**

🏧⊅**P Lafosse** (N138) ☎356247 Closed
Sep 1–15 Cit

GAILLARD
Haute-Savoie (☎50)
See also **ANNEMASSE**

☆ ☆ ☆**Mercure** (exit Annemasse-B41) r
des Jardins ☎920525 tx385815
⇌1 ▥78 **P** Lift ☽ sB ⇌ ▥200–243
dB ⇌ ▥262–301 Pool

GAILLON
Eure (☎32)

🏧⊅**Orienne** 21 av du Ml-Leclerc ☎530502
Closed Jul, Sun pm & Mon Cit Peu

🏧⊅**Poupardin** Côte des Sables ☎530337
All makes

GAP
Hautes-Alpes (☎92)

★ ★**Fons Régina** ⌷(2km S on N85)
quartier de Fontreyne ☎510253

Dec–15 Oct
rm20 ⇌5 ▥9 **P** dB75–130
dB ⇌ ▥157–168 mountains

★ ★**Grille** 2 pl F-Euzière ☎538484
rm30 ⇌12 ▥18 Lift

★ ★**Mokotel** (3km S) quartier Graffinel,
rte de Marseille (n.rest) ☎515782
rm27 ⇌22 ▥5 **P** sB ⇌ ▥122–155
dB ⇌ ▥132–167 mountains

★**Poyo** 4 pl F-Euzière (n.rest) ☎510413
rm17 ⇌6 ▥11 Lift sB ⇌ ▥107–130
dB ⇌ ▥118–140 mountains

🏧⊅**Gap Auto** av d'Embrun ☎520561
Closed Sat & Sun Ren

🏧⊅**Verdun** 4 r P-Bert ☎512618 Closed
Sat & Sun BL

At PONT-SARRAZIN (4km NE on N94)

🏧⊅**Bernard** ☎512861 Closed Sun Vlo

🏧⊅**Berta** ☎511376 Closed Sat pm, & Sun
Feb–May & Oct–Nov VW

GARDE-ST-CAST (LA) See **ST-CAST-LE-
GUILDO**

GEISPOLSHEIM See **STRASBOURG**

GÉMENOS
Bouches-du-Rhône (☎42)

★ ★ ★**Relais de la Magdaiene** rte d'Aix-
en-Provence ☎822005

15 Mar–1 Nov
rm20 ⇌18 ▥2 **P** dB ⇌ ▥250–380
Pool

GENNES
Maine-et-Loire (☎41)

★ ★**Loire** ⌷(**DPn**) ☎518103

10 Feb–27 Dec
rm11 ⇌4 ▥2 ⌂ **P**

★ ★ ★**Naulets d'Anjou** r Croix de
Mission ☎518188

Apr–Nov
⇌20 **P** sB ⇌120–150 dB140–160
dB ⇌150–170

GENTILLY See **PARIS**

GÉRARDMER
Vosges (☎29)

★ ★ ★**Grand Bragard** pl du Tilleul
☎630631 tx961408

Rest closed Nov–Apr
⇌62 ⌂ **P** Lift ☽ sB ⇌230–300
dB ⇌280–350 Pool

★ ★**Parc** ⌷12–14 av de Ville-de-Vichy
☎633243

Apr–Sep & Xmas–Feb
rm38 ⇌4 ▥18 A14rm **P** sB76
sB ⇌ ▥200 dB94–165 dB ⇌ ▥200
mountains

★**Echo de Ramberchamp** (n.rest)
☎630227

Feb–15 Nov

rm16 ⇌11 **P** sB76–89 sB ⇌101–104
dB97 dB ⇌114–123 mountains lake

At **SAUT-DES-CUVES** (3km NE on N417)

★ ★ ★**Saut-des-Cuves** ☎633046
tx961408
rm30 ⇌15 ⋔15 🏠 **P** Lift mountains

GETS (LES)
Haute-Savoie (☎50)

★ ★ ★**Marmotte ⫣ (DPn)** ☎797539
Jul–2 Sep
rm45 ⇌36 ⋔9 🏠 ▲ Lift sB ⋔200–250
dB ⇌270–340

GEX
Ain (☎50)

★**Bellevue (DPn** in season) av de la
Gare ☎415540
Feb–Nov
rm22 ⇌11 ⋔11 🏠 **P** mountains lake

GIEN
Loiret (☎38)

★ ★**Rivage ⫣** 1 quai de Nice ☎672053
rm29 ⇌17 ⋔2 🏠 **P** sB73
sB ⇌ ⋔180 dB80 dB ⇌ ⋔190 ⌂

🍴**Reverdy** rte de Bourges ☎672898
Closed Sat pm, Sun & Mon am Ren

GISORS
Eure (☎32)

★ ★**Moderne ⫣** (FAH) pl de la Gare
☎552351
Closed 20 Dec–7 Jan & 14 Jul–9 Aug
rm33 ⇌6 ⋔17 🏠 **P** dB137–177
dB ⇌ ⋔159–259

GLACERIE (LA) See **CHERBOURG**

GLÉNIC
Creuse (☎55)

★ ★**Moulin Noyé ⫣** ☎520911
rm32 ⇌12 🏠 **P** dB90–144
dB ⇌90–144

GLUGES See **MARTEL**

GONESSE
Val-d'Oise (☎3)

☆ ☆**Climat de France** la Croix St Benoît, r
d'Aulnay (off N370) ☎9874244 tx612241
⇌38 **P** dB ⇌206–226 M54–70

GOUESNIÈRE (LA) See **ST-MALO**

GOUMOIS
Doubs (☎81)

★ ★**Taillard ⫣ (DPn)** ☎442075
Mar–Oct
rm17 ⇌12 ⋔5 🏠 **P** dB125–140
dB ⇌ ⋔206 mountains

GOURNAY-EN-BRAY
Seine-Maritime (☎35)

🍴**Central** (J-Breteuil) r F-Faure
☎900075 Closed Aug 15–31 also Sun &
Mon Cit

GRAMAT
Lot (☎65)

★ ★ ★**Château de Roumégouse** (4.5km
NW on N140) ☎336381

Apr–Nov
⇌12 **P**

★ ★**Centre ⫣** pl République ☎387337
rm15 ⇌3 ⋔6 🏠 **P** sB67–162
sB ⇌ ⋔122–162 dB79–180
dB ⇌ ⋔134–180

★**Lion d'Or ⫣ (DPn)** pl République
☎387318
15 Jan–15 Dec
⇌15 Lift dB ⇌ ⋔204–264 M60–160 &
alc

GRANDE-MOTTE (LA)
Hérault (☎67)

★ ★ ★**Frantel** r du Port ☎569801
tx480241
15 Mar–10 Dec
rm135 ⇌117 ⋔18 **P** Lift sB ⇌ ⋔407
dB ⇌476

🍴**Gorin** zone Artisanale ☎565601
Closed Sun & Xmas wk Ren

GRAND-PRESSIGNY (LE)
Indre-et-Loire (☎47)

★**Espérance (DPn)** ☎949012
Closed 6 Jan–6 Feb
rm10 **P**

GRANVILLE
Manche (☎33)

★ ★**Bains** 19 r G-Clemenceau ☎501731
15 Feb–2 Jan
rm60 ⇌25 ⋔33 **P** Lift 𝄐 sea

🍴**A Harel** 5 r C-Desmaisons ☎510104
Closed Sep 8–30, Sat pm & Sun Tal

🍴**C Poulain** av des Vendéens ☎500214
Ren

GRASSE
Alpes-Maritimes (☎93)
See also **CHÂTEAUNEUF-DE-GRASSE**

★ ★**Aromes ⫣** (N85) ☎704201
Feb–1 Nov
rm7 ⇌6 sB ⇌99–144 dB ⇌145

GRAY
Haute-Saône (☎84)

★ ★ ★**Château de Rigny** ☎652501
⇌24 🏠 **P** ⌂

★ ★**Bellevue ⫣** av Carnot 1 ☎654776
1 Jan–8 Dec
rm15 ⇌7 ⋔2 🏠 **P** sB58 sB ⇌ ⋔84
dB77–90 dB ⇌ ⋔112–130

★ ★**Fer-a-Cheval ⫣** 4 av Carnot (n.rest)
☎653255
Closed 25 Dec–4 Jan & 14–22 Aug
rm39 ⇌38 🏠 **P** ⇌100 dB ⇌140–155

GRENOBLE
Isère (☎76)

★ ★ ★ ★**Mercure** 1 av d'Innsbruck
☎095427 tx980470

⇌100 🏠 **P** Lift sB ⇌305–375
dB⇌405–470 Pool mountains

★ ★ ★ ★**Park** 10 pl P-Mistral ☎872911
tx320767
Closed Xmas & New Year
rm62 ⇌57 ⋔5 🏠 **P** Lift 𝄐
sB ⇌ ⋔260–330 dB ⇌ ⋔650
mountains

★ ★ ★**Angleterre** 5 pl V-Hugo (n.rest)
☎873721 tx320297
rm70 ⇌40 ⋔30 **P** Lift
sB ⇌ ⋔220–300 dB ⇌ ⋔326–336
mountains

★ ★ ★**Grand** (Inter) 5 r de la République
☎444936 tx980882
rm70 ⇌28 ⋔42 Lift sB ⇌ ⋔155–176
dB ⇌ ⋔187–219 mountains

★ ★ ★**Terminus** 10 pl Gare (n.rest)
☎872433 tx320245
Closed Aug
rm50 ⇌12 ⋔32 Lift sB105–185
sB ⇌ ⋔185–210 dB195–210
dB ⇌ ⋔195–220

★ ★**Alpazur** 59 av Alsace-Lorraine
(n.rest) ☎464280
rm30 ⇌6 ⋔14 sB90–132 sB ⇌ ⋔150
dB161 dB ⇌ ⋔189

☆ ☆**Fimotel** 20 av J-Jaurés ☎242312
⇌42 **P** Lift sB⇌193 dB ⇌221
M49–80 mountains

★ ★**Gallia** 7 bd Ml-Joffre (n.rest)
☎873921 tx980882
20 Aug–Jul
rm35 ⇌23 ⋔5 Lift

☆ ☆**Ibis** Centre Commerciale des Trois
Dauphins, r F-Poulat ☎474849 tx320890
⇌71 **P** Lift sB ⇌193 dB ⇌231

★ ★**Paris Nice** 61 bd J-Vallier (n.rest)
☎963618
rm29 ⇌7 ⋔13 **P** 𝄐 sB99–150
sB ⇌ ⋔150–170 dB113–170
dB ⇌ ⋔150–170 mountains

🍴**Albertiny** 38 av F-Viallet ☎090087
Closed Sat pm BL

At **CLAIX** (10.5km S on N75 & D269)

★ ★ ★**Oiseaux** ☎980774 tx320871
Feb–Oct
rm20 ⇌5 ⋔10 🏠 **P** sB126–150
sB ⇌ ⋔171–191 dB182–210
dB ⇌ ⋔202–272 Pool mountains

At **MEYLAN** (3km NE on N90)

☆ ☆**Climat de France** chemin du Viend
Clêne ☎907690 tx612241
⇌38 **P** dB ⇌206–221 M54–70

At **PONT-DE-CLAIX** (8km S on N75)

★ ★**Villancourt** cours St-André
☎981854
rm33 ⇌24 ⋔9 🏠 **P** Lift
sB ⇌ ⋔107–130 dB ⇌129–170
mountains

At **VOREPPE** (12km NW by A48)

☆ ☆ ☆**Novotel** Autoroute de Lyon
☎508144 tx320273 →

⇄114 **P** Lift sB ⇄243–253
dB ⇄282–306

🕭**Echallion** ☎502385 Closed Sat & Sun
Sim Tal

GRÉOUX-LES-BAINS
Alpes-de-Hautes-Provence (☎92)

★ ★ ★**Villa Borghèse** (MAP) av des
Thermes ☎780091 tx401513
Mar–Nov
⇄70 🏥 **P** Lift 🌙 sB ⇄200
dB ⇄304–380 🏊 Pool mountains

GRIMAUD
Var (☎94)

Cheillan rte Nationale ☎432060 All
makes

At **PORT-GRIMAUD** (5.5km E)

★ ★ ★**Port** pl du Marché ☎563618
⇄50 **P** Lift sB ⇄285–400
dB⇄370–440 Pool sea

GRISOLLES
Tarn-et-Garonne (☎63)

★ ★**Relais des Garrigues** (N20)
☎303159

Closed 5 Jan–12 Feb
rm27 🏠20 🏥 **P** 🌙 sB80–160
sB 🏠 160–180 dB 🏠 180

GUÉRANDE
Loire-Atlantique (☎40)

🕭**Cottais** rte de la Turballe ☎249039
Peu

GUÉRET
Creuse (☎55)

★**Auclair** ⌐ 19 av Sénatorerie ☎520126
rm33 ⇄6 🏠15 A5rm 🏥 **P** dB82–180
dB ⇄ 🏠85–202 mountains

GUÉTHARY
Pyrénées-Atlantiques (☎59)

★ ★**Mariléna** av Mon-Mugabure (n.rest)
☎265104
Jun–Sep
rm14 ⇄4 🏠1 **P** sB65–100 dB93–140
dB ⇄ 🏠131–156 sea

GUILVINEC
Finistère (☎98)

At **LECHIAGAT** (1km E)

★ ★**Port** (FAH) (**DPn**) ☎581010
8 Jan–23 Dec
rm37 ⇄8 🏠29 dB ⇄ 🏠159–259 sea

HAM
Somme (☎22)

★**France** (**DPn**) 5 pl Hôtel-de-Ville
☎810022
Closed Feb, Aug & school hols
rm16 ⇄10 🏠 sB80–140
sB ⇄ 🏠80–140 dB110
dB ⇄ 🏠140–175

HAUCONCOURT See METZ

HAUTE-GOULAINE
Loire-Atlantique (☎40)

France

★ ★ ★**Lande St-Martin** rte de Poitiers
(N149) ☎800080
rm39 ⇄16 🏠14 **P** 🌙 🕉

HAUTEVILLE-LÈS-DIJON See DIJON

HAVRE (LE)
Seine-Maritime (☎35)

See Plan
|**AA**| agent; See page 105

★ ★ ★**Bordeaux** 147 r L-Brindeau
(n.rest) ☎226944 tx190428 Plan1
rm31 ⇄20 🏠11 Lift 🌙
sB ⇄ 🏠218–340 dB ⇄ 🏠286–356

★ ★ ★**Marley** 121 r de Paris (n.rest)
☎417248 tx190369 Plan **1A**
rm34 ⇄14 🏠19 Lift 🌙 sB121–212
sB ⇄ 🏠124–228 dB ⇄ 🏠199–239

☆ ☆ ☆**Mercure** chaussée d'Angoulême
☎212345 tx190749 Plan2
⇄96 Lift sB ⇄323–388 dB ⇄366–403
M alc

★ ★**Foch** 4 r Caligny (n.rest) ☎425069
tx190369 Plan4
rm33 ⇄20 🏠3 **P** Lift

★ ★**Grand Parisien** 1 cours de la
République (n.rest) ☎252383 tx190369
Plan7
rm22 ⇄11 🏠7 **P** Lift 🌙 sea

★ ★**Ile de France** 104 r A-France (n.rest)
☎424929 Plan 5
rm16 ⇄5 🏠11 **P** sB ⇄ 🏠68–120
dB ⇄ 🏠70–140

★ ★**Monaco** 16 r de Paris ☎422101
Plan **6**
Mar–Aug & 15 Sep–15 Feb
rm11 ⇄7 🏠2 **P** Lift sB92–190
sB ⇄ 🏠132–195 dB123–220
dB ⇄ 🏠169–253 sea

★**Petit Vatel** 86 r L-Brindeau (n.rest)
☎417207 Plan 8
rm29 ⇄3 🏠13 sB73–125
sB ⇄ 🏠103–140 dB101–150
dB ⇄ 🏠131–186

★**Voltaire** 14 r Voltaire (n.rest) ☎413091
Plan 9
rm24 🏠14 **P** sB79 sB 🏠91 dB105
dB 🏠124

Auto 91 r J-Lecesne ☎226969 Closed
Aug 15–Sep 1 & Sun BMW

At **MONTIVILLIERS** (7km NE)

☆ ☆**Climate de France** ZAC de la
Lézarde ☎304139 tx612441 Plan 3
⇄38 **P** dB ⇄193–213 M54–70

At **STE-ADRESSE** (4km NW)

★ ★**Phares** 29 r Gl-de-Gaulle (n.rest)
☎463186 Not on Plan
rm26 ⇄10 🏠8 🏥 **P** 🌙 dB90–106
dB ⇄ 🏠122–132

HAYE-DU-PUITS (LA)
Manche (☎33)

★**Gare** ⌐ (**DPn**) ☎460422
rm12 ⇄1 🏠1 **P** dB63–93 dB ⇄ 🏠120

HÉDÉ
Ille-et-Villaine (☎99)

★ ★**Hostellerie du Vieux Moulin** ⌐
(**DPn**) (N137) ☎454570
Closed 15 Dec–Feb & Sun & Mon pm
rm14 ⇄12 🏥 **P**

HENDAYE-PLAGE
Pyrénées-Atlantiques (☎59)

★ ★ ★**Lillac** 2 r des Clematites ☎200245
rm23 ⇄10 🏠13 Lift

★ ★ ★**Paris** Rond-Point (n.rest)
☎200506
Jun-Sep
rm39 ⇄5 🏠24 Lift

HENIN-BEAUMONT
Pas-de-Calais (☎21)

At **Noyelles-Godault** (3km NE)

☆ ☆ ☆**Novotel Henin Douai** (A1)
☎751601 tx110352
⇄79 **P** sB ⇄257–267 dB ⇄308–323
Pool

☆ ☆**Campanile** Zone Artisanale et
Commerciale, rte de Beaumont
dB ⇄ 🏠218–222

HERBIGNAC
Loire-Atlantique (☎40)

🕭**Thudot** ☎889174 Closed Sep, Sat pm,
Sun & Mon am ex Jul & Aug Cit

HERMIES
Pas-de-Calais (☎21)

🕭**Bachelet** 62 r d'Havrincourt ☎074184
Closed Sun Peu

🕭**Gustin** 12–13 Grand Place ☎0704010
Closed Sat pm & Sun Tal

HÉROUVILLE-ST-CLAIR See CAEN

HESDIN
Pas-de-Calais (☎21)

★ ★**Flandres** ⌐ (**DPn**) 22 r d'Arras
☎868021
15 Jan–23 Dec
rm14 ⇄5 🏠4 🏥 dB52–160
dB ⇄ 🏠52–160

HONFLEUR
Calvados (☎31)

★ ★ ★**Ferme St-Siméon** r A-Marais
☎892361
Feb–Dec
⇄19 A9rm **P** sea

★ ★**Dauphin** 10 pl P-Berthelot (n.rest)
☎891553
2 Feb–22 Dec
rm30 ⇄28 🏠2 A16rm

🕭**Nicolle** 55 r de la République
☎890164 Closed 15–30 Sep, Sat pm &
Sun Aud BL VW

🕭**Port** 15 pl A-Normand ☎891613
Closed Sat pm & Sun Peu

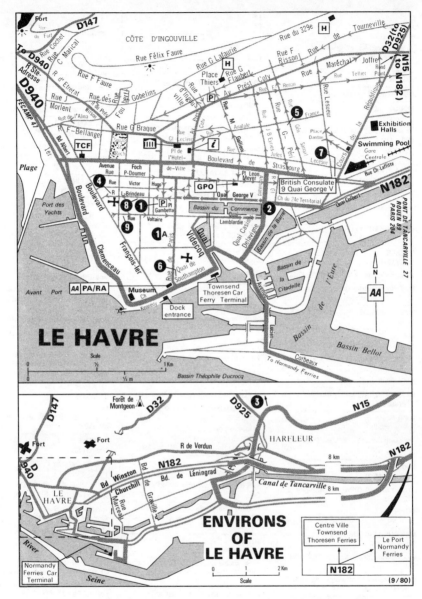

LE HAVRE

Scale

0 — ½ — 1 Km
0 — ½ m

Bassin Théophile Ducrocq

ENVIRONS OF LE HAVRE

Scale

0 — 1 — 2 Km

Centre Ville Townsend Thoresen Ferries → N182 ← Le Port Normandy Ferries

(9/80)

HOSSEGOR
Landes (☎58)

★★**Beauséjour (DPn)** av Genets par av Tour du Lac ☎435107
5 Jun–17 Sep
rm45 ⤴38 🛏7 🏠 **P** Lift
sB ⤴ 🛏143–180 dB ⤴ 🛏170–300
Pool

★★**Ermitage** 🅻 **(DPn)** allées des Pins Tranquilles ☎435222

Closed Jan
rm14 ⤴2 🛏12 **P** dB ⤴ 🛏192 🐾

HOUCHES (LES)
Haute-Savoie (☎50)

★★**Piste Bleue** rte les Chavants
☎544066
15 Dec–Etr & 15 Jun–15 Sep
rm25 ⤴16 dB121–160 dB ⤴159–176
mountains

HAVRE (LE)

1	★★★Bordeaux
1a	★★★Marly
2	☆☆☆Mercure
3	☆☆Climat de France (At Montivilliers)
4	★★Foch
5	★★Ile de France
6	★★Monaco
7	★★Grand Parisien
8	★★Petit Vatel
9	★Voltaire

149

France

HOUDAN
Yvelines (☎3)

★**St-Christopher** 🗲 (DPn) 6 pl du Gl-de-Gaulle ☎6466161

Closed Jul
rm9 🏛 **P**

HOUDEMONT See **NANCY**

HOULGATE
Calvados (☎31)

★ ★**Centre** 31 r des Bains (n.rest)
☎911815

Jun–9 Sep
rm22 ⇌4 ⋔11 dB105–178
dB ⇌ ⋔198 sea

HUELGOAT
Finistère (☎98)

★ ★**Triskel** 72 r des Cieux (n.rest)
☎997185

Closed 15 Nov–15 Dec
rm11 ⇌3 ⋔8 **P**

HYÈRES
Var (☎94)

Fleschi 7 rte de Toulon ☎650283 Fia

&🌓**M Pique** quartier de la Vilette
☎577525 Closed Sat & Sun Aud Tal VW

HYÈVRE-PAROISSE See **BAUME-LES-DAMES**

IGÉ
Saône-et-Loire (☎85)

★ ★ ★**Châteaux d'Igé** ☎333399

15 Mar–5 Nov
⇌12 🏛 **P**

ILLKIRCH-GRAFFENSTADEN See **STRASBOURG**

INOR
Meuse (☎29)

★**Faison Doré** r de l'Ecluse ☎803545
⇌13 🏛 **P**

ISIGNY-SUR-MER
Calvados (☎31)

☆ ☆**France** 🗲 (DPn) 17 r Demagny
☎220033

Feb–2 Nov
rm20 ⇌16 **P** 🌓 dB110–180 dB ⇌180

ISLE-SUR-LE-DOUBS (L')
Doubs (☎81)

&🌓**A Bouraly** 23 r du Moulin ☎927086
Frd Tal

&🌓**C Marcoux** 64 r du Magny ☎963154
Closed Sat pm & Sun Ren

ISLE-SUR-SEREIN (L')
Yonne (☎86)

&🌓**A Gentil** rte de Tonnerre ☎338414
M/c Closed Sun pm Cit

ISSOIRE
Puy-de-Dôme (☎73)

★ ★**Parlou** 🗲 18 av Kennedy ☎892211
Closed 22 Sep–15 Oct, 22 Dec–6 Jun &
Sat/Sun winter/rest closed Sat/Sun (ex
Aug)
rm29 ⇌8 ⋔15 **P**

&🌓**SA Arverne Auto** rte de Clermont
☎891631 Cit

ISSOUDUN
Indre (☎54)

★ ★**France & Commerce** 🗲 (FAH) 3r P-Brossolette ☎210065 tx751422

Mar–21 Jan
rm24 ⇌17 ⋔7 **P** 🌓

IVRY-LA-BATAILLE
Eure (☎32)

★ ★**Grand St-Martin** 🗲 9 r Erzy
☎364139

2 Feb–Dec
rm10 ⇌4 ⋔4 sB110–240 sB ⇌240
dB180 dB ⇌ ⋔180–254

JANVILLE
Eure-et-Loire (☎37)

J Godart 8 r du Moulin à Vent ☎900024
Closed 20 Dec–3 Jan Peu

JARD-SUR-MER
Vendée (☎51)

★ ★**Parc de la Grange** 🗲 (FAH) rte du
Payré ☎334488

Apr–Sep
rm55 ⇌ ⋔12 A7rm **P**
dB ⇌ ⋔153–244 ✠ Pool

JARNAC
Charente (☎45)

At **FLEURAC** (10km NE via D66 and D157)

★ ★**Domaine de Fleurac** (DPn)
☎817822

15 Mar–15 Dec
rm17 ⇌14 ⋔3 A7rm **P**
sB ⇌ ⋔110–120 dB ⇌ ⋔220–260

JARNY
Meurthe-et-Moselle (☎8)

&🌓**R Rilliard** 53 av Lafayette ☎2330486
Peu

&🌓**Rouy** r Gambetta et av Lafayette
☎2330221 Closed Aug 4–25, Sat & Sun
Cit

JOIGNY
Yonne (☎86)

★ ★ ★**Côte St-Jacques** 🗲 (DPn) 14 fbg
de Paris ☎620970

Mid Feb–Dec
⇌18 A2rm 🏛 **P** sB ⇌ ⋔250
dB ⇌ ⋔410; Pool

★ ★**Modern** 🗲 (MAP) (DPn) 17 av R-Petit ☎621628 tx801693

Closed 26 Nov–15 Dec
rm21 ⇌9 ⋔9 🏛 **P** dB300–320
dB ⇌ ⋔300–324 Pool

&🌓**R Blondeau** 6 fbg de Paris ☎620502
Closed Sun Opl

JOINVILLE
Haute-Marne (☎25)

★**Poste** 🗲 (FAH) (DPn) pl Grève
☎961263

10 Feb–10 Jan
rm11 ⇌3 ⋔2 🏛 **P** sB62–132
sB ⇌ ⋔102–132 dB84–154
dB ⇌ ⋔114–154

★**Soleil d'Or** 7 r des Capucins ☎961566

rm9 ⇌1 ⋔7 🏛 **P** sB55–90
sB ⇌ ⋔55–90 dB85 dB ⇌ ⋔108

JONZAC
Charente-Maritime (☎46)

★ ★**Club** 8 pl Église (n.rest) ☎480227

rm16 ⇌4 ⋔8 A3rm sB73 sB ⇌ ⋔90
dB105 dB ⇌ ⋔135

JOSSELIN
Morbihan (☎97)

★ ★**Château** 1 r Gl-de-Gaulle ☎222011

Closed Feb
rm36 ⇌10 ⋔17 🏛 **P** sB110–215
sB ⇌ ⋔180–215 dB130–235
dB ⇌ ⋔200–235 M50–150

JOUÉ-LÉS-TOURS
Indre-et-Loire (☎47)
See also **TOURS**

☆ ☆**Campanile** av du Lac, les
Bretonnières, rte de Chinon ☎672489
tx750806

⇌41 dB ⇌206–209 M55–80

★ ★**Château de Beaulieu** (DPn)
☎532026

rm17 ⇌9 ⋔7 A8rm **P** sB100–350
sB ⇌ ⋔200–350 dB220–350
dB ⇌ ⋔220–350

★ ★**Parc** (Inter) 17 bd Chinon (n.rest)
☎251538

Mar–Jan
rm30 ⇌20 ⋔10 🏛 **P** Lift sB ⇌203
dB ⇌225

JOUGNE
Doubs (☎81)

★**Deux Saisons** ☎490004

15 Dec–15 Apr & Jun–Sep
rm21 ⇌16 ⋔5 🏛 **P** sB ⇌ ⋔75–90
dB92–120 dB ⇌ ⋔112–151 mountains

JUAN-LES-PINS
Alpes-Maritimes (☎93)

★ ★ ★**Belles Rives** bd Littoral
☎610279 tx470984

10 Apr–Sep
rm44 ⇌41 ⋔3 Lift 🌓 M alc
DPn560–875 S15% Beach sea

★ ★ ★**Apparthotel Astor** 61 Chemin
Fournel Badine ☎610738

⇌19 **P** dB ⇌250–400

★ ★ ★**Helios** (DPn in summer) 3 av
Dautheville ☎615525 tx970906

Mar–Oct
rm70 ⇌66 ⋔4 🏛 Lift 🌓
sB ⇌ ⋔300–700 dB ⇌ ⋔520–950

★ ★ ★**Juana** (DPn in season) av G-Gallice, la Pinède ☎610870 tx470778

Mid Apr–Oct
⇌42 🏛 **P** Lift 🏛 sB ⇌ 660–905
dB ⇌ 1120–1770 M290 & alc Beach sea

★★**Alexandra** r Pauline ☎610136
Apr-Sep
rm20 ⇨7 🚪8 sB87–118
sB ⇨ 🚪123–144 dB165–273
dB ⇨ 🚪211–289 Beach

★★**Cyrano** av L-Gallet (n.rest) ☎610483
Feb–Oct
rm40 ⇨12 🚪20 Lift 🌙
sB ⇨ 🚪130–250 dB ⇨ 🚪160–320
Beach sea

★★**Emeraude** (DPn in season) 11 av
Saramartel ☎610967 tx470673
Feb–Nov
rm22 ⇨4 🚪17 🚗 P Lift sB115–160
sB ⇨ 🚪165 dB ⇨ 🚪250–290
mountains

★★**Noailles** av Gallice ☎611170
Jun–Sep
rm22 ⇨3 🚪2 🚗 P sea

★**Midi** 93 bd Poincaré ☎613516
2 Jan–15 Oct
rm22 ⇨2 🚪18 A8rm 🚗 P sB80–110
dB150 dB ⇨ 🚪185 sea

Wilson 122 bd Wilson ☎612515 Closed
Sat & Sun All makes

JULLOUVILLE
Manche (☎33)

★★**Casino**Ⓛ (DPn) r de la Mer
☎618282
28 Apr–10 May & 25 May–13 Sep
rm57 ⇨17 🚪17 P sB81–97
sB ⇨ 🚪123–174 dB141–187
dB ⇨ 🚪168–221 sea

KAYSERSBERG See **COLMAR**

LA each name preceded by 'La' is listed
under the name that follows it.

LADOIX-SERRIGNY See **BEAUNE**

LAFFREY
Isère (☎76)

★★**Grand Lac**Ⓛ ☎681290
May–Sep
rm38 ⇨15 🚪4 A19rm sB ⇨ 🚪71–91
dB ⇨ 🚪97–140 mountains lake

LALINDE
Dordogne (☎53)

★★**Château**Ⓛ (DPn) r Verdun ☎610182
Feb–Nov
rm9 ⇨1 🚪3 sB72–80 dB88
dB ⇨ 🚪202

★★**Résidence** 3 r Prof-Testut (n.rest)
☎610181
May–Sep
rm11 ⇨2 🚪9 sB ⇨ 🚪70
dB ⇨ 🚪110–150

LAMASTRE
Ardèche (☎75)

★★★**Midi** (DPn) pl Seignobos
☎064150
Mar–15 Dec
rm22 ⇨12 🚪2 🚗 sB ⇨ 🚪80–160
dB90–200 dB ⇨ 🚪150–200 mountains

LAMBALLE
Côtes-du-Nord (☎96)

France

★★**Angleterre**Ⓛ (FAH) (DPn) 29 bd
Jobert ☎310016
rm35 ⇨12 🚪10 A13rm 🚗 Lift

★★**Auberge du Manoir des Portes** La
Poterie ☎311362
Closed Feb
⇨15 P

★**Tour d'Argent**Ⓛ 2 r du Dr-Lavergne
☎310137
rm31 ⇨10 🚪12 A16rm 🚗 P
sB68–150 sB ⇨ 🚪150 dB92–190
dB ⇨ 🚪200

🏍**Clemenceau** 12 bd Clemenceau
☎310593 Closed Sep 1–20 & Sun pm Frd

LAMORLAYE See **CHANTILLY**

LANÇON-PROVENCE See **SALON-DE-PROVENCE**

LANDERNEAU
Finistère (☎98)

☆☆**Ibis** ☎213132 tx940878
⇨42 P 🌙 sB ⇨192 dB ⇨234

LANESTER See **LORIENT**

LANGEAIS
Indre-et-Loire (☎47)

★★**Hosten**Ⓛ 2 r Gambetta (n.rest)
☎967063
rm12 ⇨8 🚪2 🚗 P sB128–180
sB ⇨ 🚪188–208 dB256–266
dB ⇨ 🚪276–296

LANGON
Gironde (☎56)

🏍**Doux & Trouillot** 50 r J-Ferry ☎630047
M/c Closed Sun Peu

LANGRES
Haute-Marne (☎25)

★★**Europe** (DPn) 23 r Diderot ☎851088
Closed Oct & 1st wk May
rm28 ⇨8 🚪16 A9rm 🚗 P sB60
sB ⇨ 🚪110–120 dB110–150
dB ⇨ 🚪120–165

★★**Lion d'Or** (DPn) rte de Vesoul
☎850330
Closed Feb
rm16 ⇨5 🚪7 🚗 P sB65–100
sB ⇨ 🚪120 dB ⇨ 🚪145

★**Cheval Blanc** (DPn) 4 r de l'Estres
☎850700
Mar–Dec
rm21 ⇨7 🚪10 A7rm 🚗 P dB70–180
dB ⇨ 🚪70–180

🏍**Blosch** 2 av C-Baudoin ☎852238 M/c
Frd

🏍**Europe** rte de Charmont ☎850378
Closed Aug, Sat & Sun Aud BMW VW

At **BOURG** (9km s on N74)

🏍**Vallet** (N67) ☎852515

At **ST-GEOSMES** (4km S on N74)

🏍**Sabinus** ☎850433 Opl

LANSLEBOURG-MONT-CENIS
Savoie (☎79)

★★★**Alpazur**Ⓛ (Inter) ☎059369
20 Dec–20 Apr & Jun–20 Sep
rm21 ⇨16 🚪5 🚗 P
sB ⇨ 🚪170–200 dB ⇨ 🚪190–220
mountains

★**Relais des Deux Cols**Ⓛ 73 Val Cenis
☎059283
May–Sep
rm30 ⇨22 A10rm 🚗 P dB94–175
dB ⇨165 Pool mountains

LANSLEVILLARD
Savoie (☎79)

★★**Étoile des Neiges** ☎059041
15 Jun–15 Sep & 15 Dec–15 Apr
rm18 ⇨12 🚪4 🚗 P sB75–120
sB ⇨ 🚪95–135 dB100–150
dB ⇨ 🚪130–150 mountains

LAON
Aisne (☎23)

★★**Angleterre** 10 bd de Lyon ☎230462
24 Jan–24 Dec
rm30 ⇨16 🚪6 🚗 P Lift sB110–183
sB ⇨ 🚪183–194 dB201–256
dB ⇨ 🚪231–256

☆☆**Finotel** ZAC Ile de France (N2)
☎201811
⇨40 P Lift sB ⇨194 dB ⇨223

★**Bannière de France** (DPn) 11 r de F-Roosevelt ☎232144
20 Jan–20 Dec
rm18 ⇨5 🚪7 🚗

★**Chevaliers** 3 r Serurier ☎234378
rm15 ⇨7 🚪3

🏍**R Leroy** 16 r V-Hugo ☎235212 M/c
Closed Aug, Sun & Mon BMW Hon

LARAGNE-MONTEGLIN
Hautes-Alpes (☎92)

★★**Terrasses**Ⓛ av Provence ☎650854
May–Oct
rm17 ⇨3 🚪5 🚗 P mountains

LAROQUE-DES-ARCS See **CAHORS**

LAUMES (LES)
Côte-d'Or (☎80)

★★**Gare**Ⓛ ☎960046
Closed 2–14 Dec
rm26 ⇨6 🚪1 🚗 P 🌙

LAURIS
Vaucluse (☎90)

★★**Chaumière**Ⓛ (DPn) pl du Portail
☎680129
15 Feb–15 Nov
rm10 ⇨4 🚪6 P dB ⇨150–220
M65–80 mountains lake

LAVAL
Mayenne (☎43)

☆☆**Ibis** rte de Mayenne ☎538182
tx721094
⇨51 P sB ⇨168 dB ⇨214

151

LAVANDOU (LE)
Var (☎94)

★ ★ ★**Calanque** 62 av Gl-de-Gaulle
☎710596 tx400681
Feb−Oct
rm39 ⇄37 ⋔2 **P** Lift ⅅ sea

★ ★ ★**California** rte de St-Tropez
☎710263
Apr−Oct
⋔27 **P** sea

★ ★ ★**Résidence-Beach (Pn** in season)
bd Front-de-Mer ☎710066
20 May−20 Sep
⇄55 **P** Lift ⅅ sB ⇄250−430
dB ⇄210−450 ⤸ Beach sea

★**Petite Bohème (DPn)** av F-Roosevelt
☎711030
May−Oct
rm19 ⇄6 ⋔11 A3rm ⬛
dB ⇄140−220 sea

🍴**Central** av des Prés ☎711068 Closed
Xmas, New Year, Sat & Sun Peu

LAVAUR
Tarn (☎63)

At **ST-LIEUX-LES-LAVAUR** (11km NW by
D87 and D631)

★ ★**Château** ☎337619
⇄12 **P** ⤸ Pool

LAVERNAY See **RECOLOGNE**

LAXOU See **NANCY**

LE Each name preceded by 'Le' is listed
under the name that follows it.

LECHIAGAT See **GUILVINEC**

LECQUES (LES)
Var (☎94)

★ ★ ★**Grand** ☎262301 tx400165
Apr−Oct
rm58 ⇄53 ⋔3 **P** Lift
dB ⇄250−375 ⤸ sea

LENS
Pas-de-Calais (☎21)

At **VENDIN-LE-VIEL** (6km NE)

☆ ☆**Lensotel** Centre Commercial Lens II
☎786453 tx120324
⇄70 **P** sB ⇄185−205 dB ⇄215−235
Pool

LES Each name preceded by 'Les' is listed
under the name that follows it.

LESCAR See **PAU**

LESQUIN See **LILLE AIRPORT**

LEVERNOIS See **BEAUNE**

LEVROUX
Indre (☎54)

★ ★**Cloche et St-Jacques**ᴸ r Nationale
☎357043
rm30 ⇄9 ⋔12 A14rm **P** sBfr85
dBfr160 dB ⇄ ⋔fr160

LÉZIGNAN-CORBIÈRES
Aude (☎68)

France

★**Tassigny** Rond Point de Lattre
☎271151
Oct−Sep
⇄16 ⬛ **P** sB ⇄135−145
dB ⇄135−145 ⤸ Pool

🍴**Central** 12 av de Gaulle ☎270242
Closed Sat pm & Sun Frd

LIBOURNE
Gironde (☎56)

★ ★**Loubat** 32 r Chanzy ☎511758
rm45 ⇄21 ⋔9 A8rm ⬛ **P** ⅅ

LILLE
Nord (☎20)

★ ★ ★**Bellevue** 5 r J-Roisin ☎574586
tx120790
⇄66 **P** Lift ⅅ sB ⇄ ⋔165−256
dB ⇄ ⋔248

★ ★ ★**Carlton** (MAP) 3 r de Paris
☎552411 tx110400
rm80 ⇄70 ⋔3 Lift sB256−280
sB ⇄ ⋔256−280 dB300−350
dB ⇄ ⋔300−350

★ ★ ★**Royal** 2 bd Carnot (n.rest)
☎510511 tx820575
rm102 ⇄76 ⋔22 **P** Lift sB176
sB ⇄ ⋔243−331 dB421
dB ⇄ ⋔581−741

🍴**Delannoy** 208 r du fbg d'Arras
☎535513 M/c Closed Sat & Sun BL

🍴**Vambre** 17 r de Seclin ☎520785
Closed Sat & Sun All makes

At **ENGLOS** (7.5km W on D63)

☆ ☆ ☆**Mercure** Autoroute Lille-
Dunkerque exit Lomme ☎923015
tx820302
rm95 ⇄51 ⋔44 **P** sB ⇄ ⋔223−254
dB ⇄272−288 Pool

☆ ☆ **Novotel Lille Lomme** Autoroute
A25-exit Lomme ☎070090 tx132120
⇄115 **P** sB ⇄276 dB ⇄332 Malc Pool

At **MARQ-EN-BAROEUL** (4.5km N on
N350)

☆ ☆ ☆ ☆**Holiday Inn** bd de la Marne
☎721730 tx132785
⇄125 **P** Lift sB ⇄314 dB ⇄378 Pool

LILLE AIRPORT

At **LESQUIN** (8km SE)

☆ ☆ ☆ ☆**Holiday Inn** 110 r J-Jaurès
☎979202 tx132051
⇄ ⋔208 **P** Lift ⅅ sB ⇄ ⋔303−314
dB ⇄ ⋔366−378 Pool

☆ ☆ **Novotel Lille Aéroport** (A1)
☎979225 tx820519
⇄92 **P** sB ⇄297 dB ⇄342 Pool

🍴**Gallou** 46 r Pasteur ☎961359 Closed
Sat pm & Sun All makes

LIMOGES
Haute-Vienne (☎55)

★ ★ ★ ★**Frantel** de la République
☎346530 tx580771
⇄75 **P** Lift sB ⇄248−303
dB ⇄326−376

★ ★ ★**Luk (DPn)** 29 pl Jourdan
☎334400 tx580704
rm55 ⇄53 ⋔2 **P** Lift ⅅ
sB ⇄ ⋔190−230 dB ⇄ ⋔230−270

★ ★**Caravelle** 21 r A-Barbès (n.rest)
☎777529
rm31 ⇄6 ⋔25 ⬛ **P** Lift ⅅ

☆ **Ibis** r F-Bastiat, ZAC Industrielle Nord
2 ☎375014 tx580009
⇄76 **P** Lift sB ⇄167 dB ⇄209

★ **Jourdan** (Inter) 2 av du Gl-de-Gaulle
☎774962
rm45 ⇄30 ⋔10 Lift sB ⇄ ⋔79−220
dB ⇄ ⋔91−242

★**Relais Lamartine**ᴸ 10 r des
Cooperateurs ☎775339
rm20 ⇄2 ⋔10

🍴**Auto Sport** 14 r Dupuytren ☎371780
Closed Sat & Sun Aud VW

🍴**Bastide** 229 av du Gl-Leclerc
☎371771 Closed Sat pm & Sun Maz Vlo

LION D'ANGERS (LE)
Maine-et-Loire (☎41)

★**Voyageurs** 2 r Gl-Leclerc quai Oudon
☎913008
6 Feb−15 Nov & Dec−2 Feb
rm13 ⇄4 ⋔2 ⬛ **P**

LISIEUX
Calvados (☎31)

★ ★ ★**Grand Normandie**ᴸ (Inter) **(DPn)**
11 bis r av Char ☎621605 tx170269
May−Sep
rm90 ⇄27 ⋔27 A10rm ⬛ Lift
dB129−195 dB ⇄ ⋔189−214

★ ★ ★**Place** (MAP) 67 r H-Chéron
(n.rest) ☎311744 tx171862
rm33 ⇄19 ⋔14 ⬛ **P** Lift
sB ⇄ ⋔210−230 dB ⇄ ⋔250−280

★**Lourdes** 4 r av Char (n.rest)
☎311948
Mar−Oct
rm37 ⇄6 ⋔2 ⬛ Lift sB75
sB ⇄ ⋔100 dB75−115
dB ⇄ ⋔100−135

★**Coupe d'Or**ᴸ (FAH) 49 r Pont-Mortain
☎311684
rm16 ⇄2 ⋔10 ⬛ **P** sB101 dB185
dB ⇄ ⋔159−259

🍴**Bouley** 62 r du Gl-Leclerc ☎311614
Closed Sat pm & Sun BL BMW

🍴**Samo** 34 r du Gl-Leclerc
☎620446 Closed Sat & Sun Opl

LIVRON-SUR-DRÔME
Drôme (☎75)

🍴**Gemenez** Elf Station (N7) ☎616778
Closed Sun Sep−Mar All makes

France

LOCHES
Indre-et-Loire (☎47)

★**France (DPn)** 6 r Picois ☎590032
10 Feb–2 Jan
rm22 ⇋8 ▥6 🏛 **P** sB58–145
sB ⇋ ▥93–145 dB68–145
dB ⇋ ▥104–145

At **BRIDORÉ** (14km S via N143)

★ ★ ★**Barbe Bleue** Oizay ☎947269
15 Mar–15 Nov
rm11 ⇋1 ▥10 **P**

LODÈVE
Hérault (☎67)

★ ★**Croix Blanche (DPn)** 6 av de Fumel
(N9) ☎441087
Apr–Nov
rm32 ⇋17 ▥3 A13rm 🏛 **P** sB60–90
sB ⇋ ▥80–110 dB80–90
dB ⇋ ▥90–130 mountains

LONDE (LA) See **ELBEUF**

LONGUYON
Meurthe-et-Moselle (☎8)

★ ★**Lorraine** (Inter) face Gare
☎2395007
10 Feb–5 Jan
rm15 ⇋12 sB89 sB ⇋134 dB107
dB ⇋214 M76

LONGWY
Meurthe-et-Moselle (☎8)

☆ ☆**Fimotel** (N52) ☎2231419
⇋42 **P** Lift sB ⇋fr193 dB ⇋fr221
M47–80

LONS-LE-SAUNIER
Jura (☎84)

★ ★**Genève** 19 pl XI Novembre ☎241911
rm42 ⇋19 ▥7 🏛 **P** Lift sB110–120
sB ⇋ ▥160–230 dB130–150
dB ⇋ ▥200–280

Thevenod rte de Champagnole-Perrigny
☎244185 Closed Sat & Sun Aud VW

LORIENT
Morbihan (☎97)

★ ★ ★**Richelieu** (MAP) 31 pl J-Ferry
☎213573 tx950810
⇋58 Lift sB ⇋276 dB ⇋359

⚙**Auto du Morbihan** 20 r de
Kerolay ☎370333

⚙**Olda** 39 r C-Lefort ☎212315 Closed
Sun BL

At **LANESTER** (5km NE)

☆ ☆ ☆**Novotel** Zone Commerciale de
Bellevue ☎760216 tx950026
⇋60 **P** sB ⇋243–262 dB ⇋291–315
Pool

☆ ☆**Ibis** Zone Commerciale de Bellevue
(n.rest) ☎764022
⇋40 **P** sB ⇋176 dB ⇋216

LORMONT See **BORDEAUX**

LOUDÉAC
Côtes-du-Nord (☎96)

★**Voyageurs** 🄻 10 r Cadélac ☎280047

---

rm32 ⇋3 ▥12 🏛 **P** Lift sB69
sB ⇋ ▥178 dB94–190 dB ⇋ ▥187–222

LOUDUN
Vienne (☎49)

☆ ☆ ☆**Mercure** 40 av Leuze (n.rest)
☎981922
⇋29 **P** Lift sB ⇋172–182
dB ⇋199–209

★**Roue d'Or** 🄻 **(DPn)** 1 av d'Anjou
☎980123
20 Jan–20 Dec
rm16 ⇋5 ▥1 🏛 **P**

LOUÉ
Sarthe (☎43)

★ ★ ★**Ricordeau** 11 r Libération
☎884003 tx720410
7 Feb–5 Jan
rm22 ⇋12 ▥7 🏛 **P** dB280–340
dB ⇋ ▥316–375 M155

LOURDES
Hautes-Pyrénées (☎62)

★ ★ ★**Grotte** (MAP) 66 r de la Grotte
☎945887 tx531937
16 Apr–Oct
⇋86 🏛 **P** Lift ⚭ sB ⇋270–300
dB ⇋320–395

★ ★**Provençale** (Inter) 4 r Baron Duprat
☎943134 tx520257
rm68 ⇋24 ▥38 🏛 **P** Lift
sB ⇋ ▥266–296 dB ⇋ ▥312–332 M60
alc mountains

★ ★**St-Roche (DPn)** 6 pl J-d'Arc
☎940214
Etr–8 Dec
rm33 ▥22 Lift

LOUVIERS
Eure (☎32)

⚙**L Parsy** 28 r du 11 Novembre
☎403394 Frd

At **ST-PIERRE-DU-VAUVRAY** (8km E)

★ ★ ★**Hostellerie de St-Pierre (DPn)**
☎599329
rm15 ⇋12 **P** Lift sB130 sB ⇋330
dB ⇋250–370 lake

At **VIRONVAY** (4km SE on N182A)

★ ★**Saisons** ☎400256
Closed 28 Jan–28 Feb
⇋15 🏛 **P** ⚭

LOUVROIL
Nord (☎27)

☆ ☆ ☆**Mercure** rte d'Avesnes (N2)
☎649373 tx110696
⇋59 sB ⇋229–271 dB ⇋268–302 M
alc Pool

LUC (LE)
Var (☎94)

★**Hostellerie du Parc (DPn)** 1 r J-Jaurès
☎607001
15 Dec–15 Nov
rm12 ⇋10 ▥2 🏛 **P** sB ⇋ ▥130–215
dB ⇋ ▥160–230

⚙**M Lacoste** 14 av Barbaraux
☎735011 Closed Sat pm & Sun Ren

LUCÉ See **CHARTRES**

LUCHON
Haute-Garonne (☎61)

★ ★ ★**Poste & Golf** 29 allées d'Etigny
☎790040 tx520018
Closed Nov
rm63 ⇋50 ▥8 🏛 **P** Lift sB170
sB ⇋ ▥210 dB205 dB ⇋ ▥240
mountains

★ ★**Bains** (Inter) 75 allées d'Etigny
☎790058
20 Dec–20 Oct
rm53 ⇋15 ▥27 **P** Lift sB102–140
dB139 dB ⇋ ▥164–214 mountains

LUÇON
Vendée (☎51)

★ ★**Croissant** 1 pl du Acacias ☎561115
Closed Oct
rm40 ⇋15 ▥15 🏛 **P** ⚭

LUDE (LE)
Sarthe (☎43)

★**Maine** 🄻 **(DPn)** 24 rte Saumur
☎946054
rm18 ⇋4 ▥7 A6rm **P** dB78–160
dB ⇋ ▥185

LUDRES See **NANCY**

LUNEL
Hérault (☎67)

★**Palais (DPn)** 12 av de Lattre de
Tassigny ☎711139
15 Dec–15 Jan
rm26 ⇋2 ▥20 🏛 **P**

⚙**Auto Service 113** 21 rte de
Nîmes ☎713495 Dat Vlo

⚙**M Pons** ZI des Fournels, rte de
Montpellier ☎711059 Closed Sat &
Sun Aud VW

LUNÉVILLE
Meurthe-et-Moselle (☎8)

★ ★**Europe** 56 r d'Alsace (n.rest)
☎3741234
rm30 ⇋10 ▥10 **P**

LUS-LA-CROIX-HAUTE
Drôme (☎92)

★**Chamousset** 🄻 ☎585112
rm15 ⇋11 ▥4 A5rm **P**
dB ⇋ ▥75–135 mountains

★**Touring** 75 rte Nationale ☎585001
Apr–Sep
rm17 ⇋1 🏛 **P** mountains

LUTTERBACH
Haute-Rhin (☎89)

☆ ☆**Campanile** 100 r du Gl-de-Gaulle
☎536655 tx881432
⇋41

France

LUXEUIL-LES-BAINS
Haute-Saône (☎84)

★★**Beau Site** 🔠 18 r Thermes ☎401467
rm59 ⇆23 🍴13 A15rm 🏛 **P**
dB80–200 dB ⇆ 🍴90–220

LYON
Rhône(☎7)

See also **CHASSE-SUR-RHÔNE**

★★★★**Frantel Lyon** 129 r Servient, Part
Dieu Nord ☎8629412 tx380088
⇆245 **P** Lift sB ⇆468 dB ⇆566

★★★★**Grand Concorde** 11 r Grôlée
☎842561 tx330244
rm140 ⇆155 🍴25 🏛 **P** Lift 🌙
sB ⇆ 🍴292–422 dB ⇆ 🍴324–514

★★★★**Royal** (MAP) 20 pl Bellecour
☎8375731 tx310785
rm90 ⇆73 🍴17 Lift sB ⇆236–530
dB ⇆360–530

★★★★**Sofitel** 20 quai Gailleton
☎8427250 tx330225
⇆196 🏛 **P** Lift sB ⇆572–622
dB ⇆779–844 St%

★★★★**Terminus Lyon Perrache** 12
cours de Verdun ☎8375811 tx330500
rm140 ⇆79 🍴44 🏛 **P** Lift 🌙
sB275–363 sB ⇆ 🍴391 dB304–392
dB ⇆ 🍴448

★★★**Beaux Arts** 75 r Préc Herriot
(n.rest) ☎8380950 tx330442
⇆80 Lift sB ⇆ 🍴176–234
dB ⇆ 🍴215–258

★★★**Bordeaux et du Parc** (Inter) 1 r du
Bélier (n.rest) ☎8375873 tx330355
rm83 ⇆39 🍴36 Lift sB197–242
sB ⇆ 🍴222–242 dB244–289
dB ⇆ 🍴264–289

★★★**Carlton** (MAP) 4 r Jussieu (n.rest)
☎8425651 tx310787
rm90 ⇆52 🍴17 🏛 Lift 🌙 sB290
sB ⇆ 🍴300 dB ⇆ 🍴375

★★**Globe & Cecil** (Inter) 21 Gasparin
(n.rest) ☎8425895 tx305184
rm65 ⇆24 🍴24 Lift sB95–148
sB ⇆ 🍴166–196 dB110–175
dB ⇆ 🍴178–205

☆☆**Ibis Lyon la Part Dieu Sud** pl
Renaudel ☎895421 tx310847
⇆144 **P** Lift sB ⇆209 dB ⇆239

★★**Moderne** 15 r Dubois (n.rest)
☎8422183
rm31 ⇆2 🍴14 Lift sB76–87
sB ⇆ 🍴150–189 dB84–101
dB ⇆ 🍴152–191

At **BRON** (10km SE)

☆☆☆**Novotel Lyon Aéroport** r L-Terray
☎8269748 tx340781
⇆196 **P** Lift sB ⇆303 dB ⇆340 Pool

☆☆**Campanile** quartier Rebufer, r
Maryse-Bastie ☎8264540 tx305160
⇆50 **P** dB ⇆218–222 M55–80

☆☆**Climat de France** ☎8265076
tx612241

⇆38 **P** sB ⇆189 dB ⇆226 M54–70

☆☆**Ibis** 36 av du Doyen J-Lepine
☎8543134 tx380694

⇆140 **P** Lift sB ⇆178–228
dB ⇆226–246

At **CHARBONNIÈRES-LES-BAINS** (8km
NW on N7)

☆☆☆**Mecure** 78 bis rte de Paris (N7)
☎8347279 tx900972

⇆60 🏛 **P** sB ⇆220–237
dB ⇆264–281 Pool

At **DARDILLY** (10km on N6)

☆☆☆☆**Holiday Inn** Porte de Lyon
☎8357020 tx900006

⇆204 **P** Lift sB ⇆280–291
dB ⇆305–316 M alc Pool

☆☆☆**Mercure Lyon Nord** Autoroute A6,
Porte de Lyon ☎8352805 tx330045

⇆175 **P** sB ⇆212–256 dB ⇆256–288
M alc 🍴 Pool

☆☆☆**Novotel Lyon Nord** Porte de Lyon
(A6) ☎8351341 tx330962

⇆107 **P** Lift sB294 dB ⇆348 Pool

☆☆**Campanile** Portes de Lyon Nord
☎8354844 tx610016

⇆43 **P** dB ⇆218–222 M55–80

☆☆**Climat de France** Porte de Lyon
Nord ☎8359847 tx612241

⇆38 **P** sB ⇆189 dB ⇆221 M54–70

🔧**Technic-Auto Service** (N6)
☎8355380 Ren

At **ECULLY** (7.5km NW)

☆☆**Campanile** rte de Dardilly
☎8331693 tx610016

⇆50 **P** dB ⇆218–222 M55–80

At **ST-GENIS-LAVAL** (10km SW)

☆☆**Climat de France** chemin de
Chazelle ☎8566434 tx612241

⇆46 **P** sB ⇆189 dB ⇆226 M54–70

At **ST-PRIEST** (11km SE by D518)

🔧**Kenning's** 190 rte de
Grenoble ☎8908200 Closed Sat &
Sun BL

At **STE-FOY-LES-LYONS**(6km SW)

☆☆**Campanile** chemin de la Croix-Pivort
☎8593223

⇆50 dD ⇆218–222 M55–80

At **SATOLAS AIRPORT** (18km SW)

☆☆**Climat de France** Zone de Frêt
☎8409644 tx612241

⇆36 **P** sB ⇆189 dB ⇆226 M54–70

LYONS-LA-FORÊT
Eure(☎32)

★★**Licorn** 🔠 (DPn) pl Benserade
☎496202
rm25 ⇆14 🍴3 🏛 **P** sB160–170

sB ⇆ 🍴220–200 dB190–360
dB ⇆ 🍴220–370

MÂCON
Saône-et-Loire (☎85)

★★★★**Frantel** 26 r de Coubertin
☎382806 tx800830
rm63 ⇆47 🍴16 **P** Lift sB ⇆ 🍴326
dB ⇆ 🍴392

☆☆☆**Novotel Mâcon Nord** (7km N on
A6) ☎360080 tx800869
⇆ 🍴106 **P** 🌙 sB ⇆ 🍴259
dB ⇆ 🍴311 Pool

★★**Bellevue** (MAP) 416–420 quai
Lammartine ☎380507 tx800837
rm32 ⇆11 🍴14 **P** Lift sB290
sB ⇆ 🍴290 dB350 dB ⇆ 🍴360

★★**Champs Elysées (DPn)** 6 r V-Hugo/2
pl de la Barre ☎383657 tx801338
rm50 ⇆16 🍴5 🏛 **P** Lift 🌙
sB93–110 sB ⇆ 🍴140–190
dB113–160 dB ⇆ 🍴220–250
M55–100&alc

★★**Europe et d'Angleterre** 92–109 quai
J-Jaurès (n.rest) ☎382794 tx800762
Feb–Oct
rm32 ⇆17 🍴5 🏛

★★**Genève** 🔠 **(DPn** in summer) 1 r
Bigonnet ☎381810 tx800732
rm63 ⇆17 🍴15 🏛 Lift 🌙

★★**Terminus** 🔠 91 r V-Hugo ☎391711
tx800831
rm41 ⇆22 🍴19 🏛 Lift 🌙 M60–100
DPn158–189

🔪**Bois** 39 r Lacretelle ☎386431 closed 3
wks Aug, Sat & Sun BL

Chauvot r J-Mermoz 'Les Bruyères'
☎382859 Closed Sat pm & Sun Opl Vlo

🔪**Corsin** 25 r de Lyon ☎387333 closed 3
wks Jul–Aug, Sat & Sun Frd

🔪**Duval** 53 rte de Lyon ☎383350 Closed
Sun Fia MB

🔪**Favède** 18–20 r Lacretelle ☎384605
Closed 2 wks Aug, Sat pm & Sun BMW Lnc

🔪**Ferret** 89 rte de Lyon ☎388355 M/c
Closed Sat & Sun Cit

🔪**Gounon** 790 av Ml de Lattre de
Tassigny ☎391666 Closed Sat & Sun Peu

🔪**Mâcon Auto** 5 r du Concours
☎389320 Closed Aug 9–18, Sat pm &
Sun Opl

Quagliozzi 72 rte de Lyon ☎385442
Closed Aug, Sat pm & Sun Hon

At **CHAINTRÉ-LA-CHAPELLE-DE-
GUINCHAY** (14km SW)

☆☆**Ibis Mâcon Sud** les Bouchardes
☎365160 tx801201

⇆45 **P** sB ⇆161–207 dB ⇆219–261
Malc

At **CRÈCHES-SUR-SAÔNE** (0.5km NW on
D89)

★★**Château de la Barge** ☎371204
10 Jan–20 Dec
rm25 ⇆17 🍴5 **P** Lift

154

♨Perrin (N6) ☎371261 Closed Jun 23–Jul 14, Sat pm & Sun Ren

Romand (N6) ☎371137 Closed Sun & Mon pm Peu

At ST-ALBAIN (10km N)

☆ ☆ ☆ ☆Sofitel (A6) ☎381617 tx800881
⇌100 🏛 Lift sB ⇌310–390
dB ⇌375–443 Pool

At SANCÉ-LES-MÂCON (4km N)

☆ ☆ ☆Vielle Ferme (FAH) (N6)
☎384693
⇌32 P Pool

☆ ☆Climat de France ZAC des Platières, r du 19 Mars 1962 ☎392133 tx692844
⇌42 P dB ⇌211–231 M48–74

MAGESCQ
Landes (☎58)

★ ★Relais de la Poste **L** ☎577025
Closed 13 Nov–19 Dec
rm16 ⇌14 🍴2 🏛 P ❧ Pool

MAINTENON
Eure-et-Loir (☎37)

★Aqueduc **L** (FAH) pl Gare ☎276005
Mar–Jan
rm18 ⇌2 🍴6 P dB137–177
dB ⇌ 🍴159–259

MAISONS-LAFFITTE
Yvelines (☎3)

☆ ☆Climat de France r de Paris
☎4460123 tx692844
⇌42 P dB ⇌231

MALÈNE (LA)
Lozère (☎66)

★ ★ ★Manoir de Montesquiou
☎485112
Apr–15 Oct
rm12 ⇌5 🍴7 P mountains

MAMERS
Sarthe (☎43)

★Croix Blanche 79 r P-Bert ☎976263
Mar–20 Jan
rm10 ⇌2 🍴2 sB53–73
sB ⇌ 🍴76–96 dB53–73
dB ⇌ 🍴76–96

MANDELIEU
Alpes-Maritimes (☎93)

☆Esterel 1625 av de Fréjus ☎499220
Feb–Oct
🍴22 P mountains

★Matringe (formerly Pavillion des Sports) rte de Fréjus (n.rest) ☎495086
rm17 🍴8 A3rm P

MANOSQUE
Alpes-de-Haute-Provence (☎92)

☆ ☆Campanile rte de Voix (N96)
☎875900 tx610016
⇌30 P dB ⇌206–209 M55–80

MANS (LE)
Sarthe (☎43)

France

★ ★ ★ ★Concorde 16 av Gl-Leclerc
☎241230 tx720487
rm68 ⇌32 🍴23 P Lift ♪ sB283–323
dB356–396

★ ★ ★Moderne 14 r Bourg-Belé
☎247920
rm33 ⇌17 🍴15 🏛 P ♪

☆ ☆ ☆Novotel le Mans Est ZAC les Sabions, bd R-Schumann ☎852680
tx720706
⇌94 P Lift sB ⇌258–268
dB ⇌302–312 Pool

★ ★Central 5 bd R-Levasseur (n.rest)
☎240893
rm50 ⇌8 🍴28 🏛 P Lift

★ ★Chantecler 50 r Pelouse ☎245853
rm40 ⇌6 🍴21 P Lift
sB ⇌ 🍴165–195 dB165–195
dB ⇌ 🍴165–210

☆ ☆Ibis r C-Marot ☎861414 tx720651
⇌50 P sB ⇌181–194 dB ⇌221–234
M63

Lessul bd P-le-Faucheux, ZI ☎846170
Closed Sat & Sun Frd

At ARNAGE (9km S via N23)

☆ ☆Campanile La Gêmerie bd P-le-Faucheux ☎218121 tx722803
⇌42 P dB ⇌206–209

MANSLE
Charente (☎45)

★ ★Beaurivage Près du Pont ☎203126
Closed Feb
rm45 ⇌12 🍴13 P

♨J Gullment rte Nationale ☎203031 All makes

MANTES-LA-JOLIE
Yvelines (☎3)

☆ ☆Ibis allée des Martinets, ZAC des Brosses, Magnanville ☎0926565
⇌52 P sB ⇌184–197 dB ⇌219–232
Malc

MARCAY See CHINON

MARGNY See COMPIÉGNE

MARGUERITTES See NÎMES

MARIGNANE See MARSEILLE AIRPORT

MARLENHEIM
Bas-Rhin (☎88)

★ ★Cerf **L** 30 r du Gl-de-Gaulle
☎877373
rm19 ⇌8 🍴9 P DPn280–310

★ ★Hostellerie Reeb **L** (DPn) (N4)
☎875270
rm33 ⇌19 🍴8 🏛 P dB120–170
dB ⇌ 🍴120–170

MARQ-EN-BAROEUL See LILLE

MARSEILLE
Bouches-du-Rhône (☎91)

★ ★ ★ ★Frantel Centre Bourse, r Neuve St-Martin ☎919129 tx401886
⇌200 🏛 P Lift dB ⇌531

★ ★ ★ ★Grand & Noailles (MAP) 66 Canebière ☎549148 tx430609
⇌70 P Lift ♪ sB ⇌250–320
dB ⇌350–400

★ ★ ★Sofitel Vieux Port 36 bd C-Livon ☎529019 tx401270
⇌222 🏛 Lift sB ⇌433–698
dB ⇌526–856 Pool sea

★ ★St-Georges 10 r du Cpt-Dessemond (n.rest) ☎525692
rm27 ⇌23 🍴4 Lift ♪ sea

☆ ☆Ibis 6 r de Cassis ☎785925
tx400362
⇌119 🏛 Lift sB ⇌199 dB ⇌231

Auto Diffusicn 36 bd National ☎620805
Closed Sun Frd

♨Bonneveine 2 av J-Vidal ☎733119
Closed Sun All makes

♨Clotti 11 r J-B-Astier ☎497534 Closed Sat & Sun All makes

♨Steg-Ponteves 20 r de Ponteves ☎904663 Closed Sat & Sun Ren

♨Touchard 151 av Montolivet ☎661239
M/c All makes

At PENNE-ST-MENET (LA) (10km E of A52)

☆ ☆ ☆Novotel Marseille Est (A52)
☎439060 tx400667
⇌131 P Lift sB ⇌247–269
dB ⇌288–305 ❧ Pool

MARSEILLE AIRPORT
At MARIGNANE (8km NW)

★ ★ ★Sofitel ☎(42)899102 tx401980
⇌180 🏛 Lift sB ⇌381–451
dB ⇌466–516 Pool

☆ ☆Ibis av du 8 Mai 1945 ☎(42)883535
tx440052
⇌36 sB ⇌182 dB ⇌221 M60–90

At VITROLLES (8km N)

☆ ☆ ☆Novotel Marseille Aéroport (A7)
☎(42)899044 tx420670
⇌163 P Lift sB ⇌246–269
dB ⇌288–306 Malc Pool

☆ ☆Campanile Le Griffon, rte d'Aix-en-Provence ☎(42)892511 tx610016
⇌44 P dB⇌206–209 M55–80

☆ ☆Climat de France ZI de Couperigne (CD20) ☎(42)752300 tx692844
⇌42 P dB ⇌211–231 M48–74

MARTEL
Lot (☎65)

At GLUGES (5km SE on N681)

★ ★Falaises (DPn) ☎373359
15 Feb–Dec
rm17 ⇌5 🍴4 P sB70–85 →

---

sB ⇌ 🍴127–165 dB88–150
dB ⇌ 🍴138–165

MARTIGUES
Bouches-du-Rhône (☎42)

☆ ☆**Campanile** ZAC de Canto-Perdrix, bd
de Tholon ☎801400 tx401378
⇌42 **P** dB ⇌218–222 M55–80

MARVEJOLS
Lozère (☎66)

★**Paix**L̃ (DPn) 2 av de Brazza ☎321017
rm19 ⇌4 🍴12 🏚 **P**

MASSAT
Ariège (☎61)

★ ★**Trois Seigneurs**L̃ av de St-Girons
☎969589
Mar–Oct
rm25 ⇌20 A10rm **P** mountains

MASSIAC
Cantal (☎71)

★ ★**Poste** (FAH) (DPn) av de C-Ferrand
(N9) ☎230201 tx990989
rm35 ⇌13 🍴12 **P** Lift
dB ⇌ 🍴159–259 mountains

🛏**Richard** av de Clermont ☎230225
Closed Mon Peu

MAULÉON-LICHARRE
Pyrénées-Atlantiques (☎59)

★ ★**Bidegain** 13 r de la Navarre
☎281605
15 Jan–15 Dec
rm30 ⇌12 🍴3 🏚 **P** mountains

MAXILLY-PETITE-RIVE See **EVIAN-LES-BAINS**

MAYENNE
Mayenne (☎43)

★ ★**Grand**L̃ (FAH) 2 r Ambroise-de-Loré
(n.rest) ☎043735
8 Jan–24 Dec
rm29 ⇌7 🍴14 🏚 **P** 𝔇

★**Croix Couverte** L̃ rte de Paris
☎043248
rm11 ⇌6 🍴5 🏚 **P**

🛏**P Legros** 15 r Du Guesclin ☎041627
Closed Sat pm Frd

MAZAMET
Tarn (☎63)

★ ★ ★**Grand Balcon** sq G-Tournier
☎610115
rm25 ⇌20 🍴2 Lift mountains

MEAUX
Seine et-Marne (☎6)

★ ★**Sirène** 33 r Gl-Leclerc ☎4340780
rm16 ⇌13 🍴1 🏚 **P** 𝔇 sB83–112
sB ⇌ 🍴150–180 dB ⇌178–237

🛏**Cornillon** 45 r Cornillon ☎4340558 All
makes

🛏**Vance** 37 av F-Roosevelt ☎4332976
Closed Sat pm & Sun Ren

MEGÈVE
Haute-Savoie (☎50)

France

★ ★ ★ ★**Mont Blanc** (Inter) pl de lÉglise
☎212002 tx385854
rm68 ⇌64 🍴2 A17rm 🏚 **P** Lift 𝔇
🛁

★ ★ ★**Parc** r d'Arly (n.rest) ☎210574
Xmas, Etr & end Jun–mid Sep
⇌48 **P** Lift 𝔇 sB ⇌210–280
dB ⇌260–343 mountains

MEHUN-SUR-YEVRE
Cher (☎48)

★**Croix Blanche** (DPn) 164 r J-d'Arc
☎573001
20 Jan–20 Dec
rm20 ⇌1 🍴2 🏚 **P** 𝔇 sB70–85
sB ⇌ 🍴100–105 dB105–127
dB ⇌ 🍴125–155

MEILLY-SUR-ROUVRES See **POUILLY-EN-AUXOIS**

MELUN
Seine-et Marne (☎6)
See also **PONTHIERRY**

☆ ☆**Climat de France** 338 r R-Hervillard,
Vaux-le-Pénil ☎4527101 tx692844
⇌42 **P** dB ⇌221–243 M48–74

☆ ☆**Ibis** av de Meaux ☎0684245
tx691779
⇌74 **P** sB ⇌182 dB ⇌212

🛏**Avenue** 58 av Thiers ☎4390754
Closed Sat pm & Sun AR

At **DAMMARIE-LES-LYS** (5km SW)

☆ ☆**Campanile** 346 r C-de-Gaulle
☎4375151 tx691621
⇌50 dB ⇌206–209 M55–80

MENDE
Lozère (☎66)

★ ★**Lion d'Or** (MAP) (DPn) 12 bd Britexte
☎650646 tx480302
Mar–Dec
rm41 ⇌23 🍴18 **P** Lift 𝔇
sB ⇌210–242 dB ⇌ 🍴320–346 🛁
Pool mountains

★ ★**Paris** 2 bd du Soubeyran (n.rest)
☎650003
15 Mar–15 Nov
rm45 ⇌7 🍴15 🏚 **P** Lift mountains

Carrosserie Crespin SARL av du 11
Novembre ☎651828 Closed Sat All
makes

MENTON
Alpes-Maritimes (☎93)

★ ★**Europ** 35 av de Verdun (n.rest)
☎355992 tx470673
⇌33 🏚 Lift 𝔇 sB ⇌180–200
dB ⇌245–280

★ ★**Méditerranée** 5 r de la République
☎282525 tx461361
⇌90 **P** Lift sB ⇌180–250
dB ⇌205–290

★ ★ ★**Napoléon** 29 Porte de France
☎358950 tx470312
Closed Nov–18 Dec
rm40 ⇌39 🍴1 **P** Lift 𝔇
sB ⇌190–320 dB ⇌260–420
Pool mountains

★ ★ ★**Princess et Richmond** 32 av Gl-de-Gaulle (n.rest) ☎358020
20 Dec–3 Nov
rm45 ⇌35 🍴6 🏚 **P** Lift 𝔇 sea

★ ★**Aiglon** 7 av de la Madone (n.rest)
☎575555
20 Dec–2 Nov
rm30 ⇌22 🍴2 **P** Lift 𝔇 sB100–150
sB ⇌ 🍴150 dB200 dB ⇌ 🍴260 Pool
sea mountains

★ ★**El Paradiso** (DPn) 71 Porte de
France ☎357402
Feb–Sep
rm42 ⇌22 **P** Lift 𝔇 sB115–210
sB⇌185–210 dB135–220 dB ⇌220 sea

★ ★**Floréal** cours de Centenaire
☎357581
20 Dec–15 Oct
rm60 **P** Lift 𝔇 sea mountains

★ ★**Londres** 15 av Carnot ☎357462
10 Jan–10 Oct
rm26 ⇌8 🍴12 **P** Lift sB145
sB ⇌ 🍴155 dB ⇌ 🍴190–210

★ ★**Parc** (DPn) 11 av de Verdun
☎357174
20 Dec–10 Oct
rm75 ⇌65 🍴10 **P** Lift 𝔇

★ ★**Prince de Galles** 4 av Gl-de-Gaulle
(n.rest) ☎282121 tx470673
rm68 ⇌61 🍴7 **P** Lift 𝔇
sB ⇌ 🍴161–240 dB ⇌ 🍴204–244 sea

★ ★**Rives d'Azur** prom Ml-Joffre
☎576760
rm36 ⇌20 🍴4 **P** Lift sea

🛏**Fossan** 1 bd du Fossan ☎570307
Closed Sep–Oct, Sat pm & Sun All makes

MÉRÉVILLE
Meurthe-et-Moselle (☎8)

★ ★**Maison Carrée** L̃ ☎3470923
rm23 ⇌12 🍴10 🏚 **P**
sB ⇌ 🍴120–170 dB ⇌ **P**
M60–120 & alc

MÉRIGNAC See **BORDEAUX**

METZ
Moselle (☎8)

★ ★ ★ ★**Frantel** 29 pl St-Thiébault
☎7361769 tx930417
⇌112 **P** Lift sB ⇌321 dB ⇌382

★ ★ ★**Royal Concorde** 23 av Foch
(n.rest) ☎7668111 tx860425
rm75 ⇌43 🍴12 Lift 𝔇 sB273–333
dB ⇌346–426

★ ★ ★**Sofitel** Centre St-Jacques, pl des
Paraîges ☎7745727 tx930328
⇌115 **P** Lift 𝔇 sB⇌322–372
dB⇌404–454

★ ★**Central** 3 bis r Vauban (n.rest)
☎7755343 tx930281

rm54 ⇌36 ⋔18 🏛 P Lift

☆ ☆Ibis quartier du Pontiffroy, r
Chambière ☎7310173 tx930278

⇌79 P Lift sB ⇌183 dB ⇌218

★Lutèce Ⓛ 11 r de Paris ☎7302725

rm21 ⇌2 ⋔7 🏛 P sB52–112
sB ⇌ ⋔112 dB63–112 dB ⇌ ⋔112

⑧Ⓞ Jacquot 2 r P-Boileau ☎302440
Closed Sat & Sun Peu

At HAUCONCOURT (9.5km N on A31)

☆ ☆ ☆Novotel (A31) ☎7804111
tx860191

⇌128 P Lift sB ⇌243–278
dB ⇌286–325

At TALANGE (5km N)

☆ ☆Climat de France la Ponte, r des
Alliés ☎7721311 tx612241

⇌38 P sB ⇌189 dB ⇌221 M54–70

MEURSAULT
Côte-d'Or (☎80)

⑧Ⓞ J Hemart 14 r C-Giraud ☎212084
Closed Sun All makes

⑧Ⓞ Meyrieux rte Forges ☎212060 M/c
Closed Aug, Sat & Sun BMW Peu

MEYLAN See GRENOBLE

MEYRUEIS
Lozère (☎66)

★ ★ ★Château d'Ayres ☎456010

30 Mar–15 Oct
rm24 ⇌20 ⋔4 P sB ⇌ ⋔180–390
dB ⇌ ⋔182–390 mountains

★ ★Renaissance (Inter) (DPn) ☎456019
⇌20

MÉZIÉRE-SUR-ISSOIRE
Haute-Vienne (☎55)

⑧Ⓞ A Boos rte de Bellac ☎683028 Closed
Sun Frd

MIGENNES
Yonne (☎86)

★ ★Paris Ⓛ (DPn) 57 av J-Jaurès
☎802322

16 Jan–3 Aug & 3 Sep–1 Jan
rm10 ⇌2 ⋔2 P sB88–121
dB ⇌ ⋔116–136

⑧Ⓞ Migennes Autos 148 av J-Jaurès
☎800478 Closed Sat pm & Sun Cit

MIGNE-AUXANCES See POITIERS

MILLAU
Aveyron (☎65)

★ ★ ★International 1 pl de la Tine
☎602066 tx520629

rm110 ⇌104 🏛 P Lift Ɗ mountains

★ ★Moderne 11 av J-Jaurès ☎605923
tx520629

Apr–Sep
rm46 ⇌32 🏛 P Lift mountains

★Causses Ⓛ (DPn) 56 av J-Jaurès
☎600319

rm22 ⇌2 ⋔5 🏛

France

★Paris & Poste (DPn Jun–Aug) 10 av A-
Merle ☎600052

3 Jan–15 Nov
rm22 ⇌4 ⋔11 P sB65–75
sB ⇌ ⋔95–120 dB68–78
dB ⇌ ⋔100–125 mountains

⑧Ⓞ J Pineau 161 av de Calès ☎600855
M/c All makes

⑧Ⓞ J Vaissière 6 r L-Blanc ☎600016
Closed Sun & Mon am Vlo

MILLES (LES) See AIX-EN-PROVENCE

MILLY
Indre-et-Loire (☎47)

★Château de Milly rte de Richelieu et
Châtellerault ☎581456

15 Apr–15 Oct
rm15 ⇌12 ⋔1 P Pool

MILLY-A-FORÊT
Essonne (☎6)

⑧Ⓞ France (G Droulin) rte de
Fontainbleau ☎4988169 Closed Sun BL
Opl

MIMIZAN
Landes (☎58)

⑧Ⓞ J Poisson 48 av de Bordeaux
☎090873 Closed Sun pm Ren

At MIMIZAN-PLAGE

★ ★Côte d'Argent (DPn) 4 av M-Martin
☎091522

May–Sep
⇌ ⋔40 P Lift Ɗ sB ⇌ ⋔259–284
M94 sea

⑧Ⓞ W Kunz ☎090501 Closed Oct 1–15
Opl Vau

MIRAIL (LE) See TOULOUSE

MIRAMBEAU
Charente-Maritime (☎46)

★Union (DPn) r Principale ☎496164
rm12 ⋔1 A2rm 🏛

⑧Ⓞ Gauvin 1 a C-Jourdain ☎496185 All
makes

MIREPOIX
Ariège (☎61)

★Commerce Ⓛ (DPn) cours du Dr-
Chabaud ☎681029

Feb–10 Oct & 15 Oct–Dec
rm32 ⇌6 ⋔32 A7rm 🏛 P

MISSILLAC
Loire-Atlantique (☎40)

★ ★ ★Golf de la Bretesche (DPn in
season) ☎883005

Closed Feb
rm25 ⇌19 ⋔5 P sB242 sB ⇌ ⋔322
dB ⇌ ⋔364 M85 ⚤ ♨ lake

MODANE
Savoie (☎79)

At FOURNEAUX (3km SW)

M Bellussi 36 av de la Liberté ☎050774
Closed Sat & Sun Fia

MOISSAC
Tarn-et-Garonne (☎63)

★ ★ ★Moulin (MAP) 1 pl du Moulin
☎040355 tx521615

rm57 ⇌42 ⋔15 P Lift Ɗ
sB ⇌ ⋔250–290 dB ⇌ ⋔380–450
M80–250 lake

★Pont Napoléon (DPn) 2 allées
Montebello ☎040155

Closed Tue, 1–20 Mar & 15 Nov–15 Dec
rm15 ⇌3 ⋔6 🏛 dB83–150
dB ⇌ ⋔138–178 St15%

MONTARGIS
Loiret (☎38)

★ ★ ★Grand Post
2 pl V-Hugo ☎980068 tx78994
rm31 ⇌9 ⋔12 🏛

★Tour d'Auvergne Ⓛ 20 r J-Jaurès
☎850116

rm14 ⇌8 ⋔14 🏛 P

M Schnaldt 38 r J-Jaurès ☎932810
Closed Sat pm, Sun & Mon am MB Vlo

MONTAUBAN Tarn-et-Garonne (☎63)

★ ★Midi Ⓛ (Inter) 12r Notre-Dame
☎631723 tx531705

rm62 ⇌35 ⋔20 A10rm 🏛 P Lift Ɗ
sB83–90 sB ⇌ ⋔113–210 dB106–190
dB ⇌ ⋔136–230

★Languedoc et des Pyrénées 100 fbg
Toulousain (n.rest) ☎632215

rm42 ⇌2 ⋔5 A12rm 🏛 P dB77–131

★Orsay (FAH) (opposite station)
☎630057

Closed May & Xmas
⇌20 A33rm 🏛 P Lift sB ⇌130–160
dB ⇌160–200

⑧Ⓞ Atelier Auto Speed 23 r Lassus
☎030330 M/c P All makes

At MONTBETON (3km W)

★ ★ ★Coulandrières (DPn in season) rte
Castelsarrasin ☎031809 tx520200

Feb–Dec
rm21 ⇌20 ⋔1 P sB ⇌ ⋔252–270
dB ⇌ ⋔294–304 Pool

MONTBARD
Côte-d'Or (☎80)

★ ★Gare 10 r Ml-Foch, pl de la Gare
(n.rest) ☎920212

rm20 ⇌9 ⋔5 🏛 P sB60 sB ⇌
⋔140 dB77 dB ⇌ ⋔77–154

★Ecu Ⓛ (DPn) 7 r A-Carré ☎921166
rm24 ⇌11 ⋔12 🏛 P

MONTBAZON
Indre-et-Loire (☎47)

★ ★ ★ ★Château d'Artigny
☎262424 tx750900 →

Jan–Nov
rm55 ⇄52 🍴3 A20rm **P** Lift 🌙
dB ⇄ 🍴800 ♨ Pool

★ ★ ★ **Tortinière** (1.5km N) ☎260019
tx750806

Mar–15 Nov
rm21 ⇄20 🍴1 A10rm **P** Pool

At **MONTS** (8km W)

★ **Sporting** 🄻 ☎267015

Closed 1–15 Sep & 21 Feb–15 Mar
rm12 ⇄2 A5rm **P**

MONTBÉLIARD
Doubs (☎81)

☆ ☆ **Ibis** r J-Foillet, ZAC du Pied
d'Egouttes ☎971920 tx360724

⇄42 **P** sB⇄168 ⇄206

At **BAVANS** (2.5kmSW)

⑊**Esso** 85 Grande Rue ☎962659 Peu

MONTBETON See **MONTAUBAN**

MONTCABRIER See **PUY L'ÉVÊQUE**

MONTCHANIN See **CREUSOT (LE)**

MONT-DE-MARSAN
Landes (☎58)

★ ★ ★ **Richelieu** 🄻 3 r Wlerick ☎061020
tx550238

rm75 ⇄30 🍴20 🚗 **P** Lift 🌙
sB68–74 sB ⇄ 🍴115–141 dB98–150
dB ⇄ 🍴155–177 M60 150

MONT-DORE (LE)
Puy-de-Dôme (☎73)

★ ★ ★ **Carlina** les Pradets ☎650422

20 Dec–Nov
⇄50 🚗 **P** Lift sB ⇄228–268
dB ⇄256–296 Mfr76 Pool mountains

At **PIED-DU-SANCY** (4km S on N683)

★ ★ **Puy-Ferand** 🄻 **(DPn)** ☎651899
tx990332

15 Dec–20 Apr & 30 Sep–15 Dec
rm42 ⇄23 🍴11 **P** Lift sB140
sB ⇄ 🍴172 dB140–160
dB ⇄ 🍴171–178 mountains

MONTÉLIMAR
Drôme (☎75)

★ ★ ★ **Relais de l'Empereur** (MAP) **(DPn)**
pl M-Dormoy ☎012900 tx345537

Closed 11 Nov–21 Dec
rm40 ⇄35 🍴5 🚗 **P** 🌙
sB ⇄ 🍴306–326 dB ⇄ 🍴402–435
mountains

★ ★ **Sphinx** 19 bd Desmarais (n.rest)
☎018664

Jan–Nov
rm24 ⇄17 🍴7 🚗 **P**
sB ⇄ 🍴110–175 dB ⇄ 🍴156–195

★ **Beausoleil** 🄻 14 bd Pêcher, pl d'Armes
(n.rest) ☎011980

⇄16 **P** dB ⇄180

⑊**P Amardell** 115 av J-Jaurès ☎015821
Closed 24 Feb–2 Mar, Sat pm & Sun All
makes

France

⑊**J Brusut** (N7) ☎510658 Closed Sun
All makes

⑊**Faure** Q-Blaches, rte de Marseille
☎012767 Closed Sun Dat

⑊**G Froux** 130 av du Teil ☎015704 M/c
Closed Etr All makes

⑊**Gillet** ZI ☎011242 Closed Sat pm &
Sun MB Toy

⑊**Pelican** (N7) ☎013607 Closed Sat pm
& Sun Vlo

⑊**Peyrouse** ZI du Sud, rte de
Châteauneuf ☎013916 Closed Sat &
Sun Frd

Sud Auto rte de Marseille ☎013344
Closed 11–17 Aug, Sat & Sun Tal

At **SAUZET** (9km NE on D6)

⑊**M Chaix** ☎467170 Closed Sat pm &
Sun Ren

MONTESSON
Yvelines (☎3)

☆ ☆ **Campanile** 9 r du Chant des Oiseaux
☎0716334

⇄41 dB ⇄218–222 M55–80

MONTFAVET See **AVIGNON**

MONTIGNAC
Dordogne (☎53)

☆**Lascaux** 🄻 **(DPn)** av J-Jaurès
☎518281
rm16 ⇄2 🍴6 🚗 **P**

★ **Soleil d'Or** 🄻 **(DPn)** 16 r IV Septembre
☎518022

28 Dec–25 Nov
rm22 ⇄7 🍴7 A8rm 🚗 **P**

MONTIGNY-LA-RESLE
Yonne (☎86)

★ ★ **Soleil d'Or** 🄻 ☎418121

Jan–Nov
rm11 ⇄5 🍴5 A4rm **P**
dB ⇄ 🍴80–120

MONTIGNY-LE-ROI
Haute-Marne (☎25)

★ ★ **Moderne** (Inter) **(DPn)** av de
Neufchâteau ☎861018 tx840957
rm25 ⇄13 🍴1 **P** sB91–150
sB ⇄ 🍴146–176 dB130–190
dB ⇄ 🍴162–192

⑊**Flagex** (N74) ☎861034 Closed Sun

MONTIVILLIERS See **HAVRE (LE)**

MONTLUCON
Allier (☎70)

★ ★ ★ **Terminus** 47 av M-Dormoy
☎052893

rm48 ⇄8 🍴24 🚗 Lift 🌙 sB68
sB ⇄ 🍴140 dB75 dB ⇄ 🍴150

★ ★ **Château St-Jean** Parc St-Jean
☎050465

rm8 ⇄5 🍴3 🚗 **P**

MONTMIRAIL
Marne (☎26)

★ **Vert Galant (DPn)** 2 pl Vert Galant
☎422017

Closed Feb
rm14 🍴3 🚗 **P** sB60–74 dB 🍴94–109

MONTMORILLON
Vienne (☎49)

★ ★ **France Mercier (DPn)** 2 bd de
Strasbourg ☎910051

Closed Jan
rm25 ⇄18 🍴7 sB96–146
sB ⇄ 🍴140–180 dB140–162
dB ⇄ 🍴152–192

MONTMORT
Marne (☎26)

★ ★ **Place** 🄻 3 pl Berthelot ☎591038
rm33 ⇄16 🍴9 **P** sB79–96
sB ⇄ 🍴94–121 dB93–115
dB ⇄ 🍴108–120

MONTOIRE-SUR-LE-LOIR
Loir-et-Cher (☎54)

★ ★ **Cheval Rouge** 🄻 **(DPn)** pl Ml-Foch
☎850705

Closed Feb
rm17 ⇄10 🍴1 🚗 **P** sB60–96
sB ⇄ 🍴106–128 dB92–150
dB ⇄ 🍴122–177

MONTPELLIER
Hérault (☎67)

★ ★ ★ **Métropole** (MAP) 3 r C-René
☎581122 tx480410
rm92 ⇄58 🍴25 🚗 Lift 🌙
sB350–360 sB ⇄ 🍴350–360
dB405–430 dB ⇄ 🍴405–514

★ ★ ★ **Sofitel** le Triangle ☎540404
tx480140

⇄125 **P** Lift 🌙 sB ⇄333–393
dB ⇄426–481 S15%

★ ★ ★ **Frantel** 218 r de Bastion-
Ventadour, quartier le Polygone
☎646566 tx480362

⇄116 🚗 **P** Lift 🌙 sB ⇄341
dB ⇄392

☆ ☆ ☆ **Mercure Montpeller Est** 662 av de
Pompignane ☎655024 tx480656
rm122 ⇄116 🍴6 🚗 **P** Lift
sB ⇄ 🍴222–242 dB ⇄ 🍴291–308

☆ ☆ **Novotel** 125 bis av de Palavas
☎640404 tx490433

⇄97 Lift sB ⇄296–320 dB ⇄364–387
M alc Pool

☆ ☆ **Climat de France** r de Caducée
☎524333 tx692844

⇄42 **P** dB ⇄211–224 M48–74

☆ ☆ **Ibis** rte de Palavas ☎588230
tx480578

⇄102 **P** Lift sB ⇄183 dB ⇄240

⑊**Attard** 33 av de Pontjuvenol ☎659417
Tal

158

𝕊🅟Auto Méditérranée 26 r E-Michel ☎929729 Closed Sat pm & Sun BMW

Croix d'Argent 91 rte de Toulouse ☎428174 Closed Sun Aud VW

𝕊🅟France Auto av du M-Gare ☎926374 Closed Sat & Sun Opl Vau

𝕊🅟RNU Renault 700 r de l'Industrie ☎420075 Closed Sat pm & Sun Ren

At **PÉROLS** (8km S at Montpellier Airport)

☆ ☆ ☆**PLM Frèjorgues** rte de Carnon (D21) ☎500304 tx480652
⇥77 sB⇥211 dB⇥256 M75 Pool

At **ST-JEAN-DE-VEDAS** (5km W on N113)

Imbert rte de Sète ☎424622 Closed Sat & Sun Frd

MONTREUIL (Eure-et-Loire) See **DREUX**

MONTREUIL
Pas-de-Calais (☎21)

★ ★ ★**Château de Montreuil** 4 chaussée des Capucins ☎815304 tx135205
Feb–Nov
rm12 ⇥10 🅵2 A1rm **P** 𝄞
sB 250–450 dB ⇥350–450

★**Central (DPn)** 7–9 r du Change ☎061033
20 Jun–20 Dec
rm10 ⇥2 🅵1 🏠

𝕊🅟Lavogez 3 r St-Gengoult ☎061143 Closed Sat pm & Sun Ren

MONTREUIL-BELLAY
Maine-et-Loire (☎41)

★**Splendid 🅻🅴 (DPn)** r Dr-Gaudrez ☎523021
rm35 ⇥14 🅵16 A20rm **P** Pool

MONTRICHARD
Loir-et-Cher (☎54)

★ ★**Bellevue 🅻🅴** (Inter) quai du Cher ☎320617 21 Dec–15 Nov
rm29 ⇥26 🅵3 **P** Lift dB⇥124–234

★ ★**Tête-Noire 🅻🅴 (DPn)** rte de Tours ☎320555
Closed 2 Jan–7 Feb
rm38 ⇥26 🅵2 A9rm **P** sB38
sB ⇥🅵129 dB101–180 dB ⇥🅵200

MONTROUGE See **PARIS**

MONTS See **MONTBAZON**

MONT-ST-MICHEL (LE)
Manche (☎33)

★ ★**Digue🅻🅴** La Digue (2km S) ☎601402 tx171638
15 Mar–15 Nov
rm30 ⇥21 🅵9 **P** sB ⇥🅵148–190
dB ⇥🅵170–210

☆ ☆**K🅻🅴** (FAH) La Digue (2km S on D976) ☎601418 tx170537
Apr–Oct
⇥60 **P** DPn190

★ ★**Mère Poulard (DPn)** ☎601401
Apr–Sep
rm27 ⇥14 🅵8

France

MONTSALVY
Cantal (☎71)

★ ★**Nord🅻🅴** (Inter) pl du Barry ☎492003
22 Feb–21 Jan
rm30 ⇥8 🅵15 **P** dB70–170
dB ⇥🅵70-180

MONTSOULT
Val d'Oise (☎3)

☆ ☆ ☆**Novotel Château de Maffiers** ☎4739305 tx695701
⇥80 **P** sB ⇥285–300 dB ⇥369 🍴 Pool

MORANGIS See **ORLY AIRPORT** under **PARIS AIRPORTS**

MOREZ
Jura (☎84)

★ ★**Central Modern** 106 r de la République ☎330307
rm52 ⇥12 🅵1 A24rm 🏠 **P** mountains

MORLAIX
Finistère (☎98)

★ ★ ★**Grand Hotel d'Europe** (FAH) 1 r d'Aiguillon ☎621199 tx940696
15 Jan–15 Dec
rm68 ⇥45 🅵13 Lift dB ⇥🅵159–300

MORTAGNE-AU-PERCHE
Orne (☎33)

★**Tribunal🅻🅴 (DPn)** 4 pl du Palais ☎250477
rm15 ⇥7 🅵2 **P** sB93–149
sB ⇥🅵160 dB106–163
dB ⇥🅵123–163

MORTAGNE-SUR-SÈVRE
Vendée (☎51)

★ ★ ★**France🅻🅴** (FAH) 4 pl du Dr-Pichat ☎676337 tx11403
15 Sep–28 Aug
rm25 ⇥11 🅵10 **P** Lift dB137–177
dB ⇥🅵159–259 🍴 Pool

MORTAIN
Manche (☎33)

★**Cascades🅻🅴 (DPn)** 16 ru Bassin ☎590003
rm14 ⇥3 🅵2 sB66 dB91–140
dB ⇥🅵151

MORZINE
Haute-Savoie (☎50)

★ ★**Carlina (DPn)** av J-Plane ☎790103 tx385596
15 Dec–15 Apr & 25 Jun–31 Aug
rm24 ⇥15 🅵8 🏠 **P**
sB ⇥🅵230–250 dB ⇥🅵270–310 mountains

★ ★**Dahu** ☎791112
18 Dec–20 Apr & 30 Jun–Aug
rm26 ⇥18 🅵4 **P** Lift sB115–140

---

sB ⇥ 🅵145–160 dB205–250
dB ⇥ 🅵225–290 mountains

MOUGINS
Alpes-Maritimes (☎93)

𝕊🅟Central 723 chemin du Ferrandou ☎454746 All makes

𝕊🅟Olympique chemin de l'Oratoire ☎454646 All makes

Riviera Technil Bretelle Autoroute ☎455419 Closed Sat & Sun Aud Por VW

MOULINS
Allier (☎70)

★ ★ ★**Paris** 21 r de Paris ☎440058 tx394853
Closed Jan
rm29 ⇥19 🅵6 🏠 **P** Lift 𝄞
sB125–480 sB ⇥🅵125–480
dB ⇥🅵125–480

★ ★**Dauphin** 59 pl Allier ☎443305 tx394860
Closed Jan
rm65 ⇥27 🅵6 **P** Lift 𝄞 sB90–127
sB ⇥🅵198 dB142 dB ⇥🅵113–260 Mfr47

☆ ☆**Ibis** Angle de la rte de Lyon (N7)/bd Primaire ☎467112
⇥42 **P** sB ⇥192 dB ⇥230

★ ★**Moderne** (Inter) 9 pl J-Moulin ☎440506 tx990740
rm44 ⇥4 🅵18 🏠 **P** Lift 𝄞

★**Parc🅻🅴** 31 av Gl-Leclerc ☎441225
rm26 ⇥3 🅵23 A3rm 🏠 **P** 𝄞
sB ⇥🅵125–165 dB ⇥🅵140–200

𝕊🅟M Robin 8 C-de-Bercy ☎463282 Ren

MOUTHIER-HAUTE-PIERRE
Doubs (☎81)

★**Cascade🅻🅴 (DPn)** ☎621900
4 Jan–13 Nov
rm23 ⇥13 🅵7 🏠 **P** sB133–164
dB ⇥🅵146–188 mountains

MOÛTIERS
Savoie (☎79)

☆ ☆**Ibis** Colline de Champoulet ☎242711 tx980611
⇥62 **P** Lift sB ⇥163 dB ⇥220

MULHOUSE
Haut-Rhin (☎89)

★ ★ ★ ★**Frantel** 4 pl Gl-Gaulle ☎460123 tx881807
⇥96 **P** sB ⇥326 dB ⇥397

𝕊🅟Paris🅻 38 av de Riedisheim ☎443322 Closed Aug & Sun All makes

At **SAUSHEIM** (6km NE on D422)

★ ★ ★ ★**Sofitel** (N422A) ☎447575 tx881311
⇥100 🏠 **P** Lift ⇥327–372
dB ⇥409–454 Pool

☆ ☆ ☆**Mercure** l'Ille Napoléon ☎445440 tx881757
⇥97 **P** Lift sB ⇥244–259
dB ⇥296–308 🍴 Pool

☆ ☆ ☆**Novotel** r de l'Ille Napoléon
☎444444 tx881673

⇋77 **P** sB ⇋257–262 dB ⇋305–310
M alc Pool

☆ ☆**Ibis** rte de Sausheim es Ille Napoléon
☎543233 tx881970 ⇋76 **P**
sB ⇋188 dB ⇋224

MUREAUX (LES)
Yvelines (☎3)

☆ ☆**Climat de France** ZAC du Grand
Ouest CD43, r des Pléiades
☎(6)4460123 tx692844
⇋42 dB ⇋200–235

MUY (LE)
Var (☎94)

⊅**Depannahes Auto** quartier la
Peyrouas ☎450571 All makes

⊅**St-Roch** rte National ☎444067 BMW
Cit Fia

NAJAC
Aveyron (☎65)

★ ★**Belle Rive ᴸᴱ (DPn)** (2km NW on
D39) ☎657420

Apr–15 Oct
rm39 ⇋6 ▥23 A9rm ▩ **P**
dB ⇋ ▥139 Pool mountains

★ ★**Oustal del Barry ᴸᴱ (DPn** in season)
pl du Bourg ☎657080 tx12270

Mar–Oct
rm28 ⇋7 ▥10 A7rm ▩ **P** Lift sB70
sB ⇋ ▥115 dB90 dB ⇋ ▥145–150
mountains

NANCY
Meurthe-et-Moselle (☎8)

★ ★ ★**Frantel** 11 r R-Poincaré
☎3356101 tx960034

⇋192 ▩ **P** Lift sB ⇋321 dB ⇋387

★ ★ ★**Grand Concorde** 2 pl Stanislas
☎3350301 tx960367

rm53 ⇋34 ▥19 Lift ⅅ
sB ⇋ ▥313–433 dB ⇋ ▥426–546

★ ★**Albert 1er/Astoria** 3 r Armée-Patton
☎3403124 tx850895

rm136 ⇋100 ▩ **P** Lift sB119–185
sB ⇋204–235 dB148–215
dB ⇋238–253

★**Américain** 3 pl A-Maginot (n.rest)
☎3322853 tx961052

rm51 ⇋26 ▥25 Lift ⅅ
sB ⇋ ▥159–229 dB ⇋ ▥188–273

★**Poincaré** 81 r R-Poincaré (n.rest)
☎3402599

rm25 ▥7 **P** sB70–112 sB ▥112
dB95–112 dB ▥119

At **HOUDEMONT** (6km S)

☆ ☆ ☆**Novotel Nancy Sud** rte d'Épinal
(N57) ☎3561025 tx961124

⇋86 **P** sB ⇋257–267 dB ⇋305–315
Pool

At **LAXOU** (3km SW)

☆ ☆ ☆**Mercure** 2 r de la Saône
☎3964221 tx850036

⇋99 **P** Lift sB ⇋231–251
dB⇋292–302 Pool

☆ ☆ ☆**Novotel Nancy Ouest** (N4)
☎3966746 tx850988

⇋118 Lift sB ⇋242–267
dB ⇋290–315 Pool

At **LUDRES** (8km S)

☆ ☆**Climat de France** ZI de Ludres
☎3542113 tx692844

⇋42 **P** sB ⇋218 dB ⇋238 M48–74

NANS-LE-PINS
Var (☎94)

★ ★ ★**Châteauneuf** (N560) ☎789006
tx400747

1 Apr–1 Nov
rm32 ⇋22 ▥10 **P** sB ⇋ ▥300–380
dB ⇋ ▥310–590 ℘ Pool

NANTES
Loire-Atlantique (☎40)

★ ★ ★ ★**Sofitel** r A-Millerand ☎476103
tx710990

⇋100 **P** Lift sB ⇋350–430
dB ⇋445–525 ℘ Pool

★ ★ ★**Central** (MAP) 4 r du Couédic
☎200935 tx700666

rm143 ⇋96 ▥37 Lift ⅅ sB302
dB283 dB ⇋ ▥351 mountains

★ ★ ★**Frantal** 3 r Dr-Zamenhof
☎471058 tx711440

⇋150 ▩ **P** Lift sB ⇋329
dB ⇋360–398

★ ★ ★**Vendée** 8 allée Cdt-Charcot
(n.rest) ☎741454 tx700610

rm89 ⇋15 ▥74 ▩ **P** Lift
sB ⇋150–190 dB ⇋ ▥221–316

★ ★**Astoria** 11 r Richebourg (n.rest)
☎743990

Closed Aug
rm45 ⇋12 ▥32 ▩ **P** Lift ⅅ
sB ⇋ ▥165–210 dB ⇋ ▥170–230

★ ★**Bourgogne** 9 allée du Cdt-Charcot
(n.rest) ☎740334 tx700610

Closed Xmas
rm42 ⇋20 ▥22 ⅅ

★ ★**Graslin** 1 r Piron (off pl Graslin)
(n.rest) ☎891609

rm46 ⇋8 ▥23 Lift ⅅ sB70–147
sB ⇋ ▥70–147 dB112–172

⊅**SARL Dao** (A-Jamonières) 14r G-
Clemenceau ☎746666 All makes

At **CARQUEFOU** (4km NE on D337, off
N23)

☆ ☆ ☆**Novotel Nantes Carquefou** allée
des Sapins ☎493284 tx711175

⇋98 **P** Lift sB ⇋250–265
dB ⇋282–297 Pool

☆ ☆ ☆**PLM Carquefou** rte de Paris, Le
Petit Bel Air (N23 exit A11) ☎302924
tx710962

⇋79 **P** Lift ⅅ sB ⇋314 dB ⇋383
M alc Pool

☆ ☆**Campanile** bd des Pastureaux
☎490182

⇋50 **P** dB ⇋206–209 M55–80

☆ ☆**Climat de France** CD337, Petit Bel
Air ☎(6)4460123 tx692844

⇋42 **P** dB ⇋211–226

NANTIAT See CROUZILLE (LA)

NANTUA
Ain (☎74)

★ ★ ★**France (DPn)** 44 r Dr-Mercier
☎750055

20 Dec–Oct
⇋19 ▩ **P** mountains

★ ★**Lyon ᴸᴱ** 19r Dr-Mercier ☎751709

Dec–Oct
rm18 ⇋4 ▥6 ▩ **P** mountains

NAPOULE–PLAGE (LA)
Alpes-Maritimes (☎93)

★ ★ ★**Ermitage du Riou** (MAP) bd de
Mer ☎499566 tx470072

rm42 ⇋39 ▥3 **P** Lift ⅅ
sB ⇋315–660 dB ⇋ ▥435–855
Pool

NARBONNE
Aude (☎68)

★ ★**Midi ᴸᴱ** av de Toulouse ☎410462
tx500401

Jan–Nov
rm48 ⇋20 ▥16 ▩ **P** Lift ⅅ

☆ ☆**Novotel Narbonne Sud** quartier
Plaisance, rte d'Espagne ☎415952
tx500480

⇋96 **P** Lift sB ⇋247–267
dB ⇋299–319

★ ★**Dorade** 44 r J-Jaurès (n.rest)
☎326595

rm44 ⇋6 ▥8 ▩ **P** Lift ⅅ

☆ ☆**Ibis** quartier Plaisance (N9)
☎411441 tx500480

⇋42 ▩ Lift ⅅ sB ⇋176 dB ⇋229

★ ★**Languedoc** (MAP) **(DPn)** 22 bd
Gambetta ☎651474 tx505167

rm45 ⇋18 ▥13 **P** Lift ⅅ sB165
sB ⇋ ▥175 dB ⇋ ▥280

★ ★**Résidence** 6 r Premier-Mai (n.rest)
☎321941 tx500441

11 Feb–4 Jan
rm26 ⇋15 ▥11 ▩ **P** ⅅ

★**Lion d'Or** 39 av P-Sémard ☎320692

rm28 ⇋13 ▥7 ▩ **P**

⊅**R Deirieu** 43 r P-L-Courier ☎320838
Closed Sat pm & Sun Cit

⊅**Lopez** 180 av de Bordeaux ☎320854
Closed Sat pm & Sun Peu

⊅**Marty** 87 av du Gl-Leclerc ☎411610
Closed Sat pm & Sun Tal

&D**SANDRA** rte Perpignan ☎322720
Closed Sat & Sun Ren

At **NARBONNE-PLAGE** (1.5km E on D168)

★ ★**Caravelle** ʟᴸ (DPn in season) bd du
Front du Mer ☎498038
May–Sep
fli24 **P** sea

NAVARRENX
Pyrénées-Atlantiques (☎59)

★ ★**Commerce** r Principale ☎665016
15 Feb–25 Dec
rm30 ⇄20 fli3 A11rm

NEMOURS
Seine-et-Marne (☎6)

☆ ☆ ☆**Euromotel** (ETAP) l'Aire de Service
(2km SE on A6) (n.rest) ☎4281032
tx690243

⇄102 **P** sB⇄215 dB⇄271 M55

★ ★**Ecu de France (DPn)** 3 r de Paris
☎4281154
Seasonal
rm28 ⇄11 fli6 🏠 **P** 🌙 sB100–168
sB⇄ fli200 dB113–168 dB⇄ fli200
St15% .

☆ ☆**Ibis** r des Moines, ZI de Nemours
☎428800
⇄42 **P** sB⇄178 dB⇄211

★**Roches (DPn)** av d'Ormesson, St Pierre
☎4280143
rm17 ⇄5 fli7 A6rm 🏠 **P**

★**St-Pierre** 12 av Carnot (opp. station)
(n.rest) ☎4280157
15 Mar–28 Feb
rm25 ⇄2 fli11 🏠 **P** sB62–150
sB⇄ fli114–150 dB93–160
dB⇄ fli128–173

&D**Gambetta** 70 av Gambetta ☎4280546
Closed Sun VW

&D**Royal-Nemours** 95 r de Paris
☎4280047 M/c BL

&D**TMA** (M Carpentier) rte de Montargis
☎4280845 Closed Sun All makes

NEUF-BRISACH
Haut-Rhin (☎89)

At **VOGELGRUN** (5km E on N415)

☆ ☆**Européan (DPn)** ☎725157 tx68600
rm23 ⇄17 fli6 🏠 **P**

NEUFCHÂTEAU
Vosges (☎29)

&D**Mourot Auto** rte de Langres ☎943119
Closed Sun & Mon am Aud VW

NEUFCHÂTEL-EN-BRAY
Seine-Maritime (☎35)

★ ★**Grand Cerf (DPn)** 9 Grand Rue
☎930002
8 Jan–24 Nov
rm11 fli4 **P**

&D**Lechopier** 31, Grande Rue, St-Pierre
☎930082 Closed Sat pm & Sun Ren
&D**Lemarchand** 9 rte de Foucamont
☎930266 Closed Mon Aud VW

France

NEUILLY-SUR-SEINE See **PARIS**

NEUVÉGLISE
Cantal (☎71)

&D**Sauret** ☎238090 Closed Sun
Oct–Apr, Sun pm May–Sep All makes

NEVERS
Nièvre (☎86)

★ ★ ★**Diane** (MAP) 38 r du Midi
☎572810 tx801201
16 Jan–16 Dec
rm30 ⇄28 fli2 **P** Lift 🌙 sB⇄262
dB ⇄335

★ ★**Folie** ʟᴸ rte les Saulaies ☎570531
rm27 ⇄14 fli13 **P** sB⇄ fli109–194
dB⇄ fli143–208 Pool

★ ★**Molière** 25 r Molière (n.rest)
☎572996
rm18 ⇄3 fli15 **P** sB⇄ fli116–137
dB⇄ fli127–149

★**Morvan** 28 r Mouësse ☎611416
Closed Nov
rm11 fli7 **P** sB75–105 sB fli105–135
M55–160

★**Ste-Marie** 25 r Petit-Mouësse
☎611002
Mar–15 Jan
rm17 ⇄5 fli3 A9rm **P** sB64–110
sB⇄ fli86–110 dB76–143
dB⇄ fli108–143

&D**Verma** 4 av Colbert ☎610332 Closed
Sat & Sun BMW Opl Vau

At **VARENNES-VAUZELLES** (5km N)

☆ ☆**Routel** (N7) ☎576944 tx801059
⇄30 **P** sB⇄118–218 dB⇄211–256
🍴

NICE
Alpes-Maritimes (☎93)

See plan page 162

★ ★ ★ ★**Négresco** (SRS) 37 prom des
Anglais ☎883591 tx460040 Plan **1**
⇄150 **P** Lift sB⇄888–1325
dB⇄948–1385 Beach sea

★ ★ ★**Atlantic** 12 bd V-Hugo
☎884015 tx460840 Plan **2**
⇄122 🏠 **P** Lift sB⇄240–325
dB⇄350–450 M80–90 mountains

★ ★ ★**Frantel** 28 av Notre-Dame
☎803024 tx470662 Plan **2A**
⇄200 **P** Lift 🌙 sB⇄415 dB⇄520
Pool

★ ★ ★**Sofitel Splendid** 50 bd V-Hugo
☎886954 tx460938 Plan **3**
⇄130 **P** Lift 🌙 sB⇄420–500
dB⇄520–850 Pool mountains

★ ★ ★**Westminster Concorde** 27 prom
des Anglais ☎882944 tx460872 Plan **4**
⇄110 Lift 🌙 sB⇄410–490
dB⇄530–680 sea

★ ★ ★**Bedford** (Inter) 45 r du Ml-Joffre
(n.rest) ☎821836 tx970086 Plan **4A**
rm50 ⇄35 fli15 Lift sB⇄ fli190–260
dB⇄ fli220–320

★ ★ ★**Brice** 44 r Ml-Joffre ☎881444
tx470658 Plan **5**
rm60 ⇄55 fli15 Lift 🌙
sB⇄ fli220–260 dB⇄ fli320–370

★ ★ ★**Gounod** 3 r Gounod (n.rest)
☎882620 tx461705 Plan **6**
rm45 ⇄30 fli15 🏠 Lift 🌙
sB⇄ fli230–260 dB⇄ fli290–330
Pool

★ ★ ★**Locarno** 4 av des Baumettes
(n.rest) ☎962800 tx970015 Plan **13**
rm48 ⇄25 fli22 🏠 Lift

★ ★ ★**Malmaison** (MAP) 48 bd V-Hugo
☎876256 tx470410 Plan **6A**
⇄45 Lift sB⇄240 dB⇄350

☆ ☆ ★**Massenet** 11 r Massenet
☎871131 Plan **7**
⇄46 🏠 **P** Lift sB⇄254–314
dB⇄254–376

☆ ☆ ☆**Mercure** 2 r Halevy (n.rest)
☎823088 tx970656 Plan **7A**
⇄124 🏠 **P** Lift sB⇄293–338
dB⇄361–406 sea

★ ★ ★**Napoléon** 6 r Grimaldi (n.rest)
☎877007 tx460949 Plan **8**
rm80 ⇄75 fli5 Lift 🌙
sB⇄ fli210–250 dB⇄275–340

★ ★ ★**Windsor** 11 r Dalpozzo (n.rest)
☎885935 tx970072 Plan **10**
rm59 ⇄33 fli24 Lift sB fli210–312
dB⇄ fli240–330 Pool

★ ★**Continental Massena** 58 r Gioffredo
(n.rest) ☎854925 tx470192 Plan **12**
rm116 ⇄85 fli31 **P** Lift 🌙
sB⇄ fli170–320 dB⇄ fli255–451

Albert-1er 5 r de Cronstadt ☎883935
Closed Sat & Sun Lot Toy Vlo

&D**Côte d'Azur** 3 r Trachel ☎886717 All
makes

RMCP 297 rte de Grenoble ☎884014
Closed Sat & Sun All makes

At **ST-LAURENT-DU-VAR** (7km SW off N7)

☆ ☆ ☆**Novotel Nice Cap 3000** av de
Verdun ☎316115 tx470643 Plan **9**
⇄103 **P** Lift sB⇄310–325
dB⇄380–420 M90 Pool

NÎMES
Gard (☎66)

★ ★ ★**Imperator** (MAP) quai de la
Fontaine ☎219030 tx490635
Mar–Dec
⇄61 A3rm 🏠 Lift sB⇄250–270
dB⇄280–435

★ ★ ★**Sofitel** chemin de l'Hostellerie,
bd Périphérique Sud ☎844044 tx490644
⇄100 **P** Lift 🌙 sB⇄318–403
dB⇄399–461 🍴 Pool

★ ★**Cheval Blanc et des Arènes** 1 pl
des Arènes ☎672003 tx480856 →

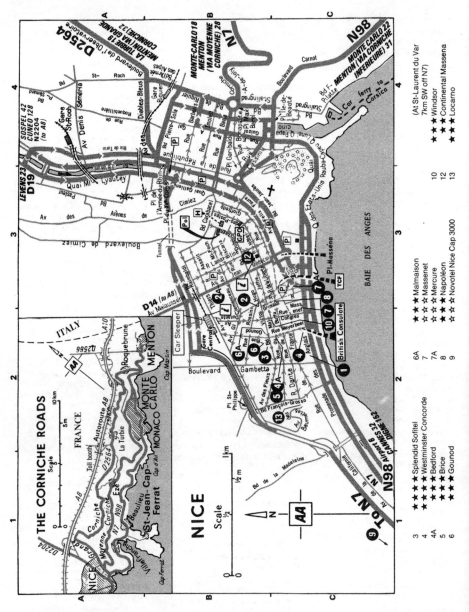

NICE

The Corniche Roads / Menton / Monte Carlo map and Nice city map (Scale ½ – 1km)

1	★★★★★	Négresco
2	★★★★	Atlantic
2A	★★★★	Frantel
3	★★★★	Splendid Sofitel
4	★★★★	Westminster Concorde
4A	★★★★	Bedford
5	★★★	Brice
6	★★★	Gounod
6A	★★★	Malmaison
7	★★★	Massenet
7A	☆☆☆☆	Mercure
8	★★★	Napoléon
9	☆☆☆	Novotel Nice Cap 3000
10	★★★	Windsor
12	★★★	Continental Massena
13	★★★	Locarno

(At St-Laurent du Var 7km SW off N7)

NICE

rm50 ←30 ⋔20 Lift ♪
sB ⇄ ⋔190–220 dB ⇄ ⋔220

☆☆☆**Novotel Nimes Ouest** 124 chemin de l'Hostellerie ☎846020 tx480675
←96 **P** sB ←237–262 dB ←293–313 Pool

★★**Carrière** (Inter) 6 r Grizot ☎672489 tx490580
rm60 ←56 ⋔4 🅿 **P** Lift sB141–181

sB ⇄ ⋔181 dB202 db ⇄ ⋔242 M52–75

☆☆**Ibis** chemin de l'Hostellerie ☎380065 tx490180
←108 **P** Lift sB ←183 dB ←240

☆☆**Louvre** 2 sq de la Couronne ☎672275 tx480218
rm35 ←25 ⋔10 🅿 **P** Lift ♪

❀**Europe** 186 rte de Montpellier ☎840440 Closed Sat pm & Sun Fia

162

🅶**Fricon** 175 rte d'Alès ☎231911 All makes

🅶**SNDA** 2543 rte de Montpellier ☎849509 Closed Sat pm & Sun Aud VW

At **CAISSARGUES BOUILLARGUES** (4km S)

☆ ☆**Campanile** chemin de la Carrèras ☎842705 tx610016

⇌50 P dB ⇌206-209 M55-80

At **MARGUERITTES** (7km NE via N86)

☆ ☆**Marguerittes** rte d'Avignon ☎260123

🅼48 P

NIORT
Deux-Sèvres (☎49)

★ ★ ★**Brèche** 8 av Bujauit ☎244178 tx790624

5 Jan-22 Dec
rm49 ⇌19 🅼17 Lift 𝔇 sB106-160
sB ⇌ 🅼136-160 dB162-230
dB ⇌ 🅼222-266

★ ★**Grand** 32 av Paris (n.rest) ☎242221 tx790624

rm40 ⇌10 🅼30 🚗 P Lift 𝔇

☆ ☆**Ibis** av de la Rochelle ☎735454 tx791635

⇌40 P sB ⇌166 dB ⇌210

★ ★ ★**Terminus**🇱 82 r de la Gare ☎240038

rm43 ⇌ 🅼36 Lift dB64-175
dB ⇌ 🅼90-200

NOEUX-LES-MINES
Pas-de-Calais (☎21)

★ ★**Tourterelles** 374 rte Nationale ☎669075

rm18 ⇌8 🅼4 🚗 P sB105-150
sB ⇌ 🅼115-200 dB180-240
dB ⇌ 🅼180-240 M60-200

NOGENTEL See **CHÂTEAU-THIERRY**

NOGENT-LE-ROTROU
Eure-et-Loir (☎37)

★ ★**Dauphin** 39 r Villette-Gate ☎521730

Mar-Dec
rm26 ⇌5 🅼6 🚗 P sB70-170
sB ⇌ 🅼180 dB100-185
dB ⇌ 🅼168-196

NOGENT-SUR-OISE
Oise (☎4)

★ ★ ★**Sarcus** (Inter) 7 r Châteaubriand ☎4740131 tx150047

rm62 ⇌34 🅼28 Lift sB ⇌ 🅼171
dB ⇌ 🅼190

NOISY-LE-GRAND See **PARIS**

NOLAY
Côte-d'Or (☎80)

★**Ste Marie**🇱 (DPn) 36 r de la République ☎217319

Feb-Dec
rm13 🅼4 A5rm 🚗 P sB80-91
sB 🅼91 dB93-130 dB 🅼104-130

NONANCOURT
Eure (☎32)

France

★**Grand Cerf**🇱 17 Grand Rue ☎581527 rm9 🅼5 P dB70-120
dB ⇌ 🅼120-130

NONTRON
Dordogne (☎53)

★**Grand**🇱 3 pl A-Agard ☎561122
rm26 ⇌12 🅼6 🚗 P Lift dB50-180
dB ⇌ 🅼80-180

NOUAN-LE-FUZELIER
Loir-et-Cher (☎54)

★**Moulin de Villiers**🇱 (DPn) (3km N by D44) rte Chaon ☎887227

26 Mar-Aug & 15 Sep-Dec
rm20 ⇌9 🅼5 P sB ⇌ 🅼88-190
dB96-165 dB ⇌ 🅼146-190

NOUVION-EN-THIÉRACHE (LE)
Aisne (☎23)

★**Paix** 37 r V-Vicary ☎970455
7 Jan-18 Dec
rm25 ⇌7 🅼5 P sB67-146 dB80-146
dB ⇌ 🅼80-146

NOVES
Bouches-du-Rhône (☎90)

★ ★ ★**Auberge de Noves (DPn)** (2km NW on D28) ☎941921 tx431312
Mar-Dec
⇌ 🅼22 A5rm 🚗 P 𝔇
dB ⇌ 🅼300-740 🏊 Pool

NOYELLES-GODAULT See **HENIN-BEAUMONT**

NOYERS-SUR-CHER
Loir-et-Cher (☎54)

★**Touraine et Sologne**🇱 (DPn) (N76 & N675) ☎751523

20 Feb-4 Jan
rm14 ⇌1 🅼11 P sB68-128
dB ⇌ 🅼100-165

NOYON
Oise (☎4)

★**St-Eloi** 81 bd Carnot ☎4440149
rm31 ⇌27 🅼2 P sB52-120
sB ⇌ 🅼120 dB62-130 dB ⇌ 🅼130

NOZAY
Loire-Atlantique (☎40)

★**Gergaud**🇱 (DPn) 12 rte Nantes ☎794754
rm8 ⇌1 🅼2 P sB60 sB ⇌ 🅼80-100
dB84 dB ⇌ 🅼100

NUITS-ST-GEORGES
Côte-d'Or (☎80)

☆ ☆**Ibis** 1 av Chambolland ☎611717 tx350954

⇌52 P sB ⇌168 dB ⇌211

Aubin rte Dijon ☎610385 Closed Aug, Sat & Sun MB

🅶**Grands Crus** rte de Dijon ☎610223 Closed Aug, Sat pm & Sun Peu

---

NYONS
Drôme (☎75)

★ ★**Colombet**🇱 pl de la Libération ☎260366
1 Jan-25 Oct
rm30 ⇌10 🅼10 🚗 Lift 𝔇
sB100-110 sB ⇌ 🅼140-180
dB120-220 dB ⇌ 🅼190-280
mountains

OBERNAI
Bas-Rhin (☎88)

★ ★**Duc d'Alsace**🇱 6 pl de la Gare ☎955534
15 Mar-15 Feb
rm17 ⇌15 🅼2 🚗 P
sB ⇌ 🅼166-215 dB ⇌ 🅼155-215

OBERSTEIGEN
Bas-Rhin (☎88)

★ ★**Belle Vue (DPn)** 16 rte de Dabo ☎873239
rm45 ⇌24 🅼10 🚗 P sB88-184
sB ⇌ 🅼184 dB184 dB ⇌ 🅼184
mountains

OLÉRON (ILE D')
Charente-Maritime (☎46)

REMIGEASSE (LA)

★ ★ ★**Grand Large (DPn** in high season) la pl de la Remigeasse ☎753789
Apr-Oct
⇌30 P Lift 🏊 Pool sea

ST-TROJAN-LES-BAINS

☆ ☆ ☆**Novotel** Plage du Gatseau (2.5km S) ☎760246 tx790910

⇌80 P Lift sB ⇌301 dB ⇌348 🏊 Pool sea

OLIVET
Loiret (☎38)

★ ★ ★**Frantel la Reine Blanche** r de la Reine Blanche ☎664051 tx760926

⇌65 Lift sB ⇌272 dB ⇌319

☆ ☆**Climat de France** ZAC de la rte de Bourges ☎692055 tx692844

⇌42 P sB ⇌182 dB ⇌218 M54-74

★ ★**Rivage** 635 r de la Reine Blanche ☎660293 tx760926
rm20 ⇌11 🅼4 P sB70 sB ⇌ 🅼170
dB ⇌ 🅼170 lake

OLORON-STE-MARIE
Pyrénées-Atlantiques (☎59)

★ ★**Béarn** 4 pl de la Mairie ☎390099
Closed Feb
rm32 ⇌16 🅼3 A6rm 🚗 Lift
sB100-160 sB ⇌ 🅼100-160
dB ⇌ 🅼110-210 mountains

ORANGE
Vaucluse (☎90)

☆ ☆ ☆**Euromotel Orange** (ETAP) rte de Caderousse ☎342410 tx431550

⇌99 P sB ⇌190 dB ⇌246 M80

★ ★**Boscotel** (Inter) rte de Caderousse ☎344750 tx431405

⇌57 P

163

★ ★**Louvre & Terminus** 89 av F-Mistral
(n.rest) ☎341008 tx431195

15 Jan – 14 Dec
rm34 ⇌21 ⋔13 ⚑ P Lift ♪
sB ⇌ ⋔99–195 dB ⇌ ⋔159–259

G Ameller 43 av Ml-Foch ☎341234 Opl
Vau VW

⏱**Auto Service** 78 av Ml-Foch ☎342435
Closed Sat & Sun Frd

⏱**H Castagne** rte de Roquemaure
☎340825 Closed Sat pm & Sun Cit

⏱**Cretalles** quartier de Condoulet
☎345305 MB

⏱**H Marquion** av C-de-Gaulle ☎346844
Closed 7–30 Jun, Sat pm & Sun Ren

ORGEVAL
Yvelines (☎3)

☆ ☆ ☆**Novotel** (N13) ☎9759760
tx697174
⇌119 P Lift sB ⇌276 dB ⇌317 ⬩
Pool

★ ★**Moulin d'Orgeval(DPn)** ☎9759574
Closed Jan
rm13 ⇌5 P Pool lake

ORLÉANS
Loiret (☎38)

See also **CHAPELLE-SAINT-MECMIN (LA)**

★ ★ ★ ★**Sofitel** 44–46 quai Barentin
☎621739 tx780073
⇌110 P Lift ♪ sB365–445
dB ⇌450–530 Pool

★ ★**Cedres** (Inter) 17 r du Ml-Foch
(n.rest) ☎622292 tx760912
rm32 ⇌21 ⋔7 Lift ♪
sB ⇌ ⋔168–205 dB185–225
dB ⇌ ⋔186–235

☆ ☆**Arcade** 4 r Ml-Foch ☎542311
tx780629
⋔125 P Lift sB ⋔158 dB ⋔169

★ ★**Marguerite** 14 pl Vieux-Marché
(n.rest) ☎537432
rm25 ⇌3 ⋔11 sBfr89 sB ⇌ ⋔fr131
dB ⇌ ⋔fr131

★ ★**Terminus** 40 r de la République
(n.rest) ☎532464
rm47 ⇌38 ⋔9 Lift sB ⇌ ⋔167–207
dB ⇌ ⋔194–234

⏱**Jousselin** 12 r Jousselin ☎536104
Closed Sat & Sun MB

⏱**Lion Fort** 51 r Porte St-Jean ☎625829
Closed Sat & Sun BL

At **SARAN** (2km NW on A10)

☆ ☆**Ibis** La Chiperie ☎733993 tx760902
⇌104 P Lift sB ⇌171 dB ⇌213

⏱**DAC** 1173 r de Montaran ☎886686

At **SOURCE (LA)** (10km S off N20)

☆ ☆ ☆**Novotel** 2 r H-de-Balzac
☎630428 tx760619
⇌ ⋔121 P Lift sB ⇌ ⋔246–272
dB ⇌ ⋔294–320 Malc ⬩ Pool

France

☆ ☆**Campanile** 326 r Châteaubriand
☎635820 tx610016
⇌42 P dB ⇌218–222 M55–80

ORLY AIRPORT See **PARIS AIRPORTS**

ORSAY
Essonne (☎6)

At **COURTABŒUF** (3km S on D35)

☆ ☆ ☆**Mercure Paris Orsay** av du
Parana, ZA ☎9076396 tx691247
⇌110 P Lift sB ⇌262–283
dB ⇌299–320 Malc Pool

☆ ☆**Climat de France** av des Andes, ZA
☎4460506 tx692844
⇌42 P sB ⇌225 dB ⇌243 M54–74

At **SACLAY** (6km N)

☆ ☆**Novotel** r C-Thomassin, Christ de
Saclay ☎9418140 tx691856
⇌136 P Lift sB ⇌289 dB ⇌332 M85
⬩ Pool

ORTHEZ
Pyrénées-Atlantiques (☎59)

☆ ★**Climat de France** r du Soulor
☎(6)4460123 tx692044
⇌24 dB ⇌208–223

⏱**Laglère** av d'Aquitaine ☎690212
Closed Sun BL Opl

⏱**Minjou** 5 r Gl-Foch ☎690937 Frd

⏱**Mousques** av F-Jammes ☎690978
Closed 28 Jul–2 Aug, Sat pm & Sun Ren

OYONNAX
Ain (☎74)

★**Nouvel** 31 r R-Nicod (n.rest) ☎772811
rm37 ⇌7 ⋔7 ⚑ Lift sB60–100
sB ⇌ ⋔95–105 dB82–127
dB ⇌ ⋔112–138

PACY-SUR-EURE
Eure (☎32)

★ ★**Etape** 1 r Isambard ☎361277
Closed 16–29 Jan
rm8 ⇌5 P sB60–100 sB ⇌60–100
dB ⇌90–160

⏱**Lepée** 98–102 r Isambard ☎360673
Closed Sat, Sun & Mon Frd

At **CHAIGNES** (5km E on N13)

⏱**Lion d'Or** (N13) ☎369404 All makes

PALAISEAU
Essonne (☎6)

☆ ☆ ☆**Novotel** 18–20 r E-Baudot, Zone
d'Activité de Massy ☎9208491 tx691595
⇌ ⋔151 P Lift sB ⇌ ⋔272–288
dB ⇌ ⋔310–326 Malc Pool

PAMIERS
Ariège (☎61)

★ ★**Parc** (DPn) 12 r Piconnières
☎670258

rm12 ⇌6 ⋔3 ⚑ dB75–180
dB ⇌ ⋔75–190

PARAMÉ See **ST-MALO**

PARAY-LE-MONIAL
Saône-et-Loire (☎85)

★ ★**Vendanges de Bourgogne** 5 r D-
Papin ☎811343
Closed 8 Feb–14 Mar
rm14 ⇌2 ⋔11 ⚑ P

★**Trois Pigeons (DPn)** 2 r d'Argaud
☎810377
10 Feb–2 Jan
rm33 ⇌6 ⋔14 A15rm ⚑ sB50–75
sB ⇌ ⋔130–150 dB75–85
dB ⇌ ⋔150–180

PARENTIS-EN-BORN
Landes ((☎58)

⏱**Larrieu** r du Stade ☎784350 Closed
Feb & Sun Ren

PARIS (☎1)
See plan pages 166 and 167
See also **AULNAY-SOUS-BOISE, BUC,
CHAMPS-SUR-MARNE, EVRY,
GONESSE, MONTESSON, MONTSOULT,
ORGEVAL, ORSAY, PALAISEAU,
PLAISIR, PONTOISE, QUEUE-EN-BRIE
(LA), RAMBOUILLET, ST-GERMAIN-EN-
LAYE, SANNOIS, SEVRAN,
SURVILLIERS-ST-WITZ, VERRIÈRES-LE-
BUISSON & VIRY-CHÂTILLON.**

1st Arrondissement Opéra, Palais-Royal,
Halles, Bourse

★ ★ ★ ★**Meurice** (Intercont) 228 r de
Rivoli ☎2603860 tx230673 Plan **45**
⇌223 Lift ♪ sB ⇌ ⋔1281–1529
dB ⇌ ⋔1662–1881 Malc

★ ★ ★ ★**Ritz** 15 pl Vendôme
☎2603830 tx220262 Plan **54**
⇌209 P Lift ♪ sB ⇌1250–1400
dB ⇌1750–2400 St%

★ ★ ★**Lotti** (Intercont) 7 r Castiglione
☎2603734 tx240066 Plan **40**
⇌130 Lift ♪ sB ⇌687–870
dB ⇌865–1132 St%

★ ★ ★**Cambon** 3 r Cambon (n.rest)
☎2603809 tx240814 Plan **16**
rm44 ⇌26 ⋔18 Lift ♪
sB ⇌ ⋔460–550 dB ⇌ ⋔530–620

★ ★ ★**Castille** 37 r Cambon (n.rest)
☎2615520 tx213505 Plan **18**
⇌75 Lift ♪ sB ⇌650 dB ⇌790

★ ★**Duminy-Vendôme** 3 r Mont-
Thabor (n.rest) ☎2603280 tx213492
Plan **21**
May–Sep
rm79 ⇌69 ⋔10 Lift ♪
sB ⇌ ⋔350–430 dB ⇌ ⋔370–450

★ ★ ★**France et Choiseul** (Comfort) 239 r
St-Honoré, pl Vendôme ☎2615460
tx680959 Plan **69**
⇌150 Lift ♪ sB ⇌490 dB ⇌620 M83

★ ★ ★**Louvre-Concorde** pl A-Malraux
☎2615601 tx220412 Plan **41**

164

rm222 ⇦150 🛏72 Lift 𝒟
sB ⇦ 🛏560-740 dB ⇦ 🛏670-850

★★Family 35 r Cambon (n.rest)
☎2615484 Plan 24

rm25 ⇦18 🛏4 Lift sB202
sB ⇦ 🛏202 dB ⇦ 🛏247

★★Montana-Tuileries 21 r St-Roch
☎2603510 tx210331 Plan 47
rm25 ⇦21 🛏4 Lift sB ⇦ 🛏270-370
dB ⇦ 🛏286-400

2nd Arrondissement Opéra, Palais-Royal,
Halles, Bourse

★★★★Westminster 13 r de la Paix
☎2615746 tx680035 Plan 68
rm102 ⇦97 🛏5 🍴 P Lift 𝒟
sB ⇦ 🛏745-820 dB ⇦ 🛏990-1150
M130-150

★★★Horset Opéra d'Antin 18 r d'Antin
(n.rest) ☎7421301 tx680564 Plan 79
rm60 ⇦55 Lift sB ⇦375 dB ⇦480

★★France 4 r du Caire (n.rest)
☎2333098 Plan 27
rm50 ⇦11 🛏9 Lift 𝒟 sB147
sB ⇦ 🛏185 dB ⇦ 🛏161-200

⚡Permanence 'Renault' 19 bd St-Denis
☎2361000

5th Arrondissement Quartier Latin,
Luxembourg, Jardin des Plantes

★★Collège de France 7 r Thénard
(n.rest) ☎3267836 Plan 76
rm29 ⇦23 🛏6 sB ⇦ 🛏243-270
dB ⇦ 🛏243-270

6th Arrondissement Quartier Latin,
Luxembourg, Jardin des Plantes

★★★★Lutetia Concorde 45 bd Raspail
☎5443810 tx270424 Plan 42
rm300 ⇦240 🛏60 Lift 𝒟
sB ⇦ 🛏620-740 dB ⇦ 🛏730-850

★★★Madison 143 bd St-Germain
(n.rest) ☎3297250 Plan 43
rm57 ⇦42 🛏15 Lift 𝒟
sB ⇦ 🛏187-254 dB ⇦ 🛏222-288

★★★Senat 22 r St-Sulpice (n.rest)
☎3254230 tx220064 Plan 59
rm32 ⇦26 P Lift 𝒟 sB ⇦296
dB ⇦296

★★★Victoria Palace 6 r Blaise-
Desgoffe ☎5443816 tx270557 Plan 67
⇦110 🍴 P Lift 𝒟 sB ⇦410-520
dB ⇦460-550

★Angleterre 44 r Jacob (n.rest)
☎2603472 Plan 4
rm31 ⇦26 Lift sB220-250
sB ⇦220-300 dB ⇦330-400

7th Arrondissement Faubourg-St-Germain,
Invalides, École Militaire

★★★Pont Royal (MAP) 7 r
Montalembert ☎5443827 tx270113
Plan 72
⇦80 P Lift 𝒟 sB ⇦555-675
dB ⇦710-830

★★★★Sofitel Bourbon 32 r St-
Dominque ☎5559180 tx250019 Not on
plan
⇦112 🛏6 🍴 P Lift
sB ⇦ 🛏710-1600 dB ⇦ 🛏870-1600

★★★Bourdonnais 111-113 av
Bourdonnais ☎7054542 tx201416
Plan 80
rm60 ⇦53 🛏7 Lift 𝒟
sB ⇦ 🛏842-882 dB ⇦ 🛏1024-1094

★★★Bourgogne & Montana 3 r de
Bourgogne ☎5512022 tx270854 Plan 12
rm35 ⇦31 🛏4 Lift 𝒟
sB ⇦ 🛏241-480 dB ⇦ 🛏385-520
M100-160

★★★Cayré 4 bd Raspail (n.rest)
☎5443888 tx270577 Plan 19
⇦131 Lift 𝒟 sB ⇦ 🛏469-481
dB ⇦ 🛏485-497

★Splendid 29 av de Tourville (n.rest)
☎5515598 tx201204 Plan 62
rm45 ⇦15 🛏9 Lift sB68-125
sB ⇦ 🛏68-125 dB113-250
dB ⇦ 🛏113-250

8th Arrondissement Champs-Élysées, St-
Lazare, Madeleine

★★★★Bristol (SRS) 112 fbg St-
Honoré ☎2669145 tx280961 Plan 15
⇦ 🛏250 🍴 P Lift 𝒟
sB ⇦ 🛏1006-1366 dB ⇦ 🛏1432-1882
t19% Pool

★★★★George V (THF) 31 av George
V ☎7235400 tx650082 Plan 30
⇦292 P Lift 𝒟 sB ⇦1100 dB ⇦1470
Malc S%

★★★★Plaza-Athénée (THF) 25 av
Montaigne ☎7237833 tx650092 Plan 51
⇦214 🍴 P Lift 𝒟 sB ⇦880-1250
dB ⇦1180-1370 S15%

★★★★Prince de Galles 33 av
George V ☎7235511 tx280627 Plan 52
⇦160 Lift 𝒟

★★★★Royal Monceau (CIGA) 35 av
Hoche ☎5619800 tx650361 Plan 57
⇦225 Lift 𝒟 sB ⇦790-917
dB ⇦950-1120

★★★Bedford 17 r de l'Arcade
☎2662232 tx290506 Plan 10
⇦150 Lift 𝒟 sB ⇦380 dB ⇦480-500

★★★Castiglione 40 r du fbg St-
Honoré ☎2650750 tx240362 Plan 17
⇦ 🛏110 Lift 𝒟 sB ⇦ 🛏655-825
dB ⇦ 🛏705-875

★★★Frantel Windsor 14 r Beaujon
☎5630404 tx650902 Plan 29
⇦135 Lift sB ⇦840 dB ⇦960

★★★Horset Astor 11 r d'Astorg
☎2665656 tx642718 Plan 6

rm144 ⇦130 🛏10 Lift sB ⇦ 🛏500
dB ⇦ 🛏600 Malc

★★★★Horset Royal Malesherbes 24
bd Malesherbes ☎2655330 tx660190
Plan 81

rm102 ⇦98 🛏4 Lift sB ⇦ 🛏500
dB ⇦ 🛏600 Malc

★★★★Lancaster 7 r de Berri
☎3599043 tx640991 Plan 38
⇦57 P Lift 𝒟 sB ⇦905 dB ⇦1210
S15%

★★★★Trémoille (THF) 14 r Trémoille
☎7233420 tx640344 Plan 64
⇦112 Lift 𝒟 sB ⇦950-1050
dB ⇦1050-1320 S%

★★★Atala 10 r Châteaubriand
☎5620162 tx640576 Plan 7
rm50 ⇦34 🛏16 Lift sB ⇦ 🛏420-520
dB ⇦ 🛏450-560

★★★Élysées Marignan 12 r de
Marignan (n.rest) ☎3595861 tx6600018
Plan 82
⇦71 Lift sB ⇦590 dB ⇦650

★★★Élysées Ponthieu 24 r de Ponthieu
(n.rest) ☎2256870 tx640053 Plan 83
⇦62 Lift sB ⇦475 dB ⇦490

★★★Royal 33 av de Friedland
☎3590814 tx280965 Plan 56
rm57 ⇦47 🛏10 Lift 𝒟
sB ⇦ 🛏460-522 dB ⇦ 🛏528-550

★★Élysée 12 r Saussaies (n.rest)
☎2652925 Plan 22
rm30 ⇦8 🛏18 Lift 𝒟 sB98-190
sB ⇦ 🛏206 dB118-222 dB ⇦ 🛏252

★★Europe 15 r Constantinople (n.rest)
☎5228080 Plan 23

Sep-Jul
rm47 ⇦18 🛏7 Lift sB99-212
sB ⇦ 🛏231 dB 153-227
dB ⇦ 🛏198-247

★★Ministère 31 r de Surène (n.rest)
☎2662143 Plan 46
rm32 ⇦26 🛏4 Lift 𝒟 sB190-250
sB ⇦ 🛏200-270 dB190
dB ⇦ 🛏210-350

★Brescia 16 r d'Edimbourg (n.rest)
☎5221431 tx660714 Plan 14
rm38 ⇦22 🛏16 Lift sB ⇦ 🛏170-210
dB ⇦ 🛏200-240

9th Arrondissement Opéra, Gare du Nord,
Gare de l'Est, Grands Boulevards

★★★★Ambassador Concorde (GT) 16
bd Haussmann ☎2469263 tx650912
Plan 3
⇦300 P Lift 𝒟 sB ⇦580-740
dB ⇦700-850

★★★★Grand (Intercont) 2 r Scribe
☎2681213 tx220875 Plan 32
⇦600 Lift 𝒟 sB ⇦860-935
dB ⇦1030-1105

★★★Blanche Fontaine 34 r Fontaine
(n.rest) ☎5267232 tx660311 Plan 11
rm49 ⇦47 🛏2 Lift 🍴 𝒟
sB ⇦ 🛏250-265 dB ⇦ 🛏290-320

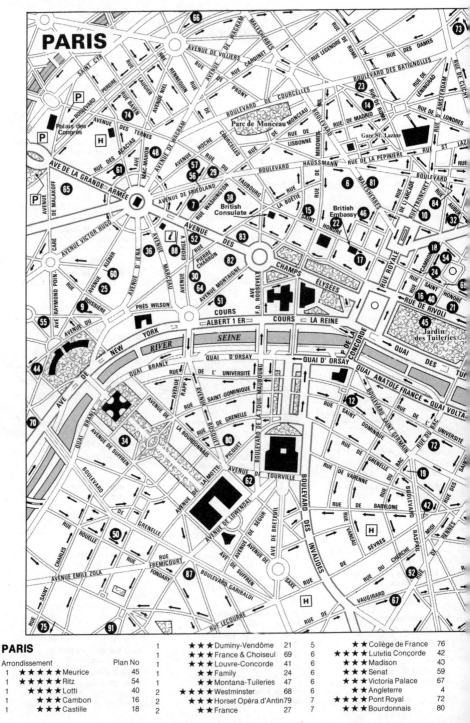

PARIS

Arrondissement		Plan No	1	★★★ Duminy-Vendôme	21	5	★★ Collège de France	76
			1	★★★ France & Choiseul	69	6	★★★★ Lutetia Conçorde	42
1	★★★★★ Meurice	45	1	★★★ Louvre-Concorde	41	6	★★★ Madison	43
1	★★★★★ Ritz	54	1	★★ Family	24	6	★★★ Senat	59
1	★★★★ Lotti	40	1	★★ Montana-Tuileries	47	6	★★ Victoria Palace	67
1	★★★ Cambon	16	2	★★★★ Westminster	68	6	★★ Angleterre	4
1	★★★ Castille	18	2	★★★ Horset Opéra d'Antin	79	7	★★★ Pont Royal	72
			2	★★ France	27	7	★★★ Bourdonnais	80

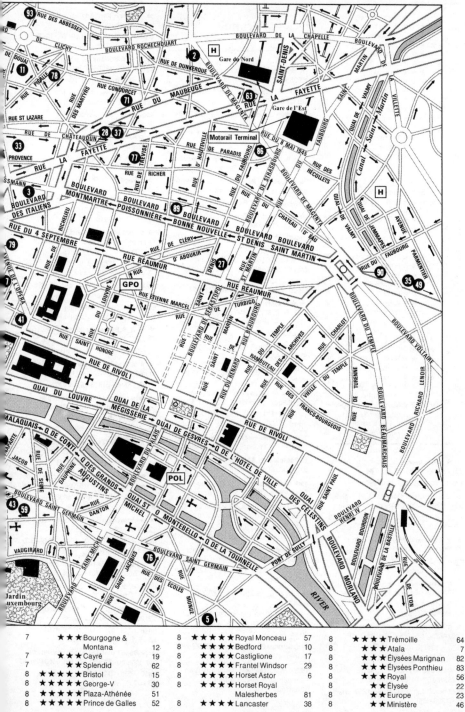

→

8	★Brescia	14
9	★★★★Ambassador-Concorde	3
9	★★★★Grand	32
9	★★★Blanche Fontaine	11
9	★★★Caumartin	84
9	★★★Franklin	28
9	★★★Havane	77
9	★★★Hélios	33
9	★★Lorette	78
9	★★Palmon	71
9	★Laffon	37
10	★★★Horset Pavillon	89
10	★★★Terminus Nord	63
10	★★Altona	2
10	★★Modern'Est	86
11	☆☆☆Holiday Inn	90
13	★Arts	5
15	★★★Hilton	34
15	☆☆☆Holiday Inn	91
15	★★★★Sofitel Paris	75
15	☆★Arcade	87
15	★★Pacific	50
15	★★Timhotel Montparnasse	92
16	★★★★Baltimore	9
16	★★Élysée Bassano	88
16	★★★Frémiet	70
16	★★★Massenet	44
16	★★Sevigné	60
16	★★Farnese	25
16	★★Keppler	36
16	★★Rond Point de Longchamp	55
16	★★Vermont	65
17	★★★★Regents' Garden	74
17	★★★★Splendid Étoile	61
17	★★Neva	48
17	★Verniquet	66
18	★★★Terrass	73
18	★★Timhotel Montmartre	93
	☆☆☆Novotel Paris Bagnolet (At Bagnolet 7km E)	49
	☆☆Ibis (At Bagnolet 7kmE)	35

★★★Caumartin 27 r Caumartin (n. rest) ☎7429595 tx680702 Plan 84
⇋40 Lift sB⇋475 dB⇋490

★★★Excelsior Opéra 5 r La Fayette (n. rest) ☎8749930 tx641312 Not on plan
rm53 ⇋30 🛏23 Lift sB⇋ 🛏225–283 dB⇋ 🛏300

★★★Franklin (MAP) 19 r Buffalt ☎2802727 tx660634 Plan 28
rm64 ⇋34 🛏30 Lift sB⇋ 🛏337–402 dB⇋ 🛏423

★★★Havane 44 r de Trévise (n.rest) ☎7707912 tx041462 Plan 77
rm49 ⇋6 🛏43 Lift sB⇋ 🛏268–305 dB⇋ 🛏320–350

★★★Hélios 75 r de la Victoire (n.rest) ☎8742864 tx641255 Plan 33
rm50 ⇋31 🛏11 P Lift ♪ sB⇋ 🛏253 dB⇋ 🛏302

★★Lorette 36 r Notre-Dame de Lorette ☎2851881 tx641877 Plan 78
rm73 ⇋70 Lift sB210 sB⇋250 dB260 dB⇋260–380

France

★★Palmon 30 r Maubeuge (n.rest) ☎2850761 tx641498 Plan 71
rm38 ⇋12 🛏24 Lift sB⇋ 🛏145–224 dB⇋ 🛏150–245

★Laffon 25 r Buffault (n.rest) ☎8784991 Plan 37
rm46 ⇋21 🛏8 Lift sB82 sB⇋ 🛏201 dB⇋ 🛏192–201

10th Arrondissement Opéra, Gare du Nord, Gare de l'Est, Grands Boulevards

★★★Horset Pavilion 38 r de l'Echiquier ☎2469275 tx641905 Plan 89
⇋89 sB⇋375 dB⇋407

★★★Terminus Nord 12 bd Denain (n.rest) ☎2802000 tx660615 Plan 63
rm230 ⇋ 🛏180 Lift sB⇋ 🛏237–378 dB⇋ 🛏305–395

★★Altona 166 r du fbg Poissonière (n.rest) ☎8786824 tx260717 Plan 2
rm58 ⇋12 🛏31 Lift sB80–155 sB⇋ 🛏165 dB208 dB⇋ 🛏219

★★Modern'Est 91 bd de Strasbourg (n.rest) ☎6072472 Plan 86
rm30 ⇋7 🛏22 Lift sB⇋ 🛏245–255 dB⇋ 🛏285–295

⋔SE St-Denis 76 r du fbg St-Denis ☎2469998 Ren

11th Arrondisement Bastille, République, Hôtel de Ville

☆☆☆☆Holiday Inn 10 pl de la République ☎3554434 tx210651 Plan 90
⇋🛏333 P Lift ♪ sB⇋ 🛏500–600 dB⇋ 🛏560–830

12th Arrondissement Bastille, Gare de Lyon, Place d'Italie, Bois de Vincennes

⋔Poniatowski SARL 57 bd Poniatowski ☎3443732 Closed Sat & Sun Ren

13th Arrondissement Bastille, Gare de Lyon, Place d'Italie, Bois de Vincennes

★Timhotel Italie 22 r Barrault ☎5806767 tx205461 Not on plan
rm73 ⇋15 🛏53 Lift sB183–187 sB⇋ 🛏266–270 dB⇋ 🛏308–316 M60

★Timhotel Tolbiac 35 r de Tolbiac (n.rest) ☎5837494 tx201309 Not on plan
rm54 ⇋12 🛏42 Lift sB⇋ 🛏226–258 dB⇋ 🛏287–295

★Arts 8 r Coypel (n.rest) ☎7077632 Plan 5
rm42 ⇋2 🛏20 Lift sB68–140 sB⇋ 🛏135–150 dB106–170 dB⇋ 🛏151–180

SOS Service 82 bd Massena ☎5846969 All makes

15th Arrondissement Vaugirard, Gare Montparnasse, Grenelle, Denfert-Rochereau

★★★★Hilton 18 av Suffren ☎2739200 tx200955 Plan 34
⇋489 🛗 Lift ♪ sB ⇋868–1042 dB ⇋1028–1229

☆☆☆☆Holiday Inn 69 bd Victor ☎5337463 tx260844 Plan 91
⇋90 P Lift ♪ sB ⇋470 dB⇋610

★★★★Sofitel Paris 8–12 r L-Armand ☎5549500 tx200432 Plan 75
⇋635 Lift ♪ sB ⇋598–718 dB ⇋706–826 Pool

☆☆Arcade 2 r Cambronne ☎5673520 tx203842 Plan 87
🛏530 P Lift sB 🛏188–200 dB 🛏199–210

★★Pacific 11 r Fondary (n.rest) ☎5752049 Plan 50
rm66 ⇋31 🛏18 Lift sB105–163 sB⇋ 🛏139–163 dB144–206 dB⇋ 🛏198–210

★★Timhotel Montparnasse 22 r de l'Arrivée (n.rest) ☎5489662 tx270625 Plan 92
rm33 ⇋6 🛏25 Lift sB183–187 sB⇋ 🛏266–270 dB⇋ 🛏308–316

⋔Allraja 366 r de Vaugirard ☎5326712 Closed Sun All makes

16th Arrondissement Passy, Auteuil, Bois de Boulogne, Chaillot, Porte Maillot

★★★★Baltimore 88 bis av Kléber ☎5538333 tx611591 Plan 9
⇋119 Lift ♪ sB⇋550 dB⇋790

★★★Élysées Bassano 24 r de Bassano (n.rest) ☎7204903 tx611559 Plan 88
⇋40 Lift sB⇋475 dB⇋490

★★★Frémiet (MAP) 6 av Frémiet (n.rest) ☎5245206 tx630329 Plan 70
rm36 ⇋23 🛏13 P Lift ♪ sB⇋ 🛏335–400 dB⇋ 🛏435–470

★★★Horset St-Cloud 21 r Gudin (n.rest) ☎6519922 tx610929 Not on plan
⇋47 Lift sB⇋330 dB⇋375

★★★Massenet (MAP) 5 bis r Massenet (n.rest) ☎5244303 tx620682 Plan 44
rm41 ⇋33 🛏2 Lift ♪ sB360 sB⇋ 🛏360 dB⇋ 🛏420

★★Sevigné 6 r de Belloy (n.rest) ☎7208890 tx610219 Plan 60
rm30 ⇋13 🛏17 Lift sB⇋ 🛏312–366 dB⇋ 🛏333–410

★★Farnese 32 r Hamelin (n.rest) ☎7205666 tx611732 Plan 25
rm40 ⇋35 🛏5 Lift ♪ sB⇋ 🛏290 dB⇋ 🛏292

★★Keppler (Inter) 12 r Keppler (n.rest) ☎7206505 tx620440 Plan 36
rm48 ⇋19 🛏25 Lift ♪ sBfr181 sB⇋ 🛏fr202 dB⇋ 🛏fr241

★★Rond Point de Longchamp 86 r de Longchamp ☎5051363 tx620653 Plan 55
rm59 ⇋35 🛏24 Lift sB⇋370 dB⇋390

★★**Vermont** 11 bis r Bois-de-Boulogne (n.rest) ☎5000497 tx612208 Plan **65**

⇆30 Lift ♪ sB275 sB ⇆ 🏠275 dB ⇆ 🏠280

17th Arrondissement Clichy, Ternes, Wagram

★★★★**Regent's Garden** (MAP) 6 r P-Demours (n.rest) ☎5740730 tx640127 Plan **74**

rm41 ⇆39 🏠2 🏠 **P** Lift sB ⇆ 🏠350–450 dB ⇆ 🏠570

★★★★**Splendid Étoile** 1 bis av Carnot ☎7664141 tx280773 Plan **61**

⇆60 Lift ♪ sB ⇆ 🏠400–590 dB ⇆ 🏠450–760

★★**Neva** 14 r Brey (n.rest) ☎3802826 Plan **48**

⇆35 Lift ♪

★**Verniquet** 3 r Verniquet (n.rest) ☎3802630 Plan **66**

rm26 ⇆11 🏠15 Lift sB ⇆ 🏠135–195 dB ⇆ 🏠187–224

Boursault 11 r Boursault ☎2936565 Closed Sat pm & Sun BL

18th Arrondissement Montmartre, La Villette, Belleville

★★★★**Terrass** 12 r J-de-Maistre ☎6067285 tx280830 Plan **73**

rm108 ⇆89 🏠19 Lift ♪ sB ⇆ 🏠330–400 dB ⇆ 🏠400–480

★**Ibis Paris Montmartre** 5 r Caulaincourt ☎2941818 tx640428 Not on plan

⇆326 **P** Lift sB ⇆299 dB ⇆364

☆☆**Pigalle Urbis Paris** 100 bd Rochechouart (n.rest) ☎6069917 tx290416 Not on plan

rm68 ⇆38 🏠30 Lift sB ⇆ 🏠232–249 dB ⇆ 🏠287

★★**Timhotel Montmartre** 11 pl E-Goudeau (n.rest) ☎2557479 tx650508 Plan **93**

rm61 ⇆4 🏠42 Lift sB146–174 sB ⇆ 🏠256–260 dB214–222 dB ⇆ 🏠289–297

The distances shown after the following locations are measured from the Place de la Concorde.

At **BAGNOLET** (7km E adj to Boulevard Périphérique)

☆☆☆**Novotel Paris Bagnolet** 1 av de la République ☎3600210 tx670216 Plan **49**

⇆611 **P** Lift sB ⇆422–440 dB ⇆462–483 Pool

☆**Ibis** r J-Jaurès ☎3600276 tx240830 Plan **35**

⇆414 **P** Lift sB ⇆228 dB ⇆261

At **BONDY** (10km NE)

⑧**B** Greuet 176–180 av Galliéni, (N3) ☎8471659 Closed Sat pm, Sun & Mon am Frd

At **BOULOGNE–BILLANCOURT** (7km W adj to Boulevard Périphérique)

France

⑧**Parc Auto** 69 r de Billancourt ☎6059100 BL Hon

At **CHILLY-MAZARIN** (20km S)

⑧**Auto Relais** 3 r du chemin de Fer ☎9344626 Closed 15 Aug–15 Sep & Sun BL MB

⑧**Mobil Station** 10–14 av P-Brossolette ☎9095427 Closed Sun All makes

At **CRÉTEIL** (12km SE off N5)

☆☆**Novotel** rte de Choissy (N186) ☎2079102 tx670396 Not on plan

⇆110 **P** Lift sB ⇆269–282 dB ⇆311–322 Pool

☆☆**Climat de France** quarter de la Brèche, r des Archives ☎8992323 tx692844 Not on plan

⇆48 **P** sB ⇆221 dB ⇆241 M54–70

At **FONTENAY-AUX-ROSES** (9.5km SE)

⑧**Marchand** 68 r Boucicaut ☎6611088 Closed Sat pm & Sun Frd

At **GENTILLY** (6km S adj to Boulevard Périphérique)

☆☆**Ibis** 13 r du Val de Marne ☎6641925 tx250733 Not on plan

⇆296 **P** Lift sB ⇆223 dB ⇆255

At **MONTROUGE** (6km S adj to Boulevard Périphérique)

☆☆**Mercure** 13 r F-Ory ☎6571126 tx202528 Not on plan

⇆192 **P** Lift sB ⇆455 dB ⇆520 M alc

☆☆**Ibis** 33 r Barbès ☎6565255 tx202527 Not on plan

⇆402 **P** Lift sB ⇆228 dB ⇆261

At **NEUILLY-SUR-SEINE** (8km W)

⑧**Atelier** 18 bd Vital Bouhot ☎7471919 Closed Sat & Sun DJ

At **NOISY-LE-GRAND** (30km E)

☆**Campanile** r du Ballon ☎3052299 tx610016 Not on plan

⇆50 **P** dB ⇆218–222 M55–80

At **VILLENEUVE-LA-GARENNE** (16km N)

☆**Climat de France** bd C-de-Gaulle ☎7995600 tx612241 Not on plan

⇆38 **P** dB ⇆206–226 M54–70

At **VINCENNES** (11km E off N34)

⑧**Wuplan** 7 av de Paris ☎8084428 Closed 4 Aug–1 Sep, Sat & Sun Aud VW

PARIS AIRPORTS
BOURGET AIRPORT (LE)

☆☆☆**Novotel** r le Pont Yblon (N2) ☎8674888 tx230115 Not on plan

⇆143 Lift sB ⇆257–287 dB ⇆289–319 M alc Pool

CHARLES-DE-GAULLE AIRPORT

At **ROISSY-EN-FRANCE** (2km E)

☆☆☆**Holiday Inn** 54 r de Paris ☎9880022 tx695143 Not on plan

⇆240 **P** Lift sB ⇆420 dB ⇆448

☆☆☆☆**Sofitel** ☎8622323 tx230166 Not on plan

⇆352 🏠 **P** Lift sB ⇆407–517 dB464–574

☆☆**Arcade** 10 r du Verseau ☎8624949 tx212989 Not on plan

🏠356 **P** Lift sB 🏠184 dB 🏠204

ORLY AIRPORT
See also **RUNGIS**

★★★★**Hilton International** 267 Orly Sud ☎6873388 tx250621 Not on plan

⇆379 **P** Lift ♪ sB ⇆505 dB ⇆635

☆☆☆**Holiday Inn** 4 av C-Lindberghe ☎6872666 tx204679 Not on plan

⇆ 🏠170 **P** Lift ♪ sB ⇆419 dB ⇆ 🏠513

☆☆**Arcade** espl Aérogare Sud ☎2682345 Not on plan 🏠220 **P** sB ⇆183 dB 🏠192

At **ATHIS-MONS** (2.5km SE)

⑧**Bidaud** 59 rte de Fontainebleau ☎9388181 Peu

At **MORANGIS** (2.5km SW)

☆**Campanile** 34 av F-de-Lesseps ☎(6)4486130 tx600832 Not on plan

⇆50 **P** dB ⇆218–222

☆**Climat de France** ZI des Sables, r Lavoisier ☎4483155 tx612241 Not on plan

⇆38 **P** dB ⇆201–221 M54–70

⑧**Orly Autos** av C-de-Gaulle, ZI Nord ☎9090897 Closed 10–25 Aug, Sun & Mon Frd

PARTHENAY
Deux-Sèvres (☎49)

★★**Grand** 85 bd de la Meilleraie ☎640016

rm26 ⇆4 🏠5 **P** sB47–143 sB ⇆ 🏠69–143 dB61 dB ⇆ 🏠143

PASSENANS See **SELLIÈRES**

PASSY
Haute-Savoie (☎50)

⑧**Savoie-Arnaud** les Ruttets ☎581189 All makes

PAU
Pyrénées-Atlantiques (☎59)

★★★**Continental** (MAP) 2 r MI-Foch ☎276931 tx570906

⇆100 Lift ♪ sB ⇆245 dB ⇆320

★★★**Roncevaux** (FAH) 25 r L-Barthou ☎270844 tx570929

rm42 ⇆19 🏠16 **P** Lift ♪ dB137–177 dB ⇆ 🏠159–259

★★★**Bristol** 3 r Gambetta (n.rest) ☎277298 tx570929

rm27 ⇆11 🏠10 **P** Lift ♪ sB ⇆103–179 sB ⇆ 🏠148–179 dB103–215 dB ⇆ 🏠175–215

☆ ☆**Campanile** bd de l'Aviation
☎803233 tx540208

⇥43 **P** dB ⇥206–209 M55–80

☆ ☆**Ibis** 45 r F-Garcia-Lorca ☎306655
tx550909

⇥83 **P** Lift sB ⇥183 dB ⇥220

★**Central** 15 r L-Daran (n.rest) ☎277275

rm27 ⇥5 🛏12 🌙 sB63–91
sB ⇥ 🛏103–140 dB98–145
dB ⇥ 🛏118–169

At **LESCAR** (7.5km NW on D945)

☆ ☆ ☆**Novotel** (N117) ☎321732
tx570939

⇥61 **P** sB ⇥218–262 dB ⇥249–294
Pool mountains

PAYRAC
Lot (☎65)

★ ★**Hostellerie de la Paix**L͡E ☎379515
Apr–Oct

rm28 ⇥16 🛏10 dB93–190
dB ⇥ 🛏128–190 M38–135

PENNE-ST-MENET (LA) See **MARSEILLE**

PÉRIGUEUX
Dordogne (☎53)

★ ★ ★**Domino** (Inter) (**DPn** in summer) 21
pl Francheville ☎082580

rm37 ⇥24 🛏7 🏛 Lift 🌙 sB100
sB ⇥ 🛏211 dB ⇥ 🛏100–292

☆ ☆**Ibis** 8 bd Saumande ☎536458
tx550159

⇥89 **P** Lift sB ⇥163 dB ⇥220

🜂**Zizard-Laroumedie** 182 rte de
Bordeaux ☎080827 Closed 1–15 Aug.
Sat pm & Sun BL

PÉROLS see **MONTPELLIER**

PÉRONNE
Somme (☎22)

★ ★**St-Claude**L͡E 42 pl L-Daudré
☎844600

rm28 ⇥5 🛏10 A4rm M57
DPn135–240

★**Remparts**L͡E (**DPn**) 21 r Beaubois
☎840122

rm16 ⇥6 🛏6 🏛

🜂**D Tutrice** 6 av Danicourt ☎840415
Closed Mon am Aud VW

At **ASSEVILLERS** (adj to autoroute A1)

☆ ☆ ☆**Mercure** (A1) ☎841276 tx140943
⇥100 **P** Lift 🌙 sB ⇥285–349
dB ⇥349–359

PÉROUGES
Ain (☎74)

★ ★ ★**Vieux Pérouges** pl du Tilleul
☎610088

⇥24 🏛 **P** sB ⇥280–350
dB ⇥280–495

PERPIGNAN
Pyrénées-Orientales (☎68)

★ ★ ★**Mondial** (MAP) 40 bd Clemenceau
(n.rest) ☎342345

France

5 Jan–24 Dec
rm43 ⇥25 🛏18 Lift

★ ★ ★**Windsor** (Inter) 8 bd Wilson
(n.rest) ☎511865 tx500024

Closed Feb
rm58 ⇥32 🛏26 **P** Lift 🌙
sB ⇥ 🛏165–250 dB ⇥ 🛏175–265

☆ ☆**Campanile** Lotissement Porte
d'Espagne, r A-Leverman, rte du Perthus
☎567575

⇥41 **P** dB ⇥206–209 M55–80
mountains

★ ★**Christina** 50 cours de Lassus (n.rest)
☎352461

rm35 ⇥20 🛏10 🏛 **P** Lift 🌙
sB104–135 sB ⇥ 🛏149 dB118–150
dB ⇥ 🛏163

🜂**Aguilar** 46 av de l'Ancien C-de-Mars
☎521864 Closed Sun All makes

🜂**Auto-Service** 14 bd St-Assiscle
☎540998 Closed Sat pm & Sun Lada
Maz Sab

🜂**Peruchet** 93 av Ml-Joffre ☎611564 All
makes

🜂**Ribert** 3 r de Thues ☎344579 M/c All
makes

SA-Europe Auto bd P-Langevin
☎850192 Closed Sat & Sun Aud VW

At **RIVESALTES** (5km NW by N9)

☆ ☆ ☆**Novotel** (N9) ☎640222 tx500851
⇥85 **P** Lift sB ⇥240 dB ⇥311 Pool

🜂**Guillouf** r E-Parés ☎641350 All makes

PERRIGNY-LÈS-DIJON See **DIJON**

PERROS-GUIREC
Côtes-du-Nord (☎96)

★ ★ ★**Printania** (FAH) (**DPn**) 12 r des
Bons-Enfants ☎232100

rm40 ⇥25 🛏10 **P** Lift 🜸

★ ★ ★**Trestraou** bd J-le-Bihan,
Trestraou ☎232405

rm71 ⇥44 🛏11 A3rm Lift dB213–304
dB ⇥ 🛏282–304 sea

★ ★**Morgane**L͡E 46 av Casino, Plage de
Trestraou ☎232280 tx740637

May–Sep
rm28 ⇥15 🛏13 A5rm **P** Lift Pool

At **PLOUMANACH** (6km NW)

★ ★ ★**Rochers** (FAH) ☎232302

Etr–Sep
⇥15 🛏8 🛏 175–220 sea

PESMES
Haute-Saône (☎84)

★ ★**France**L͡E ☎312005

8 Nov–15 Oct
⇥10 A10rm **P** 🌙 dB ⇥ 🛏96–120

PETITE-PIERRE (LA)
Bas-Rhin (☎88)

★ ★**Vosges**L͡E 30 r Principale ☎704505

Closed Nov
rm30 ⇥18 🛏11 **P** Lift sB139–219
dB ⇥ 🛏188–288 M60–180 mountains

PETIT-QUEVILLY (LE) See **ROUEN**

PEYREHORADE
Landes (☎58)

★ ★**Central** (**DPn** in season) pl A-Briand
☎730322

Jan–15 Nov
rm10 ⇥5 🛏5 🏛 **P** dB ⇥ 🛏77

PIED-DU-SANCY See **MONT DORE (LE)**

PIERRE-BUFFIÈRE
Haute-Vienne (☎55)

★**Providence** 20 r Nationale ☎006016

Mar–15 Nov & 20 Dec–3 Jan
rm11 ⇥6 🛏2 🏛

🜂**R Gauthier** 17 av de Toulouse
☎006024 Closed Sun pm Cit

PIERRELATTE
Drôme (☎75)

★ ★**Hostellerie Tom II**L͡E (**DPn** in season)
5 av Gl-de-Gaulle (N7) ☎040035

rm15 🛏12 sB ⇥ 🛏118 dB81–165
dB ⇥ 🛏131–165

🜂**Atomic** ZI ☎041286 Lada Opl

🜂**Mistral** ZI, rte de St-Paul ☎040158
M/c Closed Sat pm & Sun Frd

🜂**Notre-Dame** r N-Dame ☎040237
Closed Aug, Sat pm & Sun Aud VW

PIRIAC-SUR-MER
Loire-Atlantique (☎40)

★**Plage & Port**L͡E (**DPn**) quai de Verdun
☎235009

Mar–Sep
rm44 ⇥3 🛏8 A14rm sea

PITHIVIERS
Loiret (☎38)

★**Poste** 10 Mail Ouest ☎304030
rm10 ⇥8 🏛 **P**

PLAISIR
Yvelines (☎3)

☆ ☆**Campanile** ZI des Gâtines
☎0558150 tx697578

⇥45 **P** dB ⇥218–222 M55–80

☆ ☆**Climat de France** Lieudit le Hameau
de la Chaine ☎0557737 tx692844

⇥42 **P** dB ⇥223–243 M48–74

PLESSIS-CHENNET (LE) See **CORBEIL-
ESSONNES**

PLOËRMEL
Morbihan (☎97)

★**Commerce-Rebermina** 70 r do la
Gare ☎740532

rm19 ⇥1 🛏5 **P** sB66 sB ⇥ 🛏86
dB86–100 dB ⇥ 🛏96–120

PLOMBIÈRES-LES-BAINS
Vosges (☎29)

★**Abbesses** 6 pl de l'Église ☎660040
May–Sep

170

rm44 ⇌16 🅵2 Lift sB97 dB137−163
dB ⇌ 🅵163

PLOUGASTEL-DAOULAS See **BREST**

PLOUMANACH See **PERROS-GUIREC**

POITIERS
Vienne (☎49)

★ ★ ★**France** (MAP) 28 r Carnot
☎413201 tx790526
rm86 ⇌40 🅵36 🕭 **P** Lift 🌙
sB260−300 sB ⇌ 🅵260−325
dB340−400 dB ⇌ 🅵340−450

★ ★ ★**Royal Poitou** (3km N on N10) rte de
Paris ☎017286
rm32 ⇌30 🅵2 **P** 🌙 sB ⇌ 🅵260
dB ⇌ 🅵310 M60−65

★ ★**Europe** 39 r Carnot (n.rest)
☎881200
rm63 ⇌14 🅵27 A13rm 🕭 **P** 🌙
sB95 sB ⇌ 🅵210 dB96−236 ⇌🅵240

☆ ☆**Ibis Poitiers Sud** av du 8 Mai 1945
☎531313 tx791556
⇌83 **P** Lift sB ⇌189 dB ⇌228

☆ ☆**Ibis** ZAC de Beaulieu 'Les Mâches'
☎611102
⇌33 **P** sB ⇌183 dB ⇌220

★ ★**Relais du Stade** 84−86 r J-Coeur
(n.rest) ☎462512
rm25 🅵4 🕭 **P** Lift 🌙 sB70−139
sB ⇌ 🅵136−160 dB142−154
dB 🅵157−172

At **BIARD** (2km W)

&🔾**J P Barrault** ZI de Larnay ☎583543
Vlo

At **CHASSENEUIL-DU-POITOU** (8km N by
N21)

☆ ☆ ☆**Novotel Poitiers Nord** (N10)
☎527878
⇌89 **P** Lift sB ⇌236−253
dB ⇌282−304 🏊 Pool

☆ ☆**Relais de Poitiers** (N10)
☎529041 tx790502
rm99 ⇌42 🅵52 **P** Lift sB163−175
sB ⇌ 🅵193 dB206 dB ⇌ 🅵241 🏊
Pool

☆ ☆**Campanile** ZI de Chasseneuil-du-
Poitou, Voie Ouest ☎528540 tx791534
⇌42 **P** dB ⇌206−209 M55−80

At **MIGNE-AUXANCES** (9km NE on N147)

&🔾**Auto Sport** (N147) ☎582418 Closed
Sat AR BL

POIX-DE-PICARDIE
Somme (☎22)

★**Poste** (**DPn** in summer) 13 pl de la
République ☎900033

Closed Feb
rm18 ⇌3 🅵2 **P** sB81−100
sB ⇌ 🅵160 dB ⇌ 🅵182

POLIGNY
Jura (☎84)

★★**Hostellerie des Monts de Vaux**
(**DPn**) Monts de Vaux (4.5km SE)
☎371250

France

Jan−Oct
⇌10 🕭 **P** **DPn**600−720

★ ★**Paris**🅻🇪 7 r Travot ☎371387

Mar−9 Nov
rm24 ⇌15 🅵9 🕭 **P** 🌙 sB90
sB ⇌ 🅵130 dB150 dB ⇌ 🅵180 Pool

★ ★**Vallée Heureuse**🅻🇪 rte de Genève
☎371213
rm12 ⇌8 🅵2 A1rm 🕭 **P** sB117
sB ⇌ 🅵170 dB139−170
dB ⇌ 🅵184−224 mountains

&🔾**Poix** 10 av W-Gagneur ☎371608
Closed Sun Frd

POLISOT
Aube (☎25)

★**Seine**🅻🇪 ☎385441

Mar−Nov
rm20 ⇌2 🅵7 🕭 **P** sB86−160
sB ⇌ 🅵160 dB100−150
dB ⇌ 🅵129−160

PONS
Charente-Maritime (☎46)

★ ★**Auberge Pontoise** (**DPn** Jul−Aug) r
Gambetta ☎940099

20 Jan−20 Dec
rm22 ⇌16 🅵6 🕭 **P**
sB ⇌ 🅵150−200 dB ⇌ 🅵195−220

PONT-A-MOUSSON
Meurthe-et-Moselle (☎8)

★**Européen** 156 av Metz (n.rest)
☎3810757 tx54700
rm28 ⇌7 🅵2 A6rm 🕭 dB99−157
dB ⇌ 🅵179

★**Poste** 42 bis r V-Hugo ☎3810116

20 Jan−20 Dec
rm24 ⇌3 🅵12 🕭 **P** dB⇌ 🅵220

PONTARLIER
Doubs (☎81)

★ ★**Poste** (**DPn**) 55 r de la République
☎391812

15 Dec−15 Oct
rm55 ⇌22 🕭 **P** sB ⇌125−165
dB ⇌140−220

★ ★**Terrasse** 1 r de la République
☎390515

Dec−Oct
rm32 ⇌7 🅵6 🕭 **P** sB80−120
sB ⇌ 🅵120 dB ⇌ 🅵130

Beau Site 29 av de l'Armée de l'Est
☎392395 Closed Sat pm & Sun Peu

PONTAUBAULT
Manche (☎33)

☆ ☆ ☆**13 Assiettes**🅻🇪 (**DPn**) (1km N on
N175) ☎581403 tx170537

15 Mar−15 Nov & Wed (out of season)
rm36 ⇌2 🅵25 **P** **DPn**150

PONT-AUDEMER
Eure (☎32)

★ ★ ★**Vieux Puits** 6 r Notre-Dame du Pré
☎410148

20 Jan−2 Jul & 12 Jul−17 Dec
rm8 🅵15 **P** sB98−120 dB140−160
dB 🅵170−200

★**Palais & Poste** (**DPn**) 8 r Stanislas
☎415074
rm12 ⇌2 🅵2

★**Risle** 16 quai R-Leblanc ☎411457
rm18 sB63−79 dB92−110

&🔾**Vittecoq** 9 bd Pasteur ☎410335
Closed Sat pm & Sun All makes

At **FOURMETOT** (6 km NE on D139)

&🔾**Bacheley** ☎574069 Closed Mon All
makes

PONTAULT-COMBAULT
Seine-et-Marne (☎6)

&🔾**Audebert** 84 rte de la Libération
☎0280464 Closed Sat pm & Sun Cit

PONT-D'AIN
Ain (☎74)

★ ★**Alliés**🅻🇪 ☎390009

Dec−25 Oct
rm18 ⇌6 🅵6 🕭 **P** sB90−170
sB ⇌ 🅵151−186 dB122−210
dB ⇌ 🅵167−242

★ ★**Paris-Nice** 2 r du 1ᵉʳ Septembre 1944
(n.rest) ☎390380

Closed Nov & Tue
rm20 ⇌4 🅵2 🕭 **P** sB67 sB ⇌ 🅵123
dB95 dB ⇌ 🅵157

PONT-DE-CLAIX See **GRENOBLE**

PONT-DE-L'ISÈRE
Drôme (☎75)

☆**Portes du Midi** (N7) ☎846026

Mar−Oct
rm18 🅵11 **P** dB100 dB 🅵130
mountains

PONT-DE-PANY
Côte-d'Or (☎80)

★**Pont de Pany**🅻🇪 ☎236059

Closed 15 Nov−14 Dec
rm16 ⇌8 🅵3 **P**

PONT-DE-RHODES See **FRAYSSINET**

PONT-DE-VAUX
Ain (☎85)

★**Reconnaissance**🅻🇪 9 pl-Joubert
☎373055
rm11 ⇌3 🅵5 🕭 **P** dB150
dB ⇌ 🅵70−165

PONT-DU-GARD
Gard (☎66)

★ ★**Vieux Moulin** ☎371435

Mar−Dec
rm17 ⇌6 🅵6 **P** dB170 dB ⇌ 🅵300

At **REMOULINS** (4km E)

★ ★**Moderne** (**DPn**) pl des Grands-Jours
☎372019

Closed Nov
rm23 🅵13 🕭 **P** sB71−90 dB87−132

⊗Pretemer (N100) ☎370445 M/c All makes

PONTHIERRY
Seine-et-Marne (☎6)

⊗Tractaubat 76 av de Fontainebleau ☎0657039 Closed 1–26 Aug, Sat pm & Sun Ren

⊗Trois Sept 62 av de Fontainebleau ☎0657052 Cit

At **PRINGY** (2km SE)

☆ ☆**Ibis** 4 rte de Melun ☎0655928 tx690723

⇦32 **P** sB ⇦175 dB ⇦210 M65

PONTIVY
Morbihan (☎97)

★ ★**Porhoët** 41 av Gl-de-Gaulle (n.rest) ☎253488

rm28 ⇦9 ⋒25 **P** Lift sB86–153 sB ⇦ ⋒151–158 dB182–186

PONT-L'ÉVÊQUE
Calvados (☎31)

★**Lion d'Or**⎣ pl Calvaire ☎640038 tx171688

rm16 ⇦10 **P** sB70–110 sB ⇦160–195 dB80–190 dB ⇦175–195

⊗Dupuits 5 r Melaine ☎640186 Closed Sat pm & Sun Cit

⊗Garez 37 r de Vaucelles ☎640211 Closed Sat & Sun Tal

⊗Société van Houtte ZI de Lisieux ☎641105 Ren

PONTOISE
Val-d'Oise (☎3)

At **CERGY** (4km SW)

☆ ☆ ☆**Novotel** av de l'Ouest, Ville Nouvelle ☎0303947 tx697264

⇦194 **P** Lift sB ⇦280 dB ⇦311 Malc Pool

☆ ☆**Arcade** près Préfecture ☎0309393 tx695470

⋒140 Lift sB ⋒161–175 dB ⋒163–178

☆ ☆**Climat de France** ZAC d'Eragny, r des Pinsons ☎0378600 tx692844

⇦42 **P** dB ⇦223 M48–74

At **ST-OUEN-L'AUMÔNE** (5km SE)

★ ★ ★**Grand Cerf** 59 r Gl-Leclerc ☎4640313

⇦10 🚗 **P**

PONTORSON
Manche (☎33)

★ ★**Montgomery**⎣ (FAH) (DPn) 13 r Couesnon ☎600009

15 Apr–Oct
rm34 ⇦19 ⋒10 🚗 **P** sB61–138 sB ⇦ ⋒105–158 dB74–196 dB ⇦ ⋒171–210

⊗Galle Vettori rte d'Avranches ☎600037 Closed Sat pm & Sun Peu

PONT-SARRAZIN See **GAP**

PONTS-DE-CÉ (LES)
Maine-et-Loire (☎41)

France

☆ ☆**Campanile** chemin du Moulin-Marcille ☎683459 tx49130

⇦40 **P** dB ⇦218–222 M55–80

PONT-SUR-YONNE
Yonne (☎86)

★ ★**Ecu**⎣ 3 r Carnot ☎670100

3 Mar–3 Jan
rm8 ⇦1 ⋒5 **P** sB69–104 sB ⇦ ⋒99–104 dB88–150 dB ⇦ ⋒103–150

PORNIC
Loire-Atlantique (☎40)

⊗SARL Gaudin rte Bleue ☎820026 Closed 15 days Oct, Sun & Mon in low season only Peu

PORNICHET
Loire-Atlantique (☎40)

★ ★ ★**Sud-Bretagne**⎣ (DPn) 42 bd de la République ☎610268

15 Mar–15 Oct
rm38 ⇦34 ⋒4 **P** Lift 🌊 Pool

PORT-BLANC
Côtes-du-Nord (☎96)

★**Grand**⎣ ☎926652

Etr–Oct
rm30 ⇦7 ⋒16 **P** sB87–160 sB ⇦ ⋒fr97. dB ⇦ ⋒190–320 Mfr55 🌊 sea

PORTEL (LE)
Pas-de-Calais (☎21)

See also **BOULOGNE-SUR-MER**

★**Beau Rivage et Armada** (DPn) pl Mon-Bourgain ☎315982

Apr–Oct
rm11 ⇦2 **P** sB75–88 sB ⇦135 dB ⇦143–160 sea

⊗Bourgain & Desenclos 9 & 22 bd A-Huguet ☎317615 Peu

PORTES-LÉS-VALENCE See **VALENCE**

PORT-GRIMAUD See **GRIMAUD**

PORT-LA-NOUVELLE
Aude (☎68)

★ ★ ★**Méditerranée**⎣ (MAP) bd St-Charles ☎480308 tx500712

rm32 ⇦30 ⋒2 🚗 **P** Lift sB ⇦ ⋒180–208 dB ⇦ ⋒210–300 sea

⊗Marill ZI ☎480486 Closed Xmas, New Year & Sun Fia Lnc

⊗L Pertil r J-Jaurès ☎480064 Closed Sun All makes

PORT-LOUIS
Morbihan (☎97)

★ ★**Avel Vor**⎣ (FAH) (DPn) 25 r de Locmalo ☎824759 tx950826

15 Jan–11 Nov
rm32 ⇦23 ⋒3 A65rm Lift sB ⇦ ⋒178 dB ⇦ ⋒211–256 sea

PORTO-VECCHIO See **CORSE (CORSICA)**

POUILLY-EN-AUXOIS
Côte-d'Or (☎80)

⊗S Clair r de la Gare ☎908105 Closed Sat pm & Sun Tal

⊗J Jeannin pl des Alliés ☎908211 M/c Peu

⊗P Orset ☎908045 Closed Sun Ren

At **CHÂTEAUNEUF** (10km SE D18)

★ ★**Hostelleri du Château**⎣ (DPn) ☎330023

Mar–Nov
rm11 ⇦2 ⋒9 dB ⇦ ⋒151–236

At **MEILLY-SUR-ROUVRES** (6km S on N81)

⊗R Perrot ☎908660 Closed 15 days Sep, Sat pm & Sun Cit

POUILLY-SUR-LOIRE
Nièvre (☎86)

★ ★**Bouteille d'Or**⎣ (DPn) 13 bis rte de Paris ☎391384

Mar–Dec
rm31 ⇦11 ⋒18 A8rm

★**Relais Fleuri**⎣ (0.5km SE on N7) ☎391399

15 Feb–15 Jan
rm9 ⇦6 ⋒13 🚗 **P** dB ⇦ ⋒144

POULDU (LE)
Finistère (☎98)

★ ★**Castel Treaz** (n.rest) ☎399111

Jun–20 Sep
rm25 ⇦10 ⋒9 **P** Lift sea

★**Quatre Chemins**⎣ (DPn) ☎399044

Jun–13 Sep
rm38 ⇦4 ⋒21 **P** sB86 sB ⇦ ⋒98 dB110–170 dB ⇦ ⋒203

POUZAUGES
Vendée (☎51)

★ ★**Auberge de la Bruyère**⎣ (FAH) r Dr-Barbanneau ☎919346

rm30 ⇦15 ⋒15 **P** Lift dB ⇦ ⋒172–259

POUZIN (LE)
Ardèche (☎75)

⊗M Pheby (S on N86) ☎628016 Closed Sat & Sun Cit

⊗Renault (E-Combe) rte de Loriol ☎628022 Ren

PRAYSSAC
Lot (☎65)

★ ★**Vidal**⎣ (Inter) 3 r des Garabels ☎224178

Closed Nov–14 Dec
rm11 ⇦8 🚗 **P** dB135–151 dB ⋒175–191

PRINGY See **PONTHIERRY**

PUILBOREAU See **ROCHELLE (LA)**

PUY (LE)
Haute-Loire (☎71)

★ ★ ★**Christel** 15 bd A-Clair ☎022444
⇌30 🏠 **P** Lift ☽ sB ⇌175 dB ⇌200
mountains

PUY-L'ÉVÊQUE
Lot (☎65)

At **MONTCABRIER** (7km NW)

★ ★ ★**Relais de la Dolce** rte Villefranche
du Périgord (D28) ☎365342
(booking required Oct–Etr)
⇌12 **P** M75–175 **DPn**320 Pool ◯
mountains

PYLA-SUR-MER
Gironde (☎56)

★ ★ ★**Guitoune (DPn)** 95 bd de l'Océan
☎227010
rm22 ⇌15 ╽7 **P** ☽

★ ★**Beau Rivage** 10 bd de l'Océan
☎220182
Apr–Sep
rm17 ⇌5 ╽11 A4rm sB130
sB ⇌ ╽180 dB150 dB ⇌ ╽280

QUARRÉ-LES-TOMBES
Yonne (☎86)

★**Nord et Poste**L̶E̶**(DPn)** pl de l'Eglise
☎322455
rm35 ⇌4 ╽6 A24rm

QUÉTIGNY See **DIJON**

QUEUE-EN-BRIE (LA)
Val-de-Marne (☎1)

☆ ☆**Climat de France** (D185)
☎5946161 tx612241
⇌38 **P** sB ⇌206 dB ⇌226 M54–70

QUIBERON
Morbihan (☎97)

★ ★ ★**Sofitel Thalassa** Pointe de
Goulvas ☎502000 tx730712
⇌113 🏠 Lift **DPn**524–899 Pool sea

★ ★**Beau Rivage** 1 r de Port Maria
☎500839 tx950538
Apr–Sep
rm48 ⇌6 ╽29 Lift dB142–224
dB ⇌ ╽189–238 sea

★**Ty Breiz**L̶E̶ 23 bd Chanard ☎500990
mid Apr–Sep
rm32 ⇌5 ╽20 A4rm **P** sB ⇌120
dB ⇌ ╽70–210 sea

At **ST PIERRE-QUIBERON** (4.5km N on
D786)

★ ★**Plage**L̶E̶**(DPn)** ☎309210
Etr–Oct
rm55 ⇌21 ╽39 A5rm **P** Lift

QUILLAN
Aude (☎68)

★ ★**Chaumière**L̶E̶ (Inter) **(DPn** in season)
bd C-de-Gaulle ☎201790
rm40 ⇌30 ╽10 A22rm 🏠 **P**
mountains

★**Cartier**L̶E̶ (FAH) 31 bd C-de-Gaulle
☎200514
15 Mar–15 Dec
rm35 ⇌14 ╽14 🏠 Lift dB137–177
dB ⇌ ╽159–259

France

🍴J **Escur** av de Marides ☎200666
Closed Sat pm & Sun Ren

QUIMPER
Finistère (☎98)

★ ★ ★**Griffon** 131 rte de Bénodet
☎903333 tx940063
rm50 ⇌47 ╽3 **P** Pool

★ ★**Gradlon**L̶E̶ 30 r Brest (n.rest)
☎950439
15 Jan–20 Dec
rm25 ⇌13 ╽5

☆ ☆**Ibis Quimper** r G-Eiffel, ZI de
l'Hippodrome Secteur Ouest ☎905380
tx940007
⇌70 **P** sB ⇌178 dB ⇌221

☆ ☆**Ibis Quimper Nord** le Gourvily, rte de
Brest ☎957764 tx940749
⇌36 sB ⇌184 dB ⇌230 M63 &alc

★ ★**Tour d'Auvergne**L̶E̶ (FAH) 11–13 r
des Réguaires ☎950870 tx392853
rm47 ⇌15 ╽25 A2rm 🏠 **P** Lift ☽
dB137–201 dB ⇌ ╽159–259

🍴**Auto Secours** 28 av A-de-Bretagne
☎902805 All makes

🍴**Belleguic** 21 rte de Ceray ☎900369
Closed Sat pm MB

🍴**Kemper** 13 av de la Libération
☎901849

🍴**Ste des Garages de l'Odet** rte de
Douarnenez, ZI de Kernevez ☎956314
Closed Sat & Sun Ren

QUINCY-VOISINS
Seine-et-Marne (☎6)

★ ★**Auberge Demi Lune**L̶E̶**(DPn)** (N36)
☎0041109
rm7 Lift dB82–105

RABOT (LE)
Loir-et-Cher (☎21)

☆**Bruyères** (N20) ☎880570
rm40 ⇌30 ╽10 **P** ♨ Pool

RAMBOUILLET
Yvelines (☎3)

★**St-Charles** 1 r de Groussay (n.rest)
☎4830634
10 Jan–20 Dec
rm14 ⇌6 ╽6 A2rm **P**
sB ⇌ ╽107–142 dB ⇌ ╽139–203

🍴**Central** 15 r G-Clemenceau ☎4830187
Closed Aug, Sat pm & Sun AR Dat

RANCOURT
Somme (☎22)

★ ★**Prieuré (DPn)** (N17) ☎850443
Feb–15 Dec
rm25 ⇌12 ╽13 🏠 **P**

RAYOL (LE)
Var (☎94)

★ ★ ★ ★**Bailli de Suffren (DPn)**
☎713577 tx420535
mid May–mid Sep
⇌47 **P** Lift dB ⇌740–940 sea

RÉ (ILE DE)
Charente-Maritime (☎46)

FLOTTE (LA)

★ ★**Richelieu (DPn)** 44 av de la Plage
☎096070 tx791492
Closed Jan
⇌30 **P** sB ⇌200–450 dB ⇌250–500
sea

RECOLOGNE
Doubs (☎81)

★**Escale**L̶E̶ ☎863213
15 Nov–Sep
rm11 ⇌4 ╽7 sB67–72
sB ⇌ ╽67–89 dB84 dB ⇌ ╽123
M45–90

🍴**Muneret** rte de Noirnote ☎863181 Ren

At **LAVERNAY** (3.5km S on D13)

🍴**Pelot** ☎863362 Closed Sun Tal

REIMS
Marne (☎26)

★ ★ ★ ★**Frantel** 31 bd P-Doumer
☎885354 tx30629
⇌125 🏠 **P** Lift ☽ sB ⇌326
dB392

☆ ☆ ☆**Mercure Reims Est** ZISE Les
Essillards, rte de Châlons ☎050008
tx830782
⇌98 **P** Lift sB ⇌223–254
dB ⇌268–298 Pool

★ ★**Paix** (Inter) 9 r Buirette ☎400408
tx830974
⇌105 🏠 Lift sB ⇌214–265
dB ⇌254–324

☆ ☆**Campanile** Val de Murigny II
☎366694
⇌38 **P** dB ⇌218–222 M55–80

☆ ☆**Climat de France** r B-Russel, ZAC de
la Neuvillette ☎096273 tx612241
⇌38 **P** dB ⇌206–226 M54–70

★ ★**Continental** 93 pl Drouet d'Erlon
(n.rest) ☎403935 tx830585
5 Jan–20 Dec
rm60 ⇌32 ╽20 Lift sB100–162
sB ⇌ ╽161–195 dB128–190
dB ⇌ ╽194–222

★ ★**Europa** 8 bd Joffre (n.rest)
☎403620 tx830600
6 Jan–24 Dec
rm32 ⇌15 ╽8 **P** Lift

★ ★**Grand du Nord** 75 pl Drouet-d'Erlon
(n.rest) ☎470782
rm50 ⇌32 ╽18 Lift ☽
sB ⇌ ╽198–209 dB ⇌ ╽225

★ ★**Univers** 41 bd Foch (n.rest)
☎886808
rm40 ⇌22 Lift ☽ sB100 sB155
dB120 dB ⇌175

★ ★**Welcome** 29 r Buirette (n.rest)
☎880639 tx830600 →

173

5 Jan – 20 Dec
rm70 ⮂11 ▥36 Lift sB83–140
sB ⮂ ▥160 dB197 dB ⮂ ▥210

⊗Dauphinot 124 bd Dauphinot
☎070378 Closed Sun pm All makes

⊗Prott 40 av d'Epernay ☎080108
Closed Sun All makes

At TINQUEUX (4km W off N31)

☆ ☆ ☆Novotel rte de Soisson (N31)
☎081161 tx830034
⮂125 P sB ⮂230–260 dB ⮂270–302
M alc Pool

REMIGEASSE (LA) See OLÉRON (ILE D')

REMIREMONT
Vosges (☎29)

At ST-NABORD (5km N on N57)

★ ★ ★Montiroche (N57) (n.rest)
☎620659
Apr–Oct
rm14 ⮂13 P sB ⮂136–146
dB ⮂ ▥162–182 mountains

REMOULINS See PONT-DU-GARD

RENAISON
Loire (☎77)

★Jacques Coeur rte Vichy (n.rest)
☎659146
rm10 ⮂6 sB77–90 dB77–103
dB ⮂103

RENNES
Ille-et-Vilaine(☎99)

★ ★ ★Frantel pl du Colombier
☎795454 tx730905
⮂140 P Lift 𝄞 sB ⮂326 dB ⮂392
M90 alc

★ ★ ★Guesclin 5 pl de la Gare
☎314747 tx740748
⮂66 Lift sB ⮂fr251 dB ⮂fr304 M70 &
alc

☆ ☆ ☆Novotel Rennes Alma av du
Canada ☎506132 tx740144
⮂99 P sB ⮂305–315 dB ⮂365–375
Pool

★ ★ ★Président 27 av Janvier (n.rest)
☎654222 tx730004
rm34 ⮂26 ▥8 🛗 Lift sB ⮂190–250
dB ⮂190–270

☆ ☆Climat de France ZAC de
Beauregard Sud ☎541203 tx692844
⮂42 P dB ⮂216–231

At CESSON-SÉVIGNÉ (6km E)

☆ ☆Ibis Rennes (N 157) La Perrière
☎629393 tx740321
⮂76 P Lift sB ⮂180 dB ⮂220

☆ ☆Ibis Rennes Cesson rte de Paris
☎002172
⮂35 P sB ⮂180 dB ⮂222

RESSONS-SUR-MATZ
Oise(☎4)

⊗Blanchard ☎4425031 Closed Mon
am Ren

At CUVILLY (3km NW on N17)

France

⊗Brecqueville r Planché
☎4420016 Closed Sun All makes

RETHEL
Ardennes(☎24)

★ ★Moderne ⏚ (Inter) pl de la Gare
☎390454
rm25 ⮂5 ▥10 🛗 Lift 𝄞 dB180
dB ⮂ ▥215

RIVE-DE-GIER
Loire(☎77)

★ ★Hostellerie de la Renaissance (DPn)
41 r Marrel ☎750431
Closed 2 wks Jan–Feb
rm10 ⮂7 ▥1 🛗 P dB ⮂ ▥260

RIVESALTES See PERPIGNAN

ROANNE
Loire(☎77)

☆ ☆ ☆Ibis ZI du Côteau, le Côteau (E of
River Loire) ☎683622
⮂49 P sB ⮂180–193 dB ⮂223–244

★ ★Troisgros 22 cours de la République
☎716697
Closed 9–31 Jan, 7–22 Aug & Mon pm
⮂24 🛗 P Lift 𝄞 dB ⮂350–700

⊗Poste 56 r R-Salengro ☎683199
M/c Closed 27 Jul–17 Aug, Sat pm, Sun &
Mon am Frd

At ST-GERMAIN-LESPINASSE (10km NW
on N7)

★ ★Relais de Roanne ☎719735
Feb–5 Jan
rm32 ⮂28 ▥4 🛗 P sB ⮂ ▥155–175
dB ⮂ ▥194–231 M58–165 mountains

ROCAMADOUR
Lot(☎65)

★ ★Château ⏚ (FAH) rte de Château
☎336222 tx521871
Apr–25 Oct
⮂ ▥58 A24rm P M50–120
DPn170–190

★ ★Beau Site & Notre Dame ⏚ (MAP) r
R-le-Preux ☎336308 tx520421
Apr–Oct
rm54 ⮂27 ▥23 A4rm 🛗 P Lift
sB ▥165 dB246–273 dB ⮂ ▥246–293
M190 mountains

★ ★Ste-Marie r Grand Escalier, pl des
Sehnal ☎336307
Apr–Oct
⮂22 A5rm 🛗 P mountains

★Lion d'Or ⏚ Porte Figuier ☎336204
Apr–15 Oct
rm27 ⮂4 ▥11 P Lift mountains

ROCHEFORT
Charente-Maritime(☎46)

★ ★ ★Remparts 43 r C-Pelletan
☎871244

---

rm63 ⮂53 ▥10 Lift sB ⮂ ▥188–268
dB ⮂ ▥216–296 M45–80

ROCHELLE (LA)
Charente-Maritime(☎46)

★ ★ ★Brises chemin Digue Richelieu
(n.rest) ☎438937 tx791923
15 Jan–15 Dec
rm46 ⮂38 ▥8 🛗 P Lift
sB ⮂ ▥190–340 dB ⮂ ▥275–390 sea

★ ★ ★France et d'Angleterre (MAP) 22 r
Gargoulleau ☎413466 tx790717
rm76 🛗 P Lift 𝄞 dB300

★ ★ ★Yachtman 23 quai Valin
☎412068 tx790762
rm36 ⮂35 ▥1 🛗 Lift Pool sea

☆ ☆Campanile rte de Paris ☎340729
⮂30 dB ⮂206–209 M55–80

☆ ☆Ibis pl du Cdt-de-la-Motte-Rouge
☎416022 tx791431
⮂76 P Lift sB180 dB ⮂236

★ ★St-Nicholas (Inter) 13 r Sardinerie
(n.rest) ☎417155
⮂29 🛗 Lift

★Trianon et Plage (FAH) (DPn) 6 r de la
Monnaie ☎412135
Feb–Dec
rm19 ⮂6 ▥11 P 𝄞

⊗Auto Charente Maritime 47 r du
Lignon ☎345626 M/c All makes

At PUILBOREAU (4km NE)

☆ ☆Climat de France Zone Commerciale
de Beaulieu (N11) ☎673737 tx612241
⮂49 P dB ⮂197–207 M54–70

Chagneau ZAC de Beaulieu
☎344225 Closed Sat & Sun Frd

ROCHE-POSAY (LA)
Vienne(☎49)

★Parc av Fontaines ☎862002
2 May–Sep
rm80 ⮂20 ▥9 P Lift sB122
sB ⮂ ▥130 dB ⮂ ▥71 dB ⮂ ▥161
⸙

ROCHES-DE-CONDRIEU (LES)
Isère(☎74)

★ ★Bellevue 1 quai du Rhône ☎564142
Closed 4–14 Aug & 7–28 Feb
rm15 ⮂10 ▥5 A3rm P
dB ⮂ ▥156–216 M80–180

ROCHE-SUR-YON (LA)
Vendée(☎51)

☆ ☆Campanile Les Bazinières, rte de
Nantes ☎372786 tx610016
⮂33 P dB ⮂206–209 M55–80

⊗Aillery Ridier 3–13 rte
d'Aizenay ☎371206 Closed Sat &
Sun BL

⊗Baudry bd Lavoisier ☎372235 Closed
Sat & Sun Frd

RODEZ
Aveyron(☎65)

★ ★ ★Broussy (MAP) 1 av V-Hugo
☎681871

⇘ 🏠54 ⚓ P Lift ☽ sB75–250
sB ⇗ 🏠210 dBfr140 dB ⇗ 🏠232 M70
mountains

★ ★ ★**Tour Maje** (Inter) bd Gally (n.rest)
☎683468
rm48 ⇗24 🏠20 Lift sB131–151
sB ⇗ 🏠190 dB ⇗ 🏠190–210

★**Poste** 2 r Béteille ☎680147
rm24 ⇗5 🏠8 ⚓ P Lift

ROISSY-EN-FRANCE See **CHARLES-DE-
GAULLE AIRPORT** under **PARIS
AIRPORTS**

ROLLEBOISE
Yvelines(☎3)
🏠A **Terminarias** (N63) ☎0932128
M/c Closed Aug & Sun Lnc Ren

ROMANS-SUR-ISÈRE
Drôme(☎75)

★ ★**Terminus** 48 av P-Sémard (n.rest)
☎024688
rm32 ⇗10 🏠8 Lift dB95–160
dB ⇗ 🏠95–160

ROMILLY-SUR-SEINE
Aube(☎25)

☆ ☆**Climat de France** av Diderot (angle
N19) ☎249240 tx692844

⇗35 P dB ⇗197 M48–74

ROMORANTIN-LANTHENAY
Loir-et-Cher(☎54)

★ ★**Colombier** (DPn) 10 pl Vieux Marché
☎761276
⇗10 ⚓ P sB ⇗121–132
dB ⇗155–190 M65–130

★ ★**Lion d'Or** (DPn) 69 r G-Clemenceau
☎760028
Mid Feb–Jan
⇗10 P Lift sB ⇗283 dB ⇗396

ROQUEBRUNE-CAP-MARTIN
Alpes-Maritimes(☎93)

★ ★ ★**Victoria & Plage** 7 prom du Cap
(n.rest) ☎356590
Feb–Oct
⇗ 🏠31 ⚓ P ☽ sB ⇗ 🏠200–280
dB ⇗ 🏠240–340 mountains

★ ★ ★**Vistaëro** Grand Corniche (4km SW
on D922) ☎350150 tx461021
5 Feb–23 Nov
⇗27 P Lift ☽ sB ⇗345–385
dB ⇗500–640 Pool

★**Westminster** (DPn) 14 av L-Laurens
☎350068
Feb–15 Oct
rm26 ⇗8 🏠22 A4rm P sB95
sB ⇗ 🏠135 dB ⇗ 🏠160–190 M80 sea

ROQUE-GAGEAC (LA)
Dordogne(☎53)

★**Belle Étoile** Ⓛ ☎295144
15 Mar–15 Oct
rm15 ⇗11 🏠4 ⚓

ROSCOFF
Finistère(☎98)

★ ★ ★**Gulf Stream** Ⓛ (DPn) r Marquise
de Kergariou ☎697319

France

Apr–15 Oct
rm32 ⇗22 🏠10 P Lift sea

★**Bains** pl Église ☎612065
Etr–Oct
rm60 ⇗10 A30rm P Lift sB82 dB94
dB⇗163 sea

ROSIERS (LES)
Maine-et-Loire(☎41)

★ ★**Jeanne de Lavral** (DPn) (N152)
☎518017
Jan–15 Nov
rm15 ⇗9 🏠9 A8rm ⚓ P ⚲

ROSPORDEN
Finistère(☎98)

★ ★ ★**Bourhis** (FAH) pl Gare ☎592389
8 Mar–15 Nov
⇗27 P Lift M50–170 **DPn**205–225

ROUBAIX
Nord(☎20)

★ ★ ★**PLM Grand** 22 r J-Lebas (n.rest)
☎701590 tx132301
⇗92 P Lift sB ⇗189–234
dB ⇗249–292

At **VILLENEUVE D'ASCQ** (6km S on rte de
Lille)

☆ ☆**Campanile** La Cousinerie, av de
Canteleu ☎918310 tx610016
⇗50 P dB ⇗206–226 M55–80

☆ ☆**Climat de France** quartier du Triolo, r
Trudaine ☎050403 tx612241
⇗37 P dB ⇗206–226 M54–70

☆ ☆**Ibis Lille** quartier de l'Hôtel de Ville
Rocade Est ☎918150 tx160626
⇗80 P Lift sB ⇗197 dB ⇗218

🏠**Renault Lille-Est** Pont de
Bois ☎912035 Closed Sat & Sun Ren

ROUEN
Seine-Maritime(☎35)

★ ★ ★**Frantel** r de la Croix de Fer
☎980698 tx180949
⇗125 P Lift sB ⇗395 dB ⇗475

★ ★ ★**Dieppe** (MAP) pl B-Tissot
☎719600 tx180413
rm44 ⇗42 🏠2 P Lift ☽ sB ⇗ 285
dB ⇗ 🏠345

☆ ☆**Arcade** 20 pl de l'Eglise St-Sever
☎628182 tx770675
🏠144 P Lift sB 🏠163 dB 🏠174

★ ★**Cardinal** pl de la Cathédral (n.rest)
☎702442
Jan–15 Dec
rm22 ⇗5 🏠15 P Lift sB65–137
sB ⇗ 🏠137 dB ⇗ 🏠155

★ ★**Cathédrale** 12 r St-Romain (n.rest)
☎715795
rm23 ⇗7 🏠16 Lift sB102–163
sB ⇗ 🏠193 dB ⇗ 🏠177–198

★ ★**Europe** 87 r aux Ours (n.rest)
☎708330
rm27 ⇗6 🏠4 P Lift ☽ dB149
dB ⇗ 🏠149

★ ★**Nord** 91 r Gros-Horloge (n.rest)
☎704141 tx770668
rm64 ⇗24 🏠40 P Lift ☽
sB ⇗ 🏠170 dB ⇗ 🏠190–220

★ ★**Paris** (Inter) 12–14 r de la
Champmeslé (off quai de la Bourse)
(n.rest) ☎700926
Closed Xmas
rm23 ⇗12 🏠9 ⚓ Lift sB88–141
sB ⇗ 🏠131–176 dB ⇗ 🏠134–206

★ ★**Québec** 18–24 r Québec (off r de la
République) (n.rest) ☎700938
rm38 ⇗4 🏠23 Lift sB82–143
dB ⇗ 🏠148–197

★ ★**Viking** 21 quai du Havre (n.rest)
☎703495
rm37 ⇗26 🏠11 P Lift
sB ⇗ 🏠103–165 dB ⇗ 🏠153–191

★**Arcades** 52 r des Carmes (n.rest)
☎701030
2 Jan–Jul & 16 Aug–24 Dec
rm16 🏠4 sB66–70 sB 🏠76 dB82
dB 🏠92

★**Normandie** 19 & 21 r de Bec (off r Aux
Juis) (n.rest) ☎715577
rm23 ⇗8 🏠15 P Lift
sB ⇗ 🏠135–177 dB ⇗ 🏠159–198

★**Vieille Tour** 42 pl Haute Vieille Tour
(n.rest) ☎700327
10 Jan–26 Dec
rm23 ⇗2 🏠6 Lift ☽ sB66–124
sB ⇗ 🏠107–137 dB100–140
dB ⇗ 🏠137–180

At **BARENTIN** (17km NW)

☆ ☆**Ibis** (N15) ☎910123
⇗40 P sB ⇗163 dB ⇗192

At **PETIT-QUEVILLY (LE)**

☆ ☆**Fimotel** 112 av J-Jaurès ☎623850
⇗42 P Lift sB ⇗187 dB ⇗214

At **ST-ÉTIENNE-DU-ROUVRAY** (2km S off
N138)

☆ ☆ ☆**Novotel Rouen Sud** Le Madrillet
☎665850 tx180215
⇗133 P Lift sB ⇗300 dB ⇗264 Pool

☆ ☆**Ibis Rouen Sud** av M-Bastie
☎660363 tx771014
⇗69 ⚓ P sB ⇗183 dB ⇗121

ROUFFACH
Haut-Rhin(☎89)

☆ ☆**Campanile** (N83) ☎496632
tx610016
⇗32 P Lift dB ⇗213 M55–80

At **BOLLENBERG** (6km SW)

☆ ☆**Bollenberg** Ⓛ ☎496247 tx880896
⇗48 P

ROUFFILLAC See **ST-JULIEN-DE-
LAMPON**

ROUSSILLON
Isère(☎76)

⚶🅓**R Clemençon** 61 av G-Péri
☎862224 Closed Sat pm & Sun All
makes

⚶🅓**Guilon** 133 rte de la Chapelle
☎862436 All makes

⚶🅓**Rivoliet** 1 av G-Péri ☎862303 Closed
1–20 Aug, Sat pm & Sun Cit

At **CHANAS** (6km S on N7, Chanas exit A1)

⚶🅓**Modern** (N7) ☎842191 Closed Sat pm
& Sun Dat Lada

ROUVRAY
Côte-d'Or(☎80)

⚶🅓**J Pernot** ☎647322 Closed Sun am &
Mon am Ren

ROYAN
Charente-Maritime(☎46)

★ ★**Grand de Pontaillac** 195 av de
Pontaillac (n.rest) ☎380044

Jun–15 Sep
rm45 ⇌23 🏤17 🛁 Lift ♪ sB80
sB ⇌ 🏤180 dB ⇌ 🏤260–270 sea

⚶🅓**DE Marche** 75 av de Pontaillac
☎384888 Closed Sat pm & Sun Ren

ROYAT
Puy-de-Dôme(☎73)

★ ★ ★**Métropole** 4 bd Vaquez ☎358018

May–Sep
rm76 ⇌60 Lift ♪ sb174–250
sB ⇌220–280 dB ⇌465 mountains

ROYE
Somme(☎22)

⚶🅓**L Boitel** 16 r St-Médard
☎871021 Closed Sat pm & Sun Aud VW

⚶🅓**Dallet** 5 pl de la République
☎871089 Closed 14 Jul–8 Aug, Sat pm &
Sun Peu

⚶🅓**Pace & Dequen** 1 r St-Médard/29 r B-
Ville ☎870178 Closed Sat pm, Sun &
Mon am Frd

⚶🅓**Pellieux** 1 rte de Paris
☎871139 Closed Sun Fia

⚶🅓**Sueur** 36 r de Paris ☎870223 Closed
Aug, Sat pm & Sun Opl Vau

RUFFEC
Charente(☎45)

★**Toque Blanche** 16 r du Gl-Leclerc
☎310016

Closed Xmas & New Year
rm22 ⇌1 🏤4 A9rm P sB53–59
sB ⇌ 🏤89 dB59 dB ⇌ 🏤89

RUNGIS
Val-de-Marne(☎1)

See also **ORLY AIRPORT** under **PARIS
AIRPORTS**

★ ★ ★ ★**Frantel Paris-Orly** 20 av C-
Lindbergh ☎6873636 tx260738
⇌206 🛁 P Lift dB ⇌465 Pool

SABLES-D'OLONNE (LES)
Vendée(☎51)

★ ★**Résidence** 36 prom Clemenceau
(n.rest) ☎320666

Mar–Oct
rm35 ⇌20 🏤7 🛁 sB70–240
db70–320 sea

At **CHÂTEAU D'OLONNE** (4km E on D36)

⚶🅓**Tixier** la Mouzinère ☎324104 Closed
Sat & Sun Aud VW

SABLES-D'OR-LES-PINS
Côtes-du-Nord(☎96)

★ ★ ★**Bon Accueil** 🅛 allée des Acacias
☎414219

14 Apr–2 May & 19 May–23 Sep
rm40 ⇌29 🏤2 P Lift sB71–90
sB ⇌ 🏤88–128 dB98–231
dB ⇌ 🏤152–241

★ ★ ★**Diane** 🅛 av Brouard (n.rest)
☎414207

Etr–20 Sep
rm40 ⇌ 🏤35 A10rm P sB78–105
sB ⇌ 🏤88–128 dB106–160
dB ⇌ 🏤161–270 sea

★ ★**Ajoncs d'Or (DPn)** allée des Acasias
☎414212

May–Sep
rm75 ⇌26 🏤8 A47rm P sB68–100
sB ⇌ 🏤108–150 dB116–210
dB ⇌ 🏤126–250

★ ★**Dunes d'Armor & Mouettes**
☎414206

May–15 Sep
rm65 ⇌35 🏤4 A18rm P Lift ✔ sea

★ ★**Voile d'Or** r des Acacias ☎414249

Mar–20 Nov
rm24 ⇌9 🏤1 A4rm P dB85
dB ⇌ 🏤150 sea

SABLÉ-SUR-SARTHE
Sarthe(☎43)

☆ ☆**Campanile** 9 av Ch-de-Gaulle
☎953053 tx610016
⇌30 P dB ⇌194–197 M55–80

★**St-Martin (DPn)** 3r Haute St-Martin
☎950003

Closed Mar
rm10 ⇌1 🏤4 P

At **SOLESMES** (3km NE on D22)

★ ★ ★**Grand** (FAH) 16 pl Dom
Gueranger ☎954510 tx722903

Closed Feb
⇌35 sB ⇌fr212 dB ⇌244–344 Mfr72

SACLAY See **ORSAY**

ST-AFFRIQUE
Aveyron(☎65)

★ ★**Moderne** 🅛 54 av A-Pezet
☎492044

15 Jan–15 Dec
rm39 ⇌12 🏤15 A11rm 🛁 sB72
sB ⇌ 🏤92–131 dB84–150
dB ⇌ 🏤104–157 mountains

ST-AIGNAN
Loir-et-Cher (☎54)

★ ★**St-Aignan** 🅛 7-9 quai J-J Delorme
☎751804

Feb–Dec
rm21 ⇌2 🏤12 🛁 P M52–130
DPn155–215

ST-ALBAN See **MÂCON**

ST-AMOUR
Jura(☎84)

★**Alliance (DPn)** rte Ste-Marie ☎487494

Apr–Sep
rm16 ⇌4 🏤4 🛁 P sB65 sB ⇌ 🏤120
dB85 dB ⇌ 🏤140

★**Commerce** 🅛 pl Chevalerie ☎487305
rm16 ⇌6 🏤1 🛁 sB58–78 sB ⇌ 🏤78
dB76–100 dB ⇌ 🏤116 mountains

ST-ANDRÉ-LES-ALPES
Alpes-de-Haute-Provence(☎92)

⚶🅓**Chabot** rte de Nice ☎890001 Cit

ST-ANDRÉ-LES-VERGERS See **TROYES**

ST-APOLLINAIRE See **DIJON**

ST-AUBIN-SUR-MER
Clavados(☎31)

★**St-Aubin** 🅛 (DPn) r de Verdun
☎973039

Apr–Sep
rm26 ⇌12 sea

ST-AVOLD
Moselle(☎8)

☆ ☆ ☆**Novotel** (N3A) ☎7922593
tx860966
⇌60 P sB ⇌243–278 dB ⇌286–325
Pool

ST-BREVIN-LES-PINS
Loire-Atlantique(☎40)

⚶🅓**Charriau-Evain** 3 av de la
Saulzaie ☎274483 Closed Mon Frd

ST-BRIEUC
Côtes-du-Nord (☎96)

★ ★ ★**Alexandre 1'er** 19 pl du Guesclin
337945
⇌43 🛁 P Lift

★ ★ ★**Griffon** r de Guernsey ☎945762
rm42 ⇌30 🏤12 🛁 P Lift
sB ⇌ 🏤200 dB200–220
dB ⇌ 🏤212–222 ✔

At **YFFINIAC** (5km W)

☆ ☆**Fimotel de la Baie** Aire de Repos
(N12) ☎726410
⇌42 Lift sB ⇌198 dB ⇌226 M50–85

ST-CAST-LE-GUILDO
Côtes-du-Nord(☎96)

★**Angleterre & Panorama** 🅛 r Fosserole
☎419144

6 Jun–7 Sep
rm40 🛁 sea

At **GARDE-ST-CAST (LA)** (2km SE)

★ ★ ★**Ar Vro** 🅛 10 bd de la Plage
☎418501

rm47 ⇌42 🏛 **P** Lift M fr120
DPn230–290 1% sea

ST-CÉRÉ
Lot (☎65)

★ ★**Coq Arlequin**Ⓛ **(DPn)** 1 bd du Dr-
Roux ☎380213
Mar–Dec
rm32 ⇌20 🛏12 🏛 **P**
dB ⇌ 🛏175–260

ST-CHÉLY-D'APCHER
Lozère (☎66)

★**Lion d'Or** 132 r T-Roussel ☎310014

Closed 1 Jan–20 Jan
rm30 ⇌4 🛏1 🏛

ST-CYPRIEN
Pyrénées-Orientales (☎68)

☆ ☆**Fimotel de la Baie** Aire de Repos
(N12) ☎726410

⇌42 Lift sB ⇌198 dB ⇌fr226 M50–85

☆ ★**Ibis** Bassin Nord du Port (n.rest)
☎213030 tx500459

⇌ 🛏34 **P** Lift sB ⇌ 🛏182–212
sB ⇌ 🛏219–264 sea

ST-DENIS-SUR-SARTHON
Orne (☎33)

★ ★**Faïencerie** rte Paris-Brest ☎273016
rm18 ⇌5 🛏9 **P**   dB ⇌ 🛏85–200
mountains

ST-DIZIER
Haute-Marne (☎25)

★ ★ ★**Gambetta** 62 r Gambetta
☎052210
rm63 ⇌34 🛏29 🏛 **P** Lift 𝄢
sB ⇌ 🛏140–180 dB ⇌ 🛏160–240

★**Auberge la Bobotte** (3km W on N4)
☎562003
rm10 🛏5 🏛 **P**

★**Soleil d'Or** (MAP) 64 r Gambetta
☎056822 tx840946
⇌60 **P** Lift Pool

ST-ÉMILION
Gironde (☎57)

★ ★ ★**Hostellerie de la Plaisance** pl
Clocher ☎247232

⇌12 **P**

ST-ÉTIENNE
Loire (☎77)

★ ★ ★**Frantel** r de Woppertal ☎252275
tx300050
⇌120 🏛 **P** Lift sB ⇌299 dB ⇌349

★ ★ ★**Grand** 10 av Libération ☎329977
tx300811
rm66 ⇌39 🛏27 Lift 𝄢

★ ★ ★**Terminus du Forez** (FAH) 31 av
Denfert-Rochereau ☎324847 tx330683
rm66 ⇌21 🛏42 A1rm 🏛 **P** Lift
dB137–177 dB ⇌ 🛏159–259

ST-ÉTIENNE AIRPORT
Loire

At **ANDRÉZIEUX-BOUTHÉON** (2km W of
N82)

France

☆ ☆ ★**Novotel** Centre de Ville (N82)
☎(77)365563 tx900722

⇌98 **P** Lift sB ⇌215–245
dB ⇌252–283 Pool

ST-ÉTIENNE-DE-BAIGORRY
Pyrénées-Atlantiques (☎59)

★ ★**Arcé** ☎374014

3 Mar–2 Nov
rm24 ⇌15 🛏5 🏛 **P** mountains

ST-ÉTIENNE-DU-ROUVRÁY See **ROUEN**

ST-FLORENTIN
Yonne (☎86)

★**Est (DPn)** 7 r fbg St-Martin ☎351035
Mar–Dec
rm30 A6rm 🏛 **P** sB70–95 dB120–205

At **VENIZY** (5.5km N)

★ ★**Moulin des Pommerats**Ⓛ **(DPn)**
☎350804
rm12 ⇌11 A8rm **P** sB205 dB380

ST-FLOUR
Cantal (☎71)

★ ★ ★**Étape (DPn)** 18 av de la
République ☎601303
rm34 ⇌23 🛏11 A11rm 🏛 **P** Lift
mountains

★ ★ ★**Europe (DPn)** 12–13 cours Spy-
des-Ternes ☎600364
Feb–Dec
rm45 ⇌16 🛏12 **P** Lift sB84–194
dB98–150 dB ⇌ 🛏208 mountains

★ ★**Nouvel Bonne Table** (MAP) 16 av de
la République ☎600586 tx393160
rm48 ⇌9 🛏32 A30rm 🏛 Lift
mountains

★ ★**St-Jacques** (FAH) **(DPn)** 8 pl Liberté
☎600920
15 Jun–6 Nov
rm30 ⇌7 🛏17 🏛 dB137–177
dB ⇌ 🛏159–259 mountains

★ ★**Voyageurs** 25 r Collège ☎601551
Apr–Sep
rm39 ⇌16 🛏4 🏛 Lift sB73–145
sB ⇌ 🛏130–188 dB96–170
dB ⇌ 🛏150–190

ST-GALMIER
Loire (☎77)

★ ★**Charpinière** (FAH) ☎541020
Feb–Dec
⇌30 **P** 𝄢 Pool

ST-GAUDENS
Haute-Garonne (☎61)

★**Ferrière & France** 1 r Gl-Leclerc
☎891457
rm17 ⇌10 🛏5 **P** 𝄢 dB40
dB ⇌ 🛏250

At **VILLENEUVE-DE-RIVIÈRE** (69km W on
D117)

★ ★**Cèdres** ☎893600
rm20 ⇌15 🛏5 **P** 🌿 mountains

ST-GENIS-POUILLY
Ain (☎50)

☆ ☆**Climat de France** Lieudit le Marais
☎420520 tx692844

⇌42 **P** dB ⇌221–236

ST-GENIS-LAVAL See **LYON**

ST-GEOSMES See **LANGRES**

ST-GERMAIN-DE-JOUX
Ain (☎50)

★**Reygrobellet**Ⓛ (N84) ☎598113
Closed Oct–Nov
rm10 ⇌6 🛏4 🏛 dB ⇌ 🛏149–184
mountains

ST-GERMAIN-EN-LAYE
Yvelines (☎3)

★ ★ ★**Ermitage des Loges** (MAP) 11 av
des Loges ☎4518886 tx697112
rm24 ⇌21 🛏3 **P** Lift sB ⇌ 🛏300
dB ⇌ 🛏385

☆ ☆**Campanile** rte de Mantes, Maison
Forestière ☎515959
⇌ 🛏49 🏛 **P** dB ⇌ 🛏218–222
M55–80

At **CHAMBOURCY** (4km NW)

★ ★**Climat de France** r du Mur du Parc
☎0744261 tx692844
⇌42 **P** dB ⇌218–233 M48–74

ST-GERMAIN LESPINASSE See **ROANNE**

ST-GERVAIS-EN-VALLIÈRE
Saône-et-Loire (☎85)

★ ★**Moulin d'Hauterive**Ⓛ ☎915556
rm22 ⇌15 🛏2 🏛 **P**
dB ⇌ 🛏180–350 M80–160 river

ST-GERVAIS-LES-BAINS
Haute-Savoie (☎50)

★ ★ ★**Splendid** (n.rest) ☎782133
rm20 ⇌10 🛏5 Lift dB180–200
dB ⇌ 🛏180–220 mountains

ST-GILLES
Gard (☎66)

At **SALIERS** (4km E on N572)

★ ★ ★**Cabanettes en Camargue** (MAP)
(DPN) ☎873153 tx480451
⇌29 🏛 **P**

ST-GILLES-CROIX-DE-VIE
Vendée (☎51)

★ ★**Embruns** 16 bd de la Mer ☎551140
rm23 ⇌16 sea

ST-GIRONS
Ariège (☎61)

★ ★ ★**Eychenne** (MAP) 8 av P-Laffont
☎662055 tx530171
Feb–20 Dec
rm50 ⇌25 🛏21 🏛 **P** 𝄢 sB202–242
sB ⇌ 🛏204–242 dB ⇌ 🛏301
mountains

★ ★ ★**Hostellerie la Truite Dorée**Ⓛ (1km
S) 28 av de la Résistance ☎661689 →

177

Closed 15 Oct–15 Nov
rm12 ⇌5 🛁7 **P** 🌙 dB ⇌ 🍴165–190

&🕭**Durieux** ZI ☎640011 Closed Sun Frd Lnc

ST-JEAN-DE-MONTS
Vendée (☎51)

★ ★**Plage (DPn)** espl de la Mer ☎580035
mid May–mid Sep
rm55 ⇌37 🛁9 **P** Lift A22rm 🌙 sea

&🕭**J Simon** 2 r de Challans ☎582627
Closed 1–23 Oct, Sat pm & Sun pm AR Cit Fia

&🕭**G Vrignaud** rte de Challans ☎582674
Closed Sun out of season Ren

ST-JEAN-DE-VEDAS See MONTPELLIER

ST-JEAN-LE-THOMAS
Manche (☎33)

★ ★**Bains(DPn)** (opp Post Office)
☎488420 tx170380
25 Mar–8 Oct
rm37 ⇌19 🛁4 A8rm **P** sB85–176
dB ⇌ 🍴149–204 M48–128 Pool

ST-JEAN-PIED-DE-PORT
Pyrénées-Atlantiques (☎59)

★ ★ ★**Continental** 3 av Renaud (n.rest)
☎370025
20 Mar–5 Nov
⇌19 **P** Lift mountains

★ ★**Central** (FAH) 1 pl C-de-Gaulle
☎370022
10 Feb–22 Dec
rm14 ⇌8 🛁6 mountains lake

★ ★**Pyrénées** pl Marché ☎370101
22 Dec–12 Nov
rm31 ⇌25 **P** Lift mountains

ST-JULIEN-DE-LAMPON
Dordogne (☎53)

At **ROUFFILLAC** (N of R Dordogne)

★ ★**Cayre (DPn)** ☎297024
Closed Oct
rm15 ⇌12 🛁3 A10rm 🚗 **P** ∿ Pool mountains

ST-JULIEN-EN-BEAUCHÊNE
Hautes-Alpes (☎92)

★ ★**Bermond-Gauthier (DPn)** (N75)
☎580352
Feb–15 Dec
rm20 ⇌3 🛁7 🚗 **P** sB50 sB ⇌ 🍴100
dB ⇌ 🍴110 Pool mountains

ST-JULIEN-EN-GENEVOIS
Haute-Savoie (☎50)

★ ★**Savoyarde (DPn)** 15 rte de Lyon
☎492579
rm10 ⇌1 **P** sB65 dB65–96

ST-JULIEN-LES-VILLAS See TROYES

ST-JUNIEN
Haute-Vienne (☎55)

★ ★**Concorde**⤷ 49 av H-Barbusse
(n.rest) ☎021708

ST-GRÉGOIRE
Ille-et-Vilaine (☎99)

&🕭**Arrivée** rte de St-Malo ☎591243 Frd

ST-HILAIRE-DU-HARCOUËT
Manche (☎33)

★ ★**Cygne**⤷ (FAH) 67 r Waldeck-Rousseau ☎491184
⇌45 A25rm 🚗 **P** Lift dB137–177
dB ⇌ 🍴159–259

★**Lion d'Or**⤷**(DPn)** 120 r Avranches
☎491082
rm20 ⇌18 **P** sB85 sB ⇌ 🍴150
dB ⇌ 🍴150–170

★**Relais de la Poste (DPn)** 11 r de Mortain ☎491031
rm19 ⇌2 **P** sB67–130
sB ⇌ 🍴91–132 dB79–130
dB⇌ 🍴102–144

ST-JEAN-CAP-FERRAT
Alpes-Maritimes (☎93)

★ ★ ★ ★**Grand Cap Ferrat** bd Gl-de-Gaulle ☎010454 tx470184
14 Apr–15 Oct
rm66 ⇌62 🛁4 🚗 Lift 🌙 M alc
DPn490–995 ∿ Pool Beach sea
mountains

ST-JEAN-DE-LUZ
Pyrénées-Atlantiques (☎59)

★ ★ ★**Chantaco** rte d'Ascain ☎261476
Apr–Oct
⇌24 🚗 **P** 🌙 sB ⇌300–350
dB ⇌400–550 St15%∿ 🍴 mountains
lake

★ ★ ★**Poste** 83 r Gambetta (n.rest)
☎260453
15 Mar–15 Nov
rm35 ⇌21 🛁8 🌙 (Jun–Sep)
dB ⇌ 🍴160–220

★ ★**Paris** 1 bd Passicot ☎260062
Mar–15 Dec
rm23 ⇌19 🛁9 sB ⇌ 🍴70–140
dB ⇌ 🍴75–142 mountains lake

★**Continental (DPn)** 15 av Verdun
☎260123 tx550097
rm24 ⇌5 🛁19 Lift sB ⇌ 🍴120–141
dB ⇌ 🍴152–207 M68

&🕭**Lamerain** bd V-Hugo, Zone de Layas (N10) ☎269480 Closed Sat pm & Sun Ren

At **CIBOURE** (1km SW off N10)

★**Hostellerie de Ciboure** 10 av J-Jaurès
☎4/0057
rm22 ⇌10 🛁6 **P** dB ⇌ 🍴85–140
Pool

ST-JEAN-DE-MAURIENNE
Savoie (☎79)

★ ★**St-Georges** 334 r République (n.rest)
☎640106
rm23 ⇌16 🛁4 **P** sB72–140
sB ⇌ 🍴157 dB ⇌ 🍴105–157
mountains

---

rm26 ⇌17 🛁9 **P** sB ⇌ 🍴103–153
dB ⇌ 🍴115–178

ST-LARY-SOULAN
Hautes-Pyrénées (☎62)

★ ★**Terrasse Fleurie** (n.rest) ☎394026
tx570360
15 Dec–15 Apr & 15 May–15 Sep
rm28 ⇌12 🛁14 **P** sB66–77
sB ⇌ 🍴120–130 dB ⇌ 🍴104–215
mountains

ST-LAURENT-DE-COGNAC See COGNAC

ST-LAURENT-DU-VAR See NICE

ST-LÉONARD See BOULOGNE-SUR-MER

ST-LÉONARD-DES-BOIS
Sarthe (☎43)

★ ★ ★**Touring** (MAP) **(DPn)** ☎972803
tx720410
Feb–Dec
rm33 ⇌28 🛁5 **P** Lift dB ⇌ 🍴240

ST-LIEUX-LES-LAVAUR See LAVAUR

ST-LÔ
Manche (☎33)

★ ★**Gare et Marignan (DPn)** pl Gare
☎051515
Closed 1–20 Feb
rm18 ⇌4 🛁8 🚗 **P**

★ ★**Terminus**⤷ 3 av Briovère ☎050860
rm15 ⇌3 🛁10 **P** sB80
sB ⇌ 🍴120–130 dB80–135
dB ⇌ 🍴130–145

★ ★**Univers**⤷ 1 av Briovère ☎051084
rm24 ⇌8 🛁13 **P** sB68–93
sB ⇌ 🍴93–128 dB ⇌ 🍴195

★**Armoric** 15 r de la Marne (n.rest)
☎571747
20 Feb–26 Dec
rm21 ⇌2 🛁5 **P** Lift

★**Cremaillère** 27 r du Belle, pl de la Préfecture ☎571468
Closed end Dec
rm12 ⇌ **P**

ST-LOUIS
Haut-Rhin (☎89)

★ ★**Pfiffer** 77 r Mulhouse (n.rest)
☎697444
6 Jan–9 Aug & 26 Aug–20 Dec
rm36 ⇌15 🛁6 🚗 **P** Lift sB16
dB ⇌ 🍴230

ST-LOUP-DE-VARENNES See SENNECEY-LE-GRAND

ST-MALO
Ille-et-Vilaine (☎99)

★ ★ ★**Central** (MAP) 6 Grande Rue
☎408770 tx740802
rm46 ⇌40 🛁3 🚗 **P** Lift sB250
sB ⇌ 🍴250 dB ⇌ 🍴390

★ ★ ★**Duguesclin** 8 pl Duguesclin
(n.rest) ☎560130
rm23 ⇌9 🛁9 Lift sB85–220
sB ⇌ 🍴85–220 dB ⇌ 🍴85–220

☆ ☆ ☆**Mercure** Chaussée du Sillon
(n.rest) ☎568484 tx740583

178

⊣68 🏛 **P** Lift sB ⊣216–321
dB ⊣272–377 sea

★ ★**Louvre** 2–4 r de Marins (n.rest)
☎408662
rm45 ⊣2 🏠37 **P** Lift

★**Noguette (DPn)** 9 r de la Fosse
☎408357
rm12 ⊣6 🏠6

🕭**Corsaires** 2 av L-Martin ☎567866
Closed Sat pm & Sun Frd

At **GOUESNIÈRE (LA)** (12km SE on D4)

★ ★**Gare** (1.5km N on D76 à la Gare)
☎891046 tx740802

Closed 16 Dec–14 Jan
rm58 ⊣30 🏠18 **P** 🏊

At **PARAMÉ** (1km E)

★ ★**Rochebonne** 15 bd Châteaubriand
☎560172 tx740802
rm39 ⊣ 🏠33 Lift sea

ST-MARTIN-BELLEVUE
Haute-Savoie (☎50)

☆ ☆ ☆**Novotel Val Thorens**
☎(79)080726 tx980230
⊣104 **P** Lift sB ⊣244–280
dB ⊣377–413 Pool

ST-MAURICE-SUR-MOSELLE
Vosges (☎29)

★ ★**Relais des Ballons** 🏷 rte Bénélux-
Bâle (N66) ☎251109

Closed 2nd–3rd wk Mar & Oct
rm17 ⊣12 🏠1 8 **P** dB100–160
dB 🏠150–180 mountains

★**Bonséjour** 🏷 **(DPn)** ☎251233
rm15 ⊣2 **P** dB86–152 dB ⊣152–160
mountains

ST-MAXIMIN-LA-STE-BAUME
Var (☎94)

★**Chez Nous** 3 bd J-Jaurès ☎780257
Closed 2 Dec–15 Jan & Wed
rm7 ⊣1

🕭**Auto Real** X-rd Mont Fleury ☎780358
Closed Winter & Sun All Makes

🕭**STP** av d'Estienne d'Orves ☎780089
Frd

ST-MICHEL-DE-MAURIENNE
Savoie (☎79)

★ ★**Savoy** 🏷 25 r Gl-Ferrié ☎565512
rm22 ⊣12 🏛 **P** sB85–90
sB ⊣ 🏠135–155 dB110–140
dB ⊣ 🏠170–190 mountains

ST-MICHEL-EN-GRÈVE
Côtes-du-Nord (☎96)

★ ★**Plage** 🏷 ☎357443
3 Jan–Apr
rm38 ⊣17 🏛 🌙 **P** Lift dB120–125
dB ⊣160–180 M50–80 Sea

ST-MICHEL-SUR-ORGE
Essonne (☎6)

★ ★ ★**Delfis-Bois-des-Roches** 17 r
Berlioz ☎0154640 tx692032
⊣88 **P** Lift sB ⊣213 dB ⊣256 Mfr58

France

ST-NABORD See **REMIREMONT**

ST-NAZAIRE
Loire-Atlantique (☎40)

★ ★**Dauphin** 33 r J-Jaurès (n.rest)
☎665961
rm20 ⊣4 🏠12 🌙 sB92–167
sB ⊣ 🏠114–167 dB114–167
dB ⊣ 🏠114–167

🕭**J Barbelon** 79 r de la Ville-Huard
☎222542 M/c

ST-OMER
Pas-de-Calais (☎21)

☆ ☆**Ibis** r H-Dupuis ☎931111 tx135206
⊣41 **P** Lift sB⊣202 dB⊣239

★ ★**St-Louis** 25 r d'Arras (n.rest)
☎383521
rm20 ⊣18 🏠2 🏛 **P**

At **TILQUES** (4km NW on N43)

★ ★**Vert Mesnil** (FAH) (1.5km E of N43)
☎932899 tx133360
rm41 ⊣39 🏠2 sB ⊣ 🏠210–230
dB ⊣ 🏠230 🏊 lake

ST-OUEN-L'AUMONE See **PONTOISE**

ST-PALAIS-SUR-MER
Charente-Maritime (☎46)

★ ★ ★**Courdouan (DPn)** av Pontaillac
☎221033
Whi–15 Sep
rm35 ⊣20 🏠14 **P** dB165–220
dB ⊣ 🏠205–260 sea

ST-PARDOUX L'ORTIGIER See
DONZENAC

ST-PAUL
Alpes-Maritimes (☎93)

★ ★ ★ ★**Mas d'Artigny** rte de la Colle
(D7) ☎328454 tx470601
⊣81 🏛 **P** Lift 🌙 sB ⊣340–870
dB ⊣655–1030 M190–250 🏊 Pool sea

ST-PAUL-DE-LOUBRESSAC
Lot (☎65)

★**Relais de la Madeleine** 🏷 ☎219808
15 Jan–5 Dec
rm17 ⊣1 🏠6 **P** dB82 dB ⊣ 🏠102 🏊

ST-PÉE-SUR-NIVELLE
Pyrénées-Atlantiques (☎59)

★**Pyrénées Atlantiques** (N618)
☎540222
rm37 ⊣23 🏠12 **P** mountains

ST-PIERRE-DE-CHARTREUSE
Isère (☎76)

★ ★**Beau Site** 🏷 ☎886134
15 Dec–15 Apr & 15 May–15 Oct
rm33 ⊣28 **P** dB ⊣ 🏠180–210 Pool
mountains

ST-PIERRE-DU-VAUVRAY See
LOUVIERS

ST-PIERRE-QUIBERON See **QUIBERON**

ST-POL-DE-LÉON
Finistère (☎98)

🕭**E Charetteur** pl du Creisker ☎690208
Closed 1–21 Sep, Sat & Sun Ren

ST-POL-SUR-TERNOISE
Pas-de-Calais (☎21)

★**Lion d'Or** 🏷 (FAH) **(DPn)** 68 r Hesdin
☎031293
rm30 ⊣8 🏠15 sB83–144
sB ⊣ 🏠149–151 dB116–192
dB ⊣ 🏠189–211

ST-PONS
Hérault (☎67)

★ ★**Château de Ponderach** (1.2km S) rte
de Narbonne ☎970257
15 Apr–15 Oct
rm11 ⊣9 🏛 **P** mountains

★**Pastre** 🏷 **(DPn)** (at the station)
☎970054
15 Jan–15 Dec
rm20 ⊣2 🏠5 dB60–130 dB ⊣ 🏠130
mountains

ST-POURÇAIN-SUR-SIOULE
Allier (☎70)

★**Chêne Vert** 🏷 (FAH) 35 bd Ledru-
Rollin ☎454065
rm50 ⊣17 🏠10 A15rm 🏛
dB137–177 dB ⊣ 🏠159–259

★**Deux Ponts** 🏷 (FAH) **(DPn)** Ilot de
Tivoli ☎454114
6 Jan–20 Nov
rm28 ⊣6 🏠10 🏛 **P** dB137–177
dB ⊣ 🏠159–259

ST-PRIEST See **LYON**

ST-QUAY-PORTRIEUX
Côtes-du-Nord (☎96)

★ ★**Bretagne** 🏷 36 quai de la
République ☎704091
Mar–15 Nov
rm15 🏠5 dB70–100 dB🏠80–100 sea

★**Gerbot d'Avoine** 🏷 **(DPn)** 2 bd Littoral
☎704009

Closed 15 Nov–15 Dec
rm26 ⊣2 🏠8 **P** dB100–170
dB ⊣ 🏠100–170 sea

ST-QUENTIN
Aisne (☎23)

★ ★**Grand** 6 r Dachery (n.rest)
☎626977 tx140225
⊣41

★ ★**Paix Albert 1er** 3 pl du 8 Octobre
☎627762 tx140225
rm64 ⊣32 🏠4 **P** Lift

C Corbizet 126 r d'Espargenmailles
☎626854 Closed Sun BL

ST-QUENTIN-EN-YVELINES
Yvelines (☎3)

☆ ☆**Fimotel** Parc d'Activités de Bois-
d'Arcy ☎4605024
⊣62 **P** Lift sB⊣197 dB ⊣229

ST-RAMBERT-D'ABLON
Drôme (☎75)

☆ ☆**Ibis** 'La Champagnière', (RN7)
☎030400
⇌30 **P** sB ⇌201 dB ⇌237 M60
mountains

ST-RAPHAËL
Var (☎94)

★ ★ ★**Continental** 25 bd de la Libération
(n.rest) ☎950014 tx970809
rm49 ⇌22 ⋔11 **P** Lift ☾ sea

★ ★**Beau-Séjour** prom Prés-Coty
☎950375
Feb–15 Nov
rm52 ⇌16 ⋔5 Lift **DPn**400–460 (for 2
persons) sea

★ ★**Provençal**⊾ 197 r de la Garonne
(n.rest) ☎950152
Mid Mar–Oct
rm28 ⇌2 ⋔19 sB95–104
sB ⇌ ⋔132–186 dB109–118
dB ⇌ ⋔146–200

★**Vieux Port (DPn)** 109 av Cdt-Guilbaud
☎952312
Feb– Oct
rm16 ⇌3 ⋔4

&**R Bacchi** 658 av de Verdun ☎522736
Closed Sat pm & Sun Peu

Leruste (N98) ☎952620 Closed Sun
Hen

ST-RÉMY-DE-PROVENCE
Bouches-du-Rhône (☎90)

★ ★ ★**Antiques** 15 av Pasteur (n.rest)
☎920302
Apr–Oct
⇌27 A10rm ⋔ **P** sB ⇌232–292
dB ⇌fr324 Pool

★ ★**Castelet des Alpilles (DPn)** 6 pl
Mireille ☎920721
Mar–Nov
rm19 ⇌13 ⋔4 sB ⇌ ⋔350–400
dB ⇌ ⋔400–450

ST-SATUR
Cher (☎48)

★ ★**Laurier** r du Commerce ☎541720
Closed Feb
rm10 ⋔4 **P**

ST-SERNIN-SUR-RANCE
Aveyron (☎65)

★ ★**France**⊾ (Inter) pl de Fort ☎996026
rm20 ⇌8 ⋔10 **P** sB57–115
sB ⇌ ⋔111–140 dB69–115
dB ⇌ ⋔123–168 mountains

ST-TROJAN-LES-BAINS See **OLÉRON
(ILE D')**

ST-TROPEZ
Var (☎94)

★ ★ ★ ★**Byblos** av P-Signac ☎970004
tx470235
4 Feb–15 Oct & 12 Apr –2 Nov
⇌60 ⋔ **P** Lift ☾ sB ⇌560–920
dB ⇌650–1265 St15% Pool sea

France

★ ★ ★**Coste** Port Du Pilon ☎970064
15 Mar–Oct
rm30 ⇌25 **P** sB ⇌151–169
dB113–155 dB ⇌163–183 sea

★ ★ ★**Ermitage** av P-Signac (n.rest)
☎975233
Apr–Oct
rm29 ⇌6 ⋔23 **P** ☾ dB ⋔200–285
sea mountains

&**Auto Service des Salins** rte des Salins
☎970955 Closed 6 Oct–3 Nov, Sat &
Sun Fia Lnc

&**G Meleder** rte des Plages ☎970489
Closed 1–15 Nov ' Sun AR Ren

ST-VAAST-LA-HOUGUE
Manches (☎33)

★**France et des Fuschias**⊾ **(DPn)** 18r
Ml-Foch ☎544226
Closed Jan
rm16 ⇌11 ⋔2 A3rm **P**
sB ⇌ ⋔89–187 dB107–209
dB ⇌ ⋔184–209

ST-VALLIEZ
Drôme (☎75)

&**Brassière** av Buissonet ☎230265
Closed Sun & Mon Cit

&**Martin** 15 av Buissonet ☎231334 Chy

&**Paradis du Plein Air** La Croix des
Mailles (3km N on N7) ☎230666 Closed
Sun All makes

ST-WITZ See **SURVILLIERS-ST-WITZ**

STE-ADRESSE See **HAVRE (LE)**

STE-ANNE-LA-PALUD
Finistère (☎98)

★ ★ ★**Plage** la Plage ☎925012
1 Apr–30 Sep
rm34 ⇌ ⋔29 A4rm **P** Lift Pool sea

STE-CATHÉRINE See **BRIANÇON**

STE-ENIMIE
Lozère (☎66)

★ ★**Commerce** (FAH) (N586) ☎485001
Apr–10 Oct
rm20 ⇌7 ⋔6 A10rm ⋔ **P**

STE-FOY-LES-LYONS See **LYON**

STE-MAXIME
Var (☎94)
See also **BEAUVALLON**

★ ★ ★**Beausite (DPn** 15 Jun–15 Sep) 6
bd des Cistes ☎961953 tx970080
Feb–Oct
rm40 ⇌20 ⋔20 ⋔ **P** Lift ☾
sB ⇌ ⋔255–240 dB ⇌ ⋔280–365
Mfr75 ⧉ Pool sea

★ ★ ★**Belle Aurore** 3 la Croisette
☎960245
Mar–Oct
rm18 ⇌11 ⋔7 A4rm **P** ☾

---

dB ⇌ ⋔360–400 Beach sea

&**Arbois** av Gl-Leclerc ☎961403
Closed Nov & Sun Ren

STE-MENEHOULD
Marne (☎26)

&**J Garet** 47–49 r Florion ☎608138
Closed alternate wk-ends Opl

&**Relais L-Champagne** Esso & Total 50
Station, 52 av V-Hugo ☎608270 Closed
Jun also Wed & Sat All makes

SAINTES
Charente-Maritime (☎46)

★ ★ ★**Commerce Mancini** r des
Messageries ☎930661 tx791012
Feb–20Dec
rm40 ⇌22 ⋔9 ⋔ ☾

★ ★ ★**Relais du Bois St-Georges** r de
Royan (D137) ☎935099
⇌21 ⋔ **P** ☾ sB ⇌150–200
dB ⇌250–310

★ ★**Terminus** esp de la Gare (n.rest)
☎743503
rm36 ⇌12 ⋔2 ⋔ **P** ☾ sB67–100
sB ⇌107–142 dB98–128 dB ⇌126–156

★**Messageries** r des Messageries
(n.rest) ☎936499
rm37 ⇌10 ⋔19 ⋔ ☾ sB86–135
sB ⇌ ⋔130–150 dB104–140
dB ⇌ ⋔159

SAINTES-MARIES-DE-LA-MER (LES)
Bouches-du-Rhône (☎90)

★ ★**Mirage** 14 r C-Pelletan (n.rest)
☎978043
20 Mar–20 Oct
⋔27 dB ⋔125–150

SALBRIS
Loir-et-Cher (☎54)

★ ★ ★**Parc**⊾ (MAP) **(DPn)** 10 av
d'Orléans ☎971853 tx751164
20 Feb–20 Jan
rm27 ⇌14 ⋔13 ⋔ **P** sB ⇌ ⋔280
dB ⇌ ⋔280

★**Dauphin**⊾ **(DPn)** 57 bd de la
République ☎970483
15 Jan–Dec
rm10 ⇌3 ⋔2 **P** dB108
dB ⇌ ⋔118–208

SALERS
Cantal (☎71)

★**Beffroi** r du Beffroi (n.rest) ☎407011
3 Feb–3 Jan
⇌ ⋔10 **P** mountains

SALIERS See **ST-GILLES**

SALLANCHES
Haute-Savoie (☎50)

☆ ☆**Ibis** av de Genève ☎581442
tx385754
⇌58 **P** sB ⇌163 dB ⇌222

SALON-DE-PROVENCE
Bouches-du-Rhône (☎90)

★**Grand Poste** 1 r Prés-Kennedy
☎560194

Feb–Oct
rm28 ⇄7 🛏10 **P**

⚘**Bagnis** 35 r D-Kinet ☎562732 Closed Sat pm AR

⚘**Gutières** 3 bd Coren ☎561262 M/c Closed Sat & Sun All makes

At **BARBEN (LA)** (8km SE)

★**Touloubre** 🄻 ☎551685
Mar–15 Nov & Dec–15 Feb
rm15 ⇄7 🛏1 **P** dB90–197
dB ⇄ 🛏197

At **LANÇON-PROVENCE** (9km SE on A7)

☆ ☆ ☆**Mercure** (A7) ☎539070 tx440183
⇄100 Lift 𝄐 sB ⇄230–270
dB ⇄280–315 Pool

SALSES
Pyrénées-Orientales (☎68)

☆ ☆ ☆**Relais Rousillon** (N9) ☎386067
⇄56 **P** Pool mountains

SANARY-SUR-MER
Var (☎94)

★ ★**Tour (DPn)** quai Gl-de-Gaulle
☎741010
rm28 ⇄12 🛏16 dB134–175
dB ⇄ 🛏209 sea

⚘**Maria** quartier des Prats ☎740324
Closed Sat pm & Sun AR Fia MB Opl Peu

SANCÉ-LES-MÂCON See **MÂCON**

SANCERRE
Cher (☎48)

★ ★**Rempart** 🄻 Rampart des Dames
☎541018
Feb–Oct
⇄12 **P**

SANNOIS
Val-d'Oise (☎3)

☆ ☆**Campanile** ZUP d'Ermont-Sannois, av de la Sadernaude ☎4137957 tx697841
⇄49 dB ⇄206–209 M55–80

SANTENAY
Côte-d'Or (☎80)

★ ★ ★**Santana** av des Sources
☎206211 tx350190
⇄65 **P** Lift sB ⇄212 dB ⇄240
M90–120 mountains

SARAN See **ORLÉANS**

SARLAT-LA-CANÉDA
Dordogne (☎53)

★ ★ ★**Hostellerie de Meysset** rte des Eyzies ☎590829
18 Apr–8 Oct
rm26 ⇄22 🛏4 **P** M110–190
DPn250–260

★ ★ ★**Madeleine** 1 pl de la Petite-Rigaudie ☎591240
15 Mar–15 Nov
rm22 ⇄18 🛏4

★ ★ ★**Salamandre** r Abbé Surguier (n.rest) ☎593598 tx550059

Apr–Oct
⇄23

★ ★**St-Albert** 🄻 10 pl Pasteur ☎590109
rm50 ⇄15 🛏20 A24rm

★**Lion d'Or** 48 av Gambetta ☎590083
Mar–Dec
rm25 ⇄2 🛏5 sB65 sB ⇄ 🛏125 dB80
dB ⇄ 🛏125

⚘**Castan** av de la Dordogne ☎593679
Closed Sun & Mon Tal

⚘**Fournet** rte de Vitrac ☎590523
M/c Frd

⚘**Pechauriol** rte de Brive ☎590530
Toy

⚘**Sarlat Auto** rte de Vitrac ☎591064
Closed Sun & Mon Cit

SARREGUEMINES
Moselle (☎8)

⚘**Schwindt** 62 rte de Nancy ☎982677
Ren

SATOLAS AIRPORT See **LYON**

SAULCE-SUR-RHÔNE
Drôme (☎75)

☆ ☆**Ibis Montelimar Nord** (N7) quartier Fraysse (n.rest) ☎612822 tx345960
⇄29 **P** sB ⇄196 dB ⇄237

⚘**J P Frey** (N7) ☎610038 Closed Sun Cit

SAULIEU
Côte-d'Or (☎80)

★ ★ ★**Poste** 🄻 (Inter) 2 r Grillot (n.rest)
☎640567 tx350540
rm48 ⇄42 🛏 **P** 𝄐 sB81
sB ⇄ 161–200 dB97–230
dB ⇄177–230

⚘**J Baut** r Grillot ☎640345 Closed Sun & Mon Ren

SAUMUR
Maine-et-Loire (☎41)

★ ★ ★**Budan** 3 quai Carnot ☎512876
Apr–15 Oct
rm80 ⇄38 🛏32 🛏 **P** Lift 𝄐
sB140–240 dB ⇄ 🛏140–240
dB220–280 dB ⇄ 🛏220–280 sea

★**Croix-Verte** 49 r de Rouen ☎673931
Feb–15 Dec
rm18 ⇄3 🛏2 **P** sB72–80
sB ⇄ 🛏85–100 dB80–90
dB ⇄ 🛏95–150

At **BAGNEUX** (1.5km SW)

☆ ☆**Campanile** Côte de Bournan
☎501440 tx610016
⇄35 **P** dB ⇄206–209 M55–80

At **CHÊNEHUTTE-LES-TUFFEAUX** (8km NW)

★ ★ ★**Prieuré** ☎501531 tx720379
Mar–Jan
rm35 ⇄32 🛏2 A15rm **P** 𝄐 ✆ Pool

SAUSHEIM See **MULHOUSE**

SAUT-DES-CUVES See **GÉRARDMER**

SAUZET See **MONTÉLIMAR**

SAVERNE
Bas-Rhin (☎88)

★ ★**Geiswiller (DPn)** 17 r Côte ☎911851
rm18 ⇄2 🛏6 🛏 **P** mountains

★**Boeuf-Noir (DPn)** 22 Grande Rue
☎911053
rm20 ⇄5 🛏8 **P** mountains

★**Chez Jean** 🄻 3 r de la Gare ☎911019
rm22 ⇄15 🛏3 🛏 **P** Lift sB85–145
sB ⇄ 🛏145 dB100–160 dB ⇄ 🛏160

SAVIGNAC-LES-ÉGLISES
Dordogne (☎53)

★ ★**Parc** 🄻 ☎050811
Mar–Dec
rm14 ⇄10 🛏4 A11rm **P** ✆

SAVIGNY-SUR-CLAIRIS
Yonne (☎86)

⚘**Chapuis** les Dornets ☎863348 Ren

SÉES
Orne (☎33)

★**Cheval Blanc** 🄻 1 pl St-Pierre
☎278048
rm9 🛏2 sB52–65 sB 🛏65 dB62–81
dB 🛏72–81

★**Dauphin** 🄻 (DPn) 31 pl Halls ☎278007
rm12 ⇄2 🛏1 **P** dB55–78
dB ⇄ 🛏55–78

⚘**A Gaudiche** 60 r de la République
☎278013 Cit

SELLIÈRES
Jura (☎84)
See also **POLIGNY**

At **PASSENANS** (6km SE)

★ ★**Domaine Touristique du Revermont** 🄻 ☎446102
16 Feb–Oct & 16 Nov–Jan
rm28 ⇄24 🛏 Lift dB80–193
dB ⇄80–193 Pool

SEMUR-EN-AUXOIS
Côte-d'Or (☎80)

★ ★**Lac** 🄻 (3km S on D1036 at Lac de Pont) ☎971111
Feb–15 Dec
rm23 ⇄6 🛏12 🛏 **P** lake

★**Côte d'Or** 🄻 (DPn) 3 pl G-Gaveau
☎970313
Closed 6 Jan–14 Mar
rm15 ⇄4 🛏6 🛏 **P** sB68 dB91–130
dB ⇄ 🛏141–166

★**Gourmets (DPn)** 4 r Varenne ☎970941
Jan–25 Oct
rm15 ⇄2 🛏3 🛏

⚘**Delaveau** 3 r de Paris ☎970261
Closed Sun Frd

§⭕**Renault** (J Girard) 21 r du Cours ☎970510 Closed Sun & Mon Ren

SÉNAS
Bouches-du-Rhône (☎90)

★**Luberon (DPn)** 17 av A-Aune (N7) ☎572010

15 Dec–15 Oct
rm7 ⇄1 🏠3 **P** dB97–130
dB ⇄ 🍴108–162

§⭕**Testud** 31 av A-Aune ☎672018 Closed Sat pm & Sun All makes

SENLIS
Oise (☎4)

☆ ☆**Ibis** (N324) ☎4537050 tx140101
⇄50 **P** Lift sB ⇄195–217
dB ⇄255–277 M56–74

★ ★**Nord**⎣⎦ **(DPn)** 110 r de la République ☎4530122
rm16 ⇄3 🏠5 🏠

§⭕**Delachariery** 3–5 av Foch ☎4530968 Ren

Gare 6 (M Briziou) 16 cours Boutteville ☎4530253 Closed 3 wks Aug, Sat & Sun BL

SENNECEY-LE-DIJON See **DIJON**

SENNECEY-LE-GRAND
Saône-et-Loire (☎85)

At **ST-LOUP-DE-VARENNES** (10km N on N6)

§⭕**Desmaris** ☎442076 Closed 3 wks Aug, Sat & Sun Ren

§⭕**Varrant** ☎442065 Closed Jul, Sat pm & Sun Ren

SENONCHES
Eure-et-Loir (☎37)

★**Forêt**⎣⎦ **(DPn)** pl Champ de Foire ☎377850

Closed Feb
rm14 ⇄6 **P** sB75–100 sB ⇄90–122
dB ⇄140

SENS
Yonne (☎86)

★ ★ ★**Paris & Poste** (MAP) 97 r de la République ☎651743 tx801831
rm37 ⇄20 🏠15 🏠 **P** 𝒟 sB200–230
sB ⇄ 🍴203–273 dB ⇄ 🍴283–353

§⭕**Sens Bourgogne Autos** 5 bd de Verdun ☎655123 Closed Sat pm & Sun Frd⁴

§⭕**Vanne** (P Guiguet) 184 rte de Lyon ☎651218 Closed Sat pm & Sun Aud VW

SEPT-SAULX
Marne (☎26)

★ ★**Cheval Blanc** r du Moulin ☎616027 tx830885

15 Feb–15 Jan
rm22 ⇄10 🏠12 🏠 **P**
sB ⇄ 🍴143–153 dB ⇄ 🍴203–294
St15% 🍴

SERRES
Hautes-Alpes (☎92)

★**Alpes** av Grenoble ☎670018

France

Apr–Sep
rm19 ⇄5 🏠4 🏠 **P** sB80 sB ⇄ 🍴110
dB90 dB ⇄ 🍴110 mountains

SÈTE
Hérault (☎67)

★ ★ ★**Grand** 17 quai Ml-Lattre de-Tassigny ☎747177 tx780225
rm51 ⇄25 🏠21 Lift 𝒟
sB ⇄ 🍴163–260 dB212–365 Mfr80

★ ★ ★**Imperial** (MAP) pl E-Herriot (n.rest) ☎532832 tx480046
rm41 ⇄25 🏠12 🏠 **P** Lift 𝒟
sB ⇄ 🍴229–337 dB ⇄ 🍴248–378 St%

§⭕**14 Juillet** 27 av V-Hugo ☎488282 Closed Sep, Sat & Sun All makes

SEVRAN
Seine-et-Marne (☎1)

☆ ☆**Climat de France** av R-Dautry, ZAC de Sevran ☎3834560 tx12241
⇄43 **P** sB ⇄204 dB ⇄243 M54–70

SEVRIER
Haute-Savoie (☎50)

★**Robinson** ☎465411

Apr–Sep
rm12 ⇄2 🏠2 🏠 **P** Pool lake

SEYSSEL
Aine (☎50)

★ ★**Rhône** ☎592030

Feb–15 Nov
rm12 ⇄10 🏠2 A5rm 🏠 **P** sB90–125
sB ⇄ 🍴102–205 dB112–150
dB ⇄ 🍴124–250 M78–225

SÉZANNE
Marne (☎26)

★ ★**Croix d'Or**⎣⎦ 53 r Notre-Dame ☎806110

Closed 2 Jan–14 Jan
rm13 ⇄9 🏠2 🏠 **P** sB80 sB ⇄ 🍴97
dB95–110 dB ⇄ 🍴111–126

★ ★**France (DPn)** 25 r L-Jolly ☎805252

Closed 15 Jan–15 Feb
rm24 ⇄6 🏠10 🏠 **P**

SIORAC-EN-PÉRIGORD
Dordogne (☎53)

★**Scholly**⎣⎦ **(DPn)** r de la Poste ☎286002

Apr–Nov
rm32 ⇄14 🏠13 **P** sB112–172
sB ⇄ 🍴197–242 dB134–220
dB ⇄ 🍴219–294

SISTERON
Alpes-de-Hautes-Provence (☎92)

★ ★ ★**Grand du Cours** av de la Libération, pl de l'Église (n.rest) ☎610451

15 Mar–15 Nov
rm50 ⇄20 🏠30 🏠 **P** Lift 𝒟
sB ⇄ 🍴125–185 dB ⇄ 🍴160–217 mountains lake

---

§⭕**Provence** av J-Jaurès ☎611228 Closed Sat pm & Sun Cit

SOISSONS
Aisne (☎23)

☆ ☆**Lions** rte de Reims, ZI Soissons (3km E via N31) ☎593060
rm28 **P** sB ⇄185 dB ⇄260

★ ★**Picardie** 6 r Neuve St-Martin ☎532193
⇄33 **P** Lift 𝒟

★**Railye** 10 bd de Strasbourg (n.rest) ☎530047
rm12 ⇄1 🏠4 🏠

SOLESMES See **SABLÉ-SUR-SARTHE**

SOSPEL
Alpes-Maritimes (☎93)

★ ★**Étrangers**⎣⎦ 7 bd Verdun ☎040009

15 Jan–28 Nov
rm35 ⇄15 🏠15 A5rm **P** Lift
sB80–100 sB ⇄ 🍴135–170 dB90–120
dB ⇄ 🍴135–185 Pool mountains

SOUILLAC
Lot (☎65)

★ ★**Ambassadeurs**⎣⎦ 7–12 av Gl-de-Gaulle ☎327836

Closed Oct
rm28 ⇄15 🏠9 A10rm **P**
dB95–195 dB ⇄ 🍴137–195 mountains

★ ★**Périgord**⎣⎦ **(DPn)** 31 av Gl-de-Gaulle ☎327828

May–15 Oct
rm60 ⇄19 🏠19 A27rm 🏠 **P**

★ ★**Renaissance**⎣⎦ (FAH) **(DPn)** 2 av J-Jaurès ☎327804

Apr–2 Nov
rm24 ⇄12 🏠12 🏠 **P** Lift
dB ⇄ 🍴159–259 Pool

★ ★**Roseraie**⎣⎦ 42 av de Toulouse ☎378269

15 Apr–15 Oct
rm26 ⇄23 🏠3 🏠 **P**

★**Auberge du Puits**⎣⎦ ☎378032

Jan–Oct
rm16 ⇄4 **P**

★**Nouvel**⎣⎦ 21 av Gl-de-Gaulle ☎327958
rm25 ⇄17 🏠3 **P** sB ⇄ 🍴80 dB80
dB ⇄ 🍴155

§⭕**M Cadier** rte de Sarlat ☎378272 Closed Sat & Sun Tal

SOUPPES-SUR-LOING
Seine-et-Marne (☎6)

§⭕**Cornut Osmin** 7 av Ml-Leclerc ☎4297032 Closed Sat pm, Sun & Mon am Ren

SOURCE (LA) See **ORLÉANS**

SOUSCEYRAC
Lot (☎65)

★**Déjeuner de Sousceyrac**⎣⎦ ☎330056

Etr–Nov
rm10 ⇄2 🏠8 A4rm dB80–100
dB ⇄ 🍴120

SOUSTONS
Landes (☎58)

★ ★ *Bergerie* (DPn) av du Lac ☎480143
May – 15 Oct
⇌12 **P**

STAINVILLE
Meuse (☎29)

★ ★ ★ **Grange** ᴸ ☎786015
rm9 ⇌9 ▥2 ⋒ **P** ⚬ Pool

STRASBOURG
Bas-Rhin (☎88)

★ ★ ★ ★ **Hilton International** av
Herrenschmidt ☎371010 tx890363
⇌253 **P** Lift 🌙 dB ⇌405 – 545

☆ ☆ ☆ ☆ **Holiday Inn** 20 pl de Bordeaux
☎357000 tx890515
⇌ ▥168 **P** Lift 🌙 sB ⇌ ▥457
dB ⇌ ▥557 Pool

★ ★ ★ ★ **Sofitel** pl St-Pierre-le-Jeune
☎329930 tx870894
⇌ ▥180 ⋒ **P** Lift ⇌ ▥311 – 573
dB ⇌ ▥531 – 641

★ ★ ★ **Terminus-Gruber** (MAP) 10 pl
de la Gare ☎328700 tx870998
rm78 ⇌58 ▥12 **P** Lift 🌙
sB ⇌ ▥275 – 322 dB ⇌ ▥410

★ ★ **France** 20 r du Jeu des Enfants
(n.rest) ☎323712 tx890084
rm70 ⇌10 ▥60 ⋒ Lift

★ ★ ★ **Grand** 12 pl de la Gare (n.rest)
☎324690 tx870011
⇌90 **P** Lift 🌙 sB ⇌ ▥260 – 320
dB ⇌ ▥320 – 360

★ ★ ★ **Hannong** (FAH) 15 r du 22
Novembre (n.rest) ☎321622 tx890551
rm70 ⇌52 ▥18 **P** Lift
sB ⇌ ▥208 – 282 dB ⇌ ▥308 – 316

★ ★ ★ **Monopole-Métropole** ᴸ 16 r Kuhn
(n.rest) ☎321194 tx890366
2 Jan – 23 Dec
rm98 ⇌45 ▥47 ⋒ Lift 🌙
sB ⇌ ▥203 – 293 dB ⇌ ▥248 – 341

☆ ☆ ☆ **Novotel Centre Halles** quai
Kléber ☎221099 tx880700
⇌ ▥97 **P** Lift sB ⇌ ▥367
dB ⇌ ▥439 M alc

☆ ☆ ☆ **PLM Pont de l'Europe** Parc du
Rhin ☎610323 tx870833
⇌ ▥93 **P** sB ⇌ ▥238 – 252
dB ⇌ ▥306 – 327 M75

☆ ☆ **Arcade** 7 r de Molsheim ☎223000
tx880147
▥143 **P** Lift sB ▥184 dB ▥195

☆ ☆ **Climat de France** pl A-Maurois,
Maille Irène, ZUP Hautepierre ☎285923
tx612241
⇌38 **P** dB ⇌208 – 228 M54 – 70

☆ ☆ **Ibis** 1 r Sebastopol, quai Kléber
☎221499 tx880399
⇌97 **P** Lift sB ⇌218 – 236

★ ★ **Vendôme** (n.rest) 9 pl de la Gare
☎324523

France

rm48 ⇌14 ▥30 Lift sB90
sB ⇌ ▥170 dB ⇌ ▥200

🍴 **Straub** 34 r de la Ganzau, Neuhof
☎397160 Closed Aug, Sat & Sun BL

At **GEISPOLSHEIM** (12km SE on RN83)

☆ ☆ **Campanile** 20 r de l'Ill (N83)
☎667447 tx610016
⇌50 **P** dB ⇌218 – 222 M55 – 80

At **ILKIRCH-GRAFFENSTADEN** (7km S)

☆ ☆ ☆ **Mercure Strasbourg Sud** r du 23
Novembre, Ostwald ☎660300 tx890277
⇌91 **P** Lift sB ⇌268 – 293
dB ⇌331 – 346 M alc Pool

☆ ☆ ☆ **Novotel Strasbourg Sud** rte de
Colmar (N83) ☎662156 tx890142
⇌76 **P** sB ⇌293 dB ⇌346 M alc Pool

SULLY-SUR-LOIRE
Loiret (☎38)

★ ★ **Grand Sully** ᴸ (DPn) 10 bd Champ
de Foire ☎362756
15 Jan – 15 Dec
rm12 ⇌7 ▥1 ⋒ **P** sB94 – 168
dB ⇌185

★ ★ **Poste** (DPn) 11 r fbg St-Germain
☎352622
rm36 ⇌5 ▥7 A10rm ⋒ **P**

SURESNES
Hautes-de-Seine (☎1)

☆ ☆ **Ibis** 6 r de Bourets ☎5068844
tx614484
⇌62 ⋒ **P** Lift 🌙 sB ⇌273
dB306 M alc

SURVILLIERS-ST-WITZ
Val-d'Oise (☎3)

☆ ☆ ☆ **Mercure Paris St-Witz** chemin de
Montmélian ☎4682828 tx695917
⇌115 **P** Lift sB ⇌252 – 285
dB ⇌294 – 323 Pool

☆ ☆ ☆ **Novotel Paris Survilliers**
Autoroute A1-D16 ☎4686980 tx695910
rm79 **P** sB ⇌305 – 320 dB ⇌345 – 360
Pool

TAIN L'HERMITAGE
Drôme (☎75)

★ ★ ★ **Commerce** (Inter) 69 av J-Jaurès
☎086500 tx345573
15 Dec – 15 Nov
rm30 ⇌20 ▥10 **P** 🌙
sB ⇌ ▥210 dB ⇌ ▥210 – 243

🍴 **45e Parallele** Pont de l'Isère
☎586004 M/c Closed 28 Oct – 15 Nov,
Sat pm & Sun All makes

🍴 **Vuillerme** 126 av J-Jaurès ☎083501
Closed Sat pm & Sun Ren

TALANGE See **METZ**

TALLOIRES
Haute-Savoie (☎50)

★ ★ ★ **Cottage** rte G-Bise ☎607110
15 May – 15 Oct
rm36 ⇌26 ▥6 A14rm ⋒ **P** Lift 🌙
sB160 – 370 sB ⇌ ▥230 – 370
dB ⇌ ▥360 – 510 mountains lake

★ ★ **Beau Site** ☎607104
19 May – Sep
rm38 ⇌19 ▥8 A28rm ⋒ **P** M96
DPn174 – 253 ⚬ lake

★ ★ **Vivier** ☎607054
Apr – Oct
rm30 ⇌21 ▥9 ⋒ **P** dB ⇌ ▥126 – 175

TAMNIÈS
Dordogne (☎53)

★ ★ **Laborderie** ᴸ ☎296859 tx24620
15 Mar – 15 Nov
rm26 ⇌19 ▥5 A9rm dB100 – 220
dB ⇌ ▥130 – 220 mountains lake

TARARE
Rhône (☎74)

★ **Mère Paul** (2km on N7) ☎631457
Closed Sep
rm10 ⇌ ▥9 A4rm **P** sB ⇌ ▥102 – 122
dB ⇌ ▥120 – 150

TARASCON-SUR-ARIÈGE
Ariège (☎61)

★ ★ **Poste** ᴸ (DPn) 16 av V–Pilhès
☎646041
Closed Mon (Oct – Jun only)
rm30 ⇌14 ▥4 **P** dB90 – 172
dB ⇌ ▥90 – 172 mountains

TARASCON-SUR-RHÔNE
Bouches-du-Rhône (☎90)

★ ★ **Terminus** pl du Colonel-Berrurier
☎911895
Jan – Nov
rm24 ⇌2 ▥11 sB60 sB ⇌ ▥120
dB70 dB ⇌ ▥120

★ **Provençal** 12 cours A-Briand
☎911141
rm22 ⇌4 ▥14 ⋒ **P**

TARBES
Hautes-Pyrénées (☎62)

★ ★ ★ **Président** (MAP) 1 r G-Faure
☎939840 tx530522
rm57 ⇌45 ▥12 **P** Lift
sB ⇌ ▥222 – 262 dB ⇌ ▥304 – 349
Pool mountains

☆ ☆ **Campanile** (4km SW on N21)
Lotissement Longchamp, rte de Lourdes
☎938320 tx530571
⇌42 **P** dB ⇌206 – 209 M55 – 80

★ ★ **Croix Blanche** pl Verdun (n.rest)
☎930854
rm32 ⇌6 ▥7 sB70 – 130
dB ⇌ ▥107 – 130 dB70 – 130
dB ⇌ ▥130 – 190 dB ⇌ ▥169 – 200

★ **Henri IV** 7 bd B-Barère (n.rest)
☎340168
rm24 ⇌20 ▥4 ⋒ **P** Lift 🌙
sB ⇌ ▥130 – 190 dB ⇌ ▥169 – 200

🍴 **SA Auto Selection** 15 r F-Marque
☎936930 Closed Sun & Mon am Ren
Toy Vlo

THÉOULE-SUR-MER
Alpes-Maritimes (☎93)

★★**Guerguy la Galère** la Galère
☎754454
Feb–Oct
⇌14 🏠 **P** S15% sea

★**Hermitage Jules César** 1 av C-Dahon
☎499612
Mar–Oct
rm18 ⇌2 🍴14 dB86 dB ⇌ 🍴86–180
sea

THIERS
Puy-de-Dôme (☎73)

☆☆**Fimotel** rte de Clermont-Ferrand
(N89) ☎806440
⇌42 **P** Lift sB ⇌194 dB ⇌223
🍴⚫**Sauvagnat** 90 r de Lyon ☎800374
Closed Aug, Sat pm & Sun Cit

THIONVILLE
Moselle (☎8)

🍴⚫**R Dillmann** 81 rte de Garche
☎885950 Closed 12 Jul–4 Aug & Sun Cit

THOISSEY
Ain (☎74)

★★**Chapon Fin (DPn)** r du Champ de
Foire ☎040474
15 Feb–5 Jan
rm25 ⇌18 🍴7 🏠 **P** Lift 🌙
sB ⇌ 🍴180–280 dB ⇌ 🍴300–450

★**Beau-Rivage (DPn)** av Port ☎040166
15 Mar–15 Oct
🍴10 **P** dB 🍴130–162

THOUARS
Deux-Sèvres (☎49)

☆☆**Climat de France** les Moulins à Vent
☎681321 tx692844
rm24 dB ⇌154–174 🍴

THURY-HARCOURT
Calvados (☎31)

★**Relais de la Poste (DPn)** rte Caen
☎797212
rm11 ⇌5 🍴6 🏠 **P** sB ⇌ 🍴90–260
dB ⇌ 🍴90–260

TILQUES See **ST-OMER**

TINQUEUX See **REIMS**

TONNERRE
Yonne (☎86)

★★★**Abbaye St-Michel** L. Montée St-
Michel ☎550599
Feb–Dec
⇌11 **P** dB ⇌432–620 M160 & alc 🍴
🍴⚫**Carrosserie Auto** rte de St-Martin
☎550009 Closed Xmas, New Year &
Mon All makes

TOULON
Var (☎94)

★★★**Frantel Tour Blanche** bd Ami-
Vence ☎244157 tx400347
rm96 ⇌77 🍴19 A19rm **P** Lift
sB ⇌ 🍴338 dB ⇌ 🍴396 Pool sea

Carrefour Auto 49 av Gl-Pruneau
☎415986 Closed Sat Toy

France

🍴⚫**Soleil** (R Dulac) 31 r A-Chenièr
☎272556
At **CAMP ST-LAURENT** (7.5km W via B52-
exit Ollioules)

☆☆☆**Novotel** ☎630950 tx400759
⇌86 **P** Lift ⇌253–263
dB ⇌278–288 Pool
At **FARLÈDE (LA)** (8.5km NE)

☆☆**Climate de France** quartier de
l'Auberte ☎487427 tx612241
⇌38 **P** dB ⇌206 M54–70
At **VALETTE-DU-VAR (LA)** (4km NE)

🍴⚫**Azur** av de 1 Université ☎233648
Closed Sat & Sun Frd

TOULOUSE
Haute-Garonne (☎61)

★★★**Caravelle** (MAP) 62 r Raymond IV
(n.rest) ☎627065 tx530438
rm30 ⇌18 🍴12 🏠 🌙 sB ⇌ 🍴295
dB ⇌ 🍴369

★★★**Compagnie du Midi** Gare
Matablau ☎628493 tx530171
rm65 ⇌46 🍴19 Lift 🌙 🍴249
dB ⇌ 🍴333

★★★**Concorde** 16 bd Bonrepos (n.rest)
Sun & Aug) ☎624860 tx531686
rm97 ⇌70 🍴27 **P** Lift 🌙
sB ⇌ 🍴260–290 dB ⇌ 🌙360–390

★★★**Diane** 3 rte de St-Simon ☎075922
tx530518
⇌333 **P** sB ⇌248–299 dB ⇌298–347
M120–200 🍴 Pool

☆☆**Ibis** les Raisins, 27 bd des Minimes
☎226060 tx530437
⇌130 **P** Lift sB ⇌208 dB ⇌239

★★**Voyageurs** (Inter) 11 bd Bonrepos
(n.rest) ☎628979
rm34 ⇌5 🍴29 A9rm 🏠 Lift
🍴⚫**Vie** 57–59 allées C-de-Fitte ☎429911
Closed Sat pm & Sun Tal

At **MIRAIL (LE)**

☆☆**Climat de France** av du Mirail, ZAC
des Pradettes ☎448644 tx692844
⇌42 **P** sB ⇌216 dB ⇌236 M54–70

☆☆**Ibis** r J-Babinet ☎408686 tx520805
⇌89 **P** Lift sB ⇌180 dB ⇌205
🍴⚫**Smeca St-Michel** 123 r Vauquelin
☎401010 Closed Sat & Sun BL

TOULOUSE AIRPORT

★★★**Frantel Wilson** 7 r de Labéda
(n.rest) ☎212175 tx530550
⇌95 🏠 **P** sB ⇌388 dB ⇌486

☆☆☆**Novotel Toulouse Purpan** 23 r de
Maubec ☎493410 tx520640
⇌123 **P** Lift sB ⇌279–291
dB ⇌318–329 🍴 Pool

At **BLAGNAC** (7km NE)

☆☆**Campanile** av D-Daurat 3 ☎710340
tx610016
⇌42 **P** dB ⇌218–222 M55–80

TOUQUES See **DEAUVILLE**

TOUQUET-PARIS-PLAGE (LE)
Pas-de-Calais (☎21)

★★★**Côte d'Opale (DPn)** 99 bd Dr J-
Pouget, bd de la Mer ☎050811
15 Mar–15 Nov
rm28 ⇌19 🍴2 🌙 sB126–260
sB ⇌ 🍴165–260 dB146–260
dB ⇌ 🍴185–260 St% sea

☆☆☆**Novotel-Thalamer** La Plage
☎052400 tx160480
⇌104 **P** Lift sB ⇌335–422
dB ⇌394–592

★★★**Westminster** av Verger (n.rest)
☎051966 tx160439
Apr–11 Nov
⇌145 **P** Lift 🌙 sB ⇌365–540
dB ⇌405–575 St15%

★★**Forêt** 73 r de Moscou (n.rest)
☎050988
⇌10 sB ⇌150 dB ⇌165–180

☆☆**Ibis** Front de Mer ☎053690
tx134273
⇌72 **P** Lift sB ⇌252–282
dB ⇌294–324 sea

★★**Plage** 13 bd de la Mer (n.rest)
☎050322
15 Mar–15 Nov
rm26 ⇌8 🍴10 🌙 sB96–218
sB ⇌ 🍴186–218 dB112–218
dB ⇌ 🍴202–218 St% sea

★★**Windsor-Artois** 7 r St-Georges (off r
de la Paix) ☎050544
rm56 ⇌12 🍴23 A6rm Lift sB66
sB ⇌ 🍴185 dB114 dB ⇌ 🍴290

★**Chalet** 15r de la Paix ☎051299
Apr–15 Nov
rm15 ⇌5 🍴2

★**Robert's (DPn)** 66 r de Londres
☎051198
Apr–Sep
rm14 ⇌3

★**Touquet** 17 r de Paris (n.rest) ☎052254
rm16 ⇌1 🍴8

At the **GOLF LINKS** (3km S)

★★★**Manoir (DPn)** av du Golf
☎052022
Apr–Dec
rm45 ⇌43 A6rm **P** 🌙 sB ⇌234–375
dB ⇌300–375 St% Pool 🐾

TOURCOING
Nord (☎20)

☆☆**Novotel Neuville** Autoroute Lille-
Grand (N near Halluin interchange)
☎940770 tx131656
⇌118 **P** Lift sB ⇌257–276
dB ⇌298–315 M alc Pool

☆☆**Ibis** centre Gl-de-Gaulle, r Carnot
☎248458 tx132695

⇔102 **P** Lift sB180 dB ⇔214

TOUR-DU-PIN (LA)
Isère (☎74)

At **FAVERGES-DE-LA-TOUR** (10km NE)

★ ★ ★ ★**Château de Faverges**
☎974252 tx300372
12 May–Oct
rm40 ⇔29 ▥11 A20 **P** Lift 𝄐
DPn370–750 S% ⇩ Pool

TOURETTES See **FAYENCE**

TOURNUS
Saône-et-Loire (☎85)

★ ★ ★**Rempart (DPn** in summer) 2 & 4 av
Gambetta (N6) ☎511056
⇔30 ▥ **P** Lift

★ ★ ★**Sauvage** (MAP) pl du Champ de
Mars ☎511445 tx800726
15 Dec–15 Nov
rm30 ⇔25 ▥ Lift sB195 sB ⇔195
dB ⇔250

★**Terrasses**ᴸᴱ**(DPn)** 18 av du 23 Janvier
☎510174
rm12 ⇔3 ▥3 ▥ **P** dB79–144
dB ⇔ ▥109–144

⍫❍**M Pageaud** 3 rte de Paris ☎510705
Closed Sat pm & Sun Ren

⍫❍**Scavardo** (N6, exit Sud) ☎510-320
Closed Sat pm & Sun Cit

TOURS
Indre-et-Loire (☎47)

See also **JOUÉ-LÊS-TOURS**

★ ★ ★**Armor**ᴸᴱ 26 bis bd Heurteloup
(n.rest) ☎052437 tx750008
rm50 ⇔15 ▥15 ▥ Lift ❍

★ ★ ★**Bordeaux**ᴸᴱ 3 pl du Ml-Leclerc
☎054032 tx750414
rm54 ⇔22 ▥25 Lift 𝄐 sB196–256
sB ⇔ ▥240–260 dB210–276
dB ⇔ ▥276–296

★ ★ ★**Central** (FAH) 21 r Berthelot
(n.rest) ☎054644 tx750008
rm42 ⇔14 ▥18 ▥ **P** Lift 𝄐
dB137–220 dB ⇔ ▥159–259

★ ★ ★**Château de la Loire** 12 r Gambetta
(n.rest) ☎051005
15 Jan–15 Dec
rm32 ⇔12 ▥17 **P** Lift
sB ⇔ ▥87–173 dB102–194
dB ⇔ ▥194

★ ★ ★**Meridien** 292 av de Grammont
☎280080 tx750922
⇔125 **P** Lift 𝄐 sB ⇔343–388
dB ⇔431–481

★ ★ ★**Royal** 65 av de Grammont
☎647178 tx750289
⇔35 ▥ **P** Lift sB ⇔234 dB ⇔293

★ ★ ★**Univers** 5 bd Heurteloup
☎053712 tx750806
rm91 ⇔76 ▥15 ▥ Lift 𝄐
sB ⇔ ▥267–315 dB ⇔ ▥317–410 M90

☆ ☆**Arcade** 1 r G-Claude ☎614444
tx751201

France

▥139 Lift **P** sB ▥173 dB ▥187

☆ ☆**Climat de France** ZI les Granges
Galand (N76), St-Avertin ☎277117
tx612241
⇔38 **P** dB ⇔208–236 M54–74

★ ★**Cygne** 6 r du Cygne (off r Colbert)
(n.rest) ☎666641 tx750008
rm21 ⇔6 ▥6 A1rm ▥

★ ☆**Ibis** la Petitite Arche, av A-Maginot
☎543220 tx751592
⇔49 **P** sB ⇔183 dB ⇔220

★ ★**Mondial**ᴸᴱ 3 pl de la Résistance
(n.rest) ☎056268
rm18 ⇔4 ▥9 **P**

★**Balzac** 47 r de la Scellerie (n.rest)
☎054087 tx750008
rm18 ⇔7 ▥5 𝄐 sB73–160
sB ⇔ ▥103–160 dB91–160
dB ⇔ ▥126–166

★**Choiseul** 12 r de la Rôtisserie (n.rest)
☎208576
rm16 ⇔11 ▥8 sB89–109
sB ⇔ ▥99–124 dB118–148
dB ⇔ ▥123–158

★**Colbert** 78 r Colbert (n.rest) ☎666156
rm17 ⇔6 ▥6

★**Foch** 20 r Ml-Foch (n.rest) ☎057059
rm16 ⇔3 ▥6 A2rm ▥ sB84–122
dB ⇔ ▥137 dB115–164
dB ⇔ ▥115–164

⍫❍**Autotouraine** 151 av A-Maginot
☎411515

⍫❍**Nouveau Tours** 16 r Constantine
☎057492 Closed Sat & Sun Maz

⍫❍**G Pont** ZI du Menneton ☎202533
Closed Aug 2–24 & Sat Frd

At **CHAMBRAY-LES-TOURS** (6km S)

☆ ☆ ☆**Novotel Tours Sud** N10–ZAC de la
Vrillonerie ☎274138 tx751206
⇔91 **P** Lift sB ⇔286–296
dB ⇔362–372 M alc Pool

☆ ☆**Ibis** (N10) La Vrillonnerie (n.rest)
☎282528 tx751297
⇔60 **P** sB ⇔186 dB ⇔221

TRÉBEURDEN
Côtes-du-Nord (☎96)

★ ★**Family**ᴸᴱ (Inter) 85 r des Plages
☎235031
Apr–15 Oct
rm25 ⇔12 ▥6 **P** sB ⇔ ▥157–240
dB104–207 dB ⇔ ▥104–207

★ ★**Ker an Nod**ᴸᴱ r Pors Termen
☎235021
Apr–Nov
rm20 ⇔10 ▥4 sea

TRÉGASTEL-PLAGE
Côtes-du-Nord (☎96)

★**Beau Séjour**ᴸᴱ (Inter) ☎238802
Apr–Sep
rm20 ⇔12 **P** sea

★**Belle Vue**ᴸᴱ (FAH) **(DPn)** 20 r des
Calculots ☎238818
15 Apr–Sep
rm33 ⇔15 ▥17 A9rm **P** sea

★**Mer et Plage** ☎238803
1 Jun–25 Sep
rm40 ⇔18 ▥6 **P** sB90 sB ⇔ ▥105
dB120 dB ⇔ ▥200 sea

TRÉGUIER
Côtes-du-Nord (☎96)

★ ★**Kastell Dinec'h** (FAH) ☎924939
Mar–14 Oct & 28 Oct–Dec
rm15 ⇔10 ▥2 sB ⇔ ▥167
dB ⇔ ▥227 Mfr59

TRÉPORT (LE)
Seine-Maritime (☎35)

★**Rex** 50 quai François-1ᵉʳ ☎862655
rm17 ⇔3 ▥1 **P** dB83–120
dB ⇔ ▥120–167 sea

TRETS
Bouches-du-Rhône (☎42)

⍫❍**Rosso** 3 C-Mirabeau ☎292031
Closed Sat pm & Sun Frd

TRÉVOL
Allier (☎70)

☆ ☆**Relais d'Avrilly** (N7) ☎426143
tx990229
⇔42 **P** Lift sB ⇔282 dB ⇔384

TRIMOUILLE (LA)
Vienne (☎49)

★**Paix (DPn)** pl Église et de la Mairie
☎916050
15 Mar–Sep
rm12 ⇔4 ▥4 sB77–140
sB ⇔ ▥114–140 dB128–154
dB ⇔ ▥128–175

TRINITÉ-SUR-MER (LA)
Morbihan (☎97)

★ ★**Rouzic** 17 cours de Quais ☎557206
15 Dec–15 Nov
rm30 ⇔16 ▥14 Lift sea

TROIS-ÉPIS (LES)
Haut-Rhin (☎89)

★ ★ ★**Grand** (MAP) ☎498065
tx880229
⇔48 **P** Lift 𝄐 sB ⇔385–485
dB ⇔ ▥520–720 M alc Pool mountains

TROUVILLE-SUR-MER
Calvados (☎31)

★ ★**Flaubert** r G-Flaubert ☎883823
Closed Jan
rm33 ⇔17 ▥10 Lift 𝄐 sB ⇔ ▥100
dB140–280 dB ⇔ ▥140–280 sea

★ ★**Reynita** 29 r Carnot (n.rest)
☎881513
Closed Jan
rm25 ⇔7 ▥11 sB73 sB ⇔ ▥133–167
dB ⇔ ▥167

TROYES
Aube (☎25)

★★★**Grand** 4 av Ml-Joffre (opp station)
☎799090 tx840582

⇋100 **P** Lift dB ⇋277–302

★★**Paris** 54 r R-Salengro (n.rest)
☎433713 tx840809

rm27 ⇋1 🛏10 🚗 sB71 sB ⇋ 🛏123
dB82 dB ⇋ 🛏140–168

🕃**Contant Autos** 15 bd Danton
☎434819 Closed Sat & Sun Ren

At **ST-ANDRE-LES-VERGERS** (4km SW)

🕃**SARL Juszak** 37 rte d'Auxerre
☎824655 Closed Sat pm & Sun BL

At **ST-JULIEN-LES-VILLAS** (2km SE)

🕃**Sud Auto** 139 bd de Dijon ☎820376
Closed Sat pm & Sun BMW

TROYES AIRPORT

At **BARBEREY** (6km NW on N19)

☆☆☆**Novotel Troyes Aéroport** (N19)
☎745995 tx840759

⇋61 **P** Lift sB ⇋242–262
dB ⇋288–313 Pool

TULLE
Corrèze (☎55)

★★★**Limouzi** 19 quai République
☎264200

⇋50 🚗 **P** Lift ♪ sB ⇋90–130
dB ⇋130–190

URY See **FONTAINEBLEAU**

UZERCHE
Corrèze (☎55)

★★**Ambroise** av de Paris ☎731008
Closed Nov
rm20 ⇋4 🛏16 🚗 **P**

★★**Teyssier** r Pont-Turgot ☎731005
15 May–15 Oct
rm17 ⇋10 🚗 **P** sB72–84
sB ⇋94–132 dB84 dB ⇋94–156

🕃**Renault** (J-de Castro) rte de Limoges
☎732866 Ren

UZÈS
Gard (☎66)

★**Provençale** 3 r Grande Bourgade
☎221106
🛏10

VAIRES-SUR-MARNE
Seine-et-Marne (☎6)

🕃**Central Service** 73 r de la Gare
☎0201518 All makes

VAISON-LA-ROMAINE
Vaucluse (☎90)

★★**Beffroi** r de l'Evêché ☎360471
15 Mar–3 Nov
rm21 ⇋6 🛏9 A10rm **P** sB72
sB ⇋ 🛏224 dB126 dB ⇋ 🛏264

VAL-ANDRÉ (LE)
Côtes-du-Nord (☎96)

★**Bains (DPn)** 7 pl Gl-de-Gaulle
☎722011

Etr–20 Sep
rm25 ⇋3 🛏4 **P**

VALBONNE
Alpes-Maritimes (☎93)

☆☆☆**Novotel Sophia Antipolis**
☎333800 tx970914
⇋97 **P** Lift sB ⇋308–318
dB ⇋406–426 ✍ Pool mountains

☆☆**Ibis Sophia Antipolis** r A-Caquot
☎335060 tx461363
⇋99 **P** Lift sB ⇋206 dB ⇋245 M50
mountains

VALDAHON
Doubs (☎81)

★★**Relais de Franche Comté** 🛗 (Inter)
☎562318
20 Jan–20 Dec
⇋20 🚗 **P** sB ⇋130 dB ⇋149–164
mountains

VAL D'ISÈRE
Savoie (☎79)

★★★★**Sofitel** ☎060830 tx980558
27 Nov–3 May & Jul & Aug
⇋52 🚗 Lift **DPn**470–610 Pool
mountains

★★★**Aigion (DPn)** ☎060405
1 Dec–5 May
rm22 ⇋16 🛏6 dB ⇋ 🛏198–268
mountains

★★**Savoie (DPn** in winter) ☎061507
Jul & Aug, Dec–Apr
rm36 ⇋24 🛏12 Lift sB ⇋ 🛏185–227
dB ⇋ 🛏290 mountains

★**Vieux Village** 🛗 (**DPn** in season)
☎060379
Dec–Apr & Jul–Aug
rm23 ⇋20 🛏3 **P** dB ⇋ 🛏165–232
mountains

VALENÇAY
Indre (☎54)

★★★**Espagne** 8 r du Château
☎000002 tx751675
Mar–Nov
⇋18 **P** sB ⇋220–350 dB ⇋380–650

★★**Lion d'Or** 🛗 pl Marché ☎000087
Rest. closed Jan & Feb
rm15 ⇋6 🛏2 **P**

VALENCE
Drôme (☎75)

☆☆☆**Novotel Valence Sud** 217 av de
Provence (N7) ☎422015 tx345823
⇋107 **P** Lift sB ⇋257–258
dB ⇋298–309 M alc Pool

☆☆**Ibis** 355 av de Provence ☎444254
tx345384
⇋78 **P** Lift sB ⇋186 dB ⇋251

★★**Pic (DPn)** 285 av V-Hugo ☎441532

⇋5 🚗 **P** dB ⇋270–450

🕃**Anayan** 170 r du Châteauvert
☎441685 Cit

🕃**Brun Valence Motors** 73 & 79 av de
Verdun ☎430791 Closed Sat pm & Sun
Opi Vau

🕃**Costechareyre** 31 av des Auréats
☎440109 Closed 2 wks Sep, Sat pm &
Sun All makes

J Jaurès 410 av de Chabeuil ☎421266
Closed Sat pm & Sun Aud VW

🕃**Minodier** rte de Beauvallon, ZI
☎443124 Cit

🕃**Royal** (M Habrard) av de Provence
☎421200 Closed Sat & Sun MB

At **BOURG-LÈS-VALENCE** (1km N)

☆☆**Climat de France** rte de
Châteauneuf-sur-Isère (CD67) ☎427746
tx692844
⇋42 **P** dB ⇋225–245 M48–74

★★**Seyvet** 🛗 24 av M-Urtin ☎432651
Closed Jan
rm33 ⇋17 🛏16 🚗 **P** Lift
dB ⇋ 🛏152–216

At **PORTES-LÈS-VALENCE** (5km S)

🕃**Pietri** r J-Jaurès ☎570564 Closed Sat
pm All makes

VALENCE-D'AGEN
Tarn-et-Garonne (☎63)

★★**Tout-Va-Bien** 35–39 r de la
République ☎395483 tx560800
rm22 ⇋19 🛏2 🚗 **P** ♪

VALENCIENNES
Nord (☎27)

★★★**Grand** (MAP) 8 pl de la Gare
☎463201 tx110701
rm97 ⇋34 🛏33 Lift sB ⇋ 🛏230
dB ⇋ 🛏302

☆☆☆**Novotel Valenciennes Ouest**
Autoroute Paris–Bruxelles, ZI No2
☎442080 tx120970
⇋75 **P** sB ⇋257–276 dB ⇋298–323
M alc Pool

☆☆**Ibis** Autoroute A2 (Valenciennes
Ouest exit) ☎442986 tx160737
⇋60 sB ⇋188 dB ⇋221

VALETTE-DU-VAR (LA) See **TOULON**

VALLOIRE
Savoie (☎79)

★★**Grand de Valloire et Galibier** (Inter)
☎643266 tx980553
15 Jun–15 Sep & 20 Dec–15 Apr
rm43 ⇋30 🛏11 **P** Lift **Pn**230–310
mountains

VALOGNES
Manche (☎33)

★**Louvre** 28 r Réligieuses ☎400007
3 Jan–Nov
rm20 ⇋3 🛏3 🚗 **P** sB62–75
sB ⇋ 🛏87–102 dB80–120
dB ⇋ 🛏114–144

VALS-LES-BAINS
Ardèche (☎75)

★ ★ ★**Vivarais** (MAP) 5 r C-Expilly
☎374263 tx345866
Jan–15 Nov
rm40 ⇌20 ⋒20 **P** Lift sB ⇌ ⋒259
dB ⇌ ⋒324

★ ★**Europe** ᴸ (FAH) 86 r J-Jaurès
☎374394
12 Apr–Sep
rm36 ⇌26 Lift dB137–177
dB ⇌ ⋒159–259

VAL-SUZON
Côte-d'Or (☎80)

★ ★ ★**Hostellerie Val Suzon (DPn)**
(N71) ☎316015
Closed Jan
rm18 ⇌5 ⋒13 A10rm **P**
sB ⇌ ⋒98–148 dB ⇌ ⋒166–186

VANNES
Morbihan (☎97)

★ ★ ★**Marebaudière** 4 r A-Briand
☎473429
6 Jan–25 Dec
rm40 ⇌17 ⋒23 **P** sB ⇌ ⋒167–195
dB ⇌ ⋒187–212

☆ ☆**Ibis** r E-Jourdan, ZI de Ménimur Est
☎636111 tx950521
⇌59 **P** sB ⇌188 dB ⇌221

★**Image Ste-Anne** (FAH) **(DPn)** 8 pl de la
Libération ☎632736 tx950352
rm30 ⇌25 **P** Lift

★**Marée Bleue (DPn)** 8 pl Bir-Hakeim
☎472429
6 Jan–25 Dec
rm16 ⋒4 **P** sB77–95 sB ⋒99 dB52
dB ⋒99

⑧**Beauséjour** rte de Vannes ☎418412
Closed Sun & Mon Ren

⑧**Benelux** rte de Ste-Anne ☎631376
Aud VW

⑧**Poulichet** 13 r A-Briand ☎474546
Closed Sat & Sun Tal

VANVES
Haut-de-Seine (☎1)

☆ ☆ ☆**Mercure Paris-Vanves** r du
Moulin ☎6429322 tx202195
⇌391 ⋒ **P** Lift sB ⇌468–485
dB ⇌535–552 M alc

VARCES
Isère (☎76)

★**Escale** pl de la République ☎728019
25 Jan–2 May, 9 May–21 Sep & 27 Sep–1
Jan
⇌12 ⋒ **P** sB ⇌240 dB ⇌420
mountains

VARENGEVILLE-SUR-MER
Seine-Maritime(☎35)

★ ★**Terrasse** ᴸ (DPn) ☎851254
Mar–Oct
rm28 ⇌8 ⋒10 **P** dB55–180
dB ⇌ ⋒55–160 ⇔ sea

VARENNES-VAUZELLES See **NEVERS**

France

VARETZ See **BRIVE-LA-GAILLARDE**

VATAN
Indre(☎54)

⑧**R Monière** av de la Libération
☎497529 M/c Closed Sun Dat

VENCE
Alpes-Maritimes(☎93)

★ ★ ★**Domaine St-Martin** rte de
Coursegoules ☎580202 tx470282
Mar–Nov
⇌25 ⋒ ⅅ dB ⇌950–1250 Pool sea

☆ ☆**Diana** av Poilus (n.rest) ☎582856
⇌25 ⋒ **P** Lift dB ⇌190–210
mountains

⑧**Sporting** (J Bortali) 11 av du Gl-
Leclerc ☎580528 Closed Sun Fiat Lnc

VENDIN-LE-VIEL See **LENS**

VENDÔME
Loir-et-Cher(☎54)

★**Vendôme** ᴸ (FAH) **(DPn)** 15 fbg
Chartrain ☎770288 tx750383
rm33 ⇌11 ⋒22 ⋒ Lift
dB ⇌ ⋒159–269

VENIZY See **ST-FLORENTIN**

VERDUN
Meuse(☎29)

⑧**Capucins** (G Louis) 8 r L-Maury
860453 Closed Jul or Aug & Sat Peu

⑧**M Carré** 41 av de Paris ☎862097 Dat
Tal

⑧**F Martin** 61 bis r du Coulmier
☎841087 Closed Aug & Sat pm Fia Frd
MB

⑧**M Rochette** r V- Schleiter
☎865049 Closed Sun Frd

At **CHATTANCOURT** (14km NW on D38)
⑧**M Riboizi** ☎861513 Closed Mon
am Ren

VERDUN-SUR-LE-DOUBS
Saône-et-Loire(☎85)

⑧**M Geunot** av G-d'Estaing
☎425170 Closed Mon Cit

VERETZ
Indre-et-Loire(☎47)

★**St-Honoré (DPn)** ☎503006
Closed Feb
rm9 ⇌4 ⋒3 dB80 dB ⇌ ⋒110–165

VERNET-LES-BAINS
Pyrénées-Orientales(☎68)

★ ★**Angleterre (DPn)** 9 av de Burnay
☎055058
2 May–26 Oct
rm20 ⇌11 mountains

VERNEUIL-SUR-AVRE
Eure(☎32)

★ ★**Clos (DPn)** 98 Ferté Vidame
☎322181
15 Jan–12 Dec
rm12 ⇌9 ⋒3 **P** sB ⇌ ⋒230
dB ⇌ ⋒320–428

★ ★**Saumon** (FAH) 89 pl de la Madeleine
☎320236 tx172770
rm24 ⇌12 ⋒4 A10rm **P** sB75–95
sB ⇌ ⋒160 dB110 dB ⇌ ⋒175–210
M40–80

VERRIÈRES-LE-BUISSON
Essonne(☎6)

☆ ☆**Climat de France** ZAC des Prés
Houts, av G-Pompidou ☎9307070
tx692844
⇌38 **P** dB ⇌223–243 M54–74

VERSAILLES
Yvelines(☎3)

★ ★ ★ ★**Trianon Palace** 1 bd de la Reine
☎9503412 tx698863
rm130 ⇌86 ⋒28 **P** Lift ⅅ
sB367–567 dB ⇌ ⋒504–709

★ ★**Clagny** 6 Impasse Clagny (n.rest)
☎9501809
rm20 ⋒18 sB ⋒73 dB ⋒120–163

★ ★**St-Louis** 28 r St-Louis (n.rest)
☎9502355 tx698958
rm27 ⇌8 ⋒15 ⅅ sB ⇌ ⋒110–170
dB ⇌ ⋒140–180

★**Cheval Rouge** 18 r A-Chenier
☎9500303
15 Jan–20 Dec
rm41 ⇌11 ⋒11 **P** sB84–114
sB ⇌ ⋒143–165 dB100–120
dB ⇌ ⋒158–264

VERVINS
Aisne(☎23)

★ ★**Tour du Roy** 45 r Gl-Leclerc
☎980011
Closed 16 Jan–14 Feb
rm15 ⇌11 ⋒4 **P** sB ⇌ ⋒120–200
dB ⇌ ⋒160–320

★**Cheval Noir** 33 r de la Liberté ☎980416
Closed Xmas
rm15 ⇌3 ⋒4 ⋒ **P** sB62–92
sB ⇌ ⋒90–112 dB ⇌ ⋒124–134

VESOUL
Haute-Saône(☎84)

★ ★**Nord** 7 r Aigle Noir ☎750256
rm35 ⇌25 ⋒7 **P** Lift ⋒
sB ⇌ ⋒130–150 dB148–178
dB ⇌ ⋒178

★ ★**Relais N19** (Inter) **(DPn)** rte de Paris
(N19) ☎764242
15 Jan–22 Dec
rm26 ⇌14 ⋒12 ⋒ **P**
sB ⇌ ⋒160–210 dB ⇌ ⋒200–250

⑧**Vesoul Auto Service** av Pasteur,
Echenoz la Méline ☎752801 Closed
Sun All makes

VEURDRE (LE)
Allier(☎70)

★ ★**Pont Neuf** ᴸ (FAH) rte de Lurcy
Lévis ☎664012 tx202080 →

Closed Sun pm & Tue am 15 Oct–Mar
rm26 ⇥10 ▥10 🏦 P dB137–177
dB ⇥ ▥159–259

VEYRIER-DU-LAC
Haute-Savoie(☎50)

★**Auberge du Colvert** ☎601023

Apr–18 Nov
⇥10 Lift dB ⇥262–282 lake mountains

VICHY
Allier(☎70)

★ ★ ★ ★**Pavillon Sévigné** (MAP) 10 pl
Sévigné ☎321622 tx990246

2 May–Sep
rm48 ⇥34 ▥10 Lift sB ⇥ ▥376
dB ⇥ ▥580 ✈ Pool

★ ★ ★**Albert-1er** av P-Doumer (n.rest)
☎318110

Etr–Nov
rm33 ⇥20 ▥6 🏦 P Lift ♪

⑧**St-Blaise** 2–6 rte de Lisbonne
☎986371 Closed Sat pm & Sun BL

VIC-SUR-CÈRE
Cantal(☎71)

★ ★**Beauséjour** Ⅱ av du Parc
☎475027

Apr–Sep
rm100 ⇥40 ▥17 A20rm P Lift

At **COL DE CUREBOURSE** (6km SE on
D54)

★**Auberge des Monts** ☎475171

May–1 Oct
⇥ ▥27 P sB ⇥ ▥100–160
dB ⇥ ▥160 mountains

VIENNE
Isère(☎74)

★ ★**Nord** (Inter) 11 pl Miremont
☎857711

rm43 ⇥10 ▥23 🏦 Lift ♪

⑧**Avignon** 20 av du Gl-Leclerc
☎534825 Closed 15–30 Aug, Sat pm &
Sun AR BL MB

⑧**Fréty** rte du 11 Novembre
☎531040 M/c Closed Sun All makes

⑧**Ménender** le Péage du Vizille
☎680541 Closed Sat am Peu

At **CHONAS-L'AMBALLAN** (9km S on N7)

☆ ☆**Relais 500 de Vienne (DPn)** (N7)
☎588144 tx380343

⇥ ▥43 P Pool

VILLEDIEU-LES-POÊLES
Manche (☎33)

★ ★**St-Pierre & St-Michel** Ⅱ 12 pl de la
République ☎610011

Closed 15–31 Dec
rm25 ⇥8 ▥4 🏦 P sB57 dB73–127
dB ⇥ ▥100–142

VILLEFRANCHE-SUR-MER
Alpes-Maritimes(☎93)

★ ★ ★**Versailles** av Ml-Foch
☎808956 tx970433

Closed 24 Oct–22 Dec
rm50 ⇥44 ▥6 P Lift ♪ Pool sea

France

★ ★ ★**Provençal (DPn)** 4 av Ml-Joffre
☎807142 tx970433

rm43 ⇥40 A3rm Lift ♪ dB120–211
dB ⇥ ▥194–233 ✈ Pool sea
mountains

★ ★ ★**Welcome** (MAP) 1 quai Courbet
☎552727 tx470281

Closed Nov–14 Dec
rm32 ⇥28 🏦 Lift ♪ sB ⇥260–400
dB280–470 sea

★ ★**Coq-Hardi** Ⅱ 8 bd de la Corne d'Or
☎807106

Closed Nov
rm20 ⇥14 ▥6 🏦 P Pool sea
mountains

VILLEFRANCHE-SUR-SAÔNE
Rhône(☎74)

★ ★ ★**Plaisance** 96 av de la Libération
☎653352

Closed Xmas & New Year
rm63 ⇥30 ▥33 A6rm P Lift
sB154 sB ⇥ ▥188–206
dB ⇥ ▥211–224

☆ ☆**Campanile** r G-Mangin ☎680758
tx610016

⇥43 P dB ⇥206–209 M55–80

☆ ☆**Ibis** Le Péage-Commune de Limas
☎682223 tx370777

⇥118 P Lift sB ⇥172 ⇥229

★**Ecu de France** 35 r d'Anse ☎683448
rm30 ⇥15 ▥15 🏦 P
sB ⇥ ▥135–170 dB ⇥ ▥150–185
S12%

Europe r Ampère ☎655059 Closed Sat
pm & Sun Aud VW

M Thivolle 695 av T-Braun
☎652609 Closed Sat Cit

VILLENEUVE D'ASCQ See **ROUBAIX**

VILLENEUVE-DE-MARSAN
Landes(☎58)

★**Europe** Ⅱ **(DPn)** 1 pl Foirai ☎582008
rm15 ⇥5 ▥7 P Pool

VILLENEUVE-DE-RIVIÉRE See **ST-
GAUDENS**

VILLENEUVE-LÈS-AVIGNON
Gard(☎90)

★ ★ ★**Prieuré** 7 pl Chapitre ☎251820
tx431042

3 Mar–1 Nov
⇥35 P Lift ♪ sB ⇥300–700
dB ⇥350–900 ✈ Pool

★ ★**Magnaneraie** Ⅱ **(DPn** in summer) 37
r Camp de Bataille ☎251111
rm21 ⇥16 ▥5 🏦 P ♪ Pool

VILLENEUVE-LA-GARENNE See **PARIS**

VILLENEUVE-LOUBET-PLAGE See
CAGNES-SUR-MER

VILLENEUVE-SUR-LOT
Lot-et-Garonne(☎53)

★ ★ ★**Parc** Ⅱ (MAP) 13 bd de la Marine
☎700106 tx550379

rm42 ⇥16 ▥26 🏦 P Lift ♪
sB ⇥ ▥279–359 dB ⇥ ▥330–395

★ ★**Prune d'Or** pl de la Gare ☎700095
rm17 ⇥9 ▥2 🏦 P sB67–117
sB ⇥ ▥82–117 dB94–129 dB ⇥ ▥144

VILLENEUVE-SUR-YONNE
Yonne(☎86)

★**Dauphin** 14 r Carnot ☎871855
rm8 ⇥6 🏦 sB66 sB ⇥127–167
dB117–184 dB ⇥174–184

VILLERS-COTTERÉTS
Aisne(☎23)

☆ ☆**Ibis** rte de Vivières (CD81) ☎962680
tx145363

⇥62 P sB ⇥218 dB ⇥252

VILLERS-LES-POTS See **AUXONNE**

VILLERS-SEMEUSE See **CHARLEVILLE-
MÉZIÈRES**

VILLERS-SUR-MER
Calvados(☎31)

★ ★ ★**Bonne Auberge** Ⅱ **(DPn)** 1 r du
Ml-Leclerc ☎870464

Apr–Sep
⇥24 P Lift sB ⇥200–300
dB ⇥283–323 sea

⑧**Méridien** 13 r du Gl-Leclerc
☎870213 Closed Wed in winter Tal

VINAY See **ÉPERNAY**

VINCENNES See **PARIS**

VINEUIL See **BLOIS**

VIRE
Calvados(☎31)

★ ★**Cheval Blanc** Ⅱ (FAH) 2 pl du 6 Juin
1944 ☎680021 tx170428

10 Feb–Dec
rm22 ⇥12 ▥2 ♪ dB200 dB ⇥ ▥259

VIRONVAY See **LOUVIERS**

VIRY-CHÂTILLON
Essonne(☎6)

☆ ☆**Climat de France** r Octave-Longuet
☎9442121 tx612241

⇥38 P dB ⇥203–223 M54–70

VITRAC
Dordogne(☎53)

★**Plaisance** Ⅱ au Port (N703)
☎283304

Feb–Nov
rm38 ⇥21 ▥4 🏦 P dB90–160
dB ⇥ ▥170

VITRÉ
Ille-et-Vilaine(☎99)

★**Chêne Vert** 2 pl du Gl-de-Gaulle
☎750058

Closed Oct & Sat
rm22 ⇥4 ▥4 🏦 P sB54–71
sB ⇥ ▥90–100 dB71–78
dB ⇥ ▥100–155

VITROLLES See **MARSEILLE AIRPORT**

VITRY-LE-FRANÇOIS
Marne(☎26)
★**Cloche** 34 r A-Briand ☎740384
rm24 ⇌6 🏠2 🏛 **P**

★**Nancy** 22 Grand Rue de Vaux
☎740937
24 Jan–24 Dec
rm15 🏠3 🏛 sB72–82 sB ⇌82
dB ⇌115

At **FRIGNICOURT** (3km S)
🐾**C Loeb** 138 r du Gl-Lecerc
☎741794 All makes

VIZILLE
Isère(☎76)
★**Parc** 25 av A-Briand ☎680301
rm25 ⇌7 🏠10 mountains

VOGELGRUN See **NEUF-BRISACH**

VOREPPE See **GRENOBLE**

VOUVRAY
Indre-et-Loire(☎47)
★**Grand Vatel** 🄻 (DPn) av Brûlé
☎527032
rm7 ⇌5 🏠2 **P** dB ⇌ 🏠150–180

VRINE (LA)
Doubs(☎81)

Monaco

★**Ferme de la Vrine** 🄻 ☎382004
rm60 ⇌40 🏠10 A60rm 🏛 **P**
mountains

WALHEIM See **ALTKIRCH**

WIMEREUX
Pas-de-Calais(☎21)
★ ★**Atlantic** Digue le Mer ☎324101
Closed Feb
rm11 ⇌6 🏠5 🏛 **P** Lift dB ⇌216
Beach sea
★**Centre** 78 r Carnot ☎324108
Closed 20 Dec–10 Jan & 6–21 Jun
rm25 ⇌11 🏠7 🏛 sB86–112
sB ⇌ 🏠150 dB ⇌ 🏠124–195

YENNE
Savoie(☎79)
★**Logis Savoyard** pl C-Dullin ☎367038
rm13 A4rm **P**

YFFINIAC See **ST-BRIEUC**

Monaco
Prices are in French Francs

MONTE CARLO
(☎93)
★ ★ ★ ★ ★**Paris** pl du Casino
☎508080 tx469925
⇌300 **P** Lift 𝄞 sB ⇌700–1100
dB ⇌805–1300 ✍ Pool ♪ sea

★ ★ ★ ★**Hermitage** sq Beaumarchais
☎506731 tx479432
⇌200 **P** Lift 𝄞 sB ⇌580–1050
dB ⇌750–1200 ✍ Pool ♪ sea

★ ★ ★**Alexandra** 35 bd Princesse
Charlotte (n.rest) ☎506313
rm55 ⇌38 🏠3 Lift 𝄞
sB ⇌ 🏠193–275 dB170
dB ⇌ 🏠194–325

🐾**Bristol** 48 r Grimaldi ☎300376 Closed
Sat pm & Sun BMW

At **MONTE-CARLO BEACH**
★ ★ ★ ★**Beach** ☎782140 tx479413
Apr–Oct
⇌48 **P** Lift 𝄞 ✍ Pool Beach ♪ sea

▲Above: Rochen des Mees, Coen

▶Right: Chateau de Versailles,
le Hameau

GERMANY

The German Federal Republic (West Germany), with its fairy-tale castles and ancient towns, is a country offering legend and tradition among its many attractions. It is bordered by nine countries, Austria, Belgium, Czechoslovakia, Denmark, German Democratic Republic, France, Luxembourg, the Netherlands and Switzerland and is a country of forests, rivers and mountains. The Rhine Valley boasts magnificent cliffs and woods whilst the Black Forest has some fine valley scenery with countless waterfalls and gorges.

The climate is temperate and variable, with hotter summers than in Britain.

Area (Federal Republic)
95,965 sq miles
Population 61,400,000
Local time GMT + 1
(Summer GMT + 2)

National flag Horizontal stripes of even width starting from top, black, red and gold

How to get there

If you use one of the short-crossing Channel ferries and travel via Belgium, the German Federal Republic is just within a day's drive. The distance from Calais to Köln (Cologne) is just under 260 miles.

Stuttgart: Palace Square (Schlossplatz)

By driving through northern France and entering Germany near Strasbourg, the journey usually takes two days. This entry point is also used if travelling by the longer Channel crossings: Cherbourg, Dieppe or Le Havre to southern Germany. The distance from Le Havre to Strasbourg is just under 430 miles, a journey which will take at least one or two days. The longer-crossing ferries operating across the North Sea to the Netherlands can be an advantage if visiting northern Germany. Alternatively, it is possible to use the ferry operating between Harwich and Hamburg.

Motoring regulations and general information

This information should be read in conjunction with the general content of the European ABC (pages 6–27). **Note** As certain regulations and requirements are common to many countries they are covered by one entry in the ABC and the following headings represent some of the subjects dealt with in this way:
AA Agents
Crash or safety helmets
Customs regulations for European countries
Drinking and driving
Fire extinguisher
First-aid kit
Insurance
International distinguishing sign
Medical treatment
Overtaking
Police fines
Radio telephones/Radio transmitters
Rear view mirror
Seat belts
Tyres
Visitors' registration

Accidents
Dial 112 for **fire**, 110 **police** and **ambulance** in most areas.

You are generally required to call the police when individuals have been injured or considerable damage has been caused. Not to give aid to anyone injured will render you liable to a fine. See also *Accidents* page 7.

Accommodation
There is a good selection of hotels, many of which are listed in the official Hotel Guide. This is obtainable from the Tourist Office in London, which can also provide details of accommodation in castles and stately homes. Regional and local tourist organisations also have details of inns and boarding houses.

For a nominal charge, tourist information offices will usually assist in finding hotel accommodation (see page 197). Enquiries by post should be accompanied by an international reply coupon (obtainable from the post office).

There is also a reservations service operated by the ADZ (Allgemeine Deutsche Zimmerreservierung). This organisation will make instantly confirmed bookings at hotels throughout the country. Full information about this service, including details of the hotels concerned, may be obtained from ADZ, Beethovenstrasse 61, 6000 Frankfurt/Main 1 ☎(0611)740767; tx416666. Reduced prices apply to children under ten year of age sharing a room with their parents.

Reservations are not normally held after 18.00hrs.

Automatic hotel reservation facilities are available in Frankfurt at the airport, the main railway station and at the ADAC office, Frankfurt West, by the Wiesbaden-Frankfurt autobahn.

Berlin
Documents required for travel through the German Democratic Republic to West Berlin.

Be sure you have a valid, standard passport (children over 16 years of age must have a separate passport), national driving licence and vehicle registration document. The Green Card is now accepted, but make sure that it covers you for the GDR (DDR) before you depart from the United Kingdom. Third party insurance can be arranged at the border crossings. Transit visas for journeys to West Berlin can be obtained at the frontier crossings at a cost of *DM5* per person (each way). Tourists travelling directly between the German Federal Republic and West Berlin are exempt from paying road tax.

Customs crossings The main frontier Customs Houses between the German Federal Republic and the German Democratic Republic officially open for transit from the Federal Republic to West Berlin are listed below. The names printed in italics are within the GDR (DDR), the others outside it.

Frankfurt	*Wartha;* Herleshausen
Hamburg	*Zarrentin;* Gudow
Hannover	*Marienborn;* Helmstedt
München	*Hirschberg;* Saalebrücke; Rudolphstein

Hours: Crossings are open day and night.

Entry to West Berlin is possible at Drewitz/ Dreilinden on the routes from Frankfurt, Hannover and Munich and at Staaken on the route from Hamburg.

Entry to East Berlin for day visits from West Berlin is at Kochstrasse (Checkpoint Charlie) and Friedrichstrasse. There are no restrictions for tourists of non-German nationality who wish to make a day trip from West to East Berlin, but make sure that this is mentioned on the insurance policy. A minimum exchange (25 marks) of local currency is necessary. Entry visa for a day trip to East Berlin is *DM5* per person.

A booklet entitled *Motoring in Eastern Europe* is available to AA members.

Meersburg on Lake Constance

Boats
A Helmsman's Certificate of Competence is recommended for the German Federal Republic. See page 8 for further information about this and boat documentation.

Breakdown
If your car breaks down, try to move it to the verge of the road so that it does not obstruct traffic flow. A warning triangle must be placed to the rear of the vehicle and hazard warning lights, if fitted to the vehicle, must be used. See also *Breakdown* page 8 and *Warning triangles* page 197.

The ADAC operates a breakdown service, similar to that run by the AA, called the *Strassenwacht.* Patrol cars operate on motorways, on the more important roads and in urban areas. On motorways, patrols are notified by the Motorway Authorities, whom you can contact by using the emergency telephones. The direction of the nearest telephone is indicated by the point of the black triangle on posts alongside the motorways.

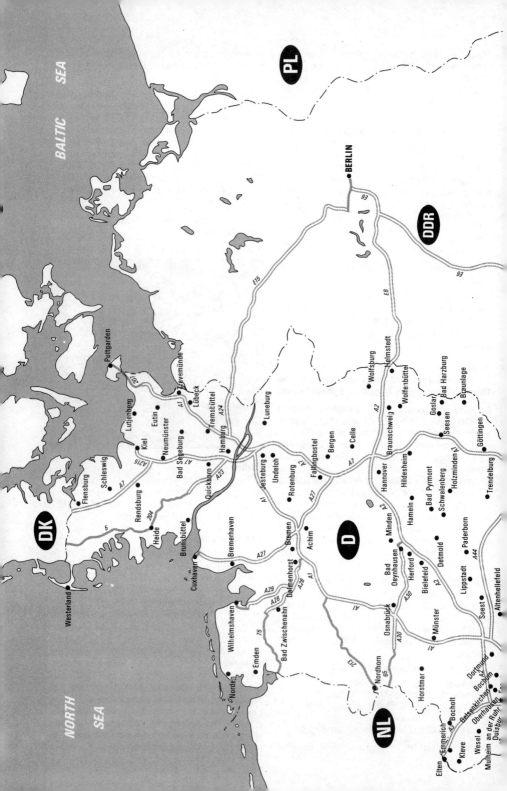

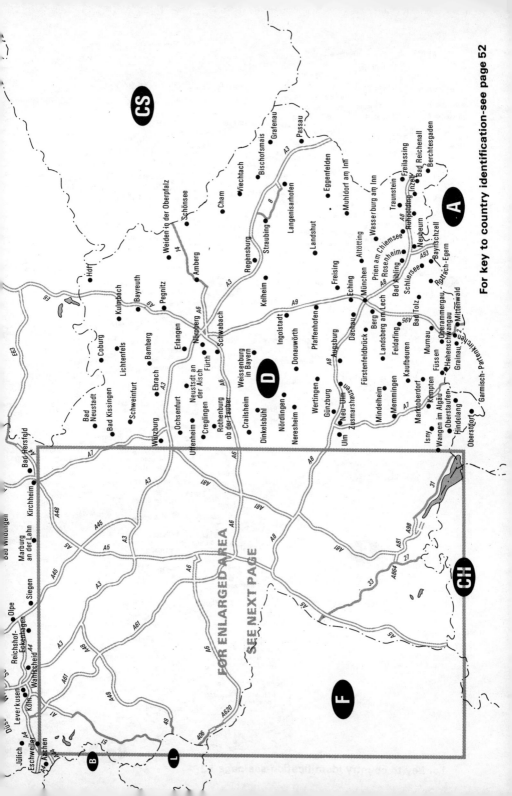

For key to country identification–see page 52

For key to country identification-see page 52

In addition, the Deutscher Touring Automobile Club (DTC), with which the AA is allied, has also introduced a patrol service. The Automobile Club of Germany (AvD) and the Auto Club Europa (ACE) also operate a patrol service. The AA is not associated with these clubs and details are not available.

British Army of the Rhine (BAOR)

Service personnel posted to Germany should consult their Standing Orders or Commanding Officer before taking a car to Germany or using it there. Although enjoying some privileges they will be regarded to some extent as residents in the country and tourist regulations (as outlined in this section) may not apply. For example, a tourist can use a warning triangle not strictly to the German regulations, but a service man will break local regulations unless his conforms.

A leaflet entitled '*Importation of Motor Vehicles into Germany by Members of the British Forces*' is available to AA members.

British Consulates

(See also page 8)
4000 Düsseldorf 30 Nordsternhaus, 14 Georg-Glock-Strasse ☎434281/5. There are also consulates in Berlin, Bremerhaven, Frankfurt/Main, Hamburg, München and Stuttgart.

Currency and banking hours

(See also page 11)
The unit of currency is the Deutsche Mark, which is divided into 100 Pfennig.

Sterling travellers cheques can be exchanged at all banks, savings banks, exchange offices at frontiers, main railway stations, and airports. There is no limit to the sum of money which may be imported or exported, either in German or in foreign currency.

Most banks are open from Monday to Wednesday and Friday 08.30–12.00hrs and 14.00–15.30hrs and Thursday 08.30–12.00hrs and 14.00–17.30hrs; closed on Saturdays. Exchange offices of the Deutsche-Verkehrs-Kredit-Bank are located at main railway stations, and road and rail frontier crossing points. Generally they are open from early morning until late at night.

Dimensions and weight restrictions

Private cars and trailers are restricted to the following dimensions – Cars height: 4 metres; width: 2.5 metres; length: Car/trailer combination 18 metres. A fully-laden trailer without an adequate braking system must not weigh more than 50% of the towing vehicle. A fully-laden trailer with an adequate braking system must not weigh more than the towing vehicle.

Driving licence

(See also page 13)
A valid British driving licence is acceptable in the German Federal Republic. The minimum age at which a visitor may drive a temporarily imported car or motorcycle is 17 years.

Emergency messages to tourists

(See also page 14)
Emergency messages to tourists are broadcast daily on German Radio.

Deutschlandfunk transmitting on 396.8 metres medium wave broadcasts these messages in German after the news at 16.00 and 23.00hrs between May and September.

Saarlandischer Rundfunk transmitting on 211 metres medium wave broadcasts the messages in German at 05.00 and 01.00hrs throughout the year.

Emergency messages are also broadcast by a variety of regional radio stations transmitting on ultra short wavelengths.

Lights

(See also page 17)
Driving on sidelights only is prohibited. When fog, falling snow, or rain substantially affect driving conditions, dipped headlights or fog lamps should be used even during daylight. The use of two fog lamps together with dipped headlamps in such conditions is required by law. Motorcycles without sidecars may use fog lamps.

Rear fog lamps may only be used if, because of fog, visibility is less than 50 metres.

Motoring clubs

(See also page 18)

The principal German motoring clubs are the **Allgemeiner Deutscher Automobil Club** (ADAC) which has its headquarters at Am Westpark 8, 8000 München 70 ☎(089) 76760 and the **Deutscher Touring Automobil Club** (DTC) whose headquarters are at Amalienburgstrasse 23, 8000 Müchen 60 ☎(089) 8111048. Both clubs have offices in the larger towns and office hours are from 08.00–17.00hrs Mon–Fri. The ADAC also has offices at major frontier crossings.

Motorways

A comprehensive motorway (Autobahn) network dominates the road system and takes most of the long distance traffic.

Orange badge scheme for disabled drivers

(See also page 19)
In the German Federal Republic special parking places reserved for disabled drivers are indicated by parking sign (white letter on blue panel) with international disabled symbol added. Provided no other parking facilities are available within the immediate vicinity badge holders may:

a park for a maximum of three hours where parking prohibited sign (red ring and bars on blue background) is displayed. The time of arrival must be shown on the parking disc;
b park beyond the permitted time where a limited duration zone sign (white panel, red ring and diagonal bar on blue background) is displayed;
c park beyond the permitted time where a parking sign (white letter on blue panel) is displayed with an additional panel restricting parking time;
d park during the permitted periods for loading and unloading in pedestrian zones;
e park without charge or time limit at parking meters.

Parking

(See also page 19)
When parking make sure you do not contravene regulations and park in the direction of the traffic flow. Parking is forbidden in the following places: on a main road or one carrying fast-moving traffic; on or near tram lines; within 15 metres (49ft) of a bus or tram stop; above man-hole covers; on the lefthand side of the road (unless the road is one-way). A vehicle is considered to be parked if the driver has left it so that it cannot be immediately removed if required or if it is stopped for more than 3 minutes. When stopping is prohibited under all circumstances, this is indicatd by an international sign. Parking metres and special areas where parking discs are used, are indicated by signs which also show the permitted duration of parking. Disabled drivers may be granted special parking concessions; application should be made to the local traffic authority. Spending the night in a vehicle is tolerated for one night, provided there are no signs to the contrary and the vehicle is lit and parked in a lay-by. The sign showing an eagle in a green triangle (wild-life reserve) prohibits parking outside parking lots.

Passengers

(See also page 19)
Children under 12 are not permitted to travel in a vehicle as front seat passengers when rear seating is available.

Petrol

(See also page 20)
Credit cards Few petrol stations will accept credit cards
Duty-free petrol In addition to the petrol in the vehicle tank up to 10 litres in a can may be imported free of customs duty and tax.
Octane rating Normal benzin (91–94) and Super benzin (98–100).

Postal information

Mail Postcards DM0.70, letters up to 20gm DM1.00.

Post offices There are 15,000 post offices in the German Federal Republic. Opening hours are from 08.00–18.00hrs Monday to Friday and 08.00–14.00hrs Saturday. In some large towns the Head Post Office is open 24hrs a day.

Postcheques

(See also page 21)
Postcheques may be cashed at all post offices for any amount up to a maximum of DM200 per cheque. Counter positions are identified by the words Auskunft, Auszahlungen or Postschecks. See above for post office opening hours.

Priority

(See also Priority including Roundabouts page 22)
On pedestrian crossings (zebra crossings) pedestrians have the right of way over all vehicles except trams. Buses have priority when leaving public bus stops and other vehicles must give way to a bus driver who has signalled his intention to leave the kerb.

Public holidays

Official public holidays in the German Federal Republic for 1985 are given below. See also Public holidays page 22.

January 1 (New Year's Day)
January 6† (Epiphany)
April 5 (Good Friday)
April 8 (Easter Monday)
May 1 (May Day)
May 16 (Ascension Day)
May 27 (Whit Monday)
June 2† (Corpus Christi)
June 17 (Berlin Day)
August 15 (Assumption)
November 1 (All Saints Day)
November 20 (Repentance Day)
December 25 (Christmas Day)
December 26 (Second day of Christmas)
†Sunday

Roads including holiday traffic
(See also *Road conditions* page 23)
The *Bundesstrassen* or state roads vary in quality. In the north and in the touring areas of the Rhine Valley, Black Forest and Bavaria the roads are good and well graded.

Traffic at weekends increases considerably during the school holidays which are from July to mid September. In order to ease congestion, heavy lorries are prohibited on all roads at weekends from approximately mid June to the end of August and generally on all Sundays and public holidays.

Road signs
(See also page 23)
A blue rectangular sign with, for example, '70/110km' in white – indicates a recommended speed range.

A blue rectangular sign with a white arrow pointing upwards and 'U' and a figure in white – indicates a diversion for motorway traffic.

Shopping hours
Generally these are: *food shops* from Monday to Friday 07.00–13.00/14.00–18.30hrs, Saturdays 07.00–13.00hrs; *department stores* from Monday to Friday 09.00–18.30hrs, Saturdays 09.00–14.00hrs. Some shops close for lunch between 13.00 and 15.00hrs.

Speed limits
(See also page 25)
The speed limit in built-up areas is 50kph (31mph) unless otherwise indicated by signs. The beginning of a built-up area is indicated by the placename sign. Outside built-up areas the limit for private cars is 100kph (62mph) unless otherwise signposted. Motorways (*Autobahnen*), dual carriageways and roads with at least two marked lanes in each direction, which are not specifically signposted have a recommended speed limit of 130kph (81mph). Vehicles towing a caravan or trailer are limited to 80kph (49mph). All lower limits must be adhered to. Anyone driving so slowly that a line of vehicles has formed behind him must permit the following vehicles to pass. If necessary he must stop at a suitable place to allow this.

Note Outside built-up areas, motor vehicles to which a special speed limit applies, as well as vehicles with trailers with a combined length of more than 7 metres (23ft), must keep sufficient distance from the preceding vehicle so that an overtaking vehicle may pull in.

Spiked, studded or snow tyres
(See also page 10)
The use of *spiked tyres* is not permitted on German registered vehicles. However, foreign registered vehicles may use them in a restricted zone near the German/Austrian border, but only on ordinary roads not motorways. The use of *snow chains* is permitted and vehicles fitted with them must not exceed 50kph (31mph).

Tourist Information offices
(See also page 25)
The UK office of the German National Tourist Office is in London at 61 Conduit Street, W1R 0EN ☎01-734 2600 (recorded message service Monday to Friday 10.00–13.00hrs and 14.00–17.00hrs). In the Federal Republic there are regional tourist associations – (DFV) whilst in most towns there are local tourist offices, usually situated near the railway station or town hall. Any of these organisations will be pleased to help tourists with information and hotel and other accommodation. The offices are usually open from 08.30 to 18.00hrs but in larger towns until 20.00hrs.

Traffic lights
(See also page 25)
At some intersections with several lanes going in different directions, there are lights for each lane; watch the light arrow for your lane.

Using the telephone
(See also page 26)
Insert coin **after** lifting receiver, dialling tone continuous tone. When making calls to subscribers within the German Federal Republic precede number with relevant area code (shown in parentheses against town entry in gazetteer). Use three pfennig coins (two in some callboxes) for local calls and *DM*1 or 5 coins for national and international calls. *International callbox identification* Green sign. *Telephone rate* Charges are based on units of time, 1 unit = 10.667 seconds, the cost is *DM*0.23. Many hotels and garages provide, as a service, direct line telephones but charges are likely to be up to double the public rate. *What to dial for the Irish Republic* 00 353. *What to dial for the UK* 00 44.

Warning triangle
The use of a warning triangle is compulsory for all vehicles except two-wheelers. The triangle must be placed on the road about 100 metres (109yds) behind the vehicle to warn following traffic of any obstruction. Vehicles over 2,500kg (2tons 9cwt 24lb) must also carry a yellow flashing light.

Although the warning triangle sold by the AA does not correspond exactly to the type prescribed for Germany, it is legally acceptable for use by *bona fide* tourists. See also *Warning triangles/Hazard warnings lights* page 26.

Wheel chains
(See also page 10)
These must not be used on some free roads. In winter months the ADAC hires out chains, either the Matic or the Endlos type, for cars and caravans. The construction of some vehicles allows only the use of the Matic chains. Chains can only be returned to ADAC offices and only during the hours of opening. On production of a valid AA membership card, chains may be hired at the following reduced charges.

Deposit   members (DM)   non-members (DM)
Matic   100   100
Endlos   100   100
Hire charge per day (days of collection and return are both counted as whole days)
            members (DM)   non-members (DM)
Matic   4.00   6.00
Endlos   3.50   5.00

If the chains are used a fee of *DM*10.00 (members) and *DM*20.00 (non-members) is payable for the Matic type and *DM*7.50 (members) and *DM*15.00 (non-members) for the Endlos type.

If chains are lost or damaged, or their wear exceeds the normal, the full selling price is charged.

If the deposit receipt is lost, the chains can be returned only to the station from which they were hired.

Chains are considered to have been used if the seal on the packaging has been removed in which case the hire charge is calculated on the basis of the fees for used chains for the whole period of hire, irrespective of the actual number of days in use. The maximum period of hire is 60 days. Reservations are not possible and the ADAC does not dispatch the chains by post.

Chains are made in several sizes, but, as foreign-made tyres may be different, it is not guaranteed that the appropriate size will be available; in this case alternative arrangements must be made. Further details may be obtained from the ADAC Head Office, department 'Strassendienste Schneeykettenverleih', 8 München 70, Am Westpark 8 ☎(089) 76760. (No wheel chains are actually hired out from head office.)

Speed must be restricted to 50kph (31mph) when using chains.

Germany

ALSFELD
Hessen (☎06631)

★*Schwalbennest* Pfarrwiesenweg 14
☎5061

🏠28 **P**

🕭*Hartman* Hersfelder Str 81 ☎4044 Opl

🕭*W Klöss* Grünbergerstr 72 ☎3005
M/c **P** Frd

ALTENA
Nordrhein-Westfalen (☎02352)

K Lienkämper Rahmedestr 141 ☎50430
M/c **P** AR BL

ALTENAHR
Rheinland-Pfalz (☎02643)

★★*Post* Brückenstr 2 ☎2098

rm55 ⇔20 🏠20 🕭 **P** Lift 𝄐
sB30−35 sB ⇔ 🏠45−55 dB60−68
dB ⇔ 🏠76−98 Pool mountains

At **MAYSCHOSS** (2km NE)

★★*Lochmühle* (BW) Bundesstr 62
☎1345 tx861766
⇔ 🏠70 🕭 **P** Lift 𝄐 Pool

ALTENHELLEFELD
Nordrhein-Westfalen (☎02934)

★★★*GutFunkenhof* ☎1012 tx7246682
⇔ 🏠32 A8rm 🕭 **P** sB ⇔ 🏠65−95
dB ⇔ 🏠110−145 M12−32 Pool

ALTGLASHÜTTEN See **FELDBERG IM SCHWARZWALD**

ALTÖTTING
Bayern (☎08671)

★★★*Post* (ROM) Kapellpl 2
☎5040 tx56962
Closed Xmas Day
rm90 ⇔12 🏠78 🕭 Lift
sB ⇔ 🏠45−88 dB ⇔ 🏠74−120

AMBERG
Bayern (☎09261)

★*Goldenes Lamm* Rathausstr 6 ☎21041
rm24 🏠5 🕭 **P**

🕭*Weiss* Bayreuther Str 26 ☎62120
M/c **P** Frd

ANDERNACH
Rheinland-Pfalz (☎02632)

★★*Rhein* Rheinpromenade ☎42240
15 Mar−Oct
rm25 ⇔19 🕭 **P** Lift sB30−35
sB ⇔ 🏠38−40 dB60−65
dB ⇔ 🏠70−75 M14−18

★*Anker* K-Adenauer Allee 21 ☎42907
rm28 ⇔2 🏠18 🕭 **P** sBfr30
sB ⇔ 🏠fr45 dBfr60 dB ⇔ 🏠fr80 lake

🕭*R-Heinemann* Koblenzerstr 56
☎46016 **P** Frd

🕭*E Kirsch* Fullscheuerweg 36 ☎492401
P Ren

AROLSEN
Hessen (☎05691)

★★★*Dorint Schlosshotel Arolsen* (GS)
Grosse Allee 1 ☎3091 tx994521

⇔ 🏠55 **P** Lift 𝄐 sB ⇔ 🏠97−111
dB ⇔ 🏠164−174 Pool

ASCHAFFENBURG
Bayern (☎06021)

★★★*Aschaffenburger Hof* Frohinnstr
11 ☎21441 tx4188736
rm62 ⇔30 🏠32 🕭 **P** Lift 𝄐

★★★*Romantik Hotel-Post*
Goldbacherstr 19 ☎21333 tx04188736
rm75 ⇔45 🏠30 🕭 **P** Lift 𝄐 Pool

🕭*Amberg* Würzburger Str 67 ☎91018
P AR BL Fia Lnc

🕭*Auto-Haus* Pappelweg 8, Nilkheim
☎8588 **P** Ren

ASENDORF See **JESTEBURG**

ASPERG
Baden-Württemberg (☎07141)

★★★*Adler* Stuttgarter Str 2 ☎63001
tx7264603
rm65 ⇔ 🏠63 🕭 **P** Lift 𝄐
sB ⇔ 🏠89−115 dB98 dB ⇔ 🏠130−210

ASSMANNSHAUSEN
Hessen (☎06722)
See also **RÜDESHEIM**

★★*Anker* Rheinstr 5 ☎2912
Apr−Oct
rm29 ⇔3 🏠31 A22rm 🕭 **P**

★★*Café Post* Rheinuferstr 2A ☎2326
Mar−Nov
rm16 ⇔7 🏠2 🕭 **P** mountains

★★*Krone* Rheinuferstr 10 ☎2036
15 Mar−15 Nov
rm80 ⇔28 🏠118 🕭 **P** Lift 𝄐 Pool

ATTENDORN
Nordrhein-Westfalen (☎02722)

★★*Burghotel Schnellenberg* (GS)
(3.5km W) ☎4081 tx876732
Closed 2−29 Jan
⇔45 🕭 **P** sB ⇔70−90 dB ⇔130−160
🕭

AUGSBURG
Bayern (☎0821)

☆☆☆☆*Holiday Inn Turmhotel*
Wittelsbacher Park ☎577087 tx533225
⇔185 **P** Lift 𝄐 sB ⇔150 dB ⇔210
Pool

★★★*Drei Mohren* (SRS) Maximillianstr
40 ☎510031 tx53710
rm110 ⇔90 🏠20 🕭 **P** Lift 𝄐
sB ⇔ 🏠109−139 dB ⇔ 🏠178−208

★★*Ost* Fuggerstr 4−6 (n.rest) ☎33088
tx533576
rm58 🏠46 **P** Lift 𝄐 sB49 sB 🏠70−80
dB84 dB 🏠110−125

★*Post* Fuggerstr 7 ☎36044
rm50 ⇔10 🏠30 🕭 **P** Lift 𝄐 sB45
sB ⇔ 🏠60−80 dB70 dB ⇔ 🏠90−120

🕭*Auto-Burger* Ulmer Str 34−38
☎414004 BL Fia Lnc

🕭*Listle* Kriegshaberstr 58 ☎403055 **P**
Ren

BACHARACH
Rheinland-Pfalz (☎06743)

★★*Altköinischer Hof* Blücherstr 2
☎1339
Apr−Oct
rm45 ⇔2 🏠14 🕭 **P** Lift sB35−50
sB ⇔ 🏠48−60 dB58−68
dB ⇔ 🏠78−85 mountains

BAD Each place preceded by 'Bad' is
listed under the name that follows it.

BADEN-BADEN
Baden-Württemberg (☎07221)

★★★★★*Brenner's Park* Schillerstr 6
☎3530 tx781261
rm109 ⇔97 🏠9 **P** Lift 𝄐
sB ⇔ 🏠176−316 dB ⇔ 🏠232−482
M65−85 Pool

★★★★*Badhotel Badischer Hof* (SRS)
Lange Str 47 ☎22827 tx781121
⇔140 🕭 𝄐 sB ⇔127−169
dB ⇔158−272

★★★★*Europälscher Hof* (SRS)
Kaiserallee 2 ☎23561 tx781188
⇔150 **P** Lift 𝄐 sB ⇔115−163
dB ⇔146−264 M42 mountains

☆☆☆☆*Holdiay Inn Sporthotel*
Falkenstr 2 ☎33011
⇔121 🕭 **P** Lift 𝄐 sB ⇔151
dB ⇔232 M25St% Pool

★★★*Golf* (2km SW) Fremersbergstr 113
☎2369 tx781174
Apr−Oct
rm85 ⇔69 🏠16 🕭 **P** Lift 𝄐
sB ⇔ 🏠95−140 dB ⇔ 🏠130−210
M30−36 🕭 Pool mountains

★★★*Hirsch* Hirschstr 1 (n.rest)
☎23896 tx781193
rm56 ⇔24 🏠32 🕭 **P** Lift 𝄐
sB ⇔ 🏠89−119 dB ⇔ 🏠145−195

★★★*Waldhotel Fischkultur* Gaisbach
91 ☎71025
15 Feb−20 Dec
rm46 ⇔17 🏠3 A16rm 🕭 **P** Lift
𝄐 sB62 sB ⇔ 🏠84 dB96 dB ⇔ 🏠143
T% mountains

★★*Allee-Hotel Bären* Haupstr 36
☎71046 tx781291
rm80 ⇔72 🕭 **P** Lift 𝄐 sB ⇔70
dB ⇔100

★★*Markt* Marktpl 17 ☎22747
rm27 ⇔3 🏠8 **P** Lift

★★*Müller* Lange Str 34 (n.rest) ☎23211
rm24 ⇔20 **P** Lift

★*Bischoff* Römerpl 2 (n.rest) ☎22378
Feb−15 Nov
🏠23 **P** Lift sB 🏠50 dB 🏠80

★*Römerhof* Sofienstr 25 (n.rest) ☎23415
Feb−15 Dec
rm27 🏠18 **P** Lift sB42 sB 🏠55−60
dB80 dB 🏠90−95

&OH *P Nagel* Lange Str 104 ☎22672 **P** BL

&OE **Scheibel** Hubertustr 19 ☎62005 Frd

At **MUMMELSEE** (29km S on Schwarzwaldhochstr)

★★**Berghotel Kandel** ☎1088
20 Dec–10 Nov
rm25 ⇄10 ⋒5 **P** sB43 sB ⇄ ⋒45
dB75 dB ⇄ ⋒85 Pool lake

BADENWEILER
Baden-Württemberg (☎07632)

★★★**Römerbad** Schlosspl 1 ☎700 tx772933
⇄114 ⋒ **P** Lift ☽ sB ⇄170–210
dB ⇄260–310 M40–50 ✆ Pool mountains

★★★**Park** (BW) E-Eisenlohrstr 15
☎710 tx17763210
2 Mar–5 Nov
rm87 ⇄80 ⋒7 ⋒ **P** Lift ☽
sB ⇄ ⋒130–145 dB ⇄ ⋒200–230
Pool mountains

★★★**Sonne** (ROM) Moltkestr 4 ☎5053
Feb–mid Nov
rm45 ⇄25 ⋒20 ⋒ **P** sB ⇄ ⋒68–75
dB ⇄ ⋒110–160

BAMBERG
Bayern (☎0951)

★★★**Bamberger Hof-Bellevue**
Schönleinspl 4 ☎22216 tx662867
rm39 ⇄24 ⋒14 ⋒ **P** Lift ☽ sB52
sB ⇄ ⋒80–100 dB72–92
dB ⇄ ⋒107–137 M alc

★★**Messerschmitt** (ROM) Langestr 41
☎27866
rm12 ⇄4 ⋒8 ⋒ **P** sB ⇄ ⋒50–60
dB ⇄ ⋒95–135 M14–34

★*Straub* Ludwigstr 31 (n.rest) ☎25838
rm38 ⇄5 ⋒2 ⋒ **P** ☽

&OSchuberth Siechenstr 87 ☎62253
M/c **P** Ren

At **BUG** (4km S)

★★**Buger Hof** am Regnitzufer 1 ☎56054
rm32 ⋒14 ⋒ **P**

BAYREUTH
Bayern (☎0921)

★★★**Bayerischer Hof** Bahnhofstr 14
☎22081 tx642737
rm62 ⇄34 ⋒18 ⋒ **P** Lift ☽ sB48
sB ⇄ ⋒60–95 dB95 dB ⇄ ⋒100–160
M alc

BAYRISCHZELL
Bayern (☎08023)

★★*Alpenrose* Schlierseestr 100 ☎5620
rm40 ⇄10 ⋒30 A4rm ⋒ **P**
mountains

BERCHTESGADEN
Bayern (☎08652)

★★★**Geiger** Stanggass ☎5055
tx56222
rm55 ⇄40 ⋒12 ⋒ **P**
sB ⇄ ⋒85–150 dB ⇄ ⋒130–260 Pool
mountains

Germany

★★*Königliche Villa* (GS) Kalbersteinstr
4 ☎5097
rm35 ⇄3 ⋒29 **P** Pool mountains

&OH **Buchwinkler** Bahnhofstr 21 ☎4087
P Aud Por VW

&OG **Köppl** Hindenburg Allee 1 ☎2615
P Aud VW

BERG
Bayern (☎08151)

At **LEONI** (1km S)

★★★**Dorint Starnberger See** ☎5911
tx0526483
⇄ ⋒70 ⋒ **P** Lift ☽ sB ⇄ ⋒99–109
dB ⇄ ⋒138–160 Pool lake

BERGEN
Niedersachsen (☎05051)

★**Kohlmann** Lukenstr 6 ☎3014
⇄14 ⋒ **P** sB ⋒35–45 dB ⋒75–80

&OK *Wehrhahn* Tilsiterstr 14 ☎4540 **P**
Frd

BERGZABERN (BAD)
Rheinland-Pfalz (☎06343)

★★★**Park** Kurtalstr 83 ☎2415
Mar–7 Jan
rm41 ⇄16 ⋒19 A6rm ⋒ **P** Lift
sB ⇄ ⋒38–45 dB45–60
dB ⇄ ⋒76–145 Pool mountains

BERLIN
(☎030)

★★★★★**Bristol Kempinski Berlin**
Kurfürstendamm 27 ☎881091 tx183553
⇄358 **P** Lift ☽ sB ⇄ ⋒170–215
dB ⇄ ⋒219–279 Pool

★★★★★**Inter-Continental Berlin**
Budapester Str 2 ☎26020 tx184380
⇄600 ⋒ **P** Lift ☽ sB ⇄ ⋒158–228
dB ⇄ ⋒221–291 M27 Pool

★★★★**Ambassador**(ETAP)Bayreuther
Str 42 ☎21902-0 tx184259
rm119 ⇄111 ⋒9 **P** ⋒ Lift ☽
sB ⇄ ⋒135–164 dB ⇄ ⋒178–208
Pool

★★★★**Berlin** (ETAP) Kurfürstenstr 62
☎269291 tx184332
rm255 ⇄170 ⋒85 **P** Lift ☽
sB ⇄ ⋒198–135 dB ⇄ ⋒150–175

★★★★**Franke** A-Achilles Str 57
☎8921097 tx0184857
⇄60 ⋒ **P** Lift ☽ sB ⇄68–80
dB ⇄126 Pool

★★★★**Ibis Europäischer Hof**
Messendamm 10 ☎302011 tx182882
⇄190 **P** Lift sB ⇄fr86 dB ⇄fr112

★★★**Plaza** Knesebeckstr 63 (n.rest)
☎88413-0 tx184181
rm131 ⇄120 ⋒11 **P** Lift ☽
sB ⇄ ⋒88 dB ⇄ ⋒126

★★★**Savoy** (BW) Fasanenstr 9–10,
Charlottenburg ☎310654 tx184292
⇄114 **P** Lift ☽ sB ⇄110–120
dB ⇄160–195

★★★★**Schweizerhof Berlin**
Budapesterstr 21–31 ☎26961 tx185501
rm431 ⇄312 ⋒81 ⋒ **P** Lift ☽
sB ⇄ ⋒122–177 dB ⇄ ⋒194–219
Mfr30 Pool

★★★**Alsterhof** Würzburger Str 1
☎219960 tx183484
⇄ ⋒140 ⋒ **P** Lift ☽ sB ⇄ ⋒129
dB ⇄ ⋒148–168 Pool

☆☆☆**Crest (See page 51)** am ADAC
Haus, Güntzelstr 14 (n.rest) ☎870241
tx182948
⇄110 **P** Lift ☽ sB ⇄ ⋒115 dB ⇄145

★★★**Eurotel Arosa** Lietzenburgerstr
79–81 ☎880050 tx183397
⇄90 ⋒ Lift sB ⇄80–98
dB ⇄120–160 M20 Pool

★★★**Hamburg** Landgrafenstr 4
☎269161 tx184974
⇄240 ⋒ **P** Lift ☽ sB ⇄103–107
dB ⇄128–156 M18

★★★**Lichtburg** Paderbornerstr 10
☎8918041 tx0184208
⇄63 ⋒ **P** Lift ☽ sB ⇄70–80
dB ⇄ ⋒122 Pool

☆☆☆**Novotel** Ohmstr 4–6 ☎381061
tx181415
⇄119 **P** Lift ☽ sB95–114
dB ⇄155–175 M alc Pool

★★★**Zoo** Kurfürstendamm 25
☎883091 tx183825
rm143 ⇄105 ⋒30 ⋒ **P** Lift ☽
sB ⇄98–110 dB ⇄160–170 M20

★★*Astrid* Bleibtreustr 20, Charlottenburg
(n.rest) ☎8815959
rm11 ⋒6 Lift

★★**Stephanie** Bleibtreustr 38–39,
Charlottenburg (n.rest) ☎8818073
tx184216
rm40 ⇄6 ⋒11 ⋒ **P** Lift ☽ sB58–63
sB ⇄ ⋒88–98 dB88–92
dB ⇄ ⋒106–126

★**Charlottenburger Hof** Stuttgarter pl 14
☎3244819
rm35 ⋒6 **P** ☽ sB36 dB72

&OW **Hinz** Naumannstr 79 ☎7843051 BL

Butenuth Forckenbeckstr 94 ☎82051
Frd

&OH **Richtzenhain** Kantstr 126
☎3122020 **P** BL

&OSturm Grünhofer Weg ☎3311075 **P**
Opl

&OF *Wachs* Stettiner Str 10 ☎4930067 **P**
BL Chy

BERNKASTEL-KUES
Rheinland-Pfalz (☎06531)

★★**Burg-Landshut** Gestade 11,
Bernkastel ☎3019 tx466422
Mar–15 Nov & 20 Dec–3 Jan

rm35 ⇔5 🛏17 🍴 P 🌙 sB30
sB ⇔ 🛏45 dB55 dB ⇔ 🛏70 mountains

★★Drei Könige Bahnhofstr 1, Kues
(n.rest) ☎2327

15 Mar–15 Nov
rm40 ⇔9 🛏31 🍴 P Lift sB ⇔ 🛏84
dB ⇔ 🛏135

★★Post Gestade 17, Bernkastel ☎3001

Closed Jan
rm17 ⇔3 🛏1 🍴

★★Sonnenlay Haupt Str 47, Wehlen
(4km NW) ☎6496

rm15 ⇔2 🛏9 A2rm P

★Graacher Tor ☎2566

Apr–Oct
rm33 ⇔5 🛏7 A12rm P

BIBERACH AN DER RISS
Baden-Württemberg (☎07351)

★★★Reith Ulmer Str ☎7828
rm43 ⇔23 🛏8 🍴 P Lift 🌙 sB40
sB ⇔ 🛏60 dB ⇔ 🛏85–98

Schwaben Steigmühlstr 34 ☎7878 M/c P
Frd Hon

BIELEFELD
Nordrhein-Westfalen(☎0521)

☆☆☆Novotel am Johannisberg 5
☎124051 tx932991

⇔119 P Lift 🌙 Pool

★★Waldhotel Brand's Busch
Furtwänglerstr 52 ☎24093
⇔65 🍴 P Lift sB ⇔65–79
dB ⇔88–120 M15–30

🅿Sparrenburg Schildescher Str
95 ☎82011 P Frd

BIERSDORF See **BITBURG**

BIESSENHOFEN See **KAUFBEUREN**

BINGEN
Rheinland-Pfalz(☎06721)

★★★Rheinhotel Starkenburger Hof
Rheinkai 1 ☎14341

15 Feb–20 Dec
rm30 ⇔17 🍴 P 🌙 sB31
sB ⇔ 🛏45–51 dB62 dB ⇔ 🛏88–98

★★Rheinterrassen Museumstr ☎12021
⇔11 🍴 P dB ⇔90

🅿Pieroth Mainzerstr 439 ☎17355 P Frd

BISCHOFSMAIS
Bayern(☎09920)

★★★Wastlsäge (BW) (DPn) L-Mueller-
Weg 3, Wastlsäg ☎216 tx69158

18 Dec–23 Oct
rm91 ⇔62 🛏29 A46rm 🍴 P Lift 🌙
sB ⇔67 dB ⇔ 🛏124 🏊 Pool

BITBURG
Rheinland-Pfalz(☎06561)

★Mosella Karenweg 11 ☎3147
rm11 🛏4 🍴 P sB29 sB ⇔ 🛏33 dB52
dB ⇔ 🛏58

🅿Auto Jegen Saarstr 46 ☎1054 Ren

🅿C Metzger Mötscherstr 49 ☎7004 P
AR BL

Germany

At **BIERSDORF** (12km NW)

★★★Dorint Sporthotel Südeifel am
Stausee ☎(06569) tx4729607
⇔ 🛏210 P Lift 🌙 sB ⇔ 🛏77–102
dB ⇔ 🛏124–164 🏊 Pool lake

BLANKENHEIM
Nordrhein-Westfalen(☎02449)

★★Schlossblick Nonnenbacher Weg
2–4 ☎238

20 Dec–15 Nov
rm34 ⇔1 🛏23 🍴 P sB30–32
sB ⇔ 🛏39–46 dB60–64 dB ⇔ 🛏76–80
Pool lake

BÖBLINGEN
Baden-Württemberg(☎07031)

☆☆☆Novotel O-Lilienthal Str 18
☎23071 tx7265438
⇔117 P Lift 🌙 sB ⇔112 dB ⇔132
M20 Pool

BOCHOLT
Nordrhein-Westfalen(☎02871)

🅿Auto Schrieber Münsterstr 11
☎8348 P BL

BOCHUM
Nordrhein-Westfalen(☎0234)

☆☆☆Novotel am Stadionsring 22
☎594041 tx825429
⇔118 P Lift 🌙 sB ⇔112–117
dB ⇔150–155 Pool

☆☆Arcade Universitätstr 3 ☎33311
🛏168 P Lift sB 🛏73 dB 🛏92–124

🅿Saurland Hanielstr 11 ☎74044 P BL
Dat

BONN
Nordrhein-Westfalen(☎0228)

★★★★ETAP Königshof Adenauerallee
9–11 ☎26010 tx886535
⇔137 🍴 P Lift 🌙 sB ⇔130–170
dB ⇔210–220 M alc

★★★Sternhotel Markt 8 ☎654455
tx886508
rm67 ⇔40 🛏27 P Lift 🌙
sB ⇔ 🛏81–99 dB ⇔ 🛏107–132 M alc

★★Beethoven Rheingasse 26
☎631411 tx886467
rm60 ⇔42 🛏6 🍴 P Lift 🌙
sB40–120 sB ⇔ 🛏120
dB ⇔ 🛏120–140 M15

★★Bergischer Hof Münsterpl 23
☎633441
rm28 ⇔5 🛏6 Lift sB42–52
sB ⇔ 🛏60–70 dB91 dB ⇔ 🛏106–114

★★Mozart Mozartstr 1 (n.rest) ☎635198
rm32 ⇔11 🛏14 P Lift 🌙

★★Savoy Berliner Freiheit 17 (n.rest)
☎651356
rm24 ⇔7 🛏9 P Lift 🌙 sB39
sB ⇔ 🛏45–55 dB65 dB ⇔ 🛏75–85

🅿Auto-Hessel Pützchen Chausee
43–53 ☎462088 P AR BL Hon

🅿J Knüfker Lievelingsweg
2–4 ☎670444 P Chy Hon Ren

Mahlberg K-Frowein Str 2 ☎636656 BL

At **GODESBERG (BAD)** (7km SW on road
No9)

★★★Godesberg auf den Godesberg 5
☎316071 tx885503
rm14 ⇔1 🛏13 P 🌙 sB ⇔ 🛏80–120
dB ⇔ 🛏110–150 M19 mountains

★★★Insel Theaterpl 5–7 ☎364082
tx885592
rm65 ⇔28 🛏37 P Lift 🌙
sB ⇔ 🛏81–94 dB ⇔ 🛏135–145 M8–25

★★★Park am Kurpark 1 (m.rest)
☎363081 tx885463
rm52 ⇔26 🛏20 P Lift 🌙
sB ⇔ 🛏80–100 dB ⇔ 🛏115–150

★★★Rheinhotel Dreesen Rheinstr
45–49 ☎349970 tx885417
⇔65 🍴 P Lift 🌙 sB ⇔ 🛏89–159
dB ⇔ 🛏140–190 M alc

★★Rheinland Rhienallee 17 ☎353087
rm30 ⇔10 🛏16 A11rm P 🌙

★Sonnenhang Mainzerstr 275 ☎346820
rm11 ⇔1 🛏5 🍴 P 🌙 sB31–33
sB ⇔ 🛏36–42 dB60 dB ⇔ 🛏69
mountains

At **RÖTTGEN** (7km S on 257)

☆☆☆Bonn Reichsstr 1 ☎251021
tx8869505

⇔43 🍴 🌙

BONN AIRPORT See **KÖLN**

BONNDORF
Baden-Württemberg(☎07703)

★★Schwarzwald Rothausstr 7 ☎421

15 Dec–15 Nov
rm68 ⇔13 🛏26 A27rm 🍴 P Lift
sBfr41 sB ⇔ 🛏48–55 dB78–86
dB ⇔ 🛏92–106 M7–32 Pool mountains

★Germania Martinstr 66 ☎281

Closed Nov
rm8 ⇔1 🛏3 P sB25 ⇔ 🛏33–50 dB50
dB ⇔ 🛏55–65

🅿O Jung Rathausstr 10 ☎588 P Frd

BOPPARD
Rheinland-Pfalz(☎06742)

★★★Bellevue (BW) Rheinallee 41–42
☎1020 tx426310
rm82 ⇔45 🛏37 P Lift 🌙
sB ⇔ 🛏80–105 dB ⇔ 🛏110–135 Mfr25
🏊 Pool

★★★Klostergut Jakobsberg (GS)
(12km N via B9 to Spay) ☎3061 tx426323
⇔ 🛏105 P Lift 🌙 sB ⇔ 🛏90–140
dB ⇔ 🛏130–220 M25–43 alc 🏊

☆☆Ebertor Heerstr (B9) ☎2081
tx426310

Apr–Oct
🛏58 🍴 P 🌙 sB 🛏fr64 dB 🛏fr86
Mfr23 🏊

★★Günther Rheinallee 40 (n.rest)
☎2335

15 Jan–16 Dec
rm19 ⇋18 P Lift sB25–30 sB ⇋30–38
dB ⇋ 🛏50–76 St%

★★Rheinkrone Mainzer Str 4 ☎5088
Apr–Oct
🛏36 P sB 🛏45–60 dB 🛏72–90

★★Rheinlust Rheinallee 27–30 ☎3001
tx426319
Apr–Oct
rm91 ⇋11 🛏62 A38rm 🏠 P Lift 𝄐

★Hunsrücker Hof Steinstr 26 ☎2433
Closed Dec
rm26 ⇋2 🛏12 A2rm P 𝄐

BRAUBACH
Rheinland-Pfalz(☎02627)

★Hammer Untermarktstr 15 ☎336
Closed Jan
rm11 ⇋1 🛏4 🏠 P

BRAUNLAGE
Niedersachsen(☎05520)

★★★★Maritim Berghotel am
Pfaffensteig ☎3051 tx96261
⇋300 🏠 P Lift 𝄐 sB ⇋104–164
dB ⇋166–276 ☞ Pool mountains

★★Tanne (ROM) Herzog-Wilhelm-Str 8
☎1034
rm22 ⇋21 A10rm P sB ⇋ 🛏60–80
dB ⇋ 🛏90–150

BRAUNSCHWEIG (BRUNSWICK)
Niedersachsen(☎0531)

★★★★Atrium (SRS) Berliner Pl 3
☎73001 tx952576
rm130 ⇋98 🛏32 P Lift 𝄐
sB ⇋ 🛏115–160 dB ⇋ 🛏165–260

★★★Forsthaus Hamburgerstr 72
☎32801
rm49 ⇋5 🛏24 🏠 P Lift 𝄐 sB60
sB ⇋ 🛏98 dB ⇋ 🛏100–135

☆☆☆Mövenpick Welfenhof ☎48170
tx952777
⇋122 🏠 P Lift 𝄐 sB ⇋127–147
dB ⇋154–174 Mfr18 Pool

★★Frühlings Bankpl 7 ☎49317
rm60 ⇋18 🛏22 🏠 P Lift 𝄐
sB ⇋ 🛏60–80 dB ⇋ 🛏90–120

☝Niedersachsen Hildesheimer Str 25
☎54052 M/c P Frd

☝Opel-Dürkop Helmstedter Str 60
☎7031 Opl Vau

BREDENEY See **ESSEN**

BREISACH
Baden-Württemberg(☎07667)

★★★Münster Münsterbergstr 23
☎7071 tx772687
Closed 7–20 Jan
rm42 ⇋21 🛏21 🏠 P Lift 𝄐
sB ⇋ 🛏63–67 dB ⇋ 🛏102–150 St25%
Pool

BREISIG (BAD)
Rheinland-Pfalz(☎02633)

Germany

★Vater & Sohn Zehnerstr 78 ☎9148
rm8 ⇋1 🛏2 P sB34–37
sB ⇋ 🛏47–50 dB68–74 dB ⇋ 🛏84–94

BREITNAU
Baden-Württemberg(☎07652)

★★★Kreuz Dorfstr 1 ☎1388
20 Dec–2 Nov
⇋ 🛏17 🏠 P

BREITSCHEID See **DÜSSELDORF**

BREMEN
Bremen(☎0421)

★★★★Park (SRS) im Bürgerpark
☎34080 tx0244343
rm150 ⇋114 🛏36 🏠 P Lift 𝄐
sB170–185 dB ⇋ 🛏230–260

★★★Columbus Bahnhofspl 5
☎314161 tx244688
rm140 ⇋79 🛏28 🏠 P Lift 𝄐
sB ⇋ 🛏110–160 dB ⇋ 🛏130–220

☆☆☆Crest (See page 51) A-Bebel Allee
4 ☎23870 tx244560
⇋ 🛏147 P Lift 𝄐 sB ⇋ 🛏139
dB ⇋ 🛏182–185

★★★Überseehotel (ETAP) Wachtstr
27–29 ☎320197 tx246501
⇋135 P Lift sB ⇋85–190
dB ⇋115–130 M alc

Auto-Handelshaus Stresemannstr
9 ☎499040 Frd
☝Deutschland Hastedter Heer Str
303–305 ☎492074 Chy

At **BRINKUM** (4km S)

☆☆Atlas G-Daimler Str 3 ☎874037
🛏30 🏠 P sB 🛏55–70 dB 🛏80–110

BREMERHAVEN
Bremen(☎0471)

★★★Nordsee-Hotel-Naber T-Heusspl
☎47001 tx238881
rm101 ⇋56 🛏41 🏠 P Lift 𝄐 sB60
sB ⇋ 🛏68–132 dB ⇋ 🛏136–159

★★Haverkamp Schlesigerstr 27
☎45031 tx238679
rm82 ⇋30 🛏52 P Lift 𝄐
sB ⇋ 🛏70–95 dB ⇋ 🛏104–140 Pool

BRINKUM See **BREMEN**

BRODENBACH
Rheinland-Pfalz(☎02605)

★★Peifer Moselstr 69 (1.5km W) ☎756
15 Jan–20 Dec
rm20 🛏11 🏠 P Lift Pool

★★Post Rhein-Mosel Str 21 ☎3048
15 Mar–15 Nov
rm28 ⇋4 🛏10 A9rm 🏠 P lake

BRUCHSAL
Baden-Württemberg(☎07251)

☝Hetzel Murgstr 12 ☎2283 P BL Lada

BRÜCKENAU (BAD)
Bayern(☎09741)

★★★Dorint Kurhotel H-von-Bibra Str
13 ☎850 tx17974
⇋113 🏠 P Lift 𝄐 sB ⇋73–85
dB ⇋110–140 Pool

BRUNSBÜTTEL
Schleswig-Holstein(☎04852)

At **ST MICHAELLSDONN** (13km N)

★★★Gardels Westerstr 19
☎(04853)566 tx28625
rm88 ⇋39 🛏34 P 𝄐 Pool

BÜDELSDORF See **RENDSBURG**

BUG See **BAMBERG**

CARTHAUSEN See **HALVER**

CELLE
Niedersachsen(☎05141)

★★Celler Hof Stechbahn 11 ☎28061
tx925117
rm58 ⇋18 🛏35 🏠 P Lift 𝄐
sB44–58 sB ⇋ 🛏98–138 dB52–116
dB ⇋ 🛏138–178

★★Hannover Wittinger str 56 ☎34870
rm13 ⇋2 🛏13 🏠 P

☝Von Maltzan & Trebeljahr Hohe
Wende 3 ☎3921 Frd

☝W Friedrich Wiesenstr 22 ☎1057 M/c
P BL

CHAM
Bayern(☎09971)

★★Randsberger Hof Randsbergerhofstr
15 ☎1916
rm85 ⇋40 🛏45 🏠 P Lift 𝄐
sB36–44 sB ⇋ 🛏40–44 sB68
dB ⇋ 🛏80–88

COBBENRODE See **ESLOHE**

COBURG
Bayern(☎09561)

☝Schamberger Kanonenweg
15 ☎7788 Frd

COCHEM
Rheinland-Pfalz(☎02671)

★★Alte Thorschenke (GS) Brückenstr 3
☎7059
15 Mar–5 Jan
rm55 ⇋35 🛏5 🏠 P Lift 𝄐 sB44–62
sB ⇋ 🛏56–75 dB81–112
dB ⇋ 🛏102–144 M alc Pool

★★Germania Moselpromenade 1
☎261 tx869422
rm28 ⇋17 🛏3 P Lift sB53–57
sB ⇋ 🛏61–67 dB84–92
dB ⇋ 🛏102–118

★★Hafen Uferstr & Zehnthausstr
☎8474
rm16 🛏23 A15rm 🏠 P sB30–45
sB ⇋ 🛏45–48 dB75 dB ⇋ 🛏80–90 sea

★Hendriks Jahnstr 8 (n.rest) ☎7261
Jan–Oct
rm16 P mountains

Autohof Cochem Sehler Anglagen
53 ☎8426 **P** Opl

⚒**M J Schneider** Industriegebiet
☎4078 Frd

CÖLBE See **MARBURG AN DER LAHN**

COLOGNE See **KÖLN**

CONSTANCE See **KONSTANZ**

CRAILSHEIM
Baden-Württemberg(☎07951)

★ ★**Post-Faber** Langestr 2–4 ☎8038
rm65 ⇆ 🏠50 A8rm 🏛 **P** Lift sB38–45
sB ⇆ 🏠48–62 dB62 dB ⇆ 🏠75–92
M10–25

CREGLINGEN
Baden-Württemberg(☎07933)

★ ★**Krone** Haupstr 12 ☎558
Feb–20 Dec
rm24 🏠10 A10rm 🏛 **P** sB26–32
sB 🏠32 dB52–58 dB 🏠66

CUXHAVEN
Niedersachsen(☎04721)

★ ★ ★**Donners** am Seedeich 2 ☎37014
rm85 ⇆69 🏠16 🏛 **P** Lift 𝄐
sB ⇆ 🏠46–92 dB ⇆ 🏠89–175 Pool
sea

DACHAU
Bayern(☎08131)

★ ★ ★**Götz** Pollnstr 6 ☎12863
🏠38 🏛 **P** Lift 𝄐 sB 🏠65–78
dB 🏠86–110 M alc Pool

DARMSTADT
Hessen(☎06151)

★ ★ ★ ★**Maritim** Rheinstr 105 ☎80041
tx176151926
⇆ 🏠312 **P** Lift sB ⇆ 🏠133–213
dB ⇆ 🏠185–295 M24–38 Pool

★ ★**Weinmichel** Schleiermacherstr
10–12 ☎26822 tx419275
10 Jan–26 Dec
rm75 ⇆24 🏠51 **P** Lift 𝄐
sB ⇆ 🏠68–98 dB ⇆ 🏠116–148

⚒**G Pöche** Eschollbrücker Str 16 ☎33234
Frd

⚒**J Wiest** Riedstr 5 ☎8640 Aud Por VW

DAUN
Rheinland-Pfalz(☎06592)

★ ★ ★**Kurfürstliches Amtshaus** (BW) auf
dem Burgberg ☎3031 tx047293
rm44 ⇆ 🏠42 **P** Lift 𝄐

★ ★**Hommes** Wirichstr 9 ☎538
22 Dec–15 Nov
rm42 ⇆12 🏠30 🏛 **P** Lift 𝄐
sB ⇆ 🏠69–73 dB ⇆ 🏠124–132 Pool
mountains

★ ★**Stadt Daun** Leopoldstr 14 ☎3555
⇆29 **P** Lift 𝄐 Pool

⚒**M Gessner** Bitburger Str ☎692 **P** Aud
VW

DECHSENDORF See **ERLANGEN**

Germany

DELMENHORST
Niedersachasen (☎04221)

★ ★**Annenriede** Annenheider Damm 129
☎6871
🏠60 🏛 **P** 𝄐

★ ★**Central** am Bahnhof ☎18019
rm44 ⇆8 🏠8 **P** 𝄐 sB30
sB ⇆ 🏠38–45 dB53 dB ⇆ 🏠68–79

⚒**Hohsmer** Syker Str 11 ☎70035 **P** Frd

DETMOLD
Nordrhein-Westfalen (☎05231)

★ ★**Detmolder Hof** Langestr 19
☎28244 tx935850
⇆21 **P** Lift 𝄐

★**Friedrichshöhe** Paderbornestr 6,
Heiligenkirchen (3km S) ☎47053
Closed 5–25 Jan
rm15 🏠8 **P** mountains

⚒**British Cars** Paderborner Str 52
☎47556 **P** BL

⚒**M Wagner** Grünstr 34 ☎28222 **P** Ren

DIEZ/LAHN
Rheinland-Pfalz (☎06432)

⚒**Auto-Müller** Wilhelmstr 44 ☎2622 **P**
Frd

DINKELSBÜHL
Bayern (☎09851)

★ ★**Goldene Kanne** Segringerstr 8
☎2363
rm24 ⇆4 🏠6 🏛 **P**

★ ★**Goldene Rose** Marktpl 4 ☎831
Mar–Oct
rm22 ⇆4 🏠16 🏛 **P** sB37
sB ⇆ 🏠47–52 dB ⇆ 🏠74–84

DONAUESCHINGEN
Baden-Württemberg (☎0771)

★ ★**Sonne** ☎3144
Closed 15 Dec–Jan
🏠20 🏛 **P**

⚒**P Greuner** Raiffeisenstr 60 ☎4730 **P**
BL

⚒**Zweibar** F-Ebert Str 51 ☎4033 **P** Frd

DONAUWÖRTH
Bayern (☎0906)

★ ★**Traube** Kapellstr 14 ☎6096
rm33 ⇆2 🏠10 🏛 **P** Lift sB35–39
sB ⇆ 🏠51–57 dB66–70
dB ⇆ 🏠92–106

⚒**J Schlicker** Berger Allee 11 ☎3001 **P**
Frd

DORTMUND
Nordrhein-Westfalen (☎0231)

★ ★ ★**Römischer Kaiser** (GT) Olpestr
2 ☎528331 tx0822441
rm160 ⇆100 🏠60 🏛 **P** Lift 𝄐

⚒**H Peters** Juchostr 25 ☎596021 **P** Frd

At **OESPEL** (6km W)

☆ ☆ ☆**Novotel Dortmund-West**
Brennaborstr 2 ☎65485 tx8227007
⇆103 **P** Lift 𝄐 sB ⇆117 dB ⇆149
M18–30 Pool

DREIEICH
Hessen (☎06103)

★ ★ ★**Dorint Kongress** Eisenbahnstr
200 ☎64041 tx417954
⇆96 **P** Lift 𝄐 sB ⇆131–170
dB ⇆180–230 Pool

DUISBURG
Nordrhein-Westfalen (☎0203)

★ ★ ★**Duisburger Hof** (SRS) Neckarstr 2,
König-Heinrich-Pl ☎331021 tx855750
rm132 ⇆32 🏠100 🏛 **P** Lift 𝄐
sB80–85 sB ⇆ 🏠119–169
dB ⇆ 🏠169–240

⚒**Schwenke** Bahnhofstr 102 ☎50371
M/c **P** BL Maz

DÜREN
Nordrhein-Westfalen (☎02421)

★ ★ ★**Germania** J-Schregel Str 20
☎15000
rm58 ⇆8 🏠39 A9rm 🏛 **P** Lift 𝄐
sB40–55 sB ⇆ 🏠60–85 dB60–70
dB ⇆ 🏠85–110

★**Nachtwächter** Kölner Landstr 12
☎74031
5 Jan–19 Dec
rm36 🏠30 A10rm **P**

At **MARIAWEILER** (3km NW)

★ ★**Mariaweiler Hof** an Gut Nazareth 45
☎87900
rm10 ⇆6 A3rm 🏛 **P** sB37–39
sB ⇆46 dB78 dB ⇆92 M6–26

DÜRKHEIM (BAD)
Rheinland-Pfalz (☎06322)

★ ★ ★**Kur Parkhotel** (BW) Schlosspl
1–4 ☎7970
rm109 ⇆75 🏠34 **P** Lift 𝄐
sB ⇆ 🏠96–105 dB ⇆ 🏠150 Pool

DÜRRHEIM (BAD)
Baden-Württemberg (☎07726)

★ ★ ★**Waldeck** Waldstr 18 ☎6630
tx07921315
⇆80 A17rm 🏛 **P** Lift

DÜSSELDORF
Nordrhein-Westfalen (☎0211)

★ ★ ★ ★**Park** (SRS) Corneliuspl 1
☎8651 tx8582331
⇆140 **P** Lift 𝄐 sB ⇆169–205
dB ⇆210–290

★ ★ ★**Hilton International** G-Glock Str
20 ☎434963 tx8584376
⇆382 **P** Lift 𝄐 sB ⇆174–314
dB ⇆228–413 M29–36 Pool

☆ ☆ ☆**Holiday Inn** G-Adolf pl 10
☎377053 tx8586359
⇆ 🏠114 **P** Lift 𝄐 sB ⇆ 🏠217
dB ⇆ 🏠270 Pool

★★★Börsen Kreuzstr 19A (n.rest)
☎363071 tx08587323
⇦26 🍴50 **P** Lift ⊅ sB ⇦ 🍴120–130
dB ⇦ 🍴190

☆☆☆**Novotel** am Schonenkamp 9
☎741092 tx8584374
⇦120 **P** Lift ⊅ sB ⇦129 dB ⇦161
M20 Pool

☆☆☆**Ramada** am Seestern 16
☎591047 tx8585575
⇦222 **P** Lift ⊅ sB ⇦155–190
dB ⇦190–260 M35 Pool

🐾**C Weber** Himmelgeisterstr 45
☎330101 **P** Frd

At **BREITSCHEID** (12 km N on A52 near
Mülheim exit)

☆☆☆**Novotel Breitscheider Kreuz**
Lintorfer Weg 75 ☎(02102) 17621
tx8585272
⇦120 **P** Lift ⊅ sB ⇦129 dB ⇦161
🏊 Pool

At **RATINGEN** (5km N. Follow signs from
exit Ratingen/Kaiserwerth on A52)

☆☆☆☆**Crest** Broichhofstr 3 **(See page
51)** ☎(02102) 46046 tx8585235
⇦200 **P** Lift ⊅ sB ⇦151–185
dB ⇦220–240 Pool

EBERBACH AM NECKAR
Baden-Württemberg (☎06271)

★★**Krone-Post** Haupstr 1 ☎2310
rm48 ⇦8 🍴30 🚗 **P** Lift sB40
sB ⇦ 🍴48–65 dB70 dB ⇦ 🍴80–120
🐾**Rosenturm** Brückenstr 9 ☎2391 M/c
Frd

EBNI-EBNISEE
Baden-Württemberg (☎07184)

★★★**Landgasthof Hirsch** ☎811
tx7246682
Feb–10 Jan
rm37 ⇦13 🍴24 🚗 **P** Lift
sB ⇦ 🍴70–80 dB ⇦ 🍴100–160 M96
🏊 Pool lake

EBRACH
Bayern (☎09553)

★**Klosterbräu** Marktpl 4 ☎212
15 Feb–15 Nov
rm19 🍴17 🚗 **P** ⊅ sB 🍴30 dBfr50
dB 🍴58 M5–28

ECHING
Bayern (☎089)

★★**Olymp** Wielandstr 3 ☎3192432
12 Jan–23 Dec
⇦32 🚗 **P** Pool

EDIGER-ELLER
Rheinland-Pfalz (☎02675)

★★**Weinhaus Oster** Moselweinstr 61
☎232
Mar–15 Nov
rm12 🍴5 **P**

EGGENFELDEN
Bayern (☎08721)

★★**Gruber Bräu** Stadtpl 27 ☎3127

Germany

rm20 ⇦2 🍴11 🚗 **P** sB29–31
sB ⇦ 🍴35–37 dB ⇦ 🍴70–74

EHLENBOGEN See **ALPIRSBACH**

EICHERSCHEID See **SIMMERATH**

ELFERSHAUSEN
Bayern (☎09704)

★★★**Ullrich** Aug–Ullrich 42 ☎281
tx0672807
rm71 ⇦49 🍴16 A5rm 🚗 **P** Lift sB45
sB ⇦ 🍴70 dB71 dB ⇦ 🍴109 Pool

ELTEN
Nordrhein-Westfalen (☎02828)

★★**Wald** Lindenallee 34 ☎2091
rm20 ⇦4 🍴14 A12rm **P** Lift 🏊 Pool

EMDEN
Niedersachsen (☎04921)

★**Goldener Adler** Neutorstr 5 ☎24055
Closed 3rd wk Sep
rm22 🍴15 **P** ⊅ sB40 sB 🍴65 dB65
dB 🍴90
🐾**Westermann Auto** Auricherstr 227
☎42051 **P** Frd

EMMERICH
Nordrhein-Westfalen (☎02822)

★★**Busch** Bahnhofstr 30 ☎70617
rm24 ⇦3 🍴11 **P**
🐾**Kummetat** Reeser Str 61 ☎3011 **P**
Frd

EMS (BAD)
Rheinland-Pfalz (☎02603)

★★★**Staatliches Kurhaus** (BW)
Römerstr 1–3 ☎3016 tx869017
rm105 ⇦34 🍴71 **P** Lift
sB ⇦ 🍴96–102 dB ⇦ 🍴132–144 Pool

★★**Russischer Hof** Römerstr 23 ☎4462
rm22 ⇦10 🍴5 **P** Lift
🐾**Gebr-Ebert** Lahnstr 47–49 ☎3028
M/c **P** Frd

ENNEPETAL
Nordrhein-Westfalen (☎02333)

★★**Burgmann** ☎71517 🍴11 **P** Lift

ENZKLÖSTERLE
Baden-Württemberg (☎07085)

★★**Parkhotel Hetschelhof** ☎273
Dec–Oct
rm18 ⇦12 🍴4 🚗 **P** Pn65–70 t%

ERFTTAL See **NEUSS**

ERLANGEN
Bayern (☎09131)

★★★★**Transmar Kongress** (GT)
Beethoven Str 3 ☎8040 tx629750
⇦ 🍴138 **P** Lift ⊅ sB ⇦ 🍴144
dB ⇦ 🍴194 Mfr8 Pool

★★★**Grille** Bunsenstr 35 ☎6136
tx629839

rm64 ⇦23 🍴41 🚗 **P** Lift ⊅
sB ⇦ 🍴70–110 dB ⇦ 🍴150

★★**Luise** Pfalzerstr 15 (n.rest) ☎32835
4 Jun–24 Dec
rm74 ⇦73 🚗 **P** Lift sB56–59
sB ⇦ 🍴79–89 dB89 dB ⇦ 🍴118–134
Pool

At **DECHSENDORF** (5km NW)

★**Rasthaus am Heusteg** Heusteg 13
☎41225
rm20 🍴4 🚗 **P**

At **TENNENLOHE** (3km S)

★★★**Transmar Motor** (GT)
Wetterkreuzstr 7 ☎6080 tx629912
⇦126 **P** Lift ⊅ Pool
🐾**Konrad** P-Gossen Str 116 ☎31025 **P**
Frd

ESCHBORN See **FRANKFURT AM MAIN**

ESCHWEILER
Nordrhein-Westfalen (☎02403)

★**Schwan** ☎6810
rm12 🍴3 **P** mountains
🐾**H Adenau** Tulpenweg 6 ☎4162 **P** BL
Maz

ESLOHE
Nordrhein-Westfalen (☎02973)

At **COBBENRODE** (7km S)

★★**Hennemann** Olperstr 28 (02970)236
rm42 ⇦4 🍴38 🚗 **P** Lift 🏊 Pool
mountains

ESPENAU See **KASSEL**

ESSEN
Nordrhein-Westfalen (☎0201)

★★★**Handelshof** (Mövenpick) am
Hauptbahnhof 2 ☎17080 tx857562
rm196 ⇦112 🍴84 **P** Lift ⊅
sB ⇦ 🍴114–144 dB ⇦ 🍴148–178 M18

☆☆**Arcade** 50 Hollestr ☎24280
tx8571133
🍴144 **P** Lift sB 🍴78 dB 🍴103 M alc

At **ESSEN-BREDENEY** (7km S on 224)

★★★**Bredeney** (BW) T-Althoff Str 5
☎714081 tx0857597
rm310 ⇦115 🍴180 🚗 **P** Lift ⊅
sB ⇦ 🍴155 dB ⇦ 🍴210 Pool

★★**Touring** Frankenstr 379 (n.rest)
☎42982 tx8571190
rm52 ⇦24 A28rm 🚗 **P** ⊅ sB42
sB ⇦61–65 dB72 dB ⇦ 🍴121

At **ESSEN-RÜTTENSCHEID** (3km S on
224)

★★★**Arosa** Rüttenscheider Str 149
☎72280 tx857354
rm68 ⇦31 🍴35 **P** Lift ⊅

ETTLINGEN
Baden-Württemberg (☎07243)

★★★**Erbprinz** Rheinstr 1 ☎12071
tx782848
⇦ 🍴50 🚗 **P** Lift ⊅ sB ⇦ 🍴155
dB ⇦ 🍴280

EUTIN
Schleswig-Holstein (☎04521)

★**Wittler** Bahnhofstr 28 ☎2347

rm29 ⇌18 🖭 **P** sB50 sB ⇌ 🍴80
dB66−78 dB ⇌ 🍴94−130

FALLINGBOSTEL
Niedersachsen (☎05162)

★ ★**Berlin** Düshorner Str 7 ☎3066

⇌ 🍴16 🖭 **P** ✌

♨⏦**F** *Kallbach* Michelsenstr 9 ☎1578 **P**
Chy Cit Lada Tal

FELDAFING
Bayern (☎08157)

★ ★**Kaiserin Elisabeth** Tutzinger Str 2
☎1013 tx526408

rm68 ⇌33 🍴15 A19rm 🖭 **P** Lift ♪
sB80 sB ⇌ 🍴110 dB130 dB ⇌ 🍴210
✌ mountains lake

FELDBERG IM SCHWARZWALD
Baden-Württemberg (☎07655)

★ ★ ★**Dorint Feldberger Hof** Seebrück
12 ☎(07676)311 tx7721124

⇌ 🍴80 🖭 **P** Lift ♪ sB ⇌ 🍴67−87
dB ⇌ 🍴104−150 ✌ Pool mountains

At **ALTGLASHÜTTEN**(9km E on 500)

★**Fernsicht** ☎392

🍴9 🖭 **P**

FINTHEN See **MAINZ**

FLENSBURG
Schleswig-Holstein (☎0461)

★ ★**Europa** Rauthausstr 1−5 ☎17522

rm74 ⇌18 **P** ♪

★ ★**Flensburger Hof** Süderhofenden 38
☎17320 tx22594

rm28 ⇌1 🍴23 🖭 **P** Lift ♪ sB65
sB ⇌ 🍴108 dB ⇌ 🍴138

At **HARRISLEE** (5km N)

★ ★**Grenze** ☎72098

⇌160 **P** Lift ♪ ✌ Pool

FRANKFURT AM MAIN
Hessen (☎0611)

Electronic room reservation facilities are
available at the airport, the main railway
station and the ADAC Service Centre,
autobahn exit 'Frankfurt West'. These
facilities are not operative during Trade
Fairs.

★ ★ ★ ★ ★**Frankfurt Intercontinental**
W-Leuschner-Str 43 ☎230561 tx413639

⇌800 🖭 **P** Lift ♪ sB ⇌240−293
dB ⇌290−346 M35−55 Pool

☆ ☆ ☆ ☆**Crest (see page 51)** Isenburger
Schneise 40, Niederrad (6km S) ☎67840
tx416717

⇌ 🍴281 **P** Lift ♪ sB ⇌ 🍴161−165
dB ⇌198−200

★ ★ ★ ★**Frankfurter Hof** (SRS) am
Kaiserpl 17 ☎20251 tx411806

⇌400 **P** Lift ♪ sB ⇌169−249
dB ⇌230−310

★ ★ ★ ★**Hessischer Hof** (GT) F-Ebert-
Anlarge 40 ☎75400 tx411776

⇌161 🖭 **P** Lift ♪ sB ⇌ 🍴160−315
dB ⇌ 🍴280−365 M alc

☆ ☆ ☆ ☆**Holiday Inn** Mailänder Str 1
☎680011 tx411805

⇌ 🍴190 **P** Lift ♪ sB ⇌ 🍴175
dB ⇌ 🍴227 Mfr18

★ ★ ★ ★**Parkhotel Frankfurt**
(Mövenpick) Wiesenhüttenpl 28−38
☎26970 tx412808

rm280 ⇌265 🍴15 **P** Lift ♪
sB ⇌ 🍴175−245 dB ⇌ 🍴219−319
M alc

★ ★ ★ ★*Savigny*(BW) Savignystr 14−16
☎75330 tx412061

3 Jan−23 Dec
rm150 ⇌40 🍴80 A30rm Lift ♪

★ ★ ★**Excelsior Monopol** Mannheimer
Str 11−13 ☎230171 tx413061

⇌ 🍴300 **P** Lift ♪ sB ⇌ 🍴95−115
dB ⇌ 🍴170

★ ★ ★**National** (BW) Baseler Str 50
☎234841 tx412570

rm95 ⇌53 🍴42 🖭 **P** Lift ♪
sB ⇌ 🍴140 dB ⇌ 🍴195

★ ★ ★**Ramada Caravelle** Oeserstr 180
☎3905-0 tx416812

rm236 ⇌166 🍴70 **P** Lift ♪
sB ⇌ 🍴140−195 dB ⇌ 🍴220−240
Pool

♨⏦**B** *Kneifel* Praunheimer Landstr 21
☎785079 **P** BL Dat

At **ESCHBORN** (12km NW)

☆ ☆ ☆**Novotel** P-Helfmann Str 10
☎(06196)42812 tx415655

⇌227 **P** Lift ♪ sB ⇌117−142
dB ⇌155−180 M18−25 Pool mountains

At **SULZBACH** (14km W via A648)

☆ ☆ ☆ ☆**Holiday Inn** am Main Taunus
Zentrum 1 ☎(06196)7878 tx410373

⇌291 **P** Lift ♪ sB ⇌155 dB ⇌205
Pool

FREIBURG IM BREISGAU
Baden-Württemberg (☎0761)

★ ★ ★**Colombi** (SRS) Rotteckring 16
☎31415 tx772750

⇌ 🍴102 🖭 Lift ♪ sB ⇌ 🍴115−155
dB ⇌ 🍴175−210

☆ ☆ ☆**Novotel** am Karlspl 1 ☎31295
tx772774

⇌ 🍴112 🖭 **P** Lift ♪ sB ⇌ 🍴129
dB ⇌ 🍴161 M18 mountains

★ ★ ★**Rappen** Münsterpl 13 ☎31353

rm20 ⇌6 🍴6 A3rm **P** Lift

★ ★**Victoria** Eisenbahnstr 54
☎31881 tx761103

rm70 ⇌20 🍴40 🖭 **P** Lift ♪ sB65
sB ⇌ 🍴105 dB90 dB ⇌ 🍴150−180

★ ★**Roten Bären** Oberlinden 12 (adj to
Schwabentor Gateway) ☎36913
tx7721574

rm33 ⇌5 🍴28 🖭 **P** Lift ♪ sB53−59
sB ⇌ 🍴69−105 dB94−120
dB ⇌ 🍴130−160 mountains

♨⏦**F** *Speck* Habsburgerstr 99−101
☎31131 M/c **P** BL

FREILASSING
Bayern (☎08654)

★ ★*Krone* Hauptstr 26 ☎9057

⇌40 🖭 **P** Lift mountains

FREISING
Bayern (☎08161)

★ ★**Bayerischer Hof** Untere Hauptstr 3
☎3037

rm68 ⇌42 🍴23 🖭 **P** Lift

FREUDENSTADT
Baden-Württemberg (☎07441)

★ ★ ★**Park-Hostellerie** (SRS) K-von-
Hahe Str 129 ☎81071 tx764266

⇌140 🖭 **P** Lift sB ⇌89−200
sB ⇌220−340 ✌ Pool

★ ★ ★**Schwarzwald Hof** Hohenrieder Str
74 ☎7421 tx0764371

rm40 ⇌20 🍴20 🖭 **P** Lift
sB ⇌ 🍴78−86 dB ⇌ 🍴140−175

★ ★ ★**Sonne am Kurpark** Turnhalle Str
63 ☎6044 tx764388

26 Dec−26 Nov
rm49 ⇌23 🍴19 🖭 **P** Lift ♪
sB ⇌ 🍴109 dB ⇌ 🍴160 Pool

★ ★**Krone** Marktpl 29 ☎2007

rm25 🍴7 🖭 **P** sB48 sB ⇌ 🍴50 dB96
dB ⇌ 🍴98

★ ★*Waldhotel Stockinger* Zollernblick 1
Ausserhalb (2kmS) ☎2187

Closed 1−14 Dec
rm45 ⇌9 🍴11 A21rm 🖭 **P**
mountains

★ ★**Württemberger Hof** Lauterbadstr 10
☎6047 tx764388

Closed 11 Nov−19 Dec
rm22 ⇌2 🍴11 🖭 **P** Lift ♪ sB41−45
sB ⇌ 🍴59−63 sB70 dB ⇌ 🍴96−114
Pool

★**See** Forststr 17 ☎2688

15 Dec−15 Nov
rm11 🍴7 A6rm 🖭 **P** Lift sB36−39
sB 🍴45 dB72−78 dB 🍴86−98 ✌

♨⏦**Hornberger & Schilling** Jetzt Deutzstr
2 ☎7084 M/c **P** Opl

Oberndorfer & Hiller Alte Poststr 3
☎7004 Frd

FRIEDBERG
Hessen (☎06031)

♨⏦**Kögler** Gilessener Str 19−21 ☎4661
M/c **P** Frd

FRIEDRICHSDORF See **HOMBURG (BAD)**

FRIEDRICHSHAFEN
Baden-Württemberg (☎07541)

★ ★**Buchorner Hof** Friedrichstr 33
☎25041 tx734210

Closed 21 Dec–9 Jan
⇌56 🏢 **P** Lift 🌒 sB⇌65–69
dB ⇌120–140

Frank Meisterhofener Str 9 ☎21617
M/c **P** Frd Hon

FULDA
Hessen (☎0661)

★ ★ ★**Lenz** Leipzigerstr 122 ☎601041
tx49733

rm48 ⇌20 🏠17 A22rm **P** Lift 🌒
sB40 sB ⇌ 🏠52–60 dB70 dB ⇌ 🏠148

🏍**W Fahr** Langebrücke Andreasberg 4
☎8161 Opl Vau

🏍**E Sorg** Kreuzbergstr 44 ☎41075 Frd

FÜSTENFELDBRÜCK
Bayern (☎08141)

★**Post** Hauptstr7 ☎24074

7 Jan–23 Dec
rm 45 ⇌11 🏠21 A9rm 🏢 **P** Lift

🏍**Auto Wolff** Am Fohlenhof 7 ☎91626
M/c BL

FÜRTH
Bayern (☎0911)

☆ ☆ ☆**Novotel Fürth** Lauberweg 6
☎791010 tx622214

⇌133 **P** Lift 🌒 sB⇌124 dB⇌156
M20 Pool

FÜSSEN
Bayern (☎08362)

🏍**G Gerhager** Oberleitnerstr 14 ☎7562

GAIMERSHEIM See **INGOLSTADT**

GARMISCH-PARTENKIRCHEN
Bayern (☎08821)

☆ ☆ ☆ ☆**Holiday Inn** Mittenwelderstr 2
☎7561 tx592415

⇌ 🏠117 **P** Lift 🌒 sB⇌ 🏠186
dB ⇌ 🏠237 Pool

★ ★ ★**Bernriederhof** von Müller Str 12
(n.rest) ☎71074 tx592421

⇌ 🏠37 🏢 **P** 🌒 sB⇌ 🏠90
dB ⇌ 🏠145

★ ★ ★**Grand Sonnenbichl** Burgstr 97
☎52052 tx59632

⇌ 🏠100 **P** Lift 🌒 sB⇌ 🏠120–145
dB ⇌ 🏠180–240 M30–50 Pool
mountains

★ ★ ★**Witteisbach** von Brugstr 24
☎53096 tx59668

20 Dec–20 Oct
rm60 ⇌45 🏠15 🏢 **P** Lift 🌒 Pool
mountains

★ ★**Garmischer Hof** Bahnhofstr 51
(n.rest) ☎51091

rm40 ⇌9 🏠7 **P** Lift 🌒 sB44
sB⇌ 🏠46–55 dB ⇌ 🏠81–99
mountains

★ ★**Partenkirchner-Hof** Bahnhofstr 15
☎58025 tx592412

Germany

15 Dec–15 Nov
rm75 ⇌65 🏠5 🏢 **P** Lift 🌒 sB60
sB ⇌ 🏠92 dB ⇌ 🏠140 Pool
mountains

🏍**Maier** Unterfeldstr 3 ☎50141 Fia Lnc

GELSENKIRCHEN
Nordrhein-Westfalen (☎0290)

★ ★ ★**Maritim** Stadtgarten 1
☎15951 tx824636

⇌250 **P** Lift 🌒 sB ⇌105 dB ⇌160
M alc Pool

🏍**A Stork** Ringstr 50–56 ☎21941 M/c **P**
Frd Hon

GERNSBACH
Baden-Württemberg (☎07224)

★**Ratsstuben** Hauptstr 34 ☎2141

rm12 🏠12 **P** sB34 sB 🏠36 dB68
dB 🏠72 mountains

GIESSEN
Hessen (☎0641)

★ ★ ★**Kübel** Bahnhofstr 47 ☎77070
tx4821754

rm47 ⇌45 🏠2 🏢 **P** 🌒
sB ⇌ 🏠65–110 dB⇌ 🏠155

☆**Lahn** Lahnstr 21 ☎73516

rm14 🏠5 🏢 **P**

GLOTTERTAL
Baden-Württemberg (☎07684)

★ ★ ★**Hirschen** Rathausweg 2 ☎215

Closed Jan & Mon
rm38 ⇌17 🏠17 **P** Lift sB40
sB ⇌ 🏠57–105 dB76 dB ⇌ 🏠97–160
M alc 🌀 mountains

GODESBERG (BAD) See **BONN**

GÖPPINGEN
Baden-Württemberg (☎07161)

★ ★**Hohenstaufen** Obere Freihofstr 64
☎70077

rm40 ⇌10 🏠30 A10rm 🏢 **P** 🌒
sB ⇌ 🏠65–80 dB ⇌ 🏠100–115

Schwabengarage Pfingstwasen 2
☎71091 M/c Frd

GOSLAR
Niedersachsen (☎05321)

At **GRAUHOF BRUNNEN** (4km NE)

★ ★**Grauhof Landhaus** ☎84001
tx953755

rm30 🏠22 A10rm 🏢 **P** Lift 🌒

At **HAHNENKLEE** (15km SW)

★ ★ ★**Dorint Harzhotel Kreuzeck** am
Kreuzeck ☎741 tx953721

⇌ 🏠96 🏢 **P** Lift 🌒 sB ⇌ 🏠143
dB ⇌ 🏠252 🌀 lake

GÖTTINGEN
Niedersachsen (☎0551)

★ ★**Sonne** Paulinerstr 10–12 ☎56798
tx96787

5 Jan–20 Dec
rm74 ⇌25 🏠28 🏢 **P** Lift 🌒

GRAFENAU
Bayern (☎08552)

★ ★ ★**Sonnenhof** (SRS) Sonnenstr 12
☎2033 tx57413

rm196 ⇌171 🏠25 🏢 **P** Lift 🌒
sB ⇌ 🏠58–86 dB ⇌ 🏠106–162 🌀
Pool mountains

GRAINAU
Bayern (☎08821)

★ ★ ★**Alpenhotel Waxenstein** Eibseestr
16 ☎8001 tx59663

⇌49 🏢 **P** Lift 🌒 sB ⇌130
dB ⇌ 250 Pool mountains

★ ★**Post** Postgasse 10 ☎8853

20 Dec–15 Oct
rm33 ⇌21 🏢 **P** sB40–42
sB ⇌ 🏠55–65 dB74–84
dB ⇌ 🏠110–124 mountains

GRAUHOF BRUNNEN See **GOSLAR**

GRIMLINGHAUSEN See **NEUSS**

GROSS-GERAU
Hessen (☎06152)

★ ★**Adler** Frankfurt Str 11 ☎2286

Closed 23–30 Dec
rm68 ⇌10 🏠45 🏢 **P** Lift sBfr40
sB ⇌ 🏠fr65 dBfr70 dB ⇌ 🏠fr98

🏍**Auto-Fritsch** Gernsheimer Str 60
☎58016 **P** Frd

GRÖTZINGEN See **KARLSRUHE**

GÜNZBURG
Bayern (☎08221)

★ ★**Goldene Traube** Marktpl 22 ☎5510

rm34 ⇌16 🏠4 🏢 **P**

★ ★**Hirsch** Marktpl 18 (n.rest) ☎5610

10 Jan–20 Nov
rm30 ⇌3 🏠9 A12rm 🏢 **P**

HAGEN
Nordrhein-Westfalen (☎02331)

☆ ☆ ☆**Crest (See page 51)** Wasserloses
Tal 4 ☎3910 tx823441

⇌148 **P** Lift sB ⇌125 dB ⇌161–165
Pool

★ ★**Deutsches Haus** Bahnhofstr 35
☎21051 tx0823640

rm41 ⇌4 🏠33 🏢 **P** Lift 🌒 sB54
sB ⇌ 🏠80–90 dB98 dB ⇌ 🏠110–142

HAGNAU
Baden-Württemberg (☎97532)

★**Landhaus Messmer** Meersburgerstr 12
(n.rest) ☎6227

Mar–Oct
rm14 ⇌6 🏠6 🏢 **P** sB43
sB ⇌ 🏠55–00 dB ⇌ 🏠98–105
mountains lake

HAHNENKLEE See **GOSLAR**

HALTINGEN
Baden-Württemberg (☎07621)

★***Rebstock*** Grosse Gasse 30 ☎62257
rm19 🚿10 A4rm 🏛 **P** ☽

HALVER
Nordrhein-Westfalen (☎02353)

At **CARTHAUSEN** (4km NE)

★★★**Frommann** ☎611
rm22 🛁9 🚿13 🏛 **P** ⚘ Pool lake

HAMBURG
Hamburg (☎040)

★★★★★**Vier Jahreszeiten** Neuer Jungfernstieg 9–14 ☎34941 tx211629
🛁187 🏛 **P** Lift ☽ sB🛁215–280 dB🛁311–386 M alc lake

★★★★**Atlantic Kempinski Hamburg** an der Alster 72 ☎248001 tx163297
🛁310 🏛 **P** Lift ☽ sB🛁210–237 dB🛁297–344 M alc Pool lake

★★★★**Hamburg Plaza** Marseiller Str 2 ☎351035 214400
🛁 🚿570 🏛 **P** Lift ☽ sB🛁 🚿267 dB🛁 🚿324 Pool lake

★★★**Berlin** Borgfeldstr 1–9 ☎251640 tx312929
rm96 🛁53 🚿27 **P** Lift ☽

☆☆☆**Crest (See page 51)** Mexikoring 1 City Nord ☎6305051 tx2174155
rm185 🛁90 🚿95 **P** Lift ☽
sB🛁 🚿161 dB🛁 🚿198–200

★★★**Europäischer Hof** (GT) Kirchenallee 45 ☎248171 tx2162493
rm350 🛁170 🚿180 **P** Lift ☽
sB🛁 🚿140–204 dB🛁 🚿208–308 Mfr15

☆☆☆**Novotel Hamburg Nord** Oldesloher Str 166, Schnelsen ☎5502073 tx212923
🛁124 **P** Lift ☽ sB🛁112 dB🛁132 Pool

★★★**Oper** Drehbahn 15 ☎35601 tx0212475
rm112 🛁53 🚿59 🏛 **P** Lift ☽
sB🛁 🚿99–124 dB🛁 🚿127–161 Mfr18 Pool

★★★**Reichshof** (SRS) Kirchenallee 34 ☎248330 tx2163396
rm350 🛁150 🚿300 🏛 Lift ☽
sB🛁 🚿135–165 dB🛁 🚿180–230

★★★**Smolka** Isestr 96, Harvestehude ☎475057 tx215275
rm40 🛁20 🚿20 🏛 **P** Lift ☽
sB🛁 🚿190–145 dB🛁 🚿165–185 M alc

☆☆**Ibis** Wandsbeker Zollstr 25–29 ☎6829021 tx2164929
🚿144 **P** Lift ☽ sB🚿97 dB🚿121–133

★★***Pacific*** Neuer Pferdemarkt 30 (n.rest) ☎4395094
rm60 🛁4 🚿16 **P** Lift ☽

☆**Hamburg** Hoheluftshaussee 119 (n.rest) ☎473067
rm37 🛁1 🚿18 🏛 **P** ☽ sB55
sB🛁 🚿98 dB🛁 🚿195

Germany

BMC Autohandelsgesellschaft Stormaner Str 26 ☎683344 **P** BL Sab

Nemeth Koppel 65 ☎244849 BL Peu RR

P Nitzschke Steinbeker Hauptstr 84 ☎7128459 BL

Vidal Angerstr 20–22 ☎257901 **P** DJ RT

HAMELN
Niedersachsen (☎05151)

★★★**Dorint Weserbergland** Dingelstedtstr 3 ☎7920 tx924716
🛁 🚿103 🏛 **P** Lift ☽ sB🛁 🚿91–96 dB🛁 🚿162–172

H Struck Hastenbeckerweg 50 ☎12052 **P** Frd

HANAU AM MAIN
Hessen (☎06181)

Millinski & Häring Moselstr 64 ☎14058 BL Vlo

Zentralgarage-Bommersheim Hernstr 21–23 ☎24551 **P** Frd

HANNOVER
Niedersachsen (☎0511)

☆☆☆**Crest (See page 51)** Tiergartenstr 117, Kirchrode ☎51030 tx922748
rm110 🛁68 🚿42 **P** Lift ☽
sB🛁 🚿151 dB🛁 🚿187

★★★**Kastens Luisenhof** (SRS) Luisenstr 1–3 ☎16151 tx922325
rm200 🛁190 🏛 **P** Lift ☽
sB🛁129–159 dB🛁178–228

☆☆☆**Parkhotel Kronsberg** (BW) Messeschnellweg ☎861086 tx923448
rm105 🛁31 🚿74 🏛 **P** Lift ☽
sB🛁 🚿98–130 dB🛁 🚿130–200

★★**Central Kaiserhof** E-August-Platz 4 ☎327811 tx922810
rm70 🛁40 🚿30 Lift ☽

☆☆**Föhrenhof** (BW) Kirchhorster Str 22 ☎61721 tx923448
rm77 🛁40 🚿37 **P** Lift ☽
sB🛁 🚿100 dB🛁 🚿200

Deisterstrasse Deisterstr 33–37 ☎444016 **P** Frd

Hentschel Vahrenwalder Str 141 ☎39030 M/c Frd

HANNOVER AIRPORT

☆☆☆☆**Holiday Inn** Petzelstr 60, Flughafen ☎730171 tx0924030
🛁145 **P** Lift ☽ sB🛁170–180 dB🛁205–215 Pool

HARRISLEE See **FLENSBURG**

HARZBURG (BAD)
Niedersachsen (☎05322)

★★★**Bodes** Stadtpark 48 ☎2041
rm82 🛁35 🚿36 A22rm 🏛 **P** Lift ☽
sB43–53 sB🛁 🚿72–80 dB86–96 dB🛁 🚿140–166 mountains

★★**Braunschweiger Hof** H-Willhelm Str 54 ☎7035 tx957821
rm70 🛁15 🚿55 🏛 **P** Lift ☽
sB🛁 🚿65–89 dB🛁 🚿148 Pool mountains

HEIDE
Schleswig-Holstein (☎0481)

W Leinweber Hamburgerstr 115 ☎3022 **P** Opl

HEIDELBERG
Baden-Württemberg (☎06221)
See also **WALLDORF**

★★★★★**Europäische Hof** (SRS) F-Ebert Anlage 1 ☎27101 tx461830
rm125 🛁106 🚿7 🏛 **P** Lift ☽
sB89–105 sB🛁 🚿119–189 dB132–142 dB🛁 🚿200–260 M40–53

★★★**Alt Heidelberg** (MIN) Rohrbacher Str 29 ☎15091 tx461897
rm65 🛁35 🚿30 🏛 **P** Lift ☽
sB🛁 🚿110 dB🛁 🚿150

★★★***Braun*** F-Ebert Anlage 32 ☎26425
rm20 🛁2 🚿17 **P** Lift ☽

☆☆☆**Crest (See page 51)** Pleikartsförsterstr 101, Kirchheim ☎71021 tx461650
rm113 🛁62 🚿51 **P** Lift ☽
sB🛁 🚿135 dB🛁 🚿161–165

★★★**Ritter** (ROM) Haupstr 178 ☎24272 tx461506
rm35 🛁20 🚿6 **P** Lift ☽ sB52–55 sB🛁 🚿58–105 dB80–85 dB🛁 🚿115–220 M20 25

★**Kohler** Goethestr 2 (n.rest) ☎24360 16 Jan–20 Dec
rm43 🛁4 🚿28 Lift ☽ sB40–46 sB🛁 🚿52–64 dB60–71 dB🛁 🚿77–98

★**Vier Jahreszeiten** Haspelgasse 2, an der alten Brücke ☎24164
15 Jan–15 Dec
rm24 🛁5 🚿9 A2rm 🏛 **P** ☽
sB45–70 sB🛁 🚿85–105 dB85–95 dB🛁 🚿120–150

Auto-Ostwald Hebelstr 6 ☎13011 **P** M/c Fia Lnc

Bosch-Dienst Karl Benz Str 2 ☎22171 M/c Lucas

Joncker Hebelstr 1 ☎20618 **P** Frd

J Pfotzer Speyerer Str 11 ☎531–0 Opl

Raichie & Baur Hebelstr 12 ☎24954 BL

HEILBRONN
Baden-Württemberg (☎07131)

★★★**Insel** F-Ebert Brücke ☎88931 tx728777
rm122 🛁103 🚿19 **P** Lift ☽
sB🛁 🚿118 dB🛁 🚿158 ⚘ Pool

★★**Kronprinz** Bahnhofstr 29 ☎83941 tx728561 →

rm35 ⇌4 🛏16 🛁 P Lift sB44
sB ⇌ 🛏56 dB82 dB ⇌ 🛏98

&⊃ASG Auto-Service Weipertstr 17
☎161850 P B

HEILIGENROTH See **MONTABAUR**

HELMSTEDT
Niedersachsen (☎05351)

★★Petzold Schöninger Str 1 ☎6001
rm28 ⇌4 🛏10 🛁 P ᗡ

&⊃Wagner K-Adenauer-Pl 3 ☎31007 P
Aud VW

HEPPENHEIM AN DER BERGSTRASSE
Hessen (☎06252)

★Goldenen Engel Grosser Markt 2
☎2563
rm35 ⇌4 🛏13 A11rm 🛁 P
mountains

&⊃Auto Eck Breslauer Str 23 ☎2237 P
Frd

HERFORD
Nordrhein-Westfalen (☎05221)

&⊃Niebaum & Hamacher Liebig Str 3–6
☎72071 P Frd

P Wiegers Waltgeriststr 71 ☎2086 AR BL
Hon

HERRENALB (BAD)
Baden-Württemberg (☎07083)

★★★Mönchs Posthotel Dobler Str 2
☎2002 tx7245123
rm50 ⇌30 🛏20 🛁 P Lift ᗡ
sB ⇌ 🛏105 dB ⇌ 🛏180 🛁 Pool 🏊
mountains

HERRENBERG
Baden-Württemberg (☎07032)

★Neue Post Wilhelmstr 48 ☎5156
9 Jan–23 Dec
rm7 🛏2 P

HERSFELD (BAD)
Hessen (☎06621)

★★Parkhotel Rose am Kurpark 9
☎14454
rm22 ⇌14 🛏6 🛁 P Lift
sB ⇌ 🛏55–89 dB ⇌ 🛏128 mountains

★★Stern (ROM) Lingg Pl 11 ☎72007
rm34 ⇌4 🛏30 A20rm 🛁 P Lift
sB ⇌ 🛏57–70 dB ⇌ 🛏120–126
M14–39 Pool

HILDESHEIM
Niedersachsen (☎05121)

Felske Automobile Porschestr 2
☎515077 P BL

HINDELANG
Bayern (☎08324)

★★★Prinz-Luitpold-Bad A-Gross Weg
☎2011
20 Dec–5 Nov
rm115 ⇌80 🛏35 🛁 P Lift ᗡ
sB ⇌ 🛏65–110 dB ⇌ 🛏106–205 🏊
Pool mountains

HINTERZARTEN
Baden-Württemberg (☎07652)

Germany

★★★Parkhotel Adler Adlepl ☎711
tx772692
⇌85 🛁 P Lift ᗡ sB ⇌ 🛏95–160
dB ⇌ 🛏495 🏊 Pool ᛢ mountains

HÖCHENSCHWAND
Baden-Württemberg (☎07672)

★★★Kurhaus Kurhauspl 1 ☎4111
tx7721212
Closed 15 Nov–20 Dec
rm90 ⇌55 🛏26 A40rm 🛁 P Lift ᗡ
sB ⇌ 🛏74 dB ⇌ 🛏140 Pool

HÖCHSTADT AN DER AISCH
Bayern (☎09193)

★★Kapuzinerbräu Hauptstr 28 ☎8327
rm16 ⇌4 🛏9 🛁 P Lift

HOCKENHEIM
Baden-Württemberg (☎06205)

★★Luxhof an der Speyerer Brücke
☎32333
rm49 ⇌30 🛁 P Pool

HOF
Bayern (☎09281)

&⊃Autoveri C-Benz Str 4 ☎9067 P Frd

HOHELEYE See **WINTERBERG**

HOHENSCHWANGAU
Bayern (☎08362)

★★Lisl und Jägerhaus
Neuschwansteinst 1 ☎81006 tx541332
rm50 ⇌26 🛏19 A21rm 🛁 P Lift
sB35 sB ⇌ 🛏50–80 dB70
dB ⇌ 🛏100–175 M alc mountains

HOLZMINDEN
Niedersachsen (☎05531)

&⊃H Friedrich Bülte 3 ☎7820
M/c P BL Cit

HOMBURG (BAD)
Hessen (☎06172)

At **FRIEDRICHSDORF** (5km NE on 455,
Exit Friedberg from autobahn A5 E4)

☆☆☆Crest im Taunus (See page 51) Im
Dammwald 1 ☎171 tx415892
⇌ 🛏134, 🛁 P Lift ᗡ sB ⇌ 🛏130
dB ⇌ 🛏172–175 Pool

HOMBURG SAAR
Saarland (☎06841)

★★★Stadt Homburg (BW) Ringstr 80
☎1331 tx44683
rm62 ⇌15 🛏47 🛁 P Lift ᗡ
sB ⇌ 🛏80–130 dB ⇌ 🛏120–190 Pool

HONNEF AM RHEIN (BAD)
Nordrhein-Westfalen (☎02224)

P Reuffel Bahnhofstr 2B ☎2406 P AR
BL

At **ZWINDHAGEN-REDERSCHEID** (8km
SE)

★★★Sporthotel Waldbrunnen
Brunnenstr 7 ☎(02645) 150 tx863020
rm54 ⇌16 🛏38 🛁 P Lift ᗡ 🏊
Pool ᛢ

HORNBERG
Baden-Wüttemberg (☎07833)

★★Schloss Hornberg auf dem
Schlossberg 1 ☎6841
Etr–Oct
rm31 ⇌2 🛏27 P sB45–55
sB ⇌ 🛏45–55 dB ⇌ 🛏90–130
M13–30 mountains

HORSTMAR
Nordrhein-Westfalen (☎02558)

★Crins Münsterstr 11 ☎02558
rm10 🛁 P

IDAR-OBERSTEIN
Rheinland-Pfalz (☎06781)

&⊃B Schwelkert Tiefensteiner Str
185–189 ☎31046 P Frd

H P Steuer Nahbollenbacherstr 90
☎(06784)565 M/c P AR BL Hon

INGOLSTADT
Bayern (☎0841)

☆☆☆Holiday Inn Goethestr 153
☎2281 tx55710
⇌ 🛏123 P Lift ᗡ Pool

★★Rappensberger Harderstr 3 ☎1625
Closed Xmas & New Year
rm90 ⇌21 🛏40 🛁 P Lift ᗡ

★Adler Theresienstr 22 (n.rest) ☎35107
Closed Jan
rm45 ⇌2 🛏20 🛁 P ᗡ sBfr34
sB ⇌ 🛏fr39 dBfr62 dB ⇌ 🛏fr70

&⊃Bacher Goethostr 56 ☎56061 P Frd

&⊃E Willner Goethestr 61 ☎56005 M/c
P Opl Vau

At **GAIMERSHEIM** (8km NW)

★★Heidehof Ingolstädter Str 121,
Friedrichshofen ☎(08458)711 tx55688
rm56 ⇌8 🛏48 🛁 P Lift Pool

INZELL
Bayern (☎08665)

★★★Dorint Inzell Lärchenstr 5 ☎851
⇌ 🛏217 P Lift ᗡ sB ⇌ 🛏133
dB ⇌ 🛏246 Pool

&⊃Sportcar Centre Baarstr 119 ☎40048
P AR BL

ISNY
Baden-Württemberg (☎07562)

★★Hohe Linde Lindauerstr 75 ☎2066
Jan–15 Oct
rm28 ⇌6 🛏10 🛁 P sB36 sB ⇌ 🛏45
dB68 dB ⇌ 🛏82 Pool

JESTEBURG
Niedersachsen (☎04183)

At **ASENDORF** (4.5km SE)

★★Heidschnucke zum Auetal 14
☎3481
rm35 ⇌26 🛏5 P Lift Pool

JÜLICH
Nordrhein-Westfalen (☎02461)

⁊⊃*Schüsseler* Römerstr 9 ☎2539 **P** BL
DJ RT

KAISERSLAUTERN
Rheinland-Pfalz (☎0631)

★ ★ ★**Dorint Pfalzerwald** St-Quentin
Ring 1 ☎66011 tx45614
⇘ 📖150 🏛 **P** Lift 𝄞
sB ⇘ 📖94−100 dB ⇘ 📖148−162 Pool

⁊⊃*Schicht* Kaiserstr 74 ☎54060 **P** BL
BMW

KAMP-BORNHOFEN
Rheinland-Pfalz (☎06773)

★**Anker** Rheinuferstr 46 ☎215
Apr−25 Oct
rm15 ⇘5 📖4 🏛 **P** mountains

KARLSRUHE
Baden-Württemberg (☎0721)

★ ★ ★**Berliner Hof** Douglasstr 7 (n.rest)
☎23981
rm55 ⇘2 📖52 🏛 **P** Lift 𝄞 sB60
sB ⇘ 📖80 dB ⇘ 📖108−115

★ ★ ★**Kaiserhof** Marktpl ☎26616
tx7825600
rm40 ⇘36 **P** Lift 𝄞 sB58 sB ⇘95
dB ⇘ 120−150

★ ★ ★**Park** (Mövenpick) Ettingerstr 23
☎60461 tx7825443
rm126 ⇘116 📖10 🏛 **P** Lift 𝄞
sB ⇘ 📖118−133 dB ⇘ 📖145−160
M alc

★ ★ ★**Ramada Renaissance**
Mendelsohnpl ☎3717-0 tx7825699
⇘216 **P** Lift 𝄞 sB ⇘149−189
dB ⇘195−248

★ ★ ★**Schloss** Bahnhofspl 2 ☎3540
tx7826746
⇘96 **P** Lift 𝄞 sB ⇘136 dB ⇘193

★ ★**Eden** Bahnhofstr 17−19 ☎28718
tx7826415
⇘65 🏛 **P** Lift 𝄞 sB ⇘110 dB ⇘160

★ ★**Hasen** Gerwigstr 47 ☎615076
rm37 ⇘1 📖7 🏛 **P** Lift 𝄞

★ ★**Markt** Kaiserstr 76(n.rest) ☎27777
rm31 ⇘24 📖4 🏛 **P** Lift 𝄞 sB58
sB ⇘ 📖60−85 dB ⇘ 📖120

⁊⊃**Böhler** Ottostr 6 ☎404051 **P** Vlo

F Opel Herman Billing Str 8−12 ☎1301
Opl

⁊⊃**Vollmer & Sack** Gottesauerstr 37
☎60471 Frd

Zentral Blumenstr 4 ☎27141 Peu Tal

At **GRÖTZINGEN** (8km E)

★ ★ ★**Schloss Augustenburg** (GS)
Kirchstr 20 ☎48555 tx7826590
rm30 ⇘4 📖26 **P** sB ⇘ 📖95−120
dB ⇘ 📖140−200 M30−50 Pool

KASSEL
Hessen (☎0561)

Germany

☆ ☆ ☆ ★**Holiday Inn** Hellingenröderstr
61 ☎52151 tx099814
⇘141 **P** Lift sB ⇘135 dB ⇘184 Pool

★ ★ ★**Dorint Reiss** W-Hilpert Str 24 (nr
Hauptbahnhof) ☎78830 tx99740
rm100 ⇘44 📖34 🏛 **P** Lift 𝄞 sB67
sB ⇘ 📖110 dB ⇘ 📖164−174

★ ★ ★**Park-Hotel Hessenland** Obere
Königsstr 2, am Rathaus ☎14974
tx099773
rm171 ⇘65 📖55 A2rm 🏛 **P** Lift 𝄞

Auto Rössler Raiffeisenstr 1 ☎21063 **P**
Frd

F Richter Schillerstr 46−48 ☎70003 Frd

At **ESPANAU** (10km NW)

★ ★**Waldhotel Schäferberg**
Wilhelmsthaler Str 14 ☎(05673)7971
rm60 ⇘5 📖55 🏛 **P** sB ⇘ 📖86−95
dB ⇘ 📖134−150 M12−30

KAUFBEUREN
Bayern (☎08341)

⁊⊃**R Langer** Neugablonzer Str 88
☎8448 Frd

At **BIESSENHOFEN** (6.5km S)

★ ★**Neue Post** Füssener Str 17 ☎8525
rm28 ⇘8 📖20 🏛 **P** mountains

KEHL
Baden-Württemberg (☎07851)

⁊⊃**Geiger** Strassburger Str 11 ☎5046 **P**
Aud Por VW

⁊⊃**Zipperer** Königsberger Str 10 ☎8077
Frd

KELHEIM
Bayern (☎09441)

★ ★**Ehrnthaller** Donaustr 22 ☎3333
Closed 1 wk Xmas
rm67 ⇘13 📖56 🏛 **P** Lift sB44−46
sB ⇘ 📖54−68 dB 69−79
dB ⇘ 📖93−111 M8−20

KEMPTEN (ALLGÄU)
Bayern (☎0831)

★ ★ ★**Fürstenhof** (BW) Rathauspl 8
☎23050
⇘75 A21rm 🏛 **P** Lift 𝄞 mountains

★ ★ ★**Peterhof** Salzstr 1 ☎25525
rm51 ⇘9 📖42 🏛 **P** Lift 𝄞
sB ⇘ 📖71−79 dB ⇘ 📖 114−134 M alc

Lander, Amman & Co Lorenzstr 24−26
☎28680 **P** BL

KIEL
Schleswig-Holstein (☎0431)

★ ★ ★**Conti-Hansa** (BW) Schlossgarten
7 ☎51244 tx292813
15 Jul−Dec
rm167 ⇘164 📖3 🏛 **P** Lift 𝄞
sB ⇘ 📖130−189 dB ⇘ 📖173−233

⁊⊃*Herold* Zum Brook 1−3 ☎74066 Cit
Fia

⁊⊃**Paulsen & Thoms** Stormarnstr 35
☎680191 **P** Frd

KIRCHHEIM
Hessen (☎06625)

☆ ☆ ☆**Motel Center** (1.5km S near
Autobahn exit) ☎631 tx0493337
rm140 ⇘108 📖32 🏛 **P** 𝄞 Pool
mountains

KISSINGEN (BAD)
Bayern (☎0971)

★ ★ ★**Bristol** Bismarckstr 8−10 ☎4031
Mar−Oct
rm110 ⇘32 📖52 🏛 **P** Lift 𝄞
sB ⇘ 📖93−99 dB ⇘ 📖152−184 Pool

★ ★ ★**Dorint** Fühlingstr 1 ☎3050
tx672910
⇘ 📖94 **P** Lift 𝄞 sB ⇘ 📖73−78
dB ⇘ 📖126−136

★ ★**Fürst Bismarck** Euerdorfer Str 4
☎1277
20 Jan−20 Dec
rm35 ⇘30 🏛 **P** Lift 𝄞 sB42
sB ⇘ 📖65 dB80 dB ⇘ 📖100−132 🏊
Pool

⁊⊃**K H Fürsch** Kapellenstr 3l ☎61413 BL

KLEVE
Nordrhein-Westfalen(☎02821)

⁊⊃**Horbelt** Kalkarer Str 41 ☎24045 **P** Frd

KLOSTERREICHENBACH
Baden-Württemberg(☎07442)

★ ★**Sonne-Post** ☎2277
Closed 2−19 Dec
rm30 ⇘12 📖17 🏛 **P** sB39−53
sB ⇘ 📖49−63 dB78−106
dB ⇘ 📖98−126 M12−40 mountains

KOBLENZ
Rheinland-Pfalz(☎0261)

★ ★ ★**Diehl's Rheinterrasse**
Ehrenbreitstein ☎72010
rm68 ⇘38 📖30 🏛 **P** Lift 𝄞
sB ⇘ 📖80−100 dB ⇘ 📖120−200 Pool
river

★ ★ ★**Kleiner Riesen** Rheinanlagen 18
(n.rest) ☎32077 tx862442
⇘ 📖27 **P** Lift 𝄞 sB ⇘ 📖70
dB ⇘ 📖120

★**Scholz** Moselweisser Str 121 ☎42488
Closed 15 Dec−15 Jan
rm33 ⇘1 📖25 **P**

⁊⊃**G Schilling** Andernacher Str
232 ☎85003 Ren

⁊⊃**P Wirtz** Andernacher Str
201 ☎83028 M/c **P** Opl Vau

KÖLN (COLOGNE)
Nordrhein-Westfalen(☎0221)
See Plan page 210

★ ★ ★ ★**Excelsior Hotel-Ernst** (SRS)
Dompl ☎2701 tx8882645 Plan **1**
⇘146 🏛 **P** Lift 𝄞 sB ⇘179−255
dB ⇘225−340

KÖLN (COLOGNE)

1	★ ★ ★ ★ ★Excelsior Hotel-Ernst
3	★ ★ ★Augustinerplatz
4	☆ ☆ ☆Crest (At Köln-Lindenthal)
5	★ ★ ★Dom
6	★ ★ ★Haus Lyskirchen
6A	★ ★ ★Mondial
7	★ ★ ★Kaiser (At Köln-Mulheim)
8	★ ★ ★Rheingold
9	★ ★Ariane
10	★ ★Berlin
11	★ ★Bremer (At Köln-Lindenthal)
12	★ ★Conti
12A	☆ ☆Intercity Ibis
13	★ ★Panorama

★ ★ ★Augustinerplatz Hohestr 30 (n.rest) ☎236717 tx8882923 Plan 3
rm56 ⇆9 🛏32 P Lift 𝒟 sB ⇆ 🛏125 dB ⇆ 🛏195

★ ★ ★Dom (BW) Domkloster 2A ☎233751 tx8882919 Plan 5
rm133 ⇆101 🛏13 🏠 P Lift 𝒟 sB ⇆ 🛏165–195 dB ⇆ 🛏325

★ ★ ★Haus Lyskirchen am Filzengraben 26–32 ☎234891 tx8885449 Plan 6
Closed 24 Dec–3 Jan
rm63 ⇆12 🛏50 🏠 P Lift 𝒟
3B ⇆ 🛏87–130 dB ⇆ 🛏169–205 Pool

★ ★ ★Mondial (ETAP) Berchergasse 10 ☎219671 tx8881932 Plan 6A
⇆205 🏠 P Lift 𝒟 sB ⇆128 dB ⇆175 M20–40

★ ★ ★Rheingold Engelbertstr 33 (n.rest) ☎236531 tx8882923 Plan 8
⇆52 🏠 P Lift 𝒟 sB ⇆ 🛏125 dB ⇆ 🛏195

★ ★Ariane Hohe Pforte 19–21 (n.rest) ☎236033 Plan 9
rm44 ⇆5 🛏29 P Lift 𝒟

★ ★Berlin Domstr 10 ☎123051 tx8885123 Plan 10
rm80 ⇆4 🛏72 P Lift 𝒟 sBfr58 sB ⇆ 🛏fr85 dB ⇆ 🛏fr140 Mfr25

★ ★Conti Brüsseler Str 42 ☎219262 tx8881644 Plan 12
4 Jan–20 Dec
⇆43 🏠 Lift 𝒟 sB ⇆78–95 dB ⇆110–150

☆ ☆Intercity Ibis Bahnhofvorpl (n.rest) ☎132051 tx8881002 Plan 12A
⇆66 🏠 Lift 𝒟 sB ⇆80–100 dB ⇆120–140

★ ★Panorama Siegburgersrstr 37 ☎884041 Plan 13
⇆30 🏠 P Lift 𝒟 sB55 sB ⇆65–80 dB ⇆100–130

🔧E Maletz Rhöndorfer Str 2 ☎448011 P Frd

At BONN AIRPORT (17km SE)

☆ ☆ ☆ ☆Holiday Inn Waldstr 255 ☎5610 tx8874665 Not on plan →

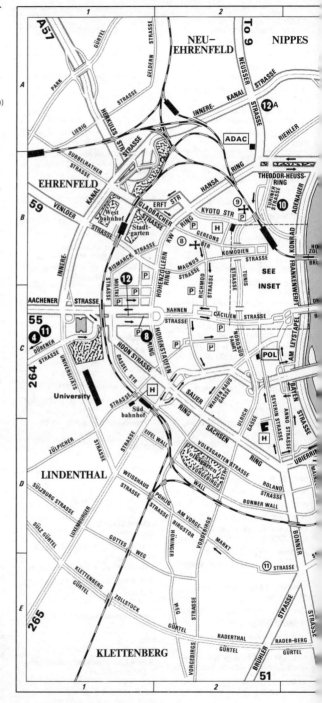

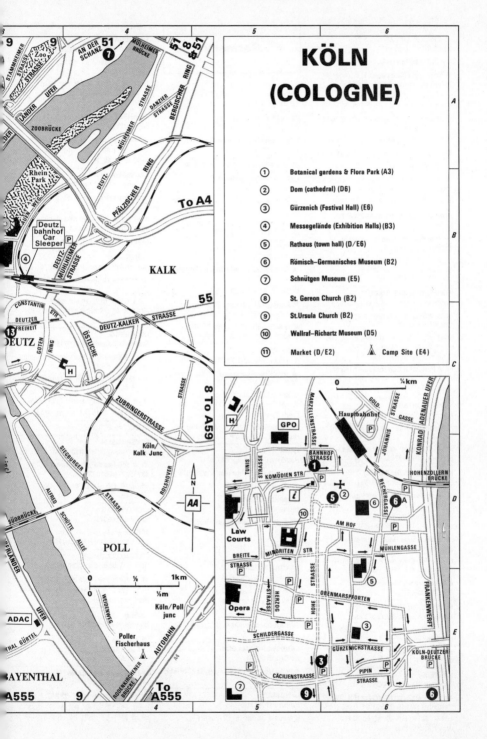

KÖLN
(COLOGNE)

1. Botanical gardens & Flora Park (A3)
2. Dom (cathedral) (D6)
3. Gürzenich (Festival Hall) (E6)
4. Messegelände (Exhibition Halls) (B3)
5. Rathaus (town hall) (D/E6)
6. Römisch–Germanisches Museum (B2)
7. Schnütgen Museum (E5)
8. St. Gereon Church (B2)
9. St.Ursula Church (B2)
10. Wallraf–Richartz Museum (D5)
11. Market (D/E2)   Camp Site (E4)

⇔ ▥113 **P** Lift ☽ sB ⇔ ▥167
dB ⇔ ▥217 Pool

At **KÖLN-LINDENTHAL**

☆ ☆ ☆**Crest (See page 51)** Dürener Str
287 ☎463001 tx8882516 Plan **4**
rm154 ⇔76 ▥78 **P** Lift ☽
sB ⇔ ▥151–175 dB ⇔ ▥198–200

★ ★**Bremer** Dürenerstr 225 ☎ 405013
tx8882063 Plan **11**
rm80 ⇔8 ▥65 ⚐ **P** Lift ☽ Pool
Klerdorf Universitätstr 91 ☎402061 Frd

At **KÖLN-MÜLHEIM**

★ ★ ★**Kaiser** Genovevastr 10–14 (n.rest)
☎623057 tx8873546 Plan **7**
rm80 ⇔7 ▥27 ⚐ **P** Lift ☽ Pool

KÖNIGSFELD IM SCHWARZWALD
Baden-Württemberg(☎07725)

★ ★ ★**Schwarzwald** H-Voland Str 10
☎7091 tx792426
rm52 ⇔16 ▥32 A31rm ⚐ **P** Lift ☽
sB62 sB ⇔ ▥74–85 dB116
dB ⇔ ▥132–172 Pool

KÖNIGSTEIN IM TAUNUS
Hessen(☎06174)

★ ★ ★**Sonnenhof** Falkensteiner Str 9
☎3051 tx0410636
rm44 ⇔31 ▥7 A22rm ⚐ **P** ☽ sB68
sB ⇔ ▥84–110 dB96 dB ⇔ ▥117–185
M20–80 Pool mountains

★ ★**Parkhotel Bender** Frankfurterstr 1
☎1005
rm34 ⇔12 ▥10 ⚐ **P**

KÖNIGSWINTER
Nordrhein-Westfalen(☎02223)

★**Siebengebirge** Haupstr 342 ☎21359
Feb–15 Dec
rm10 ▥15 ⚐ **P** sB38–44 sB ▥43–48
dB69–76 dB ▥77–82 M12–24

KONSTANZ (CONSTANCE)
Baden-Württemberg(☎07531)

★ ★ ★**Insel** (SRS) auf der Insel 1
☎25011 tx733276
rm120 ⇔105 A2rm **P** Lift ☽
sB ⇔110–140 dB ⇔165–220 M alc lake

★ ★**Deutsches Haus** Markstätte 15
(n.rest) ☎27065
rm42 ⇔6 ▥25 ⚐ **P** Lift ☽ sB48
sB ⇔ ▥50–60 dB75 dB ⇔ ▥120
⅋L Vendrame Radolfzeller Str
65 ☎79098 M/c **P** BL MG

KORNTAL-MÜNCHINGEN
Baden-Württemberg(☎07150)

☆ ☆ ☆**Mercure** Siemensstr 55 ☎131
tx723589
⇔ ▥118 **P** Lift ☽ sB ⇔ ▥94–137
dB ⇔ ▥94–157 M8–28 Pool

KREFELD
Nordrhein-Westfalen(☎02151)

★ ★ ★**Parkhotel Krefelder Hof** (BW)
Uerdinger Str 245 ☎590191 tx0853748
⇔147 ⚐ **P** Lift ☽ sB ⇔ ▥140
dB ⇔ ▥210 Pool

Germany

⅋Preckel Virchowstr 139–145
☎37110 Ren

KREUZNACH (BAD)
Rheinland-Pfalz(☎0671)

⅋E Holzhäuser Mannheimerstr
183–185 ☎30031 Frd

KREUZWERTHEIM See **WERTHEIM**

KRONBERG IM TAUNUS
Hessen(☎06173)

★ ★ ★ ★**Schloss** Hainstr 25 ☎7011
tx415424
rm53 ⇔50 ▥1 **P** Lift ☽ sB125
sB ⇔ ▥175 dB ⇔ ▥315

KULMBACH
Bayern(☎09221)

★ ★ ★**Hansa-Hotel Hönsch** Weltrichstr 2
(n.rest) ☎7995
rm29 ⇔14 ▥11 ⚐ **P** Lift

⅋A Dippold Kronacher Str 2
☎2017 Aud Por VW

⅋W Schubarth Kronacher Str 29
☎5660 BL DJ MG RT

LAHNSTEIN
Rheinland-Pfalz(☎02621)

★ ★ ★**Rhein-Lahn** (BW) Im Kurzentrum
☎151 tx869827
rm220 ⇔100 ▥120 **P** Lift ☽
sB ⇔ ▥86–96 dB ⇔ ▥140–150 ⅋
Pool mountains

⅋Autoteilehandel Frankenstr 1 Am
Hafen ☎3630 M/c **P** All makes

LAHR
Baden-Württemberg(☎07821)

★**Schulz** Alte Bahnhofstr 6 ☎22674
rm25 ⇔4 ▥16 ⚐ **P**

LAMPERTHEIM
Hessen(☎06206)

★ ★ ★**Deutsches Haus** Kaiserstr 47
☎2022
6 Jan–20 Dec
▥30 **P** Lift

LANDAU IN DER PFALZ
Rheinland-Pfalz(☎06341)

★ ★**Körber** Reiterstr 11 ☎4050
rm40 ⇔10 ▥30 ⚐ **P** ☽
sB ⇔ ▥48–55 dB ⇔ ▥80–95

⅋R Kruppenbecher Aug-Croissant Str
1–3 ☎80054 **P** Frd

LANDSBERG AM LECH
Bayern(☎08191)

A Popp Münchenerstr 34–36 ☎2020 M/c
P Opl Vau

LANDSHUT
Bayern(☎0871)

K Meusel Ottostr 15 ☎72048 Frd

LANGENARGEN
Baden-Württemberg(☎07543)

★ ★**Schiff** Marktpl 1 ☎2407
Apr–Oct
rm42 ⇔9 ▥25 ⚐ **P** Lift sB40
sB ⇔ ▥65 dB80 dB ⇔ ▥130
mountains lake

LANGENISARHOFEN
Bayern(☎09938)

☆**Buhmann** Kreuzstr 1 an der B8 ☎277
15 Jan–24 Dec
rm13 ⇔5 ⚐ **P**

LAUTENBACH
Baden-Württemberg(☎07802)

★**Sternen** Hauptstr 47 ☎3538
Closed Nov
rm42 ⇔30 ▥10 ⚐ **P** Lift sB38
sB ⇔ ▥49 dB76 dB ⇔ ▥98 mountains

LENGFELD See **WÜRZBURG**

LENZKIRCH
Baden-Württemberg(☎07653)

★ ★**Ursee** Grabenstr 18 ☎781
15 Dec–2 Nov
rm54 ⇔28 ▥22 **P** Lift sB36
sB ⇔ ▥46–52 dB68 dB ⇔ ▥80–104
t%

LEONBERG
Baden-Württemberg(☎07152)

★ ★ ★**Eiss** Neue Ramtelstr 28 (near the
Autobahn) ☎20041 tx724141
rm109 ⇔35 ▥54 ⚐ **P** Lift ☽ sB60
sB ⇔ ▥95 dB100 dB ⇔ ▥170

★ ★**Sonne** Stuttgarterstr 1 ☎27626
rm44 ⇔19 ▥15 A17rm ⚐ **P** ☽

LEONI See **BERG**

LEVERKUSEN
Nordrhein-Westfalen(☎0214)

☆ ☆ ☆**Ramada** am Büchelter Hof 11
☎41012 tx8510238
⇔202 **P** Lift ☽ sB ⇔130–220
dB ⇔190–250 Pool

LICHTENFELS
Bayern(☎09571)

⅋Szymansky Bamberg Str
125 ☎3654 M/c **P** BL Chy Hon

LIEBENZELL (BAD)
Baden-Württemberg(☎07052)

★ ★ ★**Kronen** Badweg 7 ☎2081
rm77 ⇔27 ▥33 A17rm ⚐ **P** Lift ⅋
Pool mountains

LIESER
Rheinland-Pflaz(☎06531)

★ ★**Mehn** Moselstr 2 ☎6019
15 Feb–16 Dec
rm25 ⇔2 ▥7 ⚐ **P**

LIMBURG AN DER LAHN
Hessen(☎06431)

★ ★**Dom** Grabenstr 57 ☎24077
rm59 ⇔8 ▥35 ⚐ **P** Lift ☽ sB43
sB ⇔ ▥61–67 dB81 dB ⇔ ▥81–123 M
alc

★ ★**Zimmermann** Blumenröderstr 1
☎42030 tx0484782

rm30 ⇆20 🛏10 A5rm 🍴 **P** sB45–70
sB ⇆ 🛏60–70 dB75–98 dB ⇆ 🛏80–120

★**Huss** Bahnhofpl 3 ☎25087 tx0484839
rm34 ⇆5 🛏19 🍴 **P** Lift *D* sB38–44
sB ⇆ 🛏64 dB74 dB ⇆ 🛏112

J Tritsch Industriestr–☎4601 Frd

Unterfeld Westerwaldstr 82 ☎25277 **P**
BL Hon

LINDAU IM BODENSEE
Bayern(☎08382)

★ ★ ★**Bayrischer Hof** Seepromenade
☎5055 tx054340

Apr–Oct
rm95 ⇆82 🛏13 🍴 **P** Lift *D*
sB ⇆ 🛏95–152 dB ⇆ 🛏264 Pool
mountains lake

★ ★ ★**Reutemann** Seepromenade
☎5055 tx054340
rm37 ⇆28 🛏9 🍴 **P** Lift *D*
sB ⇆ 🛏106 dB ⇆ 🛏205 Pool
mountains lake

★ ★**Kellner** Alwindstr 7 (n.rest) ☎5686
mid May–mid Sep
rm12 ⇆5 🛏1 🍴 **P**

★ ★**Seegarten** Seepromenade ☎5055
tx054340
Mar–Nov
rm29 ⇆7 🛏22 🍴 **P** Lift *D*
sB ⇆ 🛏188 dB ⇆ 🛏170 Pool
mountains lake

★**Lindauer Hof** Seehafen ☎4064
rm22 ⇆5 🛏17 **P** Lift Pool mountains
lake

LINDENTHAL See **KÖLN (COLOGNE)**

LIPPSTADT
Nordrhein-Westfalen (☎02941)

Mertens Planckstr 12 ☎14041 **P** Frd

LÖRRACH
Baden-Württemberg(☎07621)

★ ★ ★**Binoth am Markt** Baslerstr 169
☎2673
rm22 ⇆4 🛏14 **P** *D* sB40 sB ⇆ 🛏55
dB60 dB ⇆ 🛏90

🚗**Badenia** Brühlerstr 8 ☎2420 Frd

🚗*Büche & Tröndle* Tumringer Str
290 ☎8502 Aud Por VW

LÜBECK
Schleswig-Holstein(☎0451)

★ ★ ★**Lysia** (Mövenpick) auf der
Wallhalbinsel ☎15040 tx26707
rm130 ⇆17 🛏113 **P** Lift *D*
sB ⇆ 🛏162 dB ⇆ 🛏189

★**Lindenhof** Lindenstr 1A ☎84015
rm54 ⇆30 🍴 **P** Lift *D* sB45 sB ⇆65
dB75 dB ⇆100 M alc

★**Kaiserhof** Kronsforder Allee 13
☎791011
rm55 ⇆15 🛏17 A17rm 🍴 **P** Lift *D*

Germany

🚗**Albrecht & Wirth** Ratzeburger Allee
127 ☎501031 Frd

Jäckel Travemunder Allee 15–17
☎33088 **P** Ren

N Köster Heiligen-Geist-Kamp 6–8
☎32032 Cit

LÜDENSCHEID
Nordrhein-Westfalen(☎02351)

☆ ☆ ☆**Crest (see page 51)** Parkstr 66
☎1561 tx826644
⇆ 🛏195 **P** Lift *D* sB ⇆ 🛏125
dB ⇆ 🛏156–160 Pool

🚗**Märkischer Automobil** Kölner Str
88–90 ☎3711 Frd

LUDWIGSBURG
Baden-Württemberg(☎07141)

At **MONREPOS (SCHLOSS)** (5km NW)

★ ★ ★ ★**Schlosshotel Monrepos** (BW)
☎30101 tx7264720
rm83 ⇆40 🛏43 **P** Lift *D*
sB ⇆ 🛏124 dB ⇆ 🛏160–185 Pool lake

LUDWIGSHAFEN
Rheinland-Pfalz(☎0621)

★ ★ ★**City Europe** Ludwigspl
5–6 ☎519011 tx0464701
⇆ 🛏90 🍴 **P** Lift *D* 🏊 Pool

★ ★ ★**Excelsior** (BW) Lorientallee 16
☎519201 tx046450
⇆160 **P** Lift *D* sB ⇆118
dB ⇆158 Pool

LÜNEBURG
Niedersachsen(☎04131)

☆ ☆**Landwehr** Hamburgerstr 15
☎121024
20 Jan–20 Dec
rm35 ⇆12 🛏23 🍴 **P** *D* sB44
sB ⇆ 🛏56–93 dB ⇆ 🛏86–156 Pool

🚗**F Anker** Vor dem Bardowicker Tore
43 ☎31066 M/c **P** Frd

LÜTJENBURG
Schleswig-Holstein(☎04381)

🚗**J Seemann** Hindenburgstr
17 ☎7833 **P** Frd

MAINZ
Rheinland-Pfalz(☎06131)

★ ★ ★ ★**Hilton International** Rheinstr 68
☎2450 tx4187570
⇆ 🛏435 🍴 **P** Lift *D*
sB ⇆ 🛏162–298 dB ⇆ 🛏222–399

★ ★ ★**Central** Bahnhofspl 8 ☎674001
tx4187794
rm67 ⇆20 🛏47 🍴 **P** Lift *D*
sB ⇆ 🛏72–95 dB ⇆ 🛏120–190

★ ★ ★**Europa** Kaiserstr 7 ☎671091
tx4187702
⇆90 🛏60 **P** Lift *D* sB ⇆ 🛏170
dB ⇆ 🛏220 M alc

★ ★ ★**Mainzer Hof** (ETAP) Kaiserstr 98
☎233771 tx4187787
rm73 ⇆39 🛏34 **P** Lift *D*
sB ⇆ 🛏142 dB ⇆ 🛏175 M alc

☆ ☆ ☆**Novotel Mainz Süd** Essenheimer
Str ☎361054 tx4187236
⇆ 🛏121 **P** Lift *D* sB ⇆ 🛏124
dB ⇆ 🛏174 Pool

Heinz am Bismarckpl ☎676011 Frd

At **FINTHEN** (7km W)

★ ★**Kurmainz** (MIN) Flugplatzstr 44
(n.rest) ☎40056 tx4187001
3 Jan–2 Dec
rm95 ⇆7 🛏43 A7rm 🍴 **P** Lift *D*
sB ⇆ 🛏95 dB ⇆ 🛏100–135 🏊 Pool

MANDERSCHEID
Rheinland-Pfalz(☎06572)

★ ★**Zens** Kurfürststr 35 ☎769
Closed 5 Nov–20 Dec
rm46 ⇆10 🛏17 🍴 **P** Lift *D* Pool
mountains

MANNHEIM
Baden-Württemberg(☎0621)

★ ★ ★**Mannheimer Hof** (SRS) A-
Anlage 4–8 ☎45021 tx462245
⇆200 **P** Lift *D* sB ⇆ 125–175
dB ⇆190–240

★ ★**Augusta** (BW) A-Anlage 43–45
☎408001 tx462395
rm105 ⇆50 🛏55 🍴 **P** Lift *D*
sB ⇆ 🛏122–128 dB ⇆ 🛏165–195
Mfr25

☆ ☆ ☆**Novotel** auf dem Friedenspl
☎402071 tx463694
⇆ 🛏180 **P** Lift *D* sB ⇆ 🛏124
dB ⇆ 🛏155 Pool

★ ★**Intercity Mannheim** Hauptbahnhof
☎22925 tx463604
rm48 ⇆5 🛏43 **P** Lift *D* sB ⇆ 🛏73
dB ⇆ 🛏115

★ ★**Kaiserring** Kaiserring 18 (n.rest)
☎23931
rm52 ⇆16 🛏27 🍴 **P** Lift *D* sB36
sB⇆🛏46–72 dB66 dB⇆🛏86–129

★ ★**Mack** Mozartstr 14 (n.rest) ☎23888
tx0462116
10 Jan–15 Dec
rm75 ⇆16 🛏18 A6rm 🍴 **P** Lift *D*
sB38–40 sB ⇆ 🛏45–58 dB66
dB ⇆ 🛏76–92

🚗**H Kohlhoff** Obere Riedstr
117–119 ☎737005 M/c **P** Frd

🚗**Kurpfalz** Schwetzinger Str 148–152
☎441031 Frd

At **SANDHOFEN** (10km N)

☆**Weber** Frankenthaler Str 85 ☎782021
tx463537
🛏50 🍴 **P** Lift

MARBURG AN DER LAHN
Hessen(☎06421)

★ ★**Europäischer Hof** Elisabethstr 12
☎640444
rm106 ⇆17 🛏73 A40rm 🍴 **P** Lift *D* →

sB46 sB ⇄ 🛏48–75 dB65–70
dB ⇄ 🛏85–125

At **CÖLBE** (7km N)

🕭M **Feeser** Erlenring 9 ☎23038 **P** Frd

MARIA LAACH
Rheinland-Pfalz(☎02652)

★★**Seehotel** ☎4251
rm74 ⇄7 🛏16 A14rm 🚗 **P** Lift 🌙
sB39–46 sB ⇄ 🛏60 dB70–90
dB ⇄ 🛏105–115 Pool lake

MARIA WEILER See DÜREN

MARIENBERG (BAD)
Rheinland-Pfalz(☎02661)

★★★**Kneipp-Kurhotel Wildpark**
Kurallee 1 (1km W) ☎7069
20 Dec–15 Nov
rm45 ⇄20 🛏20 🚗 **P** Lift sB43
sB ⇄ 🛏60–80 dB ⇄ 🛏110–140 Pool
mountains

MARKTHEIDENFELD
Bayern(☎09391)

★★**Schöne Aussicht** Brückenstr 8
☎3455
rm47 ⇄2 🛏31 🚗 **P** Lift

★**Anker** Obertorstr 6–8 ☎4041 tx689608
rm36 ⇄28 🛏8 🚗 **P** Lift 🌙

MARKTOBERDORF
Bayern(☎08342)

★**Sepp** Bahnhofstr 13 ☎2048
rm55 ⇄4 🛏51 A24rm 🚗 **P** 🌙

MAYSCHOSS See ALTENAHR

MEERSBURG
Baden-Württemberg(☎07532)

★★**Bären** Marktpl 11 ☎6044
10 Mar–10 Nov
rm15 🛏14 🚗 **P** sB 🛏45 dB59
dB 🛏96

★★3 **Stuben** Winzergasse 1 ☎6019
Mar–Nov
rm15 ⇄2 🛏13 🚗 **P** sB ⇄ 🛏77–82
dB ⇄ 🛏108–124

★★**Weinstube Löwen** Marktpl 2 ☎6013
⇄ 🛏12 **P** sB ⇄ 🛏45–50
dB ⇄ 🛏90–130 M16–30

MEMMINGEN
Bayern(☎08331)

★★★**Adler** Maximilianstr 3 ☎87015
rm55 ⇄29 🛏15 A5rm 🚗 **P** Lift 🌙
sB45–63 sB ⇄ 🛏60–68 dB90–101
dB ⇄ 🛏115–121 M10–25

🕭**Draxler** Birkenweg 1 ☎4717 **P** Dat

Karrer Brahmstr 3 ☎87941 **P** Frd

C **Schenk** Donaustr 29 ☎86048 Opl

MERGENTHEIM (BAD)
Baden-Württemberg(☎07931)

★★★★**Victoria** Poststr 2–4 ☎5930
tx74224
rm100 ⇄65 🛏25 🚗 **P** Lift 🌙
sB65–75 sB ⇄ 🛏80–90 dB120
dB ⇄ 🛏140–160 M15–28 Pool

Germany

MERKLINGEN
Baden-Württemberg(☎07337)

★**Ochsen** Hauptstr 12 ☎483
Closed Nov
rm19 🛏12 🚗 **P** sB36 sB 🛏45–48
dB60 dB 🛏75 M11–30

MERZIG
Saarland(☎06861)

Auto-Industrie Trierer Str 197–199
☎5025 **P** Frd

MINDELHEIM
Bayern(☎08261)

🕭E **Schragl** Allgäuer Str 2 ☎8021 Aud
VW

MINDEN
Nordrhein-Westfalen(☎0571)

★★**Kruses Park** Marienstr 108 ☎46033
rm40 ⇄10 🛏24 🚗 **P** sB60
sB ⇄ 🛏93 dB112 dB ⇄ 🛏142

★★**Silke** Fischerglacis 21 (n.rest)
☎23736
rm23 ⇄8 🛏15 🚗 **P** Pool

🕭**Gössling & Böger** Ringstr 11
☎27037 **P** Frd

🕭**W Thielker** Stiftallee 27 ☎41252 M/c **P**
Frd

MITTENWALD
Bayern(☎08823)

★★**Post** Obermarkt 9 ☎1094
rm96 ⇄47 🛏21 🚗 **P** Lift 🌙
sB37–65 sB ⇄ 🛏45–80 dB60–100
dB ⇄ 🛏96–100 Pool mountains

★**Zerhoch** H-Barth-Weg 7 (n.rest)
☎1508
20 Dec–25 Oct
⇄15 🚗 **P** mountains

🕭**K Schober** ☎8442 M/c **P** Opl

MÖHRINGEN See STUTTGART

MÖNCHENGLADBACH
Nordrhein-Westfalen(☎02161)

★★★★**Dorint Mönchengladbach**
Hohenzollernstr 5 ☎86060 tx8252656
rm102 ⇄70 🛏32 **P** Lift 🌙
sB ⇄ 🛏104–129 dB ⇄ 🛏166–192 Pool

☆☆☆**Holiday Inn** am Geropl ☎31131
⇄128 Lift

🕭**Issel** Monschauer Str 34 ☎36011 Ren

🕭E **Menke** Erkelenzer Str 8 ☎58991 **P**
Fia Vau

R Rankin Druckerstr 17 ☎129128 BL DJ
RT

T Weller Hubertusstr ☎3535 Frd

At **RHEYDT** (4km S)

★★★**Besch Parkhotel** H-Junkers Str 2
☎(02166)44011 tx8529143

---

rm33 ⇄6 🛏27 🚗 **P** Lift 🌙
sB ⇄ 🛏90 dB ⇄ 🛏132

★★**Coenen** Giesenkirchener Str 41–45
☎(02166)10088
⇄ 🛏30 🚗 **P**

MONREPOS (SCHLOSS) See
LUDWIGSBURG

MONSCHAU
Nordrhein-Westfalen(☎02472)

★★**Aquarium** Heidgen 34 ☎693
rm10 ⇄3 🛏7 🚗 **P** Pool mountains

★★**Horchem** Rurstr 14 ☎490
Mar–Dec
rm14 ⇄4 🛏4 🚗 **P** sB ⇄ 🛏45 dB72
dB ⇄ 🛏84 mountains

★**Burgau** St-Vither Str 16 ☎2120
rm13 🛏7 🚗 **P** mountains

★**Haus Herrlichkelt** Haagweg 3A (n.rest)
☎3190
rm7 🛏6 🚗 **P** mountains

MONTABAUR
Rheinland-Pfalz(☎02602)

★**Post** Bahnhofstr 30 ☎3361
rm22 ⇄1 🛏6 🚗 **P** Lift 🌙

★**Schlemmer** Kirchstr 18 ☎5022
10 Jan–23 Dec
rm25 ⇄10 🚗 **P** sB31 sB 🛏42 dB62
dB 🛏72–82

At **HEILIGENROTH** (250m from
Montabaur exit Frankfurt-Köln Autobahn)

☆☆**Helligenroth** ☎5044 tx869675
🛏28 🚗 **P** Lift 🌙

MOSBACH
Baden-Württemberg(☎06261)

At **NECKARELZ** (4km SW junct 37/27)

★★★**Tannenhof** Tannenweg 12 ☎2706
rm56 ⇄6 🛏50 🚗 **P** Pool mountains

Autozentrale Waldsteige West ☎5075 **P**
Frd

MÜHLDORF AM INN
Bayern(☎08631)

★**Jägerhof** Stadpl 3 ☎4003
rm26 🛏16 🚗 **P**

MÜLHEIM See KÖLN (COLOGNE)

MÜLHEIM AN DER MOSEL
Rheinland-Pfalz(☎06534)

★★**Moselhaus Seizer** Moselstr 7 ☎707
Mar–15 Nov
rm15 ⇄7 🛏7 🚗 **P**

MÜLHEIM AN DER RUHR
Nordrhein-Westfalen(☎02133)

★★★**Noy** Schlosstr 28–30 ☎44671
rm60 ⇄15 🛏45 🚗 **P** Lift 🌙
sB67–72 sB ⇄ 🛏110–137
dB ⇄ 🛏172–184

MÜLHEIM
Baden-Württemberg(☎07631)

☆☆☆**Euro-Hotel Alte Post** (On road B3
near Autobahn exit) ☎5522 tx772916

rm57 ⇄7 🛏41 A42rm ⌂ **P** ☽
sB34–62 dB ⇄ 🛏72–80 dB66
dB ⇄ 🛏130

★★**Markgraf** Marzellerweg 18 ☎3026
rm13 ⇄7 ⌂ **P** mountains

MUMMELSEE See **BADEN-BADEN**

MÜNCHEN (MUNICH)
Bayern(☎089)
See Plan page 216

★★★**Bayerischer Hof** (SRS)
Promenadepl 2–6 ☎21200 tx523409
Plan **1**
rm442 ⇄404 🛏38 **P** Lift ☽
sB ⇄ 🛏143–188 dB ⇄ 🛏215–315 Pool

★★★★**Excelsior** Schützenstr 11
☎557906 tx522419 Plan **2**
rm105 ⇄100 🛏5 ⌂ **P** Lift ☽
sB ⇄ 🛏160 dB ⇄ 🛏190

★★★★**Hilton International** am
Tucherpark 7 ☎340051 tx5215740
Plan **2A**
⇄481 **P** Lift ☽ sB ⇄145–232
dB ⇄182–343 M33 Pool

☆☆☆**Holiday Inn München**
Leopoldstr 194 ☎340971 tx5215439
Plan **3**
⇄363 ⌂ Lift ☽ sB ⇄ 🛏130–180
dB ⇄ 🛏160–230 M alc Pool

★★★★**Vier Jahreszeiten** (Intercont)
Maximilianstr 17 ☎230390 tx523859
Plan **5**
⇄365 A172rm **P** Lift ☽ sB ⇄195–240
dB ⇄245–330 Pool

☆☆**Crest (See page 51)** Effnerstr 99
☎982541 tx524757 Plan **5A**
⇄ 🛏155 **P** Lift ☽ sB ⇄ 🛏140
dB ⇄ 🛏177–180

★★★**Deutscher Kaiser** Arnulfstr 2
☎558321 tx522650 Plan **6**
rm156 ⇄84 🛏28 **P** Lift ☽ sB84
sB ⇄ 🛏118 dB165 dB ⇄ 🛏195

★★★**Eden-Wolff** (SRS) Arnulfstr 4–8
☎558281 tx523564 Plan **7**
⇄ 🛏220 ⌂ **P** Lift ☽
sB ⇄ 🛏125–175 dB ⇄ 🛏160–260

★★★**Penta** (Forum) Hochstr 3
☎4485555 tx529046 Plan **8**
rm583 ⇄570 🛏13 ⌂ **P** Lift ☽
sB ⇄ 🛏140–171 dB ⇄ 🛏185–237 M28
Pool

★★**Daniel** Sonnenstr 5 (n.rest)
☎554945 tx523863 Plan **10**
rm81 ⇄25 🛏46 **P** Lift sB80
sB ⇄ 🛏88 dB98 dB ⇄ 🛏129

★★**Drei Löwen** (BW) Schillerstr 8
☎595521 tx523867 Plan **11**
⇄130 ⌂ **P** Lift ☽ sB ⇄105–112
dB ⇄158–178 M alc

★★**Platzl** Münzstr 8–9 ☎293101
tx522910 Plan **13**
rm100 ⇄65 🛏35 **P** Lift ☽
sB ⇄ 🛏78 dB ⇄ 🛏130

★**Leopold** Leopoldstr 119, Schwabing
☎367061 tx5215160 Plan **14**

Germany

rm82 ⇄26 🛏39 A52rm ⌂ **P** Lift ☽
sB ⇄ 🛏120 dB90 dB ⇄ 🛏150

&**Corso-Behnke** Zielstattstr
63 ☎786087 Lot Maz Peu

&**Niedermayer & Reich** Landsberger Str
20 ☎505041 Frd

H Wolff Mullerstr 50 ☎265488 **P** BL

MÜNSTER
Nordrhein-Westfalen(☎0251)

★★★**Kaiserhof** Bahnhofstr 14–16
(n.rest) ☎40059 tx892141
rm110 ⇄25 🛏85 ⌂ **P** Lift ☽
sB ⇄ 🛏95–99 dB ⇄ 🛏147–185

☆☆**Mövenpick** Kardinal-von-Galen
Ring 65 ☎89020 tx251104
⇄120 **P** Lift ☽ sB ⇄123–143
dB ⇄150–170 M alc

★★**Schloss Wilkinghege** (GS)
Steinfurterstr 374 (4km NW on B54)
☎213045
rm38 ⇄17 🛏21 A18rm ⌂ **P** ☽
sB ⇄ 🛏95 dB ⇄ 🛏120–165 ⅋ ♣

★**Conti** Berlinerpl 2A (n.rest) ☎40444
tx892113
rm62 ⇄6 🛏42 **P** Lift ☽ sB50–65
sB ⇄ 🛏65–100 dB85–95
dB ⇄ 🛏100–150

&**Ing W Brandes** Altenbergerstr
32 ☎(02533)534 **P** AR BL

&**Fischer** F-Ebertstr 71–97 ☎79931 M/c
P Frd

MURNAU
Bayern(☎08841)

★★★**Alpenhof Murnau** Ramsachstr 8
☎1045
⇄52 **P** Lift ☽ sB ⇄ 🛏85–150
dB ⇄ 🛏210 M alc Pool mountains

MURRHARDT
Baden-Württemberg(☎07192)

★★**Sonne Post** Karlstr 6–9 ☎8081
tx7245910
Closed Xmas
rm46 ⇄24 🛏13 ⌂ **P** Lift
sB ⇄ 🛏71–87 dB ⇄ 🛏112–164 Pool

NAGOLD
Baden-Württemberg(☎07452)

★★**Post** (ROM) Bahnofstr 2 ☎4048
rm20 ⇄17 🛏10 A16rm ⌂ **P** Lift ☽
sB43–80 sB ⇄ 🛏70–85 dB76–125
dB ⇄ 🛏135

NAUHEIM (BAD)
Hessen.(☎06032)

★★★**Park Hotel am Kurhaus** Nördlicher
Park 16 ☎3030 tx415514
⇄ 🛏99 ⌂ **P** Lift ☽ sB ⇄ 🛏126
dB ⇄ 🛏192

NECKARELZ See **MOSBACH**

NECKARGEMÜND
Baden-Württemberg(☎06223)

★★**Ritter** (GS) Neckarstr 40 ☎7035
tx461837
rm40 ⇄37 ⌂ **P** ☽

NECKARSTEINACH
Hessen(☎06229)

★★**Schiff** Neckargemünderstr 2 ☎324
8 Jan–15 Nov
rm22 ⇄4 🛏18 **P** Lift

NERESHEIM
Baden-Württemberg(☎07326)

★**Klosterhospiz** ☎6282
rm50 🛏13 A15rm **P** Lift

NEUASTENBERG See **WINTERBERG**

NEUBEURN
Bayern(☎08035)

★★**Burg** Marktpl 23 ☎2456
🛏16 ⌂ **P** Lift sB ⇄66 dB 🛏95
mountains

NEUENAHR (BAD)
Rheinland-Pfalz(☎02641)

★★★★**Kurhotel** (SRS) Kurgartenstr 1
☎2291 tx861812
rm246 ⇄174 🛏23 **P** Lift ☽
sB ⇄ 🛏99–135 dB ⇄ 🛏152–220 ⅋
Pool

★★★**Dorint** am Dahliengarten ☎2325
tx861805
⇄112 ⌂ **P** Lift ☽ sB ⇄107
dB ⇄fr166 Pool

★**Giffels Goldener Anker** Mittelstr 14
☎2385 tx861768
⇄60 🛏3 ⌂ **P** Lift ☽ sB65–75
sB ⇄ 🛏75–79 dB125 dB ⇄ 🛏140–150

★★**Hamburger Hof** Jesuitenstr 11
(n.rest) ☎26017
rm36 ⇄27 ⌂ **P** ☽ sB35–46
sB ⇄49–58 dB72–76 dB ⇄86–102

&**J Waldecker** Heerstr 115 ☎2366 Frd

NEUMÜNSTER
Schleswig-Holstein(☎04321)

★★**Lenz** Gasstr 11–12 (n.rest) ☎45072
⇄13 ⌂ **P** ☽ sB ⇄38–48 dB ⇄55–65

&**E Landschoof** Rungestr 5 ☎53518 **P**
BL

NEUSS
Nordrhein-Westfalen(☎02101)

At **ERFTTAL** (5km SE off A57)

☆☆☆**Novotel Neuss** am Derikumer Hof
1 ☎17081 tx8517634
⇄115 **P** Lift sB ⇄129 dB ⇄161 Pool

At **GRIMLINGHAUSEN** (4.5km SE on B9)

★★**Landhaus** Hüsenstr 17 ☎37756
tx8517891
🛏28 ⌂ **P** Lift sB 🛏65–95
dB 🛏117–170

NEUSTADT See **TITISEE-NEUSTADT**

MÜNCHEN (MUNICH)

1 ★★★★Bayerischer Hof
2 ★★★★Excelsior
2A ★★★★Hilton International
3 ☆☆☆☆Holiday Inn München
5 ★★★★Vier Jahreszeiten
5A ☆☆☆Crest
6 ★★★Deutscher Kaiser
7 ★★★Eden-Wolff
8 ★★★Penta
10 ★★Daniel
11 ★★Drei Löwen
13 ★★Platzl
14 ★Leopold

NEUSTADT AN DER AISCH
Bayern(☎09161)

★★Römerhof R-Wagnerstr 15 ☎2498
rm38 ⇄2 ⋔10 ⌂ P sB32–33
sB⇄⋔42–45 dB60 dB⇄⋔75–85

NEUSTADT AN DER SAALE (BAD)
Bayern(☎09771)

★★★Schwan & Post am Hohntor
☎5038
May–Jun
rm22 ⇄1 ⋔21 ⌂ P

NEUSTADT AN DER WEINSTRASSE
Rheinland-Pfalz(☎06321)

At SCHÖNTAL (3km W)

★Konigsmühle Schöntalstr 10 ☎83031
rm38 ⇄11 ⋔4 A13rm P Lift
mountains

⅋Naumer & Söhne A-Kolping Str
41 ☎13038 P Frd

NEU-ULM
Bayern(☎0731)

☆☆☆Mövenpick Silcherstr 40 ☎80110
tx712539
⇄109 P Lift ☾ sB⇄128–148
dB⇄155–175 Pool

NEUWIED
Rheinland-Pfalz(☎02631)

⅋Sportwagen Service Königsberger Str
12 ☎53018 P M/c

P Wirtz Allensteiner Str 15 ☎5195 P Opl

NIEFERN-ÖSCHELBRONN See
PFORZHEIM

NIERSTEIN
Rheinland-Pfalz(☎06133)

★★★Alter Vater Rhein ☎5628
Closed Xmas
rm11 ⋔10 P

★Rheinhotel Mainzerstr 16 ☎5161
15 Jan–15 Dec
rm13 ⇄1 ⋔12 ⌂ P Lift sB⇄66–88
dB⇄99–133

NONNENHORN
Bayern(☎08382)

★★★Strandhotel Nonnenhorn
Wasserburger Str 14 ☎8223
Apr–Oct →

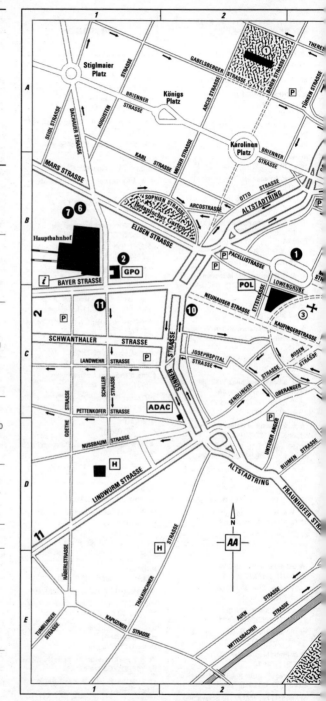

MÜNCHEN
(MUNICH) CENTRAL

Englischer Garten

National Museum

MAX JOSEPH BRÜCKE

MONTGELAS STRASSE

LUDWIG STRASSE

11 & 13

VON-DER-TANN STRASSE

GALERIE STRASSE

HOFGARTEN STRASSE

ALTSTADTRING

KARL-SCHARNAGL-RING

RESIDENZSTRASSE

PRINZREGENTEN STRASSE

PRINZREGENTEN BRÜCKE

WAGMÜLLER STRASSE

SEITZ STRASSE

LIEBIG STRASSE

ISAR

STERN STRASSE

WIDENMAYER STRASSE

THIERSCH STRASSE

TRIFT STRASSE

MARSTALL STRASSE

MAXIMILIAN STRASSE

MAXIMILIAN BRÜCKE

HILDEGARD STRASSE

THOMAS-WIMMER-RING

SPARKASSENSTRASSE

To A992

EINSTEIN STRASSE

304

FRAUEN STRASSE

ZWEIBRÜCKEN STRASSE

STEINSDORF STRASSE

INNERE WIENER STRASSE

MARIA-THERESIA-STRASSE

ISMANINGER STRASSE

MÖHL STRASSE

KLENZE STRASSE

BAADER STRASSE

CORNELIUS STR

ERHARDT STRASSE

KOHL STRASSE

LUDWIGS BRÜCKE

BOSCHE BRÜCKE

ZEPPELIN STRASSE

LILIEN STRASSE

CORNELIUS BRÜCKE

ISAR

SCHWEIGER STRASSE

OHLMÜLLER STRASSE

FALKEN STRASSE

GEBSATTEL STRASSE

ROSENHEIMER STRASSE

BALAN STRASSE

ORLEANS STRASSE

Car Sleeper

Ostbahnhof

AUERFELD STRASSE

To A8

0 ———— ½km
0 ———— ½m

ALTSTADTRING (RING ROAD) ————

KÖNIGIN STRASSE

LEUCHENFELD STRASSE

OETTINGEN STRASSE

EMIL-RIEDEL-STRASSE

WIDENMAYER STRASSE

MÖHL STRASSE

ISMANINGER STRASSE

rm27 ⇄15 ⋔5 🏛 P Pool mountains lake

NORDEN
Niedersachsen(☎04931)

★**Deutsches Haus** Neuer Weg 26 ☎4271
Closed 1–13 Jan
rm41 ⇄9 ⋔30 🏛 P Lift sB26–28
sB ⇄ ⋔37–39 dB47–49 dB ⇄ ⋔68–74
M14–28

NORDHORN
Niedersachen(☎05921)

★**Euregio** Dortmunder Str 20 ☎5077
rm26 ⋔24 🏛 P ⅅ

NÖRDLINGEN
Bayern(☎09081)

★ ★ ★**Sonne** Marktpl 3 ☎5067 tx051749
rm40 ⇄28 ⋔6 🏛 P

NOTSCHREI
Baden-Württemberg(☎07602)

★ ★**Waldhotel am Notschrei** ☎219
rm36 ⇄14 ⋔16 🏛 P Lift sB44–48
sB ⇄ ⋔54–66 dB84–92
dB ⇄ ⋔102–132 Pool mountains

NÜRBURG
Rheinland-Pfalz(☎02691)

At **NÜRBURGRING** (1km SW)

★ ★**Sporthotel Tribüne** ☎2035
tx863919
rm49 ⇄4 ⋔23 A21rm 🏛 P ⅅ

NÜRNBERG (NUREMBERG)
Bayern(☎0911)

★ ★ ★ ★ ★**Grand** Bahnhofstr 1
☎203621 tx622010
⇄185 P Lift ⅅ sB ⇄129–154
dB ⇄173–213 Mfr24

★ ★ ★**Carlton** (BW) Eilgutstr 13
☎203535 tx622329
rm120 ⇄85 ⋔35 P Lift ⅅ
sB ⇄ ⋔145 dB ⇄ ⋔192

☆ ☆ ☆ ☆**Crest (See page 51)** Münchener
Str 283 ☎49441 tx622930
rm143 ⇄90 ⋔53 P Lift ⅅ
sB ⇄ ⋔146 dB ⇄ ⋔182-185

★ ★ ★**Atrium** (BW) Münchener Str 25
☎49011 tx626167
⇄200 P Lift ⅅ sB ⇄140–150
dB ⇄158–198 M24–30 Pool

★ ★ ★**Bayerischer Hof** Gleissbühlstr 15
(n.rest) ☎209251 tx626547
⋔80 🏛 P Lift ⅅ sB ⋔73–76
dB ⋔108–115

☆ ☆ ☆**Novotel Nürnberg Süd** Münchener
Str 340 ☎86791 tx626449
⇄117 P Lift ⅅ sB ⇄124 dB ⇄156
M20 Pool

★ ★ ★**Sterntor** Tafelhofstr 8 ☎203101
tx622632
rm120 ⇄60 ⋔30 P Lift ⅅ sB55–65
sB ⇄ ⋔95–105 dB80–90
dB ⇄ ⋔130–160

Germany

★ ★ ★**Victoria** Königstr 80 (n.rest)
☎203801 tx622825
7 Jan–23 Dec
rm64 ⇄17 ⋔42 P Lift ⅅ sB50
sB ⇄ ⋔69–79 dB ⇄ ⋔120

★ ★**Drei Linden** (MIN) Äussere
Suizbacherstr 1 ☎533620
rm28 ⇄3 ⋔25 🏛 P ⅅ
sB ⇄ ⋔78–95 dB ⇄ ⋔95–120

⅋**H Greissinger** P-Henlein Str 27–31
☎442551 P Frd

⅋**F A Motus** Sandreuth Str 26
☎42000 P BL

OBERAMMERGAU
Bayern(☎08822)

★ ★**Alte Post** Dorfstr 19 ☎6691
20 Dec–Oct
rm28 ⇄27 ⋔1 A6rm 🏛 P mountains

★ ★**Böld** König-Ludwig-Str 10 ☎520
tx592406
rm63 ⇄33 ⋔30 🏛 P ⅅ sB62
sB ⇄ ⋔77–97 dB104 dB ⇄ ⋔114–144
mountains

★ ★**Friedenshöhe** König-Ludwig-Str 31
☎598
23 Dec–Oct
rm11 ⇄4 ⋔7 P mountains

★ ★**Schilcherhof** Bahnhofstr 17 ☎4740
Closed Dec–9 Jan
rm17 ⇄3 ⋔9 A10rm 🏛 P mountains

OBERHAUSEN
Nordrhein-Westfalen(☎0208)

★ ★ ★**Ruhrland** Berlinerpl 2 ☎805031
tx0856900
rm60 ⇄20 ⋔25 🏛 P Lift ⅅ
sB54–64 sB ⇄ ⋔69–100 dB118–128
dB ⇄ ⋔138–200

⅋**P Gerstmann** Wehrstr 17–33
☎870041 M/c P Frd Hon

OBERKIRCH
Baden-Württemberg(☎07802)

★ ★**Obere Linde** (ROM) Hauptstr
25–27 ☎3038
rm47 ⇄22 ⋔18 A20rm 🏛 P Lift
sB75 sB ⇄95 dB105–150
dB ⇄105–165 ⅃ mountains

⅋**L Müller** Appenweiererstr 11
☎3356 Opl

At **ÖDSBACH** (3km S)

★ ★ ★**Grüner Baum** Aimstr 33 ☎2801
tx752627
rm54 ⇄18 ⋔36 🏛 P sB ⇄ ⋔55–68
dB ⇄ ⋔95–135 M9–35 ⅃ Pool
mountains

OBERSTAUFEN
Bayern(☎08386)

★ ★**Kurhotel Einsle** Kalzhoferstr 4
(n.rest) ☎2032
rm21 ⇄8 ⋔13 🏛 P mountains

OBERSTDORF
Bayern(☎08322)

★ ★ ★**Wittelsbacher Hof** Prinzenstr 24
☎1018
18 Dec–5 Apr & 26 May–16 Oct
rm90 ⇄50 ⋔36 🏛 P Lift ⅅ
sB45–58 sB ⇄ ⋔74–85
dB ⇄ ⋔96–170 M25–30 Pool
mountains

⅋**Nebelhorn** Nebelhornstr 59 ☎4669 P
Fia

OBERWESEL
Rheinland-Pfalz (☎06744)

★ ★**Auf Schönburg** (GS) Schönburg
(1.5km SE) ☎8198
Mar–15 Dec
rm21 ⇄11 ⋔9 P sB ⇄ ⋔80–90
dB ⇄ ⋔160 M23–35

★**Goldner Pfropfenzieher** ☎207
mid Mar–Oct
rm20 ⇄9 ⋔1 A2rm 🏛 P sB30–31
sB ⇄ ⋔35 dB60 dB ⇄ ⋔76–84
M7–28

★**Römerkrug** (GS) Marktpl 1 ☎8176
Feb–Nov
rm8 ⇄5 ⋔2 P

OCHSENFURT
Bayern(☎09331)

★**Bären** Hauptstr 74 ☎2282
Feb–22 Dec
rm28 ⇄2 ⋔10 🏛 P

ÖDSBACH See **OBERKIRCH**

OESPEL See **DORTMUND**

OESTRICH
Hessen (☎06723)

★ ★ ★**Schwan** (ROM) Rheinallee 5–7
☎3001 tx42146
Mar–Nov
rm57 ⇄30 ⋔27 A20rm 🏛 P Lift ⅅ
sB ⇄ ⋔80–105 dB ⇄ ⋔160–220
Mfr25

OEYNHAUSEN (BAD)
Nordrhein-Westfalen (☎05731)

★ ★**Hahnenkamp** (2.5km NE) Alte
Reichstr 4 ☎5041
Closed 23 & 24 Dec
rm20 ⇄13 ⋔7 🏛 P sB ⇄69–98
dB ⇄109–150 M10–40 Pool

OFFENBACH
Hessen (☎0611)

☆ ☆ ☆**Novotel** Strahlenberger Str 12
☎818011 tx413047
⇄130 P Lift sB ⇄141 dB ⇄161 Pool

★ ★**Graf** Schloss Str 19 ☎811702
2 Jan–22 Dec
rm30 ⇄4 ⋔22 P sB60 sB ⇄ ⋔85
dB ⇄ ⋔125

OFFENBURG
Baden-Württemberg (☎0781)

★★★Palmengarten Okenstr 13
☎25031 tx0752849
rm70 ⇄55 ⋔15 🅐 **P** Lift 𝄓
dB ⇄ ⋔110–200 mountains

★Sonne Hauptstr 94 ☎71039
rm40 ⇄5 ⋔12 A15rm 🅐 **P** sB48–50
sB ⇄ ⋔56–58 dB78–80
dB ⇄ ⋔84–94 M13–22

A Fandrich C-Benz Str 6 ☎25200 BL

&OA Linck Freiburger Str 26 ☎25005 Opl

At **ORTENBERG** (4km SE)

★Glattfelder Finizigtalstr 20 ☎31219
rm14 ⇄14 **P**

OLPE
Nordrhein-Westfalen (☎02761)

★★Tillmanns Kölnerstr 15 ☎2607
Closed 26 Jun–14 Jul
rm15 ⇄2 ⋔6 **P**

OPPENHEIM
Rheinland-Pfalz (☎06133)

★★Kurpfalz Wormser Str 2 ☎2291
mid Jan–mid Dec
rm20 ⇄12 ⋔8 🅐 **P** sB ⇄ ⋔36–69
dB ⇄ ⋔69–99

★Oppenheimer Hof F-Ebert-Str 84
☎2495
rm25 ⇄8 ⋔9 **P** sB35 sB ⇄ ⋔55–59
dB59 dB ⇄ ⋔69–85 M alc

&OHeinz Gartenstr 15–19 ☎2055 Frd

ORTENBERG See **OFFENBURG**

OSNABRÜCK
Niedersachsen (☎0541)

★★★Hohenzollern H-Heine Str 17
☎27292 tx094776
rm100 ⇄33 ⋔59 **P** Lift 𝄓 sB60–125
sB ⇄ ⋔85–140 dB110–165
dB ⇄ ⋔130–195 M23–45 Pool

&OH Van Beers Bahlweg 16 ☎73596 AR

&OG Clupka Pferdestr 2 ☎572629 M/c
P BL

PADERBORN
Nordrhein-Westfalen (☎05251)

★★Arosa (BW) Westernmauer 38
☎2000 tx936798
⇄100 **P** Lift 𝄓 sB ⇄95–120
dB ⇄144–157 Pool

☆☆Ibis am Paderwall 1–5
☎25031 tx936972
⋔90 **P** Lift 𝄓 sB ⋔83 dB ⋔113

&OF Kleine Rathenaustr 79–83 ☎208
Frd

PASSAU
Bayern (☎0851)

★★Weisser Hase Ludwigstr 23 ☎34065
rm136 ⇄42 ⋔25 🅐 **P** Lift 𝄓
sB36–44 sB ⇄ ⋔58–66 dB68–71
dB ⇄ ⋔100–107

&OF Hofbauer Neuburgerstr 141 ☎6017
Opl

Germany

PEGNITZ
Bayern (☎09241)

★★★Pflaum's Posthotel Nürnberger Str
14 ☎404 tx0642433
⇄68 🅐 **P** Lift Pool

PFAFFENHOFEN
Bayern (☎08441)

&OF X Stigimayr Scheyererstr 70 ☎9894
P BMW

PFORZHEIM
Baden-Württemberg (☎07321)

★★★Ruf am Schlossberg ☎16011
tx783843
rm60 ⇄30 ⋔30 **P** Lift 𝄓
sB ⇄ ⋔95–110 dB ⇄ ⋔120–170

&OAutosaion R Schweickert Karlsruhe Str
40 ☎16364 **P** BL Vlo

At **NIEFERN-ÖSCHELBRONN** (6km E at
Pforzheim East exit on E11)

☆☆☆Crest (See page 51) Pforzheimer
Str ☎(07233)1211 tx783095
⇄72 **P** Lift 𝄓 sB ⇄ ⋔109–110
dB ⇄ ⋔134–140 ♨ Pool

PRIEN AM CHIEMSEE
Bayern (☎08051)

★★Bayerischer Hof Bernauerstr 3
☎1095
Closed mid–30 Nov
rm49 ⇄35 ⋔2 A12rm 🅐 **P** Lift sB44
sB ⇄ ⋔50 dB78 dB ⇄ ⋔90–94
mountains

PUTTGARDEN
Schleswig-Holstein (☎04371)

★Dänia am Fährbahnhof ☎3016
tx29814
⋔66 Lift sea

PYRMONT (BAD)
Niedersachsen (☎05281)

★★Kurhaus Heiligenangerstr 4 ☎151
tx931636
Mar–Dec
rm104 ⇄71 ⋔15 **P** Lift 𝄓 sB102
sB ⇄106–126 dB154 dB ⇄211–223 ♨

QUICKBORN
Schleswig-Holstein (☎04106)

★★★Jagdhaus Waldfrieden (ROM)
Kieler Str 1 (On B4 3km N) ☎3771
⋔17 🅐 **P**

RASTATT
Baden-Württemberg (☎07222)

★★Blume Kaiserstr 38 ☎32222
rm40 ⇄5 ⋔9 🅐 **P** 𝄓 sB46
sB ⇄ ⋔56 dB76 dB ⇄ ⋔102

★Katzenberger's Adler Jonefstr 7
☎32103
Closed Jul
rm6 🅐 **P** sB35 dB75

RATINGEN See **DÜSSELDORF**

RAVENSBURG
Bayern (☎0751)

★★Waldhorn Marienpl 15 ☎16021
rm40 ⇄27 ⋔13 A22rm **P** Lift 𝄓
sB ⇄ ⋔95 dB ⇄ ⋔165

REGENSBURG
Bayern (☎0941)

★★★Avia Frankenstr 1–3 ☎42093
tx65703
rm81 ⇄10 ⋔68 🅐 **P** Lift 𝄓
sB ⇄ ⋔82 dB ⇄ ⋔117

★★Karmeliten Dachaupl 1 ☎562256
tx65170
20 Jan–20 Dec
rm80 ⇄ ⋔62 **P** Lift 𝄓 sB50
sB ⇄ ⋔76 dB78 dB ⇄ ⋔138

★★Straubinger Hof A-Schmetzer Str 33
☎59075
3 Jan–22 Dec
rm66 ⇄1 ⋔48 🅐 **P** Lift 𝄓 sB41
sB ⇄ ⋔45 dB64–66 dB ⇄ ⋔60

★Wiendle Universitätstr 9 ☎90416
rm26 ⇄22 🅐 **P**

&OKelinberger Kirchmeierstr 24 ☎35091
P Ren

&OO Seitz Alte Straubinger Str 19
☎793377 BL

REICHENHALL (BAD)
Bayern (☎08651)

★★★Axelmannstein (SRS)
Salzburgerstr 2–6 ☎4001 tx56112
rm153 ⇄150 🅐 **P** Lift 𝄓
sB ⇄114–165 dB ⇄138–242 ♨ Pool
mountains

★★Kurhotel Luisenbad Ludwigstr 33
☎5081 tx56131
20 Dec–Oct
rm83 ⇄47 ⋔18 🅐 **P** Lift 𝄓
sB87–101 sB ⇄ ⋔113–165 dBfr174
dB ⇄ ⋔194–310 M27–30 Pool
mountains

Prechter Innsbrücker Str Angerl 6
☎2078 Frd

REICHSHOF-ECKENHAGEN
Nordrhein-Westfalen (☎02265)

★★★Haus Leyer am Aggerberg 33
☎9021
rm18 ⇄3 ⋔15 🅐 **P** Pool mountains

REMAGEN
Rheinland-Pfalz (☎02642)

★★Fürstenberg Rheinpromenade 41
☎23020
Seasonal
rm14 ⇄8 ⋔4 **P** Pool

★Fassbender Mark Str 78 ☎23472
rm24 A8rm 🅐 **P**

RENDSBURG
Schleswig-Holstein (☎04331)

★Germania Paradepl 3 ☎22997
rm16 🅐 **P**

At **BÜDELSDORF** (2km N)

J Suhr Hollerstr 9 ☎3406 Frd

REUTLINGEN
Baden-Württemberg (☎07121)

★ ★**Ernst** Leonhardspl ☎44081
tx729898
rm67 ⇄15 🛏48 A52rm 🅿 Lift
sBfr54 sB ⇄ 🛏58–86 dBfr88
dB ⇄ 🛏102–138 M5–31 Pool

Auto-Specht Weissdornweg 2 ☎54775
P BL Cit

RHEINBACH
Nordrhein-Westfalen (☎02226)

★ ★ ★**Ratskeller** vor dem Voigttor 1
☎4978

rm28 ⇄4 🛏22 **P**

R Schulz Meckenheimer Str 17–19
☎4500 **P** Frd

RHEINZABERN
Rheinland-Pfalz (☎07272)

★**Goldenes Lamm** Hauptstr 53 ☎2377
rm12 🛏4 A6rm **P** sB25 sB 🛏32 dB50
dB 🛏64

RHEYDT See **MÖNCHENGLADBACH**

ROSENHEIM
Bayern (☎08031)

★ ★ ★**Goldener Hirsch** Münchner Str 40
☎12029
rm40 ⇄15 🛏4 🅿 **P** Lift 🌙
mountains

W Hansimeier Gabelsberger Str 57
☎86777 **P** BL Hon

G Rupp Innstr 34 ☎13970 M/c **P** BL

ROTENBURG (WÜMME)
Niedersachsen (☎04261)

★**Deutsches Haus** Grosse Str 51 ☎3300
rm8 **P** sB33 dB66 M7–26

🅢**K Lengen** Harburger Str 67 ☎5409 **P**
M/c Peu Tal

ROTHENBURG OB DER TAUBER
Bayern (☎09861)

★ ★ ★ ★**Eisenhut** (SRS) Hermgasse 3
☎2041 tx61367
Mar–3 Jan
rm85 ⇄75 🛏10 🅿 **P** Lift 🌙
sB ⇄ 🛏130–150 dB ⇄ 🛏165–245

★ ★ ★**Goldener Hirsch** Untere
Schmiedgasse 16 ☎2051 tx61372
Feb–Nov
rm80 ⇄50 🛏16 A20rm 🅿 **P** Lift 🌙
sB70–75 sB ⇄ 🛏92–135 dB110–135
dB ⇄ 🛏125–220

★ ★ ★**Burg** Klostergasse 1 ☎5037
12 Dec–Oct
⇄20 🅿 **P** sB ⇄105 dB ⇄140–170

★ ★**Glocke** Plönlein 1 ☎3025
rm26 ⇄9 🛏13 A12rm 🅿 **P** Lift
sB39–41 sB ⇄ 🛏49–65 dB64–68
dB ⇄ 🛏88–106 M15–32

★ ★**Markusturm** (ROM) Rödergasse 1
☎2370

Germany

Apr–10 Jan
rm28 ⇄11 🛏16 🅿 **P**
sB ⇄ 🛏95–105 dB ⇄ 🛏130–165

★ ★**Reichsküchenmeister** Kirchpl 8
☎3406
rm35 ⇄10 🛏8 🅿 **P** Lift sB40
sB ⇄ 🛏60 dB ⇄ 🛏95

★ ★**Tilman Riemenschneider**
Georgengasse 11–13 ☎5061 tx61384
⇄65 🅿 **P** Lift 🌙 sB ⇄ 🛏65–90
dB ⇄ 🛏85–160 M9–28

🅢**Central** (H Korn) Schutzenstr 11
☎3088 **P** DJ

🅢**Döhler** Ansbacherstr 38–40 ☎2084
P Opl Vau

ROTTACH-EGERN
Bayern (☎08022)

★ ★ ★ ★**Bachmair am See** Seestr 47
☎6444 tx526920
rm253 ⇄233 🛏20 🅿 **P** Lift 🌙 Pool
mountains

RÖTTGEN See **BONN**

ROTTWEIL
Baden-Württemberg (☎0741)

★**Johanniterbad** Johannsergrasse 12
☎6083 tx762705
Closed 4–16 Jan
rm31 ⇄9 🛏20 **P** Lift sB37–39
sB ⇄ 🛏55–65 dB ⇄ 🛏82–96

RUDESHEIM *Hessen* (☎06722)
See also **ASSMANNSHAUSEN**

★ ★ ★**Waldhotel Jagdschloss
Niederwald** (GS) ☎1004 tx42152
Mar–Nov
rm46 ⇄32 🛏14 A20rm **P** 🌙
sB ⇄ 🛏110 dB ⇄ 🛏160–200 Pool

🅢**Rüdesheim** Geisenheimerstr 18
☎1085 **P** Opl

RUHPOLDING
Bayern (☎08663)

★ ★**Sporthotel am Westernberg** am
Wundergraben 4 ☎1674
15 Dec–Oct
rm46 ⇄6 🛏35 A13rm **P** 🍴 Pool
mountains

RÜTTENSCHEID See **ESSEN**

SAARBRÜCKEN
Saarland (☎0681)

★ ★ ★ ★**Haus Berlin** (ETAP) Faktoreistr
(n.rest) ☎33030 tx4420409
rm65 ⇄20 🛏40 🅿 **P** Lift 🌙

★ ★ ★**Kongress** (ETAP) Hafenstr 8
☎30691 tx4428942
⇄150 **P** Lift 🌙 sB ⇄122 dB ⇄166
M alc Pool

☆ ☆ ☆**Novotel** Zinzingerstr 9 ☎51071
tx4428836

⇄99 **P** Lift 🌙 sB ⇄114 dB ⇄146
Pool

★ ★**Christine** Gersweilerstr 39 ☎55081
tx4428736
Closed Xmas
rm65 ⇄32 🛏8 🅿 **P** Lift 🌙 sB46–53
sB ⇄ 🛏64–91 dB 76–90
dB ⇄ 🛏108–150 Pool

★ ★**Wien** Gutenbergstr 29 ☎55088
🛏31 🅿 **P** Lift 🌙

Ritz Sulzbachstr 33–35 ☎36529 **P** BL

SÄCKINGEN (BAD)
Baden-Württemberg (☎07761)

★**Kater Hiddigeigei** Tanzenpl 1 ☎4055
rm30 ⇄2 🛏8 **P**

ST-GEORGEN
Baden-Württemberg (☎07724)

★ ★**Hirsch** Bahnhofstr 70 ☎7125
rm22 ⇄7 🛏15 🅿 **P**

ST-GOAR
Rheinland-Pfalz (☎06741)

★ ★**Goldenen Löwen** Heerstr 1 ☎1674
Mar–Oct
rm11 ⇄3 🛏8 **P** sB ⇄ 🛏65
dB ⇄ 🛏80–120 river

★ ★**Schneider** am Markt 1 ☎1689
Apr–15 Dec
rm18 ⇄5 🛏4 **P** sB38–41
sB ⇄ 🛏44–54 dB75–77
dB ⇄ 🛏97–107 M6–25

★**Hauser** Heerstr 160 ☎333
Feb–15 Dec
rm15 ⇄2 🛏9 🅿 **P** sB32 sD ⇄ 🛏45
dB64 dB ⇄ 🛏76

ST-GOARSHAUSEN
Rheinland-Pfalz (☎06771)

★ ★**Erholung** Nastatterstr 161 ☎684
rm54 ⇄16 🛏2 🅿 **P** sB37–41
sB ⇄ 🛏42–47 dB72–80
dB ⇄ 🛏82–94 Mfr14 mountains

ST-MÄRGEN
Baden-Württemberg (☎07669)

★**Hirschen** Feldbergstr 9 ☎201
18 Dec–19 Nov
rm41 ⇄13 🛏27 A21rm **P** Lift
sB ⇄ 🛏34–38 dB ⇄ 🛏62–99
mountains

ST MICHAELISDONN See
BRUNSBÜTTEL

SAND
Baden-Württemberg (☎07226)

★ ★**Plättig** (1.5km N) ☎226
rm66 ⇄28 🛏21 A28rm 🅿 **P** Lift
sB35 sB ⇄ 🛏70 dB70
dB ⇄ 🛏70–160 Pool mountains

SANDHOFEN See **MANNHEIM**

SAULGAU
Baden-Württemberg (☎07581)

★ ★**Kleber-Post** Hauptstr 100 ☎3051
Nov–20 Dec

rm41 ⇌15 🛏22 🛁 P sB40
sB ⇌ 🛏59 dB64 dB ⇌ 🛏120

SCHACKENDORF See **SEGEBERG (BAD)**

SCHLANGENBAD
Hessen (☎06129)

★ ★ ★**Staatliches Kurhaus** Rheingauer Str
47 ☎41423
rm100 ⇌48 🛏47 🛁 P Lift ♪
sB65–73 sB ⇌ 🛏85–120
dB ⇌ 🛏130–170

SCHLEIDEN
Nordrhein-Westfalen (☎02445)

★**Schleidener Hof** Gemünder Str 1
☎216
rm15 🛏11 P sB24 sB 🛏28 dB48
dB 🛏56 mountains

SCHLESWIG
Schleswig-Holstein (☎04621)

★ ★**Strandhalle** am Jachthafen ☎22021
rm28 ⇌4 🛏21 🛁 P sB41 sB ⇌ 🛏70
dB ⇌ 🛏110 Pool lake

★**Weissen Schwan** Gottorfstr 1 ☎32712
rm12 🛏4 A4rm 🛁 P sB33 sB 🛏36
dB60–66 dB 🛏72 lake

&♪A **Wriedt** Flensburger Str 88 ☎25087
P Ren

SCHLIERSEE
Bayern (☎08026)

★ ★ ★**Schliersee** Kirchbichlweg 18
☎6291 tx526947
⇌91 🛁 P Lift ♪ sB ⇌85 dB ⇌150
Pool mountains

SCHMIDEN See **STUTTGART**

SCHÖNBERG See **SEELBACH**

SCHÖNMÜNZACH
Baden-Württemberg (☎07447)

★ ★**Kurhotel Schwarzwald** Murgtalstr
657 ☎1088
rm26 ⇌4 🛏15 🛁 P Lift sB32
sB ⇌ 🛏45 dB 46 dB ⇌ 🛏122
mountains

SCHÖNSEE
Bayern (☎09674)

★ ★**St-Hubertus** am Lauberberg ☎415
tx631825
rm105 ⇌55 🛏26 🛁 P Lift ℔ Pool
mountains

SCHÖNTAL See **NEUSTADT AN DER
WEINSTRASSE**

SCHRIESHEIM
Baden-Württemberg (☎06203)

★ ★**Luisenhöhe** Eichenweg 10 ☎65617
rm24 ⇌5 🛏19 🛁 P mountains

SCHWABACH
Bayern (☎09122)

&♪W **Feser** Limbacher Str 26 ☎85035 P
Aud VW

SCHWÄBISCH HALL
Baden-Württemberg (☎0791)

Germany

★ ★**Hohenlohe** Weilertor 14 ☎6116
tx74870
rm95 ⇌30 🛏65 🛁 P Lift ♪ Pool
lake

★ ★**Goldener Adler** am Markt 11 ☎6364
18 Jan–30 Dec
rm18 ⇌4 🛏7 🛁 P sB39
sB ⇌ 🛏55–60 dB60–70
dB ⇌ 🛏90–108 M12–30

SCHWALENBERG
Nordrhein-Westfalen (☎05284)

★ ★**Schloss Burg Schwalenberg** (GS)
☎5167
Mar–Dec
rm18 ⇌8 🛏6 🛁 P mountains

SCHWEINFURT
Bayern (☎09721)

★ ★**Central** Zehntstr 20 (n.rest) ☎1325
⇌40 🛁 P Lift sB ♪ sB⇌49–55
dB ⇌70–85

SCHWELM
Nordrhein-Westfalen (☎02125)

★ ★**Prinz Von Preussen** Altmarkt 8
☎13444
rm16 ⇌5 🛏8 P

SCHWETZINGEN
Baden-Württemberg (☎06202)

★ ★**Adler Post** Schlosstr 3 ☎10036
rm24 ⇌3 🛏12 🛁 P

SEELBACH
Baden-Württemberg (☎07823)

At **SCHÖNBERG** (6km E)

★ ★**Pass Höhen** ☎2044
rm29 🛏26 🛁 P Pool mountains

SEESEN
Niedersachsen (☎05381)

★ ★**Goldener Löwe** Jacobsonstr 20
☎1201 tx957316
rm22 ⇌5 🛏10 A9rm 🛁 P ♪
sB50–60 sB ⇌ 🛏78 dB82–86
dB ⇌ 🛏102–128

&♪**Hoffmann** Autobahnizubringerstr
☎1215 P Frd

SEGEBERG (BAD)
Schleswig-Holstein (☎04551)

At **SCHACKENDORF** (5km NW on B404)

★ ★**Stefanie & Motel B404** ☎3600
rm36 ⇌11 🛏11 A17rm 🛁 P sB26
sB ⇌ 🛏42 dB48 dB ⇌ 🛏70

SIEGBURG
Nordrhein-Westfalen (☎02241)

★ ★**Stern** Marktpl 14 (n.rest) ☎60021
6 Jan–24 Dec
rm36 ⇌12 🛏17 🛁 P Lift ♪

&♪M **Bässgen** Frankfurterstr 1–5
☎66001 Opl

SIEGEN
Nordrhein-Westfalen (☎0271)

☆ ☆ ☆**Crest (See page 51)** Kampenstr
83 ☎54072 tx872734
rm102 ⇌57 🛏45 🛁 P Lift ♪
sB ⇌ 🛏130 dB ⇌ 🛏156–160 Pool

★ ★ ★**Johanneshöhe** Wallhausenstr 1
☎3100088
rm25 ⇌4 🛏19 🛁 P ♪ sB47
sB ⇌ 🛏70 dB ⇌ 🛏130 mountains

SIGMARINGEN
Baden-Württemberg (☎07571)

&♪J **Zimmermann** In der Burgwiesen 18
☎1696 P Opl Vau

SIMMERATH
Nordrhein-Westfalen (☎02473)

At **EICHERSCHEID** (4km S)

★**Haus Gertud** Bachstr 4 ☎1310
rm10 P ℔ mountains

SINDELFINGEN
Baden-Württemberg (☎07031)

☆ ☆ ☆**Crest (See page 51)** W-Haspel
Str 101 ☎6150 tx7265778
⇌ 🛏145 P Lift ♪ sB ⇌ 🛏151
dB ⇌ 🛏187–190

☆ ☆ ☆**Holiday Inn** Schwertstr 65
☎61311 tx07265569
⇌185 🛁 P Lift ⇌169 dB ⇌228
M alc Pool

SOEST
Nordrhein-Westfalen (☎02921)

★ ★**Andernach Zur Börse** Thomästr 31
☎4019
Closed 1–24 Aug & 20 Dec–6 Jan
rm22 ⇌1 🛏14 A4rm 🛁 P

★ ★**Pilgrim-Haus** Jakobistr 75 ☎1828
rm12 🛏6 P sB38 sB 🛏48 dB58
dB 🛏68

H Siedler Riga Ring 15 ☎73051 M/c Frd

SPEYER
Rheinland-Pfalz (☎06232)

★**Goldener Engel** Mühlturm Str 1A
☎76732
5 Jan–23 Dec
rm39 ⇌11 🛏25 🛁 P Lift sB43
sB ⇌ 🛏56 dB75 dB ⇌ 🛏89

STAMMHEIM See **STUTTGART**

STOCKACH
Baden-Württemberg (☎07771)

★ ★**Linde** Goethestr 23 ☎2226
rm26 ⇌18 🛁 P Lift sB43 sB ⇌50
dB70 dB ⇌80

STRAUBING
Bayern (☎09421)

★ ★**Seethaler** Theresienpl 25 ☎12022
rm25 ⇌15 🛏10 🛁 P

★ ★**Wittelsbach** Stadtgraben 25 ☎1517
rm42 ⇌4 🛏20 🛁 P Lift sB30–33

221

sB ⇄ 🛏36–48 dB60–70
dB ⇄ 🛏75–90 M11–22

Germany

STUTTGART
Baden-Württemberg (☎0711)

★ ★ ★ ★ **Graf Zeppelin** (SRS) A-Klett-
Pl 7 ☎299881 tx722418
rm280 ⇌250 🛏30 **P** Lift ⅅ
sB ⇄ 🛏169–290 dB ⇄ 🛏248–300
Pool

★ ★ ★ **Schlossgarten**
Schillerstr 23 ☎299911 tx722936
rm126 ⇌81 🛏45 **P** Lift ⅅ
sB⇄ 🛏145–179 dB⇄ 🛏210–230

★ ★ **Europe** (BW) Siemensstr 26–28,
Feuerbach ☎815091 tx723650
rm147 ⇌97 🛏50 🛎 **P** Lift ⅅ
sB ⇄ 🛏130–140 dB ⇄ 🛏175

★ ★ **Intercity** A-Klett Pl 2 (n.rest)
☎299801 tx723543
rm136 ⇌39 🛏40 **P** Lift ⅅ sB70–80
sB ⇄ 🛏180–110 dB ⇄ 🛏125–145

★ ★ **Parkhotel** Villastr 21 ☎280161
tx723405
rm83 ⇌35 🛏42 **P** Lift ⅅ sB65
sB ⇄ 🛏150 dB ⇄ 🛏190

★ ★ **Rieker** Friedrichstr 3 (n.rest)
☎221311
⇌63 🛎 Lift sB ⇌92 dB ⇌140

★ ★ **Waldhotel Degerioch** Guts-Muths-
Weg 18 ☎761790 tx7255728
rm54 ⇌7 🛏37 A44rm 🛎 **P** Lift ⅅ
sB50 ⇄ 🛏115–125 dB90
dB ⇄ 🛏170–180 M alc 🕭

★ **Ketterer** Marienstr 3 ☎294151
tx722340
rm80 ⇌14 🛏58 **P** Lift ⅅ sB53–58
sB ⇄ 🛏87–98 dBfr87
dB ⇄ 🛏107–135 M16–28

&🖤**A V G Auto-Verkaufs** Chemnitzer Str 7
☎722094 **P** BL

At **MÖHRINGEN** (7km S on rd 27)

&🖤**Schwaben** Vaihingerstr 131
☎7800585 Frd

At **SCHMIDEN** (9km NE)

&🖤**Ceslik** Kanalstr 14 ☎511560 **P** DJ RT

At **STAMMHEIM** (8km N)

☆ ☆ ☆ **Novotel Stuttgart Nord** Korntaler
Str 207 ☎801065 tx7252137
⇌117 **P** Lift ⅅ sB ⇌124 dB ⇌156
M20 Pool

STUTTGART AIRPORT

☆ ☆ ☆ **Flughafen** (Mövenpick) Randstr
☎7907-0 tx7245677
⇌128 **P** Lift sB ⇌128–148
dB ⇌148–168 M18–28

SULZBACH See FRANKFURT AM MAIN

SULZBURG
Baden-Württemberg (☎07634)

★ ★ **Weldhotel Bad Sulzburg** Badstr 67
☎8270
rm42 ⇌22 **P** Lift sB40 sB ⇌70
dB68 dB ⇌120 🕭 Pool mountains

TENNENLOHE See ERLANGEN

TETTNANG
Baden-Württemberg (☎07542)

★ ★ **Rad** Lindauerstr 2 ☎6001 tx734245
Closed Xmas
⇌🛏70 🛎 **P** Lift sB ⇄ 🛏63–65
dB ⇄ 🛏116

TIEFENBRONN
Baden-Württemberg (☎07234)

★ ★ **Ochsen Post** F-J-Gall Str 13 ☎279
tx783485
Closed last 2wks Jul
rm21 ⇌8 🛏12 🛎 **P** sBfr39
sB ⇄ 🛏52–95 dB ⇄ 🛏85–120

TITISEE-NEUSTADT
Baden-Württemberg (☎07651)

At **NEUSTADT**

★ ★ **Adler-Post** (ROM) Hauptstr 16
☎5066
rm37 ⇌25 🛎 **P** sB45–55 sB ⇌60–85
dB85–95 dB ⇌110–150 M25–50 Pool
mountains

At **TITISEE**

★ ★ **Brugger** Strandbadstr 14 ☎8238
tx7722332
rm68 ⇌38 🛏18 🛎 **P** Lift ⅅ
sB53–63 sB ⇌ 🛏83–103 dB105–125
dB ⇄ 🛏135–215 M26–40 🕭 Pool
mountains lake

★ ★ **Schwarzwaldhotel am See** Seestr
12 ☎8111 tx7722341
20 Dec–Oct
rm94 ⇌82 🛎 **P** Lift ⅅ sB50–60
sB ⇌80–120 dB 80–90 dB ⇌100–200
M35–40 🕭 Pool lake

★ ★ **Seehof am See** Seestr 47 (n.rest)
☎8314
20 Dec–Oct
rm24 ⇌13 🛏5 A2rm 🛎 **P** Lift sB40
sB ⇄ 🛏54 dB80 dB ⇄ 🛏108
mountains lake

☆ **Rauchfang** Bärenhofweg 2 ☎8255
rm17 ⇌8 🛏9 🛎 **P** sB ⇄ 🛏66
dB ⇄ 🛏120 Pool mountains

★ **Seerose** Seestr 21 (n.rest) ☎8274
20 Dec–20 Oct
rm10 ⇌2 **P** sB24 dB48–52 dB ⇌60
mountains

TÖLZ (BAD)
Bayern (☎08041)

★ **Gaissacher Haus** an der
Umgehungsstr ☎9583
rm20 ⇌1 🛏17 A10rm 🛎 **P**
mountains

★ **Post-Hotel Kolberbräu** Marktstr 29
☎9158
rm57 ⇌11 🛏10 🛎 **P** Lift sB39

sB ⇄ 🛏49–59 dB78 dB ⇄ 🛏103–108
St% mountains

TRABEN-TRARBACH
Rheinland-Pfalz (☎06541)

★ ★ **Clauss-Feist** Moselufer ☎6431
15 Mar–10 Nov
rm27 ⇌3 🛏9 🛎 **P** sB29–31
sB ⇄ 🛏34–40 dB58 dB ⇄ 🛏66–78
M alc

★ ★ **Krone** an der Mosel 93 ☎6363
15 Mar–Dec
rm20 ⇌4 🛏16 🛎 **P** sB78–82
dB ⇄ 🛏112–122 M20–30 mountains

&🖤**Autohaus H Zundorf** Rissbacher Str
☎9266 Aud VW

TRAUNSTEIN
Bayern (☎0861)

★ ★ **Parkhotel Traunsteiner Hof**
Bahnhofstr 11 ☎60417
rm65 ⇌10 🛏40 🛎 **P** Lift ⅅ sB36
sB ⇄ 🛏50 dB65 dB ⇄ 🛏92

TRAVEMÜNDE
Schleswig-Holstein (☎04502)

★ ★ ★ **Golf** Helidahl 12–13 ☎4041
tx261343
19 Apr–Sep
⇌60 A32rm 🛎 **P** Lift ⅅ Pool sea

TREMSBÜTTEL
Schleswig-Holstein (☎04532)

★ ★ ★ **Schloss** (GS) ☎6544
Closed Mon
rm20 ⇌11 🛏5 🛎 **P** ⅅ 🕭

TRENDELBURG
Hessen (☎05675)

★ ★ **Burg** (GS) ☎1021 tx994812
15 Feb–Dec
rm23 ⇌9 🛏14 **P**

TRIBERG
Baden-Württemberg (☎07722)

★ ★ ★ **Parkhotel Wehrie** (ROM)
Gartenstr 24 ☎4081 tx792609
rm60 ⇌46 🛏9 A30rm 🛎 **P** Lift ⅅ
sB48–95 sB ⇄ 🛏68–96 dB 96–170
dB ⇄ 🛏130–180 Pool mountains

TRIER
Rheinland-Pfalz (☎0651)

☆ ☆ ☆ **Holiday Inn** Zurmaienerstr 164
☎23091 tx472808
⇄ 🛏215 **P** Lift ⅅ sB ⇄ 🛏114
dB ⇄ 🛏149 Pool

★ ★ ★ **Dorint Porta Nigra** Porta Nigra
Pl 11 ☎127010 tx472895
⇄ 🛏106 🛎 **P** Lift ⅅ
sB ⇄ 🛏107–109 dB ⇄ 🛏164–168

★ ★ ★ **Europa Parkhotel** (BW) Kaiserstr
28–29 ☎40011 tx472858
⇌85 **P** Lift ⅅ sB ⇄ 🛏98 dB ⇌148

★ ★ **Hügel** Beerhardstr 14 ☎33066
rm18 ⇌5 🛏13 🛎 **P** sB ⇄ 🛏55–60
dB ⇄ 🛏90–95

★ ★ **Petrisberg** Sickingenstr 11 (n.rest)
☎41181

rm30 ⇄2 🛏28 A10rm 🅿 P
sB ⇄ 🛏65 dB ⇄ 🛏90–95

இJ **Arweller** am Verteilerring ☎22041
Opl

இ**Daewel** Im Siebenbom ☎87063 AR
BL

TRITTENHEIM
Rheinland-Pfalz (☎06507)

★**Moselperle** Moselweinstr 42 ☎2221

Feb–Nov
rm14 ⇄2 🛏8 🅿 P Pool

TÜBINGEN
Baden-Württemberg (☎07122)

★ ★ ★**Bad** am Freibad 2 ☎73071

10 Jan–20 Dec
rm35 ⇄31 🅿 P 𝅘 sB42 sB⇄ 60–65
dB ⇄ 84–87 ໖ Pool lake

☆ **Stadt Tübingen** Stuttgarterstr 97
☎31071

rm39 ⇄5 🛏22 🅿 P 𝅘 sB44–55
sB ⇄ 🛏58 dB68 dB ⇄ 🛏92

TUTTLINGEN
Baden-Württemberg (☎07461)

★ ★**Schlack** Bahnhofstr 59 ☎72081

rm26 ⇄9 🛏11 🅿 P 𝅘 sB31–36
sB ⇄ 🛏45–55 dB56–60 dB ⇄ 🛏104

★**Ritter** Königstr 12 ☎8855
rm19 🛏9 🅿 P sB28 sB🛏38
dB56–68 dB 🛏74

ÜBERLINGEN
Baden-Württemberg (☎07551)

★ ★ ★**Parkhotel St-Leonard** Obere St-
Leonhardstr 83 ☎8080
rm112 ⇄25 🛏66 🅿 P Lift 𝅘 sB42
sB ⇄ 🛏 105 dB78 dB ⇄ 🛏 156 ໖
Pool mountains lake

★ ★**Alpenblick** ☎4559

10 Jan–23 Dec
rm28 🛏24 P Pool lake

★ ★**Bad** Christophstr 2 ☎61055
tx733909

Mar–Nov
rm50 ⇄24 🛏21 P Lift 𝅘 sB54–64
sB ⇄ 🛏80–105 dB98–118
dB ⇄ 🛏168 M alc lake

★ ★**Seegarten** Seepromenade 7
☎63498

Feb–Nov
rm28 ⇄🛏26 P Lift sB52 sB ⇄ 🛏87
dB116 dB ⇄ 🛏144–184 mountains
lake

UFFENHEIM
Bayern (☎09842)

★**Traube** am Marktpl 3 ☎8288

25 Jan–24 Dec
rm16 ⇄3 🛏5 🅿 P

ULM
Baden-Württemberg (☎0731)

★ ★**Goldenes Rad** Neue Str 65 (n.rest)
☎67048

rm22 ⇄3 🛏10 P Lift 𝅘 sB42–55
sB ⇄ 🛏75–78 dB70–80

Germany

dB ⇄ 🛏98–100

★ ★**Intercity Ulm** Bahnhofspl 1 ☎61221
tx712871
rm110 ⇄20 🛏70 🅿 P Lift 𝅘 sB45–66
sB ⇄ 🛏72–83 dB65–94
dB ⇄ 🛏113–155 M20–30

★ ★**Neutor Hospiz** Neuer Graben 23
☎61191 tx712401
rm90 ⇄85 🅿 P Lift 𝅘

★ ★**Stern** Sterngasse 17 ☎63091
⇄50 🅿 P Lift 𝅘 sB ⇄ 🛏70–85
dB ⇄125

★**Roter Löwe** Ulmer Gasse 8 ☎62031
rm30 ⇄6 🛏18 🅿 P Lift 𝅘 sB40–43
sB ⇄ 🛏48–71 dB74–80
dB ⇄ 🛏85–100 M8–25

Schwabengarage Marchtaler Str 23
☎1621 M/c Frd Hon

UNDELOH
Niedersachsen (☎04189)

★**Witte's** in der Nordheide ☎267

Feb–20 Dec
rm16 ⇄10 🛏6 🅿

ÜRZIG/MOSEL
Rheinland-Pfalz (☎06532)

★**Moselschild** Hauptstr 12–14 ☎3001
tx4721542
⇄14 🅿 P 𝅘 lake

★**Rotschwänzchen** Moselufer 18 ☎2183
rm14 🛏11 A4rm P

VAIHINGEN AN DER ENZ
Baden-Württemberg (☎0042)

★**Post** Franckstr 23 ☎4071
rm26 ⇄2 🛏9 🅿 P Lift

VIECHTACH
Bayern (☎09942)

★ ★**Sporthotel Schmaus** Stadtpl 5
☎1627
⇄50 🅿 Lift sB ⇄47 dB ⇄98 Pool

VIERNHEIM
Hessen (☎06204)

☆ ☆ ☆**Holiday Inn** Bürgermeister Neff
Str 12 ☎5036 tx465452
⇄ 🛏121 P Lift 𝅘 sB ⇄ 🛏 140
dB ⇄ 🛏190 Pool

VILLINGEN
Baden-Württemberg (☎07721)

★ ★**Ketterer** Brigachstr 1 ☎2095
tx792554
rm34 ⇄6 🛏28 P Lift sB ⇄ 🛏55–70
dB ⇄ 🛏90–110

WAHLSCHEID
Nordrhein-Westfalen (☎02206)

★ ★ ★**Schloss Auel** (GS) Lohmar (1.5km
NE) ☎2041 tx887510
rm23 ⇄20 🛏1 🅿 P ໖ Pool

WALDEMS-BERMBACH
Hessen (☎06126)

★ ★**Hahnberg** ☎2777

Feb–10 Jan
rm15 ⇄10 🛏1 🅿 P sB ⇄ 🛏38–45
dB ⇄ 🛏58–70

WALLDORF
Baden-Württemberg (☎06227)

See also **HEIDELBERG**

☆ ☆ ☆ ☆**Holiday Inn** Roterstr (1.5km SW
near autobahn exit) ☎62051 tx466009
⇄127 🅿 P Lift 𝅘 ⇄135–155
dB ⇄160–190 ໖ Pool

★ ★**Vorfelder** Bahnhofstr ☎2085
tx466016
rm34 ⇄18 🛏10 🅿 P Lift 𝅘
sB40–50 sB ⇄ 🛏75–90 dBfr90
dB ⇄ 🛏110–140

WANGEN IM ALLGÄU
Baden-Württemberg (☎07522)

★ ★**Alte Post** (ROM) Postpl 2 ☎4014
rm25 ⇄19 🛏16 A10rm 🅿 P 𝅘
mountains

WASSERBURG AM INN
Bayern (☎08071)

★ ★**Fletzinger** Fletzingergasse 1 ☎3876

20 Jan–15 Dec
rm30 ⇄17 🅿 P sB36 sB ⇄ 🛏52
sB68 dB ⇄ 🛏92

WEIDEN IN DER OBERPFALZ
Bayern (☎0961)

★ ★**Schmid** Obere Bachgasse 8
☎42231

10 Jan–22 Dec
rm15 ⇄7 🅿 P

இ**Friederich** Bahnhofstr 17 ☎42081 P
BMW

இ**Stegmann** Obere Bauscherstr 16
☎43055 Aud VW

WEINHEIM AN DER BERGSTRASSE
Baden-Württemberg (☎06201)

★ ★**Fuchs'sche Mühle** Birkenauer Talstr
10 ☎61031
rm28 ⇄17 🛏5 🅿 P Lift Pool

WEISSENBURG IN BAYERN
Bayern (☎09141)

★ ★**Rose** (ROM) Rosenstr 6 ☎2091
rm30 ⇄4 🛏26 🅿 P sB ⇄ 🛏58–95
dB ⇄ 🛏82–150 M13–35

Kellner Treuchtlinger Str 2A ☎2638 P
AR Cit

WERTHEIM
Baden-Württemberg (☎09342)

★ ★**Schwan** Mainpl 8 ☎1278
rm46 ⇄4 A16rm 🅿 P

At **KREUZWERTHEIM**

★**Herrnwiesen** Herrnwiesen 4 ☎37031
rm17 ⇄2 🛏13 🅿 **P** mountains

WERTINGEN
Bayern (☎08272)

★**Hirsch** Schulstr 7 ☎2055
rm29 🛏21 A17rm 🅿 **P**

WESEL
Nordrhein-Westfalen (☎0281)

★ ★ ★**Kaiserhof** Kaiserring 1 ☎21972
rm37 ⇄5 🛏32 🅿 **P** Lift ☽

WESTERLAND (Island of Sylt)
Schleswig-Holstein (☎04651)

No road connection exists between the mainland and the Island of Sylt; however there is a rail connection between Niebül and Westerland. Cars are loaded onto trains by ramps.

★ ★ ★**Stadt Hamburg** Strandstr 2
☎7058
rm75 ⇄28 🛏35 **P** Lift ☽ sB62–73
sB ⇄ 🛏130–141 dB72–92
dB ⇄ 🛏138–290 M26–36 & alc

WETZLAR
Hessen (☎06441)

★ ★**Eulerhaus** Buderuspl 1 (n.rest)
☎47016
rm30 ⇄8 🛏8 **P** Lift

WIESBADEN
Hessen (☎06121)

★ ★ ★ ★**Nassauer Hof** (SRS) Kaiser Friedrich-Pl 3-4 ☎39681 tx4186847
⇄160 🅿 Lift sB ⇄202–277
dB ⇄234–364 M alc mountains

★ ★ ★ ★**Schwarzer Bock** Kranzpl 12
☎3821 tx04186640
rm165 ⇄127 🛏32 **P** Lift ☽
sB ⇄ 🛏135–195 dB ⇄ 🛏230–380
Mfr30 Pool

★ ★**Forum** A-Lincoln Str 17 ☎77811
tx4186369
⇄157 **P** Lift sB ⇄ 150–180
dB ⇄180–220 Pool

★ ★ ★**Fürstenhof-Esplanade**
Sonnenberger Str 32 ☎522091
tx4186447
rm72 ⇄21 🛏26 🅿 **P** Lift ☽
sB40–65 sB ⇄ 🛏75–100 dB78–110
dB ⇄ 🛏100–190 M10–28

★ ★**Central** Bahnhofstr 65 ☎372001
tx4186604
rm68 ⇄23 🛏9 🅿 **P** Lift ☽ sB58
sB ⇄ 🛏81 dB85 dB ⇄ 🛏122

★**Oranien** Platter Str 2 ☎525025
tx4186217
rm85 ⇄24 🛏61 🅿 **P** Lift ☽
sB ⇄ 🛏82 dB ⇄ 🛏124

Heine Mainzer Str 141 ☎19780 **P** AR
Peu Tal

🕭🌺**Wiesbaden** Stresemannring (nr main rly station) ☎145-0 **P** Opl

At **WIESBADEN-DOTZHEIM**

Germany

H Heil Stegerwaldstr 35 ☎422088 BL
Maz

At **WIESBADEN-SONNENBERG** (6.5km NE)

★**Köhler** König-Adolf Str 6 ☎540804
Feb–Dec
rm7 **P**

WILDBAD IM SCHWARZWALD
Baden-Württemberg (☎07081)

★ ★ ★ ★**Sommerberg** Heermannsweg 5 (2.5km W) ☎1641 tx724015
⇄100 🅿 **P** Lift ☽ sB ⇄126
dB ⇄299 🌺 Pool mountains

WILDUNGEN (BAD)
Hessen (☎05621)

★ ★ ★**Staatliches Badehotel** Dr Marc Str 4 ☎860 tx994612
rm74 ⇄14 🛏35 🅿 **P** Lift ☽ sB50
sB ⇄ 🛏73–102 dB98
dB ⇄ 🛏125–180 Pool

WILHELMSHAVEN
Niedersachsen (☎04421)

★ ★**Loheyde** Eberstr 104 ☎43048
rm73 ⇄12 🛏27 A15rm 🅿 **P** Lift ☽
Pool

August Hillmann Banter Weg 5
☎202066 M/c Frd

WILLINGEN
Hessen (☎05632)

★ ★**Waldhotel Willingen** am Köhlerhagen 3 ☎6016
Closed 2 Dec–21 Dec
rm42 ⇄3 🛏39 **P** sB ⇄ 🛏50–69
dB ⇄ 🛏100–122 🌺 Pool

WIMPFEN (BAD)
Baden-Württemberg (☎07063)

★ ★**Blauer Turm** Burgviertel 5 ☎225
15 Feb–15 Dec
rm38 ⇄2 🛏10 **P** sB36–52
sB ⇄ 🛏41–52 dB66–78
dB ⇄ 🛏76–94

★ ★**Weinmann** Marktpl 3 (n.rest) ☎8582
Mar–Oct
⇄ 🛏16 🅿 **P** sB ⇄ 🛏60 dB ⇄ 🛏98

WINDHAGEN See **HONNEF AM RHEIN (BAD)**

WINTERBERG
Nordrhein-Westfalen (☎02981)

At **NEUASTENBERG** (6km SW)

★ ★ ★**Dorint Ferienpark** ☎2033
tx84539
⇄110 **P** ☽ sB ⇄75–94
dB ⇄110–148 🌺 Pool

At **WINTERBERG-HOHELEYE** (10km SE)

★**Hochsauerland** ☎(02758)313
tx875629

---

rm90 ⇄60 🛏30 **P** Lift ☽
sB ⇄ 🛏69–132 dB ⇄ 🛏118–191
M12–38 alc Pool mountains

WOLFACH
Baden-Württemberg (☎07834)

★ ★**Krone** Marktpl 33 ☎350
rm23 ⇄5 🛏9 A7rm 🅿 **P** mountains

★**Hecht** Hauptstr 51 ☎538
10 Feb–7 Jan
🛏27 A12rm 🅿 **P** mountains

WOLFENBÜTTEL
Niedersachsen (☎05331)

★**Stadtschenke** Grosse Kirchstr 9
☎2359
rm26 🛏4 🅿 **P**

WOLFSBURG
Niedersachsen (☎05361)

☆ ☆ ☆ ☆**Holiday Inn** Rathausstr 1
☎12081 tx958475
⇄207 **P** Lift ☽ sB ⇄138–145
dB ⇄173–180 M15–50 Pool

WORMS
Rheinland-Pfalz (☎06241)

★ ★ ★**Dom** Obermarkt 10 ☎6913
tx467846
rm60 ⇄30 🛏30 🅿 **P** Lift ☽
sB ⇄ 🛏57–65 dB ⇄ 🛏90–120

🕭🌺**Betriebe Berkenkamp** Speyerer Str 88
☎6343 **P** Frd

WUPPERTAL
Nordrhein-Westfalen (☎0202)

At **WUPPERTAL II-BARMEN**

H Wilke Stennert 8 ☎666517 BL Sab

At **WUPPERTAL I-ELBERFELD**

★ ★ ★**Kaiserhof** (PLM) Döppersberg 50 (n.rest) ☎459081 tx8591405
⇄84 Lift sB ⇄110–135 dB ⇄160–195
M alc

★ ★**Post** Postr 4 (n.rest) ☎450131
2 Jan–24 Dec
rm54 ⇄3 🛏50 **P** Lift ☽

★ ★**Rathaus** Wilhelmstr 7 (n.rest)
☎450148 tx8592424
rm34 ⇄10 🛏24 🅿 **P** Lift ☽

At **WUPPERTAL XXII-LANGERFELD**

★**Neuenhof** Schwelmer Str 246–8
☎602536
rm18 ⇄10 🛏4 🅿 **P** sB35–45
sB ⇄ 🛏60 dB60–100 dB ⇄ 🛏110–120

WÜRZBURG
Bayern (☎0931)

★ ★ ★**Bahnhofhotel Excelsior**
Haugerring 2–3 ☎50484 tx68435
rm49 ⇄ 🛏40 **P** Lift ☽ sB36–45
sB ⇄ 🛏65–70 dB80–90
sB ⇄ 🛏120–130 mountains

★ ★ ★**Rebstock** (BW) Neubaustr 7
☎50075 tx68684
rm81 ⇄40 🛏41 **P** Lift ☽
sB ⇄ 🛏130 dB ⇄ 🛏230

★★**Central** Koelikerstr 1 (n.rest)
☎56952

6 Jan–20 Dec
rm21 🛏9 🏛 **P** Lift 𝄡 sB47
sB 🛏55–60 dB85 dB 🛏90–100

★★**Franziskaner** Franziskanerpl 2
☎50360
rm43 🛏1 🛏26 **P** Lift 𝄡 sB40–65
sB 🛏60–70 dB60–95 dB 🛏110

★★**Walfisch** (MIN) am Pleidenturm 5
☎50055 tx068499
🛏50 🏛 **P** 𝄡 sB 🛏105 dB 🛏110–160

&🅓**W Heinsen** Mainaustr 45 ☎42046 Frd

At **LENGFELD** (4km NE on 19)

&🅓**Autohaus Stoy** Industriestr 1 ☎27646
Chy Dat

Germany

ZELL AN DER MOSEL
Rheinland-Pfalz (☎06542)

★★**Post** Schlossstr 25 ☎4217
25 Jan–Dec
rm16 🛏14 **P** Lift sB 🛏37 dB 🛏74

ZUSMARSHAUSEN
Bayern (☎08291)

★★**Post** Augsberger Str ☎302
Jan–28 Oct & 24 Nov–28 Dec
rm28 🛏3 🛏11 🏛 **P** sB34 sB 🛏 🛏44
dB61–68 dB 🛏 🛏72–82 Pool

ZWEIBRÜCKEN
Rheinland-Pfalz (☎06332)

★★★**Fasanerie** (ROM) Fasaneriestr
☎44074
🛏 🛏51 A31 🏛 **P** 𝄡 sB 🛏 🛏80
dB 🛏 🛏120 Pool
★★**Rosen** von Rosen Str 2 (n.rest)
☎2837
rm42 🛏8 🛏19 **P** Lift 𝄡
&🅓**Carbon** Zweibrückerstr 4 ☎6048 **P**
Frd

ZWISCHENAHN (BAD)
Niedersachsen (☎04403)

☆☆**Ferien-Motel** am Schlart 1 (2km E)
☎2005 tx254713
rm30 🛏8 🛏18 A4rm **P** Pool

D Mengers Windmühlenstr 2 ☎3378 **P**
BL Hon

Serpentine road in the Bavarian Forest

Traditional Whitsun festival at Schwaebisch Hall

GREECE

Greece, a country rich in history and art, offers many attractions to the tourist. It is bordered by four countries; Albania, Bulgaria, Turkey and Yugoslavia. The countryside is still largely unspoilt. Northern Greece is mountainous, Mount Olympus being one of the highest and most famous peaks. The fertile central plains area is said to contain over six thousand species of wild flowers. The islands of the Aegean Sea, among them Crete and Rhodes, are popular holiday areas. In the extreme south the Peloponnesian peninsula combines the best aspects of Greek scenery and is dominated by the Taygetos Mountains and the great plains of Argolis.

The climate is predominantly maritime and the seasons are regular and predictable with very hot, dry summers. Modern Greek is the official language but English and French are useful second languages. English will be spoken in larger towns and resort areas and it quite widely understood in many parts of Greece.

Area *mainland 40,674 sq miles, islands 9,860 sq miles*
Population *9,740,000*
Local time *GMT + 2 (Summer GMT + 3)*

National flag *Five horizontal blue stripes on white background with a white cross on blue background in the top left hand corner*

A leaflet entitled '*Motoring in the Greek Islands*' is available to AA members.

Yachts moored peacefully in quiet Aegean harbour

How to get there

The usual and most direct route for the motorist is through Belgium, West Germany Köln (Cologne) and München (Munich), Austria (Salzburg) and Yugoslavia (Belgrade). The alternative road route is via France or Switzerland, Italy (Milan and Trieste), and Yugoslavia. The third way of reaching Greece is to drive to southern Italy and use the direct ferry services. The distance to Athinai (Athens) is just under 2,000 miles and would normally require four to five overnight stops. Car sleeper services operate during the summer from Brussels and 's-Hertogenbosch to Ljubljana; from Boulogne, Brussels and Paris to Milan; and from Milan to Bari and Brindisi.

Motoring regulations and general information

This information should be read in conjunction with the general content of the European ABC (pages 6–27). **Note** As certain regulations and requirements are common to many countries they are covered by one entry in the ABC and the following headings represent some of the subjects dealt with in this way:
AA Agents
Crash or safety helmets
Customs regulations for European countries
Drinking and driving
International distinguishing sign
Medical treatment
Overtaking
Police fines
Radio telephones/Radio transmitters
Rear view mirror
Seat belts
Traffic lights
Tyres
Visitors' registration

Accidents

Fire in Athinai ☎199. In other cities the numbers are given in the local telephone directories. **Police** in most big cities ☎100; in the suburbs of

226

Athinai ☎109; elsewhere local telephone directories should be consulted. **Tourist police** ☎171. **Ambulance** in Athinai ☎166; in other cities consult local telephone directories. In the case of accidents in which private property is damaged or persons injured the police should be called. They should also be called to minor incidents that cannot be settled amicably on the spot. Your own insurance company should be informed as well as the Motor Insurers Bureau in Athinai. The Motoring Club (ELPA) should also be informed preferably at their Head Office (see under *Motoring club* for address). See also *Accidents* page 7.

Accommodation
The Hellenic Chamber of Hotels issues a comprehensive guide to hotels, which includes details of some 4,000 establishments in categories de-luxe, A, B and C. Prices, which should be exhibited in rooms, are controlled by the National Greek Tourist Office. ATV, stamp duty and local taxes are not included in quoted rates. Additional charges are sometimes made for air-conditioning.

Boats
A Helmsman's Certificate of Competence is recommended for Greece. See page 8 for further information about this and boat documentation.

Breakdown
The Automobile and Touring Club of Greece (ELPA) provides a breakdown service in most big cities and assistance can be obtained by dialling 104. See also *Breakdown* page 8 and *Warning triangles* page 230.

British Consulates
(See also page 8)
GR–105 62 Athinai 2 Karageorgi Servias Street ☎7236211. There are also consulates in Kavalla, Patrai, Thessaloniki and on the islands of Kérkira, Kríti, Rodhos and Samos.

Currency and banking hours
(See also page 11)
The unit of currency is the drachma which is divided into 100 lepta. The maximum amount of Greek currency which may be taken into or out of Greece is *Dr*3,000. There are no formalities concerning the import and export of foreign currency not exceeding the equivalent of US $500. However, if the amount is in excess of this it must be declared to the Currency Control Authorities upon arrival.

Banks are open from 08.00–14.00hrs Monday to Friday. Some foreign exchange offices are open in the afternoon.

Old forms of transport still exist in modern Greece

Dimensions and weight restrictions
Vehicles must not exceed – height: 4 metres; width: 2.5 metres; length: vehicle/trailer combinations 18 metres. Only one trailer may be towed and the axle weight must not exceed 9 metric tons.

Driving licence
A valid British driving licence is acceptable in Greece. The minimum age at which a visitor may drive a temporarily imported car or motorcycle (over 50cc) is 17 years. However, an International Driving Permit is required by the holder of a licence issued in the Republic of Ireland. See under *Driving licence and International Driving Permit* page 13 for further information.

Emergency messages to tourists
(See also page 14)
Emergency messages to tourists are broadcast daily by the National Broadcasting Institute of Greece.
ERT1 transmitting on 411 metres medium wave broadcasts these messages in English, French, German and Arabic at 07.40hrs daily throughout the year.
ERT2 transmitting on 305 metres medium wave broadcasts the messages in English and French at 14.25 and 21.15hrs daily throughout the year.

Fire extinguisher
(See also page 16)
It is compulsory for all vehicles to be equipped with a fire extinguisher.

First-aid kit
(See also page 16)
It is compulsory for all vehicles to be equipped with a first-aid kit.

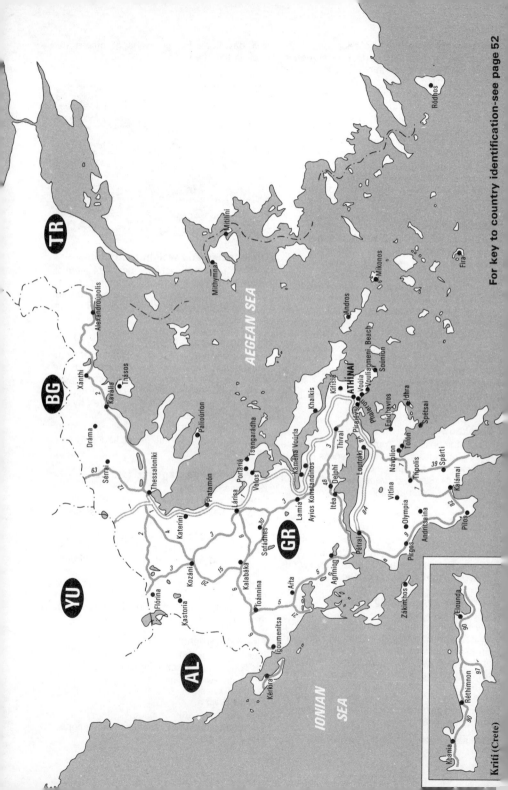

For key to country identification-see page 52

AEGEAN SEA

IONIAN SEA

TR
BG
YU
AL
GR

Ródhos
Fira
Míkonos
Mitilíni
Mithymna
Alexandroúpolis
Xánthi
Thásos
Kaválla
Dráma
Sérrai
Thessaloníki
Paliouríon
Andros
Kírissa
ATHÍNAI
Voúla
Vouliagméni Beach
Soúnion
Ídhra
Piraévs
Phaleron
Epidhavros
Spétsai
Khalkis
Tsengarádha
Kanéna Voúla
Thívai
Delphi
Loutráki
Tólon
Návplion
Tripolis
Sparti
Portariá
Vólos
Lárisa
Platamón
Katerini
Itéa
Ayios Konstandínos
Lamía
Vítina
Olympia
Kalámai
Pílos
Sofádhes
GR
Kalabáka
Árta
Agrínion
Pátrai
Andritsaína
Pírgos
Zákinthos
Ioánnina
Flórina
Kastoría
Kozáni
Kérkira
Igoumenítsa

Kríti (Crete)
Khaniá
Réthimnon
Eloúnda

63
2
72
1
2
4
3
6
3
3
20
15
6
5
5
37
3
3
3
48
8
7
7
39
82
5
90
97
80

Insurance

(See also page 16)
Short-term third-party insurance cover cannot be arranged at the frontier.

Lights

(See also page 17)
Driving on sidelights only is not permitted. It is recommended that *motorcyclists* use dipped headlights during the day.

Motoring club

(See also page 18)

 The **Automobile and Touring Club of Greece** (ELPA) has its head office at 2–4 Messogion Street, 11527 Athinai ☎(01)779 1615 and branch offices are maintained in major towns throughout the country and on Kérkira and Kríti. Office hours are 08.30–19.00hrs Monday to Friday; Saturday and Sunday 08.30–13.00hrs.

The club is able to provide general touring information and this may be obtained by telephoning 174 in Athinai and ☎(01)174 throughout the country, Monday to Saturday 08.00–22.00hrs.

Motorways

The motorways are usually only single-carriageway with some dual carriageway sections. Tolls are charged on most sections. Thessaloníki (Salonica)–Athinai (Athens) *Dr* 110 Athinai–Pátrai (Patras) *Dr* 65

Parking

(See also page 19)
Parking areas are indicated by signs. Parking is prohibited within 5 metres (16½ft) of an intersection; within 15 metres (49ft) of a bus stop or a level crossing; within 3 metres (10ft) of a fire hydrant; and where there is a continuous central white line unless there are two lanes in each direction.

Parking in Athinai can be difficult, and some garages charge high rates. *Warning* The police in Athinai are empowered to confiscate and detain the number plates from visitors' cars which are illegally parked. A heavy fine will also be imposed upon offenders and visitors are reminded that it is illegal to drive a vehicle without number plates.

Passengers

(See also page 19)
Children under 10 are not permitted to travel in a vehicle as front seat passengers.

Petrol

(See also page 20)
Credit cards Few petrol stations will accept credit cards.
Duty-free petrol The petrol in the vehicle tank may be imported free of customs duty and tax.
Octane rating Venzini Apli (91–92) and Venzini Super (96–98).
Petrol cans It is **forbidden** to carry petrol in cans in a vehicle.

Postal information

Mail Postcards *Dr*20, letters – up to 20gm *Dr*27.

Post offices There are 850 post offices in Greece. Opening hours are from 07.20–15.00hrs Monday to Friday. Post offices in central Athinai are located at: Eolou Street 100; Syntagma Square; Omonia Square.

Postcheques

(See also page 21)
Postcheques may be cashed at all post offices for a fixed sum of *Dr*6,000 per cheque. Counter positions are identified by the words *Mandats*, or *Orders*. See above for post office opening hours.

Priority

(See also *Priority including Roundabouts* page 22)
At crossroads outside cities traffic on a main road has priority.

Public holidays

Official public holidays in Greece for 1985 are given below. See also *Public holidays* page 22.

January 1 (New Year's Day)
January 6† (Epiphany)
February 25 (Clean Monday)
March 25 (Greek Independence Day)
April 12 (Orthodox Good Friday)
April 14 (Orthodox Easter Sunday)
April 15 (Orthodox Easter Monday)
May 1 (May Day)
June 3 (Orthodox Whit Monday)
August 15 (Assumption)
October 28 (Ochi or National Day)
December 25 (Christmas Day)
December 26 (Boxing Day)
†Sunday

Roads

Although the road system is reasonably comprehensive, surfaces vary and secondary roads may be poor. On long drives, a good average speed is between 30 and 40 miles an hour. The islands are best visited by sea or air. Only the larger islands – Kríti (Crete), Kérkira (Corfu)

and Rodhos (Rhodes) – have reasonably comprehensive road systems. Road on the smaller islands are generally narrow and surfaces vary from fairly good to rather poor. A leaflet entitled *'Road conditions in Greece'* is available to AA members.

Road signs
(See also page 23)
The signposting is fairly good, both Greek and English lettering are used.

Shopping hours
Food stores are open from 08.30–13.30 and from 17.30–20.30hrs on Tuesday, Thursday and Friday and from 08.30–14.30hrs on Monday, Wednesday and Saturday.

Speed limits
(See also page 25)
Unless otherwise indicated by signs, private cars with or without trailers are subject to the following restrictions: 50kph (31mph) in built-up areas; 80kph (49mph) outside built-up areas; 100kph (62mph) on motorways.

Spiked, studded or snow tyres
(See also page 10)
There are no special regulations regarding the use of *spiked tyres.*

Tourist Information offices
(See also page 25)
The National Tourist Organisation of Greece at 195–197 Regent Street, London W1R 8DL ☎01-

734 5997 will be pleased to help tourists before their departure. The organisation has offices in main towns throughout Greece.

Tourist Police
On duty in all resorts and at major frontier crossings. They all speak English and their job is to assist tourists in any way they can.

Using the telephone
(See also page 26)
Insert coin **after** lifting receiver, dialling tone same as UK. When making calls to subscribers within Greece precede number with relevant area code (shown in parentheses against town entry in gazetteer). Use *Dr*5 coin for local calls (blue/grey callbox) and *Dr*10 or 20 coins for national and international calls, but all coins must be dated 1976 or later.

International callbox identification (and national out of town calls) Orange sign round top.

Telephone rates The cost of a call between Athinai and London is *Dr*65 per minute.
What to dial for the Irish Republic 00 353.
What to dial for the UK 00 44.

Warning triangle
The use of a warning triangle is compulsory for all vehicles except two-wheelers. The triangle must be placed 20 metres (22yds) behind the vehicle in built-up areas and 50 metres (55yds) outside built-up areas. See also *Warning triangle/Hazard warning lights* page 26.

Prices are in Greek Drachmae
Abbreviations:
av   avenue
r   rue
rd   road
sq   square
st   street

AGRÍNION
Central Greece (☎0641)

☆☆*Soumells* 3 Ethniki Odos ☎23473
rm20 ⇌4 🍴 P

ALEXANDROÚPOLIS
Thrace (☎0551)

☆☆*Astir* 280 Av Komotinis ☎26448 tx26710
rm53 ⇌6 🍴21 P sB⇌ 🍴1730–2150
dB⇌ 🍴2310–2840 M650 t% Pool Beach sea

☆☆*Egnatia* ☎28661
⇌96 🏛 P ✆ Beach Sea
sB⇌1150–1250 dB⇌1800–2050
M550–660 t%

ANDRÍTSAINA
Peloponnese (☎0626)

★*Theoxenia* ☎22219
Mar–Oct
rm17 ⇌5 🍴4 P sB⇌ 🍴820–1220
dB ⇌ 🍴1440–1840 M475 t%

ANDROS
(Island of Andros) (☎0282)

★★*Xenia* ☎22270
Apr–Oct
⇌26 P sB⇌1221–1445
dB ⇌1830–2160 t%

ÁRTA
Epirus (☎0681)

★★*Xenia* Frourion ☎27413
rm22 🍴11 P ✆ sB 🍴1400 dB🍴1680
M540 t%

ATHÍNAI (ATHENS)
Attica (☎01)

See plan pages 232 and 233
★★★★★*Acropole Palace* 51 28th Octovriou ☎5223851 tx15909 Plan **1**
⇌107 sB⇌ 1470–2270
dB⇌2220–3500 M700 t%

★★★★★*Astir Palace* Athens Centre ☎3643112 tx222380 Plan **1A**
⇌78 Lift sB ⇌7800–9250
dB ⇌10350–13450 M1200 t%

★★★★*Athénée Palace* 1 Kolokotroni ☎3230791 tx6188 Plan **2**
⇌150 🏛 P Lift ℑ sB⇌2530
dB ⇌3700

★★★★*Athens Hilton* 46 Vassilissis Sofias Av ☎7220301 tx215808 Plan **2A**
⇌ 🍴473 🏛 P Lift ℑ
sB ⇌ 🍴10950–12530
dB ⇌ 🍴14200–15995 Pool mountains

★★★★*Grande Bretagne* Platia Syntagmatos ☎3230251 tx219615
Plan **3**
⇌360 P Lift ℑ sB ⇌6400–10950
dB ⇌8680–13595 t12.5% mountains

★★★★*King George* Constitution Sq ☎3230651 tx215296 Plan **4**
⇌140 P Lift ℑ sB ⇌5900–9900
dB⇌8400–20500 M1350 t%

230

Greece

★ ★ ★ ★ ★**St George Lycabettus**
2 Kleomenous ☎7290710 tx214253
Not on Plan
⇱150 🅟 P Lift 𝄞 sB⇱2854–4270
dB⇱4210–5996 M825 Pool sea

★ ★ ★ ★**Amalia** 10 Amalias Av
☎3237301 tx215161 Plan **6**
⇱98 P Lift 𝄞 sB ⇱ 🏠3010
dB ⇱ 🏠3980 M780 t%

★ ★ ★ ★**Esperia Palace** 22 Stadiou
☎3238001 tx215773 Plan **8**
⇱185 Lift sB⇱1872–2232
dB ⇱2500–3040 M700 t%

☆ ☆ ☆**Holiday Inn** Michalakopoulou
50, Ilissia 612 ☎7248322 tx218870
Plan **9**
⇱ 🏠189 P Lift 𝄞
sB ⇱ 🏠4300–4675 dB ⇱ 🏠5700–7300
Pool

★ ★ ★**King Minos** 1 Pireos
☎5231111 tx215339 Plan **10**
⇱200 P Lift 𝄞 sB ⇱1736–2360
dB ⇱2552–3400 M750 t%

★ ★ ★ ★**Olympic Palace** 16 Philellinon
☎3237611 tx215178 Plan **11**
⇱90 P Lift sB ⇱2900 dB ⇱3900
M500 t%

★ ★ ★**Acadimos** 58 Acadimias St
☎3629221 Plan **12**
rm130 ⇱105 🏠25 Lift 𝄞 mountains
sB ⇱ 🏠1235–1385 dB ⇱ 🏠1870–2120
M500 t%

★ ★ ★**Adrian** 74 Adrianou Pl (n.rest)
☎3250454 Plan **13**
15 Mar–5 Nov
⇱22 Lift dB ⇱2210–2610 t%

★ ★ ★**Asty** 2 Pireos ☎5230424 Plan **15**
rm128 ⇱112 🏠16 🅟 P Lift
sB ⇱ 🏠950–1661 dB ⇱ 🏠1278–2256
t%

★ ★ ★**El Greco** 65 Athinas ☎3244553
tx219682 Plan **18**
rm92 ⇱6 🏠86 sB ⇱ 🏠1433–2267
dB ⇱ 🏠2062–3134 M485–585 t%

★ ★ ★**Omonia** 4 Platia Omonias
☎5237210 Plan **20**
⇱ 🏠275 Lift 𝄞 sB ⇱ 🏠935–1185
dB ⇱ 🏠1320–1570 M500 t%

★ ★ ★**Stadion** 38 Vassileos
Konstantinou ☎7226054 tx215838
Plan **21**
⇱70 P Lift 𝄞 mountains
sB ⇱790–1540 dB ⇱1180–2120 M600
t%

★ ★ ★**Stanley** 1–5 Odysseos St
☎5241611 tx216550 Plan **22**
rm396 ⇱145 🏠250 🅟 P Lift 𝄞
sB ⇱ 🏠1900 dB ⇱ 🏠2700 M650 Pool

★ ★**Diomia** 5 Diomias St, Constitution Sq
☎3238034 tx215069 Plan **23**
rm71 ⇱10 🏠61 P 𝄞
sB ⇱ 🏠1700–2100 dB ⇱ 🏠2600–3200
M550

★ ★**Imperial** 46 Mitropoleos St (n.rest)
☎3227617 Plan **24**
rm21 🏠18 A5rm P Lift sB1070–1500
sB 🏠1070–1500 dB 1392–2100
dB 🏠1392–2100

★ ★**Kronos** 18 Aghiou Dimitriou (n.rest)
☎3211601 Plan **25**
rm56 ⇱28 🏠10 Lift
sB ⇱ 🏠690–1400 dB ⇱ 🏠980–1430
t%

N B Charitakis 66 Piraeus-Moschato
☎4823331 P BL

J E Condellis 10 Pladouta, Argyroymois
☎9929900 Frd

At **GILFÁDHA** (17km S)

★ ★ ★**Astir** 58 Vassileos Georgiou B, Astir
Beach ☎8946461 tx215925 Plan **14**
Apr–Oct
rm128 ⇱21 🏠107 P
dB ⇱ 🏠3667–5133 M1100 t% Beach
sea

★ ★ ★**Florida** 33 L-Metaxa ☎8945254
Plan **19**
rm86 ⇱27 P Lift sB ⇱1070–1595
dB ⇱1395–2260 M410–515 t%

AYIOS KONSTANDÍNOS
Central Greece (☎0235)

☆ ☆**Levendi** ☎31806
⇱56 P 𝄞 Beach sea

CHALKIS See **KHALKÍS**

CORFU See **KÉRKIRA**

CRETE See **KRÍTI**

DELPHÍ
Central Greece (☎0265)

★ ★ ★**Amalia** Apollonos ☎82101
tx215161
⇱185 P Lift 𝄞 sB ⇱2340 dB ⇱3430
M720 t% sea mountains

★ ★ ★**Delphi-Xenia** ☎82151
⇱44 P sB⇱1630–1980
dB ⇱2420–2940 M720 t%

★ ★ ★**Europa** ☎82353
rm46 ⇱2 🏠44 P dB⇱ 🏠2300 M700
t% sea

★**Dionyssos** 34 Vassileos Pavlou &
Frideriks (n.rest) ☎82257
Apr–Sep
rm12 sB600–660 dB750–825 sea

DRÁMA
Macedonia (☎0521)

★ ★**Xenia** 10 Ethnikis Amynis ☎23195
rm32 ⇱20 P sB ⇱1050–1100
dB ⇱1600–1700 t%

ELOUNDA See **KRÍTI (CRETE)**

EPÍDHAVROS (EPIDAURUS)
Peloponnese (☎0753)

★ ★**Xenia** ☎22003
rm24 🏠12 𝄞 dB 🏠1550–1800 M540
t% mountains

FALERON See **PHALERON**

FIRA See **THÍRA (SANTORINI)**

FLÓRINA
Macedonia (☎0385)

★ ★ ★**Tottis** ☎22645
rm32 P sB1260 dB2520 M700 t%

GLIFÁDHA See **ATHÍNAI (ATHENS)**

ÍDHRA (HYDRA)
(Island of Hydra) (☎0298)

★ ★**Hydroussa** (n.rest) ☎52217
tx219338
Apr–Oct
rm36 ⇱18 🏠18 𝄞
sB ⇱ 🏠1645–2095 dB ⇱ 🏠2160–2725
sea

★ ★**Miramare** Mandraki ☎52300
Apr–Oct
🏠28 Beach sea

IGOUMENITSA
Epirus (☎0665)

☆**Xenia** 2 Vassileos Pavlou ☎22282
Apr–Oct
🏠36 🅟 P dB ⇱ 🏠1800 M540 t%

IOÁNNINA (JANINA)
Epirus (☎0651)

★ ★ ★**Palladion** 1Pan Scoumbourdi &
28th Octovriou ☎325856 tx322212
rm135 ⇱112 P Lift sB ⇱735–1590
dB ⇱1100–2290 M480–580 t%

★ ★**Acropole** 3 Vassileos Georgiou A
(n.rest) ☎26560
rm33 ⇱10 🏠10 Lift 𝄞 sB ⇱ 🏠815
dB ⇱ 🏠1245–1485 t% lake

★ ★**Xenia (DPn** in summer) 33 Vassileos
Georgiou B ☎25087
rm60 ⇱36 🏠24 P Lift 𝄞
sB ⇱ 🏠1400 dB ⇱ 🏠1800 M540 t%
mountains lake

ITÉA
Central Greece (☎0265)

★**Xenia** ☎32263
Apr–Oct
🏠18 P dB ⇱ 🏠1530 M540 t% Beach

JANINA See **IOÁNINA**

KALABÁKA
Thessaly (☎0432)

☆**Xenia** ☎22327
Apr–Oct
⇱22 𝄞 dB ⇱2800 M620 t%

KALÁMAI (KALAMATA)
Peloponnese (☎0721)

★ ★ ★**Rex** 26 Aristomenous ☎22334
rm51 ⇱30 Lift sB ⇱899–1463
dB ⇱1374–2174 M577 t%

ATHINAI (ATHENS)

1	★★★★★	Acropole Palace
1A	★★★★★	Astir Palace
2	★★★★★	Athénée Palace
2A	★★★★★	Athens Hilton
3	★★★★★	Grande Bretagne
4	★★★★★	King George
6	★★★★	Amalia
8	★★★★	Esperia Palace
9	☆☆☆☆	Holiday Inn
10	★★★★	King Minos
11	★★★★	Olympic Palace
12	★★★	Acadimos
13	★★★	Adrian
14	★★★	Astir (At Glifádha 17km S)
15	★★★	Asty
18	★★★	El Greco
19	★★★	Florida (At Glifádha 17km S)
20	★★★	Omonia
21	★★★	Stadion
22	★★★	Stanley
23	★★	Diomia
24	★★	Imperial
25	★★	Kronos

KAMÉNA VOÚRLA
Central Greece (☎0235)

★★★★**Astir Galini** ☎22327 tx296140
⇆100 **P** Lift ⅅ **DPn**2450–3900 Pool
Beach sea mountains

KASTORÍA
Macedonia (☎0467)

★★**Xenia du Lac** pl Dexamenis ☎22565
rm26 ⇆13 🅵13 🏛 **P**
sB ⇆ 🅵1360–1580 dB ⇆ 🅵1728–2610
M540–640 t%

KATERÍNI
Macedonia (☎0351)

♫**Papoutsidis** 40 28th October St
☎29527 MB

KAVÁLLA
Macedonia (☎051)

★★**Galaxy** 51 El Venizelou ☎224605
tx452207
rm150 ⇆74 🅵76 Lift ⅅ
sB ⇆ 🅵1288–1534 dB ⇆ 🅵1894–2227
M650 t% sea

★**Panorama** 32C El Venizelou ☎224205
rm48 ⇆10 🅵6 **P** Lift
sB ⇆ 🅵845–1355 dB ⇆ 🅵1340–1802
t% sea

♫**D Hionis-G Vardavoulias** E Venizelou
77 St ☎833746 **P** BL Maz

KÉRKIRA (CORFU)
(Island of Corfu) (☎0661)

CORFU

★★★★★**CorfuPalace** L-Democratias
☎39485 tx332126

Apr–Oct
⇆114 **P** Lift ⅅ sB ⇆3175–5375
dB ⇆4300–7150 M1320 t% sea Pool

♫**Manessis** 31 Alexandra Av ☎39212
P Fia Lnc

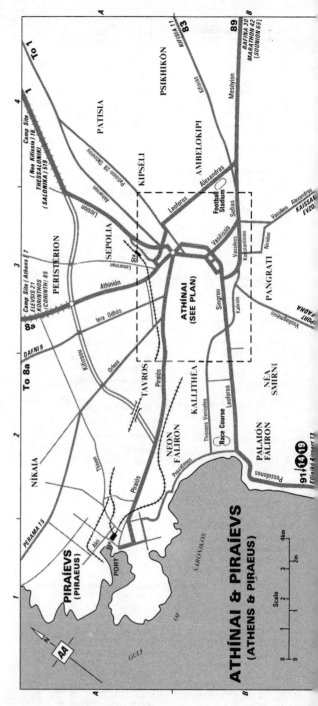

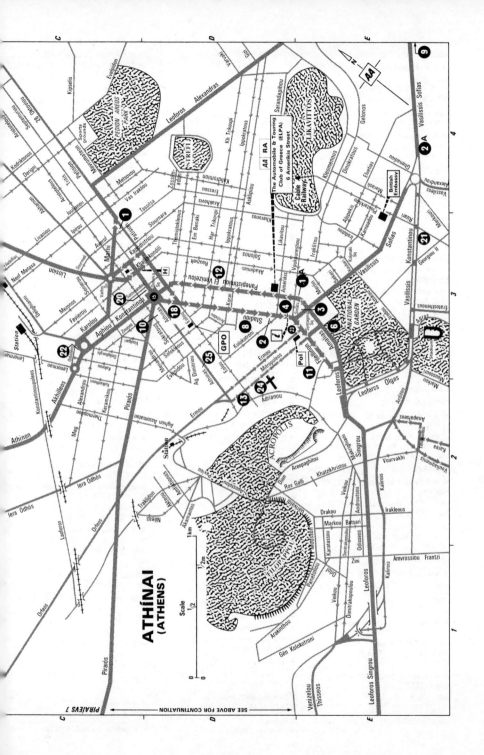

ATHÍNAI
(ATHENS)

Scale
1/2

1km

1/2cm

PEDION AREOS PARK

LIKAVITTOS

The Automobile & Touring
Club of Greece (ELPA)
6 Amerikis Street

AA RA

Cable
Railway

British
Embassy

NATIONAL
GARDEN

ACROPOLIS

FILOPAPPOU

GPO

Pol

SEE ABOVE FOR CONTINUATION
PIRAIEVS 7

KOMENO BAY (10km N of Corfu town)

★ ★ ★ ★ **AstirPalace** ☎91481 tx332169
Apr–Oct
⇋432 **P** Lift 𝒟 M1150
DPn3550–5250 t% ✹ Pool Beach sea

KHALKIS (CHALKIS)
Euboea (☎0221)

★ ★ ★ ★ **Lucy** 10 L-Voudouri ☎23831
rm92 ⇋44 ⋔36 **P** Lift
sB ⇋ ⋔850–1450 dB ⇋ ⋔1600–1980
M550 t% ✹ Beach sea

KHANIÁ See **KRÍTI (CRETE)**

KIFISIÁ
Attica (☎01)

★ ★ ★ **Aperghi** 59 Deliyanni, Kefalari
☎8013537
rm99 ⇋53 ⋔28 **P** Lift
sB ⇋ ⋔1100–1650 dB ⇋ ⋔1700–3200
M800 t% mountains

★ ★ ★ **Cecil** 7 Xenias, Kefalari
☎8013836
rm84 ⇋70 ⋔10 🖭 **P** Lift sB1730
sB ⇋ ⋔2290 dB2690 dB ⇋ ⋔3390

KOMENO BAY See **KÉRKIRA (CORFU)**

KOZÁNI
Macedonia (☎0461)

★ ★ **Hermionion** 7 Platia Nikis ☎36007
rm20 ⇋4 ⋔4 sB ⇋ ⋔890–740
dB ⇋ ⋔1080–1280 M450 t%

KRÍTI (CRETE)

ELOUNDA (☎0841)

★ ★ ★ ★ **AstirPalace** ☎41580 tx262215
Apr–Oct
⇋300 **P** Lift 𝒟 M1050
DPn4700–5450 t% ✹ Pool Beach
sea mountains

KHANIÁ (☎0821)

★ ★ ★ **Kydon** Platia Agoras ☎26190
tx291146
⇋117 **P** Lift 𝒟 sB ⇋1232–1620
dB ⇋2090–2340 M640 t% sea

☆ ☆ **Xenia** Theotokopoulou ☎24561
rm44 ⇋22 ⋔22 **P** sB ⇋ ⋔1032–1495
dB ⇋ ⋔1365–1966 M400–460 t%

RÉTHIMNON (☎0831)

★ ★ **Xenia** 30 N Pasrrou ☎29111
rm25 ⇋13 ⋔12 **P** 𝒟 ✹ Beach sea

LAMÍA
Central Greece (☎0231)

★ ★ **Apollonian** 25 Hatzopoulou, Platia
Parkou (n.rest) ☎22668
rm36 ⇋2 ⋔22 **P** Lift
sB ⇋ ⋔870–1125 dB ⇋ ⋔
1260–1612 t%

★ ★ **Leonideon** 8 Platia Eleftherias
(n.rest) ☎22822
rm31 ⋔9 **P** Lift

LÁRISA
Thessaly (☎041)

Greece

☆ **Xenia** 135 Farsaion ☎239002
⋔130 🖭 𝒟 dB ⋔1680 M540 t%

⑊**Sakellaropoulios Panachiothe** 15
Trikallon St ☎228292 **P** Fia

Saracakis 66 Farsaion ☎235501 M/c **P**
Hon Vau Vlo

LESBOS
MITHYMNA (☎2053)

★ ★ **Delphinia 1** ☎71315 tx297116
rm70 ⇋20 ⋔50 **P** 𝒟 **DPn**1376–1693
✹ Pool Beach sea

MITILINI(☎0251)

★ ★ ★ **Xenia** ☎22713
Apr–Oct
⇋74 **P** Lift 𝒟 dB ⇋2200–2600 M600
t% Pool sea mountains

LOUTRÁKI
Attica(☎0741)

★ ★ ★ **Karelion** 23 G-Lekka ☎42347
rm39 ⇋20 ⋔20 **P** sB ⇋ ⋔1300
dB ⇋ ⋔2250 t% Pool Beach

★ ★ **Pallas** 19 G-Lekka ☎42343
rm56 ⇋20 **P** Beach sea

MÍKONOS (ISLAND OF)
(☎0289)

★ ★ **Leto** ☎22207
rm25 ⇋23 ⋔2 🖭 sB ⇋ ⋔1170–1842
dB ⇋ ⋔1682–3373 M600–750 t%

★ ★ **Theoxenia** ☎22230
Apr–Oct
rm57 ⇋33 **P** sB ⇋993–2017
dB ⇋1542–2611 M500–550 t% sea

MITHYMNA See **LESBOS**

MITILÍNI See **LESBOS**

NÁVPLION (NAUPLIA)
Peloponnese(☎0752)

★ ★ ★ **Amphityron** Akti Miaouli
☎27366
rm51 ⇋32 ⋔16 **P** Lift
sB ⇋ ⋔1355–1805 dB ⇋ ⋔1990–2477
M560 t% Pool sea

★ ★ **Amalia** 93 Argous ☎27068
tx215161
⇋ ⋔175 **P** Lift 𝒟 sB ⇋ ⋔2340
dB ⇋ ⋔3430 M720 Pool mountains

★ ★ **Park** 1 Dervenaklon ☎27428
⇋70 **P** Lift sB ⇋1115–1295
dB ⇋1500–1740 M530 t% sea

★ ★ **Xenia** Acronafplia ☎28981
rm58 ⇋54 ⋔4 **P** Lift dB ⇋ ⋔3300
M700 t% Beach sea

⑊C **Antoniadis** 25 Argous St
☎28096 M/c **P**

OLYMPIA
Peloponnese(☎0624)

★ ★ ★ **Amalia** ☎22191 tx215161
⇋ ⋔147 **P** Lift 𝒟 sB ⇋ ⋔2340
dB ⇋ ⋔3430 M720 Pool sea

★ ★ ★ **Spap** ☎22514
rm51 ⇋35 ⋔16 **P** sB ⇋ ⋔2182
dB ⇋ ⋔3251 M650 mountains

★ ★ **Xenia** ☎22510
Apr–Oct
⋔36 **P** 𝒟 sB ⋔fr1705 dB ⋔fr2244
Mfr550 mountains

PALIOÚRION
Macedonia(☎0374)

☆ ☆ **Xenia** ☎92277
Jun–Sep
⋔72 **P** Lift 𝒟 dB ⋔1783–2499 M546
t% ✹ Beach

PÁTRAI (PATRAS)
Peloponnese(☎061)

★ ★ ★ **Méditérranée** 18 Aghiou Nicolaou
☎279602
rm96 ⇋56 ⋔40 Lift 𝒟 sB ⇋ ⋔960
dB ⇋ ⋔1380 M450 t%

★ ★ **Majestic** 67 Aghiou Andreou
☎272002
⇋73 **P** Lift Beach sea

PHALERON (FALERON)
Attica(☎01)

★ ★ ★ **Coral** 35 Possidonos Av
☎9816441 tx210879
⇋ ⋔89 🖭 **P** Lift 𝒟
sB ⇋ ⋔1080–2680 dB ⇋ ⋔2810–3840
M600 Pool sea

PÍLOS
Peloponnese(☎0723)

★ ★ **Nestor** 3 Tsamadou ☎22226
rm17 ⋔12 **P** 𝒟 sea

PIRAIÉVS (PIRAEUS)
Attica(☎01)

★ ★ **Arion** 109 Vassileos Pavlou, Kastella
(n.rest) ☎4121425
rm36 ⇋2 **P** Lift sB ⇋1220
dB ⇋1630–1870 t% sea

★ ★ **Phedias** 189 Kountourioti,
Passalimani (n.rest) ☎4170552
rm26 🖭 **P** Lift 𝒟 sB740–1130
dB1220–1520 t%

PÍRGOS
Peloponnese(☎0621)

⑊**Hydreos** 77 Patrou St ☎26135 M/c **P**
Dat Frd Maz Opl Toy

PLATAMÓN
Macedonia(☎0352)

★ **Olympos** 18 Frouriou ☎41380
Jul–Sep
rm23 **P** sB750 dB1100 t% Beach sea

PORTARIA
Thessaly(☎0421)

★ ★ **Xenia** ☎25922
⇋76 **P** dB ⇋1800 M540 t%

RÉTHIMNON See **KRÍTI (CRETE)**

(Island of Rhodes)(☎0241)

★ ★ ★ ★**Grand Astir Palace** Akti
Miaouli ☎26284 tx292121
⇵376 Lift ♪ M950 **DPn**2900–5100
✈ Pool sea

★ ★ ★**Ibiscus** 17 Nissyrou ☎24421
⇵170 P Lift sB ⇵1350–1844
dB ⇵1989–2889 M500–650 t% ✈
Pool Beach sea

★ ★ ★**Elafos** (Astir) Mount Profitis Elias
☎(0246)21221 tx292121
Apr–Oct
⇵68 P Lift ♪ sB ⇵1945 dB ⇵2427
M540 & alc ✈ mountains

★ ★ ★**Mediterranean** 35–37 Ko
☎24661 tx292108
rm154 ⇵72 ▥82 Lift ♪
sB ⇵ ▥1775–2575 dB ⇵ ▥2600–3710
M670 t% sea

★ ★ ★**Park** 12 Riga Ferreou ☎24611
tx292137
Apr–Oct
rm90 ⇵45 ▥45 P Lift ♪
sB ⇵ ▥1900–2950 dB ⇵ ▥2450–3780
M415–550 t% Pool

★ ★ ★**Spartalis** 2 N-Plastira (n.rest)
☎24371
⇵79 Lift sB ⇵ ▥1096–1685
dB ⇵ ▥1482–2574 sea

★ ★**Arion** 17 Ethnarhou Makariou
(n.rest) ☎20006
May–Oct
▥85 ♪ sB ▥1140–1610
dB ▥1580–2150 t% sea

★ ★**Soleil** 2 Democratias ☎28564
Jun–25 Sep
rm86 ⇵16 ▥23 P Lift
sB ⇵ ▥824–1137 dB ⇵ ▥1276–1511
M460 t%

★**Achillion** 14 Platia Vassileos Pavlou
(n.rest) ☎24604
Mar–Oct
rm50 ⇵18 ▥39 Lift

⅏**Kalliga Bros** St Kapodistriou
☎24529 M/c P Hon Vau Vlo

Zuvalas 10 Afstralias ☎23281 M/c Opl

SALONICA See THESSALONÍKI

SANTORINI See THÍRA

SÉRRAI
Macedonia(☎0321)
★ ★**Xenia** 1 Aghias Sophias ☎22931
rm32 P sB1250 dB1800 M550 t%

SOFÀDHES
Thessaly(☎0443)
⅏**G Popotas** 7 St-George's ☎22341 M/c
P

SOÙNION
Attica(☎0292)
★ ★**Aegalon** ☎39200
▥44 P Lift sB ▥1651 dB ▥2291
M700 t% Beach sea

Greece

☆**Mount Belvedere Park** ☎39102
Apr–Oct
⇵90 P ♪ ✈ Pool sea mountains

SPÁRTI (SPARTA)
Peloponnese(☎0731)
★ ★ ★**Lida** Atreidon-Ananiou ☎23601
15 Mar–Oct
⇵40 Lift ♪ sB ⇵2340 dB ⇵2900
mountains

★ ★ ★**Xenia** Lofos Dioskouron ☎26524
rm33 ⇵18 ▥15 P sB ⇵ ▥1588
dB ⇵ ▥2023–2320 M600 t%

★ ★**Dioskuri** 95 Lykourgou-Atreidon
☎28484
⇵34 Lift sB ⇵1520 dB ⇵2040 M650
t% mountains

SPÉTSAI
(Island of Spétsai)(☎0298)
★ ★ ★**Kastell** ☎72311 tx214531
Mar–Dec
⇵193 A92rm P ♪ sB ⇵2427–3055
dB ⇵3730–4600 M940 t% ✈ Beach
♦ sea

THÁSOS
(Island of Thásos)(☎0593)
★ ★**Xenia** ☎22105
Apr–Oct
rm27 ⇵6 ▥13 P sB ⇵ ▥850–1550
dB ⇵ ▥1300–2200 M600 t%

THEBES See THÍVAI

THESSALONÍKI (SALONICA)
Macedonia(☎031)
★ ★ ★ ★**Makedonia Palace** L-Megalou
Alexandrou ☎837520 tx412162
⇵287 P Lift ♪ sB ⇵3325–5275
dB ⇵4350–7950 M900 t%

★ ★ ★**Capsis** 28 Monastiriou (n.rest)
☎521321 tx412206
⇵428 P Lift ♪ Pool sB ⇵1837–3161
dB ⇵2692–4534 M600 t%

★ ★ ★**City** 11 Komninon ☎269421
tx412208
rm104 ⇵40 ▥64 Lift
sB ⇵ ▥884–1499 dB ⇵ ▥2119–3350
M650 t%

★ ★ ★**Olympic** 25 Egnatia ☎522131
rm52 ▥39 🍴 P Lift ♪
dB ⇵ ▥1400–2500 t%

★ ★ ★**Rotonda** 97 Monastiriou
☎517121 tx412322
rm79 ⇵30 ▥49 🍴 P Lift ♪
sB ⇵ ▥1330–2030 dB ⇵ ▥1860–3010
M600 mountains

★ ★ ★**Victoria** 13 Langada ☎522421
tx412145
⇵68 P Lift ♪ sB ⇵1380–2090
dB ⇵2010–2980 M600 t%

G Anastassiades 2–4 Vassileos
Georgiou ☎515209 Frd

⅏**ETEA** 142 Grammou-Bitsi,
Phoenix ☎417421 Aud VW

⅏**Saracakis** 5 Kilom Monastriou
Str ☎764802 P Hon Vlo

THIRA (SANTORINI)
(Island of Thira)(☎0286)

FIRA
★ ★**Atlantis** ☎22232 tx293113
Apr–Oct
rm25 ⇵4 ▥21 P sB ⇵ ▥2600–3080
dB ⇵ ▥3720–4400 t% sea

THÍVAI (THEBES)
Attica(☎0262)
★ ★**Dionyssion Melathron** 71 Metaxa &
Kadmou ☎27855
rm34 ⇵1 ▥3 P

TOLÓN
Peloponnese(☎0752)
★ ★**Minoa** 56 Atkis ☎59207 tx298157
18 Mar–Oct
rm62 ⇵9 ▥53 A18rm Lift
sB ⇵ ▥1030–1205 dB ⇵ ▥1400–1610
M490 t% Beach sea
★**Solon** ☎59204
15 Mar–Oct
rm28 ⇵8 ▥20 P sB ⇵ ▥1370–1465
dB ⇵ ▥2020–2180 M520–575 t% sea
mountains

TRÍPOLIS
Peloponnese(☎071)
★ ★ ★**Menalon** Platia Areos ☎222450
rm40 ⇵26 ▥26 P Lift sB ⇵ ▥1660
dB ⇵ ▥2320 M600 t%

TSANGARÁDHA
Thessaly(☎0423)
★ ★**Xenia** ☎49205
rm46 ⇵3 ▥39 P sB ⇵ ▥1400
dB ⇵ ▥1550–1800 M540 t%

VITÍNA
Peloponnese(☎0795)
☆ ☆**Xenia** ☎21218
Apr–Sep
⇵ ▥20 P ♪ dB ⇵ ▥1800 M540 t%
mountains

VÓLOS
Thessaly(☎0421)
★ ★ ★**Xenia** 1 N Plastira, Aghios
Konstantinos ☎24825
rm48 ⇵4 ▥41 P sB ⇵ ▥1765
dB ⇵ ▥2330 M510 t% Beach
★ ★**Aegli** 17A Argonafton (n.rest)
☎25691
rm40 ⇵14 P sB ⇵738–1302
dB ⇵1236–1884 t% sea
★ ★**Pallas** 44 Iassonos & Argonafton
(n.rest) ☎23510
rm50 ⇵6 ▥6 P Lift
sB ⇵ ▥950–1150 dB ⇵ ▥1700–2300
t% sea

VOÚLA
Attica(☎01)

★ ★ ★**Atlantis** 6 Aphroditis ☎8958443
rm15 ⇔8 🛏7 **P**

★**Miramare** 4 Vassileos Pavlou (n.rest)
☎8958446
rm20 **P**

VOULIAGMENI BEACH
Attica(☎01)

★ ★ ★ ★**Aphrodite Astir Palace**
☎8960211 tx223046

Greece

Apr–Nov
⇔ 🛏165 **P** Lift 🌙 M1450
DPn6200–7800 t% 🏊 Pool Beach sea

★ ★ ★ ★**Astir Palace** ☎8960211
tx215013
⇔ 🛏400 **P** Lift 🌙 M1450
DPn5000–9700 🏊 Pool Beach sea

★ ★ ★ ★ ★**Nafsika Astir Palace**
☎8960211 tx215013
⇔ 🛏384 **P** Lift 🌙 M1450
DPn6150–12800 🏊 Pool Beach sea

XÁNTHI
Thrace(☎0541)

★ ★**Xenia** 9 Vassilissis Sophias ☎24135
🛏24 **P** dB 🛏1576 M441 t%

ZÁKINTHOS
(Island of Zákinthos)(☎0695)

☆ ☆**Xenia** 66 D-Roma ☎22232
🛏39 **P** Lift Beach

ITALY

Italy, with its many beautiful cities and rich architectural heritage, is a country popular with every kind of tourist. It is bordered by four countries, Austria, France, Switzerland and Yugoslavia. The approaches are all dominated by mountains. The lakes of the north present a striking contrast with the sun-parched lands of the south and there is some beautiful countryside in the central Apennines. There are sandy beaches on the Mediterranean and Adriatic coasts. The north has a Continental climate whilst the south has an almost African climate with extremely hot summers. The language is Italian, a direct development of Latin. There are several dialect forms such as Sicilian and Sardinian, but the accepted standard is from Florence. German is spoken to a small extent in the region bordering-on the Austrian frontier.

Area *116,280 sq miles*
Population *57,426,000*
Local time *GMT + 1*
(Summer GMT + 2)

National flag *Vertical tricolour of green, white and red.*

Leaflets entitled *Motoring in Sicily* and *Motoring in Sardinia* are available to AA members.

How to get there

Although there are several ways of getting to Italy, entry will most probably be by way of France or Switzerland. The major passes, which are closed in winter, are served by road or rail tunnels. The distance to Milan from the Channel ports is approximately 650–700 miles, requiring one or two night stops. Rome is 360 miles further south. Car-sleeper services operate during the summer from Boulogne, Brussels, 's-Hertogenbosch or Paris to Milan.

La Cattolica, Stilo

Motoring regulations and general information

This information should be read in conjunction with the general content of the European ABC (pages 6–27). **Note** As certain regulations and requirements are common to many countries they are covered by one entry in the ABC and the following headings represent some of the subjects dealt with in this way:
AA Agents
Crash or safety helmets
Customs regulations for European countries
Drinking and driving
Fire extinguisher
First-aid kit
Medical treatment
Overtaking
Police fines
Radio telephones/Radio transmitters
Road signs
Traffic lights
Tyres
Visitors' registration

Accidents
Fire, police, ambulance (Public emergency service) ☎113. No particular procedure is required following an accident, excepting that a report must be made to the insurance company within three days. If the accident involves personal injury it is obligatory that medical assistance is sought for the injured party, and that the incident is reported to the police. On some *autostrade* there are emergency telephones as well as emergency push-button call boxes. See also *Accidents* page 7.

Accommodation
Hotels are classified into catagories from *4* to *de luxe*, and there are three categories of

For key to country identification-see page 52

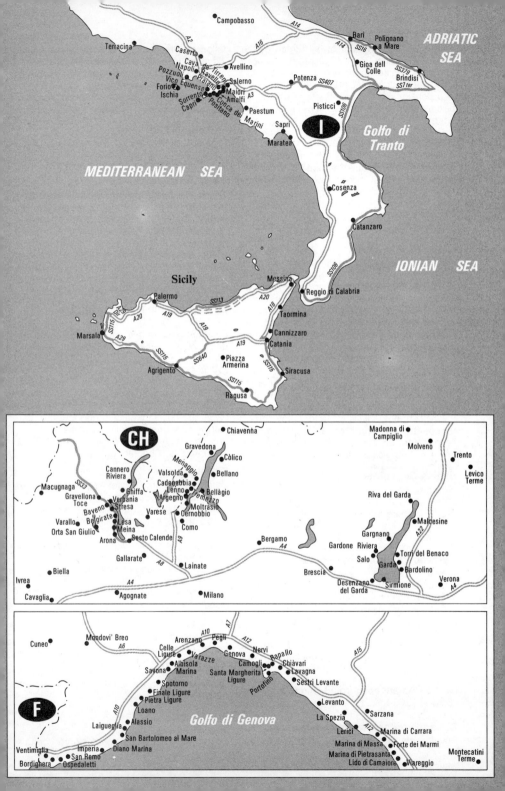

pensions. All charges must be agreed by the Provincial Tourist Board (*Ente provinciali per il Turismo*). The Italian State Tourist Office publishes every year an official list of all Italian hotels and pensions (*Annuario Alberghi*) which can be consulted at its London office or major travel agents.

Boats
A Helmsman's Certificate of Competence is recommended for Italy. See page 8 for further information about this and boat documentation.

Breakdown
Try to move the car to the verge of the road and place a warning triangle to warn following traffic of the obstruction. The Italian motoring club Automobile Club d'Italia (ACI) provides a breakdown service operated by the Breakdown Service Company of the ACI using its own staff on motorways and authorised repair garages on ordinary roads. The service can be used by any visiting motorist but must be paid for. However visiting motorists who have purchased Italian petrol coupons (see page 242) will find a 'carte carburante' coupon included in the tourist booklet which entitles them to receive emergency assistance free of charge. Assistance can be obtained by using the little telephone columns placed along motorways (every 2km) or by dialling 116 from any part of the country on ordinary roads. All services must be paid for. See also *Breakdown* page 8 and *Warning triangles* page 243.

British Consulates
(See also page 8).
00187 *Roma* Via XX Settembre 80A, ☎4755441/4755551. There are also consulates in Cagliari (Sardinia), Firenze, Genova, Milano, Napoli, Trieste and Venezia.

Currency and banking hours
(See also page 11)
The unit of currency is the Italian lira. The import of Italian lira bank notes is limited to 200,000 – but other currency is not restricted. Export of currency is restricted to Italian bank notes up to 200,000 and other currency up to the equivalent of 1 million lira. To export currency in excess of this amount it must have been declared on form V2 on entry.

Most banks are open from Monday to Friday 08.30 to 13.30 hrs.

Dimensions and weight restrictions
Private cars and trailers are restricted to the following dimensions and weights – car height: 4 metres; width: 2.5 metres; length: car/caravan combination 12 metres; weight: The maximum permitted gross weight is that stated by the manufacturers, or 80% of the gross weight of the towing vehicle – whichever is the lighter.

Driving licence
(See also page 13)
A valid British driving licence is acceptable in Italy if accompanied by an official Italian translation which may be obtained free from the AA.

The minimum age at which a visitor may drive a temporarily imported car is 18 years. However, visitors under 21 years are not permitted to drive vehicles which have a top speed in excess of 180kph (112mph). The minimum ages at which visitors may ride temporarily imported motorcycles are 17 (not exceeding 125cc), 18 (between 125cc–350cc) and 21 (exceeding 350cc).

Emergency messages to tourists
(See also page 14)
Emergency messages to tourists are broadcast daily by the Italian radio-television network (RAI).
RAI first channel transmitting on medium wave broadcasts these messages in English, German, French and Spanish at 06.58, 07.58, 09.58, 11.58, 12.58, 13.56, 14.58, 16.58, 18.58, 20.58, 22.58 and 00.28hrs daily throughout the year.
RAI third channel transmitting on medium wave broadcasts the messages in Italian at 07.00, 10.00 and 12.00hrs Monday to Saturday.

Fiscal receipt
In Italy the law provides for a special numbered fiscal receipt (ricevuta fiscale) to be issued after paying for a wide range of goods and services including meals and accommodation. This receipt indicates the cost of the various goods and services obtained and the total charge after adding VAT. Tourists should ensure that this receipt is issued as spot checks are made by the authorities and both proprietor and consumer are liable to an on-the-spot fine if the receipt cannot be produced.

Horn, use of
In built-up areas the use of the horn is prohibited except in cases of immediate danger. At night flashing headlights may be used instead of the horn. *Outside built-up areas* it is compulsory to use the horn when warning of approach is necessary.

Insurance
(See also page 16)
Third-party insurance is compulsory for certain

boats and engines in Italian waters. Short-term third-party insurance can be obtained at the frontier.

International distinguishing sign
(See also page 17)
It is compulsory for foreign-registered vehicles to display a distinctive sign at the rear of the vehicle. Failure to comply with this regulation will incur an on-the-spot fine of 10,000 lire.

Lights
(See also page 17)
Full-beam headlights can be used only outside cities and towns. Dipped headlights are compulsory when passing through tunnels and bridges even if they are well lit. Fog lamps may be used in pairs and only in fog and snow when visibility is restricted.

Motoring clubs
(See also page 18)

There are two motoring organisations in Italy the **Touring Club Italiano** (TCI) which has its head office at 10 Corso Italia, 20122 Milano ☎(02)8526 and the **Automobile Club d'Italia** (ACI) whose head office is at 8 Via Marsala, 00185 Roma ☎(06)49981. Both clubs have branch offices in most leading cities and towns.

The hours of opening of the TCI are usually between 09.00 and 19.00 hrs although some open earlier and close later. A few are closed all day on Mondays or Saturdays. However, all close for three hours for lunch between 12.00 and 16.00 hrs.

The ACI offices and those of the Provincial Automobile Clubs are open between 08.30 and 13.30 hrs Monday to Saturday. The head office in Roma opens between 08.00 and 14.00 hrs Monday to Saturday and 15.00 and 19.00 hrs Tuesday to Friday. A 24-hour information service is in operation although the interpreters are on duty only between 08.00 and 24.00 hrs. The Roma telephone number is (06)4212.

Motorways
A comprehensive motorway (autostrade) system reaching most parts of the country is available. To join a motorway follow the green signposts. Tolls are charged on most sections eg Milan to Rome is 16,200 Lire for a small car rising to 35,650 Lire for a large car. The method of calculating tolls are based either on the wheel base or the cubic capacity of the vehicle, and the distance covered.

On the majority of toll motorways a travel ticket is issued on entry and the toll is paid on leaving the motorway. The travel ticket gives all relevant information about toll charges including the toll category of the vehicle. At the exit point the ticket is handed in. On some motorways, notably A8, A9, A11, A14 (Pescara–Lanciano) and A12 (Roma–Civitavecchia) toll is paid at intermediate toll stations for each section of the motorway used. However, on a few motorways the destination must be declared and the toll paid on entering the motorway. There is no refund for a broken journey.

A leaflet entitled *Motorways in Italy* is available to AA members.

Orange badge scheme for disabled drivers
(See also page 19)
In Italy public transport is given priority in town centres and private cars may be banned. However, the local authorities are required to take special measures to allow badge holders to take their vehicles into social, cultural and recreational areas. Reserved parking bays may be provided in some areas and these will be indicated by signs featuring the international disabled symbol.

Parking
(See also page 19)
Parking is forbidden on a main road or one carrying fast-moving traffic, on or near tram lines, opposite another stationary vehicle, on or within 12 metres (39½ft) of a bus or tram stop. Violators of parking regulations are subject to heavy fines. There is a *blue zone* (*zona disco*) in most cities; in such areas parked vehicles must display a disc on the windscreen. Discs are set at the time of parking, and show when parking time expires according to the limit in the area concerned. Disc parking operates 08.00–20.00 hrs on working days. Discs can be obtained from petrol stations and automobile organisations. There are also *green zones* (*zona verde*) where parking is absolutely prohibited 08.00–09.30 hrs and 14.30–16.00 hrs. Vehicles will be towed away at the owner's expense even if they are not causing an obstruction.

Passengers
(See also page 19)
Children under 3 are not permitted to travel in a vehicle as front seat passengers.

Petrol
(See also page 20)
Credit cards A few petrol stations will accept Visa.

Duty-free petrol The petrol in the vehicle tank may be imported free of customs duty and tax.
Octane rating Benzina Normale (85–88) and Benzina Super (98–100).
Petrol cans It is **forbidden** to carry petrol in cans in a vehicle.
Petrol coupons At the time of going to press a concessionary package of Italian petrol coupons and motorways toll vouchers may be purchased from many AA Travel Agencies and AA Centres. The package is available to personal callers only and a passport and vehicle registration document must be produced at the time of application. Further information may be obtained from any AA Centre.

The package **cannot** be purchased inside Italy but may be obtained from ACI offices at main crossing points and also many ACI offices in port areas if arriving by ship.

Montalcino, Siena

Postal information
Mail Letters first 20 gm *L450*, postcards *L400* (max 5 words), Express surcharge *L1,500*.

Post offices There are 14,000 post offices in Italy. Opening hours are from 08.15–14.00hrs Monday to Friday and 08.15–12.30hrs Saturday.

Postcheques
(See also page 21)
Postcheques may be cashed at all post offices for a fixed sum of *L120,000 per cheque*. Counter positions are identified by the words *Pagamenti vaglia internazionali* or *Vaglia*. See above for post office opening hours.

Priority
(See also *Priority including Roundabouts* page 22)
Traffic on State highways (*Strade Statali*), which are all numbered and indicated by signs, has right of way, as do public service vehicles and, on postal routes, buses belonging to the service. These bus routes are indicated by a special sign.

If two vehicles are travelling in opposite directions and the drivers of each vehicle want to turn left, they must pass in front of each other (not drive round as in the UK).

Public holidays
Official public holidays in Italy for 1985 are given below. Many towns have local public holidays on the Feast Day of their Patron Saint. See also *Public holidays* page 22.
January 1 (New Year's Day)
April 8 (Easter Monday)
April 25 (Liberation Day)
May 1 (Labour Day)
August 15 (Assumption)
November 1 (All Saints' Day)
December 8† (Immaculate Conception)
December 25 (Christmas Day)
December 26 (Boxing Day)
†Sunday

Rear view mirror
Under Italian law it is obligatory for vehicles circulating on Italian roads to be fitted with a rear view mirror on the left external side. At the time of going to press this includes vehicles temporarily imported into Italy.

Roads
(See also *Road conditions* page 23)
Main roads are generally good, and there is an exceptional number of bypasses; secondary roads are often poor. Mountain roads are usually well engineered.

Seat belts
The wearing of seat belts is not compulsory in Italy. However, if your car is fitted with seat belts it is strongly recommended that you wear them in the interest of safety.

Shopping hours
Most shops are usually open Monday to Saturday; *food shops* from 08.30–13.00hrs and 16.00–20.00hrs, *other shops* from 09.00–13.00hrs and 16.00–19.30hrs. All shops close on Saturday afternoon during the summer.

Speed limits
(See also page 25)
The maximum speed limit in built-up areas, unless otherwise indicated, is 50 kph (31 mph). Mopeds are restricted to 40 kph (24 mph) on all roads unless there is a lower limit. On normal roads limits are 80 kph to 110 kph; motorways 90 kph to 140 kph depending on the cc of the vehicle's engine. Limits are signposted. Any infringement of speed regulations can result in punitive fines of up to £300, and these penalties have been enforced.

Spiked, studded or snow tyres
(See also page 10)
Snow tyres may be used on roads where wheel chains are compulsory, provided that they are used on all four wheels.

Spiked or studded tyres Vehicles with spiked tyres may be used provided that:
a they are used between 15 November and 15 March;
b they do not exceed 120 kph (74 mph) on motorways, and 90 kph (56 mph) on other roads. All signed lower limits must not be exceeded.
c they must not exceed a total weight of 3,500 kg;
d they are fitted to all wheels, including those of a trailer (if any).
Visitors are also advised to have mud flaps fitted behind the rear wheels.

Tourist information offices
(See also page 25)
The Italian State Tourist Office (ENIT) has an office in London at 1 Princes Street, W1A 7RA ☎01-408 1254. It will be pleased to assist you with any information regarding tourism. In Italy there are three organisations the Ente Nazionale Italiano per il Turismo (ENIT) with offices at frontiers and ports; the Assessorati Regionali per il Turismo (ART) and the Ente Provinciale per il Turismo (EPT) who will assist tourists through their regional and provincial offices. The Aziende Autonome di Cura Soggiorno e Turismo (AACST) have offices in places of recognised tourist interest and concern themselves exclusively with matters of local interest.

Using the telephone
(See also page 26)
Insert coins **before** lifting receiver, dialling tone short and long tones. When making calls to subscribers within Italy precede number with relevant area code (shown in parentheses against town entry in gazetteer). Use 200 lire gettoni tokens available from bars, tobacconists and slot machines or coins in new payphones.
International callbox identification Yellow sign.
Telephone rates The cost of a call to the UK if dialled direct is twelve tokens per minute.
What to dial for the Irish Republic 00 44.
What to dial for the UK 00 353.

Warning triangle
The use of a warning triangle is compulsory for all vehicles except two-wheelers. It should be used to give advance warning of any stationary vehicle which is parked on a road in fog, near a bend, on a hill or at night when the rear lights

have failed. The triangle must be placed on the road not less than 50 metres (55yds) behind the vehicle. Motorists who fail to do this are liable to an administrative fine of between 5,000 and 20,000 lire. See also Warning triangles/Hazard warning lights page 26.

Wheel chains
(See also page 10)
Roads where these are compulsory are marked by a national sign. Chains cannot be hired in Italy, but can be purchased at garages or vehicle accessory shops everywhere. Approximate prices per pair are as follows: iron L10,000−30,000; steel/iron; L20,000−40,000. Drivers of vehicles proceeding without wheel chains on road where they are compulsory are liable to prosecution.

Winter conditions
(See also page 27)
It is possible to approach northern Italy, Milan and Turin by road or rail tunnels.

From Switzerland via the Simplon rail tunnel; via the Grand St Bernard road tunnel; via the St Gotthard road tunnel; via the San Bernardino road tunnel; also via the Julier and Maloja passes.

From France via the Mont Blanc road tunnel; via the Fréjus road tunnel; in favourable weather, via the Lautaret and Montgenèvre passes; also via the French Riviera coast, entering at Ventimiglia.

From Austria via the Resia and Brenner passes; wheel chains may be necessary in severe weather.

The Plöcken pass is occasionally closed in winter, but the roads entering Italy at Dobbiaco and Tarvisio are normally free from obstruction.

Roads within the country, apart from those in the Dolomites, are not seriously affected in winter, although during January and February certain highways across the Apennines may be obstructed. Touring in the Dolomites is generally confined to the period from early May to mid October.

Cernobbio on Lake Como

San Marino

National flag *White over blue in two strips of equal breadth*

A small Republic with an area of 23 sq miles and

a population of 21,500 situated in the hills of Italy near Rimini. The official information office in the UK is the Italian State Tourist Office at 1 Princes Street, London W1A 7RA. The chief attraction is the city of San Marino on the slopes of Monte Titano. Its laws, motoring regulations and emergency telephone number are the same as Italy.

Prices are in Italian Lire
Abbreviations:
Gl   Generale
pza   piazza

ABANO TERME
Padova (☎409)

★ ★ ★ ★**Bristol Buja** via Monteortone 2
☎669390 tx430210

rm144 ⇨82 ⋔57 🏛 **P** Lift **D**
sB ⇨ ⋔48000−76000
dB ⇨ ⋔72000−105000 M26000−30000
≈ Pool

★ ★ ★ ★**Trieste & Victoria** (SRS) viale
Della Terme ☎669101 tx430250

25 Mar−Nov
⇨113 **P** Lift **D** **Pn**78000−89000 ≈
Pool

★ ★ ★**Terme Milano** viale Delle Terme
133 ☎669139

Mar−7Jan
rm102 ⇨45 ⋔28 **P** Lift **D** ≈ Pool

ACQUAPENDENTE
Viterbo (☎0763)

★**Roma** viale del Fiore 13 ☎74016

rm24 ⇨5 ⋔5 🏛 **P** ≈

ACQUI TERME
Alessandria (☎0144)

🚗**Carrara** corso Divisione Acqui 7
☎53733 **P** Aud VW

AGOGNATE
Novara (☎0321)

★ ★**Meridiana** Autostrade Torino
☎23156

Closed 9−22 Aug
⇨17 🏛 **P** Lift **D** ≈ Pool

AGRIGENTO See **SICILIA (SICILY)**

ALASSIO
Savona (☎0182)

★ ★ ★ ★**Diana** via Garibaldi 104
☎42701 tx270655

20 Mar−20 Oct

★ ★ ★ ★**Méditerranée** via Roma 63
☎42564

rm80 ⇨70 🏛 Lift **D** sea Beach

★ ★ ★**Spiaggia** via Roma 78 ☎43403
tx271617

rm82 ⇨30 ⋔52 🏛 Lift **D**
sB ⇨ ⋔58000−63000
dB ⇨ ⋔106000−111000 M30000−33000
Beach sea

★ ★ ★**Flora** Lungomare Cadorna 22
☎40336

rm37 ⇨31 ⋔3 **P** Lift **D**
sB 25000−35000 sB ⇨ ⋔35000−45000
dB40000−56000 dB ⇨ ⋔50000−60000
Mfr25000 Beach sea

★ ★ ★**Majestic** via L-da-Vinci 300
☎42721

20 Apr−8 Oct
rm77 ⇨67 ⋔10 🏛 **P** Lift **D** Beach
sea

★ ★ ★**Mare** via Boselli 24 ☎40635

rm49 ⇨48 **P** Lift Beach sea

★ ★**Toscana** via L-da-Vinci ☎40657

⇨65 Lift **D** Beach

★ ★**Villa Carlotta** via Adelasia 17
☎40463

Apr−Sep
rm16 ⇨8 **P** Beach sea

ALBA
Cuneo (☎0173)

★ ★**Savona** pza Savona ☎2381

rm110 ⇨63 🏛 **P** Lift **D** mountains

ALBISOLA MARINA
Savona (☎019)

★ ★ ★**Corallo** via M-Repetto 116
☎41784

Apr−Oct
rm24 ⇨20 🏛 **P** **D** sea

ALESSANDRIA
Alessandria (☎0131)

★ ★**Europa** via Palestro ☎42219

⇨34 🏛 **P** Lift **D** sB ⇨ ⋔41000
dB ⇨ ⋔73000 Mfr18000 St15%

ALPE DI SIUSI
Bolzano (☎0471)

★ ★**Eurotel** ☎72928 tx400181

21 Jul−28 Apr
⇨84 sB ⇨22500−52000
dB ⇨45000−88000 Pool mountains

AMALFI
Salerno (☎089)

★ ★ ★ ★**Santana Caterina** via Statale
☎871012 tx770093

⇨70 A10rm 🏛 **P** Lift **D** Pool Beach
sea

★ ★ ★**Aurora** pza Matteotti ☎871209

Apr−Oct
⇨31 🏛 **P** Lift **D** Beach sea

★ ★ ★**Luna** Lungomare ☎871002

⇨45 🏛 **P** Lift **D** Pool Beach sea

★ ★ ★**Miramalfi** ☎871247

rm44 ⇨40 **P** Lift **D** Pool Beach sea

★ ★**Bellevue** via Nazionale 163 (n.rest)
☎871846

Apr−Sep
rm25 ⇨13 ⋔12 **P** **D**

★ ★**Marina Riviera** via F-Gioia 22
☎871104

rm20 ⇨16 ⋔1 🏛 **P** **D** Beach sea

At **LONE** (2.5km W)

★ ★ ★**Caleidoscopio** via P-Leone X6
☎871220

Apr−15 Oct
rm31 ⇨20 ⋔11 A7rm **P** **D**
sB ⇨ ⋔33000−38500
dB ⇨ ⋔55000−66000 M16000 Pool
Beach sea

At **MINORI** (3km E)

★ ★**Caporal** ☎877408

⇨43 A18rm 🏛 **P** **D** Beach

★ ★**Santa Lucia** via Nazionale 44
☎877142

Apr−Sep
rm25 ⇨10 ⋔15 A12rm **D** Beach sea

ANACAPRI See **CAPRI (ISOLA DI)**

ANCONA
Ancona (☎071)

☆ ☆ ☆**AGIP** Palombina Nuova (SS 16
Adriatic km293) ☎888241 tx611627

⋔50 **P** Lift **D** dB ⋔58000

★ ★ ★**Jolly** Rupi di XXIX Settembre 14
☎201171 tx560343

⇨89 **P** Lift **D** sB63700 dB ⇨99400

At **PORTONOVO** (14km SE)

★ ★**Fortino Napoleonico** via Poggio
☎801124

May−Sep
⇨ ⋔30 **P** **D** sea

🚗**SAMET** via de Gasperi 80 ☎31568
M/c Frd

AOSTA
Aosta (☎0165)

★ ★ ★**Ambassador** via Duca degli
Abruzzi ☎42230

rm43 ⇨20 ⋔20 🏛 **P** Lift **D**
sB ⇨ ⋔30720−39000
dB ⇨ ⋔47440−55440 mountains

☆ ☆ ☆**Motelalp** ☎40007

⇨52 🏛 **P** Lift **D** mountains

Italy

★ ★ ★ Valle d'Aosta corso Ivrea 174
☎41845 tx212472

⇌102 🏨 P Lift ♪
sB ⇌60000 – 100000 dB ⇌40000 – 75000
mountains

★ ★ Gran Paradiso via Archibugio 20
☎40654

rm33 ⇌16 🛏17 P
sB ⇌🛏 28000 – 32000
dB ⇌🛏 42000 – 46000 mountains

★ ★ Mignon Strada del gran San
Bernardo 7 ☎40980 tx215013

⇌22 🏨 P ♪ sB ⇌26000 – 34000
dB ⇌42000 – 55000 M13000 t%
mountains

★ ★ Rayon de Soleil viale Gran St-
Bernardo ☎2247

Mar – Oct
⇌39 🏨 P Lift ♪ sB ⇌26000 – 32000
dB ⇌40000 – 48000 mountains

★ ★ Turin via Torino 14 ☎44593

rm51 ⇌47 🏨 P Lift sB22720 – 30720
sB ⇌30720 – 37720 dB ⇌46440 – 55440
mountains

⅋🔾F Gal via Monte Emilius 9 ☎2353 BL
RT

ARABBA
Belluno (☎0436)

★ Posta ☎79105

Dec – Apr & Jun – Sep
rm13 ⇌7 🛏6 🏨 P mountains

ARENZANO
Genova (☎010)

★ ★ ★ Miramare ☎9127325

10 Jan – Nov
rm45 ⇌15 🛏15 🏨 Lift ♪ sea

★ Europa ☎9127384

1 May – Sep
rm14 ⇌2 P sea

AREZZO
Arezzo (☎0575)

★ ★ ★ Continentale pza G-Monaco 6
☎20251

rm78 ⇌54 🛏6 Lift ♪

⅋🔾Magi Ezio di Piero & Corrado Magi via
M-Perennio 24 ☎21264 BL

ARGEGNO
Como (☎031)

★ Belvedere ☎82116

Apr – Oct
rm17 ⇌4 🛏7 P ♪ sB21000 – 26000
sB ⇌🛏27000 – 32000 dB33000 – 40000
dB ⇌40000 – 48000 M15000 lake

ARONA
Navara (☎0322)

★ ★ ★ Antares via Gramsci 9 (n.rest)
☎3438

rm50 ⇌25 🛏25 🏨 P Lift ♪
sB ⇌🛏28000 – 30000
dB ⇌42000 – 48000 lake

ARZACHENA See SARDEGNA (ISOLA) (SARDINIA)

ASOLO
Treviso (☎0423)

★ ★ ★ ★ Villa Cipriani (CIGA) ☎55444
tx411060

⇌32 🏨 P Lift ♪
sB ⇌127000 – 157000
dB ⇌184000 – 209000 t%

ASSISI
Perugia (☎075)

★ ★ ★ Glotto via Fontabella 41
☎812209 tx660122

15 Mar – 15 Nov
rm72 ⇌52 🏨 P ♪ sB27700
sB ⇌38700 dB42400 dB ⇌58400
M22000

★ ★ ★ Subasio via Frate Elia 2
☎812206 tx600311

rm70 ⇌60 🛏10 🏨 P Lift ♪
sB ⇌ 🛏45000 dB ⇌ 🛏65000
mountains

★ ★ ★ Windsor Savola porta San
Francesco 1 ☎812210 tx660122

rm33 ⇌17 🛏16 🏨 P Lift ♪

★ ★ Umbra via degli Archi 2 ☎812240

21 Dec – 5 Nov
⇌27 ♪ sB18500 sB ⇌27500
dB ⇌40000 mountains

ASTI
Asti (☎0141)

★ ★ ★ Salera via M-Marello 19 ☎211815

⇌54 🏨 P Lift ♪

⅋🔾G Vignetti via Ticino 1 ☎55016 M/c
P

AVELLINO
Avellino (☎0825)

★ ★ ★ Jolly via Tuoro Cappuccini 97A
☎32191

rm74 ⇌57 P Lift ♪ sB53000
dB ⇌83000

BADIA (LA) See ORVIETO

BARBARANO See GARDONE RIVIERA

BARDOLINO
Verona (☎045)

★ ★ ★ Vela d'Or 22 Cisano ☎7210067
tx480444

May – Sep
rm60 🛏52 A10rm 🏨 Pool lake

⅋🔾A Tortella via Gardesana 26
☎7210053

BARI
Bari (☎080)

★ ★ ★ ★ Grand Ambasciatori via
Omodeo 51 ☎410077 tx810405

rm177 ⇌90 🛏87 🏨 P Lift ♪ Pool

★ ★ ★ Palace via Lombardi 13
☎216551 tx810111

rm210 ⇌180 🛏30 🏨 P Lift ♪
sB ⇌55000 – 90000 dB ⇌17000

★ ★ ★ Boston (BW) via Piccinni 155
(n.rest) ☎216633

rm72 ⇌17 🛏55 🏨 P Lift ♪

★ ★ ★ Jolly via G-Petroni 15 ☎364366
tx810274

⇌164 🏨 Lift ♪ sB ⇌73000
dB ⇌118000

⅋🔾Autoservizio (F Losito) traversa 65
Japigia 44 ☎330158 P Frd

At TORRE A MARE (12km E)

☆ ☆ ☆ AGIP SS 16km 816 ☎300001
tx611627

🛏95 P Lift ♪ dB 🛏73000

BAVENO
Novara (☎0323)

★ ★ ★ Lido Palace Strada Statale
Sempione 30 ☎24444 tx200697

⇌ 🛏80 🏨 P Lift ♪ ✒ Pool
mountains lake

★ ★ Beau Rivage viale della Vittoria 36
☎24534

Apr – Sep
rm80 ⇌25 🏨 P Lift ♪ lake

★ ★ Simplon via Garibaldi 52 ☎24112
tx200217

15 Mar – Oct
rm96 ⇌90 🛏6 🏨 P Lift ♪
sB ⇌ 🛏44000 dB ⇌ 🛏77000 ✒ Pool
lake

★ ★ Splendid via Sempione 12 ☎24583
tx200217

15 Mar – Oct
rm100 ⇌80 🛏20 🏨 P Lift ♪ ✒
Pool lake

At FERIOLO (3km NW)

★ ★ Carillon Strada Nazionale del
Sempione 2 ☎28115

Apr – Sep
⇌ 🛏25 P ♪ lake

BELGIRATE
Novara (☎0322)

★ ★ ★ Milano (BW) via Sempione 4
☎7495 tx200490

rm60 ⇌25 🛏35 🏨 P Lift
sB ⇌ 🛏45000 dB ⇌ 🛏80000 lake

★ ★ Villa Carlotta via Sempione 119
☎7277 tx200490

rm120 ⇌110 🏨 P Lift ♪
sB35500 – 40500 sB ⇌40500 – 45500
dB47000 – 52000 dB ⇌53000 – 73000
M14000 – 19000 ✒ Pool lake

BELLAGIO
Como (☎031)

★ ★ ★ ★ Villa Serbellono via Roma 1
☎950216 tx380330

Apr – Oct
rm100 ⇌90 🛏10 🏨 P Lift ♪
sB ⇌ 🛏130000 dB ⇌ 🛏190000 ✒
Pool lake

★ ★ ★*Lac* pza Mazzini ☎950320
end Apr–Sep
rm48 ⇌41 🛏3 Lift lake

★ ★ ★*Ambassadeur Metropole* pza
Mazzini 5 ☎950409 tx380861
Mar–Oct
rm46 ⇌34 🛏7 **P** Lift sB24500–28000
sB ⇌ 🛏33500–37000 dB43000–47000
dB ⇌ 🛏53000–57000 M12000–14000
lake

★ ★*Belvedere* via Valassina 33
☎950410
Apr–10 Oct
rm50 ⇌30 🛏15 🛎 **P** Lift
sB22000–25000 sB ⇌ 🛏31000–37000
dB41000 dB ⇌ 🛏55000 Pool lake

★ ★*Florence* pza Mazzini ☎950342
Etr–5 Oct
rm48 ⇌25 🛏4 Lift sB29000–33000
sB ⇌ 🛏47000–53000 dB50000–52000
dB ⇌ 🛏56000–64000 M18000
mountains lake

BELLANO
Como (☎0341)

★ ★*Meridiana* via C-Alberto 19
☎821126
rm34 ⇌28 A4rm 🛎 **P** Lift mountains
lake

BELLARIA IGEA MARINA
Forli (☎0541)

At **IGEA MARINA**

★ ★ ★*Touring Spiaggia* via la Pinzoni
217 ☎630419
15 May–20 Sep
rm39 ⇌6 🛏30 **P** Lift Pool Beach sea

BELLUNO
Belluno (☎0437)

B Mortti via T-Veccellio 117 ☎30790 AR

BERGAMO
Bergamo (☎035)

★ ★ ★*Excelsior San Marco* pza
Repubblica 6 ☎232132 tx301295
rm151 ⇌40 🛏111 Lift 𝄞
sB ⇌ 🛏85000 dB ⇌ 🛏 134500 M26000

★ ★ ★*Grand Moderno* (MIN) viale
Papagiovanni XXIII 106 ☎233033
tx340598
rm100 ⇌15 🛏60 🛎 **P** Lift 𝄞

★ ★*Agnelo d'Oro* via Gombito 22
☎249883
rm20 ⇌5 🛏15 **P** Lift

★ ★*Moro* L-Porta Nuova 6 ☎242946
Closed 2wks Aug
⇌25 **P** Lift 𝄞 sB ⇌37000
dB ⇌60000 M alc

BIELLA
Vercelli (☎015)

★ ★ ★*Astoria* viale Roma 9 (n.rest)
☎20545 tx214083
rm50 ⇌15 🛏35 🛎 **P** Lift 𝄞
sB ⇌ 🛏58500 dB ⇌ 🛏82000

BIVIGLIANO
Firenze (☎055)

Italy

★ ★*Giotto Park* ☎406608
Mar–20 Oct
rm34 ⇌7 🛏18 A17rm **P** 𝄞
sB ⇌ 🛏38500–52000
dB ⇌ 🛏59000–84000 ⏰ mountains

BOLOGNA
Bologna (☎051)

★ ★ ★ ★ ★*Royal Carlton* (SRS) via
Montebello 8 ☎554141 tx510356
⇌250 🛎 **P** Lift 𝄞 sB ⇌145000
dB ⇌195000 M alc

★ ★ ★*Jolly* pza XX Settembre 2
☎264405 tx510076
⇌176 **P** Lift 𝄞 sB⇌95000
dB ⇌138000

☆ ☆ ☆*AGIP* via EM Lepido 203/4
☎401130
🛏60 **P** Lift 𝄞 dB 🛏76000

☆ ☆ ☆*Crest (See page 51)* pza della
Constituzione ☎372172 tx510676
rm164 ⇌159 🛏5 🛎 Lift 𝄞
sB ⇌ 🛏95800 dB ⇌ 🛏138800 Pool

★ ★ ★*Garden* via Lame 109 ☎522222
rm83 ⇌43 🛏40 🛎 **P** Lift 𝄞

🛈*AMM* via Po 2A ☎492552 M/c Ren

C Cesari via della Grada 9 ☎554554 VW

Cisa Via A-di-Vincenzo 6 ☎370434 BL

BOLSENA
Viterbo (☎0761)

★ ★*Columbus* Lungo Lago 27 ☎98009
⇌39 🛎 **P** 𝄞 dB ⇌62000
M12000–15000 ⏰ lake

BOLZANO-BOZEN
Bolzano (☎0471)

★ ★ ★*Alpi* via Alto Adige 35 ☎26671
tx400156
rm112 ⇌57 🛏37 🛎 **P** Lift 𝄞
sB ⇌ 🛏6100 dB ⇌ 🛏102000
mountains

★ ★*Grifone* pza Walther 7 ☎27057
tx400081
rm132 ⇌ 🛏101 🛎 Lift 𝄞 sB33500
sB ⇌ 🛏77500 dB 80000
dB ⇌ 🛏110000 M195000 Pool
mountains

★*Cita di Bolzano* pza Walther 21
☎25221
rm97 ⇌50 Lift sB ⇌22500 dB ⇌58000

★*Luna* via Piave 15 ☎25642 tx400309
rm84 ⇌40 🛏33 🛎 **P** Lift 𝄞
sB ⇌ 🛏40000 dB45000 dB ⇌ 🛏70000
mountains

★*Scala* via Brennero 11 ☎41111
rm60 ⇌20 🛏40 🛎 **P** Lift 𝄞
sB ⇌ 🛏40000 dB ⇌ 🛏57600 M alc
Pool mountains

🛈*M Mattevi* 6 via Roma 96 ☎36265 BL
Cit

🛈*Mich* via Galileo Galilei 6 ☎41119
M/c **P** BL DJ Hon RT

🛈*1000 Miglia* via Macello 13 ☎26340
Opl Vau

🛈*SAS Motor* via Macello 54 ☎25373
BMW

E Tasini via Roma N61B ☎916465

BORCA DI CADORE
Belluno (☎0435)

At **CORTE DI CADORE** (2km E)

★ ★ ★*Bolte* ☎82001 tx440072
Jun–Sep & 20 Dec–Mar
🛏84 Lift ⏰

BORDIGHERA
Imperia (☎0184)

★ ★ ★*Grand del Mare* portico della
Punta 34 ☎262201 tx270535
23 Dec–Oct
⇌105 🛎 **P** Lift 𝄞 ⏰ Pool Beach

★ ★ ★*Jolanda* corso Italia 85
☎261325
Closed Oct & Nov
rm48 ⇌42 🛏4 **P** Lift 𝄞 sea

★ ★*Excelsior* via Gl-Biamonti 30
☎262970
18 Dec–Oct
rm43 ⇌20 🛏10 🛎 **P** Lift 𝄞 Beach
sea

★ ★*Villa Elisa* via Romana 70 ☎261313
20 Dec–20 Oct
rm35 ⇌32 **P** Lift 𝄞 sB ⇌35000
dB43000 dB ⇌ 🛏56000 M15000–25000
Beach sea

BÒRMIO
Sondrio (☎0342)

★ ★*Posta* via Roma 66 ☎904753
tx321425
Dec 15–Apr & Jul–20 Sep
⇌55 Lift 𝄞 sB ⇌ 🛏35000
dB ⇌ 🛏60000

BRESCIA
Brescia (☎030)

☆ ☆ ☆*AGIP* viale Bornata 42 (SS 11km
236) ☎361654
🛏42 **P** 𝄞 dB 🛏52000

Brescia Motori via L-Appollonio 17A
☎50051 BL

BRESSANONE-BRIXEN
Bolzano (☎0472)

★ ★ ★*Elefante* Rio Bianco 4 ☎22288
Mar–Nov
⇌48 A14rm 🛎 **P** 𝄞 dB ⇌110000
Pool mountains

★ ★ ★*Gasser* via Giardini 19 ☎22105
Apr–20 Oct
⇌30 🛎 **P** Lift 𝄞
sB⇌ 🛏27000–42000
dB ⇌ 🛏54000–84000 M13000
mountains

★★Corona d'Oro-Goldene Krone via
Fienili 4 ☎24154 tx400491
⇄36 🏭 P Lift sB ⇄ 🍴26000
dB ⇄ 🍴36000–42000 St10%
mountains

🅢⅁F I Lanz via Stazione 32 ☎22226 P
Aud VW

🅢⅁A Pecora via V-Veneto 57 ☎23277

BREUIL-CERVINIA
Aosta (☎0166)

★★Valdôtain Lac Bleu ☎949428
tx211822

Dec–Apr & Jun–Sep
30rm ⇄10 🍴20 🏭 P Lift 🌙
sB ⇄ 🍴25000–35000
dB ⇄ 🍴45000–65000 M23000
mountains lake

BRINDISI
Brindisi (☎0831)

★★★Internazionale Lungomare
Regina Margherita ☎23475
⇄ 🍴87 🏭 P Lift 🌙 sea

Biagio via Cappuccini 70 ☎23037 M/c
Opl

🅢⅁T Marino via E-Fermi 7, Zone
Industriale ☎24094 M/c P Frd

BRUNICO-BRUNECK
Bolzano (☎0474)

★★★Posta Greben 9 ☎85127 tx400530
rm64 ⇄34 🍴15 P 🌙 sB26000–32000
sB ⇄ 🍴28500–35500 dB44000–52000
dB ⇄ 🍴50000–61000 mountains

CADENABBIA
Como (☎0344)

★Beau-Rivage via Regina 87 ☎40426
Apr–30 Oct
rm23 ⇄4 🍴6 P mountains lake

CAGLIARI See **SARDEGNA (ISOLA)**
(SARDINIA)

CAMAIORE (LIDO DI)
Lucca (☎0584)

🅢⅁L Galletti via del Termine 2 ☎90024
DJ RT Vlo

CAMOGLI
Genova (☎0185)

★★★★Cenobio del Dogi via Cuneo 34
☎770041 tx211116

31 Jan–30 Nov
rm83 ⇄70 🍴13 P Lift 🌙 ⅏ Pool
Beach sea mountains

★★Casmona via Garibaldi 103
☎770015

rm34 🍴22 🌙 sB18000 sB 🍴21000
dB18000 dB 🍴40000 sea

CAMPOBASSO
Campobasso (☎0874)

P Vitale via XXIV Maggio 95 ☎61069
Aud MB Por VW

CANAZEI
Trento (☎0462)

★★Croce Bianca via Roma 3 ☎61111
tx400012

Italy

15 Jun–10 Oct
⇄41 P Lift sB ⇄20000–27000
dB ⇄37000–52000 M18000 mountains

CANDELI See **FIRENZE (FLORENCE)**

CÀNNERO RIVIERA
Novara (☎0323)

★★Cannero Lungolago 2 ☎78046
16 Mar–30 Oct
rm32 ⇄16 🍴16 🏭 P Lift
sB ⇄ 🍴38000 dB ⇄ 🍴72000 M20000
⅏ lake

CANNIZZARO See **SICILIA (SICILY)**

CAORLE
Venezia (☎0421)

★★Excelsior viale Vespucci 1 ☎81515
15 May–Sep
rm55 ⇄45 🍴10 P Lift 🌙 Beach sea

🅢⅁G Cecotto via Strada Nuova 64
☎81315 M/c

CAPRI (ISOLA DI)
Napoli (☎081)

CAPRI

★★★★★Grand Quisisana (CIGA) via
Camerelle 2 ☎8370788 tx710520
Apr–Oct
⇄140 Lift 🌙 DPn166800–373600
Pool sea

At **ANACAPRI** (3.6km W)

★★★San Michele via G-Orlandi 1
☎8371427
Apr–Oct
rm60 ⇄40 🍴20 🏭 P Lift 🌙 sea

CARRARA (MARINA DI)
Massa Carrara (☎0585)

★★Mediterraneo via Genova 2 bis
☎635222
rm50 ⇄48 P Lift 🌙 sB25100
sB ⇄38300 dB ⇄56200 M1800 sea
mountains

CASERTA
Caserta (☎0823)

★★★Jolly viale V-Veneto 9 ☎325222
tx710548
⇄92 P Lift 🌙 sB ⇄60000 dB ⇄92000

🅢⅁Colombo via Colombo 56 ☎25268 P
Cit Lnc MB Ren

🅢⅁M Masullo via Roma 78–92 ☎26441
BL RT

CASTELLINA IN CHIANTI
Siena (☎0577)

★★Villa-Cassalecchi (DPn) (1km S)
☎740240
Apr–Oct
⇄19 A3rm P 🌙 sB ⇄ 🍴49000
dB ⇄ 🍴77000 Pool M45000 ⅏
mountains

At **RICAVO** (4km N)

★★★Tenuta di Ricavo ☎740221
Apr–Oct
⇄25 A14rm P DPn74000–102000 Pool
mountains

CASTIGLIONCELLO
Livorno (☎0586)

★★★Miramare via Marconi 8
☎752435
Etr–15 Sep
rm64 ⇄42 🍴18 A6rm P Lift 🌙
sB ⇄ 🍴35000 dB ⇄ 🍴52000 sea

★★Guerrini via Roma 12 ☎752047
Closed Nov
rm22 ⇄12

CATANIA See **SICILIA (SICILY)**

CATANZARO
Catanzaro (☎0961)

☆ ☆ ☆AGIP exit Strada due Mari
☎51791
🍴76 P Lift 🌙 dB 🍴74000

Autosabim Nuova Bellavista 35–37 M/c
P Frd

CATTOLICA
Forlì (☎0541)

★★★★Victoria Palace via Carducci 24
☎962921 tx550459
15 May–28 Sep
⇄98 P Lift 🌙 Beach sea

★★★Diplomat via del Turismo 9
☎962200
2 Jun–15 Sep
⇄80 P Lift 🌙 sB⇄27000–29000
dB ⇄43000–48000 M15000 Beach sea

★★★Europa-Monetti via Curiel 33
(n.rest) ☎961159
15 May–25 Sep
rm77 ⇄22 🍴50 🏭 🌙 P Lift Pool
Beach

★★★Gambrinus via Carducci 86
☎961347
May–Oct
rm42 🍴33 P Lift sB 🍴26000–34000
Beach sea

★★★Maxim via Facchini 7 ☎962137
May–Sep
🍴55 P Lift 🌙 sB 🍴20500–25000
dB 🍴37000–42000 M11000–15000

★★★Moderno-Majestic viale
d'Annunzio 13 ☎961169
15 May–25 Sep
⇄60 P Lift 🌙 Beach sea

★★★Rosa via Carducci 80 ☎963275
20 May–20 Sep
rm53 ⇄23 🍴30 P Lift 🌙 sea

★★Senior viale del Prete ☎963443
May–Sep
rm47 ⇄16 🍴31 A10rm P Lift 🌙 Pool

★Bellariva via Fiume 10 ☎961609
10 Apr–Sep
rm26 ⇄10 🍴6 A12rm P 🌙

⊗A **Fernando** via del Prete 4 ☎961055 M/c **P** Aud VW

CAVA DE'TIRRENI
Salerno (☎089)

★★**Victoria** corso Mazzini 4 ☎464022
rm61 ⇌13 ⋒40 ⋔ **P** Lift 𝔇 ✎ mountains

At **CORPO DI CAVA** (4km SW)

★★**Scapolatiello** ☎463838
rm48 ⇌10 ⋒38 ⋔ **P** Lift Pool mountains

CAVAGLIA
Vercelli (☎0161)

★★**Prateria** ☎96115
Mar–Nov
⇌32 ⋔ **P** mountains

CAVI See **LAVAGNA**

CELLE LIGURE
Savona (☎019)

★★★**San Michele** via Monte Tabor 26 ☎90017
Jun–19 Sep
rm57 ⇌55 **P** Lift 𝔇 Pool sea

CERNOBBIO
Como (☎031)

★★★★★**Villa d'Este** via Regina 40 ☎511471 tx380025
Apr–Oct
rm100 ⇌174 ⋒6 A40rm **P** Lift 𝔇 sB ⇌ ⋒190000 dB ⇌ ⋒305000 M alc ✎ Pool mountains lake

★★★**Regina Olga** via Regina 18 ☎510171 tx380821
rm67 ⇌50 ⋒17 ⋔ **P** Lift 𝔇 sB ⇌ ⋒48000–65500 dB ⇌ ⋒74000–96800 M20000 Pool mountains lake

★**Asnigo** pza San Stefano (n.rest) ☎510062
16 Mar–Oct
rm25 ⋒16 **P** lake

CERVIA
Ravenna (☎0544)

★★**Buenos Aires** Lungomare G-Deledda 130 ☎973174 tx50394
Apr–15 Oct
rm62 ⋒54 ⋔ **P** 𝔇 dB23500–35000 dB⇌39000 Beach sea

⊗**Opel-Cervia** via Oriani 67 ☎991390 M/c Opl

At **MILANO MARITTIMA** (3km N)

⊗**Europa** viale 2 Giugno 15 ☎92276 **P** Fia

CERVINIA-BREUIL See **BREUIL-CERVINIA**

CESENA
Forli (☎0547)

★★★**Casali** via Benedetto Croce 81 ☎22745 tx550480
rm40 ⇌35 ⋒5 ⋔ **P** Lift 𝔇 sB ⇌ ⋒34000 dB ⇌ ⋒48000

CESENATICO
Forli (☎0547)

★★★**Brittania** viale Carducci 129 ☎80041
20 May–11 Sep
⇌44 ⋔ **P** Lift 𝔇 Pool Beach sea

★★★**Internazionale** via Ferrara 7 ☎80231
Jun–Sep
rm54 ⇌31 ⋒23 **P** Lift 𝔇 ✎ Pool Beach sea

★★★**Torino** viale Carducci 55 ☎80044
20 May–20 Sep
⇌ ⋒48 **P** Lift 𝔇 sB ⇌ ⋒20500–25000 dB ⇌ ⋒35000–44000 sea

Internazionale viale Carducci 95 ☎81418 Opl

⊗**Luciano** via A-Saffi 91 ☎81347 BMW Lnc MB

CHÂTILLON
Aosta (☎0166)

★★**Marisa** via Pellissier 10 ☎61845
Closed Nov
⇌28 ⋔ **P** Lift sB ⇌ ⋒25000 dB ⇌ ⋒42000 mountains

CHIANCIANO TERME
Siena (☎0578)

★★★**Grand Capitol** viale della Libertà 492 ☎644681
Apr–Oct
⇌68 ⋔ **P** Lift 𝔇 sB⇌37250 dB ⇌581000 Pool

CHIÀVARI
Genova (☎0185)

★★**Santa Maria** via T-Groppo ☎309621
⇌34 ⋔ **P** Lift 𝔇 sea

Cantero corso Dante 90 ☎307018 **P**

G Ughini via Nazario Sauro 13–15 ☎308278 Aud MB VW

CHIAVENNA
Sondrio (☎0343)

★★★**Conradi** pza Verdi 10 ☎32300
rm34 ⇌7 ⋒11 ⋔ **P** Lift sB ⇌ ⋒22500 dB34000 dB ⇌ ⋒42000

CHIOGGIA
Venezia (☎041)

★★**Grande Italia** pza Vigo (n.rest) ☎400515
rm58 ⇌20 Lift 𝔇 sea

⊗**Autolagunare** via Orti Est 31 ☎490110 M/c **P** Fia

CHIUSA-KLAUSEN
Bolzano (☎0472)

★**Post Hotel Posta** ☎47514
rm64 ⇌21 ⋒19 **P** Lift sB ⇌ ⋒23000

dB30000 dB ⇌ ⋒38000 Pool mountains

CIVITAVECCHIA
Roma (☎0766)

SAC Lungomare Garibaldi 42 ☎21830 BL

CÒLICO
Como (☎0341)

★**Gigi** ☎940268
rm18 ⋒4 ⋔ **P** mountains

★**Risi** pza Cavour 1 ☎940123
15 Mar–20 Oct
⇌42 A17rm ⋔ **P** Lift

COLLE DI VAL D'ELSA See **SIENA**

COMACCHIO
Ferrara (☎0533)

At **LIDO DEGLI ESTENSI** (7km SE)

★★**Conca del Lido** viale G-Pascoli 42 ☎87459 tx216149
Apr–Sep
rm59 **P** Lift 𝔇 sB22000 sB ⇌ ⋒27000 dB30000 dB ⇌ ⋒39000 M18000 Pool sea

COMO
Como (☎031)

★★★**Como** via Mentana 28 (n.rest) ☎266173
rm79 ⇌60 A11rm ⋔ **P** Lift 𝔇 Pool mountains

★★★**Fiori** via per Cernobbio 12 (n.rest) ☎557642
rm49 ⇌41 ⋒7 ⋔ **P** Lift 𝔇 sB29500 sB ⇌ ⋒58500 dB58000 dB ⇌ ⋒83000

★★★**Metropole Suisse** pza Cavour 19 (n.rest) ☎269444
rm70 ⇌38 ⋒32 ⋔ Lift sB ⇌ ⋒54000–64000 dB ⇌ ⋒77000–90000

★★**Engadina** viale Rosselli 22 (n.rest) ☎550415
Mar–15 Nov
rm21 ⇌9 ⋒12 ⋔ **P** Lift 𝔇

★★**Park** viale Rosselli 20 (n.rest) ☎556782
Apr–Nov
rm42 ⇌15 ⋒15 Lift 𝔇

★★**San Gottardo** pza Volta ☎263531
rm56 ⇌21 **P** Lift 𝔇 sB28000–31500 sB ⇌45500–50500 dB46000–53000 dB ⇌66000–76000 M18000 lake

⊗**Autorimessa Dante** via Dante 59 ☎272545 **P** Ren

Grassi & Airoldi via Napoleona 50 ☎266027 BL RT

CONCA DEI MARINI
Salerno (☎089)

★★**Belvedere** (SS 163) ☎871266
Apr–15 Oct
⇌37 **P** Lift 𝔇 sB ⇌36750–44750 dB ⇌65500–80500 M25300 Pool Beach sea

CORPO DI CAVA See **CAVA DE' TIRRENI**

CORTE DI CADORE See **BORCA DI CADORE**

CORTINA D'AMPEZZO
Belluno (☎0436)

★ ★ ★**Corona** corso C-Battisti
☎3251 tx440004
20 Dec–Mar & Jul–10 Sep
rm57 ⇌36 ▥5 A11rm Lift **P** ☽
sB40000–45000 sB ⇌ ▥60000–65000
dB70000–75000
dB ⇌ ▥104000–118000 M20000
mountains

★ ★ ★**Grand Savoia** via Roma 62
☎3201 tx440811
rm142 ⇌124 ▥18 ▦ **P** Lift ☽
sB ⇌ ▥70000–112000
dB ⇌ ▥120000–196000 M28000–36000
✇ Pool mountains

☆ ☆ ☆**AGIP** via Roma 70 (SS 51km 102)
☎61400
▥28 Lift

★ ★ ★**Ancora** corso Italia 62 ☎3261
tx440004
Dec–Apr & Jun–Sep
rm82 ⇌59 ▥15 ▦ **P** Lift ☽
sB41000–58000 sB ⇌ ▥46000–77000
dB 67000–92000
dB ⇌ ▥82000–138000 M25000–30000
mountains

★ ★ ★**Concordia Parc** (**DPn** in season)
corso Italia 28 ☎4251 tx440004
22 Dec–20 Mar & 10 Jul–Aug
rm58 ⇌55 ▥3 ▦ **P** Lift ☽
sB⇌ ▥ 50000–78000
dB ⇌ ▥90000–140000 M20000–30000
mountains

★ ★ ★**Cortina** corso Italia 94 ☎4221
tx440004
Dec–Apr & Jun–Sep
⇌50 **P** Lift ☽ sB ⇌68000–71000
dB ⇌110000–126000 mountains

★ ★ ★**Cristallo** (CIGA) via R-Mandardi
42 ☎4281 tx440090
25 Jun–15 Sep & 20 Dec–31 Mar
⇌102 ▦ **P** Lift ☽ ✇ Pool ♂
mountains

★ ★ ★**Europa** corso Italia 207 ☎3221
tx440004
rm52 ⇌40 ▥12 **P** Lift ☽
sB ⇌ ▥49000–79000
dB ⇌ ▥90000–138000 mountains

★ ★ ★**Poste** pza Roma 14 ☎4271
tx440044
20 Dec–20 Oct
⇌83 ▦ **P** ☽ Mfr35000
DPn 96000–165000 ♂ mountains

★ ★**Alpes** via la Verra 2 ☎2021
20 Dec–Mar & 10 Jul–Sep
rm35 ⇌8 ▥2 **P** mountains

★ ★**San Marco** (**DPn** in season) pza
Roma 6 ☎66941
rm24 ⇌12 ▥9 **P** sB21000–38000
sB ⇌ ▥28000–48000 dB32000–46000;
dB ⇌ ▥39000–83000 M18000–24000
mountains

Italy

☾⤵**Dolomiti** Corso Italia 182 ☎61077 **P**
Fia Lnc

COSENZA
Cosenza (☎0984)

At **RENDE** (6km NW off SS107)

☆ ☆ ☆**AGIP** (SS 19-Bivio SS 107)
☎839101
▥65 **P** Lift ☽ dB ▥73000

☾⤵**AMC** via S-Pellico ☎39598 M/c BMW

COURMAYEUR
Aosta (☎0165)

★ ★ ★ ★**Royal & Golf** via Roma 87
☎84362 tx214312
Dec–Apr & Jun–Sep
⇌ ▥95 ▦ **P** Lift ☽
sB ⇌ ▥60000–100000
dB ⇌ ▥100000–200000 Pool
mountains

★ ★ ★**Palace Bron** (2km E) Verso Plan
Gorret ☎842545 tx211085
20 Dec–Apr & Jul–Sep
⇌30 **P** Lift ☽ sB ⇌60000–73000
dB ⇌106000–130000 M25000–30000
mountains

★ ★ ★ ★**Pavilion** Strada Regionale 60
☎842420 tx210541
Dec–Apr & Jun–Oct
⇌40 ▦ **P** Lift ☽ sB ⇌58000–78000
dB ⇌106000–146000 Mfr28000 Pool
mountains

CREMONA
Cremona (☎0372)

☾⤵**General Cars** via Catelleone 77–79
☎20343 Opl Vau

At **SAN FELICE** (5km E)

☆ ☆ ☆**AGIP** (exit Autostrade Piscenza/
Brescia) ☎43101
▥77 **P** Lift ☽ dB ▥70000

CUNEO
Cuneo (☎0171)

☾⤵**Cunicar** via Torino ☎66442 BL RT

DESENZANO DEL GARDA
Brescia (☎030)

★ ★ ★**Ramazzotti** viale Dal Molin 78
(n.rest) ☎9141808 tx300395
Apr–Sep
rm22 ⇌10 ▦ **P** sB26000 sB ⇌31000
dB37000 dB ⇌49000

★ ★**Europa** ☎9142333
Mar–Oct
rm37 ⇌31 ▦ **P** Lift lake

★ ★**Vittoria** Portovecchio 4 ☎9141504
rm35 ⇌20 ▥5 **P** ☽ lake

DIANO MARINA
Imperia (☎0183)

★ ★ ★ ★**Diana Majestic** via Degli
Oleandri 15 ☎495445 tx271025

15 Apr–20 Oct
rm80 ⇌72 ▥8 ▦ **P** Lift ☽ Pool
Beach sea

★ ★ ★**Bellevue & Méditerranée** via Gl-
Ardoine 2 ☎495089 tx271620
23 Dec–Oct
rm90 ⇌24 ▥43 A15rm ▦ sB51000
sB ⇌ ▥56000 dB72000 dB ⇌ ▥77000
M18000–20000 Pool Beach sea

☾⤵**G Ghiradi** via G-Ardoino 127 ☎45334
M/c **P** AR

ELBA (ISOLA D')
Livorno (☎0565)

LACONA

★ ★ ★**Capo Sud** ☎964021
15 May–Sep
rm39 ⇌2 ▥37 ▦ **P** Lift ☽
sB ⇌ ▥23000–33000
dB ⇌ ▥36000–54000 ✇ Beach sea

PORTO AZZURRO

★ ★ ★**Elba International** ☎968611
tx590669
Apr–Oct
rm242 ⇌210 ▥32 **P** Lift ☽
sB ⇌ ▥43000–51000
dB ⇌ ▥59000–72800 M15000–30000
✇ Pool Beach sea

★**Belmare** ☎95012 tx95076
⇌25 **P** ☽ sea

PORTOFERRAIO

★ ★ ★**Hermitage** ☎969932 tx500219
10 May–Sep
⇌90 **P** Lift ☽ Pool Beach sea

PROCCHIO

★ ★ ★ ★**Golfo** ☎907565 tx590690
24 May–Sep
rm95 ⇌65 ▥30 ▦ **P** Lift ☽
sB ⇌ ▥46000–71500
dB ⇌ ▥90000–99000 ✇ Pool Beach
sea

At **SPARTAIA**

★ ★ ★**Desirée** ☎907502 tx590649
May–Oct
rm69 ⇌55 ▥14 **P** ☽ sB ⇌ ▥60000
dB ⇌ ▥90000 ✇ Pool Beach sea

EMPOLI
Firenze (☎0571)

★ ★**Tazza d'Oro** via del Papa 46
☎72129
rm56 ⇌43 ▥9 ▦ **P** Lift ☽

FABRO
Umbria (☎0763)

☆ ☆**Fabro** Contrada della Stazione 70
☎82063
rm16 ⇌10 ▥10 **P** ☽

FANO
Pesaro & Urbino (☎0721)

★ ★**Excelsior** Lungomare Simonetti 17
☎82558
5 Jun–15 Sep
rm30 ▥27 **P** Beach sea

FERIOLO See **BAVENO**

FERRARA
Ferrara (☎0532)

★ ★ ★**Astra** viale Cavour 55 ☎26234
rm79 ⇄31 🏠37 🏛 Lift ♪
sB 34000–43500 sB ⇄ 🏠52500
dB76000 dB ⇄ 🏠89000 M13000

♨SIRA via Bologna 306 ☎93275 M/c
Frd

FIESOLE
Firenze (☎055)

★ ★ ★ ★**Villa San Michele** via Doccia 4
☎59451 tx570643

16 Mar–Oct
⇄30 P ♪ M65000
DPn270000–310000 Pool

★ ★**Villa Bonelli** via F-Poeti1 ☎59513
rm23 ⇄1 🏠13 🏛 Lift ♪

FINALE LIGURE
Savona (☎019)

At **VARIGOTTI** (6km SE)

★ ★ ★**Nik-Mehari** via Aurelia 104
☎698030
⇄30 🏛 P Lift ♪ sB ⇄60000
dB ⇄80000 Beach sea

FIRENZE (FLORENCE)
Firenze (☎055)

See plan

★ ★ ★ ★ ★**Excelsior Italia** (CIGA) pza
Ognissanti 3 (off Lungarno A-Vespucci)
☎294301 tx570022 Plan **1**
⇄205 🏛 P Lift sB ⇄194000–214000
dB ⇄298000–353000 t%

★ ★ ★ ★ ★**Savoy** pza della
Repubblica 7 ☎283313 tx570220 Plan **3**
⇄101 Lift ♪ sB ⇄132000–192000
dB ⇄199000–264000

★ ★ ★ ★ ★**Villa Medici** (SRS) via il Prato
42 ☎261331 tx570179 Plan **4**
⇄107 P Lift sB ⇄188200 dB ⇄296400
M alc Pool

★ ★ ★ ★**Grandhotel Baglioni** (BW) pza
Unita Italiana 6 ☎218441 tx570225
Plan **5**
rm195 ⇄185 🏠10 🏛 P Lift ♪

★ ★ ★ ★**Jolly** pza V-Veneto 4A ☎2770
tx570191 Plan **6**
⇄60 P Lift ♪ sB ⇄103350
dB ⇄148700 Pool

★ ★ ★ ★**Londra** (GT) Via Jacopo da
Diacceto 16–20 ☎262791 tx571152
Plan **7**
rm107 ⇄94 🏠13 🏛 Lift ♪
sB ⇄ 🏠124000 dB ⇄ 🏠183000 M32000

★ ★ ★ ★**Minerva** pza Santa Maria
Novella 16 ☎284555 tx570414 Plan**8**
rm112 ⇄94 🏠18 🏛 P Lift ♪
sB ⇄ 🏠94000 dB ⇄ 🏠133000 Pool

★ ★ ★**Adriatico** via Maso Finiguerra 9
☎261781 tx572265 Plan **10**
⇄ 🏠114 P Lift ♪ sB ⇄ 🏠52000
dB ⇄ 🏠84000

Italy

☆ ☆ ☆**AGIP** Autostrade del Sole
Raccordo Firenze-Mare (12km NW)
☎440081 tx570263 Plan **11**
🏠156 P Lift ♪ dB 🏠90500

☆ ☆ ☆**Crest (See page 51)** viale Europa
205 ☎686841 tx70376 Plan**13**
⇄92 P Lift ♪ sB130000 dB ⇄17000
Pool

★ ★ ★**Croce di Malta** via della Scala 7
☎282600 tx570540 Plan **14**
rm100 ⇄35 🏠65 Lift ♪ Pool

★ ★ ★**Kraft** via Solferino 2 ☎284273
tx571523 Plan **17**
rm66 ⇄63 🏠3 P Lift ♪
sB ⇄ 🏠95000 dB ⇄ 🏠133000 Pool

★ ★ ★**Regency** pza d'Azeglio 3
☎245247 tx571058 Plan **18**
rm31 ⇄23 🏠8 P ♪ sB ⇄ 🏠133000
dB ⇄ 🏠200000

★ ★ ★**Roma** pza Santa Maria Novella 8
(n.rest) ☎210366 Plan **19**
rm60 ⇄25 🏠18 P Lift ♪

★ ★ ★**Villa Belvedere** via Benedetto
Castelli 3 (n.rest) ☎222501 Plan **20**
Mar–Nov
rm27 ⇄25 🏠2 P Lift ♨ Pool

★ ★ ★**Villa Park San Domenico** via della
Piazzuola ☎576697 Plan **21**
⇄19 🏛 P Lift ♪

★ ★**Basilea** via Guelfa 41 ☎214587
tx571689 Plan **23**
rm52 ⇄10 🏠40 🏛 P Lift ♪

★ ★**Liana** via V-Alfieri 18
(n rest) ☎245304 Plan **27**
rm22 ⇄14 🏛 P ♪

★ ★**Rapallo** via Santa Caterina
d'Allessandria 7 ☎472412 tx574251
Plan **28**
rm30 ⇄20 🏛 P Lift ♪

♨**Europa** Borgognissanti 96 ☎260846
P Opl Vlo

♨**M Ronchi** via Crimea 8 ☎489855 Frd

♨**Zaniratti** viale Fratelli Rosselli 55
☎471465 BL Vlo

At **CANDELI** (6km SE on road to Bagno a
Ripoli)

★ ★ ★**Villa Massa** ☎630051
tx573555 Plan**9**
rm56 ⇄42 A14rm P Lift ♪

At **SESTO FIORENTINO** (9km NW)

★ ★ ★**Villa Villoresi** ☎4489032 Plan**30**
rm30 ⇄14 🏠14 P sB ⇄ 🏠65000
dB ⇄ 🏠123500 M28000 Pool

FOGGIA
Foggia (☎0881)

★ ★ ★**Cicolella** viale 24 Maggio 60
☎3890 tx810273

FIRENZE (FLORENCE)

1	★ ★ ★ ★ ★ Excelsior Italia
3	★ ★ ★ ★ ★ Savoy
4	★ ★ ★ ★ ★ Villa Medici
5	★ ★ ★ ★ Grandhotel Baglioni
6	★ ★ ★ ★ Holly
7	★ ★ ★ ★ Londra
8	★ ★ ★ ★ Minerva
9	★ ★ ★ ★ Villa Massa (At
	Candeli 6km SE)
10	★ ★ ★ Adriatico
11	☆ ☆ ☆ AGIP
13	☆ ☆ ☆ Crest
14	★ ★ ★ Croce di Malta
17	★ ★ ★ Kraft
18	★ ★ ★ Regency
19	★ ★ ★ Roma
20	★ ★ ★ Villa Belvedere
21	★ ★ ★ Villa Park San
	Domenico
23	★ ★ Basilea
27	★ ★ Liana
28	★ ★ Rapallo
30	★ ★ Villa Villoresi
	(At Sesto Fiorentino
	9km NW)

⇄ 🏠130 🏛 Lift ♪ sB ⇄ 🏠61500
dB ⇄ 🏠120000 M alc

FOLIGNO
Perugia (☎0742)

★ ★ ★**Umbria** via C-Battisti 3 ☎52821
rm47 ⇄40 🏠7 P Lift ♪
sB ⇄ 🏠32000 dB ⇄ 🏠45000

FORIO See **ISCHIA (ISOLA D')**

FORTE DEI MARMI
Lucca (☎0584)

★ ★ ★**Augustus** viale Morin 169
☎80202 tx590673

15 May–Sep
rm70 ⇄64 🏠6 A27rm P Lift ♪
sB ⇄ 🏠74000–100000
dB ⇄ 🏠136000–190000 M35000–40000
♨ Beach sea

★ ★ ★**Alcione** viale Morin 137 ☎89952
Jun–Sep
rm45 ⇄27 🏠14 🏛 P Lift
sB ⇄ 🏠50000–59000
dB ⇄ 🏠65000–87000 M30000 Beach
sea

★ ★ ★**Astoria Garden** (DPn) via L-da-
Vinci 10 ☎80754
May–Sep
⇄27 P Lift ♪ sB ⇄39800
dB ⇄58850 M23000 Beach

★ ★ ★**Byron** viale Morin 46 ☎80087
16 May–4 Oct
rm45 ⇄25 🏠15 A5rm P ♪
sB ⇄ 🏠49500–60500
dB ⇄ 🏠70000–110000 Pool sea

★ ★ ★**Raffaelli Park** (BW) (DPn in
season) via Mazzini 37 ☎81494 tx590239
Apr–10 Oct
rm34 ⇄32 🏠2 A6rm P Lift ♪
sB ⇄ 🏠88000–103000
dB ⇄ 🏠122000–150500 M25000–34000
♨ Pool Beach

250

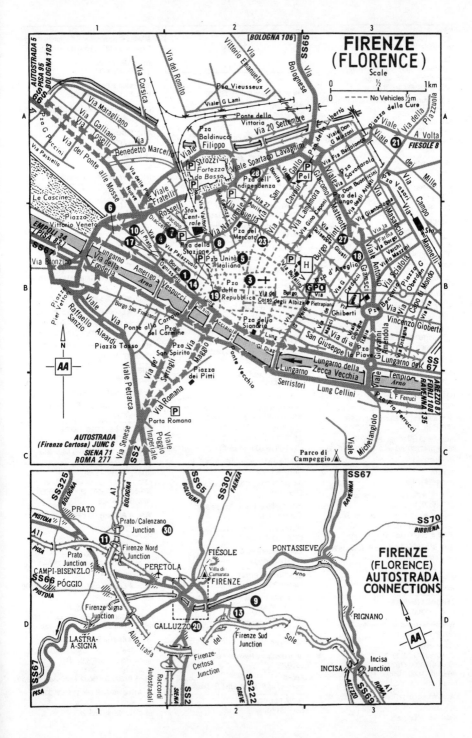

FIRENZE (FLORENCE)

★ ★ ★**Raffaelli Villa Angela** via G-
Mazzini 64 ☎80652 tx590239

May–Dec
rm48 ⇌33 ⋔15 A15rm **P** Lift ☽
sB ⇌ ⋔55000 dB ⇌ ⋔90000
M25000–30000 ⋙ Pool Beach

★ ★ ★**Adams Villa Maria** Lungomare
110 ☎80901

Jun–Sep
rm44 ⇌18 ⋔22 A6rm **P** Lift ☽
sB35000–45000 dB ⇌ ⋔50000–70000
Pool sea

FROSINONE
Frosinone (☎0775)

★ ★**Palace Hasser** via Brighindi 1
☎852747

⇌60 🏠 **P** Lift ☽

GABICCE MARE
Pesaro & Urbino (☎0541)

★ ★ ★**Alexander** via Panoramica 35
☎961166 tx550535

May–Sep
⇌ ⋔50 **P** Lift ☽
sB ⇌ ⋔21000–25000
dB ⇌ ⋔32000–38000 Pool Beach sea

★ ★**Club de Bona** via Panoramica 33
☎962622 tx550535

May–Sep
rm50 ⇌10 ⋔40 🏠 **P** Lift ☽ ⋙
Pool Beach sea

★ ★**Valbruna** via Redipuglia 1 ☎961843

20 May–20 Sep
rm36 ⇌7 ⋔23 **P** Lift ☽

GALLARATE
Varese (☎0331)

★ ★**Astoria** pza Risorgimento 9A
☎791043

rm50 ⇌30 ⋔20 🏠 **P** Lift ☽
sB ⇌ ⋔42250 dB ⇌ ⋔59000 M22000
mountains

GARDA
Verona (☎045)

★ ★ ★**Eurotel** via Gardesana 18
☎7255107 tx431299

rm150 ⇌120 ⋔30 🏠 **P** Lift ☽
sB ⇌ ⋔29500–45500
dB ⇌ ⋔52000–65300 Pool lake

★ ★ ★**Regina Adelaide Palace** via 20
Settembre ☎7255013 tx341078

rm54 ⇌10 ⋔44 **P** Lift ☽
sB ⇌ ⋔37800–42000
dB ⇌ ⋔64800–72000

GARDONE RIVIERA
Brescia (☎0365)

★ ★ ★ ★**Grand** via Zanardelli 72
☎20261 tx300254

20 Apr–6 Oct
rm180 ⇌141 ⋔39 **P** Lift ☽
sB ⇌ ⋔48000–75000
dB ⇌ ⋔79000–129000 M27000 Pool
lake

★ ★ ★**Lac** corso Repubblica 58 ☎20124

Apr–15 Oct
rm30 ⇌17 Lift lake

★ ★ ★**Monte Baldo** ☎20951

May–Sep
rm46 ⇌17 ⋔18 A15rm **P** Lift ☽
Pool lake

★ ★**Bellevue** via Zanardelli 44 ☎20235

Apr–10 Oct
rm31 ⇌4 ⋔27 🏠 **P** Lift lake

At **BARBARANO** (1km W)

★ ★ ★**Astoria** (**DPn** in season) ☎20761
tx301088

rm120 ⇌ ⋔95 🏠 **P** Lift ☽
sB30000–35000 sB ⇌ ⋔45000–52000
dB62000–68000 dB ⇌ ⋔85000–92000
M22000 t% Pool mountains lake

GARGNANO
Brescia (☎0365)

★**Europa** ☎71191

Apr–30 Oct
rm20 ⇌2 ⋔18 **P** lake

GENOVA (GENOA)
Genova (☎010)

★ ★ ★ ★**Colombia** (CIGA) via Balbi 40
☎261841 tx270423

⇌172 **P** Lift ☽ sB ⇌133000–153000
dB ⇌191000–216000 t%

★ ★ ★ ★**Plaza** via M-Piaggio 11
☎893642 tx213142

rm97 ⇌58 ⋔33 **P** Lift ☽

★ ★ ★ ★**Savola Majestic** (SRS) via
Arsenale di Terra 5, Stazione Centrale
Principe ☎261641 tx270426

⇌ ⋔170 A50rm Lift ☽
sB ⇌ ⋔100000 dB ⇌ ⋔150000 M34000

&♪**ARA** via Marsilio de Padova 6
☎317388 Chy

Dilla viale Carlo-E-Mello Rosselli 18
☎300430 Frd

&♪**B Koelliker** Corso Europa 810
☎3993241 BL

&♪**Oram** via G-Bandi 10 Quarto
☎384653 DJ Vlo

XX-Settembre via D-Fiasella 19
☎511941 **P** Cit

GENZANO DI ROMA
Roma (☎06)

★ ★**Villa Robinia** viale Frattelli Rosselli
19 ☎9396409

⇌30 **P** Lift mountains lake

GHIFFA
Novara (☎0323)

★ ★**Ghiffa** via Belvedere 88–90 ☎59285
tx200285

Apr–Sep
rm24 ⇌ ⋔9 🏠 **P** Lift ☽ lake

GIOIA DEL COLLE
Bari (☎080)

&♪**Auto Carrozzeria** (F Capurso) via
Santeramo 120 ☎830417 M/c **P** Ren

GIULIANOVA LIDO
Teramo (☎085)

&♪**Ubaldo & Forlini** via G-Galilei 180
☎862771 M/c Opl Vau

GOLFO ARANCI See **SARDEGNA (ISOLA)**
(SARDINIA)

GRAVEDONA
Como (☎0344)

★**Turismo** ☎85227

Mar–Nov
rm14 ⇌7 🏠 **P** mountains lake

GRAVELLONA TOCE
Novara (☎0323)

★**Helios** ☎848096

rm19 ⇌11 **P** mountains

GRIGNANO See **TRIESTE**

GROSSETO
Grosseto (☎0564)

☆ ☆ ☆**AGIP** (SS 1km 179 exit Roma)
☎24100

⋔32 **P** dB ⋔48000

★ ★**Lorena** via Trieste 3 ☎25501

rm66 ⇌12 ⋔54 🏠 **P** Lift ☽
sB ⇌ ⋔43700 dB ⇌ ⋔75400

&♪**Morelli** via Privata dei Curiazi 13
☎23000 BL Vlo

GUBBIO
Perugia (☎075)

★ ★**Tre Ceri** via Benamati 6 ☎9273304

⇌32 🏠 **P** Lift ☽ sB ⇌29000
dB ⇌43000

IESOLO (JESOLO) (LIDO DI)
Venezia (☎0421)

★ ★ ★**Las Vegas** via Mascagni 3
☎971515 tx410433

10 May–Sep
⇌110 **P** Lift ☽ sB ⇌37000–47000
dB ⇌65000–75000 M20000–21000
Pool Beach sea

★ ★ ★**Anthony** via Padova 25 ☎971711
tx410433

May–Sep
rm68 ⇌4 ⋔64 **P** Lift ☽
sB ⇌ ⋔57000–72000
dB ⇌ ⋔84000–109000 M25000–30000
⋙ Pool Beach sea

★ ★ ★**London** via Dalmazia 64 ☎90988

May–Sep
rm84 ⇌74 ⋔8 **P** Lift ☽
sB ⇌ ⋔23000–40000 dB35000–50000
dB ⇌ ⋔40000–65000 Beach sea

★ ★ ★**Ritz** via Zanella 2 ☎90861

May–Sep
rm48 ⇌3 ⋔45 **P** Lift ☽
sB ⇌ ⋔38500–48000
dB ⇌ ⋔60000–75000 Pool Beach sea

★ ★**Regina** via Bafile 115 ☎90383

May–Sep
⇌ ⋔53 🏠 **P** Lift ☽

Italy

sB ⇄ 🍴 22000–40000
dB ⇄ 🍴 40000–72000 Beach sea

★ ★Termini via Altinate 32 ☎90488
tx410433

18 Apr–Sep
⇄44 P Lift ♪ sB ⇄30000–38000
dB ⇄ 40000–62000 Pool Beach sea

&♪Brusa pza Mazzini ☎91344 Frd

At IESOLO PINETA (6km E)

★ ★Danmark via Oriente 170 ☎961013
tx410433

May–Sep
rm50 ⇄38 🍴10 P ♪ Pool Beach
sea

IGEA MARINA See BELLARIA IGEA
MARINA

IMPERIA
Imperia (☎0183)

&♪Riviera Motori viale Matteotti 175
☎20297 BL

ISCHIA (ISOLA D')
Napoli (☎081)

FORIO

★Splendid (1km N) ☎997165

10 Apr–30 Oct
rm40 ⇄8 🍴32 P ♪
sB ⇄31800–34800
dB ⇄ 🍴52600–140000 M22000 Pool
sea mountains

ISCHIA

★ ★ ★Jolly via A-de Luca 42
☎991744 tx710267
⇄208 P Lift ♪ sB ⇄101000
dB ⇄180000 Pool

IVREA
Torino (☎0125)

★ ★Eden corso Massimo d'Azeglio 67
(n.rest) ☎424741
⇄36 🚗 P Lift ♪ mountains

&♪M Peroni via S Lorenzo 10 ☎422022
VW

JESOLO See IESOLO

LACONA See ELBA (ISOLA D')

LAIGUEGLIA
Savona (☎0182)

★ ★ ★Aquilia via Asti 1 ☎49040
⇄40 🚗 P Lift sB ⇄35000–50000
dB ⇄45000–54000 M15000 Beach sea

★ ★Mariolina via Concezione 15
☎49024
🍴22 P Beach sea

★ ★Splendid pza Badaro 4 ☎49325

Etr–Sep
rm50 ⇄30 🍴20 P Lift ♪
sB ⇄ 🍴45000 dB ⇄ 🍴70000 Pool
Beach

★ ★Windsor pza 25 Aprile 7 ☎49000

15 Apr–Sep
rm70 ⇄35 🍴35 P Lift ♪ Beach sea

LAINATE
Milano (☎02)

☆ ☆Italmotel via Manzoni 43 ☎9370869
tx324354
rm34 ⇄8 🍴26 P ♪ dB ⇄ 🍴87150
M14500 🏊 Pool

LAVAGNA
Genova (☎0185)

★ ★Tiguilio via Matteotti 3 ☎321521

Apr–15 Nov
rm42 ⇄17 🍴10 P Lift sea

At CAVI (3km SE)

★Scogliera (n.rest) ☎390072

Jun–Sep
🍴21 P ♪ Beach sea

&♪G Cordano corso Buenos Aires
☎301101 P Fia

LEGHORNE See LIVORNO

LENNO
Como (☎0344)

★ ★San Giorgio via Regina 81 ☎40415

Apr–Oct
rm29 ⇄21 🍴3 🚗 P Lift ♪ sB29000
sB ⇄47000 dB51000 dB ⇄75000 🏊
lake

LERICI
La Spezia (☎0187)

★ ★ ★Doria via A-Doria ☎967124
rm42 ⇄15 🍴16 P Lift ♪ sea

★ ★Italia ☎967108
🍴16 P sea

LESA
Novara (☎0322)

★ ★Cavalieri di Malta ☎7283

Mar–Oct
rm40 ⇄28 🍴12 🚗 P ♪ Pool
mountains

LEVANTO
La Spezia (☎0187)

★ ★ ★Crystal via Vallesanta ☎808261

15 Jun–Sep
rm16 ⇄1 🍴13 A9rm P ♪
sB ⇄ 🍴36000 dB ⇄ 🍴62000 sea
mountains

★ ★Cara via M-della Liberta 28
☎808275
🍴36 P sB 🍴18000 dB 🍴32000

★Garden corso Italia 6 ☎808173

Apr–Sep
rm18 A3rm Lift sea

LEVICO TERME
Trento (☎0461)

★ ★ ★Bellavista via V-Emanuele 2
☎706136 tx400856

May–30 Oct
rm78 ⇄69 🍴9 P Lift

LIDO DEGLI ESTENSI See COMACCHIO

LIDO DI CAMAIORE See CAMAIORE
(LIDO DI)

LIDO DI IESOLO (JESOLO) See IESOLO
(JESOLO) (LIDO DI)

LIGNANO SABBIADORO
Udine (☎0431)

At LIGNANO PINETA (5km SW)

★ ★ ★Medusa Splendid Arco dello
Scirocco 13 ☎422211

20 May–15 Sep
rm56 ⇄8 🍴48 P Lift ♪ Pool Beach
sea

At LIGNANO RIVIERA (7km SW)

★ ★ ★Eurotel calle Mendelssohn 13
☎(049)428991 tx460890

May–Sep
⇄ 🍴95 P Lift ♪
sB ⇄ 🍴30000–43000
dB ⇄ 🍴61000–86000 M19000 Pool
Beach 🦌 ◯ sea

LIVORNO (LEGHORN)
Livorno (☎0586)

★ ★ ★Giappone via Grande 65 ☎24751
rm60 ⇄21 🍴39 🚗 Lift ♪
sB ⇄ 🍴33000 dB ⇄ 🍴51500

At STAGNO (5km N on SS1)

☆ ☆ ☆AGIP (SS 1km 320) ☎943067
tx611627
🍴50 P Lift ♪ dB ⇄ 🍴60000

LOANO
Savona (☎019)

★ ★ ★Garden Lido Lungomare N-Sauro
9 ☎669666 tx213178
rm92 ⇄70 🍴22 🚗 P Lift ♪
sB ⇄ 🍴48000 dB ⇄ 🍴76000 Pool sea

LONE See AMALFI

LUCCA
Lucca (☎0583)

At MASSA PISANA (4.5km S on SS12R)

★ ★ ★Villa la Principessa ☎370037
tx590068

21 Dec–Nov
⇄43 🚗 P Lift ♪
sB ⇄100500–110500
dB ⇄151000–211000 M35000–55000
Pool

MACERATA
Macerata (☎0733)

☆ ☆ ☆AGIP via Roma 149B (SS 77km 89)
☎34248 tx611627
🍴51 P Lift ♪ dB ⇄ 🍴56000

MACOMER See SARDEGNA (ISOLA)
(SARDINIA)

MACUGNAGA
Novara (☎0324)

★ ★Cristallo Franzione Pacetto
☎65139

Jun–Sep & Dec–20 Apr
rm21 ⇄17 P mountains

MADONNA DI CAMPIGLIO
Trento (☎0465)

★ ★ ★**Savoia** ☎41004 tx300254
3 Dec–10 Apr
rm57 ⇄47 ⋔10 🏛 **P** Lift ☽
sB ⇄ ⋔62000 dB ⇄ ⋔112000
mountains

★ ★**Golf** ☎41003 tx400882
23 Dec–12 Apr
rm124 ⇄64 ⋔60 **P** Lift ☽ ⚓ ♂
mountains

MAIORI
Salerno (☎089)

★ ★ ★**San Francesco** via S-Tecia 54
☎877070
15 Mar–15 Oct
⇄ ⋔44 🏛 **P** Lift ☽
sB ⇄ ⋔27000–31000
dB ⇄ ⋔42000–54000 M16000 Beach
♂ sea

MALCESINE
Verona (☎045)

★ ★ ★**Lac** via Gardesana 18 ☎600156
tx430567
May–Sep
rm40 ⇄39 🏛 **P** Lift ☽ dB ⇄50000
mountains lake

☆ ☆**Vega** via Roma 10 ☎600151
tx480448
Apr–Oct
rm20 ⇄10 ⋔10 **P** Lift mountains lake

MANTOVA
Mantova (☎0376)

★ ★**Apollo** pza Don Leoni 16 (n.rest)
☎323745
⇄35 **P** Lift ☽ sB ⇄41000 dB ⇄68000

Filipini via Curtatone & Montanara 58
☎29696 Aud Por VW

MARATEA
Potenza (☎0973)

★ ★ ★ ★**Santavenere** ☎876160
Mar–Oct
rm49 ⇄40 ⋔4 A5rm **P** ☽
sB⇄ ⋔54500–64500
dB⇄ ⋔84000–103000 ⚓ Pool Beach
sea

MARGHERA See **MESTRE**

MARINA DI CARRARA See **CARRARA**
(MARINA DI)

MARINA DI MASSA See **MASSA**
(MARINA DI)

MARINA DI PIETRASANTA See
PIETRASANTA (MARINA DI)

MARSALA See **SICILIA (SICILY)**

MASSA (MARINA DI)
Massa Carrara (☎0585)

★ ★ ★**Marina** viale Magliano 3 ☎21092
Jun–Sep
⇄32 **P** ☽ sB ⇄30000–45000
dB⇄40000–60000 M10000–15000
Beach

Italy

★**Internazionale** via Siena 1 ☎309243
20 May–20 Sep
rm12 **P** sea

MATELICA
Macerata (☎0737)

☆ ☆ ☆**AGIP** (SS256 Muccese km29)
☎82381 tx611627
⋔16 **P** dB ⋔47000

MAZZARÒ See **TAORMINA** under
SICILIA (SICILY)

MEINA
Novara (☎0322)

★**Bel Sit** via Sempione 76 ☎6483
Dec–Oct
rm12 ⇄3 ⋔9 🏛 **P** lake

MENAGGIO
Como (☎0344)

★ ★ ★**Bella Vista** via IV Novembre 9
☎32136
Apr–15 Oct
rm38 ⇄22 ⋔15 **P** Lift lake

★ ★**Loveno** via N-Sauro 37 ☎39110
Apr–Oct
rm14 ⇄8 ⋔4 🏛 **P** lake

At **NOBIALLO** (1km N)

★ ★**Miralago** via Diaz 26 ☎32363
Apr–Oct
rm28 ⇄9 ⋔14 🏛 **P** sB ⇄ ⋔29000
dB ⇄ ⋔53000 lake

MERANO-MERAN
Bolzano (☎0473)

★ ★ ★ ★**Grand Bristol** via O-Huber 14
☎49500 tx400662
Apr–Nov
rm150 ⇄114 ⋔36 🏛 **P** Lift ☽
sB ⇄ ⋔49500–75900
dB ⇄ ⋔81400–138600 M18000–22000
Pool mountains

★ ★ ★**Augusta** via O-Huber 2 ☎49570
tx400632
Apr–Oct
⇄26 🏛 **P** Lift ☽ sB ⇄34000–42000
dB ⇄66000–82000 mountains

☆ ☆ ☆**Eurotel Merano** via Garibaldi 5
☎34900 tx400471
rm123 ⇄62 ⋔62 🏛 **P** Lift ☽
sB ⇄ ⋔38500–44500
dB ⇄ ⋔68000–77000 mountains

★ ★ ★**Mirabella** via Garibaldi 35
☎26112
26 Mar–Oct
rm30 ⇄16 ⋔14 🏛 Lift ☽
sB ⇄ ⋔28500–32500
dB ⇄ ⋔5400–62000 Pool mountains

★ ★ ★**Palace** via Cavour ☎34734
tx400256
⇄124 **P** Lift ☽ sB ⇄95000
dB ⇄160000 Pool mountains

★ ★ ★**Savoy** via Rezia 1 ☎47719
tx400632
Apr–Oct
⇄50 **P** Lift ☽ sB ⇄77000
dB ⇄114000 Pool mountains

★ ★**Adria** via Gilm 2 ☎36610
Mar–Oct
rm51 ⇄28 ⋔23 A9rm **P** Lift ☽
sB ⇄ ⋔49000 dB ⇄ ⋔220000 Pool

★ ★**Irma** via Belvedere 17 ☎30124
5 Mar–7 Nov
⇄55 **P** Lift ☽ ⚓ Pool mountains

★ ★**Regina** via Cavour 101 ☎33432
tx440195
16 Mar–Oct
rm79 ⇄32 ⋔41 🏛 **P** Lift ☽
sB27000 sB ⇄ ⋔41000 dB46000
dB ⇄ ⋔65000 Pool mountains

★**Westend** ☎47654
Apr–Oct
rm22 ⇄4 ⋔9 **P** ☽ mountains

🐾**Merano** (O Montoili) via Roma 288
☎32074 M/c Ren

MESSINA See **SICILIA (SICILY)**

MESTRE
Venezia (☎041)

See also **VENEZIA (VENICE)**

★ ★ ★**Ambasciatori** corso del Popolo
221 ☎926699 tx410445
rm104 ⇄24 ⋔80 🏛 **P** Lift ☽
sB ⇄ ⋔57000–80000
dB ⇄ ⋔88000–119000 M28000

★ ★ ★**Bologna & Stazione** pza Stazione,
via Piave 214 ☎931000 tx410678
rm131 ⇄24 ⋔101 **P** Lift ☽
sB ⇄ ⋔43000–50000
dB ⇄ ⋔65000–75000

★ ★ ★**Plaza** pza Stazione
☎929388 tx410490
rm222 ⇄130 ⋔90 🏛 Lift ☽
sB ⇄ ⋔52000 dB⇄ ⋔81000

★ ★ ★**President** via Forte Marghera 99
(n.rest) ☎985655
⇄51 **P** Lift ☽ sB ⇄52000
dB ⇄81000

★ ★ ★**Sirio** via Circonvallazione 109
☎949194 tx410626
⋔100 **P** Lift ☽ sB ⋔59000
dB ⋔92000 M24000

★ ★ ★**Tritone** pza Stazione 16 ☎930955
Mar–Nov
rm67 ⇄30 ⋔24 🏛 **P** Lift ☽
sB ⇄ ⋔50000 dB ⇄ ⋔75000

★ ★**Aurora** pza G-Bruno 15 (n.rest)
☎989832
rm33 ⇄15 ⋔4 **P** Lift ☽ sB 29000
sB ⇄ ⋔39500 dB51000 dB ⇄ ⋔52000

★ ★**Venezia** pza XXVII Ottobre
☎972400 tx410693
rm100 ⇄90 🏛 **P** Lift ☽ sB29000
sB ⇄39000 dB51000 dB ⇄61500
M16000

Autolambro SAS corso del Popolo 7
☎929922 Cit

♻Damiami & Giorgio via Torino 40
☎932844 M/c Frd

♻S Lorenzo via Giustizia27 ☎926722
P Op Vau

Roma/Caldera via Piave 182 ☎929611
Fia

At MARGHERA (1km S)

★★Lugano via Rizzardi 11 ☎936777
tx411155
⇄62 🖚 P Lift ♪ sB ⇄42000-49000
dB ⇄66000-79000 Pool

MILANO (MILAN)
Milano (☎02)

See plan page 256
★★★★Excelsior-Gallia (SRS) pza
Duca d'Aosta 9 ☎6277 tx311160 Plan 2
rm252 ⇄240 🗒12 🖚 Lift ♪
sB ⇄ 🗒188500-213500
dB ⇄ 🗒257000-302000 M40000-45000

★★★★Palace (CIGA) pza della
Repubblica 20 ☎6336 tx311026 Plan 3
⇄199 🖚 P Lift ♪
sB ⇄168000-188000
dB ⇄256000-286000 t%

★★★★Principe&Savoia (CIGA) pza
della Repubblica 17 ☎6230 tx310052
Plan 4
⇄302 🖚 P Lift ♪
sB ⇄204000-258000
dB ⇄308000-358000 M alc t%

★★★★Diána Majestic (CIGA) viale
Piáve 42 (n.rest) ☎203404 tx333047
Plan 4A
⇄102 P Lift ♪ sB ⇄116000-121000
dB ⇄166000-177000 t%

★★★★Duomo via San Raffaele 1
☎8833 tx312086 Plan 4B
rm160 ⇄135 🗒25 P Lift ♪
sB ⇄ 🗒134000 dB ⇄ 🗒203000

★★★★Hilton International via Galvani
12 ☎6983 tx330433 Plan 4C
rm346 ⇄342 🗒4 🖚 P Lift
sB ⇄ 🗒155000-257000
dB ⇄ 🗒209000-334000

★★★★Jolly President Largo Augusto
☎7746 tx312054 Plan 5
rm201 🖚 Lift ♪ sB ⇄150000
dB ⇄190000

★★★★Jolly Touring via U-Tarchetti 2
☎665653 tx320118 Plan 8
⇄267 P Lift ♪ sB ⇄125000
dB ⇄170000

★★★★Select (BW) via Baracchini 12
(n.rest) ☎8843 tx312256 Plan 7
rm140 ⇄70 🗒70 P Lift ♪

☆☆☆AGIP Milano Tangenziale Ovest,
Assago (14km SW) ☎8463441 tx320132
Plan 9
🗒222 P Lift ♪ dB 🗒87900 Pool

★★American (BW) via Finocchiaro
Aprile 2 ☎666441 tx312150 Plan 11
rm382 ⇄100 🗒282 🖚 P Lift ♪

Italy

★★★Manin via Manin 7 ☎667251
tx320385 Plan 12
⇄110 P Lift ♪ sB ⇄118000
dB ⇄158000

☆☆Dei Fiori Ingresso Autostrada per
Genova (n.rest) ☎8436441 Plan 13
rm55 ⇄40 🗒12 🖚 P Lift ♪

☆☆Eur via L-da-Vinci 36A (n.rest)
☎4451951 Not on plan
rm41 🗒39 🖚 P Lift ♪

☆☆Fini via del Mare 93 (n.rest)
☎8464041 Plan 14
rm98 ⇄24 🗒48 🖚 P Lift ♪

★★Gamma via V-Peroni 85 (n.rest)
☎2141118 Plan 15
rm55 ⇄10 🗒45 🖚 Lift ♪

♻Forlanini via Mecenate 84 ☎5060340
Fia

At SAN DONATO MILANESE (8km SE on
road N9)

☆☆☆AGIP Ingresso Autostrada del
Sole ☎512941 tx320132 Plan 10
🗒270 P Lift ♪ dB 🗒93700

At SEGRATE (6km E)

★★★★Jolly Milano 2 via F. lli Cervi
☎21606 tx321266 Not on plan
⇄149 🖚 P Lift ♪ sB ⇄118000
dB ⇄144000

MILANO MARITTIMA See CERVIA

MINORI See AMALFI

MISANO ADRIATICO
Forlì (☎0541)

★★Gala via Pascoli 8 ☎615109
15 May-20 Sep
⇄27 P Lift ♪ sea

MODENA
Modena (☎059)

★★★★Fini via E-Est 441 ☎238091
tx510285
Closed 28 Jul-22 Aug & 23 Dec-1 Jan
⇄100 Lift ♪

☆☆☆AGIP (SS 9 via Tre Olmi-Autosole
Raccordo Brennero) ☎518221 tx611627
🗒184 P Lift ♪ dB 🗒75900

♻Barbieri Auto via E-Est 1040
☎360260 P BL

Bellei via E-Est 1127 ☎366271 Frd

MOGLIANO VENETO
Treviso (☎041)

★★★★Villa Condulmer via Zermanese
1 ☎457100
rm54 ⇄48 🗒6 P ♪ sB ⇄ 🗒47500
dB ⇄ 🗒104500 ⚘ Pool ♂ ♫

MOLTRASIO
Como (☎031)

★★Caramazza via Besana 50 ☎290050
Apr-30 Oct
rm20 ⇄ 🗒17 🖚 P Lift lake

MALVENO
Trento (☎0461)

★★Miralago pza Scuole 4 ☎586935
Jun-Sep
⇄55 P Lift ♪ sB⇄24000 dB ⇄38000
Pool lake

★Cima Tosa via Scuole 3 ☎586928
Jun-Sep
rm34 ⇄8 🗒26 P Lift
sB ⇄ 🗒17000-21500
dB ⇄ 🗒32000-39000 M12000-15000
mountains lake

MONDOVI' BREO
Cuneo (☎0174)

♻F Govone via Piava 4 ☎40355 P Cit
Fia

MONTALTO DI CASTRO
Viterbo (☎0766)

☆☆☆AGIP via Aurelia (SS 1km 108)
☎89090
🗒32 P ♪ dB 🗒52000

MONTECATINI TERME
Pistoia (☎0572)

★★★Croce di Malta (SRS) via IV
Novembre 18 ☎79381 tx574041
rm110 ⇄100 🗒10 P Lift ♪
sB ⇄ 🗒64500-78500
dB ⇄ 🗒116000-157000 mountains

★Astoria via Fedeli ☎71191
Apr-Oct
rm65 ⇄ 🗒59 P Lift ♪ Pool
mountains

★Lido Palace Risorgimento via IV
Novembre 14 ☎70731
Apr-Oct
rm56 ⇄52 Lift ♪

MONTEGROTTO TERME
Padova (☎049)

★★★International Bertha Largo
Traiano ☎793100 tx430277
⇄200 P Lift ♪ sB ⇄65000-75000
dB ⇄120000-130000 M35000 t%1
Pool ♂ mountains

MONTESILVANO MARINA See PESCARA

MUCCIA
Macerata (☎0737)

☆☆☆AGIP Bivio Maddalena (SS77
km44) ☎43138
🗒37 P Lift ♪ dB 🗒47700

NAPOLI (NAPLES)
Napoli (☎081)

★★★★Excelsior (CIGA) via
Partenope 48 ☎417111 tx710043
⇄137 🖚 Lift ♪ sB ⇄148000-163000
dB ⇄216000-256000 t% sea

★★★★Vesuvio (SRS) via Partenope 45
☎417044 tx710127
rm179 ⇄114 🗒64 🖚 Lift ♪ →

sB ⇌ ⋔ 86000–118000
dB ⇌ ⋔ 124000–166000

★★★**Jolly Ambassador's** via Medina
70 ☎416000 tx720335
rm278 ⇌251 🍴 Lift 𝄐 dB ⇌120000

★★★**Parker's** corso V-Emmanuele 135
☎684866 tx710578
rm87 ⇌56 ⋔ 10 🍴 P Lift 𝄐 sea

★★★**Royal** via Partenope 38 ☎400244
tx710167
⇌490 🍴 P Lift 𝄐 sB ⇌ ⋔ 86800
dB ⇌ ⋔ 142700 Pool sea

⋈**S Luigi** via G-Francesco Pinto 59
☎514865 Ren

⋈**SVAI** via S-Veniero 17–20 ☎611122
Frd

At **SECONDIGLIANO** (8km N)

☆☆☆**AGIP** (SS7 bis km24) ☎7540560
⋔ 57 P Lift 𝄐 dB ⋔ 83200

NERVI
Genova (☎010)

★★★**Giardino Rivera** Passegiata a
Mare ☎328581
rm35 ⇌20 ⋔ 6 🍴 P Lift 𝄐 sea

☆★**Milano** via Somma Donato 39
☎328292
rm50 ⇌25 ⋔ 5 A19rm 🍴 P Lift 𝄐
sea

NOBIALLO See **MENAGGIO**

MILANO (MILAN)			
2	★★★★★	**Excelsior-Gallia**	8	★	**Jolly Touring**
3	★★★★★	**Palace**	9	☆☆☆	**AGIP**
4	★★★★	**Principe & Savoia**	10	☆☆☆	**AGIP** (At San Donato Milanese/8km SE)
4A	★★★★	**Diana Majestic**	11	★★★	**American**
4B	★★★★	**Duomo**	12	★★★	**Manin**
4C	★★★★	**Hilton International**	13	☆☆	**Dei Fiori**
5	★★★★	**Jolly President**	14	★★	**Fini**
7	★★★	**Select**	15	★★	**Gamma**

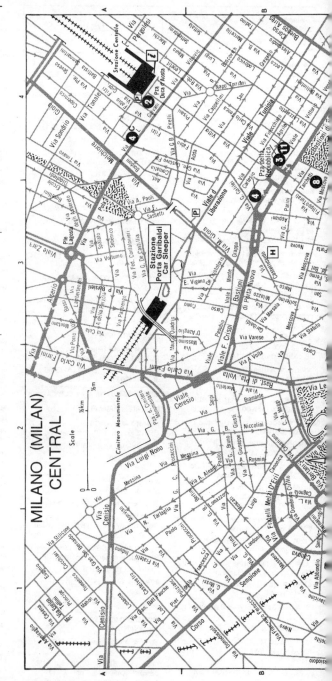

MILANO (MILAN)
CENTRAL

Scale ½km
0   1km

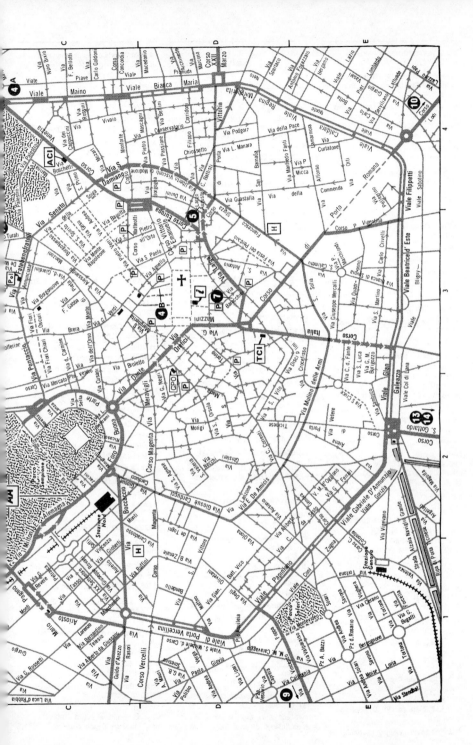

NOVA LEVANTE-WELSCHNOFEN
Bolzano (☎0471)

★ ★ ★**Posta Cavallino Bianco** via
Carezza 30, Strada Dolomiti ☎613113
tx400555

17 Dec–Etr & 20 May–20 Oct
rm47 ⇄40 ⋔7 🚗 **P** Lift 𝔇
sB ⇄ ⋔53000 dB ⇄ ⋔116000 ⭑
Pool mountains

NUMANA
Ancona (☎071)

★ ★**Numana Palace** via Litoranea 10
☎930155

15 May–15 Sep
rm90 ⇄3 ⋔87 **P** Lift 𝔇
dB ⇄ ⋔80000 ⭑ Pool Beach sea

NUORO See **SARDEGNA (ISOLA)**
(SARDINIA)

ORA-AUER
Bolzano (☎0471)

★ ★**Elefant** pza Principale 45 ☎80129
⇄32 🚗 **P** Lift dB ⇄34000 mountains

ORTA SAN GIULIO
Novara (☎0322)

★ ★ ★**San Rocco** via Gippini de Verona
11 ☎90222
rm41 ⇄36 ⋔5 🚗 **P** Lift 𝔇 lake

★ ★**Bussola** via Panoramica 24 ☎90198

Closed 2 wks Jan
rm16 ⇄11 ⋔5 **P** Lift
sB ⇄ ⋔39500–44500
dB ⇄ ⋔59000–69000 M21000–24000
Pool mountains lake

ORTISEI-ST ULRICH
Bolzano (☎0471)

★ ★ ★**Aquila** via Rezia 7 ☎76203

Dec–Oct
rm85 ⇄70 🚗 **P** Lift 𝔇
dB82000–133000 dB ⇄93000–157000
⭑ Pool mountains

ORVIETO
Terni (☎0763)

★ ★ ★**Maitani** via L-Maitani 5 ☎33001
rm44 ⇄32 ⋔12 Lift 𝔇
sB ⇄ ⋔54000–61000
dB ⇄ ⋔98000–108000 M24000

At **BADIA (LA)** (5km S)

★ ★ ★**Badia** (DPn in season) ☎90359
Mar–Dec
⇄24 🚗 **P** 𝔇 sB ⇄72000–78000
dB ⇄101000–120000 M29000 ⭑ Pool

OSPEDALETTI
Imperia (☎0184)

★ ★ ★**Floreal** corso R-Margherita 83
☎59638
rm26 ⇄20 Lift 𝔇 sea mountains

★ ★ ★**Rocce del Capo** Lungomare C-
Columbo (n.rest) ☎59733
Dec–Sep
rm22 ⇄3 ⋔19 🚗 Lift 𝔇 Pool
Beach sea

★ ★**Petit Royal** via Regina Mergherita 86
☎59026

Italy

20 Dec–Sep
rm30 ⇄9 ⋔15 **P** Lift sB 22000–33000
sB ⇄ ⋔25000–37000 dB43000–51000
dB ⇄ ⋔49000–61000 M15000–25000
sea

PADOVA (PADUA)
Padova (☎049)

★ ★ ★**Park Hotel Villa Altichiero**
Altichiero (6km N on SS47) ☎615111
⇄ ⋔70 **P** Lift 𝔇 Pool

PAESTUM
Salerno (☎0828)

★ ★**Calypso** via Licinella 35, Zona Pineta
☎811031
⇄40 𝔇 dB ⇄32000–42000 sea

PALERMO See **SICILIA (SICILY)**

PALLANZA See **VERBANIA**

PARMA
Parma (☎0521)

★ ★ ★**Palace Maria Luigia** viale
Mentaria 140 ☎21032 tx531008
rm70 ⇄16 ⋔54 **P** Lift 𝔇
sB ⇄ ⋔65000–75000
dB ⇄ ⋔90000–110000 M28000

★ ★**Button** via 3-Vitale 7 ☎208039
Closed Jul
rm44 ⇄26

★ ★**Milano** viale Ponte Bottego 9
☎773031
rm47 ⇄32 ⋔3 🚗 **P** Lift 𝔇

⭑○**Bottesini** via Golese 30 ☎24219 M/c
Hon Vlo

PASSO DEL TONALE See **TONALE**
(PASSO)

PASSO DI ROLLE See **ROLLE**

PEGLI
Genova (☎010)

★ ★ ★**Mediterranée** Lungomare 69
(n.rest) ☎683041
⇄72 **P** Lift 𝔇 sB ⇄ ⋔58200
dB ⇄ ⋔83900 sea

PERUGIA
Perugia (☎075)

★ ★ ★**Rosetta** pza Italia 19 ☎20841
rm108 ⇄49 ⋔33 🚗 **P** 𝔇
sB ⇄ ⋔33600 dB30450 dB ⇄ ⋔47250

⭑○**Negri & Ricci** via Romana 35, Piscille di
Perugia (strada di P S Giov) ☎395044
M/c BMW

PESARO
Pesaro & Urbino (☎0721)

★ ★ ★**Mediterraneo Ricci** viale Trieste
199 ☎31556 tx56006
rm47 ⇄6 ⋔41 A4rm **P** Lift 𝔇
sB ⇄ ⋔34000 dB ⇄ ⋔53000

★ ★ ★**Vittoria** pza della Libertá 2 (rest 12
Jun–12 Sep only) ☎34343 tx560062
rm27 ⇄10 ⋔17 🚗 Lift 𝔇
sB ⇄ ⋔7100 dB ⇄ ⋔97000 sea

★ ★**Atlantic** viale Trieste 365 ☎61911
tx560062
10 May–Sep
rm40 ⇄25 ⋔15 **P** Lift 𝔇 Beach sea

A Gabellini Strada Romagna 119
☎39124 Aud Por VW

Paolo del Monte via Porta Rimini
☎32919 BL

PESCARA
Pescara (☎085)

☆ ☆ ☆**AGIP** Autostrada Adriatica Casello
Pescara Nord (SS 16) ☎95321
⋔85 **P** Lift 𝔇 dB ⋔57500

★ ★ ★**Carlton** viale Riviera 35 ☎26373
rm71 ⇄19 ⋔52 **P** Lift 𝔇
sB ⇄ ⋔43000 dB ⇄ ⋔68500 sea

⭑○**MADA** via Tiburtina Valeria ☎51342
Frd

At **MONTESLIVANO MARINA** (8km NW on
SS16)

★ ★ ★ ★**Grand Monteslivano** via Riviera
28 ☎838251 tx600118
⇄140 🚗 **P** Lift 𝔇 sB ⇄14000
dB ⇄56000 Beach sea

★ ★ ★**Serena Majestic** viale Kennedy
☎835142 tx600186
Apr–Sep
rm216 ⇄120 ⋔96 **P** Lift 𝔇
Pn46500–90000 ⭑ Pool Beach

PIACENZA
Piacenza (☎0523)

★ ★ ★**Grande Albergo Roma** via
Cittadella 14 ☎23201 tx530874
⇄90 🚗 Lift 𝔇

⭑○**Agosti & Lunardi** via Perletti 5
☎28920 BL

Mirani & Toscani via E-Parmense 6
☎62721 M/c Frd

PIAZZA ARMERINA See **SICILIA (SICILY)**

PIETRA LIGURE
Savona (☎019)

★ ★ ★ ★**Royal** via Don Bado 129
tx647192
rm105 ⇄88 ⋔20 🚗 **P** Lift 𝔇 Beach
sea

PIETRASANTA (MARINA DI)
Lucca (☎0584)

★ ★**Palazzo della Spiaggia** (DPn)
Lungomare Roma-Faocette ☎21195
May–Sep
⇄50 **P** Lift 𝔇 sB ⇄67000
dB ⇄115000 Pool Beach sea

★ ★**Battelli** viale Versilia 189, Motrone
☎20010 tx590403
Jun–Sep
⇄42 🚗 **P** Lift 𝔇 sB ⇄47000
dB ⇄74000 ⭑ Beach sea

★★**Esplanade** viale Roma 235 Tonfano
☎21151 tx590403
⇌33 **P** Lift ☽ dB ⇌58850 sea

★★**Venezia** via Firenze 48 ☎20731
⇌34 **P** Lift ☽ sB ⇌39800
dB ⇌58850 sea

PINETA (LIGNANO) See **LIGNANO SABBIADORO**

PIOMBINO
Livorno (☎0565)

★★**Centrale** pza Verdi 2 ☎32581
rm38 ⇌6 ⋔27 Lift ☽

E Bianchetti pza Constituzione 54
☎33017 Frd

PISA
Pisa (☎050)

★★★★**Cavalieri** (CIGA) pza Stazione 2
☎43290 tx590663
rm102 ⇌58 ⋔44 🏛 **P** Lift ☽
sB ⇌ ⋔111000–126000
dB ⇌ ⋔167000–177000 t%

☆ **California** via Surelia (4km NW on SS67) ☎890726 tx500119
Apr–Oct
⋔74 **P** ☽ sB ⋔53000 dB ⋔89000
Pool

⅋**G Finocchi** via Galcesana ☎86147
Aud VW

PISTICCI
Matera (☎0835)

☆☆☆**AGIP** (SS407 Basentana km137)
☎462007 tx611627
⇌64 **P** ☽ dB ⇌6100

POLIGNANO A MARE
Bari (☎080)

★**Grotta Palazzese** via Narciso 59
☎740261
rm14 ⇌11 ⋔3 A4rm 🏛 ☽ sea

PONTASSIEVE
Firenze (☎055)

★★★**Moderno** (n.rest) ☎8315541
tx574381
rm120 ⇌6 ⋔114 🏛 **P** Lift ☽

PORDENONE
Pordenone (☎0434)

Automobile viale Grigoletti ☎32591 BL

⅋**Cossetti & Vatta** viale Venezia
☎31474 Ren

PORT' ERCOLE
Grosseto (☎0564)

★★★★**Pelicano** Cale del Santi (4.5km SW on Strada Panoramica) ☎833801
tx500131
⇌34 **P** ☽ M46000
DPn108000–262000 ⅋ Pool Beach
sea

★**Don Pedro** via Panoramica ☎833914
Mar–Sep
rm44 ⇌16 ⋔28 🏛 **P** Lift ☽ sea

PORTO AZZURRO See **ELBA (ISOLA D')**

Italy

PORTOFERRAIO See **ELBA (ISOLA D')**

PORTOFINO
Genova (☎0185)

★★★★**Splendido** viale Baratta 13
☎69551 tx331057
29 Mar–29 Oct
⇌67 🏛 **P** Lift ☽
sB ⇌146000–196000
dB ⇌252000–312000 Mfr60000 ⅋
Pool sea

★★**Piccolo** via Duca degli Abruzzi 31
☎69015
Mar–2 Nov
rm27 ⇌6 ⋔19 🏛 **P** ☽ Beach sea

PORTONOVO See **ANCONA**

PORTO SAN GIORGIO
Ascoli Picerno (☎0734)

★**Terrazza** via A-Costa ☎379005
rm21 ⇌12 **P** Lift ☽ Beach sea

⅋**Petracci** via Nazionale Adriatica 235
☎4248

POSITANO
Salerno (☎089)

★★★**Savoia** via C-Colombo 29
☎875003
Apr–15 Oct
rm44 ⇌27 ⋔12 Lift ☽
sB ⇌ ⋔26000–30000 dB47000–50000
dB ⇌ ⋔62000–66000 M16000–18000
sea mountains

★★**Buca di Bacco & Buca Résidence** via Colombo 21 ☎875699
Jan–Oct
rm31 ⋔8 Lift sea

★★**Maresca** ☎825140
15 Mar–30 Oct
rm19 ⇌12 ⋔5 **P** sea

POTENZA
Potenza (☎0971)

⅋**L Olita** via del Gallitello ☎26477 **P**
Opl Vau

POZZUOLI
Napoli (☎081)

Pelli via E-Scarfoglio ☎7605322 M/c Opl
Vau

PRAIANO
Salerno (☎089)

★★**Grand Tritone** via Campo 1
☎874005 tx770025
10 Apr–10 Oct
⇌73 **P** Lift ☽ Pool Beach sea

★★**Tramonto d'Oro** via G-Capriglione
119 ☎874008
⇌ ⋔60 🏛 **P** Lift ☽ Pool sea

PRATO
Firenze (☎0574)

★★**Fiora** via Cairoli 31 (n.rest) ☎20021
tx571358
rm30 ⇌18 ⋔8 🏛 **P** Lift

PROCCHIO See **ELBA (ISOLA D')**

PUGNOCHIUSO See **VIESTE**

PUNTA ALA
Grosseto (☎0564)

★★★★**Gallia Palace** via delle Sughere
☎922022 tx590454
20 May–Sep
rm98 ⇌72 ⋔26 **P** Lift ☽
sB ⇌ ⋔114000–164000
dB ⇌ ⋔158000–268000 M31000–39000
⅋ Pool Beach ⓢ ◠ sea

RAGUSA See **SICILIA (SICILY)**

RAPALLO
Genova (☎0185)

★★★**Eurotel** via Aurelia Ponente 22
☎60981 tx213851
rm62 ⇌47 ⋔15 🏛 **P** Lift ☽
sB ⇌ ⋔48000–54000
dB ⇌ ⋔74000–82000 Pool sea

★★★**Grande Italia & Lido** Lungomare
Castello 1 ☎50030
rm59 ⇌34 ⋔25 **P** Lift ☽
sB ⇌ ⋔30000–40000
dB ⇌ ⋔45000–65000 Beach sea

★★★**Miramare** Lungomare V-Veneto
27 ☎50293
rm28 ⇌16 ⋔5 **P** Lift ☽ sea

★★★**Riviera** pza IV Novembre 2
☎50248
Closed 5 Nov–20 Dec
rm26 ⇌25 ⋔1 🏛 **P** Lift ☽ sea

★**Brandoni** via Marsala 24 ☎50423
rm16 ⇌6 Lift sea

⅋ **E Massa** via G-Mameli 182
☎50689 BL

⅋**Ratto & Cordano** via Arginati 33
☎51419 M/c **P**

RAVELLO
Salerno (☎089)

★★★**Caruso Belvedere** via Toro 52
☎857111
rm26 ⇌18 ⋔2 **P** ☽ sB30100
sB ⇌ ⋔43000 dB55600 dB ⇌ ⋔75300
sea

★★★**Palumbo** (**DPn**) via Toro 28
☎857244 tx770101
rm20 ⇌19 ⋔1 A7rm 🏛 **P** ☽ sea

★★**Parsifal** via d'Anna 5 ☎857144
22 Mar–10 Oct
rm19 ⇌15 🏛 **P** ☽ sea

RAVENNA
Ravenna (☎0544)

★★★★**Jolly** pza Mameli 1 ☎35762
tx550575
⇌75 Lift ☽ sB ⇌75000 dB ⇌113000

★★★**Bisanzio** via Salara 30 (n.rest)
☎27111
⇌36 Lift ☽ sB ⇌67000 dB ⇌139000

★ ★**Centrale Byron** via IV Novembre 14
☎22225 tx551070
rm57 ⇄ ⋔54 Lift 𝒟 sB ⇄ ⋔34000
dB46000 dB ⇄ ⋔56000

☆**Romea** (2.5km S on SS16) ☎61247
rm39 ⇄2 ⋔37 **P** Lift 𝒟
sB ⇄ ⋔34000 dB ⇄ ⋔56000

&⊃**C Ravennate** via M-Perilli 40
☎421579 **P** Fia Ren

REGGIO DI CALABRIA
Reggio di Calabria (☎0965)

C Mazzone via San Caterina 12 ☎48600
M/c Aud Por VW

REGGIO NELL'EMILIA
Reggio Nell'Emilia (☎0522)

★ ★ ★**Grand Astoria** via L-Nobili 4
☎35245 tx530534
⇄112 🏠 **P** Lift 𝒟 sB ⇄fr71000
dB ⇄fr102000 Mfr25000

★ ★**Posta** pza C-Battisti 4 (n.rest)
☎32944
rm54 ⇄13 ⋔32 🏠 Lift 𝒟

RENDE See **COSENZA**

RICAVO See **CASTELLINA IN CHIANTI**

RICCIONE
Forlì (☎0541)

★ ★ ★**Atlantic** Lungomare della
Libertá 15 ☎601155 tx550192
18 May–Sep
rm65 ⇄40 ⋔25 🏠 Lift 𝒟
dB ⇄ ⋔300000 Pool Beach sea

★ ★ ★**Saviolo Spiaggia** via G-
d'Annunzio 2–6 ☎43252 tx551038
10 May–20 Sep
rm100 ⇄80 ⋔20 🏠 **P** Lift 𝒟 Pool
Beach sea

★ ★ ★**Abner's** Lungomare Repubblica
☎600601 tx550153
⇄ ⋔50 🏠 **P** Lift 𝒟
sB ⇄ ⋔56000–72000
dB ⇄ ⋔88000–118000 M18000–30000
🖙 Beach sea

★ ★ ★**Arizona** via G-d'Annunzio 22
☎48520
10 May–Sep
rm52 ⇄36 **P** Lift 𝒟 Beach sea

★ ★ ★**Lungomare** viale Milano 7
☎41601
11 May–30 Sep
rm62 ⇄30 ⋔32 **P** Lift 𝒟 Beach sea

★ ★ ★**Vienna & Touring** viale Gramsci
79 ☎601700 tx550153
May–Sep
⇄94 🏠 Lift 𝒟 sB ⇄42000–57000
dB ⇄69000–99000 M18000–30000 🖙
Pool Beach sea

★ ★**Alexandra Plaza** viale Torino 61
☎615344 tx550153
Apr–Sep
⇄ ⋔50 **P** Lift 𝒟 M18000–30000

DPn37000–63000 Beach sea

★ ★**Nevada** via Milano 54 ☎601245

Italy

May–Sep
⇄ ⋔50 🏠 **P** Lift 𝒟 sB ⇄ ⋔29000
dB ⇄ ⋔58000 M15000 Beach sea

&⊃**Morelli & Mucciolo** via R-Molari 26
☎600806 M/c **P** VW

RIMINI
Forlì (☎0541)

★ ★ ★**Ambasciatori** viale Vespucci 22
☎27642 tx550132
⇄70 **P** Lift 𝒟 sB ⇄93460
dB ⇄165620 Pool Beach sea

★ ★ ★**President** via Tripoli 270 ☎25741
May–Sep
⇄50 🏠 Lift 𝒟 sB ⇄27000
dB ⇄50000

★ ★**Alpen** viale Regina Élena 203
☎80662
May–Sep
rm56 ⇄5 ⋔51 **P** Lift 𝒟 sea

&⊃**Grattacielo** viale P-Amedeo 11
☎24610 **P** Opl

&⊃**Sartini** viale P–Amedeo 13 ☎27548 **P**
Fia

At **RIVAZZURRA** (4km SE)

★ ★ ★**France** viale Regina Margherita 48
☎31551
20 May–Sep
⇄65 **P** 𝒟 Pool Beach sea

★ ★ ★**Grand Meeting** viale Regina
Margherita 46 ☎32123
Apr–Sep
rm38 ⇄20 ⋔18 **P** Lift 𝒟 sB ⇄20000
dB ⇄34000 sea

★ ★ ★**Little** via Gubbio 16 ☎33258
20 May–Sep
⋔45 **P** Lift 𝒟

RIVA DEL GARDA
Trento (☎0464)

★ ★ ★**Lac & Parc** (BW) viale Rovereto 38
☎513344 tx400258
Apr–15 Oct
rm170 ⇄130 ⋔40 🏠 **P** Lift 𝒟 🖙
Pool mountains lake

RIVAZZURRA See **RIMINI**

RIVIERA (LIGNANO) See **LIGNANO
SABBIADORO**

ROCCARASO
L'Aquila (☎0864)

☆ ☆ ☆**AGIP** (SS17 dall'Appennino
l'Abruzzese km136) ☎62443
⋔57 **P** Lift 𝒟 mountains

ROLLE (PASSO DI)
Trento (☎0439)

★**Passo Rolle** ☎68216
rm27 ⇄7 **P** mountains

ROMA (ROME)
Roma (☎06)

See Plan page 262

★ ★ ★ ★**Cavalieri Hilton** via Cadlolo
101 ☎3151 tx610296 Plan **1**
⇄400 🏠 **P** Lift 𝒟
sB ⇄174000–208300
dB ⇄246700–295100 M alc 🖙 Pool

★ ★ ★**Excelsior** (CIGA) via Vittorio
Veneto 125 ☎4708 tx333047 Plan **1A**
⇄394 🏠 **P** Lift 𝒟
sB ⇄204000–224000
dB ⇄283000–328000 t%

★ ★ ★ ★**Grand** (CIGA) via Vittorio E-
Orlando 3 ☎4709 tx610210 Plan **2**
⇄175 Lift 𝒟 sB ⇄210000–250000
dB ⇄305000–350000 t%

★ ★ ★ ★**Grand Flora** via V-Veneto 191
(n.rest) ☎497821 tx680494 Plan **2A**
⇄200 🏠 Lift 𝒟

★ ★ ★ ★**Hassler Villa Medici** pza
Trinità dei Monti 6 ☎672651 tx610208
Plan **3**
⇄100 🏠 **P** Lift 𝒟 sB ⇄170000
dB ⇄240000

★ ★ ★ ★**Jolly V-Veneto** cordo d'Italia
1 ☎8495 tx612293 Plan **4**
⇄200 🏠 **P** Lift 𝒟 sB ⇄131000
dB ⇄181000

★ ★ ★**Eliseo** (BW) via di Porta
Pinciana 30 ☎460556 tx610693 Plan **6**
rm60 ⇄55 ⋔5 **P** Lift 𝒟

☆ ☆ ☆**Holiday Inn Parco dei Medici**
viale Castello della Magliana 65 (10km W
of autostrada to Fiumicino [Airport])
☎5475 tx613302 Plan **6A**
⇄331 **P** Lift 𝒟 🖙 Pool

☆ ☆ ☆**Holiday Inn St-Peter's** via
Auselia Antica 415 ☎5872 tx680195
Plan **8A**
⇄350 **P** Lift 𝒟 sB ⇄100500
dB ⇄153080 Pool

★ ★ ★**Quirinale** (SRS) via Nazionale 7
☎4707 tx610332 Plan **8**
⇄ ⋔200 🏠 Lift 𝒟 sB ⇄ ⋔118000
dB ⇄ ⋔170000

★ ★ ★**Sheraton** viale del Pattinaggio
☎65453 tx614223 Plan **8B**
⇄700 **P** Lift 𝒟 sB ⇄125000–165000
dB ⇄165000–220000 St% Pool

★ ★ ★**Ville** (Forum) via Sistina 69
☎6733 tx620836 Plan **9**
rm189 **P** Lift 𝒟 sB121000 dB178000

☆ ☆ ☆**AGIP** via Aurelia (6km W on SS1)
☎626843 tx613699 Plan **10**
⋔222 **P** Lift 𝒟 dB ⋔79000 Pool

★ ★ ★**Bernini-Bristol** (SRS) pza
Barberini 23 ☎463051 tx610554 Plan **10A**
⇄124 **P** Lift 𝒟 sB ⇄180000
dB ⇄230000 M alc t%

★ ★ ★**Boston** (ETAP) via Lombardia 47
☎473951 tx680460 Plan **10B**
rm121 ⇄88 ⋔33 🏠 **P** Lift 𝒟

sB ⇄ 🏨75000–110000
dB ⇄ 🏨115000–180000 M alc

★ ★ ★Britannia via Napoli 65 (n.rest)
☎465785 tx611292 Plan **11**
⇄32 **P** Lift ♪ sB ⇄85000
dB ⇄122000

★ ★ ★Columbus via della Concillazione
33 ☎475144 Plan **12**
rm120 ⇄60 🏨15 **P** Lift ♪

★ ★ ★Commodore via Torino 1 (n.rest)
☎4754112 tx612170 Plan **13**
⇄ 🏨65 **P** Lift ♪ sB ⇄ 🏨60250
dB ⇄ 🏨97500

★ ★ ★Lord Byron via G-de Notaris 5
☎3609541 tx611217 Plan **15**
rm50 ⇄48 🏨2 **P** Lift ♪
sB ⇄ 🏨205000 dB ⇄ 🏨260000

★ ★ ★Nord-Nuova via G-Amendola 3
☎465051 tx610556 Plan **16**
⇄150 Lift ♪

★ ★ ★Piccadilly (BW) via Magnagrecia
122 (n.rest) ☎777017 Plan **18A**
rm55 ⇄23 🏨32 **P** Lift ♪

★ ★ ★Regina-Carlton via V-Veneto 72
☎4758841 tx611684 Plan **19**
⇄134 🚗 Lift ♪ sB ⇄114000–134000
dB ⇄173000–198000 Mfr35000

★ ★ ★Rivoli via Torquato Taramelli 7,
Parioli ☎870141 tx614615 Plan **20**
⇄ 🏨50 Lift sB ⇄ 🏨60000
dB ⇄ 🏨76000 m18000

★ ★ ★Savoy via Ludovisi 15 ☎4744141
tx611339 Plan **21**
⇄ 🏨115 Lift ♪ sB ⇄ 🏨98000
dB ⇄ 🏨157000 Mfr21500

★ ★Alba via Leonina 12 (n.rest)
☎484471 Plan **22**
rm25 ⇄6 🏨19 Lift ♪

★ ★Hilberia via 24 Maggio 7 (n. rest)
☎6782662 tx621399 Not on plan
rm22 ⇄21 Lift ♪

★Margutta via Laurina 34 (n.rest)
☎6798440 Plan **28**
rm25 ⇄7 🏨18 Lift ♪

☆Scalinata di Spagna pza Trinita del
Monti 17 (n.rest) ☎67930006 Plan **29**
rm14 ⇄6 🏨7 ♪

⅋DMarchir Orlando Circonvallazione
Trionfale 133 ☎3599893 M/c DJ Sko
Toy

At **STORTA (LA)** (16km NW on SS2)
☆Bela via Cassia 1801 ☎3790232
Plan **25**
rm44 ⇄24 🏨20 **P** ♪ 🏊 Pool

ST-VINCENT
Aosta (☎0166)

★ ★ ★ ★Billia viale Piemonte 18 ☎3446
tx212144
⇄134 🚗 **P** Lift ♪ 🏊 Pool
mountains

⅋DFabris pza Zerbion ☎2619 **P** Cit

Italy

SALERNO
Salerno (☎089)

★ ★ ★ ★Jolly Lungomare Trieste 1
☎225222 tx770050
rm105 ⇄100 **P** Lift ♪ sB ⇄67000
dB ⇄105000

G Jannone via Picenza 12 ☎351229 BL
DJ RT

At **VIETRI SUL MARE** (3km W)
★ ★ ★Lloyd's Bala (SRS) (**Pn** in
season) via de Marinis ☎210145
tx770043
rm120 ⇄114 🏨6 🚗 **P** Lift ♪
sB ⇄ 🏨75000 dB ⇄ 🏨107000 Pool
sea

SALÓ
Brescia (☎0365)

★ ★ ★Duomo via Duomo 18 ☎21026
tx303028
Mar–15 Jan
rm27 ⇄17 🏨10 🚗 **P** Lift
sB ⇄ 🏨52000 dB ⇄ 🏨89000 M30000
lake

SALSOMAGGIORE TERME
Parma (☎0524)

★ ★ ★ ★Porro viale Porro 10 ☎78221
tx530639
⇄85 **P** Lift ♪ Pool

SAN BARTOLOMEO AL MARE
Imperia (☎0183)

★ ★ ★Mayola ☎400739
Mar–Sep
rm80 ⇄8 🏨72 🚗 **P** Lift ♪ Pool sea

SAN BENEDETTO DEL TRONTO
Ascoli Piceno (☎0735)

⅋DE G Tomassini corso Mazzini 249
☎5608 Aud VW

SÁN CÁNDIDO-INNICHEN
Bolzano (☎0474)

★ ★Park Sole Paradiso via Sesto 11
☎73120 tx400329
22 Dec–20 Apr & Jun–Sep
⇄ 🏨45 A4rm 🚗 **P** Lift
⇄20000–40000
dB ⇄ 🏨40000–80000 M11000–18000
♪ Pool mountains

SAN DONATO MILANESE See **MILANO**
(MILAN)

SAN FELICE See **CREMONA**

SAN GIMIGNANO
Siena (☎0577)

★ ★Cisterna pza della Cisterna 23
☎940328
⇄46 Lift ♪ sB ⇄36800 dB ⇄67200

SAN MAMETE See **VALSOLDA**

SAN MARINO follows **ITALY**

SAN MARTINO DI CASTROZZA
Trento (☎0439)

★ ★ ★San Martino ☎68011 tx44043
20 Dec–20 Apr & Jul–20 Sep
rm46 ⇄38 🏨8 🚗 **P** ♪ Pool
mountains

★ ★Savoia via Passo Rolle 233 ☎68094
tx440043
20 Dec–10 Apr & Jul–15 Sep
⇄73 🚗 **P** Lift ♪ mountains

★Belvedere via Passo Rolle 247
☎68000 tx440046
20 Dec–Mar & 25 Jun–Aug
⇄32 **P** Lift sB ⇄29500–44500
dB ⇄52500–75000 M17000 mountains

SAN REMO
Imperia (☎0184)

★ ★ ★ ★ ★Royal corso Imperatrice 80
☎79991 tx270511
18 Dec–23 Sep
⇄140 🚗 **P** Lift ♪
sB ⇄100000–130000
dB ⇄160000–210000 M40000 🏊 sea

★ ★ ★ ★Miramare corso Matuzia 9
☎882381 tx270620
20 Dec–20 Sep
rm57 ⇄50 🏨7 **P** Lift ♪ Pool sea

★ ★ ★Astoria West End corso Matuzia 8
☎70791 tx213834
⇄112 **P** Lift ♪ sB ⇄68000–88000
dB ⇄116000–152000 M35000

★ ★ ★Europa & Pace corso Imperatrice
27 ☎70605
rm80 ⇄ 🏨40 🚗 **P** Lift ♪
sB31500–36500 sB ⇄ 🏨41500–52500
dB59000–67000 dB ⇄ 🏨73000–85000
M25000 sea

★ ★ ★Residence Principe via
Asquasciati 48 ☎83565
rm56 ⇄40 🏨16 🚗 **P** Lift ♪
sB ⇄ 🏨26000–49000
dB ⇄ 🏨52000–78000 M15000–25000
Pool sea

★ ★Beaurivage corso Trieste 49
☎85146
20 Dec–10 Oct
🏨30 Lift ♪ sB ⇄ 🏨23000 dB 🏨44000
M15000 sea

☆ ☆Bobby Motel via Marconi 208 (2.5km
W on SS1) ☎60255
22 Dec–20 Oct
rm75 ⇄20 🏨55 A10rm 🚗 **P** Lift ♪
sea

★ ★King corso Cavallotti 92 ☎880167
rm26 **P** ♪ sea

★ ★Morandi corso Matuzia 25 ☎73686
rm32 ⇄17 🏨15 🚗 **P** Lift ♪ sea

★ ★Paradiso corso Imperatrice ☎85112
txd270620
rm41 ⇄22 🏨19 🚗 **P** Lift ♪ sea

SANTA CATERINA VALFURVA
Sondrio (☎0342)

★ ★Sobretta ☎935510 →

261

Dec–Apr & Jul–15 Sep
rm30 ⇄22 ⌂ P sB18000
dB26000–32000 dB ⇄32000–36000
M13000 mountains

SANTA CRISTINA VAL GARDENA-ST CHRISTINA IN GRÖDEN
Bolzano (☎0471)

★★Posta ☎76678

15 Dec–7 Apr & 6 Jun–25 Oct
rm79 ⇄71 ⋔6 A19 P Lift 𝄞
sB ⇄ ⋔30000 dB ⇄ ⋔60000 ⚓ Pool
mountains

SANTA MARGHERITA LIGURE
Genova (☎0185)

★★★★★Imperial Palace via Pagana
19 ☎88991 tx271398

Apr–6 Jan
rm102 ⇄97 ⋔5 ⌂ Lift 𝄞
sB ⇄ ⋔97000–129000
dB ⇄ ⋔154000–224000 Pool Beach
sea

★★★Miramare (SRS) via M-Ignoto
30 ☎87014 tx270437

⇄79 ⋔5 A5rm ⌂ P Lift 𝄞
sB ⇄ ⋔74000–102000
dB ⇄ ⋔136000–192000 Pool sea
mountains

★★★Continental via Pagana 8
☎86512 tx271601

22 Dec–2 Nov
⇄ ⋔71 A5rm ⌂ P Lift 𝄞
sB ⇄ ⋔59000–82000 →

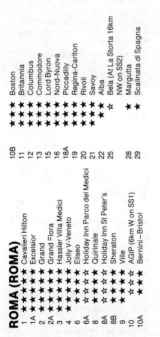

		ROMA (ROMA)		
1	★★★★★	Cavalieri Hilton		
1A	★★★★★	Excelsior	10B	★ Boston
2	★★★★★	Grand	11	★ Britannia
2A	★★★★★	Grand Flora	12	★ Columbus
3	★★★★★	Hassler Villa Medici	13	★ Commodore
4	★★★★★	Jolly V-Veneto	15	★ Lord Byron
6	★★★★	Eliseo	16	★ Nord-Nuova
6A	★★★★	Holiday Inn Parco dei Medici	18A	★ Piccadilly
8	★★★★	Quirinale	19	★ Regina-Carlton
8A	☆☆☆☆	Holiday Inn St Peter's	20	★ Rivoli
8B	☆☆☆☆	Sheraton	21	★ Savoy
9	★★★	Ville	22	☆ Alba
10	☆	AGIP (6km W on SS1)	25	☆ Bela (At La Storta 16km NW on SS2)
10A	★★	Bernini–Bristol	28	★ Margutta
			29	★ Scalinata di Spagna

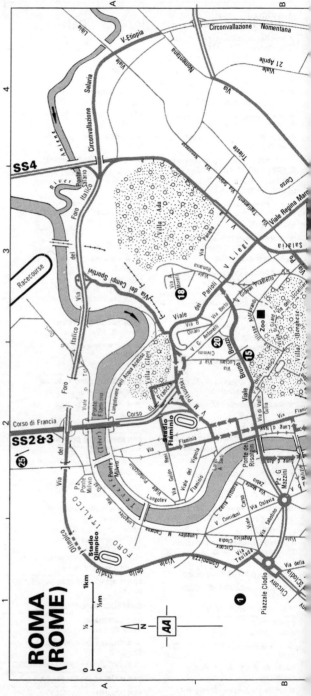

ROMA (ROME)

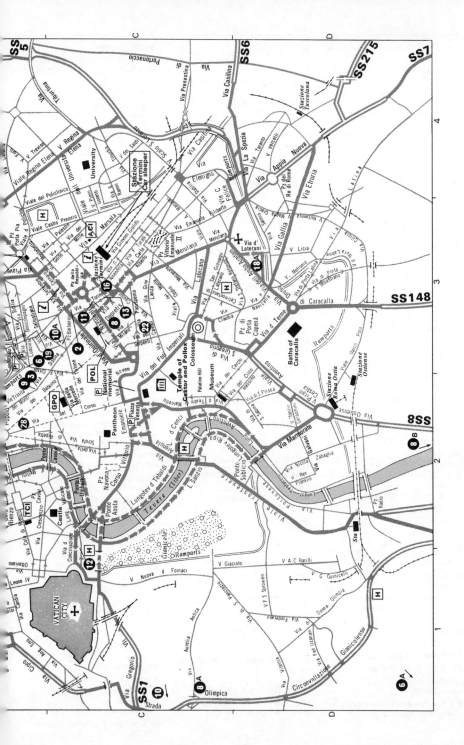

dB ⇄ 🛏102000–144000 M28000–39000
Beach sea

★ ★ ★*Laurin* corso Marconi 3 ☎89971
tx271646

21 Dec–19 Nov
⇄41 Lift sea

★ ★ ★*Metropole* via Pagana 2 ☎86134
Closed 1 Nov–20 Dec
⇄50 A12rm 🍴 P Lift D sB ⇄51000
dB ⇄84000 Beach sea

★ ★ ★*Park Suisse* via Favale 31
☎89571 tx271549
rm79 ⇄70 🛏9 P D sB ⇄ 🛏65000
dB ⇄ 🛏115000 Pool sea

★ ★ ★*Regina Elena* Lungomare M-
Ignoto 44 ☎87004 tx271563
rm86 ⇄73 🛏13 A22rm 🍴 P Lift D
sB ⇄ 🛏80100 dB ⇄ 🛏138800 sea

★ ★*Villa Anita* viale Minerva ☎86543
21 Dec–20 Oct
rm20 ⇄4 🛏7 A5rm 🍴 P D sea

★*Europa* via Trento 5 ☎87187
rm16 ⇄2 🍴 P

SAPRI
Salerno (☎0973)

৪০*Comisso* via Pisacane 22 ☎31370 P
Frd

SARDAGNA See **TRENTO**

SARDEGNA (ISOLA) (SARDINIA)
ARZACHENA
Sassari (☎079)

· ★ ★ ★ ★*Romazzino* Costa Smeralda
☎96020 tx790059
16 May–14 Oct
⇄100 P Lift D DPn148000–303000
t% ৬ Pool Beach sea

CAGLIARI
Cagliari (☎070)

☆ ☆ ☆AGIP Circonvallazione Nuova
☎561645 tx611627
🛏57 P Lift D dB 🛏60000

GOLFO ARANCI
Sassari (☎0789)

★ ★*Margherita* ☎46906
Apr–Oct
rm30 ⇄8 🛏16 P D sB32500
sB ⇄ 🛏47500 dB ⇄ 🛏73000 sea

MACOMER
Nuoro (☎0785)

☆ ☆ ☆AGIP corso Umberto 1 (SS131 di C-
Felice km 145) ☎71066 tx611627
🛏96 P Lift D dB 🛏49500

NUORO
Nuoro (☎0784)

☆ ☆ ☆AGIP via Trieste ☎34071
🛏51 P Lift D dB 🛏49500

SASSARI
Sassari (☎079)

★ ★ ★ ★Jolly Grazia Deledda viale
Dante 47 ☎271235 tx790056

Italy

⇄140 P Lift D sB ⇄59000
dB ⇄96000 Pool

☆ ☆ ☆AGIP Serra Secca ☎271440
tx611627
🛏57 P Lift D dB 🛏73000

VILLASIMIUS
Cagliari (☎070)

★ ★ ★*Timi Ama* (3km S) ☎791228
5 Jun–20 Sep
⇄65 P D sB ⇄45000–55000
dB ⇄62000–76000 Mfr23000 ৬ Beach

SARZANA
Le Spezia (☎0187)

☆ ☆ ☆AGIP Circonvallazione Aurelia 32
☎621491 tx611627
🛏51 P Lift D dB 🛏69000

SASSARI See **SARDEGNA (ISOLA)**
(SARDINIA)

SAVONA
Savona (☎019)

☆ ☆ ☆AGIP Via Nizza, Zinola ☎801961
tx611627
🛏60 P Lift D dB 🛏75000

★ ★ ★*Miramare* via Giordano 5
☎803333
rm16 ⇄14 🛏2 🍴 P Lift D sea

★ ★*Riviera-Suisee* via Palesocapa 24
(n.rest) ☎20683
rm68 ⇄59 🛏1 P Lift D

৪০M Spirito corso Viglienzoni 8F
☎806860 Chy

SECONDIGLIANO See **NAPOLI (NAPLES)**

SEGRATE See **MILANO (MILAN)**

SELVA DI VAL GARDENA-
WOLKENSTEIN IN GRÖDEN
Bolzano (☎0471)

★ ★*Solaia* via Centro 142 ☎75104
tx400359
15 Jun–20 Sep & Dec–20 Apr
rm30 ⇄26 🛏4 P sB ⇄ 🛏41800
dB ⇄ 🛏84000 Pool mountains

SENIGALLIA
Ancona (☎071)

★ ★*City* Lungomare Dante Alighieri 12
☎63464
rm60 ⇄10 🛏50 P Lift D
sB ⇄ 🛏34000–45000
dB ⇄53000–65000 M15000–22000
Beach sea

★ ★ ★*Ritz* Lungomare Dante Alighieri
142 ☎63563 tx560044
Jun–Sep
rm150 ⇄75 🛏75 P Lift D sea

৪০G E Luzi & Figli via Podesti 156
☎62035 P Aud Por VW

SESTO CALENDE
Varese (☎0331)

★ ★*Tre Re* pza Garibaldi 25 ☎924229
Mar–Nov
rm36 ⇄32 🛏4 🍴 P Lift D lake

SESTO FIORENTINO See **FIRENZE**
(FLORENCE)

SESTRI LEVANTE
Genova (☎0185)

★ ★ ★ ★*Villa Balbi* viale Rimembranze 1
☎42941
5 Apr–5 Oct
rm100 ⇄80 🛏20 P Lift D Pool
Beach

★ ★*Vis à Vis* via della Chiusa 28
☎42661
Closed Nov
rm45 ⇄28 🛏17 P Lift D Pool sea

★ ★*Helvetia* via Cappuccini 17 ☎41175
Apr–Sep
⇄28 P Lift D

SETTIMO See **TORINO (TURIN)**

SICILIA (SICILY)

AGRIGENTO
Agrigento (☎0922)

★ ★ ★*Jolly del Templi* Parco Angeli,
Villaggio Mosè (SS115) ☎76144 tx910086
⇄146 P Lift D sB ⇄60500
dB ⇄92500

P Capizzi viale della Vittoria 115 ☎65854
M/c BL

CANNIZZARO
Catania (☎095)

★ ★ ★*Grand Baia Verde* (BW) via della
Scogliera 8–10 ☎491522 tx970285
rm127 ⇄101 🛏26 🍴 P Lift D
sB ⇄ 🛏82000 dB ⇄ 🛏124000 M25000
৬ Pool Beach sea

CATANIA
Catania (☎095)

☆ ☆ ☆AGIP Ognina (SS114 km92)
(n.rest) ☎492233 tx611627
🛏 56 P Lift D dB 🛏79600

★ ★ ★*Jolly* pza Trento 13 ☎316933
tx970080
⇄159 P Lift D sB ⇄75000
dB ⇄120000

MARSALA
Trapani (☎0923)

☆ ☆ ☆AGIP Uscita per Mazara del Vallo
(SS115 km31) ☎951611
🛏32 P Lift D dB 🛏52000

MESSINA
Messina (☎090)

★ ★ ★*Jolly* via Garibaldi 126
☎43401 tx980074
⇄99 P Lift D sB ⇄60000
dB ⇄96000 sea

PALERMO
Palermo (☎091)

★ ★ ★*Jolly* Foro Italico ☎235842
tx910076

⤺290 **P** Lift ☽ sB ⤺70000
dB ⤺98000 Pool sea

☆ ☆ ☆**AGIP** via della Regione Siciliana
2620 ☎552033 tx611627

🏠100 **P** Lift ☽ dB 🏠71000

PIAZZA ARMERINA
Enna (☎0935)

★ ★ ★**Jolly** via C-Altacura ☎81446
rm58 ⤺53 **P** Lift ☽ sB ⤺48000
dB ⤺78000

RAGUSA
Ragusa (☎0932)

🏠CAI via R-Morandi ☎24047 Cit

SIRACUSA (SYRACUSE)
Siracusa (☎0931)

★ ★ ★**Grand Villa Politi** via M-P-
Laudlen 3 ☎32100 tx970205

⤺98 **P** Lift ☽ 🏊 Pool sea

☆ ☆ ☆**AGIP** viale Teracati 30–32
☎66944 tx611627

🏠76 **P** Lift ☽ dB 🏠60400

★ ★ ★**Jolly** corso Gelone 43 ☎64744
tx970108

⤺102 **P** Lift ☽ sB ⤺58000
dB ⤺89000

TAORMINA
Messina (☎0942)

★ ★ ★**Jolly** via Bagnoli Croce 75
☎23312 tx980028

⤺103 **P** Lift ☽ dB ⤺130000 Pool sea

★ ★**Villa Paradiso** via Roma 2 ☎23922
tx980062

21 Dec–Oct
rm33 ⤺28 🏠5 **P** Lift ☽
sB ⤺ 🏠31500–41000
dB ⤺ 🏠65000–82000 M23000–25000
Beach sea

At **MARRARÒ** (4.5km NE)

★ ★ ★ ★**Mazzarò Sea Palace** (SRS) via
Nazionale 16 ☎24004 tx980041
Apr–Oct
rm81 ⤺52 🏠29 🏠 **P** Lift ☽
sB ⤺ 🏠90000–129000
dB ⤺ 🏠133000–218000 M45500 Pool
Beach sea

★ ★ ★ ★**Villa Sant'Andrea** via Nazionale
Santandrea 137 ☎23125 tx980077
Apr–Oct
rm50 ⤺42 🏠8 A15rm 🏠 Beach sea
mountains

SIENA
Siena (☎0577)

★ ★ ★ ★**Jolly Excelsior** pza della Lizza
☎288448 tx573345
⤺126 **P** Lift ☽ sB⤺75000
dB ⤺122000

★ ★ ★ ★**Park** (CIGA) via Marciano 16
☎44803 tx571005
⤺69 **P** Lift ☽ sB ⤺107000–127000
dB ⤺159000–184000 t% 🏊 Pool
mountains

★ ★ ★**Palazzo Ravizza** piano dei
Mantellini 34 ☎280462

Italy

rm28 ⤺18 🏠 **P** Lift ☽

At **COLLE DI VAL D'ELSA** (22km NW)

★ ★**Arnolfo** via F-Campana 8 ☎922020
🏠28 **P** Lift ☽ sB 🏠26600 dB 🏠43450

SIRACUSA (SYRACUSE) See **SICILIA (SICILY)**

SIRMIONE
Brescia (☎030)

★ ★ ★**Florida** via Colombare ☎919018
tx300395
Mar–25 Oct
⤺28 🏠 **P** ☽ Pool lake

★ ★ ★**Grand Terme** viale Marconi 1
☎916211 tx300395
6 Apr–28 Oct
⤺57 **P** Lift sB ⤺89000
dB ⤺138000–158000 M33000 Pool lake

★ ★ ★**Sirmione** pza Castello ☎916331
tx300395
Apr–6 Nov
rm76 ⤺55 🏠16 A24rm Lift ☽
sB ⤺ 🏠46000 dB ⤺ 🏠76000 Pool lake

★ ★**Lac** via XXV Aprile 60 ☎916026
30 Mar–28 Oct
rm28 ⤺20 🏠9 A7rm **P** sB24000
sB ⤺ 🏠35000 dB42000
dB ⤺ 🏠50000–56000 M25000 lake

SORRENTO
Napoli (☎081)

★ ★ ★ ★**Excelsior Vittoria** pza Tasso 34
☎8781900 tx720368
rm125 ⤺123 🏠2 🏠 **P** Lift ☽ Pool
sea

★ ★ ★**Imperial Tramontano** via V-
Veneto 1 ☎8781940 tx710345
rm104 ⤺75 🏠29 Lift Pool Beach

★ ★ ★**Aminta Grand** via Nastro Verde 7
☎8781821
Apr–Oct
rm73 ⤺66 🏠7 🏠 Lift ☽ Pool sea

★ ★ ★**Cocumella** via Cocumella 7
☎8782933 tx720370
⤺50 **P** Lift ☽ sB ⤺50000–65000
dB ⤺90000–100000 M25000 🏊 Pool
Beach sea

★ ★ ★**Eden** via Correale 25 ☎8781909
Apr–Oct
⤺60 **P** Lift Beach sea

★ ★ ★**Grand Ambasciatori** via Califano
16 ☎8782025 tx710645
⤺105 🏠 **P** Lift ☽
sB ⤺40800–48300 dB ⤺70100–91600
M25500 Pool Beach sea

★ ★ ★**Grand Capodimonte** via del Capo
14 ☎8784076 tx710645
Apr–Oct
⤺150 **P** Lift ☽ sB ⤺40800–48300
dB ⤺65100–86600 M25500 Pool sea

SPARTAIA See **ELBA (ISOLA D')** under **PROCCHIO**

SPEZIA (LA)
La Spezia (☎1087)

★ ★ ★**Jolly** via XX Settembre 2
☎27200 tx331047
⤺110 **P** Lift ☽ sB ⤺66000
dB ⤺98000

🏠**Cozzani & Rossi** pza Caduti per La
Liberta 6 ☎25386 BL

SPOLETO
Perugia (☎0743)

☆ ☆ ☆**AGIP** Uscita per Foligno (SS3
km127) ☎49340 tx611627
🏠57 **P** Lift ☽ dB 🏠53500

SPOTORNO
Savona (☎019)

★ ★ ★**Royal** Lungomare Kennedy
☎745074 tx213867
May–10 Oct
rm90 ⤺54 🏠36 **P** Lift ☽ Beach sea

★ ★**Ligure** pza della Vittoria ☎745118
Apr–15 Oct
⤺37 **P** ☽ sea

★**Villa Teresina** via Imperia ☎745160
Apr–Sep
⤺24 🏠 **P**

STAGNO See **LIVORNO (LEGHORN)**

STORTA (LA) See **ROMA (ROME)**

STRESA
Novara (☎0323)

★ ★ ★ ★**Grand des Iles Borromées**
(CIGA) Lungolago Umberto 1ᵉʳ 63
☎30431 tx200377
⤺120 🏠 **P** Lift ☽
sB ⤺123000–158000
dB ⤺186000–226000 t% 🏊 Pool 🏌
lake

★ ★ ★**Bristol** via Nazionale del
Sempione 73 ☎32601 tx200217
15 Mar–15 Nov
rm250 ⤺200 🏠50 **P** Lift ☽
sB ⤺ 🏠49000–81000
dB ⤺ 🏠78000–127000 M24000–32000
🏊 Pool mountains lake

★ ★ ★**Regina Palace** Lungolago
Umberto 1ᵉʳ 27 ☎30171 tx200381
Apr–Nov
rm175 ⤺165 🏠10 🏠 **P** Lift ☽
sB ⤺ 🏠110580 dB ⤺ 🏠170160 🏊
Pool mountains lake

★ ★ ★**Astoria** Lungolago Umberto 1ᵉʳ 31
☎30259 tx200381
20 Mar–Oct
rm107 ⤺71 🏠36 A9rm 🏠 **P** Lift ☽
sB ⤺ 🏠59000–85000
dB ⤺ 🏠88000–110000 M28000 🏊
Pool lake

★ ★ ★**Palma** Lungolago Umberto 1ᵉʳ
☎32151 tx200541
Mar–Nov
⤺128 🏠 **P** Lift ☽ sB ⤺ 🏠68500
dB ⤺ 🏠105000 Pool

★ ★Italia & Svizzera pza Imbercadero
☎30540
15 Mar–15 Nov
rm36 ⇋11 🍴8 P Lift sB ⇋ 🛏28000
dB ⇋ 🛏44000 lake

★ ★Lido la Perla Nera pza Stazione
Funivia ☎30384 (31323 in winter)
tx200396
Apr–15 Oct
rm27 ⇋21 🍴4 P D sB32000–35000
sB ⇋🛏41000–50000 dB46000–55000
dB ⇋ 🛏62000–75000 M20000 lake

★ ★Milano & Speranza au Lac pza
Imbarcadero ☎31190 tx200381
20 Mar–Oct
rm171 ⇋145 🛏26 🍴 P Lift D
sB ⇋ 🛏35000–47000
dB ⇋ 🛏58000–76000 M23000–25000
lake

★ ★Parc via Gignous 1 ☎30335
Apr–Oct
rm38 ⇋35 A16rm🍴 Lift lake

★ ★Royal via Nazionale del Sempione
☎32777 tx200396
Apr–Oct
rm45 ⇋35 🛏10 P Lift D
sB ⇋ 🛏30000–46000
dB ⇋ 🛏50000–67000 M15000 20000
t% lake

SUSA
Torino (☎0122)
★ ★Napoleon via Mazzini 44 ☎2704
⇋37 🍴 P Lift mountains

SYRACUSE See SIRACUSA under
SICILIA (SICILY)

TAORMINA See SICILIA (SICILY)

TERRACINA
Latina (☎0773)
★ ★Palace Lungomare Matteotti 2
☎727285
rm71 ⇋19 🛏52 🍴 P Lift D
sB ⇋ 🛏2800 dB ⇋ 🛏49000 Beach sea

TIRRENIA
Pisa (☎050)
★ ★ ★Golf via dell'Edera 29 (n.rest
Oct–Apr) ☎37545
⇋85 🍴 P Lift D sB ⇋68000
dB ⇋121000 🏊 Pool Beach sea

TOLMEZZO
Udine (☎0433)
🅱Automezzi Tolmezzo via Paluzza 3
☎2151 Fia

TONALE (PASSO)
Brescia (☎0364)
★ ★Redivalle ☎91349
rm52 ⇋24 🛏25 🍴 P D mountains

TORINO (TURIN)
Torino (☎011)
★ ★ ★ ★ ★Jolly Principi di Piemonte via
P-Gobetti 15 ☎519693 tx221120
⇋107 P Lift D sB ⇋127200
dB ⇋162500

Italy

★ ★ ★ ★Jolly Ambasciatori corso V-
Emanuele 104 ☎5752 tx221296
⇋197 🍴 P Lift D sB ⇋114500
dB ⇋140600

★ ★ ★ ★Turin Palace (SRS) via Sacchi 8
☎515511 tx221411
⇋125 🍴 P Lift D sB ⇋130000
dB ⇋170000

★ ★ ★Patria via Cernaia 42 (n.rest)
☎519903
rm108 ⇋78 🛏8 🍴 Lift D

★ ★Alexandra Lungo Dora Napoli 14
(n.rest) ☎858327 tx221562
⇋50 🍴 P Lift D sB ⇋61000
dB ⇋ 🛏82000

B Koeliker via Barletta 133–135
☎353632 BL DJ RT

At SETTIMO (8km NE on Autostrade to
Ivres)
☆ ☆ ☆AGIP ☎8001855 tx611627
🛏100 dB 🛏72500

TORRE A MARE See BARI

TORRI DEL BENACO
Verona (☎045)
★ ★Continental via Gardesana, San
Felice (2.5km N on SS249) (n.rest)
☎7225195
Apr–15 Oct
⇋ 🛏30 🍴 P Beach lake

TREMEZZO
Como (☎0344)
★ ★ ★Grand Tremezzo Grande Parco
☎40446 tx380128
Apr–Oct
rm100 ⇋80 🛏20 🍴 P Lift D
sB ⇋ 🛏57500 dB ⇋ 🛏85000 🏊 Pool
lake

★ ★Bazzoni via Regina ☎40403
Apr–Oct
⇋120 🛏10 P Lift D sB ⇋ 🛏45000
dB ⇋ 🛏75000 M16000–45000 lake

TRENTO
Trento (☎0461)
★ ★Venezia pza Duomo 45 ☎26257
rm80 ⇋70 🛏5 P Lift D
sB17000–18900 sB ⇋ 🛏23500–25900
dB31000–34800 dB ⇋ 🛏37500–40800
M12000

🅱E Franceschi via Brennero 264
☎980110 Opl Vau

At SARDAGNA (4km W)
☆ ☆ ☆AGIP via Brennero, 168 Uscita per
Bolzano (SS12) ☎981117 tx611627
🛏45 P Lift D dB 🛏65000

TREVISO
Treviso (☎0422)

★ ★ ★Continental via Roma 16
☎57216 tx311814
⇋26 🛏55 P Lift D sB ⇋ 🛏40000
dB ⇋ 🛏75000

Bobbo via della Repubblica 270 ☎62396
BL DJ RT

Sile Motori viale della Repubblica 278
☎62743 M/c BL

SOCAART viale della Repubblica 19
☎63725 M/c Frd

🅱Trevisauto viale Felissent 58 ☎63265
Opl Vau

TRIESTE
Trieste (☎040)
★ ★ ★Duchi d'Aosta (CIGA) via
dell'Orologio 2 ☎62081 tx460358
⇋52 P Lift D sB ⇋97000–107000
dB ⇋138000–149000 t%

★ ★ ★ ★Jolly corso Cavour 7 ☎7694
tx460139
⇋177 🍴 P Lift D sB ⇋85000
dB ⇋120000

☆ ☆ ☆AGIP Duino Service Area (On
Autostrada A42 4km NW via SS14)
☎208273
🛏80 P Lift D sB 🛏78000

🅱F Antonucci via Villan de Bacchino 2
☎414396 Peu

Filotecnica Giuliana via F-Severo 42–48
☎569121 BL Vlo

A Grandi viale Flavia 120 ☎817201 Fia

🅱Regina via Raffineria 6 ☎725045 M/c
P BMW Opl Vau

At GRIGNANO (8km NW)
★ ★ ★ ★Adriatico Palace ☎224241
tx460449
20 Mar–20 Oct
rm102 ⇋72 🛏30 🍴 P Lift D 🏊
Pool Beach sea

TURIN See TORINO

UDINE
Udine (☎0432)
★ ★Astoria Italia pza XX Settembre 24
☎207091 tx450120
⇋80 🍴 P Lift D sB ⇋60900
dB ⇋103900

★ ★Cristallo piazzale G-d'Annunzio
43 ☎205951
⇋81 🍴 P Lift D

Autofriuiana viale Europa Unita 33
☎266330 P BL

🅱Edera via della Cisterna 18 ☎204422
Chy Sim

🅱Furgiuele & Baidelli viale Venezia 383
☎32168 P Frd

🅱Nord viale L-da-Vinci ☎55669 Ren

VALSOLDA
Como (☎0344)
At SAN MAMETE
★ ★Stella d'Italia ☎68139
10 Apr–10 Oct
⇋35 🍴 P Lift lake mountains

VARALLO
Vercelli (☎0163)

☆ ☆ ☆**AGIP** (SS299 d'Alagna – km26)
☎52447
🏢38 **P** Lift 𝄞 dB 🏢53000 mountains

VARAZZE
Savona (☎019)

★ ★**Delfino** via Colombo 48 ☎97073
rm25 ⇋22 🏢3 A14rm 🛁 **P** Lift 𝄞
Beach sea

VARESE
Varese (☎0332)

★ ★ ★**Palace** via L-Manara 11
☎312600 tx380163
Mar–Oct
rm110 ⇋55 🏢55 **P** Lift 𝄞 ☘ lake

VARIGOTTI See **FINALE LIGURE**

VENEZIA (VENICE)
Venezia (☎041)
See also **MESTRE**

No road communications in city. Vehicles
may be left in garages in piazzale Roma or at
the mainland end of the causeway or at
open parking places on the mainland
approaches. Garages will not accept
advance bookings. Transport to hotels by
waterbus, etc, for which there are fixed
charges for fares and porterage. Hotel
rooms overlooking the Grand Canal
normally have a surcharge.

★ ★ ★ ★ ★**Danieli** (CIGA) Riva degli
Schiavoni 4191 ☎26480 tx10077
⇋250 Lift 𝄞 sB ⇋199000–244000
dB ⇋293000–348000 t% sea

★ ★ ★ ★**Gritti Palace** (CIGA) campo
Santa Maria del Giglio 2467 ☎26044
tx410125
⇋101 Lift 𝄞 sB ⇋249000–299000
dB ⇋343000–388000 t% Pool ♂ ♁

★ ★ ★ ★**Europa & Regina** (CIGA) Canal
Grande-San Marco 2159 ☎700477
tx410123
⇋200 Lift 𝄞 sB ⇋133000–173000
dB ⇋203000–266000 t% ☘ Pool
Beach ♂ ♁ sea

★ ★ ★**Cavalletto** calle del Vacelletto, pza
San Marco ☎700955 tx410684
rm81 ⇋56 🏢25 Lift 𝄞
sB ⇋61000–76000
dB ⇋ 🏢88500–109000 sea

★ ★ ★**Concordia** (GT) calle Larga, San
Marco 367 ☎706866 tx411069
rm60 ⇋50 🏢10 Lift 𝄞
sB ⇋ 🏢60000–88000
dB ⇋ 🏢90000–133500

★ ★ ★**Gabrielli-Sandwirth** Riva degli
Schiavoni 4110 ☎31580 tx410228
Mar–10 Nov
rm111 ⇋90 Lift 𝄞 sB75000
sB ⇋140000 dB 110000 dB ⇋230000
M45000 sea

★ ★ **Metropole** riva degli Schiavoni
4149 ☎705044 tx410340
rm65 ⇋54 🏢11 Lift 𝄞

Italy

sB ⇋ 🏢140000 dB ⇋ 🏢230000 ☘
Pool

★ ★ ★**Saturnia & International** via XXIII
Marzo San Marco 2399 ☎708377
tx410355
rm96 ⇋56 🏢40 Lift 𝄞
sB ⇋ 🏢95000–154000
dB ⇋ 🏢140000–226000

★ ★**Flora** via XXII Marzo 2283A
☎705844 tx2283a
15 Feb–15 Nov
⇋44 Lift 𝄞 sB ⇋68000 dB ⇋103000

★ ★**Giorgione** Santa Apostoli 4587
☎25810
⇋56 Lift 𝄞 sB ⇋84000 dB ⇋125000

★ ★**Panada** (GT) calle Larga San Marco
656 ☎709088 tx410153
⇋50 Lift 𝄞 sB ⇋60000–88000
dB ⇋90000–133500 M27000

★**Basilea** S.Croce-Rio Marin 817 (n.rest)
☎718477
rm30 ⇋5 🏢24 𝄞 sB ⇋ 🏢43500
dB59000 dB ⇋ 🏢75000

VENEZIA LIDO
Venezia (☎041)

There is a car ferry service from Venice
(piazza Roma).

★ ★ ★ ★ ★**Excelsior**(CIGA) Lungomare
Marconi 41 ☎760201 tx410023
Apr–Oct
⇋245 **P** Lift 𝄞 sB ⇋224000–284000
dB ⇋318000–358000 t% ☘ Pool
Beach ♂

★ ★ ★ ★**Bains** (CIGA) Lungomare
Marconi 17 ☎765921 tx410142
Apr–Oct
⇋ 🏢270 **P** Lift 𝄞
sB ⇋ 🏢127500–157500
dB ⇋ 🏢200000–24500 t% ☘ Pool ♂

★ ★ ★**Adria-Urania & Villa Nora & Ada**
viale Dandolo 24, 27 & 29 ☎760120
tx410666
15 Apr–15 Oct
rm100 ⇋60 🏢30 A17rm **P** Lift 𝄞
sB ⇋ 🏢65000–80000 dB90000–110000
dB ⇋ 🏢110000–130000 Mfr25000
Beach

VENTIMIGLIA
Imperia (☎0184)

★ ★**Posta** via Sottoconvento 15
☎351218
5 Feb–3 Jan
rm18 ⇋3 🏢15 Lift 𝄞

🅟**G Revelli** via Nervia 2 ☎352459 BMW
Sab

VERBANIA
Novara (☎0323)

At **PALLANZA** (1km SW)

★ ★ ★**Astor** via V-Veneto 17B ☎504261
tx200644
rm52 ⇋14 🏢38 **P** Lift 𝄞 lake

★ ★**Belvedere** pza IV-Novembre 10
☎503202 tx200269
Apr–Oct
rm56 ⇋32 🏢12 A36rm **P** Lift 𝄞 lake

★ ★**San Gottardo** viale dell Magnolie 4
☎503212 tx200269
Mar–Oct
rm40 ⇋5 🏢35 **P** Lift 𝄞

VERCELLI
Vercelli (☎0161)

★ ★ ★**Viotti** via Marsala 7 (n.rest)
☎61602
rm61 ⇋28 🏢33 **P** Lift 𝄞

VERONA
Verona (☎045)

★ ★ ★ ★**Colomba d'Oro** via C-Cattaneo
10 (n.rest) ☎595300 tx480872
rm60 ⇋42 🏢18 🛁 **P** Lift 𝄞
sB ⇋ 🏢59000–72000
dB ⇋ 🏢86000–106000

★ ★ ★ ★**Due Torri** (SRS) pza
Sant'Anastasia 4 ☎595044 tx480524
rm100 ⇋50 🏢50 🛁 **P** Lift 𝄞
sB ⇋ 🏢130000 dB ⇋ 🏢200000

★ ★ ★**Accademia** via Scala 12
☎596222 tx480874
rm116 ⇋33 🏢83 🛁 **P** Lift 𝄞
sB ⇋ 🏢62800–71800
dB ⇋ 🏢85600–105600 M alc

☆ ☆ **AGIP** via Unità d'Italia 346 (SS11km
307) ☎972033 tx611627
🏢68 **P** Lift 𝄞 dB 🏢50600

★ ★ ★**San Pietro** via Santa Teresa 1
(n.rest) ☎582600 tx480523
rm58 ⇋10 🏢48 🛁 **P** Lift 𝄞
sB⇋ 🏢43000–60000
dB ⇋ 🏢67000–88000

★ ★**Capuleti** via del Pontiere 26 ☎32970
rm36 ⇋25 **P** Lift 𝄞 sB27000
sB ⇋34000 dB44000 dB ⇋55000
M14000–23000

★ ★**Italia** via G-Mameli 54 ☎918088
rm50 ⇋3 🏢47 🛁 **P** Lift 𝄞

🅟**Auto Motor** Stradone Santa Lucia 21
☎500344 Aud Por VW

🅟**SVAE** via Torricelli-Z.A.I. ☎508088
Frd

VIAREGGIO
Lucca (☎0584)

★ ★ ★ ★**Palace** via F-Gioia 2 ☎46134
tx624044
rm68 ⇋46 🏢22 Lift 🏢
sB ⇋ 🏢79000 dB ⇋ 🏢138000 sea

★ ★ ★**Plaza & de Russie** Longomare
Manin 1 (n.rest) ☎46546
⇋50 **P** Lift 𝄞 sB ⇋28500–57000
dB ⇋48500–97000 sea

★ ★**Garden** ☎44025 tx590403 →

267

rm41 ⇔38 Lift ⟩ sB25000–32200
sB ⇔30000–39800 dB ⇔45000–58850

Autosalone Lupori via Galvani 9
☎42266 **P** Cit

≋F Fazioli via Buonarroti 67 ☎42580 **P**
Opl Vau

≋Pecchia viale del Tigli 8 ☎443312 Cit

VICENZA
Vicenza (☎0444)

☆ ☆ ☆**AGIP** via degli Scoligerri, Fiera
☎564711 tx611627
🏤123 **P** Lift ⟩ dB 🏤78400

Americana viale San Lazzaro 15
☎463101 M/c Opl Vau

Sabema viale della Pace 50 ☎500348
M/c **P** BMW

VICO EQUENSE
Napoli (☎081)

★ ★**Oriente** ☎8798143 tx721051
rm72 🏛 **P** ⟩ sea

VIESTE
Foggia (☎0884)

★ ★ ★ ★**Pizzomunno Vieste Palace**
☎78741 tx810267

Italy

18 Apr–Sep
⇔ 🏤183 🏛 **P** Lift ⟩
sB ⇔ 🏤54700–71900
dB ⇔ 🏤109400–23000 M25000–45000
≋ Pool Beach δ sea

At **PUGNOCHIUSO** (22km S)

★ ★ ★**Faro** ☎79011
⇔191 **P** Lift

★ ★ ★**Ulivi** ☎79061 tx810122
🏤202 **P** Lift ≋ Pool Beach

VIETRI SUL MARE See **SALERNO**

VILLASIMUS See **SARDEGNA (ISOLA)
(SARDINIA)**

VITERBO
Viterbo (☎0761)

★ ★**Leon d'Oro** via della Cava 36
☎31012

---

rm47 ⇔39 🏛 Lift ⟩

≋Tedeschi via L-Garbini 84 ☎32109
M/c Frd

Prices are in Italian Lire

SAN MARINO (☎0541)

★ ★ ★**Grand** via Antonio Onofri 31
☎992400 tx505555
28 Mar–7 Nov
rm55 ⇔40 🏤15 🏛 **P** Lift ⟩
sB ⇔ 🏤44800 dB ⇔ 🏤63600
M14000–40000 mountains

★ ★ ★**Titano** Contrada del Collegio 21
☎991007
15 Mar–15 Nov
rm50 ⇔26 🏤24 Lift ⟩
sB ⇔ 🏤34200 dB ⇔ 🏤49400

★ ★**Excelsior** via J-Istriani ☎991163
rm24 ⇔12 🏤12 🏛 **P** Lift mountains

★**Tre Penne** via Giovanni de Simone delle
Penne ☎992437
⇔ 🏤24 Lift ⟩ dB ⇔ 🏤37500
mountains

Sirmione in Brescia

Polignano A Mare

268

LUXEMBOURG

Luxembourg, the tiny Grand Duchy only 1,000 square miles in size, offers a wide range of facilities to the visitor.

Entirely land-locked, it is bordered by three countries, Belgium, France and the German Federal Republic. One third of the country is occupied by the hills and forests of the Ardennes, while the rest is taken up by wooded farmland and, in the south-east, the rich wine-growing valley of the Moselle.

The Grand Duchy enjoys a temperate climate, the summer often extending from May to late October. The official languages are French and German, but most of the people speak Luxembourgeois as an everyday language.

Area *999 sq miles*
Location map See page 80
Population *365,500*
Local time *GMT + 1 (Summer GMT + 2)*
National flag *Horizontal tricolour of red, white and blue*

Pétrusse valley, Luxembourg city

How to get there

Luxembourg is easily approached through either Belgium or France. Luxembourg City is just over 200 miles from Oostende or Zeebrugge, about 260 miles from Boulogne, Calais or Dunkerque, and is therefore within a day's drive of the Channel coast.

Motoring regulations and general information

This information should be read in conjunction with the general content of the European ABC pages 6–27). **Note** As certain regulations and requirements are common to many countries they are covered by one entry in the ABC and the following headings represent some of the subjects dealt with in this way:
AA Agents
Crash or safety helmets
Drinking and driving
Fire extinguisher
First-aid kit
Insurance
Medical treatment
Police fines
Radio telephones/Radio transmitters
Road signs
Rear view mirror
Seat belts
Traffic lights
Tyres
Visitors' registration

Accidents
Fire, police, ambulance ☎012 – Civil Defence emergency service (*Secours d'urgence*).

There are no firm rules to adopt following an accident, however anyone requested to give assistance must do so, in most cases the recommendations under *Accidents* on page 7 are advisable.

Accommodation
A national guide to hotels, inns, restaurants, and boarding houses in the Grand Duchy can be obtained free of charge from the National Tourist Office.

Details of holiday flats and chalets are also available from this source.

Boats

When temporarily importing boats into Luxembourg, documentation, in addition to the *Customs regulations* referred to below, may be required if your route takes you through France. See *Boats* page 8 for further information.

Breakdown

The Automobile Club de Grand-Duché de Luxembourg (ACL) operates a 24-hour road assistance service throughout the whole country. The vehicles of the ACL are yellow in colour and bear a black inscription '*Automobile Club, Service Routier*'. This service should not be confused with the '*Depannage Automobile Luxembourg*' or '*DAL*' which is a commercial enterprise not connected with the AA or any other organisation. See also *Breakdown* page 8 and *Warning triangles* page 272.

British Consulate

(See also page 8)
Luxembourg 28 Boulevard Royal ☎29864.

Currency and banking hours

(See also page 11)
The unit of currency is the Luxembourg franc, divided into 100 centimes. There are no restrictions on the amount of foreign or local currency which can be taken into or out of the country, but because of the limited market for Luxembourg notes in other countries, it is advisable to change them before leaving. Belgian currency is also used in Luxembourg.

Banks are open from Monday to Friday 08.00–12.00hrs and 13.30–16.30hrs or 14.00–17.00hrs. Banks are usually closed on Saturdays.

Customs regulations

A *Customs Carnet de Passages en Douane* is required for all temporarily imported boats unless entering and leaving by water. See also *Customs regulations for European countries* page 11 for further information.

Dimensions and weight restrictions

Private cars and trailers are restricted to the following dimensions – car height: 4 metres; width: 2.50 metres; cars and trailer overall length: 12 metres; caravan weight: 75% of towing vehicle.

Driving licence

(See also page 13)
A valid British driving licence is acceptable in Luxembourg. The minimum age at which a visitor may drive a temporarily imported car or motorcycle is 17 years.

Emergency messages to tourists

(See also page 14)
Emergency messages to tourists are broadcast during the summer on the German RTL programme. These messages are transmitted on 208 metres medium wave and may be given at any time between 06.00–01.00hrs.

Horn, use of

In built-up areas it is prohibited to use the horn except to avoid an accident.

Outside built-up areas use the horn instead of the lights only, during the day, to warn of approach.

International distinguishing sign

(See also page 17)
It is compulsory for foreign-registered vehicles to display a distinctive sign at the rear of the vehicle. Failure to comply with this regulation will incur a fine of *Fr*600.

Lights

(See also page 17)
It is prohibited to drive on sidelights only. At night and also during the day when necessary, vehicles parked on a public road must have their sidelights on if the public lighting does not enable them to be seen from a sufficient distance. Vehicles equipped with a side parking light may use this instead of sidelights. Should fog or snow reduce visibility to less than 100 metres, vehicles stopped or parked outside a built-up area must be illuminated by dipped headlights or fog lamps. Two fog lamps may be used at the same time as dipped headlights but full headlights together with fog or spot lamps may not be used at the same time. At night it is compulsory to flash one's headlights before overtaking another vehicle, at places where visibility is restricted, and whenever road safety requires it. It is compulsory for *motorcyclists* to use dipped headlights during the day.

Motoring club

(See also page 18)

The **Automobile Club du Grand-Duché de Luxembourg** (ACL) has its head office at 13 Route de Longwy, Helfenterbruck/Bertrange, Luxembourg ☎311031.

ACL office hours are 08.30–12.00hrs and 13.30–18.00hrs from Monday to Friday; closed Saturday and Sunday.

Motorways
Only short sections totalling 64 km (40 miles) are at present open, but a future network of 160 km is planned.

Orange badge scheme for disabled drivers
(See also page 19)
In Luxembourg parking places reserved for disabled drivers are indicated by a parking sign (white letter on blue panel) or a parking prohibited sign (red ring and bars with blue background) both with the international disabled symbol added. However, badge holders are not permitted to exceed the parking time limit.

Overtaking
(See also page 19)
Outside built-up areas at night it is compulsory to flash one's headlights before overtaking another vehicle. During the day use the horn instead of lights.

Esch-sur-Sûre

Parking
(See also page 19)
Spending the night in a vehicle or trailer on the roadside is prohibited. In towns parking is controlled by parking discs, parking meters and persons who issue tickets. Discs are availble from the ACL, the Luxembourg Communal Administration, principal banks, petrol companies and other firms.

Discs must be displayed on the windscreen and are set at the time of parking and show when parking time expires.

Park on the right-hand side of the road in the direction of the traffic flow unless parking is prohibited on this side.

A disabled driver may obtain special concessions for parking if he/she applies to the Administration Communale or police station.

Passengers
(See also page 19)
Children under 10 are not permitted to travel in a vehicle as front seat passengers when rear seating is available.

Petrol
(See also page 20)
Credit cards A few petrol stations will accept Visa.
Duty-free petrol In addition to the petrol in the vehicle tank up to 10 litres in a can may be imported free of customs duty and tax.
Octane rating Normal (90–93) and Super (98).

Postal information
Mail Postcards *Fr*7, letters up to 20 gm *Fr*10.

Post offices There are 100 post offices in Luxembourg. Opening hours are generally from 08.00–12.00hrs and 14.00–17.00hrs Monday to Friday, but smaller offices may have different opening hours which will be listed at the entrance. The head post office in Esch-sur-Alzette opens on Saturday. In the city of Luxembourg the post office at 1 Place de la Gare provides a 24hr service and the airport post office is open from 07.00–21.30hrs.

Postcheques
(See also page 21)
Postcheques may be cashed at all post offices for any amount up to a maximum of *Fr*4,000 per cheque. Counter positions are identified by the words *Chèques* or *Mandats à encaisser*. See above for post office opening hours.

Priority
(See also *Priority including Roundabouts* page 22)
All road users must yield right of way to other road users when entering a public road, starting from the kerb or reversing.

Public holidays
Official public holidays in Luxembourg for 1985 are given below. See also *Public holidays* page 22.
January 1 (New Year's Day)
April 8 (Easter Monday)
May 1 (Labour Day)
May 16 (Ascension Day)
May 27 (Whit Monday)

June 2† (Pentecost)
June 23† (National Day)
August 15 (Assumption)
November 1 (All Saints' Day)
December 25 (Christmas Day)
December 26 (Boxing Day)
† Sunday

Roads

There is a comprehensive system of good main and secondary roads.

Shopping hours

Some shops close on Monday mornings but the usual hours of opening for *food shops* are from Monday to Saturday 08.00–12.00hrs and 14.00–18.00hrs. However, *supermarkets* open from 09.00–20.00hrs but close at 18.00hrs on Saturdays.

Speed limits

(See also page 25)
The placename indicates the beginning and end of a built-up area. The following speed limits for cars are in force if there are no special signs: built-up areas 60 kph (37 mph); main roads 90 kph (56 mph); motorways 120 kph (74 mph). All lower signposted speed limits must be adhered to.

Spiked, studded or snow tyres

(See also page 10)
Spiked tyres may be used between December and March, however they must be fitted to all four wheels and speeds must not exceed 60 kph (37 mph) on ordinary roads and 90 kph (56 mph) on motorways. A disc must be attached to the rear of the vehicle indicating "60".

Tourist information offices

(See also page 25)
The National Tourist Office in London is at 36–37 Piccadilly (entrance Swallow Street), W1V 9PA ☎01-434 2800 (recorded message service out of office hours). In Luxembourg the Office National du Tourisme (National Tourist Office), local authorities and tourist information societies) (*Syndicats d'Initiatives*) organise information offices and will be pleased to assist you with information regarding tourism.

Using the telephone

(See also page 26)
Insert coin **after** lifting receiver, dialling tone same as the UK. Use *Fr*5 coins for local calls and *Fr*5 or 20 (Lux. or Belg.) for national and international calls.
International callbox identification Roadside callboxes.
Telephone rates A telephone call to the UK costs *Fr*75 for three minutes and *Fr*25 for each additional minute.
What to dial for the Irish Republic 00 353
What to dial for the UK 00 44.

Warning triangles

The use of a warning triangle is compulsory for all vehicles except two-wheelers. The triangle must be placed on the road about 100 metres (109 yds) behind the vehicle to warn following traffic of any obstruction. See also *Warning triangles/Hazard warning lights* page 26.

Prices are in Belgian Francs
See French section for abbreviations

BEAUFORT

★ ★**Meyer (DPn)** Grand r 120 ☎86262 tx1524
Closed 16 Jan–19 Mar
rm44 ⇌28 ⋒16 ⋒ **P** Lift
sB ⇌ ⋒1000–1100 dB ⇌ ⋒1900–2100 St8%

BERDORF

★ ★**Ermitage** rte de Grundhof 44 ☎79184
3 Apr–3 Oct
rm16 ⇌11 ⋒5 ⋒ **P** sB ⇌ ⋒1170 dB ⇌ ⋒1900–1970 St8%

CLERVAUX

★ ★**Abbaye** r Principale 80 ☎91049
Apr–24 Oct & 20–30 Dec
rm50 ⋒10 ⋒ **P** Lift sB700–850
sB ⇌ ⋒1000–1150 dB 1000–1375
dB ⇌ ⋒1300–1800 St8%

★ ★**Claravallis** r de la Gare 3 ☎90134 tx3134
Closed 16 Jan–14 Mar
rm36 ⇌22 ⋒2 **P** Lift sB850
sB ⇌ ⋒1250 dB1100–1250
dB ⇌ ⋒1400–1850 St10%

★ ★**Grand Central** pl du Marché 109 ☎91105
Mar–Dec
rm26 ⇌22 ⋒1 **P** Lift sB800 dB1000
dB ⇌ ⋒1300–1600

DIEKIRCH

★**Beau Séjour** Esplanade 10–12 ☎83403
Closed 16 Oct–14 Nov
rm27 ⇌4 ⋒14 **P** Lift sB740–890
sB ⇌ ⋒850–890 dB1140–1350
dB ⇌ ⋒1290–1350 St8% ✍

DOMMELDANGE

☆ ☆ ☆**Novotel Luxembourg** rte d'Echternach (E42) ☎435643 tx1418
⇌173 **P** Lift sB ⇌2200 dB ⇌2600 ♂
Pool ⌒

ECHTERNACH

★ ★ ★**Bel Air** rte Berdorf 1 ☎729383 tx2640
Closed 13 Nov–9 Dec
⇌42 ⋒ **P** Lift sB⇌1700–2200
dB ⇌2500–3300 St8% ✍

★ ★**Commerce** pl du Marché 16 ☎72301
Mar–15 Nov & 20 Dec–1 Jan
rm56 ⇌11 ⋒20 ⋒ **P** Lift sB700
dB1050 dB ⇌ ⋒1180–1400 St8%

★ ★**Parc** rue de l'Hôpital 9 ☎729481
25 Mar–15 Nov
rm32 ⇌24 ⋒4 **P** sB800–900
sB ⇌ ⋒1200–1500 dB1200–1400
dB ⇌ ⋒1600–2000 St8% Pool

★**Universel & Cheval Blanc** r de Luxembourg 40 ☎729991
Apr–Oct
rm35 ⇌ ⋒30 **P** Lift sB900–1100
sB ⇌ ⋒1100 dB1200
dB ⇌ ⋒1500–1600 St8%

EHNEN

★★**Simmer** rte du Vin 117 ☎76030
Closed 16 Jan–14 Mar
rm22 ⇌13 🏛4 🏛 **P** sB1050
sB ⇌ 🏠1450 dB1550
dB ⇌ 🏠1850–1950

★**Moselle** rte du Vin 131 ☎76022
17 Jan–1 Dec
rm18 ⇌7 🏠6 🏛 **P** Lift sB800
sB ⇌ 🏠1500 dB1200
dB ⇌ 🏠1800–2000 St8%

ESCH·SUR·ALZETTE

Muller Esch bd Kennedy 122–4
☎544844 Opl

ETTELBRUCK

⏀**Grand Garage P Wengler** av des Alliés
36 ☎82157 Frd

FINDEL See **LUXEMBOURG**

GREVENMACHER

★**Poste** 26 r de Tréves (n.rest) ☎75136
rm12 ⇌1 🏛 **P** sB620–650
dB870–920 dB ⇌1200–1220 St8%

GRUNDHOF

★★**Brimer** ☎862551 tx1308
15 Feb–10 Nov
⇌23 **P** Lift sB ⇌ 🏠1350
dB ⇌ 🏠1850 St8%

★**Ferring** rte Beaufort 4 ☎86015
25 Mar–15 Nov
rm27 ⇌13 🏠11 🏛 **P** Lift
sB ⇌ 🏠1100 dB 1200
dB ⇌ 🏠1400–1700 St8%

HALLER

★★**Hallerbach** r des Romains 2
☎86151
Closed 11 Jan–18 Mar
⇌18 **P** Lift sB 1150–1250
dB ⇌1650–2300 St8% 🌭 Pool

HEINERSCHEID

★**Wagener** r de Stavelot 29 ☎98503
rm10 🏛 **P** sB410 dB710 Pool

KAUTENBACH

★**Hatz** (**DPn**) ☎96561

Luxembourg

Closed 18 Nov–16 Dec
rm12 🏠6 **P**

KIRCHBERG See **LUXEMBOURG**

LAROCHETTE

★★**Château** (**DPn**) r de Medernach 1
☎87009
Closed 6–31 Jan
rm45 ⇌18 🏠3 **P** sB600–650
sB ⇌ 🏠950–1200 dB950–1050
dB ⇌ 🏠1300–1800 St8%

★★**Poste** pl Bleiche 11 ☎87006
Closed Jan
rm27 ⇌16 🏠2 **P** sB1120
sB ⇌ 🏠1400 dB1425 dB ⇌ 🏠1925
St8%

LUXEMBOURG

★★★★**Kons** pl de la Gare 24
☎486021 tx2306
rm141 ⇌59 🏠56 Lift sB1050–1250
sB ⇌ 🏠1650–1850 dB ⇌ 🏠2900 St8%

★★★**Central Molitor** (GT) av de la
Liberté 28 ☎489911 tx2613
⇌36 🏛 Lift sB ⇌ 🏠1900 dB ⇌2500

★★★**Dauphin** av de la Gare 42
☎488282
rm37 ⇌20 🏠17 Lift sB880–1270
sB ⇌ 🏠1270–1790 dB1140–1530
dB ⇌ 🏠1530–1980 St8%

★**Français** pl d'Armes 14 ☎23009
rm26 🏠23 Lift sB1400–1600
dB 🏠20000

⏀**Grand Garage de la Pétrusse** r des
Jardiniers 13–15 ☎442324 BL DJ RR RT

Hubert Fréres r d'Esch 106 ☎442555
Lnc

⏀**P Lentz** rte d'Arlon 257 ☎444545 Dat

M Losch 88 rte de Thionville ☎488121
Aud Por VW

At **FINDEL** (8km NW)

★★★★**Aerogolf Sheraton** rte de
Tréves ☎34571 tx2662
⇌150 **P** Lift 🌙 sB ⇌2635–3185
dB ⇌3420–4170 M545–2000

At **KIRCHBERG**

☆☆☆☆**Holiday Inn** European Centre
☎435051 tx2751
⇌260 **P** Lift sB ⇌2800–3200
dB ⇌3600–4400 M alc Pool

At **STRASSEN** (2km W on N9)

★★**Dany** rte d'Arlon 72 ☎318062
rm17 ⇌6 🏠11 🏛 **P**
dB ⇌ 🏠1300–1700

MERSCH

★7 **Châteaux** d'Arlon 3 ☎32255
May–Oct
rm23 🏠6

★**Marisca** (**DPn**) pl de l'Étoile 1 ☎328456
rm20 ⇌2 🏠5 🏛 **P** sB800–900
sB ⇌ 🏠1100–1300 dB1200–1400
dB ⇌ 🏠1700–1900 St5%

MONDORF-LES-BAINS

★★★**Grand Chef** av des Bains 36
☎68122 tx1840
23 Apr–20 Oct
rm46 ⇌27 🏠14 🏛 **P** Lift
sB ⇌ 🏠1105–1245 dB ⇌ 🏠1605–1905

STRASSEN See **LUXEMBOURG**

VIANDEN

★★**Collette** Grand 68–70 ☎84004
12 Apr–Oct
rm30 ⇌5 🏠9 🏛 **P** sB900–1000
sB ⇌ 🏠1100–1400 dB1400–1600
dBL ⇌ 🏠2000–2300

★★**Heintz** Grande r 55 ☎84155
28 Mar–4 Nov
rm30 ⇌25 🏛 **P** Lift sB900
sB ⇌1200–1300 dB1200–1500
dB ⇌1600–1900

★**Oranienburg** Grand r 16 ☎84153
Closed Jan–14 Feb
rm42 ⇌20 🏠13 🏛 sB650
sB ⇌ 🏠750 dB1000 dB ⇌ 🏠1300
St5%

NETHERLANDS

The Netherlands, large areas of which have been won from the sea, is bordered by two countries, Belgium and the German Federal Republic. One fifth of this flat, level country criss-crossed by rivers and canals, lies below sea-level. The areas reclaimed from the sea, known as polders, are extremely fertile. The landscape is broken up by the forests of Arnhem, the bulb fields, for which the country is so famous, in the west, the lakes in the central and northern areas, and the coastal dunes which are the most impressive in Europe.

The climate is generally mild and tends to be damp. The summers are moderate with changeable weather and are seldom excessively hot. The language, Netherlandish or Dutch, is fairly gutteral and closely allied to the low German dialect. One form of the Dutch language is spoken in the northern districts of Belgium and is known as Flemish. Other dialect forms exist throughout the Netherlands.

Area *15,900 sq miles*
Population *14,340,000*
Local time *GMT + 1*
(Summer GMT + 2)

National flag *Horizontal tricolour of red, white and blue*

How to get there

There are direct ferry services to the Netherlands. Services operate from Harwich to the Hook of Holland, Hull to Rotterdam (Europoort) and Sheerness to Vlissingen (Flushing); the sea journey can take between 7 and 14hrs depending on the port of departure. Alternatively one of the short Channel crossings can be used, and the Netherlands can be easily reached by driving through France and Belgium. The distance from Calais to Den Haag is just 210 miles and is within a day's drive.

Motoring regulations and general information

This information should be read in conjunction with the general content of the European ABC (pages 6–27). **Note** As certain regulations and requirements are common to many countries they are covered by one entry in the ABC and the following headings represent some of the subjects dealt with in this way:
AA Agents
Crash or safety helmets
Customs regulations for European countries
Drinking and driving
Fire extinguisher
First-aid kit
Insurance
Medical treatment
Overtaking
Police fines
Radio telephones/Radio transmitters
Rear view mirror
Seat belts
Traffic lights
Tyres
Visitors' registration

A land of windmills and canals

Accidents

Police and **ambulance** Amsterdam and Den Haag ☎222222, Rotterdam ☎141414; **Fire** Amsterdam ☎212121, Den Haag ☎222333, Rotterdam ☎292929. Numbers for other towns are in the front of the local telephone directories.

If necessary, contact the State Police Emergency Centre ☎(03438)14321. See also *Accidents* page 7.

In the event of a serious or complicated accident, especially when personal injury has been sustained, the police should be called before the vehicles are removed.

Accommodation

The official hotel guide includes details of most hotels in the Netherlands. Information on other types of accommodation such as guest houses, furnished rooms, and bungalows can be obtained from tourist information offices (VVV).

Hotels are officially classified and the category is exhibited outside each. Room prices must by law be indicated in hotel receptions and in each bedroom but they are not subject to official control. The service charge amounts to 15%, and it is usual for this to be included in the charges as well as the value added tax.

The National Reservation Centre will secure accommodation free of charge. Application may be made direct, by post, telephone or telex to NRC Amsterdam, PO Box 3387, 1001 AD Amsterdam ☎(020)211211 (if calling this number from the UK refer to your *Telephone Dialling Codes* booklet) or telex 15754. For those already in the Netherlands the VVV offices will book a room for a small charge.

Boats

A Helmsman's Certificate of Competence is recommended for the Netherlands. See page 8 for further information about this and boat documentation.

Breakdown

If your car breaks down, try to move it to the verge of the road so that it obstructs the traffic flow as little as possible, and place a warning triangle behind the vehicle to warn following traffic of the obstruction.

The Royal Dutch Touring Club (ANWB) maintains a 24hr road patrol service (Wegenwacht) which operates throughout the country. See also *Breakdown* page 8 and *Warning triangles* page 279.

British Consulate

(See also page 8)
1075 AE Amsterdam Koningslaan 44 ☎764343.

Currency and banking hours

(See also page 11)
The unit of currency is the gulden (*Fl*), which is also known as the guilder and is divided into 100 cents. There are no restrictions limiting the import of currency. All imported currency may be freely exported, as well as any currency exchanged in, or drawn on an account established in, the Netherlands.

Banks are open from Monday to Friday 09.00–15.00hrs and closed on Saturday. At all ANWB offices, money can be exchanged from Monday to Friday 08.45–16.45hrs, and on Saturdays 08.45–12.00hrs; there are also exchange offices at the principal railway stations (eg Amsterdam, Arnhem, Eindhoven, Den Haag, Hoek van Holland, Maastricht, Rosendaal, Rotterdam, Utrecht and Venlo).

Dimensions and weight restrictions

Private cars are restricted to the following dimensions – Cars height: 4 metres; width: 2.20 metres on 'B' roads, 2.50 metres on 'A' roads; cars and trailers: overall length 18 metres. Maximum weight for caravan/luggage trailers without brakes 750 kg or 75% of weight of towing vehicle; with brakes 100% of weight of towing vehicle.

Driving licence

(See also page 13)
A valid British driving licence is acceptable in the Netherlands. The minimum age at which a visitor may drive a temporarily imported car or motorcycle is 18 years.

Emergency messages to tourists

(See also page 14)
Emergency messages to tourists are broadcast daily on Dutch radio.

Radio Hilversum 1 transmitting on 298 metres medium wave broadcasts these messages in Dutch, German and English as necessary at 17.55hrs on Sunday throughout the year.

Emergency messages are also broadcast in Dutch by a variety of regional local radio stations.

Firearms

The Dutch laws concerning the possession of firearms are the most stringent in Europe. Any person crossing the frontier with any type of firearm will be arrested. The law applies also to any object which, on superficial inspection, shows any resemblance to real firearms (eg plastic imitations etc). if you wish to carry firearms, real or imitation, of any description into the Netherlands, seek the advice of the Netherlands Consulate.

International distinguishing sign

(See also page 17)
It is compulsory for foreign registered vehicles to display a distinctive sign at the rear of the vehicle. Failure to comply with this regulation will incur a fine of *Fl* 55.00.

NORTH

SEA

Groningen *A7*
Leeuwarden *N7*
Eernewoude *A7* Haren
Drachten Veendam
De Koog
Sneek Assen
A7
Den Helder Beetsterzwaag
Heerenveen
N99 Dwingeloo Emmen
N9 Giethoorn
Bergen Enkhuizen Emmeloord Hoogeveen
Hoorn
Bergen-aan-Zee Alkmaar Lelystad Ommen
Heiloo
Egmond-aan-Zee Edam Dronten Kampen
Beverwijk Zwolle
Bloemendaal Zaandam Volendam Raalte Nijverdal Ootmarsum
Overveen Almelo
Zandvoort Haarlem Amsterdam Haderwijk Deventer Hengelo Oldenzaal
Heemstede Vierhouten Hoften Delden De Lutte
Noordwijk-aan-Zee Sassenheim Laren Leuvenum Apeldoorn Enschede
Katwijk Bussum Baarn Lochem Boekelo
Aalsmeer Hilversum Amersfoort Zutphen Warnsveld
Wassenaar Leiden Woerden Leusden Lunteren Rozendaal
Boskoop Ede
DEN HAAG Zoetermeer *A12* Zeist Doetinchem
Delft Utrecht Maarsbergen *A12*
Gouda Scherpenzeel Arnhem Zeddam
Rotterdam Wageningen
Schiedam Heusum Oosterbeek
Papendrecht Nijmegen
Noordgouwe Gorinchem Oss Berg-en-Dal
Middelharnis Dordrecht Groesbeek
Zierikzee *N59* Mook-en-Middelaar
Domburg S-Hertogenbosch
Veere Venray
Goes Roosendaal Breda Oisterwijk
Middelburg Bergen-op- Arcen en Velden
Vlissingen Zoom Tilburg Helmond
Breskens Hoogerheide Eindhoven
Cadzand Venlo
Oostburg Terneuzen Tegelen
Sluis
Roermond

Born

Beek Heerlen
Maastrich Valkenburg
Epen

NL

D

B

For key to country identification-see page 52

Lights
(See also page 17)
Driving on sidelights only is prohibited. Dipped headlights must be used at all times in built-up areas. In fog or falling snow, fog lamps may be used in pairs in conjunction with sidelights only. Headlights should be flashed as a warning of approach at night provided that they do not inconvenience other traffic. All vehicles parked on a public road must have their sidelights on if not within 30 metres (33 yds) of a street lamp.

Motoring club
(See also page 18)

 The **Koninklijke Nederlandse Toeristenbond** (ANWB) has its headquarters at Wassenaarseweg 220, Den Haag, and offices in numerous provincial towns. They will assist motoring tourists generally and supply road and touring information. Offices are usually open between 08.45 and 16.45 hrs Monday to Friday, and 08.45 to 12.00 hrs on Saturdays. Traffic information can be obtained from the ANWB by phoning (070)313131 (24 hrs service).

Motorways
There is a network of Motorways (*Autosnelweg*) carrying most inter-city and long-distance traffic.

Orange badge scheme for disabled drivers
(See also page 19)
In the Netherlands badge holders may:
a park in special car parks set aside for the handicapped where there is no time limit;
b park for an indefinite period in blue zones;
c park for an indefinite period where parking sign (white letter on blue panel with an additional panel stating parking times) is displayed;
d park for a maximum of two hours where parking prohibited (red ring and bars on blue background) or alternative parking (red ring and bars on blue background with white upright 'line' symbol) signs appear. A handicapped person's parking disc must be used. However, this concession does not apply when other parking facilities are to be found within a reasonable distance.

Parking
(See also page 19)
You can stop provided that you keep to the extreme right of the road and do not interfere with other traffic. You are allowed to stop to let passengers in and out at bus stops. Parking meters and/or parking discs are used in many towns. Discs can be obtained from police stations and must be displayed on the windscreen. They must be set at the time of parking and show when parking time lapses according to the limit in the area concerned. Failure to observe zonal regulations could result in a fine or the vehicle being towed away.

Spending the night in a vehicle or trailer on the roadside is **not** permitted.

The Begijnhof in Amsterdam

Passengers
(See also page 19)
Children under 12 are not permitted to travel in a vehicle as front seat passengers with the exception of children over 4 using a hip safety belt and children under 4 a safety seat of approved design.

Petrol
(See also page 20)
Credit cards The use of credit cards to obtain petrol is not available to visiting motorists.
Duty-free petrol In addition to the petrol in the vehicle tank up to 10 litres in a can may be imported free of customs duty and tax.
Octane rating Normal Benzine (90–93) and Super Benzine (98–100).

Postal information
Mail Postcards *Fl* 0.60, letters up to 20 gm *Fl* 0.70.
Post offices There are 2,600 post offices in the Netherlands. Opening hours of main post offices are from 08.30–19.00hrs Monday to Friday and 09.00–12.00hrs Saturday. Smaller offices are open from 08.30–17.00hrs Monday to Friday.

Postcheques
(See also page 21)
Postcheques may be cashed at all post offices for any amount up to a maximum of *Fl* 200 per cheque. Counter positions are identified by the words *Alle Lokethandelingen* or *Post-giro/rijks-postspaarbank*. See above for post office opening hours.

Priority
(See also *Priority including Roundabouts* page 22)
Regulations in the Netherlands take account of the very large numbers of cyclists for whom special tracks are provided on a number of roads. Motor vehicles generally have priority over this slower moving traffic except when controlled by the appropriate road signs. However, cyclists proceeding straight ahead at intersections have priority over all turning traffic. Visitors should be particularly alert.

Public holidays
Official public holidays in the Netherlands for 1985 are given below. See also *Public holidays* page 22.
January 1 (New Year's Day)
April 8 (Easter Monday)
April 30 (HM Queen Beatrix's Official Birthday)
May 5† (Liberation Day)
May 16 (Ascension Day)
May 27 (Whit Monday)
December 25 (Christmas Day)
December 26 (Boxing Day)
†Sunday

Religious services
(See also page 23)
The Intercontinental Church Society welcomes visitors from any denomination to English language services in the following centres:
1011 HW Amsterdam The Revd Brian Eaves, Christ Church, Groenburgwal 42 ☎248877. *2588 HA Den Haag* The Revd Canon Alan Lindsay, 2 Riouwstraat ☎555359. *3024 Rotterdam* The Revd Canon John Taylor, 133 Pieter de Hoochweg ☎765025. *Utrecht* The Revd Douglas Beukes, Holy Trinity Church, Van Hogendorpstraat 26 ☎513424.

Roads
Main roads usually have only two lanes but they are well surfaced. The best way to see the countryside is to tour along minor roads, often alongside canals.

Road signs
(See also page 23)
Signposting is good; in some places there are special by-way tours signposted by the ANWB. In residential areas the sign *'woonerven'* indicates that bumps (silent policemen) have been installed across the roads to oblige drivers to reduce speed.

Shopping hours
Stores Monday 13.00–18.00hrs, Tuesday –Friday 09.00–18.00hrs (17.00 on Saturday); *Food shops* 08.30–18.00hrs (17.00 Saturday).

Most *food shops* close for one half day per week. This varies according to location.

Speed limits
(See also page 25)
The placename indicates the beginning and end of a built-up area. The following speed limits for cars are in force if there are no special signs. Built-up areas 50 kph (31 mph). Outside built-up areas it is 100 kph (62 mph) on motorways and 80 kph (49 mph) on other roads. Car/trailer combinations are limited to 80 kph (49 mph).

Spiked, studded or snow tyres
(See also page 10)
Although residents are not permitted to use *spiked tyres*, visitors may do so provided that they do not exceed 80 kph (49 mph), and only if spikes are allowed in their home country.

Toll bridges and tunnels
Toll bridges: **Zeeland** (Oosterschelde) bridge; car *Fl*3.50 car/caravan *Fl*5.00 Waalbrug (near Tiel); car *Fl*2.50 car/caravan *Fl*3.00.

Toll tunnels: **Kiltunnel** ('s–Gravendeel-Dordrecht); car *Fl*3.50 car/caravan *Fl*10.

Tourist information offices
(See also page 25)

The Netherlands National Tourist Office (NBT), Savory & Moore House, 2nd floor, 143 New Bond Street (no sign outside), London W1Y 0QS ☎01-499 9367/8/9 will be pleased to assist you with any information regarding tourism and has branch offices (VVV) in all towns and large villages in the Netherlands. They can be recognised by the sign illustrated on the left (blue with white lettering).

There are three types of these branch offices: Travel Offices giving detailed information about the whole of the Netherlands; Information Offices giving general information about the Netherlands and detailed information about their own region, and Local Information Offices giving detailed information about that locality.

Using the telephone
(See also page 26)
Insert coin **after** lifting receiver (instructions in English in all public callboxes). When making calls to subscribers within the Netherlands precede number with relevant area code (shown in parentheses against town entry in gazetteer). Use 25 cent coin for local calls and *FI2.50* coins for national and international calls.
International callbox identification All callboxes.
Telephone rates The cost of a call to the UK is *FI0.95* for each minute. Local calls cost 25 cents. The cheap rate operates from 18.00–07.00hrs on Saturday and Sunday, the charge being *FI0.70* per minute.
What to dial for the Irish Republic 09 *353.
What to dial for the UK 09 *44.
*Wait for second dialling tone.

Warning triangles
The use of a warning triangle is compulsory for all vehicles except two-wheelers. The triangle must be used to warn following traffic of any obstruction and also if a parked vehicle is insufficiently illuminated either by its own or street lighting. See also *Warning triangles/Hazard warning lights* page 26.

Prices are in Dutch Florins (Guiden or Guilder)
Abbreviations:
pl   plein
st   straat

AALSMEER
Noord-Holland (☎02977)

★★**Schouwsehof** Raadhuispl 16 ☎25551
rm11 ⇌1 ffl10

⑧⑩**Boom** Oosteindweweg 220 ☎25667
P BL

ALKMAAR
Noord-Holland (☎072)

☆ ☆**Alkmaar** (Comfort) Arcadialaan 2 ☎120744 tx57658
rm90 ⇌6 ffl84 **P** ⅅ sB ⇌ ffl56
dB ⇌ ffl96 M17–60

⑧⑩**Klaver** Helderseweg 29–30 ☎127033
P BL

⑧⑩**N Schmidt** Nassaupl 1 ☎113545 Frd

ALMELO
Overijssel (☎05490)

☆ ☆**Postiljon** (BW) Aalderinkssingel 2 ☎26655 tx44817
rm50 ⇌4 ffl46 **P** dB ⇌ ffl90–120

⑧⑩**Autobedrijf Almelo** Wierdensestr 107 ☎12442 M/c Frd

⑧⑩**Konink** H-R-Holst Laan 1 ☎11064
Aud Por VW

AMERSFOORT
Utrecht (☎033)

★★★**Witte** Utrechtseweg 2 ☎14142
rm17 ⇌10 ffl5 **P** sB52 sB ⇌ ffl75
dB90 dB ⇌ ffl105

★★**Berg** (GT) Utrechtseweg 225 ☎620444 tx79213
rm52 ⇌38 ffl14 ⚙ **P** Lift
sB ⇌ ffl87–99 dB ⇌ ffl127–168

⑧⑩**Stam Amersfoort** Kapelweg 12 ☎635104 Ren

AMSTERDAM
Noord-Holland (☎020)
See plan on page 280

★★★★**Amstel** (Intercont) Prof-Tulppl 1 ☎226060 tx11004 Plan **1**
⇌114 ⚙ **P** Lift sB ⇌350
dB ⇌371–477

★★★★**Amsterdam Hilton**
Apollolaan 138–140 ☎780780 tx11025
Plan **2**
⇌264 **P** Lift

★★★★★**Apollo** (THF) Apollolaan 2 ☎735922 tx14084 Plan **3**
⇌229 **P** Lift sB ⇌215–265
dB ⇌250–295

★★★★★**Europe** (ETAP) Nieuwe Doelenstr 2–4 ☎234836 tx12081 Plan **4**
rm82 ⇌78 ffl4 Lift ⅅ
sB ⇌ ffl213–313 dB ⇌ ffl290–390 M65

★★★★**American** (Forum)
Leidsekade 97 ☎245322 tx11379 Plan **5**
rm185 ⇌180 ffl5 Lift sB ⇌ ffl fr156
dB ⇌ ffl fr225

★★★**Caransa** (Crest **See page 51**)
Rembrandtspl 19 ☎229455 tx13342
Plan **6**
⇌66 Lift ⅅ sB ⇌178 dB 242

★★★**Carlton** (Crest **See page 51**)
Vijzelstr 2–18 (n.rest) ☎222266 tx11670
Plan **7**
⇌156 **P** Lift ⅅ sB ⇌178 dB ⇌242

☆ ☆ ☆**Crest** (**See page 51**) de Boelelaan 2, Europa Boulevard ☎429855 tx13647 Plan **8**
⇌260 **P** Lift ⅅ sB ⇌191 dB ⇌242

★★★★**Doelen** (Crest **See page 51**)
Nieuwe Doelenstr 24 ☎220722 tx14399
Plan **9**
rm85 ⇌82 ffl3 **P** Lift ⅅ sB ⇌ ffl178
dB ⇌ ffl249

★★★**Krasnapolsky** (SRS) Dam 9 ☎5549111 tx2262 Plan **10**
rm283 ⇌230 ffl18 ⚙ dB240 Lift
sB ⇌ ffl190 dB ⇌ ffl320

★★★★**Memphis** (Comfort) de Lairessestr 87 ☎733141 tx12450 Not on plan

⇌80 **P** Lift ⅅ sB ⇌152 dB ⇌217
M25

★★★**Park** (Comfort)
Stadhouderskade 25–29 ☎730961
tx11999 Plan **10A**
⇌184 ⚙ **P** Lift ⅅ sB ⇌147
dB ⇌207 M25

★★★**Port van Cleve** (ETAP) N.Z.
Voorburgwal 178 ☎244860 tx13129
Plan **11**
⇌110 Lift sB ⇌121–132
dB ⇌143–224 M40

★★★**Pulitzer** (GT) Prinsengracht 315–331 ☎28333 tx16508 Plan **12**
⇌194 Lift sB ⇌195 dB ⇌240

★★★**Victoria** (Forum) Damrak 1–6 ☎234255 tx16625 Plan **12A**
⇌160 Lift ⅅ sB ⇌164 dB ⇌236

★★★**Apollofirst** Apollolaan 123–125 ☎730333 tx13446 Plan **13**
rm33 ⇌31 Lift sB ⇌147 dB ⇌155

★★★**Centraal** (GT) Stadhouderskade 7 ☎185765 tx12601 Plan **14**
⇌116 Lift sB ⇌136 dB ⇌198 M alc

★★★**Delphi** Apollolaan 101–105 ☎795152 tx16699 Plan **15**
⇌50 Lift sB ⇌85–108 dB ⇌110–150

☆ ☆ ☆**Euromotel E9** (ETAP)
J Muyskenweg 10 ☎658181 tx13382
Plan **16**
rm140 ffl128 **P** sB78 sB ffl83 dB ffl125

☆ ☆ ☆**Euromotel B10** (ETAP) Oude Haagseweg 20 ☎179005 tx15524
Plan **17**
⇌157 **P** Lift sB ⇌100 dB ⇌133 M22

★★★**Jan Luyken** Jan Luykenstr 58 ☎764111 tx16254 Plan **17A**
rm63 ⇌48 ffl15 Lift sB ⇌ ffl110–140
dB ⇌ ffl130–170 Mfr20

☆ ☆ ☆**Novotel** Europa Boulevard 10 ☎5411123 tx13375 Plan **18**
⇌600 **P** Lift ⅅ sB 165–175
dB ⇌200–215 Mfr25

279

★★★**Rembrandt** (Crest **See page 51**)
Herengracht 255 (n.rest) ☎221727
tx15424 Plan **18A**
⇌111 Lift 𝄞 sB ⇌169 dB ⇌215

★★★**Schiller** (Crest **See page 51**)
Rembrandtspl 26–36 ☎231660 tx14058
Plan **18B**
⇌🍴97 **P** Lift 𝄞 sB ⇌🍴178
dB ⇌ 🍴242

★★**Ams Hotel Terdam** (BW)
Tesselschadestr 23–29 ☎733918
tx1275 Plan **19**
rm61 ⇌18 🍴25 Lift

★★**Atlanta** Rembrandtspl 8–10 (n.rest)
☎253585 tx15528 Plan **19A**
rm30 ⇌8 🍴9 sB55 sB ⇌🍴95 dB80
dB ⇌🍴120

★★**Cordial** Rokin 62 ☎235574 tx15621
Plan **20**
🍴44 Lift sB 🍴93 dB 🍴78–120

★★**Hoksbergen** Singel 30 ☎266043
Not on plan
🍴14 dB 🍴60–80 dB 🍴90–120

★★**Piet Hein** Vossiusstr 53 ☎628375
tx16443 Plan **20A**
rm31 ⇌1 🍴22 sB58 sB 🍴88 dB98
dB 🍴128

★★**Roode Leeuw** Damrak 93–94
☎240396 Plan**21**
rm85 ⇌54 🍴3 Lift sB68 sB ⇌ 🍴82
dB100 dB ⇌ 🍴136

AMSTERDAM		
1	★★★★★ Amstel	15
2	★★★★★ Amsterdam Hilton	16
3	★★★★★ Apollo	17
4	★★★★★ Europe	17A
5	★★★★★ American	18
6	★★★★★ Caransa	18A
7	★★★★ Carlton	18B
8	☆☆☆☆ Crest	19
9	★★★★ Doelen	19A
10	★★★★ Krasnapolsky	20
10A	★★★★ Park	20A
11	★★★★ Port van Cleve	21
12	★★★★ Pulitzer	21A
12A	★★ Victoria	22
13	★★★★ Apollofirst	23
14	★★★★ Centraal	23A
		24

★★★ Delphi	15
☆☆☆ Euromotel E9	16
☆☆☆ Euromotel E10	17
☆☆☆ Jan Luyken	17A
★★★ Novotel	18
★★★ Rembrandt	18A
★★★ Schiller	18B
★★ Ams Hotel Terdam	19
★★ Atlanta	19A
★★ Cordial	20
★★ Piet Hein	20A
★★ Roode Leeuw	21
★ Sander	21A
★ Amstel	22
★ Hemonyhof	23
★ Sphinx	23A
★ Leydsche Hof	24

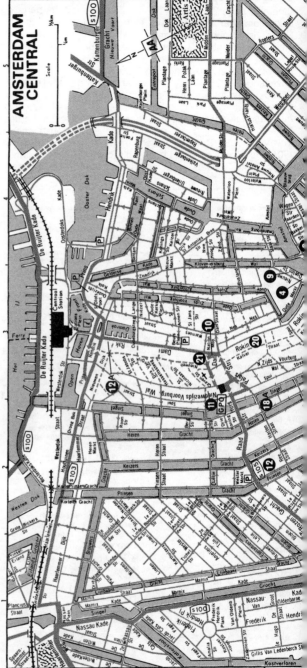

AMSTERDAM
CENTRAL

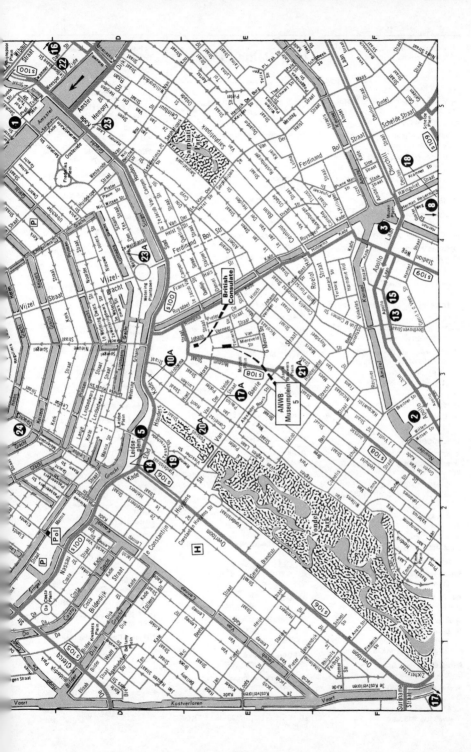

★★Sander J-Obrechstr 69 (n.rest)
☎735429 tx18456 Plan **21A**
Mar-Nov
▥15 **P** sB ⇔ ▥80-95
dB ⇔ ▥90-125

★Amstel Weesperzijde 28 ☎946407
Plan **22**
rm16 sB40 dB66-99

★Asterisk de Texstr 14-16 (n.rest)
☎262396 Not on plan
rm19 ⇔4 ▥9 sB42 sB ⇔ ▥55 dB65
dB ⇔ ▥115

★Hemonyhof Hrmonystr 7 ☎714241
Plan **23**
rm14

★Leydsche Hof Leidsegracht 14
☎232148 Plan **24**
rm12 ▥5 sB39 dB68 dB ▥78

★Sphinx Weteringschans 82 ☎273680
Plan **23A**
rm17 ⇔2 ▥6

⋈Asmoco J-Rebelstr 26 ☎101949 **P**
BMW

⋈J C Doorn Dorpstr 74 ☎02908 Chy
Sab Sim

AMSTERDAM AIRPORT
At **SCHIPHOL** (10km SW)

☆ ☆ ☆ ☆Sheraton Kruisweg 495
☎(02503)15851 tx41646 Not on plan
⇔167 **P** Lift ♪ sB ⇔201-216
dB ⇔247-307 Mfr35

☆ ☆Ibis Schipholweg 181
☎(02968)1234 tx16491 Not on plan
⇔ ▥392 **P** Lift ♪ sB ⇔ ▥114
dB ⇔ ▥145

APELDOORN
Gelderland (☎055)

★ ★ ★Bloemink (ETAP) Loolaan 56
☎214141 tx49253
rm90 ⇔68 ▥16 **P** Lift sB39-55
sB ⇔ ▥52-256 dB65 dB ⇔ ▥91-266
Mfr35 Pool

★ ★ ★Keizerskroon (GT) Koningstr 7
☎217744 tx49221
rm67 ⇔61 ▥6 **P** Lift sB ⇔ ▥145
dB ⇔ ▥170-235 M40 & alc Pool

⋈Bakker Gazellestr 21 ☎214208 **P** Ren

⋈Nefkens-Apeldoorn Wagenhakershoek
2/Edisonlaan 270 ☎414222 Peu

ARCEN-EN-VELDEN
Limburg (☎04703)

★Maas Schans 18 ☎1556
15 Mar-15 Dec
rm15 ⇔4 ▥9 ⋒ **P** sB40 sB ⇔ ▥75
dB100 dB ⇔ ▥125 M40 & alc Pool

ARNHEM
Gelderland (☎085)

★ ★ ★Haarhuis (BW) Stationspl 1
☎427441 tx45357
rm96 ⇔54 ▥42 **P** Lift sB ⇔ ▥75-85
dB ⇔ ▥102 M15 & alc

Netherlands

☆ ☆ ☆Postiljon (BW) Europaweg 25
☎453741 tx45028 rm30 ▥28 **P**
db ▥102

★ ★Leeren Doedel Amsterdamseweg
467 ☎332344
rm11 ⇔3 **P** sB38-45 sB ⇔48-55
dB70-75 dB ⇔95-100 M18-33 & alc

⋈J Reymes Amsterdamseweg 5A
☎423204 **P**

⋈Rosler & Meijer Boulevard Heuvelink
5a ☎435984 Frd

At **VELP** (2km NE)

☆ ☆ ☆ ☆Crest (**See page 51**) Pres-
Kennedylaan 102 ☎629210 tx45527
rm74 ⇔38 ▥36 **P** Lift ♪
sB ⇔ ▥129 dB ⇔ ▥160

ASSEN
Drenthe (☎05920)

★ ★ ★Overcingel Stationspl 10 ☎11333
rm42 ⇔8 ▥24 **P** Lift

⋈AZA Europaweg ☎55944 **P** MB

BAARN
Utrecht (☎02154)

★Prom Amalialaan 1 ☎12913
rm43 ⇔8 ▥35

⋈M Kooy Eemnesser 57a ☎12619 Chy
Sim

⋈Splinter Eemland Eemneserweg
16-22 ☎15555 **P** Frd

BEATRIXHAVEN See **MAASTRICHT**

BEEK
Limburg (☎04402)

☆ ☆ ☆Euromotel Limburg (ETAP)
Vliegveldweg 19 ☎72462 tx56059
rm61 ⇔60 ▥1 **P** sB ⇔ ▥79
dB ⇔ ▥114 M22

BEETSTERZWAAG
Friesland (☎05126)

★ ★ ★Leuswolt Van Harinxmaweg 10
☎1245
rm22 ⇔17 ▥5 ⋒ **P**
sB ⇔ ▥102-135 dB ⇔ ▥125-185
M75-85 & alc ✆ ◯

BERGEN
Noord-Holland (☎02208)

★ ★Park Breelaan 19 ☎2223
rm26 ▥18 **P** sB40 sB ▥44 dB80
dB ▥88

BERGEN-AAN-ZEE
Noord-Holland (☎02208)

★ ★ ★Nassau-Bergen van der Wyckpl 4
☎97541
5 Jan-22 Dec
rm45 ⇔8 ▥25 **P** sB77
sB ⇔ ▥85-145 dB 130 dB ⇔ ▥200
Pool

★Prins Maurits van Hasseltstr 7 ☎2364
Mar-Oct
rm24 ▥18 ⋒ **P** dB ▥108

BERG-EN-DAL
Gelderland (☎08895)

★ ★ ★Park Val Monte (GT) Oude
Holleweg 5 ☎1704 tx48428
rm92 ⇔53 ▥37 **P** sB53 sB ⇔ ▥105
dB115 dB ⇔ ▥133

BERGEN-OP-ZOOM
Noord-Brabant (☎01640)

★ ★ ★Gouden Leeuw Fortuinstr 14
☎35000 tx78265
rm24 ⇔4 ▥20 sB ⇔ ▥52-78
dB ⇔ ▥103-120

★Draak Grote Markt 37-38 ☎33661
rm26 ⇔4 ▥1 sB39 sB ⇔ ▥65 dB78
dB ⇔ ▥100

⋈Difoga Bredasestr 25 ☎50200 Frd

⋈Swagemakers Korenbeurspl 16
☎36285 **P** AR

⋈Vos Ravelstr 10-12 ☎42050 Cit

BEVERWIJK
Noord-Holland (☎02510)

⋈Admiraal & Zn Laan der Nederlanden
1 ☎36050 **P** Cit

Wijkeroog Bullerlaan 6 ☎41664 **P** BL

BLOEMENDAAL
Noord-Holland (☎023)

★ ★Lepenhove Hartenlustlaan 4
☎258301
rm44 ⇔4 ▥31 **P** Lift

⋈Van Loon's Korte Kleverlaan 30-44
☎259311 **P** Lnc Ren Sab

BOEKELO
Overijssel (☎05428)

★ ★ ★Boekelo (Crest **See page 51**)
Oude Deldenerweg 203 ☎1444 tx44301
rm78 ⇔76 ▥2 **P** Lift ♪ sB ⇔ ▥140
dB ⇔ ▥181 ✆ Pool

BORN
Limburg (☎04498)

☆ ☆ ☆Crest (**See page 51**) Langereweg
21 ☎51666 tx36048
rm50 ⇔17 ▥33 **P** Lift ♪ sB ⇔ ▥97
dB ⇔ ▥135 M alc

BOSKOOP
Zuid-Holland (☎01727)

★ ★Neuf Barendstr 10 ☎2031
rm12 ⇔51 ▥11 **P** sB32 sB ⇔ ▥78
dB64 dB ⇔ ▥95

⋈Eerste Boskoops Plankier 2-6
☎2110 **P** MB Opl

BREDA
Noord-Brabant (☎076)

☆ ☆ ☆Euromotel Brabant (ETAP)
Heerbaan 4-6 ☎224666 tx54263
rm80 ⇔20 ▥60 **P** Lift sB ⇔ ▥89
dB ⇔ ▥99 M22 Pool

☆ ☆ ☆**Novotel** Dr-Batenburglaan 74
☎659220 tx74016
⇌ 🍴80 **P** Lift ⟶ sB ⇌ 🍴111–115
dB ⇌ 🍴135–239 Mfr15 ಿ Pool

☆ ☆ **Euromotel Breda** (ETAP) Roskam 20
☎222177 tx54126
rm130 ⇌70 🍴60 🏥 **P** Lift
sB ⇌ 🍴50–125 dB ⇌ 🍴122–135 M22
Pool

⅋**Nefkens-Breda** Loevesteinstr 20
☎659211 **P** Peu

⅋**Tigchelaar** Boeimersingel 6 ☎224400
P Frd

⅋**Van Nunen** Hagweg 442–444
☎224920 **P** RT

⅋**Valkenberg** Spinvelo 74 ☎222371 Cit

At **GINNEKEN** (2km S)

★ ★ ★**Mastbosch** (GT) Burg-
Kerstenslaan 20 ☎650050 tx54406
rm40 ⇌34 🍴5 **P** Lift sB ⇌ 🍴102
dB ⇌ 🍴165

BRESKENS
Zeeland (☎01172)

★ ★**Wapen van Breskens** Grote Kade 33
☎1401
rm20 🍴6 **P** sB35 sB 🍴55 dB70
dB 🍴110 M20–45 & alc

⅋**Van de Ree** Rermuriusstr 11–13
☎1729 **P** Frd

BUNNIK See **UTRECHT**

BUSSUM
Noord-Holland (☎02159)

★**Goolland** Stationsweg 16–22 ☎43724
rm12 🍴4 sB30 sB 🍴45 dB70 dB 🍴90
M20

⅋**Hogguer Bussum** Vlietlaan 58–66
☎18651 Frd

⅋**Van Meurs** Huizerweg 84–86
☎34047 Ren

⅋**Van Meurs** Noorderweg 2 ☎30024 **P**
Opl

CADZAND
Zeeland (☎01179)

★ ★**Schelde** Scheldestr 1 ☎1720
rm26 ⇌10 🍴16 **P** sB60 sB ⇌ 🍴65
dB120 dB ⇌ 🍴130 M28–45 & alc Pool

DELDEN
Overijssel (☎05407)

★ ★**Zwaan** Langestr 2 ☎1206
rm13 ⇌1 🍴8 **P** sB48–85
sB ⇌ 🍴fr70 dBfr90 dB ⇌ 🍴fr110
M25–30 & alc

DELFT
Zuid-Holland (☎015)

★ ★**Leeuwenburg** Koornmarkt 16
(n.rest) ☎123062 tx16443
rm31 ⇌8 🍴23 Lift sB ⇌ 🍴110–130
dB ⇌ 🍴115–145

Netherlands

★**Central** Wijnhaven 6–9 ☎123442
rm36 ⇌9 🍴21 sB40 sB ⇌ 🍴65 dB70
dB ⇌ 🍴90

⅋**Kinesis** Vulcenusweg 281 ☎569202
Frd

DEN HAAG See **HAAG (DEN) (HAGUE, THE)**

DEN HELDER See **HELDER (DEN)**

DEVENTER
Overijssel (☎05700)

☆ ☆ ☆**Postiljon** (BW) Deventerweg 1221
☎24022 tx49028
rm103 ⇌48 🍴55 **P** Lift
dB ⇌ 🍴95–120

⅋**Hardonk's** Gl-Gibsonstr 6 ☎13945
Fia MB Vau

DOETINCHEM
Gelderland (☎08340)

⅋**Martens** Edison Str 1 ☎33250 **P** Frd

DOMBURG
Zeeland (☎01188)

★ ★**Duinheuvel** Badhuisweg 2 ☎1282
Etr–Oct
rm16 ⇌2 🍴7 **P** sB45 dB66
dB ⇌ 🍴110 M28

DORDRECHT
Zuid-Holland (☎078)

★ ★ ★**Bellevue Groothoofdspoort**
Boomstr 37 ☎137900
rm18 ⇌9 🍴9 **P** sB ⇌ 🍴53–83
dB ⇌ 🍴110–130 M20–59

⅋**Dubbeesteyn** Dubbelsteynlaan 51
☎161155 **P** BMW

⅋**Kern's** Copernicusweg 1 ☎171633
Ren

⅋**J Van den Berg** Blekersdijk 96
☎143088 Frd

⅋**H W Van Gorp & Zonnen** A-Cuypsingel
296 ☎142044 Peu

DRACHTEN
Friesland (☎05120)

☆ ☆ ☆**Crest (See page 51)** Zonnedauw 1
☎20705 tx46693
rm48 ⇌42 🍴6 **P** Lift ⟶ sB ⇌ 🍴121
dB ⇌ 🍴165

⅋**Siton** de Knobben 25 ☎14455 Opl

DRONTEN
Gelderland (☎03210)

⅋**Visser** de Ketting 1 ☎3114 Opl Vau

DWINGELOO
Drenthe (☎05219)

At **LHEE** (1.5km SE)

★ ★**Borken** ☎7200
rm24 ⇌9 🍴6 🏥 **P** dB ⇌ 🍴68–80
ಿ Pool 🍴

EDAM
Noord-Holland (☎02993)

★**Dam** Keizersgracht 1 ☎71766
Apr–Sep
rm12 🍴1 sB30–35 dB50 dB 🍴65
m17–23

⅋**Evodam** D-Poschlaan ☎65551 Ren

EDE
Gelderland (☎083380)

⅋**Van der Kolk** Klaphekweg 30 ☎30201
Frd

⅋**Van Silthout** Proosdijweg 1–5
☎14041 **P** Ren

At **VEENENDAAL** (8km W)

☆ ☆**Ibis** Vendelier 8 ☎(08385) 22222
tx37210
⇌41 **P** Lift ⟶ sB ⇌70 dB ⇌85

⅋**Langendijk** Hofstede 27 ☎10546 **P**
Vau

EEMNES See **LAREN**

EERNEWOUDE
Friesland (☎05117)

★ ★ ★**Princenhof** P-Miedemaweg 15
☎9206
rm45 ⇌23 🍴15 **P** sB44 sB ⇌ 🍴fr73
dB85 dB ⇌ 🍴fr135 M25–48 & alc

EGMOND-AAN-ZEE
Noord-Holland (☎02206)

★ ★ ★**Bellevue** Boulevard Noord (A7)
☎1387
rm51 ⇌12 🍴36 Lift sB47–97
sB ⇌ 🍴fr80 dB90–97 dB ⇌ 🍴fr164
M28–33 & alc

⅋**J A Karels** Trompstr 17 ☎1250 BL

EINDHOVEN
Noord-Brabant (☎040)

★ ★ ★ ★ ★**Cocagne** (SRS) Vestdijk 47
☎444755 tx51245
⇌ 🍴207 🏥 **P** Lift sB ⇌ 🍴156–165
dB ⇌ 🍴200–210

☆ ☆ ☆**Holiday Inn** Veldmaarschalk
Montgomerylaan 1 ☎433222 tx51775
⇌200 **P** Lift sB ⇌140–150
dB ⇌ 🍴190–200 Pool

☆ ☆ ☆**Eindhoven** Aalsterweg 322
☎116033 tx51999
⇌ 🍴186 **P** Lift Pool

⅋**Driessen** Pieterbergweg 31 ☎422335
Sab

⅋**Van Laarhoven's Auto** Hondsruglaan
99 ☎413615 **P** BL

⅋**L Lang** Keiser Karel V Singel 57
☎518402 Fia Lnc

⅋**OBAM** Aalsterweg 135 ☎116444 Frd

EMMELOORD
Overijseel (☎05270)

⅋**Gorter** Kampwai 50 ☎3541 BL Opl
Vau

EMMEN
Drenthe (☎05910)

🛏Jong Statenweg 5–7 ☎22330 Cit

🛏Misker Oordoornerweg 4 ☎18288 BL
Chy

ENKHUIZEN
Noord-Holland (☎02280)

★★Wapen van Enkhuizen Breedstr 59
☎13434
rm24 🛏11 P sB35 dB65 dB 🛏73
M alc

🛏Watses Westerstr 273–275 ☎2708
Frd

ENSCHEDE
Overijssel (☎053)

★★★Memphis M-H-Tromplaan 55
☎318244 tx44702
rm37 ⇌25 🛏10 P Lift sB40
sB ⇌ 🛏fr85 dB78 dB ⇌ 🛏fr130

🛏Auto Fischer Oldenzaalsestr 137
☎354555 Frd

🛏Oldenhof Europalaan 23 ☎310961
BMW

🛏Ruinemans de Reulver 30 ☎770077
Hon

EPEN
Limburg (☎04455)

★Gerardushoeve Julianastr 23 ☎1793
rm6 P dB84 M alc

FLUSHING See **VLISSINGEN**

GIETHOORN
Overijssel (☎05216)

☆☆☆Giethoorn Beulakerweg 128
☎1216
rm20 ⇌10 🛏10 P sB ⇌ 🛏55–65
dB ⇌ 🛏80–100 M alc

GINNEKEN See **BREDA**

GOES
Zeeland (☎01100)

★Ockenburgh van de Spiegelstr 104
☎16303
Closed Sunday
rm7 ⇌1 🛏4 P sB38 sB ⇌ 🛏75
dB100 M alc

🛏Adria West Havendyk 150 ☎20440 P
Frd

🛏Van Frassen Voorstad 79 ☎27353
M/c P Cit

🛏B Oeveren A-Plasmanweg 2 ☎12730
P MB

🛏Van Strien Van de Spiegelstr 92
☎14840 P Aud VW

GORINCHEM
Zuid-Holland (☎01830)

⇌15 P sB ⇌ 🛏80 dB ⇌125 M18–60 &
alc

🛏Van Mill Banneweg 1–3 ☎32344 Fia
Opl Vau

Netherlands

GOUDA
Zuid-Holland (☎01820)

★Zalm Markt 34 ☎12344
rm23 ⇌1 🛏22 sB ⇌ 🛏58 dB ⇌ 🛏90
M alc

🛏J L Hulleman Burg Jamessingel 2
☎12977 P Frd

GROESBEEK
Gelderland (☎08891)

★★Wolfsberg Mooksebaan 12 ☎1327
rm20 ⇌1 🛏14 P sB37 sB ⇌ 🛏42
dB70–74 dB ⇌ 🛏86–90 M24–30 & alc

GRONINGEN
Groningen (☎050)

☆☆☆Crest (see page 51) Donderslaan
156 ☎252040 tx53394
rm59 ⇌10 🛏49 P Lift D
sB ⇌ 🛏83–94 dB ⇌ 🛏118–131
M18–35 & alc

☆☆☆Euromotel Groningen (ETAP)
Expositielaaan 7 ☎258400 tx53795
⇌157 🛉 P Lift sB ⇌82–89 dB ⇌120
M22–65 Pool

🛏A–Z Friesestraatweg 22 ☎120012 P
Hon

🛏Geba Flemingstr 1 ☎250015 BL

🛏Gronam Rijksweg 130,
Oosterhoogeburg ☎411552 Frd

🛏B Oosterhuis Protonstr ☎182223 Toy

HAAG (DEN) (HAGUE, THE)
Zuid-Holland (☎070)

★★★★★Promenade Van Stolkweg 1
☎574121 tx31162
⇌ 🛏100 P Lift sB ⇌ 🛏170
dB ⇌ 🛏175–275 M alc

★★★★Bel Air (GT) J-de-Wittlaan 30
☎502021 tx31444
⇌350 P Lift sB ⇌130 dB ⇌180

★★★★Grand Central (ETAP) Lange
Poten 6 ☎469414 tx32000
rm137 ⇌123 🛏14 🛉 Lift
sB ⇌ 🛏104–118 dB ⇌ 🛏151–180 M25

★★★Indes (Crest see page 51)
Lange Voorhout 54–56 ☎469553
tx31196
⇌ 🛏72 P Lift D sB ⇌ 🛏205
dB ⇌ 🛏265 M alc

★★★Corona Buitenhof 41–42
☎637930
rm23 ⇌3 🛏7 🛉 Lift sB65–80
sB ⇌ 🛏fr95 dB90–95 dB ⇌ 🛏fr135
M30–58 & alc

★★★Parkhotel de Zalm Molenstr 53
☎624371 tx33005
rm132 ⇌92 🛏21 🛉 Lift sB53
sB ⇌ 🛏95 dB ⇌ 🛏155–170

★Esquire Van Aerssenstr 59–61
☎522341 tx34329
rm16 ⇌5 🛏7 sB55 sB 🛏75 dB80
dB 🛏100

🛏Auto Haag Calandpl 2 ☎889255 Ren

🛏Case Pletterijstr 6 ☎858780

🛏Central Auto Bedrijf Prinses
Megrietplantsoen 10 ☎814131 Frd

🛏National Automobiel Bedrijf Scheldestr
2 ☎850300 Hon

🛏Zoet Meteorstr 87–89 ☎814751 Chy

At **RIJSWIJK**

☆☆☆Hoornwijk J-Thijssenweg 2
☎903130 tx32538
🛏70 P sB 🛏80–90 dB 🛏110–120
M alc

At **SCHEVENINGEN**

★★★★Europa (Crest see page 51)
Zwolsestr 2 ☎512651 tx33138
rm174 ⇌112 🛏62 🛉 Lift D
sB ⇌ 🛏137 dB ⇌ 🛏215 M alc ⚲
pool sea

★★★Badhotel Gevers Deynootweg 15
☎512221 tx31592
rm96 ⇌20 🛏76 Lift sB ⇌ 🛏80
dB ⇌ 🛏125 M28 & alc

★★★Eurotel Gevers Deynootweg 63
☎512821 tx32799
rm83 ⇌59 🛏24 P Lift sB ⇌ 🛏95–98
dB ⇌ 🛏180–190 M30

★★Bali Badhuisweg 1 ☎501234
rm36 ⇌6 🛏2 P sBfr33 sB ⇌ 🛏fr44
dBfr61 dB ⇌ 🛏fr83 M alc

★★Van der Spek Antwerpsestr 18
☎556831

3 Jan–23 Dec
rm12 ⇌1 🛏11 sB ⇌ 🛏65
dB ⇌ 🛏100

HAARLEM
Noord-Holland (☎023)

★★★Lion d'Or (GT) Kruisweg 34–36
☎321750 tx71101
rm33 ⇌16 🛏13 Lift sBfr70
sB ⇌ 🛏125 dB90–95 dB ⇌ 🛏135–140
Mfr35 & alc

🛏Kimman Zijlweg 35 ☎339069 M/c P
BL DJ RT

HAGUE (THE) See **HAAG (DEN)**

HARDERWIJK
Gelderland (☎03410)

★★Baars Smeepoortstr 52 ☎12007
rm17 ⇌2 🛏13 P sBfr48 sB ⇌ 🛏fr60
dBfr73 dB ⇌ 🛏fr93 M25–50 & alc

🛏Gelderse Auto Service Handelsweg 4
☎13800 P Frd

HAREN
Groningen (☎050)

☆☆☆Postiljon Emmalaan 33 ☎347041
tx53688
rm97 ⇌24 🛏73 P Lift
dB ⇌ 🛏90–120

HEELSUM
Gelderland (☎08373)

★ ★ ★**Klein Zwitserland** Klein
Zwitserlandlaan 5 ☎19104 tx45627
rm62 ⇆35 ⋔26 **P** Lift
sB ⇆ ⋔110–130 dB ⇆ ⋔170–210
Mfr40 ✍

HEEMSTEDE
Noord-Holland (☎023)

⏶**Barnhoorn** Roemer Visscherspl 21
☎242250 Toy

HEERENVEEN
Friesland (☎05130)

☆ ☆ ☆**Postijon** (BW) Schans 65 ☎24041
tx46591
rm61 ⇆16 ⋔45 **P** Lift
dB ⇆ ⋔95–120

HEERLEN
Limburg (☎045)

★ ★ ★**Grand** (GT) Groene Boord 23
☎713846 tx56920
rm112 ⇆76 ⋔36 **P** Lift sB ⇆ ⋔fr125
dB ⇆ ⋔150–300 M30–85 & alc

⏶**Canton-Reiss** Valkenburgerweg 34
☎718040 BL

⏶**Van Haaren** Schandelerboord 25
☎721152 Frd

⏶**Heijnen Heerlen** Frankenlaan 1
☎713600 **P** Ren

⏶**Sondagh** ☎223300 **P** Cit

⏶**Vencken** Heesbergstr 60–64
☎412641 **P** Aud VW

HEILOO
Noord-Holland (☎02205)

☆ ☆ ★**Heiloo** Kennemerstraatweg 425
☎1340
⇆ ⋔22 sB ⇆ ⋔60 dB ⇆ ⋔90

HELDER (DEN)
Noord-Holland (☎02230)

⏶**Ceres** Baljuwstr 139 ☎30000 Peu

At **NIEUW DEN HELDER** (2km SW)

☆ ☆**Den Helder** Marsdiepstr 2 ☎22333
⋔74 **P**

HELMOND
Noord-Brabant (☎04920)

★ ★ ★**West Ende** Steenweg 1 ☎24151
rm47 ⇆33 ⋔10 **P** Lift sB43–63
sB ⇆ ⋔90 dB99 dB ⇆ ⋔135 M alc

⏶**Alards** Gerwenseweg 31 ☎22608 **P**
BL RT

⏶**J Gorp** Engelseweg 220 ☎39670 Cit

HENGELO
Overijssel (☎074)

★ ★ ★**Lansink** C-T-Storkstr 14–18
☎910066
rm25 ⇆6 ⋔19 **P** sB ⇆ ⋔52–75
dB ⇆ ⋔93 M alc

★ ★**Ten Hoopen** Burg Jansenpl 20
☎910265
⋔20 sB ⋔58–65 dB ⋔93–105 M20

Netherlands

⏶**G Ter Haar** Braemarsweg 140
☎913901 BL

⏶**W Noordegraaf** Oldenzaalsestr 19–23
☎914444 M/c Frd

'S-HERTOGENBOSCH
Noord-Brabant (☎073)

★ ★ ★**Europhotel** (BW) Hinthamerstr 63
☎137777 tx50014
⇆47 🍴 Lift sB ⇆80–85 dB ⇆98–105
M24–40 & alc

⏶**Rietvelden** Rietvelderweg 34
☎130636 Fia Sko

HILVERSUM
Noord-Holland (☎035)

★ ★**Hilfertsom** Koninginneweg 28–30
☎232444
rm37 ⇆8 ⋔19 **P** sBfr48 sB ⇆ ⋔fr95
dBfr78 dB ⇆ ⋔fr125 M27–32 & alc

★ ★**Hof van Holland** (BW) Kerkbrink 1–7
☎46141 tx43399
rm59 ⇆39 ⋔20 **P** Lift
sB ⇆ ⋔99–115 dB ⇆ ⋔130–195 M alc

⏶**H Koster** Langestr ☎41156 BMW

⏶**J K Poll** Zoverijnstr 2 ☎47841 Frd

HOLTEN
Overijssel (☎05483)

★ ★**Hoog Holten** Forthaarsweg 7
☎1306
rm22 ⇆3 ⋔10 **P** Lift ☽ sB42
sB ⇆ ⋔55 dB84 dB ⋔110 M alc

★ ★**Losse Hoes** Holterbergweg 14
☎1353
rm12 ⋔8 **P** Pool

HOOGERHEIDE
Noord-Brabant (☎01646)

★ ★**Pennehuis** Atwerpsestraatweg 100
☎4552
rm21 ⋔12 **P** sBfr37 sB ⋔fr53 dBfr74
dB ⋔fr90 M28–45 & alc

HOOGEVEEN
Drenthe (☎05280)

☆ ☆ ☆**Hoogeveen** (ETAP) Mathijsenstr 1
☎63303
⇆39 **P** sB ⇆75 dB ⇆100 M alc

⏶**J Kip** van Limburg Stirumstr ☎66666
P Frd

HOORN
Noord-Holland (☎02290)

★**Keizerskroon** Breed 33 ☎12717
rm20 ⇆3 ⋔17

⏶**Koopmans** Dampten 5 ☎17912 **P**
Hon

⏶**Van der Linden & Van Sprankhuizen**
Berkhouterweg 11 ☎36464 **P** Opl Vau
Vlo

KAMPEN
Overijssel (☎05202)

★ ★ ★**Stadsherberg** Ijsselkade 48
☎12645 tx42110
rm16 ⇆6 ⋔10 sB ⇆ ⋔50–63
dB ⇆ ⋔85–95 M20–65 & alc

★ ★**Van Dijk** Ijsselkade 30–31 ☎14925
rm22 ⇆8 ⋔1 sBfr45 sB ⇆ ⋔fr60
dBfr60 dB ⇆ ⋔fr90

⏶**J H R Van Noort** Nijverheidsstr 35
☎12241 Frd

KATWIJK AAN ZEE
Zuid-Holland (☎01718)

★ ★**Noordzee** Boulevard 72 ☎13450
rm44 ⇆22 Lift sBfr45 dB ⇆fr75
dBfr90 dB ⇆fr130 M20–45 & alc

⏶**Rijnland West** Kon Wilhelminastr 16
☎72743 Frd

KOOG (DE)
Texel (☎02228)

★ ★ ★**Opduin** Ruyslaan 22 ☎445
tx57555
Closed 10 Jan–10 Feb
rm52 ⇆23 ⋔20 🍴 **P** Lift sB63–133
sB ⇆ ⋔123 dB125–133 dB ⇆ ⋔254
M28–98 & alc Pool

LAREN
Noord-Holland (☎02153)

At **EEMNES** (2km E)

☆ ☆ ★**Witte Bergen** Rijksweg A1
☎86754 tx73041
rm62 ⇆43 ⋔19 **P** sB ⇆ ⋔53–64
dB ⇆ ⋔58–70 M alc

LEEUWARDEN
Friesland (☎058)

★ ★ ★**Orange** (GT) Stationsweg 4
☎126241 tx46528
rm80 ⇆45 ⋔26 🍴 Lift sB ⇆ ⋔125
dB ⇆ ⋔165

★ ★**Eurohotel** Europapl 20 ☎131113
rm56 ⇆12 ⋔38 Lift sBfr53 dBfr89
dB ⇆ ⋔fr115 M17–39 & alc

⏶**Molenaar** Keidam 2 ☎(058)661115 **P**
Toy

⏶**Nagelhout** Brademeer 2
☎(058)663633 Chy Dat Toy

⏶**Zeeuw** Valerinsstr 2–11
☎(058)131444 M/c Frd

LEIDEN
Zuid-Holland (☎071)

☆ ☆ ☆**Holiday Inn** (GT) Haagse
Schouwweg 10 ☎769310 tx39213
⇆ ⋔192 **P** Lift sB ⇆ ⋔140–160
dB ⇆ ⋔200–220 ✍ Pool

⏶**Keidse Autoboxen** (LAG) Van
Oldenbamereldstr 37 ☎172679 BL RT

⏶**Rijnland** Vijf Meilaan 7 ☎310031 Frd

LELYSTAD
Gelderland (☎03200)

★ ★ ★**Lelystad** (ETAP) Agoraweg 11
☎42444 tx70311 →

⇔86 **P** Lift ☾ sB ⇔87-92
dB ⇔115-128 Mfr23.50

LEUSDEN
Utrecht (☎03498)

★ ★**Huize den Treek** Trekenweg 23
☎1425
Closed Xmas & New Yr
rm20 ⇔3 🛏9 **P** Lift sB48 sB ⇔ 🛏55
dB95 dB ⇔ 🛏140

LEUVENUM
Gelderland (☎05770)

★ ★**Roode Koper** Jhr-Sandbergweg 82
☎7393 tx49633
rm24 ⇔11 🛏11 **P** ✆ Pool

LHEE See **DWINGELOO**

LOCHEM
Gelderland (☎05730)

★ ★**Lochemse Berg** Lochemseweg 42
☎1377
🛏15 **P** Lift dB 🛏86 M28

🕭**Van de Straat** Tramstr 36 ☎1652 M/c
P BL

LUNTEREN
Gelderland (☎08388)

★ ★ ★**Lunterse Boer** Boslaan 87 ☎3657
rm18 ⇔13 🛏15 **P** sB ⇔ 🛏78-88
dB ⇔ 🛏110-130 M36 & alc

LUTTE (DE)
Overijssel (☎05415)

★ ★ ★**Lutt** Beuningerstr 20 ☎1309
rm19 ⇔4 🛏15 **P** sB ⇔ 🛏68-83
dB ⇔ 🛏105-150 M25-30 & alc ☂

MAARSBERGEN
Utrecht (☎03433)

☆ ☆**Maarsbergen** Woudenbergseweg 44
☎341 tx47986
🛏11 dB 🛏60

MAASTRICHT
Limburg (☎043)

★ ★ ★ ★ ★**Maastricht** De Ruiterij 1
☎54171 tx56822
⇔ 🛏11 **P** Lift sB ⇔ 🛏150-172
dB ⇔ 🛏205-428 Mfr45

★ ★ ★**Casque** Vrijhof 52 Helmstr 14
☎14343 tx56657
rm40 ⇔21 🛏14 🏬 Lift sB58-63
sB ⇔ 🛏90-100 dB ⇔ 🛏150

🕭**Straten** via Regia 170 ☎34500 Aud
VW
At **BEATRIXHAVEN** (4km N)

🕭**Feyts Autos** Korvetweg 20-22
☎16755 **P** Frd

MIDDELBURG
Zeeland (☎01180)

★ ★ ★**Commerce** Loskade 1 ☎36051
rm45 ⇔15 🛏22 Lift sB ⇔ 🛏68-78
dB ⇔ 🛏110-116

★ ★ ★**Nieuwe Doelen** Loskade 3-7
☎12121

Netherlands

rm29 🛏12 Lift sBfr48 sB 🛏fr60
dBfr95 B 🛏fr20 M30-50 & alc

★**Hulfkar** Markt 19 ☎12998
🛏4 sB 🛏53-65 dB 🛏73-80 M17-63
& alc

🕭**Louisse** Kalverstr 1 ☎25851 Opl

MIDDLEHARNIS
Zuid-Holland (☎01870)

🕭**Auto Service** Kastanjelaan 41-43
☎3094 Chy Sim

🕭**Knöps** Langeweg 113 ☎2222 Opl Vau

MOOK-EN-MIDDELAAR
Limburg (☎08896)

★ ★ ★**Plasmolen** Rijksweg 170 ☎1444
rm29 ⇔17 🛏10 🏬 **P** sBfr40
sB ⇔ 🛏fr80 dBfr90 dB ⇔ 🛏fr105
M25-80 & alc ✆

★ ★**Schans** Rijksweg 95 ☎1209
rm9 ⇔1 🛏4 **P**

NIEUW DEN HELDER See **HELDER (DEN)**

NIJMEGEN
Gelderland (☎080)

★ ★ ★**Nijmegen** (ETAP) Stationspl 29
☎238888 tx48670
⇔100 **P** Lift ☾ sB ⇔78-84 dB ⇔105
M22

🕭**Britcar** Muldersweg 15 ☎5770144 **P**
BL

🕭**Jansen & Ederveen** ☎224800 Ren

NIJVERDAL
Overijssel (☎05486)

🕭**Blokken** Bergleidingweg 27 ☎12959
BL

NOORDGOUWE
Zeeland (☎01112)

🕭**Akkerdaas** Kloosterweg 2 ☎1347 **P**
Opl Vau

NOORDWIJK AAN ZEE
Zuid-Holland (☎01719)

★ ★ ★**Noordzee** (Comfort) Kon-
Wilhelmina Boulevard 8 ☎19205 tx39206
⇔90 **P** Lift ☾ sB ⇔105 dB ⇔201
M25 Pool sea

★ ★**Palace** Parallelboulevard 7
☎19231 tx39116
🛏36 Lift

★ ★**Alwine** Jan van Henegouwenweg 7
☎12213
🛏27 Lift sB 🛏55-60 dB 🛏100-110
M13-18 Pool

★ ★**Clarenwijck** Kon-Astrid Boulevard
46 ☎12727
15 Jan-20 Dec
rm25 ⇔2 🛏16 **P** sB35 sB ⇔ 🛏fr48
dB70-75 dB ⇔ 🛏fr95 Mfr28

★**Duinlust** Koepelweg 1 ☎12916
Mar-Oct
rm25 **P** sB30-45 dB60-90

🕭**Beuk** Golfweg 19 ☎19213 Fia Lnc

🕭**Rijnland West** Beeklaan 5 ☎14300
Frd

OISTERWIJK
Noord-Brabant (☎04242)

★ ★ ★**Swaen** de Lind 47 ☎19006
tx52617
Closed 2 wks Jul
⇔19 **P** Lift sB ⇔fr145 dB ⇔fr183
M100-155 & alc
★**Spoormaker** Kerkstr 80 ☎84683 Fia

OLDENZAAL
Overijssel (☎05410)

🕭**Munsterhuis** Oliemolenstr 4 ☎15661
Ren

🕭**Olde Monnikhof** Vos de Waelstr 20
☎14451 Opl

OMMEN
Overijssel (☎05291)

★ ★**Zon** Voorbrug 1 ☎1141
rm16 ⇔8 🛏8 **P** sB ⇔ 🛏fr58
dB ⇔ 🛏105 M35-90 & alc

🕭**Leerentveld** Hammerweg 1 ☎2500
Dat

OOSTBURG
Zeeland (☎01170)

★**Commerce** Markt 24 ☎2912
rm20 ⇔4 🛏16 sB ⇔ 🛏43-48
dB ⇔ 🛏85-95 M alc

OOSTERBEEK
Gelderland (☎085)

★ ★ ★**Bilderberg** Utrechtseweg 261
☎340843 tx45484
⇔146 **P** Lift Pool

★ ★**Strijland** Stationsweg 6-8 ☎343034
rm31 ⇔9 🛏22 **P** sB ⇔ 🛏56-77
dB ⇔ 🛏86-135 Pool

★**Dreyeroord** Gr-van Rechterenweg 12
☎333169
rm28 ⇔10 🛏15 **P** Lift

🕭**Hoog en laag** Utrechtseweg 84
☎334757 Toy

OOTMARSUM
Overijssel (☎05419)

★ ★ ★ ★**Wiemsel** Winhofflaan 2
☎2155
⇔ 🛏31 **P** ✆ Pool

★ ★**Wapen van Ootmarsum** Almelosestr
20 ☎1500
Closed 31 Dec & 1 Jan
rm16 🛏15 **P** sBfr41 dB 🛏81-85
M18-31

OSS
Noord-Brabant (☎04120)

★**Alem** Molenstr 81 ☎22114
rm12 ⇔11 **P**

🕭**J Putters** Hertogensingel 38 ☎23600
P AR MB

&Uyting & Smits Oude Molenstr 27
☎26925 **P** Opl Vau

OVERVEEN
Noord-Holland (☎023)

★ ★ **Roozendaal** Bloemendaalseweg 260
☎324517
rm12 ⇋3 ▥9 **P** sB ⇋ ▥50–60
dB ⇋ ▥90–150 M35–50

PAPENDRECHT
Zuid-Holland (☎078)

☆ ☆ ☆ **Crest (See page 51)** Lange
Tiendweg 2 ☎152099 tx29331
rm83 ⇋66 ▥17 **P** Lift 🅓
sB ⇋ ▥131 dB ⇋ ▥187

RAALTE
Overijssel (☎05720)

★ ★ ★ **Zwaan** Kerkstr 2 ☎3122
rm20 ⇋5 ▥11 **P** sB38 sB ⇋ ▥55
dB70 dB ⇋ ▥98 M21–45 Pool

RIJSWIJK See **HAAG (DEN) (HAGUE,
THE)**

ROERMOND
Limburg (☎04750)

&Nedam Maasbrug ☎15962 **P** Opl
Vau

&Opheij II Singel 29–31 ☎12125 BL
Hon

ROOSENDAAL
Noord-Brabant (☎01650)

★ ★ **Central** Stationspl 9 ☎35657
rm20 ⇋12 ▥5 sBfr49 sB ⇋ ▥fr84
dBfr91 dB ⇋ ▥115 M alc

&Hennekam Amri-Lonckestr 1 ☎26924
Frd

&Van Poppel Van Beefhovenlaan 9
☎36566 BL RT

ROTTERDAM
Zuid-Holland (☎010)
See also **SCHIEDAM**

★ ★ ★ ★ ★ **Hilton International** Weena
10 ☎144044 tx22666
⇋ ▥259 Lift 🅓 sB ⇋ ▥216–306
dB ⇋ ▥262–372 Mfr28

★ ★ ★ **Atlanta** (GT) Aert van Nesstr 4
☎110420 tx21595
rm170 ⇋140 ▥25 Lift

★ ★ ★ **Central** Kruiskade 12
☎140744 tx24040
rm64 ⇋29 ▥35 Lift sB ⇋ ▥105–160
dB ⇋ ▥150–190

★ ★ ★ **Park** (BW) Westersingel 70–72
☎363611 tx22020
⇋95 **P** Lift sB ⇋107–187
dB ⇋176–222 M33

★ ★ ★ **Rijn** Schouwburgpl 1
☎333800 tx21640
rm140 ⇋20 ▥120 🚗 Lift
sB ⇋ ▥99–173 dB ⇋ ▥181–197 M alc

★ ★ **Savoy** (GT) Hoogstr 81 ☎139280
tx21525
rm94 ⇋18 ▥76 Lift sB ⇋ ▥104–113
dB ⇋ ▥124–138 M alc

Netherlands

★ ★ **Baan** Rochussenstr 345 ☎7700555
rm14 ▥9 sB43–60 dB ▥73–90

★ ★ **Pax** Schiekade 658 ☎663344
rm31 ⇋5 ▥21 **P** Lift sB48 sB ▥85
dB79 dB ▥105

★ ★ **Walsum** Mathenesserlaan 199
☎363275 tx20010
rm29 ⇋6 ▥18 sB ⇋ ▥70–90 dB72
dB ⇋ ▥100 M25

★ **Holland** Provenierssingel 7 ☎653100
rm24 sB48 dB80

&Dunant Dunantstr 22–40 ☎760166
Toy

&Excelsior Boezemsingel 12 ☎144644
BL RT

&Gam Rotterdam Smirnoffweg 21–23
☎298844 Aud WV

&Hoogenboom Geijssendorfferweg
5–15 ☎298844 **P** Aud VW

At **VLAARDINGEN**

★ ★ ★ ★ **Delta** (Crest **See page 51**)
Maasboulevard 15 ☎345477 tx23154
rm78 ⇋70 ▥8 **P** Lift 🅓 sB ⇋ ▥129
dB ⇋ ▥174 M alc Pool

ROZENDAAL
Gelderland (☎085)

★ ★ ★ **Residence Roosendael**
Beekhuizenseweg 1 ☎629123
Closed 28 Dec–3 Jan
rm14 ⇋10 **P** sB50 sB ⇋95–100 dB85
dB ⇋175 Mfr45 & alc

SASSENHEIM
Zuid-Holland (☎02522)

☆ ☆ ☆ **Sassenheim** Warmonderweg 8
☎19019
⇋57 **P** Lift 🅓 sB ⇋68 dB ⇋76

SCHERPENZEEL
Gelderland (☎03497)

★ ★ **Witte Holevoet** Holevoetpl 282
☎1336
Closed 28 Dec–18 Jan
rm11 ⇋5 ▥3 **P**

SCHEVENINGEN See **HAAG (DEN)
(HAGUE, THE)**

SCHIEDAM
Zuid-Holland (☎010)
See also **ROTTERDAM**

☆ ☆ ☆ **Novotel** Hargalaan 2 ☎713322
tx22582
⇋138 **P** Lift sB ⇋123–128
dB ⇋149–154 Pool

SCHIPHOL See **AMSTERDAM AIRPORT**

SLUIS
Zeeland (☎01178)

★ **Sanders de Pauw** Kade 44 ☎1224
Closed 29–31 Dec

rm10 ▥5 **P** dB80 dB ▥120 M25–70 &
alc

SNEEK
Friesland (☎05150)

★ ★ **Wijnberg** Marktstr 23 ☎12421
rm23 ⇋6 ▥13 sBfr39 sB ⇋ ▥fr65
dB79–83 dB ⇋ ▥113 M17–29 & alc

★ **Bonnema** Stationsstr 62–66 ☎13175
Closed New Year
rm23 ▥5 **P**

&Fritsma Frittomalaan 3 ☎12030 M/c
Opl Vau

&F Ozinga's Parkstr 16 ☎13344 Frd

&H de Vries Oosterkade 26 ☎13291
P Ren

TEGELEN
Limburg (☎077)

&Linssen Roermondseweg 139
☎31421 M/c **P** Fia

TERNEUZEN
Zeeland (☎01150)

★ ★ **Milliano** Nieuwstr 11 (n.rest)
☎12342
▥20 **P** sB ⇋ ▥50 dB ▥80

TEXEL (ISLAND OF) See **KOOG (DE)**

TILBURG
Noord-Brabant (☎013)

★ ★ ★ **Heuvelpoort** (ETAP) Heuvelpoort
300 ☎354675 tx52722
⇋63 **P** Lift 🅓 sB ⇋95 dB ⇋125 M23

★ **Postelse Hoeve** Dr-Deelenlaan 10
☎636335 tx52788
rm22 ⇋4 ▥18 **P** sB73 sB ▥100
dB90 dB ▥125 M20–30 & alc

&W A Holland Hart Van Brabanlaan 100
☎422600 **P** BL DJ RT

UTRECHT
Utrecht (☎030)

☆ ☆ ☆ ☆ **Holiday Inn** Jaarbeurspl 24
☎910555 tx47745
⇋280 🏨 Lift sB ⇋160–195
dB ⇋200–235 M alc Pool

★ ★ ★ **Pays Bas** (GT) Janskerkhof 10
☎333321 tx47485
⇋47 🏨 Lift sB ⇋95–115
dB ⇋168–210 M alc

★ ★ ★ **Smits** (ETAP) Vredenburg 14
(n.rest) ☎331232 tx47557
rm46 ⇋18 ▥24 Lift 🅓 sB ⇋ ▥90
dB ⇋ ▥115 M alc

★ ★ **Hes** Maliestr 2 ☎316424 tx70870
rm19 ⇋9 ▥9 Lift

&Van Meeuwen's Weerdsingel 42–44
☎719111 AR Hon Vau

&Stichtse Leidseweg128 ☎931744 Frd

At **BUNNIK** (7km SE)

☆ ☆ ☆ **Postiljon** (BW) Motorestoweg 8
☎(03405)69222 tx70298
rm84 ⇋15 ▥69 **P** Lift
dB ⇋ ▥107–120

VALKENBURG
Limburg (☎04406)

★★★★**Prinses Juliana** Broekhem 11
☎12244

rm34 ⇄19 🛏15 🚗 **P** Lift
sB ⇄ 🕮80–85 dB ⇄ 🕮95–190
M65–90 & alc

★★**Atlanta** Neerhem 20 ☎12193

rm36 ⇄20 🕮10 **P** Lift sBfr35 sB ⇄59
dBfr77 dB ⇄ 🕮fr82 M25–35

★★**Apollo** Nieuweweg 7 ☎15341

rm37 ⇄1 🕮35 **P**

★**Lindenhorst** Broekhem 130 ☎13444

15 Jan–Jun & Aug–Dec
rm10 ⇄5 sB75 dB ⇄110 Mfr55

&D**Auto-Caubo** Neerham 25 ☎15041

&D**Nerum** Neerham 25 ☎15041 **P** Aud
VW

VEENDAM
Groningen (☎05987)

&D**Bakker** Dr-Bosstr 71 ☎12288 **P** AR

VEENENDAAL See **EDE**

VEERE
Zeeland (☎01181)

★**Campveerse Toren** Kade 2 (n.rest)
☎291

rm18 ⇄6 **P** sB40–83 dB70–80
dB ⇄130 M48–90 & alc

VELP See **ARNHEM**

VENLO
Limburg (☎077)

★★★★**Bovenste Molen** Bovenste
Molenweg 12 ☎41045 tx58393

rm65 ⇄62 🕮3 **P** Lift
sB ⇄ 🕮105–190 dB ⇄ 🕮160–290
Mfr58 & alc Pool

☆ ☆ ☆**Novotel** Nijmeegseweg 90
☎44141 tx58229

⇄ 🕮88 **P** Lift 𝄞 sB ⇄ 🕮101–116
dB ⇄ 🕮123–128 Mfr25 Pool

★★**Wilhelmina** Kaldenkerkerweg 1
☎16251

Closed Xmas Day
rm41 ⇄25 🕮7 **P** Lift sB42
sB ⇄ 🕮fr54 dBfr88 dB ⇄ 🕮fr117
M23–78 & alc

★**Grolsch Quelle** Eindhovensestr 3–8
☎13560

rm20 sB30 dB60

&D**AML** Wezelseweg 53E ☎96666 **P** MB

&D**Van Gorp** Ferd Bolstr 10 ☎16752 Cit

&D**L Van den Hombergh** Straelsewog 18
☎11441 Frd

&D**J B Nefkens & Zonen** Staelseweg 52
☎12474 Peu

&D**Peters** Burg Bloemartsstr 30 ☎10455
Vlo

VENRAY
Limburg (☎04780)

&D**J Gop** Horsterweg 10a ☎86825 Cit

Netherlands

&D**Van Haren** Raadhuisstr 38 ☎85300 **P**
Frd

VIERHOUTEN
Gelderland (☎05771)

★★★**Mallejan** Nunspeterweg 70 ☎241

⇄42 🚗 **P** Lift sB ⇄70–75
dB ⇄120–140 M35–50 & alc

VLAARDINGEN See **ROTTERDAM**

VLISSINGEN (FLUSHING)
Zeeland (☎01184)

★★★**Britannia** bd Evertsen 244
☎13255 tx36219

⇄35 **P** Lift sB ⇄86–95 dB ⇄113–133
M18–98 & alc

★★★**Strand** (GT) bd Evertsen 4
☎12297 tx37878

rm40 ⇄10 🕮30 **P** Lift sB ⇄ 🕮130
dB ⇄ 🕮150 M40–100 & alc

&D**Dijkwel Vlissingen** Pres-Rooseveltlaan
745 ☎12008 Chy Peu

VOLENDAM
Noord-Holland (☎02993)

★★**Van Diepen** Haven 35 ☎63705

15 Mar–15 Nov
rm19 ⇄2 🕮8 **P** sB43 sB ⇄ 🕮48
dB80 dB ⇄ 🕮90 Mfr15 & alc

WAGENINGEN
Gelderland (☎08373)

&D**Van der Kolk** Station Str 2 ☎19055
Frd

WARNSVELD
Gelderland (☎05750)

★**Het Jachthuis** Vordenseweg 2 ☎23328

rm11 ⇄1 🕮2 **P**

WASSENAAR
Zuid-Holland (☎01751)

★★**Bianca** Gravestr 1 ☎19206

rm11 🕮9 🚗 sB70 dB85 dB 🕮95
Mfr23

★★**Duinoord** Wassenaarse Slag 26
☎12961 tx34383

rm20 ⇄18 🕮2 **P** sB ⇄ 🕮59–108
dB ⇄ 🕮105–129 M28–55 & alc

&D**A Blankespoor** Oostdorperweg 29–31
☎12405 BL DJ RT

&D**Jansen** Rijksstraatweg 773 ☎79941
Aud VW

WOERDEN
Zuid-Holland (☎03480)

★★★**Eenhoorn** (GT)
Utrechtsestraatweg 33 ☎12515 tx76151

rm69 ⇄7 🕮62 A10rm 🚗 **P** 𝄞
sB ⇄ 🕮81–86 dB ⇄ 🕮111–126
M10–30

ZAANDAM
Noord-Holland (☎075)

&D**Verenigde** Zeemanstr 43 ☎172751
Frd

ZANDVOORT
Noord-Holland (☎02507)

★★★★**Bouwes** (GT) Badhuispl 7
☎15041 tx41096

rm58 ⇄6 🕮52 **P** Lift sB ⇄ 🕮85–120
dB ⇄ 🕮146–170 Mfr30 & alc

★★★**Palace** Burg van Fenemapl 2
☎12911 tx41812

🕮45 **P** Lift sB 🕮55–65 dB 🕮100–170
Mfr30

★★**Hoogland** Westerparkstr 5 ☎15541

rm26 ⇄1 🕮24 sBfr50 sB 🕮70 dBfr90
dB 🕮fr135

ZEDDAM
Gelderland (☎08345)

★★**Aaldering** s'Heerenbergseweg 1
☎1273 rm24 ⇄6 🕮8 **P**
sB ⇄ 🕮35–37 dB ⇄ 🕮80 M19–35 &
alc Pool

ZEIST
Utrecht (☎03404)

★★★**Hermitage** Het Rond 7 ☎24414

🕮14 **P** Lift sB 🕮78–100
dB 🕮100–130 M alc

&D**J Molenarr's** 2e Hogeweg 109
☎18041 **P** AR

&D**A F Phillippo** Laan Van Cattenbroeck
23 ☎14529 Toy

ZIERIKZEE
Zeeland (☎01110)

★★**Mondragon** Havenpark 21 ☎3051

rm9 ⇄4 🕮5 🚗 sB ⇄ 🕮60
dB ⇄ 🕮80–130

ZOETERMEER
Zuid-Holland (☎079)

★★★**City** Boerhaavelaan ☎219228
tx36726

⇄60 **P** Lift sB ⇄98–130
dB ⇄137–137

ZUTPHEN *Gelderland* (☎05750)

★★**Gravenhof** Kuiperstr 11 ☎18222

🕮12 **P** sB 🕮67–80 dB 🕮126 M30–37
& alc

☆ ☆**Ibis** de Stoven 14 ☎25555 tx49701

⇄40 **P** Lift 𝄞 sB ⇄72–82
dB ⇄93–112 ⅋⃝

&D**H Nijendijk** Spittaalstr 32–34 ☎15257
BL

&D**Weimers** H-Dunentweg 2 ☎12537 **P**
Fia

ZWOLLE *Overijssel* (☎038)

☆ ☆ ☆**Postiljon** Hertsenbergweg 1
☎216031 tx42180

rm72 ⇄8 🕮64 **P** dB ⇄ 🕮95–120

★★★**Wientjes** (GT) Stationsweg 7
☎211200 tx42640

rm50 ⇄46 🕮4 🚗 **P**
sB ⇄ 🕮120–135 dB ⇄ 🕮165–200
Mfr23 & alc

288

NORWAY

The fjords between Stavanger and Trondheim are the most outstanding feature of Norway's landscape. Many of them, such as Hardanger, Sogne and Romsdal, are between fifty and a hundred miles long and they are all extraordinarily deep and surrounded by towering mountains. Much of northern Norway is beyond the Arctic Circle and experiences perpetual daylight during the summer. In the south the landscape is less stark, notably the lakes and forests around Telemark.

Despite its northerly position Norway has a favourable climate. The coastal areas have cool summers, but inland temperatures are more extreme, with hot summers. Norwegian is the official language and is closely allied to Danish and Swedish and, to a lesser degree, to Dutch, English and German. English is taught in all schools and spoken throughout Norway.

Area *125,000 sq miles*
Population *4,070,000*
Local time *GMT + 1*
(Summer GMT + 2)

National flag *Red with a white-bordered, blue, upright cross.*

Bergen, set at the foot of seven hills

How to get there

Norway can be reached direct by ferry. Services perate from Newcastle to Bergen or Harwich to Kristiansand. Crossing times vary between 20 and 23 hours, depending on the departure point. Another way of reaching Norway is by using one of the short Channel crossings to France or Belgium, then driving through the Netherlands and northern Germany to Denmark, then either using one of the direct ferry links to southern Norway or travelling via Sweden. Crossing from Harwich to Hamburg gives a shorter overland journey via Germany and Denmark.

The distance from the Channel ports to Oslo via Sweden is about 1,000 miles, and would normally require three night stops.

Motoring regulations and general information

This information should be read in conjunction with the general content of the European ABC (pages 6–27). **Note** As certain regulations and requirements are common to many countries they are covered by one entry in the ABC and the following headings represent some of the subjects dealt with in this way.:
AA Agents
Crash or safety helmets
Customs regulations for European countries
Drinking and driving
Fire extinguisher
First-aid kit
Insurance
Medical treatment
Overtaking
Police fines
Radio telephones/Radio transmitters
Rear view mirror
Road signs
Seats belts
Traffic lights
Tyres
Visitors' registration

Accidents

In Oslo emergency telephone numbers are **Fire** 429900, **Police** 110011, **Ambulance** 201090. For other towns see inside front cover of the local telephone directory. See also *Accidents* page 7.

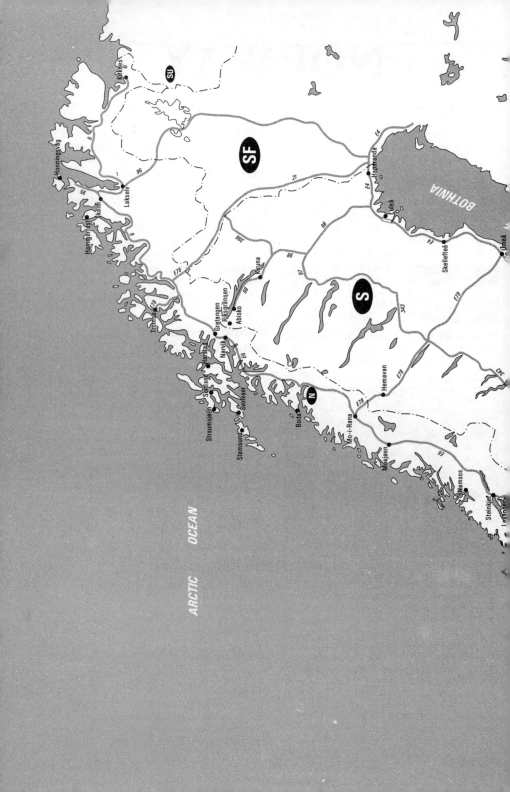

There are no firm rules of procedure, except when personal injuries are sustained, in which case, the police must be called. Under such circumstances you should obtain medical assistance for the injured person. It is also obligatory to place a warning triangle on the road to notify following traffic of the obstruction.

Accommodation

There is no official classification of hotels, but the term hotel is protected by law. Such establishments must be easily recognisable as hotels and must have adequate amenities.

Establishments mainly catering for international tourist traffic which must satisfy the more rigorous requirements may qualify for the description of 'tourist' and 'mountain' hotels (turist – and høyfjells – hoteller). In most towns of any size there is a range of hotels from the simple to the more luxurious. Higher standards are required of these hotels than is generally the case with country hotels.

Lists of establishments which are members of the Norway Travel Association are available from the National Tourist Board. Full details of prices and facilities are given.

Pensionater and hospitser are too small to be classed as hotels but they provide electricity, modern sanitation and, frequently, hot and cold water in bedrooms. Turiststasjoner (tourist stations) and fjellstuer (mountain inns) provide comfortable rooms but often there is no electricity or modern sanitation. Nevertheless, they are scrupulously clean.

Breakdown

The Norwegian Motoring Club (NAF) operates a limited road patrol service between about 20 June and 1 September. The service operates from 10.00 to 19.00hrs daily but in view of its limitations a local garage may offer help more quickly. See also Breakdown page 8 and Warning triangles page 294.

British Consulates

(See also page 8)
Oslo 2 Thomas Heftyesgate 8 ☎563890/7.
There are also consulates in Ålesund, Bergen, Haugesund, Kristiansund(N), Kristiansand(S), Narvik, Stavanger, Tromsø and Trondheim.

Currency and banking hours

(See also page 11)
The unit of currency is the Krone which is divided into 100 øre. There is no restriction on

the amount of Norwegian currency which may be imported, but visitors may be requested to declare all foreign currency, travellers cheques, letters of credit, etc, in their possession. Visitors may export up to the total amount of foreign currency imported, but not exceeding 10,000 Kroner. Not more than 2,000 Kroner in Norwegian currency may be exported. However, banknotes of a higher denomination than 100 Kroner may not be imported or exported.

Banks are open 08.30–15.00hrs Monday to Friday and closed on Saturday. Currency may usually be exchanged at railway stations and airports. Their opening hours vary, but are usually 08.00–21.00hrs from Monday to Friday and 08.00–14.00hrs Sunday. At Bogstad Camping (a well-equipped NAF site near Oslo) there is an exchange office open from June to August on weekdays with opening hours as ordinary banks, closed on Saturday and Sunday.

Dimensions

(See also page 13)
Vehicles must not exceed – height: no restriction; width car 2.50 metres; trailer/caravan: 2.30 metres*; length: 18/15 metres (depending on category of State Highway). The maximum axle load permitted is 10 metric tons but this can be lower on certain roads depending on road conditions. The lower weight restriction will be indicated by a road sign.

*A special permit can be granted for caravans exceeding 2.30 metres but not 2.35 metres, on condition that the difference in width between the motor vehicle and caravan does not exceed 30 cm. Applications for the permit should be sent to Vegdirektoratet, Postboks 8109, Oslo 1.

Driving licence

(See also page 13)
A valid British driving licence is acceptable in Norway. The minimum age at which a visitor may drive a temporarily imported car or motorcycle is 17 years.

Emergency messages to tourists

(See also page 14)
Emergency messages to tourists are broadcast in English by Norwegian State Radio (NRK) in the programme Reiseradio (Travel Radio). The messages are transmitted in medium wave on 228 metres and 1376 metres at 09.00hrs Monday to Friday.

International distinguishing sign

(See also page 17)
It is compulsory for foreign registered vehicles

to display a distinctive sign at the rear of the vehicle. Failure to comply with this regulation will incur an on-the-spot fine of *Krn*50.

Lights
(See also page 17)
Dipped headlights should be used in towns and built-up areas.

Motoring club
(See also page 18)

The **Norwegian Motoring Club** (NAF) which has its headquarters at 2 Storgaten, Oslo 1 ☎(02)429400 has offices or agents in main towns. Office hours are generally 08.30–16.00hrs Monday to Friday and 08.30–13.00hrs on Saturday.

Motorways
Several main roads incorporate stretches of motorway (*motorvei*), mainly around Oslo, with short stretches at Bergen, Stavanger, and Moss. Motorways are divided into two classes, Motorvei Klasse A and Motorvei Klasse B. The first is the usual two-lane dual carriageway and the second is a two-lane road from 20ft to 25ft wide with limited access points.

Parking
(See also page 19)
Do not park by signs bearing the incription "*All stans forbudt*" which means stopping prohibited. Parking meters are in use in the main towns.

Spending the night in a vehicle or trailer on the roadside is **not** permitted.

Passengers
(See also page 19)
Children under 12 are not permitted to travel in a vehicle as front seat passengers.

Petrol
(See also page 20)
Credit cards The use of credit cards to obtain petrol is not available to visiting motorists.
Duty-free petrol In addition to the petrol in the vehicle tank up to 15 litres in a can may be imported free of customs duty and tax.
Octane rating Normal Benzin (93) and Super Benzin (99).

Postal information
Mail Postcards *krn*2.75, letters 5–20gm *Krn*3.00.
Post offices There are 2,700 post offices in Norway. Opening hours are from 09.00–

16.00hrs Monday to Friday and 09.00–13.00hrs Saturday.

Postcheques
(See also page 21)
Postcheques may be cashed at all post offices for any amount up to a maximum of *Krn*500 per cheque. Counter positions are identified by the words *Postgiro* or *Inn-og Utbetalinger*. See above for post office opening hours.

Priority
(See also page 22)
In Norway trams always have right of way.

Public holidays
Official public holidays in Norway for 1985 are given below. See also *Public holidays* page 22.
January 1 (New Year's Day)
April 4 (Maundy Thursday)
April 5 (Good Friday)
April 8 (Easter Monday)
May 1 (Labour Day)
May 16 (Ascension Day)
May 17 (National Day)
May 27 (Whit Monday)
December 25 (Christmas Day)
December 26 (Boxing Day)

Historic ships in Oslo harbour

Roads
In southern and eastern Norway, the most important routes have modern surfaces. In the west and north, some road surfaces are oil bound (partly water-bound) grit. Vehicles with a high ground clearance are more suitable on mountain roads than those with low ground clearance. As a courtesy to other road users, you should fit mudguard flaps. The roads sometimes have soft edges – a great inconvenience to motorcyclists. Watch for warnings signs *Løse Veikanter* and *Svake Kanter*. In the fjord district and often in other areas, careful and confident driving is necessary, although gradients are seldom excessive and hairpin bends can usually be easily negotiated. The

region is mainly unsuitable for large vehicles or caravans. There are sometimes ferry crossings and a reasonable touring maximum is 100 to 150 miles a day.

Shopping hours

Monday to Friday 08.30–17.00hrs (09.00–19.00hrs Thursdays). Saturday 08.30–14.00hrs. During the month of July some shops restrict their opening times to 09.00–15.00hrs.

Speed limits

(See also page 25)
In built-up areas all vehicles are restricted to 50kph (31mph) unless there are signs to the contrary. Outside built-up areas private vehicles are restricted to 80kph (49mph) and on certain motorways the speed limit is 90kph (56mph). Vehicles towing caravans are limited to 80kph (49mph) if the trailer is equipped with a braking system, 60 kph (37mph) if not.

Spiked, studded or snow tyres

(See also page 10)
These may be used from 15 October to 30 April. If *spiked tyres* are used, they must be fitted to all four wheels.

Tourist information offices

(See also page 25)
Local tourist information is available from tourist offices and kiosks throughout Norway. The Norwegian Tourist Board operates from 20 Pall Mall (entrance St James's Square), London SW1Y 5NE ☎01-839 6255 (recorded message service between 09.00–11.00hrs and 14.00–17.00hrs).

Trams

(See also page 25)
Stationary trams may be overtaken on the right at moderate speed, or on the left where there is no room on the right. Moving trams may normally be overtaken only on the right, but overtaking is permitted on the left in one-way streets or where there is no room on the right.

Using the telephone

(See also page 26)
Insert coin **after** lifting receiver (instructions in English in many callboxes). When making calls to subscribers within Norway precede number with relevant area code (shown in parentheses against town entry in gazetteer). Use *Krn*1 coins for local calls and *Krn*5 coins for national and international calls.
International callbox identification Most callboxes.

Telephone rates The cost of a direct dialled call to the UK is *Krn*0.90 for 9 seconds. An operator assisted call costs *Krn*12.60 for 3 minutes and *Krn*4.80 for each additional minute. An extra charge of *Krn*9.60 is made for a personal call. Local calls cost *Krn*1.
What to dial for the Irish Republic 095 353.
What to dial for the UK 095 44.

Warning triangles

The use of a warning triangle is compulsory for all vehicles except two-wheelers. See also *Warning triangles/Hazard warning lights* page 26,

Wheel chains

(See also page 10)
Chains may be necessary if tyre equipment is not adequate for driving under winter conditions.

Winter conditions

Roads to the Swedish frontier (leading to Stockholm and Göteborg) are kept clear. The western fjord district is generally unsuitable for motoring between mid October and late May, and in places until mid June. During this period, the road from Bergen to Oslo via Haukeli remains open but the road via Eidfjord and Geilo is obstructed; It is possible to take cars by train between Voss and Ål (see below) or to motor via Voss, Gudvangen (ferry to Revsnes), Laerdal, and Fagernes. On this stretch it is necessary to use spiked tyres or chains during the winter.

The road from Stavanger to Oslo and the Oslo–Trondheim–Mo-i-Rana road is always open. The possibility of motoring further north depends on the weather. Ålesund and Kristiansund can be approached from Dombås and Oppdal. A map showing roads passable in winter can be obtained from the Norwegian Tourist Board in London.

In winter only, cars may be conveyed by rail between certain stations, provided space is booked at least 24 hours in advance (at Narvik and Kiruna, by 12.00hrs the day before loading). Cars must be available at the station at least three hours before departure (at Narvik and Kiruna two hours before departure).

Bergen railway – between Ål and Voss. Vehicle rates are calculated at time of booking. Narvik––Kiruna railway – (Swedish State Railways). There are two services daily taking $3\frac{1}{2}$–4 hours. Wagons carrying cars are normally attached to passenger trains. Vehicle rates are calculated at time of booking.

Prices are in Norwegian Kroner
In Norwegian ø is the equivalent to œ. The
Norwegian alphabet differs from the
English one in that the last letters after Z
are Æ, Ø, Å; this must be borne in mind
when using Norwegian reference books.
**According to our information garages
with no specific service agencies will
handle any make of car.**
Abbreviations:
gt   gaten
pl   plads

AKKERHAUGEN
Telemark (☎036)

★ ★**Norsjø Turisthotel** ☎66211
⇌🛏36 ☽ sB ⇌ 🛏190 dB ⇌ 🛏280
M75–90 lake

ÅL
Buskerud (☎067)

★ ★ ★**Bergjøstølen** ☎84618
Feb–Apr & 21 Jun–Sep
rm30 ⇌13 dB240–260 dB ⇌300–320
Beach sea mountains lake

★ ★**Sundre** (n.rest) ☎81100
rm28 ⇌12 **P** sB150 sB ⇌200 dB240
dB ⇌290 M170 mountains

ÅLESUND
Møre og Romsdal (☎071)

★ ★**Noreg** Kongensgate 27 ☎22938
tx40440
rm120 ⇌85 🏧 **P** Lift ☽ sB285
sB ⇌430–485 dB ⇌595–645 M75–90
Pool

🛢☽**Ødegårds Karosserifabrikk** ☎42079

🛢☽**Vestlandske Auto** Vaagav 27 ☎25500
Frd

ÅNDALSNES
Møre og Romsdal (☎072)

★ ★**Grand Bellevue** ☎21011
rm45 ⇌40 **P** ☽ sB295 sB ⇌375
dB490 dB ⇌640 M75–105 🏖 sea
mountains

🛢☽**I Sylte** ☎21477

ARENDAL
Aust-Agder (☎041)

★ ★ ★**Phönix** Tyholmen ☎25160
⇌83 **P** Lift ☽ sB ⇌400–500
dB ⇌550–650

🛢☽**Josephsens Auto** ☎26200

ASKIM
Østfold (☎02)

🛢☽**Martiniussen Bilservice** ☎887776

BALESTRAND
Sogn og Fjordane (☎056)

★ ★ ★**Kvikne's** Balholm ☎91101
tx42858
10 May–24 Sep
rm212 ⇌165 **P** Lift ☽ sB ⇌316
dB ⇌520 M100 Beach sea mountains

★ ★**Kringsjå** ☎91303
5 Jan–28 Aug

Norway

rm30 ⇌17 **P** sB180 sB ⇌215 dB200
dB ⇌290 sea

★**Balestrand Pensionat** ☎91138
Lift Beach sea

★**Midtnes Pensionat** ☎91138
rm38 ⇌30 Lift sB 142–147
sB ⇌192–207 dB214–224
dB ⇌269–279 M65–70 Beach sea

BERGEN
Hordaland (☎05)

★ ★ ★**Center** Torgalmenning 11 (n.rest)
☎232300 tx42190
rm65 ⇌58 Lift ☽ sB 225 sB ⇌335
dB360 dB ⇌480–660

★ ★ ★**Grand Terminus** Kong Oscarsgt
71 ☎311655 tx42262
rm130 ⇌125 🏧 **P** Lift ☽ sB240
sB ⇌ 🛏440–500 dB350
dB ⇌ 🛏530–600 M98

★ ★ ★**Norge** (SRS) Ole Bulls Pl 4
☎323090 tx42129
rm241 ⇌125 🛏116 🏧 **P** Lift ☽
sB ⇌ 🛏495–555 dB ⇌ 🛏640–710

★ ★ ★**Orion** Bradbenken 3 ☎318080
tx42442
rm110 ⇌105 A6rm **P** Lift ☽ sea
mountains

☆ ☆ ☆**Scandic** Kokstadflaten 2,
Blomsterdalenn ☎227150 tx40840
🛏150 **P** Lift ☽ Pool

★ ★**Hordahelmen** C-Sundtsgt 18
☎232320 tx40926
rm78 ⇌ 🛏45 A6rm **P** Lift ☽ sB210
sB ⇌280 dB350 dB ⇌430 M65–80

★ ★**Neptun** Walckendorffsgt 8
☎326000 tx40040
rm109 ⇌63 🛏46 Lift ☽
sB ⇌ 🛏480–520 dB ⇌ 🛏565–650

★ ★**Rosenkrantz** Rosenkrantzgt 7
☎315000 tx42427
rm100 ⇌51 🛏37 **P** Lift ☽ sB260
sB ⇌435–545 dB395 dB572–643
M94–125 sea

★ ★**Slottsgården** Sandbrogt 3 ☎316155
rm31 ⇌23 Lift ☽ sea

★**Park** H-Hårfagresgt 35 (n.rest)
☎320960
rm29 ⇌23 **P** ☽ sB195 sB ⇌270
dB290 dB ⇌350 mountains

🛢☽**Vikingservice** ☎292222 BL Cit CJ MG
RT

BESSHEIM
Oppland (☎062)

★**Fjellstue** (n.rest) ☎38913
Feb–25 May & Jun–Sep
rm61 ⇌19 A28rm **P** sB140 sB ⇌180
dB200 dB ⇌220 mountains lake

BØ
Telemark (☎036)

★ ★**Bø** ☎60111 tx21119
⇌65 **P** ☽ sB ⇌250–310
dB ⇌400–440 M90–120 🏖 Pool
mountains lake

★ ★**Lifjell Turist** (8km N of railway
station) ☎60011
rm74 ⇌68 **P** ☽ 🏖 Pool mountains
lake

BODØ
Nordland (☎081)

★ ★ ★**Grand** Storgt 3 ☎20000
rm52 ⇌48 ☽ sB ⇌ 🛏360
dB ⇌ 🛏510–560 M70

★ ★**SAS Royal** Storgt 2 ☎24100
tx64031
rm300 ⇌246 A112rm **P** Lift ☽
sB ⇌590 dB ⇌780 M120 sea

BOLKESJØ
Telemark (☎036)

★ ★ ★**Bolkesjø** ☎18600 tx21007
⇌123 **P** Lift ☽ Pool sea

BØVERDALEN
Oppland (☎062)

★**Jutunheimen Fjellstue** ☎12910
tx11954
rm49 ⇌2 🛏22 A10rm sB170–225
sB ⇌ 🛏170–225 dB250–270
dB ⇌ 🛏350–370 M55–65 lake

At **ELVESETER** (4km SW)

★ ★ ★**Elveseter Turist** ☎12000
Jun–20 Sep
⇌90 **P** Lift sB120–170 sB ⇌140–170
dB200–250 dB ⇌240–330 M75 🏖
Pool mountains

BRUMUNDDAL
Hedmark (☎065)

★ ★ ★**Hedemarken** ☎440011
⇌ 🛏57 sB ⇌ 🛏375–425
dB ⇌ 🛏475–525

BRYNE
Rogaland (☎04)

★ ★**Jæren Turist Rica** ☎482488
⇌51 **P** ☽ sB ⇌470–510
dB ⇌670–720 Pool

BYGDIN
Oppland (☎061)

★ ★**Bygdin Hoyfjellshotell** ☎53813

BYGLANDSFJORD
Aust-Agder (☎043)

★ ★**Revsnes Turisthotell** ☎34105
rm43 ⇌9 🛏34 **P** sB ⇌ 🛏228–245
dB ⇌ 🛏356–390 M70–90 mountains
lake

BYKLE
Aust-Agder (☎043)

★**Bykle** ☎38120
rm15 A10rm **P** Lift sB95–165
dB190–280 M alc mountains

DOKKA
Oppland (☎061)

★ ★ ★ **Spatind Høyfjellshotell** ☎19506
rm96 ⇌30 🍴66 A12rm **P** 𝄐
sB ⇌ 🍴225 dB ⇌ 🍴290–350
M90–110 ✈ Pool mountains lake
⑂**Dokka Bilberging** ☎10558

DOMBÅS
Oppland (☎062)

★ ★ ★ **Dombås Turisthotell** ☎41001
tx19959
rm110 A24rm **P** Lift 𝄐 mountains

★ ★ ★ **Dovrefjell** ☎41005 tx76573
rm91 ⇌15 🍴43 𝄐 sB275
sB ⇌ 🍴300 dB410 dB ⇌ 🍴460 M85
mountains
⑂**Storrusten** ☎41009

DRAMMEN
Buskerud (☎03)

★ ★ ★ **Park** Gamie Kirkpl 3 ☎838280
rm104 ⇌24 🍴80 🚗 **P** Lift 𝄐
sB ⇌ 🍴495 dB ⇌ 🍴530

⑂**Bilberging** ☎824930

DRANGEDAL
Telemark (☎036)

★ ★ **Gautefall** ☎36600 tx21756
rm75 ⇌12 🍴63 **P** 𝄐
sB ⇌ 🍴240–270 dB ⇌ 🍴360–410
M115 ✈ Pool mountains
⑂**BWR Stenberg** ☎36154

EDLAND
Telemark (☎036)

★ ★ **Vågslid** ☎70532 tx21441
18 May–Oct
⇌48 **P** 𝄐 sB ⇌330 dB ⇌470 M90 &
alc

EGERSUND
Rogaland (☎04)

★ ★ **Elger** J-Feyers gt 3 ☎491811
⇌27 Lift sB ⇌225 dB ⇌325 Malc

EIDFJORD
Hordaland (☎054)

★ ★ **Voringfoss** ☎65184
rm58 ⇌14 🍴31 A28rm **P** 𝄐 sB180
sB ⇌ 🍴225–250 dB340 dB ⇌ 🍴400
M75–85 Beach sea mountains

EIKEN
Vest-Agder (☎043)

★ ★ **Eiken Feriesenter** ☎48200
🍴24 **P** sB 🍴290–340 dB 🍴410–460
M65–75 mountains lake

ELVERUM
Hedmark (☎064)

⑂**E Kristiansen** ☎11827 & 12738

ELVESETER See **BØVERDALEN**

ESPEDALEN
Oppland (☎062)

★ ★ **Dalseter Høyfjellshotell** ☎ 99910
tx76722

Norway

26 Dec–Apr & 10 Jun–Sep
rm90 ⇌19 🍴62 **P** Lift 𝄐 sBfr245
sB 🍴fr294 dB ⇌450–475 M100–110
✈ Pool 🛁 ∩ mountains lake

★ **Espedalen Fjellstue** (n.rest) ☎99912
18 Dec–23 Apr & Jun–Sep
🍴29 sB 🍴161–180 dB 🍴322–360
M62–75 mountains lake

EVJE
Aust-Agder (☎043)

☆ ☆ **Grenaderen** ☎30400
⇌28 **P** 𝄐 sB ⇌225 dB ⇌275 Pool
mountains
⑂**Lanz Auto** ☎043-30301

FAGERNES
Oppland (☎061)

★ ★ **Fagernes** ☎31100 tx76562
⇌109 **P** Lift 𝄐 sB ⇌410–435
dB ⇌495–540 M100 Pool Beach sea
mountains

★ ★ **Sanderstolen** (28km SW on road
to Gol) ☎34000 tx19061
sB ⇌ 🍴325–370 dB ⇌ 🍴450–675
M100 ✈ Pool lake

★ **Fagerlund** ☎30600
rm25 ⇌6 A8rm **P** 𝄐 sB155–185
sB ⇌250 dB210–250 dB ⇌315 lake
mountains
⑂**Autoservice** ☎32266

FARSUND
Vest-Agder (☎043)

★ ★ **Fjordhotel** ☎91022 tx21678
⇌54 **P** Lift 𝄐 sB ⇌375–425
dB ⇌490–530 Beach sea
⑂**Kjell Ore Bill & Oljesenter** ☎93111

FEVIK
Aust-Agder (☎041)

★ ★ **Strand** ☎47322 tx21098
rm39 ⇌35 🍴5 A11rm **P** Lift 𝄐 ✈
Beach ∩ sea

FLÅM
Sogn og Fjordane (☎(056)32200

★ ★ **Fretheim** ☎(056)32200
10 May–25 Sep
rm85 ⇌54 A16rm 🚗 𝄐 Pool sea

FLORØ
Sogn og Fjordane (☎057)

★ ★ **Victoria** ☎41033 tx42186
rm85 ⇌55 **P** Lift 𝄐 sB 184–219
sB ⇌234–314 dB278–298
dB ⇌418–568 M80 sea mountains

FØRDE
Sogn og Fjordane (☎057)

★ ★ **Sunnfjord** ☎21622 tx42217
⇌160 **P** Lift 𝄐 dB ⇌295–495
dB ⇌426–465 ✈ Pool mountains

⑂**Autoservice** ☎25311 Fia

FREDRIKSTAD
Østfold (☎032)

★ ★ ★ **City** ☎17750 tx17072
⇌104 🚗 **P** Lift 𝄐

⑂**Fredrikstad Automobil-Forr**
Mosseveien 3 ☎11260 Frd

GAUSA
Oppland (☎062)

★ ★ **Skeikampen Høyfjellshotell**
☎28505 tx18601
⇌76 🚗 **P** Lift 𝄐 ✈ Pool
mountains lake

GEILO
Buskerud (☎067)

★ ★ ★ **Bardøla** ☎85400 tx18771
rm100 ⇌96 **P** Lift 𝄐 sB ⇌370
dB ⇌760 M110–130 ✈ Pool
mountains

★ ★ ★ **Highland** ☎85600 tx18401
rm96 **P** Lift 𝄐 sB ⇌ 🍴420–460
dB ⇌ 🍴530–570 Pool mountains

★ ★ **Vestlia Hoyfjellshotell & Sportell**
☎85611 tx19874
⇌71 **P** 𝄐 ✈ Pool mountains lake

★ ★ **Alpin** ☎85544 tx16558
rm31 🍴11 🚗 **P** 𝄐 sB170 sB 🍴190
dB270 dB 🍴295 sea mountains lake

★ **Gello** ☎85511
⇌73 **P** 𝄐 sB ⇌325 dB ⇌430 M110
mountains lake
⑂**Gello Bil & Bensin** ☎85790

GEIRANGER
Møre og Romsdal (☎071)

★ ★ ★ **Geiranger** ☎63005
15 Apr–15 Oct
rm82 ⇌72 sB ⇌345–375
dB ⇌470–530 M105–125 Pool sea

★ ★ ★ **Union** ☎63000 tx42339
⇌140 **P** Lift 𝄐 sB ⇌390–410
dB ⇌520–560 M100–130 ✈ Pool 🛁
sea

★ ★ **Grande** ☎63067
May–Sep
rm15 🍴10 **P** sB120–145 Beach sea

★ ★ **Meroks Fjord** ☎63002 tx40670
May–Sep
⇌54 **P** Lift 𝄐 sea mountains

GJØVIK
Oppland (☎061)

★ ★ **Strand Rica** ☎72120 tx11110
rm86 ⇌74 **P** Lift 𝄐 sB ⇌340–420
dB ⇌550–590 Pool lake

★ ★ **Nye Grand** Jernbanegt 5 (n.rest)
☎72180
rm32 ⇌4 🍴7 **P** 𝄐 sB ⇌ 🍴330
dB ⇌ 🍴460 M70–85
⑂**Carhos Bilberging** ☎73386

GODØYSUND
Hordaland (☎054)

★★**Godøysund Fjord** ☎31100 tx42137
May–Sep
rm50 🛁14 🚿34 A33rm ☽
sB🛁🚿325 dB🛁🚿500 M110–140
🎾 Beach ⛳ sea mountains

GOL
Buskerud (☎067)

★★★**Oset Høyfjellshotell** (20km N) ☎77920
🛁105 **P** sB🛁345–375 dB🛁490–550 M80 Pool mountains lake

★★★**Pers** ☎4500 tx18472
🛁135 Lift ☽ sB🛁435 dB🛁640 Pool mountains

★★**Storefjell Høyfjellshotell** ☎77930
sB285–305 sB🛁🚿335–375 dB370–390 dB🛁🚿510–550 Pool

★**Eidsgard** ☎74955
rm28 🚿14 **P** sB195–205 sB🚿265–290 dB295–300 dB🚿420–470 M90 mountains

☆**Thorstens** (n.rest) ☎74062
🛁26 **P** sB🛁180–240 dB🛁270–340

GOLÅ
Oppland (☎062)

★★★**Golå Høyfjellshotell**
Gudbrandsdalen ☎98109 tx18601
20 Dec–Sep
rm36 🛁15 🏠 **P** ☽ sB🛁205 dB🛁410 M85–95 🎾 Pool ∩ mountains lake

GRANVIN
Hordaland (☎055)

★★**Granvin Fjordhotell** ☎25106
rm40 🛁25 🏠 **P** ☽ sB160–180 dB320–360 dB🛁370–390 M85–95 sea mountains

GRATANGEN
Troms (☎082)

★***Gratangen Turiststasjoen*** ☎20108

GROTLI
Oppland (☎062)

★★**Grotli Høyfjellshotell** ☎13912 tx71954
12 Feb–Sep
rm55 🛁51 **P** ☽ sB🛁285 dB410 dB🛁410–445 M88–98 mountains lake

GUDVANGEN
Sogn og Fjordane (☎055)

★★**Gudvangen** ☎31921
15 May–15 Sep
rm38 🛁3 🚿8 Beach sea mountains

HALDEN
Østfold (☎031)

★★***Grand*** Jarnbanetorvet ☎80211
rm36 🛁2 🚿10 **P** ☽ sea

🔧**H Thanstrøm** Augustaborg ☎81122 Maz Vau

HAMAR
Hedmark (☎065)

Norway

★★★**Olrud Rica** ☎50100
sB🛁🚿430 dB🛁🚿560

★★★**Victoria** Strandgt 21 ☎30500 tx18568
rm118 Lift ☽ sB🛁🚿460–485 dB🛁🚿600–700

🔧**Furnes Bilberging** ☎50300

HAMMERFEST
Finnmark (☎084)

★★**Grand Rica** ☎11333
rm78 🛁65 **P** ☽ sB🛁495 dB🛁696 M alc sea mountains

HANKØ
Østfold (☎032)

★★**Hankø Nye Fjord** ☎(032) 32105 tx74950
Mar–20 Dec
🛁🚿67 **P** ☽ sB🛁🚿350 dB🛁🚿475 M125 🎾 Pool Beach

HARPEFOSS
Oppland (☎062)

★★★**Wadahl Høyfjellshotell** (5km S of railway station) ☎98300 tx72534
Dec–Apr & Jun–Oct
rm95 🛁40 🚿55 **P** Lift ☽ sB🛁🚿295–375 dB🛁🚿410–490 M100–120 🎾 Pool ⛳ ∩ mountains lake

HARSTAD
Troms (☎082)

★★★**Grand Nordic** ☎62170 tx64152
sB🚿510 dB🚿615

★★★**Viking Nordic** ☎64080 tx64322
🚿97 **P** Lift ☽ sB🚿520 dB🚿615 Pool sea

HAUGESUND
Rogaland (☎047)

★★★**Saga** ☎14044 tx42691
🛁90 🏠 **P** Lift ☽ sB495–560 dB🛁595–675 M alc sea

★★***Haugaland*** Rutebilstasjonen (n.rest) ☎13466 tx42691
rm22 🚿16 **P** ☽

★★**Park** ☎12000
🛁105 🏠 Lift ☽ sB🛁470–500 dB🛁550–600 Pool sea

🔧**Førland Bilberging** ☎31000

HAUKELIFJELL
Telemark (☎(036)70100)

★**Haukeliseter Fjellstue** ☎70100
rm15 🚿6 A23rm **P** sB190 sB🛁🚿250 dB270 sB🛁🚿380 M80 alc mountains lake

HEMSEDAL
Buskerud (☎067)

★★**Hemsedal** ☎79102 tx18472
🛁55 **P** sB🛁335 dB🛁275–375 M80–90 mountains

★★**Skogstad** ☎78333
rm65 🛁35 🚿16 **P** Lift ☽ sB🛁🚿175–350 dB🛁🚿250–500 M65–85 🎾 Pool mountains lake

HERMANSVERK
Sogn og Fjordane (☎056)

★★**Sognefjord Turist** ☎53444 tx40654
🛁38 **P** Lift ☽ sB🛁300 dB🛁400–470 M95 Pool Beach sea

HJERKINN
Oppland (☎062)

★**Hjerkinn Fjellstue** ☎42927
Jun–Sep
rm34 🛁7 A23rm **P** sB230 dB295 M alc mountains lake

HØNEFOSS
Buskerud (☎067)

★★**Grand** (n.rest) ☎22722
rm46 🛁27 A7rm 🏠 **P** ☽ sB180–190 sB🛁🚿280 dB320–330 dB🛁🚿380–410

At **KLEKKEN** (3km E)

★★★**Klaekken Turisthotell** ☎32200 tx18838
🛁77 **P** Lift ☽ sB🛁205 dB🛁410 M75–95 Pool ∩ mountains

HONNINGSVÅG (MAGERØYA ISLAND)
Finnmark (☎084)
(Access by ferry from KÅFJORD)

★★★**SAS Nordkapp** ☎72333 tx64346
rm133 🛁3 🚿97 **P** Lift ☽ sB240–270 sB🛁410–440 dB380 dB🛁520–555 M90 mountains

HOVDEN
Aust-Agder (☎043)

★★★**Hovden Høyfjellshotell** ☎39600 tx21698
🛁85 **P** Lift ☽ sB🛁310 dB🛁420 M100 Pool mountains

★★★**Hovdestøylen** ☎39552 tx21257
🛁41 **P** Lift ☽ sB🛁355 dB🛁510 M100–130 & alc Pool lake

HOVET
Buskerud (☎067)

★★★***Hallingskarvet*** ☎88525
rm34 🛁11 🚿23 **P** ☽ Pool

HØVIK See **OSLO**

HØVRINGEN
Oppland (☎062)

★★***Brekkeseter Fjelistue*** ☎33711 tx11954
15 Feb–20 Apr & 20 Jun–Sep
rm66 🛁14 🚿40 **P**

★★**Hovringen Høyfjellshotell** ☎33722 tx11954
24 Jun–Sep
rm64 🛁50 **P** ☽ sB145–160 →

sB ⇆185-210 dB210-290
dB ⇆240-280 mountains

HØYANGER
Sogn og Fjordane (☎057)

★★Øren ☎12606
sB160-190 sB ⇆ ▥250-320
dB ⇆ ▥400-460 sea

KINSARVIK
Hordaland (☎054)

★★★Kinsarvik Fjord ☎63100 tx42292
15 Jan-20 Dec
rm79 ⇆ ▥62 P Lift ☽ sB ▥275-300
dB ⇆ ▥390-440 M90-100 sea
mountains

KIRKENES
Finnmark (☎085)

★★★Kirkenes Rica Turist ☎901491
rm68 ⇆42 P Lift ☽ sB ⇆409
dB ⇆610 ⅏ sea

KLEKKEN See **HØNEFOSS**

KOLBOTN
Oslo (☎02)

★★★Müller Lienga 1 ☎807500
⇆150 P Lift ☽ sB ⇆525 dB ⇆625
mountains

KONGSBERG
Buskerud (☎03)

★★★Grand ☎732029 tx72991
⇆94 P Lift ☽ sB ⇆440-480
dB ⇆540-680 Pool

★★★Gyldenløve ☎731744
rm66 ⇆33 P Lift ☽ sB200-375
sB ⇆300-375 dBfr350 dB ⇆350-475
M35-100 mountains

KONGSVINGER
Hedmark (☎066)

⅏Kristiansen Bilberging ☎15180

KOPERVIK
Rogaland (☎047)

★★★Karmøy ☎50400
⇆55 P Lift ☽ sB ⇆390-400
dB ⇆510 M60-70 sea

KRISTIANSAND S
Vest-Agder (☎042)

★★★Caledonien V-Strandgt 7
☎29100 tx21222
rm205 ☎135 ▥70 ⛺ P Lift ☽
sB ⇆ ▥560-570 dB ⇆ ▥625-670
M alc sea

★★★Christian Quart ☎22210 tx21126
⇆99 P Lift ☽ sB ⇆415
dB ⇆535-580 M65-80

★★★Ernst Rådhusgt 2 ☎21400
tx21104
rm70 ⇆40 ▥30 ⛺ P Lift ☽
sB ⇆ ▥390-456 dB ⇆ ▥567-622

★★★Fregatten Rica Dronningensgt 66
☎21500 tx21792
rm50 ⇆45 ⛺ P Lift ☽ sB ⇆460
dB ⇆580 M alc

Norway

★Norge Dronningensgt 5-9 ☎23320
tx21369
⇆65 ⛺ P Lift ☽ sB ⇆420 dB ⇆550
M70-85

⅏Nygaards Auto ☎23810

KRISTIANSUND N
Møre og Romsdal (☎073)

★★★Grand Bernsdorffredet 1 ☎73011
tx55488
⇆115 P Lift ☽ sB ⇆485-505
dB ⇆610-650

⅏Moblistasjonen ☎74680 & 75218

KVAM
Oppland (☎062)

☆☆Vertshuset Sinclair ☎94024
rm16 P sB ⇆ ▥218-278
dB ⇆ ▥296-356

KVINESDAL
Vest-Agder (☎043)

★★Rafoss (n.rest) ☎50388
Closed Xmas & New Year
rm22 ⇆5 ▥12 P sBfr190
sB ⇆ ▥250-280 dBfr270
dB ⇆ ▥330-370 Mfr80 mountains lake

☆☆Utslkten Turlst ☎50444
sB195-245 sB ⇆ ▥260-370
dB280-345 dB ⇆ ▥390-490

KVITESEID
Telemark (☎036)

★Brokefjell (n.rest) ☎53222
rm36 ⇆6 ▥2 A10rm P ☽ mountains
lake

LAERDAL
Sogn og Fjordane (☎056)

★★★Lindstøm Turisthotell ☎66202
Apr-15 Oct
rm90 ⇆84 A40rm P Lift ☽
sB ⇆310-335 dB ⇆460-510 M90-115
mountains

LAKSELV
Finnmark (☎084)

★★Banak ☎61377
rm48 ⇆2 ▥28 A13rm P ☽ sea
mountains

⅏Lakselv Bilberging ☎61744

LARVIK
Vestfold (☎034)

★★★Grand Storgt 38 ☎03000 tx21024
rm117 ⇆91 P Lift ☽ sB ⇆405-450
dB ⇆570-610 M75 sea

⅏Larvik Auto Nansetgt 36/38 ☎81212
Frd

LEIKANGER
Sogn og Fjordane (☎056)

★★Leikanger Fjord ☎53622
rm40 A5rm P sB235 sB ⇆335-350
dB350-400 dB ⇆360-480 Beach sea

LEVANGER
Nord Trøndelag (☎076)

★★Backlund Kirkegt 41 ☎81600
rm60 ▥57 Lift ☽ sB295
sB ⇆ ▥345-400 dB470 dB ▥565-580
M85-95

⅏Nilsen Bilberging ☎82522

LILLEHAMMER
Oppland (☎062)

★★★Kronen Storgt 89 ☎51600
tx16384
⇆66 ⛺ P Lift ☽

★★★Lillehammer ☎54800 tx19592
rm163 ⇆125 ▥38 P Lift ☽
sB ⇆ ▥430 dB ⇆ ▥660 M87-98
Pool mountains

★★★Oppland ☎51528
⇆ ▥83 A10rm P Lift ☽ sB ⇆ ▥330
dB ⇆ ▥460 M80-95 Pool lake

★★★Victoria Rica Storgt 82 ☎50049
tx19806
⇆94 P Lift ☽ sB ⇆428-497
dB ⇆596-690

★★Ersgaard ☎50684
rm38 ▥16 A9rm P ☽ sB150
sB ▥190 dB260 dB ▥320

★Breiseth Jerbanegt 5 ☎50060
rm3 ⇆1 ▥1 ⛺ P ☽ sB140 dB265
M alc

⅏Furnes Bil & Karosseriverkstad
☎51016

At **NORDSETER** (14km NE)

★★★Nevra (n.rest) ☎64001 tx19598
rm70 ⇆23 ▥32 P ☽ sB180
sB ⇆ ▥205 dB260 dB ⇆ ▥310 M65
⅏ Pool mountains

★★★Nordseter Høyfjellshotell
☎64008 tx19706
⇆46 ☽ sB ⇆235-235 dB ⇆370-440
M65-90 Pool mountains lake

LOEN
Sogn og Fjordane (☎057)

★★★★Alexandra ☎77660 tx42665
20 Jan-20 Dec
⇆201 P Lift ☽ sB ⇆405-455
dB ⇆550-730 M100-135 ⅏ Pool
Beach ♪ sea mountains

☆☆Richards ☎77661 tx42665
⇆23 P ☽ sB ⇆335-395
dB ⇆460-540 M75-95 Pool sea
mountains

★Rake ☎Stryn 1534

LOFTHUS
Hordaland (☎054)

★★★Ullensvang ☎61100 tx42659
rm130 ⇆120 ▥10 ⛺ P Lift ☽
sB ⇆ ▥390-450 dB ⇆520-640 M145 &
alc Pool

LOM
Oppland (☎062)

★ ★**Fossberg Turiststasjon** ☎11073
rm22 ▥7 A2rm **P** sB120 dB160–180
dB ▥210–220 M65 mountains

★ ★**Fossheim** ☎11005
Feb–Nov
rm55 ⇆31 ▥11 A22rm **P** mountains

⅋☉**S Skaansar** ☎11041

MANDAL
Vest-Agder (☎043)

★ ★ ★**Solborg Turisthotell** ☎61311
rm65 ⇆25 ▥30 **P** Lift ⅅ
sB ⇆ ▥350–400 dB ⇆ ▥450–520
M66–90 Pool sea

★**Bondehelmen** Elvegt 23A ☎61422

⅋☉**Malmø Bensinstasjon** ☎62888

MARIFJØRA
Sogn og Fjordane (☎056)

★ ★**Tørvis** ☎87200 tx40654
⇆43 A8rm **P** ⅅ sB ⇆231
dB ⇆267–347 M80 Beach sea
mountains

MO-I-RANA
Nordland (☎087)

★ ★ ★**Meyergården** ☎50555 tx55649
rm125 ⇆100 ♨ **P** Lift ⅅ sB235–285
sB ⇆385–415 dB365 dB ⇆490–550
M55–80

⅋☉**Rana Transportservice** ☎52220

MOLDE
Møre og Romsdal (☎072)

★ ★ ★**Alexandra** ☎51133 tx42847
⇆115 **P** Lift ⅅ sB ⇆485–495
dB ⇆615–625 Pool sea

☆**Knausen** ☎51577
rm50 ⇆30 **P** Lift ⅅ sB150
sB ⇆200–300 dB200–250
dB ⇆250–350 M55 sea mountains

⅋☉**Bj-Rødseth** ☎56755 & 52767

MORGEDAL
Telemark (☎036)

★ ★**Morgedal** ☎54144 tx21712
⇆70 **P** Lift ⅅ sB ⇆280–340
dB ⇆400–520 M140 ⅍ Pool Ω

MOSJØEN
Nordland (☎087)

★ ★**Fru Haugans** ☎70477
rm85 ⇆41 A26rm **P** ⅅ sB120–190
sB ⇆ ▥235–310 dB215–290
dB ⇆ ▥385–450 M alc

★ ★**Lyngengården** ☎70622
rm29 ▥20 **P** ⅅ sBfr225
sB ▥300–350 dBfr370 dB ⇆ ▥fr485
M60 mountains

⅋☉**Sparby Bilberging** ☎71023

MOSS
Østfold (☎032)

Norway

★ ★ ★**Refsnes-Gods** Godset 5 Jeløy
☎70411
⇆60 **P** Lift ⅅ Pool Beach sea

⅋☉**Moss Bil Vulkan** Oreveien 37 ☎54040
Hon Vau

NAMSOS
Nord-Trøndelag (☎077)

★ ★**Grand Bondehelmen** Kirkegt 7–9
☎73155
rm48 ▥12 sB220–240 sB ▥270–290
dB340–380 dB ▥430–480 M70–90

⅋☉**Bugges Karosseriverksted** ☎72150

NARVIK
Nordland (☎082)

★ ★ ★**Grand Royal** Kongensgt 64
☎41500 tx64032
⇆110 **P** Lift ⅅ sB ⇆475 dB ⇆595
M90 sea mountains

⅋☉**A Olsen Bil & Kranservice** ☎44208

NESBYEN
Buskerud (☎067)

★ ★ ★**Østenfor Turisthotell** ☎71530
rm74 ⇆5 ▥59 Lift ⅅ
sB ⇆ ▥250–265 dB ⇆ ▥365–480 ·
M90–115 Pool mountains lake

★ ★**Ranten Fjellstue Mykingstølen**
☎73445

★ ★**Smedsgarden Pensonat** (n.rest)
☎73125
sB75–85 sB ⇆100–110 dB140–150
dB ⇆ ▥170–180 M60 Pool

★**Svenkerud** ☎71260
⇆ ▥51 **P** Lift ⅅ sB ⇆ ▥210–235
dB ⇆ ▥295–320 mountains

⅋☉**Nesbyen Auto** ☎71066 Aud VW

NORDFJORDEID
Sogn og Fjordane (☎057)

★ ★ ★**Nordfjord Turist** ☎60433
⇆55 **P** ⅅ sB ⇆275–335
dB ⇆400–500 ⅍ sea mountains

NORDSETER See **LILLEHAMMER**

NOREFJELL
Buskerud (☎067)

★ ★**Fjellhvil** ☎46174
rm59 ⇆32 A8rm ⅅ sB240 sB ⇆270
dB350 dB ⇆380 M90–100 mountains
lake

★**Sandum Seter** ☎46155

NORHEIMSUND
Hordaland (☎055)

★ ★ ★**Fjord** ☎51522 tx42757
⇆36 **P** sB ⇆255–300 dB ⇆375–450
Beach sea

★ ★**Sandven** ☎51911
15 Jan–15 Dec
rm46 ⇆14 ▥14 **P** mountains

★**Turisthelm** ☎51264
rm12 **P** ⅅ mountains lake

NYSTOVA
Oppland (European Highway E68/5)
(☎061)

★ ★ ★**Nystuen** ☎37710 tx16562
rm50 ▥45 **P** ⅅ sB ▥200–250
dB ▥300–370 lake

ODDA
Hordaland (☎054)

★ ★ ★**Hardanger** ☎42133 tx42245
rm56 ⇆40 **P** ⅅ

⅋☉**Moe Motor** ☎42364 Fia

⅋☉**Nå Auto** ☎42700

OLDEN
Sogn og Fjordane (☎057)

★ ★ ★**Yris Turisthotell** ☎73240
May–Sep
rm39 ⇆34 ⅅ sB ⇆250–350
dB ⇆350–420 Pool sea mountains

★ ★**Olden Fjord** ☎73235 tx40560
15 May–24 Sep
rm40 ⇆34 ♨ ⅅ sB ⇆350 dB ⇆460
M80–125 & alc sea mountains

★**Olden Krotell** ☎73296 tx42609
▥15 sB ▥155–170 dB ▥245–270
Pool sea

OPPDAL
Sør Trøndelag (☎074)

★ ★**Müllerhotel Oppdal** ☎21611
rm52 ⇆50 **P** ⅅ mountains

★ ★**Oppdal Turisthotell** ☎21111
rm80 ⇆60 ▥20 A14rm **P** Lift ⅅ
sB ⇆ ▥295 dB ⇆ ▥470–500
M90–100 Pool mountains

☆**Fagerhaug** ☎23646
rm27 ⇆16 A11rm ⅅ sB ⇆135–195
dB ⇆210–295 mountains

⅋☉**Prøven Bil** ☎21888 Peu

ØRSTA
Møre-og-Romsdal (☎070)

★ ★**Viking Fjord** ☎66800 tx42945
rm42 ⇆8 ▥34 **P** Lift ⅅ sea
mountains

⅋☉**Mur Bil** ☎66514 & 66094

OS
Hordaland (☎05)

★ ★ ★**Solstrand** ☎300099 tx42050
⇆116 **P** Lift ♨ sB ⇆420–470
dB ⇆580–680 M90–130 ⅍ Pool
Beach sea

OSLO
Oslo (☎02)
See plan pages 300 and 301

★ ★ ★ ★**Bristol** Kristian IV-des gt 7
☎415840 tx71668 Plan **1** →

299

rm143 ⮜76 Lift ☽ sB ⮜600–700
dB ⮜800–1000 M alc

★★★★**Continental** Stortingsgt 24
☎419060 tx71012 Plan **2**
⮜170 🕭 **P** Lift ☽ sB ⮜600–650
dB ⮜750–850

★★★★**Grand** (SRS) K-Johansgt 31
☎429390 tx71683 Plan **3**
⮜310 **P** Lift ☽ sB ⮜665–705
dB ⮜845–1095 M alc 🏊 Pool

★★★★**KNA** (GT) Parkvelen 68
☎562690 tx71763 Plan **3A**
⮜48 🕭 **P** Lift ☽ sB ⮜640–695
dB ⮜815 M alc

★★★★**SAS Scandinavia** Holbergstgt
30 ☎113000 tx19090 Not on plan
⮜500 🕭 **P** Lift ☽ sB ⮜655–725
dB ⮜863 M alc Pool mountains

★★★**Ambassadeur** C-Colletsvej 15
☎441835 tx71446 Not on plan
⮜33 Lift ☽ sB ⮜375–475 dB ⮜725
Pool

★★★**Astoria** Akersgt 21 ☎426900
tx18754 Plan **5**
rm99 ⮜91 Lift ☽ sB ⮜525 dB ⮜717
M alc

★★★**Carlton Rica** Parkveien 78
☎563090 tx17902 Plan **4**
⮜50 Lift ☽ sB ⮜450–515 dB ⮜650
M95–350

★★★**SAS Globetrotter** Fornebuparken
☎120220 tx18745 Plan **6**
⮜150 **P** Lift ☽ sB ⮜560 dB ⮜740
Beach sea

OSLO

1	★★★ Bristol
2	★★★★ Continental
3	★★★★ Grand
3A	★★★★ KNA
4	★★★ Carlton Rica
5	★★★ Astoria
6	★★★ SAS Globetrotter
7	★★★ Smestad
8	★ Voksenåsen
9	★★★ Forbunds
10	★★★ Nye Helsfyr
10a	★★★ IMI
11	★★★ Panorama
12	★★★ Stefan
14	★★★ Sara Oslo
15	★★★ Ansgar

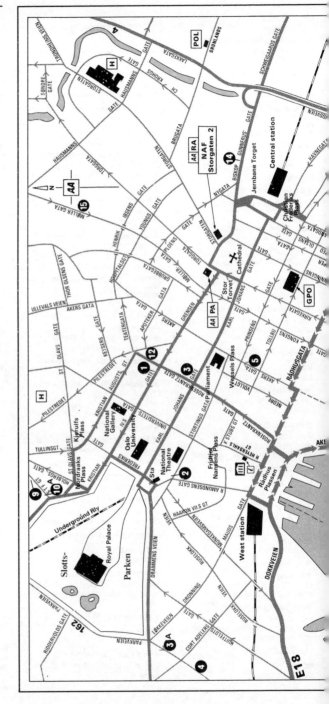

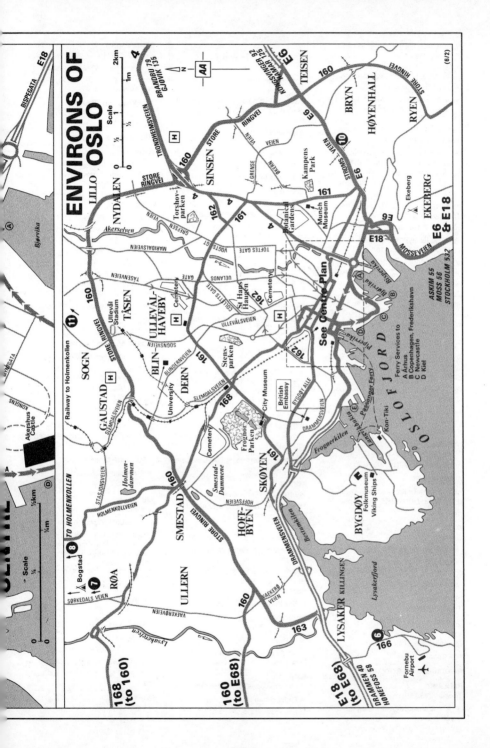

ENVIRONS OF OSLO

★★★Smestad Sørkedalsveien 93
☎146490 Plan 7
rm31 ⇔19 ⓜ12 A3rm
sB ⇔ ⓜ425-515 dB ⇔ ⓜ530-655
M85-125 sea mountains

★★★Voksenåsen (SARA) Ullveien 4,
Voksenkollveien ☎143090 tx17450
Plan 8
rm72 ⇔28 ⓜ44 P D sB ⇔ ⓜ450
dB ⇔ ⓜ550 Pool lake

★★Forbunds (Temperance) Holbergs
Plass 1 ☎208855 tx19413 Plan 9
rm107 ⇔100 🛁 P Lift D sB275
sB ⇔375-425 dB350-375 dB ⇔510
M95

★★IMI (Temperance) Staffeldtsgt 4
☎205330 tx18142 Plan 10A
⇔60 🛁 P Lift D

★★Nye Helsfyr Strømsveien 108
☎672380 tx6776 Plan 10
⇔115 P Lift D sB ⇔565-615
dB ⇔715-810 M alc

★★Panorama Sognsveien 218
☎187080 tx18432 Plan 11
Jun-Aug
rm414 Lift D sB225 sB ⇔ ⓜ290-320
dB320-350 dB ⇔ ⓜ430-500
mountains lake

★★Sara Oslo (SARA) Biskop
Gunnerusgt 3 ☎429410 tx71342 Plan 14
⇔319 P Lift D sB ⇔505 605
dB ⇔750-850

★★Stefan Rosenkrantzgt 1 ☎429250
tx19809 Plan 12
rm127 Lift D sB440 sB ⇔ ⓜ540-590
dB540 dB ⇔ ⓜ640-660 M115
mountains

★Ansgar (Temperance) Møllergt 26
☎204735 tx19602 Plan 15
rm59 ⇔14 🛁 P Lift D

At HØVIK (10km W)
☆☆☆Scandic Ramstadsletta 12-14
(E18) ☎121740 tx72430 Not on plan
rm51 P D

OTTA
Oppland (☎062)
★★★Otta Turist ☎30033
rm85 ⇔40 ⓜ45 🛁 P Lift D
sB ⇔ ⓜ375 dB ⇔ ⓜ495 Pool

🅟Otta Auto ☎30111

PORSGRUNN
Telemark (☎035)
★★Vic Skelegt 1 ☎55580 tx21450
⇔100 P Lift D sB ⇔430-470
dB ⇔565-585 M alc

🅟A Goberg ☎97499

RANDABERG See STAVANGER

RAULAND
Telemark (☎036)
★★★RaulandHøgfjellshotell ☎73222
tx21580

rm80 ⇔60 ⓜ20 P D sB ⇔ ⓜ290
dB ⇔ ⓜ330-500 M80-110 Pool
mountains

★Rauland Fjellstoge ☎73425
Jun-7 Oct & 22 Dec-April
rm33 ⇔22 D sB205 sB ⇔235 dB260
dB ⇔270-300 M90 mountains lake

🅟Rauland Servicesenter ☎73103

RINGEBU
Oppland (☎062)
★★Venabu Høfjellshotell ☎84055
rm63 P Lift D sB ⇔ ⓜ285-315
dB ⇔ ⓜ530 M90-110 sea mountains
lake

RISØR
Aust-Agder (☎041)
★★★Risør ☎50020

RJUKAN
Telemark (☎036)
★★★Gaustablikk Høyfjellshotell
☎91422 tx21677
rm90 ⇔5 ⓜ85 P D
sB ⇔ ⓜ280-300 dB ⇔ ⓜ440-480
M100 ♨ Pool mountains lake

★★★Skinnarbu Høyfjellshotell
Mosvatn ☎95461 tx21633
rm60 ⇔50 sB ⇔265-335
dB ⇔490-530 M80-100 Pool
mountains lake

★Rjukan Fjellstue ☎95162 tx16186
rm50 A35rm P D sB210 dB200-350
mountains

🅟B Berge Bilforretning Sam Ejdesgate
265 ☎90422 Vlo

RØROS
Sør Trøndelag (☎074)
★★★Bergstadens Turisthotell
☎11111 tx55617
rm76 ⇔71 🛁 P D sB ⇔330-350
dB ⇔455-450 M85 Pool mountains

★★★Røros Turisthotell ☎11011
tx55570
⇔108 ⓜ55 A10rm P Lift D
sB ⇔ ⓜ395-450 dB ⇔ ⓜ410-480 ♨
Pool mountains

🅟Nye Røros Auto ☎11855 Frd

ROSENDAL
Hordaland (☎054)
★★Fjord ☎81511
⇔40 P D sB ⇔375 dB ⇔590 M100
Beach sea

SANDANE
Sogn og Fjordane (☎(057)66000)
★Firdahelmen ☎66177
sB185 sB ⇔ ⓜ215 dB ⇔ ⓜ315

SANDEFJORD
Vestfold (☎034)
★★★Park ☎65550 tx21055
⇔166 🛁 P Lift D sB ⇔350-500
dB ⇔408-650 Pool

★★Kong Carl ☎63117
⇔27 🛁 P D sB ⓜ210-275
dB ⇔300-375

🅟Gustavsens ☎75792

SARPSBORG
Østfold (☎031)
★★★Saga Sannesundsveien 1
☎56080 tx18544
⇔70 🛁 P Lift D sB ⇔320-425
dB ⇔510-590

★★St-Olav ☎52055 tx18744
rm78 ⇔64 🛁 P Lift D sB150-250
sB ⇔195-340 dB250-350
dB ⇔295-450 M48-60

★Victoria ☎54500
rm18 ⇔22 ⓜ6 P sB ⇔190
sB ⇔ ⓜ200-260 dB300
dB ⇔ ⓜ340-400

🅟Bilservice Astridsgt 42 ☎53000

SAUDA
Rogaland (☎047)
At SAUDASJØEN (5km SW)
★★Sauda Fjord ☎93208
rm40 ⇔12 A4rm P D sB300
sB ⇔400 dB460 dB ⇔560 M80-105
♨ sea mountains

SELJESTAD
Hordaland (☎054)
★★Seljestad ☎45155
rm47 ⇔4 ⓜ24 P sB200 sB ⇔250
dB ⇔400 mountains

At SOLFONN (2.5km NW)
★★Solfonn ☎45122
Lift Pool

SJUSJØEN
Oppland (☎065)
★★Rustad Fjellstue (n.rest) ☎63408
Closed May, Nov & 1-20 Dec
rm47 A28rm P sB160 sB ⇔175-215
dB270 dB ⇔320-370 Beach
mountains lake

SKAIDI
Finnmark (☎084)
★Repparfjord ☎16121
rm52 ⇔21 A20rm P

🅟Kolmgrens Transport ☎16145

SKÅNEVIK
Hordaland (☎047)
★★Skånevik Fjord ☎65255
⇔49 P D sB ⇔265 dB ⇔400 M95
sea mountains

SKIEN
Telemark (☎035)
★★Høyer ☎20540
rm73 P Lift D

★ ★ ★Ibsen Kuerndalen 10 ☎24990
tx21136

⊷119 ⋒ P LIft 𝄇 sB ⊷450
dB ⊷556 Pool

🅢A Goberg ☎97500

SKJOLDEN
Sogn og Fjordane (☎056)

★ ★Skjolden ☎86606

6 May–Aug
rm55 ⊷30 ⋒5 P Lift 𝄇 sB ⊷ ⋒252
dB ⊷ ⋒359–634 M90 Beach sea
mountains

SOGNDAL
Sogn og Fjordane (☎056)

★ ★ ★Sogndal ☎72311 tx42727
rm110 ⊷83 ⋒27 Lift 𝄇 sB ⊷ ⋒300
dB ⊷ ⋒446–488 M125 & alc Pool

★ ★Hofslund Fjord ☎71022
rm47 ⊷19 ⋒28 P 𝄇 sB ⋒210
dB ⊷ ⋒310 M80 Pool Beach
mountains

🅢Sogn Maskinservice ☎72244

SOLFONN See **SELJESTAD**

SOLVORN
Sogn of Fjordane (☎056)

★ ★Walaker ☎84207 tx40654

May–Sep
rm25 ⊷20 A17rm P sB130 sB ⊷160
dB160–190 dB ⊷200–270 M90–100 &
alc Beach sea mountains

SORTLAND
Nordland (☎088)

No road connection: rail services from
HARSTAD

★ ★Sortland Nordic Vesterålsgt 59
☎21833 tx75845
rm65 ⊷14 ⋒46 P Lift 𝄇
sB ⊷ ⋒425 dB ⊷ ⋒525 sea

STALHEIM
Hordaland (☎055)

★ ★ ★ ★Stalheim ☎22122

10 May–25 Sep
⊷130 P Lift 𝄇 sB ⊷335
dB ⊷570–690 M115–120 mountains

STAMSUND
Nordland (☎088)

★ ★ ★SAS Lofoten ☎89300 tx64011
rm38 ⋒26 A10rm ⋒ P Lift 𝄇 Pool
sea

STAVANGER
Rogaland (☎04)

★ ★ ★ ★SAS Royal Atlantic
Jarnbaneveien 1 ☎527520 tx33095
⊷280 P Lift 𝄇 sB ⊷595–695
dB ⊷825 M135–185 sea lake

★ ★ ★KNA (GT) Lagårdsvegen 61
☎528500 tx33385
rm102 ⊷92 A4rm P Lift 𝄇
sB ⊷430–610 dB ⊷550–720 M74–120
ᵹ

Norway

★ ★ ★St-Svithun (Temperance) Klubbgt
3 ☎533020 tx73646
rm70 ⊷24 ⋒26 P Lift 𝄇

☆ ☆ ☆Scandic Elganesveien 181
☎526500 tx33144
⊷ ⋒154 P Lift 𝄇 Pool

★ ★Alstor Tjensvoll 4 ☎527020 tx40756
⊷80 P 𝄇 Pool lake mountains

🅢Bilberging ☎582900

At RANDABERG (8.5km NW)

★ ★ ★Viste Strand ☎597022 tx33161
rm52 ⊷51 P 𝄇 sB ⊷360 dB ⊷ 480
🌣 Beach sea

STAVERN
Vestfold (☎034)

★Wassiloff ☎98311
rm31 ⊷10 ⋒17 ⋒ P 𝄇
sB ⊷ ⋒290–310 dB ⊷ ⋒360–450
M90 sea

🅢Stavern Auto ☎99489

STEINKJER
Nord Trøndelag (☎077)

★ ★Grand Kongensgt 37 ☎64700
tx55518
⊷80 P Lift 𝄇 sB ⊷388–425
dB ⊷500–575

🅢Sortvik og Øyen ☎61472

STRONGFJORD
Sogn og Fjordane (☎(057)30100)

🅢Strongfjord Auto ☎31675 Hon

STØREN
Sør-Trøndelag (☎074)

★ ★ ★Støren ☎31118
⊷32 P Lift 𝄇 sB ⊷280–340
dB ⊷320–420 M65–110 mountains

STRANDA
Møre og Romsdal (☎071)

★ ★ ★Müllerhotell Stranda ☎60000
rm70 ⊷55 ⋒40 P Lift 𝄇
sB ⊷ ⋒375 dB335 dB ⊷ ⋒495 🌣
Pool sea mountains

STRAUMSJØEN
Nordland (☎088)

🅢K Strømme ☎38259 Vau

STRYN
Sogn og Fjordane (☎057)

🅢Karstad ☎71011 Maz

SUNDVOLLEN
Buskerud (☎067)

★ ★Sundvolden ☎39140 tx72960
⋒115 Lift 𝄇 sB ⊷ ⋒250–370
dB ⊷ ⋒370–375 M alc Pool
mountains lake

SUNNDALSØRA
Møre og Romsdal (☎073)

★ ★Müllerhotell Sunndalen ☎91655
rm65 ⊷ ⋒47 ⋒ P Lift 𝄇
sB ⊷ ⋒280–315 dB ⊷ ⋒495–505 🌣
mountains

SURNADAL
Møre og Romsdal (☎073)

★ ★Surnadal ☎61544
rm70 ⊷47 P 𝄇 sB ⊷330
dB ⊷400–460 M90–130 Beach sea
mountains

SVOLVAER
Nordland (☎088)

☆ ☆ ☆Lofoten Nordic ☎71200 tx64451
rm68 ⊷63 Lift 𝄇 sB ⊷415 dB ⊷530
sea mountains

TINN AUSTBYGDA
Telemark (☎036)

🅢Marumsrud Bilverksted ☎97166

TØNSBERG
Vestfold (☎033)

🅢Bergans Auto ☎12703

TRETTEN
Oppland (☎062)

★ ★ ★Gausdal ☎28500
⊷120 ⋒ P 𝄇 sB ⊷245 dB360
dB ⊷450 🌣 Pool ∩ mountains

★Glomstad Gard (n.rest) ☎76257

16 Dec–Apr & Jun–10 Oct
rm27 sB130–140 dB220–240

TROMSØ
Troms (☎083)

★ ★ ★SAS Royal Sjogt 7 ☎56000
tx64260
⊷ ⋒200 P Lift 𝄇 sB ⊷ ⋒575
dB ⊷ ⋒690 M80–190 sea mountains

★ ★Grand Nordic Storgt 44 ☎85500
tx64204
rm170 ⊷12 ⋒136 P Lift 𝄇
sB ⊷ ⋒525 dB ⊷ ⋒670 mountains

🅢Bilredningstjenesten ☎70700

TRONDHEIM
Sør Trøndelag (☎07)

★ ★ ★Astoria Nordregt 24 ☎529550
tx55154
rm52 ⊷48 Lift 𝄇 sB ⊷450 dB ⊷645

★ ★ ★Britannia Dronningensgate 5
☎530040 tx55451
rm120 ⊷112 P Lift 𝄇
sB ⊷ ⋒350–485 dB ⊷ ⋒580–695
M alc

★ ★ ★Prinsen Kongensgt 30 ☎530650
tx55324
rm60 ⊷10 ⋒45 P Lift 𝄇
sB ⊷ ⋒515 dB ⊷ ⋒660–770

☆ ☆ ☆Scandic Brøsetveien 186
☎939500 tx55420
⊷ ⋒165 P Lift 𝄇

★★**Larssens** T-Angellsgt 106 ☎528851
rm35 Lift sB245–280 sB ⌂390–410
dB ⌂490–510

⚹Prøven Bil ☎935540

TURTAGRØ
Sogn og Fjordane

★★*Turtagrø* ☎Skjolden 6616

TYIN
Oppland (☎061)

★★★**Tyin Høyfjelshotell (DPn** in
winter) ☎37712
Jan–Oct
rm100 ⇔17 ⌂83 Lift ☽
sB ⇔ ⌂fr255 dB ⇔ ⌂fr410 M75–85
Pool mountains lake

TYNSET
Hedmark (☎064)

★★**Tynset** ☎80600
rm42 ⇔13 ☽ sB175–280
sB⇔225–325 dB300–420
dB⇔375–495 M alc mountains

ULVIK
Hordaland (☎055)

★★★**Brakanes** ☎26105 tx42955
Apr–15 Dec
⇔100 **P** Lift ☽ ⛵ Beach 𝛿 sea

★★**Strand** ☎26305
May–Sep
⇔58 **P** ☽ 3B ⇔340 rlB ⇔560
M85–95 Pool Beach sea mountains

★★**Ulvik Turist** ☎26200
Closed Jan
rm63 ⇔33 ⌂18 Lift ☽ sB230
sB ⇔ ⌂290–330 dB360
dB ⇔ ⌂430–570 M110 sea

★*Bjotvelt* ☎26300
sea

Norway

USTAOSET
Buskerud (☎067)

★**Ustaoset Fjellstue** ☎87123
15 Jun–Sep
rm26 ⌂7 **P** sB158–175 dB226–250
dB ⌂276–300 M60–70 mountains

UTNE
Hordaland (☎055)

★★**Utne** ☎66983
rm26 ⇔2 ⌂11 **P** sB200 dB340
dB ⇔ ⌂390 M80–90 sea

VÅGÅMO
Oppland (☎062)

★★★**Villa** ☎37071 tx18876
⇔63 **P** ☽ sB ⇔384 dB ⇔533–563
M95 Pool mountains

VIKI I SOGN
Sogn og Fjordane (☎056)

☆☆**Hopstock** ☎95102
rm34 ⇔6 ⌂28 **P** ☽ sB ⌂276–315
dB ⇔ ⌂430–530 M115 & alc Pool sea

VINSTRA
Oppland (☎(062)81100)

★★★**Fefor Høyfjellshotell** ☎90099
rm115 ⇔40 ⌂l7U Llft ☽
sB ⇔ ⌂185–225 dB ⇔ ⌂280–370 ⛵
Pool 𝛿 Ω mountains lake

★★**Sødorp Gjestgivengård** ☎91000
rm16 **P** sB220–260 dB310–350
M40–75 mountains

★★*Vinstra* ☎90199

VOSS
Hordaland (☎055)

☆☆☆**Fleischer's** ☎11155 tx40470
rm71 ⇔34 ⌂37 ☽ sB ⇔380
dB ⇔590 Pool lake

★★★**Park Voss** ☎11322
⇔48 🅶 **P** Lift ☽ sB ⇔375
dB ⇔500–600 M100 mountains lake

☆☆☆**Voss** ☎12006
⇔23 dB ⇔310 M alc mountains

★★**Jarl** ☎11933
rm64 ⇔51 **P** Lift ☽ sB ⇔340
dB ⇔560 M85–95 Pool mountains lake

★*Nøring Pensjonat* ☎11211
⇔23 **P** M alc mountains lake

⚹**Motor Service** ☎12700 Frd Ren

⚹**J Seims** ☎11622 Frd Ren

VRÅDAL
Telemark (☎036)

★★★**Strand Turisthotel** ☎056100
tx21762
rm87 ⇔75 A12m **P** ☽ sBfr270
sB ⇔fr320 dBfr380 dB ⇔480–680
M105–115 ⛵ Pool Ω mountains lake

★★**Vrådal** ☎56127
rm70 ⇔6 ⌂45 **P** Lift ☽ sB235
sB ⇔295 dB360 dB ⇔420 mountains
lake

VRÅLIOSEN
Telemark (☎036)

★★**Vråliosen** ☎55111
rm24 ⇔2 ⌂2 A8rm **P** ☽ sB185
dB295 dB ⇔345 M80 Pool Beach
mountains lake

The glacier Suphellebreen

Holmenkollen, Oslo

PORTUGAL

Portugal, a relatively small country lying in the south-western corner of the Iberian peninsula, has as its only land frontier the Spanish border in the east. The country is perhaps best known for its five hundred miles of coastline. The Algarve in the extreme south is one of the finest stretches of coastline in Europe, with unique caves and a remoteness which has been preserved by the lack of development in the area. Inland the cool valleys and pastures of the River Tagus contrast sharply with the wooded mountain slopes of the Minho area in the north.

Generally the country enjoys a mild climate, with the Algarve being very hot in the summer. The language is Portuguese, which was developed from Latin and closely resembles Spanish.

The Rio Douro, Costa Verde

Area *34,700 sq miles*
Location map *See pages 318 and 319*
Population *9,800,000*
Local time *GMT (Summer GMT +1)*
National flag *Divided vertically, green in the hoist, red in the fly with the arms of the former monarchy superimposed on the gold armillary in the centre.*

How to get there

The usual approach to Portugal is via France and Spain, entering Spain on the Biarritz to San Sebastian road at the western end of the Pyrénées. The distance from the Channel ports to Lisboa (Lisbon), the capital, is about 1,300 miles, a distance which will require three or four night stops. The driving distance can be shortened by using one of the car/sleeper service from Boulogne or Paris to Biarritz, or Paris to Madrid. Alternatively you can ship you vehicle to Spain by the Plymouth to Santander car ferry, then travel onwards by road. Santander to Lisboa is about 550 miles and this will require one or two night stops.

Motoring regulations and general information

This information should be read in conjunction with the general content of the European ABC (pages 6–27). **Note** As certain regulations and requirements are common to many countries they are covered by one entry in the ABC and the following headings represent some of the subjects dealt with in this way:
AA Agents
Crash or safety helmets
Customs regulations for European countries
Drinking and driving
Fire extinguisher
First-aid kit
Insurance
Medical treatment
Police fines
Radio telephones/Radio transmitters
Rear view mirror
Road signs
Seat belts
Traffic lights
Tyres
Visitors' registration

Accidents
Fire, police and **ambulance** Public emergency service ☎115. There are no firm rules of procedure after an accident; however, the recommendations under *Accidents* page 7 are advised.

Accommodation
A list of hotels is available from the Tourist Office in London. Hotels are officially approved and classified by the office of the Secretary of

State for Information and Tourism. Details of officially authorised charges and the classification of the hotel must be exhibited in every bedroom. The cost of meals served in bedrooms, other than breakfast, is subject to an increase of 10%. Children under eight years of age are granted a discount of 50% on prices of meals.

While commendations and complaints about hotels are an important source of information to us, members may also like to know that an official complaint book, which must be kept in all establishments, enables guests to record their comments.

Complaints may also be made to local Tourism Delegations and Boards or to the State Tourism Department, Palácio Foz, Praça dos Restaudores, Lisboa. The Government has encouraged the building of well-equipped hotels, particularly in the Algarve region. Tourist inns known as *pousadas* and *estalagens* are controlled by the *Direcçao General de Turismo*, the official Portuguese tourist organisation; details of most of these are included in the gazetteer.

Pousadas are Government-owned but privately run. They have been specially built or converted, and are often located in the more remote touring areas where there is a lack of other hotels. Visitors may not usually stay more than five nights.

Estalagens are small, well-equipped wayside inns (although there are some in towns), privately-owned and run, and normally in the one- or two-star category.

Breakdown
The Portuguese motoring club Automóvel Club de Portugal (ACP) operates a road patrol service and roadside assistance may be obtained by telephoning Porto 29271 in the north and Lisboa 775475 in the south. See also *Breakdown* page 8 and *Warning triangles* page 309.

Should you break down or need assistance on the Ponte 25 de Abril (on the southern approach to Lisboa), keep the vehicle as near to the right-hand side of the bridge as possible, remain in the vehicle and hang a white handkerchief out of the window. You must wait inside the vehicle until the road patrol arrives. Vehicles must not be towed, except by purpose-built towing vehicles, or pushed by hand on the bridge. If you run out of petrol on the bridge you will be fined *Esc*600 and have to buy 10 litres

(2gal 1½pt) of petrol from the bridge authorities at the official price.

British Consulates
(See also page 8)
1200 Lisboa Rua de São Domingos Là Lapa ☎661191. There are also consulates in Porto and Portimão.

Currency and banking hours
(See also page 11)
The unit of currency is the escudo, which is divided into 100 centavos; 1,000 escudos are known as 1 conto; one escudo is written 1$00 (with the dollar sign). One escudo fifty centavos is written 1$50.

It is prohibited to import or export more than *Esc*5,000 in Portuguese currency. There is no restriction on the importation of foreign currencies or travellers cheques, which must be declared at the Customs on entry if the total exceeds *Esc*70,000. Amounts in excess of this figure may only be exported if they tally with the amount declared on entry.

Banks are usually open from Monday to Friday 08.30–11.45hrs and 13.00–14.45hrs, closed on Saturdays.

Dimensions and weight restrictions
Private cars and trailers are restricted to the following dimensions and weights – Car height: 4 metres; width: 2.5 metres; car/caravan combination – length: 18 metres; weight (unladen): 750kg (14cwt 85lb) if the towing vehicle's engine is 2,500cc or less; 1,500kg (1ton 9cwt 59lb) for vehicles with an engine capacity in excess of 2,500 but under 3,500cc.

Driving licence
A valid British driving licence is acceptable in Portugal. The minimum age at which a visitor may drive a temporarily imported car or motorcycle (over 50cc) is 17 years. See also page 13 and *Speed limits* page 308.

Emergency messages to tourists
(See also page 14)
Emergency messages to tourists are broadcast all year by Portuguese Radio.

Radiodifusão Portuguesa (RDP1) transmitting on 383 metres and 451 metres medium wave broadcasts these messages in English, French, German, Italian, Portuguese and Spanish every hour during the news Monday to Saturday.

Radiodifusão Portuguesa (RDP2) transmitting

on 290 metres and 397 metres medium wave broadcasts the messages as RDP1 above.

International distinguishing sign
(See also page 17)
The penalty for failure to display a nationality plate, or for displaying one of the wrong size or type, is a fine of between *Esc*1000–5000.

Lights
(See also page 17)
The use of full headlights is prohibited in built-up areas.

Motoring club
(See also page 18)

The **Automovel Club de Portugal** (ACP) which has its headquarters at rua Rosa Araújo 24, Lisboa 1200 ☎563931 has offices in a number of provincial towns. They will assist motoring tourists generally and supply information on touring and other matters. ACP offices are normally open 09.30–12.45 and 14.30–17.00hrs Monday to Friday; English and French are spoken. Offices are closed on Saturday and Sunday.

Motorways
About 113 miles of motorway (Auto-Estrada) are open, and more stretches are under construction. A 200 mile network is planned. Tolls are charged on most sections. A leaflet entitled *Motorways in Portugal* is available to AA members.

Orange badge scheme for disabled drivers
(See also page 19)
In Portugal parking places reserved for disabled drivers are indicated by signs displaying the international disabled symbol. However, badge holders are not allowed to park in places where parking is otherwise prohibited.

Overtaking
(See also page 19)
Vehicles more than 2 metres wide must stop, if need be, to facilitate passing.

Parking
(See also page 19)
Parking is forbidden, except where parking signs are displayed, and on a main road outside a built-up area, also on a road carrying fast-moving traffic. At night, parking is prohibited on all roads outside built-up areas. Always park in the direction of the traffic flow except where regulations decree otherwise or where parking is allowed on only one side of the road. Parking lights must be used in badly-lit areas and when visibility is poor. Spending the night in a vehicle by the roadside is not advisable.

Passengers
(See also page 19)
It is recommended that children do not travel in a vehicle as front seat passengers.

Petrol
(See also page 20)
Credit cards Petrol stations do not accept credit cards.
Duty-free petrol The petrol in the vehicle tank may be imported free of customs duty and tax.
Octane ratings Gasolina Normal (85) and Gasolina Super (98).
Petrol cans It is **forbidden** to carry petrol in cans in a vehicle.

Postal information
Mail Postcards *Esc*40.00, Letters 5–220gm *Esc*40.00.
Post offices There are 1,045 post offices in Portugal. Opening hours are from 09.00–19.00hrs Monday to Friday, with the smaller offices closing between 12.30–14.00hrs.

Amarante on the River Tâmega

Postcheques
(See also page 21)
Postcheques may be cashed at all post offices for any amount up to a maximum of *Esc5,000* per cheque. Counter positions are identified by the *Postcheque* sign. See above for post office opening hours.

Priority
(See also *Priority including Roundabouts* page 22)
Vehicles on motorways have right of way over all vehicles approaching from the respective slip roads.

Public holidays
Official public holidays in Portugal for 1985 are given below. See also *Public holidays* page 22.

January 1 (New Year's Day)
February 19 (Carnival Day)
April 5 (Good Friday)
April 25 (Revolution Day)
May 1 (Labour Day)
June 2† (Corpus Christi)
August 15 (Assumption)
October 5* (Republic Day)
November 1 (All Saints' Day)
December 1† (Independence Day)
December 8† (Immaculate Conception)
December 25 (Christmas Day)
*Saturday   †Sunday

Registration document
If the vehicle is not registered in your name a special certificate is required authorising you to use it. This certificate is available free from the AA. See also page 22.

Roads
Main roads and most of the important secondary roads are good as are the mountain roads of the north-east. A leaflet entitled '*Road conditions in Spain and Portugal*' is available to AA members.

Shopping hours
Shops are usually open Monday to Friday 09.00–13.00hrs and 15.00–19.00hrs and Saturdays 09.00–13.00hrs.

Speed limits
(See also page 25)
The beginning of a built-up area is marked by a sign bearing the placename; there are no signs showing the end – the only indication is the sign for the beginning of the area (on the other side of the road) for motorists coming from the other

direction. In built-up areas the limit is 60kph (37mph), or 50kph (31mph) for vehicles towing trailers. Outside built-up areas private vehicles must not exceed 120kph (74mph) on motorways and 90kph (56mph) on other roads. Vehicles towing trailers must not exceed 70kph (43mph) outside built-up areas. There is a minimum speed limit of 40kph (24mph) on motorways, except where otherwise signposted.

Visitors to Portugal who have held a full driving licence for less than one year are restricted to driving at a top speed of 90kph (56mph). They must also display a yellow disc bearing the figure '90' at the rear of their vehicle (obtainable from ACP frontier office at Valenca, Vilar Formoso and Caia).

Leaflets giving details in English are handed to visitors at entry points.

Spiked, studded or snow tyres
(See also page 10)
The use of *spiked tyres* is prohibited in Portugal.

Toll bridges
Lisbon Tagus Bridge	Esc
Cars	60
Caravans/trailers	plus 60
Motorcycles – over 50cc	60
under 50cc not permitted	

Pedestrians, bicycles, and bicycles with auxiliary motors of less than 50cc, are prohibited. Drivers must maintain a speed of 40–70kph (24–43mph) on the bridge. Speed is checked by radar. Heavy vehicles must keep at least 20 metres (66ft) behind the preceding vehicle. Toll payable in one direction only, when travelling from Lisbon to the south. There are no charges for vehicles travelling northbound, into Lisbon.

Tourist Information offices
(See also page 25)
The Portuguese National Tourist Office, New Bond Street House, 1/5 New Bond Street (above National Westminster Bank, entrance in Burlington Gardens opposite Burlington Arcade), London W1Y 0NP, ☎01-493 3873, will be pleased to assist you with information regarding tourism. There is an office of the Direccão Geral de Turismo in Lisboa and local information offices will be found in most provincial towns under this name or one of the following Comissão Municipal de Turismo, Junta de Turismo or Câmara Municipal.

Using the telephone

(See also page 26)

Insert coin **after** lifting receiver, dialling tone same as the UK. When making calls to subscribers within Portugal precede number with relevant area code as necessary (shown in parentheses against town entry in gazetteer). Use *Esc*2.50, 5 or 25 centavos coins for local calls and *Esc*5 for national and international calls.

International callbox identification Selected boxes in Lisbon and Porto.

Telephone rates The cost of an 8 second call to the UK is *Esc*5.50. Local calls cost *Esc*5.50. *What to dial for the Irish Republic** 07 353. *What to dial for the UK** 00 44.

*or see local instructions.

Warning triangles

The use of a warning triangle is compulsory for all vehicles except two-wheeled vehicles. The triangle must be placed on the road 30 metres (33yds) behind the vehicle and must be clearly visible from 100 metres (109yds). See also *Warning triangles/Hazard warning lights* page 26.

Prices are in Portuguese Escudos
According to our information garages
with no specific service agencies will
handle any make of car.
Abbreviations:
av   avenida
Capt   Capitão
esp   esplanada
Gen   General
r   rua

ABRANTES
Ribatejo (☎043)

★ ★ ★**Turismo** Largo de Santo António
☎21261

⇌24 🏛 sB ⇌1730 dB ⇌2850 ⅋
Pool lake

A Ferreira r Brito Capelo 482 ☎129 BL

Sosepor Largo de Chafariz ☎22127 Cit

ALBERGARIA A VELHA
Beira Litoral (☎0034)

☆**Alameda** Estrada Naciónal 1 ☎52402
⇌18 sB1730 dB ⇌2850 mountains

ALBUFEIRA
Algarve (☎0089)

★ ★ ★ ★**Balaia** (SRS) Praia M-Luisa
☎52681 tx56278

⇌193 🏛 P Lift ♪ sB ⇌4769–10492
dB ⇌5723–11445 Mfr1717 ⅋ Pool
Beach ◠ sea

★ ★ ★**Sole e Mar** r J-Bernardino de
Sousa ☎52121 tx56217
⇌74 Lift

★ ★**Estalagem do Cerro** r B-Cerro da
Piedade ☎52191 tx56211
rm83 ⇌77 🏠6 P Lift ♪
sB⇌ 🍴1730 dB ⇌ 🍴4800 sea

★ ★**Estalagem Mar á Vista** Cerro da
Piedade ☎52154
⇌29 Lift dB ⇌ 🍴4800

ALCÁCER DO SAL
Baixo Alentejo (☎065)

★ ★**Estalagem da Barrosinha** Estrada
Naciónal 5 ☎62363
rm10 ⇌9 🏠 P dB ⇌ 🍴3800
mountains

ALJCOBAÇA
Estremadura (☎0044)

T Marques Praça 25 de Abril 48 ☎42175
BL

ALPEDRINHA
Beira Baize (☎0052)

★**Estalagem São Jorge** ☎57154
⇌14 sB ⇌2750 dB ⇌ 🍴3800

AMARANTE
Douro Litoral (☎0025)

At **SERRA DO MARÃO** (25km E on N15 to
Vila Real)

★**Pousada de São Gonçalo** ☎46123
rm18 ⇌14 🏠

ARMAÇÃO DE PÊRA
Algarve (☎0082)

★ ★ ★**Estalagem Algar** av Beira-Mar
☎32353
Mar–Oct
⇌19 dB ⇌4800

★ ★ ★**Garbe** av Marginal ☎32187
tx57485
⇌102 🍴9 P Lift ♪ dB ⇌ 🍴4800
Pool sea

AVEIRO
Beira Litoral (☎0034)

★ ★**Arcada** r Viana do Castelo 4 (n.est)
☎23001 tx37460
⇌52 P Lift ♪ sB ⇌1050–1300
dB ⇌1650–1950

Riauto av 5 de Outubro 18 ☎22031 BL

AZEITÃO
Estremadura

★**Estalagem Quintas das Torres** Quinta
das Torres ☎2080001
rm12 ⇌11 A2rm P sB ⇌2750
dB ⇌3755

BARCELOS
Minho (☎0023)

Castro (M Gonçalves de Castro) r F-
Borges ☎82008 BL

BEJA
Baixo Alentejo (☎0079)

Acail av M-Fernandes 27 ☎22191 BL
BMW

J Pinto Caeiro av da Boavista 1 & 7
☎23031 Frd

BRAGA
Minho (☎0023)

Ranhada & Taixeira Largo 1 de
Dezembro 20 ☎22912 Frd

BRAGANÇA
Tras-Os-Montes Alto Douro (☎0092)

★ ★**Pousada de São Bartolomeu**
Estrada de Turismo ☎22493
⇌12 🏛 P dB ⇌3350 mountains

Chamauto r A-Herculano ☎22478 Dat

CALDAS DA RAINHA
Estremadura (☎062)

★**Central** Largo do Dr J-Barbosa 22
(n.rest) ☎22078
rm40 ⇌7 🏠2 P ♪ sB900
sB ⇌ 🍴1700 dB1600 dB ⇌ 🍴2400

⇌◐**Auto-Leiria** r Capt Filipe de Sousa 89
☎22561

Auto-Mechânica das Caldas (JL
Morgado) r P-Proença ☎22947 Cit

CANAS DE SENHORIM
Beira Atla (☎0032)

At **URGEIRÇA** (1km NE on N234)

★ ★ ★**Urgeiriça** ☎67267
⇌53 P ♪ sB ⇌1730 dB ⇌2850 ⅋
Pool mountains

CANIÇADA
Minho

★ ★**Pousada de São Bento** Cerdeirinhas-
Soengas ☎57190
⇌ 🍴10 🏛 P ♪ dB ⇌ 🍴3350 ⅋
Pool mountains lake

CARCAVELOS
Estremadura

★ ★ ★**Praia-Mar** r do Gurué 16
☎2473131 tx42283
rm158 ⇌44 🍴14 P Lift ♪
sB ⇌3030–4230 dB ⇌3510–4785 Pool

CASCAIS
Estremadura

★ ★ ★**Estoril Sol** Estrada Marginal
☎282831 tx15102 →

309

⊷400 🏠 **P** Lift ☽ sB ⊷4100–5000
dB ⊷5000–5900 Pool ♂ sea

★ ★ ★**Baia** Estrada Marginal ☎281034
tx16001

⊷87 **P** Lift dB ⊷175–2285 sea

★ ★ ★**Estalagem Albatroz** r F-Aronca
100–102 ☎282821 tx16052

⊷40 🏠 **P** Lift ☽ dB ⊷ 🍴3755 sea

★ ★ ★**Nau** r Dr Iracy Doyle Lote 14
☎282861 tx42289

⊷53 Lift ☽ dB ⊷2285 sea mountains

★ ★**Estalagem Solar do Carlos** r Latino
Coelho 8 ☎2868463

rm8 ⊷

J Jorge av E-Navarro 32 ☎280112

Reparadora de Cascais r das
Amendoeiras-Torre ☎289045 BL

At **PRAIA DO GUINCHO** (4km W)

★ ★ ★ ★**Guincho** ☎2850491 tx12624

⊷36 🏠 Lift dB ⊷3250 ♨ Beach sea

★ ★**Estalagem Mar do Guincho** Praia do
Guincho ☎2850251

rm13 ⊷14 A2rm **P** ☽ sea

CASTELO BRANCO
Beira Baixa (☎72)

⊷**Avenida de Castelo Branco** av Gen H-
Delgado 75–79 ☎421 BL

⊷**S Cristóvão** av Gen H-Delgado ☎283

CASTELO DO BODE See **TOMAR**

CHAVES
Tras-Os-Montes Alto Douro (☎0091)

★ ★**Estalagem Santiago** r do Olival
(n.rest) ☎22545

⊷31

Império de Chaves av 5 de Outubro
☎22133 Dat

COIMBRA
Beira Litoral (☎0039)

★ ★ ★**Bragança** Largo das Ameias 10
☎22171

rm83 ⊷57 🍴26 Lift

Brinca & Morais r do Arnadod 19–21
☎29096 Dat

P Irmãos r de Sofia 171 ☎25493 Frd

S José av Fernão de Magalhães 216
☎25578 BL

COLARES
Estremadura

★**Estalagem do Conde** Quinta do Conde
☎9291652

Closed Dec

⊷10 **P** dB ⊷3755 sea mountains

At **PRAIA DAS MACÁS** (4km NW by N375)

★ ★ ★**Miramonte** ☎929 1230 tx13221

⊷ 🍴90 **P** ☽ dB ⊷3200 M750 Pool
mountains

COSTA DA CAPARICA
Estremadura

Portugal

★ ★**Estalagem Colobri** ☎2400776

⊷ 🍴25 Lift dB ⊷ 🍴3755

COVILHÃ
Beira Baixa (☎0075)

Auto Representações da Covilhã Largo
das Forças Armadas ☎22048 Cit

CURIA
Beira Litoral (☎0031)

★ ★ ★**Palace** ☎52131

Apr–15 Oct
rm125 ⊷107 🍴18 **P** Lift ☽
sB ⊷ 🍴3434 dB ⊷ 🍴3815 M1145 ♨
Pool mountains

ELVAS
Alto Alentejo

★ ★**Estalagem D Sancho II** Praça da
Sancho II ☎22686

⊷ 🍴26 Lift ☽ dB⊷ 🍴3800

★**Pousada de Santa Luzia** (outside town
on Borba-Badajoz road) ☎22194

rm11 **P** ☽ dB ⊷ 🍴3350

Antunes & Guerra av de Badajoz ☎170

ERICEIRA
Estremadura (☎061)

★ ★**Estalagem Morais** r M-Bombarda 3
(n.rest) ☎62611

Closed Nov

⊷40 Lift dB ⊷3755 Pool sea

ESPINHO
Douro Litoral (☎02)

★ ★ ★**Praia Golfe** r 6 ☎720630 tx23727

⊷119 🏠 **P** Lift ☽ dB ⊷3755 Pool
sea

ESPOSENDE
Minho (☎0023)

★ ★**Suave-Mar** av E-Duarto Pacheco
☎(053)89445

⊷61 🏠 **P** ☽ sB ⊷1500–2200
dB ⊷1800–3200 ♨ Pool sea
mountains

ESTORIL
Estremadura

★ ★ ★ ★**Palacio Estoril** Parque
Estoril ☎2680400 tx12757

⊷68 **P** Lift ☽ sB ⊷4550–6500
dB ⊷4175–8125 Pool ♂ sea

★ ★ ★**Cibra** ☎2681811 tx16007

⊷05 **P** Lift ☽ dB ⊷3755 sea

★ ★**Estalagem Claridade** r Mouzinho de
Albuquerque 14 ☎2683434

⊷10 dB ⊷3755

★ ★**Founder's Inn (Albergaria do
Fundador)** r D-A-Henriques 11
☎2682221

⊷12 **P** ☽ dB ⊷4600

ESTREMOZ
Alto Alentejo

★ ★ ★**Pousada Rainha Santa Isabel**
Castelo de Estremoz ☎22618

⊷23 **P** Lift ☽ mountains

Ago Comercial Estremoz av de Santo
António, Estrada Nacional 4 & Rossió
Marquês de Pombal 33 ☎22215 Cit

ÉVORA
Alta Alentejo (☎0069)

★ ★ ★**Pousada dos Loios** ☎24051
tx43288

⊷32 ☽ sB ⊷4100 dB ⊷4540

★ ★**Planicle** r M-Bombarda 40
☎24026

rm33 Lift sea

R Cruz r do Raimundo 99C ☎24096 Cit

FARO
Algarve (☎0089)

★ ★ ★ ★**Eva** av da República ☎24054
tx56524

⊷150 🍴40 Lift ☽ dB ⊷ 🍴4800
Pool sea

★ ★ ★**Faro** Praça D F-Gomes 2
☎22076

rm52 ⊷36 🍴16 Lift ☽
sB ⊷ 🍴1715–2505 dB ⊷ 🍴1845–3205
M750–800 ♂ ∩

★ ★**Albacor** r Brites de Almeida 25
(n.rest) ☎22093

⊷ 🍴38 **P** Lift ☽ sB ⊷1850
dB ⊷ 🍴2400

A Baptista r do Alportel 121A ☎23071
Cit

FIAAL Largo do Mercado 2–6 ☎23061
Frd Vlo

At **PRAIA DE FARO** (8km SW)

★ ★**Estalagem Aeromar** ☎23542

Feb–Nov

⊷20

FÁTIMA
Beira Litoral (☎0049)

★ ★ ★**Fatima** r Jacinta Marto ☎97751
tx43750

⊷76 **P** Lift ☽ sB ⊷2400 dB ⊷3900
M800 mountains

★ ★**Trés Pastorinhas** Cova da Iria
☎97629

⊷92 🏠 **P** Lift ☽ dB ⊷2850

FIGUEIRA DA FOZ
Beira Litoral (☎0033)

★ ★ ★**Figueira** av Dr O-Salazar
☎22146 tx16086

⊷91 Lift ☽ sea

★ ★**Portugal** r da Liberdade 41 (n.rest)
☎22176

rm52 ⊷29 🏠 dB ⊷ 🍴1950

FUNDÁO
Beira Baixa

Industrias do Fundão Estrada Nacional
18 ☎52375

GUARDA
Beira Alta (☎0051)

★ ★ ★Turismo Largo de São Francisco
☎22206 tx18760

⇔105 🏤 P Lift 🌙 dB ⇔2850 Pool
mountains

★ ★Alicança r V-da-Gama ☎22135
rm30 ⇔16 🏤 🌙 dB ⇔2850
mountains

★ ★Filipe r V-de-Gama 9 ☎22659
rm25 ⇔7 Lift 🌙 dB ⇔ 🍴3800
mountains

Auto Neofor r 31 de Janeiro 20 ☎21348
Frd

D José r Batalha Reis 2 ☎22947 Cit

LAGOS
Algarve (☎0082)

★ ★ ★Meia Praia Meia Praia (4km NE)
☎62001 tx57489

⇔65 Lift dB ⇔3150 ⚓ Pool Beach
☊ sea

★ ★Pensão Dona Ana Praia de Dona
Ana ☎62322
Apr–Oct
rm11 ⇔5 dB ⇔3150

★ ★Residential Mar Azul r 25 de Abril 13
(n.rest) ☎62181
rm17 ⇔12 🍴1 sB700 sB ⇔ 🍴1000
dB1700 dB ⇔ 🍴1100 sea

LECA DO BALIO
Douro Litoral

★ ★ ★Estalagem via Norte Estrada via
Norte ☎9480294

⇔12 🏤 P 🌙 dB ⇔5700

LEIRIA
Beira Litoral(☎0044)

★ ★ ★Euro Sol r D J-Alves da Silva
☎24101 tx42031

⇔54 🏤 P Lift 🌙 dB ⇔2850 Pool

🅿Auto-Leiria r Machado Santos
10B ☎24191 Frd

🅿Lubrigaz r Capt Mousinho
Albuquerque 38–42 ☎22135

LISBOA (LISBON)
Estremadura(☎01)
See plan page 312

★ ★ ★ ★Ritz (Intercont) r R-da-
Fonseca 88A ☎684131 tx12589 Plan 1

⇔290 🏤 P Lift dB ⇔ 🍴8125

★ ★ ★ ★ ★Sheraton r L-Coelho 1
☎575757 tx12774 Plan 1A

⇔401 P Lift 🌙 sB ⇔5300–6000
dB ⇔6700–7400 Pool

★ ★ ★Avenida Palace r 1 de
Dezembro 123 ☎360151 tx12815 Plan 2

⇔96 P Lift dB ⇔7300

★ ★ ★Eduardo VII av Fontes Pereira
de Mello 5 ☎530141 tx18340 Plan 3

⇔68 P Lift 🌙 dB ⇔2285

★ ★ ★Fénix Praça Marqûes de
Pombal 8 ☎535121 tx12170 Plan 4

⇔ 🍴125 Lift 🌙 dB ⇔ 🍴3755

★ ★ ★ ★Florida (ETAP) r Duque de
Palmela 32 ☎567145 tx12256 Plan 5

⇔120 Lift 🌙 sB ⇔2950–3660
dB ⇔3760–4475

★ ★ ★Mundial r D-Duarte 4
☎863101 tx12308 Plan 6

⇔150 P Lift 🌙 dB ⇔3755

★ ★ ★Plaza Travessa do Salitre 7 (Off
av da Liberdade) ☎363922 tx16402
Plan 7

⇔93 P Lift 🌙 dB ⇔3755

★ ★ ★Tivoli (SRS) av da Liberdade
185 ☎530181 tx12588 Plan 8

⇔344 P Lift 🌙 dB ⇔4320 dB ⇔8125
lake

★ ★Flamingo (GT) r Castilho 41
☎532191 tx14736 Plan 9

⇔39 Lift 🌙 dB ⇔3250

★ ★Torre dos Jeronimos 8 ☎630161
Plan 10

⇔52 P Lift 🌙 dB ⇔2285 sea

★ ★Borges r Garrett 108 ☎846574
tx15825 Plan 12

⇔198 Lift 🌙 dB ⇔1950

★ ★Jorge V r Mouzinho da Silveira 3
☎562525 Plan 13

⇔52 P Lift 🌙 dB ⇔2285

★ ★Miraparque av Sidonio Pais 12
☎578070 tx16745 Plan 14

⇔100 Lift 🌙 dB ⇔2285

★ ★Principe av Duque d'Avila 201
☎536151 Plan 15

⇔68 P Lift 🌙 dB ⇔2285

Auto Montes Claros av Marçoni
6A ☎801066

🅿Auto Palma Estrada das Laranjeira
196–198 ☎786914

Auto Rail r C-Mardel 12 ☎562061 Frd

Fernandes & Santos av Duque de Loulè
56 ☎42807

🅿Flamingo r L-Cordeiro 4A ☎534627

Sorel r F-Folque 12A ☎563441 Cit

LUSO
Beira Litoral(☎0031)

★ ★ ★Termas r dos Banhos ☎93450
Apr–Oct
rm157 ⇔81 🍴76 P Lift 🌙 ⚓ Pool
mountains lake

MACEDO DE CAVALAIEROS
Tras-Os-Montes Alto Douro(☎0093)

★Estalagem Caçador Largo Pinto de
Azevedo ☎42356
rm22 ⇔8 dB ⇔3800

MANGUALDE
Beira Alta(☎0032)

★ ★Estalagem Cruz de Mata Estrada
Nacional ☎62556
⇔13 dB ⇔3800

MANTEIGAS
Beira Alta(☎0059)

★ ★Pousada de São Laurenco (13km N
on road to Gouveia) ☎(075)47150
⇔ 🍴12 🏤 sB ⇔ 🍴1820–4500
dB ⇔ 🍴2150–3880 M650–1100
mountains

MIRANDA DO DOURO
Tras-Os-Montes Alto Douro

★ ★Pousada de Santa Catarina
☎42255
⇔12 🏤 P dB ⇔3350

MONTE GORDO
Algarve(☎0081)

★ ★ ★Das Caravelas r Diogo Cão
☎44458 tx560
⇔87 P Lift dB ⇔3150 ⚓ Pool Beach
sea

★ ★ ★Dos Navegadores r Gancaiso
Velho ☎42490 tx56054
⇔103 Lift 🌙 dB ⇔3150 Pool sea

★ ★ ★Vasco da Gama av Infante D-
Henrique ☎44321 tx56020
⇔180 P Lift 🌙 dB ⇔4800 ⚓ Pool
Beach sea

MONTES DE ALVOR See **PORTIMÃO**

NAZARÉ
Estremadura(☎062)

★ ★ ★Dom Fuas Estrada Dom Fuas
☎46351 tx13889
Apr–Oct
⇔40 P Lift 🌙 dB ⇔1950 sea

★ ★Nazaré Largo A-Zuquete
☎46311 tx16116
⇔ 🍴52 P Lift 🌙 sB ⇔ 🍴1900
dB ⇔ 🍴2900 M690 sea

★ ★Praia av V-Guimaraes 39 (n.rest)
☎46423
⇔40 P Lift 🌙

ÓBIDOS
Estremadura(☎062)

★ ★Estalagem do Convento r Dr-J-de-
Ornelas ☎95217
rm13 ⇔14 A1rm P 🌙 dB ⇔3800

★Pousada do Castelo (on the Caldas da
Rainhatorres Vedras-Lisbon rd) ☎95105
rm6 ⇔3 🌙 dB ⇔3350

OFIR
Minho(☎0023)

★ ★Estalagem do Parque do Rio
☎89521
Apr–Oct
⇔36 P Lift 🌙 ⚓ Pool 🏌

★ ★Pinhal Estrada do Mar ☎89473
tx32857
⇔ 🍴90 P Lift 🌙 sB ⇔ 🍴1550–2200
dB ⇔ 🍴2600–3300 M500–850 ⚓
Pool sea

LISBOA (LISBON)

1	★★★★★Ritz
1A	★★★★★Sheraton
2	★★★★Avenida Palace
3	★★★★Eduardo VII
4	★★★★Fénix
5	★★★★Florida
6	★★★★Mundial
7	★★★★Plaza
8	★★★★Tivoli
9	★★★Flamingo
10	★★★Torre
12	★★Borges
13	★★Jorge V
14	★★Miraparque
15	★★Principe

OLHÃO
Algarve

★**Calque** r Dr O Salazar 37 ☎72167
⇌40 🏠

OLIVEIRA DO HOSPITAL
Beira Alta(☎0037)

At **POVOA DAS QUARTAS** (7km E on N17)

★★**Pousada Santa Bàrbara** ☎52252
⇌16 🏠 P dB⇌3350 mountains

OPORTO See **PORTO**

PAREDES
Douro Litoral(☎0025)

Ruão Serpa Pinto ☎22164 BL

PENAFIEL
Douro Litoral

Egas Moniz av Egas Moniz
155 ☎22032 Vlo

PORTALEGRE
Alto Alentejo(☎0045)

★**Alto Alentejo** 19 de Junho 59 (n.rest)
☎22290
rm15 ⇌2 P Lift 🌙 dB⇌ 🍴1950
mountains

🐾**Auto-Portalegre** r de Maio 94 ☎23540

PORTIMÃO
Algarve(☎0082)

★★★★**Alvor Praia** Praia dos Tres
Irmaos ☎24021 tx57399
⇌241 P Lift 🌙 Pool Beach sea

★★**Miradoiro** r Machado dos Santos 13
(n.rest) ☎23011
⇌25 dB⇌4800

★**Estalagem Mira-Foia** V Vaz das
Vacas 33 ☎22011
⇌23 Lift dB⇌4800

J F C Alexandre av D-A-Henriques BL

At **MONTES DE ALVOR** (5km W on N125)

★★★★**Penina Golf** Montes de Alvor
☎22051 tx57307
⇌209 P Lift 🌙 sB⇌4197 7630
dB⇌5723–9919 M1813 🍴 Pool ⚡
mountains

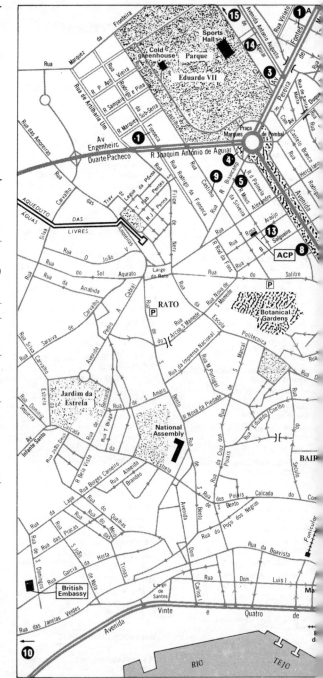

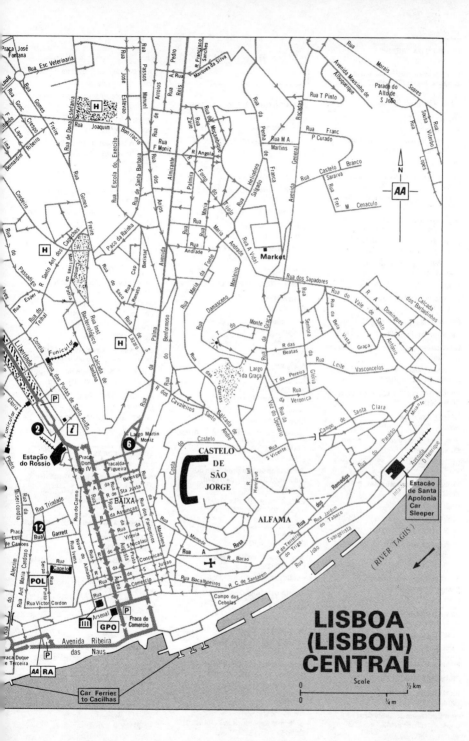

LISBOA (LISBON) CENTRAL

CASTELO DE SÃO JORGE

BAIXA

ALFAMA

Estação do Rossio

Estação de Santa Apolonia Car Sleeper

Market

Largo da Graça

Largo Martin Moniz

Praca do Comercio

GPO

POL

Avenida Ribeira das Naus

Car Ferries to Cacilhas

(RIVER TAGUS)

Scale
0 .... ½ km
0 .... ¼ m

PORTINHO DA ARRÁBIDA
Estremadura(☎019)

★★**Residencia de Santa Maria de Arrábida** (n.rest) ☎2080527
Apr–Oct
rm33 ⌐24 **P** dB ⌐2285

PORTO (OPORTO)
Douro Litoral(☎02)

★★★★**Infante de Sagres** Praça Filipa de Lencastre 62 ☎28101 tx22378
⌐83 Lift 𝄂 dB ⌐8125

★★★**Grande da Batalha** Praça da Batalha 116 ☎20571 tx25131
⌐147 Lift 𝄂 sB ⌐4960 dB ⌐5914 M1336

★★★**Grande do Porto** r da Santa Catarina 197 ☎28176 tx22553
⌐100 🍴 Lift 𝄂 sB ⌐2000–3000 dB ⌐2400–3400 M700–850

★★★**Império** Praça da Batalha 130 (off r São Lidefosa) ☎26861 tx26060
⌐95 **P** Lift 𝄂 dB ⌐2850

Almerindo F de A-Ferreira av dos Combatentes 627 ☎485258

Batalha r A-Herculano ☎23024 Vlo

Filinto Mota r do Godim ☎562202 Cit

Lab-Vitorino Fer da Silva r Nau Trindade 154 ☎482782

Pereira de Castro & Ferreira r Antero Quental 591 ☎480759

POVOA DAS QUARTAS See **OLIVEIRA DO HOSPITAL**

PRAIA DA ROCHA
Algarve(☎0082)

★★★★★**Algarve** av T-Cabreira ☎24001 tx57347
⌐218 **P** Lift 𝄂 dB ⌐8125 🏊 Pool sea

★★★**Estalagem Mira Sol** r E-F-Bivar ☎24046
rm38 dB4800

★★★**Belavista** av T-Cabreira ☎24055
rm25 ⌐23 Lift dB ⌐3150

★★**Estalagem Alcaia** av Marginal ☎24062
⌐20 dB ⌐4800 sea

★★**Estalagem São José** r A-de-Albuguerque ☎24037
rm23 ⌐25 A14rm **P** sB ⌐4800 sea

PRAIA DA SALEMA
Algarve(☎0082)

★★**Estalagem Infante do Mar** ☎65137
⌐30 **P** 𝄂 sB ⌐4800 Pool sea

PRAIA DAS MACÀS See **COLARES**

PRAIA DE FARO See **FARO**

PRAIA DE SANTA CRUZ
Estremadura(☎063)

★★**Estalagem de Santa Cruz** r J-P Lopes (n.rest) ☎97142
⌐32 Lift dB3800 sea

Portugal

PRAIA DO GUINCHO See **CASCAIS**

SAGRES
Algarve(☎0082)

★★★**Baleeira** ☎64212 tx57467
⌐114 **P** 𝄂 dB ⌐3150 Pool sea

★★**Estalagem Descobertas** Estrade Marginal ☎64251 ⌐17

★★**Pousada do Infante** Ponta da Atalaia ☎64222 tx57491
⌐21 🍴 **P** 𝄂 dB ⌐3350 sea

SANTA CLARA-A-VELHA
Baixo Alentejo(☎0083)

★★**Pousada de Santa Clara** Barragem de Santa Clara ☎52250
⌐6 **P** dB ⌐3350 Pool mountains lake

SANTA LUZIA See **VIANA DO CASTELO**

SANTARÉM
Ribatejo(☎0043)

★**Abidis** r Guilherme de Azevedo 4 ☎22017
rm28 ⌐66🍴 𝄂 sB ⌐ 🍴1050–1300 dB ⌐ 🍴2212

Autogirar r P-de Santaťem 47 ☎24077 Dat

SANTIAGO DO CACÉM
Baxio Alentejo(☎0017)

★**Pousada de São Tiago** Estrada National ☎22459
rm7 ⌐4 A3rm **P** 𝄂 dB ⌐3350 Pool

SÃO BRAS DE ALPORTEL
Algarve(☎0089)

★**Pousada de São Bras** Serro do Caldeirao (5km N on main road) ☎42305 tx56786
⌐23 A8rm **P** 𝄂 sB ⌐1600–3310 dB ⌐1850–3500 M850–1100 mountains lake

SERPA
Baixo Alentejo(☎0079)

★★**Pousada de São Gens** Alto de São Gens ☎52327
⌐ 🍴17 **P** 𝄂 dB ⌐ 🍴3350

SERRA DO MARÃO See **AMARANTE**

SESIMBRA
Estremadura

★★★★**Do Mar** ☎2233326 tx13883
⌐119 **P** Lift 𝄂 dB ⌐2480–6677 M954–1336 Pool sea

★★★★**Espadarte** Esplanada do Altantico ☎2233189 tx14699
⌐80 Lift 𝄂 dB ⌐1950

SETÚBAL
Estremadura(☎065)

★★★★**Esperança** av L-Todi 220 ☎25151

rm76 ⌐52 🍴24 Lift 𝄂 dB ⌐2285 sea

★★**Pousada de São Filipe** ☎23844
⌐15 𝄂 dB ⌐3350

🍴**Setubauto** av dos Combatentes da Grande Guerra 81 ☎23131 Frd

SINES
Baixo Alentejo(☎0017)

★★★**Malhada** do Farol ☎62105
⌐27 dB ⌐3800

SINTRA
Estremadura

★★★★**Palàcio de Seteais** r do Bocage 8 ☎2933200
⌐18 **P** Lift 𝄂 dB ⌐fr7600 Mfr1400 sea mountains

Sintra r do DF de Almeido 1 ☎2932353 Frd

TAVIRA
Algarve(☎0081)

★★★**Eurotel-Tavira** Quinta das Oliveiras ☎22042 tx56068
⌐80 **P** Lift 𝄂 dB ⌐3150–4000 🏊 Pool Beach sea mountains

TOMAR
Ribatejo(☎0049)

J Antunes Oliveira & Alves av D Nuno Alvares Pereira, Loto 8 & 9 ☎33637 Dat

Auto Mecânica Tomarense av D Nuno Alvares Pereira 15 ☎33144 Frd

At **CASTELO DO BODE** (14km SE, near Dam)

★★**Pousada de São Pedro** (☎38159
⌐15 A7rm **P** dB ⌐3350 mountains lake

TORRES VEDRAS
Estremadura (☎061)

Auto-Torreense r Santos Bernardes ☎22021 Chy Sim

Foroestre Parque do Choupal ☎23115 Frd

URGEIRIÇA See **CANAS DE SENHORIM**

VALE DO LOBO
Algarve(☎0089)

★★★★**Dona Filipa** (THF) ☎94141 tx56848
⌐ 🍴129 **P** Lift 𝄂 sB ⌐ 🍴4197–8584 dB ⌐ 🍴5723–12399 M2289–2480 🏊 Pool Beach sea

VALENÇA DO MINHO
Minho(☎0021)

★★**Pousada de São Teotónio** ☎22252
⌐ 🍴16 A4rm 🍴 **P** dB ⌐ 🍴3350 mountains

VIANA DO CASTELO
Minho(☎0028)

★★★★**Parque** Azenhas do D-Prior ☎24151 tx32511
⌐ 🍴123 **P** Lift 𝄂

dB ⇌ ▥3800–4350 Pool sea mountains

★★**Alianca** av dos Combatentes da Grande Guerra ☎23001

rm29 ⇌15 **P** ☽ dB ⇌1050 sea

★★**Rail** av Afonso III 180 (n.rest) ☎22176 tx22699

⇌39 **P** Lift ☽ dB ⇌1950 Pool mountains

Auto-Vianense av Camões 25–27 ☎22092 Chy VW

At **SANTA LUZIA** (2km NW: also funicular connection)

★★★★**Santa Luzia** ☎22192 tx32420 ⇌48 **P** Lift ☽ dB ⇌3800 ✆ Pool sea

VILA DO CONDE
Douro Litoral(☎0022)

Traditional Algarve fishing boats

★★**Estalagem do Brasão** r J-M-de Melo ☎64016

⇌28 **P** ☽ dB ⇌3800

VILA FRANCA DE XIRA
Ribatejo(☎013)

Auto Nascimento r A-L-Batista 2 ☎23122 Cit

⅋⅊**Auto-Vilafranquense** r Curado 8 ☎22830

VILA REAL
Tras-Os-Montes Alto Douro(☎0099)

★★**Tocaio** av Carvalho Araujo 45 ☎23106

⇌52 🏛 Lift ☽ dB ⇌1950 mountains

A Camilo Fernandes r Visconde de Carnaxide 26 ☎22151 Frd

VILA REAL DE SANTO ANTÓNIO
Algarve(☎0081)

★★★**Eurotel** Praia da Altura ☎95450 tx56068

⇌135 **P** Lift ☽ dB ⇌2000–4000 M600–750 ✆ Pool Beach sea

VISEU
Beira Alta(☎0032)

★★★**Grão Vasco** r G-Barreiros ☎23511

⇌ ▥90 **P** Lift ☽ sB ⇌ ▥2500–3800 dB ⇌ ▥4000–5000 M alc Pool mountains

GAVIS av E-Navarro ☎22966 Aud BMW VW

⅋⅊**Lopes & Figueiredo** av da Bélgica 52 ☎25151 BL

Armacao de Pera, Algarve

SPAIN
AND ANDORRA

Spain is a country rich in history and natural beauty. It is bordered by two countries, France in the north and Portugal in the west. Central Spain is mountainous and barren and the coastline is extremely rocky. Some of the most popular holiday areas in Europe are in Spain, the best known being the Costa Brava, the Costa Blanca, the Costa Dorada and the Costa del Sol. All have fine, sandy beaches.

Spain has a varied climate; temperate in the north, dry and hot in the south and in the Balearic Islands. The Canary Islands are warm and dry for most of the year. The language is Spanish and has developed from the Castilian dialect. Certain words are of Arabic origin and there are many local dialects spoken throughout the provinces, for example Catalan in the north-east.

Area *mainland 189,950 sq miles Balearic Islands 1,935 sq miles* **Population** *37,100,000* **Local time** *GMT + 1 (Summer GMT + 2)*
National flag *Horizontal tricolour of red, yellow and red*

Leaflets entitled '*Motoring in the Balearics*' and '*Motoring in the Canary Islands*' are available to AA members

Church of San Salvador in Guetaria.

How to get there

From the Channel ports, Spain is approached via France. The two main routes are at either end of the Pyrenean mountains, the Biarritz to San Sebastiàn–Donostia road, or motorway, at the western end for central and southern Spain, or the Perpignan to Barcelona road, or motorway, at the eastern end for the Costa Brava. The distance from Calais to Madrid is about 990 miles and usually requires two or three night stops. It is possible to shorten the journey by using the car sleeper services between Boulogne or Paris and Biarritz or Narbonne, or Paris to Madrid. There is also a direct ferry service from Plymouth to Santander which takes about 24 hours.

Motoring regulations and general information

This information should be read in conjunction with the general content of the European ABC (pages 6–27). **Note** As certain regulations and requirement are common to many countries they are covered by one entry in the ABC and the following headings represent some of the subjects dealt with in this way:
Crash or safety helmets
Drinking and driving
Fire extinguisher
First-aid kit
Insurance
Medical treatment
Police fines
Radio telephones/Radio transmitters
Rear view mirror
Seat belts
Tyres
Visitors' registration

AA Port agent

(See also *AA Agents* page 7)
Santander Viajes Ecuador SA, Calle Lealtad 21
☎(942)215708.

Accidents

Fire, police, ambulance. In Madrid and Barcelona dial 091 for **police**, and 2323232 for **fire** service; in other towns call the operator.

There are no firm rules of procedure after an accident; however, in most cases the recommendations under *Accidents* on page 7 are advisable.

There is an assistance service for the victims of traffic accidents which is run by the Central Traffic Department. At the moment the service operates day and night on the N1 Madrid—Irún road, on the N11 road in the province of Lerida, on some roads in the provinces of Valencia (N111, N340, N332, and N430) and Vizcaya (N625, N634, N240, C639, C6211, C6315, C6318, and C6322).

There is an SOS telephone network on these roads; motorists in need of help should ask for *auxilio en carretera* (road assistance). The special ambulances used are in radio contact with the hospitals participating in the scheme.

Accommodation

Spain has some of the most attractively furnished hotels in Europe – especially luxury hotels converted from former monasteries or palaces. Provincial hotels are pleasantly old-fashioned; usually the plumbing and lavatories are just about adequate, and do not compare with those in modern hotels in coastal resorts. Hotels are officially classified, and the category exhibited outside each. Establishments are now permitted to charge for breakfast whether taken or not.

While commendations or complaints about hotels are an important source of information to us, AA members may also like to know that Spanish hotels must keep official complaint forms and if these are unobtainable at the hotel, they are available from Tourist Information offices.

Paradores are fully-appointed tourist hotels, usually on the outskirts of towns or in the country. Some are newly built, but others are converted country houses, palaces, or Moorish castles. They offer very good value for money. A stay must normally be limited to ten days. Bookings for Paradores should be addressed to: Central de Reservas de los Paradores del

Esta do Apartado de Correos 50043, Madrid 1 ☎(91)4359700 (if calling this number from the UK refer to your *Telephone Dialling Codes* booklet) or telex 46865. Alternatively, you may contact their London Office on ☎(01) 402 8182.

Bail Bond

An accident in Spain can have very serious consequences, including the impounding of the car, and property, and the detention of driver pending bail. A Bail Bond can often facilitate release of person and property, and you are advised to obtain one of these from your insurer, for a nominal premium, together with your Green Card. A Bail Bond is a written guarantee that a cash deposit of usually up to £1,500 will be paid to the Spanish Court as surety for bail, and as security for any fine which may be imposed, although in such an event you will have to reimburse any amount paid by your insurer. In very serious cases the Court will not allow bail and it has been known for a minor Spanish court to refuse Bail Bonds, and to insist on cash being paid by the driver. Nevertheless, motorists are strongly advised to obtain a Bail Bond and to ensure that documentary evidence of this (in Spanish) is attached to the Green Card.

Boats

A Helmsman's Certificate of Competence is recommended when temporarily importing boats into Spain. See page 8 for further information about this and boat documentation.

Breakdown

If your car breaks down, try to move it to the verge of the road so that it obstructs the traffic flow as little as possible and place a warning triangle 30 metres behind the vehicle to warn following traffic. A 24-hour breakdown service is run by the Spanish Motoring Club (RACE) in the Madrid area only. To obtain assistance telephone 4412222. Elsewhere in Spain there is no road patrol service and if you need help you must make your own arrangements with a garage. See also *Breakdown* page 8 and *Warning triangles* page 323.

British Consulates

(See also page 8)
Madrid 4 Calle de Fernando el Santo 16 ☎(91)4190200. There are also consulates in Algeciras, Alicante, Barcelona, Bilbao, Islas de Baleares (Ibiza, Mallorca & Menorca), Malaga, Santander, Sevilla, Tarragona and Vigo.

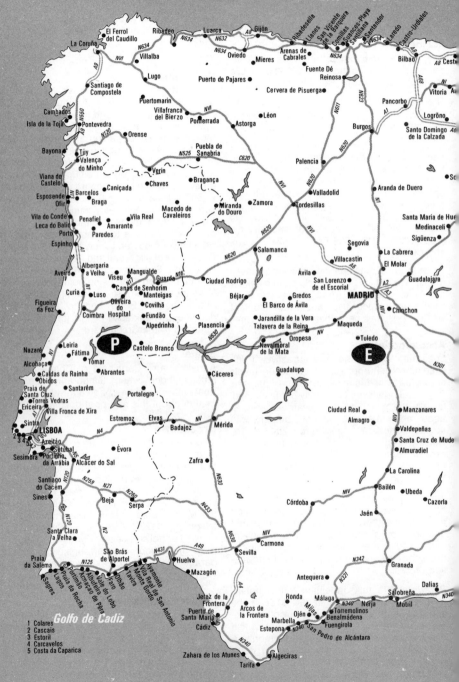

Currency and banking hours
(See also page 11)
The unit of currency is the peseta, which is divided into 100 centimos.

There are no restrictions on the importation of foreign and Spanish currency or travellers cheques, etc, if a declaration is made to the Customs on entry. Travellers cheques, etc, may only be changed at banks, authorised travel agencies or hotels. A tourist may export up to 20,000 pesetas in Spanish banknotes and a larger amount if:
a the documents from the Spanish bank confirming the exchange of foreign currency into pesetas are produced;
b the tourist produces evidence of declaration made to Customs on entry for a larger amount.

Banks are usually open 09.00–1400hrs Monday to Saturday. There are exchange offices at travel agents which are open 09.00–13.00hrs and 16.00–19.00hrs from Monday to Friday, and 09.00–13.00hrs on Saturday.

Customs regulations
A television set, radio, pocket calculator or tape recorder may be temporarily imported, but only against a deposit of duty and a permit valid for three months issued by the Spanish Customs. See also Customs regulations for European countries page 11 for further information.

Dimensions and weight restrictions
Private cars and trailers are restricted to the following dimensions – car height: 4 metres; width: 2.5 metres; vehicle/trailer combinations length: 16 metres. Trailers with an unladen weight exceeding 750kg must have an independent braking system.

Granada: Alhambra Palace

Driving licence
A valid British driving licence is acceptable in Spain but only if accompanied by an official translation stamped by a Spanish Consulate. The minimum age at which a visitor may drive a temporarily imported car or motorcycle (over 75cc) is 18 years. However, it is recommended that you carry an International Driving Permit which costs less than the official stamping and translation. see under Driving Licence and International Driving Permit page 13 for further information.

Emergency messages to tourists
(See also page 14)
Emergency messages to tourists are broadcast daily throughout the year by Radio Nacional de España. The messages are transmitted in Spanish, French and occasionally English and German on 513 metres medium wave at 5 minutes past the hour beginning 05.05hrs and ending 00.05hrs.

Garages
Garages are officially classified. Blue signs displayed outside garages indicate the classification I to III as well as the type of work that can be dealt with, by means of symbols. There must be set prices for common repair jobs and these must be available to customers so that they may authorise repairs. They are also required by law to keep and produce complaint forms on request by a customer. If you are unable to obtain one they are available from Tourist Information offices, or write to the Delegado de Turismo in the capital of the province concerned, or to the Dirección General de Servicios, Sección de Inspección y Reclamaciones enclosing all factual evidence. This should be done as soon as possible and whilst still in Spain.

International distinguishing sign
(see also page 17)
The penalty for failure to display a nationality plate, or for displaying one of the wrong size or type, is a fine of approximately Pta500.

Lights
(See also page 17)
It is compulsory for visiting motorists to equip their vehicle with a set of replacement bulbs.

Passing lights (dipped headlights) are compulsory on motorways and fast dual carriageways even if they are well lit. The use of full headlights in built-up areas is prohibited but it is also an offence to travel with faulty sidelights. It is

compulsory for *motorcyclists* to use dipped headlights during the day.

Motoring club
(See also page 18)

The **Real Automovil Club de España** (RACE) which has its headquarters at c José Abascal 10 Madrid 3 ☎4473200 is associated with local clubs in a number of provincial towns. Motoring club offices are normally open from 09.00–14.00hrs only and are closed on Sundays and public holidays. Some, including Madrid, are closed on Saturdays.

Motorways
There are approximately 1,240 miles of motorway (Autopista) open, and more are under construction. A network of 1,800 miles is planned.

Apart from a few stretches of motorway in the Madrid and Barcelona areas, tolls are charged on most of the motorways eg La Jonquera (French–Spanish border) to Valencia is 2,275 *Ptas* for a car and 4,000 *Ptas* for a car towing a caravan.

The majority of toll motorways issue a travel ticket on entry and the toll is paid on leaving the motorway. The travel ticket gives all relevant information about the toll charges including the toll category of the vehicle. The ticket is handed in at the exit point and the toll paid. On some toll motorways the toll collection is automatic; have the correct amount ready to throw into the collecting basket. If change is required use the separate lane marked accordingly.

A leaflet entitled *Motorways in Spain* is available to AA members.

Orange badge scheme for disabled drivers
(See also page 19)
There is no national system of parking concessions in operation. However, many large cities and towns operate their own individual schemes and it is understood that consideration is shown to badge holders from other countries.

Overtaking
(See also page 19)
Both at night and during the day, drivers who are about to be overtaken must operate their righthand indicator light to show the driver following that his intention to overtake has been understood. Outside built-up areas drivers about to overtake must sound their horn during the day and flash their lights at night. Stationary trams must not be overtaken while passengers are boarding or alighting.

Parking
(See also page 19)
Parking is forbidden in the following places: within 5 metres (16½ft) of cross-roads or an intersection; near a level crossing; within 5 metres of the entrance to a public building; on a main road or one carrying fast-moving traffic; on or near tram lines; within 7 metres (23ft) of a tram or bus stop. You must not park on a two-way road if it is not wide enough for three vehicles. In one-way streets, vehicles are parked alongside buildings with even numbers on even dates and on the opposite side on odd dates; any alteration to this system is announced by signs or notices in the press. Drivers may stop their vehicles alongside another parked vehicle if there is no space free nearby and the flow of traffic is not obstructed, but only long enough to let passengers in or out or to load or unload goods.

A special parking zone has been established in the centre of Madrid and motorists wishing to park in this zone may obtain tickets from tobacconists. The tickets must be displayed on the windscreen and cost 20 pesetas for ½hr, 40 pesetas for 1hr and 60 pesetas for 1½hrs.

Passengers
(See also page 19)
It is recommended that children do not travel in a vehicle as front seat passengers.

Petrol
(See also page 20)
Credit cards The use of credit cards to obtain petrol is not available to visiting motorists.
Duty-free petrol In addition to the petrol in the vehicle tank up to 5 litres in a can may be imported free of customs duty and tax.
Octane rating Gasolina Normal (90) and Gasolina Super (96–98).

Postal information
Mail Postcards *Pta23*, letters up to 20gm *Pta33*.
Post offices There are 1,550 post offices in Spain. Opening hours are from 08.00–14.00hrs Monday to Saturday.

Postcheque
(See also page 21)
Postcheques may be cashed for a fixed sum of

*Pta*11,000 per cheque, but only at main post offices. Counter positions are identified by the words *Caja Postal de Ahorros* or *Reintegros.* See page 321 for post office opening hours.

Priority

(See also *Priority including Roundabouts* page 22)
Drivers on secondary roads must give way to vehicles in both directions when entering a main road.

Public holidays

Official public holidays in Spain for 1985 are given below. In addition there are many local and regional holidays throughout mainland Spain. See also *Public holidays* page 22.
January 1 (New Year's Day)
January 6† (Epiphany)
March 19 (Saint Joseph)
April 5 (Good Friday)
April 8 (Easter Monday)
May 1 (May Day)
June 2† (Corpus Christi)
June 29* (St Peter and St Paul)
July 25 (St James the Apostle)
August 15 (Assumption)
October 12* (Day of our Lady of El Pilar)
November 1 (All Saints' Day)
December 8† (Immaculate Conception)
December 25 (Christmas Day)
* Saturday
† Sunday

Religious services

(See also page 23)
The Intercontinental Church Society welcomes visitors from any denomination to English language services in the following centres: *Barcelona 22* The Revd Ben Eaton, San Juan de la Salle 41, Horacio 38 tel 478867;
Ibiza The Revd Joe Yates-Round, Aptdo 6, San Antonio Abad

Roads including holiday traffic

The surfaces of the main roads vary, but on the whole are good; traffic is light. The roads are winding in many places and at times it is not advisable to exceed 30–35 mph. Secondary roads are often rough, winding, and encumbered by slow, horse-drawn traffic. A leaflet entitled *Road conditions in Spain and Portugal* is available to AA members.

Holiday traffic, particularly on the coast road to Barcelona and Tarragona and in the San Sebastián–Donostia area, causes congestion which may be severe at weekends.

Road signs

(See also page 23)
All main roads are prefixed 'N', six of those radiating from Madrid are numbered in Roman numerals. Secondary roads are prefixed 'C'.

In the Basque area local versions of some placenames appear on signposts together with the national version used in current AA gazetteers and maps. Some local names differ considerably from the national spelling – *eg* San Sebastián = Donostia. In the Catalonia area some local spellings are used exclusively on signposts but most of these are recognisable against the national version – *eg* Gerona = Girona, Lérida = Lleida.

Shopping hours

Shops are open Mondays to Saturday: *food shops* 09.00/10.00–13.00/13.30 and 15.00/15.30–19.30/20.00hrs; *stores* 10.00–20.00hrs; however, some close earlier.

Speed limits

(See also page 25)
In built-up areas all vehicles are limited to 60kph (37mph) except where signs indicate a lower limit. Outside built-up areas cars are limited to 120kph (74mph) on motorways and *90kph (56mph) or **100kph (62mph) on other roads. Vehicles towing a caravan or trailer are limited to 80kph (49mph) on motorways and *70kph (43mph) or **80kph (49mph) on other roads.
*On ordinary roads.
**On roads with more than one lane in each direction, a special lane for slow moving vehicles or wide lanes.

Spiked, studded or snow tyres

(See also page 10)
Spikes on tyres must be 10mm in diameter and not more than 2mm in length.

Tourist information offices

(See also page 25)
The Spanish National Tourist Office, Metro House, 57–58 St James's Street, London SW1A 1LD ☎01-499 0901, will be pleased to assist you with information regarding tourism and there are branch offices in most of the leading Spanish cities, towns and resorts. Local offices are normally closed at lunchtime.

Traffic lights

(See also page 25)
In some cases the green light remains on with the amber light when changing from green to red. Two red lights, one above the other, mean

'no entry'. Usually, lights on each side of crossroads operate independently and must be obeyed independently.

A policeman with a whistle may over-ride the traffic lights, and he must be obeyed.

Turning
Unless there is a 'turning permitted' sign, three-point turns and reversing into side streets are prohibited in towns.

Using the telephone
(See also page 26)
Insert coin **before** lifting receiver. When making calls to subscribers within Spain precede number with relevant area code (shown in parentheses against town entry in gazetteer). Use Pta5, 25 or 50 coins for local calls and Pta50 for national and international calls. The internal telephone system connects all principal towns, but long delays on trunk calls are not unusual. *International callbox identification* Light green sign.
Telephone rates A call to the UK costs Pta261 for the first 3 minutes and Pta97 for each additional minute. The cost of local calls is determined by the distance (within the town limits) and the time taken. Hotels, restaurants etc., usually make an additional charge.
What to dial for the Irish Republic 07 *353.
What to dial for the UK 07 *44.
*Wait for second dialling tone

Warning triangles
The use of two warning triangles is compulsory for vehicles weighing more than 3,500kg (3 tons 8cwt 100lbs) and passenger vehicles with more than nine seats (including the driver's). The triangles must be placed on the road in front of and behind the vehicle at a distance of 30 metres (33yds). However, it is recommended that all other vehicles except two-wheelers carry a warning triangle. See also *Warning triangles/Hazard warning lights* page 26.

Winter conditions
(See also page 10)
Most roads across the Pyrénées are either closed or affected by winter weather, but the roads or motorways to Biarritz and Perpignan in France avoid the mountains. The main routes into Portugal are unaffected. Within the country, motoring is not severely restricted although certain roads may be temporarily blocked, particularly in January and February. The most important roads likely to be affected are San Sebastián (Donostia) – Burgos – Madrid, Madrid – Granada, Zaragoza – Teruel and Granada – Murcia, but these are swept immediately there is a snowfall. On the Villacastin–Madrid road there is a tunnel under the Guadarrama Pass. Roads likely to be affected by heavy snowfall are:

Pass	Road
Pajares	León–Gijon
Reinosa	Santander–Palencia
Escudo	Santander–Burgos
Somosierra	Burgos–Madrid
Orduña	Bilbao (Bilbo)–Burgos
Barazar	Bilbao (Bilbo)–Vitoria
Piqueras	(Gasteiz)
Navacerrada	Logroño–Madrid
	Madrid–Le Granja

The Real Automóvil Club de España will give you up-to-date information about road conditions. See also *Major road tunnels* pages 38–39, and *Major rail tunnels* pages 39–40.

Andorra

National flag
Vertical tricolour blue, yellow and red.
Andorra is an independent Principality covering 190 sq miles with a population of 32,700. It is situated high in the Pyrénées between France and Spain and jointly administered by the two co-princes (the President of France, the Bishop of La Seu d'Urgell) and the Andorrans. French and Spanish are both·spoken and the currency of either country is accepted. General regulations for France and Spain apply to Andorra with the following exceptions.

Accidents
Fire and **ambulance** ☎18 **police** ☎17. There are no firm rules of procedure after an accident; however, in most cases the recommendations under *Accidents* on page 7 are advisable.

Breakdown
The Automobile Club d'Andorra ☎(078)20890 will offer advice and assistance in the event of a breakdown. However, owing to many unnecessary journeys made in the past, the motorist is now asked to go to the garage and personally accompany the mechanic or breakdown vehicle to his car. See also *Breakdown* page 8.

British Consulate
(See also page 8)
Andorra comes within the Consular District of the British Consul-General at Barcelona.

Dimensions

The maximum height for vehicles where tunnels are involved is 3.5m.

Motoring club

(See also page 18)

 The Automobil Club d'Andorra has its head office at Carrer Babot Camp 4, Andorra la Vella ☎(078)20890.

Passengers

(See also page 19)
Children under 10 years of age are not permitted to travel in a vehicle as front seat passengers.

Roads

Andorra can be approached from France via the Pas de la Casa (6,851ft), then from the frontier over the Envalira Pass (7,897ft). Roads may occasionally be closed for short periods between November and April. The approach from Spain via La Seu d'Urgell is always open. The three main roads radiating from the town are prefixed N and numbered; side roads are prefixed V.

Speed limits

(See also page 25)
The following speed limits apply to Andorra. Car, car/caravan combination *Built-up areas* 40 kph (25 mph); *Other roads* 70 kph (43 mph). Some villages have a speed limit of 20 kph (12 mph).

Weather information

(See also page 27)
The condition of the Envalira pass may be obtained by ☎21166 or 21055.

Wheel chains

(See also page 10)
These must be used on the Envalira pass whenever conditions require it.

Prices are in Spanish Pesetas
Abbreviations:
av   avenida
c   calle
Cdt   Commandant
Cpt   Capitán
ctra   carretera
Gl   Generalísimo
pl   plaza
ps   paseo

AIGUA-BLAVA See **BEGUR**

ALARCÓN
Cuenca (☎966)

★ ★**Parador del Marques de Villena**
☎331350

19 Dec–Oct
⇆11 **P** ⅅ dB ⇆5200 M1300
mountains

ALBACETE
Albacete (☎967)

★ ★ ★**Lianos** av Rodrigues Acosta 9
☎223750

⇆103 🏛 **P** Lift ⅅ sB ⇆3900–4220
dB ⇆5100–5500

★ ★ ★**Parador Nacional de la Mancha**
☎229450

⇆70 **P** Lift ⅅ dB ⇆4700 M1300 ⅙
Pool

ALBARRACIN
Teruel (☎974)

★ ★ ★**Albarracin** Azagra ☎710011
⇆36 **P** sB ⇆ 📶3715 dB ⇆4850 t5%
Pool mountains

ALBUFERETA (LA) See **ALICANTE**

ALCANAR
Tarragona (☎977)

★ ★**Biarritz** (n.rest) ☎737025

15 Jun–15 Sep
⇆24 **P** ⅙ Pool Beach sea

ALCAÑIZ
Teruel (☎974)

★ ★**Parador Nacional de la Concordia** ☎830400

Mar–13 Jan
⇆12 Lift ⅅ dB ⇆5200 M1300
mountains

Auto-Recambios Teruel Rondas de
Castelseras 4 ☎830777 MB

ALGECIRAS
Cádiz (☎956)

★ ★ ★**Reina Cristina** (THF) ps de las
Conferencias ☎650061 tx78057
⇆135 **P** Lift ⅅ dB ⇆5405–8670 ⅙
Pool sea

★ ★ ★**Alarde** Alfonso XI–4 (n.rest)
☎660408 tx78009
⇆68 🏛 Lift dB ⇆3485–4000

🖏**Automecanicos 'Baltanas'** ctra Cádiz-
Málaga 21 ☎660950 BL (Landrover
only)

🖏**M G Gaggero** c Zorrilla 34 ☎664488

ALICANTE
Alicante (☎965)

★ ★ ★**Meliá Alicante** Playa de El
Postiguet ☎205000 tx66131
⇆545 **P** Lift ⅅ sB ⇆3610–4300
dB ⇆6250–7420 M1100 Pool sea

★ ★**Palas** pl del Ayuntamiento 6
☎206690

⇆53 🏛 Lift ⅅ dB ⇆3520–4310 t5%
⅙ Pool

★ ★**Gran Sol** Méndez Núñez 3 ☎203000
⇆150 Lift ⅅ sea sB ⇆4750
dB ⇆5350 t5%

🖏**Nuevo** Tal Aznar Domenech 7
☎283932

At **ALBUFERETA (LA)** (3km N)

★ ★ ★**Villa Linda** ☎262208
rm34 ⇆29 📶5 **P** Pool mountains

ALMAGRO
Ciudad Real (☎926)

★ ★ ★**Parador Nacional** Ronda de San
Francisco ☎860100
⇆55 **P** ⅅ sB ⇆3950–4350
dB ⇆5200–5700 M1350 t4% Pool

ALMERÍA
Almería (☎951)

★ ★ ★**Gran** av Reina Regente 4
(n.rest) ☎238011
⇆ 📶124 🏛 **P** Lift ⅅ
sB ⇆ 📶3175–3575 dB ⇆ 📶4500–5950
Pool sea

★ ★**Costasol** Generalisimo 58 (n.rest)
☎234011
rm55 ⇆35 📶20 **P** Lift ⅅ
dB ⇆ 📶4500–5950

★ ★**Peria** pl del carmen 1 ☎238877
⇆44 ⅅ dB ⇆2720–3030 t5%

🖏**Automecanica Almeriense** Paraje los
Callejones N340 KM117,4 ☎237033 **P**
Frd

ALMURADIEL
Ciudad Real (☎926)

★ ★**Podencos** ctra NIV–Km232
☎339000

⊷64 🏠 P 🌙 sB ⇄2375 dB ⇄4025
M900 Pool mountains

ALSASUA
Navarra (☎948)

★ ★ **Alaska** ctra Madrid – Irún Km402
☎562802
Mar – Oct
⊷30 🏠 P 🌙 dB ⇄3100 – 3600 M900
Pool mountains

🏷️P **Celaya Urrestarazu** ctra GI-Irún
Madrid ☎560233 M/c Cit Ren Vlo

ANDRAITX See **MALLORCA**
under **BALEARES (ISLAS DE)**

ANTEQUERA
Málaga (☎952)

☆ ☆ **Parador Nacional** Parque M-
Christina ☎840901
⊷55 P 🌙 dB ⇄4700 – 5200 M1300
Pool mountains

ARANDA DE DUERO
Burgos (☎947)

☆ ☆ ☆ **Bronces** ctra Madrid – Irún Km161
☎500850
rm29 ⊷26 📶3 🏠 P 🌙
sB ⇄ 📶2014 – 2435 dB ⇄4001 M1205
mountains

★ ★ ★ **Montehermoso** ctra Madrid – Irún
Km163 ☎501550
⊷60 🏠 P Lift 🌙 dB ⇄2750 – 3050
M1050

Electro-Sanz av Castilla 49 ☎501134 BL

ARCOS DE LA FRONTERA
Cádiz

★ ★ ★ **Parador Nacional Casa del**
Corregidor pl d'España ☎700460
⊷21 Lift dB ⇄5700 M1300

ARENAS DE CABRALES
Asturias

★ **Naranjo de Buines** ctra General
☎845119
rm38 ⊷21 📶1 A18rm dB1650 – 1800
dB ⇄ 📶2100 – 2400 M750 mountains

ARENYS DE MAR
Barcelona (☎93)

★ ★ ★ **Raymond** ps Xifré ☎7921700
⊷73 🏠3 P Lift 🌙 sB ⇄1800 – 2050
dB ⇄3000 – 4200 M865 – 1050 sea

★ ★ **Floris** Playa Cassá 78 ☎7920384
⊷31 P Lift 🌙 dB ⇄2215 – 2470 M725
sea

★ **Impala** Apartado 20 (n.rest) ☎7921504
rm52 ⊷14 📶38 P 🌙
dB ⇄ 📶2300 – 2560 M750 Pool sea

ARGOMANIZ
Alava

★ ★ ★ **Parador Nacional de Argomaniz**
☎282200
⊷48 P Lift 🌙 dB ⇄4700 – 5200
M1300 mountains

ARTIES
Lleida (☎973)

Spain

★ ★ ★ **Parador Nacional Don Gaspar de**
Portola ☎640801
⊷40 A10rm 🏠 P Lift 🌙
dB ⇄5200 – 5700 M1300 mountains

ASTORGA
León (☎987)

🏷️M **Alonso** ctra Madrid-Coruña 60
☎615259 P BL

ÁVILA
Ávila (☎918)

★ ★ ★ **Palacio Valderrabanos** pl
Catedral 9 ☎211023
⊷73 P Lift 🌙 dB ⇄4960 – 5630 M1180

★ ★ ★ **Parador Nacional Raimundo de**
Borgona Marques de Canales de Chozas
16 ☎211340
⊷62 🏠 P Lift sB ⇄2750 – 3150
dB ⇄5500 – 6000 M1300 St%

★ ★ **Cuatro Postes** ctra Salamanca 23
☎212944
⊷36 P Lift 🌙 dB ⇄3000 – 3400 M850
mountains

AYAMONTE
Huelva (☎955)

★ ★ ★ **Parador Nacional Costá de la Luz**
☎320700
⊷20 dB ⇄4700 – 5700 M1300 Pool sea

BADAJOZ
Badajoz (☎924)

★ ★ ★ **Gran Zurbaran** ps Castelar
☎223741 tx48818
⊷215 🏠 P Lift 🌙 dB ⇄5200 – 5650
M1300 t5% 🏊 Pool

BAGUR See **BEGUR**

BAILEN
Jaén (☎953)

☆ ☆ ☆ **Don Lope de Sosa** KM295 ctra
Madrid – Cádiz ☎670058
⊷27 P 🌙

☆ ☆ ☆ **Parador Nacional** (1km S on N1)
☎670100
⊷40 dB ⇄4700 M1300

BALAGUER
Lleida (☎973)

★ ★ ★ **Parador Colaborador Conde**
Jaime de Urgel c Urgel 2 ☎445604
⊷60 🏠 P Lift 🌙 dB ⇄3950 – 4250
M1000 Pool

BALEARES (ISLAS DE)
IBIZA
SAN ANTONIO (☎971)

★ ★ ★ **Tanit** Cala Gracio ☎341300
tx69221
Apr – Oct
⊷386 P Lift 🌙 sB ⇄1725 – 3300
dB ⇄2130 – 5364 M800 🏊 Pool sea

MALLORCA (MAJORCA)
CALA RATJADA (☎971)

★ ★ ★ **Son Moll** Playa Son Moll
☎563100 tx69012
Apr – Oct
rm118 ⊷108 📶10 Lift 🌙
dB ⇄ 📶4500 M1000 Pool sea

FORMENTOR (☎971)

★ ★ ★ ★ ★ **Formentor** ☎531300
tx68523
⊷131 P Lift 🌙 dB ⇄12450 M2900
🏊 Pool Beach ∩ sea

MAGALUF (☎971)

★ ★ ★ **Magaluf Playa Sol** ☎681050
tx69175
⊷242 P Lift dB ⇄ 📶7000 M1400 t5%
🏊 Pool sea

PAGUERA (☎971)

★ ★ ★ **Villamil** (THF) ☎686050
tx68841
⊷102 P Lift 🌙 dB ⇄6600 – 11000
M1500 🏊 Pool sea mountains

PALMA DE MALLORCA (☎971)

★ ★ ★ ★ ★ **Son Vida Sheraton**
☎451011 tx68651
⇄ 📶173 P Lift 🌙
sB ⇄ 📶6500 – 8850
dB ⇄ 📶8700 – 16300 M2500 🏊 Pool
♪ ∩ sea mountains

★ ★ ★ ★ ★ **Victoria-Sol** av J-Miró 21
☎234342 tx68558
⊷171 P Lift 🌙 dB ⇄12100 M2100
t5% Pool sea

★ ★ ★ **Alcina** ps Maritimo 26 ☎231140
⊷89 Lift dB ⇄3000 – 3200 M750 sea
mountains

★ ★ ★ **Maricel** C'as Catala Beach
☎402712
⊷55 A8rm P Lift 🌙 🏊 Pool sea

★ ★ ★ **Nixe Palace** Calvo Sotelo 537
☎403811 tx68569
⊷131 🏠 P Lift 🌙 Pool sea

★ ★ **Paso** Alvaro de Bazán 3
☎237602 tx68652
⊷260 P Lift 🌙 dB ⇄2100 – 2400
M650 Pool

🏷️T **Minaco** Gran via Asima 11
☎200111 BL (Landrover) Cit

🏷️T **Oliver** G-Llabre 12 – 14 ☎275503 All
makes

At **PLAYA DE PALMA (CA'N PASTILLA)**

★ ★ **Oasis** B-Riutort 25 ☎260150
tx69103
⊷110 🏠 P Lift 🌙 dB ⇄3040 – 3890
M680 Pool sea mountains

At **PLAYA DE PALMA NOVA** (16km SW)

★ ★ ★ **Hawaii** ☎681150 tx68670
Mar – Dec
⊷2 P Lift 🌙 dB ⇄1700 – 3700 M750
Pool Beach sea

POLLENSA (☎971)

At **CALA SAN VINCENTE**

★ ★ ★ ★**Molins** ☎530200 tx69109

5 Feb–27 Nov
rm100 ⇆97 ▥3 **P** Lift ☽
dB ⇆ ▥3710–5095 M1870 ⇘ Pool
sea

At **PUERTO DE POLLENSA** (6km NE)

★ ★ ★**Miramar** ps de Anglada Camarasa
39 ☎531400

Apr–Oct
⇆70 Lift dB ⇆2880–3840 M1020 ⇘
Beach

SON SERVERA (☎971)

At **COSTA DE LOS PINOS** (7.5km NE)

★ ★ ★ ★**Eurotel Golf Punta Rotja**
☎567600 tx68666

⇆250 sB ⇆4070–5220
dB ⇆5310–6750

MENORCA (MINORCA)
MAHÓN (☎971)

At **VILLACARLOS** (3km W)

★ ★ ★ ★**Agamenon** Fontanillas
☎362150

Apr–Oct
⇆75 **P** Lift ☽ dB ⇆3500–4535
M1050 t5% Pool Beach sea

BARAJAS See **MADRID**

BARCELONA
Barcelona (☎93)
See plan page 328

★ ★ ★ ★ ★**Avenida Palace** (SRS) av
Gran via de les Corts Catalones 605–607
☎3019600 tx54734 Plan **1**

⇆229 **P** Lift ☽ sB ⇆8030 dB ⇆10300

★ ★ ★ ★**Ritz** av Gran via de les Corts
Catalones 668 ☎3185200 tx52739
Plan **2**

⇆203 **P** Lift ☽ sB ⇆8750–10750
dB ⇆13500–15500 M3600 t%

★ ★ ★**Condado** Aribau 201
☎2002311 tx54535 Plan **4**

⇆89 Lift ☽ sB ⇆2535–2810
dB ⇆4565–5115 M1100

★ ★ ★**Diplomatic** (GT) carrer de Pau
Claris ☎3173200 tx54701 Plan **6**

⇆225 ▥ **P** Lift ☽ sB ⇆9000–10900
dB ⇆11800–14150 Mfr2600 Pool

★ ★ ★**Majestic** (GT) ps de Gracia 70
☎2154512 tx52211 Plan **7**

⇆350 **P** Lift ☽ dB ⇆9500 M2000
Pool

★ ★ ★ ★**Manila** Rambla Estudios III
☎3186206 tx54634 Plan **8**

Spain

⇆200 ▥ **P** Lift ☽ sB ⇆4990
dB ⇆6460 t5%

★ ★ ★ ★**Presidente** av Diagonal 570
☎2002111 tx52118 Plan **9**

⇆161 ▥ **P** Lift ☽ sB ⇆7575
dB ⇆9750 t5% Pool

★ ★ ★ ★**Princesa Sofia** pl Papa Pio XII
☎3307111 tx51032 Plan **9A**

⇆496 ▥ **P** Lift ☽ sB ⇆8875
dB ⇆11450 Pool

★ ★ ★**Regente** Rambla de Cataluña
76 ☎2152570 tx51939 Plan **10**

⇆78 Lift ☽ Pool sB ⇆4800–5300
dB ⇆6900

★ ★ ★**Arenas** Capitan Arenas 20 (n.rest)
☎2040300 Plan **11**

⇆62 ▥ **P** Lift ☽ sB ⇆4800
dB ⇆7400 t5%

★ ★ ★**Astoria** c de Paris 203 (n.rest)
☎2098311 tx97429 Plan **12**

rm109 ⇆32 ▥77 **P** Lift ☽
sB ⇆ ▥2975 dB ⇆ ▥4650–5150

★ ★ ★**Calderón** Rambla de Cataluñ 26
☎3010000 tx51549 Plan **13**

⇆244 ▥ Lift ☽ Pool

★ ★ ★**Cristal** Diputación 257
☎3016600 tx54560 Plan **14**

⇆ ▥150 ▥ **P** Lift ☽ dB ⇆ ▥5900
M1550

★ ★ ★**Dante** c Mallorca 181 (n.rest)
☎3232254 tx52588 Plan **15**

⇆81 ▥ Lift ☽ sB ⇆5500 dB ⇆7100

★ ★ ★**Derby** c de Loreto 21 ☎2393007
tx97429 Plan **16**

⇆116 ▥ **P** Lift ☽ sB ⇆5150
dB ⇆8250

★ ★ ★**Expo** (GT) c Mallorca 1
☎3251212 tx54147 Plan **17**

rm432 ⇆384 ▥48 ▥ **P** Lift ☽
dB ⇆ ▥5695 t5% Pool

★ ★ ★**Gaudi** ctra Nou de la Rambla 12
☎3017780 tx50111 Not on plan

rm71 ⇆47 ▥24 **P** Lift ☽
sB ⇆ ▥2100–2300 dB ⇆ ▥3500–4000
M1050

★ ★ ★**Regina** c Vergara 4 ☎301323
tx50705 Plan **19**

⇆102 Lift dB ⇆4850

★ ★ ★**Wilson** av Diagonal 568 (n.rest)
☎2092511 tx52180 Plan **20**

⇆55 ▥ Lift ☽ sB ⇆3275 dB ⇆5350

☷**Benedito** Corcega 418 ☎2572443 **P**
Opl

☷**British Motors** c Calabria ☎2232924
BL DJ RT

☷**California** c Mallorca 419
☎2363545 **P**

☷**Layetana** Travesera de Gracia
17–29 ☎3212327 Frd

☷**F-Roca** Diputación 43 ☎3251550 M/c
Aud Chy DJ RR RT Sim VW

☷**Romagosa** c Bolivia 243–245
☎3071957 BL (Landrover) Opl

☷**Ryvesa** Aragón 179 ☎2531600 MB

At **MONT-TIBIDABO** (12km NW)

★ ★ ★**Florida** ☎2475000 Plan **18**

Jun–Aug
⇆52 Lift

BARCO DE ÁVILA (EL)
Ávila(☎918)

★ ★ ★**Manila** ctra de Plasencia Km 69
☎340844

⇆50 ▥ **P** Lift ☽ sB ⇆1500–1850
dB ⇆24000–29000 M850 mountains

BAYONA
Pontevedra(☎986)

★ ★ ★**Parador Nacional Conde de
Gondomar** ☎355000

⇆128 ▥ **P** ☽ sB ⇆3650–4750
dB ⇆6200–8200 M1300 ⇘ Pool
Beach sea

BEGUR
Girona(☎972)

★ ★ ★**Begur** De Coma y Ros 8 ☎622207

Apr–Sep
⇆37 **P** ☽ dB ⇆2400–3200 M800

★ ★**Sa Riera** Playa de Sa Riera ☎623000

Mar–Oct
rm41 ⇆19 ▥41 **P** ☽
dB ⇆ ▥2840–3730 M860 Pool sea

At **AIGUA BLAVA** (3.5km SE)

★ ★ ★**Algua-Blava** (DPn in season)
Playa de Fornells ☎622058

25 Mar–17 Oct
rm85 ⇆78 ▥7 ▥ **P** ☽
dB ⇆ ▥4300–4900 M1600 ⇘ Pool
sea

★ ★ ★**Parador Nacional Costa Brava**
☎622162

⇆80 **P** ☽ sB ⇆3250–4250
dB ⇆5200–6700 M1300 ⇘ Pool ♨
∩

BÉJAR
Salamanca(☎923)

★★★**Colón** c Colón 42 ☎400650
⇌54 **P** Lift ☽ sB ⇌1700–2200
dB ⇌2800–3300 Mfr1000 t4%
mountains

BENALMÁDENA
Málaga(☎952)

★★★★**Riviera** ctra Cadiz-Málaga
Km288 ☎441240 tx77041
⇌189 **P** Lift ☽ dB ⇌4620–6620
M1400 t5% ✆ Pool sea

★★★**Siroco** ctra de Cádiz Km228
☎443040 tx77135
⇌252 **P** Lift dB ⇌2685–4900 M1300
t5% ✆ Pool sea

★★**Puerto Benalmádena** ctra de Cádiz
Km229 ☎441640
⇌78 Lift dB ⇌3025 M625 Pool sea

BENICARLO
Castellón(☎964)

☆☆☆**Parador Costa del Azahar** ctra de
Peñiscola ☎470100
⇌108 **P** ☽ dB ⇌5200–6700 M1300
✆ Pool sea

★★**Sol** av Magallanes 90 (n.rest)
☎471349
Jul–Aug
⇌16 🍴 **P** ☽ dB ⇌2000 sea
mountains

BENICASIM
Castellón(☎964)

★★★★**Azor** ps Maritimo ☎300350
tx65503
Mar–Nov
⇌88 **P** Lift ☽ sB ⇌2300–2800
dB ⇌3000–4000 M1250 ✆ Pool ∩
sea mountains

★★★**Voramar** ☎300150
17 Apr–Sep
⇌55 🍴 Lift ☽ sB ⇌1800–2250
dB ⇌2800–3500 M720–900 ✆ Beach
sea

★★**Bonaire** ps Maritimo ☎300800
tx65503
Mar–Oct
⇌87 **P** ☽ sB ⇌1960–2360
dB ⇌2920–3470 M1100 ✆ Pool ∩
sea mountains

BENIDORM
Alicante(☎965)

★★★★**Gran Delfin (DPn)** Playa de
Poniente ☎853400
14 Apr–Sep
⇌99 **P** Lift ☽ dB ⇌6840–7440
M1800 ✆ Pool sea

★★**Presidente** av Filipinas ☎853950
tx66365
rm228 ⇌216 🏠12 Lift ☽
dB ⇌2700–3200 M600 ✆ Pool
mountains

🍴**Autonautica** ctra Alicante-Valencia
Km116.700 ☎853562 Frd

BIELSA
Huesca(☎974)

Spain

At **VALLE DE PINETA** (14km NW)

★★★**Parador Nacional Monte Perdido**
☎501011
⇌16 **P** Lift ☽ dB ⇌4700–5700
M1300 t4% mountains

BILBAO (BILBO)
Vizcaya(☎94)

★★★★★**Villa de Bilbao** Gran Via 87
☎4416000 tx32164
⇌142 🍴 **P** Lift ☽ dB ⇌10400 t5%

★★★★**Aránzazu** R-Arias 66
☎4413200 tx32164
⇌171 🍴 **P** Lift ☽ dB ⇌7000 t5%

★★★★**Avenida** av H-de-Saracho 2
☎4124300 tx32164
⇌116 **P** Lift ☽ dB ⇌4600 mountains

★★★★**Carlton** pl F-Moyua 2 (n.rest)
☎4162200 tx32233
⇌150 Lift ☽ sB ⇌fr5350 dB ⇌fr6950
t4%

★★★★**Ercilla** (GT) Ercilla 37 (n.rest)
☎4438800 tx32449
⇌350 **P** Lift ☽ dB ⇌8100

🍴**Aubisa** Alameda de Urquijo
85 ☎4419900 Cit

BLANES
Girona(☎972)

★★★★**Park** ☎330250
May–Oct
⇌131 **P** Lift ☽ sB ⇌3255–4155
dB ⇌5310–6710 Mfr1000 ✆ Pool
Beach sea

★**Horitzo** ps Marítimo 11 ☎330400
15 Apr–Oct
rm122 ⇌95 🏠27 **P** Lift ☽
dB ⇌ 🏠2600–3200 M900 sea

★★**San Antonio** ps del Mar 63 ☎331150
May–Sep
⇌ 🏠156 Lift ☽ dB ⇌2100–2700
M600

★★**San Francisco** (DPn in season) ps del
Mar 72 ☎330477
May–Oct
⇌32 Lift ☽ dB ⇌2000–2310 M610
sea

BURGOS
Burgos(☎947)

★★★★**Almirante Bonifaz** Vitoria 22–24
(n.rest) ☎206943 tx39430
⇌79 Lift ☽ dB ⇌4670–5520 t5%

★★★★**Landa Palace** (2km S on N1)
ctra de Madrid–Irún Km230 ☎206343
⇌ 🏠39 🍴 **P** Lift ☽
sB ⇌ 🏠6600–7000 dB ⇌ 🏠8900–9500
M2800 Pool

★★★**Asubio** Carmen 6 (n.rest)
☎203445

⇌30 Lift ☽ dB ⇌3300–3800

🍴**J Barrios** c de Vitoria 113
☎224900 Fia Lnc

🍴**Mecanico 'Sulzo'** San Agustin 5
☎202364 **P** Aud VW

🍴**Pedro** ctra Madrid/Irún Km247
☎280300 **P** Peu Tal

BURRIANA
Castellón(☎964)

★★★**Aloha** (2.5km E) av Mediterraneo
75 ☎510104
Mar–Sep
⇌30 **P** Lift ☽ dB ⇌2917 M840 Pool
sea mountains

CABRERA (LA)
Madrid(☎91)

★★**Mavi** ctra de Madrid–Irún 58
☎8688000
rm43 ⇌15 🏠28 **P** ☽ dB ⇌ 🏠2400
M900 mountains

CÁCERES
Cáceres(☎927)

★★★**Alcántara** av Virgen de Guadalupe
14 ☎228900
⇌67 Lift ☽ dB ⇌3820–4105 t5%

★**Alvarez** Moret 20 ☎246400
rm37 ⇌17 🏠20 **P** Lift ☽
dB ⇌ 🏠2760 M525 t5%

CADAQUES
Girona(☎972)

★★★**Plays-Sol** (n.rest) ☎258100
Mar–Dec
rm50 ⇌40 🏠10 🍴 **P** Lift ☽
dB ⇌ 🏠5500–6500 ✆ Pool sea

CÁDIZ
Cádiz(☎956)

★★★**Atlantico** Parque Genovés 9
☎212301
⇌155 🍴 **P** Lift ☽ dB ⇌5700–6700
M1300 t5% Pool

🍴**Saina** av del Puente ☎231604 Ren

CALAFELL
Tarragona(☎977)

★★★**Kursaal** av San J-de-Dios
☎692300
Mar–Oct
⇌39 🍴 **P** Lift ☽ sB ⇌2100–2300
dB ⇌4950–5550 M1400 sea

★★★**Miramar** Rambla Costa Dorada 1
☎690700
26 Mar–15 Oct
rm200 ⇌180 🏠20 🍴 **P** Lift ☽
dB ⇌ 🏠4340 M800 Pool

CALAHORRA
La Rioja(☎941)

★★★**Parador Nacional Marco Fabio
Quintiliano** av Generalisimo ☎130358
⇌67 Lift ☽ sB ⇌3550–3950
dB ⇌4700–4850 M1300 t4%

CALA RATJADA See **BALEARES (ISLAS
DE)** under **MALLORCA**

BARCELONA

1	★ ★ ★ ★ ★ Avenida Palace
2	★ ★ ★ ★ ★ Ritz
4	★ ★ ★ ★ Conado
6	★ ★ ★ ★ Diplomatic
7	★ ★ ★ ★ Majestic
8	★ ★ ★ ★ Manilla
9	★ ★ ★ ★ Presidente
9A	★ ★ ★ ★ Princesa Sofia
10	★ ★ ★ ★ Regente
11	★ ★ ★ Arenas
12	★ ★ ★ Astoria
13	★ ★ ★ Calderón
14	★ ★ ★ Cristal
15	★ ★ ★ Dante
16	★ ★ ★ Derby
17	★ ★ ★ Expo
18	★ ★ ★ Florida (At Mont-Tibidabo 12km NW)
19	★ ★ ★ Regina
20	★ ★ ★ Wilson

CALA SAN VICENTE See **BALEARES (ISLAS DE)** under **POLLENSA, MALLORCA**

CALATAYUD
Zaragoza(☎976)

★ ★**Calatayud** (2km NE on N11 at Km237) ☎881323
rm63 ⇌35 ▥28 A33rm 🏠 P ♪
sB ⇌1600–2450 dB ⇌2500–4200
M925 mountains

CALDES D'ESTRAC
Barcelona(☎93)

★ ★ ★ ★**Colón (DPn)** ps 16 ☎7910351
Apr–15 Oct
rm83 ⇌70 ▥13 🏠 P Lift ♪
sB ⇌ ▥2550–3050 dB ⇌ ▥4800–5700
Mfr1150 Pool sea mountains

CALELLA DE LA COSTA
Barcelona(☎93)

★ ★ ★**Las Vegas** ctra de Francia
☎7690850 tx97338
May–Oct
rm115 ⇌48 ▥62 P Lift ♪
dB ⇌ ▥2150–3950 M525 Pool sea

★ ★ ★ ★**Mont-Rosa** ps de las Rocas
☎7690508
May–25 Oct
⇌120 P Lift ♪ dB ⇌3010–4835
M955 Pool sea

★ ★**Fragata** ps de las Rocas ☎7692112
15 May–15 Oct
⇌72 P Lift ♪ dB ⇌2350–2700 sea

CALELLA DE PALAFRUGELL See
PALAFRUGELL

CALPE
Alicante(☎965)

★ ★ ★**Paradero Ifach** Explanada del
Puerto 81 ☎830300
Mar–Nov
rm29 ⇌15 ▥14 🏠 P ♪ dB ⇌4100
M800 🏖 Beach sea

★ ★**Venta la Chata** (4km N) ☎830308

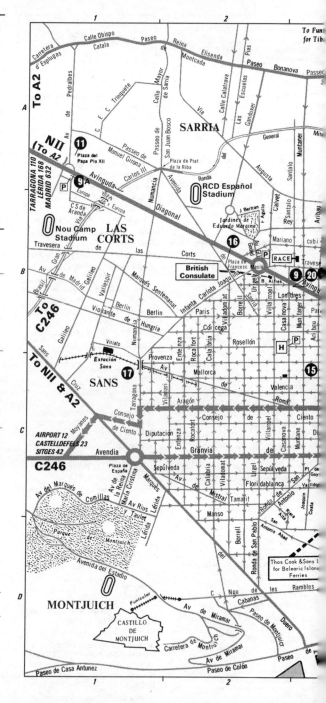

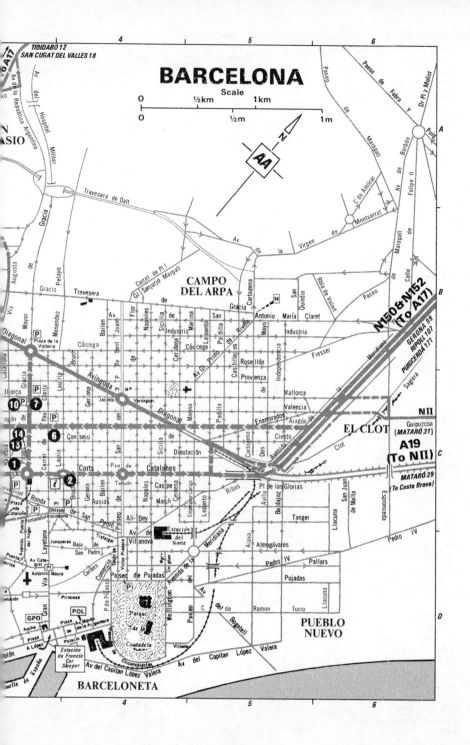

BARCELONA

Scale

TIBIDABO 12
SAN CUGAT DEL VALLES 18

CAMPO
DEL ARPA

EL CLOT

PUEBLO
NUEVO

BARCELONETA

⌂18 ⏚ P ☽ dB ↵4430 M1180 ⚲
sea mountains

CAMBADOS
Pontevedra(☎986)

★ ★ ★Parador Nacional del Albariño ps
de Cervantes ☎542250
↵63 P Lift ☽ dB ↵4700–6700
M1300 sea

CARDONA
Barcelona(☎93)

★ ★ ★Parador Nacional Duques de
Cardona ☎8691275
↵65 P Lift ☽ dB ↵4700–5200
M1300 mountains

CARMONA
Sevilla(☎954)

★ ★ ★ ★Parador Nacional Aicázar Rey
Don Pedro ☎141010
rm55 ↵50 ▥5 P Lift ☽
dB ↵ ▥5700 M1300 Pool

CAROLINA (LA)
Jaén(☎953)

★ ★ ★Perdiz (ctr a N IV) ☎660300
tx28315
↵89 ⏚ P dB ↵3980–4480 M1200
t5% Pool

CARTAGENA
Murcia(☎968)

★ ★ ★Cartagonova Marcos Redondo 3
☎504200 tx6771
rm126 ↵100 ▥26 ⏚ P Lift ☽
sB ↵ ▥2890–3565 dB ↵ ▥3800–4640
t5% sea

★ ★ ★Mediterráneo Puerta de Murcia
11 ☎507400
↵46 Lift ☽ sB↵1685–2390
dB ↵2920–3610 M650–1000 t%

CASTELLCIUTAT See SEU
D'URGELL(LA)

CASTELLDEFELS
Barcelona(☎93)

★ ★ ★Neptuno ps Garbi 74 ☎6651450
↵40 P Lift ☽ dB ↵4350–5100
M1380 ⚲ Pool

★ ★ ★Rancho ps de la Marina 212
☎6651900 tx57638
↵40 ▥20 Lift ☽ dB ↵ ▥4600
M1300 ⚲ Pool sea

CASTELLÓN DE LA PLANA
Castellón(☎964)

★ ★ ★Mindoro Moyano 4 ☎222300
↵114 ⏚ P Lift ☽ dB ↵ ▥5920

⭗Tagerbaf Hnos Vilafana
13 ☎216653 P All makes

At GRAO DE CASTELLÓN (5km E)
★ ★ ★ ★Golf Playa del Pinar ☎221950
Apr–Sep
↵127 ⏚ P Lift ☽ dB ↵4050–4550
M850

CASTILLO DE SANTA CATALINA See
JAÉN

Spain

CASTRO-URDIALES
Cantabria(☎924)

★ ★ ★Rocas av de la Playa ☎860404
↵ ▥61 ⏚ P Lift ☽
dB ↵ ▥4000–5500 M1250

CAZORLA
Jaén(☎953)

★ ★Parador Nacional el Adelantado
(25km SE) ☎721075
rm30 ↵16 A8rm ⏚ dB ↵4700–5200
M1300 ⟲

CERVERA DE PISUERGA
Palencia(☎988)

★ ★ ★Parador Nacional de Fuentes
Carrionas ☎870075
25 Dec–2 Nov
↵80 ⏚ P Lift ☽ dB ↵5200–6200
M1300 mountains lake

CESTONA
Guipúzcoa(☎943)

★ ★ ★ ★Arocena ☎867040
Jul–Sep
rm109 ↵84 ▥25 ⏚ P Lift ☽
dB ↵ ▥3900 M1150 t5% ⚲ Pool
mountains

CHINCHÓN
Madrid(☎91)

★ ★ ★Parador Nacional av Generalisimo
1 ☎8940836
↵38 ☽ dB ↵5700 M1300 t4% Pool

CIUDAD REAL
Ciudad Real(☎926)

⭗Calatrave ctra Carrion
Km242 ☎220315 All makes

CIUDAD RODRIGO
Salamanca(☎923)

★ ★ ★Parador Nacional Enrique II pl del
Castillo 1 ☎460150
↵27 P ☽ sB ↵3550–3950
dB ↵4700–5200 M1300 t5% mountains

⭗Auto Sprint Salamanca S/N
☎460945 All makes

COMA-RUGA
Tarragona(☎977)

★ ★ ★Gran Europa av Palfurina
☎680411 tx56681
Apr–Oct
rm155 ↵124 ▥31 A3rm ⏚ P Lift ☽
dB ↵ ▥4880–5880 M1550 ⚲ Pool
Beach sea

COMILLAS
Cantabria(☎942)

★ ★ ★Casal del Castro San Jeronimo
☎720036
15 Jun–15 Sep
rm45 ↵42 ▥3 P Lift ☽
dB ↵ ▥3450 M1250 mountains

CONTRERAS
Cuenca

★ ★Venta de Contreras ☎(96)2170050
rm14 ↵3 ▥4 A4rm P ☽ ⚲ Pool
mountains lake

CÓRDOBA
Córdoba(☎957)

★ ★ ★ ★Gran Capitan av America 3–5
☎221955
↵97 P Lift ☽ sB ↵4250
dB ↵5800 t5%

★ ★ ★ ★Mellá Córdoba Jàrdines de la
Victoria ☎298066 tx76591
↵106 P Lift ☽ sB ↵3920 dB ↵7230
M1870 Pool

★ ★ ★Parador Nacional de la
Arruzafa av de la Arruzafa ☎275900
↵82 P Lift ☽ dB ↵6800 M1300 ⚲
Pool mountains

★ ★Marisa Cardenal Herrero 6 (n.rest)
☎473144
rm28 ↵10 ▥18 ☽ dB ↵ ▥3130

★Brilliante av del Brilliante 97 ☎275800
rm27 ↵9 ▥8 ☽ dB1850
dB ↵ ▥2300 M800 mountains

CORUÑA (LA) (CORUNNA)
La Coruña (☎981)

★ ★ ★ ★Finisterre ps del Parrote 2
☎205400 tx84089
↵127 P Lift ☽ sB ↵3500–4620
dB ↵4600–6000 t5% ⚲ Pool Beach
sea

⭗L R Amado Gl-Sanjurjo 117–119
☎283400 BL (Landrover)

COSTA DE LOS PINOS See BALEARES
(ISLAS DE) under SON SERVERA,
MALLORCA

CUENCA
Cuenca (☎966)

★ ★ ★Torremangana San Ignacio de
Loyola 9 ☎223351 tx23400
↵115 ⏚ P Lift ☽ dB ↵5000–5550
M1150 t5% mountains

CULLERA
Valencia (☎96)

★ ★ ★Sicania ctra El Faro, Playa del
Raco ☎1520143 tx64774
↵117 ⏚ P Lift ☽ dB ↵4150–4750
M1200 Beach sea

DALIAS
Almeria

★ ★ ★ ★Golf Almerimar ☎480950
tx78933
↵38 P Lift ☽ dB ↵5200–7100 M130
t5% ⚲ Pool ♉ sea

DENIA
Alicante (☎965)

At PLAYA DE LES MARINAS (1km N)
★ ★Angeles Playa de las Marinas 649
☎780458
Apr–Sep

330

rm60 ⇌30 🗐30 **P** ☽
dB ⇌ 🗐2680–3080 M825 ⚲ sea

EL Each name preceded by 'EL' is listed under the name that follows it.

ELCHE
Alicante (☎965)

★ ★ ★**Huerto del Cura** F-G-Sanchiz 14
☎458040 tx48452
⇌59 🏛 **P** ☽ dB ⇌5690–6425
M1325 ⚲ Pool

ESCALA (L')
Girona (☎972)

★ ★ ★**Barca** E-Serra 25 ☎770162
13 Jun–17 Sep
rm26 ⇌23 🗐3 ☽ dB ⇌1600–2000
M550 sea

ESCORIAL (EL) See **SAN LORENZO DE EL ESCORIAL**

ESTARTIT (L')
Girona (☎972)

★**Vila** Santa Ana 34 ☎758113
Jun–Sep
rm58 ⇌7 🗐28 A20rm ☽
dB1710–1950 dB ⇌ 🗐2200–2600 M600

ESTEPONA
Málaga (☎952)

★ ★ ★**Robinson Clubhotel Atalaya Park** (SRS) ☎781300 tx77210
11 Nov–14 Dec
⇌416 **P** Lift ☽ dB ⇌5950–6950 ⚲
Pool Beach ♂ ∩ sea mountains

★ ★ ★**Santa Marta** Apartado 2
☎780716
Apr–Sep
⇌37 **P** ☽ dB ⇌3600–3900 M1200
t5% Pool Beach sea mountains

★**Buenavista** ps Maritimo ☎800137
⇌38 **P** Lift ☽ dB ⇌2900–3300 M750
sea

FERROL DEL CAUDILLO (EL)
La Coruña (☎981)

৪ত**Castelos** ctra a la Cándara 11/17
☎312417 Frd

FIGUERES
Girona (☎972)

★ ★ ★ ★**President** crte Nacional 11 de
Madrid-Francia ☎501700
rm77 ⇌56 🗐21 🏛 **P** Lift ☽
dB ⇌ 🗐4100–4400 M1100

☆ ☆ ☆**Ampurdan** ctra Madrid-Francia
Km763 ☎500562
⇌48 🏛 **P** Lift ☽ dB ⇌3600–4300
M2100 mountains

Spain

★ ★ ★**Durán** c Lasuaca 5 ☎501250
⇌70 🏛 Lift ☽ dB ⇌3450–3950 M975
৪ত**Central** av J-Antonio, Zone Rally Sur
☎500667 Frd
৪ত**Victoria** ctra de Rosas ☎500293 BL
(Landrover)

FORMENTOR See **BALEARES (ISLAS DE)** under **MALLORCA**

FORNELLS DE LA SELVA See **GIRONA (GERONA)**

FUENGIROLA
Málaga (☎952)

★ ★ ★**Mare Nostrum** ctra de Cádiz
☎471100/27578
May–Oct
⇌246 dB ⇌3760–4560 M825 Pool
Beach sea

★ ★ ★ ★**Palmeras** ps Marítimo
☎472700 tx77202
⇌530 🏛 **P** Lift ☽ dB ⇌5200–7700
M1200 ⚲ Pool ♂ sea

★ ★ ★ ★**Pirámides** ps Marítimo
☎470600 tx77315
⇌320 🏛 **P** Lift ☽ dB ⇌4250–6250
t5% ⚲ Pool ♂ ∩ sea

★ ★ ★**Florida** Playa Florida ☎476100
tx77791
rm116 ⇌106 🗐10 **P** Lift ☽
dB ⇌ 🗐3100–3700 M925 t5% Pool
Beach sea

FUENTE DÉ
Cantabria (☎942)

★ ★**Parador Nacional del Rio Deva**
☎730001
Nov–15 Dec
⇌78 **P** ☽ dB ⇌4700–5700 M1300
mountains

FUENTERRABÍA (HONDARRIBIA)
Guipúzcoa (☎943)

★ ★**Guadalupe** Puntal de España
(n.rest) ☎641650
Jun–Sep
rm35 ⇌22 🗐13 **P** ☽ dB ⇌ 🗐4300
t5% Pool

★ ★**Parador Nacional el Emperador** pl
de Armas del Castillo ☎642140
⇌16 dB ⇌5200 M1300 ⸱

At **JAIZKÍBEL** (8km SW)

★ ★ ★**Jaizkibel** Monte Jaizkibel
☎641100
rm13 ⇌6 🗐7 dB1656–2016
dB ⇌ 🗐2256–2616

GANDÍA
Valencia (☎96)

★ ★**Ernesto** ctra de Valencia 40
☎2864011
⇌ 🗐86 **P** Lift ☽ dB ⇌ 🗐1900 M650

GERONA See **GIRONA**

GIJÓN
Asturias (☎985)

★ ★ ★**Robledo** A-Trúan 2 (n.rest)
☎355940
⇌138 Lift ☽ dB ⇌5100 t5%

★ ★**Parador Nacional Molino Viejo** parc
de Isabel la Catolica 19 ☎370511
⇌6 **P** ☽ dB ⇌6700 M1300

GIRONA (GERONA)
Girona (☎972)

★ ★**Europa** J-Garreta 23 (n.rest)
☎202750
rm26 ⇌12 🗐14 🏛 **P** Lift ☽
dB ⇌ 🗐2800

At **FORNELLA DE LA SELVA** (5km S off N11)

★ ★ ★**Fornella Park** ☎476125
⇌31 **P** Lift dB ⇌4145–4595 M1325
t5% Pool mountains
৪ত**Blanch** ctra N11 KM718 ☎476028 Opl

GRANADA
Granada (☎958)

★ ★ ★ ★**Alhambra Palace** Peña Partida
2 ☎221468 tx78400
⇌117 **P** Lift ☽ dB ⇌6650 M1500
t5% mountains

★ ★ ★ ★**Brasilia** Recogidas 7 (n.rest)
☎258450
⇌68 **P** ☽ dB ⇌3780–4130 t5%

★ ★ ★**Carmen** av J-Atonio 62
☎258300 tx78546
⇌207 🏛 **P** Lift ☽ sB ⇌4670
dB ⇌7112 M1540 t4%

★ ★ ★**Meliá Granada** A-Garnivet 7
☎227400 tx78429
⇌221 Lift ☽ sB ⇌3795–4795
dB ⇌5690–7090 M1400

★ ★ ★**Guadalupe** av de los Alijares
☎223423
⇌86 **P** Lift ☽ dB ⇌4450 M1200 t5%

★ ★ ★**Kenia** Molinas 65 ☎227506
⇌19 **P** ☽ dB ⇌3880 M1110 t5%
mountains

★ ★ ★Parador Nacional de San Francisco (in the Alhambra) ☎221462
⇋32 **P** ☽ dB ⇋8200 M1300 mountains

★ ★Inglaterra Cetti Merien 4 (off Gran Via de Colon) (n.rest) ☎221558
rm50 ⇋45 🅵5 🅼 Lift ☽ dB ⇋ 🅵2960

★América Real Alhambra 53 ☎227471
Mar–9 Nov
rm14 ⇋8 🅵2 **P** ☽ dB ⇋3350 M1000 mountains

⅏Autiberia av Andalucia ☎2065602 BL (& Landrover)

⅏Auto Dibesa av Andalucia Km3 ☎276750 **P** Cit

⅏Baquero Motor c Cisne 5 ☎203011 M/c Peu Tal

At **SIERRA NEVADA** (40km SE)

★ ★ ★Meliá Sierra Nevada Pradollano ☎480400 tx78507
Apr–Dec
⇋221 **P** Lift ☽ sB ⇋ 4770–5740 dB ⇋8390–9700 M1725–1895 Pool mountains

★ ★ ★Meliá Sol y Nieve Pradollano ☎480300 tx78507
Dec–May
⇋200 **P** Lift ☽ sB ⇋2790–3570 dB ⇋5120–6050 M1150–1265 Pool mountains

★ ★ ★Parador Nacional Sierra Nevada ☎480200
Closed Nov
rm32 ⇋20 🅵12 🅼 **P** ☽ dB ⇋ 🅵4700–5700 M1300 ✍
mountains

GRAO DE CASTELLÓN See **CASTELLÓN DE LA PLANA**

GREDOS
Avila (☎918)

★ ★ ★Parador Nacional de Gredos ☎348048
⇋ 🅵77 🅼 **P** Lift ☽ dB ⇋ 🅵4700–5700 M1300 ◯
mountains

GUADALAJARA
Guadalajara (☎911)

★ ★ ★Husa (formerly Pax) ctra Madrid-Barcelona Km57 ☎221800
⇋61 🅼 **P** Lift ☽ sB ⇋2055 dB ⇋3700 M1100 t4% ✍ Pool

⅏Taberne Ingeniere Mariñvo 27 ☎211038 Landrover

GUADALUPE
Cáceres (☎927)

Hospederiá de Real Monasterio
(Monastery where accommodation is provided by the monks) pl J-Carlos 1 ☎367000
15 Feb–15 Jan
rm40 ⇋32 🅵1 **P** ☽ dB2000 dB ⇋3300 M1100 t5% mountains

Spain

★ ★Parador Nacional de Zurbarian Marques de la Romana 10 ☎367075
⇋20 **P** ☽ dB ⇋5200 M1300 Pool mountains

HUELVA
Huelva (☎955)

★ ★ ★Luz Huelva av Sundheim 26 (n.rest) ☎250011 tx75527
⇋105 🅼 Lift dB ⇋6390

★ ★Tartessos av M-A-Pinzon 13–15 ☎245611
⇋105 Lift dB ⇋4100

HUESCA
Huesca (☎974)

★ ★Pedro I de Aragón ps de Gl-Franco 34 ☎220300 tx58626
⇋52 **P** Lift ☽ dB ⇋4500 M950 t5% mountains

⅏Tumasa ctra Zaragoza ☎213294 BL (Landrover) Peu Tal

IBIZA See **BALEARES (ISLAS DE)**

IGUALADA
Barcelona (☎593)

★ ★ ★América ctra N11 Km557 ☎8031000
rm52 ⇋38 🅵14 **P** Lift ☽ dB ⇋ 🅵4550–4850 M1050 Pool mountains

IRÚN
Guipúzcoa (☎943)

★ ★Alcázar av Iparralde 11 ☎620900
⇋50 **P** Lift ☽ dB ⇋3800–4300 M1000

★ ★Lizaso Marires de Guadaloupe 5 (n.rest) ☎611660
rm20 ⇋6 🅵5 ☽ dB1850 dB ⇋ 🅵2600

★París ps de Colón 94–96 (n.rest) ☎616545
rm22 ⇋1 🅵6 dB 1800 dB ⇋ 🅵2650

JACA
Huesca (☎974)

★ ★Gran ps del Gl-Franco 1 ☎360900
May–Oct
rm80 ⇋35 🅵45 🅼 **P** Lift ☽ sB ⇋ 🅵1450–2400 dB ⇋ 🅵2500–4500 ✍ Pool mountains

JAÉN
Jaén (☎953)

⅏Lopez Poligono de las Olivas Ortega Nieto 16 ☎220132 Sko

At **CASTILLO DE SANTA CATALINA** (4km W)

★ ★ ★Parador Nacional ☎232287
⇋43 Lift ☽ sB ⇋3950 dB ⇋56200 M1300 t4% mountains

JAIZKÍBEL See **FUENTERRABIA**

JARANDILLA DE LA VERA
Cáceres (☎927)

★ ★ ★ ★Parador Nacional de Carlos-V ☎560117
⇋6 **P** ☽ dB ⇋4700–5200 M1300 Pool mountains

JÁVEA
Alicante (☎965)

★ ★ ★Parador Nacional Costa Blanca ☎790200
⇋65 🅼 **P** Lift ☽ sB ⇋3950–5150 dB ⇋5200–6700 M1300 t5% Pool sea

⅏Auto Jávea av de Ondara 11 ☎790178 All makes

JEREZ DE LA FRONTERA
Cádiz (☎956)

★ ★ ★Jerez, av A-Domecq 41 ☎330600 tx75059
⇋120 **P** Lift ☽ dB ⇋7600–8750 M2000 t5% Pool

☆ Aloha (On western bypass) ☎332500
⇋30 🅼 **P** dB ⇋3505 M850 Pool

JONQUERA (LA)
Girona (☎972)

★ ★Porta Catalana (2km SW on A17-service area) ☎540640
⇋80 **P** Lift ☽ sB ⇋3275–4575 dB ⇋4750–6650 M1000 mountains

★ ★Puerta de España ctra Nacional II ☎540120
⇋26 **P** ☽ sB ⇋1690–2030 dB ⇋2650–3160 M950 t4% mountains

★ ★Mercé Park ctra National II ☎549038
rm48 ⇋39 🅵9 **P** Lift ☽ mountains lake

LA Each name preceded by 'La' is listed under the name that follows it.

LAREDO
Cantabria (☎942)

★ ★ ★Cosmopol av de la Victoria ☎605400
15 Jun–15 Sep
⇋60 **P** Lift ☽ dB ⇋4820 M1280 Pool sea mountains

★Remona av J-Antonio 4 ☎605336
rm31 ⇋20 🅼 dB1895–2120 dB ⇋2220–2520 M875 sea

LECUMBERRI
Navarra (☎948)

★ ★Ayestaran ctra San Juan 64 ☎504127
rm120 ⇋50 🅵15 A94rm 🅼 **P** Lift dB1260–1410 dB ⇋1910 M600 Pool mountains lake

LEÓN
León (☎987)

★ ★ ★Conde Luna Inepencia 7 ☎206512 tx89888
⇋150 🅼 **P** Lift sB ⇋5150–5650 t5% Pool

★ ★ ★ ★**San Marcos** pl San Marcos
☎237300 tx89809

⇨200 **P** Lift sB ⇦5250–5550
dB ⇦8100–9000 M1700 t4%

★ ★ ★**Oliden** Playa de Santo Domingo 4
☎227500

rm50 ⇦40 🅵5 **P** Lift *D*
dB ⇨ 🅵3535–3950 t5%

★ ★ ★**Riosol** av de Palencia 3 ☎223650

⇨141 Lift *D* dB ⇦2905–3235 t5%
mountains

★ ★**Quindos** av J-Antonio 24 ☎236200

⇨96 **P** Lift *D* dB ⇦3325–3630 t5%

LÉRIDA See **LLEIDA**

LLANÇÁ
Girona (☎972)

At **PUERTO DE LLANÇÁ** (2km NE)

★ ★ ★**Mendisol** Playa de Grifeu
☎380100

Jun–Sep
⇨32 🅼 **P** *D* dB ⇦3630–6310
M1250 sea mountains

★ ★**Berna** ps Marítimo 5 ☎380150

15 May–Sep & Xmas wk
⇨38 **P** *D* dB ⇦2575–2625 M950
Beach sea

★**Miramar** ps Marítimo 2 ☎380132

Apr–Sep
rm31 dB1200–1800 M700

LLANFRANCH See **PALAFRUGELL**

LLANES
Asturias (☎985)

★ ★**Peñablanca** Pidal 1 (n.rest)
☎400166

15 Jun–15 Sep
⇨31 *D* dB ⇦3400–3600 t5%

LLANSA See **LLANÇÁ**

LLEIDA (LÉRIDA)
Lleida (☎973)

★ ★ ★**Condes de Urgel** av de Barcelona
17–27 ☎202300

⇨105 **P** Lift *D* dB ⇦5200

🕭**Mancasi** av de las Garrigas 38
☎2021650 **P** All makes

LLORET DE MAR
Girona (☎972)

★ ★ ★**Monterrey** ctra de Tossa
☎364050 tx57374

15 Mar–5 Nov
⇨229 **P** Lift *D* M1700
DPn3000–4800 🕭 Pool sea

Spain

★ ★ ★ ★**Rigat Park** Playa de Fanals
☎365200 tx57015

Mar–Nov
rm108 ⇦104 🅵4 **P** Lift *D*
dB7000–9000 M2000 🕭 Pool Beach
sea mountains

★ ★ ★ ★**Santa Marta** Playa de Santa
Cristina ☎364904

15 Jan–15 Dec
rm78 ⇦74 🅵4 A18rm 🅼 **P** Lift *D*
dB ⇨ 🅵7300–9300 M3000 🕭 Pool
Beach sea mountains

★ ★**Anabel** Feliciá Serra 10 ☎364108
tx57380

Closed Nov–22 Dec & 4 Jan–19 Feb
⇨230 **P** Lift *D* dB ⇦3800 M850 Pool
mountains

★ ★**Excelsior** ps M-J-Verdaguer 16
☎364137 tx97061

Apr–Oct
⇨45 Lift *D* dB ⇦3350–4050 M950
sea

★ ★**Fanals** ctra de Blanes ☎364112
tx57362

Apr–Oct
⇨80 🅼 **P** Lift *D* dB ⇦4580 M1060
🕭 Pool mountains

★ ★**Mañana** ctra Tossa ☎364180

15 Jun–Sep
rm17 ⇦12 **P** *D* dB1100 dB ⇦1500
M450 sea mountains

🕭**Celler** av Vidreras 22–26 ☎365397
Peu Tal

LOGROÑO
Rioja (☎941)

★ ★ ★**Carlton Rioja** av Rey-J-Carlos 5
☎242100

⇨120 🅼 **P** Lift *D* dB ⇦5135–5430

★ ★**El Cortijo** crta del Cortijo Km2
☎225050

⇨40 **P** *D* dB ⇦2860–3360 M950
t5% Pool mountains

LOS Each name preceded by 'Los' is listed
under the name that follows it.

LUARCA
Asturias (☎985)

★**Gayoso** ps de Gómez 4 ☎640054

⇨28 **P** Lift *D* dB ⇦4700–5360 t5%

LUGO
Lugo (☎982)

★ ★**Méndez Nuñez** Reina 1 (n.rest)
☎230711

⇨100 Lift *D* dB ⇦2900–4000

MADRID
Madrid (☎91)
See plan page 334

★ ★ ★ ★ ★**Meliá Madrid** c de la Princesa
27 ☎2418200 tx22537 Plan **2**

⇨266 **P** Lift *D* sB ⇦8570
dB11340–11740 M2600

★ ★ ★ ★**Palace** pl de las Cortes 7
☎4297551 tx22272 Plan **3**

⇨ 🅵525 🅼 **P** Lift *D*
sB ⇨ 🅵9650–11650
dB ⇨ 🅵12550–15050 M3125

★ ★ ★ ★**Princesa Plaza** (SRS) c de la
Princesa 40 ☎2422100 tx44378 Plan **4A**

⇨406 🅼 **P** Lift *D* sB ⇦9050
dB 🅵11770 M2760

★ ★ ★ ★**Ritz** (THF) pl de la Lealtad 5
☎2212857 tx 43985 Plan **5**

⇨156 **P** Lift *D* dB ⇦20800 M5000
t5%

★ ★ ★ ★**Villa Magna** ps e la
Castellana 22 ☎2614900 tx22914
Plan **6**

⇨200 **P** Lift *D* k dB ⇦20200 M4100
t5%

★ ★ ★**Alcalá** c de Alcalá 66
☎4351060 tx48094 Plan **7**

rm153 ⇦107 🅵46 🅼 **P** Lift *D*
dB ⇦ 🅵6305

★ ★ ★**Castellana** (Intercont) ps de la ·
Castellana 57 ☎4100200 tx27686 Plan **8**

⇨322 **P** Lift *D* dB ⇦11500–13500

★ ★ ★**Emperador** Gran Vía 53
☎2472800 tx27521 Plan **9**

⇨ 🅵231 Lift dB ⇦ 🅵6675 Pool

★ ★ ★**Emperatriz** López de Hoyos 4
☎4136511 tx43640 Plan **10**

⇨ 🅵170 🅼 **P** Lift *D* dB ⇨ 🅵7690

★ ★ ★**Meliá Castilla** Cpt Haya 43
☎2708000 tx23142 Plan **11**

⇨1000 **P** Lift *D* sB ⇦7475–9150
dB ⇦9800–11650 M2350 Pool

★ ★ ★**Plaza** (SRS) pl de España 8
(n.rest) ☎2471200 tx27383 Plan **11A**

⇨354 🅼 **P** Lift *D* sB ⇦6780
dB ⇦8840 Pool

★ ★ ★**Sanvy** c de Goya 3 (n.rest)
☎2760800 Plan **12** →

MADRID

2	★ ★ ★ ★ ★	Meliá Madrid
3	★ ★ ★ ★ ★	Palace
4A	★ ★ ★ ★ ★	Princesa Plaza
5	★ ★ ★ ★ ★	Ritz
6	★ ★ ★ ★ ★	Villa Magna
7	★ ★ ★ ★	Alcalá
8	★ ★ ★ ★	Castellana
9	★ ★ ★ ★	Emperador
10	★ ★ ★ ★	Emperatriz
11	★ ★ ★ ★	Meliá Castilla
11A	★ ★ ★ ★	Plaza
12	★ ★ ★ ★	Sanvy
13	★ ★ ★ ★	Velázquez
14	★ ★ ★	Carlos-V
15	★ ★ ★	Carlton
15A	★ ★ ★	Gran Via
16	★ ★ ★	Lope de Vega
17	★ ★ ★	Miguel Angel
18	★ ★ ★	Príncipe Pio
19	★ ★ ★	Residenciá Madrid
20	★ ★ ★	Tirol
21	★ ★	Mercator

⇌109 🚗 **P** Lift ⅅ dB ⇌8100 t5% Pool

★ ★ ★ **Velázquez** Velázquez 62
☎2752800 tx22779 Plan **13**
⇌140 🚗 Lift ⅅ dB ⇌6525 M1400 t5%.

★ ★ ★ **Carlos V** c Maetro Vitoria 5 (n.rest)
☎2314100 tx48547 Plan **14**
⇌67 Lift ⅅ sB ⇌3200 dB ⇌4350

★ ★ ★ **Carlton** ps de las Delicias 28
☎2397100 tx42598 Plan **15**
rm133 ⇌94 ▥39 **P** Lift ⅅ
sB ⇌ ▥2775 dB ⇌ ▥4650

★ ★ ★ **Centro Norte** Mauricio Ravel 10
☎7333400 tx42598 Not on plan
⇌ ▥200 🚗 **P** Lift ⅅ sB ⇌ ▥3635
dB ⇌ ▥4750 Pool

★ ★ ★ **Gran Vía** Gran Vía 25 (n.rest)
☎2221121 tx44173 Plan **15A**
⇌162 Lift dB ⇌5170 t5%

★ ★ ★ **Lope de Vega** Gran Vía 59 (n.rest)
☎2477000 Plan **16**
⇌50 Lift ⅅ dB ⇌3040

★ ★ ★ **Miguel Angel** c de Miguel Angel
29–31 ☎4420022 tx44235 Plan **17**
⇌305 🚗 ⅅ sB ⇌10200 dB ⇌13300 t5%

★ ★ ★ **Príncipe Pio** ps de Onesimo
Redondo 16 ☎2470800 tx42183 Plan **18**
⇌157 🚗 **P** Lift ⅅ dB ⇌4115–4570 M950

★ ★ ★ **Residonciá Madrid** Carretas 10
(off Puerto del Sol) (n.rest) ☎2216520
Plan **19**
⇌71 Lift ⅅ dB ⇌3700 t5%

★ ★ ★ **Tirol** Marqués de Urquijo 4 (n.rest)
☎2481900 Plan **20**
rm92 ⇌84 🚗 Lift dB ⇌3565

★ ★ **Mercator** c de Atocha 123 (n.rest)
☎4290500 tx46129 Plan **21**
⇌90 🚗 **P** Lift dB ⇌3950

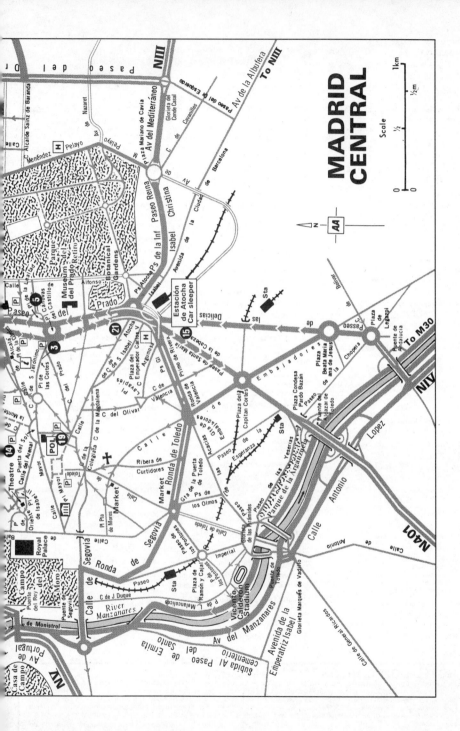

MADRID CENTRAL

At **BARAJAS** (15km N on N1)

★ ★ ★ ★ ★**Barajas**(GT)avLogroño305
☎7477700 tx22255 Not on plan
⇌230 🅿️ **P** Lift 𝄢 sB ⇌7395
dB ⇌11890 M2150 Pool

★ ★ ★**Eurotel** Galéon 27 ☎7471355
tx45688 Not on plan
⇌271 **P** Lift sB ⇌4685 dB ⇌6040

MAGALUF See **BALEARES (ISLAS DE)**
under **MALLORCA**

MAHÓN See **BALEARES (ISLAS DE)**
under **MENORCA**

MÁLAGA
Málaga (☎952)

★ ★ ★ ★**Málaga Palacio** av Cortina del
Muelle 1 (n.rest) ☎215185 tx77021
⇌223 Lift 𝄢 dB ⇌6000–7700 t5%
Pool sea

★ ★ ★**Las Vegas** ps de Sancha 28
☎217712
⇌73 **P** Lift 𝄢 dB ⇌3700–4000
M1150 Pool sea

★ ★ ★**Naranjos** ps Sancha 29
☎224316 tx77030
rm41 ⇌34 🏠7 🅿️ **P** Lift 𝄢
dB ⇌4470–4770 sea

★ ★**Parador Nacional de Gibralfaro**
☎221902
⇌12 **P** 𝄢 dB ⇌5700 M1300 sea

MALLORCA See **BALEARES (ISLAS DE)**

MANZANARES
Ciudad Real (☎926)

☆ ☆**Parador Nacional** (2km S) ☎610400
⇌50 **P** Lift 𝄢 dB ⇌4700 M1100 Pool

★**Cruce** ctra Madrid-Cádiz KM173
☎611900
rm37 ⇌33 🏠4 𝄢 dB ⇌3680–4080
M1100 Pool

🕭**Serrano-Calvillo** ctra Madrid-Cádiz
Km171 ☎611192 **P** Fia Lnc

MAQUEDA
Toledo

★ ★ ★**Cazador** ctra Madrid-Badajoz
Km74 ☎20
⇌30 **P** Lift 𝄢 dB ⇌2250 M750 Pool
mountains lake

MARBELLA
Malaga (☎952)

★ ★ ★ ★ ★**Meliá Don Pepe** ctra de
Cádiz-Málaga Km186 ☎770300 tx77055
⇌218 **P** Lift 𝄢 sB ⇌7850–10250
dB ⇌12100–16800 M2950 🏊 Pool
Beach sea

Spain

★ ★ ★ ★ ★**Monteros** ctra de Cádiz
☎771700 tx77059
⇌ 🏠163 **P** Lift 𝄢 dB ⇌23000 M4500
t5% 🏊 Beach ♂ ∩ sea mountains

★ ★ ★ ★**Chapas** ctra de Cádiz
☎831375 tx77057
⇌ 🏠117 **P** Lift 𝄢
sB ⇌ 🏠2300–2875 dB ⇌ 🏠3220–4370
🏊 Pool sea mountains

★ ★ ★**Guadalpin** ctra Cádiz-Málaga
Km186 ☎771100
⇌103 **P** 𝄢 dB ⇌3000–4700 M950
t5% Pool

★ ★ ★**Artola** (SRS) ctra de Cádiz Km201
☎831390 tx77654
⇌18 🅿️ **P** Lift 𝄢 dB ⇌3700–5200
🏊 Pool ♂ sea

★ ★ ★**Estrella del Mar** ctra Cádiz-
Málaga Km197 ☎831275 tx77086
⇌98 **P** Lift dB ⇌4610–5300 M1400
🏊 Pool sea

★ ★ ★**Fuerté** Castillo de San Luis
☎771500 tx77523
⇌146 Lift 𝄢 dB ⇌6000–7000 M1400
t5% 🏊 Pool sea

MATARÓ
Barcelona (☎93)

★ ★ ★**Castell de Mata** (N11) ☎7901044
⇌52 **P** Lift 𝄢 dB ⇌3650–4250
M1100 🏊 Pool Beach sea mountains

MAZAGÓN
Huelva (☎955)

★ ★ ★**Parador Nacional Cristóbal
Colón** ☎376000
⇌20 A10rm dB ⇌5200–6700 M1300
Pool sea

MEDINACELI
Soria (☎975)

★ ★**Duque de Medinaceli** rte N11
☎32611
rm12 ⇌2 🏠3 🅿️ **P** dB1120–1485
dB ⇌ 🏠1466–1863 Pool mountains

🕭**Vicente Martinex Medina** ctra Madrid-
Zaragoza Km150 ☎326029 **P** All makes

MENORCA See **BALEARES (ISLAS DE)**

MÉRIDA
Badajoz (☎924)

★ ★ ★**Emperatriz** pl España 19
☎302640

⇌41 𝄢 sB ⇌1750–1950
dB ⇌3300–3650 M975

★ ★ ★**Parador Nacional 'Via de la Plata'**
pl de Queipo de Llano 3 ☎301540
⇌50 🅿️ **P** dB ⇌6200 M1300

★ ★**Texas** ctra Madrid Km341 ☎302940
⇌44 **P** Lift 𝄢 dB ⇌3100–3200

MIERES
Asturias

🕭**Tunon** Poligno Industrial ☎463323
Peu Tal

MIJAS
Málaga (☎952)

★ ★ ★**Mijas** Tamisa ☎485800 tx77393
⇌10 **P** 𝄢 dB ⇌7535–8220 M1925
🏊 Pool mountains

MOJÁCAR
Almeria (☎951)

★ ★ ★**Moresco** ☎478025
Apr–Oct
⇌147 **P** Lift 𝄢 sB ⇌2720–3245
dB ⇌4165–4815 M1400 Pool sea
mountains

★ ★ ★**Parador Nacional Reyes
Catolicos** ☎478250
⇌98 **P** 𝄢 dB ⇌5200–6700 M1300
Pool sea

MOLAR (EL)
Madrid (☎91)

🕭**M Sato** ctra de Francia Km42
☎8410081 **P** Ren

MONTILLA DEL PALANCAR
Cuenca (☎966)

★ ★ ★**Sol** ctra Madrid-Valencia 11
☎331025
rm37 ⇌20 🏠17 🅿️ **P** 𝄢 dB ⇌2500
M900 mountains

MONT-TIBADABO See **BARCELONA**

MOTRIL
Granada (☎958)

🕭**Litoral** ctra de Almeria Km1.4
☎601950 BL (Landrover) Peu Tal

MURCIA
Murcia (☎968)

★ ★ ★**7 Coronas Meliá** Ronda de Garay
3 ☎217771
⇌121 **P** Lift 𝄢 sB ⇌3840 dB ⇌6280
M1650

🕭**T Gullen** ctra de Alicante 119
☎241212 **P** Peu

NAVALMORAL DE LA MATA
Cáceres (☎927)

HOTEL DON CARLOS ★ ★ ★ ★ ★ Set within 6.5 ha of private subtropical garden, reaching the sea, provides
an atmosphere of tranquility and leisure whilst offering exceptional facilities. HOTEL DON CARLOS, recently fully modernized,
has 231 rooms, equipped with all the 5-star hotel luxuries — 2 top class restaurants, a beach restaurant and a choice of bars provide
exciting evening entertainment — Recreational facilities available include golf, miniture golf and driving range on our premises,
horse-back riding, 2 swimming-pools (heated in winter), 11 tennis courts, 4 of them floodlit. European headquarters for Womens
Tennis Association, with all the latest techniques and equipment for coaching available, windsurfing, water skiing, sauna and
gymnasium.
                                              KM 198,000, Ctra. (Road) Cádiz-Málaga, Marbella (Málaga), Costa del sol
                                                      Phone: 831140 — Telex: 77015 and 77481 — Cable: Don Carlos

★**Moya** Apartado 110 ☎530500
rm40 ⇌16 ▥5 **P** dB1380
dB ⇌ ▥1780 M600 t5% mountains
⬡**Moya** ctra Talayuela ☎551179 **P** Ren

NAVARREDONDA DE LA SIERRA See
GREDOS

NERJA
Málaga (☎952)

★ ★ ★ ★**Parador Nacional** ☎520050
⇌60 **P** Lift ♪ dB ⇌5700–6700
M1300 ▥ Pool sea

NUÉVALOS
Zaragoza (☎976)

★ ★ ★**Monasterio de Piedra** (3km S)
☎849011
⇌61 **P** ♪ sB ⇌2650 dB ⇌4100
M900 ▥ mountains

OJÉN
Málaga (☎952)

★**Refugio N de Juanar** Sierra Blanca
(10km NW) ☎881000
⇌16 **P** dB2465–2765 dB ⇌3600–4100
M1100 mountains

OLITE
Navarra (☎948)

★ ★ ★**Parador Principe de Viana**
☎740000
⇌39 **P** Lift ♪ dB ⇌4700–5200 M1300

OLOT
Girona (☎972)

⬡**Ferran** ctra de Ripolll ☎261546 All
makes

⬡**Maso** av Gerona 7 ☎262340 AR BL
Opl

ORENSE
Orense (☎988)

★ ★**Barcelona** av Pontevedra 13
☎220800
rm50 ⇌10 ▥10 Lift ♪ dB2130–2180
dB ⇌ ▥2880–3080 M800

OROPESA
Toledo (☎925)

★ ★ ★**Parador Nacional de Virrey
Toledo** pl del Palacio 1 ☎430000
⇌44 **P** Lift ♪ dB ⇌5700 M1300
mountains

OVIEDO
Asturias (☎985)

★ ★ ★ ★ ★**Reconquista** Gil de Jaz 16
☎241100 tx87328
⇌141 ⬥ **P** Lift ♪ sB ⇌5426–6400
dB ⇌7876–9100 t5%

★ ★ ★**Gruta** Alto de Buenavista
☎232450
⇌55 **P** Lift ♪ dB ⇌4900 t5%
mountains

★ ★**Principado** San Francisco 6
☎217792
rm55 ⇌48 ▥7 Lift ♪
dB ⇌ ▥4550–5050 M1350 t5%
mountains

Spain

PAGUERA See **BALEARES (ISLAS DE)**
under **MALLORCA**

PAJARES (PUERTO DE)
Asturias (☎985)

★ ★**Parador Nacional Puerto de
Pajares** ☎496023
rm29 ⇌7 ▥3 ⬥dB ⇌ ▥4100 M1000

PALAFRUGELL
Girona (☎972)

⬡**J M Suquet** Bagur 45–47
☎300248 Cit

At **CALELLA DE PALAFRUGELL** (5km SE)

★ ★ ★ ★**Alga** ☎300058
⇌54 **P** Lift sB ⇌2175–4285
dB ⇌3950–6050 ▥ Pool Beach sea

★ ★ ★**Garbi** (**DPn** in Jul & Aug)
☎300100
Apr–15 Oct
⇌36 A6rm **P** Lift ♪ sB ⇌1800–2500
dB ⇌2900–4400 Pool sea

★ ★**Mediterráneo** Playa Baños
☎300150
20 May–Sep
rm38 ⇌20 ▥18 **P** ♪
dB ⇌ ▥2750–3850 M850 ▥ Beach
sea

At **LLAFRANCH** (6km E)

★ ★ ★**Paraiso** ☎300450
18 May–17 Sep
⇌55 **P** Lift ♪ dB ⇌4200–4800
M1000 ▥ Pool mountains

★ ★ ★**Terramar** ps de Cypsele 1
☎300200
May–Sep
rm56 ⇌53 ▥3 ⬥ **P** Lift ♪
dB ⇌ ▥4750–5350 M1500 sea

★ ★**Lindranch** ps Cypsele 16 ☎300208
rm28 ⇌24 **P** ♪ dB ⇌2640–3890
M880 sea

★**Levante** San Francisco de Blanes
☎300366
24 Feb–15 Jan
rm20 ⇌10 ▥10 dB ⇌ ▥3735–4920
M900 sea

At **TAMARIU** (4km SE)

★ ★ ★**Hostalillo** Bellavista 22 ☎300158
9 Jun–20 Sep
⇌70 ⬥Lift ♪ dB ⇌4600–6300 M950
t5% sea

★ ★ ★**Tamariu** ps del Mar 3 ☎300108
15 May–Sep
rm83 ⇌52 ▥2 A29rm ⬥ ♪
dB ⇌ ▥2500–2800 M950 sea

PALAMÓS
Girona (☎972)

★ ★ ★**Trias** (**DPn** in season) ps del Mar
☎314100

14 Apr–17 Oct
rm80 ⇌70 ▥10 ⬥ **P** Lift ♪
sB ⇌ ▥2350–2700 dB4700–5400
dB ⇌ ▥5300–5800 M1600–1700 Pool
sea

★ ★**Marina** av 11 de Septembre 48
☎314250
rm62 ⇌34 ▥28 ⬥ **P** Lift ♪
dB ⇌ ▥2730–3050 M725

★ ★**San Juan** (**DPn** in season) av de la
Victoria ☎314208
Apr–Sep
rm31 ⇌19 ▥12 ♪
dB ⇌ ▥2480–2680 M780 Pool sea

⬡**Central** ctra a San Feliú 6
☎314466 Aud VW

At **SAN ANTONIO DE CALONGE** (2.5km S)

★ ★ ★**Lys** ctra de San Feliú ☎314150
Jun–Sep
⇌70 ⬥ **P** Lift ♪ dB ⇌2015 M885
Beach sea

★ ★ ★**Rosa dels Vents** ps del Mar
☎314216
15 Apr–Sep
⇌70 ⬥ **P** Lift ♪ dB ⇌6000 M850
▥ Beach sea

★ ★ ★**Rosamar** ps del Mar 33 ☎314165
15 Apr–15 Oct
⇌62 **P** Lift ♪ dB ⇌2600–4900 M750
sea

PALENCIA
Palencia (☎988)

★ ★ ★**Rey Sancho de Castilla** av Ponce
de Leon ☎725300
⇌100 ⬥ **P** Lift ♪ sB ⇌2025–2525
dB ⇌3850–4350 t5% ▥ Pool

PALMA DE MALLORCA See **BALEARES
(ISLAS DE)** under **MALLORCA**

PAMPLONA
Navarra (☎948)

★ ★ ★ ★**Tres Reyes** Jardines de la
Taconera ☎226600 tx37720
⇌180 ⬥ **P** Lift ♪ dB ⇌5600–9600
dB ⇌6200–8200 t% Pool mountains

★ ★**Yoldi** av San Ignacio 11 ☎224800
⇌50 ⬥ **P** Lift dB ⇌3370–6405 M975

★**Hostal Valerio** av de Zaragoza 5
(n.rest) ☎245466
rm16 ⇌1 Lift dB2000–2850
dB ⇌2650–3350

PANCORBO
Burgos (☎947)

★ ★ ★**El Molino** ctra G-Madrid-Irún
Km306 ☎354050
⇌48 **P** ♪ sB ⇌1450–1850
dB ⇌2400–3000 M850 ▥ Pool
mountains

PEÑISCOLA
Castellón (☎964)

★ ★ ★**Hosteria del Mar** ctra de Benicarló
Km6 ☎480600 tx65750
⇌85 **P** Lift ♪ dB ⇌4270–6070
M1175 ▥ Beach sea

PINEDA DE MAR
Barcelona(☎93)

★ ★ **Mont Palau** c Mayor 21 ☎7623387

Mar–Nov
rm109 ⇋90 ▥10 A17rm **P** Lift *♪*
sB ⇋ ▥1075–2200 dB ⇋ ▥1750–2200
M450–550 sea

★ ★ **Sorrabona** (n.rest) ps Maritimo 10
☎7623250

15 May–Sep
rm103 ⇋55 ▥40 **P** Lift *♪*
dB1300–2750 dB ⇋ ▥1700–3150
M500 Pool sea

PLASENCIA
Cáceres(☎927)

★ ★ ★ **Alfonso VIII** c Alfonso VIII 32
☎410250 tx28290

⇋56 ▥ Lift *♪* sB ⇋2425–2650
dB ⇋4100–4450 M1150 t4% mountains

PLATJA D'ARO (LA)
Girona(☎972)

★ ★ ★ **Cliper** ☎81700

15 May–Sep
rm40 ⇋30 ▥10 *♪* sB ⇋ ▥800–950
dB ⇋ ▥1600–1900 M575–625 sea

★ ★ ★ **Miramar** Verge del Carme N12
☎817150

15 May–Sep
⇋45 ▥ **P** Lift *♪* dB ⇋2400–3400
Beach sea

★ ★ ★ **Rosamar** pl Mayor ☎817304

15 May–15 Oct
⇋65 ▥ **P** Lift *♪* dB ⇋3500 M700
sea mountains

★ ★ ★ **Xaloc** Playa de Rovira ☎817300

May–Sep
⇋45 **P** Lift ▥ **Pn** 1900–2800

★ ★ **Els Pins** ☎817219

Apr–Oct
⇋60 ▥ Lift *♪* dB ⇋2510–4660 M625

★ ★ **Residencia Japet** ctra de Palamós
18–20 ☎817366

4 Dec–14 Oct
rm48 ⇋26 ▥22 **P** *♪*
dB ⇋ ▥1800–3400 M900

PLAYA DE GANDÍA See **GANDÍA**

PLAYA DE PALMA (CA'N PASTILLA) See
BALEARES (ISLAS DE) under **PALMA DE
MALLORCA, MALLORCA**

PLAYA DE PALMA NOVA See **BALEARES
(ISLAS DE)** under **PALMA DE
MALLORCA, MALLORCA**

POLLENSA See **BALEARES (ISLAS DE)**
under **MALLORCA**

Spain

PONFERRADA
Léon(☎987)

★ ★ **Madrid** J-Antonio 50 ☎411550

rm54 ⇋42 ▥12 ▥ **P** Lift *♪*
sB ⇋ ▥1675–1925 dB ⇋ ▥2850–3150
Mfr750 t4%

PONTEVEDRA
Pontevedra(☎986)

★ ★ **Parador Nacional Casa del Barón**
Maceda 21 ☎855800

⇋47 **P** Lift *♪* dB ⇋4700–6200 M1300

PORTBOU
Girona(☎972)

★ **Costa Brava** Rambla Cataluña 26
☎390003

Jun–Sep
rm34 **P** sB1050–1180 dB1850–2080
M700–820

PREMIÀ DE MAR
Barcelona(☎93)

★ ★ **Premiá** c San Miguel 46 ☎7510336

⇋22 *♪* dB ⇋1500 M500 mountains

PUEBLA DE SANABRIA
Zamora(☎988)

☆ ☆ **Parador Nacional de Puebla de
Sanabria** ☎620001

rm24 ⇋18 ▥ dB ⇋4700–5200 M1300

PUERTO DE LLANÇA See **LLANÇA**

PUERTO DE POLLENSA See **BALEARES
(ISLAS DE)** under **POLLENSA,
MALLORCA**

PUERTO DE SANTA MARIA (EL)
Cádiz(☎956)

☆ ☆ ☆ ☆ **Meliá el Caballo Blanco** Playa
de Valdelagrana (2.5km S on ctra de
Cádiz) ☎863745 tx76070

⇋94 **P** *♪* sB ⇋4010–6400
dB ⇋5320–8300 M1400–1500 Pool Ω

★ ★ ★ **Fuentebravia** ctra de Rota
☎851717

Apr–Sep
⇋ ▥90 **P** Lift *♪* dB ⇋ ▥5260–5960
M1495 t5% Pool Beach sea

PUERTO LUMBRERAS
Murca(☎968)

☆ ☆ **Parador Nacional de Puerto
Lumbreras** ☎402025

PUERTOMARIN
Lugo(☎982)

★ ★ ★ **Parador Nacional de
Puertomarin** ☎545025

⇋10 **P** *♪* dB ⇋4200–4700 M1300
mountains lake

PUIGCERDÁ
Girona(☎972)

★ ★ **María Victoria** Florenza 9. ☎880300

rm50 ⇋29 ▥21 *♪* **P** Lift *♪*
dB ⇋ ▥3300 M1100 mountains

★ ★ **Martinez** ctra de Llivia (n.rest)
☎880250

⇋14 **P** *♪* sB ⇋1675 dB ⇋2350
M800 Pool mountains

PUZOL
Valencia(☎96)

★ ★ ★ ★ **Monte Picayo** Paraje
Denominado Monte Picayo (Autoroute 7,
Exit 6) ☎1420100 tx62087

⇋82 **P** Lift *♪* dB ⇋10150 M2300 ⅙
Pool Ω sea mountains

REINOSA
Cantabria(☎942)

★ ★ **Vejo** av Cantabria 15 ☎751510

⇋71 **P** Lift *♪* dB ⇋3670–4320
M1120 mountains

★ ★ **Fontibre-Iberia** Nestares ☎750450

⇋ ▥51 ▥ **P** Lift *♪*
dB ⇋ ▥2370–3470 mountains

⬥Ω**Hermanos Hidalgo** Pozo Pozmeo,
Requejo ☎751883 **P** All makes

REUS
Tarragona(☎977)

★ ★ **Gaudi** Arrabal Robuster 49 (n.rest)
☎305545

⇋73 ▥ **P** Lift *♪* sB ⇋1755
dB ⇋2870

⬥Ω**Petrubial** c Rosé 25 ☎3044605 All
makes

RIBADEO
Lugo(☎982)

★ ★ **Eo** av de Asturias 5 (n.rest) ☎110750

Apr–Sep
rm24 ⇋23 ▥1 **P** *♪*
dB ⇋ ▥2900–3400 Pool sea

☆ ☆ **Parador Nacional** ☎110825

⇋47 ▥ **P** Lift *♪* dB ⇋4700–5700
M1300 sea

RIBADESELLA
Asturias(☎985)

★★★**Gran del Sella** la Playa ☎860150
Apr–Sep
↩74 **P** Lift ♪ dB ↩5160–6500
M1500 t5% ✱ Pool sea mountains

RIBES DE FRESER
Girona(☎972)

★★**Montagut** (3km S on N152) Aguas de
Ribas ☎727021
Jul–15 Sep
rm100 ↩33 🍴19 🚗 **P** ✱ Pool
mountains

★★**Prats** San Quintin 20 ☎727001
↩25 **P** dB1300–1700 dB ↩1900–2300
M850 mountains

RIUDELLOTS DE LA SELVA
Girona(☎72)

☆☆☆**Novotel Gerona** Autopista
A17–Salida 8 ☎477100 tx57238
↩82 **P** ♪ sB ↩4350–5700
dB ↩5700–7100 t4% Pool

RONDA
Málaga(☎952)

★★★**Reina Victoria** c Jerez 39
☎871240
rm89 ↩78 🍴11 **P** Lift ♪
dB ↩ 🍴5450–6000 M1500 Pool
mountains

ROSES
Girona(☎972)

★★★**Almadraba Park** Playa de
Almadraba ☎256550 tx57032
29 Apr–15 Oct
↩66 🚗 **P** Lift ♪ dB ↩4340–5440
M1600 ♉ Pool sea

★★★**Coral Playa** ctra Playa ☎256250
tx57191
Apr–Oct
rm133 ↩121 🍴12 **P** Lift ♪
dB ↩ 🍴3000–4400 M775

★★★**Vistabella** Playa de Cañyellos
Petites ☎256200
15 Dec–15 Oct
↩43 🚗 **P** ♪ sB ↩2340–3140
dB ↩3985–5270 Mfr1680 ✱ Pool
Beach sea

★★**Terraza** Playa ☎256154
Mar–Nov
rm110 ↩103 🍴7 🚗 **P** Lift ♪
dB ↩ 🍴5400–6900 ✱ Pool sea

SABIÑANIGO
Huesca(☎974)

★★**Pardina** ☎480975
↩64 **P** Lift ♪ dB ↩3400–3600 M850
Pool mountains

Spain

✤♦**Arranz** Zaragoza 5 ☎480083 BL (&
Landrover) Frd

S'AGARÓ
Girona(☎972)

★★★★★**Gavina** ☎321100 tx57132
Apr–Oct
rm74 ↩72 🍴2 **P** Lift ♪
sB ↩ 🍴7550–13550
dB ↩ 🍴9700–16700 M2950 t4% ♉
Pool 🐟 sea

★★★**Caleta Park** (**DPn** Jul & Aug) Platja
de Sant Pol ☎320012 tx57366
14 Apr–25 Oct
rm105 ↩95 🍴10 🚗 **P** Lift ♪ sea

SALAMANCA
Salamanca(☎923)

★★★**Monterrey** Azafranal 21
☎214400 tx26809
rm89 ↩66 🍴23 Lift ♪
dB ↩ 🍴4700–5700 t5%

★★★**Parador Nacional** ☎228700
↩108 🚗 **P** Lift ♪ sB ↩3950–4850
dB ↩5700–6700 M1300 t5% Pool

✤♦**Vicente Sanchez Marcos** av de las
Comuneros 30 ☎222450 Cit Peu

At **SANTA MARTA DE TORMES** (4km E)

★★★**Jardin Regio** ☎200250 tx22895
↩118 🚗 **P** Lift ♪ sB ↩2475–2875
dB ↩3950–4850 M1200 Pool

SALER (EL) See **VALENCIA**

SALOBREÑA
Granada(☎958)

★**Salambina** (1km W) ☎610037
↩14 **P** ♪ dB ↩1920–2220 M800
t5% sea

SALOU
Tarragona(☎977)

★★★**Calaviña** (**DPn**) ctra
Tarragona–Salou Km10 ☎380848
tx56501
15 May–15 Oct
rm70 ↩60 🍴10 **P** Lift ♪
dB ↩ 🍴1440–3840 M650 Pool sea

★★★**Picnic** ctra Salou-Reus Km1
☎380158
↩45 **P** ♪ dB ↩2700–3300 M800
Pool sea

★★★**Salou Park** Burselas 35, Cala
Capellens ☎380208
↩102 **P** Lift ♪ dB ↩2900–7500
M1000

★★**Planas** pl Bonet 2 ☎380108
Apr–Oct
↩100 Lift ♪ dB ↩2700–3250 M850
sea

✤♦**Internaciónal** c P-Martel ☎380614 **P**

SAN ANTONIO See **BALEARES (ISLAS
DE)** under **IBIZA**

SAN ANTONIO DE CALONGE See
PALAMÓS

SAN LORENZO DE EL ESCORIAL
Madrid(☎91)

★★★★**Victoria Palace** J-de-Toledo 4
☎8901511
rm90 ↩83 🍴8 **P** Lift ♪
sB ↩ 🍴2690–4570 dB ↩ 🍴4060–5930
M1550 Pool mountains

SAN PEDRO DE ALCÁNTARA
Málaga(☎952)

★★★★**Golf Guadalmina** ☎811744
tx77058
↩75 **P** ♪ ✱ Pool Beach 🐟 ♉ sea

SAN SEBASTIÁN (DONOSTIA)
Guipúzcoa (☎943)

★★★**Costa Vasca** av Pio Baroja 9
☎211011 tx36551
↩203 🚗 **P** Lift ♪ dB ↩7600 t5%
✱ Pool mountains

★★★**Gudamendi** (4km W) ☎214111
↩24 **P** Lift ♪ dB ↩3100–4200 M900
sea mountains

★★★**Monte Igueldo** ☎210211
↩121 🚗 **P** Lift ♪ sB ↩3485–3885
dB ↩6570–7270 t5% ✱ Pool sea

✤♦**Gruas España** av Isabel II 15
☎458352 **P**

✤♦**Ingels** av A-Elosegui 78 ☎396516 Opl

SANTA CHRISTINA D'ARO
Girona (☎972)

★★★**Costa Brava Golf** ☎837052
tx57252
Apr–Sep
↩92 **P** Lift ♪ dB ↩4250–7750
M1100 t5% ✱ Pool 🐟 mountains
lake

SANTA CRUZ DE MUDELA
Ciudad Real

✤♦**Izquierdo** ctra Madrid-Cádiz Km217
☎342022 **P** Cit

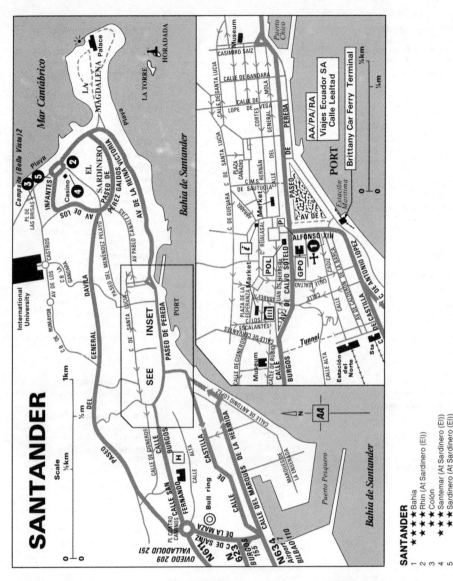

SANTANDER

1	★ ★ ★ ★ ★ Bahia
2	★ ★ ★ ★ Rhin (At Sardinero (El))
3	★ ★ ★ ★ Colón
4	★ ★ ★ Santemar (At Sardinero (El))
5	★ ★ Sardinero (At Sardinero (El))

SANTA MARIA DE HUERTA
Soria (☎975)

★ ★ ★ **Parador Nacional de Santa Maria de Huerta** ☎327011

15 Jun–Feb
⇆40 🏠 ♪ dB ⇆4700 M1300
mountains

SANTA MARTA DE TORMES See **SALAMANCA**

SANTANDER
Cantabria (☎942)
See plan

★ ★ ★ ★ **Bahia** av de Alfonso XIII 6
☎221700 tx35859 Plan **1**
rm181 ⇆162 🏠19 Lift ♪
dB ⇆ 🏠4800–6450 sea mountains

★ ★ **Colón** pl de las Brisas 1 (n,rest)
☎(943)272300 Plan **3**

Jul–15 Sep
rm43 ⇆6 ♪ sB1020 dB1800
dB ⇆2500 t4% sea

🛇🅾**Sancho Motor** c Castilla 62 ☎370017
Frd

🛇🅾**J Vidal de la Pena** ps de Pereda 5, ctra
Parayas ☎336200 Ren

At **SARDINERO (EL)** (3.5km NE)

★ ★ ★ **Rhin** Reina Victoria 153 ☎274300
Plan **2**
⇆95 🏠 P Lift ♪ dB ⇆3200–4250

★ ★ ★ **Santemar** Joaquin Costa 28
☎272900 tx35963 Plan **4**
⇆350 🏠 P Lift sB ⇆3130–4580
dB ⇆4610–6760 t% 🍽 sea

★ ★ **Sardinero** pl Italia 1 ☎271100
Plan **5**
⇆112 Lift ♪ sB ⇆2100–2800
dB ⇆3100–4250 t4% sea

340

Spain

SANT FELIÚ DE GUIXOLS
Girona (☎972)

★ ★ ★ ★**Muriá Park** ps Dels Guixols
21–23 (n.rest Nov–Mar) ☎320450
tx57364
rm86 ᗡ75 ₥11 Lift ♪
dB ᗡ ₥3970–4540 M1105 Pool sea

★ ★ ★**Montecarlo** Montaña de San Elmo
☎320000
Jun–Sep
ᗡ61 **P** Lift ♪ dB ᗡ2574–3294 M875
sea

★ ★ ★**Montjoi** San Elmo ☎320300
May–Sep
ᗡ64 **P** Lift ♪ dB ᗡ2400–4000
M1000 Pool sea

★ ★ ★**Rex** Rambla Portalet 18 (n.rest)
☎320312
Jun–15 Sep
rm25 ᗡ23 ₥2 Lift ♪
dB ᗡ ₥2280–2580

★ ★**Noles** Rambla J-Antonio 10
☎320400
May–Sep
ᗡ45 A10rm Lift ♪ sB ᗡ1600–1700
dB ᗡ2600–2700 M800 ⌀ sea

★ ★**Turist** San Ramón 39 ☎320841
May–Oct
rm20 ᗡ8 🏠 ♪ dB1950–2350
dB ᗡ2350–2850 M800 sea mountains

⌀**Metropol Comercial** ctra Gerona 7
☎320982 Ren

SANTIAGO DE COMPOSTELA
La Coruña (☎981)

★ ★ ★ ★**Los Reyes Catolicos** pl de
España 1 ☎582300 tx86004
rm157 ᗡ105 ₥52 🏠 **P** Lift ♪
dB ᗡ9900–11300 M2000 t5%

★ ★ ★**Peregrino** av R-de-Castro
☎591850 tx82352
ᗡ ₥150 **P** Lift ♪ sB ᗡ ₥2400–2900
dB ᗡ ₥4100–5100 M1250 t% Pool

SANTILLANA DEL MAR *Cantabria* (☎942)

★ ★ ★**Parador de Gil Blas** ☎818000
rm45 ᗡ24 A21rm 🏠 **P** ♪
dB ᗡ4700–6200 M1300

★ ★**Altamira** Cantón 1 ☎818025
rm28 ᗡ17 ₥11 **P** 🏠
dB ᗡ ₥2900–3500 M700

SANT POL DE MAR *Barcelona* (☎93)

★ ★ ★**Gran Sol** ctra de Francia Km670
☎7600051
ᗡ41 **P** Lift ♪ dB ᗡ2950–4150
M1050 ⌀ Pool sea

SANTO DOMINGO DE LA CALZADA
Rioja (☎941)

★ ★**Parador Nacional** ☎340300
ᗡ20 **P** ♪ dB ᗡ4700–5200 M1300

SAN VICENTE LA BARQUERA
Cantabria (☎942)
★ ★**Miramar** La Barquera (1km N)
☎710075
Mar–15 Dec

---

rm30 ᗡ17 A15rm **P** ♪
dB ᗡ2900–3300 M875 sea mountains

SARDINERO (EL) See **SANTANDER**

SEGOVIA
Segovia (☎911)

★ ★ ★**Linajes** Dr-Velasco 9 (n.rest)
☎431712
ᗡ55 🏠 **P** Lift ♪ sB ᗡ2530–2935
dB ᗡ4315–5010 t5% mountains

★ ★ ★**Parador Nacional de Segovia**
☎430462
ᗡ80 🏠 **P** Lift ♪ dB ᗡ5700 M1300
Pool

★ ★ ★**Puerta de Segovia** ctra de Soria
(N110) ☎437161
ᗡ100 **P** Lift ♪ sB ᗡ2275–2530
dB ᗡ3510–3910 Mfr1050 t4% ⌀ Pool
mountains

★ ★ ★**R Las Sirenas** J-Bravo 30 (n.rest)
☎411897
rm39 ᗡ35 ₥4 **P** Lift ♪
dB ᗡ ₥2500–3000 mountains

SEU D'URGELL (LA)
Lleida (☎973)

★ ★**Parador Nacional** Santo Domingo
☎352000
ᗡ86 🏠 **P** Lift ♪ sB ᗡ3550–4350
dB ᗡ4700–5700 M1300 t% Pool
mountains

★**Avenida** av Gl-Franco 18 ☎350104
rm40 ᗡ8 ₥30 **P** Lift ♪
dB 1604–1716 dB ᗡ ₥2101–2321
M740 mountains

⌀**Carillo** av Guillermo Graeli 9
☎350570 BL (Landrover & Rangerover)
At **CASTELLICIUTAT** (1km SE)
☆ ☆ ☆**Castell** ctra C1313 ☎350704
ᗡ40 **P** ♪ dB ᗡ4300–4500 M alc
Pool mountains

SEVILLA (SEVILLE)
Sevilla (☎954)

★ ★ ★ ★ ★**Alfonso XIII** San Fernando 2
☎222850 tx72725
ᗡ148 **P** Lift ♪ sB ᗡ7450–8250
dB ᗡ10200–11550 M2000 t4% Pool

★ ★ ★ ★**Colón** J-Canalejas 1 ☎222900
tx72726
rm268 Lift ♪ dB ᗡ6100–10000
M1450 t5%

★ ★ ★ ★**Inglaterra** pl Nueva 7
☎224970 tx72244
ᗡ120 🏠 Lift ♪ dB ᗡ6600–9600
M1400 t5%

★ ★ ★**Fleming** Sierra Nevada 3
☎416661 tx72417
ᗡ90 🏠 **P** Lift ♪ dB ᗡ4000–5400
M1200 t5%

★ ★ ★**Porta Coeli** av E-Dato 49–51
☎251800 tx72913
ᗡ246 **P** Lift ♪ sB ᗡ4700–6900
dB ᗡ6100–8850 St5%

★ ★**Doña Maria** Don Remondo 19
(n.rest) ☎224990
ᗡ61 Lift ♪ dB ᗡ6100–7200 t5%
Pool

SIERRA NEVADA See **GRANADA**

SIGÜENZA *Guadalajara* (☎911)

★ ★ ★**Parador Nacional Castillo de
Sigüenza** ☎390100
ᗡ77 Lift dB ᗡ5700 M1300

SITGES
Barcelona (☎93)

★ ★ ★ ★**Calipolis** ps Marítimo
☎8941500 tx53067
Jan–Oct
rm175 ᗡ160 ₥15 **P** Lift ♪
sB ᗡ3745–4615 dB ᗡ ₥5990–7400
sea

See page 342 for advertisement

★ ★ ★ ★**Terramar** ps Calvo Sotelo
☎8940050 tx53186
May–Oct
ᗡ209 **P** Lift ♪ dB ᗡ5100–6950 t5%
⌀ Pool Beach 🛇 sea mountains

★ ★ ★**Antemare** av Nuestra Señora de
Montserrat ☎8940600 tx57599
28 Mar–Oct
ᗡ ₥110 A38rm 🏠 **P** Lift ♪
dB ᗡ ₥5000–6600 M1400 Pool Beach
sea

★ ★ ★**Platjador** ps Ribera 35
☎8940312 tx57599
May–Oct
ᗡ44 Lift ♪ dB ᗡ2210–3445 M750
sea

★ ★**Arcadia** c Socias 22–24 (n.rest)
☎8940900 tx52962
7 Apr–Oct
ᗡ38 🏠 **P** Lift ♪ dB ᗡ3200–5000
Pool Beach sea

★ ★**Luna Playa** Puerto Alegre 51
☎9040430
ᗡ12 **P** Lift ♪ dB ᗡ3508 sea

★ ★**Sitges Residencia** San Gaudencio 5
(n.rest) ☎8940072 tx52962
Jun–Sep
rm52 ᗡ11 ₥17 Lift ♪ dB1900–2280
dB ᗡ2480–2910

★**Romantic** San Isidro 23 ☎8940643
tx52962
Apr–Oct
rm55 ᗡ3 ₥50 ♪ dB3180–3430
dB ᗡ ₥3580–3780 M750

SON SERVERA See **BALEARES (ISLAS
DE)** under **MALLORCA**

SORIA
Soria (☎975)

★ ★**Caballero** E-Saavedra 4
☎220100
ᗡ84 Lift ♪ dB ᗡ2600–3300

★ ★ ★Mesón Leonor ps del Mirón
☎220250

⇋32 🏛 **P** 𝄐 dB ⇋2925–3200 M865
mountains

★ ★Les Heras pl Ramóny Cajal 5
☎213346

rm24 ⇋8 🍴9 **P** 𝄐 dB1700–2650
dB ⇋ 🍴2200–3150 M625

★ ★Parador Nacional Antonio Machado
Parque del Castillo ☎213445

⇋14 sB ⇋3750 dB ⇋5200 M1300

SOS DEL REY CATÓLICO
Zaragoza (☎948)

**★ ★ ★Parador Nacional Fernando de
Aragón** ☎888011

⇋66 🏛 **P** Lift 𝄐 sB ⇋3550–4350
dB ⇋4700–6200 M1300 t5% mountains

SUANCES-PLAYA
Cantabria (☎942)

★Lumar ctra de Tagle ☎810214
Jun–15 Sep
rm29 ⇋23 🍴4 **P** dB1500–1800
dB ⇋ 🍴3000–3300 M720 sea
mountains

TALAVERA DE LA REINA
Toledo (☎925)

★ ★Auto-Estacion av Toledo 1
☎800300

rm40 ⇋31 🍴9 🏛 𝄐
dB ⇋ 🍴2070–2320 M575 mountains

TAMARIU See **PALAFRUGELL**

TARIFA
Cádiz (☎956)

★ ★ ★Mesón de Sancho ctra Cádiz-
Málaga ☎684900

⇋45 **P** 𝄐 dB ⇋2980–3430 M975
t5% ⚊ Pool mountains

☆ ☆**Balcón de España** ctra Cádiz
☎684326
Apr–25 Oct
⇋38 **P** 𝄐 dB ⇋4060–4660 M1400
⚊ Pool ∩ mountains

★ ★Dos Mares ctra Cádiz-Málaga Km78
☎684035
Apr–Nov

Spain

⇋17 **P** 𝄐 dB ⇋4000–4500 M1150
⚊ Pool Beach ∩ sea

TARRAGONA
Tarragona (☎977)

★ ★ ★ ★Imperial Tarraco Rambla de
San Carlos ☎233040 tx56441

⇋170 🏛 **P** Lift 𝄐 sB ⇋4300
dB ⇋5600 ⚊ Pool sea

★ ★ ★Astari via Augusta 95 ☎236911
May–15 Oct
rm83 ⇋59 🍴24 🏛 **P** Lift 𝄐
sB ⇋ 🍴2790–3490 M800 Pool sea

★ ★ ★Lauria Lauria 4 ☎236712
rm72 ⇋62 🍴10 **P** Lift 𝄐
dB ⇋ 🍴3400–3900 Pool sea

★ ★Nuria via Augusta 217 ☎235011
Apr–Sep
⇋ 🍴61 🏛 **P** Lift 𝄐
dB ⇋ 🍴2270–2670 M750 sea

⛽**Minicar Pons** c Gasometro 40–42
☎216169 Maz

⛽**Tarrauto** ctra de Valencia Km246.8
☎540870 Peu Tal

TERUEL
Teruel (☎974)

⛽**J Z Coll** ctra Sagunto-Burgos Km 123
☎601061 Frd

TOJA (ISLA DE LA)
Pontevedra (☎986)

★ ★ ★ ★ ★Gran ☎730025 tx88042
⇋201 🏛 **P** Lift sB ⇋9500–10700
dB ⇋12100–13300 M2250 St% ⚊
Pool Beach 𝛿 sea

TOLEDO
Toledo (☎925)

★ ★ ★Parador Conde de Orgaz
☎221850 tx47998

⇋57 **P** Lift 𝄐 dB ⇋6700 M1300

★ ★Maravilla Barrio Rey 5–7 ☎223300

⇋18 Lift 𝄐 dB ⇋3450 M900

TORDESILLAS
Valladolid (☎983)

★ ★ ★Montico ctra N122 Km145
☎770651 tx26575

⇋34 🏛 **P** 𝄐 dB ⇋3650–4250
M1050 ⚊ Pool

★ ★ ★Parador Nacional de Tordesillas
ctra N620 Km153 ☎770051 tx26215

rm73 ⇋65 🍴8 🏛 **P** Lift 𝄐
dB ⇋ 🍴5200–5700 M1300 Pool

TORREMOLINOS
Málaga (☎952)

★ ★ ★ ★Meliá Torremolinos av de C-
Alessandri 109 ☎380500 tx77060
Apr–Oct
⇋284 **P** Lift 𝄐 sB ⇋4845–5885
dB ⇋6340–7710 M1770 ⚊ Pool

★ ★ ★ ★Parador Nacional del Golf
☎381255
⇋40 **P** 𝄐 sB ⇋3950–5150
dB ⇋5200–6700 M1300 t5% ⚊ Pool
Beach 𝛿 sea

★ ★ ★Pez Espada via Imperial
☎380300 tx77655
Apr–Oct
⇋149 **P** Lift 𝄐 dB ⇋7000–9000
M1700 t5% ⚊ Pool Beach sea

★ ★ ★Isabel ps Marítimo 97, Playa del
Lido (n.rest) ☎381744
Apr–Oct
⇋40 **P** Lift 𝄐 dB ⇋3140–3390 t5%
Pool Beach sea

★ ★Meliá Costa del Sol ps Marítimo,
Playa de Bajondilla ☎386677 tx77326
⇋540 **P** Lift 𝄐 sB ⇋3150–3900
dB ⇋4850–6350 M1350 Pool sea

★ ★Nidos c Los Nidos ☎384633
tx77151
Jun–Sep
⇋70 **P** 𝄐 sB ⇋2550 dB ⇋4000
M950 ⚊ Pool

★ ★Tropicana Trópico 6 ☎386600
tx77107

⇋86 Lift 𝄐 dB ⇋4425–5575 M1325
Pool Beach sea

⛽**Salamanca** av C-Alessandri 27
☎381151 BL RR

TORREVIEJA
Alicante (☎965)

★ ★ **Berlin** Torre del Moro ☎711537
⇌30 🏛 **P** Lift ☽ dB ⇌3580–4330
M1140 Pool sea

TORTOSA
Tarragona (☎977)

★ ★ ★ **Parador Nacional Castillo de la
Zuda** Castillo de la Zuda ☎444450
⇌82 **P** Lift ☽ dB ⇌5200–5700
M1300 Pool mountains

TOSSA DE MAR
Girona (☎972)

★ ★ ★ ★ **Gran Reymar** Playa de Mar
Menuda ☎340312
May–15 Oct
⇌131 **P** Lift ☽ dB ⇌4750–6150
M1500 t5% ⤶ Pool Beach sea

★ ★ ★ **Ancora** av de la Palma 25
☎340299
Jun–Sep
rm60 ⇌30 🛏30 🏛 **P** ☽
dB ⇌ 🛏3900–4500

★ ★ ★ **Florida** av de la Palma 21
☎340308
May–Oct
⇌47 **P** Lift ☽ dB ⇌2600–3900
M1100 ⤶

★ ★ ★ **Mar Menuda** Playa de Mar
Menuda ☎341000
14 Apr–Sep
⇌40 🏛 **P** Lift ☽ dB ⇌4780–5005
M1350 ⤶ Pool ∩ sea mountains

★ ★ **Corsico** ps del Mar (n. rest)☎340174
Apr–Sep
rm28 ⇌19 🛏9 Lift ☽
dB⇌3260–3650

🕭**Nautica** ctra San Feliá ☎341021 Aud
VW

TUDELA
Navarra (☎948)

★ ★ **Morase** ps de Invierno 2 ☎812700
rm22 ⇌16 🛏6 🏛 **P** ☽
dB ⇌3230–3430 M1025

★ **Tudela** ctra de Zaragoza ☎820558
rm16 ⇌12 🛏4 **P** ☽
dB ⇌ 🛏2720–2840 M920

🕭**Auto Variante Zaragoza-Logroño** Km6
Poligno Industriel ☎820209 MB

TUY
Pontevedra (☎986)

★ ★ ★ **Parador Nacional San Telmo**
☎600309
⇌16 **P** ☽ sB ⇌3550–4350
dB ⇌4700–5700 M1300 t5% Pool

ÚBEDA
Jaén (☎953)

★ ★ ★ **Parador Nacional Condestable
Dávalos** pl Váquez de Molina 1 ☎750345
⇌25 🏛 dB ⇌4700–5200 M1300

VALDEPEÑAS
Ciudad Real (☎926)

☆ ☆ ☆ **Meliá el Hildalgo** ctra Andalucía
Km194 ☎323254
⇌ 🛏54 🏛 **P** sB ⇌ 🛏3220
dB ⇌ 🛏4250–4600 M1400 Pool

VALENCIA
Valencia (☎96)

★ ★ ★ ★ **Reina Victoria** c de las Barcas 4
☎3520487 tx64755
⇌100 **P** Lift ☽ sB ⇌4180 dB ⇌6060
M1200

★ ★ ★ ★ **Rey Don Jaima** av Baleares 2
☎3607300 tx64252
⇌314 **P** Lift ☽ dB ⇌8980–12980
M2300 t5% Pool

★ ★ ★ **Dimar** Gran vía Marques del Tuna
80 (n.rest) ☎3341807 tx62952
⇌95 **P** Lift ☽ sB ⇌5000 dB ⇌6550

★ ★ ★ **Excelsior** Barcelonina 5 (n.rest)
☎3514612
⇌65 Lift ☽ sB ⇌ 🛏2570–2840
dB ⇌fr4520

★ ★ **Bristol** Abadía de San Martín 3
(n.rest) ☎3521176
15 Jan–Nov
rm40 ⇌22 🏛18 Lift ☽ dB ⇌ 🛏3820

🕭**Auto-Montalt** c San Vicente 118
☎3703150 Frd

🕭**Basset** c San Vicente 79–81
☎3515612 Aud VW

At **SALER (EL)** (12km S)

★ ★ ★ **Parador Nacional Luis Vives**
☎3236850
⇌58 **P** Lift ☽ dB ⇌6700 M1300 ⤶
Pool Beach ♭ sea mountains lake

VALLADOLID
Valladolid (☎983)

★ ★ ★ ★ **Olid Meliá** pl San Miguel 10
☎357200 tx26312
⇌237 **P** Lift ☽ sB ⇌3480–3580
dB ⇌5965–6165 M1075

★ ★ ★ **Conde Ansurez** María de Molina 9
(n.rest) ☎351800

⇌76 Lift ☽ dB ⇌5160–5808 t5%

★ ★ ★ **Meliá Parque** Joaquin-Garaia-
Morato 17 ☎470100 tx26312
⇌306 🏛 **P** Lift sB ⇌2750 dB ⇌4910

VALLE DE PINETA See **BIELSA**

VERÍN
Orense (☎988)

★ ★ **Parador Nacional de Monterrey**
☎410075
⇌23 🏛 dB ⇌4700–5200 M1300

VIC
Barcelona (☎93)

★ ★ ★ **Parador Nacional** (15km NE)
☎8887211
⇌31 🏛 **P** Lift ☽ dB ⇌5200–5700
M1300 ⤶ Pool mountains lake

★ ★ **Colón** Rambla ps 1 ☎8860220
rm40 ⇌30 🛏4 🏛 **P** ☽ dB1650
dB ⇌ 🛏1900 M600

VIELLA
Lleida (☎973)

★ ★ ★ **Parador Nacional Valle de Ara¹n**
Estación de la Tüca ☎640100
⇌135 🏛 **P** Lift ☽ dB ⇌5200–5700
M1300

VILAFRANCA DEL PENEDÈS
Barcelona (☎93)

🕭**Romeu** av Barcelona 56 ☎8900592 **P**

VILLACARLOS See **BALEARES (ISLES
DE)** under **MAHÓN, MENORCA**

VILLACASTÍN
Segovia (☎911)

☆ ☆ ☆ **Parador Nacional** ☎107000
⇌13 **P** ☽ dB ⇌4200–4700 M1300

VILLAFRANCA DEL BIERZO
León (☎987)

☆ ☆ ☆ **Parador Nacional Villafranca del
Bierzo** ☎540175
⇌40 A12rm 🏛 dB ⇌4700–5200
M1300

VILLAJOYOSA
Alicante (☎965)

★ ★ ★ ★ **Montiboli** ctra N332, Km 108.6
☎890250 tx67712
⇌52 A14rm 🏛 **P** Lift ☽
dB ⇌8800–12000 M2300 ⤶ Pool
Beach sea

VILLALBA
Lugo (☎982)

★ ★ **Parador Nacional Condes de
Villalba** ☎510011 →

⇆6 P Lift ♪ dB ⇆6700 M1300 mountains

VILANOVA I LA GELTRÚ
Barcelona (☎93)

★**Solvi 70** ps Ribes Roges 1 ☎8933243
11 Nov–10 Oct
rm30 ⇆24 ▥6 🏛 P
dB ⇆ ▥2050–2350 M750 ◠

VIÑAROZ
Castellón (☎964)

★★**Duc de Vendôme** ctra N340 Km 144
☎450944
⇆12 🏛 P ♪ dB ⇆2410–2570 M815
sea mountains

★★**Roca** ctra Valencia-Barcelona Km
140.7 ☎450350
⇆36 🏛 P ♪ dB ⇆2130–2380 M650
🏊 sea mountains

🐾**Opel Borsa** ctra Valencia-Barcelona
Km 141 ☎452012 P Opl

VITORIA (GASTEIZ)
Alva (☎945)

★★★★**Canciller Ayala** Ramóny Cajal
6 ☎220800 tx35441
⇆ ▥185 🏛 P Lift ♪ dB ⇆ ▥6700

★★★**General Álava** av de Gasteiz 53
(n.rest) ☎222200 tx35468
⇆105 🏛 P Lift ♪ dB ⇆4700

ZAFRA
Badajoz (☎924)

★★★**Parador Nacional Hernán Contés**
pl de Maria Cristina ☎550200 ˙
16 Dec–Oct
rm28 ⇆23 ▥5 ♪ dB ⇆5200 M1300
Pool

On **N432 Badajoz road** (16km NW)
🐾**F Alvarez Rulz** Passaje de Feria, ctra
Badajoz-Granada Km 73.200 ☎551160
P Cit

ZAHARA DE LOS ATUNES
Cádiz

★★★**Cortijo la Plata** Calso de Plata
☎430901
15 Apr–15 Oct
rm14 ⇆10 ▥4 P sea

ZAMORA
Zamora (☎988)

★★**Cuatro Naciones** av J-António 7
☎512275
rm40 ⇆30 ▥10 P Lift ♪
dB ⇆ ▥2860–3260 M700

★★**Parador Nacional Condes de Alba &
Aliste** pl de Cánovas I ☎514497
⇆19 🏛 P ♪ dB ⇆5700 M1300 Pool

Andorra

ZARAGOZA
Zaragoza (☎976)

★★★**Goya** Cinco de Marzo 5 (off ps de
la Independencia) ☎229331
⇆150 🏛 Lift dB ⇆3600–4500 M1025

★**Conde Bianco** Predicadores 84 (n.rest)
☎441411
⇆83 🏛 P Lift ♪ dB ⇆3020

On **N11 Madrid road** (8km SW)

★★**Cisne** ctra Madrid, Barcelona Km
309 ☎332000
rm61 ⇆47 ▥4 P ♪ dB ⇆ ▥4670
Pool mountains

ZARAUZ (ZARAUTZ)
Guipúzcoa (☎943)

★★★**Zarauz** av de Navarra 4 ☎830200
15 Jan–15 Dec
⇆82 P Lift ♪ sB ⇆2440–3240
dB ⇆3780–4680 M980 t4% sea
mountains

★★**Alameda** Travesia Alameda
☎830143
rm26 ▥4 P ♪ dB2570 dB ▥2970
M690

Andorra

Prices are in Spanish pesetas
(☎from France 16078
☎from Spain 9738)

ANDORRA LA VELLA

★★★**Andorra Center** ctra Dr-Nequi 12
☎24999 tx203
⇆150 🏛 P Lift ♪ dB ⇆3750–5130
M930–1100 🏊 Pool mountains

★★★**Andorra Palace** Prat de la Creu
☎21072 tx208
⇆140 🏛 P Lift ♪ dB ⇆ ▥4090
M1490 S10% 🏊 Pool mountains

★★★**Andorra Park** (MAP) ☎20979
tx203
rm80 ⇆45 ▥35 A40rm P ♪
sB ⇆2825–5415 dB ⇆ ▥3550–6670
M1925 🏊 Pool mountains

★★★**Mercure** av Méritxell 58 ☎20773
tx208
⇆70 🏛 P Lift ♪ sB ⇆4362
dB ⇆5847 🏊 Pool mountains

★★★**Sasplugas** av del Princep Iglesias
☎20311

⇆26 🏛 Lift ♪ DPn1700–2300
mountains

★★**Internacional** ctra Mossen Tremosa
2 ☎21422
rm50 ⇆30 ▥20 Lift dB ⇆ ▥2325
M850

★★**Pyrénées** av Princep Benlloch 20
☎20508 tx209
rm82 ⇆32 ▥20 P Lift
dB ⇆ ▥1600–2300 M950 mountains

🐾**CIMEX** av Dr Mitjavila 5 ☎23190 P
Fia

Auto Servel av Principe Beniloch 3
☎30023 Frd

ENCAMP

★**Residencia Belvedere** ctra Bellavista
☎31263
16 Dec–14 Oct
rm10 ⇆1 P sB1068–1311
dB1844–3050 dB ⇆2300–3050
M975–1340 mountains

ESCALDES (LES)

★★★**Roc Blanc** (MAP) pl dels Co-
Princeps 5 ☎21486 tx224
⇆100 🏛 P Lift ♪ sB ⇆3980–4480
dB ⇆5660–6160 M1680 S15% 🏊
Pool mountains

★★**Pia** (n.rest) ☎21432
Jul–25 Aug
rm32 ⇆15 Lift sBfr1500 sB ☎fr2000
dBfr2800 S10% mountains

Ets Becler 105 av Charlemagne ☎21462
Ren

SANTA COLOMA

★★★**Roureda** av d'Enclar 18 ☎20681
Jun–Sep
▥36 P ♪ Pool mountains

SANT JULIÀ DE LÒRIA

★★★**Co-Princeps** ctra de Hué 1
☎41002
Apr–Oct
⇆80 P Lift ♪ dB ⇆2750 M890
mountains

★★**Sardana** pl Major 2-4 ☎41018
Apr–Sep
rm25 ⇆23 ▥2 dB ⇆ ▥2030 M alc
mountains

SOLDEU

At **TARTER (EL)** (3 km W)

★★★**Tarter** ☎51165
Dec–Oct
⇆35 🏛 P Lift mountains

SWEDEN

Sweden is a smart, clean land of modern towns and cities, and beautiful lakes and forest scenery. It is bordered by two countries, Norway in the west and Finland in the north-east. About half the country is forested and most of the many thousands of lakes are situated in the southern central area. Vanern, the largest, occupies 2,140 sq miles. Swedish Lapland, to the north, is mountainous and enters the Arctic Circle.

In spite of its northerly position, Sweden has a mild climate although its great length does lead to variations. The summers can be very hot, but the further north you travel the shorter they become. The midnight sun can be seen during June and July above the Arctic Circle. The language is based on Old Norse and is allied to Norwegian and Danish. There are local variations; the Lapps have their own language.

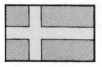

Area *173,624 sq miles*
Location map *See page 290*
Population *8,318,000*
Local time *GMT + 1 (Summer GMT + 2)*

National flag *Gold cross on a blue field*

How to get there

Sweden can be reached by direct ferry services operating from Harwich or Newcastle to Göteborg (Gothenburg). The crossing takes 23–26 hours. It is also possible to reach Sweden via Denmark, using the Newcastle or Harwich to Esbjerg car ferry services; sailing time is about 19 hours. Alternatively you can take one of the short Channel crossings to France or Belgium, then drive through the Netherlands, northern Germany, and Denmark to Sweden, using the ferry connections between Puttgarden–Rødbyhavn, and Helsingør––Helsingborg. Crossing from Harwich to Hamburg gives a shorter overland journey via Germany or Denmark. The distance from Calais to Stockholm, the capital, is about 1,000 miles and would normally require three night stops.

Stockholm, built on 14 islands

Motoring regulations and general information

This information should be read in conjunction with the general content of the European ABC (pages 6–27). **Note** As certain regulations and requirements are common to many countries they are covered by one entry in the ABC and the following headings represent some of the subjects dealt with in this way:

AA Agents
Crash or safety helmets
Customs regulations for European Countries
Drinking and driving
Fire extinguisher
First aid kit
Insurance
International distinguishing sign
Medical treatment
Overtaking
Police fines
Radio telephones/Radio transmitters
Rear view mirror
Road signs
Seat belts
Traffic lights
Tyres
Visitors' registration

Accidents

Fire, police and **ambulance** ☎90000. The emergency telephone number should only be used in the case of personal injury or illness. See also *Accidents* page 7.

In the case of an accident it is not necessary to call the police, but the driver is required to give information regarding his name and address to other persons concerned. He is not allowed to leave the scene of the accident before this is

done, no matter how slight the damage. If a driver goes away he may be sentenced to imprisonment or be fined. However, as a general rule, report the matter to the police in your own interests.

Accommodation

Swedish hotels have a particularly good reputation for cleanliness. A full list is published by the Swedish Tourist Board, but there is no official classification.

In many places summer chalets can be rented. In the south it is possible to holiday on a farm or as paying guest at a manor house. The Swedish Touring Club has over fifty lodges at which families can be accommodated. They provide from 4 to 6 beds, hot and cold water, and showers.

Breakdown

The Swedish motoring clubs Motormännens Riksförbund (M) and Svenska Turistföreningen (STF) do not operate road patrol services. There are alarm centres organised by Larmtjanst AB (Alarm Services Ltd) or garages which are open day and night to help motorists in difficulties. The service is restricted to breakdowns and accidents and is not free. See also *Breakdown* page 8 and *Warning triangles* page 348.

British Consulates

(See also page 8)
11527 Stockholm Skarpögatan 6–8 ☎(08)670140. There are also consulates in Gävle, Göteborg and Malmö.

Currency and banking hours

(See also page 11)
The unit of currency is the Krona divided into 100 öre. Travellers from abroad may import an unlimited sum in foreign banknotes and coins as well as other forms of currency, such as travellers cheques, letters of credit, etc. Visitors may import and export Swedish banknotes and coins up to the sum of *Kr*6,000.

In towns, banks are generally open 09.30–15.00hrs but some may be open until 18.00hrs Monday to Friday. In the country banks are usually open from 10.00hrs to 14.00hrs Monday to Friday.

Dimensions and weight restrictions

(See also page 13)
Height: no restriction; width: 2.60 metres; length (car/caravan/trailer): 24 metres. One or two trailers may be towed, but the maximum weight of the trailer(s) must not exceed twice the maximum weight of the towing vehicle.

Driving licence

(See also page 13)
A valid British driving licence is acceptable in Sweden. The minimum age at which a visitor may drive a temporarily imported car is 18 years and a temporarily imported motorcycle 17 years.

Emergency messages to tourists

(See also page 14)
Emergency messages to tourists are broadcast daily throughout the year by Swedish Radio. *Sveriges Radio* (Programme 1) transmitting on medium wave 245 metres, 255 metres, 306 metres, 388 metres, 417 metres and 506 metres broadcasts these messages in English, French, German and Swedish at 08.10, 13.10, 16.45 and 21.50hrs. *Sveriges Radio* (Programme 3) transmitting as above, but messages broadcast at 11.55 and 19.02hrs.

Lights

(See also page 17)
It is compulsory for all motorists including motorcyclists to use dipped headlights during the day.

Motoring clubs

(See also page 18)

The **Motormännens Riksförbund** (M) has its headquarters at Sturegatan 32, 10240 Stockholm ☎(08)7823800 and the **Svenska Turistforeningen** (STF) at Vasagatan 48, 10120 Stockholm ☎(08)227200. Both have branch offices and agents in main towns.

Motorways

Several main roads, mainly E3, E4, E6 and E18 incorporate stretches of motorway (motorväg). There are 834 miles open in all and further sections are under construction or in the planning stage. No tolls are charged.

Orange badge scheme for disabled drivers

(See also page 19)
Although concessions are available to disabled drivers in Sweden, they have not yet been extended to include visiting disabled drivers.

Parking

(See also page 19)
In Stockholm and a few of the larger towns

there are parking restrictions which are connected with road cleaning and are decided locally. A sign (blue disc with red border and red diagonal) is placed under the street name and gives the day and times when parking is prohibited. The restriction applies only to the side of the street on which the sign is displayed.

Gränna on Lake Vättern

Passengers
(See also page 19)
It is recommended that children do not travel in a vehicle as front seat passengers unless seated in a special child restraint.

Petrol
(See also page 20)
Credit cards International credit cards are rarely accepted by petrol stations.
Duty-free petrol The petrol in the vehicle tank may be imported free of customs duty and tax. However, as an additional concession, the customs authorities generally allow a reasonable quantity of petrol to be imported in a spare can.
Octane rating Regular (93) and Premium (96–98).

Postal information
Mail Postcards *Kr*1.60; letters up to 20gm *Kr*4.
Post offices There are 2,500 post offices in Sweden. Opening hours of the larger offices are from 09.00–18.00hrs Monday to Friday and 09.00–13.00hrs Saturday. Smaller offices open 10.00–16.00hrs Monday to Friday and 10.00–13.00hrs Saturday. In Stockholm the Head Post Office is open from 08.00–21.00hrs and 11.00–13.00hrs on Sunday. The Central Station post office is open from 07.00–22.00hrs on weekdays.

Postcheques
(See also page 21)
Postcheques may be cashed for any amount up to a maximum of *Kr*600 per cheque at all post offices except those in smaller villages.

Counter positions are identified by the words *All slags expedition/inoch utbetalingar*. See above for post office opening hours.

Priority
(See also *Priority including Roundabouts* page 22)

Buses have priority when leaving bus stops in areas where speed is restricted to 50 kph (32 mph).

Public holidays
Official public holidays in Sweden for 1985 are given below. See also *Public holidays* page 22.
January 1 (New Year's Day)
January 6† (Epiphany)
April 5 (Good Friday)
April 8 (Easter Monday)
May 1 (May Day)
May 16 (Ascension Day)
May 27 (Whit Monday)
June 6 (Swedish Flag Day)
June 22* (Midsummer Day)
November 2* (All Saints' Day)
December 24 (Christmas Eve)
December 25 (Christmas Day)
December 26 (Boxing Day)
*Saturday †Sunday

Roads
There is a comprehensive network of numbered, well-signposted highways but minor roads are not numbered. Although many roads in the south are being improved, others – particularly in central and northern Sweden – are still surfaced with loose gravel.

In various parts, chiefly along the Baltic coast, there are protected areas where only certain roads are open to motorists, and in these areas visitors may stay only at certain places and for a limited time. The two areas likely to concern visitors are around Boden and Kalix in the provinces of Norrbotten. Warning notices are displayed in English and other languages on the boundaries of these areas.

Shopping hours
Shopping hours vary, especially in large cities, but most are open 09.00–18.00hrs from Monday to Friday, and 09.00–14.00hrs or 16.00hrs on Saturday.

Speed limits
(See also page 25)
There are maximum speed limits indicated by signs on all roads in Sweden. In built-up areas 50 kph (31 mph); on all minor roads and roads

with a high traffic density 70 kph (43 mph); on all other roads 90 kph (56 mph) and 110 kph (62 mph) on motorways. Cars towing caravans fitted with brakes 70 kph (43 mph); without brakes 40 kph (24 mph).

Spiked, studded or snow tyres

(See also page 10)
Spiked tyres are permitted from 1 October to 30 April. They may be used during the rest of the year if weather conditions require their use, and if the relevant special decision is announced by the authorities. When spiked tyres are used they must be fitted on all wheels. If a vehicle with spiked tyres tows a trailer, the trailer must be fitted with spiked tyres.

Tourist information offices

(See also page 25)
Local tourist information is available from tourist offices throughout Sweden. Persons requiring information in the UK should contact the Swedish National Tourist Office, 3 Cork Street, London W1X 1HA ☎01-437 5816.

Trams

(See also page 25)
Trams should be overtaken on the right if the position of the tracks permits this. If there is no refuge at a tram stop, drivers should stop and give way to passengers alighting from and boarding the tram. All road users must give way to trams.

Using the telephone

(See also page 26)
Insert coin **after** lifting receiver (instructions in English in many callboxes). When making calls to subscribers within Sweden precede number with relevant area code (shown in parentheses against town entry in gazetteer). Use *Kr*1 coin for local calls and *Kr*1 or 5 coins for national and international calls.

International callbox identification Callboxes with 1/3 slots.

Telephone rates A call to the UK costs *Kr*4.15 per minute. Local calls cost *Kr*1.

What to dial for the Irish Republic 009 353*
What to dial for the UK 009 44*
*Wait for second dialling tone

Warning triangles

The use of a warning triangle is compulsory for all vehicles except two-wheelers. See also *Warning triangles/Hazard warning lights* page 26.

Winter conditions

During winter there is usually no difficulty in driving to Stockholm from Göteborg, Oslo, and Denmark. Farther north, motoring is also possible subject to prevailing conditions, as the main roads are cleared as quickly as possible. Generally, however, the touring season is from May to September.

Prices are in Swedish Kroner
Abbreviations:
gt gatan

ABISKO
Lappland (☎0980)
No road connection: rail service from Kiruna

★ ★Abisko Turistation ☎40000

25 Feb–13 May & 9 Jun–16 Sep
rm100 ⇌2 sB110–150 dB140–230
dB ⇌220–270

ALINGSÅS
Västergötland (☎0322)

☆ ☆ ☆Scandic Bankgt 1 ☎14000
⇌ 🏠66 **P** ⅅ sB 🏠310 dB ⇌ 🏠400

&⊘Allbägning Burman Åkareg 5 ☎36200

&⊘O Bjöklund Ö Ringgt 1 ☎15950 Frd

&⊘F W Börjesson Häradsvägen ☎14030 VW

ALVESTA
Småland (☎0472)

☆ ☆ ☆Scandic Stargt ☎11350 tx12636
🏠48 **P** Lift ⅅ sB 🏠310 dB 🏠400

ÅMÅL
Dalsand (☎0532)

★ ★Stadshotellet Kungsgt 9 ☎12020
rm49 ⇌8 🏠31 A12rm 🏠 **P** Lift
sB150 sB ⇌ 🏠250 dB200 dB ⇌ 🏠360
&⊘ Pool

&⊘Dalslands Vänersborgsvägen 45
☎12090 VW

&⊘Perrolf Bil & Transport AB
Vänersborgsvägen 15 ☎13006 All makes

ÄNGELHOLM
Skåne (☎0431)

☆Erikslunds N Varalov ☎22114
rm15 ⇌6 🏠 ⅅ **P**

ÅRE
Jämtland (☎0647)

★ ★Diplomat Åre-Aregarden ☎50205 tx44050

23 Dec–2 May & 20 Jun–Aug
rm100 ⇌50 **P** sB220–275
sB ⇌250–330 dB370–460
dB ⇌430–570 Pool mountains lake

ÅRJÄNG
Värmland (☎0573)

☆ ☆ ☆Scandic Arikavägen ☎11070 tx12636
⇌ 🏠40 **P** ⅅ sB ⇌ 🏠300
dB ⇌ 🏠390 Pool

ARLÖV See **MALMÖ**

ARVIKA
Värmland (☎0570)

★ ★ ★Bristol Kyrkogt 25 (n.rest)
☎13280
rm40 ⇌20 🏠20 🏠 **P** Lift
sB ⇌ 🏠195–450 dB ⇌ 🏠250–600

★ ★Stadshotellet Torggt 9 ☎13120
rm36 🏠10 🏠 ⅅ

&⊘Ola By Bilbärgning Rosendalsvägen ☎11057

&⊘Södergvists Industrigt 4 ☎13270 Aud VW

ASKERSUND
Närke (☎0583)

☆ ☆ ☆Scandic Marieborg Sundsbrogt ☎12010 tx12636
⇌ 🏠36 **P** ⅅ sB ⇌ 🏠300
dB ⇌ 🏠390 Pool

★★Vättern Torgparken 3 ☎11155
rm24 ⇦18 P sB ⇦175 dB175
dB ⇦200

ÅTVIDABERG
Östergötland (☎0120)

★★★Stallet Östantorpsvägen 2
☎11940 tx5586
⇦68 P Lift ☽ Pool

BÅSTAD
Skåne (☎0431)

★★Enehall Stationsterrassen 10
☎70212
Etr–Nov
rm58 ⇦2 ▥35 A50rm P sB115–125
sB ⇦ ▥150 dB180–230
dB ⇦ ▥250–290 M35–45 mountains

☆☆Hallandsås ☎(0430)24270
rm22 ▥17 P sB ▥175 dB160
dB ▥220–250 ✍

BOLLNÄS
Hälsingland (☎0278)

★★Frimurarehotellet Stationsgt 15
☎13220 tx17930
rm67 ⇦ ▥42 ▥ Lift

⅏HB Kajos Autobärgning Alftav 10C
☎16882

⅏Motorcentr Söderhamn-Bollnäs AB
Edelbergsvägen 18 ☎13040 Opl Peu

BORÅS
Västergötland (☎033)

★★★Grand (SARA) Hallbergsgt 14
☎108200 tx36182
⇦166 P Lift ☽ sB ⇦470 dB ⇦625
lake

☆☆☆Scandic Hultasjögt 7 ☎157000
⇦ ▥95 P Lift ☽ sB ⇦ ▥310
dB ⇦ ▥400 Pool

BORGHOLM
Öland (☎0485)

⅏Lundgren Södra Länggt ☎10068 Dat

BORLÄNGE
Dalarna (☎0243)

☆☆☆Scandic Stationsgt 21–23
☎28120
⇦ ▥111 ▥ P Lift ☽ sB ⇦ ▥310
dB ⇦ ▥400 Pool

★★Brage (SARA) Stationsgt 1 ☎24150
rm90 ⇦42 P Lift ☽ sB ⇦410
dB ⇦540

⅏Bilherman I Borlänge Mästargt 2
☎28025 Dat

DEGEBERGA
Skåne (☎0450)

⅏Degeberga-Auto Tingsvägen 48
☎50002 BL

ENKÖPING
Uppland (☎0171)

★★Stadshotellet Stora Torget ☎20010
rm67 ▥63 P Lift ☽ sB260 sB ▥340
dB ▥415 Pool ♂

Sweden

ESKILSTUNA
Södermanland (☎016)

★★★Eskilstuna (SARA) Hamngt 11
☎137225 tx460465
⇦120 ▥ P Lift ☽ sB ⇦460
dB ⇦605 Pool

FAGERSTA
Västmanland (☎0223)

☆☆Scandic Blomstervägen ☎17060
⇦ ▥148 P Lift ☽ sB ⇦ ▥310
dB ⇦ ▥400 Pool

FALKENBERG
Halland (☎0346)

⅏A Olssons Storgt 3 ☎10531 Ren

FALUN
Dalarna (☎023)

★★★Grand (SARA) Trotzgt 9–11
☎18700 tx84141
▥183 ▥ P Lift ☽ sB ▥390
dB ▥500 Pool

☆☆☆Scandic Norslund ☎22160
⇦ ▥84 P ☽ sB ⇦ ▥310
dB ⇦ ▥400 Pool

⅏Dala Bilcentrum Tegelvägen 2
☎19220 Lnc Sab

⅏Falu Bilbägning Kongstvaktareg 13
☎10017

FÄRJESTADEN
Öland (☎0485)

⅏A B Lasses Gärdby ☎33057

FILIPSTAD
Värmland (☎0590)

☆☆☆Scandic Lasarettsgt 2 ☎12530
⇦ ▥47 P ☽ sB ⇦ ▥300
dB ⇦ ▥390 Pool

FINSPÅNG
Östergötland (☎0122)

★★Geer (SARA) Vallonvägen 8 ☎13150
▥61 P Lift ☽ sB ▥335 dB ▥485
Pool

FLEN
Södermanland (☎0157)

☆☆Scandic Brogt 5 ☎13940 tx12636
⇦ ▥49 P Lift ☽ sB ⇦ ▥300
dB ⇦ ▥390

FLENINGE See **HELSINGBORG**

GAMLEBY
Smårland (☎0493)

☆Tjust ☎11550
rm17 ⇦7 ☽

GÄVLE
Gästrikland (☎026)

★★★★Grand Central (Inter S) Nygt 45
☎129060 tx47103

⇦150 ▥ P Lift ☽ sB ⇦390–450
dB ⇦495–525

☆☆Scandic (3 km S on E4)
Hemmlingby ☎188060 tx47355
⇦ ▥145 P Lift ☽ sB ⇦ ▥310
dB ⇦ ▥400 Pool

⅏Dahlboms Bomhusvägen 55
☎100400 AR Ren

GETÅ
Östergötland (☎011)

★★Turisthotell ☎62050
Closed Sun (Sep–May)
rm48 ⇦4 ▥40 A22rm ▥ P ✍ Pool
mountains lake

GISLAVED
Småland (☎0371)

☆☆Scandic Riksväg 26 ☎11540
tx12636
⇦ ▥54 P Lift ☽ sB ⇦ ▥300
dB ⇦ ▥390

GLUMSLÖV
Skåne (☎0418)

★★★Örenäs Slott ☎70250 tx72759
⇦128 A18rm P Lift ☽ sB ⇦350
dB ⇦420 ✍ Pool ♂

GÖTEBORG (GOTHENBURG)
Bohuslän (☎031)

★★★★★Park Avenue (SRS)
Kungsports Avenyn 36–38 ☎176520
tx2320
⇦320 ▥ P Lift ☽ sB ⇦570–730
dB ⇦810–865 Pool

★★★★Europa (THF) Köpmansgt 38
☎801280 tx21374
⇦462 ▥ P Lift ☽ sB ⇦620
dB ⇦720 Pool

★★★★Opalen Engelbrektsgt 73
☎810300 tx2215
⇦230 ▥ P Lift ☽ sB ⇦450–490
dB ⇦600

★★★Eggers Drottningtorget 1
☎171570 tx27273
rm90 ⇦20 ▥20 Lift ☽ sB 225
sB ⇦ ▥395 dB325 dB ⇦ ▥495

☆☆☆O K Motor Kaggeledsgt 43
☎250450 tx21895
Closed Xmas
▥114 P ☽ sB ▥225–380
dB ▥330–480 Pool

★★★Rubinen Kungsports Avenyn 24
☎810800 tx20837
⇦189 ▥ P Lift ☽ sB ⇦525–580
dB ⇦600–650

☆☆☆Scandic Bäckobolsvägen
☎520060 tx27767
⇦ ▥180 ▥ P Lift ☽ sB ⇦ ▥330
dB ⇦ ▥420 Pool

★★★Scandinavia (THF) Kustgt 10
☎417000 tx21522
⇦317 ▥ P Lift ☽ sB ⇦450–485
dB ⇦600–630 Pool

★★Frålsningsarméns Ritz
(Temperance) Burggrevegt 25 ☎175260
rm110 ⇦55 **P** Lift *D* sB180–200
sB ⇦260–290 dB310 dB ⇦485–450

★★Örgryte Danska Vagen 68 ☎197620
tx27565
⇦ 🏛80 🏛 **P** Lift *D*
dB ⇦ 🏛275–305 dB ⇦ 🏛365–415

★Liseberg Heden Sten Sturegt
☎200280 tx27450
⇦147 **P** Lift *D* sB ⇦350 dB ⇦485

★Örnen Lorensbergsgt 6 (off Vasagt)
☎182380
rm30 **P** Lift sB135–160 dB200–250

Bivahuset Vågmåstareplatsen ☎500200
Maz Opl

⊛Motorverken Odinsgt 6–8 ☎175060
Frd

GRÄNNA
Småland (☎0390)
☆ ☆ ☆*Scandic* Gyllene Uttern ☎10800
⇦ 🏛56 **P** Lift *D* lake

HÄGERSTEN See **STOCKHOLM**

HALMSTAD
Halland (☎035)
★★★★**Hallandia** Rädhusgt 2
☎118800 tx38030
⇦92 **P** Lift *D* sB⇦425 dB ⇦525–600
☆ ☆ ☆**O K Motor** Strandvallen 3
☎104300 tx38279
Closed Xmas
⇦118 **P** Lift *D* sB ⇦225–375
dB ⇦330–475 Pool
★★★**Mårtenson** Storgt 52 ☎118070
Closed Xmas
rm72 ⇦16 🏛8 **P** Lift *D* sB160–280
sB ⇦ 🏛320–360 dB290–395
dB ⇦ 🏛430–540 M alc

⊛**Bilexpo** Furuviksringen 2 ☎102030
Toy

HAPARANDA
Norrbotten (☎0922)
★★**Stadshotellet** Torget 7 ☎11490
rm40 ⇦ 🏛28 🏛 Lift sB300
sB ⇦ 🏛350 dB350 dB ⇦ 🏛400 Pool

HÄRNÖSAND
Ångermanland (☎0611)
☆ ☆ ☆*Scandic* Ådalsvägen ☎19560
⇦ 🏛51 **P** sB ⇦ 🏛300 dB ⇦ 🏛390
Pool
★★**Stattshotellet** (SARA) Skeppsbron 9
☎10510
⇦73 🏛 **P** Lift *D* sB ⇦353 dB ⇦470
Pool

HÄSSLEHOLM
Skåne (☎0451)
★★**Göingehof** Frykholmsgt 23 ☎14330
rm47 ⇦14 🏛 Lift sB255–275
sB ⇦295 dB415 dB ⇦430

HELSINGBORG
Skåne (☎042)

Sweden

☆ ☆ ☆**Scandic** Florettgt 41 ☎151560
tx72149
⇦ 🏛175 **P** *D* sB ⇦310 dB ⇦400
Pool

☆ ☆**Kronan** Ängelholmsvagen 35
☎127965
⇦24 **P** sB ⇦190–250 dB ⇦222–270

★★**Mollberg** Stortorget 18 (Off Södra
Storgt) ☎120270 tx72234
⇦80 🏛 **P** Lift *D*

⊛**Hadströms Skånemotor** Garnisonsgt
4 ☎151010 Maz

⊛**Motorami** Ängelhomsvägen 10
☎120250 Vau

⊛**Motor Rep** Drottninggt 26 ☎111928
Vau

⊛**Scania** Muskötgt 1 ☎151410 VW

At **FLENINGE** (10km NE)
☆ ☆**Fleninge** ☎205155
⇦24 **P** *D* sB ⇦185 dB ⇦200

HEMAVAN
Lappland (☎0954)
★★**Hemavans Fjällhotell** ☎30150
26 Dec–13 May & 10 Jun–16 Sep
rm72 ⇦10 A12rm **P** *D* dBfr320
dB ⇦fr480 M35–85 mountains lake

HOFORS
Gästrikland (☎0290)
☆ ☆ ☆**Scandic** R80 Skolgt 11 ☎23010
tx12636
⇦ 🏛40 **P** Lift *D* sB ⇦ 🏛300
dB ⇦ 🏛390

HOK
Småland (☎0393)
★★**Hook Manor** ☎21080 tx70419
rm102 ⇦10 🏛80 **P** sB250
sB ⇦ 🏛310 dB330 dB ⇦ 🏛450–810
Pool 💍 lake

HUDIKSVALL
Hälsingland (☎0650)
★★**Stadshotellet** (Inter S) Storgt 36
☎15060 tx71534
rm140 ⇦60 🏛75 🏛 **P** Lift *D*
sB ⇦ 🏛445 dB ⇦ 🏛524 Pool

HYLTEBRUK
Småland (☎0345)
⊛**Hylte Bilverkstad** Gamia Nissastigen
☎10206 Opl

INSJÖN
Dalarna (☎0247)
★★**Insjön Turisthotell** Hotellvägen
☎40200
rm33 🏛9 A9rm **P** *D* sB155–185
sB 🏛230 dB240–250 dB 🏛280 ‰ 💍

JOHANNESHOV See **STOCKHOLM**

JÖNKÖPING
Småland (☎036)

★★★★**Portalen** Västra Storgt 9
☎118200 tx70037
⇦173 **P** Lift *D* sB ⇦395–415
dB ⇦515
★★★**City** Västra Storgt 25 ☎119280
rm65 ⇦25 🏛35 🏛 **P** Lift *D*
sB260–270 sB ⇦ 🏛315–390
dB ⇦ 🏛415–500 lake
★★★**Savoy** Brunnsgt 15 ☎119480
rm60 ⇦33 sB175–250 sB ⇦285–325
dB325 dB ⇦375–425
☆ ☆ ☆**Scandic** Rosenlund ☎119160
⇦ 🏛170 **P** Lift sB ⇦ 🏛310
dB ⇦ 🏛400 ‰ Pool
★★★**Stora** (Inter S) ☎119300 tx70057
⇦111🏛 **P** Lift *D* sB ⇦410–550
dB ⇦480–650 M alc alke
★★**Grand** Hovrättstorget ☎119600
rm60 ⇦16 🏛 **P** Lift sB170–235
sB ⇦270–295 dB285–320
dB ⇦390–420 mountains lake

⊛**Atteviks** J-Bauersgt 1 ☎169100 Aud
Por VW

⊛**Autolarm Börje Linden** Ö Stradgatan
5 ☎114048 All makes

⊛**Föenade** Hästhovsvägen ☎119700
BMW Chy Hon

⊛**Holmgrens** Osterängsvägen 8
☎119920 AR BL Ren

⊛**A Karige** Hästhovsvägen ☎119620
Opl Vau

KALMAR
Småland (☎0480)
☆ ☆ ☆**Scandic** (3km W) Dragonvagen 7
☎22360 tx43007
⇦ 🏛149 **P** *D* sB ⇦310 dB ⇦400 ‰
Pool 💍
★★★**Witt** (SARA) Södra Langgt 42
☎15250 tx43133
rm113 ⇦98 🏛 **P** Lift *D*
sB ⇦335–445 dB ⇦620–670 Pool

⊛**Autodelta** S Vägen70 ☎16244 AR Fia

KARLSBORG
Västergötland (☎0505)
★★★**Kanalhotellet** Storgt 94 ☎10021
rm25 ⇦2 🏛5 A20rm **P** sB140–150
sB ⇦ 🏛195–250 dBfr210
dB ⇦ 🏛270–340 mountains lake

KARLSHAMN
Blekinge (☎0454)
☆ ☆ ☆**Scandic** Strömmavägen ☎16660
⇦ 🏛194 **P** *D* sB ⇦ 🏛310
dB ⇦ 🏛400 Pool

⊛**E Andersson** Sölvesborgsv 15
☎10863 All makes

⊛**Ingemansson** Kungsgt 48 ☎14330
Frd

KARLSKOGA
Värmland (☎0586)

☆ ☆ ☆**Scandic** Hyttåsen ☎50460
⇦ 🏠77 **P** Lift ⅅ sB ⇦ 🏠310
dB ⇦ 🏠400 Pool

KARLSKRONA
Blekinge (☎0455)

☆ ☆ ☆**OK Motor** Ronnebyvägen 1
☎23040

Closed Xmas
🏠48 **P** Lift ⅅ sB 🏠225–350
dB 🏠330–450

KARLSTAD
Värmland (☎054)

☆ ☆ ☆**OK Motor** Höjdgt 3 ☎131000
tx66083

Closed Xmas
rm165 ⇦5 🏠100 **P** Lift ⅅ
sB ⇦ 🏠225–365 dB ⇦. 🏠330–465
Pool

☆ ☆ ☆**Scandic** Sandbäcksgt 6 ☎187120
⇦ 🏠93 **P** ⅅ sB ⇦ 🏠310
dB ⇦ 🏠400 Pool

★ ★**Stads** (Inter S) Kungsgt 22
☎115220 tx66024
⇦ 🏠140 **P** Lift ⅅ sB ⇦ 🏠395–510
dB ⇦ 🏠510–650 Pool

★ ★**Gösta Berling** Drottninggt 1
☎150190
rm75 ⇦20 🏠55 🍴 **P** Lift ⅅ
sB ⇦ 🏠295–315 dB ⇦ 🏠400–430
M35–45 Pool

★ ★**Ritz** Västra Torggt 20 (n.rest)
☎115140

Closed Xmas & New Year
⇦62 **P** Lift ⅅ sB ⇦320–350
dB ⇦410–440

★**Drott** Järnvägsgt 1 ☎115635 tx66329
rm38 ⇦ 🏠6 Lift sB ⇦ 🏠320
dB ⇦ 🏠400

&ᗡ**GDG Service** Ö Infarten 1 ☎180130
All makes

KIRUNA
Lappland (☎0980)

★ ★**Ferrum** Köpmansgt 1 ☎18600
tx8746
⇦170 🍴 **P** Lift ⅅ sB ⇦425
dB ⇦510–575

&ᗡ**Maskintjänst** Österleden 4 ☎11125
Peu

KÖPING
Västmanland (☎0221)

☆ ☆ ☆**OK Motor** Hultgrensgt 10
☎18120 tx40423
Closed Xmas
rm112 ⇦2 🏠60 **P** ⅅ
sB ⇦ 🏠190–415 dB ⇦ 🏠260–515

&ᗡ**A Falks** Fabriksgt 8 ☎14111 BL Ren

KRAMFORS
Ångermanland (☎0612)

★ ★**Kramm** Torggt 14 ☎13160
tx71325
rm110 ⇦50 🏠60 🍴 **P** Lift ⅅ
sB ⇦ 🏠395 dB ⇦ 🏠450 mountains

Sweden

KRISTIANSTAD
Skåne (☎044)

★ ★**Grand** Östra Storgt 18 ☎115315
rm90 ⇦50 🍴 **P** Lift ⅅ sBfr275
sB ⇦fr350 dBfr375 dB ⇦fr450

&ᗡ**Kristianstads Bilcentrum**
Blekringevägen 2 ☎115890 Aud VW

KRISTINEHAMN
Värmland (☎0550)

&ᗡ**E Andersson Bil & Maskin** 1a Indstrigt
3 ☎15540 BMW Frd RR

KUNGÄLV
Bohuslän (☎0303)

★ ★**Fars Hatt** ☎10970 tx2415
rm115 ⇦103 🏠12 🍴 **P** Lift ⅅ
sB ⇦ 🏠360–450 dB ⇦ 🏠480–550
mountains

&ᗡ**Inlands** Smedmästaregt 1 ☎15030
BMW Ren

KUNGENS KURVA
Stockholm (☎08)

☆ ☆**Scandic** Ekgardsvägen 2
☎7100460 tx13830
⇦ 🏠266 **P** Lift ⅅ sB ⇦ 🏠370
dB ⇦ 🏠460 Pool

LANDSKRONA
Skåne (☎0418)

★ ★**Öresund** Kungsgt 15 ☎16315
rm60 ⇦55 **P** Lift ⅅ Pool

&ᗡ**Maskin & Motorrenoveringer**
Landskronav 3 ☎18574 All makes

&ᗡ**Scania-Bilar 1 Helsingborg**
Malmövagen 29 ☎26055 VW

LAXA
Närka (☎0584)

☆ ☆ ☆**Scandic** ☎15540
⇦ 🏠42 **P** sB ⇦ 🏠300 dB ⇦ 🏠390

LEKSAND
Dalarna (☎0247)

★ ★**Tre Kullor** Hjortnäsv 2 ☎11350
rm40 ⇦ 🏠13 🍴 sB173 dB280
dB ⇦ 🏠305

LIDKOPING
Västergötland (☎0510)

&ᗡ**Per Bengtsson** Wennerbergsvägen 27
☎22470 Hon Opl Vau

&ᗡ**E Bjöstig** Wennerbergsvägen 33
☎22480 Por

LINKÖPING
Östergötland (☎013)

★ ★**Ekoxen** Klostergt 68 ☎146070
tx50142
rm118 ⇦30 🏠88 A23rm 🍴 **P** Lift ⅅ
sB ⇦ 🏠195–560 dB ⇦ 🏠270–620
Pool

★ ★**Frimurarehotellet** St-Larsgt 14
☎129180 tx50053
🏠122 **P** Lift ⅅ sB 🏠395–425
dB 🏠495–525

★ ★**Rally** (SARA) Storgt 72 ☎130200
tx50055
rm135 ⇦68 🏠67 **P** Lift 🏠
sB ⇦370–430 dB ⇦ 🏠475–525 M35

☆ ☆ ☆**Scandic** Rydsvagen ☎171060
⇦ 🏠87 **P** sB ⇦ 🏠310 dB ⇦ 🏠400
Pool

★ ★**Stora** Stora Torget 9 ☎129630
tx50053
rm100 ⇦20 🏠75 **P** Lift ⅅ sB250
sB ⇦ 🏠345–400 dB ⇦ 🏠475–525

LJUNGBY
Småland (☎3072)

★ ★**Terraze** (Inter S) Stora Torget 1
☎13560 tx52046

Closed Jul
rm75 ⇦10 🏠65 🍴 **P** Lift ⅅ
sB ⇦ 🏠395–425 dB ⇦ 🏠475–525

&ᗡ**Sunnerbo** Vislandavägen ☎81000 AR
BL Dat

LJUSDAL
Hälsingland (☎0651)

★ ★**Stads** N-Järvägsgt 41 ☎11750
rm36 ⇦ 🏠4 🍴Lift sB195–220
sB ⇦ 🏠245 dB320 dB ⇦ 🏠350

&ᗡ**Bilbolaget I Ljusdal Persson** Kyrkogt 9
☎11770 Vlo

LULEÅ
Norrbotten (☎0920)

★ ★ ★ ★**SAS Globetrotter** Storgt 17
☎94000 tx80406
⇦214 🍴 **P** Lift ⅅ Pool

☆ ☆ ☆**Scandic** Mjölkudden ☎28360
tx80253
⇦ 🏠158 **P** Lift ⅅ sB ⇦ 🏠310
dB ⇦ 🏠400 Pool

★ ★**Stads** (Inter S) Storgt 15 ☎10410
tx80413
⇦115 🍴 sB ⇦405–450
dB ⇦480–550 sea

&ᗡ**A Myller** Banvägen 2 ☎10340 VW

LUND
Skåne (☎046)

★ ★**Lundia** (Inter S) Knut den Stores
Gata 2 ☎124140 tx32761
rm97 ⇦95 🍴 **P** Lift ⅅ sB ⇦525
dB ⇦610

LYSEKIL
Bohuslän (☎0523)

★ ★**Lysekil** Rosvikstorgt 1 ☎11860
rm90 ⇦12 🏠60 A40rm **P** Lift ⅅ
sB ⇦ 🏠300 dB ⇦ 🏠450 sea

&ᗡ**Winthers** Landsvägsgt 50 ☎11178
VW

MALMÖ
Skåne (☎040)

★ ★ ★ ★**Savoy** (Inter S) N Vallgt 62
☎70230 tx32383 →

⊄100 🏠 P Lift 🌙 sB ⊄465-515
dB ⊄570-640 M52 & alc sea

★★★Scandinavia (Inter S)
Drottninggt 1F ☎936700 tx32235

⊄214 🏠 P Lift 🌙 sB ⊄475
dB ⊄595 M alc

★★★Kramer Stortorget 7 ☎70120
tx32159

rm100 ⊄85 P Lift 🌙 sB290
sB ⊄420-480 dB ⊄550

★★★St-Jörgen Stora Nygt 35 ☎77300
tx32404

rm285 ⊄260 🛏25 🏠 P Lift 🌙
sB ⊄ 🛏360-580 dB ⊄ 🛏605-660

★★Tunnein Adelgt 4 ☎101930
rm49 ⊄17 🛏18 🏠 P Lift 🌙 sB195
sB ⊄345 dB345 dB ⊄435

★★Winn (SARA) Jörgen Kocksgt 3
(n.rest) ☎101800 tx33295
🛏101 P Lift 🌙 sB 🛏380 dB 🛏510

🅢Auto-Linden St Trådgärdsgt 30-34
☎72270 Fia

🅢Hedbergs Lundavägen 48-50
☎934260 Frd

🅢Malmö Scanauto Lundavägen 72
☎934630 BL DJ RT

🅢Motorami Hanögt 10 ☎73270 Opl
Vau
At **ARLÖV** (7km NW)

☆☆**Scandic** Kronetorpsvägen
☎433620

⊄ 🛏73 P 🌙 sB ⊄ 🛏330
dB ⊄ 🛏420 Pool

At **SEGEVÅNG** (5km E)

☆☆**Scandic** Segesvängen ☎180120
tx33478

⊄ 🛏158 P 🌙 sB ⊄ 🛏330
dB ⊄ 🛏420 Pool

MALUNG
Dalarna (☎0280)

★Nya Skinnargäden Grönlandsvägen
☎11750

rm55 ⊄7 🛏22 P sB ⊄ 🛏300
dB ⊄ 🛏345 mountains

MARKARYD
Småland (☎0433)

★★Stora ☎10730
rm44 ☎5 ⊄36 A20rm P

MÖLLE
Skåne (☎042)

★Grand Bökebolsv 11 ☎47280
Etr-Sep
rm50 ⊄30 P 🌙 sB140-217
sB ⊄220-242 dB209-254
dB ⊄330-324 sea mountains

MÖLNDAL
Västergötland (☎031)

☆☆**Scandic** Abro ☎275060 tx12636
⊄ 🛏172 P Lift 🌙 sB ⊄ 🛏330
dB ⊄ 🛏420 Pool

🅢Bivahuset
Mölndalsvägen ☎813560 Opl Maz Vau

Sweden

MORA
Dalarna (☎0250)

☆☆☆**Scandic** Kristinebergsgt ☎15070
⊄ 🛏79 A32rm P 🌙 sB ⊄ 🛏310
dB ⊄ 🛏400 Pool

🅢Björks Kniploksvägen 13 ☎13187

MOTALA
Östergötland (☎0141)

★★★Stads (Inter S) Stora Torget
☎16400 tx5561
rm80 ⊄ 🛏78 🏠 P Lift 🌙
sB ⊄ 🛏305-380 dB ⊄ 🛏470-520
sea lake

🅢Jansén Motor Vadstenavägen
30-34 ☎16230 Frd

🅢Wahlstedts Vintergt 17 ☎16030 VW

NÄSSJÖ
Småland (☎0380)

★★Högland (SARA) Esplanaden 4
☎13100 tx35289
⊄105 🏠 P Lift 🌙 sB ⊄355-415
dB ⊄455-490

🅢Höre Bil Höregt 12 ☎13170 BL
🅢Syrens Bäckgt 9 ☎13320 Frd

NORRKÖPING
Östergötland (☎011)

☆☆**Scandic** (3km N) Järngt ☎100380
⊄ 🛏148 P 🌙 sB ⊄310 dB ⊄400 🎑
Pool 𝛿

★★Standard (SARA) Slottsgt 99
☎129220 tx64171
⊄176 🏠 P Lift 🌙 sB ⊄385-440
dB ⊄530-720

🅢Automobilf (A D Carlsson)
Fredriksdalsgt 45 ☎186290 Dat Peu

🅢L E Ringborg Dagsbergsvägen
33 ☎139630 Fia Vau

🅢Zetterbioms
Grundverksgt ☎100440 AR BL Fia

NORRTÄLJE
Uppland (☎0176)

☆☆☆**O K Motor** Stockholmsvägen 53
☎17180 tx14307
Closed Xmas
rm167 ⊄5 🛏102 P Lift 🌙
sB ⊄ 🛏190-405 dB ⊄ 🛏260-505
Pool

🅢Lundqvists Bil & Motor
Stockholmsvägen 17 ☎12850 Opl Vau

🅢Norrtälje Bilcentral Trädgärdsgt
3 ☎12510 Frd

NYBRO
Småland (☎0481)

★★Stora Stadshusplan ☎11935
tx17930

rm32 ⊄ 🛏8 Lift sB ⊄ 🛏260-275
dB ⊄ 🛏400-450

NYKÖPING
Södermandland (☎0155)

☆☆**Scandic** Gumsbacken ☎89000
⊄ 🛏96 P Lift 🌙 sB ⊄ 🛏310
dB ⊄ 🛏400 Pool mountains

🅢E Källander V Kvarngt
52-54 ☎17170 Opl Vau

🅢Saab-Ana Stockholmsvägen
10 ☎17560 Chy Sab Sim

ÖREBRO
Närke (☎019)

★★★Grev Rosen Södra Grev Rosengt
2 ☎130240 tx73557
Closed Xmas
rm74 ⊄15 🛏50 🏠 P Lift 🌙 sB235
sB ⊄ 🛏275 dB285-330
dB ⊄ 🛏320-360

☆☆**Scandic** Västhagagt 1 ☎130480
tx73581
⊄ 🛏205 P Lift 🌙 sB ⊄ 🛏310
dB ⊄ 🛏400 Pool

★★★Stora Drottninggt 1 ☎124360
tx73230
rm108 ⊄37 🛏32 🏠 P Lift 🌙 sB270
sB ⊄ 🛏370-450 dB390 dB ⊄ 🛏540

★★Bergsmannen Drottninggt 42
☎130320
Closed Jul
rm66 ⊄36 🏠 P Lift 🌙 sB210
sB ⊄250 dB ⊄340-415

🅢AB T-Bil Södermalmsplan
5 ☎124790 Dat Vau

🅢Bilovalen & Örebro Nastagt
14 ☎140400 Frd

ÖRKELLJUNGA
Skåne (☎0435)

🅢Yngves Bil
Ängelholmsvägen ☎50980 BL Toy

ÖRNSKÖLDSVIK
Ångemanland (☎0660)

☆☆**Scandic** Häsmarksvägen 4
☎82870
⊄ 🛏173 🏠 P Lift sB ⊄ 🛏310
dB ⊄ 🛏400 Pool

★★Statt (SARA) Lasarettsgt 2 ☎10110
rm54 ⊄47 🏠 P Lift 🌙 sB ⊄395
dB ⊄550 lake

OSKARSHAMN
Småland (☎0491)

🅢Ekelunds Ringplatsen 11 ☎14330 BL
Fia Vau

🅢C E Holström Nygräd 13
☎15050 BMW Cit

ÖSTERSUND
Jämtland (☎063)

☆☆**Scandic** Krondikesvägen 97
☎127560
⊄ 🛏12 P 🌙 sB ⊄ 🛏310
dB ⊄ 🛏400 Pool

★ ★Winn (SARA) Prästgt 16 (n.rest)
☎127740 tx44038
⇋140 🛗 P Lift 𝄐 sB ⇋390
dB ⇋495 Pool lake

RÄTTVIK
Dalarna(☎0248)

☆ ☆ ☆OK Motor Storgt ☎11070
Closed Xmas
🍴32 P 𝄐 sB 🍴225-315
dB 🍴330-375

☆ ☆Rättvikshästen Nyåkersvägen
☎11015
rm40 🍴20 P sB200 sB 🍴225 dB250
dB 🍴260-300 Pool
&ↃW Olofssons ☎10527 All makes

RIKSGRÄNSEN
Lappland(☎0980)

★Lappiandia Sporthotel ☎43120
⇋ 🍴95 A9rm Pn160-485 lake

RONNEBY
Blekinge(☎0457)

★ ★ ★Ronneby Brunn ☎12750 tx4505
rm320 ⇋260 🍴16 P Lift 𝄐
sB ⇋ 🍴280-390 dB ⇋ 🍴360-460 &ↄ
Pool

SÄFFLE
Värmland(☎0533)

☆ ☆ ☆Scandic O-Trätäljagt 2 ☎12660
tx12636
⇋ 🍴64 P 𝄐 sB ⇋ 🍴310
dB ⇋ 🍴400 Pool

SALTSJÖBADEN See STOCKHOLM

SEGEVÅNG See MALMÖ

SIGTUNA
Uppland(☎0760)

★ ★Stads St Nygt 3 ☎50100
rm25 ⇋11 🍴12 sB300 sB ⇋ 🍴400
dB ⇋ 🍴500 lake

SKELLEFTEÅ
Västerbotten(☎0910)

★ ★Statt (SARA) Stationsgt 8-10
☎14140
rm67 ⇋55 🛗 P lift 𝄐 sB ⇋375-470
dB ⇋500-600
&ↃC Thylin Tjärnvägen 1 ☎17060 Fia
Opl Vau

SKÖVDE
Västergötland(☎0500)

★ ★ ★Billingehus (SARA)
Asbotorpsvägen ☎83000 tx67006
⇋240 P Lift 𝄐 sB ⇋460 dB ⇋610
Pool

☆ ☆ ☆O K Motor Gamia Kungsvägen 51
☎83030
Closed Xmas
🍴49 P 𝄐 sB 🍴190-350
dB 🍴260-450

★ ★Billingen (SARA) Trädgårdgt 10
☎10790

Sweden

Closed Jul & wknds
⇋92 🛗 P Lift 𝄐 sB ⇋455
dB ⇋580-665 Pool
&ↃSkövde Bil & Motor Hjovägen
3 ☎84250 Toy

SÖDERHAMN
Hälsingland(☎0270)

☆ ☆ ☆Scandic Montörsbacken
☎18020 tx12636
⇋ 🍴87 P Lift 𝄐 sB ⇋ 🍴310
dB ⇋ 🍴400 Pool

SÖDERTÄLJE
Södermanland(☎0755)

☆ ☆ ☆Scandic Verkstadsvägen ☎34260
⇋ 🍴126 P Lift 𝄐 sB ⇋ 🍴310
dB ⇋ 🍴400 Pool

SOLNA See STOCKHOLM

STOCKHOLM
Stockholm(☎08)
See plan page 354

★ ★ ★ ★Grand Södra
Blasieholmshamnen 8 ☎221070 tx19500
Plan 2
⇋ 🍴352 Lift 𝄐 sB ⇋ 🍴545-775
dB ⇋ 🍴770-935

★ ★ ★Mornington (Inter S) Nybrogt53
☎631240 tx10145 Plan 5
Closed Xmas & New Year
rm123 ⇋100 🍴23 🛗 P Lift 𝄐
sB ⇋ 🍴455-475 dB ⇋ 🍴585-595

★ ★ ★Park (Inter S) Karlavägen 43
☎229620 tx10666 Plan 5A
Closed Xmas
rm205 ⇋200 🍴5 🛗 P Lift 𝄐
sB ⇋ 🍴595-770 dB ⇋ 🍴800-850 M
alc

★ ★ ★Amaranten (THF) Kungsholmsgt
31 ☎541060 tx17498 Plan 7
rm363 ⇋257 🍴106 🛗 P Lift 𝄐
sB ⇋ 🍴570 dB ⇋ 🍴710 Pool

★ ★ ★Bromma Brommaplan 1
☎252920 tx13125 Plan 8
rm139 ⇋7 🍴132 P Lift 𝄐
sB ⇋ 🍴390 dB ⇋ 🍴470-510

★ ★ ★Continental Vasagt ☎244020
tx10100 Plan 9
rm132 ⇋100 🍴32 P Lift 𝄐
sB ⇋ 🍴460-730 dB ⇋ 🍴730-850

★ ★ ★Diplomat Strandvägen 7 C
☎635800 tx177119 Plan 10
rm132 ⇋100 🍴32 P Lift 𝄐
sB ⇋ 🍴460-730 dB ⇋ 🍴730-850

★ ★ ★Malmen Götgt 49-51 ☎226080
tx19489 Plan 11
⇋279 🛗 P Lift 𝄐 sB ⇋400-450
dB ⇋500-550

★ ★ ★Palace St-Eriksgt 115 ☎241220
tx19877 Plan 12

Closed Xmas & New Year
⇋ 🍴215 🛗 P Lift 𝄐
sB ⇋ 🍴495-525 dB ⇋ 🍴595-625

★ ★ ★Reisen (THF) Skeppsbron 12-14
☎223260 tx17494 Plan 13
⇋125 Lift 𝄐 sB ⇋710-735
dB ⇋810-835 Pool sea

★ ★ ★Sjotartshotellet Katarinavagen 26
☎226960 tx19020 Plan 14
rm184 ⇋16 🍴168 🛗 Lift 𝄐
sB ⇋ 🍴390-450· dB ⇋ 🍴490-550

★ ★ ★Terminus (Inter S) Vasagt 20
☎222640 tx11749 Plan 15
Closed Xmas
rm138 ⇋93 🍴40 🛗 P Lift 𝄐
sB ⇋ 🍴510-550 dB ⇋ 🍴650-725

★ ★Adlon Vasagt 42 (n.rest) ☎245400
tx11543 Plan 16
rm64 ⇋34 🛗 P Lift 𝄐 sB235-295
sB ⇋350 dB365 dB475-525

★ ★Eden Sturegt 10 ☎223160 tx10570
Plan 18
⇋60 🛗 P Lift 𝄐 sB ⇋340-575
dB ⇋395-825

★ ★Frälsningsarméns (Temperance)
Drottninggt 66 ☎222250 tx12487 Plan 19
rm154 ⇋ 🍴22 Lift

★Kung Carl Birger Jarlsgt 23 (n.rest)
☎221240 tx12262 Plan 21
⇋ 🍴88 🛗 P Lift 𝄐 sB ⇋ 🍴425
dB ⇋ 🍴595

&ↃW Kindwall Roslagsgt 4
Järfälla ☎970820 All makes
&ↃPhillipsons Norr Regeringsgt
109 ☎340000 MB Sim

At HÄGERSTEN (15km SW on E3)

☆ ☆Scandic Vantörsvägen 285, Gyllene
Ratten ☎462660 Plan 20

At JOHANNESHOV

☆ ☆ ☆OK Motor Marksnadsvägen 6
☎810600 tx15804 Plan 11A
Closed Xmas
rm104 ⇋4 🍴100 P Lift 𝄐
sB ⇋ 🍴225-395 dB ⇋ 🍴330-495

At SALTSJÖBADEN (20km SE road No
228)

★ ★ ★Grand ☎7170020 tx10210
Plan 4
rm100 ⇋96 🍴4 P Lift 𝄐
sB ⇋ 🍴525-575 dB ⇋ 🍴650-750 sea

At SOLNA (5km N)

★ ★ ★Flamingo Hotellgt 11 ☎830800
tx10060 Plan 10A
rm129 ⇋45 🍴84 🛗 P Lift 𝄐
sB ⇋ 🍴230-295 dB ⇋ 🍴350-370

☆ ☆ ☆Scandic Jarva Krog, Uppsalar
Ullriksdale ☎850360 tx13767 Not on
plan
⇋ 🍴198 P Lift 𝄐 sB ⇋ 🍴370
dB ⇋ 🍴460 Pool

STOCKHOLM

2	★★★★★ Grand
4	★★★★ Grand (At Saltsjöbaden 20km SE on road no.228)
5	★★★★ Mornington
5A	★★★★ Park
7	★★★ Amaranten
8	★★★ Bromma
9	★★★ Continental
10	★★★ Diplomat
10A	★★★ Flamingo (At Solna 5km N)
11	★★★ Malmen
11A	☆☆☆ OK Motor (At Johanneshov)
12	★★★ Palace
13	★★★ Reisen
14	★★★ Sjöfartshotellet
15	★★★ Terminus
16	★★ Adlon
18	★★ Eden
19	★★ Frälsningsarméns
20	☆☆ Scandic (At Hägersten 15km SW on E3)
21	★ Kung Carl

STORLIEN
Jämtland (☎0647)

★★**Storliens Högfjällshotellet** ☎70170 tx44051

11 Nov–5 May & 25 Jun–Sep
rm215 ⇔56 🛍 Lift Pool lake

SUNDSVALL
Medelpad (☎060)

★★★**Bore** (Inter S) Trädgårdsgt 31–33
☎150600 tx71280

Closed Xmas
rm112 ⇔4 🏨108 sB ⇔ 🏨450
dB ⇔ 🏨575

☆☆☆**OK Motor** Esplanaden 29
☎171600 tx71254

rm201 ⇔8 🏨193 🛍 P Lift ♪
sB ⇔ 🏨190–430 dB ⇔ 🏨260–530
Pool sea lake

☆☆☆**Scandic** Vardshusbacken 6
☎566860 tx71092

⇔🏨160 P ♪ sB ⇔ 🏨310
dB ⇔ 🏨400 Pool

★★★**Strand** (SARA) Strandgt 10
☎121800 tx71340

⇔113 🛍 P Lift ♪ sB⇔465–485
dB⇔570–710 sea

TÄLLBERG
Dalarna (☎0247)

★★★**Green** ☎50250
rm88 ⇔18 🏨70 P sB ⇔ 🏨200–350
dB ⇔ 🏨360–700 Pool mountains

★★**Dalecarlia** ☎50255
rm50 🏨15 sB ⇔ 🏨290
dB ⇔ 🏨440 ◐ Pool lake

★★**Långbers** ☎50290
rm52 ⇔15 🏨37 A39rm P sB ⇔ 🏨205
dB ⇔ 🏨350 ◐ lake

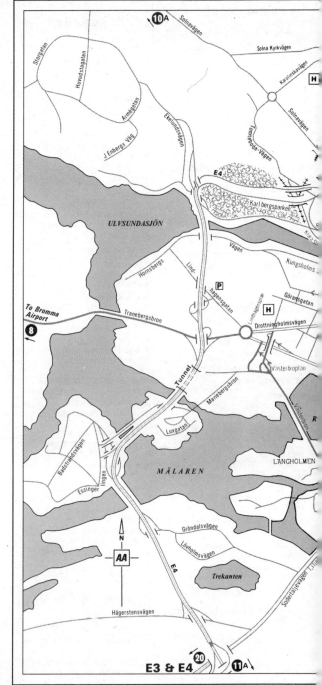

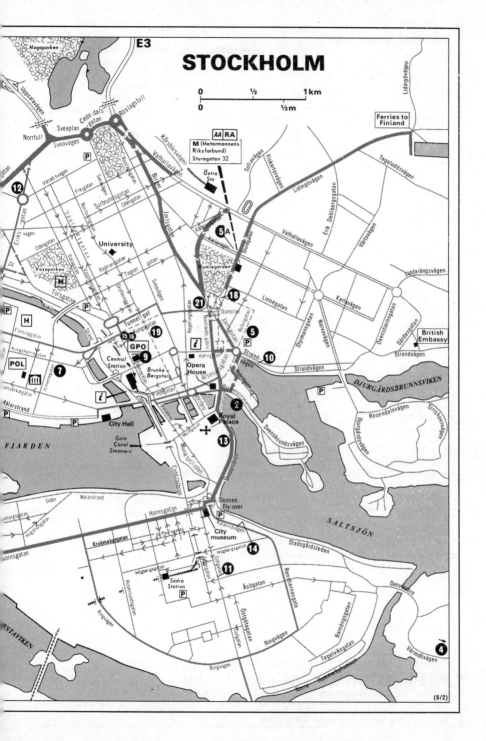

STOCKHOLM

★ ★Siljansgården ☎50040 tx74088
22 Dec–Sep
rm25 ⇥12 A18rm 🏛 **P** sB94–140
sB ⇥145–170 dB138–205
dB ⇥216–300 ⚓ lake

TORSBY
Värmland (☎0560)

★ ★Björnidet Kyrkogt 2 ☎11910
rm26 ▥17 **P** 𝄞 sB150–170
sB ▥160–190 dB 185–200
dB ▥195–230 Pool mountains lake

TRANÅS
Småland (☎0140)

★ ★ ★Scandic Storgt 22 ☎14160
⇥ ▥73 Lift 𝄞 sB ⇥ ▥310
dB ⇥ ▥400

TRELLEBORG
Skåne (☎0410)

ⓈⓄG Larsson V-Vallgt 5 ☎15380 Opl VW

TROLLHÄTTEN
Hästergötland (☎0520)

★ ★ ★Swania (Inter S) Storg 49
☎12570 tx42225
⇥ ▥56 Lift sB ⇥ ▥395–485
dB ⇥ ▥495–585 Pool

ⓈⓄF Anderssons Garvaregt 13 ☎13395
All makes

TYLÖSAND
Halland (☎035)

★ ★Tylösands ☎30500 tx38209
⇥ ▥136 sB ⇥ ▥355–370
dB ⇥ ▥440–450 Pool Beach sea

UDDEVALLA
Bohuslän (☎0522)

★ ★ ★Carlia N-Drottninggt 20–22
☎14140 tx42224
rm66 ⇥ ▥32 **P** Lift 𝄞 sB ⇥ ▥320
dB ⇥ ▥410 M alc

★Viking Strömstadsvägen 25 (n.rest)
☎14550
rm21 ☎5 A2rm **P**

ⓈⓄE Hansson Strömstadsvägen 15
☎14470 Vau

ULRICEHAMN
Västergötland (☎0321)

☆ ☆ ☆Scandic Nyboholm ☎12040
⇥ ▥58 **P** 𝄞 sB ⇥ ▥300
dB ⇥ ▥390

Sweden

UMEÅ
Västerbotten (☎090)

☆ ☆ ☆Scandic Yrkesvägen 8 ☎135250
⇥ ▥134 **P** 𝄞 sB ⇥ ▥310
dB ⇥ ▥400 Pool

★ ★ ★Strand V-Strandgt 11 (n.rest)
☎129020

Closed Xmas & New Year
⇥ ▥44 Lift sB ⇥ ▥325–350
dB ⇥ ▥400

★ ★ ★Winn (SARA) Skolgt 64 ☎122020
tx54118
▥148 🏛 **P** Lift 𝄞 sB ▥240–440
dB ▥360–565

ⓈⓄH Åströms Maskin Storgt 6A
☎122220 RR Sab Toy

ⓈⓄBilovalen I Umeå Rothoffsvägen 16
☎118470 Frd

UPPSALA
Uppland (☎018)

★ ★ ★ ★Uplandia (Inter S)
Dragarbrunnsgt 32 ☎102160 tx76125
rm105 ⇥98 ▥6 🏛 **P** Lift 𝄞 sB280
sB ⇥ ▥425 dB ⇥ ▥515–540

☆ ☆ ☆Scandic Gamla Uppsalagt 48
☎100280
⇥ ▥125 𝄞 sB ⇥ ▥310 dB ⇥ ▥400
Pool

★ ★Gillet (SARA) Dragarbrunnsgt 23
☎155360 tx76028
⇥171 🏛 **P** Lift 𝄞 sB ⇥440
dB ⇥ ▥590 M alc

VÄNERSBORG
Västergötland (☎0521)

☆ ☆ ☆Scandic Nabbensberg ☎62120
⇥ ▥83 **P** Lift sB ⇥ ▥310
dB ⇥ ▥400 Pool

ⓈⓄSundin Bilar Östravägen 18 ☎12180
Por VW

VARBERG
Halland (☎0340)

★ ★Statt (SARA) Kungsgt 24–28
☎16100 tx3481

rm126 ⇥122 Lift 𝄞 sB ⇥405
dB ⇥520 sea

ⓈⓄVarberge Bilcentral Susvindsvägen 21
☎80070 Frd

VÄRNAMO
Småland (☎0370)

★ ★ ★Värnamo (SARA) Storgt 20
☎11530
⇥125 **P** Lift 𝄞 sB ⇥390–440
dB ⇥525–585

ⓈⓄThitusons Margretelundsvägen 2
☎11830 MB Sim

VASSMOLÖSA
Småland (☎0480)

★Wassmolösa Gästgivaregård ☎32065
Jan–22 Dec
rm9 **P** sBfr170 dBfr225 St13%

VÄSTERÅS
Västmanland (☎021)

★ ★ ★Park (Inter S) Gunnibogt 2
☎110120 tx40477
rm139 ⇥5 ▥134 **P** Lift 𝄞
sB ⇥ ▥425–450 dB ⇥ ▥530–560 lake

VÄXJÖ
Småland (☎0470)

☆ ☆ ☆OK Motor Sandviksvägen 1
☎29050 tx52277

Closed Xmas
rm148 ⇥5 ▥100 **P** Lift 𝄞
sB ⇥ ▥190–365 dB ⇥ ▥260–465
Pool

☆ ☆ ☆Scandic Hejaregt 15 ☎22070
⇥ ▥106 **P** 𝄞 sB ⇥ ▥310
dB ⇥ ▥400 Pool

★ ★ ★Statt (SARA) Kungsgt 6 ☎13400
tx52139
rm139 🏛 **P** Lift 𝄞 sB405–440 dB 555
Pool

ⓈⓄHolmquist & Strömberg Hj Petris V 57
☎28090 BL Ren

VISBY
Gotland (☎0498)

ⓈⓄBilcity Färjeleden 7 ☎11940 VW

YSTAD
Skåne (☎0411)

★ ★ ★Ystads Saltsjöbad ☎13630
tx32342
rm112 ▥69 **P** 𝄞 sB ▥350 dB ▥460
⚓ Beach sea

SWITZERLAND AND LIECHTENSTEIN

Switzerland and Liechtenstein offer some of the most beautiful scenery in Europe. Switzerland is bordered by France in the west, the German Federal Republic in the north, Austria in the east, and Italy in the south. It has the highest mountains in Europe and some of the most awe-inspiring waterfalls and lakes, features that are offset by picturesque villages set amid green pastures and an abundance of Alpine flowers covering the valleys and lower mountain slopes during the spring. The highest peaks are Monte Rosa (15,217 ft) on the Italian border, the Matterhorn (14,782 ft), and the Jungfrau (13,669 ft). Some of the most beautiful areas are the Via Mala Gorge, the Falls of the Rhine near Schaffhausen, the Rhône Glacier, and the lakes of Luzern and Thun.

The Alps cause many climatic variations throughout Switzerland, but generally the climate is said to be the healthiest in the world. In the higher Alpine regions temperatures tend to be low, whereas the lower land of the northern area has higher temperatures and hot summers. French is spoken in the western cantons, German in the central and northern cantons and Italian in Ticino. Romansch is spoken in Grisons and there are numerous regional dialects throughout the country of which the Swiss-German dialects are a notable example.

The principality of Liechtenstein lies between the upper reaches of the Rhine valley and the Austrian Alps. The scenery is typically Alpine and the country is noted for its fine vineyards.

Area *15,953 sq miles*
Population *6,400,000*
Local time *GMT + 1*
(Summer GMT + 2)

National flag *A white cross on a red field*

How to get there

From Great Britain, Switzerland is usually approached via France. The distance from the Channel ports to Bern, the capital, is approximately 470 miles, a distance which will normally require only one night stop.

Monte Brè, overlooking Lake Lugano

Motoring regulations and general information

This information should be read in conjunction with the general content of the European ABC (pages 6–27). **Note** As certain regulations and requirements are common to many countries they are covered by one entry in the ABC and the following headings represent some of the subjects dealt with in this way:
AA Agents
Crash or safety helmets
Customs regulations for European countries
Drinking and driving
Fire extinguisher
First-aid kit
Insurance
Medical treatment
Overtaking
Police fines
Radio telephones/Radio transmitters
Rear view mirror
Road signs
Seat belts
Traffic lights
Tyres
Visitors' registration

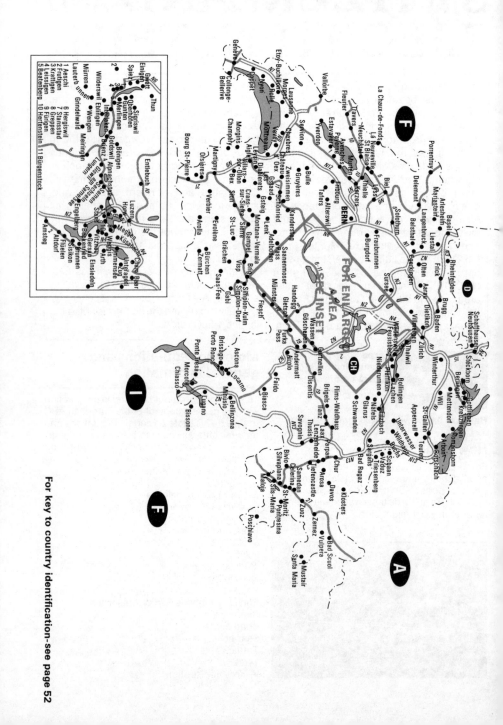

For key to country identification–see page 52

Accidents

Fire ☎118 **Police, Ambulance** ☎117. In provincial areas ☎111; this connects you with the postal services, who will then connect you with the police, giving you precedence over other callers.

The most important principle is that all persons involved in an accident should ensure, as far as is possible, that the traffic flow is maintained. Should the accident have caused bodily injuries, the police must be called immediately. Those injured should be assisted by the persons at the scene of the accident until the arrival of medical help. It is not necessary to call the police if the accident has only caused material damage, although the driver(s) concerned should immediately report the incident to the owner of the damaged property and exchange particulars. If this is not possible, the police must be informed. See also *Accidents* page 7.

Accommodation

Hotel classifications are indicated in the *Guide to Swiss Hotels*, published annually by the Swiss Hotel Association. The guide, which also contains details of spas and facilities for sports, is available from the Swiss National Tourist Office in London and local tourist offices issue hotel guides on a regional basis.

Prices generally include all service, taxes and heating. Some hotels offer reduced prices for children not requiring separate rooms. Children up to and including six years of age pay at the discretion of the hotel, children up to and including 12 years, pay 50% of the adult rate and children up to and including 16, pay 70% of the adult rate.

The Swiss Hotel Association operates a service for dealing with complaints which should be addressed to them at PO Box 2657, 3001 Berne and marked *Complaints Service*.

Breakdown

The major motoring club, Touring Club Suisse, operates a patrol service and a day and night breakdown service but it is likely that you will be charged for any service. The service (*Secours routier*) operates from several centres throughout the country and can be summoned by telephone.

When calling, give the operator the password *Touring Secours, Touring Club Suisse*, and state your location and if possible the nature of the trouble. The operator will state within a short time whether it will be a black and yellow patrol car or garage assistance, and how soon help can be expected. See also *Breakdown* page 8. *Motorways* page 360 and *Warning triangles* page 363.

British Consulates

(See also page 8)
3005 Berne Thunstrasse 50 ☎(031)445021/6. There are also consulates in Genève, Lugano, Montreux and Zürich.

Currency and banking hours

(See also page 11)
The unit of currency is the Swiss franc, divided into 100 centimes or Rappen. There are no restrictions on the import or export of currency.

Generally banking hours are as follows: in Basel 08.15–17.00 hrs (Wednesday 18.30); Bern 08.00–16.30 hrs (Thursday 18.00); Genève 08.30–16.30 hrs; Lausanne 08.30–12.00, 13.30–16.30 hrs (Friday 17.00); Lugano 09.00–12.30, 13.00/13.30–16.00 hrs; Zürich 08.15/09.00–16.30, 17.00 hrs (Thursday 18.00 hrs). All banks close on Saturday.

There are exchange offices in nearly all TCS offices open during office hours. At railway stations in large towns, and at airports, exchange offices are open 08.00–20.00 hrs (these hours may vary from place to place).

Dimensions and weight restrictions

Private cars and trailers are restricted to the following dimensions – car height: 4 metres; width: 2.30 metres; caravan–length: 6 metres including tow bar; width 2.10 metres.

The fully-laden weight of trailers which do not have an independent braking system should not exceed 50% of the unladen weight of the towing vehicle, but trailers which have an independent braking system can weigh up to 100% of the unladen weight of the towing vehicle.

Luggage trailers may not be wider than the towing vehicle. Special regulations apply to four-wheel-drive vehicles towing trailers.

The Swiss Customs Officials can authorise slightly larger limits for foreign caravans for direct journeys to their destination and back, eg: width: maximum 2.20 metres (7ft 4in) if Alpine passes are used; maximum 7.00 metres (23ft) if no Alpine passes are used.

A charge is made for these special permits.

It is dangerous to use a vehicle towing a trailer on some mountain roads; motorists should

ensure that roads on which they are about to travel are suitable for the conveyance of car/trailer combinations.

Driving licence
(See also page 13)
A valid British driving licence is acceptable in Switzerland. The minimum age at which a visitor may drive a temporarily imported car is 18 years and a temporarily imported motorcycle (exceeding 125cc) 20 years.

Emergency messages to tourists
(See also page 14)
Emergency messages to tourists are broadcast daily throughout the year by Swiss Radio. Any messages broadcast in English or Spanish will be grouped together after the last news bulletin. *Radio Suisse Romande* transmitting on 392 metres medium wave broadcast these messages in French at 12.25 and 18.30hrs.
Radio Suisse Alémanique transmitting on 192 metres medium wave broadcasts the messages in German at 18.40hrs and on 565 metres medium wave at 12.25 and 18.40hrs.
Radio Suisse Italienne transmitting on 538 metres medium wave broadcasts the messages in italian at 12.25 and 18.55hrs.
Radio Suisse Internationale transmitting on short wave broadcasts in Italian at 13.35hrs on 31.46 metres, in French at 12.35hrs on 48.66 metres and in German at 13.05hrs on 75.28 metres.

International distinguishing sign
(See also page 17)
If no plate or sticker is displayed on a foreign, temporarily imported vehicle the police will impose an on-the-spot fine of up to *Fr*100. British visitors should display the standard GB sign.

Lights
(See also page 17)
Driving on sidelights only is prohibited. Spotlights are forbidden. Fog lamps can be used only in pairs of identical shape, brilliance and colour, dipped headlights must be used in cities and towns. Dipped headlights must be used at all times in tunnels, whether they are lit or not, and failure to observe this regulation can lead to a fine. Switzerland has a '*tunnel*' road sign (a red triangle showing a tunnel entrance in the centre) which serves to remind drivers to turn on their dipped headlights. In open country, headlights must be dipped: at least 200 metres (20yds) in front of any pedestrian or oncoming vehicle (including trains

parallel to the road); when requested to do so by the driver of an oncoming vehicle flashing his lights; or when reversing, travelling in lines of traffic or stopping. Dipped headlights must be used when waiting at level crossings, or near roadworks. They must also be used in badly-lit areas when visibility is poor.

It is recommended that *motorcyclists* use dipped headlights during the day.

Motoring club
(See also page 18)

The **Touring Club Suisse** has branch offices in all important towns and has its head office at 9 rue Pierre-Fatio, 1211 Genève 3 ☎(022) 371212. The TCS will extend a courtesy service to all motorists but their major services will have to be paid for. TCS offices are usually open from 08.30 to 12.00 hrs and 13.30 to 17.00 hrs, during the week and between 08.00 and 11.30 hrs on Saturday mornings (summer only). They are not open on Sunday.

Bundeshaus (Parliament Building), Berne

Motorways
There are approximately 842 miles of motorway (Autobahn or Autoroute) and more are under construction. A network of 1,143 miles is planned.

Motorways are numbered N (national road) and are divided into classes 1, 2 and 3; they vary from the usual two-lane (sometimes three) dual carriageway to 25ft wide two-lane roads with limited access points. To join a motorway follow the green and white signposts or signposts with the motorway symbol.

Motorway telephones are placed 2km ($1\frac{1}{4}$ m) apart along all motorways, and give an automatic connection with the motorway control police. Ask for TCS patrol assistance. A patrol will normally be sent, but if one is not available, help will be sent from a TCS affiliated office.

Motorway tax In 1985 the Swiss authorities will be charging motorway tax. A vehicle sticker (costing SFr30 for vehicles up to 3.5 tons) will have to be displayed by all vehicles using Swiss motorways. Motorists may purchase the sticker from AA Centres and AA Port Service Centres or at the Swiss frontier.

Orange badge scheme for disabled drivers

(See also page 19)
In Switzerland badge holders may:

a park without time limit at parking places where time limits are in force or within a blue or red zone;

b park without time limit at parking meters on payment of the minimum charge;

c park where parking is otherwise banned, provided no obstruction or danger is caused and that no other parking spaces are available. Parking is not allowed where stopping is prohibited;

d park at reserved parking places indicated by parking sign (white on blue panel) displaying the international disabled symbol.

Parking

(See also page 19)
Parking restrictions are indicated by international signs or by broken yellow lines or crosses at the side of the road, or yellow markings on pavements or poles. Parking is forbidden where it would obstruct traffic or view on a main road or one carrying fast-moving traffic, and on or within 1.5 metres (5 ft) of tram lines. Stopping is forbidden, even for passengers to get in or out of a vehicle, for unloading goods, in places marked by a continuous yellow line at the side of the road or red markings on pavements or poles. When parked on a slope or incline, use the handbrake and place chocks or wedges under the wheels. If you have to stop in a tunnel you must immediately switch off your engine. Spending the night in a vehicle or trailer on the roadside may be tolerated in some Cantons but make sure you do not contravene local regulations.

In some large towns, there are short-term parking areas known as *blue zones*. In these areas parked vehicles must display a disc on the windscreens; discs are set at the time of parking, and show when parking time expires. Restrictions apply 08.00–19.00hrs on weekdays throughout the year. Discs can be obtained from the TCS, the police, some large shops, or tobacconists' shops. Failure to observe zonal

regulations could result in a fine or the vehicle being towed away.

In Lausanne, a *red zone* system is in operation; for this, adjustable discs entitling up to 15 hours' parking are available from the local TCS office or the tourist information office. These discs may be used for either *red* or *blue zones*, one side of the disc to be used for the *blue zone* and the other for the *red zone*. Failure to observe zonal regulations could result in a fine or in the vehicle being towed away.

Passengers

(See also page 19)
Children under 12 are not permitted to travel in a vehicle as front seat passengers when rear seating is available.

Petrol

(See also page 20)
Credit cards It is unlikely that garages will accept credit cards in payment for petrol.
Duty-free petrol In addition to the petrol in the vehicle tank up to 25 litres in a can may be imported free of customs duty and tax.
Octane rating Normale (90–94) and Super (98–99).

Postal information

Mail Postcards *Fr*0.70, letters 5–20 gm *Fr*0.90.
Post offices There are 4,000 post offices in Switzerland. Opening hours are from 07.30–12.00hrs and 13.30–18.30hrs Monday to Friday and 07.30–11.00hrs Saturday.

Postcheques

(See also page 21)
Postcheques may be cashed at all post offices for a fixed sum of *Fr*150 per cheque. Counter positions are identified by the words *Paeiments/Auszahlungen/Pagamenti*. See above for post office opening hours.

Priority

(See also *Priority including Roundabouts* page 22)
When the road is too narrow for two vehicles to pass, vehicles towing trailers have priority over other vehicles; heavy vehicles over light vehicles. If two vehicles of the same category cannot pass, the vehicle nearest to the most convenient stopping point or lay-by must reverse. On mountain roads if there is no room to pass, the descending vehicle must manoeuvre to give way to the ascending vehicle – unless the ascending vehicle is obviously near a lay-by. If two vehicles are travelling in opposite

directions and the driver of each vehicle wants to turn left, they must pass in front of each other (not drive round). Drivers turning left may pass in front of traffic islands in the centre of an intersection.

Lanes reserved for buses have been introduced; these are marked with either a continuous or broken yellow line and the word 'bus'. Bus lanes may be supplemented with the sign 'Bus lane only – *Voie réservée aux bus*' (a circular blue sign with the white silhouette of a bus superimposed on it). Only the broken yellow line may be crossed, either at a junction when turning or to enter the premises of a company.

Public holidays
Official public holidays in Switzerland for 1985 are given below. There are other official public holidays such as Epiphany, Corpus Christi and All Saints' Day, but they vary from canton to canton. See also *Public holidays* page 22.
January 1 (New Year's Day)
January 2 (Bank Holiday)
April 5 (Good Friday)
April 8 (Easter Monday)
May 1 (Labour Day)
May 16 (Ascension Day)
May 27 (Whit Monday)
August 1 (Swiss National Day)
December 25 (Christmas Day)
December 26 (Boxing Day)

Religious services
(See also page 23)
The Intercontinental Church Society welcomes visitors from any denomination to English language services in the following centres:
4051 Basel The Revd Canon Tom Roberts, Chaplain's Flat, Henric Petri Strasse 26 *tel* (061)235761
1807 Blonay (near Vevey) The Revd Timothy Barlow, La Parsonage, Champsavaux *tel* (021)532239

Roads including holiday traffic
The road surfaces are generally good, but some main roads are narrow in places.

Traffic congestion may be severe at the beginning and end of the German school holidays (See page 197).

On any stretch of mountain road, the driver of a private car may be asked by the driver of a postal bus, which is painted yellow, to reverse, or otherwise manoeuvre to allow the postal bus to pass.

Postal bus drivers often sound a distinctive three note horn and no other vehicles may use this type of horn in Switzerland.

Shopping hours
Shops are open in general 08.30–18.30hrs from Monday to Friday, and 08.30–16.00hrs on Saturdays with the exception of *food stores* which close at 17.30hrs. In large towns some stores close on Monday morning.

Speed limits
(See also page 25)
Because the country is mountainous with many narrow and twisting roads, it is not safe to maintain a high speed. Built-up areas are indicated by signs bearing the placename and in these areas the speed limit is 50 kph (31 mph) for all vehicles.

Outside built-up areas the limit is 100 kph (62 mph) except on motorways where vehicles are subject to a limit of 130 kph (80 mph). Car/caravan or luggage trailer combinations are restricted to 80 kph (49 mph) on all roads outside built-up areas. These limits do not apply if another limit is indicated by signs or if the vehicle is subject to a lower general speed limit.

Spiked, studded or snow tyres
(See also page 10)
Spiked or studded tyres may be used on light vehicles and on trailers drawn by such vehicles from 1 November to 31 March provided they are fitted to all four wheels and a speed of 80 kph (49 mph) is not exceeded. They are prohibited on motorways and semi-motorways with the exception of the N13 between Thusis and Mesocco and between Göschenen and Airolo on the N2 (St Gothard road tunnel). Spiked or studded tyres may not be substituted for wheel chains when these are compulsory. On-the-spot fines of *Fr* 30 are imposed for the use of spiked or studded tyres after 31 March.

Tourist information offices
(See also page 25)
The Swiss Government maintains an excellent information service in London at the Swiss National Tourist Office, 1 New Coventry Street, W1V 8EE ☎01-734 1921. In all provincial towns and resorts throughout the country there are tourist information offices who are pleased to help tourists with local information and advice.

Using the telephone
(See also page 26)
Insert coin **after** lifting receiver, dialling tone

continuous tone. When making calls to subscribers within Switzerland precede number with relevant area code (shown in parentheses against town entry in gazetteer). Use coins to the value of 40 cents for local calls and *Fr*1 or 5 coins for national and international calls.

International callbox identification All callboxes.
Telephone rates A direct dial call to the UK costs *Fr*1.80 per minute. Local calls are cheaper at weekends.
What to dial for the Irish Republic 00 353.
What to dial for the UK 00 44.

Warning triangles/Hazard warning lights

The use of a warning triangle is compulsory for all vehicles except two-wheelers. The triangle must be placed on the road at least 50 metres (55yds) behind the vehicle on ordinary roads and at least 150 metres (164yds) on motorways. Hazard warning lights may be used in conjunction with the triangle on ordinary roads, but on motorways and semi-motorways they must be switched off as soon as the warning triangle is erected. If this is not done the police may impose an *on-the-spot* fine (see page 21). See also *Warning triangles/Hazard warning lights* page 26.

Weather services

The Touring Club Suisse operates a weather service to give up-to-the-minute conditions of mountain passes. The information appears on notices placed at strategic points along the roads leading up to the passes. When the weather is exceptional, special bulletins are issued by the TCS through the press and broadcasting services. You can also get road/weather reports in French, German or Italian, according to the canton from which the call is made on the national telephone system by dialling 162 (weather) or 163 (road conditions).

Locarno, on Lake Maggiore

Wheel chains

(See also page 10)
These are generally necessary on journeys to places at high altitudes. Roads with a sign 'chains compulsory' (a tyre with chains on it drawn on a white board which also includes the name of the road) are closed to cars without wheel chains. It is a punishable offence to drive without this equipment.

Winter conditions

(See also page 27)
Entry from France and Germany: the main entries are seldom affected, although the Faucille pass on the Dijon–Genève road, and also minor routes through the Jura, Vosges, and Black Forest may be obstructed.

To Italy: from western Switzerland – during the winter months this is via the Grand St Bernard road tunnel or the Simplon rail tunnel (see page 39); wheel chains are sometimes necessary on the approach to the Grand St Bernard road tunnel. From central Switzerland use the St Gotthard road tunnel. From eastern Switzerland, the San Bernardino tunnel (see page 38) or the Julier or Maloja passes can be used.

To Austria: the route across northern Switzerland via Liechtenstein is open all the year.

Within the country: the main highways linking Basel, Zürich, Luzern, Bern, Lausanne, and Genève are unaffected. The high passes are usually closed in the winter months but it is generally possible to drive within reasonable distance of all winter sports resorts. According to weather conditions, wheel chains may be compulsory or snow tyres necessary.

Liechtenstein

National flag Blue over red in two strips of equal breadth

The principality of Liechtenstein has a population of 23,000 and an area of 65 sq miles. Although it is an independent state it is represented in diplomatic and other matters by Switzerland. Vaduz is the capital.

Traffic regulations, insurance laws, and the monetary unit are the same as for Switzerland and prices are adjusted to match those in the major country.

Prices are in Swiss Francs
Abbreviations:
pl   place, platz
pza   piazza
r   rue
rte   route
str   strasse

AARAU
Aargau (☎064)

⏚F Brack Buchserstr 19 ☎221851 P
Frd

⏚F Glaus Entfelderstr 8 ☎221332 Dat

ADELBODEN
Bern (☎033)

★ ★ ★ ★Nevada Palace ☎732131
tx922184
15 Dec – 15 Apr & 15 Jun – 15 Sep
rm72 ⇌55 ᠓6 ♨ P Lift ☽
sB 57 – 77 sB ⇌ ᠓167 – 127 dB 114 – 154
dB ⇌ ᠓134 – 254 M30 ⤶ Pool
mountains

★ ★Parkhotel Bellevue ☎731621
Dec – Apr & Jun – Oct
rm60 ⇌35 ᠓10 P Lift sB65 – 105
sB ⇌ ᠓80 – 130 dB ⇌ ᠓240 M20 – 30
Pool mountains

★Alpenrose ☎731161
Jun – Sep & Mid Dec – Apr
rm37 ⇌8 ᠓3 A5rm ♨ P sB42 – 56
sB ⇌ ᠓55 – 72 dB84 – 112
dB ⇌ ᠓108 – 136 M20 – 25 mountains

★Bären ☎732151
rm12 sB42 – 58 sB ⇌ ᠓52 – 68
dB84 – 116 dB ⇌ ᠓104 – 136

ADLISWIL See ZÜRICH

AESCHI
Bern (☎033)

★ ★Baumgarten ☎544121
rm23 ⇌5 ᠓14 ♨ P sB28 – 35
sB ⇌ ᠓38 – 47 dB50 – 60
dB ⇌ ᠓70 – 90 mountains

AIGLE
Vaud (☎025)

★ ★Nord r Colomb 4 ☎261055 tx76703
⇌13 ᠓6 P Lift sB ⇌70 – 95
dB ⇌100 – 140 mountains

AIROLO
Ticino (☎094)

⏚Airolo (A.Piccinonno) ☎881765 AR
Cit

⏚S Gottardo ☎881177 P Toy

⏚Wolfisberg via San Gottardo
☎881055 M/c BL Chy Vlo

ALPNACHSTAD
Obwalden (☎041)

★ ★Rössli ☎961181
rm49 ⇌18 ᠓20 ♨ P Pool
mountains lake

ALTDORF
Uri (☎044)

★Schwarzer Löwen Gothardstr ☎21007
rm19 ⇌5 ♨ Lift mountains

Switzerland

⏚Central (B.Musch) Gothardstr 54
☎21120 M/c P Cit Dat Vlo

ALTERSWIL
Fribourg (☎037)

⏚A Piller Hofmatt ☎441237 BL

AMSTEG
Uri (☎044)

★ ★ ★Stern & Post (ROM) Gothardstr
☎64440 tx866385
rm40 ⇌20 ♨ P Lift sB37 sB ⇌52
dB68 – 83 dB ⇌113 – 143 M12 – 30
mountains

ANDERMATT
Uri (☎044)

★ ★Badus ☎67286
Closed Nov
rm23 ⇌11 ᠓9 ♨ P Lift sB28 – 37
sB ⇌ ᠓34 – 42 dB68 – 74
dB ⇌ ᠓68 – 84 mountains

★ ★Helvetia (MIN) ☎67515 tx868608
rm33 ⇌18 ᠓12 P Lift sB ⇌ ᠓43 – 52
dB68 – 84 dB ⇌ ᠓82 – 100 M8 – 40
mountains

★ ★Ideal Krone ☎67206 tx868605
Closed Nov
rm49 ⇌14 ᠓25 P Lift sB33 – 53
sB ⇌ ᠓41 – 64 dB66 – 106
dB ⇌ ᠓82 – 128 M12 – 30 mountains

★ ★Monopol Metropol ☎67575
tx868606
Jun – Oct & Dec – Apr
rm31 ⇌18 ᠓12 ♨ P Lift
sB ⇌ ᠓41 – 64 dB ⇌ ᠓82 – 128 M aic
Pool mountains

⏚L Loretz Gotthardstr 38 ☎67243 P
Ren

APPENZELL
Appenzell (☎071)

★ ★ ★Hecht (Amb) Hauptgasse 9
☎871025
Closed 24 Nov – 22 Dec
rm42 ⇌14 ☽19 P Lift sB35 – 45
sB ⇌ ᠓45 – 65 dB60 – 75
dB ⇌ ᠓85 – 120 M7 – 60

★ ★Mettien ☎871246
rm44 ᠓29 A15rm P sB30 – 35
sB ᠓35 – 40 dB68 – 76 dB ᠓78 – 90
mountains

★ ★Santis (ROM) ☎872644
Closed 11 Jan – 9 Feb
rm33 ⇌22 ᠓11 P Lift sB35 – 75
sB ⇌ ᠓50 – 70 dB65 – 80
dB ⇌ ᠓85 – 135 mountains

⏚W Baumann Weissbadstr 11
☎871466 M/c Cit Dat Peu

ARBON
Thurgau (☎071)

★ ★ ★Metropol (Amb) Bahnhofstr 49
☎463535 tx77247
rm42 ⇌18 ᠓24 P Lift ☽
sB ⇌ ᠓87 – 104 dB ⇌ ᠓140 Pool
lake mountains

★Frohsinn Romanshornerstr 15
☎461046
rm7 ⇌1 P Lake

★Rotes Kreuz ☎461914
Closed Jan
rm26 ⇌2 ᠓7 P mountains lake

ARLESHEIM
Basel (☎061)

★Ochsen ☎725225
rm27 ⇌3 ᠓11 ♨ P sB33 – 35
sB ⇌ ᠓53 – 58 dB65 – 70
dB ⇌ ᠓85 – 90

AROLLA
Valais (☎027)

★ ★Grand Hotel & Kurhaus ☎831161
Jul – Aug & 20 Dec – 20 Apr
rm79 ⇌25 ᠓40 P Lift sBfr36
sB ⇌ ᠓35 – 61 dBfr56 dB ⇌ ᠓60 – 104
mountains

AROSA
Graubünden (☎081)

★ ★ ★Kulm ☎310131 tx74279
24 Jun – Sep & 26 Nov – 24 Apr
rm146 ⇌116 ᠓30 P Lift ☽
sB ⇌ ᠓80 – 290 dB ⇌ ᠓140 – 500 ⤶
Pool mountains

★ ★ ★Alexandra-Palace ☎310111
tx74261
rm163 ⇌158 ᠓5 ♨ P Lift ☽
sB ⇌ ᠓92 – 200 dB ⇌180 – 400 M18
Pool mountains

★ ★ ★Cristallo ☎312261 tx74270
15 Jul – 10 Oct & Dec – 20 Jun
⇌40 P Lift ☽ sB ⇌ ᠓65 – 165
dB ⇌ ᠓120 – 290 mountains

★ ★Seehof ☎311541 tx74277
Dec – Apr
rm90 ⇌70 ♨ P Lift ☽ lake

★ ★ ★Sporthotel Valsana (Amb)
☎310275 tx74232
26 Nov – 24 Apr & 23 Jun – 13 Oct
rm86 ⇌62 ᠓24 ♨ P Lift ☽
sB ⇌ ᠓80 – 105 dB ⇌ ᠓140 – 190
mountains lake

⏚Grand Dosch ☎312222 M/c P AR
Chy MB Opl Vau

ARTH-AM-SEE
Schwyz (☎041)

⏚Rigi Zugerstr 17 – 23 ☎821223 M/c P
Chy Peu

ASCONA
Ticino (☎093)

★ ★ ★ ★Acapulco au Lac Lago di
Maggiore ☎354521 tx846135
Mar – Oct
rm42 ⇌37 ᠓4 P Lift ☽
sB ⇌ ᠓74 – 145 dB ⇌ ᠓112 – 212
M alc Pool lake

★ ★ ★ ★Eden Roc via Albarelle
☎350171 tx846164

Closed 16 Mar – 4 Apr
↰45 🏛 P Lift ☾ dB ↰240–36
M34–44 Pool lake

★ ★ ★Ascona (Amb) via Collina
☎351135 tx846035

Mar – Dec
rm75 ↰45 🍴30 🏛 P Lift ☾
sB ↰ 🍴90–135 dB ↰ 🍴180–260
M alc Pool mountains lake

★ ★ ★Schweizerhof via Locarno
☎351214

Mar – Oct
rm43 ↰21 🍴22 P Lift sB ↰ 🍴55–77
dB ↰ 🍴110–154 Pool mountains

★ ★ ★Tamaro au Lac ☎350282
tx846132

Mar – 25 Nov
rm54 ↰21 🍴22 A9rm Lift sB42–52
sB ↰ 🍴62–72 dB84–104
dB ↰ 🍴124–144 M18–23 Pool lake

★Piazza au Lac ☎351181

Mar – Nov
rm10 🍴15 A5rm P sB 🍴50–70
dB 🍴86–130 mountains lake

&ⓋC Buzzini via Locarno 124 ☎352414
Aud VW

&ⓋCristallina via Circonvallazione
☎354585 P AR BL Maz

&ⓋStorell via Cantonale ☎352196 MB
Toy

AVENCHES
Vaud (☎037)

&ⓋJ P Divorne rte de Berne 6 ☎751263
P Opl

BAAR
Zug (☎042)

★ ★Lindenhof Dorfstr ☎311220

rm8 ↰3 🍴2 P Lift sB30–35
sB ↰ 🍴45–48 dB50 dB ↰ 🍴65–70
M15–35

BADEN
Aargau (☎056)

★ ★ ★Parc (Amb) Haselstr 9 ☎201311
tx53911

rm73 ↰26 🍴47 P Lift ☾
sB ↰ 🍴80–98 dB ↰ 🍴116–116

★ ★Verenahof Kurpl ☎225251

rm130 ↰90 🍴15 🏛 P Lift ☾
sB65–87 sB↰🍴92–135 dB130–162
dB↰🍴162–227 Pool mountains

&ⓋKappelerhof (J Miller) ☎227326 P
Aud VW

BAD-RAGAZ-PFÄFERS See **RAGAZ-PFÄFERS (BAD)**

BAD SCUOL See **SCUOL (BAD)**

BÂLE See **BASEL**

BALSTHAL
Solothurn (☎062)

Switzerland

★Kreuz Hauptstr ☎713412

rm18 ↰3 🍴7 🏛 Lift sB25
dB ↰ 🍴35–45 dB50 dB ↰ 🍴60–70

★Rössli ☎715858

🍴6 P sB22 sB 🍴25–30 dB44
dB 🍴50–60

BASEL (BÂLE) (☎061)
See plan page 366

★ ★ ★ ★ ★Basel Hilton Aeschengraben
31 ☎226622 tx62055 Plan **2A**

↰ 🍴226 P Lift ☾ sB ↰ 🍴120–175
dB ↰ 🍴180–245 Pool mountains

★ ★ ★ ★ ★Drei Könige Blumenrain 8
☎255252 tx62937 Plan **1**

↰80 🏛 P Lift ☾ sB ↰ 🍴130–180
dB ↰190–280

★ ★ ★ ★Euler Centralbahnpl 14
☎234500 tx62215 Plan **2**

↰66 🏛 P Lift ☾ sB ↰ 🍴108–160
dB ↰165–240 M28

★ ★ ★International (Amb)
Steinentorstr 25 ☎221870 tx62370
Plan **3**

rm200 ↰188 🍴12 🏛 P Lift ☾
sB ↰ 🍴100–165 dB ↰ 🍴140–230
M15–30 Pool

★ ★ ★ ★Schweizerhof Centralbahnpl 1
☎222833 tx62369 Plan **4**

↰75 P Lift ☾ sB ↰95–140
dB ↰145–190 M alc

★ ★ ★Bernina Basel Innere
Margarethenstr 14 (n.rest) ☎237300
tx63813 Plan **5**

rm36 ↰20 🍴16 🏛 P Lift ☾
sB50–75 sB ↰ 🍴70–120 dB 70–105
dB ↰ 🍴110–180 M15–20

★ ★ ★Cavalier (MIN) Reiterstr 1
☎392262 Plan **6**

15 Jan – 20 Dec
rm27 ↰21 🍴6 P Lift sB ↰ 48–80
dB ↰82–120

★ ★ ★Drachen Aeschenvorstadt 24
☎239090 tx62346 Plan **7**

rm38 ↰18 🍴17 🏛 P Lift ☾
sB44–56 sB ↰ 🍴62–78
dB ↰ 🍴105–125

★ ★ ★Europe (ETAP) Clarastr 35–43
☎268080 tx64103 Plan **8**

rm170 ↰40 🍴130 P Lift ☾
sB ↰ 🍴118–138 dB ↰ 🍴158–178
M alc

★ ★ ★Excelsior Aeschengraben 13
(n.rest) ☎225300 tx62303 Plan **9**

↰36🏛 P Lift ☾

★ ★ ★Merian am Rhein (KA) Rheingasse
2 ☎259466 tx63537 Plan **10**

rm54 ↰29 🍴17 🏛 P Lift sB45–55
sB ↰ 🍴85–98 dB ↰ 🍴130–160

★ ★Greub Centralbahnstr 11 ☎231840
Plan **11**

rm50 ↰7 P Lift ☾ sB38–48
sB ↰50–70 dB60–80 dB ↰120–150

★ ★Jura Centralbahnpl 11 ☎231800
Plan **12**

rm80 ↰7 🍴30 P Lift ☾ sB47–62
sB ↰ 🍴72–92 dB78–103
dB ↰ 🍴113–163

★ ★Krafft Rheingasse 12 ☎268877
tx64360 Plan **13**

rm52 ↰16 🍴29 P Lift ☾ sB 42–54
sB ↰ 🍴66–80 dB73–93
dB ↰ 🍴90–130 M9–26

★ ★Merkur Theaterstr 24 ☎233740
Plan **14**

rm22 P sB35–50 sB ↰ 🍴55–80
dB65–90 dB ↰ 🍴85–120

★ ★Rochat Petersgraben 23 ☎258140
Plan **14A**

rm48 ↰18 🍴6 P Lift ☾ sB48
sB ↰ 🍴48–72 dB80 dB ↰ 🍴80–120
M9–15

★ ★St-Gotthard-Terminus
Centralbahnstr 13 ☎225250 Plan **15**

rm38 ↰9 🍴4 P Lift ☾ sB35–50
sB ↰ 🍴55–80 dB65–90
dB ↰ 🍴85–120

★ ★Victoria am Bahnhof Centralbahnpl
3–4 ☎225566 tx62362 Plan **16**

rm115 ↰15 🍴84 🏛 P Lift ☾
sB50–65 sB ↰ 🍴80–98 dB80–90
dB ↰ 🍴130–150 M alc

★Bristol Centralbahnstr 15 ☎223822
Plan **17**

rm30 ↰3 🍴1 P Lift ☾ sB35–50
sB ↰ 🍴65–80 dB65–90
dB ↰ 🍴85–120 Mfr9

★Engelhof Ecke Nadelberg/Stiftsgasse 1
(n.rest) ☎252244 Plan **19**

rm47 ↰6 🍴3 🏛 P Lift sB32–44
sB ↰ 🍴52–59 dB64–75
dB ↰ 🍴84–90

&ⓋAutavia Hardstr 14 ☎427878 Frd

&ⓋDelta Münchenstein ☎466288 Hon

Dreispitz (G. Kenk) Reinacherstr 28
☎501550 BL Chy

&ⓋDufour Dufourstr 36 ☎231214

&ⓋGrosspeter Grosspeterstr 12
☎507000 P Opl

&ⓋOlympic Vladuktstr 45 ☎230126 BMW
Chy

&ⓋSt-Johann Ruffstr 16 ☎438450 BL Fia

&ⓋC Schlotterbeck Viaduktstr 40
☎220050 BL Cit

&ⓋSettelen Turkheimerstr 17 ☎383800
BL RT Toy

&ⓋG Uecker Nafelserstr 19 ☎385076
Chy Sim

BEATENBERG
Bern (☎036)

★Beauregard ☎411341

Dec – Apr & May – Oct →

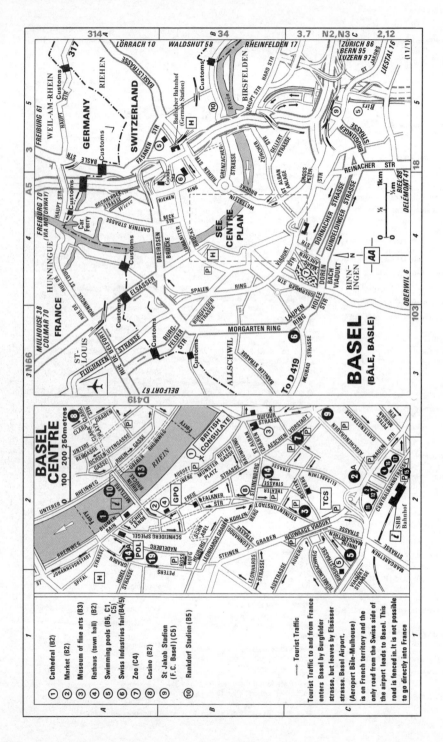

BASEL (BÂLE, BASLE)

① Cathedral (B2)
② Market (B2)
③ Museum of fine arts (B3)
④ Rathaus (town hall) (B2)
⑤ Swimming pools (B5, C1, C5)
⑥ Swiss Industries fair (B4/5)
⑦ Zoo (C4)
⑧ Casino (B2)
⑨ St Jakob Stadion (F.C. Basel) (C5)
⑩ Rankdorf Stadion (B5)

→ Tourist Traffic

Tourist Traffic to and from France enters Basel by Burgfelder strasse, but leaves by Elsasser strasse. Basel Airport. (Aeroport Bâle-Mulhouse) is on French territory and the only road from the Swiss side of the airport leads to Basel. This road is fenced in. It is not possible to go directly into France

BASEL CENTRE
0 100 200 250metres

rm22 ⇌6 sB25-35 sB ⇌35-42
dB50-70 dB ⇌70-80 lake
★Jungfraublick (MIN) ☎411581
rm13 ▥10 sB25-38 sB ⇌ ▥35-47
dB50-70 dB ⇌ ▥60-80 mountains lake

BECKENRIED
Nidwalden (☎041)
★★Edelweiss ☎641252
rm25 ⇌4 ▥3 🆒 P sB31-36
dB ⇌ ▥51 dB52-92 dB ⇌ ▥82-92
M17-20 mountains lake
★Mond ☎641204
rm34 P Lift sB30 sB ▥40 dB60
dB ▥78 M12-16 mountains lake
★Sonne ☎641205
rm34 P sBfr25 dBfr50 mountains lake

BELLINZONA
Ticino(☎092)
★★★Unione Gl-Guisan ☎255577 tx846277
rm35 ⇌21 ▥8 P Lift sB30-35
sB ⇌ ▥50-60 dB60-70
dB ⇌ ▥85-95 mountains
♫Ferrari via Lugano 31 ☎251668 P Toy
♫Gottardo viale Portone 6 ☎252818 BL Hon
♫Pedrini via Lugano 18 255274 Peu

BASEL (BÂLE)
- 1 ★★★★ Drei Könige
- 2 ★★★★ Euler
- 2A ★★★★ Basel Hilton
- 3 ★★★★ International
- 4 ★★★★ Schweizerhof
- 5 ★★★★ Bernina Basel
- 6 ★★★★ Cavalier
- 7 ★★★★ Drachen
- 8 ★★★★ Europe
- 9 ★★★★ Excelsior
- 10 ★★★ Merian am Rhein
- 11 ★★★ Greub
- 12 ★★★ Jura
- 13 ★★★ Krafft
- 14 ★★★ Merkur
- 14A ★★★ Rochat
- 15 ★★★ St-Gotthard-Terminus
- 16 ★★★ Victoria am Bahnhof
- 17 ★ Bristol
- 19 ★ Engelhof

Switzerland

BERLINGEN
Thurgau(☎054)
★Seestern ☎82404
Feb-Dec
rm9 ▥1 sB35-40 dB ▥35-45
dB48-55 dB ▥65-70 lake

BERN (BERNE)
Bern(☎031)
★★★★★Bellevue Palace
Kochergasse 3-5 ☎224581 tx32124
⇌150 🆒 P Lift ♪ sB ⇌ ▥140-165
dB ⇌ ▥210-260 mountains river
★★★★★Schweizerhof (Amb)
Bahnhofpl 11 (Nr Station) ☎224501 tx32188
⇌90 P Lift ♪ sB ⇌115-160
dB ⇌185-260
★★★★City Mövenpick Bubenbergpl 7 ☎225377 tx22323
rm47 ⇌25 ▥22 P Lift ♪
sB ⇌ ▥90-110 dB ⇌ ▥118-138 M alc
★★★★Savoy Neuengasse 26 (n.rest) ☎224405 tx32445
rm55 ⇌17 ▥33 P Lift ♪ sB55-70
sB ⇌ ▥80-105 dB90-105
dB ⇌ ▥110-140
★★★Bären (Amb) Schauplatzgasse 4 ☎223367 tx33199
rm57 ⇌23 ▥34 Lift ♪
sB ⇌ ▥80-105 dB ⇌ ▥110-140·
★★★Bern Zeughausgasse 9 ☎211021 tx33055
rm100 ⇌20 ▥80 Lift ♪
sB ⇌ ▥93-113 dB ⇌ ▥126-150 M15
★★★Bristol Schauplatzgasse 10 (off Bärenpl) (n.rest) ☎220101 tx33199
rm83 ⇌16 ▥36 P Lift ♪ sB55-65
sB ⇌ ▥80-105 dB ⇌ ▥110-140
★★★Touring Eigerpl ☎458666 tx33356
rm56 ⇌16 ▥31 Lift sB45
sB ⇌ ▥55-75 dB ⇌ ▥84-115
★★★Wächter (Mövenpick) Neuengasse 44 ☎220866 tx33232
rm44 ⇌8 ▥27 Lift ♪ sB46-53
sB ⇌ ▥82-103 dB ⇌ ▥110-130
★★Continental Zeughausgasse 27 (n.rest) ☎222626 tx33611
rm38 ⇌5 ▥17 P Lift ♪ sB40-52
sB ⇌ ▥58-75 dB72-85
dB ⇌ ▥86-110
★Goldener Schlüssel Rathausgasse 72 ☎220216
rm29 P Lift ♪ sB36-42 sB ▥48-55
dB65-72 dB ▥84-90
♫Auto Marti Eigerpl 2 ☎451515 BMW
♫Citroën (Suisse) Freiburgstr 447 ☎553311 P Cit

♫Egghölzli Egghölzlistr 1 ☎446366 P Hon Peu Vau
♫Schultheiss Hofweg 5 ☎427742 P Frd
♫Willy Freiburgstr 443 ☎552511 P Fia Frd
At **GÜMLIGEN** (6km E)
♫Schwarz ☎523636 P Vlo
At **MURI** (3km SE on N6)
☆☆Krone ☎521666
rm28 ⇌4 ▥9 🆒 P sB35-48
sB ⇌ ▥82-100 dB58-86
dB ⇌ ▥100-125 M14-32
♫Bigler & Bürki Thunstr 25 ☎521600 P BL
At **WABERN** (2km S)
♫Wabern Seftigenstr 198 ☎542622 P BL Maz

BEX-LES-BAINS
Vaud(☎025)
☆St-Christophe ☎652979
rm18 ▥10 A4rm P sB40 sB ▥50
dB60 dB ▥90
♫Rallye (W Dreier) r Servannaz ☎631225 Sab Toy

BIASCA
Ticino(☎092)
★★Poste via Stazione ☎722121
rm10 🆒 P ♪ mountains
♫Maggetti via San Gottardo ☎721266 Chy Peu

BIEL (BIENNE)
Bern(☎032)
★★★★Élite pl Gl-Guisan ☎225441 tx34101
rm62 ⇌45 ▥15 🆒 Lift ♪
sB ⇌ ▥75-98 dB;⇌ ▥100-140
★★★Continental (Amb) r d'Aarberg 29 ☎223255 tx34440
rm80 ⇌50 ▥30 🆒 P Lift ♪
sB ⇌62-86 dB ⇌86-125
♫W Mühle Heilmannstr 16 ☎222201 M/c P BL Ren
♫Progress Portstr 32 ☎259666 AR Hon

BISSONE
Ticino(☎091)
★★★Lago di Lugano ☎688591 tx79378
Mar-Dec
⇌80 🆒 P Lift ♪ sB ⇌60-160
dB ⇌95-185 M25-45 Pool mountains lake

BIVIO
Graubünden(☎081)
★★★Post ☎751275
Closed Nov
rm50 ⇌18 ▥14 A20rm 🆒 P ♪
sB28-35 sB ⇌ ▥50-60 dB50-70
dB ⇌ ▥100-120 M12-25 mountains

BOLLINGEN
St-Gallen(☎055)

☆ ☆ **Schiff** am Oberen Zürichsee
☎283888

🏠15 🏨 **P** 🌙 mountains lake

BÖNIGEN
Bern(☎036)

★ ★ ★**Seller au Lac** (Amb) ☎223021
tx923164

15 Dec–15 Nov
rm50 ⇆32 🏠15 🏨 **P** 🌙 Lift
sB ⇆ 🏠85–124 dB ⇆ 🏠150–221
M20–35 mountains lake

BOURG ST PIERRE
Valais(☎026)

⚡Tunnel du Grand St-Bernard (R
Ellenberger) ☎49124

BRÉ See **LUGANO**

BRIENZ
Bern(☎036)

★ ★**Bären** ☎512412
rm33 ⇆4 🏠6 🏨 Lift sB28–38
sB ⇆ 🏠36–42 dB56–72
dB ⇆ 🏠70–104 Pool

★ ★**Gare** ☎512712
rm10 🏠3 **P** sB28–30 dB56–60
dB 🏠66–70 M10–30 mountains

★ ★**Schönegg** (n.rest) ☎511113
rm15 ⇆4 🏠2 **P** sB38 dB50
dB ⇆84–96 mountains lake

BRIG (BRIGUE)
Valais(☎028)

★ ★ ★**Sporting** (n.rest) ☎232363
rm33 ⇆6 🏠15 🏨 Lift sB28–39
sB ⇆ 🏠35–48 dB50–65
dB ⇆ 🏠60–80

★ ★ ★**Viktoria-Terminus** (Amb)
Bahnhofstr 2 ☎231503 tx473861
Closed Nov
rm40 ⇆19 🏠15 🏨 **P** Lift 🌙
sB42–54 sB ⇆ 🏠50–70
dB ⇆ 🏠85–120 M22–36 mountains

★ ★**Brigerhof** Rhonesandstr 18 (n.rest)
☎231607
Feb–Oct
rm30 ⇆5 🏠18 🏨 **P** Lift sB38–48
dB ⇆ 🏠70–80

At **GILS** (2km E)
⚡**Saltina** (H Schwery) ☎232562 Toy

BRIGELS
Graubünden(☎086)

★ ★ ★**Eurotel** la Val Breil ☎41252
tx74577
⇆40 **P** Lift sB ⇆40–90 dB ⇆64–150
M15 Pool mountains

BRISSAGO
Ticino(☎093)

★ ★**Mirto au Lac** ☎651328
Apr–Nov
rm28 ⇆14 🏠14 🏨 **P** Lift sB ⇆fr45
dB ⇆80–104 Mfr15 lake

Switzerland

BRUGG
Aargau(☎056)

★ ★ ★**Rotes Haus** Haupstr 7 ☎411479
tx53084
rm24 ⇆6 🏠18 🏨 **P** Lift 🌙
sB ⇆ 🏠39–46 dB ⇆ 🏠70–78

BRUNNEN
Schwyz(☎043)

★ ★ ★**Waidstätterhof** (Amb) ☎331133
tx78378
Mar–20 Jan
rm100 ⇆75 🏠25 🏨 **P** Lift 🌙
sB ⇆ 🏠79–119 dB ⇆ 🏠138–198
M25–30 🏊 mountains lake

★ ★**Bellevue** Vierwaldstratterisee
☎311318 tx78313
Etr–15 Oct
⇆50 🏨 **P** Lift 🌙 sB ⇆70–75
dB ⇆120–130 mountains lake

★ ★**Élite & Aurora** ☎311024
6 Jan–Oct
rm90 ⇆34 🏠24 A22rm **P** Lift
sB35–50 sB ⇆ 🏠50–61 dB60–92
dB ⇆ 🏠90–116 M19 mountains lake

★ ★**Metropole au Lac** ☎311039
Mar–Nov
rm21 ⇆1 🏠8 🏨 Lift sB35–45
sB ⇆ 🏠46–56 dB60–90
dB ⇆ 🏠82–112 lake

★ ★**Schmid** ☎311882
Mar–Nov
rm20 ⇆9 🏨 **P** Lift sB43–53
dB80–105 dB ⇆95–155 M alc
mountains lake

★ ★**Weisses-Rössli** ☎311022
rm30 ⇆3 🏠1 **P** sB30–38
sB ⇆ 🏠36–50 dB54–70
dB ⇆ 🏠66–94 M19–25

★**Alpina** ☎311813
rm22 ⇆2 🏠8 🏨 **P** sB30–38
sB ⇆ 🏠36–50 dB54–76
dB ⇆ 🏠66–100 M15 mountains

⚡**Inderbitzin** Gersauerstr 17
☎311313 Aud VW

BUCHS
St-Gallen(☎085)

⚡**Sulser** St Gallerstr 19 ☎61414 Opl
Vau

BULLE
Fribourg(☎029)

★ ★**Rallye** rte de Riaz 8 ☎28498
tx940017
🏠15 🏨 **P** Lift 🌙 sB 🏠43 dB 🏠80
mountains

BÜRCHEN
Valais(☎028)

★ ★ ★**Bürchnerhof** ☎442434
Dec–mid Apr & May–Nov

⇆ 🏠18 **P** sB ⇆ 🏠44–50
dB ⇆ 🏠76–88 mountains

BURGDORF
Bern(☎034)

⚡**Central** ☎228288 **P** Cit Vau

BÜRGENSTOCK
Nidwalden(☎041)

★**Waldheim** (MIN) ☎641306
rm55 ⇆8 🏠31 🏨 **P** Lift sB30
sB ⇆ 🏠47–57 dB60 dB ⇆ 🏠94–114
Pool mountains

BUSSIGNY See **LAUSANNE**

CASSARATE See **LUGANO**

CASTAGNOLA See **LUGANO**

CELERINA
Graubünden(☎082)

★ ★ ★**Cresta Palace** (Amb) ☎33564
tx74461
23 Jun–22 Sep & 17 Dec–23 Apr
rm98 ⇆52 🏠29 🏨 **P** Lift 🌙
sB77–105 sB ⇆ 🏠95–165 dB148–200
dB ⇆ 🏠222–320 Pool mountains

★ ★**Cresta Kulm** ☎33373
Dec–Apr & Jun–Sep
rm50 ⇆27 🏠6 A5rm 🏨 **P** Lift 🌙
sB70–100 sB ⇆ 🏠80–110 dB140–200
dB ⇆ 🏠160–220 mountains

CHAM
Zug(☎042)

⚡**Ettmüller** Steinhauserstr ☎363133 **P**
Cit

CHAMPÉRY
Valais(☎025)

★ ★**Alpes** ☎791222
15 Dec–15 Apr & 10 Jun–20 Sep
rm25 ⇆21 sB33–54 sB ⇆ 🏠43–78
dB56–92 dB ⇆ 🏠73–133

★ ★**Beau-Séjour** ☎791701
Dec–Apr & Jun–Sep
rm22 ⇆6 🏠16 **P** Lift sB ⇆ 🏠48–68
dB ⇆ 🏠80–120 mountains

★ ★**Parc** ☎791313
Jun–Sep, Dec–Apr
rm30 ⇆8 🏠15 sB33–54
sB ⇆ 🏠43–78 dB56–92
dB ⇆ 🏠73–133 Pool mountains

CHÂTEAU-D'OEX
Vaud(☎029)

★ ★ ★**Beau-Séjour** ☎47423 tx940022
Dec–Nov
rm44 ⇆21 🏠4 **P** Lift 🌙 sB35–50
sB ⇆ 🏠42–65 dB66–98
dB ⇆ 🏠80–120 mountains

★ ★ ★**Hostellerie du Bon Accueil**
☎46320 tx940083
Jun–15 Oct & 15 Dec–Apr
⇆12 **P** sB ⇆ 🏠70 dB66–98
dB ⇆ 🏠120 mountains

★ ★**Victoria** ☎46434
Dec–Apr & May–Oct
rm18 ⇆15 🏠3 🏨 **P** Lift

368

sB ⇋ 🍴42–65 dB ⇋ 🍴80–120 Pool
mountains

🕭Burnand ☎47539 P BL Cit Toy Vlo

🕭Pont Petit Pré ☎46173 M/c P Opl Vau

CHÂTELET (LE) See GSTEIG

CHAUX-DE-FONDS (LA)
Neuchâtel(☎39)

★ ★ ★Club r du Parc 71 ☎235300
tx35548
⇋40 Lift sB ⇋65–70 dB ⇋109–130

🕭E Frey r F-Courvoisier 28 ☎231362 P
Chy Sim

🕭Metropole r du Locle 64 ☎269595 AR
BL DJ Frd

🕭Trois Rois bd des Eplatures 8
☎268181 Frd Lnc

CHERNEX See MONTREAUX

CHEXBRES
Vaud(☎021)

★ ★ ★Bellevue ☎561481
rm20 ⇋18 🍴2 P Lift sB50
sB ⇋ 🍴70 dB60–85 dB ⇋ 🍴75–110
mountains lake

★ ★ ★Signal ☎562525
Mar–Nov
rm82 ⇋64 🍴18 🏠 P Lift ⅅ
sB ⇋ 🍴55–95 dB ⇋ 🍴108–164 Pool
mountains lake

★ ★Cécil ☎561292
rm25 ⇋10 🍴2 P Lift sB35–45
sB ⇋ 🍴45–60 dB60–80
dB ⇋ 🍴75–100 Pool mountains lake

CHIASSO
Ticino(☎091)

★ ★ ★Albergo Touring (Mövenpick) pza
Indipendenza ☎441541 tx842493
rm60 ⇋30 🍴30 P Lift ⅅ
sB ⇋ 🍴89–98 dB ⇋ 🍴128–137 M alc

CHUR (COIRE)
Graubünden(☎081)

★ ★ ★Duc de Rohan (Amb) Masanserstr
44 ☎221022 tx74161
rm35 ⇋32 🍴1 🏠 P Lift ⅅ sB55
sB ⇋ 🍴56–68 dB ⇋ 🍴95–112 M alc
Pool mountains

★ ★A.B.C. Bahnhofpl (n.rest) ☎226033
tx74580
rm36 ⇋8 🍴20 🏠 P Lift ⅅ
sB ⇋ 🍴56–70 dB ⇋ 🍴92–112

★ ★Drei Könige Reichsgasse 18
☎221725
rm30 ⇋4 🍴8 🏠 P Lift sB32–36
sB ⇋ 🍴40–46 dB58–62
dB ⇋ 🍴74–82 M12–28 mountains

☆ ☆Sommerau Emserstr 4 ☎225545
tx74172
rm90 ⇋45 🍴45 P sB ⇋ 🍴55–65
dB ⇋ 🍴95–110 M8–40 mountains

★ ★Stern (Rom) Reichsgasse 11
☎223555 tx74198
rm55 ⇋14 🍴41 🏠 P Lift ⅅ

Switzerland

sB ⇋ 🍴65 dB ⇋ 🍴98 M14–28
mountains

🕭Auto Center Tribolet Rossbodenstr
14 ☎221212 BL Frd Toy

🕭Calanda & Montalin Kasernenstr
30 ☎221414 Fia Lnc

🕭Comminot Rossbodenstr
24 ☎223737 P Peu RT

🕭Grand Garage Dosch Kasernenstr
☎215171 Opl Vau

🕭Lidoc St Margrethenstr 9 ☎221313 P
AR MB Vau

COLLONGE-BELLERIVE
Genève

★ ★Bellerive ☎521420
Feb–15 Dec
rm11 ⇋8 A4rm P lake

COPPET
Vaud (☎022)

🕭Port (P Keller) rte de Suisse ☎761212
BL Maz

CORNAREDO See LUGANO

CRANS-SUR-SIERRE
Valais (☎027)

★ ★ ★Alpine & Savoy ☎412142
tx473134
Dec–Apr & Jun–Sep
⇋60 🏠 P Lift ⅅ sB ⇋60–150
dB ⇋100–250 Pool mountains

★ ★ ★Élite ☎4114301
Closed Nov
⇋26 P Lift ⅅ sB31–71 sB ⇋40–93
dB53–121 dB ⇋68–158 Mfr22 Pool
mountains

★ ★ ★Eurotel Christina ☎431891
tx473295
17 Dec–24 Sep
⇋63 P sB ⇋61–125 dB ⇋102–230
Pool

★ ★Robinson ☎411353
rm16 ⇋12 🍴4 P Lift sB ⇋ 🍴46–93
dB ⇋ 🍴80–158

★ ★Royal ☎413931 tx38227
Dec–Apr & Jun & Oct
rm69 ⇋61 🍴7 P Lift ⅅ
sB ⇋ 🍴157–148 dB ⇋ 🍴97–252

★ ★Splendide ☎412056
Dec–Apr & Jun–Oct
rm32 ⇋30 P Lift ⅅ sB31–71
sB ⇋40–93 dB53–121 dB ⇋68–158
mountains lake

CULLY See LAUSANNE

DAVOS
Graubünden (☎083)

At DAVOS DORF

★ ★ ★Alpes (KA) Promenade 136
☎61261 tx74341

Closed Nov
rm56 ⇋46 🍴3 🏠 P Lift ⅅ sB48–85
sB ⇋ 🍴58–95 db76–150
dB ⇋ 🍴96–170 mountains

★ ★ ★Melerhof Promenade ☎61285
tx74363
Dec–May & Jun–Oct
rm43 ⇋19 🏠 P Lift ⅅ sB55–95
sB ⇋70–145 dB110–190
dB ⇋130–270 M20–35 mountains

At LARET (8km NE)

★Tischiery's im Landhaus ☎52121
Dec–Apr & Jun–Oct
rm30 ⇋6 🏠 P mountains

At DAVOS PLATZ

★ ★ ★Morosani Post (Amb) Promenade
42 ☎21161 tx74350
Dec–Apr & Jun–Oct
rm90 ⇋75 🍴15 A24rm 🏠 P Lift ⅅ
sB ⇋ 🍴110–160 dB ⇋ 🍴110–170
Mfr35 Pool mountains

★ ★ ★Schweizerhof (Amb) Promenade
50 ☎21151 tx74324
4 Dec–23 Apr & 26 May–27 Sep
rm103 ⇋91 🍴9 🏠 P Lift ⅅ
sB45–55 sB ⇋ 🍴65–83
dB ⇋ 🍴114–150 M20–25 Pool
mountains

★Belmont Tanzbuhlstr 2 ☎35032
Dec–15 Apr & Jun–15 Sep
rm25 P sB25–50 dB100 mountains

DELÉMONT
Jura (☎066)

★ ★ ★National rte de Bâle 25 ☎229622
tx349522
Closed Jan
⇋27 🏠 P Lift sB ⇋ 🍴61–76
dB ⇋ 🍴101–121 M10

★Bonne Auberge (MIN) r du 23 Juin 32
☎221758
rm10 ⇋1 🍴5 🏠 P Lift

🕭Mercay r de la Maltière 20 ☎221745
BMW Fia MB

🕭Willemin rte de Moutier 65 ☎222461
P Ren Vlo

DIABLERETS (LES)
Vaud (☎025)

★ ★ ★Eurotel ☎531721 tx456174
⇋115 P Lift sB ⇋41–117
dB ⇋92–204 Pool

DIETIKON
Zürich (☎01)

★ ★Krone (ROM) Zürcherstr 3
☎7406011
rm20 ⇋7 🍴13 🏠 P sB ⇋ 🍴55–65
dB ⇋ 🍴97–125 M20

DISENTIS
Graubünden (☎086)

★ ★ ★Park Baur (KA) Sontga Catrina
☎74545 tx74585
Closed Nov
⇋54 🏠 P Lift ⅅ sB ⇋77–134
dB ⇋79–174 M20 🐾 Pool mountains

DÜRRENAST See **THUN (THOUNE)**

EBIKON See **LUZERN (LUCERNE)**

EBLIGEN
Bern (☎036)

★**Hirschen** ☎511551
rm12 ⇆3 ⋔5 sB30−40
sB ⇆ ⋔35−45 dB50−60
dB ⇆ ⋔60−80 M14−18 Pool lake
mountains

EGERKINGEN
Solothurn (☎062)
See also **OLTEN**

☆ ☆**AGIP** (Autobahn crossroads N1/N2)
☎612121 tx68644
rm68 ⇆34 ⋔34 **P** 𝄞 sB ⇆ ⋔57−74
dB ⇆ ⋔97

⁂**Reinhart** Oltenstr 102 ☎611250 Frd
Toy

EINIGEN
Bern (☎033)

☆ ☆**Hirschen** Hauptstr ☎543733
⋔20 🏰 **P** 𝄞 mountains lake

EINSIEDELN
Schwyz (☎055)

★ ★ ★**Drei Könige** ☎532441 tx875293
⇆51 🏰 **P** Lift 𝄞 sB ⇆57−62
dB ⇆97−133 M15−30

EMMENBRÜCKE See **LUZERN
(LUCERNE)**

ENGELBERG
Obwalden (☎041)

★ ★ ★**Bellevue Terminus** ☎941213
tx78555
Jan−Sep & Dec
rm90 ⇆45 ⋔35−60 A3rm **P** Lift 𝄞
dB ⇆ ⋔60−100 dB ⇆ ⋔60−100
M12−15 🏊 mountains

★ ★ ★**Dorint Regina Titlis** Dorstr
☎942828 tx72304
⋔127 🏰 **P** Lift 𝄞 sB ⋔60−145
dB ⋔ 100−280 Pool mountains

★ ★ ★**Hess** ☎941366 tx866270
Closed Nov
rm58 ⇆33 ⋔11 **P** Lift sB68
sB ⇆ ⋔60−100 dB70−117
dB ⇆ ⋔110−190 mountains

★**Engelberg** Dorfstr 14 ☎941168
Closed Nov
rm33 ⇆10 ⋔14 **P** Lift 𝄞 sB33−48
sB ⇆ ⋔40−66 dB66−86
dB ⇆ ⋔80−124 M18−28 mountains

ENTLEBUCH
Luzern (☎041)

★ ★**Drei Könige** ☎721227
rm12 ⇆4 ⋔3 🏰 **P** Lift 𝄞 sB22−26
sB ⇆ ⋔32−38 dB44−50
dB ⇆ ⋔60−66 M10−70 mountains

ESTAVAYER-LE-LAC
Fribourg (☎037)

★**Lac** ☎631343
Mar−Oct

Switzerland

rm17 ⇆6 **P** sB32−38 sB ⇆46−52
dB52−64 dB ⇆72−84 🏊 Pool lake

ETOY-BUCHILLON
Vaud (☎021)

☆ ☆**Pêchers-Etoy** rte du Lac Genéve-
Lausanne ☎763277
rm14 ⇆2 ⋔12 🏰 **P** 𝄞 Pool lake
mountains

EVOLÈNE
Valais (☎027)

★ ★**Hermitage** (MIN) ☎831232
Jun−Sep & Dec−Apr
rm22 ⇆12 🏰 sB23−35 sB ⇆32−45
dB46−66 dB60−84

★**Dent-Blanche** ⇆831105
rm50 **P** sB36−47 dB62−84 Mfr15
mountains

★**Eden** ☎831112
Closed Nov
rm18 🏰 sB20−35 sB ⇆ ⋔27−41
dB32−45 dB ⇆ ⋔46−72

★**Evolène** ☎831151
rm45 ⇆15 ⋔3 **P** Lift 𝄞 sB24−37
sB ⇆ ⋔32−45 dB41−70
dB ⇆ ⋔54−77 🏊 Pool mountains

FAIDO
Ticino (☎094)

★ ★**Milan** ☎381307
Mar−Oct
rm41 ⇆20 ⋔1 🏰 **P** Lift sB37
sB ⇆ ⋔47 dB62 dB ⇆ ⋔80 mountains

FERNEY VOLTAIRE See **GENÈVE
AIRPORT**

FEUSISBERG
Zürich (☎01)

★ ★ ★**Panorama** Tagungszentrum
☎7842464 tx765825
⇆65 **P** Lift 𝄞 sB ⇆75−85
dB ⇆110−130 mountains lake

FIESCH
Valais (☎028)

★**Glacier & Poste** ☎711301
rm40 ⇆5 ⋔10 🏰 **P** 🏊 mountains

FILZBACH
Glarus (☎058)

★**Seeblick** ☎321455
rm10 **P** lake mountains

FLEURIER
Neuchâtal (☎038)

★**Commerce** ☎611190
rm10 **P** Lift mountains

⁂**C Duthe** r de Temple 34 ☎611637 **P**
Aud VW

⁂**C Hotz** r de l'Industrie 19 ☎612922 Cit
Peu Tal

FLIMS-WALDHAUS
Graubünden (☎081)

★ ★ ★ ★**Park-Hotels Waldhaus**
☎390181 tx74125
19 Dec−Mar & 20 May−Sep
rm172 ⇆157 ⋔15 🏰 **P** Lift 𝄞
sB ⇆ ⋔95−170 dB ⇆ ⋔190−340
M40−78 🏊 Pool 〇 mountains

★ ★ ★**Schloss** ☎391245
Dec−mid Apr & May−Oct
rm41 ⇆18 ⋔17 A19rm 🏰 **P** Lift
sB55−72 sB ⇆ ⋔61−96 dB110−144
dB ⇆ ⋔122−192 mountains

★ ★ ★**Segnes** ☎391281 tx74125
Dec−Apr & May−Oct
rm70 ⇆37 ⋔11 **P** Lift 𝄞 sB61−80
sB ⇆77−109 dB144−168
dB ⇆ ⋔144−220 🏊 Pool mountains

★ ★**Alpes** Hauptstr ☎390101 tx74565
Closed May & Nov
⇆80 🏰 **P** Lift 𝄞 sB ⇆78−125
dB ⇆136−230 Mfr11 Pool mountains

★ ★**Guardaval** (n.rest) ☎391119
May−Oct & Dec−Apr
rm10 ⇆6 **P** sB27−36 sB ⇆32−50
dB50−72 dB ⇆62−96 mountains

★ ★**National** ☎391224
Closed May
rm24 ⇆6 ⋔6 🏰 **P** Lift 𝄞
sB ⇆ ⋔57−79 dB ⇆ ⋔108−158
mountains

FLÜELEN
Uri (☎044)

★**Weisses Kreuz** ☎21717
Apr−Nov
rm33 ⇆1 ⋔12 🏰 **P** sB28−30
sB ⇆ ⋔42−44 sB52−56
dB ⇆ ⋔64−72 M alc mountains lake

⁂**Sigrist** ☎21260 **P** Ren

FRAUBRUNNEN
Bern (☎031)

★ ★**Löwen** ☎967219
rm5 ⇆1 ⋔3 A1rm **P**

FRIBOURG
Fribourg (☎037)

★ ★ ★**Eurotel** Grand-Places 14
☎813131 tx36439
⇆131 **P** Lift sB ⇆65−95
dB ⇆115−135 Pool

⁂**Central** r de l'Industrie 7 ☎243520 Frd

⁂**Gendre** rte de Villars 105 ☎240331
Aud VW

⁂**Piller** r Guillimann 24−26 ☎223092
Cit Lnc

FRICK
Aargau (☎064)

★**Engel** ☎611314
⋔15 🏰 **P** sB ⋔40 dB ⋔65
mountains

FRUTIGEN
Bern (☎033)

370

★**Simplon** ☎711041
rm15 ⇌1 ▥3 **P** mountains

⇖**Niederfeld** (F Kanel) ☎711414 **P** Aud
VW

FÜRIGEN
Nidwalden (☎041)

★★**Fürigen & Bellevue** ☎611254
tx866257
rm110 ⇌50 ▥40 **P** Lift ♪ sB45–50
sB ⇌ ▥55–65 dB80–90
dB ⇌ ▥100–120 M20–25 ✍
mountains lake

FURKA PASS
Uri (☎044)

★**Furkablick** ☎67297

Jun–Sep
rm20 🏛 sB30–36 dB60–72 mountains

GABI
Valais (☎028)

★★**Weissmies** Simplonstr ☎291116
rm15 ⇌3 ▥3 A2rm 🏛 **P** sB24–31
sB ⇌ ▥32–42 dB41–53
dB ⇌ ▥54–71 M12–23 mountains

GAMPEL
Valais (☎028)

☆☆**Vallesia** ☎421283
rm30 ⇌8 ▥11 🏛 **P** mountains

GENÈVE (GENEVA) (☎022)
See plan page 372

★★★★★**Bergues** (THF) quai des
Bergues 33 ☎315050 tx23383 Plan **1**
⇌117 🏛 **P** Lift ♪ sB ⇌144–209
dB ⇌278–348 M alc mountains lake

★★★★★**Noga Hilton International**
quai du Mont-Blanc 19 ☎319811
tx289704 Plan **1A**
⇌316 Lift ♪ sB ⇌185–270
dB ⇌265–385 Mfr36 Pool mountains
lake

★★★★★**Président** quai Wilson 47
☎311000 tx22780 Plan **2**
⇌190 🏛 **P** Lift ♪ sB ⇌183–220
dB ⇌281–341 M45 & alc mountains
lake

★★★★★**Rhône** quai Turrettini 3
☎319831 tx22213 Plan **3**
rm300 ⇌250 ▥50 **P** Lift ♪
sB ⇌ ▥135–170 dB ⇌ ▥210–265
M alc mountains lake

★★★★★**Richemond** Jardin Brunswick
☎311400 tx22598 Plan **4**
rm150 ⇌130 ▥20 🏛 **P** Lift ♪
sB ⇌ ▥120–180 dB ⇌ ▥200–300
mountains lake

★★★★**Beau Rivage** (Amb) quai du
Mont-Blanc 13 ☎310221 tx23362 Plan **5**
rm120 ⇌110 ▥10 **P** Lift ♪
sB ⇌ ▥130–190 dB ⇌ ▥210–300
mountains lake

★★★★**Paix** quai du Mont-Blanc 11
☎326150 tx22552 Plan **6**
⇌106 Lift ♪ sB ⇌110–165
dB ⇌ ▥240–300 M alc mountains lake

Switzerland

★★★**Ambassador** quai des Bergues 21
pl Chevelu ☎317200 tx23231 Plan **7**
⇌ ▥92 🏛 Lift sB ⇌ ▥75–115
dB ⇌ ▥115–160 lake

★★★**Angleterre** quai du Mont-Blanc 17
☎328180 tx22668 Plan **8**
⇌65 **P** Lift ♪ sB ⇌135–200
dB ⇌195–295 mountains lake

★★★**Berne** r de Berne 26 ☎316000
tx22764 Plan **9**
⇌80 Lift ♪ sB ⇌115 dB ⇌150 M20

★★★**Century** (Amb) av de Frontenex 24
(n.rest) ☎368095 tx2323 Plan **10**
rm139 ⇌90 ▥35 **P** Lift
sB ⇌ ▥80–112 dB ⇌ ▥130–170

★★★**Cornavin** (KA) bd J-Fazy 33
(n.rest) ☎322100 tx22853 Plan **11**
rm175 ⇌65 ▥50 **P** Lift ♪ sB75–85
sB ⇌ ▥85–125 dB90–100
dB ⇌ ▥125–170 mountains

★★★**Cristal** 4 r Pradier ☎313400
tx289926 Plan **11A**
rm79 ⇌40 ▥39 Lift ♪

★★★**Eden** r de Lausanne 135
☎326540 tx23962 Plan **12**
⇌54 🏛 **P** Lift ♪ sB ⇌80–100
dB ⇌105–135 lake

★★★**Grand Pré** r du Grand Pré 35
(n.rest) ☎339150 tx23284 Plan **13**
rm100 ⇌50 ▥50 🏛 Lift sB40–55
sB ⇌ ▥80–120 dB ⇌ ▥120–170

★★★**Lutetia** r de Carouge 12
☎204222 tx28845 Plan **14**
⇌42 Lift

★★★**Warwick** (Amb) r de Lausanne 14
☎316520 tx23630 Plan **15**
⇌168 **P** Lift ♪ sB ⇌110–150
dB ⇌150–220 mountains lake

★★**Montbrilliant** r de Montbrillant 2
☎337784 Plan **19**
rm44 ⇌6 ▥2 **P** Lift

★★**Touring-Balance** pl Longemalle 13
☎287122 tx427634 Plan **21**
rm54 Lift ♪ sB ⇌ ▥100
dB ⇌ ▥120–135 lake mountains

★**Adris** Gevray 6–8 (n.rest) ☎315225
Plan **22**
rm22 ⇌9 ▥10 Lift

⇖**Acacias Motors** r Boissonnas 11
☎433600 Chy Sim

⇖**Athénée** rte de Meyrin 122 ☎960044
P BMW MB RR

⇖**Autohall Metropole** rte du Pont Butin
☎921322 Frd

⇖**Auto Import** Viguet 1 Acacias
☎425804 **P** BMW

⇖**Bouchet** (R. Claude) rte de Meyrin
54–56 ☎968900 BL Peu

⇖**E Frey** rte des Acacias 23 ☎421010
BL MB Toy

⇖**Nouveau** r Pré Jérome 21–23
☎202111 M/c BMW

Tranches (Blanc & Paiche) bd des
Tranchées 50 ☎468911 Maz

At **MIES** (10km N on N1)

☆**Buna** ☎551535 Plan **23**
⇌6 **P** mountains

At **VÉSENAZ** (6km NE on No 37)

★★**Tourelle** rte d'Hermance 26 (n.rest)
☎521628 Plan **24**
15 Jan–15 Dec
rm24 ⇌10 ▥8 A2rm **P** sB40–45
sB ⇌ ▥65–75 dB65–75
dB ⇌ ▥80–110 mountains lake

GENÈVE AIRPORT (7km N)

At **FERNEY VOLTAIRE** (in France, 4km
from airport)

☆☆☆**Novotel Genève Aéroport** rte de
Meyrin ☎(50)408523 tx385046 Plan **15A**
⇌79 **P** Lift sB ⇌194–260
dB ⇌262–317 M alc ✍ Pool
mountains

☆☆**Campanile** chemin de la Planche
Brûlee ☎(50)407479 tx610016 Plan **17A**
⇌42 **P** dB ⇌206–209 M55–80
mountains

GERSAU
Schwyz (☎041)

★★★**Beau-Rivage** ☎841223 tx72588
Apr–Oct
rm35 ⇌6 ▥2 🏛 **P** Lift sB38–43
sB ⇌ ▥53–58 dB75–85
dB ⇌ ▥85–115 Pool mountains

★★★**Seehof du Lac** ☎841245 tx72588
Apr–Oct
▥32 🏛 **P** Lift sB ▥40–52
dB ⇌80–104 mountains lake

★**Bellevue** (n.rest) ☎841120
rm15 ⇌5 **P** sB35 dB68 dB ⇌80 Pool
mountains lake

GISWIL
Obwalden (☎041)

★**Krone** Brünigstr ☎681151
rm100 ▥60 🏛 **P** Lift sB45 sB ▥50
dB70 dB ▥80 mountains

GLARUS
Glarus (☎058)

★★**Glarnerhof** Bahnhofstr 2 ☎614106
rm30 ⇌16 🏛 **P** Lift sB34–44
sB ⇌ ▥44–56 dB68–88 dB ⇌88–112
M10–25 mountains

⇖**K Enz** Bahnhofpl ☎611770 Cit

⇖**Schielly** Landsgemeisepl ☎611834 **P**
Opl

GLATTBRUGG See ZÜRICH AIRPORT

GLETSCH
Valais (☎028)

★★**Glacier du Rhône** ☎731515
Jun–Sep
rm64 A32rm 🏛 **P** ♪ sB27–40

GENÈVE (GENEVA)

1	★★★★★	Bergues
1A	★★★★★	Noga Hilton International
2	★★★★★	Président
3	★★★★★	Rhône
4	★★★★	Richemond
5	★★★★	Beau Rivage
6	★★★★	Paix
7	★★★	Ambassador
8	★★★	Angleterre
9	★★★	Berne
10	★★★	Century
11	★★★	Cornavin
11A	★★★	Cristal
12	★★★	Eden
13	★★★	Grand Pré
14	★★★	Lutetia
15	★★★	Warwick
15A	☆☆☆	Novotel Genève Aéroport (At Ferney Voltaire, in France under GENÈVE AIRPORT)
17A	☆☆	Campanile (At Ferney Voltaire, in France under GENÈVE AIRPORT)
19	★★	Montbrillant
21	★★	Touring-Balance
22	★	Adris
23	☆	Buna (At Mies 10km N on N1)
24	★★	Tourelle (At Vésenaz 6km NE on No 37)

sB ⇌ 🛏 138–58 dB51–74
dB ⇌ 🛏 74–114 ⋒ mountains

GLION See **MONTREUX**

GLIS See **BRIG (BRIGUE)**

GOLDSWIL
Bern (☎036)

★**Park** ☎222942

rm55 ⇌2 A7rm **P** sB27 dB50 dB ⇌65
M12 mountains

🍴**Burgseell** Brienzerseestr ☎221043
Sab Toy

GÖSCHENEN
Uri (☎044)

★**St-Gotthard** ☎65263

rm25 ⇌2 🛏2 🏛 **P** sB24–26
sB ⇌ 🛏 28–30 dB42–44
dB ⇌ 🛏 50–54

GOTTLIEBEN
Thurgau (☎072)

★★**Krone** (ROM) ☎692323

rm20 ⇌10 🛏10 **P** Lift sB ⇌ 🛏 60–70
dB ⇌ 🛏 100–120 lake

GRÄCHEN
Valais (☎028)

★★**Beausite** ☎562656
Dec–Apr, Jun–Oct
rm42 ⇌6 🛏3 🏛 Lift sB48–66
sB ⇌ 🛏 57–75 dB88–110
dB ⇌ 🛏 103–130 Pool

★**Grächerhof & Schönegg** (Amb)
☎562515
Jun–Oct & Dec–Apr

rm35 sB53–71 sB ⇌ 🛏 62–80
dB98–120 dB ⇌ 🛏 113–140

GREPPEN
Luzern (☎041)

★**St-Wendelin** ☎811016
Apr–Nov
rm10 🏛 **P** mountains lake

GRINDELWALD
Bern (☎036)

★★★★**Grand Regina** ☎545455
tx923263
Closed Nov
rm120 ⇌108 🛏12 🏛 **P** Lift ☽

sB ⇌ 🛏 120–150 dB ⇌ 🛏 220–280 M45
& alc 🏊 Pool mountains

★★★**Belvédère** ☎531818 tx923244
18 Dec–24 Apr & Jun–10 Oct
rm60 ⇌40 🛏11 **P** Lift sB50–70
sB ⇌ 🛏 60–90 dB110–126
dB ⇌ 🛏 130 190 M6 30alc Pool
mountains

★★★**Gletschergarten** ☎531721
Closed Nov
rm28 ⇌12 🛏12 **P** Lift sB ⇌ 🛏 50–80
dB ⇌ 🛏 90–150 M20 mountains

★★★**Parkhotel Schönegg** ☎531853
tx923245

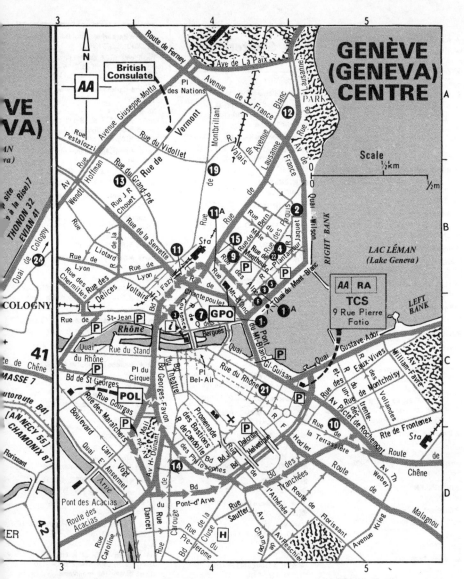

GENÈVE (GENEVA) CENTRE

Scale ½km

LAC LÉMAN
(Lake Geneva)

RIGHT BANK

LEFT BANK

AA RA
TCS
9 Rue Pierre
Fatio

British Consulate

AA

Dec–Apr & May–Oct
rm60 ⇋40 ▥6 ⌂ **P** Lift sB40–70
sB ⇋ ▥50–80 dB70–130
dB ⇋ ▥90–150 M20–30 Pool
mountains

★★★**Schweizerhof** ☎532202
Dec–May & Jun–Oct
⇋40 ▥5 **P** Lift sB ⇋ ▥93
dB ⇋ ▥110–175 Mfr30 Pool
mountains

★★★**Sunstar** ☎545417 tx923230
May–Oct & Dec–Apr
rm135 ⇋110 ▥25 ⌂ **P** Lift ♪

sB ⇋ ▥65–110 dB ⇋ ▥120–220 ✆
Pool mountains

★★**Derby** ☎545461 tx923277
Closed Nov
rm80 ⇋47 ▥27 **P** Lift ⌂
sB ⇋ ▥50–80 dB ⇋ ▥90–150
mountains

☆☆**Grindelwald** ☎532131
rm22 ⇋18 A10rm ⌂ **P**
sB ⇋ ▥76–100 dB ⇋100–135
mountains

★★**Hirschen** ☎532777
rm33 ⇋8 ▥12 ⌂ **P** Lift sB40–65

sB ⇋ ▥50–80 dB70–120
dB ⇋ ▥90–150 M20–36alc mountains

★**Alpenblick** (n.rest) ☎531105
rm22 **P** mountains

⯐**Rothenegg** Rothenegg ☎531507 Aud
VW

GRUYÈRES
Fribourg (☎029)

★★**Hostellerie des Chevaliers** ☎61933
Closed 11 Jan–9 Feb
⇋34 ⌂ **P** Lift sB ⇋75–105
dB ⇋105–160 mountains

★★**Hostellerie St-Georges** ☎62246
Mar–Nov
rm14 sB30–45 sB ⇄ ▥40–50
dB60–75 dB ⇄ ▥65–80

GSTAAD
Bern (☎030)

★★★**Bellevue Grand** (Amb) (**DPn**
Xmas) ☎43264 tx922232
15 Dec–Mar & 8 Jun–Sep
rm55 ⇄47 ▥8 **P** Lift ☽
sB ⇄ ▥90–135 dB ⇄ ▥180–270
mountains

★★**National-Rialto** Hauptstr ☎43474
rm33 ⇄11 ▥6 ▥ **P** Lift ☽ sB50–68
sB ⇄ ▥60–90 dB100–136
dB ⇄ ▥120–180 mountains

★★**Olden** ☎43444 tx922211
rm16 ⇄14 ▥2 ▥ **P** sB ⇄ ▥60–125
dB ⇄ ▥120–250 mountains

★**Rössli** ☎43412
Closed May
rm23 ⇄10 A4rm **P** mountains

GSTEIG (LE CHÂTELET)
Bern (☎030)

★**Viktoria** ☎51034
rm12 ⇄3 ▥5 ▥ **P** mountains

GUMLIGEN See **BERN**

GUNTEN
Bern (☎033)

★★★**Hirschen am See** (Amb)
☎512244 tx922100
11 May–23 Oct
rm68 ⇄39 ▥29 ▥ **P** Lift
sB ⇄ ▥68–113 dB ⇄ ▥132–220
M20–26 mountains lake

★**Bellevue** ☎511121
Mar–Oct
rm38 ⇄5 ▥5 ▥ **P** sB35–45
dB60–80 ⇄ ▥80–100 M12–25
mountains lake

GURTNELLEN
Uri (☎044)

★**Gotthard** ☎65110
rm12 ⇄1 ▥5 ▥ **P** mountains

GWATT
Bern (☎033)

★**Lamm** ☎362233
rm16 **P** mountains

HANDEGG
Bern (☎036)

★★**Handeck** ☎731131 tx923257
May–Oct
rm40 ⇄10 ▥10 A20rm ▥ **P**
mountains

HERGISWIL
Nidwalden (☎041)

★★★**Belvédère** (Amb) ☎951185
tx78444
rm53 ⇄20 ▥33 **P** sB ⇄ ▥60–75
dB ⇄ ▥96–125 mountains lake

Switzerland

★★★**Pilatus** ☎951555 tx72527
rm69 ⇄46 ▥23 **P** Lift ▥
sB ⇄62–90 dB ⇄110–160 Pool
mountains lake

★★**Friedhelm** Kantonstr ☎951282
rm30 ⇄3 A1rm **P** Lift sB28–34
sB ⇄36–48 dB56–68 dB ⇄72–96
mountains lake

HERTENSTEIN
Luzern (☎041)

★★★**Hertenstein** ☎931444 tx72284
Mar–Nov
rm70 ⇄57 Lift ☽ sB53–89
sB ⇄70–118 dB102–174
dB ⇄134–220 Pool lake

HORW
Luzern (☎041)

★★**Waldhaus** ☎471754
rm17 ⇄5 ▥12 A12 **P** sB ⇄ ▥85
dB ⇄ ▥120–140 M alc Pool lake
mountains

HÜNIBACH See **THUN**

ILANZ
Graubünden (☎086)

★**Casutt** ☎21131
rm15 ▥8 **P** sB30 ▥35 dB50–60
dB ▥60–70 M10–20 mountains

☾**Spescha** ☎21424 **P** Cit Frd

IMMENSEE AM ZUGERSEE
Schwyz (☎041)

★★**Rigi-Royal** ☎811161
rm35 ⇄22 ▥12 ▥ **P** sB28–44
sB ⇄ ▥45–59 dB56–88
dB ⇄ ▥90–118 lake mountains

INTERLAKEN
Bern (☎036)

★★★★**Beau Rivage** Höheweg 211
☎224621 tx923122
Mar–Nov
rm110 ⇄87 ▥ **P** Lift ☽
sB ⇄80–180 dB ⇄135–180 Pool
mountains

★★★**Metropole** Höheweg 37
☎212151 tx923191
rm100 ⇄67 ▥27 ▥ **P** Lift ☽
sB ⇄ ▥75–120 dB ⇄ ▥120–205
mountains

★★★★**Victoria-Jungfrau** Höheweg 41
☎212171 tx923121
Apr–Nov & Dec–Mar
⇄220 ▥ **P** Lift ☽ sB ⇄80–180
dB ⇄135–290 ☝ Pool mountains

★★★**Bellevue Garden** Marktgasse 59
(n.rest) ☎224431
Apr–Oct
rm60 ⇄30 Lift ☽ sB43–61
sB ⇄56–61 dB66–110 dB ⇄93–172
mountains

★★★**Bernerhof** (Amb) Bahnhofstr 16
☎223131 tx923138
rm36 ⇄9 ▥27 ▥ **P** Lift
sB ⇄ ▥54–78 dB ⇄ ▥86–130
mountains

★★★**Carlton** (MIN) Höheweg 92
☎223821
15 Apr–15 Oct
rm50 ⇄17 ▥8 ▥ **P** Lift sB38–54
sB ⇄ ▥54–78 dB62–94
dB ⇄ ▥86–130 M18–26 mountains

★★★**Eden-Nova** Bahnhofpl 45
☎228812
rm37 ⇄9 ▥28 **P** Lift sB ⇄ ▥50–78
dB ⇄ ▥80–130 M13–30 mountains

★★★**Eurotel** Rugenparkstr 13 (n.rest)
☎226233
Closed Nov
rm37 ⇄21 ▥11 **P** Lift sB34–54
sB ⇄ ▥50–78 dB56–94
dB ⇄ ▥80–130 mountains

★★★**Goldey** Goldey 85 Unterseen
☎224445 tx923114
May–15 Oct
rm35 ⇄25 ▥10 **P** Lift sB ⇄ ▥60–86
dB ⇄ ▥99–148 M20–25 mountains
lake

★★★**Interlaken** Höheweg 74 ☎212211
rm65 ⇄24 ▥8 **P** Lift ☽ sB55
sB ⇄ ▥50–78 dB56–94
dB ⇄ ▥80–130 mountains

★★★**Krebs** Bahnhofstr 4 ☎227161
tx923150
May–Oct
rm51 ⇄42 ▥6 **P** Lift ☽
sB ⇄ ▥56–94 dB ⇄ ▥93–172
mountains

★★★**Lac** (Amb) Höheweg 225
☎222922 tx923100
rm43 ⇄27 ▥4 **P** Lift ☽ sB43–61
sB ⇄ ▥56–94 dB66–110
dB ⇄ ▥93–172 mountains lake

★★★**Merkur** ☎226655 tx923153
rm36 ⇄16 ▥20 **P** Lift ☽
sB ⇄ ▥50–78 dB ⇄ ▥80–130
M15–22 mountains

★★★**Royal St-Georges** Höheweg 139
☎227575 tx923175
Apr–Oct
rm120 ⇄66 ▥35 ▥ **P** Lift ☽
sB41–59 sB ⇄ ▥54–92 dB64–110
dB ⇄ ▥106–168 mountains

★★**Beau Site** Seestr 16 ☎228181
tx923131
12 Dec–15 Oct
rm50 ⇄30 ▥ **P** Lift ☽ sB37–44
sB ⇄70 dB80–94 dB ⇄112–130
M18–28 mountains

☆☆**Marti** Brienzstr 38 ☎222602
Apr–Oct
rm46 ▥38 **P** Lift sB26–32
sB ▥30–64 dB45–60 dB ▥70–110
Mfr18 mountains lake

★★**National** Jungfraustr 46 ☎223621
tx923187

374

rm46 ⇄40 🛗6 **P** Lift ⫶
sB ⇄ 🛗70–95 dB ⇄ 🛗110–170
mountains

★★**Nord** Höheweg 70 ☎222631
tx923101
rm58 ⇄22 🛗19 **P** Lift ⫶ sB33–54
sB ⇄ 🛗50–78 dB56–94
dB ⇄ 🛗80–130 M15–25 mountains

★★**Oberland** Postgasse 1 ☎229431
rm68 ⇄6 🛗10 **P** Lift ⫶
sB ⇄ 🛗48–75 dB ⇄ 🛗78–126
mountains

★★**Splendid** Höheweg 33 ☎227612
tx923189
rm38 ⇄8 🛗11 **P** Lift sB34–54
sB ⇄50–78 dB ⇄ 🛗80–130 mountains

★★**Strand Hotel Neuhaus** Seestr 121
☎228282 tx923196
Apr–Oct & Dec–Mar
rm57 ⇄9 🛗48 **P** sB ⇄ 🛗50–78
dB ⇄ 🛗80–130 Pool Beach
mountains lake

★★**Weisses Kreuz** Höheweg ☎225951
tx923166
Closed Nov
rm100 ⇄25 🛗15 **P** Lift ⫶ dB56–94
dB ⇄ 🛗80–130

★**Harder-Minerva** Harderstr 15
☎222361 tx923361
rm33 ⇄16 🛗16 🏠 **P** Lift ⫶
sB31–46 sB ⇄ 🛗42–70 dB50–86
dB ⇄ 🛗70–112 M8–30 & alc
mountains

⬥🄾**Auto Zimmermann** Seestr 109
☎221515 Toy Vlo

⬥🄾**Bohren & Urfer** Rugenparkstr 34
☎223231 **P** Cit

⬥🄾**Hilbergarage** Harderstr 25
☎223651 MB Vau

⬥🄾**National** Centralstr 34 ☎222143 **P**
Chy

⬥🄾**Waldegg** (H Oertel-Balmer) Waldeggstr
34a ☎221939 **P** BL RT

JONGNY See **VEVEY**

KANDERSTEG
Bern(☎033)

★★★★★**Royal Bellvue** ☎751212
tx922192
mid May–mid Oct
rm45 ⇄35 A10 **P** Lift ⇄80–170
dB ⇄140–320 M40–65 & alc ⬥
mountains

★★★**Parkhotel Gemmi** ☎751117
tx922171
Closed Nov
rm42 ⇄14 🛗2 🏠 **P** Lift sB40–65
sB ⇄50–85 dB80–120 dB ⇄100–160
Pool mountains

★★★**Schweizerhof** ☎751241
Dec–Apr & May–Oct
rm47 ⇄13 🛗6 🏠 **P** Lift ⫶ sB45–65
sB ⇄ 🛗55–85 dB80–120
dB ⇄ 🛗100–160 ⬥ mountains

Switzerland

★★**Adler** (MIN) ☎751121 tx922169
Closed 26 Oct–Dec
rm20 ⇄10 🛗8 🏠 **P** sB45–65
sB ⇄ 🛗55–85 dB80–120
dB ⇄ 🛗100–160 M4–33 mountains

★★**Alpenrose** ☎751170
May–Sep
rm36 ⇄3 🛗8 A18rm **P** sB37–41
dB70–76 dB ⇄ 🛗88–98 Mfr16
mountains

★**Doldenhorn** ☎751251 tx922110
rm29 ⇄10 🛗15 🏠 **P** sB45–65
sB ⇄ 🛗55–85 dB80–120
dB ⇄ 🛗100–160 M12–20 mountains

KERZERS
Fribourg(☎031)

★**Löwen** ☎955117
rm16 ⇄1 🛗2 sB25 sB ⇄ 🛗26–30
dB44–46 dB ⇄ 🛗60 M9–18 mountains

KLOSTERS
Graubünden(☎083)

★★★★**Grand Vereina** ☎41161
tx74359
Jun–Sep & Dec–Mar
rm95 ⇄85 🛗4 **P** Lift ⫶
sB ⇄ 🛗95–155 dB150–220
dB ⇄ 🛗180–280 ⬥ Pool mountains

★★★**Silvretta** ☎41353 tx74336
Dec–Apr
rm120 ⇄100 🛗6 **P** Lift ⫶ sB90–120
sB ⇄ 🛗105–155 dB160–210
dB ⇄ 🛗190–280 mountains

★★**Sport Ferienzentrum** ☎42921
Closed Dec
rm60 ⇄30 **P** Lift M14 sB45–78
sB ⇄ 🛗50–86 dB90–156
dB ⇄ 🛗100–172 ⬥ Pool mountains

★**Waiserhof Sporthof** ☎44242
rm11 ⇄8 🛗5 A2rm 🏠 **P** Lift
sB ⇄ 🛗75–125 dB ⇄ 🛗160–230
mountains

KRATTIGEN BEI SPIEZ
Bern(☎033)

★★**Bellevue-Bären** ☎543929
rm25 ⇄3 🛗12 A8rm **P** Lift sB40–48
sB ⇄ 🛗52–58 dB90–96
dB ⇄ 🛗104–116 M8–30 mountains
lake

KREUZLINGEN
Thurgau(☎072)

⬥🄾**Amag** Hauptstr 99 ☎722424 Aud VW

KRIENS See **LUZERN (LUCERNE)**

KÜSSNACHT AM RIGI
Schwyz(☎041)

★★**Hirschen** (KA) ☎811027
rm32 ⇄9 🛗23 **P** Lift sB ⇄ 🛗50–60
dB ⇄ 🛗80–100 Mfr10 alc mountains

⬥🄾**Aebi** Hürtelstr ☎811050 Aud VW

LA Each place preceded by 'La' is listed
under the name that follows it.

LAAX
Graubünden(☎086)

★★★**Sporthotel Laax** (KA) ☎20133
tx74721
26 Nov–20 Oct
⇄83 **P** Lift ⫶ sB ⇄60–130
dB ⇄100–280 mountains

LACHEN
Schwyz(☎055)

★★**Bären** ☎631602
rm16 ⇄8 🛗8 **P** Lift

LANGENBRÜCK
Basel(☎062)

★**Bären** ☎601414 tx680330
rm21 ⇄16 A4rm 🏠 **P** sB28
sB ⇄ 🛗41–60 dB54 dB ⇄ 🛗76–92
mountains

LARET See **DAVOS**

LAUSANNE
Vaud(☎021)

★★★★★**Palace** r du Grand Chêne
7–9 ☎203711 tx24171
⇄160 🏠 **P** Lift ⫶ sB ⇄120–180
dB ⇄160–240 lake

★★★★**Continental** pl de la Gare 2
☎201551 tx24500
⇄120 **P** Lift ⫶ sB ⇄90–130
dB ⇄140–180

★★★**Alpha-Palmiers** r de la Petit Chêne
34 ☎230131 tx24999
rm133 ⇄112 🛗21 **P** Lift ⫶
sB ⇄ 🛗80–120 dB ⇄ 🛗120–170 M15

★★**Carlton** (Amb) av de Cour 4
☎263235 tx24800
⇄50 **P** Lift ⫶ sB ⇄105–120
dB ⇄150–205 mountains

★★★**City** r Caroline 5 (n.rest)
☎202141 tx24400
rm57 ⇄33 🛗24 Lift ⫶
sB ⇄ 🛗40–80 dB ⇄ 🛗60–120 M15 &
alc

★★★**Jan** av de Beaulieu 8 ☎361161
tx25744
rm60 ⇄45 🏠 **P** Lift ⫶ sB45–60
sB ⇄ 🛗80–110 db70–90
dB ⇄ 🛗120–150 Mfr10

★★★**Mirabeau** ☎206231 tx25030
rm68 ⇄39 🛗22 🏠 Lift ⫶
sB ⇄90–120 dB ⇄130–160 M alc
mountains lake

★★★**Paix** av de Benjamin Constant 5
☎207171 tx24080
rm117 ⇄68 🛗45 🏠 **P** Lift ⫶
sB ⇄ 🛗100–140 dB ⇄ 🛗140–200
M30 lake

☆☆**Victoria** av de la Gare 46 (n.rest)
☎205771 tx26644
rm65 ⇄45 🛗9 🏠 **P** Lift ⫶
sB ⇄ 🛗90–120 dB ⇄ 🛗130–160 M25
mountains

At **BUSSIGNY** (7km NW)

☆ ☆ ☆**Novotel** r des Condémines
☎892871 tx25752 (to be superseded by
459531)
⇋100 **P** Lift sB ⇋86 dB ⇋100 Mfr12
Pool mountains lake

At **CULLY** (8.5km SE)

☆ ☆**Intereurop** ☎992091 tx25973
Closed Jan
⇋60 **P** Lift 𝄐 sB ⇋60–80
dB ⇋80–120 M12–30 lake

At **OUCHY**

★ ★ ★ ★ ★**Beau-Rivage** chemin-de-
Beau-Rivage ☎263831 tx24341
⇋220 🏛 **P** Lift 𝄐 sB ⇋110–200
dB ⇋160–340 M alc 🏊 Pool
mountains lake

★ ★ ★ ★**Royal Savoy** av d'Ouchy 40
☎264201 tx24640
rm110 ⇋96 🍴14 🏛 **P** Lift
sB ⇋120 dB ⇋190 M30 Pool
mountains lake

★ ★ ★**Aulac** pl de la Navigation 4
☎271451 tx25823
rm69 ⇋54 🍴15 **P** Lift sB ⇋80–120
dB ⇋120–170 M10–28 lake

☆ ☆ ☆**Parking** av du Rond-Point 9
☎271211 tx25300
⇋100 🏛 **P** Lift 𝄐 sB ⇋80–120
dB ⇋120–170

★ ★**Angleterre** pl du Port 9 ☎264145
rm40 ⇋15 🍴4 **P** 𝄐 sB40–55
sB ⇋60–80 dB60–80
dB ⇋80–120 mountains lake

★**France** r de Mauborget 1 (n.rest)
☎233131
rm49 **P** Lift 𝄐

🛇🔧**Auto Jan** Petit-Rocher 6 ☎361921
M/c **P** BL Fia Toy

🛇🔧**Autonor Garage de Bellevaux** rte A-
Fauquez 91 ☎373960 **P** BL Lada

🛇🔧**City** (E Frey) rte de Genève
60 ☎242600 RT

🛇🔧**Edelweiss** av de Morges
139 ☎253131 Vau

🛇🔧**E Frey** chemin du Martinet
12 ☎253722

🛇🔧**Gare** (E Frey) ☎203761 **P** BL BMW

🛇🔧**Occidental** av de Morges 7 ☎258225

🛇🔧**Tivoli** av Tivoli 3 ☎203071 BL BMW
DJ RT

At **PULLY** (2km SE)

★ ★ ★**Montillier** av de Lavaux 35
☎287585 tx25747
rm45 ⇋15 🍴15 🏛 **P** Lift 𝄐
sB40–55 sB ⇋60–80 dB60–80
dB ⇋80–120 mountains lake

At **RENENS** (5km NW)

🛇🔧**Étoile** rte de Cossonay
101 ☎349691 Fia Lnc MB

At **ST-SULPICE** (7km SW)

Switzerland

☆**Pierrettes** ☎254215

🍴21 **P** Pool mountains lake

LAUTERBRUNNEN
Bern(☎036)

★ ★**Jungfrau** ☎553434 tx923215
Dec–Oct
rm25 ⇋5 🍴13 A3rm 🏛 **P** 𝄐
sB31–50 sB ⇋ 🍴38–60 dB60–90
dB ⇋ 🍴71–110 Pool mountains

★ ★**Silberhorn** ☎551471
rm30 ⇋15 🍴15 **P** sB31–50
sB ⇋ 🍴38–60 dB60–90
dB ⇋ 🍴72–110 M12–30 mountains

★ ★**Staubbach** ☎551381 tx923255
Closed Nov–14 Dec
rm31 ⇋15 🍴9 🏛 **P** Lift sB35–50
sB ⇋ 🍴50–70 dB70–100
dB ⇋ 🍴96–130 mountains

★**Oberland** ☎551241 tx923285
Closed Nov
rm25 ⇋8 🍴9 **P** sB28–42
sB ⇋ 🍴37–54 dB54–76
dB ⇋ 🍴66–94 mountains

LE Each name preceded by 'Le' is listed
under the name that follows it.

LEISSIGEN
Bern(☎036)

★**Kreuz** ☎471231
rm30 ⇋8 🍴22 **P** Lift sB ⇋ 🍴48–58
dB ⇋ 🍴76–92 M14–30 & alc Beach
lake mountains

LENK
Bern(☎030)

★ ★ ★**Parkhotel Bellevue** ☎31761
tx922246
17 Dec–Apr & Jun–6 Oct
rm59 ⇋34 🍴11 🏛 **P** Lift sB60–80
sB ⇋ 🍴80–115 dB124–170
dB ⇋ 🍴160–230 Pool mountains

★ ★ ★**Wildstrubel** ☎31506
15 Dec–23 Apr & 21 May–9 Oct
rm57 ⇋31 🍴3 A4rm **P** Lift sB55–85
sB ⇋ 🍴70–114 dB124–170
dB ⇋ 🍴140–227 Pool mountains

LENZERHEIDE
Graubünden(☎081)

★ ★ ★**Palanca** (KA) ☎343131
16 Dec–14 Apr & 2 Jun–19 Oct
rm35 ⇋5 🍴27 🏛 **P** Lift 𝄐 sB45–62
sB ⇋ 🍴62–77 dB66–90
dB ⇋ 🍴100–130 M12–40 mountains

LEYSIN
Vaud(☎025)

★ ★ ★**Central Residence** (Amb)
☎341211 tx456132
17 Dec–Mar & 26 May–14 Oct
⇋94 **P** Lift sB ⇋80–134

---

dB ⇋120–188 Mfr28 🏊 Pool
mountains

★**Mont-Riant** ☎341235 tx456166
Dec–Apr & Jun–Sep
rm19 ⇋2 🍴11 **P** Lift 𝄐 sB27–46
sB ⇋ 🍴40–59 dB50–74
dB ⇋ 🍴65–112 M15–22 mountains

LIESTAL
Basel(☎061)

★ ★ ★**Engel** (Amb) Kasernenstr 10
☎912511 tx966040
rm36 ⇋20 🍴14 🏛 **P** 𝄐 sB40–54
sB ⇋ 🍴66–90 dB77–90
dB ⇋ 🍴90–130

★ ★**Radackerhof** Rheinstr 93 ☎943222
rm27 ⇋2 🍴20 🏛 **P** Lift sB29–44
sB ⇋ 🍴43–65 dB49–74
dB ⇋ 🍴69–105

★**Bahnhof** Bahnhofpl 14 ☎910072
rm14 ⇋2 🍴12 **P** sB ⇋48–60
dB ⇋70–95 M alc

🛇🔧**Peter Auto** Gasstr 11 ☎919140 M/c **P**
Frd

🛇🔧**Rheingarage Buser** Rheinstr 95
☎945025 **P** Cit Vlo

LOCARNO
Ticino(☎093)
See also **MINÚSLO**

★ ★ ★ ★**Palma au Lac** viale Verbano
29 ☎330171 tx846124
rm106 ⇋85 🍴11 🏛 **P** Lift 𝄐
sB50–70 sB ⇋ 🍴100–150 dB82–170
dB ⇋ 🍴170–310 Pool lake

★ ★ ★**Reber au Lac** via Verbano
☎330202 tx846074
rm93 ⇋66 🍴13 A18 🏛 **P** Lift 𝄐
sB60–90 sB ⇋ 🍴82–140 dB104–170
dB ⇋ 🍴156–260 M35–60 🏊 Pool
lake

★ ★**Lac** pza Grande ☎312921
Closed Nov
rm33 ⇋17 🍴15 🏛 Lift 𝄐 sB40–45
sB ⇋ 🍴40–59 dB ⇋ 🍴90–118
mountains lake

★ ★**Quisisana** via-del-Sole 17
☎330141 tx846020
rm70 ⇋42 🍴18 **P** Lift 𝄐
sB ⇋ 🍴60–105 dB ⇋ 🍴110–200
M20–40 Pool mountains lake

★**Belvédère** via al Sasso ☎311154
15 Mar–Nov
rm50 ⇋25 🏛 **P** Lift lake

★ ★**Montaldi** pza Stazione ☎330222
rm65 ⇋24 🍴20 A6rm **P** Lift 𝄐
sB25–38 sB ⇋ 🍴40–59 dB ⇋ 🍴50–76
dB ⇋ 🍴76–112 mountains

🛇🔧**Alfa Romeo** pza 5 Vie ☎311616 Cit

Léomotor via Ciseri 19 ☎314880 Clt Fia

At **MURALTO** (1km W)

🛇🔧**Autostar** via Sempione 12
☎333355 Chy

🛇🔧**Starnini** via Sempione 11 ☎333355 BL
RT

LUCERNE See **LUZERN**

LUGANO
Ticino(☎091)

★ ★ ★ ★**Arizona** via S. Gottardo 58
☎229343 tx79087
rm56 ⇌50 🏛 Lift ♪ sB ⇌55–80
dB ⇌100–150 Pool mountains lake

★ ★ ★ ★**Excelsior** riva-V-Vela
☎228661 tx79151
rm81 ⇌65 🏦16 **P** Lift ♪
sB ⇌ 🏦95–115 dB ⇌ 🏦135–145
Mfr35 ⅋ Pool ♂ ⋂ mountains lake

★ ★ ★ ★**Splendide-Royal** riva A-Caccia
7 ☎542001 tx73032
rm115 ⇌100 🏦15 🏛 **P** Lift ♪
sB ⇌ 🏦120–170 dB ⇌ 🏦100–300
M38–46 Pool lake

★ ★ ★**Bellvue au Lac** riva A-Caccia 10
☎543333 tx79440
14 Apr–15 Oct
rm70 ⇌58 🏦12 **P** Lift ♪
sB ⇌ 🏦95–115 dB ⇌ 🏦160–210
M20–50 Pool lake

★ ★ ★**Gotthard-Terminus** via Gl-Maraini
1 ☎227777 tx73761
17 Feb–13 Nov
rm40 ⇌12 🏦13 **P** Lift sB35–50
sB ⇌65–85 dB70–100 dB ⇌95–140
M12–25 lake

★ ★ ★**Holiday Select** (KA) Salita del Frati
5 ☎236172 tx79131
Mar–Dec
⇌42 🏛 **P** Lift ♪ sB ⇌58–78
dB ⇌95–128 M15–18 mountains lake

★ ★ ★**International** via Nassa 68
☎227541 tx840017
Apr–Oct
rm80 ⇌65 🏦2 🏛 **P** Lift ♪ sB38–50
sB ⇌ 🏦57–85 dB66–90
dB ⇌ 🏦99–148 M18–24 mountains
lake

★ ★ ★**Ticino** (ROM) pza Cioccaro 1
☎227772
Mar–Dec ⇌23 **P** Lift ♪
sB ⇌110–120 dB ⇌160–170

★ ★**Continental Beauregard** Basilea
28–30 ☎561112 tx79222
20 Mar–10 Nov
rm100 ⇌80 🏦10 A20rm **P** Lift
sB40–60 sB ⇌60–90 dB60–90
dB ⇌100–150 M17 lake

★ ★**Everest** via Ginevra 7 (n.rest)
☎229555 tx840057
rm45 ⇌12 🏦16 **P** Lift ♪ sB45–49
sB ⇌ 🏦65–90 dB75–85
dB ⇌ 🏦100–140

&🛇**Cencini** via Ceresio 2 ☎512826 **P**
BMW DJ

&🛇**Centro Mercedes** via Cantonale
24 ☎220732 MB

&🛇**N Crescionini** via Franscini 8
☎228343 Opl

&🛇**Stazione** via San Gottardo 13
☎228251 **P** Hon Vau

Switzerland

At **BRÈ** (5km E)
★**Brè Paese** ☎514761
Mar–Nov
rm16 ⇌5 🏦5 **P** sB37–42
sB ⇌ 🏦47–52 dB64–74
dB ⇌ 🏦84–94 mountains

At **CASSARATE**

★ ★ ★ ★**Villa Castagnola au Lac**
☎512213
15 Apr–Oct
rm76 ⇌56 🏦5 🏛 **P** Lift ♪ sB50–60
sB ⇌ 🏦80–120 dB100–110
dB ⇌ 🏦160–240 M25–35 & alc ⅋
Pool mountains lake

★**Atlantico** via Concordia 12 (n.rest)
☎512921
15 Jan–15 Dec
rm18 ⇌4 **P** Lift sB30–32 dB60–64
dB ⇌70–76

&🛇**M Vismara** via Concordia 2
☎512614 Frd

At **CASTAGNOLA** (2km E)
★ ★**Carlton** ☎513812 tx840003
Mar–Oct
rm60 ⇌20 🏦32 🏛 **P** Lift ♪
sB40–48 sB ⇌ 🏦55–66 dB90
dB ⇌ 🏦98–128 M8–26 & alc Pool lake

At **CORNAREDO**
&🛇**R Camenisch** Pista del
Ghiaccio ☎519725 M/c BL Maz RT

At **MELIDE** (6km S)
★ ★**Riviera** (MIN) ☎687912
Apr–Oct
rm25 ⇌20 🏦5 **P** Lift sB ⇌ 🏦45–58
dB ⇌ 🏦80–120 M18 Pool lake

At **PARADISO** (2km S)
★ ★ ★ ★**Admiral** (SRS) via Geretta 15
☎542324 tx73177
rm92 ⇌81 🏦11 🏛 **P** Lift ♪
sB ⇌ 🏦90–135 dB ⇌ 🏦140–200
M25–35 Pool

★ ★ ★**Grand Eden** riva Paradiso 7
☎550121 tx79150
rm130 ⇌110 🏦20 🏛 **P** Lift ♪
sB ⇌130 dB ⇌220–300 Mfr40 Pool
lake mountains

★ ★ ★**Conca d'Oro** riva Paradisco 7
☎543131
Mar–Oct
rm35 ⇌18 **P** sB ⇌55–80
dB ⇌100–140 Pool mountains lake

★ ★ ★**Flamingo** viale San Salvatore 10
☎541321 (n.rest)
Feb–Oct
rm20 ⇌6 🏦6 **P** Lift mountains

★ ★ ★**Lac Seehof** ☎541921 tx79555
6 Apr–2 Jan
rm54 ⇌30 🏦24 🏛 Lift ♪

---

sB ⇌ 🏦74–86 dB ⇌ 🏦134–194
M17–45 Pool lake

★ ★ ★**Meister** via San Salvatore 11
☎541412 tx79365
7 Apr–20 Oct
rm80 ⇌50 🏦30 **P** Lift ♪
sB ⇌ 🏦70–105 dB ⇌ 🏦110–160
M25–30 Pool

★ ★ ★**Paix** (Amb) via Cattori 18
☎542331 tx73949
rm80 ⇌70 🏦10 **P** Lift ♪
sB ⇌ 🏦70–100 dB ⇌ 🏦120–180 Pool
mountains

&🛇**Mazzuchelli-Auto** riva Paradiso 26
☎543412 **P** Lnc RR

At **VEZIA** (3km NW)
☆ ☆**Vezia** ☎563631 tx843046
Mar–15 Nov
rm64 ⇌3 🏦32 🏛 **P** sB45–57
sB ⇌ 🏦63–85 dB60–79
dB ⇌ 🏦92–119 M12–18alc Pool

LUNGERN AM SEE
Obwalden (☎041)
★**Rössli** ☎691171
Nov–Oct
rm12 ⇌2 A6rm **P** sB25–30
sB ⇌30–35 dB50–60 dB ⇌60–70
mountains

LUZERN (LUCERNE)
Luzern (☎041)
See plan page 378

★ ★ ★ ★**Carlton-Tivoli** (Amb)
Haldenstr 57 ☎513051 tx72456 Plan **1**
15 Apr–Oct
rm100 ⇌95 🏦5 🏛 **P** Lift ♪
sB ⇌95–140 dB ⇌ 🏦50–242 M34–38
⅋ mountains lake

★ ★ ★ ★**Grand National** (SRS)
Haldenstr 4 ☎501111 tx78130 Plan **2**
⇌78 **P** Lift ♪ sB ⇌100–135
dB ⇌180–230 Pool mountains lake

★ ★ ★ ★**Palace** Haldenstr 10
☎502222 tx78155 Plan **3**
rm164 ⇌161 🏦3 🏛 Lift ♪
sB ⇌ 🏦120–160 dB ⇌ 🏦220–340
mountains lake

★ ★ ★ ★**Schweizerhof** Schweizerhof
quai 3 ☎502211 tx78277[Plan **4**
rm157 ⇌117 **P** Lift ♪ sB ⇌85–160
dB ⇌220–290 lake

★ ★ ★**Astoria** Pilatusstr 29 ☎235323
tx78220 Plan **5**
rm106 ⇌55 🏦51 **P** Lift ♪
sB ⇌ 🏦60–100 dB ⇌ 🏦100–160
mountains

★ ★ ★**Balances** (Amb) Weinmarkt 7
☎511851 tx78183 Plan **6**
Apr–Oct
⇌80 **P** Lift ♪ sB ⇌72–110
dB ⇌130–196 mountains lake

★ ★ ★**Montana** Adigenswilerstr 22
☎516565 tx78591 Plan **7**
Apr–Oct
rm65 ⇌54 🏦11 🏛 **P** Lift ♪ →

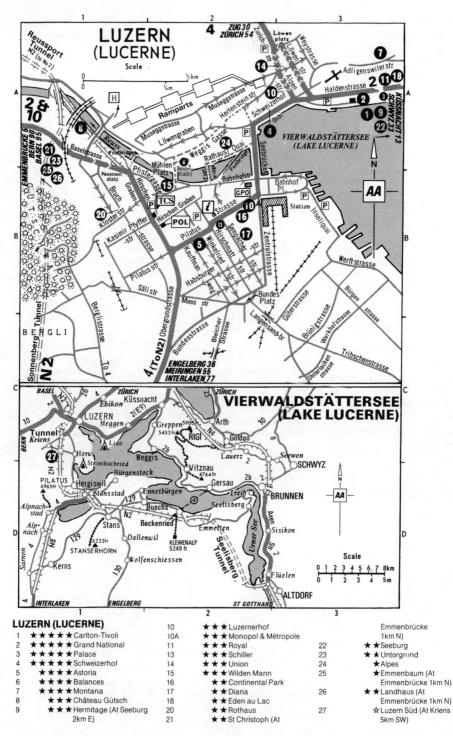

LUZERN (LUCERNE)

1	★★★★★ Carlton-Tivoli	10	★★★ Luzernerhof		Emmenbrücke
2	★★★★★ Grand National	10A	★★★ Monopol & Métropole		1km N)
3	★★★★★ Palace	11	★★★ Royal	22	★★ Seeburg
4	★★★★★ Schweizerhof	13	★★★ Schiller	23	★★ Untorgrund
5	★★★★ Astoria	14	★★★ Union	24	★ Alpes
6	★★★★ Balances	15	★★★ Wilden Mann	25	★ Emmenbaum (At
7	★★★★ Montana	16	★★ Continental Park		Emmenbrücke 1km N)
8	★★★ Château Gütsch	17	★★ Diana	26	★★ Landhaus (At
9	★★★ Hermitage (At Seeburg	18	★★ Eden au Lac		Emmenbrücke 1km N)
	2km E)	20	★★ Rothaus	27	☆ Luzern Süd (At Kriens
		21	★★ St Christoph (At		5km SW)

378

sB ⇌ 🏨83–110 dB ⇌ 🏨142–196
M14–35 mountains lake

★ ★ ★Château Gütsch (GS) Kanonenstr
☎220272 tx72455 Plan 8
rm40 ⇌37 🏨3 P Lift ♪
sB ⇌ 🏨69–100 dB ⇌ 🏨110–175 Pool
mountains lake

★ ★ ★Luzernerhof Alpenstr 3 ☎514646
tx72435 Plan 10
rm63 ⇌47 🏨27 P Lift ♪ sB42–61
sB⇌ 🏨53–80 dB ⇌ 🏨69–110
dB ⇌ 🏨95–159 M alc

★ ★ ★Monopol & Métropole (KA)
Pilatusstr 1 ☎230866 tx78192 Plan 10A
rm105 ⇌92 🏨13 P Lift ♪
sB ⇌ 🏨77–97 dB ⇌ 🏨134–174
mountain lake

★ ★ ★Royal Rigistr 22 ☎511233 Plan 11
Apr–Oct
rm50 ⇌45 P Lift ♪ sB40–54
sB⇌53–75 dB66–92 dB ⇌90–127
mountains lake

★ ★ ★Schiller Sempacherstr 4
☎235155 tx78621 Plan 13
rm70 ⇌42 🏨28 ⛴ P Lift ♪
sB ⇌ 🏨54–85 dB ⇌ 🏨88–150
M20–27

★ ★ ★Union Löwenstr 16 ☎513651
tx78163 Plan 14
rm92 ⇌92 P Lift ♪ sB45–55
sB ⇌80–95 dB70–90 dB ⇌120–170
M18–20 mountains

★ ★ ★Wilden Mann (ROM) Bahnhofstr
30 ☎231666 tx78233 Plan 15
rm50 ⇌40 🏨3 ⛴ P Lift ♪ sB40–75
sB ⇌ 🏨58–75 dB ⇌ 🏨96–175 M alc
🍴 Pool

★ ★Continental Park Morgartenstr 4 13
☎237566 tx78553 Plan 16
rm65 ⇌10 🏨55 P Lift ♪
sB ⇌ 🏨48–72 dB ⇌ 🏨82–126

★ ★Diana Sempacherstr 16 ☎232623
Plan 17
Apr–Oct
rm39 ⇌5 🏨34 P Lift ♪
sB ⇌ 🏨61–72 dB ⇌ 🏨106–128
mountains

★ ★Eden au Lac Haldenstr 47 ☎513806
tx78160 Plan 18
rm50 ⇌18 🏨8 ⛴ P Lift ♪ sB35–54
sB ⇌ 🏨46–68 dB56–95
dB ⇌ 🏨78–123 lake mountains

★ ★Rothaus Klosterstr 4 ☎224522
Plan 20
rm52 ⇌20 🏨32 P Lift ♪ sB47–60
sB ⇌ 🏨51–65 dB77–99
dB ⇌ 🏨92–118 M10–22

★ ★Seeburg ☎311922 tx78270 Plan 22
rm120 ⇌75 🏨17 ⛴ P Lift ♪
sB40–52 sB ⇌55–67 dB67–90
dB ⇌98–121 M23–34 mountains lake

★ ★Untergrund Baselstr 57 (n.rest)
☎224751 Plan 23
rm80 ⇌50 🏨1 Lift sB ⇌ 🏨45–58
dB ⇌ 🏨81–105

Switzerland

★Alpes Ratausquai 5 ☎515825 Plan 24
🏨41 P Lift sB 🏨50–71 dB 🏨86–127
mountains lake

🍴Epper Luzern Horwerstr 81 ☎411122
DJ Peu

🍴Koch Panorama Luzern Löwenstr 18
☎502250 Chy

🍴Macchi Maihofstr 61 ☎363344 BL
Maz Sab

🍴Ottiger Spitalstr 8 ☎365555 Fia MB
Por

🍴Schwerzmann Kauffmannweg 24 &
Habsburgerstr 29 ☎238181 BL MG RT

At EBIKON (4.5km NE)

🍴J Windin Luzernerstr 57 ☎367500
Dat MB

At EMMENBRÜCKE (1km N)

★ ★Landhaus ☎531737 Plan 26
rm30 ⇌5 🏨25 ⛴ P Lift sB42
sB ⇌ 🏨58 dB ⇌ 🏨98 mountains

★ ★St-Christoph ☎531308 Plan 21
Closed Jan
rm14 ⇌4 🏨2 P sB32–41
sB ⇌ 🏨41–50 dB54–73
dB ⇌ 🏨74–90 M10–25

★Emmenbaum Gerliswilstr 8 ☎552960
Plan 25
rm12 ⇌4 🏨4 ⛴ P sB35–37
sB ⇌ 🏨35–37 dB69–74
dB ⇌ 🏨69–74 Mfr16

At KRIENS (5km SW)

☆Luzern Süd Autobahn Luzern-Süd
☎413546 Plan 27
⇌35 ⛴ P Lift sB ⇌55 dB ⇌110

At SEEBURG (2km E)

★ ★ ★Hermitage (KA) Seeburgstr 72
☎313737 tx862709 Plan 9
rm33 ⇌7 🏨22 A24rm P Lift sB32–42
sB ⇌ 🏨53–63 dB68–84
dB ⇌ 🏨86–106 M18 mountains lake

LYSS
Bern (☎032)

🍴Aebi Bernstr 38–40 ☎844995 M/c P
Cit

MALOJA
Graubünden (☎082)

★ ★Maloja-Kulm ☎43105
16 Dec–20 Oct
rm30 ⇌12 🏨12 ⛴ P Lift sB45–65
sB ⇌ 🏨60–80 dB90–130
dB ⇌ 🏨110–170 M14–30 mountains

★Sporthotel Maloja ☎43126
Dec–Apr
rm18 ⇌6 🏨4 P sB40–60

sB ⇌ 🏨55–80 dB80–130
dB ⇌ 🏨100–170 mountains lake

MARIASTEIN
Solothurn (☎061)

★ ★ ★Engelbad (KA) ☎753111 tx64071
rm27 ⇌13 🏨14 P Lift sB ⇌ 🏨65–90
dB ⇌ 🏨90–120 Malc Pool mountains

MARTIGNY
Valais (☎026)

★ ★ ★Central pl Centrale ☎21184
tx473841
rm30 ⇌22 P Lift ♪ sB ⇌43–61
dB ⇌73–104 mountains

★ ★ ★Forclaz av du Léman 15 ☎22710
tx473591
rm36 🏨22 ⛴ Lift sB43–61
dB 🏨73–104

★ ★ ★Poste ☎21444
rm32 ⇌22 🏨10 P Lift ♪
sB ⇌ 🏨43–61 dB ⇌ 🏨73–104
mountains

★ ★ ★Rhône (Amb) av du Grand St-
Bernard ☎21717 tx473341
6 Dec–6 Nov
⇌55 🏨 P Lift ♪ sB ⇌50–70
dB ⇌85–120 M20 mountains

★ ★Kluser ☎22641 tx473641
rm48 ⇌14 🏨25 ⛴ P Lift sBsB37–52
sB ⇌48–70 dB63–88 dB ⇌82–119
M17–25 mountains

🍴Mont-Blanc av du Grand St-Bernard
☎21181 P Ren

MEGGEN
Luzern (☎041)

★ ★Balm ☎371135
mid Jan–mid Dec
rm20 ⇌4 🏨8 ⛴ sB35–45
sB ⇌70–80 dB65–75 dB ⇌100–120
lake mountains

MEIRINGEN
Bern (☎036)

★ ★Löwen ☎711407
rm20 P sB27–37 sB ⇌ 🏨40–45
dB54–74 dB ⇌ 🏨66–90 mountains

★Weisses Kreuz ☎711216 tx923264
rm30 ⇌1 🏨15 P Lift sB ⇌ 🏨35–47
dB ⇌ 🏨64–94 mountains

🍴E Boss ☎711631 P Frd MB

MELIDE See LUGANO

MERLIGEN
Bern (☎033)

★ ★ ★ ★Beatus ☎512121 tx922147
Apr–Nov
rm78 ⇌53 🏨25 ⛴ P Lift ♪
sB ⇌ 🏨95–160 dB ⇌ 🏨170–300
M32–42 Pool mountains lake

☆Mon Abri ☎511399
rm24 🏨19 P mountains

🍴K Wittwer ☎512222 Cit Sab

METTENDORF
Thurgau (☎054)

⚠W **Debrunner** Hauptstr 90 ☎651119
P Toy

MEYRIEZ See **MÜRTEN**

MIES See **GENÈVE**

MINÚSIO
Ticino (☎093)

See also **LOCARNO**

★ ★ ★**Esplanade** via delle Vigne
☎332121 tx846146
rm85 ⊷39 ᠗22 🏠 **P** Lift ☽ sB60
sB ⊷ ᠗60–115 dB70–120
dB ⊷ ᠗100–210 M32–40 ⤶ Pool
lake

★ ★**Remorino** (n.rest) ☎331033
Mar–Oct
⊷45 **P** Lift ☽ sB ⊷ ᠗60–80
dB ⊷ ᠗120–160 Pool lake

⚠**Rivaplana** via R-Simen 56 ☎334056
BMW

MONTANA-VERMALA
Valais (☎027)

★ ★ ★**Mirabeau** (Amb) ☎413912
tx473365
Dec–May & Jun–Oct
rm54 ⊷30 ᠗16 **P** Lift ☽
sB ⊷ ᠗57–148 dB ⊷ ᠗97–252 Mfr25
mountains

★ ★ ★**St-Georges** ☎412414 tx473854
Closed May & Nov
rm50 ⊷25 ᠗25 🏠 **P** Lift ☽
sB ⊷ ᠗45–116 dB ⊷ ᠗77–196
M25–30 Pool mountains

★ ★**Eldorado** ☎411333 tx473203
rm34 ⊷26 ᠗1 **P** Lift sB30–71
sB ⊷ ᠗40–93 dB53–121
dB ⊷ ᠗68–158 M18–28 ⤶ Pool
mountains

⚠**Lac** Crans ☎411818 **P** AR Frd

MONTREUX
Vaud (☎021)

★ ★ ★ ★**Eurotel** Grand Rue 81
☎634951 tx453120
rm170 ⊷130 ᠗40 **P** Lift ☽
sB ⊷80–140 dB ⊷130–210 M30–38
Pool mountains lake

★ ★ ★**Excelsior** r Bon Port 21
☎633231 tx453133
15 Jan–15 Dec
⊷70 🏠 Lift ☽ sB ⊷ ᠗120–160
dB ⊷ ᠗180–260 M45 Pool mountains
lake

★ ★ ★ ★**Palace** (SRS) Grand Rue 100
☎635373 tx453101
⊷230 **P** Lift ☽ sB ⊷130–210
dB ⊷220–330 M45–75 ⤶ Pool
mountains lake

★ ★ ★**Eden au Lac** (Amb) r du Thèâtre
11 ☎635551 tx453151
⊷105 🏠 **P** Lift ☽ sB180
dB ⊷130–210 M38 lake mountains

Switzerland

★ ★ ★**Golf** r Bon Port 35 ☎634631
tx453255
⊷60 🏠 **P** Lift ☽ sB ⊷63–85
dB ⊷102–140 M25 lake mountains

★ ★ ★**National** (Amb) chemin du
National 2 ☎634911 tx453118
⊷60 **P** Lift ☽ sB ⊷80–140
dB ⊷130–210 M30–40 Pool
mountains lake

★ ★ ★**Suisse & Majestic** av des Alpes 43
☎635181 tx453126
rm150 ⊷130 ᠗20 🏠 **P** Lift ☽
sB ⊷ ᠗80–140 dB ⊷ ᠗130–210 M25
mountains lake

★ ★**Bon Acceuil** (KA) Grand Rue 80
☎630551 tx453245
rm39 ⊷24 ᠗15 🏠 Lift ☽
sB ⊷ ᠗85–95 dB ⊷ ᠗140–150 M18
mountains lake

★ ★**Europe** (MIN) av des Alpes ☎634541
Apr–Nov
⊷103 🏠 **P** Lift ☽ sB ⊷55–81
dB ⊷140 mountains

★ ★**Parc & Lac** Grand Rue 38 ☎633738
Mar–Oct
rm50 ⊷14 Lift sB35–50 sB ⊷50–75
dB60–80 dB ⊷90–137 lake

★ ★**Terminus** r de la Gare ☎631071
tx453155
rm60 ⊷33 **P** Lift ☽ sB38–55
sB ⊷55–85 dB90 dB ⊷95–137 Malc
mountains lake

⚠**Central** Grande Rue 106 ☎633261
Vau

⚠**Kursaal** av du Thèâtre 7 ☎633491
DJ Frd

At **CHERNEX** (2km NE)

★**Pension les Iris** (MIN) ☎64252
rm23 ᠗6 🏠 **P** sB30–40 sB ᠗40–55
dB50–65 dB ᠗75–95 mountains lake

At **GLION** (3km E)

★ ★ ★**Victoria** ☎633131 tx453102
rm55 ⊷32 ᠗13 🏠 **P** Lift ☽
sB41–70 sB ⊷ ᠗80–140
dB ⊷ ᠗130–210 ⤶ Pool mountains
lake

MORAT See **MÜRTEN**

MORCOTE
Ticino (☎091)

★**Rivabella** ☎691314
Apr–Oct
rm15 ⊷10 A6rm **P** sB30–38
sB ⊷38–45 dB56–64 dB ⊷76–90
mountains lake

MORGES
Vaud (☎021)

★ ★**Lac** (Amb) St-Jean ☎716371
tx458147

Closed 23 Dec–21 Jan
rm28 ⊷19 ᠗7 **P** Lift mountains lake

MORGINS
Valais (☎025)

★**Beau-Site** ☎771138
rm15 **P** sB29–30 dB54–56

MÜNSTER
Valais (☎028)

⚠**Grimsel** ☎731350 M/c **P** Frd

MURALTO See **LOCARNO**

MURI See **BERN**

MÜRREN
Bern (☎036)

No road connections: take funicular from
LAUTERBRUNNEN or **STECHELBERG**

★ ★ ★**Eiger** ☎551331 tx923262
17 Dec–22 Apr & 9 Jun–20 Sep
rm41 ⊷38 ᠗3 🏠 **P** Lift
sB ⊷ ᠗65–125 dB ⊷ ᠗110–210
M alc Pool mountains

MURTEN (MORAT)
Fribourg (☎037)

★ ★**Bâteau** ☎712701
Mar–Oct
rm15 ⊷9 ᠗6 **P** ⤶ lake mountains

★ ★**Weisses Kreuz** Rathausgasse
☎712641
Mar–15 Dec
rm31 ⊷9 ᠗10 A22rm 🏠 **P** Lift
sB37–52 sB ⊷ ᠗57–77 dB69–84
dB ⊷ ᠗99–139 M15–30 lake

⚠W **Näf** Ryffstr 59 ☎711238 **P** Frd

At **MEYRIEZ** (1km S)

★ ★ ★**Vieux Manoir au Lac**
☎711283 tx942026
Feb–Nov
rm23 ⊷15 ᠗2 **P** Lift sB ⊷ ᠗65–85
dB ⊷ ᠗120–180 ⤶ Pool Beach lake

MUSTAIR
Graubünden (☎082)

★ ★**Münsterhof** ☎85541
rm20 ⊷1 ᠗8 🏠 **P** mountains

NÄFELS
Glarus (☎058)

★ ★**Schwert** ☎343373
rm7 ⊷5 ᠗2 🏠 **P** Lift ☽ sB35
sB ⊷ ᠗45–55 dB65–70
dB ⊷ ᠗85–95 mountains

⚠J **Felber** Haupfstr ☎343440 **P** Frd

NEUCHÂTEL
Neuchâtel (☎038)

★ ★ ★**Eurotel** av de la Gare 15–17
☎212121 tx35515
⊷107 **P** Lift sB ⊷70–95
dB ⊷120–140 M25 Pool

★ ★**Beaulac** (Amb) quai L-Robert 2
☎258822 tx35122
rm46 ⊷18 ᠗28 **P** Lift ☽
sB ⊷ ᠗102 dB ⊷ ᠗140 lake

★★★Touring (MIN) ☎255501 tx35127
rm50 ⇆40 ⋔3 P Lift ♪ sB35–40
sB ⇆ ⋔63–68 dB80 dB ⇆ ⋔95–100
mountains lake

★★City pl Piaget 12 ☎255412
rm35 ⇆3 Lift sB32–40 sB ⇆55–70
dB60–70 dB ⇆90–120

&ⓄM Facchinetti av Portes Rouges 1–3
☎242133 Closed wknds Fia

&ⓄTrois Rois P-A-Mazel 11 ☎258301
Frd Lnc

At PESEUX (3km W)

&ⓄCôte (R Waser) r de Neuchâtel 15
☎317573 BL MG RT

NEUHAUSEN AM RHEINFALL
Schaffhausen (☎053)

★★★Bellevue ☎22121
rm27 ⇆10 ⋔10 P Lift ♪ sB38–45
sB ⇆ ⋔70–85 dB72–84
dB ⇆ ⋔110–130 M alc

NEUVEVILLE (LA)
Bern (☎038)

★Faucon Grand Rue ☎513125
Closed Jan
rm12 ⋒ lake

☆Neuveville ☎512060
Closed Feb
rm21 ⋔18 P mountains lake

NIEDERURNEN
Glarus (☎058)

★Mineralbad Badstr 43 ☎211703
rm6 ⇆6 ⋒ P sB25–27 sB ⋔27–29
dB54–58 dB ⋔54–58 M10–35
mountains

NYON
Vaud (☎022)

★★★Clos de Sadex rte de Lausanne
☎612831
Closed Feb
rm18 ⇆12 ⋔2 A5rm P sB48–55
sB ⇆ ⋔93–120 dB84–92
dB ⇆ ⋔128–180 lake

★★★Nyon r de Rive 15 ☎611931
tx23591
Closed Nov
rm40 ⇆10 ⋔15 P Lift sB28–40
sB ⇆ ⋔40–55 dB50–65
dB ⇆ ⋔65–96 mountains lake

&ⓄL Jacques rte de Lausanne ☎612902
AR Fia Lnc

Quai (R Dubler) quai des Alpes
☎614133 Chy Lnc Sim

OBERHOFEN
Bern (☎033)

★★★Moy Staatstr ☎431514
15 May–Sep
rm30 ⇆5 ⋔12 ⋒ P Lift sB32–50
sB ⇆ ⋔45–62 dB60–84
dB ⇆ ⋔80–120 M8–25 Pool
mountains lake

★★Montana ☎431661
Apr–Oct

Switzerland

rm30 ⇆2 ⋒ Lift sB43–48
sB ⇆51–60 dB78–80 dB ⇆90–100

★Kreuz Haupstr ☎431448
Mar–Dec
rm17 ⇆4 ⋔8 P Lift sB33–38
dB58–88 dB ⇆ ⋔90–104 M9–20
mountains lake

OERLIKON See ZÜRICH

OLTEN
Solothurn (☎062)

See also EGERKINGEN

★★★Schweizerhof Bahnhofquai 18
☎214571
rm60 ⇆10 P Lift sB32 sB ⇆40 dB56
dB ⇆70 ⤴

&ⓄCity (F Widmer) Baslerstr 90 ☎321422
AR BL

&ⓄMoser Baslerstr 47 ☎328280

At STARRKIRCH (2km)

&ⓄPilloud Aarauerstr 235 ☎353232 Frd

ORSIÈRES
Valais (☎026)

★★Catogne ☎41230
Closed Nov
rm30 ⇆20 ⋔5 P sB25–30
sB ⇆ ⋔35–40 dB50–55
dB ⇆ ⋔60–65 M13–52 mountains

OUCHY See LAUSANNE

PARADISO See LUGANO

PARPAN
Graubünden (☎081)

★Alpina Haupfstr ☎351184
Jun–Oct & 15 Dec–Apr
rm45 ⇆7 ⋔11 ⋒ P Lift ♪
Sb43–59 sB ⇆ ⋔53–76 dB86–118
dB ⇆ ⋔106–152 M18–24 mountains

PAYERNE
Vaud (☎037)

&ⓄPromenade (A Ischi) pl du Gl-Guisan 1
☎612505 P Frd

PESEUX See NEUCHÂTEL

PFÄFFIKON
Schwyz (☎055)

★Sternen ☎481291
rm15 ⇆13 ⋔13 ⋒ P

PONT TRESA
Ticino (☎091)

★★★Zita ☎711825
Mar–Dec
rm30 ⇆8 ⋔14 A6rm ⋒ P Lift
sB26–36 sB ⇆ ⋔32–42 dB52–76
dB ⇆ ⋔64–88 Pool mountains lake

PONTRESINA
Graubünden (☎082)

★★★Kronenhof-Bellavista ☎66333
tx74488
Dec–Apr & Jun–Sep
rm120 ⇆116 ⋔4 ⋒ P Lift ♪
sB ⇆ ⋔130–180 dB ⇆ ⋔240–340
M30–40 ⤴ Pool mountains

★★Müller (DPn in season) ☎66341
17 Dec–25 Apr & 30 May–5 Oct
rm48 ⇆15 ⋔19 A11rm ⋒ P Lift
sB40–50 sB ⇆ ⋔60–80 dB76–104
dB ⇆ ⋔104–150 M20–24 mountains

★★★Palü ☎66688
rm37 ⇆6 ⋔29 ⋒ P sB ⇆ ⋔66–95
dB ⇆ ⋔120–180 mountains

★★★Schweizerhof Berninastr
☎66412 tx74442
Dec–Apr & Jun–Oct
rm90 ⇆60 ⋔30 ⋒ P Lift ♪
sB ⇆ ⋔90–135 dB ⇆ ⋔170–260
mountains

PORRENTRUY
Jura (☎066)

&ⓄJ Moutarou r Cuenin 21 ☎661408 P
Ren

&ⓄPonts rte de Courgenay ☎661206 P
Opl

&ⓄL Vallat r du Jura 5 ☎661913 M/c P
Frd

PORTO-RONCO
Ticino (☎093)

★Eden (n. rest) ☎355142
Mar–Oct
rm14 ⇆2 P mountains lake

POSCHIAVO
Graubünden (☎082)

At PRESE (LE) (4.5km S)

★★★Prese ☎503333
May–Oct
rm29 ⇆23 ⋔4 ⋒ P Lift sB63–94
sB ⇆74–110 dB ⇆150–220 M26–30
⤴ Pool lake mountains

PULLY See LAUSANNE

RAGAZ-PFÄFERS (BAD)
St-Gallen (☎085)

★★★★Quellenhof ☎90111 tx855897
rm135 ⇆96 ⋔32 ⋒ Lift ♪
sB115–165 sB ⇆ ⋔125–185
dB ⇆ ⋔250–370 M45–70 ⤴ Pool ♿
lake mountains

☆☆TM Schloss Ragaz ☎92355
rm62 ⇆8 ⋔46 P sB44–70
sB ⇆ ⋔58–91 dB88–140
dB ⇆ ⋔108–170 M24–28 Pool
mountains

★Park ☎92244
Apr–Oct
rm65 ⇆4 ⋔35 ⋒ P Lift ♪ sB49–74
sB ⇆ ⋔66–99 dB 92–138
dB⇆ ⋔118–177 M23–28 mountains

REGENSDORF See ZÜRICH

RENENS See LAUSANNE

RHEINFELDEN
Aargau (☎061)

★ ★ ★Schwanen Kaiserstr 8 ☎875344

15 Jan – 20 Dec
rm65 ⇌27 ▥10 ♨ P Lift sB58–82
sB ⇌ ▥84–94 dB118–160
dB ⇌ ▥160–184 M23–27 Pool

★Ochsen ☎875101

Mar – Nov
rm30 ▥3 ♨ sB30–40 sB ▥40–50
dB60–80 dB ▥80–100

★Storchen Marktgasse 61 ☎875322

rm30 ▥15 ♨ P Lift sB42–55
sB ▥50–65 dB61–85 dB ▥80–105

☼Grell Kaiserstr 30 ☎875051 P Frd

ROLLE
Vaud (☎021)

★ ★Tête Noir ☎752251

rm20 ⇌15 sB30–35 sB ⇌40–50
dB60–70 dB ▥70–90 lake

ROMANSHORN
Thurgau (☎071)

★ ★Bodan ☎631502

rm18 ⇌4 ▥2 ♨ P 𝔻 lake

RORSCHACH
St-Gallen (☎071)

★ ★ ★Anker Hauptstr 71 ☎414243

rm32 ⇌10 ▥14 P Lift sB40–45
sB ⇌45–60 dB60–70
dB ⇌ ▥80–100 M22 lake mountains

☼Meyer ☎412222 P Aud VW

SAANENMOSER PASS
Bern (☎030)

★ ★ ★Golf & Sporthotel ☎43222
tx922220

Dec – Apr & Jun – Sep
rm55 ⇌35 ▥6 ♨ P Lift 𝔻 ♨ ♂
mountains

SAAS-FEE
Valais (☎028)

★ ★Bergfreude ☎572137

Jun – Oct & Dec – Apr
rm25 ⇌5 sB65 sB ⇌42–68 dB72–120
dB ⇌84–136 mountains

SACHSELN AM SARNERSEE
Obwalden (☎041)

☆ ☆ ★Kreuz ☎661466 tx72643

15 Mar – Jan
rm50 ⇌40 P Lift sB ⇌40–55
dB ⇌70–110 mountains lake

ST-BLAISE
Neuchâtel (☎038)

★Cheval Blanc Grande Rue 18
☎333007

rm12 ⇌1 ▥11 P sB ⇌ ▥35–38
dB ⇌ ▥55–80 mountains

ST-GALLEN
St-Gallen (☎071)

★ ★ ★ ★Walhalla (Amb) Poststr 27
☎222922 tx77160

Switzerland

⇌52 ♨ P Lift 𝔻 sB ⇌85–95
dB ⇌130–180 M alc

★ ★ ★Hecht Marktpl ☎226502 tx77173

rm59 ⇌18 ▥15 P Lift 𝔻 sB50–60
sB ⇌ ▥85–95 dB80–90
dB ⇌ ▥130–180

★ ★ ★Im Portner Bankgasse 12
☎229744

⇌25 ♨ Lift sB ⇌85–95
dB ⇌130–180

☼Capitol Rorschacherstr 239 ☎351414
BL RT

☼Citroën St-Gallen Fürstenlandstr 25
☎282121 Cit

☼City ☎291131 P Aud Por VW

☼H Erb Fürstenlandstr 149 ☎273333

Lutz Vadianstr 57 ☎232382

ST-LUC
Valais (☎027)

★ ★Belle-Tola ☎651444

Jun – Sep & Dec – Feb
rm42 ⇌21 ♨ P Lift sB37–52
sB ⇌48–70 dB63–88
dB ⇌ ▥82–119 mountains

ST-MORITZ
Graubünden (☎082)

★ ★ ★ ★Kulm (DPn in winter) ☎2151
tx7447?

26 Nov – 15 Apr & 25 Jun – 10 Sep
⇌215 ♨ P Lift 𝔻 sB ⇌95–255
dB ⇌180–435 M35–45 ♨ Pool
mountains lake

★ ★ ★Carlton (SRS) ☎21141 tx74454

Dec – Apr & Jun – Sep
⇌115 ♨ P Lift 𝔻 sB ⇌105–300
dB ⇌170–560 ♨ Pool mountains lake

★ ★ ★Crystal ☎21165 tx74449

Dec – Apr May – Oct
⇌110 Lift sB ⇌85–160 dB ⇌160–300
Pool

★ ★ ★Suvretta House ☎21121
tx74491

3 Dec – Mar & Jul – 9th Sep
⇌230 ♨ P Lift sB ⇌110–300
dB ⇌220–600 M40–55 ♨ Pool ♂
lake mountains

★ ★ ★Bellevue (KA) via dal Bagn 18
☎22161 tx74428

rm42 ⇌10 ▥30 ♨ P Lift 𝔻
sB ⇌ ▥58–105 dB ⇌ ▥105–179
M7–33 & alc mountains lake

★ ★ ★Belvédère ☎33905 tx74435

Dec – Apr & Jun – Oct
rm70 ⇌45 ▥25 P Lift 𝔻 sB60–110
dB ⇌120–220 ♨ Pool mountains lake

★ ★ ★Neues Posthotel ☎22121
tx74430

rm83 ⇌46 ▥17 ♨ P Lift sB55–110

---

sB ⇌ ▥70–160 dB110–220
sB ⇌ ▥140–320 M20–40 mountains
lake

★ ★Bären Hauptstr ☎33656

Closed May
rm62 ⇌54 ▥8 P Lift sB ⇌ ▥55–110
dB ⇌ ▥110–220 Pool mountains

★ ★Margna Bahnhofst ☎22141
tx74402

Jun Sep & Dec – Apr
rm64 ⇌38 ▥26 ♨ P Lift 𝔻
sB ⇌ ▥80–155 dB ⇌ ▥140–290
mountains lake

☼M Conrad ☎33788 Fia Lnc

☼Grand Dosch ☎33333 P AR MB Opl

At **ST-MORITZ-BAD** (1km S)

★National ☎33274

Dec – Apr & Jun – Sep
▥22 ♨ P 𝔻 Lift sB40–60
sB ▥45–70 dB80–120 dB ▥90–140
mountains

At **ST-MORITZ CHAMPFÉR** (3km SW)

★ ★ ★ ★Europa ☎21175 tx74458

Jun – Sep & Nov – Apr
rm137 ⇌109 ▥16 ♨ P Lift 𝔻
sB70–110 sB ⇌ ▥85–175 dB140–220
dB ⇌ ▥150–350 ♨ Pool mountains

ST-SULPICE See LAUSANNE

SAMEDAN
Graubünden (☎082)

★ ★ ★Bernina (Amb) Haupstr ☎65421
tx74482

Jun – Oct & Dec – Apr
rm80 ⇌60 ▥10 ♨ P Lift 𝔻
sB65–86 sB ⇌ ▥176–120 dB120–170
dB ⇌ ▥114–240 ♨ mountains

☼Gebrüder Pfister ☎65666 Toy Vlo

☼Palü Hauptstr ☎64743 P BL DJ MB
Frd

SANTA MARIA
Graubünden (☎082)

★Schweizerhof Hauptstr ☎85124
tx74715

15 May – Oct
rm30 ⇌13 ▥12 ♨ P Lift sB46–60
sB ⇌ ▥55–85 dB92–120
dB ⇌ ▥110–170 M9–18 mountains

SARGANS
St-Gallen (☎085)

★ ★Post ☎21214

rm15 ⇌3 ▥8 A11rm ♨ P mountains

SARNEN
Obwalden (☎041)
At **WILEN** (2km SW)

★ ★Wilerbad ☎661292

rm67 ⇌20 ▥8 ♨ P Lift sB26–34
sB ⇌ ▥34–48 dB44–61
dB ⇌ ▥61–87 Pool

SAVOGNIN
Graubünden (☎081)

☆ ☆ Berg ☎741444

382

24 Dec–Mar & 15 Jun–15 Sep
⇌44 🏠 **P** mountains

SCHAFFHAUSEN
Schaffhausen (☎053)

★★**Bahnhof** Bahnhofstr 46 ☎54001 tx76800
rm44 ⇌30 ▥14 🏠 **P** Lift 🌙
sB ⇌60–80 dB ⇌90–120

★★**Kronenhof** Kirchhofpl 7 (off Vordergasse) ☎56631
rm35 ⇌14 ▥12 **P** Lift 🌙 sB55
sB ⇌ ▥85 dB75–85 dB ⇌ ▥130–150
M20–30

★★**Parkvilla & Schwyzerhüsli** Parkstr 18 ☎52737
rm32 ⇌20 ▥5 A10rm **P** sB50
sB ⇌55–60 dB65–70 dB ⇌120
M18–24 ⚓

⑧**Auto-Ernst** Schweizerbildstr 61 ☎33322 **P** BMW Frd

SCHÖNRIED
Bern (☎030)

★★★**Ermitage & Golf** ☎42727 tx922213
Dec–Apr & May–Oct
rm50 ⇌40 ▥7 🏠 **P** Lift 🌙 sB60–80
sB ⇌ ▥75–145 dB50–70
dB ⇌ ▥65–175 ⚓ Pool mountains

SCHWANDEN
Glarus (☎058)

★**Adler** ☎811171
28 Jan–28 Dec
▥8 sB ▥38–45 dB ▥75–85 M12–20 mountains

SCUOL (BAD)
Graubünden (☎084)

★★★**Kurhotel Belvedere** ☎91041 tx74474
17 Dec–Oct
rm60 ⇌ ▥45 🏠 **P** Lift sB45–67
sB ⇌ ▥65–90 dB80–124
dB ⇌ ▥120–180 Mfr20 mountains

SEEBURG See **LUZERN (LUCERNE)**

SERVION
Vaud (☎021)

☆☆**Fleurs** ☎932054
rm31 ▥14 **P** 🌙 sB30–45 sB ▥43–45
dB59 dB ▥50–65 M9 mountains

SIERRE (SIDERS)
Valais (☎027)

★★**Arnold** rte de Sion ☎551721 tx38439
rm32 ⇌3 ▥16 🏠 **P** Lift sB31–37
sB ⇌ ▥40–50 dB53–63
dB ⇌ ▥68–85 M alc

★**Victoria-Jardin** rte de Sion 5 ☎551007
rm13 ⇌2 **P** sB31–37 sB ⇌40–50
dB53–63 dB ⇌68–85 M12–25
mountains

⑧**International** rte de Noës ☎551436 **P** Peu Tal

⑧**Rawyl** (F Durret) rte du Simplon ☎550308 **P** Frd

Switzerland

SIGRISWIL
Bern (☎033)

★**Adler** ☎512424
rm28 ⇌12 ▥10 **P** Lift sB41–50
sB ⇌ ▥47–70 dB80–96
dB ⇌ ▥90–126 M17–30 lake mountains

SILS-MARIA
Graubünden (☎082)

★★★★**Waldhaus** ☎45331 tx74444
Jun–20 Oct & mid-Dec–25 Apr
rm150 ⇌120 ▥5 🏠 **P** Lift 🌙
sB90–130 sB ⇌ ▥110–180
dB150–230 dB ⇌ ▥186–340 M26–45
Pool mountains lake

★**Privata** ☎45247
Dec–Apr & Jun–Oct
rm20 sB ⇌ ▥65–82 dB ⇌ ▥130–155

At **SILS-BASEGLIA**

★★★**Margna** ☎45306 tx74496
Dec–Apr & Jun–Oct
rm72 ⇌68 ▥4 **P** Lift 🌙
sB ⇌ ▥90–150 dB ⇌ ▥180–300
M20–45 ⚓ lake mountains

SILVAPLANA
Graubünden (☎082)

★★★**Sonne** ☎48152 tx75649
rm50 ⇌34 🏠 **P** Lift 🌙 sB50–82
sB ⇌59–95 dB100–164 dB ⇌118–190
⚓ mountains lake

★**Corvatsch** ☎48162
Jun–Oct & Nov–Apr
rm16 **P** sB50–70 dB100–140
mountains lake

SIMPLON-DORF
Valais (☎028)

★**Poste** ☎29112
rm26 ▥8 🏠 **P** sB32–34 sB ▥34–36
dB54–60 dB ▥60–66 M alc mountains

SIMPLON-KULM
Valais (☎028)

★★**Bellevue** Simplon Pass ☎291331
Mar–Oct
rm45 ⇌3 🏠 **P** Lift 🌙 sB30–40
dB50–70 dB ⇌70–90 M20–35
mountains

SION (SITTEN)
Valais (☎027)

★★★**Rhône** (KA) r du Sex 10 ☎228291 tx38104
⇌44 **P** Lift 🌙 sB ⇌48–66
dB ⇌88–114 mountains

★★**Continental** rte de Lausanne 116 ☎224641
Closed 1–20 Aug
▥24 **P** sB ▥37–44 dB ▥63–75 M&alc mountains

★★**Touring** av de la Gare 6 ☎231551
rm30 ⇌13 ▥11 🏠 **P** Lift sB40–58
sB ⇌ ▥48–66 dB ⇌ ▥88–114

⑧**Aviation** rte Cantonale-Corbassières ☎223924 Maz Vlo

⑧**Hediger** Batasse ☎220131 Chy MB

⑧**Kasper** r du Tunnel 22 ☎221271 Frd

⑧**Nord** av Ritz 35 ☎223413 Ren

⑧**Tourbillon** av de Tourbillon 23 ☎222077 Peu

SISIKON
Uri (☎044)

★★★**Tellsplatte** ☎21612
Apr–15 Oct
rm50 ⇌9 ▥32 🏠 **P** Lift Pool mountains lake

SOLOTHURN (SOLEURE)
Solothurn (☎065)

★★★**Krone** (Amb) Hauptgasse 64 ☎224412
rm42 ⇌15 ▥26 🏠 **P** Lift
sB ⇌ ▥100 dB ⇌ ▥150

⑧**Howald Otto** Engistr 13 ☎223718 DJ Ren

SPIEZ
Bern (☎033)

★★★**Eden** Seestr 58 ☎541154
May–Oct
rm60 ⇌50 🏠 **P** Lift sB48–68
sB ⇌54–78 dB80–116 dB ⇌90–146
M18–32 ⚓ Pool mountains lake

★★**Alpes** Seestr 38 ☎543354
rm40 ⇌11 ▥29 🏠 **P** Lift
sB ⇌ ▥38–56 dB ⇌ ▥76–112 M20
mountains

★★**Terminus** Bahnhofpl ☎543121
rm65 ⇌30 **P** Lift sB30–44
sB ⇌42–58 dB58–85 sB ⇌78–110
M8–20 lake mountains

STANS
Nidwalden (☎041)

★★**Stanserhof** Stansstaderstr 20 ☎614122
rm45 ⇌8 ▥3 Lift sB ⇌ ▥30–35
dB ⇌ ▥56–64 mountains

STANSSTAD
Nidwalden (☎041)

★★★**Freienhof** ☎613531
rm50 ⇌35 🏠 **P** Lift sB30–40
sB ⇌37–52 dB60–80 dB ⇌74–104
mountains

★★★**Schützen** (Amb) Stanserstr 23 ☎611355 tx866256
rm50 ⇌28 🏠 **P** Lift sB44–48
sB ⇌68–83 dB85–91 dB ⇌125–155
M15–50 mountains

STARRKIRCH See **OLTEN**

STECKBORN
Thurgau (☎054)

⑧**Bürgl's Erben** Bahnhofstr ☎611251
P Dat Sab

SURSEE
Luzern (☎045)

★ ★**Hirschen** Obserstadt 10 ☎211048
rm12 ⇌2 ⌂4 ⌂ **P** Lift sB28–30
sB ⇌ ⌂32–35 dB45–50
dB ⇌ ⌂56–64 M7–30

★**Bellevue** Mariazell ☎211844
rm15 ⌂2 A1rm **P** sB26 sB ⌂30 dB52
dB ⌂60 mountains lake

&⚬**Centrai** (L Muller) Luzernstr 18
☎211144 Frd

TAFERS
Fribourg (☎037)

&⚬**Schweingruber** ☎441750 M/c Opl

TARASP-VULPERA See **VULPERA**
(TARASP)

TEUFEN
Appenzell (☎071)

★**Ochsen** ☎332188
rm13 ⇌2 **P** mountains

THALWIL
Zürich (☎01)

★ ★**Thalwilerhof** Bahnhofstr 16
☎7200603
rm26 ⇌3 ⌂7 **P** Lift sBfr47
sB ⇌ ⌂52–58 dB73–96
dB ⇌ ⌂98–116 M9–15 mountains lake

THIELLE
Neuchâtel (☎038)

☆ ☆ ☆**Novotel Neuchâtel Est** rte de
Berne ☎335757 tx35402
⇌60 **P** ⅅ sB ⇌70 dB ⇌110 M9–35
Pool mountains

THUN (THOUNE)
Bern (☎033)

★ ★ ★ ★**Elite** Bernstr 1–3 ☎232823
tx921214
rm39 ⇌14 ⌂25 ⌂ **P** Lift ⅅ
sB ⇌ ⌂52–80 dB ⇌ ⌂95–125
mountains lake

★ ★ ★**Beau Rivage** ☎222236
May–20 Oct
rm30 ⇌20 ⌂1 ⌂ **P** Lift sB37–53
sB ⇌ ⌂53–82 dB69–92
dB ⇌ ⌂99–134 Pool mountains

★ ★**Freienhof** (Amb) Freienhofgasse3
☎224672 tx921190
rm63 ⇌31 ⌂32 ⌂ **P** Lift ⅅ
sB ⇌ ⌂46–80 dB ⇌ ⌂85–125
M10–30

★**Metzgern** Rathauspl ☎222141
Closed Oct
rm8 **P** mountains

&⚬**City** (G Wenger) Kyburgstr ☎229578
Cit Maz

&⚬**Moser** Gwattstr 24 ☎341515 Aud Por
VW Vlo

&⚬**Touring** Schlossmattstr 10 ☎224455
MB Toy

At **DÜRRENAST** (2km S)

Switzerland

☆ ☆ ☆**Holiday** Gwattstr 1 ☎365757
⇌57 **P** Lift ⅅ sB ⇌70–87
dB ⇌124–139 Mfr17 lake

At **HÜNIBACH** (1km SE)

&⚬**K Schick** Staatsstr 134 ☎433131
BMW Ren

THUSIS
Graubünden (☎081)

Central ☎811154 **P** Frd

&⚬**Viamala** Hauptstr ☎811822 **P** Frd
Opl Vau

TIEFENCASTEL
Graubüden (☎081)

★ ★**Posthotel Julier** Julierstr ☎771415
rm50 ⇌17 ⌂22 ⌂ **P** Lift sB30–35
sB ⇌ ⌂41–46 dB47–55
dB ⇌ ⌂62–80 M16 mountains

★**Albula** ☎711121
⇌30 ⌂ **P** Lift sB34–38 sB ⇌41–44
dB62–66 dB ⇌72–82 M15 mountains

TRAVERS
Neuchâtel (☎038)

★**Crêt** ☎631178
Closed Feb
rm6 ⚬ mountains

UNTERÄGERI
Zug (☎042)

★ ★**Seefeld** (KA) Seestr 8 ☎722727
tx864981
rm36 ⇌9 ⌂25 A6rm **P** Lift sB45
sB ⇌ ⌂70–75 dB90 dB ⇌ ⌂120–130
M18–25 ⚬ mountains lake

UNTERWASSER
St-Gallen (☎074)

★ ★**Sternen** ☎52424 tx884148
rm55 ⇌25 **P** Lift mountains

VALLORBE
Vaud (☎021)

☆**Jurats** ☎831991
⌂16 **P** mountains

&⚬**Moderne** r de l'Ancien Poste
41 ☎831156 **P** Aud VW

VERBIER
Valais (☎026)

★ ★**Farinet** ☎76626
22 Dec–27 Apr & 26 May–11 Sep
rm25 ⇌16 ⌂9 **P** Lift sB30–90
sB ⇌ ⌂50–110 dB40–150
dB ⇌ ⌂80–190 Mfr20 mountains

★ ★**Grand Combin** ☎75515 tx38795
Jun–Sep & Dec–Apr
rm35 ⇌25 ⌂1 **P** Lift ⅅ sB48–66
sB ⇌ ⌂60–104 dB ⇌ ⌂116–200

★ ★**Rhodania** (Amb) ☎70121
tx473392
22 Dec–27 Apr & 26 May–11 Sep

⇌ ⌂45 **P** Lift ⅅ sB ⇌ ⌂58–120
dB ⇌ ⌂96–200 Mfr20 mountains

&⚬**Verbier** (M A Stuckelberger) ☎76666

VÉSENAZ See **GENÈVE**

VEVEY
Vaud (☎021)

★ ★ ★**Trois Couronnes** r d'Italie 49
☎513005 tx451148
⇌90 **P** Lift ⅅ sB ⇌110–160
dB ⇌190–270 M50 mountains lake

★ ★**Lac** (Amb) r d'Italie 1 ☎511041
tx451161
rm56 ⇌44 ⌂ **P** Lift ⅅ sB40–60
sB ⇌80–120 dB70–100 dB ⇌125–190
Pool mountains lake

★**Familie** ☎513931 tx451181
rm62 ⇌24 ⌂21 **P** Lift sB32–42
sB ⌂38–52 dB60–76 dB ⌂112
M12–15 Pool

At **JONGNY** (3km N)

★ ★ ★**Léman** (KA) ☎510544 tx451198
rm60 ⇌7 ⌂40 A29rm ⌂ **P** Lift ⅅ
sB50–65 sB ⇌ ⌂65–80 dB90–120
dB ⇌ ⌂120–150 M20–30 mountains
lake

VEZIA See **LUGANO**

VILLARS-SUR-OLLON
Vaud (☎025)

★ ★ ★**Eurotel** ☎353131 tx456206
⇌171 **P** Lift sB ⇌71–126
dB ⇌102–222 M23 Pool

★ ★**Montesano & Regina** ☎352551
tx456217
15 Dec–Etr & Jun–Sep
rm50 ⇌30 ⌂6 ⌂ **P** Lift sB65
sB ⇌80 dB120 dB ⇌150 ⚬ Pool
mountains

VILLMERGEN
Schwyz(☎057)

&⚬**R Huber** Hauptstr ☎221379 **P** Aud MB
VW

VISP
Valais(☎028)

&⚬**Moderne** ☎464333 **P** Fia MB

&⚬**Touring** Kantonstr ☎461040 **P** Aud
Por VW

VITZNAU
Luzern(☎041)

★ ★ ★**Park** ☎831322 tx78340
mid Apr–mid Oct
rm84 ⇌62 ⌂16 A19rm ⌂ **P** Lift ⅅ
sB ⇌ ⌂134–174 dB ⇌ ⌂248–318
M48–52 ⚬ Pool

★ ★**Kreuz** ☎831305 tx72524
Apr–Dec
rm53 ⇌33 ⌂ Lift sB34–43
sB ⇌40–54 dB56–70 dB ⇌70–90
M17–22 Pool mountains lake

★ ★ ★**Vitznauerhof** ☎831315 tx72241
10 Apr–10 Oct
rm60 ⇌45 ⌂9 ⌂ **P** Lift ⅅ sB38–50

sB ⇌ ⋔60–75 dB ⇌ ⋔144 M22–34
🏊 mountains lake

★★**Terasse am See** ☎831033
rm30 ⇌16 P Lift sB33–51
sB ⇌41–59 dB54–81 dB ⇌74–114
mountains lake

VULPERA (TARASP)
Graubünden(☎084)

★★★**Schweizerhof** ☎91331 tx74427
Closed May & Nov
rm80 🏨 Lift ☽ sB95–115
sB ⇌ ⋔115–135 dB160–200
dB ⇌ ⋔200–240 🏊 Pool ♪ lake

WABERN See BERN (BERNE)

WÄDENSWIL
Zürich(☎01)

★★★**Lac** Seestr 100 ☎780031
rm22 ⇌4 ⋔9 P Lift sB65
sB ⇌ ⋔34–42 dB65 dB ⇌ ⋔85–105
mountains

🛢**Zentrum** (B & C Weber) Seestr
114 ☎7808080

WASSEN
Uri(☎044)

★★*Krone* Gottharstr ☎65334
Apr–Oct
rm15 ⇌4 ⋔1 🏨 P mountains

★**Alpes** (MIN) ☎65233
rm11 ⇌6 🏨 P sBfr35 sB ⇌ ⋔fr40
dBfr60 dB ⇌ ⋔fr80 M5–30 mountains

Gotthardgarage (K Calagni) ☎65663 P
BMW Frd MB

WEGGIS
Luzern(☎041)

★★★**Albana** ☎932141 tx78637
Apr–Oct
⇌70 🏨 P Lift sB ⇌65–113
dB ⇌127–208 M25–30 🏊 lake

★★★**Beau Rivage** Gottardstr
☎931422 tx72525
mid Mar–mid Oct
rm42 ⇌30 ⋔12 🏨 P Lift
sB ⇌ ⋔65–113 dB ⇌ ⋔127–208
M28–35 Pool lake mountains

★★★**Park** ☎931313
Apr–Oct
rm64 ⇌46 ⋔4 Lift ☽ sB50–80
sB ⇌ ⋔65–113 dB98–151
dB ⇌ ⋔127–208 🏊 mountains lake

★★★**Waldstätten** (KA) ☎931341
tx72428
⇌42 P Lift sB ⇌ ⋔65–113
dB ⇌ ⋔127–208

★★**Central am See** ☎931317
Feb–Nov
rm50 ⇌10 ⋔33 🏨 P Lift sB43–68
sB ⇌ ⋔61–87 dB93–127
dB ⇌ ⋔93–168 M17–24 Pool
mountains lake

★★**Rigi** Seestr ☎932151 tx78395
May–Sep
rm50 ⇌6 ⋔30 A30rm P sB43–68
sB ⇌ ⋔48–87 dB81–127

Switzerland

dB ⇌ ⋔93–168 M15–20 mountains
lake

★★**Rössli** Seestr ☎931106 tx78395
Mar–Nov
rm50 ⇌35 P Lift sB ⇌ ⋔48–87
dB ⇌ ⋔93–168 M8–25 mountains lake

★**Frohburg** (n.rest) ☎931022
Apr–10 Oct
rm22 ⇌20 P sB ⇌55–75
dB ⇌100–150 mountains lake

★**National** Seestr ☎931225 tx78292
Apr–15 Oct
rm38 ⇌32 ⋔4 🏨 P Lift
sB ⇌ ⋔48–87 dB76–118
dB ⇌ ⋔93–168 M14–18 mountains
lake

★**Seehotel du Lac** (MIN) ☎931151
tx78395
Mar–Nov
rm29 ⇌11 ⋔11 P Lift sB45–52
sB ⇌52–78 dB81–114 dB ⇌96–149 M
alc mountains lake

WENGEN
Bern(☎036)

★★★**Victoria-Lauberhorn** ☎565151
tx923232
Dec–Apr & end May–Sep
rm71 ⇌62 P Lift sB ⇌62–75
dB ⇌106–132 mountains

★★★**Waldrand** ☎552855
10 Sec–29 Sep
rm50 ⇌42 ⋔3 Lift ☽ sB57–77
sB ⇌ ⋔66–100 dB ⇌ ⋔129–194
M18–20 mountains

WIL
St-Gallen(☎073)

★★★**Derby** Bahnhofpl 1 ☎222626
tx883206
rm22 ⇌9 ⋔4 🏨 P Lift

🛢**Bahnhof** Untere Bahnhofstr 9
☎221112 BL Ren RT

WILDERSWIL
Bern(☎036)

★★**Bären** ☎223521 tx923137
rm45 ⇌10 ⋔30 A7rm 🏨 P ☽
sB38–48 sB ⇌ ⋔40–65 dB76–96
dB ⇌ ⋔80–130 M15–19 mountains

☆☆**Luna** ☎228414
rm30 ⇌8 ⋔8 P mountains

★**Alpenrose** ☎221024
rm40 ⇌14 P sB28–38 sB ⇌ ⋔36–48
dB54–74 dB ⇌ ⋔70–94 M15–24
mountains

★**Viktoria** ☎221670
rm15 ⋔2 P sB21–24 dB38–44
dB ⇌ ⋔50–56 M8–12 mountains

WILDHAUS
St-Gallen(☎074)

★★★**Acker** ☎59111 tx71208
rm100 ⇌60 ⋔40 A50rm 🏨 P Lift ☽
sB ⇌ ⋔60–105 dB ⇌ ⋔100–170 Pool
mountains

★★**Hirschen** ☎52252 tx884139
rm80 ⇌24 ⋔48 P Lift sB80
sB ⇌ ⋔70–100 dB90–125
dB ⇌ ⋔120–178 M20–25 mountains

WILEN See SARNEN

WINTERTHUR
Zürich(☎052)

★★★★**Garten** Stadthausstr 4
☎232231 tx896201
⇌55 🏨 P Lift ☽ sB ⇌88–96
dB ⇌130–144

★★★**Krone** Marktgasse 49 ☎232521
rm38 ⇌18 ⋔15 🏨 P Lift ☽
sB40–45 sB ⇌ ⋔53–65 dB ⇌ ⋔85–95
🛢**Eulach** Technikumstr 67
☎222333 Opl

🛢**Riedbach** Frauenfeldstr 9 ☎272222 P
BL BMW Ren

🛢**A Siegenthaler** Frauenfeldstr 44
☎272900 Chy Sim

YVERDON
Vaud(☎024)

★★**Prairie** av des Bains 9 ☎231330
tx457136
rm36 ⇌17 ⋔8 P Lift sB40–45
sB ⇌ ⋔75–90 dB ⇌ ⋔110–130 🏊
mountains

🛢**Belair** av des Sports 13 ☎218595 Frd

🛢**Remparts** Champs Louats 1
☎213535 Peu Tal

ZERMATT
Valais(☎028)
No road connection; take train from
TÄSCH or **VISP**

★★★★**Mont Cervin Seiler** Bahnhofstr
☎661121 tx38329 (fr mid 84 472129)
Dec–Apr & Jun–Oct
rm129 ⇌102 ⋔10 A17rm Lift ☽
sB65–120 sB ⇌ ⋔84–178 dB130–240
dB ⇌ ⋔168–356 M30–42 🏊 Pool
mountains

★★★**Julen** (ROM) ☎672481 tx472111
⇌34 P Lift sB ⇌40–100 dB ⇌80–200
mountains

★★★**Parkhotel Beau Site** ☎671271
tx38361
3 Dec–Apr & Jun–8 Oct
⇌67 🏨 P Lift sB ⇌67–136
dB ⇌134–272 M26–35 🏊 Pool
mountains

★★**Schweizerhof** ☎661155 tx38201
Jun–Oct & 3 Dec–Apr
rm104 ⇌78 ⋔26 Lift ☽
sB ⇌ ⋔84–178 dB ⇌ ⋔168–356
Mfr30 🏊 Pool mountains

★★★**Zermatterhof** ☎661101 tx38275
26 Nov–6 Oct
rm95 ⇌69 ⋔11 Lift ☽ sB65
sB ⇌ ⋔84–178 dB130–240 →

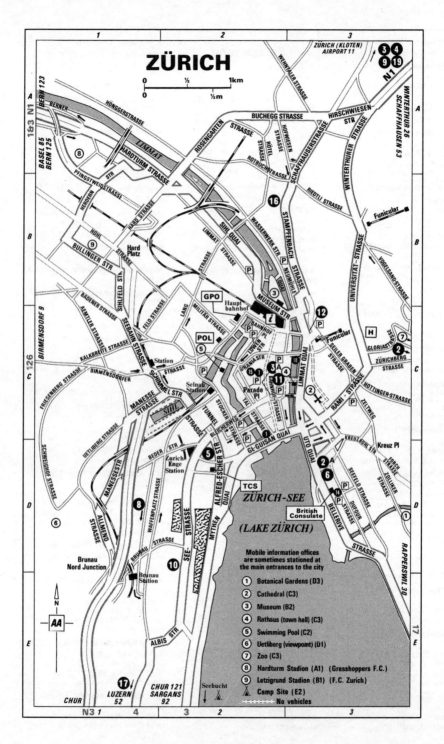

ZÜRICH

0 ½ 1km

0 ½m

Mobile information offices are sometimes stationed at the main entrances to the city

① Botanical Gardens (D3)

② Cathedral (C3)

③ Museum (B2)

④ Rathaus (town hall) (C3)

⑤ Swimming Pool (C2)

⑥ Uetliberg (viewpoint) (D1)

⑦ Zoo (C3)

⑧ Hardturm Stadion (A1) (Grasshoppers F.C.)

⑨ Letzigrund Stadion (B1) (F.C. Zurich)

⚑ Camp Site (E2)

┅┅┅┅ No vehicles

ZÜRICH-SEE

British Consulate

(LAKE ZÜRICH)

ZÜRICH

1 ★ ★ ★ ★ ★Baur au Lac
2 ★ ★ ★ ★ ★Dolder
2A ★ ★ ★ ★ ★Eden au Lac
3 ★ ★ ★ ★ ★Hilton International
(At Glattbrugg 8km NE
on N4 under ZÜRICH
AIRPORT)
3A ★ ★ ★ ★ ★Savoy Bauer en Ville
4 ★ ★ ★ ★Airport (At Glattbrugg,
8km NE on N4 under
ZÜRICH AIRPORT)
5 ★ ★ ★ ★Ascot
6 ★ ★ ★ ★Bellerive au Lac
7 ★ ★ ★ ★Carlton Elite
8 ★ ★ ★ ★Engematthof
9 ☆ ☆ ☆ ☆Mövenpick (At
Glattbrugg 8km
NE on N4 under
ZÜRICH AIRPORT)
11 ★ ★ ★Zum Storchen
12 ★ ★ ★Central
14 ★ ★ ★Excelsior
15 ★ ★ ★Glockenhof
16 ★ ★Burma
17 ☆ ☆Jolie Ville Motor In (At
Adiswil 4km SE on N4)
18 ★ ★Krone
19 ★ ★Sternen Oerlikon
At Oerlikon 4km N)

dB ⇄ ▥168–356 M18–20 ⸎ pool
mountains

★ ★Dom ☎671371

Dec–Apr & Jun–Oct
rm40 ⇄35 P Lift sB41–80
sB ⇄ ▥57–110 dB82–160
dB ⇄ ▥114–220 Mfr10 mountains

ZERNEZ
Graubünden(☎082)

★ ★Baer & Post Curtinstr ☎81141
Dec–Oct
rm19 ⇄5 ▥14 A12rm ▥
sB ⇄ ▥54–60 dB ⇄ ▥96–110 Pool

ZUG
Zug(☎042)

★ ★ ★City Ochsen Kolinpl ☎213232
⇄35 P Lift sB ⇄ ▥75–90
dB ⇄ ▥130–160 M25–30

★Guggital Zugerbergstr ☎212821
tx865134
rm33 ⇄23 ▥9 ▥ P Lift
sB ⇄ ▥65–90 dB ⇄ ▥100–145
M13–30 lake mountains

★Rössli Vorstadtstr 8 ☎210394
15 Jan–20 Dec
rm18 ▥10 P Lift sB33–38
sB ▥40–48 dB54–60 dB ▥61–72
mountains lake

🖐Kaiser Baarestr 50 ☎212424 Fia Lnc
MB RT

🖐C Keiser Grabenstr 18 ☎218148 P
Ren

ZUOZ
Graubünden(☎082)

★ ★ ★Engladina Haupstr ☎71021

Switzerland

Jun–Oct & Dec–Apr
rm40 ⇄20 ▥15 P Lift sB67–81
sB ⇄ ▥86–108 dB123–150
dB ⇄ ▥142–197 ⸎ Pool mountains

ZÜRICH
Zürich(☎01)
See plan

★ ★ ★ ★ ★Baur au Lac Taistr 1
☎2211650 tx813567 Plan 1
⇄170 ▥ P Lift ⅅ sB ⇄150–210
dB ⇄240–320 M42–46 lake

★ ★ ★ ★ ★Dolder (Amb) Kurhaus Str 65
☎2516231 tx53449 Plan 2
⇄200 ▥ P Lift ⅅ sB ⇄150–210
dB ⇄240–320 M35–100 ⸎ Pool lake

★ ★ ★ ★ ★Eden au Lac Utoquai 45
☎479404 tx52440 Plan 3
rm53 ⇄47 ▥6 P Lift ⅅ
sB ⇄ ▥135–160 dB ⇄ ▥230–280 M
alc mountains lake

★ ★ ★ ★ ★Savoy Bauer en Ville Poststr
12 ☎2115360 tx812845 Plan 3A
⇄112 P Lift ⅅ sB ⇄140–180
dB ⇄230–280 M alc

★ ★ ★ ★Ascot Lavaterstr 15 ☎2011800
tx52783 Plan 5
⇄60 P Lift ⅅ sB ⇄130 dB ⇄180
M12 & alc

★ ★ ★ ★Bellerive au Lac Utoquai 47
☎2517010 tx53272 Plan 6
rm60 ⇄50 ▥10 P Lift ⅅ
sB ⇄ ▥98–130 dB ⇄ ▥150–180 M
alc mountains lake

★ ★ ★ ★Carlton Elite Bahnhofstr 41
☎2116560 tx812781 Plan 7
rm72 ⇄68 ▥4 P Lift ⅅ sB ⇄180
dB ⇄240

★ ★ ★ ★Engematthof (KA) Engimattstr
14 ☎2012504 tx56327 Plan 8
rm79 ⇄35 ▥44 ▥ P ⅅ
sB ⇄ ▥80–103 dB ⇄ ▥120–145
M19–25 ⸎

★ ★ ★Zum Storchen Weinpl 2
☎2115510 tx813354 Plan 11
rm77 ⇄55 ▥22 P Lift ⅅ
sB ⇄ ▥110–170 dB ⇄ ▥180–260 M
alc lake

★ ★ ★Central Central Pl ☎2515555
tx54909 Plan 12
⇄99 ▥ P Lift ⅅ sB ⇄120–180
dB ⇄180–270

★ ★ ★Excelsior (GT) Dufourstr
☎2525000 tx59295 Plan 14
rm50 ⇄41 ▥9 P Lift
sB ⇄ ▥110–130 dB ⇄ ▥180–197
M13–20

★ ★ ★Glockenhof (Amb) Sihlstr 31
☎2115650 tx812466 Plan 15
rm106 ⇄92 ▥14 P Lift ⅅ

---

sB ⇄ ▥85–115 dB ⇄ ▥120–160
M10–30

★ ★Burma Schindlerstr 26 ☎3611008
Plan 16
rm32 ⇄8 P Lift ⅅ sB40–45
dB65–70 dB ⇄85–90

★ ★Krone Limmatquai 88 ☎2514222
Plan 18
rm25 ⇄2 Lift ⅅ sB38–46 dB72–80
dB ⇄85–95 M alc

🖐AMAG Auto & Motoren Überlandstr
166 ☎412222

🖐Canonica Albisriederstr 401
☎4919824 P BL Hon

🖐E Frey Badenerstr 600 ☎4952411 P
BL DJ RT

🖐J H Keller Vulkanstr 120
☎642410 Hon

🖐Riesbach Dufourstr 182 ☎552211 P
Frd

At ADLISWIL (4km SE on N4)

☆ ☆Jolie Ville Motor Inn (Mövenpick)
Zürichstr 105 ☎7108585 tx52507
Plan 17
rm70 ⇄38 ▥32 P ⅅ sB ⇄ ▥72–82
dB ⇄ ▥100–110 M10–25

At OERLIKON (4km N)

★ ★Sternen Oerlikon Schaffhauserstr
335 ☎3117777 Plan 19
rm55 ⇄15 ▥22 ▥ Lift ⅅ sB45–50
sB ⇄ ▥62–70 dB80–90
dB ⇄ ▥100–110 M14–20

At REGENSDORF (8km NW)

☆ ☆ ☆ ☆Holiday Inn Mövenpick
Watterstr, Zentrum ☎8402520 tx53658
Not on plan
⇄149 ▥ P Lift ⅅ sB ⇄107–122
dB ⇄fr148 M alc Pool

ZÜRICH AIRPORT
At GLATTBRUGG (8km NE on N4)

★ ★ ★ ★ ★Hilton International
Hohenbuhlstr 10 ☎8103131 tx55135
Plan 3
⇄287 ▥ Lift ⅅ sB ⇄120–140
dB ⇄159–195 M & alc Pool

★ ★ ★ ★Airport Oberhauserstr 30
☎8104444 tx53287 Plan 4
rm48 ⇄28 ▥20 ▥ P Lift ⅅ
sB ⇄ ▥100 dB ⇄ ▥130–140

☆ ☆ ☆ ☆Mövenpick W-Mittelholzerstr 8
☎8101111 tx57979 Plan 9
⇄335 P Lift ⅅ sB ⇄129–154
dB ⇄157–182 M12–55 Pool

ZWEISIMMEN
Bern(☎300)

★ ★Krone Lenkstr ☎22626
Closed Nov
rm40 ⇄30 ▥6 ▥ Lift sB28–38
sB ⇄ ▥38–53 dB56–76
dB ⇄ ▥76–106

☆Sport Saanenstr ☎21431
▥20 P sB ▥40 dB ▥68 lake

Liechtenstein

Liechtenstein

Prices are in Swiss Francs

SCHAAN
(☎075)

★★**Linde** Lindenpl ☎21704
10 Jan–20 Dec
rm23 ⇌6 🍴15 **P** sB ⇌ 🍴38–40
dB ⇌ 🍴58–68 Mfr10 mountains

♨**Fanal** (A Netzer) Feldkircherstr
52 ☎24604 Chy Sim

TRIESENBERG
(☎075)

★**Masescha** Masescha ☎22337
rm6 🏚 **P** Lift sB27–32 sB ⇌ 🍴32–37

Cable car from Locarno to Cardada

---

dB63 dB ⇌ 🍴63–68 M11–24
mountains

VADUZ
(☎075)

★★★**Park Sonnenhof** (Amb) Mareestr,
29 ☎21192 tx77781
mid Feb–mid Jan
⇌29 🏚 **P** Lift sB ⇌90–120
dB ⇌140–240 Pool mountains

☆ ☆ ☆ *Triesen* ☎22666
Feb–Oct
rm32 ⇌7 🍴25 🏚 **P** mountains

★★**Real** ☎22222 tx77809
rm10 ⇌6 🍴4 **P** Lift sB ⇌ 🍴80–110
dB ⇌ 🍴95–140 mountains

★**Engel** ☎21057
Closed Xmas
rm19 ⇌9 🍴6 **P** Lift 𝄞
sB ⇌ 🍴55–70 dB65–75
dB ⇌ 🍴75–90 Pool mountains

★**Löwen** Herrengasse ☎21408
11 Dec–9 Nov
rm11 ⇌1 **P** 𝄞 sB24 dB52 dB ⇌70
mountains

♨**Muhleholzgarage** Landstr 126
☎21668 **P** AR Ren

The River Rhine, Basel

YUGOSLAVIA

Yugoslavia, set on the Balkan peninsula and still largely uncommercialised, is bordered by Italy, Austria and Hungary in the north, Romania and Bulgaria in the east, Albania and Greece in the south, and the Adriatic in the west. The mountains in the north follow the Alpine pattern, with wooded slopes, lakes, waterfalls, and gorges, whilst the southern ranges are bare and desolate. The Carpathian Mountains, on the Romanian border, are especially rich in woods and pastures. The rocky Adriatic coast stretches for some 390 miles, with many islands off the shore. The River Danube crosses the Hungarian border and flows through the Panonian Plain, where the famous Iron Gates Canyon is located. The Adriatic coastal strip has a Mediterranean climate with warm summers, but the higher mountainous regions have an Alpine climate with short, cool summers. The remainder of the country has a Central European climate with hot summers. The main languages of Yugoslavia are Serbo-Croat, which predominates, Slovene and Macedonian. In the north the Latin alphabet is used, in the south the Cyrillic. The most common second languages are German in the north and French in the south.

The picturesque town of Piran

Area 98,766 sq miles
Population 22,681,000
Local time GMT +1
(Summer GMT + 2)

National flag Horizontal tricolour of blue, white and red, with a red 5-pointed star in the centre

How to get there

Yugoslavia is usually approached via Belgium, West Germany (Köln/Cologne and München/Munich) and Austria (Salzburg), or alternatively via France or Switzerland and Italy (Milan and Trieste). The distance from Calais via German to Beograd (Belgrade), the capital, is just over 1,200 miles, a distance which will normally require three or four overnight stops. Car sleeper services operate during the summer from Brussels and 's-Hertogenbosch to Ljubljana; and from Boulogne, Brussels and Paris to Milan.

Motoring regulations and general information

This information should be read in conjunction with the general content of the European ABC (pages 6–27). **Note** As certain regulations and requirements are common to many countries they are covered by one entry in the ABC and the following headings represent some of the subjects dealt with in this way:
AA Agents
Crash or safety helmets
Customs regulations for European countries
Drinking and driving
Fire extinguisher
Insurance
International distinguishing sign
Medical treatment
Overtaking
Police fines
Radio telephones/Radio transmitters
Rear view mirror
Seat belts
Traffic lights
Tyres
Visitor's registration

Accidents

Fire ☎93. **Police** ☎92 and **ambulance** ☎94 in main towns, but elsewhere the number will be found in the front of the local telephone directory. See also *Accidents* page 7.

It is obligatory for the driver of a passing vehicle to assist persons injured in a traffic accident.

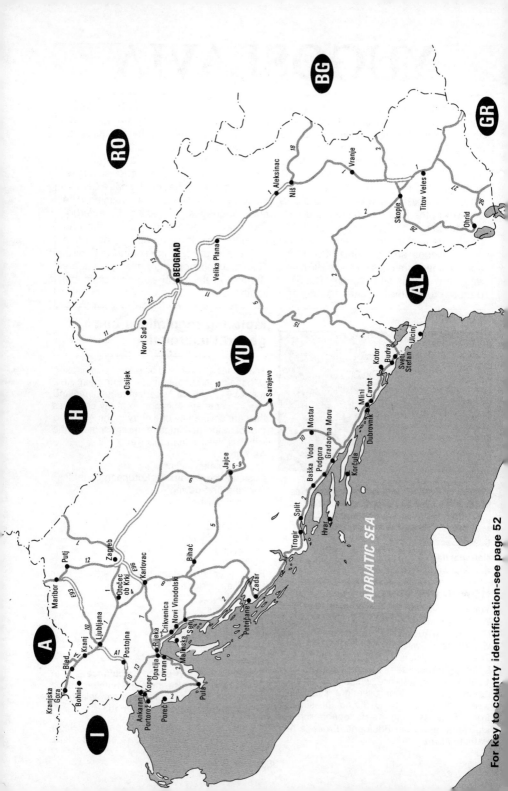

For key to country identification-see page 52

The driver of a vehicle involved in an accident should inform the traffic police (*Saobracajna Milicija*) immediately and wait for an on-the-spot investigation and the completion of a written report on the accident and damage.

Any damage to a vehicle entering Yugoslavia must be certified at the time of entry at the frontier. When leaving the country, certificates must be produced to cover any visible damage, otherwise the vehicle and driver will be detained until the circumstances of the damage have been ascertained.

Accommodation
Many good hotels will be found in the tourist centres and main towns; the majority of those on the coast are relatively new. There is also a good coverage of motels along the country's main roads. The Yugoslav National Tourist Office issues a comprehensive hotel guide.

The summer tourist season generally lasts from mid June to mid September and the winter sports season from December to March, with local differences and variations in prices. Rates normally include a service charge but a tourist tax is payable per person per day which varies according to locality and period of stay. Special reductions are allowed for children under 7 years. Accommodation in private homes is available in every resort and may be booked locally at tourist offices (*Turisticki Biro*).

Boats
A Helmsman's Certificate of Competence is recommended for Yugoslavia. See page 8 for further information about this and boat documentation.

Breakdown
The Yugoslav motoring club Auto-Moto Savez Jugoslavije (AMSJ) operates a breakdown and road information service which covers the whole of the country. ☎987. See also *Breakdown* page 8 and *Warning triangles* page 393.

British Consulates
(See also page 8)
1100 Beograd Generala Zdanova 46, ☎(011)645055/34. There are also consulates in Split and Zagreb.

Currency and banking hours
(See also page 11)
The unit of currency is the dinar which is divided into 100 para. A maximum of 1,500 dinars per person in Yugoslav currency may be imported or exported on your first trip to

Yugoslavia in any one year. For each subsequent trip during that year a maximum of 200 dinars per person is allowed.

There is no restriction on the importation and exportation of foreign currencies or travellers cheques; visitors may exchange these freely at exchange offices, banks, hotels, tourist offices and some offices of the Yugoslav motoring organisation into dinar banknotes or dinar-denominated cheques. All exchange receipts should be retained until you leave the country. The dinar cheques may be used to pay for certain goods and services entitling the holder to a discount. They are easily re-converted into foreign currency unlike dinar banknotes and coins.

Most banks are open 08.00–19.00hrs from Monday to Friday and some on Saturday morning.

Dimensions
Vehicles must not exceed–height: 4 metres; width: 2.5 metres; length; vehicle/trailer combinations 15 metres.

Driving licence
(See also page 13)
A valid British driving licence is acceptable in Yugoslavia. The minimum age at which a visitor may drive a temporarily imported car or motorcycle (exceeding 125cc) is 18 years.

Emergency messages to tourists
(See also page 14)
Emergency messages to tourists are broadcast by the Yugoslav radio network.
Radio Zagreb transmitting on medium wave 189 metres, 202 metres, 221 metres, 347 metres, 358 metres, 388 metres and 407 metres broadcast these messages in English, German and Italian between 11.00–11.30hrs Monday to Friday from 15 June to 15 September.
Radio Ljubljana transmitting on 326.8 metres medium wave broadcasts the messages in Dutch, English, French, German and Italian between 09.45–10.00hrs Monday to Saturday from May to September.
Radio Yugoslavia transmitting on 333 metres medium wave broadcasts the messages in the mother tongue of the tourist between 17.00–18.00hrs Monday to Saturday throughout the year.

First aid kit
(See also page 16)
It is *compulsory* for visiting motorists to carry a first-aid kit in their vehicles.

Lights
(See also page 17)

It is *compulsory* for visiting motorists to equip their vehicle with a set of replacement bulbs.

Dipped headlights must be used by motorcyclists during the day when travelling outside built-up areas.

Motoring club
(See also page 18)

 The **Auto-Moto Savez Jugoslavije** (AMSJ) has its headquarters at 11000 Beograd, Ruzveltova 18 ☎(011)401-699 and is represented in most towns either direct or through regional and associated clubs.

Motorways
Several single and dual carriageway sections of motorway (autoput or avtocesta) are now available. There are 440 miles open in all and further stretches are under construction. Tolls are charged on most sections.

Parking
(See page 19)

Between 08.00–19.00hrs (Mon–Sat) parking meters are in use in some towns.

Passengers
(See also page 00)

Children under 12 and persons visibly under the influence of alcohol are not permitted to travel in a vehicle as front seat passengers.

Petrol
(See also page 20)

Duty free petrol The petrol in the vehicle tank may be imported free of customs duty and tax.

Octane rating Normal Benzin (86) and Super Benzin (98).

Petrol coupons At the time of going to press coupons are compulsory to obtain supplies of fuel including diesel. Two types of coupon are available 'Tourist' and 'Commercial'. Tourist coupons provide a discount on pump prices and may be purchased at road border crossings, but only with freely convertible currency. They cannot be purchased in Yugoslavia. The border crossings are at Škofije, Kozina, Fernetiči, Nova Gorica, Rateče, Korensko sedlo, Ljubelj, Vič, Šentilj and Gornja Radgona provide tourist services on a 24-hr basis. However visitors arriving by Motorail cannot purchase tourist petrol coupons at Jesenice, the border crossing for rail traffic, but may obtain them in Ljubljana from the Kompas agency in the airport bank. Commercial coupons do not provide a dis-

count and may be purchased in all large Yugoslav towns from banks, exchange offices, travel agencies, AMSJ offices and some petrol stations in Slovenia and Croatia. They cannot be purchased with dinars, only with freely convertible currency. Both types of coupon are available to tourists.

Petrol cans Petrol in cans may be imported in limited quantities but only on payment of customs duty.

Postal information
Mail Postcards *Din* 5.60, Letters *Din* 8.00

Post offices There are 3,500 post offices in Yugoslavia. Opening hours of main post offices are from 08.00–19.00hrs with the smaller offices opening 08.00–12.00hrs and 18.00–20.00hrs.

Postcheques
(See also page 21)

Postcheques may be cashed at all post offices for any amount up to a maximum of *Din* 8,000 per cheque. Counter positions are identified by the words *Isplata-uplata*. See above for post office opening hours.

Priority
(See also *Priority including Roundabouts* page 22)

Trams have priority over all vehicles at all times.

The Plitvice Lakes form a series of fine cascades

Public holidays
Official public holidays in Yugoslavia for 1985 are given below. See also *Public holidays* page 22.

January 1/2 (New Year)
April 27 (National holiday in Slovenia)
May 1/2 (Labour Day)
July 4 (Veterans' Day)
July 7† (National holiday in Serbia)
July 13* (National holiday in Montenegro)
July 22 (National holiday in Slovenia)
July 27* (National holiday in Croatia and Bosnia-Herzegovina)

August 2 (National holiday in Macedonia)
October 11 (National holiday in Macedonia)
November 29/30 (Republic Day)
* Saturday
† Sunday

Registration documents

(See also page 22)
If the vehicle is not registered in your name you should have a letter from the owner authorising you to use it; this letter must be countersigned by a motoring organisation.

Roads

Roads have improved considerably in the last few years and many have been rebuilt. The main roads in the extreme north-west are good, and so is the road from Rijeka to Dubrovnik and beyond. It is wise, when making a tour off the beaten track, to enquire at the local tourist agencies for the latest information on the next stage of the journey. Make sure your car is in good order before you go, as telephones and service stations are far apart. A leaflet entitled *Road conditions in Yugoslavia* is available to AA members.

Road signs

(See also page 23)
The words *Jedan Smer* on a blue and white arrow indicate a one-way street in the direction the arrow is pointing.

Shopping hours

08.00–12.00hrs and 16.00–20.00hrs from Monday to Friday, 08.00–15.00hrs Saturday. Some *food shops* also open on Sunday 06.00–10.00hrs.

Speed limits

(See also page 25)
In built-up areas 60kph (37 mph); outside built-up areas 80 kph (49 mph) but 100 kph (62 mph) on dual carriageways and 120 kph (74 mph) on motorways.

Vehicle trailer combinations not exceeding 750 kg in weight are restricted to 80 kph (49 mph) on all roads outside built-up areas.

Spiked, studded or snow tyres

(See also page 10)
The use of *spiked tyres* is prohibited. *Snow tyres* may be used but they must have grooves with a depth of at least 4 mm.

Tourist information offices

(See also page 25)
The Yugoslav National Tourist Office has an office at 143 Regent Street, London W1R 8AE telephone 01-734 5243/8714 and 01-439 0399. They will be pleased to help tourists before their departure to Yugoslavia. Additionally, many resorts have their own tourist bureau where local information may be obtained.

Using the telephone

(See also page 26)
Insert coin **after** lifting receiver, dialling tone long and short tones. When making calls to subscribers within Yugoslavia precede number with relevant area code (shown in parentheses against town entry in gazetteer). Use *Din2* coins for local calls and *Din10* for national and international calls.
International callbox identification Certain boxes with 3/4 coin slots.
Telephone rates A direct dial call to the UK costs *Din192.72* for 3 minutes and *Din75* for each additional minute.
What to dial for the Irish Republic 99 353.
What to dial for the UK 99 44.

Warning triangles

The use of a warning triangle is compulsory for all vehicles except two wheelers. The triangle must be placed on the road 50 metres (55 yds) behind the vehicle to warn following traffic of any obstruction. Two triangles (placed side by side) are required for vehicle/trailer combinations. See also *Warning triangles/Hazard warning lights* page 26.

Prices are in Yugoslav Dinars
Abbreviations:

pl   plaza

The province names are as follows with their better known forms:
Bosna/Hercegovina – Bosnia and Herzegovina
Crna Gora – Montenegro
Hrvatska – Croatia
Makedonija – Macedonia
Slovenija – Slovenia
Srbija – Serbia

ALEKSINAC
Srbija (☎018)

☆**Morava** ☎72222 tx16179
⇆ 🏠104 🏨 dB ⇆ 🏠2272–2777
Beach

ANKARAN
Slovenija (☎066)

★★**Bor** ☎51820
Apr–Oct
⇆ 🏠96 🏨 sB ⇆ 🏠1689–2315
dB ⇆ 🏠2599–3658 Beach

BAŠKA VODA
Hrvatska (☎058)

★★**Slavija** ☎620155
Apr–Oct
rm50 ⇆ 🏠30 **FPn**1203–2262 sea

BEOGRAD (BELGRADE)
Srbija (☎011)

★★★★**Metropol** Bulevar Revolucije
69 ☎330910 tx11349
⇆ 🏠200 🏨 **P** Lift 𝄞 sB ⇆6311
dB ⇆10097 M alc

★ ★ ★ Excelsior Kneza Miloša 5
☎331381 tx12299

⊷81 **P** Lift ☽ sB ⊷5040–5545
dB ⊷6675–7560 M alc

★ ★ ★ Jugoslavia (SRS) Bulevar E-
Kardelja 3 ☎600222 tx11349

⊷500 🍴 **P** Lift ☽ sB ⊷6307
dB ⊷11353 Pool River

★ ★ ★ ★ Majestic ☎636022 tx11345

⊷ 🏠92 Lift sB ⊷ 🏠5545
dB ⊷ 🏠6300–7560

★ ★ ★ Balkan ☎687466
rm95 ⊷45 🏠5 **P** Lift ☽ sB2900
sB ⊷ 🏠4035 dB2530
dB ⊷ 🏠3780–4790

★ ★ ★ Kasina pl Terazi 25 ☎335574
tx11865

⊷ 🏠96 Lift sB ⊷ 🏠4163
dB ⊷ 🏠2500

★ ★ ★ National ☎601122 tx11774
🏠70 **P** ☽ sB 🏠3780 dB 🏠4540
mountains

★ ★ ★ Putnik ☎697225 tx12434
⊷118 Lift

★ ★ ★ Slavija Svetog Save 9 ☎450842
tx11545

rm509 ⊷182 🍴 **P** Lift ☽
sB ⊷ 🏠4163 dB ⊷5803

★ ★ ★ Toplice ☎626426
⊷110 **P** Lift ☽ sB ⊷3406–4163
dB ⊷5046

⚭Auto-moto Turing Društvo Ruzveltova
19–21 ☎987 All makes

Dvadesetprvi MAJ Patrijarha Dimitrija 24
☎592111 Fia

Interkomerc-Kontinental Omiadinskih
Brigada 31 ☎154660 Frd Opl

Zastava-Auto Mije Kavacevića 6
☎764699 Fia

BIHAĆ
Bosna I Hercegovina (☎077)

★ ★ Park ☎229400
rm110 ⊷ 🏠76 🍴 Lift sB1298–1443
dB2405 dB ⊷ 🏠3078 sea

BLED
Slovenija (☎064)

★ ★ ★ ★ Golf Cankarjeva 4 ☎77591
tx34531

⊷150 **P** Lift ☽ sB ⊷2397–3911
dB ⊷3784–6812 Pool mountains lake

★ ★ ★ Grand Hotel Toplice (SRS)
☎77222 tx34588

⊷ 🏠121 Lift sB ⊷ 🏠2283–4037
dB ⊷ 🏠3936–7190 Pool

★ ★ Jelovica ☎77316
rm146 ⊷ 🏠39 🍴 Lift sB1425–2069
sB ⊷ 🏠2068–3292 dB2573–3999
dB ⊷ 🏠2863–4718 lake

★ ★ Park ☎77945 tx34504

⊷86 **P** Lift ☽ sB ⊷2270–3784 Pool
mountains lake

Yugoslavia

★ Krim Ljubilianska Cesta 7 ☎77418
rm99 🍴 ⊷ 🏠69 sB1425–2069
sB ⊷ 🏠2220–3153 dB2497–3934
dB ⊷ 🏠2863–4503

BOHINJ
Slovenija (☎064)

★ ★ Zlatorog Bohinjsko Jezero ☎76381
tx34619

⊷43 **P** Lift ☽ sB ⊷1731–2068
dB ⊷3126–3752 Pool mountains

BORIK See **ZADAR**

BUDVA
Crna Gora (☎086)

★ ★ ★ International ☎41044
⊷ 🏠295 Lift ⚭ Pool Beach sea

CAVTAT
Hrvatska (☎050)

★ ★ ★ Cavtat ☎78226 tx27537
⊷ 🏠109 Lift sB ⊷ 🏠1122–2409
dB ⊷ 🏠2018–4667 Beach sea

★ ★ ★ Epidaurus ☎78144 tx27537
Apr–Oct
rm192 ⊷ 🏠175 Lift
dB ⊷ 🏠1387–4692 Beach sea

CRIKVENICA
Hrvatska (☎051)

★ ★ ★ Esplanade Stronsmajerovo
Setalište ☎781133
Apr–Oct
⊷ 🏠89 sB ⊷ 🏠1058–2309
dB ⊷ 🏠1924–3848

★ ★ ★ International Setalište VI Bakarica
☎781324
⊷ 🏠53 Lift

★ ★ Therapia ☎781511
⊷ 🏠115 Lift sB ⊷ 🏠1202–2405
dB ⊷ 🏠1683–4810 Pool

Automehanika Selska 1 ☎831205

DUBROVNIK
Hrvatska (☎050)

★ ★ ★ ★ Argentina put Frana Supila 20
☎23855 tx27558
rm155 ⊷145 🍴 **P** Lift ☽
sB ⊷2333–6055 dB ⊷4666–12110
Pool Beach sea

★ ★ ★ ★ Excelsior put Frana Suplia 3
☎23566 tx27523
⊷ 🏠211 Lift sB ⊷ 🏠1892–6307
dB ⊷ 🏠2270–10092 Pool Beach sea

★ ★ ★ Libertas Lavceviceva 1
☎27444 tx27588
⊷360 **P** Lift ☽ sB ⊷2964–7758
dB ⊷3910–10470

★ ★ Imperial Mise simoni 2 ☎23688
⊷ 🏠108 **P** Lift sB ⊷ 🏠1766–5550
dB ⊷ 🏠2775–3710 sea

★ ★ ★ Neptun Dalmatinski put ☎23755
tx27523
Apr–Oct
⊷ 🏠220 Lift dB ⊷ 🏠2396–5298
Beach sea

★ ★ ★ Splendid ☎24733
Apr–Oct
⊷ 🏠61 Lift sB ⊷ 🏠1892–5
dB ⊷ 🏠1650–3150 Beach sea

★ ★ ★ Sumratin (5km from Station) Aleja
Ive Loie Ribara ☎24722
Apr–Oct
⊷ 🏠70 A2rm Lift sB ⊷ 🏠1387–3784
dB ⊷ 🏠21446–5046 sea

★ ★ ★ Villa Dubrovnik Vlaha Bukovca 8
☎22933 tx27503
Apr-Oct
⊷ 🏠56 A9rm **P** Lift
sB ⊷ 🏠2350–6183 dB ⊷ 🏠2843–8038
t% Beach

★ ★ Bellevue put Pera Cingrie ☎25075
Apr–Oct
rm51 ⊷ 🏠47 Lift sB ⊷ 🏠1766–3910
dB ⊷ 🏠2270–5803 Beach sea

Auto-Dubrovnik put Mihaila 1 ☎23728
Cit Frd Opl Ren

Dubrovkinja OOUR Auto-servis
Masarikov PUT 3 ☎23178 Aud VW

GORICA See **OHRID**

GRADAC NA MORU
Hrvatska (☎058)

★ ★ Laguna ☎70614
⊷ 🏠70 **P** Lift sB ⊷ 🏠1195–2030
dB ⊷ 🏠2210–3824 Beach sea

HALUDOVO See **MALINSKA**

HVAR (ISLAND OF)
Hrvatska (☎058)

★ ★ ★ Adriatic ☎74024 tx26235
⊷ 🏠63 Lift sB ⊷ 🏠1513–3153
dB ⊷ 🏠 fr 3161 Pool sea

★ ★ Dalmacija ☎74120
⊷ 🏠70 sB ⊷ 🏠1135–2775
dB ⊷ 🏠2018–4289 Beach sea

★ ★ Pharos ☎74028
⊷ 🏠175 sB ⊷ 🏠1135–2775
dB ⊷ 🏠2018–5046

JAJCE
Bosna I Hercegovina (☎070)

★ ★ Turist ☎33268
rm54 ⊷ 🏠20 sB1261 sB ⊷ 🏠1513
dB2270 dB ⊷ 🏠2775

KARLOVAC
Hrvatska (☎047)

Automehanika Ilovac 29 ☎23510 Aud
VW

KOPER
Slovenija (☎066)

Trgoavto Tozd Servis Is Istarska Cesta
12 ☎22771 MB Ren

KORČULA (ISLAND OF)
Hrvatska (☎050)

★ ★ ★Marko Polo ☎711100 tx27556
⇋113 P Lift ☽ sB ⇋1639–3784
dB ⇋2523–6055 ⚓ Pool Beach sea

★ ★ ★Park ☎711004 tx27556
Apr–Oct
rm225 ⇋100 🛏70 A75rm P ☽
sB1009–1766 sB ⇋ 🛏1261–3027
dB2018–3153 dB ⇋ 🛏2144–5046 ⚓
Beach sea

KOSTRENA See **RIJEKA**

KOTOR
Crna Gora

Autoremont put Prvoboraca 188
☎25388 Fia Opl Ren

KRANJ
Slovenija (☎064)

★ ★ ★Creina ☎23650 tx34556
⇋ 🛏91 P Lift ☽ sB ⇋ 🛏2523–2901
dB ⇋ 🛏4163 Pool mountains

Gasilsko Resevaina Sluzba Oldhamska
Cesta 4 ☎24253

KRANJSKA GORA
Slovenija (☎064)

☆ ☆Kompas (9km on Ratece-Jesenice
road) ☎88661 tx34611
⇋ 🛏155 🏛 Lift sB ⇋ 🛏2018–3216
dB ⇋ 🛏3027–4289 Pool

★ ★Prisank ☎88472
⇋ 🛏64 sB ⇋ 🛏1639–2270
dB ⇋ 🛏2270–3532

LJUBLJANA
Slovenija (☎061)

★ ★ ★ ★Lev Vosnjakova 1 ☎310555
tx31350
⇋209 🏛 P ☽ sB ⇋ 🛏2838–4036
dB ⇋ 🛏4352–5361 mountains

★ ★ ★ ★Sion Titova 10 ☎211232
tx31254
⇋ 🛏185 Lift sB ⇋ 🛏2901–4036
dB ⇋ 🛏4163–4541

★ ★ ★Grand Union Miklosoceva Cesta 1
☎212133 tx31295
⇋270 P Lift sB ⇋3431 dB ⇋4819

★ ★ ★Turist Dalmationova 15
☎322043 tx31317
rm192 ⇋55 🛏50 P Lift ☽
sB ⇋ 🛏1361–2844 dB ⇋ 🛏2721–3957
M742

★ ★Ilirijg Trg Prekomorskin Brigad 4
☎551173 tx31574
rm134 ⇋10 🛏110 P Lift ☽ sB1639
sB ⇋ 🛏2270 dB2396 dB ⇋ 🛏3279

Agrostroj Koseska 11 ☎555366 Sab Sim

Automontaza Celovska Cesta 182
☎556451 AR

Autotehna Celovska 228 ☎573555 Frd
Opl Vau

Cimos-Citroen Servis Cilenskova 13
☎442917 Cit

PAP Autoservis Celovska 258 ☎572640
BMW

Yugoslavia

LOVRAN
Hrvatska (☎051)

★ ★Beograd ☎731022
May–Dec
⇋ 🛏102 Lift sB ⇋ 🛏1202–2838
dB ⇋ 🛏1828–5099 Beach sea

★ ★Miramar ☎731124
May–Oct
⇋ 🛏32 Lift sB ⇋ 🛏1106–1972
dB ⇋ 🛏1731–3944 sea

MALINSKA
Hrvatska (☎051)

At **HALUDOVO** (0.5km N)

★ ★ ★ ★Palace ☎885566 tx24142
⇋ 🛏220 Lift sB ⇋ 🛏1804–3511
dB ⇋ 🛏1804–3511 ⚓ Pool

★ ★ ★Tamaris ☎885566
May–Oct
⇋ 🛏289 Lift sB ⇋ 🛏914–2020
dB ⇋ 🛏1707–3511 Beach

MARIBOR
Slovenija (☎062)

★ ★Slavija Vita Kraigherja 3 ☎23661
tx33141
rm143 ⇋8 🛏101 P Lift ☽
sB1924–2164 sB ⇋ 🛏2645–2934
dB 🛏3704–4137

★ ★Orel Grajski Trg 3 ☎2617 tx33244
⇋ 🛏100 🏛 P Lift☽ sB1979–2473
sB ⇋ 🛏2597–2968 dB2721–2968
dB ⇋ 🛏3957–4328 M371–619 ⚓
mountains

Auto-Servis Cesta XIV Divizije 89
☎513092 Chy Sim
Ferromoto Minska Cesta 13 ☎21441 Fia

MLINI
Hrvatska (☎050)

★ ★Mlini ☎86053
⇋ 🛏90 🏛 sB ⇋ 🛏1387–3784
dB ⇋ 🛏2018–5046 Beach sea

MOSTAR
Bosna I Hercegovina (☎088)

★ ★Bristol ☎32921 tx46136
rm56 ⇋ 🛏45 Lift sB1513
sB ⇋ 🛏1892 dB 2523 dB ⇋ 🛏2901

★ ★Mostar ☎32941 tx46136
rm27 ⇋3 🛏24 P sB ⇋ 🛏1892
dB ⇋ 🛏2901

★ ★Neretva ☎32330
rm40 ⇋ 🛏24 sB1513 sB ⇋ 🛏1892
dB2523 dB ⇋ 🛏2901

🛢Auto-Moto Drustvo Splitska 66 ☎987
All makes

NIŠ
Srbija (☎018)

★ ★ ★Ambassador ☎25650 tx16256

⇋ 🛏162 P Lift sB ⇋ 🛏2396
dB ⇋ 🛏3279

★ ★Park 7 Julia 4 ☎23296
⇋87 🛏6 Lift sB1766 sB ⇋ 🛏2018
dB2523

☆ ☆Mediana ☎337161
rm54 ⇋ 🛏22 sB1135 dB1766
dB ⇋ 🛏2523

🛢Auto-Moto Drustvo Marka Oreskovića
15 ☎987 Fia

Zastava-Auto Kragujevac N Stojanovića
☎65628 Fia

NOVISAD
Srbija (☎021)

★ ★ ★Park Hadjuk Veljkova 2 ☎611711
⇋ 🛏315 P Lift ☽ Pool

🛢Auto-Moto Drustvo Lenjinov trg 10
☎29389 All makes

Autovojvodina Kosovska 54 ☎28168
Aud VW

NOVI VINOLDOLSKI
Hrvatska (☎051)

★ ★Horizont ☎791329
Apr–Oct
rm73 ⇋ 🛏63 Lift sB1058–1779
sB ⇋ 🛏1539–2309 dB1924–2886
dB ⇋ 🛏2405–3848 sea

★ ★Lisanj ☎791330
Apr–Oct
rm49 ⇋ 🛏6 sB1058–1779
dB1924–2886 dB ⇋ 🛏2405–3848 sea

OHRID
Makedonija (☎096)

★ ★ ★Grand Palace ☎25030 tx53878
⇋ 🛏13 A88rm P Lift
sB ⇋ 🛏2270–2523 dB ⇋ 🛏4163–4541
lake

At **GORICA** (2.5km S)

★ ★Inex Gorica ☎22020
Apr–Oct
⇋110 A20rm P ☽
sB ⇋ 🛏2586–2964 dB ⇋ 🛏4036–4856
Beach

OPATIJA
Hrvatska (☎051)

★ ★ ★Ambassador ☎712211
tx24184
⇋271 🏛 P Lift ☽ sB ⇋1731–4666
dB ⇋2501–6350 Pool Beach Sea

★ ★ ★Kvarner Park 1, Maja 4
☎711211 tx24341
rm86 ⇋ 🛏86 A30rm P Lift ☽
sB ⇋ 🛏1539–3415 dB ⇋ 🛏2501–6253
Pool Beach sea

★ ★Belvedere Maršala Tita 89
☎712433
May–Oct
rm171 ⇋100 Lift sB ⇋1443–2838
dB ⇋1828–5099 ⚓ Pool Beach sea

★ ★ ★Slavija Maršala Tita 200
☎711811

5 Jan–23 Dec →

⊷ 🏠106 Lift sB ⊷ 🏠1539-2934
dB ⊷ 🏠2309-5099 Pool

★ ★Dubrovnik Maršala Tita 201
☎711611

5 Jan-23 Dec
⊷ 🏠42 Lift sB ⊷ 🏠962-2405
dB ⊷ 🏠1539-4233 Beach sea

★ ★Palme Maršala Tita 166 ☎711823

May-Oct
rm103 ⊷ 🏠61 Lift sB817-1972
dB1346-2886 dB ⊷ 🏠1635-3944

Automotor-40 Box Spinčićeva 21
☎711439 Aud Opl VW

OSIJEK
Srbija (☎054)

Remontservis Vinkovacka 7 ☎24366
Fia

OTOČEC OB KRKI
Slovenija (☎068)

★ ★Grad Otočec ☎21830 tx35740
rm21 ⊷10 P ♪ sB1972 dB2982-3367
dB ⊷3944 Pool Beach

☆ ☆Otočec ☎21830 tx35740
rm151 ⊷ 🏠A61rm P Lift ♪
dB ⊷2405 Pool beach

PETRČANE
Hrvatska (☎057)

★ ★ ★Pinija ☎73062 tx27136
May-Oct
⊷ 🏠302 Lift Beach

PODGORA
Hrvatska (☎058)

★ ★ ★Mediteran ☎625155 tx26320
Apr-Oct
⊷ 🏠131 A sea

★ ★Podgorka ☎625266
Apr-Oct
rm19 A

POREČ
Hrvatska (☎053)

★ ★Riviera Obala Maršala Tita 25
☎32422
Apr-Oct
rm84 ⊷34 Lift sB832-1385
dB1472-2482 dB ⊷1760-3396 Beach
sea

Riviera Autoremont M Vlašića 66
☎31344 Cit Ren

PORTOROŽ
Slovenija (☎066)

★ ★ ★Palace ☎73541 tx34156
rm39 ⊷135 🏠474 P Lift ♪
sB ⊷ 🏠2212-4233 dB ⊷ 🏠3175-6253
Pool

POSTOJNA
Slovenija (☎067)

★ ★Kras Titov Trg ☎21071 tx34181
May-Dec
rm108 ⊷ 🏠54 P Lift
sB ⊷ 🏠1513-2018 dB ⊷ 🏠2270-3279

Yugoslavia

PTUJ
Slovenija (☎062)

★ ★Poetovio ☎772621
⊷33 🏠13 🏠 sB1346 sB ⊷ 🏠1587
dB2453 dB ⊷ 🏠2645

PULA
Hrvatska (☎052)

★ ★ ★Verudela ☎22871
Apr-Oct
rm376 ⊷328 sB914-1537
sB ⊷1034-1727 dB1419-2621
dB 🏠1580-2956 Beach sea

Auto-Servis Takop Veruda 39 ☎22450
Aud Ren VW

RIJEKA
Hrvatska (☎051)

★ ★ ★Bonavia ☎33744 tx24129
⊷ 🏠161 Lift sB ⊷ 🏠2649-2775
dB ⊷ 🏠4036-4541

★ ★ ★Jadran ☎421600
rm82 ⊷ 🏠72 Lift sB1250
sB ⊷ 🏠1683-2261 dB2164
dB ⊷ 🏠2597-3078 Pool Beach sea

★ ★Park ☎421155
rm47 ⊷ 🏠16 Lift sB1443-1539
sB ⊷ 🏠1683 dB2212-2501
dB ⊷ 🏠2838 Beach sea

Autoservis Barčićeva 3 ☎30388 Cit Frd
At **KOSTRENA** (6km E)
☆Lucija ☎441886
rm81 ⊷ 🏠48 P sB1539 dB2501
dB ⊷ 🏠2934 Beach sea

SARAJEVO
Bosna I Hercegovina (☎071)

★ ★Evropa Vase Pelagiča 5 ☎532722
tx41213
⊷ 🏠225 Lift

Bosna-Auto Obala 27 jula 35 ☎43143
MB Ren

SENJ
Hrvatska (☎051)

★ ★Nehaj Titova Obala ☎881285
rm93 🏠21 Lift sB997-1187
dB2089-2563 t% sea

SKOPJE
Makedonija (☎091)

★ ★Continental ☎220122 tx51318
⊷200 🏠 P Lift ♪ sB ⊷3406-3658
dB ⊷5803-6307

Gradska Zaednica & Auto-Moto
Drustvata Ivo Lola Ribar 51 ☎222361

SPLIT
Hrvatska (☎058)

★ ★ ★Marjan Obala Jna 5 ☎42866
tx26102

⊷311 🏠 P Lift ♪ sB ⊷3532-4919
dB ⊷5424-7316 Pool sea

★ ★ ★Park Maja 15 Setalište II
☎515411 tx26316
⊷ 🏠60 Lift sB ⊷ 🏠2901-4919
dB ⊷ 🏠3658-6307

Auto-Dlamacija Mosorskog Odrena 1
☎47277 Aud MB VW

STOBI See **TITOV VELES**

SVETI STEFAN
Crna Gora (☎086)

★ ★ ★ ★Sveti Stefan ☎41333 tx61188
May-Oct
⊷ 🏠118 🏠 ♪ sB ⊷ 🏠4576-7419
dB ⊷ 🏠7419-15828 M1484 ⊷ Pool
Beach sea mountains

★ ★ ★Maestral ☎41333 tx61188
⊷ 🏠157 A30rm 🏠 P Lift ♪ ⊷
Pool Beach sea mountains

★ ★ ★Miločer ☎41333 tx61188
May-Sep
rm46 ⊷26 🏠46 A24rm 🏠 P Lift ♪
⊷ Beach sea mountains

TITOV VELES
Makedonija (☎093)

At **STOBI** (26km SE)
★Stobi ☎70036
⊷ 🏠20 🏠 sB1766-1892
sB ⊷ 🏠2018-2270 dB3027-3279
dB ⊷ 🏠4036-4541

TROGIR
Hrvatska (☎058)

★ ★ ★Medena ☎73788 tx26204
⊷ 🏠663 Lift sB ⊷ 🏠1491-2405
dB ⊷ 🏠2212-3848 ⊷ Pool Beach
sea

ULCINJ
Crna Gora (☎085)

★ ★Grand Lido ☎81354
Apr-Oct
⊷ 🏠52 Lift sB ⊷ 🏠1766-2775
dB ⊷ 🏠2775-4541 ⊷ Pool Beach
sea

★ ★Mediteran ☎81411
Apr-Oct
rm244 ⊷ 🏠202 sB756-1135
sB ⊷ 🏠883-1261 dB1261-1892
dB ⊷ 🏠1513-2018 Beach sea

VELIKA PLANA
Srbija (☎011)

☆Velika Plana ☎52253
⊷36 P ♪ sB ⊷1892 dB ⊷3027

VRANJE
Srbija (☎017)

☆ ☆Vranje ☎23863
⊷ 🏠64 sB ⊷ 🏠1507-1633
dB ⊷ 🏠2661-2794

ZADAR
Hrvatska (☎057)

At **BORIK** (On coast 4km NW)

★★★*Novi Park* ☎22177 tx27145

⇌170 **P** ☽ ✆ Pool Beach sea

★★*Barbara* ☎24299 tx27145

Apr–Nov

⇌177 **P** Lift ☽ ✆ Pool Beach sea

★★*Slavija* ☎23244

May–Oct

⇌ ▥127 Lift ☽ ✆ Beach sea

Autorvatska Benkovacka 6 ☎22690 Aud
Cit Frd MB Peu

ZAGREB
Hrvatska (☎041)

★★★★*Esplanade* Minhanoviceva 1
☎512222 tx21395

Yugoslavia

⇌ ▥197 Lift sB ⇌ ▥5676–8704
dB ⇌ ▥7947–11101

★★★**International** Miramarška
☎511511 tx21184

⇌ ▥420 ♨ Lift sB1639
sB ⇌ ▥2270–4163 dB ⇌ ▥3784–5046

★★**Dubrovnik** Gajeva 1 (n.rest)
☎424222 tx21670

⇌ ▥279 Lift sB ⇌ ▥2586–3027
dB ⇌ ▥4541–5298

☆☆**Zagreb** av V-Holjevca ☎513255

Apr–Oct
rm51 sB ⇌ ▥2119–2543
dB ⇌ ▥3576–4291

PTT Autoradionica Folnegovićeva 6b
☎519868 Opl Peu

Autosanitarija Heinzelova 53 ☎212622
BL Ren RT

Autoservis-Borongaj Borongajska 75
☎215222

Opel Servis Samoborska 222a
☎576257 Opl

Skolski Centar za Cestovni Saobraćaj
Kraljevićava 24 ☎210320 Peu

Harbour at Korcula

The peaceful lake at Bohinj

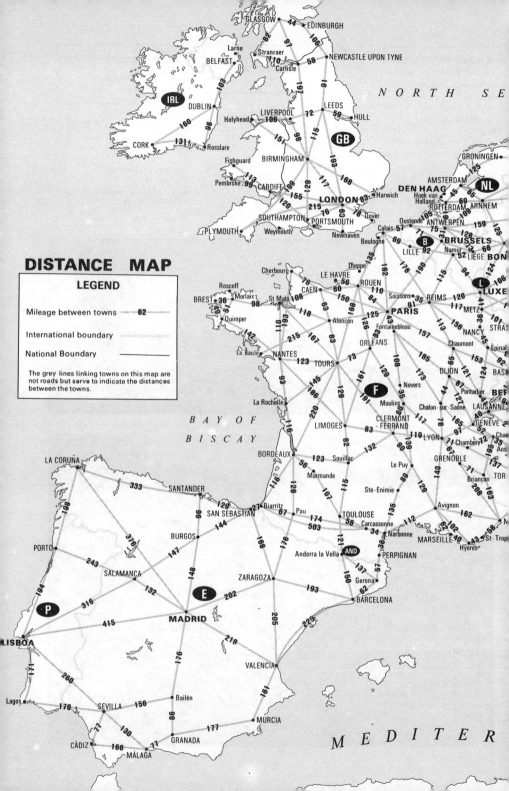

DISTANCE MAP

LEGEND

Mileage between towns ···· **62**

International boundary

National Boundary

The grey lines linking towns on this map are
not roads but serve to indicate the distances
between the towns.

NORTH SEA

BAY OF BISCAY

MEDITERR

Measurement Conversions

metres	Length yds or metres	yards		km	Length miles or km	miles
0.914	1	1.094		1.609	1	0.621
1.829	2	2.187		3.219	2	1.243
2.743	3	3.281		4.828	3	1.864
3.658	4	4.374		6.437	4	2.485
4.572	5	5.468		8.047	5	3.107
5.486	6	6.562		9.656	6	3.728
6.401	7	7.655		11.27	7	4.350
7.315	8	8.749		12.87	8	4.971
8.230	9	9.843		14.48	9	5.592
9.144	10	10.94		16.09	10	6.214
18.29	20	21.87		32.19	20	12.43
27.43	30	32.81		48.28	30	18.64
36.58	40	43.74		64.37	40	24.85
45.72	50	54.68		80.47	50	31.07
54.86	60	65.62		96.56	60	37.28
64.01	70	76.55		112.65	70	43.50
73.15	80	87.49		128.75	80	49.71
82.30	90	98.42		144.84	90	55.92
91.44	100	109.36		160.93	100	62.14
228.60	250	273.40		402.34	250	155.34
457.20	500	546.80		804.67	500	310.68

D@n't Drink and Drive

Capacity			Pressure		Weight		
litres	gallons or litres	gallons	lb per sq in	kg per sq cm	kg	lb or kg	lb
4.546	1	0.22	18	1.266	0.454	1	2.205
9.092	2	0.44	20	1.406	0.907	2	4.409
13.64	3	0.66	22	1.547	1.361	3	6.614
18.18	4	0.88	24	1.687	1.814	4	8.818
22.73	5	1.10	26	1.828	2.268	5	11.02
27.28	6	1.32	28	1.969	2.722	6	13.23
31.82	7	1.54	30	2.109	3.175	7	15.43
36.37	8	1.76	32	2.250	3.629	8	17.64
40.91	9	1.98	34	2.390	4.082	9	19.84
45.46	10	2.2	36	2.531	4.536	10	22.05
90.92	20	4.4	38	2.672	9.072	20	44.09
136.38	30	6.6	40	2.812	13.61	30	66.14
181.84	40	8.8	42	2.953	18.14	40	88.18
227.30	50	11.0	44	3.093	22.68	50	110.23
272.76	60	13.2	46	3.234	27.22	60	132.28
318.22	70	15.4	48	3.375	31.75	70	154.32
363.68	80	17.6	50	3.515	36.29	80	176.37
409.14	90	19.8	52	3.656	40.82	90	198.42
454.60	100	22.0	54	3.797	45.36	100	220.46
909.20	200	44.0	56	3.937	90.72	200	440.92
			58	4.078			
			60	4.218			

Road report

to The Automobile Association,
Overseas Routes,
Fanum House, Basingstoke,
Hants RG21 2EA.

section of road
from   to

passing through   road no.

names shown on signposts

remarks: *ie* surface, width, estimated gradient, description of landscape

section of road
from   to

passing through   road no.

names shown on signposts

remarks: *ie* surface, width, estimated gradient, description of landscape

vehicle used   date of journey

name (block letters)

address (block letters)

membership no.   for office use only
                                  acknowledged   recorded

Road report

to The Automobile Association,
Overseas Routes,
Fanum House, Basingstoke,
Hants RG21 2EA.

section of road
from   to

passing through   road no.

names shown on signposts

remarks: *ie* surface, width, estimated gradient, description of landscape

section of road
from   to

passing through   road no.

names shown on signposts

remarks: *ie* surface, width, estimated gradient, description of landscape

vehicle used   date of journey

name (block letters)

address (block letters)

membership no.   for office use only
                                        acknowledged   recorded

Garage report

to The Automobile Association,
Hotel & Information Services,
Fanum House, Basingstoke,
Hants RG21 2EA.

Town, country, garage

address

telephone no.

agents for   were AIT vouchers   recommended
                          used for payment

remarks

town, country, garage

address

telephone no.

agents for   were AIT vouchers   recommended
                          used for payment

remarks

town, country, garage

address

telephone no.

agents for   were AIT vouchers   recommended
                          used for payment

remarks

name (block letters)

address (block letters)

membership no.   for office use only   recorded
                          acknowledged

Garage report

to The Automobile Association,
Hotel & Information Services,
Fanum House, Basingstoke,
Hants RG21 2EA.

Town, country, garage

address

telephone no.

agents for
were AIT vouchers
used for payment
recommended

remarks

town, country, garage

address

telephone no.

agents for
were AIT vouchers
used for payment
recommended

remarks

town, country, garage

address

telephone no.

agents for
were AIT vouchers
used for payment
recommended

remarks

name (block letters)

address (block letters)

membership no.
for office use only
acknowledged
recorded

Accommodation report

to The Automobile Association,
Hotel & Information Services,
Fanum House, Basingstoke,
Hants RG21 2EA.

town, country, hotel

your star rating   location   date of stay

food   rooms

service   sanitary arrangements   value for money

general remarks

town, country, hotel

your star rating   location   date of stay

food   rooms

service   sanitary arrangements   value for money

general remarks

town, country, hotel

your star rating   location   date of stay

food   rooms

service   sanitary arrangements   value for money

general remarks

name (block letters)

address (block letters)

membership no.   for office use only
                                      acknowledged   recorded

Accommodation report

to The Automobile Association,
Hotel & Information Services,
Fanum House, Basingstoke,
Hants RG21 2EA.

town, country, hotel

your star rating   location   date of stay

food   rooms

service   sanitary arrangements   value for money

general remarks

town, country, hotel

your star rating   location   date of stay

food   rooms

service   sanitary arrangements   value for money

general remarks

town, country, hotel

your star rating   location   date of stay

food   rooms

service   sanitary arrangements   value for money

general remarks

name (block letters)

address (block letters)

membership no.   for office use only
acknowledged   recorded

Accommodation report

to The Automobile Association,
Hotel & Information Services,
Fanum House, Basingstoke,
Hants RG21 2EA.

town, country, hotel

your star rating   location   date of stay

food   rooms

service   sanitary arrangements   value for money

general remarks

town, country, hotel

your star rating   location   date of stay

food   rooms

service   sanitary arrangements   value for money

general remarks

town, country, hotel

your star rating   location   date of stay

food   rooms

service   sanitary arrangements   value for money

general remarks

name (block letters)

address (block letters)

membership no.

Accommodation report

to The Automobile Association,
Hotel & Information Services,
Fanum House, Basingstoke,
Hants RG21 2EA.

town, country, hotel

your star rating   location   date of stay

food   rooms

service   sanitary arrangements   value for money

general remarks

town, country, hotel

your star rating   location   date of stay

food   rooms

service   sanitary arrangements   value for money

general remarks

town, country, hotel

your star rating   location   date of stay

food   rooms

service   sanitary arrangements   value for money

general remarks

name (block letters)

address (block letters)

membership no.   for office use only   acknowledged   recorded

MOTORING IN EUROPE?

IF SO YOU NEED
AA 5 STAR SERVICE

If you are taking a European motoring holiday let AA 5-Star Service give you the added peace of mind of knowing that you, your family and your car are well cared for by the world's No. 1 motoring organisation.

AA 5 Star Service give you roadside assistance, vehicle recovery, medical expenses and lots more besides – no wonder over 235,000 cars and 500,000 people were covered last year.

So why not contact your local AA Centre or AA Travel Agency or phone 021-550 7648 and ask for details now.

HAVE THE BEST
DON'T HOPE FOR THE BEST

Symbols and Abbreviations

English

★ ★ ★
☆ ☆ ☆   Hotel classification
⇌   Private baths
🚿   Private showers
P   Parking for cars
🅿   Garage and/or lock-up
☽   Night porter
🎾   Tennis court(s) (private)
⚡   Golf (private)
∩   Riding stables (private)
🛠   Breakdown service
☎   Telephone number. Where there is a dialling code it is shown in parentheses against the town entry
sB   Single room per person per night*
sB ⇌ 🚿   Single with private bath/shower per person per night*
dB   Double room (two persons)*
dB ⇌ 🚿   Double room (two persons) with private bath/shower*
M   Main meal
alc   à la carte
DPn   Demi-pension
Pn   Full pension
St%   Service and/or tax charge (service and tax is included unless otherwise stated)
(n. rest)   Hotel does not have own restaurant
tx   Telex
rm   Number of bedrooms (including annexe)
A   Annexe followed by number of rooms
Ⅼ   Logis de France
M/c   Motorcycle repairs undertaken
Beach   Hotel has private beach
Pool   Hotel has private pool
Sea/   Rooms overlook sea,
moun-   mountain(s) or a lake
tains/lake
→   Entry continued overleaf
Plan   Number gives location of hotel on town plan

*in most cases this price includes breakfast.

For a more detailed explanation refer to 'About the Gazetteer' (see contents page).

Français

★ ★ ★
☆ ☆ ☆   Classement des hôtels
⇌   Salles de bain privées
🚿   Douches privées
P   Parking pour voitures
🅿   Garage et/ou garage avec serrure
☽   Portier de nuit
🎾   Cour(s) de tennis (privés)
⚡   Golf (privé)
∩   Equitation (privée)
🛠   Service dépannage
☎   Numéro de téléphone. Lorsqu'il y a un indicatif, celui-ci est indiqué entre parenthèses à côté du nom de la ville

sB   Chambre à un lit, par personne, pour un nuit*
sB ⇌ 🚿   Chambre à un lit avec bain/douche privés par personne, pour une nuit*
dB   Chambre à deux lits (deux personnes)*
dB ⇌ 🚿   Chambre à deux lits (deux personnes) avec bain/douche privé*
M   Repas principal
alc   à la carte
DPn   Demi-pension
Pn   Pension complète
St%   Charge pour service et/ou taxe (service et taxe sont compris sauf indication spéciale)
(n. rest)   Hôtel ne fait pas restaurant
tx   Télex
rm   Nombre de chambres (annexes comprises)
A   Annexe suivie par nombre de chambres
Ⅼ   Logis de France
M/c   Réparations de cyclomoteurs possibles
Beach   Hôtel a une plage privée
Pool   Hôtel a une piscine privée
Sea/   Chambres avec vue sur la mer,
moun-   les montagnes ou un lac
tains/lake
→   Suite au verso
Plan   Chiffre indique l'emplacement de l'hôtel sur le plan de la ville

*ce prix comprend généralement le petit-déjeuner
Pour plus amples informations veuillez vous référer à 'About the Gazetteer' (voir la table de matières).

Deutsch

★ ★ ★
☆ ☆ ☆   Hotelklassifzierung
⇌   Privatbad
🚿   Privatdusche
P   Parken
🅿   Garage bzw verschliessbare Parkeinheit
☽   Nachtportier
🎾   Tennisplatz (Privat)
⚡   Golfplatz (Privat)
∩   Reitgelegenheiten (Privat)
🛠   Pannendienst
☎   Telefonnummer Wenn Vorwahlnummer vorhanden wird sie in Klammern zusammen mit Stadtangaben aufgeführt
sB   Einzelzimmer pro Person pro Nacht*
sB ⇌ 🚿   Einzelzimmer mit Privatbad/Dusche pro Person pro Nacht*
dB   Doppelzimmer (2 Personen)*
dB ⇌ 🚿   Doppelzimmer (2 Personen) mit Privatbad/Dusche*
M   Hauptessen
alc   à la carte
Dpn   Demipension
Pn   Vollpension
St%   Dienst-bzw. Steuergebühren (Dienst-bzw. Steuergebühren sind, wenn keine Gegenangaben, einbegriffen)
(n. rest)   Hotel ohne eigenes Restaurant
tx   Telex

412

rm   Zimmeranzahl (einschliesslich Nebengebäude
A   Nebengebäude und danach Zimmeranzahl
L   Logis de France
M/c   Motorradreparaturen
Beach   Hotel hat Privatstrand
Pool   Hotel hat Privatschwimmbad
Sea/   Zimmer mit einem Blick auf das
moun-   Meer, die Gebirge oder einen
tains/lake   See
→   Fortsetzung siehe umseitig
Plan   Nummer gibt den Standort des Hotels auf dem Stadtplan

*in den meisten Fällen sind die Preise einschl des Frühstücks.
Für weitere Angaben beziehen Sie sich auf 'About the Gazetteer' (siehe Inhaltsverzeichnis).

Italiano

★ ★ ★
☆ ☆ ☆   Classificazione alberghi
⇨   Bagni privati
🚿   Docce private
P   Parcheggio macchine
🏛   Garage e/o box
D   Portiere notturno
🎾   Campi da tennis (privati)
🏌   Golf (privato)
○   Scuola d'equitazione (privata)
🆘   Servizio assistenza stradale
☎   Numero telefonico. I prefissi figurano tra parentesi vicino al norme della città
sB   Prezzo per persona di una camera singola (a notte)*
sB ⇨ 🚿   Prezzo per persona di una camera singola con bagno/doccia privati (a notte)*
dB   Camera per due persone*
dB ⇨ 🚿   Camera per due persone con bagno/doccia privati*
M   Pasto principale
alc   Alla carta
DPn   Mezza pensione
Pn   Pensione completa
St%   Servizio e/o tassa (compresi, salvo indicazione contraria)
(n. res)   Albergo senza ristorante
tx   Telex
rm   Numero di camere (compresa la dependance)
A   Dependence, seguita dal numero di camere
L   Logis de France
M/c   Si riparano motociclette
Beach   L'albergo é provvisto di spiaggia privata
Pool   L'albergo é provvisto di piscina
Sea/   Le camere guardano sul mare/i
moun-   monti/il lago
tains/lake
→   La lista delle voci continua a tergo

Plan   Il numero indica la posizione dell'albergo sulla cartina della città

*Nella maggioranza dei casi nel prezzo é inclusa la prima. colazione

Per una spiegazione piú dettagliata, consultare la sezione 'About the Gazetteer' (vedi indice).

Español

★ ★ ★
☆ ☆ ☆   Clasificación de hoteles
⇨   Baños en cada habitación
🚿   Duchas en cada habitación
P   Aparcamiento para automóviles
🏛   Garaje y/o garaje individual con cerradura
D   Conserje nocturno
🎾   Canchas de tenis (privadas)
🏌   Golf (privado)
○   Escuela hípica (privada)
🆘   Servicio de asistencia averias
☎   Número de teléfono. Si hay prefijo, ésto figura entre paréntesis junto al nombre de la ciudad
sB   Precio por persona de una habitación individual (por noche)*
sB ⇨ 🚿   Precio por persona de una habitación individual con baño/ducha (por noche)*
dB   Precio de una habitación para dos personas*
dB ⇨ 🚿   Precio de una habitación para dos personas con baño/ducha*
M   Comida principal
alc   A la carta
DPn   Media pensión
Pn   Pensión completa
St%   Servicio y/o impuesto (Ambos incluidos, a menos que se indique lo contrario)
(n. rest)   El hotel no tiene restaurante
tx   Telex
rm   Número de habitaciones (incluso el edificio anexo)
A   Edificio anexo, seguido por el número de habitaciones
L   Logis de France
M/c   Se reparan motocicletas
Playa   El hotel tiene playa privada
Pool   El hotel tiene piscina privada
Sea/   Las habitaciones tienen vista al
moun-   mar/a las montañas/al lago
tains/lake
→   La lista de símbolos continúa a la vuelta
Plan   El número indica la ubicación del hotel en el plano de la ciudad

*El la mayoría de los casos, en este precio está incluido el desayuno.

Para una explicación más detallada, consúltese la sección 'About the Gazetteer' (véase el índice de materias).

Index

*See under *Country sections*
†See also *Country sections*

Acknowledgements

The Automobile Association would like to thank the National Tourist Boards of the following countries for kindly giving us permission to reproduce the photographs used in this book: Austria, pp. 57, 59, 78; Belgium, pp. 79, 82, 92; Denmark, pp. 93, 95, 104; France, pp. 105, 112, 189; Germany, pp. 190, 191, 225; Greece, pp. 226, 227, 236; Italy, pp. 237, 242, 243, 268; Luxembourg, pp. 269, 271; Netherlands, pp. 274, 277; Norway, pp. 289, 293, 304; Portugal, pp. 305, 307, 315; Spain, pp. 316, 320; Sweden, pp. 345, 347; Switzerland, pp. 357, 360, 363, 388; Yugoslavia, pp. 389, 392, 297.